The Original Home Schooling Series by Charlotte Mason

The Original Home Schooling Series by Charlotte Mason

Start Publishing PD LLC

Cover art: Shutterstock/Taisiya Kozorez

Cover design: Jennifer Do

ISBN 979-8-8809-1884-3

Home Education

Table of Contents

Home Education

Table of Contents

Preface to the Home Education Series

The educational outlook is rather misty and depressing both at home and abroad. That science should be a staple of education, that the teaching of Latin, of modern languages, of mathematics, must be reformed, that nature and handicrafts should be pressed into service for the training of the eye and hand, that boys and girls must learn to write English and therefore must know something of history and literature; and, on the other hand, that education must be made more technical and utilitarian—these, and such as these, are the cries of expedience with which we take the field. But we have no unifying principle, no definite aim; in fact, no philosophy of education. As a stream can rise no higher than its source, so it is probable that no educational effort can rise above the whole scheme of thought which gives it birth; and perhaps this is the reason of all the fallings from us, vanishings, failures, and disappointments which mark our educational records.

Those of us, who have spent many years in pursuing the benign and elusive vision of Education, perceive her approaches are regulated by a law, and that this law has yet to be evoked. We can discern its outlines, but no more. We know that it is pervasive; there is no part of a child's home life or school work which the law does not penetrate. It is illuminating, too, showing the value, or lack of value, of a thousand systems and expedients. It is not only a light, but a measure, providing a standard whereby all things, small and great, belonging to educational work must be tested. The law is liberal, taking in whatsoever things are true, honest, and of good report, and offering no limitation or hindrance save where excess should injure. And the path indicated by the law is continuous and progressive, with no transition stage from the cradle to the grave, except that maturity takes up the regular self direction to which immaturity has been trained. We shall doubtless find, when we apprehend the law, that certain German thinkers—Kant, Herbart, Lotze, Froebel—are justified; that, as they say, it is necessary to believe in God; that, therefore, the knowledge of God is the principal knowledge, and the chief end of education. By one more character shall we be able to recognise this perfect law of educational liberty when it shall be made evident. It has been said that The best idea which we can form of absolute truth is that it is viable to meet every condition by which it can be tested. This we shall expect of our law—that it shall meet every test of experiment and every test of rational investigation.

Not having received the tables of our law, we fall back upon Froebel or upon Herbart; or, if we belong to another School, upon Locke or Spencer; but we are not satisfied. A discontent, is it a divine discontent? Is upon us; and assuredly we should hail a workable, effectual philosophy of education as a deliverance from much perplexity. Before this great deliverance comes to us it is probable that many tentative efforts will be put forth, having more or less of the characters of a philosophy; notably, having a central idea, a body of thought with various members working in vital harmony.

Such a theory of education, which need not be careful to call itself a system of psychology, must be in harmony with the thought movements of the age; must regard education, not as a shut off compartment, but as being as much a part of life as birth or growth, marriage or work; and it must leave the pupil attached to the world at many points of contact. It is true that educationalists are already eager to establish such contact in several directions, but their efforts rest upon an axiom here and an idea there, and there is no broad unifying basis of thought to support the whole.

Fools rush in where angels fear to tread; and the hope that there may be tentative efforts towards a philosophy of education, and that all of them will bring us nearer to the magnum opus, encourages me to launch one such attempt. The central thought, or rather body of thought, upon which I found, is the somewhat obvious fact that the child is a person with all the possibilities and powers included in personality. Some of members which develop from this nucleus have been exploited from time to time by educational thinkers, and exist vaguely in the general common sense, a notion here, another there. One thesis, which is, perhaps, new, that Education is the Science of Relations, appears to me to solve the question of curricula, as showing that the object of education is to put a child in living touch as much as may be of the life of Nature and of thought. Add to this one or two keys to self knowledge, and the educated youth goes forth with some idea of self management, with some pursuits, and many vital interests. My excuse for venturing to offer a solution, however tentative and passing, to the problem of education is twofold. For between thirty and forty years I have laboured without pause to establish a working and philosophic theory of education; and in the next place, each article of the educational faith I offer has been arrived at by inductive processes; and has, I think, been verified by a long and wide series of experiments. It is, however, with sincere diffidence that I

venture to offer the results of this long labour; because I know that in this field there are many labourers far more able and expert than I—the angels who fear to tread, so precarious is the footing!

But, if only pour encourager les autres, I append a short synopsis of education theory advanced in the volumes of the Home Education Series.

The treatment is not methodic, but incidental; here a little, there a little, as seemed to me most likely to meet the occasions of parents and teachers. I should add that in the course of a number of years the various essays have been prepared for the use of the Parents National Education Union in the hope that that Society might witness for a more or less coherent body of educational thought.

"The consequence of truth is great; therefore the judgment of it must not be negligent."—Whichcote

1. Children are born persons.

2. They are not born either good or bad, but with possibilities for either good or evil.

3. The principles of authority on the one hand and obedience on the other, are natural, necessary and fundamental; but

4. These principles are limited by the respect due to the personality of children, which must not be encroached upon, whether by fear or love, suggestion or influence, or undue play upon any one natural desire.

5. Therefore we are limited to three educational instruments—the atmosphere of environment, the discipline of habit, and the presentation of living ideas.

6. By the saying, Education is an atmosphere, it is not meant that a child should be isolated in what may be called a 'child environment,' especially adapted and prepared; but that we should take into account the educational value of his natural home atmosphere, both as regards persons and things, and should let him live freely among his proper conditions. It stultifies a child to bring down his world to a 'child's' level.

7. By Education is a discipline, is meant the discipline of habits formed definitely and thoughtfully, whether habits of mind or body. Physiologists tell us of the adaptation of brain structure to habitual lines of thought—i.e. to our habits.

8. In the saying that Education is a life, the need of intellectual and moral as well as of physical sustenance is implied. The mind feeds on ideas, and therefore children should have a generous curriculum.

9. But the mind is not a receptacle into which ideas must be dropped, each idea adding to an 'apperception mass' of its like, the theory upon which the Herbartian doctrine of interest rests.

10. On the contrary, a child's mind is no mere sac to hold ideas; but is rather, if the figure may be allowed, a spiritual organism, with an appetite for all knowledge. This is its proper diet, with which it is prepared to deal, and which it can digest and assimilate as the body does foodstuffs.

11. This difference is not a verbal quibble. The Herbartian doctrine lays the stress of education—the preparation of knowledge in enticing morsels, presented in due order—upon the teacher. Children taught upon this principle are in danger of receiving much teaching with little knowledge; and the teacher's axiom is, 'What a child learns matters less than how he learns it.'

12. But, believing that the normal child has powers of mind that fit him to deal with all knowledge proper to him, we must give him a full and generous curriculum; taking care, only, that the knowledge offered to him is vital—that is, the facts are not presented without their informing ideas. Out of this conception comes the principle that,

13. Education is the Science of Relations; that is, that a child has natural relations with a vast number of things and thoughts: so we must train him upon physical exercises, nature, handicrafts, science and art, and upon many living books; for we know that our business is, not to teach him all about anything, but to help him make valid, as many as may be of 'Those first born affinities, 'That fit our new existence to existing things.'

14. There are also two secrets of moral and intellectual self management which should be offered to children; these we may call the Way of the Will and the Way of the Reason.

15. The Way of the Will.—Children should be taught (a) 'To distinguish between 'I want' and 'I will.' (b) That the way to will effectively is to turn our thoughts from that which we desire but do not will. (c) That the best way to turn our thoughts is to think of or do some quite different thing, entertaining or interesting. (d) That, after a little rest in this way, the will returns to its work with new vigour. (This adjunct of the will is familiar to us as diversion, whose office is to ease us for a time from will effort, that we may 'will' again with

added power. The use of suggestion—even self suggestion—as an aid to the will, is to be deprecated, as tending to stultify and stereotype character. It would seem that spontaneity is a condition of development, and that human nature needs the discipline of failure as well as of success.)

16. The Way of the Reason.—We should teach children, too, not to 'lean' (too confidently) 'unto their own understanding,' because of the function of reason is, to give logical demonstration (a) of mathematical truth; and (b) of an initial idea, accepted by the will. In the former case reason is, perhaps, an infallible guide, but in the second it is not always a safe one, for whether that initial idea be right or wrong, reason will confirm it by irrefragable proofs.

17. Therefore children should be taught, as they become mature enough to understand such teaching that the chief responsibility which rests on them as persons is the acceptance or rejection of initial ideas. To help them in this choice we should give them principles of conduct and a wide range of the knowledge fitted for them. These three principles (15, 16 and 17) should save children from some of the loose thinking and heedless action which cause most of us to live at a lower level than we need.

18. We should allow no separation to grow up between the intellectual and 'spiritual' life of children; but should teach them that the divine Spirit has constant access to their spirits, and is their continual helper in all the interests, duties and joys of life.

The 'Home Education' Series is so called from the title of the first volume, and not as dealing, wholly or principally with 'Home' as opposed to 'School" education.

Preface to the Fourth Edition

My attempt in the following volume is to the suggest to parents and teachers a method of education resting upon a basis of natural law; and to touch, in this connection, upon a mother's duties to her children. In venturing to speak on this latter subject, I do so with the sincerest deference to mothers, believing that, in the words of a wise teacher of men, "the woman receives from the Spirit of God Himself the intuitions into the child's character, the capacity of appreciating its strength and its weakness, the faculty of calling forth the one and sustaining the other, in which lies the mystery of education, apart from which all its rules and measures are utterly vain and ineffectual." But just in proportion as a mother has this peculiar insight as regards her own children she will, I think, feel her need of a knowledge of the general principles of education, founded upon the nature and the needs of all children. And this knowledge of the science of education, not the best of mothers will get from above, seeing that we do not often receive as a gift that which we have the means of getting by our own efforts.

I venture to hope that teachers of young children, also, may find this volume of use. This period of a child's life between his sixth and his ninth year should be used to lay the basis of a liberal education, and of the habit of reading for instruction. During these years the child should enter upon the domain of knowledge, in a good many directions, in a reposeful, consecutive way, which is not to be attained through the somewhat exciting medium of oral lessons. I hope that teachers may find the approach (from a new standpoint), to the hackneyed "subjects of instruction" proper for little children at any rate interesting and stimulating; and possibly the methods which this fresh standpoint indicates may prove suggestive and helpful.

The particular object of this volume, as a member of the 'Home Education' Series, is to show the bearing of the physiology of habit upon education; why certain physical, intellectual, and moral habits are a valuable asset to a child, and what may be done towards the formation of such habits. I beg to acknowledge my indebtedness to Dr Carpenter's Mental Physiology for valuable teaching on the subject of habits contained in some two or three chapters of that work. Also, I would renew my grateful thanks to those medical friends who have given careful and able revision to such parts of the work as rest upon a physiological basis.

I should add that some twenty years ago (1885) the greater part of this volume was delivered as 'Lectures to Ladies,' in which form the papers were originally published (1886) under the title which is still retained.

Lectures VII. and VIII. and the Appendix of the original volume have been transferred from this to other volumes of the Series. The whole has been very carefully revised, and much new matter introduced, especially in Part V., 'Lessons as Instruments of Education,' which now offers a fairly complete introduction to methods of teaching subjects fit for children between the ages of six and nine.

The rest of the volume attempts to deal with the whole of education from infancy until the ninth year of life.

C. M. Mason
Scale How, Ambleside.
1905

Part I
Some Preliminary Considerations

Not the least sign of the higher status they have gained, is the growing desire for work that obtains amongst educated women. The world wants the work of such women; and presently, as education becomes more general, we shall see all women with the capacity to work falling into the ranks of working women, with definite tasks, fixed hours, and for wages, the pleasure and honour of doing useful work if they are under no necessity to earn money.

Children are a Public Trust.—Now, that work which is of most importance to society is the bringing up and instruction of the children—in the school, certainly, but far more in the home, because it is more than anything else the home influences brought to bear upon the child that determine the character and career of the future man or woman. It is a great thing to be a parent: there is no promotion, no dignity, to compare with it. The parents of but one child may be cherishing what shall prove a blessing to the world. But then, entrusted with such a charge, they are not free to say, "I may do as I will with mine own." The children are, in truth, to be regarded less as personal property than as public trusts, put into the hands of parents that they may make the very most of them for the good of society. And this responsibility is not equally divided between the parents: it is upon the mothers of the present that the future of the world depends, in even a greater degree than upon the fathers, because it is the mothers who have the sole direction of the children's early, most impressible years. This is why we hear so frequently of great men who have had good mothers—that is, mothers who brought up their children themselves, and did not make over their gravest duty to indifferent persons.

Mothers owe a 'thinking love' to their Children.—"The mother is qualified," says Pestalozzi, "and qualified by the Creator Himself, to become the principal agent in the development of her child; ... and what is demanded of her is—a thinking love ... God has given to the child all the faculties of our nature, but the grand point remains undecided—how shall this heart, this head, these hands be employed? to whose service shall they be dedicated? A question the answer to which involves a futurity of happiness or misery to a life so dear to thee. Maternal love is the first agent in education."

We are waking up to our duties and in proportion as mothers become more highly educated and efficient, they will doubtless feel the more strongly that the education of their children during the first six years of life is an undertaking hardly to be entrusted to any hands but their own. And they will take it up as their profession—that is, with the diligence, regularity, and punctuality which men bestow on their professional labours.

That the mother may know what she is about, may come thoroughly furnished to her work, she should have something more than a hearsay acquaintance with the theory of education, and with those conditions of the child's nature upon which such theory rests.

The training of Children 'dreadfully defective.'—"The training of children, says Mr. Herbert Spencer—"physical, moral and intellectual—is dreadfully defective. And in great measure it is so, because parents are devoid of that knowledge by which this training alone can be rightly guided. What is to be expected when one of the most intricate of problems is undertaken by those who have given scarcely a thought to the principle on which its solution depends? For shoemaking or housebuilding, for the management of a ship or of a locomotive engine, a long apprenticeship is needful. Is it, then, that the unfolding of a human being in body and mind is so comparatively simple a process that any one may superintend and regulate it with no preparation whatever? If not—if the process is, with one exception, more complex than any in Nature, and the task of ministering to it one of the surpassing difficulty—is it not madness to make no provision for such a task!? Better sacrifice accomplishments than omit this all essential instruction ... Some acquaintance with the first principles of physiology and the elementary truths of psychology is indispensable for the right bringing up of children. ... Here are the indisputable facts: that the development of children in mind and body follows certain laws; that unless these laws are in some degree conformed to by parents, death is inevitable; that unless they are in a great degree conformed to, and that only when they are completely conformed to, can a perfect maturity be reached. Judge, then, whether all who may one day be parents should not strive with some anxiety to learn what these laws are." (Herbert Spencer, Education)

How Parents Usually Proceed.—The parent begins instinctively by regarding his child as an unwritten tablet, and is filled with great resolves as to what he shall write thereon. By-and-by, traits of disposition appear, the child has little ways of his own; and, at first, every new display of personality is a delightful surprise. That the infant should show pleasure at the sight of his father, that his face should cloud in sympathy with his mother, must always be wonderful to us. But the wonder stales; his parents are used to the fact by the time the child shows himself as a complete human being like themselves, with affections, desires, powers; taking to his book, perhaps, as a duck to the water; or to the games which shall make a man of him. The notion of doing all for the child with which the parents began gradually recedes. So soon as he shows that he has a way of his own he is encouraged to take it. Father and mother have no greater delight than to watch the individuality of their child unfold as a flower unfolds. But Othello loses his occupation. The more the child shapes his own course, the less do the parents find to do, beyond feeding him with food convenient, whether of love, or thought, or of bodily meat and drink. And here, we may notice, the parents need only supply; the child knows well enough how to appropriate. The parents' chief care is, that that which they supply shall be wholesome and nourishing, whether in the way of picture books, lessons, playmates, bread and milk, or mother's love. This is education as most parents understand it, with more of meat, more of love, more of culture, according to their kind and degree. They let their children alone, allowing human nature to develop on its own lines, modified by facts of environment and descent.

Nothing could be better for the child than this 'masterly inactivity,' so far as it goes. It is well he should be let grow and helped to grow according to his nature; and so long as the parents do not step in to spoil him, much good and no very evident harm comes of letting him alone. But this philosophy of 'let him be,' while it covers a part, does not cover the serious part of the parents' calling; does not touch the strenuous incessant efforts upon lines of law which go to the producing of a human being at his best.

Nothing is trivial that concerns a child; his foolish-seeming words and ways are pregnant with meaning for the wise. It is in the infinitely little we must study in the infinitely great; and the vast possibilities, and the right direction of education, are indicated in the open book of the little child's thoughts.

A generation ago, a great teacher amongst us never wearied of reiterating that in the Divine plan "the family is the unit of the nation": not the individual, but the family. There is a great deal of teaching in the phrase, but this lies on the surface; the whole is greater than the part, the whole contains the part, owns the part, orders the part; and this being so, the children are the property of the nation, to be brought up for the nation as is best for the nation, and not according to the whim of individual parents. The law is for the punishment of evil doers, for the praise of them that do well; so, practically, parents have very free play; but it is as well we should remember that the children are a national trust whose bringing up is the concern of all—even of those unmarried and childless persons whose part in the game is the rather dreary one of 'looking on.'

I.—A Method of Education

Traditional Methods of Education.—Never was it more necessary for parents to face for themselves this question of education in all its bearings. Hitherto, children have been brought up upon traditional methods mainly. The experience of our ancestors, floating in a vast number of educational maxims, is handed on from lip to lip; and few or many of these maxims form the educational code of every household.

But we hardly take in how complete a revolution advancing science is effecting in the theory of education. The traditions of the elders have been tried and found wanting; it will be long before the axioms of the new school pass into the common currency; and, in the meantime, parents are thrown upon their own resources, and absolutely must weigh principles, and adopt a method, of education for themselves.

For instance, according to the former code, a mother might use her slipper now and then, to good effect and without blame; but now, the person of the child is, whether rightly or wrongly, held sacred and the infliction of pain for moral purposes is pretty generally disallowed.

Again, the old rule of the children's table was, 'the plainer the better, and let hunger bring sauce'; now the children's diet must be at least as nourishing and as varied as that of their elders; and appetite, the cravings for certain kinds of food, hitherto a vicious tendency to be repressed, is now within certain limitations the parents' most trustworthy guide in arranging a dietary for their children.

That children should be trained to endure hardness, was a principle of the old regime. "I shall never make a sailor if I can't face the wind and rain," said a little fellow of five who was taken out on a bitter night to see a torchlight procession; and, though, shaking with cold, he declined the shelter of a shed. Nowadays, the shed is everything; the children must not be permitted to suffer from fatigue or exposure.

That children should do as they are bid, mind their books, and take pleasure as it offers when nothing stands in the way, sums up the old theory; now, the pleasures of children are apt to be made more account than their duties.

Formerly, they were brought up in subjection; now, the elders give place, and the world is made for the children.

English people rarely go so far as the parents of that story in French Home Life, who arrived an hour late at a dinner party, because they had been desired by their girl of three to undress and go to bed when she did, and were able to steal away only when the child was asleep. We do not go so far, but that is the direction in which we are now moving; and how far the new theories of education are wise and humane, the outcome of more widely spread physiological and psychological knowledge, and how far they just pander to child worship to which we are all succumbing, is not a question to be decided off hand.

At any rate, it is not too much to say that a parent who does not follow reasonably a method of education, fully thought out, fails—now, more than ever before—to fulfil the claims his children have upon him.

Method a Way to an End.—Method implies two things—a way to an end, and a step by step progress in that way. Further, the following of a method implies an idea, a mental image, of the end of object to be arrived at. What do you propose that education shall effect in and for your child? Again, method is natural; easy, yielding, unobtrusive, simple as the ways of Nature herself; yet, watchful, careful, all pervading, all compelling. Method, with the end of education in view, presses the most unlikely matters into service to bring about that end; but with no more tiresome mechanism than the sun employs when it makes the winds to blow and the waters to flow only by shining. The parent who sees his way—that is, the exact force of method—to educate his child, will make use of every circumstance of the child's life almost without intention on his own part, so easy and spontaneous is a method of education based upon Natural Law. Does the child eat or drink, does he come, or go, or play—all the time he is being educated, though he is as little aware of it as he is of the act of breathing. There is always the danger that a method, a bona fide method, should degenerate into a mere system. The Kindergarten Method, for instance, deserves the name, as having been conceived and perfected by large hearted educators to aid the many sided evolution of the living, growing, most complex human being; but what a miserable wooden system does it become in the hands of ignorant practitioners!

A System easier than a Method.—A 'system of education' is an alluring fancy; more so, on some counts, than a method, because it is pledged to more definite calculable results. By means of a system certain developments may be brought about through the observance of given rules. Shorthand, dancing, how to pass examinations, how to become a good accountant, or a woman of society, may all be learned upon systems.

System—the observing of rules until the habit of doing certain things, of behaving in certain ways, is confirmed, and, therefore, the art is acquired—is so successful in achieving precise results, that it is no wonder there should be endless attempts to straiten the whole field of education to the limits of a system.

If a human being were a machine, education could do more for him than to set him in action in prescribed ways, and the work of the educator would be simply to adopt a good working system or set of systems.

But the educator has to deal with a self-acting, self-developing being, and his business is to guide, and assist in, the production of the latent good in that being, the dissipation of the latent evil, the preparation of the child to take his place in the world at his best, with every capacity for good that is in him developed into a power.

Though system is a highly useful as an instrument of education, a 'system of education' is mischievous, as producing only mechanical action instead of the vital growth and movement of a living being.

It is worth while to point out the differing characters of a system and a method, because parents let themselves be run away with often enough by some plausible 'system,' the object of which is to produce development in one direction—of the muscles, of the memory, of the reasoning faculty—were a complete all-round education. This easy satisfaction arises from the sluggishness of human nature, to which any definite scheme is more agreeable than the constant watchfulness, the unforeseen action, called for when the whole of a child's existence is to be used as the means of his education. But who is sufficient for an education so comprehensive, so incessant? A parent may be willing to undergo any definite labours for his child's sake; but to be always catering to his behoof, always contriving that circumstances shall play upon him for his good, is the part of a god and not of a man! A reasonable objection enough, if one looks upon education as an endless series of independent efforts, each to be thought out and acted out on the spur of the moment; but the fact is, that a few broad essential principles cover the whole field, and these once fully laid hold of, it is as easy and natural to act upon them as it is to act upon our knowledge of such facts as that fire burns and water flows. My endeavour in this and the following chapters will be to put these few fundamental principles before you in their practical bearing. Meantime, let us consider one or two preliminary questions.

II.—The Child's Estate

The Child in the Midst.—And first, let us consider where and what the little being is who is entrusted to the care of human parents. A tablet to be written upon? A twig to be bent? Wax to be moulded? Very likely; but he is much more—a being belonging to an altogether higher estate than ours; as it were, a prince committed to the fostering care of peasants. Hear Wordsworth's estimate of the child's estate:—

"Our birth is but a sleep and a forgetting:
The soul that rises with us, our life's star,
Hath had elsewhere in its setting,
And cometh from afar;
Not in entire forgetfulness,
And not in utter nakedness,
But in trailing clouds of glory do we come
From God, who is our home:
Heaven lies about us in our infancy!

Thou, whose exterior semblance doth belie
Thy soul's immensity;
Thou best philosopher, who yet dost keep
Thy heritage; thou eye among the blind,
That, deaf and silent, read'st the eternal deep,
Haunted for ever by the eternal mind
Mighty Prophet! Seer blest!
On whom those truths do rest,
Which we are toiling all our lives to find
Thou, over whom they immortality
Broods like a day, a master o'er a slave,
A presence which is not be put by;
Thou little child, yet glorious in the might
Of heaven born freedom, on they being's height"—

and so on, through the whole of that great ode [Intimiations of Immortality from Reflections of Early Childhood], which next after the Bible, shows the deepest insight into what is peculiar to the children in their nature and estate. "Of such is the kingdom of heaven." "Except ye become as little children ye shall in no case enter the kingdom of heaven." "Who is the greatest in the kingdom of heaven?" "And He called a little child, and set him in the midst." Here is the Divine estimate of the child's estate. It is worth while for parents to ponder every utterance in the Gospels about these children, divesting themselves of the notion that these sayings belong, in the first place, to the grown up people who have become as little children. What these profound sayings are, and how much they may mean, it is beyond us to discuss here; only they appear to cover far more than Wordsworth claims for the children in his sublimest reach

"Trailing clouds of glory do we come
From God, who is our home."

Code of Education in the Gospels.—It may surprise parents who have not given much attention to the subject to discover also a code of education in the Gospels, expressly laid down by Christ. It is summed up in three commandments, and all three have a negative character, as if the chief thing required of grown-up people is that they should do no sort of injury to the children: Take heed that ye *offend* not—*despise* not—*hinder* not—one of these little ones.

So run the three educational laws of the New Testament, which, when separately examined, appear to me to cover all the help we can give the children and all the harm we can save them from—that is, whatever is included in training up a child in the way he should go. Let us look upon these three great laws as prohibitive, in order to clear the ground for the consideration of a method of education; for if we once settle with ourselves what we may not do, we are greatly helped to see what we may do, and must do. But, as a matter of fact, the positive is included in the negative, what we are bound to do for the child in what we are forbidden to do to his hurt.

III.—Offending the Children

Offences.—The first and second of the Divine edicts appear to include our sins of commission and of omission against the children: we offend them, when we do by them that which we ought not to have done; we despise them, when we leave undone those things which, for their sakes, we ought to have done. An offence, we know, is literally a stumbling-block, that which trips up the walker and causes him to fall. Mothers know what it is to clear the floor of every obstacle when a baby takes his unsteady little runs from chair to chair, from one pair of loving arms to another. The table-leg, the child's toy on the floor, which has caused a fall and a pitiful cry, is a thing to be deplored; why did not somebody put it out of the way, so that the baby should not stumble? But the little child is going out into the world with uncertain tottering steps in many directions. There are causes of stumbling not so easy to remove as an offending footstool; and woe to him who causes the child to fall!

Children are born Law-abiding.—'Naughty baby!' says the mother; and the child's eyes droop, and a flush rises over neck and brow. It is very wonderful; very 'funny,' some people think, and say, 'Naughty baby!' when the baby is sweetly good, to amuse themselves with the sight of the infant soul rising visibly before their eyes. But what does it mean, this display of feeling, conscience, in the child, before any human teaching can have reached him? No less than this, that he is born a law abiding being, with a sense of may, and must not, of right and wrong. That is how children are sent into the world with the warning, "Take heed that ye offend not one of these little ones." And—this being so—who has not met big girls and boys, the children of right-minded parents, who yet do not know what must means, who are not moved by ought, whose hearts feel no stir at the solemn name of Duty, who know no higher rule of life than 'I want,' and 'I don't want,' 'I like,' and 'I don't like'? Heaven help parents and children when it has come to that!

But how has it been brought about that the babe, with an acute sense of right and wrong even when it can understand little of human speech, should grow into the boy or girl already proving 'the curse of lawless heart'? By slow degrees, here a little and there a little, as all that is good or bad in character comes to pass. 'Naughty!' says the mother, again, when a little hand is thrust into the sugar bowl; and when a pair of roguish eyes seek hers furtively, to measure, as they do unerringly, how far the little pilferer may go. It is very amusing; the mother 'cannot help laughing'; and the little trespass is allowed to pass: and, what the poor mother has not thought of, an offence, a cause of stumbling, has been cast into the path of her two-year-old child. He has learned already that which is 'naughty' may yet be done with some impunity, and he goes on improving his knowledge. It is needless to continue; everybody knows the steps by which the mother's 'no' comes to be disregarded, her refusal teased into consent. The child has learned to believe that he has nothing to overcome but his mother's disinclination; if she choose to let him do this and that, there is no reason why she should not; he can make her choose to let him do the next thing forbidden, and then he may do it. The next step in the argument is not too great for childish wits: if his mother does what she chooses, of course he will do what he chooses, if he can; and henceforward the child's life becomes an endless struggle to get his own way; a struggle in which a parent is pretty sure to be worsted, having many things to think of, while the child sticks persistently to the thing which has his fancy for the moment.

They must perceive that their Governors are Law-compelled.—Where is the beginning of this tangle, spoiling the lives of parent and child alike? In this: that the mother began with no sufficient sense of duty; she thought herself free to allow and disallow, to say and unsay, at pleasure, as if the child were hers to do what she liked with. The child has never discovered a background of must behind is mother's decisions; he does not know that she must not let him break his sister's playthings, gorge himself with cake, spoil the pleasure of other people, because these things are not right. Let the child perceive that his parents are law-compelled as well as he, that they simply cannot allow him to do the things which have been forbidden, and he submits with the sweet meekness which belongs to his age. To give reasons to a child is usually out of place, and is a sacrifice of parental dignity; but he is quick enough to read the 'must' and 'ought' which rule her, in his mother's face and manner, and in the fact that she is not to be moved from a resolution on any question of right and wrong.

Parents may Offend their Children by Disregarding the Laws of Health.—This, of allowing him in what is wrong, is only one of the many ways in which the loving mother may offend her child. Through ignorance, or wilfulness, which is worse, she may not only allow wrong in him, but do wrong by him. She may cast a stumbling-block in the way of physical life by giving him unwholesome food, letting him sleep and live in ill-ventilated rooms, by disregarding any or every of the simple laws of health, ignorance of which is hardly to be excused in the face of the pains taken by scientific men to bring this necessary knowledge within the reach of every one.

And the Intellectual Life.—Almost as bad is the way the child's intellectual life may be wrecked at its outset by a round of dreary, dawdling lessons in which definite progress is the last thing made or expected, and which, so far from educating in any true sense, stultify his wits in a way he never gets over. Many a little girl, especially, leaves the home schoolroom with a distaste for all manner of learning, an aversion to mental effort, which lasts her lifetime, and that is why she grows up to read little but trashy novels, and to talk all day about her clothes.

And of the Moral Life.—And her affections—the movements of the outgoing tender child-heart—how are they treated? There are few mothers who do not take pains to cherish the family affections; but when the child comes to have dealings with outsiders, do not worldly maxims and motives ever nip the buds of childish love? Far worse than this happens when the child's love finds no natural outlets within her home: when she is the plain or the dull child of the family, and is left out in the cold, while the parents' affection is lavished on the rest. Of course she does not love her brothers and sisters, who monopolise what should have been hers too. And how is she to love her parents? Nobody knows the real anguish which many a child in the nursery suffers from this cause, nor how many lives are embittered and spoiled through the suppression of these childish affections. "My childhood was made miserable," a lady said to me a while ago, "by my mother's doting fondness for my little brother; there was not a day when she did not make me wretched by coming into the nursery to fondle and play with him, and all the time she had not a word nor a look nor a smile for me, any more than if I had not been in the room. I have never got over it; she is very kind to me now, but I never feel quite natural with her. And how can we two, brother and sister, feel for each other as we should if we had grown up together in love in the nursery?"

IV.—Despising the Children

Children should have the best of their Mothers.—Suppose that a mother may offend her child, how is it possible that she should not despise him? "Despise: to have a low opinion of, to undervalue"—thus the dictionary; and, as a matter of fact, however much we may delight in them, we grown-up people have far too low an opinion of children. If the mother did not undervalue her child, would she leave him to the society of an ignorant nursemaid during the early years when his whole nature is, like the photographer's sensitive plate, receiving momently indelible impressions? Not but that his nurse is good for the child. Very likely it would not answer for educated people to have their children always about them. The constant society of his parents might be too stimulating for the child; and frequent change of thought, and the society of other people, make the mother all the fresher for her children. But they should have the best of their mother, her freshest, brightest hours; while, at the same time, she is careful to choose her nurses wisely, train them carefully, and keep a vigilant eye upon all that goes on in the nursery.

'Nurse.'—Mere coarseness and rudeness in his nurse does the tender child lasting harm. Many a child leaves the nursery with his moral sense blunted, and with an alienation from his heavenly Father set up which many last his lifetime. For the child's moral sense is exceedingly quick; he is all eyes and ears for the slightest act or word of unfairness, deception, shiftiness. His nurse says, "If you'll be a good boy, I won't tell"; and the child learns that things may be concealed from his mother, who should be to him as God, knowing all his good and evil. And it is not as if the child noted the slips of his elders with aversion. He knows better, it is true, but then he does not trust his own intuitions; he shapes his life on any pattern set before him, and with the fatal tint of human nature upon him he is more ready to imitate a bad pattern than a good. Give him a nurse who is coarse, violent, and tricky, and before the child is able to speak plainly he will have caught these dispositions.

Children's Faults are Serious.—One of many ways in which parents are apt to have too low an opinion of their children is in the matter of their faults. A little child shows some ugly trait—he is greedy, and gobbles up his sister's share of the goodies as well as his own; he is vindictive, ready to bite or fight the hand that offends him; he tells a lie;—no, he did not touch the sugar-bowl or the jam-pot. The mother puts off the evil day: she knows she must sometime reckon with the child for those offences, but in the meantime she says, "Oh, it does not matter this time; he is very little, and will know better by-and-by." To put the thing on no higher grounds, what happy days for herself and her children would the mother secure if she would keep watch at the place of the letting out of waters! If the mother settle it in her own mind that the child never does wrong without being aware of his wrong-doing, she will see that is not too young to have his fault corrected or prevented. Deal with a child on his first offence, and a grieved look is enough to convict the little transgressor; but let him go on until a habit of wrong-doing is formed, and the cure is a slow one; then the mother has no chance until she has formed in him a contrary habit of well-doing. To laugh a ugly tempers and let them pass because the child is small, is to sow the wind.

V.—Hindering the Children

A Child's Relationship with Almighty God.—The most fatal way of despising the child falls under the third educational law of the Gospels; it is to overlook and make light of his natural relationship with Almighty God. "Suffer the little children to come unto Me," says the Saviour, as if that were the natural thing for the children to do, the thing they do when they are not hindered by their elders. And perhaps it is not too beautiful a thing to believe in this redeemed world, that, as the babe turns to his mother though he has no power to say her name, as the flowers turn to the sun, so the hearts of the children turn to their Saviour and God with unconscious delight and trust.

Nursery Theology.—Now listen to what goes on in many a nursery:—'God does not love you, you naughty, wicked boy!' 'He will send you to the bad, wicked place!,' and so on; and this is all the practical teaching about the ways of his 'almighty Lover' that the child gets!—never a word of how God does love and cherish the little children all day long, and fill their hours with delight. Add to this, listless perfunctory prayers, idle discussions of Divine things in their presence, light use of holy words, few signs whereby the child can read that the things of God are more to his parents than any things of the world, and the child is hindered, tacitly forbidden to "come unto Me,"—and this, often, by parents who in the depths of their hearts desire nothing in comparison with God. This mischief lies in that same foolish undervaluing of the children, in the notion that the child can have no spiritual life until it please his elders to kindle the flame.

VI.—Conditions of Healthy Brain-Activity

Having just glanced at the wide region of forbidden ground, we are prepared to consider what it is, definitely and positively, that the mother owes to her child under the name of Education.

All Mind Labour means Wear of Brain.—And first of all, the more educable powers of the child—his intelligence, his will, his moral feelings—have their seat in his brain; that is to say, as the eye is the organ of sight, so is the brain, or some part of it, the organ of thought and will, of love and worship. Authorities differ as to how far it is possible to localise the functions of the brain; but this at least seems pretty clear—that none of the functions of mind are performed without real activity in the mass of grey and white nervous matter named 'the brain.' Now, this is not a matter for the physiologist alone, but for every mother and father of a family; because that wonderful brain, by means of which we do our thinking, if it is to act healthily and in harmony with the healthful action of the members, should act only under such conditions of exercise, rest, and nutrition as secure health in every other part of the body.

Exercise.—Most of us have met with a few eccentric and a good many silly persons, concerning whom the question forces itself, Were these people born with less brain power than others? Probably not; but if they were allowed to grow up without the daily habit of appropriate moral and mental work, if they were allowed to dawdle through youth without regular and sustained efforts of thought or will, the result would be the same, and the brain which should have been invigorated by daily exercise has become flabby and feeble as a healthy arm would be after carried for years in a sling. The large active brain is not content with entire idleness; it strikes out lines for itself and works fitfully, and the man or woman becomes eccentric, because wholesome mental effort, like moral, must be carried on under the discipline of rules. A shrewd writer suggests that mental indolence may have been in some measure the cause of those pitiable attacks of derangement and depression from which poor Cowper suffered; the making of graceful verses when the 'maggot bit' did not afford him the amount of mental labour necessary for his well being.

The outcome of which is—Do not let the children pass a day without distinct efforts, intellectual, moral, volitional; let them brace themselves to understand; let them compel themselves to do and to bear; and let them do right at the sacrifice of ease and pleasure: and this for many higher reasons, but, in the first and lowest place, that the mere physical organ of mind and will may grow vigorous with work.

Rest.—Just as important is it that the brain should have due rest; that is, should rest and work alternately. And here two considerations come into play. In the first place, when the brain is actively at work it is treated as is every other organ of the body in the same circumstances; that is to say, a large additional supply of blood is attracted to the head for the nourishment of the organ which is spending its substance in hard work. Now, there is not an indefinite quantity of what we will for the moment call surplus blood in the vessels. The supply is regulated on the principle that only one set of organs shall be excessively active at one time—now the limbs, now the digestive organs, now the brain; and all the blood in the body that can be spared goes to the support of those organs which, for the time being, are in a state of labour.

Rest after Meals.—The child has just had his dinner, the meal of the day which most severely taxes his digestive organs; for as much as two or three hours after, much labour is going on in these organs, and the blood that can be spared from elsewhere is present to assist. Now, send the child out for a long walk immediately after dinner—the blood goes to the labouring extremities, and the food is left half digested; give the child a regular course of such dinners and walks, and he will grow up a dyspeptic. Set him to his books after a heavy meal, and the case is as bad; the blood which should have been assisting in the digestion of the meal goes to the labouring brain.

It follows that the hours for lessons should be carefully chosen, after periods of mental rest—sleep or play, for instance—and when there is no excessive activity in any other part of the system. Thus, the morning, after breakfast (the digestion of which lighter meal is not a severe task), is much the best time for lessons and every sort of mental work; if the whole afternoon cannot be spared for out-of-door recreation, that is the time for mechanical tasks such as needlework, drawing, practising; the children's wits are bright enough in the evening, but the drawback to evening work is, that the brain, once excited, is inclined to carry on its labours beyond bed-time, and dreams, wakefulness, and uneasy sleep attend the poor child who has been at work until the last minute. If the elder children must work in the evening, they should have at least one or two pleasant social hours before they go to bed; but, indeed, we owe it to the children to abolish evening 'preparation.'

Change of Occupation.—"There is," says Huxley, "no satisfactory proof at present, that the manifestation of any particular kind of mental faculty is especially allotted to, or connected with, the activity of any particular region or the cerebral hemispheres," a dictum against the phrenologists, but coming to us on too high authority to be disputed. It is not possible to localise the 'faculties'—to say you are cautious with this fraction of your brain, and music-loving with another; but this much is certain, and is very important to the educator: the brain, or some portion of the brain, becomes exhausted when any given function has been exercised too long. The child has been doing sums for some time, and is getting unaccountably stupid: take away his slate and let him read history, and you find his wits fresh again. Imagination, which has had no part in the sums, is called into play by the history lesson, and the child brings a lively unexhausted power to his new work. School time-tables are usually drawn up with a view to give the brain of the child variety of work; but the secret of weariness children often show in the home school room is, that no such judicious change of lessons is contrived.

Nourishment.—Again, the brain cannot do its work well unless it be abundantly and suitably nourished; somebody has made a calculation of how many ounces of brain went to the production of such a work—say Paradise Lost—how many to such another, and so on. Without going into mental arithmetic of this nature, we may say with safety that every sort of intellectual activity wastes the tissues of the brain; a network of vessels supplies an enormous quantity of blood to the organ, to make up for this waste of material; and the vigour and health of the brain depend upon the quality and quantity of this blood-supply.

Certain Causes affect the Quality of the Blood.—Now, the quality of the blood is affected by three or four causes. In the first place, the blood is elaborated from the food; the more nutritious and easy of digestion the food, the more vital will be the properties of the blood. The food must be varied, too, a mixed diet, because various ingredients are required to make up for the various waste in the tissues. The children are shocking spendthrifts; their endless goings and comings, their restlessness, their energy, the very wagging of their tongues, all mean expenditure of substance: the loss is not appreciable, but they lose something by every sudden sally, out of doors or within. No doubt the gain of power which results from exercise is more than compensation for the loss of substance; but, all the same, this loss must be promptly made good. And not only is the body of the child more active, proportionately, than that of the man: the child's brain as compared with a man's is in a perpetual flutter of endeavour. It is calculated that though the brain of a man weighs no more than a fortieth part of his body, yet a fifth or sixth of his whole complement of blood goes to nourish this delicate and intensely active organ; but, in the child's case, a considerably larger proportion of the blood that is in him is spent on the sustenance of his brain. And all the time, with these excessive demands upon him, the child has to grow! not merely to make up for waste, but to produce new substance in brain and body.

Concerning Meals.—What is the obvious conclusion? That the child must be well fed. Half the people of low vitality we come across are the victims of low-feeding during their childhood; and that more often because their parents were not alive to their duty in this respect, then because they were not in a position to afford their children the diet necessary to their full physical and mental development. Regular meals at, usually, unbroken intervals—dinner, never more than five hours after breakfast; luncheon, unnecessary; animal food, once certainly, in some lighter form, twice a day—are the suggestions of common sense followed out in most well-regulated households. But it is not the food which is eaten, but the food which is digested, that nourishes body and brain. And here so many considerations press, that we can only glance at two or three of the most obvious. Everybody knows that children should not eat pastry, or pork, or fried meats, or cheese, or rich, highly-flavoured food of any description; that pepper, mustard, and vinegar, sauces and spices, should be forbidden, with new bread, rich cakes and jams, like plum or gooseberry, in which the leathery coat of the fruit is preserved; that milk, or milk and water, and that not too warm, or cocoa, is the best drink for children, and that they should be trained not to drink until they have finished eating; that fresh fruit at breakfast is invaluable; that, as serving the same end, oatmeal porridge and treacle, and the fat of toasted bacon, are valuable breakfast foods; and that a glass of water, also, taken the last thing at night, and the first thing in the morning, is useful in promoting those regular habits on which much of the comfort of life depends.

Talk at Meals.—All this and much of the same kind it is needless to urge; but again let me say, it is digested food that nourishes the system, and people are apt to forget how far mental and moral conditions affect the processes of digestion. The fact is, that the gastric juices which act as solvents to the viands are only secreted freely when the mind is in a cheerful and contented frame. If the child dislike his dinner, he swallows it, but the digestion of that distasteful meal is a laborious, much-impeded process: if the meal be eaten in silence, unrelieved by pleasant chat, the child loses much of the 'good' of his dinner. Hence it is not a matter of pampering them at all, but a matter of health, of due nutrition, that the children should enjoy their food, and that their meals should be eaten in gladness; though, by the way, joyful excitement is as mischievous as its opposite in destroying that even, cheerful tenor of mind favourable to the processes of digestion. No pains should be spared to make the hours of meeting round the family table the brightest hours of the day. This is supposing that the children are allowed to sit at the same table with their parents; and, if it is possible! to let them do so at every meal excepting a late dinner, the advantage to the little people is incalculable. Here is the parents' opportunity to train them in manners and morals, to cement family love, and to accustom the children to habits, such as that of thorough mastication, for instance, as important on the score of health as on that of propriety.

Variety in Meals.—But, given pleasant surroundings and excellent food, and even then the requirements of these exacting little people are not fully met: plain as their food should be, they must have variety. A leg of mutton every Tuesday, the same cold on Wednesday, and hashed on Thursday, may be very good food; but the child who has this diet week after week is inadequately nourished, simply because he is tired of it. The mother should contrive a rotation for her children that will last at least a fortnight, without the same dinner recurring twice. Fish, especially if the children dine off it without meat to follow, is excellent as a change, the more so as it is rich in phosphorus—a valuable brain food. The children's puddings deserve a good deal of consideration, because they do not commonly care for fatty foods, but prefer to derive the warmth of their bodies from the starch and sugar of their puddings. But give them a variety; do not let it be 'everlasting tapioca.' Even for tea and breakfast the wise mother does not say, 'I always give my children' so and so. They should not have anything 'always'; every meal should have some little surprise. But is this the way, to make them think overmuch of what they shall eat and drink? On the contrary, it is the underfed children who are greedy, and unfit to be trusted with any unusual delicacy.

Air as important as Food.—The quality of the blood depends almost as much on the air we breathe as on the food we eat; in the course of every two or three minutes, all the blood in the body passes through the endless ramifications of the lungs, for no other purpose than that, during the instant of its passage, it should be acted upon by the oxygen contained in the air which is drawn into the lungs in the act of breathing. But what can happen to the blood in the course of an exposure of so short duration? Just this- the whole character, the very colour, of the blood is changed: it enters the lungs spoiled, no longer capable of sustaining life; it leaves them, a pure vital fluid. Now, observe, the blood is only fully oxygenated when the air contains its full proportion of oxygen, and every breathing and burning object withdraws some oxygen from the atmosphere. Hence the importance of giving the children daily airings, and abundant exercise of limb and lung in unvitiated, unimpoverished air.

The Children Walk every Day.—'The children walk every day; they are never out less than an hour when the weather is suitable.' That is better than nothing; so is this: An East London school mistress notices the pale looks of one of her best girls. "Have you had any dinner, Nellie?" "Ye-es" (with hesitation). "What have you had?" "Mother gave Jessie and me a halfpenny to buy our dinners, and we bought a haporth of aniseed drops—they go further than bread"—with an appeal in her eyes against possible censure for extravagance. Children do not develop at their best upon aniseed drops for dinner, nor upon an hour's 'constitutional' daily. Possibly science will bring home to us more and more the fact that animal life, pent under cover, is supported under artificial conditions, just as is plant life in a glass house. Here is where most Continental nations have the advantage over us; they keep up the habit of out-of-door life; and as a consequence, the average Frenchman, German, Italian, Bulgarian, is more joyous, more simple, and more hardy than the average Englishman Climate? Did not Charles II—and he knew—declare for the climate of England because you could be abroad "more hours in the day and more days in the year" in England than "in any other country"? We lose sight of the fact that we are not like the historical personage who live upon "nothing but victuals and drink." "You can't live upon air!" we say to the invalid who can't eat. No; we cannot live upon air; but, if we must choose among the three sustainers of life, air will support us the longest. We know all about it; we are deadly weary of the subject; let but the tail of your eye catch 'oxygenation' on a page, and the well trained organ skips that paragraph of its own accord. No need to tell Macaulay's schoolboy, or anybody else, how the blood of the body is brought to the lungs and there spread about in a huge extent of innumerable 'pipes' that it may be exposed momentarily to the oxygen of the air; how the air is made to blow upon the blood, so spread out in readiness, by the bellows-like action of breathing; how the air penetrates the very thin walls of the pipes; and then, behold, a magical (or chemical) transmutation; the worthless sewage of the system becomes on the instant the rich vivifying fluid whose function it is to build up the tissues of muscle and nerve. And the Prospero that wears the cloak? Oxygen, his name!; and the marvel that he effects within us some fifteen times in the course of a minute is possibly without parallel in the whole array of marvels which we 'tot up' with easy familiarity, setting down 'life,' and carrying—a cypher!

Oxygenation has its Limitations.—We know all about it; what we forget, perhaps, is, that even oxygen has its limitation: nothing can act but where it is, and, waste attends work, hold true for this vital gas as for other matters. Fire and lamp and breathing beings are all consumers of the oxygen which sustains them. What follows? Why, that this element, which is present in the ration of twenty-three parts to the hundred in pure air, is subject to an enormous drain within the four walls of a house, where the air is more or less stationary. I am not speaking just now of the vitiation of air—only of the drain upon its life-sustaining element. Think, again, of the heavy drain upon the oxygen which must support the multitudinous fires and many breathing beings congregated in a large town! 'What follows?' is a strictly vital question. Man can enjoy the full measure of vigorous joyous existence possible to him only when his blood is fully aerated; and this takes place when the air he inhales contains its full complement of oxygen. Is it too much to say that vitality is reduced, other things being equal in proportion as persons are house dwellers rather than open-air dwellers? The impoverished air sustains life at a low and feeble level; wherefore in the great towns, stature dwindles, the chest contracts, men hardly live to see their children's children. True, we must needs have houses for shelter from the weather by day and for rest at night; but in proportion as we cease to make our houses 'comfortable,' as we regard them merely as necessary shelters when we cannot be out of doors, shall we enjoy to the full the vigorous vitality possible to us.

Unchanged Air.—Parents of pale faced town children, think of these things! The gutter children who feed on the pickings of the streets are better off (and healthier looking) in this one respect than your cherished darlings, because they have more of the first essential of life—air. There is some circulation of air even in the slums of the city, and the child who spends its days in the streets is better supplied with oxygen than he who spends most of his hours in the unchanged air of a spacious apartment. But it is not the air of the streets the children want. It is the delicious life-giving air of the country. The outlay of the children in living is enormously in excess of the outlay of the adult. The endless activity of the child, while it develops muscle, is kept up at the expense of very great waste of tissue. It is the blood which carries material for the reparation of this loss. The child must grow, every part of him, and it is the blood which brings material for the building up new tissues. Again, we know the brain is, out of all proportion to its size, the great consumer of the blood supply, but the brain of the child, what with its eager activity, what with its twofold growth, is insatiable in its demands!

'I feed Alice on beef tea.'—'I feed Alice on beef tea, cod-liver oil, and all sorts of nourishing things; but it's very disheartening, the child doesn't gain flesh!' It is probable that Alice breathes for twenty-two of the twenty-four hours the impoverished and more or less vitiated air pent within the four walls of a house. The child is practically starving; for the food she eats is very imperfectly and inadequately converted into the aerated blood that feeds the tissues of the body.

And if she is suffering from bodily inanition, what about the eager, active, curious, hungering mind of the little girl? 'Oh, she has her lessons regularly every day.' Probably: but lessons which deal with words, only the signs of things, are not what the child wants. There is no knowledge so appropriate to the early years of a child as that of the name and look and behaviour in situ of every natural object he can get at. "He hath so done His marvellous works that they ought to be had in remembrance."

"Three years she grew in sun and shower,
Then Nature said, 'A lovelier flower
On earth was never sown:
This child I to myself will take:
She shall be mine, and I will make
A lady of my own.

" 'She shall be sportive as the fawn,
That wild with glee across the lawn
Or up the mountain springs;
And hers shall be the breathing balm,
And hers the silence and the calm
Of mute, insensate things.

" 'The stars of midnight shall be dear
To her; and she shall lean her ear
In many a secret place
Where rivulets dance their wayward round,
And beauty born of murmuring sound
Shall pass into her face.' "

Indoor Airings.—About out-of-door airings we shall have occasion to speak more fully; but indoor airings are truly as important, because, if the tissues be nourished upon impure blood for all the hours the child spends in the house, the mischief will not be mended in the shorter intervals spent out of doors. Put two or three breathing bodies, as well as fire and gas, into a room, and it is incredible how soon the air becomes vitiated unless it be constantly renewed; that is, unless the room be well ventilated. We know what is to come in out of the fresh air and complain that a room feels stuffy; but sit in the room a few minutes, and you get accustomed to its stuffiness; the senses are no longer a safe guide.

Ventilation.—Therefore, regular provision must be made for the ventilation of rooms regardless of the feelings of their inmates; at least an inch of window open at the top, day and night, renders a room tolerably safe, because it allows the escape of the vitiated air, which, being light, ascends, leaving room for the influx of colder, fresher air by cracks and crannies in doors and floors. An open chimney is a useful, though not a sufficient, ventilator; it is needless to say that the stopping-up of chimneys in sleeping-rooms is suicidal. It is particularly important to accustom children to sleep with an inch or two, or more, of open window all through the year—as much more as you like in the summer.

Night Air Wholesome.—There is a popular notion that night air is unwholesome; but if you reflect that wholesome air is that which contains its full complement of oxygen, and no more than its very small complement of carbonic acid gas, and that all burning objects—fire, furnace, gas-lamp—give forth carbonic acid gas and consume oxygen, you will see that night air is, in ordinary circumstances, more wholesome than day air, simply because there is a less exhaustive drain upon its vital gas. When the children are out of a room which they commonly occupy, day nursery or breakfast room, then is the opportunity to air it thoroughly by throwing windows and doors wide open and producing a thorough draught.

Sunshine.—But it is not only air, and pure air, the children must have if their blood is to be of the 'finest quality,' as the advertisements have it. Quite healthy blood is exceedingly rich in minute, red disc-like bodies, known as red corpuscles, which in favourable circumstances are produced freely in the blood itself. Now, it is observed that people who live much in the sunshine are of a ruddy countenance—that is, a great many of these red corpuscles are present in their blood; while the poor souls who live in cellars and sunless alleys have skins the colour of whity-brown paper. Therefore, it is concluded that light and sunshine are favourable to the production of red corpuscles in the blood; and, therefore—to this next 'therefore' is but a step for the mother—the children's rooms should be on the sunny side of the house, with a south aspect if possible. Indeed, the whole house should be kept light and bright for their sakes; trees and outbuildings that obstruct the sunshine and make the children's rooms dull should be removed without hesitation.

Free Perspiration.—Another point must be attended to, in order to secure that the brain be nourished by healthy blood. The blood receives and gets ride of the waste of the tissues, and one of the most important agents by means of which it does this necessary scavenger's work is the skin. Millions of invisible pores perforate the skin, each the mouth of a minute many-folded tube, and each such pore is employed without a moment's cessation, while the body is in health, in discharging perspiration—that is, the waste of the tissues—upon the skin.

Insensible Perspiration.—When the discharge is excessive, we are aware of moisture upon the skin; but, aware of it or not, the discharge is always going on; and, what is more, if it be checked, or if a considerable portion of the skin be glazed, so that it becomes impervious, death will result. This is why people die in consequence of scalds or burns which injure a large surface of the skin, although they do not touch any vital organ; multitudes of minute tubes which should carry off injurious matters from the blood are closed, and, though the remaining surface of the skin and the other excretory organs take extra work upon them, it is impossible to make good the loss of what may be called efficient drainage over a considerable area. Therefore, if the brain is to be duly nourished, it is important to keep the whole surface of the skin in a condition to throw off freely the excretion of blood.

Daily Bath and Porous Garments.—Two considerations follow: of the first, the necessity for the daily bath, followed by vigorous rubbing of the skin, it is needless to say a word here. But possibly it is not so well understood that children should be clothed in porous garments which admit of the instant passing off of the exhalations of the skin. Why did delicate women faint, or, at any rate, 'feel faint,' when it was the custom to go to church in sealskin coats? Why do people who sleep under down, or even under silk or cotton quilts, frequently rise unrefreshed? From the one cause: their coverings have impeded the passage of the insensible perspiration, and so have hindered the skin in its function of relieving the blood of impurities. It is surprising what a constant loss of vitality many people experience from no other cause than the unsuitable character of their clothing. The children cannot be better dressed throughout than in loosely woven woollen garments, flannels and serges, of varying thicknesses for summer and winter wear. Woollens have other advantages over cotton and linen materials besides that of being porous. Wool is a bad conductor, and therefore does not allow of the too free escape of the animal heat; and it is absorbent, and therefore relieves the skin of the clammy sensations which follow sensible perspiration. We should be the better for it if we could make up our minds to sleep in wool, discarding linen or cotton in favour of sheets made of some lightly woven woolen material.

We might say much on this one question, the due nutrition of brain, upon which the very possibility of healthy education depends. But something will have been effected if the reason why of only two or three practical rules of health is made so plain that they cannot be evaded without a sense of law-breaking.

I fear the reader may be inclined to think that I am inviting his attention for the most part to a few physiological matters—the lowest round of the educational ladder. The lowest round it may be, but yet it is the lowest round, the necessary step to all the rest. For it is not too much to say that, in our present state of being, intellectual, moral, even spiritual life and progress depend greatly upon physical conditions. That is to say, not that he who has a fine physique is necessarily a good and clever man; but that the good and clever man requires much animal substance to make up for the expenditure of tissue brought about in the exercise of his virtue and his intellect. For example, is it easier to be amiable, kindly, candid, with or without a headache or an attack of neuralgia?

VII—'The Reign of Law' in Education

Common Sense and Good Intentions.—Besides, though this physical culture of the brain may be only the groundwork of education, the method of it indicates what should be the method of all education; that is, orderly, regulated progress under the guidance of Law. The reason why education effects so much less than it should effect is just this—that in nine cases out of ten, sensible good parents trust too much to their common sense and their good intentions, forgetting that common sense must be at the pains to instruct itself in the nature of the case, and that well-intended efforts come to little if they are not carried on in obedience to divine laws, to be read in many cases, not in the Bible, but in the facts of life.

Law-abiding Lives often more blameless than Pious Lives.—It is a shame to believing people that many whose highest profession is that they do not know, and therefore do not believe, should produce more blameless lives, freer from flaws of temper, from the vice of selfishness, than do many sincerely religious people. It is a fact that will confront the children by-and-by, and one of which they require an explanation; and what is more, it is a fact that will have more weight, should it confront them in the person of a character which they cannot but esteem and love, than all the doctrinal teaching they have had in their lives. This appears to me the threatening danger to that confessed dependence upon and allegiance to Almighty God which we recognise as religion—not the wickedness, but the goodness of a school which refuses to admit any such dependence and allegiance.

My sense of this danger is my reason for offering the little I have to say upon the subject of education,—my sense of the danger, and the assurance I feel that it is no such great danger after all, but one that parents of the cultivated class are competent to deal with, and are precisely the only persons who can deal with it.

Mind and Matter equally governed by Law.—As for this superior morality of some non-believers, supposing we grant it, what does it amount to? Just to this, that the universe of mind, as the universe of matter, is governed by unwritten laws of God; that the child cannot blow soap bubbles or think his flitting thoughts otherwise than in obedience to divine laws; that all safety, progress, and success in life come out of obedience to law, to the laws of mental, moral or physical science, or of that spiritual science which the Bible unfolds; that it is possible to ascertain laws and keep laws without recognising the Lawgiver, and that those who do ascertain and keep any divine law inherit the blessing due to obedience, whatever be their attitude towards the Lawgiver; just as the man who goes out into blazing sunshine is warmed, though he may shut his eyes and decline to see the sun. Conversely, that they who take no pains to study the principles which govern human action and human thought miss the blessings of obedience to certain laws, though they may inherit the better blessings which come of acknowledged relationship with the Lawgiver.

Antagonism to Law shown by some Religious Persons.—These last blessings are so unspeakably satisfying, that often enough the believer who enjoys them wants no more. He opens his mouth and draws in his breath for the delight he has in the law, it is true; but it is the law of the spiritual life only. Towards the other laws of God which govern the universe he sometimes takes up an attitude of antagonism, almost of resistance, worthy of an infidel.

It is nothing to him that he is fearfully and wonderfully made; he does not care to know how the brain works, nor how the more subtle essence we call mind evolves and develops in obedience to laws. There are pious minds to which a desire to look into these things savours of unbelief, as if it were to dishonour the Almighty to perceive that He carries on His glorious works by means of glorious Laws. They will have to do with no laws excepting the laws of the kingdom of grace. In the meantime, the non-believer, who looks for no supernatural aids, lays himself out to discover and conform to all the laws which regulate natural life—physical, mental, moral; all the laws of God, in fact, excepting those of the spiritual life which the believer appropriates as his peculiar inheritance. But these laws which are left to Esau are laws of God also, and the observance of them is attended with such blessings, that the children of the believers say, Look, how is it that these who do not acknowledge the Law as of God are better than we who do?

Parents must acquaint themselves with the Principles of Physiology and Moral Science.—Now, believing parents have no right to lay up this crucial difficulty for their children. They have no right, for instance, to pray that their children may be made truthful, diligent, upright, and at the same time neglect to acquaint themselves with those principles of moral science the observance of which will guide into truthfulness, diligence, and uprightness of character. For this, also, is the law of God. Observe, not into the knowledge of God, the thing best worth living for: no mental science, and no moral science, is pledged to reveal that. What I contend for is, that these sciences have their part to play in the education of the human race, and that the parent may not disregard them with impunity. My endeavour in this and the following volumes of the series will be to sketch out roughly a method of education which, as resting upon a basis of natural law, may look, without presumption, to inherit the Divine blessing. Any sketch I can offer in this short compass must be very imperfect and very incomplete; but a hint here and there may be enough to put intelligent parents on profitable lines of thinking with regard to the education of their children.

Part II
Out-of-Door Life for the Children

I.—A Growing Time

Meals out of Doors.—People who live in the country know the value of fresh air very well, and their children live out of doors, with intervals within for sleeping and eating. As to the latter, even country people do not make full use of their opportunities. On fine days when it is warm enough to sit out with wraps, why should not tea and breakfast, everything but a hot dinner, be served out of doors? For we are an overwrought generation, running to nerves as a cabbage runs to seed; and every hour spent in the open is a clear gain, tending to the increase of brain power and bodily vigour, and to the lengthening of life itself. They who know what it is to have fevered skin and throbbing brain deliciously soothed by the cool touch of the air are inclined to make a new rule of life, Never be within doors when you can rightly be without.

Besides, the gain of an hour or two in the open air, there is this to be considered: meals taken al fresco are usually joyous, and there is nothing like gladness for converting meat and drink into healthy blood and tissue. All the time, too, the children are storing up memories of a happy childhood. Fifty years hence they will see the shadows of the boughs making patterns on the white tablecloth; and sunshine, children's laughter, hum of bees, and scent of flowers are being bottled up for after refreshment.

For Dwellers in Towns and Suburbs.—But it is only the people who live, so to speak, in their own gardens who can make a practice of giving their children tea out of doors. For the rest of us, and the most of us, who live in towns or the suburbs of towns, that is included in the larger question—How much time daily in the open air should the children have? And how is it possible to secure this for them? In this time of extraordinary pressure, educational and social, perhaps a mothers first duty to her children is to secure for them a quiet growing time, a full six years of passive receptive life, the waking part of it spent for the most part out in the fresh air. And this, not for the gain in bodily health alone—body and soul, heart and mind, are nourished with food convenient for them when the children are let alone, let to live without friction and without stimulus amongst happy influences which incline them to be good.

Possibilities of a Day in the Open.—I make a point, says a judicious mother, of sending my children out, weather permitting, for an hour in the winter, and two hours a day in the summer months. That is well; but it is not enough. In the first place, do not send them; if it is anyway possible, take them; for, although the children should be left much to themselves, there is a great deal to be done and a great deal to be prevented during these long hours in the open air. And long hours they should be; not two, but four, five, or six hours they should have on every tolerably fine day, from April till October. Impossible! Says an overwrought mother who sees her way to no more for her children than a daily hour or so on the pavements of the neighbouring London squares. Let me repeat, that I venture to suggest, not what is practicable in any household, but what seems to me absolutely best for the children; and that, in the faith that mothers work wonders once they are convinced that wonders are demanded of them. A journey of twenty minutes by rail or omnibus, and a luncheon basket, will make a day in the country possible to most town dwellers; and if one day, why not many, even every suitable day?

Supposing we have got them, what is to be done with these golden hours, so that every one shall be delightful? They must be spent with some method, or the mother will be taxed and the children bored. There is a great deal to be accomplished in this large fraction of the children's day. They must be kept in a joyous temper all the time, or they will miss some of the strengthening and refreshing held in charge for them by the blessed air. They must be let alone, left to themselves a great deal, to take in what they can of the beauty of earth and heavens; for of the evils of modern education few are worse than this—that the perpetual cackle of his elders leaves the poor child not a moment of time, nor an inch of space, wherein to wonder—and grow. At the same time, here is the mother's opportunity to train the seeing eye, the hearing ear, and to drop seeds of truth into the open soul of the child, which shall germinate, blossom, and bear fruit, without further help or knowledge of hers. Then, there is much to be got by perching in a tree or nestling in heather, but muscular development comes of more active ways, and an hour or two should be spent in vigorous play; and last, and truly least, a lesson or two must be got in.

No Story-Books.—Let us suppose mother and children arrived at some breezy open wherein it seemeth always afternoon. In the first place, it is not her business to entertain the little people: there should be no story-books, no telling of tales, as little talk as possible, and that to some purpose. Who thinks to amuse children with tale or talk at a circus or pantomime? And here, is there not infinitely more displayed for their delectation? Our wise mother, arrived, first sends the children to let off their spirits in a wild scamper, with cry, hallo, and hullaballo, and any extravagance that comes into their young heads. There is no distinction between big and little; the latter love to follow in the wake of their elders, and, in lessons or play, to pick up and do according to their little might. As for the baby, he is in bliss: divested of his garments, he kicks and crawls, and clutches the grass, laughs soft baby laughter, and takes in his little knowledge of shapes and properties in his own wonderful fashion—clothed in a woollen gown, long and loose, which is none the worse for the worst usage it may get.

II.—Sight-Seeing

By-and-by the others come back to their mother, and, while wits are fresh and eyes are keen, she sends them off on an exploring expedition—Who can see the most, and tell the most, about yonder hillock or brook, hedge, or copse. This is an exercise that delights children, and may be endlessly varied, carried on in the spirit of a game, and yet with the exactness and carefulness of a lesson.

How to See.—Find out all you can about that cottage at the foot of the hill; but do not pry about too much. Soon they are back, and there is a crowd of excited faces, and a hubbub of tongues, and random observations are shot breathlessly into the mother's ear. 'There are bee-hives.' 'We saw a lot of bees going into one.' 'There is a long garden.' 'Yes, and there are sunflowers in it.' 'And hen-and-chicken daisies and pansies.' 'And there's a great deal of pretty blue flowers with rough leaves, mother; what do you suppose it is?' 'Borage for the bees, most likely; they are very fond of it.' 'Oh, and there are apple and pear and plum trees on one side; there's a little path up the middle, you know.' 'On which hand side are the fruit trees?' 'The right—no, the left; let me see, which is my thimble-hand? Yes, it is the right-hand side.' 'And there are potatoes and cabbages, and mint and things on the other side.' 'Where are the flowers, then?' 'Oh, they are just the borders, running down each side of the path.' 'But we have not told mother about the wonderful apple tree; I should think there are a million apples on it, all ripe and rosy!' 'A million, Fanny?' 'Well, a great many, mother; I don't know how many.' And so on, indefinitely; the mother getting by degrees a complete description of the cottage and its garden.

Educational Uses of Sight-Seeing.—This is all play to the children, but the mother is doing invaluable work; she is training their powers of observation and expression, increasing their vocabulary and their range of ideas by giving them the name and the uses of an object at the right moment,—when they ask, 'What is it?' and 'What is it for?' And she is training her children in truthful habits, by making them careful to see the fact and to state it exactly, without omission or exaggeration. The child who describes, 'A tall tree, going up into a point, with rather roundish leaves; not a pleasant tree for shade, because the branches all go up,' deserves to learn the name of the tree, and anything her mother has to tell her about it. But the little bungler, who fails to make it clear whether he is describing an elm or a beech, should get no encouragement; not a foot should his mother move to see his tree, no coaxing should draw her into talk about it, until, in despair, he goes off, and comes back with some more certain note—rough or smooth bark, rough or smooth leaves,—then the mother considers, pronounces, and, full of glee, he carries her off to see for himself.

Discriminating Observation.—By degrees the children will learn discriminatingly every feature of the landscapes with which they are familiar; and think what a delightful possession for old age and middle life is a series of pictures imaged, feature by feature, in the sunny glow of the child's mind! The miserable thing about the childish recollections of most persons is that they are blurred, distorted, incomplete, no more pleasant to look upon than a fractured cup or a torn garment; and the reason is, not that the old scenes are forgotten, but that they were never fully seen. At the time, there was no more than a hazy impression that such and such objects were present, and naturally, after a lapse of years those features can rarely be recalled of which the child was not cognisant when he saw them before him.

III.—'Picture-Painting'

Method of.—So exceedingly delightful is this faculty of taking mental photographs, exact images, of the beauties of Nature we go about the world for the refreshment of seeing, that it is worth while to exercise children in another way towards this end, bearing in mind, however, that they see the near and the minute, but can only be made with an effort to look at the wide and the distant. Get the children to look well at some patch of landscape, and then to shut their eyes and call up the picture before them, if any bit of it is blurred, they had better look again. When they have a perfect image before their eyes, let them say what they see. Thus: 'I see a pond; it is shallow on this side, but deep on the other; trees come to the waters edge on that side, and you can see their green leaves and branches so plainly in the water that you would think there was a wood underneath. Almost touching the trees in the water is a bit of blue sky with a soft white cloud; and when you look up you see that same little cloud, but with a great deal of sky instead of a patch, because there are no trees up there. There are lovely little water-lilies round the far edge of the pond, and two or three of the big round leaves are turned up like sails. Near where I am standing three cows have come to drink, and one has got far into the water, nearly up to her neck,' etc.

Strain on the Attention.—This, too, is an exercise children delight in, but, as it involves some strain on the attention, it is fatiguing, and should only be employed now and then. It is, however, well worth while to give children the habit of getting a bit of landscape by heart in this way, because it is the effort of recalling and reproducing that is fatiguing; while the altogether pleasurable act of seeing, fully and in detail, is likely to be repeated unconsciously until it becomes a habit by the child who is required now and then to reproduce what he sees.

Seeing Fully and in Detail.—At first the children will want a little help in the art of seeing. The mother will say, 'Look at the reflection of the trees! There might be a wood under the water. What do those standing up leaves remind you of?' And so on, until the children have noticed the salient points of the scene. She will even herself learn off two or three scenes, and describe them with closed eyes for the children's amusement; and such little mimics are they, and at the same time so sympathetic, that any graceful fanciful touch which she throws into her descriptions will be reproduced with variations in theirs.

The children will delight in this game of picture-painting all the more if the mother introduce it by describing some great picture gallery she has seen—pictures of mountains, of moors, of stormy seas, of ploughed fields, of little children at play, of an old woman knitting,—and goes on to say, that though she does not paint her pictures on canvas and have them put in frames, she carries about with her just such a picture gallery; for whenever she sees anything lovely or interesting, she looks at it until she has the picture in her mind's eye; and then she carries it away with her, her own for ever, a picture on view just when she wants it.

A Means of After-Solace and Refreshment.—It would be difficult to overrate this habit of seeing and storing as a means of after-solace and refreshment. The busiest of us have holidays when we slip our necks out of the yoke and come face to face with Nature, to be healed and blessed by

"The breathing balm,
The silence and the calm
Of mute, insensate things."

This immediate refreshment is open to everybody according to his measure; but it is a mistake to suppose that everybody is able to carry away a refreshing image of that which gives him delight. Only a few can say with Wordsworth, of scenes they have visited

"Though absent long,
These forms of beauty have not been to me
As is a landscape to a blind mans eye;
But oft, in lonely rooms, and mid the din
Of towns and cities, I have owed to them,
In hours of weariness, sensations sweet,
Felt in the blood, and felt along the heart;
And passing even into my purer mind,
With tranquil restoration.

And yet this is no high poetic gift which the rest of us must be content to admire, but a common reward for taking pains in the act of seeing which parents may do a great deal to confer upon their children.

The mother must beware how she spoils the simplicity, the objective character of the child's enjoyment, by treating his little descriptions as feats of cleverness to be repeated to his father or to visitors; she had better make a vow to suppress herself, 'to say nothing to nobody,' in his presence at any rate, though the child should show himself a born poet.

IV. Flowers and Trees

Children should know Field-crops.—In the course of this 'sight-seeing' and 'picture-painting,' opportunities will occur to make the children familiar with rural objects and employments. If there are farm-lands within reach, they should know meadow and pasture, clover, turnip, and corn field, under every aspect, from the ploughing of the land to the getting in of the crops.

Field Flowers and the Life-History of Plants.—Milkwort, eyebright, rest-harrow, lady's-bedstraw, willow-herb, every wild flower that grows in their neighbourhood, they should know quite well; should be able to describe the leaf—its shape, size, growing from the root or from the stem; the manner of flowering—a head of flowers, a single flower, a spike, etc. And, having made the acquaintance of a wild flower, so that they can never forget it or mistake it, they should examine the spot where they find it, so that they will know for the future in what sort of ground to look for such and such a flower. 'We should find wild thyme here!' 'Oh, this is the very spot for marsh marigolds; we must come here in the spring.' If the mother is no great botanist, she will find Miss Ann Pratt's Wild Flowers [see Appendix] very useful, with its coloured plates, like enough to identify the flowers, by common English names, and pleasant facts and fancies that the children delight in. To make collections of wild flowers for the several months, press them, and mount them neatly on squares of cartridge paper, with the English name, habitat, and date of finding each, affords much happy occupation and, at the same time, much useful training: better still is it to accustom children to make careful brush drawings for the flowers that interest them, of the whole plant where possible.

The Study of Trees.—Children should be made early intimate with the trees, too; should pick out half a dozen trees, oak, elm, ash, beech, in their winter nakedness, and take these to be their year-long friends. In the winter, they will observe the light tresses of the birch, the knotted arms of the oak, the sturdy growth of the sycamore. They may wait to learn the names of the trees until the leaves come. By-and-by, as the spring advances, behold a general stiffening and look of life in the still bare branches; life stirs in the beautiful mystery of the leaf-buds, a nest of delicate baby leaves lying in downy warmth within many waterproof wrappings; oak and elm, beech and birch, each has its own way of folding and packing its leaflets; observe the 'ruby budded lime' and the ash, with its pretty stag's foot of a bud, not green but black—

"More black than ash-buds in the front of March."

The Seasons should be followed.—But it is hard to keep pace with the wonders that unfold themselves in the 'bountiful season bland.' There are the dangling catkins and the little ruby eyed pistil-late flowers of the hazel—clusters of flowers, both of them, two sorts on a single tree; and the downy staminate catkins of the willow; and the festive breaking out of all the trees into lovely leafage; the learning the patterns of the leaves as they come out, and the naming of the trees from this and other signs. Then the flowers come, each shut up tight in the dainty casket we call a bud, as cunningly wrapped as the leaves in their buds, but less carefully guarded, for these 'sweet nurslings' delay their coming for the most part until earth has a warm bed to offer, and the sun a kindly welcome.

Leigh Hunt on Flowers.—"Suppose," says Leigh Hunt, "suppose flowers themselves were new! Suppose they had just come into the world, a sweet reward for some new goodness... Imagine what we should feel when we saw the first lateral stem bearing off from the main one, and putting forth a leaf. How we should watch the leaf gradually unfolding its little graceful hand; then another, then another; then the main stalk rising and producing more; then one of them giving indications of the astonishing novelty—a bud! then this mysterious bud gradually unfolding like the leaf, amazing us, enchanting us, almost alarming us with delight, as if we knew not what enchantment were to ensue, till at length, in all its fairy beauty, and odorous voluptuousness, and the mysterious elaboration of tender and living sculpture, shines forth the blushing flower." The flowers, it is true, are not new; but the children are; and it is the fault of their elders if every new flower they come upon is not to them a Picciola, a mystery of beauty to be watched from day to day with unspeakable awe and delight.

Meanwhile, we have lost sight of those half-dozen forest-trees which the children have taken into a sort of comradeship for the year. Presently they have the delight of discovering that the great trees have flowers, too, flowers very often of the same hue as their leaves, and that some trees have put off having their leaves until their flowers have come and gone. By-and-by there is the fruit, and the discovery that every tree—with exceptions which they need not learn yet—and every plant bears fruit, 'fruit and seed after his kind.' All this is stale knowledge to older people, but one of the secrets of the educator is to present nothing as stale knowledge, but to put himself in the position of the child, and wonder and admire with him; for every common miracle which the child sees with his own eyes makes of him for the moment another Newton.

Calendars.—It is a capital plan for the children to keep a calendar—the first oak-leaf, the first tadpole, the first cowslip, the first catkin, the first ripe blackberries, where seen, and when. The next year they will know when and where to look out for their favourites, and will, every year, be in a condition to add new observations. Think of the zest and interest, the object, which such a practice will give to daily walks and little excursions. There is hardly a day when some friend may not be expected to hold a first 'At Home.'

Nature Diaries.—As soon as he is able to keep it himself, a nature-diary is a source of delight to a child. Every day's walk gives him something to enter: three squirrels in a larch tree, a jay flying across such a field, a caterpillar climbing up a nettle, a snail eating a cabbage leaf, a spider dropping suddenly to the ground, where he found ground ivy, how it was growing and what plants were growing with it, how bindweed or ivy manages to climb. Innumerable matters to record occur to the intelligent child. While he is quite young (five or six), he should begin to illustrate his notes freely with brush drawings; he should have a little help at first in mixing colours, in the way of principles, not directions. He should not be told to use now this and now that, but, 'we get purple by mixing so and so,' and then he should be left to himself to get the right tint. As for drawing, instruction has no doubt its time and place; but his nature diary should be left to his own initiative. A child of six will produce a dandelion, poppy, daisy, iris, with its leaves, impelled by the desire to represent what he sees, with surprising vigour and correctness.

An exercise book [Nature note-books may be had at the P.N.E.U Office. See Appendix] with stiff covers serves for a nature diary, but care is necessary in choosing paper that answers both for writing and brush drawing.

'I can't stop thinking.'—'But I can't stop thinking; I can't make my mind to sit down!' Poor little girl! All children owe you thanks for giving voice to their dumb woes. And we grown up people have so little imagination, that we send a little boy with an over-active brain to play by himself in the garden in order to escape the fag of lessons. Little we know how the brain-people swarm in and out and rush about!

"The human (brain) is like a millstone, turning ever round and round;
If it have nothing else to grind, it must itself be ground."

Set the child to definite work by all means, and give him something to grind. But, pray, let him work with things and not with signs—the things of Nature in their own places, meadow and hedgerow, woods and shore.

V. 'Living Creatures'

A Field of Interest and Delight.—Then, as for the 'living creatures,' here is a field of unbounded interest and delight. The domesticated animals are soon taken into kindly fellowship by the little people. Perhaps they live too far from the 'real country' for squirrels and wild rabbits to be more to them than a dream of possible delights. But surely there is a pond within reach—by road or rail—where tadpoles may be caught, and carried home in a bottle, fed, and watched through all their changes—fins disappearing, tails getting shorter and shorter, until at last there is no tail at all, and a pretty pert little frog looks you in the face. Turn up any chance stone, and you may come upon a colony of ants. We have always known that it becomes us to consider their ways and be wise; but now, think of all Lord Avebury has told us to make that twelve-year-old ant of his acquaintance quite a personage. Then, there are the bees. Some of us may have heard the late Dean Farrar describe that lesson he was present at, on 'How doth the little busy bee'—the teacher bright, but the children not responsive; they took no interest at all in little busy bees. He suspected the reason, and questioning the class, found that not one of them had ever seen a bee. 'Had never seen a bee! Think for a moment,' said he, 'of how much that implies'; and then we were moved by an eloquent picture of the sad child-life from which bees and birds and flowers are all shut out. But how many children are there who do not live in the slums of London, and yet are unable to distinguish a bee from a wasp, or even a 'humble' from a honey-bee!

Children should be encouraged to Watch.—Children should be encouraged to watch, patiently and quietly, until they learn something of the habits and history of bee, ant, wasp, spider, hairy caterpillar, dragon-fly, and whatever of larger growth comes in their way. 'The creatures never have any habits while I am looking!' a little girl in some story-book is made to complain; but that was her fault; the bright keen eyes with which children are blest were made to see, and see into, the doings of creatures too small for the unaided observation of older people. Ants may be brought under home observation in the following way: Get two pieces of glass 1 foot square, three strips of glass 11 1/2 inches long, and one strip 11 inches long, these all 1/4 inch wide. The glass must be carefully cut so as to fit exactly. Place the four strips of glass upon one of the sheets of glass and fix in an exact square, leaving a 1/2 inch opening, with seccotine or any good fixer. Get from an ant-hill about twelve ants (the yellow ants are best, as the red are inclined to be quarrelsome), a few eggs, and one queen. The queen will be quite as large as an ordinary ant, and so can be easily seen. Take some of the earth of the ant-hill. Put the earth with your ants and eggs upon the sheet of glass and fix the other sheet above, leaving only the small hole in one corner, made by the shorter strip, which should be stopped with a bit of cotton-wool. The ants will be restless for perhaps forty-eight hours, but will then begin to settle and arrange the earth. Remove the wool plug once a week, and replace it after putting two or three drops of honey on it. Once in three weeks remove the plug to drop in with a syringe about ten drops of water. This will not be necessary in the winter while the ants are asleep. This 'nest' will last for years.

With regard to the horror which some children show of beetle, spider, worm, that is usually a trick picked up from grown-up people. Kingsley's children would run after their 'daddy' with a 'delicious worm,' a 'lovely toad,' a 'sweet beetle' carried tenderly in both hands. There are real antipathies not to be overcome, such as Kingsley's own horror of a spider; but children who are accustomed to hold and admire caterpillars and beetles from their babyhood will not give way to affected horrors. The child who spends an hour in watching the ways of some new 'grub' he has come upon will be a man of mark yet. Let all he finds out about it be entered in his diary—by his mother, if writing be a labour to him,—where he finds it, what it is doing, or seems to him to be doing; its colour, shape, legs: some day he will come across the name of the creature, and will recognise the description of an old friend.

The Force of Public Opinion in the Home.—Some children are born naturalists, with a bent inherited, perhaps, from an unknown ancestor; but every child has a natural interest in the living things about him which it is the business of his parents to encourage; for, but few children are equal to holding their own in the face of public opinion; and if they see that the things which interest them are indifferent or disgusting to you, their pleasure in them vanishes, and that chapter in the book of Nature is closed to them. It is likely that the Natural History of Selborne would never have been written had it not been that the naturalist's father used to take his boys on daily foraging expeditions, when not a moving or growing thing, not a pebble nor a boulder within miles of Selborne, escaped their eager examination. Audubon, the American ornithologist, is another instance of the effect of this kind of early training. "When I had hardly learned to walk," he says, "and to articulate those first words always so endearing to parents, the productions of Nature that lay spread all around were constantly pointed out to me . . . My father generally accompanied my steps, procured birds and flowers for me, and pointed out the elegant movements of the former, the beauty and softness of their plumage, the manifestations of their pleasure, or their sense of danger, and the always perfect forms and splendid attire of the latter. He would speak of the departure and return of the birds with the season, describe their haunts, and, more wonderful than all, their change of livery, thus exciting me to study them, and to raise my mind towards their great Creator."

What Town Children can Do.—Town children may get a great deal of pleasure in watching the ways of sparrows—knowing little birds, and easily tamed by a dole of crumbs,—and their days out will bring them in the way of new acquaintances. But much may be done with sparrows. A friend writes:—"Have you seen the man in the gardens of Tuileries feeding and talking to dozens of them? They sit on his hat, his hands, and feed from his fingers. When he raises his arms they all flutter up and then settle again on him and round him. I have watched him call a sparrow from a distance by name and refuse food to all others till 'petit chou,' a pretty pied sparrow, came for his destined bit. Others had their names and came at call, but I could not see any distinguishing feature; and the crowd of sparrows on the walk, benches and railing, formed a most attentive audience to the bright French talk which kept them in constant motion as they were, here one and there another, invited to come for a tempting morsel. Truly a St. Francis and the birds!"

The child who does not know the portly form and spotted breast of the thrush, the graceful flight of the swallow, the yellow bill of the blackbird, the gush of song which the skylark pours from above, is nearly as much to be pitied as those London children who 'had never seen a bee.' A pleasant acquaintance, easy to pick up, is the hairy caterpillar. The moment to seize him is when he is seen shuffling along the ground in a great hurry; he is on the look-out for quiet quarters in which to lie up: put him in a box, then, and cover the box with net, through which you may watch his operations. Food does not matter—he has other things to attend to. By-and-by he spins a sort of white tent or hammock, into which he retires; you may see through it and watch him, perhaps at the very moment when his skin splits asunder, leaving him, for months to come, an egg-shaped mass without any sign of life. At last the living thing within breaks out of this bundle, and there it is, the handsome tiger-moth, fluttering feeble wings against the net. Most children of six have had this taste of a naturalist's experience, and it is worth speaking of only because, instead of being merely a harmless amusement, it is a valuable piece of education, of more use to the child than the reading of a whole book of natural history, or much geography and Latin. For the evil is, that children get their knowledge of natural history, like all their knowledge, at second hand. They are so sated with wonders, that nothing surprises them; and they are so little used to see for themselves, that nothing interests them. The cure for this blasé condition is, to let them alone for a bit, and then begin on new lines. Poor children, it is no fault of theirs if they are not as they were meant to be—curious eager little souls, all agog to explore so much of this wonderful world as they can get at, as quite their first business in life.

"He prayeth best who loveth best
All things both great and small;
For the dear God who loveth us,
He made and loveth all."

Nature Knowledge the most important for Young Children.—It would be well if we all persons in authority, parents and all who act for parents, could make up our minds that there is no sort of knowledge to be got in these early years so valuable to children as that which they get for themselves of the world they live in. Let them once get touch with Nature, and a habit is formed which will be a source of delight through life. We were all meant to be naturalists, each in his degree, and it is inexcusable to live in a world so full of the marvels of plant and animal life and to care for none of these things.

Mental Training of a Child Naturalist.—Consider, too, what an unequalled mental training the child-naturalist is getting for any study or calling under the sun—the powers of attention, of discrimination, of patient pursuit, growing with his growth, what will they not fit him for? Besides, life is so interesting to him, that he has no time for the faults of temper which generally have their source in ennui; there is no reason why he should be peevish or sulky or obstinate when he is always kept well amused.

Nature Work especially valuable for Girls.—I say 'he' from force of habit, as speaking of the representative sex, but truly that she should be thus conversant with Nature is a matter of infinitely more importance to the little girl: she it is who is most tempted to indulge in ugly tempers (as child and woman) because time hangs heavy on her hands; she, whose idler, more desultory habits of mind want the spur and bridle of an earnest absorbing pursuit; whose feebler health demands to be braced by an out-of-door life full of healthy excitement. Moreover, is it to the girls, little and big, a most true kindness to lift them out of themselves and out of the round of petty personal interests and emulations which too often hem in their lives; and then, with whom but the girls must it rest to mould the generations yet to be born?

VI.—Field-Lore and Naturalists' Books

Reverence for Life.—Is it advisable, then, to teach the children the elements of natural science, of biology, botany, zoology? on the whole, no: the dissection even of a flower is painful to a sensitive child, and, during the first six or eight years of life, I would not teach them any botany which should necessitate the pulling of flowers to bits; much less should they be permitted to injure or destroy any (not noxious) form of animal life. Reverence for life, as a wonderful and awful gift, which a ruthless child may destroy but never can restore, is a lesson of first importance to the child:—

"Let knowledge grow from more to more;
But more of reverence in us dwell."

The child who sees his mother with reverent touch lift an early snowdrop to her lips, learns a higher lesson than the 'print-books' can teach. Years hence, when the children are old enough to understand that science itself is in a sense sacred and demands some sacrifices, all the 'common information' they have been gathering until then, and the habits of observation they have acquired, will form a capital groundwork for a scientific education. In the meantime, let them consider the lilies of the field and the fowls of the air.

Rough Classification at First Hand.—For convenience in describing they should be able to name and distinguish petals, sepals, and so on; and they should be encouraged to make such rough classifications as they can with their slight knowledge of both animal and vegetable forms. Plants with heart-shaped or spoon-shaped leaves, with whole or divided leaves; leaves with criss-cross veins and leaves with straight veins; bell-shaped flowers and cross-shaped flowers; flowers with three petals, with four, with five; trees which keep their leaves all the year, and trees which lose them in autumn; creatures with a backbone and creatures without; creatures that eat grass and creatures that eat flesh, and so on. To make collections of leaves and flowers, pressed and mounted, and arranged according to their form, affords much pleasure, and, what is better, valuable training in the noticing of differences and resemblances. Patterns for this sort of classification of leaves and flowers will be found in every little book for elementary botany.

The power to classify, discriminate, distinguish between things that differ, is amongst the highest faculties of the human intellect, and no opportunity to cultivate it should be let slip; but a classification got out of books, that the child does not make for himself, cultivates no power but that of verbal memory, and a phrase or two of 'Tamil' or other unknown tongue, learnt off, would serve that purpose just as well.

Uses of 'Naturalists' ' Books.—The real use of naturalists' books at this stage is to give the child delightful glimpses into the world of wonders he lives in, to reveal the sorts of things to be seen by curious eyes, and fill him with desire to make discoveries for himself. There are many [Kingsley's Water Babies and Madam How and Lady Why. All Mrs. Brightwen's books. Miss Buckley's (Mrs. Fisher) 'Eyes and no Eyes' Series. Life and her Children, etc. All Seton-Thompson's books. Long's The School of the Woods, The Little Brother of the Bear. Kearton's Wild Nature's Ways. Living Animals of the World.] to be had, all pleasant reading, many of them written by scientific men, and yet requiring little or no scientific knowledge for the enjoyment.

Mothers and Teachers should know about Nature.—The mother cannot devote herself too much to this kind of reading, not only that she may read tit-bits to her children about matters they have come across, but that she may be able to answer their queries and direct their observations. And not only the mother, but any woman, who is likely ever to spend an hour or two in the society of children, should make herself mistress of this sort of information; the children will adore her for knowing what they want to know, and who knows but she may give its bent for life to some young mind designed to do great things for the world.

VII.—The Child Gets Knowledge By Means Of His Senses

Nature's Teaching.—Watch a child standing at gaze at some sight new to him—a plough at work, for instance—and you will see he is as naturally occupied as is a babe at the breast; he is, in fact, taking in the intellectual food which the working faculty of his brain at this period requires. In his early years the child is all eyes; he observes, or, more truly, he perceives, calling sight, touch, taste, smell, and hearing to his aid, that he may learn all that is discoverable by him about every new thing that comes under his notice. Everybody knows how a baby fumbles over with soft little fingers, and carries to his mouth, and bangs that it may produce what sound there is in it, the spoon or doll which supercilious grown-up people give him to 'keep him quiet.' The child is at his lessons, and is learning all about it at a rate utterly surprising to the physiologist, who considers how much is implied in the act of 'seeing,' for instance: that to the infant, as to the blind adult restored to sight, there is at first no difference between a flat picture and a solid body,—that the ideas of form and solidity are not obtained by sight at all, but are the judgments of experience.

Then, think of the vague passes in the air the little fist makes before it lays hold of the object of desire, and you see how he learns the whereabouts of things, having as yet no idea of direction. And why does he cry for the moon? Why does he crave equally, a horse or a house-fly as an appropriate plaything? Because far and near, large and small, are ideas he has yet to grasp. The child has truly a great deal to do before he is in a condition to 'believe his own eyes'; but Nature teaches so gently, so gradually, so persistently, that he is never overdone, but goes on gathering little stores of knowledge about whatever comes before him.

And this is the process the child should continue for the first few years of his life. Now is the storing time which should be spent in laying up images of things familiar. By-and-by he will have to conceive of things he has never seen: how can he do it except by comparison with things he has seen and knows? By-and-by he will be called upon to reflect, understand, reason; what material will he have, unless he has a magazine of facts to go upon? The child who has been made to observe how high in the heavens the sun is at noon on a summer's day, how low at noon on a day in mid-winter, is able to conceive of the great heat of the tropics under a vertical sun, and to understand the climate of a place depends greatly upon the mean height the sun reaches above the horizon.

Overpressure.—A great deal has been said lately about the danger of overpressure, of requiring too much mental work from a child of tender years. The danger exists; but lies, not in giving the child too much, but in giving him the wrong thing to do, the sort of work for which the present state of his mental development does not fit him. Who expects a boy in petticoats to lift half a hundredweight? But give the child work that Nature intended for him, and the quantity he can get through with ease is practically unlimited. Whoever saw a child tired of seeing, of examining in his own way, unfamiliar things? This is the sort of mental nourishment for which he has an unbounded appetite, because it is that food of the mind on which, for the present, he is meant to grow.

Object Lessons.—Now, how far is this craving for natural sustenance met? In infant and kindergarten schools, by the object lesson, which is good so far as it goes, but is sometimes like that bean a day on which the Frenchman fed his horse. The child at home has more new things brought under his noticed, if with less method. Neither at home nor at school is much effort made to set before the child the abundant 'feast of eyes' which his needs demand.

A Child learns from 'Things.'—We older people, partly because of our maturer intellect, partly because of our defective education, get most of our knowledge through the medium of words. We set the child to learn in the same way, and find him dull and slow. Why? Because it is only with a few words in common use that he associates a definite meaning; all the rest are no more to him than the vocables of a foreign tongue. But set him face to face with a thing, and he is twenty times as quick as you are in knowledge about it; knowledge of things flies to the mind of a child as steel filings to magnet. And, pari passu with his knowledge of things, his vocabulary grows; for it is a law of the mind that what we know, we struggle to express. This fact accounts for many of the apparently aimless questions of children; they are in quest, not of knowledge, but of words to express the knowledge they have. Now, consider what a culpable waste of intellectual energy it is to shut up a child, blessed with this inordinate capacity for seeing and knowing, within the four walls of a house, or the dreary streets of a town. Or suppose that he is let run loose in the country where there is plenty to see, it is nearly as bad to let this great faculty of the child's dissipate itself in random observations for want of method and direction.

The Sense of Beauty comes from Early Contact with Nature.—There is no end to the store of common information, got in such a way that it will never be forgotten, with which an intelligent child may furnish himself before he begins his school career. The boy who can tell you off-hand where to find each of the half-dozen most graceful birches, the three or four finest ash trees in the neighbourhood of his home, has chances in a life a dozen to one compared with the lower, slower intelligence that does not know an elm from an oak—not merely chances of success, but chances of a larger, happier life, for it is curious how certain feelings are linked with the mere observation of Nature and natural objects. "The aesthetic sense of the beautiful," says Dr. Carpenter, "of the sublime, of the harmonious, seems in its most elementary form to connect itself immediately with the Perceptions which arise of out of the contact of our minds with external Nature"; while he quotes Dr. Morrell, who says still more forcibly that "All those who have shown a remarkable appreciation of form and beauty date their first impressions from a period lying far behind the existence of definite ideas or verbal instruction."

Most Grown Men lose the Habit of Observation.—Thus, we owe something to Mr. Evans for taking his little daughter Mary Anne with him on his long business drives among the pleasant Warwickshire lanes; the little girl stood up between her father's knees, seeing much and saying little; and the outcome was the scenes of rural life in Adam Bede and The Mill on the Floss. Wordsworth, reared amongst the mountains, becomes a very prophet of Nature; while Tennyson draws endless imagery from the levels of the eastern counties where he was brought up. Little David Copperfield was "a very observant child, though," says he, "I think the memory of most of us can go farther back into such times than many of us suppose; just as I believe the power of observation in numbers of very young children to be quite wonderful for its closeness and accuracy. Indeed, I think that most grown men who are remarkable in this respect may with greater propriety be said not to have lost the faculty, than to have acquired it; the rather, as I generally observe such men to retain a certain freshness, and gentleness, and capacity of being pleased, which are also an inheritance they have preserved from their childhood";—in which remark Dickens makes his hero talk sound philosophy as well as kindly sense.

VIII.—The Child Should Be Made Familiar With Natural Objects

An Observant Child should be put in the way of Things worth Observing.—But what is the use of being a 'very observant child,' if you are not put in the way of things worth observing? And here is the difference between the streets of a town and the sights and sounds of the country. There is plenty to be seen in a town and children accustomed to the ways of the streets become nimble-witted enough. But the scraps of information to be picked up in a town are isolated fragments; they do not hang on to anything else, nor come to anything more; the information may be convenient, but no one is the wiser for knowing which side of the street is Smith's, and which turning leads to Thompson's shop.

Every Natural Object a Member of a Series.—Now take up a natural object, it does not matter what, and you are studying one of a group, a member of a series; whatever knowledge you get about it is so much towards the science which includes all of its kind. Break off an elder twig in the spring; you notice a ring of wood round a centre of pith, and there you have at a glance a distinguishing character of a great division of the vegetable world. You pick up a pebble. Its edges are perfectly smooth and rounded: why? you ask. It is water-worn, weatherworn. And that little pebble brings you face to face with disintegration, the force to which, more than to any other, we owe the aspects of the world which we call picturesque—glen, ravine, valley, hill. It is not necessary that the child should be told anything about disintegration or dicotyledon, only that he should observe the wood and pith in the hazel twig, the pleasant roundness of the pebble; by-and-by he will learn the bearing of the facts with which he is already familiar—a very different thing from learning the reason why of facts which have never come under his notice.

Power will pass, more and more, into the hands of Scientific Men.—It is infinitely well worth of the mother's while to take some pains every day to secure, in the first place, that her children spend hours daily amongst rural and natural objects; and, in the second place, to infuse into them, or rather to cherish in them, the love of investigation. "I say it deliberately," says Kingsley, "as a student of society and of history: power will pass more and more into the hands of scientific men. They will rule, and they will act—cautiously, we may hope, and modestly, and charitably—because in learning true knowledge they will have learnt also their own ignorance, and the vastness, the complexity, the mystery of Nature. But they will also be able to rule, they will be able to act, because they have taken the trouble to learn the facts and the laws of Nature."

Intimacy with Nature makes for Personal Well-being.—But to enable them to swim with the stream is the least of the benefits this early training should confer on the children; a love of Nature, implanted so early that it will seem to them hereafter to have been born in them, will enrich their lives with pure interests, absorbing pursuits, health, and good humour. "I have seen," says the same writer, "the young man of fierce passions and uncontrollable daring expend healthily that energy which threatened daily to plunge him into recklessness, if not into sin, upon hunting out and collecting, through rock and bog, snow and tempest, every bird and egg of the neighbouring forest . . . I have seen the young London beauty, amid all the excitement and temptation of luxury and flattery, with her heart pure, and her mind occupied in a boudoir full of shells and fossils, flowers and seaweeds, keeping herself unspotted from the world, by considering the lilies of the fields of the field, how they grow."

IX.—Out-Of-Door Geography

Small Things may teach Great.—After this long digression, intended to impress upon mothers the supreme importance of stirring up in their children a love of Nature and of natural objects—a deep-seated spring to send up pure waters into the driest places of after-life—we must return to the mother whom we have left out of doors all this time, waiting to know what she is to do next. This pleasant earth of ours is not to be overlooked in the out-of-door education of the children. 'How do you get time for so much?' 'Oh, I leave out subjects of no educational value; I do not teach geography, for instance,' said an advanced young theorist with all sorts of certificates.

Pictorial Geography.—But the mother, who knows better, will find a hundred opportunities to teach geography by the way: a duck-pond is a lake or an inland sea; any brooklet will serve to illustrate the great rivers of the world; a hillock grows into a mountain—an Alpine system; a hazel-copse suggests the mighty forests of the Amazon; a reedy swamp, the rice-fields of China; a meadow, the boundless prairies of the West; the pretty purple flowers of the common mallow is a text whereon to hang the cotton fields of the Southern States: indeed, the whole field of pictorial geography—maps may wait until by-and-by—may be covered in this way.

The Position of the Sun.—And not only this: the children should be taught to observe the position of the sun in the heavens from hour to hour, and by his position, to tell the time of day. Of course they will want to known why the sun is such an indefatigable traveller, and thereby hangs a wonderful tale, which they may as well learn in the 'age of faith,' of the relative sizes of sun and earth, and of the nature and movements of the latter.

Clouds, Rain, Snow, and Hail.—"Clouds and rain, snow and hail, winds and vapours, fulfilling His Word"—are all everyday mysteries that the mother will be called upon to explain faithfully, however simply. There are certain ideas which children must get from within a walking radius of their own home if ever they are to have a real understanding of maps and of geographical terms.

Distance is one of these, and the first idea of distance is to be attained by what children find a delightful operation. A child walks at his usual pace; somebody measures and tells him the length of his pace, and then he measures the paces of his brothers and sisters. Then such a walk, such a distance, here and there, is solemnly paced, and a little sum follows—so many inches or feet covered by each pace equals so many yards in the whole distance. Various short distances about the child's home should be measured in this way; and when the idea of covering distance is fully established, the idea of times as a means of measurement should be introduced. The time taken to pace a hundred yards should be noted down. Having found out that it takes two minutes to pace a hundred yards, children will be able for the next step—that if they have walked for thirty minutes, the walk should measure fifteen hundred yards; in thirty-five minutes they would have walked a mile, or rather seventeen hundred and fifty yards, and then they could add the ten yards more which would make a mile. The longer the legs the longer the pace, and most grown people can walk a mile in twenty minutes.

Direction.—By the time they have got somewhat familiar with the idea of distance, that of direction should be introduced. The first step is to make children observant of the progress of the sun. The child who observes the sun for a year and notes down for himself, or dictates, the times of his rising and setting for the greater part of the year, and the points of his rising and setting, will have secured a basis for a good deal of definite knowledge. Such observation should take in the reflection of the sun's light, the evening light reflected by east windows, the morning light by west windows, the varying length and intensity of shadows, the cause of shadows, to be learned by the shadow cast by a figure between the blind and a candle. He should associate, too, the hot hours of the day with the sun high overhead, and the cool hours of the morning and evening with a low sun; and should be reminded, that if he stands straight before the fire, he feels the heat more than if he were in a corner of the room. When he is prepared by a little observation in the course of the sun, he is ready to take in the idea of direction, which depends entirely upon the sun.

East and West.—Of course the first two ideas are that the sun rises in the east and sets in the west; from this fact he will be able to tell the direction in which the places near his own home, or the streets of his own town, lie. Bid him stand so that his right is towards the east where the sun rises, and his left towards the west where the sun sets. Then he is looking towards the north and his back is towards the south. All the houses, streets and towns on his right hand are to the east of him, those on the left are to the west. The places he must walk straight forward to reach are north of him, and the places behind him are to the south. If he is in a place new to him where he has never seen the sun rise or set and wants to know in what direction a certain road runs, he must notice in what direction his own shadow falls at twelve o'clock, because at noon the shadows of all objects fall towards the north. Then if he face the north, he has, as before, the south behind him, the east on his right hand, the west on his left; or if he face the sun at noon, he faces south.

Practice in finding Direction.—This will throw an interesting light for him on the names of our great railways. A child may become ready in noticing the directions of places by a little practice. Let him notice how each of the windows of his schoolroom faces, or the windows of each of the rooms in his home; the rows of houses he passes in his walks, and which are north, south, east and west sides of the churches he knows. He will soon be prepared to notice the direction of the wind by noticing the smoke from the chimneys, the movement of branches, corn, grass, etc. If the wind blow from the north—'The north wind doth blow and we shall have snow.' If it blow from the west, a west wind, we expect rain. Care must be taken at this point to make it clear to the child that the wind is named after the quarter it comes from, and not from the point it blows towards—just as he is English because he was born in England, and not French because he goes to France. The ideas of distance and direction may now be combined. Such a building is two hundred yards to the east of a gate, such a village two miles to the west. He will soon come across the difficulty, that a place is not exactly east or west, north or south. It is well to let him give, in a round-about way, the direction of places as—'more to the east than the west, 'very near the east but not quite,' 'half-way between east and west.' He will value the exact means of expression all the more for having felt the need of them.

Later, he should be introduced to the wonders of the mariner's compass, should have a little pocket compass of his own, and should observe the four cardinal and all other points. These will afford him the names for directions that he has found it difficult to describe.

Compass Drill.—Then he should do certain compass drills in this way: Bid him hold the N of the compass towards the north. "Then, with the compass in your hand, turn towards the east, and you will see a remarkable thing. The little needle moves, too, but moves quite by itself in just the other direction. Turn to the west, and again the needle moves in the opposite direction to that in which you move. However little you turn, a little quiver of the needle follows your movement. And you look at it, wondering how the little thing could perceive you had moved, when you hardly knew it yourself. Walk straight on in any direction, and the needle is fairly steady; only fairly steady, because you are sure, without intending it, to move a lttle to the right or left. Turn round very slowly, a little bit at a time, beginning at the north and turning towards the east, and you may make the needle also move round in a circle. It moves in the opposite direction to yourself, for it is trying to get back to the north from which you are turning."

Boundaries.—The children having got the idea of direction, it will be quite easy to introduce that of boundaries—such and such a turnip field, for instance, is bounded by the highroad on the south, by a wheat crop on the south-east, a hedge on the north-east, and so on; the children getting by degrees the idea that the boundaries of a given space are simply whatever touches it on every side. Thus one crop may touch another without any dividing line, and therefore one crop bounds the other. It is well that children should get clear notions on this subject, or, later, they will be vague when they learn that such a county is 'bounded' by so and so. In connection with bounded spaces whether they be villages, towns, ponds, fields, or what not, children should be led to notice the various crops raised in the district, why pasture-lands and why cornfields, what manner of rocks appear, and how many sorts of tree grow in the neighbourhood. For every field or other space that is examined, that they should draw a rude plan in the sand, giving the shape roughly and lettering the directions as N, S, W, etc.

Plans.—By-and-by, when they have learned to draw plans indoors, they will occasionally pace the length of a field and draw their plan according to scale, allowing an inch for five or for ten yards. The ground-plans of garden, stables, house, etc. might follow.

Local Geography.—It is probable that a child's own neighbourhood will give him opportunities to learn the meaning of hill and dale, pool and brook, watershed, the current, bed, banks, tributaries of a brook, the relative positions of villages and towns; and all this local geography he must be able to figure roughly on a plan done with chalk on a rock, or with walking stick in the gravel, perceiving the relative distances and situations of the places he marks.

X.—The Child And Mother-Nature

The Mother must refrain from too much Talk.—Does so wide a programme alarm the mother? Does she with dismay see herself talking through the whole of those five or six hours, and, even at that, not getting through a tithe of the teaching laid out for her? On the contrary, the less she says the better; and as for the quantity of educational work to be got through, it is the fable of the anxious pendulum over again: it is true there are countless 'ticks' to be ticked, but there will be always be a second of time to tick in, and no more than a single tick is to be delivered in any given second.

Making a New Acquaintance.—The rapid little people will have played their play, whether of 'sight-seeing' or 'picture-painting,' in a quarter of an hour or so; for the study of natural objects, an occasional 'Look!' an attentive examination of the object on the mother's own part, a name given, a remark—a dozen words long—made at the right moment, and the children have begun a new acquaintance which they will prosecute for themselves; and not more than one or two such presentations should occur in a single day.

Now, see how much leisure there is left! The mother's real difficulty will be to keep herself from much talk with the children, and to hinder them from occupying themselves with her. There are few things sweeter and more precious to the child than playful prattle with her mother; but one thing is better—the communing with the larger Mother, in order to which the child and she should be left to themselves. This is, truly, a delightful thing to watch: the mother reads her book or knits her sock, checking all attempts to make talk; the child stares up into a tree, or down into a flower—doing nothing, thinking of nothing; or leads a bird's life among the branches, or capers about in aimless ecstasy;—quite foolish, irrational doings, but, all the time a fashioning is going on: Nature is doing her part, with the vow—

"This child I to myself will take:
She shall be mine, and I will make
A lady of my own." [Wordsworth]

Two Things permissible to the Mother.—There is one thing the mother will allow herself to do as interpreter between Nature and the child, but that not oftener than once a week or once a month, and with look and gesture of delight rather than with flow of improving words—she will point out to the child some touch of especial loveliness in colouring or grouping in the landscape or the heavens. One other thing she will do, but very rarely, and with tender filial reverence (most likely she will say her prayers, and speak out of her prayer, for to touch on this ground with hard words is to wound the soul of the child): she will point to some lovely flower or gracious tree, not only as a beautiful, but a beautiful thought of God, in which we may believe He finds continual pleasure, and which He is pleased to see his human children rejoice in. Such a seed of sympathy with the Divine thought sown in the heart of the child is worth many of the sermons the man may listen to hereafter, much of the 'divinity' he may read.

XI.—Out-Of-Door Games, etc.

The bright hours fly by; and there is still at least one lesson on the programme, to say nothing of an hour or two for games in the afternoon. The thought of a lesson is uninviting after the discussion of much that is more interesting, and, truly, more important; but it need only be a little lesson, ten minutes long, and the slight break and the effort of attention will give the greater zest to the pleasure and leisure to follow.

The French Lesson.—The daily French lesson is that which should not be omitted. That children should learn French orally, by listening to and repeating French words and phrases; that they should begin so young that the difference of accent does not strike them, but they repeat the new French word all the same as if it were English and use it as freely; that they should learn a few—two or three, five or six—new French words daily, and that, at the same time, the old words should be kept in use—are points to be considered more fully hereafter: in the meantime, it is so important to keep tongue and ear familiar with French vocables, that not a lesson should be omitted. The French lesson may, however, be made to fit in with the spirit of the other out-of-door occupations; the half-dozen words may be the parts—leaves, branches, bark, trunk of a tree, or the colours of the flowers, or the movements of bird, cloud, lamb, child; in fact, the new French words should be but another form of expression for the ideas that for the time fill the child's mind.

Noisy Games.—The afternoon's games, after luncheon, are an important part of the day's doings for the elder children, though the younger have probably worn themselves out by this time with the ceaseless restlessness by means of which Nature provides for the due development of muscular tissue in them; let them sleep in the sweet air, and awake refreshed. Meanwhile, the elders play; the more they run, and shout, and toss their arms, the more healthful is the play. And this is one reason why mothers should carry their children off to lonely places, where they may use their lungs to their hearts' content without risk of annoying anybody.

The muscular structure of the organs of voice is not enough considered; children love to indulge in cries and shouts and view-halloos, and this 'rude' and 'noisy' play, with which their elders have not much patience, is no more than Nature's way of providing for the due exercise of organs, upon whose working power the health and happiness of the child's future largely depend. People talk of 'weak lungs,' 'weak chest,' 'weak throat,' but perhaps it does not occur to everybody that strong lungs and strong throat are commonly to be had on the same terms as a strong arm or wrist—by exercise, training, use, work. Still, if the children can 'give voice' musically, and more rhythmically to the sound of their own voices, so much the better. In this respect French children are better off than English; they dance and sing through a hundred roundelays—just such games, no doubt, mimic marryings and buryings, as the children played at long ago in the market place of Jerusalem.

'Rondes.'—Before Puritan innovations made us a staid and circumspect people, English lads and lasses of all ages danced out little dramas on the village green, accompanying themselves with the words and airs of just such rondes as the French children sing to-day. We have a few of them left still—to be heard at Sunday-school treats and other gatherings of the children,—and they are well worth preserving: 'There came three dukes a-riding, a-riding, a-riding': 'Oranges and lemons, say the bells of St. Clement's'; 'Here we come gathering nuts in May'; 'What has my poor prisoner done?' and many more, all set to delightful sing-song airs that little feet trip to merrily, the more so for the pleasant titillation of the words—dukes, nuts, oranges,—who could not go to the tune of such ideas?

The promoters of the kindergarten system have done much to introduce games of this, or rather of a more educational kind; but is it not a fact that the singing games of the kindergarten are apt to be somewhat inane? Also, it is doubtful how far the prettiest plays, learnt at school and from a teacher, will take hold of the children as do the games which have been passed on from hand to hand through an endless chain of children, and are not be found in the print-books at all.

Skipping-rope and Shuttlecock.—Cricket, tennis, and rounders are the games par excellence if the children are old enough to play them, both as giving free harmonious play to the muscles, and also as serving the highest moral purpose of games in bringing the children under the discipline of rules; but the little family we have in view, all of them under nine, will hardly be up to scientific games. Races and chases, 'tag,' 'follow my leader,' and any romping game they may invent, will be more to their minds: still better are the hoop, the ball, the shuttlecock, and the invaluable skipping-rope. For the rope, the very best use is to skip with her own, throwing it backwards rather than forwards, so that the tendency of the movement is to expand the chest. Shuttlecock is a fine game, affording scope for ambition and emulation. Her biographer thinks it worth telling that Miss Austen could keep up in 'cup and ball' over a hundred times, to the admiration of nephews and nieces; in like manner, any feat in keeping up the shuttle-cock might be noted down as a family event, so that the children may be fired with ambition to excel in a game which affords most graceful and vigorous play to almost every muscle of the upper part of the body, and has this great recommendation, that it can be as well played within doors as without. Quite the best play is to keep up the shuttlecock with a battledore in each hand, so that the muscles on either side are brought equally into play. But to 'ordain' about children's games is an idle waste of words, for here fashion is as supreme and as arbitrary as in questions of bonnet or crinoline.

Climbing.—Climbing is an amusement not much in favour with mothers; torn garments, bleeding knees, and boot-toes rubbed into holes, to say nothing of more serious risks, make a strong case against this form of delight. But, truly, the exercise is so admirable—the body being thrown into endless graceful postures which bring every muscle into play,—and the training in pluck, daring, and resource so invaluable that it is a pity trees and cliffs and walls should be forbidden even to little girls. The mother may do a good deal to avert serious mishaps by accustoming the younger children to small feats of leaping and climbing, so that they learn, at the same time, courage and caution from their own experiences, and are less likely to follow the lead of too-daring playmates. Later, the mother had best make up her mind to share the feelings of the hen that hatched a brood of ducklings, remembering that a little scream and sudden 'Come down instantly!' 'Tommy, you'll break your neck!' gives the child a nervous shock, and is likely to cause the fall it was meant to hinder by startling Tommy out of all presence of mind. Even boating and swimming are not without the reach of town-bred children, in days when everybody goes for a summer outing to the neighbourhood of the sea or of inland waters; and then, there are swimming baths in most towns. It would be well if most children of seven were taught to swim, not only for the possible usefulness of the art, but as giving them an added means of motion, and, therefore, of delight.

Clothing.—The havoc of clothes need not be great if the children are dressed for their little excursions, as they should be, in plainly made garments of some loosely woven woollen material, serge or flannel. Woollen has many advantages over cotton, and more over linen, as a clothing material; chiefly, that it is a bad conductor; that is to say, it does not allow the heat of the body too free an exit, nor the heat of the sun too free an entrance. Therefore the child in woollen, who has become heated in play, does not suffer a chill from the sudden loss of this heat, as does the child in linen garments; also, he is cooler in the sunshine, and warmer in the shade.

XII.—Walks In Bad Weather

Winter Walks as necessary as Summer Walks.—All we have said hitherto applies to the summer weather, which is, alas for us! a very limited and uncertain quantity in our part of the world. The question of out-of-door exercise in winter and in wet weather is really more important; for who that could would not be abroad in the summer time? If the children are to have what is quite the best thing for them, they should be two or three hours every day in the open air all through winter, say an hour and a half in the morning and as long in the afternoon.

Pleasures connected with Frost and Snow.—When frost and snow are on the ground children have very festive times, what with sliding, snow-balling, and snow-building. But even on the frequent days when it is dirty under foot and dull over head they should be kept interested and alert, so that the heart may do its work cheerfully, and a grateful glow be kept up throughout the body in spite of clouds and cold weather.

Winter Observations.—All that has been said about 'sight-seeing' and 'picture painting,' the little French talk, and observations to be noted in the family diary, belongs just as much to winter weather as to summer; and there is no end to the things to be seen and noted. The party come across a big tree which they judge, from its build, to be an oak—down it goes in the diary; and when the leaves are out, the children come again to see if they are right. Many birds come into view the more freely in the cold weather that they are driven forth in search of food.

"The cattle mourn in corners where the fence screens them."

"The sun, with ruddy orb
Ascending, fires the horizon."

"Every herb and every spiry blade
Stretches a length of shadow o'er the field."

"The sparrows peep, and quit the sheltering eaves.

"The redbreast warbles still, but is content
With slender notes, and more than half suppress'd;
Pleased with his solitude, and flitting light
From spray to spray, wheree'er he rests he shakes
From many a twig the pendent drops of ice
That tinkle in the wither'd leaves below."

There is no reason why the child's winter walk should not be as fertile in observations as the poet's; indeed, in one way, it is possible to see the more in winter, because the things to be seen do not crowd each other out.

Habit of Attention.—Winter walks, too, whether in town or country, give great opportunities for cultivating the habit of attention. The famous conjurer, Robert Houdin, relates in his autobiography, that he and his son would pass rapidly before a shop window, that of a toy shop, for instance, and each cast an attentive glance upon it. A few steps further on each drew paper and pencil from his pocket, and tried which could enumerate the greater number of the objects momentarily seen in passing. The boy surprised his father in quickness of apprehension, being often able to write down forty objects, whilst his father could scarcely reach thirty; yet on their returning to verify his statement, the son was rarely found to have made a mistake. Here is a hint for a highly educational amusement for many a winter's walk.

Wet Weather Tramps.—But what about the wet days? The fact is, that rain, unless of the heaviest, does the children no harm at all if they are suitably clothed. But every sort of water proof garment should be tabooed, because the texture which will not admit rain will not allow of the escape of the insensible perspiration, and one secret of health for people who have no organic disease is the prompt carrying off of the decayed and harmful matters discharged by the skin.

Outer Garments for.—Children should have woollen rain-garments—made of coarse serge, for instance,—to be changed the moment they return from a walk, and then there is no risk of catching cold. This is the common-sense of the matter. Wet cloths are put upon the head of a fever patient; by-and-by the cloths dry, and are dipped again: what has become of the water? It has evaporated, and, in evaporating, has carried off much heat from the fevered head. Now, that which eases the hot skin of fever is just the one thing to be avoided in ordinary circumstances. To be wet to the skin may do a child no more harm than a bath would do him, if the wet clothes do not dry upon him—that is, if the water does not evaporate, carrying off much heat from his body in the process. It is the loss of animal heat which is followed by 'colds,' and not the 'wetting,' which mothers are ready to deplore. Keep an child active and happy in the rain, and he gets nothing but good from his walk. The case is altered if the child has a cold already; then active exercise might increase any inflammation already set up.

I do not know whether it is more than a pretty fancy of Richter's, that a spring shower is a sort of electric bath, and a very potent means of health; certainly rain clears the atmosphere—a fact of considerable importance in and about large towns. But it is enough for our purpose to prove that the rain need do no harm; for abundant daily exercise in the fresh air is of such vital importance to the children, that really nothing but sickness should keep them within doors. A mere time and distance tramp is sufficiently joyous for a wet day, for, taken good-humouredly, the beating rain itself is exhilarating. The 'long run' of the schoolboy, that is, a steady trot, breaking now and then into a run, is capital exercise; but regard must be had to the powers of the children, who must not be overdone.

Precautions.—At the same time, children should never be allowed to sit or stand about in damp clothes; and here is the use of waterproof rain-wraps—to keep them dry on short journeys to church, or school, or neighbour's house, where they cannot very well change their garments.

XIII.—'Red Indian' Life

Scouting.—Baden Powell's little book about Scouting set us upon a new track. Hundreds of families make joyous expeditions, far more educative than they dream, wherein scouting is the order of the day.

For example, one party of four or more lies in ambush,—the best ambush to be had, which is pitched upon after much consideration. The enemy scouts; first he finds the ambush, and then his skill is shown in getting within touch of the alert foe without being discovered. But every family should possess Scouting in default of the chance of going on the war-path with a Red Indian. The evil of the ready-made life we lead is that we do not discern the signs of the times. An alert intelligence towards what goes on in the open-air world is a great possession, and, strongly as we sympathise with the effort made to put down bird's-nesting, we shall lose, if we are not careful, one of the few bits of what we may call 'Red Indian' training still within our reach.

Bird-stalking.—But bird 'stalking,' to adapt a name, is a great deal more exciting and delightful than bird's nesting, and we get our joy at no cost of pain to other living things. All the skill of a good scout comes into play. Think, how exciting to creep noiselessy as shadows behind river-side bushes on hands and knees without disturbing a twig or pebble till you get within a yard of a pair of sandpipers, and then, lying low, to watch their dainty little runs, pretty tricks of head and tail, and to hear the music of their call. And here comes the real joy of bird-stalking. If in the winter months the children have become fairly familiar with the notes of our resident birds, they will be able in the early summer to 'stalk' to some purpose. The notes and songs in June are quite bewildering, but the plan is to single out those you are quite sure of, and then follow up the others. The key to a knowledge of birds is knowledge of their notes, and the only way to get this is to follow any note of which you are not sure. The joy of tracking a song or note to its source is the joy of a 'find,' a possession for life.

But bird-stalking is only to be done upon certain conditions. You must not only be 'most mousy-quiet,' but you must not even let a thought whisper, for if you let yourself think about anything else, the entirely delightful play of bird-life passes by you unobserved; nay, the very bird notes are unheard.

Here are two bird walks communicated by a bird lover:—

"We heard a note something like a chaffinch's, only slower, and we looked up in the boughs of the ash to try and track the bird by the sudden quiver of one twig here, another, there. We found a steep, rocky path which brought us almost level with the tree tops, and then we had a good view of the shy little willow wren busily seeking food. A note from the next tree like a bubbling of song drew us farther on, and then we found the wood wren and watched him as with up-turned head and bubbling throat he uttered his trill."

"A joyous burst of song came from a bush near by, and we crept on, to find a blackcap warbler with upraised crest turning excitedly round and round in the ecstasy of song. We waited, and traced him to his next station by his light touch on the branches. A hoarse screech from another tree announced a green-finch, and we had a long chase to get a glimpse of him; but he came to an outstanding twig, and then we heard his pretty song, which I should never have guessed to be his had we not seen him at it. A little squeaky note made us watch the tree trunks, and, sure enough, there was a tree-creeper running up and round and round an ash, uttering his note all the time.

"Another day we got behind a wall from which we could examine a field that lay beside the lake. There was the green plover with his jaunty crest, running and pecking, and, as he pecked, we caught sight of the rosy flash under his tail. We waited, hoping for more, for the plovers stand so still that they are lost in their surroundings. But someone coughed, and up went the plovers, a dozen of them, with their weary taunt, 'Why don't you let us alone?' Their distress roused other birds, and we saw a snipe rise from the water edge, a marshy place, with hasty zigzag flight; it made a long round and settled not much further than where it rose. The sandpipers rose, two flying close to the water's edge, whistling all the time. By the side of a little gully we watched a wagtail, and presently a turn in the sunshine showed us the yellow breast of the yellow wagtail. A loud 'tis-sic' near us drew our eyes to the wall, and there stood a pied wagtail with full beak, waiting to get rid of us before visiting his nest in the wall. We crept away and sheltered behind a tree, and after a few minutes' waiting we saw him go into his hole. An angry chatter near by (like a broom on Venetian blinds!) directed our eyes to a little brown wren on the wall with cocked-up tail, but in a minute he disappeared like a mouse over the side."

This from another bird-lover:—

"Now, they (the children) are beginning to care more for the birds than the eggs, and their first question, instead of being, 'What is the egg like?' is usually 'What is the bird like?' We have great searching through Morris's British Birds [John's British Birds, which costs as many shillings as Morris's does guineas, is better for beginners] to identify birds we have seen and to make quite sure of doubtful points.

"But now for the birds. Stonechats abound on the heaths. I pricked myself up to my knees standing in a gorse-patch watching and listening to the first I saw, but I was quite rewarded, and saw at least four pairs at one time. Do you know the birds? The cock-birds are such handsome little fellows, black head and mask, white collar, rufous breast and dark grey or brown back. They have a pretty little song, rather longer than a chaffinch's, besides the chit-chat cry when they are disturbed. They do not make a long flight, and will hover in the air like a flycatcher. The sandmartins have numbers of holes in the cliffs. We tried to see how deep they burrowed to build their nests, but though I put my arm in up to the elbows in several deserted holes, I could not reach the end. I think my favourites are the reed-warblers. I know of at least four pairs, and when I could induce the children to both stop talking for a few minutes, we were able to watch them boldly hopping up and down the reeds and singing in full view of us."

This is the sort of thing bird-stalkers come upon—and what a loss have those children who are not brought up to the gentle art wherein the eye is satisfied with seeing, and there is no greed of collecting, no play of the hunter's instinct to kill, and yet a lifelong joy of possession.

XIV.—The Children Require Country Air

The Essential Proportion of Oxygen.—Every one knows that the breathing of air which has lost little of its due proportion of oxygen is the essential condition of vigorous life and of a fine physique; also, that whatever produces heat, whether it be animal heat, or the heat of fire, candle, gas-lamp, produces that heat at the expense of the oxygen in the atmosphere—a bank which is drawn upon by every breathing and burning object; that in situations where much breathing and burning are going on, there is a terrible drain upon this vital gas; that the drain may be so excessive that there no longer sufficient oxygen in the air to support animal life, and death results; that where the drain is less excessive but still great, animal life may be supported, and people live in a flaccid, feeble life in a state of low vitality.

Excess of Carbonic Acid Gas.—Also we know that every breathing and every burning object expels a hurtful gas—carbonic acid. A very small proportion of this gas is present in the purest atmospheric air, and that small proportion is healthful; but increase that quantity by the action of furnaces, fires, living beings, gas-lamps, and the air is rendered unwholesome, just in proportion to the quantity of superfluous carbonic-acid gas it contains. If the quantity be excessive—as when many people are huddled together in a small unventilated room—speedy death by suffocation is the result.

Unvitiated, Unimpoverished Air.—For these reasons, it is not possible to enjoy fulness of life in a town. For grown-up people, the stimulus of town life does something to make up for the impurity of town air; as, on the other hand, country people too often forfeit their advantages through the habit of mental sluggishness they let themselves fall into: but, for the children—who not only breathe, but grow; who require, proportionately, more oxygen than adults need for their vital processes—it is absolutely cruel not to give them very frequent, if not daily, copious draughts of unvitiated, unimpoverished air, the sort of air that can be had only remote from towns.

Solar Light.—But this is only one of the reasons why, for health's sake alone, it is of the first importance to give children long days in the open country. They want light, solar light, as well as air. Country people are ruddier than town folk; miners are sallow, so are the dwellers in cellars and in sunless valleys. The reason is, that, to secure the ruddy glow of perfect health, certain changes must take place in the blood—the nature of which it would take too long to explain here—and that these changes in the blood, marked by free production of red corpuscles, appear to take place most favourably under the influence of abundant solar light. What is more, men of science are beginning to suspect that not only the coloured light rays of the solar spectrum, but the dark heat rays, and the chemical rays, minister to vitality in ways not yet fully understood.

A Physical Ideal for a Child.—There was a charming picture in Punch some time ago, of two little boys airing their English-French on their mother's new maid; two noble little fellows, each straight as a dart, with no superfluous flesh, eyes well opened, head erect, chest expanded, the whole body full of spring even in repose. It was worth looking at, if only as suggesting the sort of physique we delight to see in a child. No doubt the child inherits the most that he is in this respect as in all others; but this is what bringing-up may, with some limitations, effect:—The child is born with certain natural tendencies, and, according to his bringing-up, each such tendency may run into a blemish of person or character, or into a cognate grace. Therefore, it is worth while to have even a physical ideal for one's child; not, for instance, to be run away with by the notion that a fat child is necessarily a fine child. The fat child can easily be produced: but the bright eyes, the open regard, the springing step; the tones, clear as a bell; the agile, graceful movements that characterise the well-brought-up child, are the result, not of bodily well being only, but of 'mind and soul according well,' of a quick, trained intelligence, and of a moral nature habituated to the 'joy of self control.'

Part III: 'Habit Is Ten Natures'

I.—Education Based Upon Natural Law

A Healthy Brain.—What I desire to set before the reader is a method of education based upon natural law. In the first place, we have considered some of the conditions to be observed with a view to keep the brain in healthy working order; for it is upon the possession of an active, duly nourished brain that the possibility of a sound education depends.

Out-of-Door Life.—The consideration of out-of-door life, in developing a method of education, comes second in order; because my object is to show that the chief function of the child—his business in the world during the first six or seven years of his life—is to find out all he can, about whatever comes under his notice, by means of his five senses; that he has an insatiable appetite for knowledge got in this way; and that, therefore, the endeavour of his parents should be to put him in the way of making acquaintance freely with Nature and natural objects; that, in fact, the intellectual education of the young child should lie in the free exercise of perceptive power, because the first stages of mental effort are marked by the extreme activity of this power; and the wisdom of the educator is to follow the lead of Nature in the evolution of the complete human being.

The next subject for consideration—a rather dry psycho-physiological one—seems to me, all the same, to be very well worthy of attention as striking the keynote of a reasonable method of education.

Habit the Instrument by which Parents Work.—'Habit is *ten* natures!' If I could but make others see with my eyes how much this saying should mean to the educator! How habit, in the hands of the mother, is as his wheel to the potter, his knife to the carver—the instrument by means of which she turns out the design she has already conceived in her brain. Observe, the material is there to begin with; his wheel will not enable the potter to produce a porcelain cup out of coarse clay; but the instrument is as necessary as the material or the design. It is unpleasant to speak of one's self, but if the reader will allow me, I should like to run over the steps by which I have been brought to look upon habit as the means whereby the parent may make almost anything he chooses of his child. That which has become the dominant idea of one person's life, if it be launched suddenly at another, conveys no very great depth or weight of meaning to the second person—he wants to get at it by degrees, to see the steps by which the other has travelled. Therefore, I shall venture to show how I arrived at my present position, which is, from one of the three possible points of view—The formation of habits is education, and Education is the formation of habits.

II.—The Children Have No Self-Compelling Power

An Educational Cul-de-sac.—Some years ago I was accustomed to hear, 'Habit is *ten* natures,' delivered from the pulpit on at least one Sunday out of four. I had at the time just begun to teach, and was young and enthusiastic in my work. It was to my mind a great thing to be a teacher; it was impossible but that the teacher should leave his stamp on the children. His own was the fault if anything went wrong, if any child did badly in school or out of it. There was no degree of responsibility to which youthful ardour was not equal. But, all this zeal notwithstanding, the disappointing thing was, that nothing extraordinary happened. The children were good on the whole, because they were the children of parents who had themselves been brought up with some care; but it was plain that they behaved very much as twas their nature to.' The faults they had, they kept; the virtues they had were exercised just as fitfully as before. The good, meek little girl still told fibs. The bright, generous child was incurably idle. In lessons it was the same thing; the dawdling child went on dawdling, the dull child became no brighter. It was very disappointing. The children, no doubt, 'got on'—a little; but each one of them had the makings in her of a noble character, of a fine mind, and where was the lever to lift each of these little worlds? Such a lever there must be. This horse-in-a-mill round of geography and French, history and sums, was no more than playing at education; for who remembers the scraps of knowledge he laboured over as a child? and would not the application of a few hours in later life effect more than a year's drudgery at any one subject in childhood? If education is to secure the step-by-step progress of the individual and the race, it must mean something over and above the daily plodding at small tasks which goes by the name.

Love, Law, and Religion as Educational Forces.—Looking for guidance to the literature of education, I learned much from various sources, though I failed to find what seemed to me an authoritative guide, that is, one whose thought embraced the possibilities contained in the human nature of a child, and, at the same time, measured the scope of education. I saw how religious teaching helped the children, gave them power and motives for continuous effort, and raised their desires towards the best things. I saw in how far law restrained from evil, and love impelled towards good. But with these great aids from without and from above, there was still the depressing sense of labouring at education in the dark; the advance made by the young people in moral, and even in intellectual, power was like that of a door on its hinges—a swing forward to-day and back again to-morrow, with little sensible progress from year to year beyond that of being able to do harder sums and read harder books.

Why Children are incapable of Steady Effort.—Consideration made the reason of the failure plain: there was a warm glow of goodness at the heart of every one of the children, but they were all incapable of steady effort, because they had no strength of will, no power to make themselves do that which they knew they ought to do. Here, no doubt, come in the functions of parents and teachers; they should be able to make the child do that which he lacks the power to compel himself to. But it were poor training that should keep the child dependent upon personal influence. It is the business of education to find some way of supplementing that weakness of will which is the bane of most of us as well as of the children.

Children should be saved the Effort of Decision.—That the effort of decision is the most exhausting effort of life, has been well said from the pulpit; and if that remain true about ourselves, even when the decision is about trifling matters of going or coming, buying or not buying, it surely is not just to leave the children all the labour of an effort of will whenever they have to choose between the right and the wrong.

III.—What Is 'Nature'?

'Habit is *ten* natures,' went on being proclaimed in my ears; and at last it came home to me as a weighty saying, which might contain the educational 'Open, sesame!' I was in quest of. In the first place, what is Nature, and what, precisely, is Habit?

It is an astonishing thing, when we consider, what the child is, irrespective of race, country, or kindred, simply in right of his birth as a human being.

All Persons born with the same Primary Desires.—That we all have the same instincts and appetites, we are prepared to allow, but that the principles of action which govern all men everywhere are primarily the same, is a little startling; that, for instance, the same desires stir in the breasts of savage and of sage alike; that the desire of knowledge, which shows itself in the child's curiosity about things and his eager use of his eyes, is equally active everywhere; that the desire of society, which you may see in two babies presented to one another and all agog with glee and friendliness, is the cause, alike, of village communities amongst savage tribes and of the philosophical meeting of the learned; that everywhere is felt the desire of esteem—a wonderful power in the hands of the educator, making a word of praise or blame more powerful as a motive than any fear or hope of punishment or reward.

And Affections.—And it is not only the same desires; all people, everywhere, have the same affections and passions which act in the same way under similar provocation: joy and grief, love and resentment, benevolence, sympathy, fear, and much else, are common to all of us. So, too, of conscience, the sense of duty.

Content of the most Elemental Notion of Human Nature.—Dr Livingstone mentions that the only addition he felt called upon to make to the moral code of certain of the Zambesi tribes (however little they observed their own law) was, that a man should not have more than one wife. "Evil speaking, lying, hatred, disobedience to parents, neglect of them," were all known to be sin by these dark peoples whom civilised or Christian teaching had never before reached. Not only is a sense of duty common to mankind, but the deeper consciousness of God, however vague such consciousness may be. And all this and much more goes to make up the most elemental notion of human nature.

Nature plus Heredity.—Then, heredity comes in, and here, if you please, is ten natures: who is to deal with the child who is resentful, or stubborn, or reckless, because it is born in him, his mother's nature or his grandfather's? Think of the trick of the eye, the action of the hand, repeated from father to son; the peculiar character of the handwriting, traceable, as Miss Power Cobbe tells us is the case in her family, for instance, through five generations; the artistic temperament, the taste for music or drawing, running in families: here you get Nature with a twist, confirmed, sealed, riveted, utterly proof, you would say, against any attempt to alter or modify it.

Plus Physical Conditions.—And, once more, physical conditions come into force. The puny, feeble child and the sturdy urchin who never ails must necessarily differ from one another in the strength of their desires and emotions.

Human Nature the Sum of certain Attributes.—What, then, with the natural desires, affections, and emotions common to the whole race, what with the tendencies which each family derives by descent, and those peculiarities which the individual owes to his own constitution of body and brain,—human nature, the sum of all these, makes out for itself a strong case; so much so, that we are inclined to think the best that can be done is to let it alone, to let every child develop unhindered according to the elements of character and disposition that are in him.

The Child must not be left to his Human Nature.—This is precisely what half the parents in the world, and three-fourths of the teachers, are content to do; and what is the consequence? That the world is making advances, but the progress is, for the most part, amongst the few whose parents have taken their education seriously in hand; while the rest, who have been allowed to stay where they were, be no more, or no better than Nature made them, act as a heavy drag: for, indeed, the fact is, that they do not stay where they were; it is unchangeably true that the child who is not being constantly raised to a higher and a higher platform will sink to a lower and a lower. Wherefore, it is as much the parent's duty to educate his child into moral strength and purpose and intellectual activity as it is to feed him and clothe him; and that in spite of his nature, if it must be so. It is true that here and there circumstances step in and 'make a man' of the boy whose parents have failed to bring him under discipline; but this is a fortuitous aid which the educator is no way warranted to count upon.

I was beginning to see my way—not yet out of the psychological difficulty, which, so far as I was concerned, blocked the way to any real education; but now I could put my finger on the place, and that was something. Thus: -

The will of the child is pitifully feeble, weaker in the children of the weak, stronger in the children of the strong, but hardly ever to be counted upon as a power in education.

The nature of the child—his human nature—being the sum of what he is as a human being, and what he is in right of the stock he comes of, and what he is as the result of his own physical and mental constitution—this nature is incalculably strong.

Problem before the Educator.—The problem before the educator is to give the child control over his own nature, to enable him to hold himself in hand as much in regard to the traits we call good, as to those we call evil:—many a man makes shipwreck on the rock of what he grew up to think his characteristic virtue—his open-handedness, for instance.

Divine Grace works on the Lines of Human Effort.—In looking for a solution of this problem, I do not undervalue the Divine grace—far otherwise; but we do not always make enough of the fact that Divine grace is exerted on the lines of enlightened human effort; that the parent, for instance, who takes the trouble to understand what he is about in educating his child, deserves, and assuredly gets, support from above; and that Rebecca, let us say, had no right to bring up her son to be "thou worm, Jacob," in the trust that Divine grace would, speaking reverently, pull him through. Being a pious man, the son of pious parents, he was pulled through, but his days, he complains at the end, were "few and evil."

The Trust of Parents must not be Supine.— And indeed this is what too many Christian parents expect: they let a child grow free as the wild bramble, putting forth unchecked whatever is in him—thorn, coarse flower, insipid fruit,—trusting, they will tell you, that the grace of God will prune and dig and prop the wayward branches lying prone. And their trust is not always misplaced; but the poor man endures anguish, is torn asunder in the process of recovery which his parents might have spared him had they trained the early shoots which should develop by-and-by into the character of their child.

Nature then, strong as she is, is not invincible; and, at her best, Nature is not to be permitted to ride rampant. Bit and bridle, hand and voice, will get the utmost of endeavour out of her if her training be taken in hand in time; but let Nature run wild, like the forest ponies, and not spur nor whip will break her in.

IV.—Habit May Supplant 'Nature'

'Habit is ten natures.' If that be true, strong as nature is, habit is not only as strong, but tenfold as strong. Here, then, have we a stronger than he, able to overcome this strong man armed.

Habit runs on the Lines of Nature.—But habit runs on the lines of nature: the cowardly child habitually lies that he may escape blame; the loving child has a hundred endearing habits; the good-natured child has a habit of giving; the selfish child, a habit of keeping. Habit, working thus according to nature, is simply nature in action, growing strong by exercise.

But Habit may be a Lever.—But habit, to be the lever to lift the child, must work contrary to nature, or at any rate, independently of her.

Directly we begin to look out for the working of habit on these lines, examples crowd upon us: there are the children trained in careful habits, who never soil their clothes; those trained in reticent habits, who never speak of what is done at home, and answer indiscreet questions with 'I don't know'; there are the children brought up in courteous habits, who make way for their elders with gentle grace, and more readily for the poor woman with the basket than for the well-dressed lady; and there are children trained in grudging habits, who never offer to yield, or go, or do.

A Mother forms her Children's Habits involuntarily.—Such habits as these, good, bad, or indifferent, are they natural to the children? No, but they are what their mothers have brought them up to; and as a matter of fact, there is nothing which a mother cannot bring her child up to, and there is hardly a mother anywhere who has not some two or three—crotchets sometimes, principles sometimes—which her children never violate. So that it comes to this—given, a mother with liberal views on the subject of education, and she simply cannot help working her own views into her children's habits; given, on the other hand, a mother whose final question is, 'What will people say? what will people think? how will it look?' and the children grow up with habits of seeming, and not of being; they are content to appear well-dressed, well-mannered, and well-intentioned to outsiders, with very little effort after beauty, order, and goodness at home, and in each other's eyes.

Habit forces Nature into New Channels.—The extraordinary power of habit in forcing nature into new channels hardly requires illustration; we have only to see a small boy at a circus riding two barebacked ponies with a foot on the back of each, or a pantomime fairy dancing on air, or a clown behaving like an indiarubber ball, or any of the thousand feats of skill and dexterity which we pay our shillings to see—mental feats as well as bodily, though, happily, these are the rarer—to be convinced that exactly anything may be accomplished by training, that is, the cultivation of persistent habits. And the power of habit is not seen in human beings alone. The cat goes in search of her dinner always at the same time and to the same place—that is, if it is usual to feed her in one spot. Indeed, the habit of place is so much to the cat, that she will often rather die of famine than forsake the house to which she is accustomed. As for the dog, he is still more a 'bundle of habits' than his master. Scatter the crumbs for the sparrows at nine o'clock every morning, and at nine o'clock they will come for their breakfast, crumbs or no crumbs. Darwin inclines to think that the terror and avoidance shown towards man by the wild birds and lesser animals is simply a matter of transmitted habit; he tells us how he landed upon certain of the Pacific islands where the birds had never seen man before, and they lighted upon him and flew about him with utter fearlessness. To come nearer home, what evidence of the mastery of habit is more sad and more overwhelming than the habits of the drunkard, for instance, persisted in, in spite of reason, conscience, purpose, religion, every motive which should influence a thinking being?

Parents and Teachers must lay down Lines of Habit.—All this is nothing new; we have always known that 'use is second nature,' and that 'man is a bundle of habits.' It was not the fact, but the application of the fact, and the physiology of habit, that were new and exceedingly valuable ideas to me, and I hope they may be of some use to the reader. It was new to me, for instance, to perceive that it rests with parents and teachers to lay down lines of habit on which the life of the child may run henceforth with little jolting or miscarriage, and may advance in the right direction with the minimum of effort.

V.—The Laying Down Of Lines Of Habit

'Begin it, and the thing will be completed!' is infallibly true of every mental and moral habitude: completed, not on the lines you foresee and intend, but on the lines appropriate and necessary to that particular habitude. In the phrase 'unconscious cerebration' we are brought face to face with the fact that, whatever seed of thought or feeling you implant in a child—whether through inheritance or by early training—grows, completes itself, and begets after its kind, even as does a corporeal organism. It is a marvellous and beautiful thing to perceive an idea when the idea itself is a fine one—developing within you of its own accord, to find your pen writing down sentences whose logical sequence delights you, and yet in the conception of which you have had no conscious part. When the experienced writer 'reels off' in this fashion, he knows that so far as the run of the words, the ordering of the ideas, go, his work will need no revision. So fine a thing is this, that the lingering fallacy of the infallible reason established itself thereupon. The philosopher, who takes pleasure in observing the ways of his own mind, is a thinker of high thoughts, and he is apt to forget that the thought which defiles a man behaves in precisely the same way as that which purifies: the one, as the other, develops, matures, and increases after its kind.

We Think, as we are accustomed to Think.— How does this bear on the practical work of bringing up children? In this way. We think, as we are accustomed to think; ideas come and go and carry on a ceaseless traffic in the rut—let us call it—you have made for them in the very nerve substance of the brain. You do not deliberately intend to think these thoughts; you may, indeed, object strongly to the line they are taking (two 'trains' of thought going on at one and the same time!), and objecting, you may be able to barricade the way, to put up 'No Road' in big letters, and to compel the busy populace of the brain-world to take another route. But who is able for these things? Not the child, immature of will, feeble in moral power, unused to the weapons of the spiritual warfare. He depends upon his parents; it rests with them to initiate the thoughts he shall think, the desires he shall cherish, the feelings he shall allow. Only to initiate; no more is permitted to them; but from this initiation will result the habits of thought and feeling which govern the man—his character, that is to say. But is not this assuming too much, seeing that, to sum up roughly all we understand by heredity, a child is born with his future in his hands? The child is born, doubtless, with the tendencies which should shape his future; but every tendency has its branch roads, its good or evil outcome; and to put the child on the right track for the fulfilment of the possibilities inherent in him, is the vocation of the parent.

Direction of Lines of Habit.—This relation of habit to human life—as the rails on which it runs to a locomotive—is perhaps the most suggestive and helpful to the educator; for just as it is on the whole easier for the locomotive to pursue its way on the rails than to take a disastrous run off them, so it is easier for the child to follow lines of habit carefully laid down than to run off these lines at his peril. It follows that this business of laying down lines towards the unexplored country of the child's future is a very serious and responsible one for the parent. It rests with him to consider well the tracks over which the child should travel with profit and pleasure; and, along these tracks, to lay down lines so invitingly smooth and easy that the little traveller is going upon them at full speed without stopping to consider whether or no he chooses to go that way. Habit and Free-will—But,—supposing that the doing of a certain action a score or two of times in unbroken sequence forms a habit which it is as easy to follow as not; that, persist still further in the habit without lapses, and it becomes second nature, quite difficult to shake off; continue it further, through a course of years, and the habit has the strength of ten natures, you cannot break through it without doing real violence to yourself;—grant all this, and also that it is possible to form in the child the habit of doing and saying, even of thinking and feeling, all that it is desirable he should do or say, think or feel,—and do you not take away the child's free-will, make a mere automaton of him by this excessive culture?

Habit rules ninety-nine in a hundred of our Thoughts and Acts.—In the first place, whether you choose or no to take any trouble about the formation of his habits, it is habit, all the same, which will govern ninety-nine one-hundredths of the child's life: he is the mere automaton you describe. As for the child's becoming the creature of habit, that is not left with the parent to determine. We are all mere creatures of habit. We think our accustomed thoughts, make our usual small talk, go through the trivial round, the common task, without any self-determining effort of will at all. If it were not so—if we had to think, to deliberate, about each operation of the bath or the table—life would not be worth having; the perpetually repeated effort of decision would wear us out. But, let us be thankful, life is not thus laborious. For a hundred times we act or think, it is not necessary to choose, to will, say, more than once. And the little emergencies, which compel an act of will, will fall in the children's lives just about as frequently as in our own. These we cannot save them from, nor is it desirable that we should. What we can do for them is to secure that they have habits which shall lead them in ways of order, propriety, and virtue, instead of leaving their wheel of life to make ugly ruts in miry places.

Habit powerful even where the Will decides.—And then, even in emergencies, in every sudden difficulty and temptation that requires an act of will, why, conduct is still apt to run on the lines of the familiar habit. The boy who has been accustomed to find both profit and pleasure in his books does not fall easily into idle ways because he is attracted by an idle schoolfellow. The girl who has been carefully trained to speak the exact truth simply does not think of a lie as a ready means of getting out of a scrape, coward as she may be.

But this doctrine of habit, is it, after all, any more than an empirical treatment of the child's symptoms? Why should the doing of an act or the thinking of a thought, say, a score of times in unbroken succession, have any tendency to make the doing of that act or the thinking of that thought a part of the child's nature? We may accept the doctrine as an act of faith resting on experience; but if we could discover the raison d'être of this enormous force of habit it would be possible to go to work on the laying down of habits with real purpose and method.

VI.—The Physiology Of Habit

A work of Dr. Carpenter's was perhaps the first which gave me the clue I was in search of. In his Mental Physiology—a most interesting book, by the way—he works out the analogy between mental and physical activity, and shows that the correspondence in effect is due to a correspondence in cause.

Growing Tissues form themselves to Modes of Action.—To state roughly the doctrine of the school Dr Carpenter represents—the tissues, as muscular tissue, for instance, undergo constant waste and as constant reparation. Even those modes of muscular action which we regard as natural to us, as walking and standing erect, are in reality the results of a laborious education; quite as much so as many modes of action which we consciously acquire, as writing or dancing; but the acquired modes become perfectly easy and natural. Why? Because it is the law of the constantly growing tissues that they should form themselves according to the modes of action required of them. In a case where the brain is repeatedly sending down to the muscles, under nervous control as they are, the message to have a certain action done, that action becomes automatic in the lower centre, and the faintest suggestion from outside comes to produce it without the intervention of the brain. Thus, the joints and muscles of the child's hand very soon accommodate themselves to the mode of action required of them in holding and guiding the pen. Observe, it is not that the child learns with his mind how to use his pen, in spite of his muscles; but that the newly growing muscles themselves take form according to the action required of them. And here is the explanation of all the mountebank feats which appear simply impossible to the untrained looker-on. They are impossible to him, because his joints and muscles have not the same powers which have been produced in the mountebank by a process of early training.

Therefore Children should learn Dancing, Swimming, etc., at an Early Age.—So much for mere bodily activities. And here we have the reason why children should learn dancing, riding, swimming, calisthenics, every form of activity which requires a training of the muscles, at an early age: the fact being, that muscles and joints have not merely to conform themselves to new uses, but to grow to a modified pattern; and this growth and adaptation take place with the greatest facility in early youth. Of course, the man whose muscles have kept the habit of adaptation picks up new games, new muscular exercises, without very great labour. But teach a ploughman to write, and you see the enormous physical difficulty which unaccustomed muscles have in growing to any new sort of effort. Here we see how important it is to keep watch over the habits of enunciation, carriage of the head, and so on, which the child is forming hour by hour. The poke, the stoop, the indistinct utterance, is not a mere trick to be left off at pleasure 'when he is older and knows better,' but is all the time growing into him becoming a part of himself, because it is registered in the very substance of his spinal cord. The part of his nervous system where consciousness resides (the brain) has long ago given a standing order, and such are the complications of the administration, that to recall the order would mean the absolute re-making of the parts concerned. And to correct bad habits of speaking, for instance, it will not be enough for the child to intend to speak plainly and to try to speak plainly; he will not be able, to do so habitually until some degree of new growth has taken place in the organs of voice whilst he is making efforts to form the new habit.

Moral and Mental Habits make their Mark upon Physical Tissues.—But, practically, everybody knows that the body, and every part of the body, accommodates itself very readily to the uses it is put to: we know that if a child accustom herself to stand on one foot, thus pushing up one shoulder, the habit will probably end in curvature of the spine; that to permit drooping shoulders, and, consequently, contracted chest, is to prepare the way for lung disease. The physical consequences of bad habits of this sort are so evident, that we cannot blind ourselves to the relation of cause and effect. What we are less prepared to admit is, that habits which do not appear to be in any sense physical—a flippant habit, a truthful habit, an orderly habit—should also make their mark upon a physical tissue, and that it is to this physical effect the enormous strength of habit is probably due. Yet when we consider that the brain, the physical brain, is the exceedingly delicate organ by means of which we think and feel and desire, love and hate and worship, it is not surprising that that organ should be modified by the work it has to do; to put the matter picturesquely, it is as if every familiar train of thought made a rut in the nervous substance of the brain into which the thoughts run lightly of their own accord, and out of which they can only be got by an effort of will.

Persistent Trains of Thought.—Thus, the mistress of the house knows that when her thoughts are free to take their own course, they run to cares of the house or the larder, to to-morrow's dinner or the winter's clothing; that is, thought runs into the rut which has been, so to speak, worn for it by constant repetition. The mother's thoughts run on her children, the painter's on pictures, the poet's on poems; those of the anxious head of the house on money cares, it may be, until in times of unusual pressure the thoughts beat, beat, beat in that well-worn rut of ways and means, and decline to run in any other channel, till the poor man loses his reason, simply because he cannot get his thoughts out of that one channel made in the substance of his brain. And, indeed, "that way madness lies" for every one of us, in the persistent preying of any one train of thought upon the brain tissue. Pride, resentment, jealousy, an invention that a man has laboured over, an opinion he has conceived, any line of thought which he has no longer the power to divert, will endanger a man's sanity.

Incessant Regeneration of Brain Tissue.—If we love, hate, think, feel, worship, at the expense of actual physical effort on the part of the brain, and consequent waste of tissue, how enormous must be the labour of that organ with which we, in fact, do everything, even many of those acts whose final execution falls to the hands or feet! It is true: and to repair this excessive waste, the brain consumes the lion's share of the nourishment provided for the body. As we have already seen, fully a sixth or a fifth of all the blood in the body goes to repair the waste in the king's house; in other words, new brain tissue is being constantly formed at a startlingly rapid rate: one wonders at what age the child has no longer any part left of that brain with which he was born.

The new tissue repeats the old, but not quite exactly, just as a new muscular growth adapts itself to any now exercise required of it, so the new brain tissue is supposed to 'grow to' any habit of thought in force during the time of growth—'thought' here including, of course, every exercise of mind and soul. "The cerebrum of man grows to the modes of thought in which it is habitually exercised," says an able physiologist; or, in the words of Dr Carpenter, "Any sequence of mental action which has been frequently repeated, tends to perpetuate itself; so that we find ourselves automatically prompted to think, feel, or do what we have been before accustomed to think, feel, or do, under like circumstances, without any consciously formed purpose or anticipation of results. For there is no reason to regard the cerebrum as an exception to the general principle, that whilst each part of the organism tends to form itself in accordance with the mode in which it is habitually exercised, this tendency will be specially strong in the nervous apparatus, in virtue of that incessant regeneration which is the very condition of its functional activity. It scarcely, indeed, admits of a doubt, that every state of ideational consciousness which is either very strong or is habitually repeated, leaves an organic impression on the cerebrum, in virtue of which the same state may be reproduced at any future time in correspondence to a suggestion fitted to excite it."

Artificial Reflex Actions may be Acquired.—Or, to take Huxley's way of putting the case:

"By the help of the brain we may acquire an infinity of artificial reflex actions; that is to say, an action may require all our attention and all our volition for its first, second, or third performance, but by frequent repetition it becomes, in a manner, part of our organisation, and is performed without volition or even consciousness.

"As every one knows, it takes a soldier a long time to learn his drill—for instance, to put himself into the attitude of 'attention' at the instant the word of command is heard. But after a time the sound of the word gives rise to the act, whether the soldier be thinking of it or not. There is a story, which is credible enough, though it may not be true, of a practical joker who, seeing a discharged veteran carrying home his dinner, suddenly called out 'Attention!' whereupon the man instantly brought his hands down, and lost his mutton and potatoes in the gutter. The drill had been thorough, and its effects had become embodied in the man's nervous structure.

"The possibility of all education (of which military drill is only one particular form) is based upon the existence of this power which the nervous system possesses, of organising conscious actions into more or less unconscious, or reflex, operations. It may be down laid as a rule, that if any two mental states be called up together, or in succession, with due frequency and vividness, the subsequent production of the one of them will suffice to call up the other, and that whether we desire it or not.

Intellectual and Moral Education.—"The object of intellectual education is to create such indissoluble associations of our ideas of things, in the order and relation in which they occur in nature; that of a moral education is to unite as fixedly, the ideas of evil deeds with those of pain and degradation, and of good actions with those of pleasure and nobleness."

But it is the intimate interlocking of mind and matter which is more directly important to the educator—the idea which we have put broadly under the (by no means scientifically accurate) figure of a rut.

Given, that the constant direction of the thoughts produces a certain set in the tissues of the brain, this set is the first trace of the rut or path, a line of least resistance, along which the same impression, made another time, will find it easier to travel than to take another path. So arises a right-of-way for any given habit of action or thought.

Character affected by Acquired Modification of Brain Tissue.—What follows? Why, that the actual conformation of the child's brain depends upon the habits which the parents permit or encourage; and that the habits of the child produce the character of the man, because certain mental habitudes once set up, their nature is to go on for ever unless they should be displaced by other habits. Here is an end to the easy philosophy of, 'It doesn't matter,' 'Oh, he'll grow out of it,' 'He'll know better by-and-by,' 'He's so young, what can we expect?' and so on. Every day, every hour, the parents are either passively or actively forming those habits in their children upon which, more than upon anything else, future character and conduct depend.

Outside Influence.—And here comes in the consideration of outside influence. Nine times out of ten we begin to do a thing because we see some one else do it; we go on doing it, and—there is the habit! If it is so easy for ourselves to take up a new habit, it is tenfold as easy for the children; and this is the real difficulty in the matter of the education of habit. It is necessary that the mother be always on the alert to nip in the bud the bad habit her children may be in the act of picking up from servants or from other children.

VII.—The Forming Of A Habit—'Shut The Door After You'

"Do Ye Next Thinge."

"Lose this day loitering, and 'twill be the same story
To-morrow; and the next, more dilatory:
The indecision brings its own delays,
And days are lost, lamenting o'er lost days,"

says Marlowe, who, like many of us, knew the misery of the intellectual indolence which cannot brace itself to "Do ye next thinge." No question concerning the bringing up of children can, conceivably, be trivial, but this, of dilatoriness, is very important. The effort of decision, we have seen, is the greatest effort of life; not the doing of the thing, but the making up of one's mind as to which thing to do first. It is commonly this sort of mental indolence, born of indecision, which leads to dawdling habits. How is the dilatory child to be cured? Time? She will know better as she grows older? Not a bit of it: "And the next, more dilatory" will be the story of her days, except for occasional spurts. Punishments? No; your dilatory person is a fatalist. 'What can't be cured must be endured,' he says, but he will endure without any effort to cure. Rewards? No; to him a reward is a punishment presented under another aspect: the possible reward he realises as actual; there it is, within his grasp, so to say; in foregoing the reward he is punished; and he bears the punishment. What remains to be tried when neither time, reward, nor punishment is effectual? That panacea of the educationist: 'One custom overcometh another.' This inveterate dawdling is a habit to be supplanted only by the contrary habit, and the mother must devote herself for a few weeks to this cure as steadily and untiringly as she would to the nursing of her child through measles. Having in a few—the fewer the better—earnest words pointed out the miseries that must arise from this fault, and the duty of overcoming it, and having so got the (sadly feeble) will of the child on the side of right-doing, she simply sees that for weeks together the fault does not recur. The child goes to dress for a walk; she dreams over the lacing of her boots—the tag in her fingers poised in mid air—but her conscience is awake; she is constrained to look up, and her mother's eye is upon her, hopeful and expectant. She answers to the rein and goes on; midway, in the lacing of the second boot, there is another pause, shorter this time; again she looks up, and again she goes on. The pauses become fewer day by day, the efforts steadier, the immature young will is being strengthened, the habit of prompt action acquired. After that first talk, the mother would do well to refrain from one more word on the subject; the eye (expectant, not reproachful), and, where the child is far gone in a dream, the lightest possible touch, are the only effectual instruments. By-and-by, 'Do you think you can get ready in five minutes to-day without me?' 'Oh yes, mother.' 'Do not say "yes" unless you are quite sure.' 'I will try.' And she tries, and succeeds. Now, the mother will be tempted to relax her efforts—to overlook a little dawdling because the dear child has been trying so hard. This is absolutely fatal. The fact is, that the dawdling habit has made an appreciable record in the very substance of the child's brain. During the weeks of cure new growth has been obliterating the old track, and the track of a new habit is being formed. To permit any reversion to the old bad habit is to let go all this gain.

To form a good habit is the work of a few weeks; to guard it is a work of incessant, but by no means anxious care. One word more,—prompt action on the child's part should have the reward of absolute leisure, time in which to do exactly as she pleases, not granted as a favour, but accruing (without any words) as a right.

Habit a Delight in itself.—Except for this one drawback, the forming of habits in the children is no laborious task, for the reward goes hand in hand with the labour; so much so, that it is like the laying out of a penny with the certainty of the immediate return of a pound. For a habit is a delight in itself; poor human nature is conscious of the ease that it is to repeat the doing of anything without effort; and, therefore, the formation of a habit, the gradually lessening sense of effort in a given act, is pleasurable. This is one of the rocks that mothers sometimes split upon: they lose sight of the fact that a habit, even a good habit, becomes a real pleasure; and when the child has really formed the habit of doing a certain thing, his mother imagines that the effort is as great to him as at first, that it is virtue in him to go on making this effort, and that he deserves, by way of reward, a little relaxation—she will let him break through the new habit a few times, and then go on again. But it is not going on; it is beginning again, and beginning in the face of obstacles. The 'little relaxation' she allowed her child meant the forming of another contrary habit, which must be overcome before the child gets back to where he was before.

As a matter of fact, this misguided sympathy on the part of mothers is the one thing that makes it a laborious undertaking to train a child in good habits; for it is the nature of the child to take to habits as kindly as the infant takes to his mother's milk.

Tact, Watchfulness, and Persistence.—For example, and to choose a habit of no great consequence except as a matter of consideration for others: the mother wishes her child to acquire the habit of shutting the door after him when he enters or leaves a room. Tact, watchfulness, and persistence are the qualities she must cultivate in herself; and, with these, she will be astonished at the readiness with which the child picks up the new habit.

Stages in the Formation of a Habit.—'Johnny,' she says, in a bright, friendly voice, 'I want you to remember something with all your might: never go into or out of a room in which anybody is sitting without shutting the door.' 'But if I forget, mother?' 'I will try to remind you.' 'But perhaps I shall be in a great hurry.' 'You must always make time to do that.' 'But why, mother?' 'Because it is not polite to the people in the room to make them uncomfortable.' 'But if I am going out again that very minute?' 'Still, shut the door, when you come in; you can open it again to go out. Do you think you can remember?' 'I'll try, mother.'

'Very well; I shall watch to see how few "forgets" you make.'

For two or three times Johnny remembers; and then, he is off like a shot and half-way downstairs before his mother has time to call him back. She does not cry out, 'Johnny, come back and shut the door!' because she knows that a summons of that kind is exasperating to big or little. She goes to the door, and calls pleasantly, 'Johnny!' Johnny has forgotten all about the door; he wonders what his mother wants, and, stirred by curiosity, comes back, to find her seated and employed as before. She looks up, glances at the door, and says, 'I said I should try to remind you.' 'Oh, I forgot,' says Johnny, put upon his honour; and he shuts the door that time, and the next, and the next.

But the little fellow has really not much power to recollect, and the mother will have to adopt various little devices to remind him; but of two things she will be careful—that he never slips off without shutting the door, and that she never lets the matter be a cause of friction between herself and the child, taking the line of his friendly ally to help him against that bad memory of his. By and by, after, say, twenty shuttings of the door with never an omission, the habit begins to be formed; Johnny shuts the door as a matter of course, and his mother watches him with delight come into a room, shut the door, take something off the table, and go out, again shutting the door.

The Dangerous Stage.—Now that Johnny always shuts the door, his mother's joy and triumph begin to be mixed with unreasonable pity. 'Poor child,' she says to herself, 'it is very good of him to take so much pains about a little thing, just because he is bid!' She thinks that, all the time, the child is making an effort for her sake; losing sight of the fact that the habit has become easy and natural, that, in fact, Johnny shuts the door without knowing that he does so. Now comes the critical moment. Some day Johnny is so taken up with a new delight that the habit, not yet fully formed, loses its hold, and he is half-way downstairs before he thinks of the door. Then he does think of it, with a little prick of conscience, strong enough, not to send him back, but to make him pause a moment to see if his mother will call him back. She has noticed the omission, and is saying to herself, 'Poor little fellow, he has been very good about it this long time; I'll let him off this once.' He, outside, fails to hear his mother's call, says, to himself—fatal sentence!—'Oh, it doesn't matter,' and trots off.

Next time he leaves the door open, but it is not a 'forget.' His mother calls him back in a rather feeble way. His quick ear catches the weakness of her tone, and, without coming back, he cries, 'Oh, mother, I'm in such a hurry,' and she says no more, but lets him off. Again he rushes in, leaving the door wide open. 'Johnny!'—in a warning voice. 'I'm going out again just in a minute, mother,' and after ten minutes' rummaging he does go out, and forgets to shut the door. The mother's mis-timed easiness has lost for her every foot of the ground she had gained.

VIII.—Infant 'Habits'

The whole group of habitudes, half physical and half moral, on which the propriety and comfort of everyday life depend, are received passively by the child; that is, he does very little to form these habits himself, but his brain receives impressions from what he sees about him; and these impressions take form as his own very strongest and most lasting habits.

Some Branches of Infant Education.—Cleanliness, order, neatness, regularity, punctuality, are all 'branches' of infant education. They should be about the child like the air he breathes, and he will take them in as unconsciously. It is hardly necessary to say a word about the necessity for delicate cleanliness in the nursery. The babies get their share of tubbing, and unlimited washing is done on their behalf; but, indeed, scrupulous as mothers of the cultured class are, a great deal rests with the nurses, and it needs much watchfulness to secure that there shall not be the faintest odour about the infant or anything belonging to him, and that the nurseries be kept sweet and thoroughly aired. One great difficulty is, that there are still some nurses who belong to a class to which an open window is an abomination; and another is, they do not all know the meaning of odours: they cannot see 'a smell,' and, therefore, it is not easy to persuade them that a smell is matter, microscopic particles which the child takes into him with every breath he draws.

A Sensitive Nose.—By the way, a very important bit of physical education for a child is to train in him a sensitive nose—nostrils which sniff out the least 'stuffiness' in a room, or the faintest odour attached to clothes or furniture. The sense of smell appears to have been given us not only as an avenue of pleasure, but as a sort of danger-signal to warn us of the presence of noxious matters: yet many people appear to go through the world without a nose at all; and the fact tends to show that a quick sense of smell is a matter of education and habit. The habit is easily formed. Encourage the children to notice whether the room they enter 'smells' quite fresh when they come in out of the open air, to observe the difference between the air of the town and the fresher air beyond; and train them to perceive the faintest trace of pleasant or harmless odours.

The Baby is Ubiquitous.—To return to the nursery. It would be a great thing if the nurse could be impressed with the notion that the baby is ubiquitous, and that he not only sees and knows everything, but will keep, for all his life, the mark of all he sees:—

"If there's a hole in a'your coats,
I pray ye, tent it;
A chiel's amang ye takin' notes,
And, faith, he'll prent it":—

'prent it' on his own active brain, as a type for his future habits. Such a notion on the nurse's part might do something to secure cleanliness that goes beyond that of clean aprons. One or two little bits of tidiness that nurses affect are not to be commended on the score of cleanliness—the making up of the nursery beds early in the morning, and the folding up of the children's garments when they take them off at night. It is well to stretch a line across the day nursery at night, and hang the little garments out for an airing, to get rid of the insensible perspiration with which they have been laden during the day. For the same reason, the beds and bedclothes should be turned down to air for a couple of hours before they are made up.

Personal Cleanliness as an Early Habit.— The nursery table, if there be one, should be kept as scrupulously nice as that of the dining-room. The child who sits down to a crumpled or spotted tablecloth, or uses a discoloured metal spoon, is degraded—by so much. The children, too, should be encouraged to nice cleanliness in their own persons. We have all seen the dainty baby-hand stretched out to be washed; it has got a smudge, and the child does not like it. May they be as particular when they are big enough to wash their own hands! Not that they should be always clean and presentable; children love to 'mess about' and should have big pinafores for the purpose. They are all like that little French prince who scorned his birthday gifts, and entreated to be allowed to make dear little mud-pies with the boy in the gutter. Let them make their mud-pies freely; but that over, they should be impatient to remove every trace of soil, and should do it themselves. Young children may be taught to take care of their fingernails, and to cleanse the corners of eyes and ears. As for sitting down to table with unwashed hands and unbrushed hair, that, of course, no decent child is allowed to do. Children should be early provided with their own washing materials, and accustomed to find real pleasure in the bath, and in attending to themselves. There is no reason why a child of five or six should not make himself thoroughly clean without all that torture of soap in the eyes and general pulling about and poking which children hate, and no wonder. Besides, the child is not getting the habit of the daily bath until he can take it for himself, and it is important that this habit should be formed before the reckless era of school-life begins.

Modesty and Purity.—The operations of the bath afford the mother opportunities to give necessary teaching and training in habits of decency, and a sense of modesty. To let her young child live and grow in Eden-like simplicity is, perhaps, the most tempting and natural course to the mother. But alas! we do not live in the Garden, and it may be well that the child should be trained from the first to the conditions under which he is to live. To the youngest child, as to our first parents, there is that which is forbidden. In the age of unquestioning obedience, let him know that not all of his body does Almighty God allow him to speak of, think of, display, handle, except for purposes of cleanliness. This will be the easier to the mother if she speak of heart, lungs, etc., which, also, we are not allowed to look at or handle, but which have been so enclosed in walls of flesh and bone that we cannot get at them. That which is left open to us is so left, like that tree in the Garden of Eden, as a test of obedience; and in the one case, as in the other, disobedience is attended with certain loss and ruin.

The Habit of Obedience and the Sense of Honour.—The sense of prohibition, of sin in disobedience, will be a wonderful safeguard against knowledge of evil to the child brought up in habits of obedience; and still more effective will be the sense of honour, of a charge to keep—the motive of the apostolic injunctions on this subject. Let the mother renew this charge with earnestness on the eve, say, of each birthday, giving the child to feel that by obedience in this matter he may glorify God with his body; let her keep watch against every approach of evil; and let her pray daily that each one of her children may be kept in purity for that day. To ignore the possibilities of evil in this kind is to expose the child to frightful risks. At the same time, be it remembered that words which were meant to hinder may themselves be the cause of evil, and that a life full of healthy interests and activities is amongst the surest preventives of secret vice.

Order Essential.—What has been said about cleanliness applies as much to order—order in the nursery, and orderly habits in the nurse. One thing under this head: the nursery should not be made the hospital for the disabled or worn-out furniture of the house; cracked cups, chipped plates, jugs and teapots with fractured spouts, should be banished. The children should be brought up to think that when once an article is made unsightly by soil or fracture it is spoiled, and must be replaced; and this rule will prove really economical, for when children and servants find that things no longer 'do,' after some careless injury, they learn to be careful. But, in any case, it is a real detriment to the children to grow up using imperfect and unsightly makeshifts.

The pleasure grown-up people take in waiting on children is really a fruitful source of mischief;—for instance, in this matter of orderly habits. Who does not know the litter the children leave to be cleared up after them a dozen times a day, in the nursery, garden, drawing-room, wherever their restless little feet carry them? We are a bit sentimental about scattered toys and faded nosegays, and all the tokens of the children's presence; but the fact is, that the lawless habit of scattering should not be allowed to grow upon children. Everybody condemns the mother of a family whose drawers are chaotic, whose possessions are flung about heedlessly; but at least some of the blame should be carried back to her mother. It is not as a woman that she has picked up a miserable habit which destroys the comfort, if not the happiness, of her home; the habit of disorder was allowed to grow upon her as a child, and her share of the blame is, that she has failed to cure herself.

The Child of Two should put away his Playthings.—The child of two should be taught to get and to replace his playthings. Begin early. Let it be a pleasure to him, part of his play, to open his cupboard, and put back the doll or the horse each in its own place. Let him always put away his things as a matter of course, and it is surprising how soon a habit of order is formed, which will make it pleasant to the child to put away his toys, and irritating to him to see things in the wrong place. If parents would only see the morality of order, that order in the nursery becomes scrupulousness in after life, and that the training necessary to form the habit is no more, comparatively, than the occasional winding of a clock, which ticks away then of its own accord and without trouble to itself, more pains would be taken to cultivate this important habit.

Neatness Akin to Order.—Neatness is akin to order, but is not quite the same thing: it implies not only 'a place for everything, and everything in its place,' but everything in a suitable place, so as to produce a good effect; in fact, taste comes into play. The little girl must not only put her flowers in water but arrange them prettily, and must not be put off with some rude kitchen mug or jug for them, or some hideous pink vase, but must have jar or vase graceful in form and harmonious in hue, though it be but a cheap trifle. In the same way, everything in the nursery should be 'neat'—that is, pleasing and suitable; and children should be encouraged to make neat and effective arrangements of their own little properties. Nothing vulgar in the way of print, picture-book, or toy should be admitted—nothing to vitiate a child's taste or introduce a strain of commonness into his nature. On the other hand, it would be hard to estimate the refining, elevating influence of one or two well-chosen works of art, in however cheap a reproduction.

Regularity.—The importance of Regularity in infant education is beginning to be pretty generally acknowledged. The young mother knows that she must put her baby to bed at a proper time, regardless of his cries, even if she leave him to cry two or three times, in order that, for the rest of his baby life, he may put himself sweetly to sleep in the dark without protest. But a good deal of nonsense is talked about the reason of the child's cries—he is supposed to want his mother, or his nurse, or his bottle, or the light, and to be 'a knowing little fellow,' according to his nurse, quite up to the fact that if he cries for these things he will get them.

Habits of Time and Place.—The fact is, the child has already formed a habit of wakefulness or of feeding at improper times, and he is as uneasy at his habits being broken in upon as the cat is at a change of habitation; when he submits happily to the new regulation, it is because the new habit is formed, and is, in its turn, the source of satisfaction. According to Dr Carpenter, "Regularity should begin even with infant life, as to times of feeding, repose, etc. The bodily habit thus formed greatly helps to shape the mental habit at a later period. On the other hand, nothing tends more to generate a habit of self-indulgence than to feed a child, or to allow it to remain out of bed, at unseasonable times, merely because it cries. It is wonderful how soon the actions of a young infant (like those of a young dog or horse) come into harmony with systematic 'training' judiciously exercised." The habit of regularity is as attractive to older children as to the infant. The days when the usual programme falls through are, we know, the days when the children are apt to be naughty.

IX.—Physical Exercises

Importance of Daily.—The subject of the natural training of eye and muscles was taken up pretty fully in treating of 'Out-of-door Life.' I will only add, that to give the child pleasure in light and easy motion—the sort of delight in the management of his own body that a good rider finds in managing his horse—dancing, drill, calisthenics, some sort of judicious physical exercise, should make part of every day's routine. Swedish drill is especially valuable, and many of the exercises are quite suitable for the nursery. Certain moral qualities come into play in alert movements, eye-to-eye attention, prompt and intelligent replies; but it often happens that good children fail in these points for want of physical training.

Drill of Good Manners.—Just let them go through the drill of good manners: let them rehearse little scenes in play,—Mary, the lady asking the way to the market; Harry, the boy who directs her, and so on. Let them go through a position drill—eyes right, hands still, heads up. They will invent a hundred situations, and the behaviour proper to each, and will treasure hints thrown in for their guidance; but this sort of drill should be attempted while children are young, before the tyranny of mauvaise honte sets in. Encourage them to admire and take pride in light springing movements, and to eschew a heavy gait and clownish action of the limbs.

Training of the Ear and Voice.—The training of the ear and voice is an exceedingly important part of physical culture. Drill the children in pure vowel sounds, in the enunciation of final consonants; do not let them speak of 'walkin and 'talkin',' of a 'fi-ine da-ay,' 'ni-ice boy-oys.' Drill them in pronouncing difficult words —'imperturbability,' 'ipecacuanha,' 'Antananarivo,'—with sharp precision after a single hearing; in producing the several sounds of each vowel and the sounds of the consonants without attendant vowels. French, taught orally, is exceedingly valuable as affording training for both ear and voice.

The Habit of Music.—As for a musical training, it would be hard to say how much that passes for inherited musical taste and ability is the result of the constant hearing and producing of musical sounds, the habit of music, that the child of musical people grows up with. Mr. Hullah maintained that the art of singing is entirely a trained habit—that every child may be, and should be, trained to sing. Of course, transmitted habit must be taken into account. It is a pity that the musical training most children get is of a random character; that they are not trained, for instance, by carefully graduated ear and voice exercises, to produce and distinguish musical tones and intervals.

Let Children Alone.—In conclusion, let me say that the education of habit is successful in so far as it enables the mother to let her children alone, not teasing them with perpetual commands and directions—a running fire of Do and Don't; but letting them go their own way and grow, having first secured that they will go the right way, and grow to fruitful purpose. The gardener, it is true, 'digs about and dungs,' prunes and trains, his peach tree; but that occupies a small fraction of the tree's life: all the rest of the time the sweet airs and sunshine, the rains and dews, play about it and breathe upon it, get into its substance, and the result is—peaches. But let the gardener neglect his part, and the peaches will be no better than sloes.

Part IV
Some Habits Of Mind — Some Moral Habits

A Science of Education.—Allow me to say once more, that I venture to write upon subjects bearing on home education with the greatest deference to mothers; believing, that in virtue of their peculiar insight into the dispositions of their own children, they are blest with both knowledge and power in the management of them which lookers on can only admire from afar. At the same time, there is such a thing as a science of education, that does not come by intuition, in the knowledge of which it is possible to bring up a child entirely according to natural law, which is also Divine law, in the keeping of which there is great reward.

Education in Habit favours an Easy Life.—We have seen why Habit, for instance, is such a marvellous force in human life. I find this view of habit very encouraging, as giving a scientific reasonableness to the conclusions already reached by common experience. It is pleasant to know that, even in mature life, it is possible by a little persistent effort to acquire a desirable habit. It is good, if not pleasant, to know, also, with what fatal ease we can slip into bad habits. But the most comfortable thing in this view of habit is, that it falls in with our natural love of an easy life. We are not unwilling to make efforts in the beginning with the assurance that by-and-by things will go smoothly; and this is just what habit is, in an extraordinary degree, pledged to effect. The mother who takes pains to endow her children with good habits secures for herself smooth and easy days; while she who lets their habits take care of themselves has a weary life of endless friction with the children. All day she is crying out, 'Do this!' and they do it not; 'Do that!' and they do the other. 'But,' you say, 'if habit is so powerful, whether to hinder or to help the child, it is fatiguing to think of all the habits the poor mother must attend to. Is she never to be at ease with her children?'

Training in Habit Becomes a Habit.—Here, again, is an illustration of that fable of the anxious pendulum, overwhelmed with the thought of the number of ticks it must tick. But the ticks are to be delivered tick by tick, and there will always be a second of time to tick in. The mother devotes herself to the formation of one habit at a time, doing no more than keep watch over those already formed. If she be appalled by the thought of overmuch labour, let her limit the number of good habits she will lay herself out to form. The child who starts life with, say, twenty good habits, begins with a certain capital which he will lay out to endless profit as the years go on. The mother who is distrustful of her own power of steady effort may well take comfort in two facts. In the first place, she herself acquires the habit of training her children in a given habit, so that by-and-by it becomes, not only no trouble, but a pleasure to her. In the second place, the child's most fixed and dominant habits are those which the mother takes no pains about, but which the child picks up for himself through his close observation of all that is said and done, felt and thought, in his home.

Habits inspired in the Home Atmosphere.—We have already considered a group of half physical habits—order, regularity, neatness—which the child imbibes, so to speak, in a way. But this is not all: habits of gentleness, courtesy, kindness, candour, respect for other people, or—habits quite other than these, are inspired by the child as the very atmosphere of his home, the air he lives in and must grow by.

I. The Habit of Attention

Let us pass on, now, to the consideration of a group of mental habits which are affected by direct training rather than by example.

First, we put the habit of Attention, because the highest intellectual gifts depend for their value upon the measure in which their owner has cultivated the habit of attention. To explain why this habit is of such supreme importance, we must consider the operation of one or two of the laws of thought. But just recall, in the meantime, the fixity of attention with which the trained professional man—the lawyer, the doctor, the man of letters—listens to a roundabout story, throws out the padding, seizes the facts, sees the bearing of every circumstance, and puts the case with new clearness and method; and contrast this with the wandering eye and random replies of the uneducated;—and you see that to differentiate people according to their power of attention is to employ a legitimate test.

A Mind at the Mercy of Associations.—We will consider, then, the nature and the functions of attention. The mind—with the possible exception of the state of coma—is never idle; ideas are for ever passing through the brain, by day and by night, sleeping or walking, mad or sane. We take a great deal too much upon ourselves when we suppose that we are the authors and intenders of the thoughts we think. The most we can do is to give direction to these trains of thought in the comparatively few moments when we are regulating the thoughts of our hearts. We see in dreams—the rapid dance of ideas through the brain during lighter sleep—how ideas follow one another in a general way. In the wanderings of delirium, in the fancies of the mad, the inconsequent prattle of the child, and the babble of the old man, we see the same thing, i.e.—the law according to which ideas course through the mind when they are left to themselves. You talk to a child about glass—you wish to provoke a proper curiousity as to how glass is made, and what are its uses. Not a bit of it; he wanders off to Cinderella's glass slipper; then he tells you about his godmother who gave him a boat; then about the ship in which Uncle Harry went to America; then he wonders why you do not wear spectacles, leaving you to guess that Uncle Harry does so. But the child's ramblings are not whimsical; they follow a law, the law of association of ideas, by which any idea presented to the mind recalls some other idea which has been at any time associated with it—as glass and Cinderella's slipper; and that, again some idea associated with it. Now this law of association of ideas is a good servant and a bad master. To have this aid in recalling the events of the past, the engagements of the present, is an infinite boon; but to be at the mercy of associations, to have no power to think what we choose when we choose, but only as something 'puts it into our head,' is to be no better than an imbecile.

Wandering Attention.—A vigorous effort of will should enable us at any time to fix our thoughts. Yes; but a vigorous self-compelling will is the flower of a developed character; and while the child has no character to speak of, but only natural disposition, who is to keep humming-tops out of a geography lesson, or a doll's sofa out of a French verb? Here is the secret of the weariness of the home schoolroom—the children are thinking all the time about something else than their lessons; or rather, they are at the mercy of the thousand fancies that flit through their brains, each in the train of the last. "Oh, Miss Smith," said a little girl to her governess, "there are so many things more interesting than lessons to think about!"

Where is the harm? In this: not merely that the children are wasting time, though that is a pity; but that they are forming a desultory habit of mind, and reducing their own capacity for mental effort.

The Habit of Attention to be Cultivated in the Infant.—The help, then, is not the will of the child but in the habit of attention, a habit to be cultivated even in the infant. A baby, notwithstanding his wonderful powers of observation, has no power of attention; in a minute, the covered plaything drops from listless little fingers, and the wandering glance lights upon some new joy. But even at this stage the habit of attention may be trained: the discarded plaything is picked up, and, with 'Pretty!' and dumb show, the mother keeps the infant's eyes fixed for fully a couple of minutes—and this is her first lesson in attention. Later, as we have seen, the child is eager to see and handle every object that comes in his way. But watch him at his investigations: he flits from thing to thing with less purpose than a butterfly amongst the flowers, staying at nothing long enough to get the good out of it. It is the mother's part to supplement the child's quick observing faculty with the habit of attention. She must see to it that he does not flit from this to that, but looks long enough at one thing to get a real acquaintance with it.

Is little Margaret fixing round eyes on a daisy she has plucked? In a second, the daisy will be thrown away, and a pebble or buttercup will charm the little maid. But the mother seizes the happy moment. She makes Margaret see that the daisy is a bright yellow eye with white eyelashes round it; that all the day long it lies there in the grass and looks up at the great sun, never blinking as Margaret would do, but keeping its eyes wide open. And that is why it is called daisy, 'day's eye,' because its eye is always looking at the sun which makes the day. And what does Margaret think it does at night, when there is no sun? It does what little boys and girls do; it just shuts up its eye with its white lashes tipped with pink, and goes to sleep till the sun comes again in the morning. By this time the daisy has become interesting to Margaret; she looks at it with big eyes after her mother has finished speaking, and then, very likely, cuddles it up to her breast or gives it a soft little kiss. Thus the mother will contrive ways to invest every object in the child's world with interest and delight.

Attention to 'Things'; Words a Weariness.—But the tug of war begins with the lessons of the schoolroom. Even the child who has gained the habit of attention to things, finds words a weariness. This is a turning point in the child's life, and the moment for mother's tact and vigilance. In the first place, never let the child dawdle over copybook or sum, sit dreaming with his book before him. When a child grows stupid over a lesson, it is time to put it away. Let him do another lesson as unlike the last as possible, and then go back with freshened wits to his unfinished task. If mother or governess have been unwary enough to let the child 'moon' over a lesson, she must just exert her wits to pull him through; the lesson must be done, of course, but must be made bright and pleasant to the child.

Lessons Attractive.—The teacher should have some knowledge of the principles of education; should know what subjects are best fitted for the child considering his age, and how to make these subjects attractive; should know, too, how to vary the lessons, so that each power of the child's mind should rest after effort, and some other power be called into play. She should know how to incite the child to effort through his desire of approbation, of excelling, of advancing, his desire of knowledge, his love of his parents, his sense of duty, in such a way that no one set of motives be called unduly into play to the injury of the child's character. But the danger she must be especially alive to, is the substitution of any other natural desire for that of knowledge, which is equally natural, and is adequate for all the purposes of education.

Time-table; Definite Work in a Given Time.—I shall have opportunities to enter into some of these points later; meantime, let us look in at a home schoolroom managed on sound principles. In the first place, there is a time-table, written out fairly, so that the child knows what he has to do and how long each lesson is to last. This idea of definite work to be finished in a given time is valuable to the child, not only as training him in habits of order, but in diligence; he learns that one time is not 'as good as another'; that there is no right time left for what is not done in its own time; and this knowledge alone does a great deal to secure the child's attention to his work. Again, the lessons are short, seldom more than twenty minutes in length for children under eight; and this, for two or three reasons. The sense that there is not much time for his sums or his reading, keeps the child's wits on the alert and helps to fix his attention; he has time to learn just so much of any one subject as it is good for him to take in at once: and if the lessons be judiciously alternated—sums first, say, while the brain is quite fresh; then writing, or reading—some more or less mechanical exercise, by way of a rest; and so on, the program varying a little from day to day, but the same principle throughout—a 'thinking' lesson first, and a 'painstaking' lesson to follow,—the child gets through his morning lessons without any sign of weariness.

Even with regular lessons and short lessons, a further stimulus may be occasionally necessary to secure the attention of the child. His desire of approbation may ask the stimulus, not only of a word of praise, but of something in the shape of a reward to secure his utmost efforts. Now, rewards should be dealt out to the child upon principle: they should be the natural consequences of his good conduct.

A Natural Reward.—What is the natural consequence of work well and quickly done? Is it not the enjoyment of ampler leisure? The boy is expected to do two right sums in twenty minutes: he does them in ten minutes; the remaining ten minutes are his own, fairly earned, in which he should be free for a scamper in the garden, or any delight he chooses. His writing task is to produce six perfect m's: he writes six lines with only one good m in each line, the time for the writing lesson is over and he has none for himself; or, he is able to point out six good m's in his first line, and he has the rest of the time to draw steamboats and railway trains. This possibility of letting the children occupy themselves variously in the few minutes they may gain at the end of each lesson, is compensation which the home schoolroom offers for the zest which the sympathy of numbers, and emulation, are supposed to give to schoolwork.

Emulation.—As for emulation, a very potent means of exciting and holding the attention of children, it is often objected that a desire to excel, to do better than others, implies an unloving temper, which the educator should rather repress than cultivate. Good marks of some kind are usually the rewards of those who do best, and it is urged that these good marks are often the cause of ungenerous rivalry. Now, the fact is, the children are being trained to live in the world, and in the world we all do get good marks of one kind or another, prize, or praise, or both, according as we excel others, whether in football or tennis, or in picture painting or poem-making. There are envyings and heart burnings amongst those who come in second best; so it has been from beginning, and doubtless will be to the end. If the child is go out into an emulous world, why, it may be possibly be well that he should brought up in an emulous school. But here is where the mother's work comes in. She can teach her child to be first without vanity, and to be last without bitterness; that is, she can bring him up in such a hearty outgoing of love and sympathy that joy in his brother's success takes the sting out of his own failure, and regret for his brother's failure leaves no room for self glorification. Again, if a system of marks be used as a stimulus to attention and effort, the good marks should be given for conduct rather than for cleverness—that is, they should be within everybody's reach: every child may get his mark for punctuality, order, attention, diligence, obedience, gentleness; and therefore, marks of this kind may be given without danger of leaving a rankling sense of injustice in the breast of the child who fails. Emulation becomes suicidal when it is used as the incentive to intellectual effort, because the desire for knowledge subsides in proportion as the desire to excel becomes active. As a matter of fact, marks of any sort, even for conduct, distract the attention of children from their proper work, which is in itself interesting enough to secure good behaviour as well as attention.

Affection as a Motive.—That he ought to work hard to please his parents who do so much for him, is a proper motive to bring before the child from time to time, but not too often: if the mother trade on her child's feelings, if, 'Do this or that to please mother,' 'Do not grieve poor mother,' etc., be brought too frequently before the child as the reason for right doing, a sentimental relation is set up which both parent and child will find embarrassing, the true motives of action will be obscured, and the child unwilling to appear unloving, will end in being untrue.

Attractiveness of Knowledge.—Of course, the most obvious means of quickening and holding the attention of children lies in the attractiveness of knowledge itself, and in the real appetite for knowledge with which they are endowed. But how successful faulty teachers are in curing children of any desire to know, is to be seen in many a school room. I shall later, however, have an opportunity for a few words on this subject.

What is Attention?—It is evident that attention is no 'faculty' of the mind; indeed, it is very doubtful how far the various operations of the mind should be described as 'faculties' at all. Attention is hardly even an operation of the mind, but is simply the act by which the whole mental force is applied to the subject in hand. This act, of bringing the whole mind to bear, may be trained into a habit at the will of the parent or teacher, who attracts and holds the child's attention by means of a sufficient motive.

Self-Compelled.—As the child gets older, he is taught to bring his own will to bear; to make himself attend in spite of the most inviting suggestions from without. He should be taught to feel a certain triumph in compelling himself to fix his thoughts. Let him know what the real difficulty is, how it is the nature of his mind to be incessantly thinking, but how the thoughts, if left to themselves, will always run off from one thing to another, and that the struggle and the victory required of him is to fix his thoughts upon the task in hand. 'You have done your duty,' with a look of sympathy from his mother, is a reward for the child who has made this effort in the strength of his growing will. But it cannot be too much borne in mind that attention is, to a great extent, the product of the educated mind; that is, one can only attend in proportion as one has the intellectual power of developing the topic.

It is impossible to overstate the importance of this habit of attention. It is, to quote words of weight, "within the reach of everyone, and should be made the primary object of all mental discipline"; for whatever the natural gifts of the child, it is only so far as the habit of attention is cultivated in him that he is able to make use of them.

The Secret of Overpressure.—If it were only as it saves wear and tear, a perpetual tussle between duty and inclination, it is worth while for the mother to lay herself out to secure that her child never does a lesson into which he does not put his heart. And that is no difficult undertaking; the thing is, to be on the watch from the beginning against the formation of the contrary habit of inattention. A great deal has been said lately about overpressure, and we have glanced at one or two of the causes whose effects go by this name. But truly, one of the most fertile causes of an overdone brain is a failure in the habit of attention. I suppose we are all ready to admit that it is not the things we do, but the things we fail to do, which fatigue us, with the sense of omission, with the worry of hurry in overtaking our tasks. And this is almost the only cause of failure in the work in the case of the healthy schoolboy or schoolgirl: wandering wits hinder a lesson from being fully taken in at the right moment; that lesson becomes a bugbear, continually wanted henceforth and never there; and the sense of loss tries the young scholar more than would the attentive reception of a dozen such lessons.

The Schoolboy's Home Work.—In the matter of home work, the parents may still be of great use to their boys and girls after they begin to go to day-school; not in helping them, that should not be necessary; but let us suppose a case: 'Poor Annie does not her finish her lessons till half past nine, she really has so much to do'; 'Poor Tom is at his books till ten o'clock; we never see anything of the children in the evening,' say the distressed parents; and they let their children go on in a course which is absolutely ruinous both to bodily health and brain power.

Wholesome Home Treatment for Mooning.—Now, the fault is very seldom in the lessons, but in the children; they moon over their books, and a little wholesome home treatment should cure them of that ailment. Allow them, at the utmost, an hour and a half for their home-work; treat them tacitly as defaulters if they do not appear at the end of that time; do not be betrayed into word or look of sympathy; and the moment the time for lessons is over, let some delightful game or storybook be begun in the drawing room. By-and-by they will find that it is possible to finish lessons in time to secure a pleasant evening afterwards, and the lessons will be much the better done for the fact that concentrated attention has been bestowed upon them. At the same time the custom of giving home-work, at any rate to children under fourteen, is greatly to be deprecated. The gain of a combination of home and school life is lost to the children; and a very full scheme of school work may be carried through in the morning hours.

Rewards and Punishments should be relative Consequences of Conduct.—In considering the means of securing attention, it has been necessary to refer to discipline—the dealing out of rewards and punishments,—a subject which every tyro of a nursery maid or nursery governess feels herself very competent to handle. But this, too, has its scientific aspect: there is a law by which all rewards and punishments should be regulated: they should be natural, or, at any rate, the relative consequences of conduct; should imitate, as nearly as may be without injury to the child, the treatment which such and such conduct deserves and receives in after life. Miss Edgeworth, in her story of Rosamond and the Purple Jar, hits the right principle, though the incident is rather extravagant. Little girls do not often pine for purple jars in chemists' windows; but that we should suffer for our wilfulness in getting what is unnecessary by going without what is necessary, is precisely one of the lessons of life we all have to learn, and therefore is the right sort of lesson to teach a child.

Natural and Elective Consequences.—It is evident that to administer rewards and punishments on this principle requires patient consideration and steady determination on the mother's part. She must consider with herself what fault of disposition the child's misbehaviour springs from; she must aim her punishment at that fault, and must brace herself to see her child suffer present loss for his lasting gain. Indeed, exceedingly little actual punishment is necessary where children are brought up with care. But this happens continually—the child who has done well gains some natural reward (like that ten minutes in the garden), which the child forfeits who has done less well; and the mother must brace herself and her child to bear this loss; if she equalise the two children she commits a serious wrong, not against the child who has done well, but against the defaulter, whom she deliberately encourages to repeat his shortcoming. In placing her child under the discipline of consequences, the mother must use much tact and discretion. In many cases, the natural consequence of the child's fault is precisely that which it is her business to avert, while, at the same time, she looks about for some consequence related to the fault which shall have an educative bearing on the child: for instance, if a boy neglects his studies, the natural consequences is that he remains ignorant; but to allow him to do so would be criminal neglect on the part of the parent.

II. The Habits of Application, Etc.

Rapid Mental Effort—The habits of mental activity and of application are trained by the very means employed to cultivate that of attention. The child may plod diligently through his work who might be trained to rapid mental effort. The teacher herself must be alert, must expect instant answers, quick thought, rapid work. The tortoise will lag behind the hare, but the tortoise must be trained to move, every day, a trifle quicker. Aim steadily at securing quickness of apprehension and execution, and that goes far towards getting it.

Zeal must be Stimulated.—So of application. The child must not be allowed to get into the mood in which he says, 'Oh, I am so tired of sums,' or 'of history.' His zeal must be stimulated; and there must be always a pleasing vista before him; and the steady, untiring application to work should be held up as honourable, while fitful, flagging attention and effort are scouted.

III. The Habit of Thinking

'A Lion' Operations included in Thinking.—The actual labour of the brain is known to psychologists under various names, and divided into various operations: let us call it thinking, which, for educational purposes, is sufficiently exact; but, by 'thinking,' let us mean a real conscious effort of mind, and not the fancies that flit without effort through the brain. This sort of thing, for instance, an example quoted by Archbishop Thompson in his Laws of Thought [This example, offered by so able a psychologist, is so admirable that I venture to quote it more than once]:—"when Captain Head was travelling across the pampas of South America, his guide one day suddenly stopped him, and pointing high into the air, cried out 'A lion!' Surprised at such an exclamation, accompanied with such an act, he turned up his eyes, and with difficulty perceived, at an immeasurable height, a flight of condors, soaring in circles in a particular spot. Beneath this spot, far out of sight of himself of himself or guide, lay the carcass of a horse, and over that carcass stood, as the guide well knew, a lion, whom the condors were eyeing with envy from their airy height. The signal of the birds was to him what the sight of the lion alone would have been to the traveller—a full assurance of its existence.

Here was an act of thought which cost the thinker no trouble, which was easy to him as to cast his eyes upward, yet which from us, unaccustomed to the subject, would require many steps and some labour. The sight of the condors convinced him that there was some carcass or other; but as they kept wheeling far above it, instead of swooping down to their feast, he guessed that some beast had anticipated them. Was it a dog, or a jackal? No; the condors would not fear to drive away, or share with, either: it must be some large beast, and as there were lions in the neighbourhood, he concluded that one was here." And all these steps of thought are summed in the words 'A lion.'

This is the sort of thing that the children should go through, more or less, in every lesson—a tracing of effect from cause, or of cause from effect; a comparing of things to find out wherein they are alike, and wherein they differ; a conclusion as to causes or consequences from certain premisses.

IV. The Habit of Imagining

The Sense of Incongruous.—All their lessons will afford some scope for some slight exercise of the children's thinking power, some more and some less, and the lessons must be judiciously alternated, so that the more mechanical efforts succeed the more strictly intellectual, and that the pleasing exercise of the imagination, again, succeed efforts of reason. By the way, it is a pity when the sense of the ludicrous is cultivated in children's books at the expense of better things. Alice in Wonderland is a delicious feast of absurdities, which none of us, old or young, could afford to spare; but it is doubtful whether the child who reads it has the delightful imaginings, the realising of the unknown, with which he reads The Swiss Family Robinson.

This point is worth considering in connection with Christmas books for the little people. Books of 'comicalities' cultivate no power but the sense of the incongruous; and though life is the more amusing for the possession of such a sense, when cultivated to excess it is apt to show itself a flippant habit. Diogenes and the Naughty Boys of Troy is irresistible, but it is not the sort of thing the children will live over and over, and 'play at' by the hour, as we have all played at Robinson Crusoe finding the footprints. They must have 'funny books,' but do not give the children too much nonsense reading.

Commonplace Tales: Tales of Imagination—Stories, again, of the Christmas holidays, of George and Lucy, of the amusements, foibles, and virtues of children in their own condition of life, leave nothing to the imagination. The children know all about everything so well that it never occurs to them to play at the situations in any one of these tales, or even to read it twice over. But let them have tales of the imagination, scenes laid in other lands and other times, heroic adventures, hairbreadth escapes, delicious fairy tales in which they are never roughly pulled up by the impossible—even where all is impossible, and they know it, and yet believe.

Imagination and Great Conceptions.—And this, not for the children's amusement merely: it is not impossible that posterity may write us down a generation blest with little imagination, and, by so far, the less capable of great conceptions and heroic efforts, for it is only as we have it in us to let a person or a cause fill the whole stage of the mind, to the exclusion of self occupation, that we are capable of large hearted action on behalf of that person or cause. Our novelists say there is nothing left to imagine; and that, therefore, a realistic description of things as they are is all that is open to them. But imagination is nothing if not creative, unless it see, not only what is apparent, but what is conceivable, and what is poetically fit in given circumstances.

Imagination Grows.—Now imagination does not descend, full grown, to take possession of an empty house; like every other power of the mind, it is the merest germ of a power to begin with, and grows by what it gets; and childhood, the age of faith, is the time for its nourishing. The children should have the joy of living in far lands, in other persons, in other times—a delightful double existence; and this joy they will find, for the most part, in their story books. Their lessons, too, history and geography, should cultivate their conceptive powers. If the child do not live in the times of his history lesson, be not at home in the climes of his geography book describes, why, these lessons will fail of their purpose. But let lessons do their best, and the picture gallery of the imagination is poorly hung if the child have not found his way into the realms of fancy.

Thinking comes by Practice.—How the children's various lessons should be handled so as to induce habits of thinking, we shall consider later; but this for the present: thinking, like writing or skating, comes by practice. The child who has never thought, never does think, and probably never will think; for are there not people enough who go through the world without any deliberate exercise of their own wits? The child must think, get at the reason why of things for himself, every day of his life, and more each day than the day before. Children and parents both are given to invert this educational process. The child asks 'Why?' and the parent answers, rather proud of this evidence of thought in his child. There is some slight show of speculation even in wondering 'Why?' but it is the slightest and most superficial effort the thinking brain produces. Let the parent ask 'Why?' and the child produce the answer, if he can. After he has turned the matter over and over in his mind, there is no harm in telling him—and he will remember it—the reason why. Every walk should offer some knotty problem for the children to think out—"Why does that leaf float on the water, and this pebble sink?" and so on.

V. The Habit of Remembering

Remembering and Recollecting.—Memory is the storehouse of whatever knowledge we possess; and it is upon the fact of the stores lodged in the memory that we take rank as intelligent beings. The children learn in order that they may remember. Much of what we have learned and experienced in childhood, and later, we cannot reproduce, and yet it has formed the groundwork of after knowledge; later notions and opinions have grown out of what we once learned and knew. That is our sunk capital, of which we enjoy the interest though we are unable to realise. Again, much that we have learned and experienced is not only retained in the storehouse of memory, but is our available capital, we can reproduce, recollect upon demand. This memory which may be drawn upon by the act of recollection is our most valuable endowment.

A 'Spurious' Memory.—There is a third kind of (spurious) memory—facts and ideas floating in the brain which yet make no part of it, and are exuded at a single effort; as when a barrister produces all his knowledge of a case in his brief, and then forgets to tell about it; or when the schoolboy 'crams' for an examination, writes down what he has thus learned, and behold, it is gone from his gaze for ever: as Ruskin puts it, "They cram to pass, and not to know, they do pass, and they don't know." That this barrister, the physician, should be able thus to dismiss the case on which he has ceased to be occupied, the publisher the book he has rejected, is well for him, and this art of forgetting is not without its uses: but what of the schoolboy who has little left after a year's work but his place in a class list?

Memory a Record in the Brain Substance.—To say anything adequate on the subject of memory is impossible here; but let us try to answer two or three queries which present themselves on the surface. How do we come to 'remember' at all? How do we gain the power to utilise remembered facts—that is, to recollect? And under what conditions is knowledge acquired that neither goes to the growth of brain and mind, nor is available on demand, but is lightly lodged in the brain for some short period, and is then evacuated at a single throw? We are interested in a wonderful invention—an instrument which records spoken words, and will deliver, say a century hence, speech or lecture on the very words and in the very tones of the speaker. Such an instrument is that function of the brain called memory, whereby the impressions received by the brain are recorded mechanically—at least, such is the theory pretty generally received now by physiologists. That is, the mind takes cognisance of certain facts, and the nerve substance of the brain records that cognisance.

Made under what Conditions.—Now, the questions arise, Under what conditions is such an imprint of fact or event made upon the substance of the brain? Is the record permanent? And is the brain capable of receiving an indefinite number of such impressions? It appears, both from common experience and from an infinite number of examples quoted by psychologists, that any object or idea which is regarded with attention makes the sort of impression on the brain which is said to fix it in the memory. In other words, give an instant's undivided attention to anything whatsoever, and that thing will be remembered. In describing this effect, the common expression is accurate beyond its intention. We say, "Such and such a sight or sound, or sensation, made a strong impression on me." And that is precisely what has happened: arrest the attention upon any fact or incident, that fact or incident is remembered; it is impressed, imprinted upon the brain substance. The inference is plain. You want a child to remember? Then secure his whole attention, the fixed gaze of his mind, as it were, upon the fact to be remembered; then he will have it: by a sort of photographic (!) process, that fact or idea is 'taken' by his brain, and when he is an old man, perhaps, the memory of it will flash across him.

Recollection and the Law of Association.—But it is not enough to have a recollection flash across one incidentally; we want to have the power of recalling at will: and for this, something more is necessary than an occasional act of attention producing a solitary impression. Supposing, for instance, that by good teaching you secure the child's attention to the verb avoir, he will remember it; that is to say, some infinitely slight growth of brain tissue will record and retain that one French verb. But one verb is nothing; you want the child to learn French, and for this you must not only fix his attention upon each new lesson, but each must be so linked into the last that it is impossible for him to recall one without the other following in its train. The physical effect of such a method appears to be that each new growth of the brain tissue is, so to speak, laid upon the last; that is, to put it figuratively, a certain tract of the brain may be conceived of as being overlaid with French. This is to make a practical use of that law of association of ideas of which one would not willingly become the sport; and it is the neglect of this law which invalidates much good teaching. The teacher is content to produce a solitary impression which is only recalled as it is acted upon by a chance suggestion; whereas he should forge the links of a chain to draw his bucket out of the well. Probably the reader may have heard, or heard of, a Dr Pick, who grounded a really philosophical system of mnemonics on these two principles of attention and association. Whatever we may think of his application of it, the principle he asserted is the right one.

Every Lesson must recall the Last.—Let every lesson gain the child's entire attention, and let each new lesson be so interlaced with the last that the one must recall the other; that again, recalls the one before it, and so on to the beginning.

No Limit to the Recording Power of the Brain.—But the 'lightly come, lightly go' of a mere verbal memory follows no such rules. The child gets his exercise 'by heart,' says it off like a parrot, and behold, it is gone; there is no record of it upon the brain at all. To secure such a record, there must be time; time for that full gaze of the mind we call attention, and for the growth of the brain tissue to the new idea. Given these conditions, there appears to be no limit of quantity to the recording power of the brain. Except in this way: a girl learns French, and speaks it fairly well; by the time she is a grandmother she has forgotten it entirely, has not a word left. When this is the case, her French has been disused; she has not been in the habit of reading, hearing, or speaking French from youth to age. Whereby it is evident that, to secure right-of-way to that record of French imprinted on her brain, the path should have been kept open by frequent goings and comings.

But Links of Association a Condition of Recollection.—To acquire any knowledge or power whatsoever, and then to leave it to grow rusty in a neglected corner of the brain, is practically useless. Where there is no chain of association to draw the bucket out of the well, it is all the same as if there were no water there. As to how to form these links, every subject will suggest a suitable method. The child has a lesson about Switzerland to-day, and one about Holland to-morrow, and the one is linked to the other by the very fact that the two countries have hardly anything in common; what the one has, the other has not. Again, the association will be of similarity, and not of contrast. In our own experience we find that colours, places, sounds, odors recall persons or events; but links of this sensuous order can hardly be employed in education. The link between any two things must be found in the nature of the things associated.

VI. The Habit of Perfect Execution

The Habit of turning out Imperfect Work.—'Throw perfection into all you do' is a counsel upon which a family may be brought up with great advantage. We English, as a nation, think too much of persons, and too little of things, work, execution. Our children are allowed to make their figures or their letters, their stitches, their dolls' clothes, their small carpentry, anyhow, with the notion that they will do better by-and-by. Other nations—the Germans and the French, for instance—look at the question philosophically, and know that if children get the habit of turning out imperfect work, the men and women will undoubtedly keep that habit up. I remember being delighted with the work of a class of about forty children, of six and seven, in an elementary school at Heidelberg. They were doing a writing lesson, accompanied by a good deal of oral teaching from a master, who wrote each word on the blackboard. By-and-by the slates were shown, and I did not observe one faulty or irregular letter on the whole forty slates. The same principle of 'perfection' was to be discerned in a recent exhibition of school-work held throughout France. No faulty work was shown, to be excused on the plea that it was the work of children.

A Child should Execute Perfectly. No work should be given to a child that he cannot execute perfectly, and then perfection should be required from him as a matter of course. For instance, he is set to do a copy of strokes, and is allowed to show a slateful at all sorts of slopes and all sorts of intervals; his moral sense is vitiated, his eye is injured. Set him six strokes to copy; let him, not bring a slateful, but six perfect strokes, at regular distances and at regular slopes. If he produces a faulty pair, get him to point out the fault, and persevere until he has produced his task; if he does not do it to-day, let him go on to-morrow and the next day, and when the six perfect strokes appear, let it be an occasion of triumph. So with the little tasks of painting, drawing, or construction he sets himself—let everything he does be well done. An unsteady house of cards is a thing to be ashamed of. Closely connected with this habit of 'perfect work' is that of finishing whatever is taken in hand. The child should rarely be allowed to set his hand to a new undertaking until the last is finished.

VII. Some Moral Habits—Obedience

It is disappointing that, in order to cover the ground at all, we must treat those moral habits, which the mother owes it to her children to cultivate in them, in a slight and inadequate way; but the point to be borne in mind is, that all has been already said about the cultivation of habit applies with the greatest possible force to each of these habits.

The Whole Duty of a Child—First and infinitely the most important, is the habit of obedience. Indeed, obedience is the whole duty of the child, and for this reason—every other duty of the child is fulfilled as a matter of obedience to his parents. Not only so: obedience is the whole duty of man; obedience to conscience, to law, to Divine direction.

It has been well observed that each of the three recorded temptations of our Lord in the wilderness is a suggestion, not of an act of overt sin, but of an act of wilfulness, that state directly opposed to obedience, and out of which springs all that foolishness which is bound up in the heart of a child.

Obedience no Accidental Duty.—Now, if the parent realise that obedience is no mere accidental duty, the fulfilling of which is a matter that lies between himself and the child, but that he is the appointed agent to train the child up to the intelligent obedience of the self compelling, law-abiding human being, he will see that he has no right to forego the obedience of his child, and that every act of disobedience in the child is a direct condemnation of the parent. Also, he will see that the motive of the child's obedience is not the arbitrary one of, 'Do this, or that, because I have said so,' but the motive of the apostolic injunction, "Children, obey your parents in the Lord, for this is right."

Children must have the Desire to Obey.—It is only in proportion as the will of the child is in the act of obedience, and he obeys because his sense of right makes him desire to obey in spite of temptations to disobedience—not of constraint, but willingly—that the habit has been formed which will, hereafter, enable the child to use the strength of his will against his inclinations when these prompt him to lawless courses. It is said that the children of parents who are most strict in exacting obedience often turn out ill; and that orphans and other poor waifs brought up under strict discipline only wait their opportunity to break into license. Exactly so; because, in these cases, there is no gradual training of the child in the habit of obedience; no gradual enlisting of his will on the side of sweet service and a free will offering of submission to the highest law: the poor children are simply bullied into submission to the will, that is, the wilfulness, of another; not at all, 'for it is right'; only because it is convenient.

Expect Obedience.—The mother has no more sacred duty than that of training her infant to instant obedience. To do so is no difficult task; the child is still "trailing clouds of glory...from God, who is his home"; the principle of obedience is within him, waiting to be called into exercise. There is no need to rate the child, or threaten him, or use any manner of violence, because the parent is invested with authority which the child intuitively recognises. It is enough to say, 'Do this,' in a quiet, authoritative tone, and expect it to be done. The mother often loses her hold over children because they detect in the tone of her voice that she does not expect them obey her behests; she does not think enough of her position; has not sufficient confidence in her own authority. The mother's great stronghold is in the habit of obedience. If she begin by requiring that her children always obey her, why, they will always do so as a matter of course; but let them once get the thin end of the wedge in, let them discover that they can do otherwise than obey, and a woeful struggle begins, which commonly ends in the children doing that which is right in their own eyes.

This is the sort of thing which is fatal: The children are in the drawing room, and a caller is announced. 'You must go upstairs now.' 'Oh, mother dear, do let us stay in the window-corner; we will be as quiet as mice!' The mother is rather proud of her children's pretty manners, and they stay. They are not quiet, of course; but that is the least of the evils; they have succeeded in doing as they chose and not as they were bid, and they will not put their necks under the yoke again without a struggle. It is in little matters that the mother is worsted. 'Bedtime, Willie!' 'Oh, mamma, just let me finish this'; and the mother yields, forgetting that the case in point is of no consequence; the thing that matters is that the child should be daily confirming a habit of obedience by the unbroken repetition of acts of obedience. It is astonishing how clever the child is in finding ways of evading the spirit while he observes the letter. 'Mary, come in.' 'Yes, mother'; but her mother calls four times before Mary comes. 'Put away your bricks'; and the bricks are put away with slow reluctant fingers. 'You must always wash your hands when you hear the first bell.' The child obeys for that once, and no more.

To avoid these displays of wilfulness, the mother will insist from the first on an obedience which is prompt, cheerful, and lasting—save for lapses of memory on the child's part. Tardy, unwilling, occasional obedience is hardly worth the having; and it is greatly easier to give the child the habit of perfect obedience by never allowing him in anything else, than it is to obtain this mere formal obedience by a constant exercise of authority. By-and-by, when he is old enough, take the child into confidence; let him know what a noble thing it is to be able to make himself do, in a minute, and brightly, the very thing he would rather not do. To secure this habit of obedience, the mother must exercise great self-restraint; she must never give a command which she does not intend to see carried out to the full. And she must not lay upon her children burdens, grievous to be borne, of command heaped upon command.

Law Ensures Liberty.—The children who are trained to perfect obedience may be trusted with a good deal of liberty: they receive a few directions which they know they must not disobey; and for the rest, they are left to learn how to direct their own actions, even at the cost of some small mishaps; and are not pestered with a perpetual fire of 'Do this' and 'Don't do that!'

VIII.—Truthfulness

It is unnecessary to say a word of the duty of Truthfulness; but the training of the child in the habit of strict veracity is another matter, and one which requires delicate care and scrupulosity on the part of the mother.

Three Causes of Lying—All Vicious.—The vice of lying causes: carelessness in ascertaining the truth, carelessness in stating the truth, and a deliberate intention to deceive. That all three are vicious, is evident from the fact that a man's character may be ruined by what is no more than a careless mis-statement on the part of another; the speaker repeats a damaging remark without taking the trouble to sift it; or he repeats what he has heard or seen with so little care to deliver the truth that his statement becomes no better than a lie.

Only One Kind visited on Children.—Now, of the three kinds of lying, it is only, as a matter of fact, the third which is severely visited upon the child; the first and the second he is allowed in. He tells you he has seen 'lots' of spotted dogs in the town—he has really seen two; that 'all the boys' are collecting crests—he knows of three who are doing so; that 'everybody' says Jones is a 'sneak'—the fact is he has heard Brown say so. These departures from strict veracity are on matters of such slight importance that the mother is apt to let them pass as the 'children's chatter'; but, indeed, ever such lapse is damaging to the child's sense of truth—a blade which easily loses its keenness of edge.

Accuracy of Statement.—The mother who trains her child to strict accuracy of statement about things small and great fortifies him against temptations to the grosser forms of lying; he will not readily colour a tale to his own advantage, suppress facts, equivocate, when the statement of the simple fact has become a binding habit, and when he has not been allowed to form the contrary vicious habit of playing fast and loose with words.

Exaggeration and Ludicrous Embellishments.—Two forms of prevarication, very tempting to the child, will require great vigilance on the mother's part—that of exaggeration and that of clothing a story with ludicrous embellishments. However funny a circumstance may be as described by the child, the ruthless mother must strip the tale of everything over and above the naked truth: for, indeed, a reputation for facetiousness is dearly purchased by the loss of that dignity of character, in child or man, which accompanies the habit of strict veracity; it is possible, happily, to be humorous, without any sacrifice of truth.

Reverence, etc.—As for reverence, consideration for others, respect for persons and property, I can only urge the importance of a sedulous cultivation of these moral qualities—the distinguishing marks of a refined nature—until they become the daily habits of the child's life; and the more, because a self assertive, aggressive, self seeking temper is but too characteristic of the times we live in.

Temper—Born in a Child.—I am anxious, however, to a say a few words on the habit of sweet temper. It is very customary to regard temper as constitutional, that which is born in you and is neither to be helped nor hindered. 'Oh, she is a good tempered little soul; nothing puts her out!' 'Oh, he has his father's temper; the least thing that goes contrary makes him fly into a passion,' are the sorts of remarks we hear constantly.

Not Temper, but Tendency.—It is no doubt true that children inherit a certain tendency to irascibility or to amiability, to fretfulness, discontentment, peevishness, sullenness, murmuring, and impatience; or to cheerfulness, trustfulness, good-humour, patience, and humility. It is also true that upon the preponderance of any of these qualities—upon temper, that is—the happiness or wretchedness of child and man depends, as well as the comfort or misery of the people who live with him. We all know people possessed of integrity and of many excellent virtues who make themselves intolerable to their belongings. The root of evil is, not that these people were born sullen, or peevish, or envious—that might have been mended; but that they were permitted to grow up in these dispositions. Here, if anywhere, the power of habit is invaluable: it rests with the parents to correct the original twist, all the more so if it is from them the child gets it, and to send their child into the world best with an even, happy temper, inclined to make the best of things, to look on the bright side, to impute the best and kindest motives to others, and to make no extravagant claims on his own account—fertile source of ugly tempers. And this, because the child is born with no more than certain tendencies.

Parents must correct Tendency by New Habit of Temper.—It is by force of habit that a tendency becomes a temper; and it rests with the mother to hinder the formation of ill tempers, to force that of good tempers. Nor is it difficult to do this while the child's countenance is as an open book to his mother, and she reads the thoughts of his heart before he is aware of them himself. Remembering that every envious, murmuring, discontented thought leaves a track in the very substance of the child's brain for such thoughts to run in again and again—that this track, this rut, so to speak, is ever widening and deepening with the traffic in ugly thoughts—the mother's care is to hinder at the outset the formation of any such track. She sees into her child's soul—sees the evil temper in the act of rising: now is her opportunity.

Change the Child's Thoughts.—Let her change the child's thoughts before ever the bad temper has had time to develop into conscious feeling, much less act: take him out of doors, send him to fetch or carry, tell him or show him something of interest,—in a word, give him something else to think about; but all in a natural way, and without letting the child perceive that he is being treated. As every fit of sullenness leaves place in the child's mind for another fit of sullenness to succeed it, so every such fit averted by the mother's tact tends to obliterate the evil traces of former sullen tempers. At the same time, the mother is careful to lay down a highway for the free course of all sweet and genial thoughts and feelings.

I have been offering suggestions, not for a course of intellectual and moral training, but only for the formation of certain habits which should be, as it were, the outworks of character. Even with this limited programme, I have left unnoticed many matters fully as important as those touched upon. In the presence of an embarrassment of riches, it has been necessary to adopt some principle of selection; and I have thought it well to dwell upon considerations which do not appear to me to have their full weight with educated parents, rather than upon those of which every thoughtful person recognises the force.

Part V

Lessons as Instruments of Education

I. The Matter and Method of Lessons

It seems to me that we live in an age of pedagogy; that we of the teaching profession are inclined to take too much upon ourselves, and that parents are ready to yield the responsibility of direction, as well as of actual instruction, more than is wholesome for the children.

Parents must reflect on the Subject-matter of Instruction.—I am about to invite your attention to a subject that parents are accustomed to leave very much in the hands of the schoolmaster or governess when they do not instruct their children themselves—I mean the choice of subjects of instruction, and the ways of handling those subjects. Teachers are the people who have, more than others, given themselves to the consideration of what what a child should learn and how he should learn it; but the parent, also, should have thought on this subject, and even when he does not profess ot teach his children, should have his own carefully formed opinions as to the subject-matter and the method of their intellectual education: and this for the sake of the teacher as well as for that of the children. Nothing does more to give vitality and purpose to the work of the teacher than the certainty that the parents of his pupils go with him.

Even when children go to schools taught by qualified persons, some insight on the part of fathers and mothers is useful as hindering the teacher from dropping into professional grooves, valuing proficiency in this or that subject for its own sake, and not as it affects the children. But in the early days of the home schoolroom, it is iniquitous to leave the young governess, with little qualification beyond her native French or German, or scanty English, to chalk out a course for herself and her charges. That the children waste their time is the least of the evils that accrue: they are forming habits dead against intellectual effort; and by-and-by, when they go to school, the lessons go over their heads, the work slips through their fingers, and their powers of passive resistance baffle the most strenuous teachers.

Home the best Growing-ground for Young Children.—All the same, whatever be the advantages of Kindergarten or other schools for little children, the home schoolroom ought to be the best growing-ground for them. And doubtless it would be so, were the mother at liberty to devote herself to the instruction of her children; but this she is seldom free to do. If she can live in a town, she can send them to school when they are six; if in the country, she must have a governess; and the difficulty is to get a woman who is not only acquainted with the subjects she undertakes to teach, but who understands in some measure the nature of the child and the art and objects of education; a woman capable of making the very most of the children without waste of power or of time. Such a rara avis does not present herself in answer to every advertisement; and in default of a trained teacher, the mother must undertake to train the governess—that is, she may supplement with her own insight the scanty knowledge and experience of the young teacher. 'I wish the children to be taught to read, thus and thus, because ________': or, 'to learn and history in such a way that the lessons may have such and such effects.' Half an hour's talk of this kind with a sensible governess will secure a whole month's work for the children, so well directed that much is done in little time, and the widest possible margin secured for play and open-air exercise.

Three Questions for the Mother.—But if the mother is to inoculate the governess with her views as to the teaching of writing, French, geography, she must, herself, have definite views. She must ask herself seriously, Why must the children learn at all? What should they learn? And, How should they learn it? If she take the trouble to fiind a definite and thoughtful answer to each of these three queries, she will be in a position to direct her children's studies; and will, at the same time, be surprised to find that three-fourths of the time and labour ordinarily spent by the child at his lessons is lost time and wasted energy.

Children learn, to Grow.—Why must the child learn? Why do we eat? Is it not in order that the body may live and grow and be able to fulfil its functions? Precisely so must the mind be sustained and developed by means of the food convenient for it, the mental pabulum of assimilated knowledge. Again, the body is developed not only by means of proper sustenance, but by the appropriate exercise of each of its members. A young mother remarked to me the other day, that before her marriage she had such slender arms she never liked to exhibit them; but a strong five-months-old baby had cured her of that; she could toss and lift him with ease, and could now show well-rounded arms with anybody: and just as the limbs grow strong with exercise, so does intellectual effort with a given power of the mind make that power effective. People are apt to overlook the fact that mind must have its aliment—we learn that we may know, not that we may grow; hence the parrot-like saying of lessons, the cramming of ill-digested facts for examinations, all the ways of taking in knowledge which the mind does not assimilate.

Doctoring of the Material of Knowledge.—Specialists, on the other hand, are apt to attach too much importance to the several exercise of the mental 'faculties.' We come across books on teaching, with lessons elaborately drawn up, in which certain work is assigned to the perspective faculties, certain work to the imagination, to the judgment, and so on. Now this doctrine of the faculties, which rests on a false analogy between the mind and the body, is on its way to the limbo where the phrenologist's 'bumps' now rest in peace. The mind would appear to be one and indivisible, and endowed with manifold powers; and this sort of doctoring of the material of knowledge is unnecessary for the healthy child, whose mind is capable of self-direction, and of applying itself to its proper work upon the parcel of knowledge delivered to it. Almost any subject which common sense points out as suitable for the instruction of children will afford exercise for all their powers, if properly presented.

Children learn, to get Ideas.—The child must learn, in the second place, in order that ideas may be freely sown in the fruitful soil of his mind. 'Idea, the image or picture formed by the mind of anything external, whether sensible or spiritual.'—so, the dictionary; therefore, if the business of teaching be to furnish the child with ideas, any teaching which does not leave him possessed of a new mental image has, by so far, missed its mark. Now, just think of the listless way in which the children too often drag through reading and tables, geography and sums, and you will see that it is a rare thing for any part of any lesson to flash upon them with the vividness which leaves a mental picture behind. It is not too much to say that a morning in which a child receives no new idea is a morning wasted, however closely the little student has been kept at his books.

Ideas Grow and Produce after their Kind.—For the dictionary appears to me to fall short of the truth in its definition of the term 'idea.' An idea is more than an image or picture; it is, so to speak, a spiritual germ endowed with vital force—with power, that is, to grow, and to produce after its kind. It is the very nature of an idea to grow: as the vegetable germ secretes that it lives by, so, fairly implant an idea in the child's mind, and it will secrete its own food, grow, and bear fruit in the form of a succession of kindred ideas. We know from our own experience that, let our attention be forcibly drawn to some public character, some startling theory, and for days after we are continually hearing or reading matter which bears on this one subject, just as if all the world were thinking about what occupies our thoughts: the fact being, that the new idea we have received is in the act of growth, and is reaching out after its appropriate food. This process of feeding goes on with peculiar avidity in childhood, and the growth of an idea in the child is proportionably rapid.

Scott and Stephenson worked with Ideas.—Scott got an idea, a whole group of ideas, out of the Border tales and ballads, the folklore of the country-side, on which his boyhood was nourished: his ideas grew and brought forth, and the Waverley novels are the fruit they bore. George Stephenson made little clay engines with his playmate, Thomas Tholoway; by-and-by, when he was an engineman, he was always watching his engine, cleaning it, studying it; an engine was his dominant idea, and it developed into no less a thing than the locomotive.

Value of Dominant Ideas.—But how does this theory of the vital and fruitful character of ideas bear upon the education of the child? In this way: give your a child a single valuable idea, and you have done more for his education than if you had laid upon his mind the burden of bushels of information; for the child who grows up with a few dominant ideas has his self-education provided for, his career marked out.

Lessons must furnish Ideas.—In order for the reception of an idea, the mind must be in an attitude of eager attention, and how to secure that state we have considered elsewhere. One thing more: a single idea may be a possession so precious in itself, so fruitful, that the parent cannot fitly allow the child's selection of ideas to be a matter of chance; his lessons should furnish him with such ideas as shall make for his further education.

Children learn to get Knowledge.—But it is not only to secure due intellectual growth and the furnishing his mind with ideas, that the child must learn: the common notion, that he learns for the sake of getting knowledge, is also a true one so much so, that no knowledge should be so precious as that gained in childhood, no later knowledge should be so clearly chronicled on the brain, nor so useful as the foundation of that to follow. At the same time, the child's capacity for knowledge is very limited; his mind is, in this respect at least, but a little phial with a narrow neck; and, therefore, it behooves the parent or teacher to pour in only of the best.

Diluted Knowledge.—But, poor children, they are too often badly used by their best friends in the matter of the knowledge offered them. Grown-up people who are not mothers talk and think far more childishly than the child does in their efforts to approach his mind. If a child talk twaddle, it is because his elders are in the habit of talking twaddle to him; leave him to himself, and his remarks are wise and sensible so far as his small experience guides him. Mothers seldom talk down to their children; they are too intimate with the little people, and have, therefore, too much respect for them: but professional teachers, whether the writers of books or the givers of lessons are too apt to present a single grain of pure knowledge in a whole gallon of talk, imposing upon the child the labour of discerning the grain and of extracting it from the worthless flood.

Dr. Arnold's Knowledge as a Child.—On the whole, the children who grow up amongst their elders and are not provided with what are called children's books at all, fare the better on what they are able to glean for themselves from the literature of grown-up people. Thus it is told of Dr. Arnold that when he was three years old he received as a present from his father of Smollett's History of England as a reward for the accuracy with which he went through the stories connected with the portraits and pictures the successive reigns—an amusement which probably laid the foundation of the great love for history which distinguished him in after life. When occupying the professorial chair at Oxford, he made quotations, we are told, from Dr Priestley's Lectures on History—verbally accurate quotations, we may believe, for such was the habit of his mind; besides, a child has little skill in recasting his matter—and that, though he had not had the book in his hands since he was a child of eight. No doubt he was an exceptional child; and all I maintain is, that had his reading been the sort of diluted twaddle which is commonly thrust upon children, it would have been impossible for him to cite passages a week, much less some two score years, after the reading.

Literature Proper for Children.—This sort of weak literature for the children, both in any story and lesson books, is the result of a reactionary process. Not so long ago the current impression was that the children had little understanding, but prodigious memory for facts; dates, numbers, rules, catechisms of knowledge, much information in small parcels, was supposed to be the fitting material for a child's education. We have changed all that, and put into the children's hands lesson-books with pretty pictures and easy talk, almost as good as story-books; but we do not see that, after all, we are but giving the same little pills of knowledge in the form of a weak and copious diluent. Teachers, and even parents, who are careful enough about their children's diet, are so reckless as to the sort of mental aliment offered to them, that I am exceedingly anxious to secure consideration for this question, of the lessons and literature proper for the little people.

Four Tests which should be applied to Children's Lessons.—We see, then, that the children's lessons should provide material for their mental growth, should exercise the several powers of their minds, should furnish them with fruitful ideas, and should afford them knowledge, really valuable for its own sake, accurate, and interesting, of the kind that the child may recall as a man with profit and pleasure. Before applying these tests to the various subjects in which children are commonly instructed, may I remind you of two or three points which I have endeavoured to establish in the preceding pages:—

Resume of Six Points already considered.—

(a) That the knowledge most valuable to the child is that which he gets with his own eyes and ears and fingers (under direction) in the open air.

(b) That the claims of the schoolroom should not be allowed to encroach on the child's right to long hours daily for exercise and investigation.

(c) That the child should be taken daily, if possible, to scenes—moor or meadow, park, common, or shore—where he may find new things to examine, and so add to his store of real knowledge. That the child's observation should be directed to flower or boulder, bird or tree; that, in fact, he should be employed in gathering the common information which is the basis of scientific knowledge.

(d) That play, vigorous healthful play, is, in its turn, fully as important as lessons, as regards both bodily health and brain-power.

(e) That the child, though under supervision, should be left much to himself—both that he may go to work in his own way on the ideas that he receives, and also that he may be the more open to natural influences.

(f) That the happiness of the child is the condition of his progress; that his lessons should be joyous, and that occasions of friction in the schoolroom are greatly to be deprecated.

Promising so much, let us now consider—What the child should learn, and how they should be taught.

II. The Kindergarten As A Place of Education

The Mother the best Kindergartnerin.—It is hardly necessary, here, to discuss the merits of the Kindergarten school. The success of such a school demands rare qualities in the teacher—high culture, some knowledge of psychology and of the art of education; intense sympathy with the children, much tact, much common sense, much common information, much 'joyousness of nature,' and much governing power;—in a word, the Kindergarten method is nicely contrived to bring the child en rapport with a superior intelligence. Given such a superior being to conduct it, and the Kindergarten is beautiful—'tis like a little heaven below'; but put a commonplace woman in charge of such a school, and the charmingly devised gifts and games and occupations become so many instruments of wooden teaching. If the very essence of the Kindergarten method is personal influence, a sort of spiritual mesmerism, it follows that the mother is naturally the best Kindergartnerin; for who so likely as she to have the needful tact, sympathy, common sense, culture?

The Nursery need not therefore be a Kindergarten.—Though every mother should be a Kindergartnerin, in the sense in which Froebel would employ the term, it does not follow that every nursery should be a regularly organised Kindergarten. Indeed, the machinery of the Kindergarten is no more than a device to ensure the carrying out of certain educational principles, and some of these it is the mother's business to get at, and work out according to Froebel's methods—or her own. For instance, in the Kindergarten the child's senses are carefully and progressively trained: he looks, listens, learns by touch; gets ideas of size, colour, form, number; is taught to copy faithfully, express exactly. And in this training of the senses, the child is made to pursue the method the infant shapes for himself in his early studies of ring or ball.

Field of Knowledge too circumscribed.—But it is possible that the child's marvellous power of obtaining knowledge by means of his senses may be undervalued; that the field may be too circumscribed; and that, during the first six or seven years in which he might have become intimately acquainted with the properties and history of every natural object within his reach, he has obtained, exact ideas, it is true—can distinguish a rhomboid from a pentagon, a primary from a secondary colour, has learned to see so truly that he can copy what he sees in folded paper or woven straw,—but this at the expense of much of that real knowledge of the external world which at no time of his life will he be so fitted to acquire. Therefore, while the exact nicely graduated training of the Kindergarten may be of value, the mother will endeavour to give it by the way, and will by no means let it stand for that wider training of the senses, to secure which for her children is a primary duty.

Again, the child in the Kindergarten is set to such tasks only as he is competent to perform, and then, whatever he has to do, he is expected to do perfectly. I have seen a four-years-old child blush and look as self-condemend, because he had folded a slip of a paper irregularly, as if found out in a falsehood. But mother or nurse is quite able to secure that the child's small offices are perfectly executed; and, here is an important point, without that slight strain of distressful anxiety which may be observed in children labouring to please that smiling goddess, their 'Kindergarnerin.'

Training of a Just Eye and Faithful Hand.—The Kindergarten 'Occupations' afford opportunities for training in this kind of faithfulness; but in the home a thousand such opportunities occur; if only in such trifles as the straightening of a tablecloth or of a picture, the hanging of a towel, the packing of a parcel—every thoughtful mother invents a thousand ways of training in her child a just eye and a faithful hand. Nevertheless, as a means of methodical training, as well as of happy employment, the introduction of some of the games and occupations of the Kindergarten into the nursery may be allowed; provided that the mother does not depend upon these, but makes all the child's occupations subserve the purposes of his education.

'Sweetness and Light' in the Kindergarten—The child breathes an atmosphere of 'sweetness and light' in the Kindergarten. You see the sturdy urchin of five stiffen his back and decline to be a jumping frog, and the Kindergartnerin comes with unruffled gentleness, takes him by the hand, and leads him out of the circle,—he is not treated as an offender, only he does not choose to do as the others do, therefore he is not wanted there: the next time, he is quite content to be a frog. Here we have the principle for the discipline of the nursery. Do not treat the child's small contumacy too seriously; do not assume that he is being naughty: just leave him out when he is not prepared to act in harmony with the rest. Avoid friction; and above all, do not let him disturb the moral atmosphere in all gentleness and serenity, remove him from the company of others, when he is being what nurses call 'tiresome.'

Once more, the Kindergarten professes to take account of the joyousness of the child's nature: to allow him full and free expression for the glee that is in him, without the 'rampaging' which follows if he is left to himself to find an outlet for his exuberant life. This union of joy and gentleness is the very temper to be cultivated in the nursery. The boisterous behaviour sometimes allowed in children is unnecessary—within doors, at any rate: but even a momentary absence of sunshine on the faces of her children will be a graver cause of uneasiness to the mother. On the whole, we may say that some of the principles which should govern Kindergarten training are precisely those in which every thoughtful mother endeavours to bring up her family; while the practices of the Kindergarten, being only ways, amongst others, of carrying out these principles, and being apt to become stereotyped and wooden, are unnecessary, but may be adopted so far as they fit in conveniently with the mother's general scheme for the education of her family.

III. Further Consideration Of The Kindergarten

The Childhood of Tolstoi—There is possibly no known field of research in which so little available work has been done as in that covered by the word 'children.' The 'fair lande' lies under our very eyes, but whoso would map it out must write 'Unexplored' across vast tracts. Thoughtful persons begin to suspect that the mistakes we make through this ignorance are grievous and injurious. For example, are not all our schemes of education founded on the presumption that a child's mind—his 'thinking, feeling man'—begins 'very small,' and grows great with the growth of his body? We cannot tell if this is indeed the case. The children keep themselves to themselves in a general way, their winning ways and frank confidences notwithstanding; but if one of us do, by chance, get a child revealed to him, he is startled to find that the child has by far the keener intelligence, the wiser thoughts, the larger soul of the two. When genius is able to lift the veil and show us a child, it does a service which, in our present state of thought, we are hardly able to appraise; and when genius or simplicity, or both, shall have given us enough such studies to generalise upon, we shall doubtless reconsider the whole subject, and shall be dismayed at the slights we have been putting upon children in the name of education. Count Tolstoi gives us, in Childhood, Boyhood, Youth [see Appendix], unmistakable child-portraiture, a miniature in which a mother may see her child and recognise what and how much there is in him:—

"Like our own dear mother," the little fellow writes, in the verses he makes for his grandmother's birthday; and then, when the verses come to be read, ah! The humiliation of the soul he goes through, and how surely he expects father and grandmother to find him out for a hypocrite. "Why did I write it? She's not here, and it was not necessary to mention her; I love grandma, it's true; I reverence her, but still she is not the same. Why did I write it? Why have I lied?" This is the sort of thing there is in children. We recognise it as we read, and remember the dim, childish days when we, too, had an 'organ of truth' just so exquisitely delicate; and the recollection should quicken our reverence of the tender consciences of children.

"The Story of a Child."—I should like while speaking of this subject to mention another book which contains the self-revelation of a child,—a child that once was summoned, to give evidence, out of the dark abysm of time. This is the sort of study of a child that is really precious, because it is to be had on no other terms than by harking back to our own childhood, vivifying it, reproducing it, by mere force of imaginative power. This is absolutely the only way to get into sympathy with a child, for children, with all their frank confidences and ready chatter, are quite inscrutable little persons, who never tell anyone the sort of things that read in this 'Story.' There is no need to tell each other, for other children know, and, as for telling the grown-ups, children are fully persuaded that no grown-up, not even mother, could understand; Otto might, perhaps, and confidences will be poured into the ear of a dog which the loving mother lays herself out for in vain.

"Each in his hidden sphere of joy or woe,
Our hermit spirits dwell, and range apart,
Our eyes see all around in gloom or glow—
Hues of their own, fresh borrow'd from the heart."

And this is even more notably the case with children than with ourselves. It is a law of our nature with which it is absolutely useless to contend, and our only means of true intimacy with a child is the power of recovering our own childhood—a power which we are apt to let slip as of no vital importance. This, Miss Margaret Deland helps us to do: we recognise our old selves, with a difference, in Ellen. Just so irrational, inconsequent, loving and heroic, and generally tiresome to the grown-up world were our own impulses that long ago, on which we look back with tenderness, but seldom with complacency. If we rise, after reading, The Story of a Child [See Appendix], a little more humble, a little more diffident, ready to believe more than we see, why, it will do us no harm, and should bless and help the children. From one word of the author's we should like to differ. Miss Deland thinks that it may be wholesome for the elders to understand children better, but for the children, why, she thinks that most of us grow up wonderfully well in spite of this and all other difficulties. In a sense this is true, but, in another sense, one of the saddest things in life is the issue of splendid child-material into common place, uninteresting maturity, of a kind that the world seems to be neither the best nor the worse for.

Tolstoi's childhood and that of Miss Deland's little heroine would appear to be a far cry from the 'Kindergarten'; but as a matter of fact these two revelations of what children are bring our contention to a point.

We are told that, "but yesterday, in the University of Edinburgh, the greatest figure in the Faculty was Sir James Simpson, the discoverer of chloroform. The other day his successor and nephew, Professor Simpson, was asked by the librarian of the University to go to the library and pick out the books on his subject that were no longer needed. And his reply to the librarian was this: 'Take every text-book that is more than ten years old, and put it down in the cellar.'" So far as education is a science, the truth of even ten—much more, a hundred—years ago is not the whole truth of to-day.

"Thought beyond their thoughts to those high seers were given"; and, in proportion as the urgency of educational effort presses upon us, will be the ardour of our appreciation, the diligence of our employment, of those truths which the great pioneers, Froebel and the rest, have won for us by no less than prophetic insight. But, alas, and alas, for the cravings of lazy human nature—we may not have an educational pope; we must think out for ourselves, as well as work out, those things that belong to the perfect bringing-up of our children.

What we Owe to Froebel.—We reverence Froebel. Many of his great thoughts we share; we cannot say borrow, because some, like the child's relations to the universe, are at least as old as Plato; others belong to universal practice and experience, and this shows their psychological rightness. Froebel gathered diffused thought and practice into a system, but he did a greater thing than this. He raised an altar to the enthusiasm of childhood upon which the flame has never since gone out. The true Kindergartnerin is the artist amongst teachers; she is filled with the inspiration of her work, and probably most sincere teachers have caught something from her fervour, some sense of the beauty of childhood, and of the enthralling delight of truly educational work.

Requirements of a Person.—And yet I enter a caveat. Our first care should be to preserve the individuality, to give play to the personality, of children. Now persons do not grow in a garden, much less in a greenhouse. It is a doubtful boon to a person to have conditions too carefully adapted to his needs. The exactly due sunshine and shade, pruning and training, are good for a plant whose uses are subordinate, so to say, to the needs and pleasures of its owner. But a person who has other uses in the world, and mother or teacher who regards him as a plant and herself as the gardener, will only be saved from grave mistakes by the force of human nature in herself and in her child.

Nature as an Educator.—The notion of supplementing Nature from the cradle is a dangerous one. A little guiding, a little restraining, much reverent watching, Nature asks of us; but beyond that, it is the wisdom of parents to leave children as much as may be to Nature, and "to a higher Power than Nature itself."

Danger of undervaluing Children's Intelligence.—Those of us who have watched an urchin of seven making Catherine-wheels down the length of a street, or a group of little girls dancing to a barrel organ, or small boys and girls on a door-step giving what Dickens calls 'dry nourishment' to their babies, or a small girl sent by her mother to make four careful purchases out of sixpence and bring home the change—are not ready to believe that physical, mental, and moral development waits, so to speak, upon Kindergarten teaching. Indeed, I am inclined to question whether, in the interest of carrying out a system, the charming Kindergartnerin is not in danger sometimes of greatly undervaluing the intelligence of her children. I know a person of three who happened to be found by a caller alone in the drawing room. It was spring, and the caller thought to make himself entertaining with talk about the pretty 'baa-lambs.' But a pair of big blue eyes were fixed upon him and a solemn person made this solemn remark, "Isn't it a dwefful howid thing to see a pig killed!" We hope she had never seen or even heard of the killing of a pig, but she made as effective a protest against twaddle as would any woman of Society. Boers and kopjes, Russians and Japs, Treasure Island, Robinson Crusoe and his man Friday, the fight of Thermopylae, Ulysses and the Suitors—these are the sorts of things that children play at by the month together; even the toddlers of three and four will hold their own manfully with their brothers and sisters. And, if the little people were in the habit of telling how they feel, we should learn perhaps that they are a good deal bored by the nice little games in which they frisk like lambs, flap their fins, and twiddle their fingers like butterflies.

We all like to be Humoured.—'But,' says the reader, 'children do all these things so pleasantly and happily in the Kindergarten!' It is a curious thing about human nature that we all like to be managed by persons who take the pains to play on our amiabilities. Even a dog can be made foolishly sentimental; and, if we who are older have our foibles in this kind, it is little wonder that children can be wooed to do anything by persons whose approaches to them are always charming. It is true that 'W.V.,' the child whom the world has been taught to love, sang her Kindergarten songs with little hands waving in the 'air so blue'! but that was for the delectation and delusion of the elders when bedtime came. 'W.V.' had greater thoughts at other times.

Teachers mediate too much.—There are still, probably, Kindergartens where a great deal of twaddle is talked in song and story, where the teacher conceives that to make poems for the children herself and to compose tunes for their singing and to draw pictures for their admiration, is to fulfil her function to the uttermost. The children might echo Wordsworth's complaint of 'the world,' and say, the teacher is too much with us, late and soon. Everything is directed, expected, suggested. No other personality out of book, picture, or song, no, not even that of Nature herself, can get at the children without the mediation of the teacher. No room is left for spontaneity or personal initiation on their part.

Danger of Personal Magnetism.—Most of us are misled by our virtues, and the entire zeal and enthusiasm of the Kindergartnerin is perhaps her stone of stumbling. 'But the children are so happy and good!' Precisely; the home-nursery is by no means such a scene of peace, but I venture to think it a better growing place. I am delighted to see that an eminent Froebelian protests against the element of personal magnetism in the teacher; but there is, or has been, a good deal of this element in the successful Kindergartner, and we all know how we lose vigour and individuality under this sort of influence. Even apart from this element of charm, I doubt if the self-adjusting property of life in the Kindergarten is good for the children.

'Kindergarten' a False Analogy.—The world suffered that morning when the happy name of 'Kindergarten' suggested itself to the greatest among educational 'Fathers.' No doubt it was simple and fit in its first intention as meaning an out-of-door garden life for the children; but, a false analogy has hampered, or killed, more than one philosophic system—the child became a plant in a well-ordered garden. The analogy appealed to the orderly, scientific German mind, which does not much approve of irregular, spontaneous movement in any sort. Culture, due stimulus, sweetness and light, became the chief features of a great educational code. From the potting-shed to the frame and thence to the flower-bed, the little plant gets in due proportion what is good for him. He grows in a seemly way, in ordered ranks; and in fit season puts forth his flower.

Now, to a figure a person by any analogy whatsoever is dangerous and misleading; there is nothing in nature commensurable with a person. Because the analogy of the garden plant is very attractive, it is the more misleading; manifestations of purpose in a plant are wonderful and delightful, but in a person such manifestations are simply normal. The outcome of any thought is necessarily moulded by that thought, and to have a cultivated garden as the ground-plan of our educational thought, either means nothing at all, which it would be wronging the Master to suppose, or it means undue interference with the spontaneous development of a human being.

Mother-games too strenuous for a Child.—To begin with the 'Mother-games,' a sweet conception, most lovingly worked out. But let us consider; the infant is exquisitely aware of every mood of his mother, the little face clouds with grief or beams with joy in response to the expression of hers. The two left to themselves have rare games. He jumps and pulls, crows and chuckles, crawls and kicks and gurgle with joy; and, amid all the play, is taught what he may not do. Hands and feet, legs and arms, fingers and toes, are continually going while he is awake; mouth, eyes and ears are agog. All is play without intention, and mother plays with baby as glad as he. Nature sits quietly by and sees to it that all the play is really work; and development of every sort is going on at a greater rate during the first two years of life than at any like period of after life—enough development and not too much, for baby is an inordinate sleeper. Then comes in the educator and offers a little more. The new games are so pretty and taking that baby might as well be doing these as his own meaningless and clumsy jumpings and pattings. But a real labour is being put upon the child in addition to the heaviest two years' work that his life will know. His sympathy with his mother is so acute that he perceives something strenuous in the new play, notwithstanding all the smiles and pretty talk; he answers by endeavour, great in proportion as he is small. His nerve centres and brain power have been unduly taxed, some of the joy of living has been taken from him, and though his baby response to direct education is very charming, he has less latent power left for the future calls of life.

The Society of his Equals too stimulating for a child.—Let us follow the little person to the Kindergarten, where he has the stimulus of classmates of his own age. It certainly is stimulating. For ourselves, no society is so much so as that of a number of persons of our own age and standing; this is the great joy of college life; a wholesome joy for all young people for a limited time. But persons of twenty have, or should have, some command over their inhibitory centres. They should not permit the dissipation of nerve power caused by too much social stimulus; yet even persons of twenty are not always equal to the task of self-management in exciting circumstances. What then, is to be expected of persons of two, three, four, five? That the little person looks rather stolid than otherwise is no guarantee against excitement within. The clash and sparkle of our equals now and then stirs up to health; but for everyday life, the mixed society of elders, juniors and equals, which we get in a family, gives at the same time the most repose and the most room for individual development. We have all wondered at the good sense, reasonableness, fun and resourcefulness shown by a child in his own home as compared with the same child in school life.

Danger of supplanting Nature.—Danger lurks in the Kindergarten, just in proportion to the completeness and beauty of its organisation. It is possible to supplement Nature so skilfully that we run some risk of supplanting her, depriving her of space and time to do her own work in her own way. 'Go and see what Tommy is doing and tell him he mustn't,' is not sound doctrine. Tommy should be free to do what he likes with his limbs and his mind through all the hours of the day when he is not sitting up nicely at meals. He should run and jump, leap and tumble, lie on his face watching a worm, or on his back watching the bees in a lime tree. Nature will look after him and give him promptings of desire to know many things; and somebody must tell as he wants to know; and to do many things, and somebody should be handy just to put him in the way; and to be many things, naughty and good, and somebody should give direction.

Importance of Personal Initiative.—Here we come to the real crux of the Kindergarten question. The busy mother says she has no leisure to be that somebody, and the child will run wild and get into bad habits; but we must not make a fetish of habit; education is a life as well as a discipline. Health, strength, and agility, bright eyes and alert movements, come of a free life, out-of-doors, if it may be and as for habits, there is no habit or power so useful to man or woman as that of personal initiative. The resourcefulness which will enable a family of children to invent their own games and occupations through the length of a summer's day is worth more in after life than a good deal of knowledge about cubes and hexagons, and this comes, not of continual intervention on the mother's part, but of much masterly inactivity.

Parents and Teachers must sow Opportunities.—The educational error of our day is that we believe too much in mediators. Now, Nature is her own mediator, undertakes, herself, to find work for eyes and ears, taste and touch; she will prick the brain with problems and the heart with feelings; and the part of the mother or teacher in the early years (indeed, all through life) is to sow opportunities, and then to keep in the background, ready with a guiding or restraining hand only when these are badly wanted. Mothers shirk their work and put it, as they would say, into better hands than their own, because they do not recognise that wise letting alone is the chief thing asked of them, seeing that every mother has in Nature an all-sufficient handmaid, who arranges for due work and due rest of mind, muscles, and senses.

In one way the children of the poor have better chances than those of the rich. Poor children get education out of household ways; but there is a great deal of teaching to be got out of a wisely ordered nursery, and their own small persons and possessions should, as I have said, afford much 'Kindergarten' training to the little family at home. At six or seven, definite lessons should begin, and these need not be watered down or served with jam for the acute intelligences that will in this way be brought to bear on them.

'Only' Children.—But what of only children, or the child too old to play with her baby brother? Surely the Kindergarten is a great boon for these! Perhaps so; but a cottage-child as a companion, or a lively young nursemaid, might be better. A child will have taught himself to paint, paste, cut paper, knit, weave, hammer and saw, make lovely things in clay and sand, build castles with his bricks; possibly, too, will have taught himself to read, write, and do sums, besides acquiring no end of knowledge and notions about the world he lives in, by the time he is six or seven. What I contend for is that he shall do these things because he chooses (provided that the standard of perfection in his small works be kept before him).

The Child should be allowed some Ordering of his Life.—The details of family living will give him the repose of an ordered life; but, for the rest, he should have more free-growing time than is possible in the most charming school. The fact that lessons look like play is no recommendation: they just want the freedom of play and the sense of his own ordering that belongs to play. Most of us have little enough opportunity for the ordering of our own lives, so it is well to make much of the years that can be given to children to gain this joyous experience.

Helen Keller.—I think what I have said of natural development as opposed to any too carefully organised system is supported by a recent contribution, of unique value, to the science of education—I mean the autobiography of Helen Keller.

When she was nineteen months old, Helen had a severe illness, in which she lost sight and hearing, and consequently speech. She never recovered the lost senses and here, we should say, was a soul almost inviolably sealed, to which there was no approach but through the single sense of touch; yet, this lady's book, written with her own unaided hands (she used a typewriter), with hardly any revision, should rank as a classic for the purity and pregnancy of the style, independently of the vital interest of the matter. How was the miracle accomplished? Of her childhood Helen says herself that, save for a few impressions, "the shadows of the prison-house" enveloped it. But there were always roses, and she had the sense of smell; and there was love—but she was not loving then. When she was seven Miss Sullivan came to her. This lady herself had been blind for some years, and had been at the Perkins Institute, founded by that Dr Howe who liberated the intelligence of Laura Bridgman. But Miss Sullivan is no mere output of any institution. She is a person of fine sanity and wholesomeness, trusting to her personal initiative, and aware from the first that her work was to liberate the personality of her little pupil and by no means to superimpose her own. "Thus I came up out of Egypt," says Miss Keller of the arrival of her teacher, and the voice which she heard from Sinai said, "Knowledge is love and light and vision"; and then follows that amazing and enthralling epic which tells how it was all done, how the one word water was the key which opened the doors of the child's mind, while the word love opened those of the closed heart. Thenceforth, many new words came every day with crowds of ideas; and it is not too much to say that this imprisoned and desolate child entered upon such a large inheritance of thought and knowledge, of gladness and vision, as few of us of the seeing and hearing world attain to. The instrument in this great liberation was nothing more than the familiar manual alphabet, followed in course of time by raised books and 'Braille.'

Miss Sullivan on Systems of Education.—Like all great discoveries, this, of a soul, was, in all its steps, marked by simplicity. Miss Sullivan had little love for psychologists and all their ways; would have no experiments; would not have her pupil treated as a phenomenon, but as a person. "No," she says, "I don't want any more Kindergarten materials . . . I am beginning to suspect all elaborate and special systems of education. They seem to me to be built up on the supposition that every child is a kind of idiot who must be taught to think, whereas if the child is left to himself he will think more and better, if less showily. Let him go and come freely, let him touch real things, and combine his impressions for himself, instead of sitting indoors at a little round table, while a sweet-voiced teacher suggests that he build a stone wall with his wooden blocks, or make a rainbow out of strips of coloured paper, plant straw trees in bead flower-pots. Such teaching fills the mind with artificial associations that must be got rid of before the child can develop independent ideas out of actual experiences." It is a great thing to have a study of education as it were de novo, in which we see the triumph of mind, not only over apparently insuperable natural obstacles, but over the dead wall of systematised education—a more complete hindrance to any poor child than her grievous defects proved to Helen Keller.

The Kindergarten in the United States.—This question of the Kindergarten, as the proper place for the education of young children, is so important that I should like to recommend to parents and teachers the examination of the subject contained in the Special Reports published by the Board of Education. [See Appendix]

We must go to the United States to witness the apotheosis of educational theory; I say theory rather than practice, because the American mind, like the French, seems to me severely logical as well as generously impulsive. A theory arrives, is liberally entertained, and is set to work with due appliances on a magnificent scale to do that which in it lies for the education of a great people. To say, educational science in America appears to be deductive rather than inductive; theories are translated into experiments with truly imposing zeal and generosity. An inductive theory of education is, on the other hand, arrived at by means of long, slow, various, and laborious experiments which disclose, here a little, and there a little, of universal truth. The Americans have chosen, perhaps, the easier way, and in the end, they too experiment upon their theory. The Kindergarten system illustrates what I mean; notwithstanding its German name, the Kindergarten is not a common product in the Fatherland; it is in America that the ideas of Froebel have received their greatest development, that the Kindergarten has become a cult, and the great teacher a prophet. But the impulse has worn itself out; any way, it is waxing weak.

Mr Thistleton Mark on the Kindergarten.—According to Mr Thistleton Mark—whose able paper on 'Moral Education in American Schools' offers matter for much profitable reflection—"Even a stationary Froeblian is driven to have some better holdfast than the ipse dixit of the great reformer. The word Kindergarten is no longer a proper noun signifying always and everywhere the one, sole, original, and identical thing. It is a common noun, and as such is assured of a more permanent place in American speech." That is to say, educational thought in America is tending towards the broad and natural conception expressed in the phrase 'education is a life.' But I wish that educationalists would give up the name Kindergarten. I cannot help thinking that it is somewhat of a strain to conscientous minds to draw the cover of Froeblian doctrine and practice over the broader and more living conceptions that are abroad to-day. Even revolutionised Kindergarten practice must suffer from the memory and habit of weaknesses such as are pointed out by Dr Stanley Hall in the following words:—

Dr Stanley Hall on the Kindergarten.—"The most decadent intellectual new departure of the American Froebelists is the emphasis now laid upon the mother-plays as the acme of Kindergarten wisdom. These are represented by very crude poems, indifferent music and pictures, illustrating certain incidents of child life believed to be of fundamental and typical significance. I have read these in German and in English, have strummed the music, and have given a brief course of lectures from the sympathetic standpoint, trying to put all the new wine of meaning I could think of into them. But I am driven to the conclusion that, if they are not positively unwholesome and harmful for the child, and productive of anti-scientific and unphilosphical intellectual habits in the teacher, they should nevertheless be superseded by the far better things now available." [quoted by Mr Thistleton Mark].

"Another cardinal error of the Kindergarten is the intensity of its devotion to gifts and occupations. In devising these Froebel showed great sagacity; but the scheme as it left his own hands was a very inadequate expression of his educational ideas, even for his time. He thought it a perfect grammar of play and an alphabet of industries; and in this opinion he was utterly mistaken. Play and industry were then relatively undeveloped; and while his devices were beneficent for the peasant children in the country, they lead in the interests of the modern city a child a very pallid and unreal life." With these important utterances I must conclude a superficial examination of the very important question,—Is the Kindergarten the best training-ground for a child?

IV.—Reading

Time of Teaching to Read, an Open Question.—Reading presents itself first amongst the lessons to be used as instruments of education, although it is open to discussion whether the child should acquire the art unconsciously, from his infancy upwards, or whether the effort should be deferred until he is, say, six or seven, and then made with vigour. In a valuable letter, addressed to her son John, we have the way of teaching to read adopted by that pattern mother, the mother of the Wesleys:—

Mrs Wesley's Plan.—"None of them was taught to read till five years old, except Kezzy, in whose case I was overruled; and she was more years in learning than any of the rest had been months. The way of teaching was this: the day before a child began to learn, the house was set in order, every one's work appointed them, and a charge given that no one should come into the room from nine to twelve, or from two to five, which were our school hours. One day was allowed the child wherein to learn its letters, and each of them did in that time know all its letters, great and small, except Molly and Nancy, who were a day and a half before they knew them perfectly, for which I thought them then very dull; but the reason I thought them so was because the rest learned them so readily; and your brother Samuel, who was the first child I ever taught, learned the alphabet in a few hours. He was five years old the tenth of February; the next day we began to learn, and as soon as he knew the letters, began at the first chapter of Genesis. He was taught to spell the first verse, then to read it over and over until he could read it off-hand without hesitation; so on, to the second verse, etc., till he took ten verses for a lesson, which he quickly did. Easter fell low that year, and by Whitsuntide he could read a chapter very well; for he read continually, and had such a prodigious memory, that I cannot remember to have told him the same word twice. What was yet stranger, any word he had learnt in his lesson he knew wherever he saw it, either in his Bible or any other book, by which means he learned very soon to read an English author well." [Southey's Life of Wesley].

It is much to be wished that thoughtful mothers would more often keep account of the methods they employ with their children, with some definite note of the success of this or that plan.

Many persons consider that to learn to read a language so full of anomalies and difficulties as our own is a task which should not be imposed too soon on the childish mind. But, as a matter of fact, few of us can recollect how or when we learned to read: for all we know, it came by nature, like the art of running; and not only so, but often mothers of the educated classes do not know how their children learned to read. 'Oh, he taught himself,' is all the account his mother can give of little Dick's proficiency. Whereby it is plain, that this notion of the extreme difficulty of learning to read is begotten by the elders rather than by the children. There would be no little books entitled Reading Without Tears, if tears were not sometimes shed over the reading lesson; but, really, when that is the case, the fault rests with the teacher.

The Alphabet.—As for his letters, the child usually teaches himself. He has his box of ivory letters and picks out p for pudding, b for blackbird, h for horse, big and little, and knows them both. But the learning of the alphabet should be made a means of cultivating the child's observation: he should be made to see what he looks at. Make big B in the air, and let him name it; then let him make round O, and crooked S, and T for Tommy, and you name the letters as the little finger forms them with unsteady strokes in the air. To make the small letters thus from memory is a work of more art, and requires more careful observation on the child's part. A tray of sand is useful at this stage. The child draws his finger boldly through the sand, and then puts a back to his D; and behold, his first essay in making a straight line and a curve. But the devices for making the learning of the 'A B C' interesting are endless. There is no occasion to hurry the child: let him learn one form at a time, and know it so well that he can pick out the d's, say, big and little, in a page of large print. Let him say d for duck, dog, doll, thus: d-uck, d-og, prolonging the sound of the initial consonant, and at last sounding d alone, not dee, but d', the mere sound of the consonant separated as far as possible from the following vowel.

Let the child alone, and he will learn the alphabet for himself: but few mothers can resist the pleasure of teaching it; and there is no reason why they should, for this kind of learning is no more than play to the child, and if the alphabet be taught to the little student, his appreciation of both form and sound will be cultivated. When should he begin? Whenever his box of letters begins to interest him. The baby of two will often be able to name half a dozen letters; and there is nothing against it so long as the finding and naming of letters is a game to him. But he must not be urged, required to show off, teased to find letters when his heart is set on other play.

Word-making. The first exercises in the making of words will be just as pleasant to the child. Exercises treated as a game, which yet teach the powers of the letters, will be better to begin with than actual sentences. Take up two of his letters and make the syllable 'at': tell him it is the word we use when we say 'at home,' 'at school.' Then put b to 'at'— bat; c to 'at'—cat; fat, hat, mat, sat, rat, and so on. First, let the child say what the word becomes with each initial consonant to 'at,' in order to make hat, pat, cat. Let the syllables all be actual words which he knows. Set the words in a row, and let him read them off. Do this with the short vowel sounds in combination with each of the consonants, and the child will learn to read off dozens of words of three letters, and will master the short-vowel sounds with initial and final consonants without effort. Before long he will do the lesson for himself. 'How many words can you make with "en" and another letter, with "od" and another letter?' etc. Do not hurry him.

Word-making with Long Vowels, etc.—When this sort of exercise becomes so easy that it is no longer interesting, let the long sounds of the vowels be learnt in the same way: use the same syllables as before with a final e; thus 'at' becomes 'ate,' and we get late, pate, rate, etc. The child may be told that a in 'rate' is long a; a in 'rat' is short a. He will make the new sets of words with much facility, helped by the experience he gained in the former lessons.

Then the same sort of thing with final 'ng'—'ing,' 'ang,' 'ong,' 'ung'; as in ring, fang, long, sung: initial 'th,' as then, that: final 'th,' as with, pith, hath, lath, and so on, through endless combinations which will suggest themselves. This is not reading, but it preparing the ground for reading; words will be no longer unfamiliar, perplexing objects, when the child meets with them in a line of print. Require him to pronounce the words he makes with such finish and distinctness that he can himself hear and count the sounds in given way.

Early Spelling.—Accustom him from the first to shut his eyes and spell the word he has made. This is important. Reading is not spelling, nor is it necessary to spell in order to read well; but the good speller is the child whose eye is quick enough to take in the letters which compose it, in the act of reading off a word, and this is a habit to be acquired from the first: accustom him to see the letters in the word, and he will do without effort.

If words were always made on a given pattern in English, if the same letter always represented the same sounds, learning to read would be an easy matter; for the child would soon acquire the few elements of which all words would, in that case, be composed. But many of our English words are, each, a law unto itself: there is nothing for it, but the child must learn to know them at sight; he must recognise 'which,' precisely as he recognises 'B,' because he has seen it before, been made to look at it with interest, so that the pattern of the word is stamped upon his retentive brain. This process should go on side by side with the other—the learning of the powers of the letters; for the more variety you can throw into his reading lessons, the more will the child enjoy them. Lessons in word-making help him to take intelligent interest in words; but his progress in the art of reading depends chiefly on the 'reading at sight' lessons.

Reading at Sight.—The teacher must be content to proceed very slowly, securing the ground under her feet as she goes. Say—

"Twinkle, twinkle, little star,
How I wonder what you are,"

is the first lesson; just those two lines. Read the passage for the child, very slowly, sweetly, with just expression, so that it is pleasant to him to listen. Point to each word as you read. Then point to 'twinkle,' 'wonder,' 'star,' 'what,'—and expect the child to pronounce each word in the verse taken promiscuously; then, when he shows that he knows each word by itself, and not before, let him read the two lines with clear enunciation and expression: insist from the first on clear, beautiful reading, and do not let the child fall into a dreary monotone, no more pleasant to himself than to his listener. Of course, by this time he is able to say the two lines; and let him say them clearly and beautifully. In his after lesson he will learn the rest of the little poem.

The Reading of Prose.—At this stage, his reading lessons must advance so slowly that he may just as well learn his reading exercises, both prose and poetry, as recitation lessons. Little poems suitable to be learned in this way will suggest themselves at once; but perhaps prose is better, on the whole, as offering more of the words in everyday use, of Saxon origin, and of anomalous spelling. Short fables, and such graceful, simple prose as we have in Mrs Gatty's Parables from Nature, and, still better, in Mrs Barbauld's prose poems, are very suitable. Even for their earliest reading lessons, it is unnecessary to put twaddle into the hands of children.

But we have not yet finished the reading lesson on 'Twinkle, twinkle little star.' The child should hunt through two or three pages of good clear type for 'little,' star,' you,' are,' each of the words he has learned, until the word he knows looks out upon him like the face of a friend in a crowd of strangers, and he is able to pounce upon it anywhere. Lest he grow weary of the search, the teacher should guide him, unawares, to the line or paragraph where the word he wants occurs. Already the child has accumulated a little capital; he knows eight or ten words so well that he will recognise them anywhere, and the lesson has occupied probably ten minutes.

The next 'reading at sight' lesson will begin with a hunt for the familiar words, and then—

"Up above the world so high,
Like a diamond in the sky,"

should be gone through in the same way. As spelling is simply the art of seeing, seeing the letters in a word as we see the features of a face—say to the child, 'Can you spell sky?'—or any of the shorter words. He is put on his mettle, and if he fails this time, be sure he will be able to spell the word when you ask him next; but do not let him learn to spell or even say the letters aloud with the word before him.

As for understanding what they read, the children will be full of bright, intelligent remarks and questions, and will take this part of the lesson into their own hands; indeed, the teacher will have to be on her guard not to let them carry her away from the subject.

Careful Pronunciation.—The little people will probably have to be pulled up on the score of pronunciation. They must render 'high,' sky,' 'like,' 'world,' with delicate precision; 'diamond,' they will no doubt wish to hurry over, and say as 'di'mond,' just as they will reduce 'history' to 'hist'ry.' But here is another advantage of slow and steady progress—the saying of each word receives due attention, and the child is trained in the habit of careful enunciation. Every day increases the number of words he is able to read at sight, and the more words he knows already, the longer his reading lesson becomes in order to afford the ten or dozen new words which he should master every day.

A Year's Work.—'But what a snail's progress!' you are inclined to say. Not so slow, after all: a child will thus learn, without appreciable labour, from two to three thousand words in the course of a year; in other words, he will learn to read, for the mastery of this number of words will carry him with comfort through most of the books that fall in his way.

Ordinary Method.—Now, compare the steady progress and constant interest and liveliness of such lessons with the deadly weariness of the ordinary reading lesson. The child blunders through a page or two in a dreary monotone without expression, with imperfect enunciation. He comes to a word he does not know, and he spells it; that throws no light on the subject, and he is told the word: he repeats it, but as he has made no mental effort to secure the word, the next time he meets with it the same process is gone through. The reading lesson for that day comes to an end. The pupil has been miserably bored, and has not acquired one new word. Eventually, he learns to read, somehow, by mere dint of repetition; but consider what an abuse of his intelligence is a system of teaching which makes him undergo daily labour with little or no result, and gives him a distaste for books before he has learned to use them.

V.—The First Reading Lesson

[It is so important that children should be taught to read in a rational way, that I introduce two papers—by the writer—which have appeared in Parents' Review, in the hope that they will make the suggested method fairly clear & familiar.]

(Two Mothers Confer)

"You don't mean to say you would go plump into words of three or four syllables before a child knows his letters?"

"It is possible to read words without knowing the alphabet, as you know a face without singling out its features; but we learn not only the names but the sounds of the letters before we begin to read words."

"Our children learn their letters without any teaching. We always keep by us a shallow table drawer, the bottom covered half an inch deep with sand. Before they are two, the babies make round O and crooked S, and T for Tommy, and so on, with dumpy, uncertain little fingers. The elder children teach the little ones by way of a game."

"The sand is capital! We have various devices, but none so good as that. Children love to be doing. The funny, shaky lines the little finger makes in the sand will be ten times as interesting as the shapes the eye sees."

"But the reading! I can't get over three syllables in the first lesson. Why, it's like teaching a twelve-months old child to waltz."

"You say that because we forget that a group of letters is no more than the sign of a word, while a word is only the vocal sign of a thing or an act. This is how the child learns. First, he gets the notion of the table; he sees several tables; he finds they have legs, by which you can scramble up; very often covers which you may pull off; and on them many things lie, good and pleasant for a baby to enjoy; sometimes, too, you can pull these things off the table, and they go down with a bang, which is nice. The grown-up people call this pleasant thing, full of many interests, 'table,' and, by-and-by, baby says 'table' too; and the word 'table' comes to mean, in a vague way, all this to him. 'Around table,' 'on the table,' and so on, form part of the idea of 'table' to him. In the same way baby chimes in when his mother sings. She says, 'Baby, sing,' and, by-and-by, notions of 'sing,' 'kiss,' 'love,' dawn on his brain."

"Yes, the darlings! and it's surprising how many words a child knows even before he can speak them; 'pussy,' 'dolly,' 'carriage,' soon convey interesting ideas to him."

"That's just it. Interest the child in the thing, and he soon learns the sound-sign for it—that is, its name. Now, I maintain that, when he is a little older, he should learn the form-sign—that is, the printed word—on the same principle. It is far easier for a child to read plum-pudding than to read 'to, to,' because 'plum-pudding' conveys a far more interesting idea."

"That may be, but when he gets into words of three or four syllables; but what would you do while he's in words of one syllable—indeed, of two or three letters?"

"I should never put him into words of one syllable at all. The bigger the word, the more striking the look of it, and, therefore, the easier it is to read, provided always that the idea it conveys is interesting to a child. It is sad to see an intelligent child toiling over a reading lesson infinitely below his capacity—ath, eth, ith, oth, uth—or, at the very best, 'The cat sat on the mat.' How should we like to begin to read German, for example, by toiling over all conceivable combinations of letters, arranged on no principle but similarity of sound; or, worse still, that our readings should be graduated according to the number of letters each word contains? We should be lost in a hopeless fog before a page of words of three letters all drearily like one another, with no distinctive features for the eye to seize upon; but the child? 'oh, well—children are different;

no doubt it is good for the child to grind in this mill!' But this is only one of many ways in which children are needlessly and cruelly oppressed!"

"You are taking high moral ground! All the same, I don't think I am convinced. It is far easier for a child to spell cat, cat, than to spell plum-pudding, plum-pudding."

"But spelling and reading are two things. You must learn to spell in order to write words, not to read them. A child is droning over a reading-lesson, spells c o u g h; you say 'cough,' and she repeats. By dint of repetition, she learns at last to associate the look of the word with the sound, and says 'cough' without spelling it; and you think she has arrived at 'cough' through c o u g h. Not a bit of it; c o f spells cough!"

"Yes; but 'cough' has a silent u, and a gh with the sound of f. There, I grant, is a great difficulty. If only there were no silent letters, and if all letters had always the same sound, we should, indeed, have reading made easy. The phonetic people have something to say for themselves."

"You would agree with the writer of an article in a number of a leading review: 'Plough ought to be written and printed plow; through, thru; enough, enuf; ought, aut or ort'; and so on. All this goes on the mistaken idea that in reading we look at the letters which compose a word, think of their sounds, combine these, and form the word. We do nothing of the kind; we accept a word, written or printed, simply as the symbol of a word we are accustomed to say. If the word is new to us we may try to make something of the letters, but we know so well that this is a shot in the dark, that we are careful not to say the new word until we have heard someone else say it."

"Yes, but children are different."

"Children are the same, 'only more so.' We could, if we liked, break up a word into its sounds, or put certain sounds together to make a word. But these are efforts beyond the range of children. First, as last, they learn to know a word by the look of it, and the more striking it looks the easier it is to recognise; provided always that the printed word is one which they already know very well by sound and by sense."

"It is not clear yet; suppose you tell me, step by step, how you would give your first reading lesson. An illustration helps so much."

"Very well: Bobbie had his first lesson yesterday—on his sixth birthday. The lesson was part of the celebration. By the way, I think it's rather a good idea to begin a new study with a child on his birthday, or some great day; he begins by thinking the new study a privilege."

"That is a hit. But go on; did Bobbie know his letters?"

"Yes, he had picked them up, as you say; but I had been careful not to allow any small readings. You know how Susanna Wesley used to retire to her room with the child who was to have his first reading-lesson, and not to appear again for some hours, when the boy came out able to read a good part of the first chapter of Genesis? Well, Bobbie's first reading-lesson was a solemn occasion, too, for which we had been preparing for a week or two. First, I bought a dozen penny copies of the 'History of Cock Robin'—good bold type, bad pictures, that we cut out.

Then we had a nursery pasting day—pasting the sheets on common drawing-paper, six one side down, and six the other; so that now we had six complete copies, and not twelve.

Then we cut up the first page only, of all six copies, line by line, and word by word. We gathered up the words and put them in a box, and our preparations were complete.

Now for the lesson. Bobbie and I are shut in by ourselves in the morning room. I always use a black-board in teaching the children. I write up, in good clear 'print' hand, **Cock Robin**. Bobbie watches with more interest because he knows his letters. I say, pointing to the word, 'cock robin,' which he repeats.

"Then the words in the box are scattered on the table, and he finds half a dozen 'cock robins' with great ease.

We do the same thing with 'sparrow,' 'arrow,' 'said,' 'killed,' 'who,' and so on, till all the words in the verse have been learned. The words on the black-board grow into a column, which Bob reads backwards and forwards, and every way, except as the words run in the verse.

Then Bobbie arranges the loose words into columns like that on the board.

Then into columns of his own devising, which he reads off.

Lastly, culminating joy (the whole lesson has been a delight!), he finds among the loose words, at my dictation,

'Who killed Cock Robin
I said the sparrow
With my bow and arrow
I killed Cock Robin,'

Arranging the words in verse form. Then I had still one unmutilated copy, out of which Bob had the pleasure of reading the verse, and he read it forwards and backwards. So long as he lives he will know those twelve words."

"No doubt it was a pleasant lesson; but, think of all the pasting and cutting!"

"Yes, that is troublesome. I wish some publisher would provide us with what we want—nursery rhymes, in good bold type, with boxes of loose words to match, a separate box, or division, for each page, so that the child may not be confused by having too many words to hunt amongst. The point is that he should see, and look at, the new word many times, so that its shape becomes impressed upon his brain."

"I see; but he is only able to read 'Cock Robin'; he has no general power of reading."

"On the contrary, he will read those twelve words wherever he meets with them. Suppose he learns ten words a day, in half a year he will have at least six hundred words; he will know how to read a little."

"Excellent, supposing your children remember all they learn. At the end of a week, mine would remember 'Cock Robin,' perhaps, but it the rest would be gone!"

"Oh, but we keep what we get! When we have mastered the words of the second verse, Bob runs through the first in the book, naming words here and there as I point to them. It takes less than a minute, and the ground is secured."

"The first lesson must have been long?"

"I'm sorry to say it lasted half an hour. The child's interest tempted me to do more than I should."

"It all sounds very attractive—a sort of game—but I cannot be satisfied that a child should learn to read without knowing the powers of the letters. You constantly see a child spell a word over to himself, and then pronounce it; the more so, if he has been carefully taught the sounds of the letters—not merely their names."

"Naturally; for though many of our English words are each a law unto itself, others offer a key to a whole group, as arrow gives us sp arrow, m arrow, h arrow; but we have alternate days—one for reading, the other for word-building—and that is one way to secure variety, and, so, the joyous interest which is the real secret of success."

VI—Reading By Sight And Sound

Learning to read is Hard Work.—Probably that vague whole which we call 'Education' offers no more difficult and repellent task than that to which every little child is (or ought to be) set down—the task of learning to read. We realise the labour of it when some grown man makes a heroic effort to remedy shameful ignorance, but we forget how contrary to Nature it is for a little child to occupy himself with dreary hieroglyphics—all so dreadfully alike!—when the world is teeming with interesting objects which he is agog to know. But we cannot excuse our volatile Tommy, nor is it good for him that we should. It is quite necessary he should know how to read; and not only so—the discipline of the task is altogether wholesome for the little man. At the same time, let us recognise that learning to read is to many children hard work, and let us do what we can to make the task easy and inviting.

Knowledge of Arbitrary Symbols—In the first place, let us bear in mind that reading is not a science nor an art. Even if it were, the children must still be the first consideration with the educator; but it is not. Learning to read is no more than picking up, how we can, a knowledge of certain arbitrary symbols for objects and ideas. There are absolutely no right and necessary 'steps' to reading, each of which leads to the next; there is no true beginning, middle, or end. For the arbitrary symbols we must know in order to read are not letters, but words. By way of illustration, consider the delicate differences of sound represented by the letter 'o' in the last sentence; to analyse and classify the sounds of 'o' in 'for,' 'symbols,' 'know,' 'order,' 'to,' 'not,' and 'words,' is a curious, not especially useful, study for a philologist, but a laborious and inappropriate one for a child. It is time we faced the fact that the letters which compose an English word are full of philological interest, and that their study will be a valuable part of education by-and-by; but meantime, sound and letter-sign are so loosely wedded in English, that to base the teaching of reading on the sounds of the letters only, is to lay up for the child much analytic labour, much mental confusion, due to the irregularities of the language; and some little moral strain in making the sound of a letter in a given word fall under any of the 'sounds' he has been taught.

Definitely, what is it we propose in teaching a child to read? (a) that he shall know at sight, say, some thousand words; (b) That he shall be able to build up new words with the elements of these. Let him learn ten new words a day, and in twenty weeks he will be to some extent able to read, without any question as to the number of letters in a word. For the second, and less important, part of our task, the child must know the sounds of the letters, and acquire power to throw given sounds into new combinations.

What we want is a bridge between the child's natural interests and those arbitrary symbols with which he must become acquainted, and which, as we have seen, are words, and not letters.

These Symbols should be Interesting.—The child cares for things, not words; his analytic power is very small, his observing faculty is exceedingly quick and keen; nothing is too small for him; he will spy out the eye of a fly; nothing is too intricate, he delights in puzzles. But the thing he learns to know by looking at it, is a thing which interests him. Here we have the key to reading. No meaningless combinations of letters, no cla, cle, cli, clo, clu, no ath, eth, ith, oth, uth, should be presented to him. The child should be taught from the first to regard the printed word as he already regards the spoken word, as the symbol of fact or idea of full of interest. How easy to read 'robin redbreast,' 'buttercups and daisies'; the number of letters in the words is no matter; the words themselves convey such interesting ideas that the general form and look of them fixes itself on the child's brain by the same law of association of ideas which makes it easy to couple the objects with their spoken names. Having got a word fixed on the sure peg of the idea it conveys, the child will use his knowledge of the sounds of the letters to make up other words containing the same elements with great interest. When he knows 'butter' he is quite ready to make 'mutter' by changing the b for an m.

Tommy's First Lesson—But example is better than precept, and more convincing than the soundest reasoning. This is the sort of reading lesson we have in view. Tommy knows his letters by name and sound, but he knows no more. To-day he is to be launched into the very middle of reading, without any 'steps' at all, because reading is neither an art nor a science, and has, probably, no beginning. Tommy is to learn to read to-day—

"I like little pussy,
Her coat is so warm" -

And he is to know those nine words so well that he will be able to read them wherever they may occur henceforth and for evermore.

"Oh, yes," says a reader, "as in the 'Cock Robin' lesson; grant that the principle is sound—and there is much to be said on both sides of that question—but grant it, who in the world could get through all the pasting and cutting and general messing preparatory to the great lesson? No; the method of the books may be only second-best, but ready-made books must do for me. I have no time to make my own apparatus."

I must own that the cutting and pasting was very clumsy, but the lesson served its purpose because it induced a good friend to education [Miss Miller, founder of a Training College at Oxford] to have a delightful 'Little Pussy' box prepared for us, loose words, nice big type, two lines in a bag. Whoso learns "Little Pussy' as it should be learned will know at least one hundred words—not a bad stock-in-trade for a beginner—all of them good useful words that we want every day. There is one objection; such contractions as 'I'll' are ugly at the best, and I hope that in the word-lessons based upon 'Little Pussy,' pieces will be chosen in which this fault is avoided.

Steps.—And now, we begin. Material: Tommy's box of loose letters, the new 'Little Pussy' box, pencil and paper, or much better, blackboard and chalk. We write up in good big print hand 'Pussy.' Tommy watches with interest: he knows the letters, and probably says them as we write. Besides, he is prepared for the great event of his life; he knows he is going to begin to learn to read to-day. But we do not ask anything yet of his previous knowledge. We simply tell him that the word is 'pussy.' Interest at once; he knows the thing, pussy, and the written symbol is pleasant in his eyes because it is associated with an existing idea in his mind. He is told to look at the word 'pussy' until he is sure he would know it again. Then he makes 'pussy' from memory with his own loose letters. Then the little bag containing our two lines in loose words is turned out, and he finds the word 'pussy'; and, lastly, the little sheet with the poem printed on it is shown to him, and he finds 'pussy,' but is not allowed yet to find out the run of the rhyme. 'Coat, little, like, is, her, warm, I, so,' are taught in the same way, in less time than it takes to describe the lesson. When each new word is learned, Tommy makes a column of the old ones, and reads up and down and cris-cras, the column on the blackboard.

Reading Sentences—He knows words now, but he cannot yet read sentences. Now for the delight of reading. He finds at our dictation, amongst his loose words, 'pussy—is—warm,' places them in 'reading' order, one after the other, and then reads off the sentence. Joy, as of one who has found a new planet! And Tommy has indeed found a new poet. Then, 'her-little-coat-is-warm,' 'Pussy-is-so-little,' 'I-like-pussy,' 'Pussy-is-little-like-her-coat,' and so on through a dozen more little arrangements. If the rhyme can be kept a secret till the whole is worked out, so much the better. To make the verses up with his own loose words will give Tommy such a delicious sense that knowledge is power, as few occasions in after life will afford. Anyway, reading is to him a delight henceforth, and it will require very bad management indeed to make him hate it.

Tommy's Second Lesson.—Tommy promises himself another reading lesson next day, but he has instead a spelling lesson, conducted somewhat in this way:

He makes the word 'coat' with his letters, from memory if he can; if not, with the pattern word. Say 'coat' slowly; give the sound of the c. 'Take away c, and what have we left?' A little help will get 'oat' from him. How would you make 'boat' (say the word very slowly, bringing out the sound of b). He knows the sounds of the letters, and says b-oat readily; fl-oat, two added sounds, which you lead him to find out; g-oat, he will give you the g, and find goat a charming new word to know; m-oat, he easily decides on the sound of m; a little talk about moat; the other words are too familiar to need explanation. Tommy will, no doubt, offer 'note' and we must make a clean breast of it and say, 'No, note is spelt with other letters'; but what other letters we do not tell him now. Thus he comes to learn incidentally and very gradually that different groups of letters may stand for the same sounds. But we do not ask him to generalise; we only let him have the fact that n-oat does not spell the symbol we express by 'note.' 'Stoat'—he will be able to give the sounds of the initial letters, and stoat again calls for a little talk—another interesting word. He has made a group of words with his letters, and there they are on the black-board in a column, thus

c-oat
m-oat
g-oat
fl-oat
st-oat
b-oat

He reads the column up and down and cris-cras; every word has a meaning and carries an idea. Then the loose words he knows are turned out, and we dictate new sentences, which he arranges: 'I-like-her-goat'; 'her-little-stoat-is-warm,' and so on, making the new words with loose letters.

Unknown Words—Now for a new experience. We dictate 'pussy in the boat.' Consternation! Tommy does not know 'in' nor 'the.' 'Put counters for the words you don't know; they may soon come in our lessons,' and Tommy has a desire and a need—that is, an appetite for learning.

Like Combinations have Different Sounds.—We deal with the remaining words in the same way—'little' gives brittle, tittle, skittle: pussy, is, I, and her, give no new words. 'Like' gives mike and pike. 'so' gives no, do (the musical 'do'), and lo! From 'warm' we get arm, harm, charm, barm, alarm; we pronounced warm as arm. Tommy perceives that such a pronunciation is wrong and vulgar, and sees that all these words are sounded like 'arm,' but not one of them like 'warm'—that is, he sees that the same group of letters need not always have the same sound. But we do not ask him to make a note of this new piece of knowledge; we let it grow into him gradually, after many experiences.

By this time he has eighteen new words on the blackboard of which to make sentences with the nine loose words of 'pussy.' Her skittle is little, her charm is brittle, her arm is warm, and so on. But we take care that the sentences make sense. Her goat is brittle, is 'silly,' and not to be thought of at all. Tommy's new words are written in his 'note-book' in print hand, so that he can take stock of his possessions in the way of words.

Moral Training in Reading Lessons—The next day we do the last two lines of the stanza, as at first. These lines afford hardly any material for a spelling lesson, so in our next lesson we go on with the second verse. But our stock of words is growing; we are able, as we go on, to make an almost unlimited number of little sentences. If we have to use counters now and then, why, that only whets our appetite for knowledge. By the time Tommy has worked 'Little Pussy' through he has quite a large stock of words; has considerable power to attack new words with familiar combinations; what is more, he has achieved; he has courage to attack all 'learning,' and has a sense that delightful results are quite within reach. Moreover, he learns to read in a way that affords him some moral training. There is no stumbling, no hesitation from the first, but bright attention and perfect achievement. His reading lesson is a delight, of which he is deprived when he comes to his lesson in a lazy, drawling mood. Perfect enunciation and precision are insisted on, and when he comes to arrange the whole of the little rhyme in his loose words and read it off (most delightful of all the lessons) his reading must be a perfect and finished recitation. [Spirited nursery rhymes form the best material for such reading lessons. A 'Delightful Reading Box' has been issued on similar plan to the 'Pussy' Box, whose one fault is that the verses are a little dull. But this 'Box' should be of great use]. I believe that this is a practical common-sense way to teach reading in English. It may be profitable for the little German child to work through all possibly dreary combinations of letters before he is permitted to have any joy in 'reading,' because wherever these combinations occur they will have the sounds the child has learned laboriously. The fact that English is anomalous as regards the connection between sign and sound, happily exonerates us from enforcing this dreary grind. [It is desirable that 'Tommy' should not begin to 'read' until his intelligence is equal to the effort required by these lessons. Even then, it may be well to break up one into two, or half a dozen, as he is able to take it].

VII.—Recitation

'The Children's Art' On this subject I cannot do better than refer the reader to Mr Arthur Burrell's Recitation. This book purports to be a handbook for teachers in elementary schools. I wish that it may be very largely used by such teachers, and may also become a family hand-book; though many of the lessons will not be called for in educated homes. There is hardly any 'subject' so educative and so elevating as that which Mr Burrell has happily described as 'The Children's Art.' All children have it in them to recite; it is an imprisoned gift waiting to be delivered, like Ariel from the pine. In this most thoughtful and methodical volume we are possessed of the fit incantations. Use them duly, and out of the woodenness of even the most commonplace child steps forth the child-artist, a delicate sprite, who shall make you laugh and make you weep. Did not the great Sir Walter "sway to and fro, sobbing his fill," to his little 'Pet's' speaking of—

"For I am sick, and capable of fears,
Oppressed with wrong, and therefore full of fears;
A widow, husbandless, subject to fears;
A woman, naturally born to fears"?

Marjorie Fleming was, to be sure, a child-genius; but in this book we learn by what carefully graduated steps a child who is not a genius, is not even born of cultivated parents, may be taught the fine art of beautiful and perfect speaking; but that is only the first step in the acquisition of 'The Children's Art.' The child should speak beautiful thoughts so beautifully, with such delicate rendering of each nuance of meaning, that he becomes to the listener the interpreter of the author's thought. Now, consider what appreciation, sympathy, power of expression this implies, and you will grant that 'The Children's Art' is, as Steele said of the society of his wife, "a liberal education in itself." It is objected— 'Children are such parrots! They say a thing as they hear it said; as for troubling themselves to 'appreciate' and 'interpret,' not a bit of it!" Most true of the 'My name is Norval' style of recitation; but throughout this volume the child is led to find the just expression of thought for himself; never is the poor teacher allowed to set a pattern—'say this as I say it.' The ideas are kept well within the child's range, and the expression is his own. He is caught with guile, his very naughtiness is pressed into service, he finds a dozen ways of saying 'I shan't,' is led cunningly up to the point of expressing himself, and—he does it, to his own surprise and delight. The pieces given here for recitation are a treasure-trove of new joys. 'Winken, Blinken, and Nod,' "Miss Lilywhite's Party,' and 'The Two Kittens,' would compel any child to recite. Try a single piece over with the author's markings and suggestions, and you will find there is as much difference between the result and ordinary reading aloud as there is in a musical composition played with and without the composer's expression marks. I hope that my readers will train their children in the art of recitation; in the coming days, more even than in our own will it behove every educated man and woman to be able to speak effectively in public; and, in learning to recite you learn to speak.

Memorising.—Recitation and committing to memory are not necessarily the same thing, and it is well to store a child's memory with a good deal of poetry, learnt without labour. Some years ago I chanced to visit a house, the mistress of which had educational notions of her own, upon which she was bringing up a niece. She presented me with a large foolscap sheet written all over with the titles of poems, some of them long and difficult: Tintern Abbey, for example. She told me that her niece could repeat to me any of those poems that I liked to ask for, and that she had never learnt a single verse by heart in her life. The girl did repeat several of the poems on the list, quite beautifully and without hesitation; and then the lady unfolded her secret. She thought she had made a discovery, and I thought so too. She read a poem through to E.; then the next day, while the little girl was making a doll's frock, perhaps, she read it again; once again the next day, while E.'s hair was being brushed. She got in about six or more readings, according to the length of the poem, at odd and unexpected times, and in the end E. could say the poem which she had not learned.

I have tried the plan often since, and found it effectual. The child must not try to recollect or to say the verse over to himself, but, as far as may be, present an open mind to receive an impression of interest. Half a dozen repetitions should give children possession of such poems as 'Dolly and Dick,' 'Do you ask what the birds say?' Little lamb, who made thee?' and the like. The gains of such a method of learning are, that the edge of the child's enjoyment is not taken off by weariful verse by verse repetitions, and, also, that the habit of making mental images is unconsciously formed.

I remember once discussing this subject with the late Miss Anna Swanwick in some connection with Browning of which I do not recall, but in the course of talk an extremely curious incident transpired. A lady, a niece of Miss Swanwick's, said that after a long illness, during which she had not been allowed to do anything, she read 'Lycidas' through, by way of a first treat to herself as a convalescent. She was surprised to find herself then next day repeating to herself long passages. Then she tried the whole poem and found she could say it off, the result of this single reading, for she had not learned the poem before her illness, nor read it with particular attention. She was much elated by the treasure-trove she had chanced upon, and to test her powers, she read the whole of 'Paradise Lost,' book by book, and with the same result,—she could repeat it book by book after a single reading! She enriched herself by acquiring other treasures during her convalescence; but as health returned, and her mind became preoccupied with many interests, she found she no longer had this astonishing power. It is possible that the disengaged mind of a child is as free to take and as strong to hold beautiful images clothed in beautiful words as was that of this lady during her convalescence. But, let me again say, every effort of the kind, however unconscious, means wear and tear of brain substance. Let the child lie fallow till he is six, and then, in this matter of memorising, as in others, attempt only a little, and let the poems the child learns be simple and within the range of his own thought and imagination. At the same time, when there is so much noble poetry within a child's compass, the pity of it, that he should be allowed to learn twaddle!

VIII—Reading for Older Children

In teaching to read, as in other matters, c'est le premier pas qui coute. The child who has been taught to read with care and deliberation until he has mastered the words of a limited vocabulary, usually does the rest for himself. The attention of his teachers should be fixed on two points—that he acquires the habit of reading, and that he does not fall into slipshod habits of reading.

The Habit of Reading.—The most common and the monstrous defect in the education of the day is that children fail to acquire the habit of reading. Knowledge is conveyed to them by lessons and talk, but the studious habit of using books as a means of interest and delight is not acquired. This habit should be begun early; so soon as the child can read at all, he should read for himself, and to himself, history, legends, fairy tales, and other suitable matter. He should be trained from the first to think that one reading of any lesson is enough to enable him to narrate what he has read, and will thus get the habit of slow, careful reading, intelligent even when it is silent, because he reads with an eye to the full meaning of every clause.

Reading Aloud.— He should have practice, too, in reading aloud, for the most part, in the books he is using for his term's work. These should include a good deal of poetry, to accustom him to the delicate rendering of shades of meaning, and especially to make him aware that words are beautiful in themselves, that they are a source of pleasure, and are worthy of our honour; and that a beautiful word deserves to be beautifully said, with a certain roundness of tone and precision of utterance. Quite young children are open to this sort of teaching, conveyed, not in a lesson, but by a word now and then.

Limitation—In this connection the teacher should not trust to setting, as it were, a copy in reading for the children's imitation. They do imitate readily enough, catching tricks of emphasis and action in an amusing way; but these are mere tricks, an aping of intelligence. The child must express what he feels to be the author's meaning; and this sort of intelligent reading comes only of the habit of reading with understanding.

Reading to Children—It is a delight to older people to read aloud to children, but this should be only an occasional treat and indulgence, allowed before bedtime, for example. We must remember the natural inertness of a child's mind; give him the habit of being read to, and he will steadily shirk the labour of reading for himself; indeed, we all like to be spoon-fed with our intellectual meat, or we should read and think more for ourselves and be less eager to run after lectures.

Questions on the Subject-Matter—When a child is reading, he should not be teased with questions as to the meaning of what he has read, the signification of this word or that; what is annoying to older people is equally annoying to children. Besides, it is not of the least consequence that they should be able to give the meaning of every word they read. A knowledge of meanings, that is, an ample and correct vocabulary, is only arrived at in one way—by the habit of reading. A child unconsciously gets the meaning of a new word from the context, if not the first time he meets with it, then the second or the third: but he is on the look-out, and will find out for himself the sense of any expression he does not understand. Direct questions on the subject-matter of what a child has read are always a mistake. Let him narrate what he has read, or some part of it. He enjoys this sort of consecutive reproduction, but abominates every question in the nature of a riddle. If there must be riddles, let it be his to ask and the teacher's to direct him the answer. Questions that lead to a side issue or to a personal view are allowable because these interest children—'What would you have done in his place?'

Lesson-Books—A child has not begun his education until he has acquired the habit of reading to himself, with interest and pleasure, books fully on a level with his intelligence. I am speaking now of his lesson-books, which are all too apt to be written in a style of insufferable twaddle, probably because they are written by persons who have never chanced to meet a child. All who know children know that they do not talk twaddle and do not like it, and prefer that which appeals to their understanding. Their lesson-books should offer matter for their reading, whether aloud or to themselves; therefore they should be written with literary power. As for the matter of these books, let us remember that children can take in ideas and principles, whether the latter be moral or mechanical, as quickly and clearly as we do ourselves (perhaps more so); but detailed processes, lists and summaries, blunt the edge of a child's delicate mind. Therefore, the selection of their first lesson-books is a matter of grave importance, because it rests with these to give children the idea that knowledge is supremely attractive and that reading is delightful. Once the habit of reading his lesson-book with delight is set up in a child, his education is—not completed, but—ensured; he will go on for himself in spite of the obstructions which school too commonly throws in his way.

Slipshod Habits; Inattention—I have already spoken of the importance of a single reading. If a child is not able to narrate what he has read once, let him not get the notion that he may, or that he must, read it again. A look of slight regret because there is a gap in his knowledge will convict him. The power of reading with perfect attention will not be gained by the child who is allowed to moon over his lessons. For this reason, reading lessons must be short; ten minutes or a quarter of an hour of fixed attention is enough for children of the ages we have in view, and a lesson of this length will enable a child to cover two or three pages of his book. The same rule as to the length of a lesson applies to children whose lessons are read to them because they are not yet able to read for themselves.

Careless Enunciation—It is important that, when reading aloud, children should make due use of the vocal organs, and, for this reason, a reading lesson should be introduced by two or three simple breathing exercises, as, for a example, a long inspiration with closed lips and a slow expiration with open mouth. If a child read through his nose, it is well to consult a doctor; an operation for adenoids may be necessary, which is rarely distressing, and should be performed while children are young. Provincial pronunciation and slipshod enunciation must be guarded against. Practice in pure vowel sounds, and the respect for words which will not allow of their being hastily slurred over, should cure these defects. By the way, quite little children commonly enunciate beautifully, because a big word is a new acquirement which they delight in and make the most of; our efforts should be directed to make older children hold words in like esteem.

The habit of 'minding your stops' comes of intelligent reading. A child's understanding of the passage will lead him to correct pointing.

IX.—The Art of Narrating

Children Narrate by Nature.—Narrating is an art, like poetry-making or painting, because it is there, in every child's mind, waiting to be discovered, and is not the result of any process of disciplinary education. A creative fiat calls it forth. 'Let him narrate'; and the child narrates, fluently, copiously, in ordered sequence, with fit and graphic details, with a just choice of words, without verbosity or tautology, so soon as he can speak with ease. This amazing gift with which normal children are born is allowed to lie fallow in their education. Bobbie will come home with a heroic narrative of a fight he has seen between 'Duke' and a dog in the street. It is wonderful! He has seen everything, and he tells everything with splendid vigour in the true epic vein; but so ingrained is our contempt for children that we see nothing in this but Bobbie's foolish childish way! Whereas here, if we have eyes to see and grace to build, is the ground-plan of his education.

Until he is six, let Bobbie narrate only when and what he has a mind to. He must not be called upon to tell anything. Is this the secret of the strange long talks we watch with amusement between creatures of two, and four, and five? Is it possible that they narrate while they are still inarticulate, and that the other inarticulate person takes it all in? They try us, poor dear elders, and we reply 'Yes,' 'Really!' 'Do you think so?' to the babble of whose meaning we have no comprehension. Be this as it may; of what goes on in the dim region of 'under two' we have no assurance. But wait till the little fellow has words and he will 'tell' without end to whomsoever will listen to the tale, but, for choice, to his own compeers.

This Power should be used in their Education.— Let us take the goods the gods provide. When the child is six, not earlier, let him narrate the fairy-tale which has been read to him, episode by episode, upon one hearing of each; the Bible tale read to him in the words of the Bible; the well-written animal story; or all about other lands from some such volume as The World at Home [See Appendix]. The seven-years-old boy will have begun to read for himself, but must get most of his intellectual nutriment, by ear, certainly, but read to him out of books. Geography, sketches from ancient history, Robinson Crusoe, The Pilgrim's Progress, Tanglewood Tales, Heroes of Asgard, and much of the same calibre, will occupy him until he is eight. The points to be borne in mind are, that he should have no book which is not a child's classic; and that, given the right book, it must not be diluted with talk or broken up with questions, but given to the boy in fit proportions as wholesome meat for his mind, in the full trust that a child's mind is able to deal with its proper food.

The child of eight or nine is able to tackle the more serious material of knowledge; but our business for the moment is with what children under nine can narrate.

Method of Lesson.—In every case the reading should be consecutive from a well-chosen book. Before the reading for the day begins, the teacher should talk a little (and get the children to talk) about the last lesson, with a few words about what is to be read, in order that the children may be animated by expectation; but she should beware of explanation and, especially, of forestalling the narrative. Then, she may read two or three pages, enough to include an episode; after that, let her call upon the children to narrate,—in turns, if there be several of them. They not only narrate with spirit and accuracy, but succeed in catching the style of their author. It is not wise to tease them with corrections; they may begin with an endless chain of 'ands,' but they soon leave this off, and their narrations become good enough in style and composition to be put in a 'print book'!

This sort of narration lesson should not occupy more than a quarter of an hour.

The book should always be deeply interesting, and when the narration is over, there should be a little talk in which moral points are brought out, pictures shown to illustrate the lesson, or diagrams drawn on the blackboard. As soon as children are able to read with ease and fluency, they read their own lesson, either aloud or silently, with a view to narration; but where it is necessary to make omissions, as in the Old

Testament narratives and Plutarch's Lives, for example, it is better that the teacher should always read the lesson which is to be narrated.

X.—Writing

Perfect Accomplishment.—I can only offer a few hints on the teaching of writing, though much might be said. First, let the child accomplish something perfectly in every lesson—a stroke, a pothook, a letter. Let the writing lesson be short; it should not last more than five or ten minutes. Ease in writing comes by practice; but that must be secured later. In the meantime, the thing to be avoided is the habit of careless work—humpy 'm's, angular o's.

Printing.—But the child should have practice in printing before he begins to write. First, let him print the simplest of the capital letters with single curves and straight lines. When he can make the capitals and large letters, with some firmness and decision, he might go on to the smaller letters—'printed' as in the type we call 'italics,' only upright,—as simple as possible, and large.

Steps in Teaching.—Let the stroke be learned first; then the pothook; then the letters of which the pothook is an element—n, m, v, w, r, h, p, y; then o, and letters of which the curve is an element a, c, g, e, x, s, q; then looped and irregular letters—b, l, f, t, etc. One letter should be perfectly formed in a day, and the next day the same elemental forms repeated in another letter, until they become familiar. By-and-by copies, three or four of the letters they have learned grouped into a word—'man,' 'aunt'; the lesson to be the production of the written word once without a single fault in any letter. At this stage the chalk and blackboard are better than pen and paper, as it is well that the child should rub out and rub out until his own eye is satisfied with the word or letter he has written.

Of the further stages, little need be said. Secure that the child begins by making perfect letters and is never allowed to make faulty ones, and the rest he will do for himself; as for 'a good hand,' do not hurry him; his 'handwriting' will come by-and-by out of the character that is in him; but, as a child, he cannot be said, strictly speaking, to have character.

Set good copies before him, and see that he imitates his model dutifully: the writing lesson being not so many lines, or 'a copy'—that is, a page of writing—but a single line which is as exactly as possible a copy of the characters set. The child may have to write several lines before he succeeds in producing this.

Text-Hand—If he write in books with copperplate headlines (which are, on the whole, to be eschewed), discrimination should be exercised in the choice of these; in many of them the writing is atrocious, and the letters are adorned with flourishes which increase the pupil's labour but by no means improve his style. One word more; do not hurry the child into 'small hand'; it is unnecessary that he should labour much over what is called 'large hand,' but 'text-hand,' the medium size, should be continued until he makes the letters with ease. It is much easier for the child to get into an irregular scribble by way of 'small-hand,' than to get out of it again. In this, as in everything else, the care of the educator must be given, not only to the formation of good, but to the prevention of bad habits.

A 'New Handwriting.'—Some years ago I heard of a lady who was elaborating, by means of the study of old Italian and other manuscripts, a 'system of beautiful handwriting' which could be taught to children. I waited patiently, though not without some urgency, for the production of this new kind of 'copy-book.' The need for such an effort was very great, for the distinctly commonplace writing taught from existing copy-books, however painstaking and legible, cannot but have a rather vulgarising effect both on the writer and the reader of such manuscript. At last the lady, Mrs Robert Bridges, has succeeded in her tedious and difficult undertaking, and this book for teachers will enable them to teach their pupils a style of writing which is pleasant to acquire because it is beautiful to behold. It is surprising how quickly young children, even those already confirmed in 'ugly' writing, take to this 'new handwriting.'

But Mrs Bridges' purpose in A New Handwriting will be better understood by some passages quoted, with her permission, from her preface: "The accompanying ten plates are intended chiefly for those who teach writing: a few words, both of apology and explanation, are needed to introduce them. I was always interested in handwriting, and after making acquaintance with the Italianised Gothic of the sixteenth century, I consciously altered my hand towards some likeness with its forms and general character. The script happening to please, I was often asked to make alphabets and copies, and begged by professional teachers to have such a book as this printed, that they might use it in their schools. One can never quite satisfy oneself in the making of models for others to copy, but these plates are very much what I intended, though, owing to my inexperience, some of them have suffered in the reproduction...

A child must first learn to control his hand and constrain it to obey his eye; at this earliest stage, any simple forms will serve the purpose; and hence it might be further argued that the forms are always indifferent, and that full mastery of the hand can be as well attained by copying bad models as good; but this can hardly be: the ordinary copybook, the aim of which seems to be to economise the component parts of the letters, cannot train the hand as more varied shapes will; nor does this uniformity, exclusive of beauty, offer as good training to the eye. Moreover, I should say that variety and beauty of form are attractive, even to little children, and that the attempt to create something which interests them, cheers and crowns their stupendous efforts with a pleasure that cannot be looked for in the task of copying monotonous shapes. But whether such a hand as that here shown lends itself as easily as the more uniform model to the development of a quick, useful cursive, I cannot say; and it is possible that the degradations, inevitable in the habit of quick writing, might produce a mere untidiness, almost the worst reproach of penmanship. Some of the best English hands of to-day are as good a quick cursive as one can desire, and show points of real beauty; but such hands are rare, and are only those which have, as we say, character; which probably means that the writer would have done well for himself under any system: whereas the average hands, which are the natural outcome of the old copybook writing, degraded by haste, seem to owe their common ugliness to the mean type from which they sprang; and the writers, when they have occasion to write well, find they can do but little better, and only prove that haste was not the real cause of their bad writing."

How to Use.—The method of using Mrs Bridges' Handwriting [see Appendix], which we find most effectual, is to practise each form on the blackboard from the plate, and later to use pencil, and still later pen and ink. By-and-by the children will be promoted to transcribe little poems, and so on, in this very pleasing script.

Set headlines are to be avoided, as children fail to use the forms of the headline in their ordinary writing. It is sometimes objected that this rather elaborate and beautiful handwriting will interfere with a characteristic 'hand,' but it seems to me that to have a beautiful, instead of a commonplace, basis for handwriting is a great gain.

XI.—Transcription

Value of Transcription—The earliest practice in writing proper for children of seven or eight should be, not letter writing or dictation, but transcription, slow and beautiful work, for which the New Handwriting is to be preferred, though perhaps some of the more ornate characters may be omitted with advantage.

Transcription should be an introduction to spelling. Children should be encouraged to look at the word, see a picture of it with their eyes shut, and then write from memory.

Children should Transcribe favourite Passages.—A certain sense of possession and delight may be added to this exercise if children are allowed to choose for transcription their favourite verse in one poem and another. This is better than to write a favourite poem, an exercise which stales on the little people before it is finished. But a book of their own, made up of their own chosen verses, should give them pleasure.

Small Text-Hand—Double-ruled Lines—Double ruled lines, small text-hand, should be used at first, as children are eager to write very minute 'small hand,' and once they have fallen into this habit it is not easy to get good writing. A sense of beauty in their writing and in the lines they copy should carry them over this stage of their work with pleasure. Not more than ten minutes or a quarter of an hour should be given to the early writing-lessons. If they are longer the children get tired and slovenly.

Position in Writing.—For the writing position children should sit so that light reaches them from the left, and desk or table should be at a comfortable height.

It would be a great gain if children were taught from the first to hold the pen between the first and second fingers, steadying it with the thumb. This position avoids the uncomfortable strain on the muscles produced by the usual way of holding a pen—a strain which causes writer's cramp in later days when there is much writing to be done. The pen should be held in a comfortable position, rather near the point, fingers and thumb somewhat bent, and the hand resting on the paper. The writer should also be allowed to support himself with the left hand on the paper, and should write in an easy position, with bent head but not with stooping figure. It would be unnecessary to say that the flat of the nib should be used if children had not a happy gift for making spider marks with the nib held sideways. In all writing lessons, free use should be made of the black-board by both teacher and children by way of model and practice.

Desks.—The best desks I know are those recommended by Dr Roth, single desks which may be raised or lowered, moved backwards or forwards, with seat, back, and a back pad, and rests for the feet. There may be others as good, even better, in the market, but these seem to answer every purpose.

Children's Table.—For little children it is a good plan to have a table of the right height made by the house carpenter, to the top of the table consisting of two leaves with hinges. These leaves open in the middle, and disclose a sort of box in the space which is often used for a drawer, the table-top itself making the lids of the box. Such a receptacle for the children's books, writing materials, etc., is more easily kept neat by themselves than is an ordinary drawer or box.

XII.—Spelling And Dictation

Of all the mischievous exercises in which children spend their school hours, dictation, as commonly practised, is perhaps the most mischievous; and this, because people are slow to understand that there is no part of a child's work at school which some philosophic principle does not underlie.

A Fertile Cause of Bad Spelling.—The common practise is for the teacher to dictate a passage, clause by clause, repeating each clause, perhaps, three of our times under a fire of questions from the writers. Every line has errors in spelling, one, two, three, perhaps. The conscientious teacher draws her pencil under these errors, or solemnly underlines them with red ink. The children correct in various fashions; sometimes they change books, and each corrects the errors of another, copying the word from the book or from the blackboard. A few benighted teachers still cause children to copy their own error along with the correction, which last is written three or four times, learned, and spelt to the teacher. The latter is astonished at the pure perversity which causes the same errors to be repeated again and again, notwithstanding all these painstaking efforts.

The Rationale of Spelling.—But the fact is, the gift of spelling depends upon the power the eye possesses to 'take' (in a photographic sense) a detailed picture of a word; and this is a power and habit which must be cultivated in children from the first. When they have read 'cat,' they must be encouraged to see the word with their eyes shut, and the same habit will enable them to image 'Thermopylae.' This picturing of words upon the retina appears to be to be the only royal road to spelling; an error once made and corrected leads to fearful doubt for the rest of one's life, as to which was the wrong way and which is the right. Most of us are haunted by some doubt as to whether 'balance,' for instance, should have one 'l' or two; and the doubt is born of a correction. Once the eye sees a misspelt word, that image remains; and if there is also the image of the word rightly spelt, we are perplexed as to which is which. Now we see why there could not be a more ingenious way of making bad spellers than 'dictation' as it is commonly taught. Every misspelt word is in image in the child's brain not to be obliterated by the right spelling. It becomes, therefore, the teacher's business to prevent false spelling, and, if an error has been made, to hide it away, as it were, so that the impression may not become fixed.

Steps of a Dictation Lesson.—Dictation lessons, conducted in some such way as the following, usually result in good spelling. A child of eight or nine prepares a paragraph, older children a page, or two or three pages. The child prepares by himself, by looking at the word he is not sure of, and then seeing it with his eyes shut. Before he begins, the teacher asks what words he thinks will need his attention. He generally knows, but the teacher may point out any word likely to be a cause of stumbling. He lets his teacher know when he is ready. The teacher asks if there are any words he is not sure of. These she puts, one by one, on the blackboard, letting the child look till he has a picture, and then rubbing the word out. If anyone is still doubtful he should be called to put the word he is not sure of on the board, the teacher watching to rub out the word when a wrong letter begins to appear, and again helping the child to get a mental picture. Then the teacher gives out the dictation, clause by clause, each clause repeated once. She dictates with a view to the pointing, which the children are expected to put in as they write; but they must not be told 'comma,' 'semicolon,' etc. After the sort of preparation I have described, which takes ten minutes or less, there is rarely an error in spelling. If there be, it is well worth while for the teacher to be on the watch with slips of stamp-paper to put over the wrong word, that its image may be erased as far as possible. At the end of the lesson, the child should again study the wrong word in his book until he says he is sure of, and should write it correctly on the stamp-paper.

A lesson of this kind secures the hearty co-operation of children, who feel they take their due part in it; and it also prepares them for the second condition of good spelling, which is—much reading combined with the habit of imaging the words as they are read.

Illiterate spelling is usually a sign of sparse reading; but, sometimes, of hasty reading without the habit of seeing the words that are skimmed over.

Spelling must not be lost sight of in the children's other studies, though they should not be teased to spell. It is well to write a difficult proper name, for example, on the blackboard in the course of history or geography readings, rubbing the word out when the children say they can see it. The whole secret of spelling lies in the habit of visualising words from memory, and children must be trained to visualise in the course of their reading. They enjoy this way of learning to spell.

XIII.—Composition

George Osborne's Essay—"What a prodigiously well-read and delightful person the Reverend Lawrence Veal was, George's Master! 'He knows everything,' Amelia said. 'He says there is no place in the bar or the senate that Georgy may not aspire to. Look here,' and she went to the piano-drawer and drew out a theme of George's composition. This great effort of genius, which is still in the possession of Georgy's mother, is as follows:

" 'On Selfishness.—Of all the vices which degrade the human character, Selfishness is the most odious and contemptible. An undue love of Self leads to the most monstrous crimes and occasions of the greatest misfortunes both in States and Families. As a selfish man will impoverish his family and often bring them to ruin; so a selfish king brings ruin on his people and often plunges them into war. Example: The selfishness of Achilles, as remarked by the poet Homer, occasioned a thousand woes to the Greeks—[a sentence in Greek follows here, from Homer's Illiad, A. 2]. The selfishness of the late Napoleon Bonaparte occasioned innumerable wars in Europe, and caused him to perish, himself, in a miserable island—that of St. Helena in the Atlantic Ocean.

" 'We see by these examples that we are not to consult our own interest and ambition, but that we are to consider the interests of others as well as our own.—George S. Osborne.

" 'Athene House, 24 April 1827.'

" ' 'Think of him' (George was 10) 'writing such a hand, and quoting Greek too, at his age,' the delighted mother said."

And well might Mrs George Sedley be delighted. Would not many a mother to-day triumph in such a literary effort? What can Thackeray be laughing at? Or does he, in truth, give us this little 'theme' as a tour de force?

An Educational Futility.—I think this great moral teacher here throws down the gauntlet in challenge of an educational fallacy which is accepted, even in the twentieth century. That futility is the extraction of original composition from schoolboys and schoolgirls. The proper function of the mind of the young scholar is to collect material for the generalisations of after-life. If a child is asked to generalise, that is, to write an essay upon some abstract theme, a double wrong is done him. He is brought up before a stone wall by being asked to do what is impossible to him, and that is discouraging. But a worse moral injury happens to him in that, having no thought of his own to offer on the subject, he puts together such tags of commonplace thought as have come in his way and offers the whole as his 'composition,' an effort which puts a strain upon his conscience while it piques his vanity. In these days masters do not consciously put their hand to the work of their pupils as did that 'prodigiously well-read and delightful' master who had the educating of George Osborne. But, perhaps, without knowing it, they give the ideas which the cunning schoolboy seizes to 'stick' into the 'essay' he hates. Sometimes they do more. They deliberately teach children how to 'build a sentence' and how to 'bind sentences' together.

Lessons in Composition.—Here is a series of preliminary exercises (or rather a part of a series, which numbers 40) intended to help a child to write an essay on 'An Umbrella,' from a book of the hour proceeding from one of our best publishing houses: -

"Step I.

"1. What are you? "2. How did you get your name? "3. Who uses you? "4. What were you once? "5. What were like then? "6. Where were you obtained or found? "7. Of what stuff or materials are you made? "8. From what sources do you come? "9. What are your parts? "10. Are you made, grown, or fitted together?

"Step II.

"I am an umbrella, and am used by many people, young and old. "I get my name from a word which means a shade. "The stick came perhaps from America, and is quite smooth, even, and polished, so that the metal ring may slide easily up and down the stick. "My parts are a frame and a cover. My frame consists of a stick about a yard long, wires, and a sliding metal band. At the lower end of the stick is a steel ferrule or ring. This keeps the end from wearing away when I am used in walking.

"Step III.

"Now use it, is, and was, instead of I, have, my, and am.

"Exercise.

"Now write your own description of it."

Such Teaching a Public Danger.—And this is work intended for Standards VI. And VII.! That is to say, this kind of thing is the final literary effort to be exacted from children in our elementary schools!

The two volumes (I quote from near the end of the second and more advanced volume) are not to be gibbeted as exceptionally bad. A few years ago the appalling discovery was made that, both in secondary and elementary schools, 'composition' was dreadfully defective, and, therefore, badly taught. Since then many volumes have been produced, more or less on the lines indicated in the above citation, and distinguished publishers have not perceived that to offer to the public, with the sanction of their name, works of this sterilising and injurious character, is an offence against society. The body of a child is sacred in the eye of the law, but his intellectual powers may be annihilated on such starvation diet as this, and nothing said! The worst of it is, both authors and publishers in every case act upon the fallacy that well intentioned effort is always excusable, if not praiseworthy. They do not perceive that no effort is permissible towards the education of children without an intelligent conception, both of children, and of what is meant by education.

'Composition' comes by Nature.—In fact, lessons on 'composition' should follow the model of that famous essay on "Snakes in Ireland"—"There are none." For children under nine, the question of composition resolves itself into that of narration, varied by some such simple exercise as to write a part and narrate a part, or write the whole account of a walk they have taken, a lesson they have studied, or of some simple matter that they know. Before they are ten, children who have been in the habit of using books will write good, vigorous English with ease and freedom; that is, if they have not been hampered by instructions. It is well for them not even to learn rules for the placing of full stops and capitals until they notice how these things occur in their books. Our business is to provide children with material in their lessons, and leave the handling of such material to themselves. If we would believe it, composition is as natural as jumping and running to children who have been allowed due use of books. They should narrate in the first place, and they will compose, later readily enough; but they should not be taught 'composition.'

XIV.—Bible Lessons

Children Enjoy the Bible.—We are apt to believe that children cannot be interested in the Bible unless its pages be watered down—turned into the slipshod English we prefer to offer them. Here is a suggestive anecdote of the childhood of Mrs Harrison, one of the pair of little Quaker maidens introduced to us in the Autobiography of Mary Howitt, the better known of the sisters. "One day she found her way into a lumber room. There she caught sight of an old Bible and turning over its yellow leaves she came upon words that she had not heard at the usual morning readings, the opening chapters of St Luke—which her father objected to read aloud—and the closing chapter of Revelation. The exquisite picture of the Great Child's birth in the one chapter and the beauty of the description of the New Jerusalem in the other, were seized upon by the eager little girl of six years old with a rapture which, she used to say, no novel in after years ever produced."

And here is a mention of a child of five. "The little ones read every day the events of Holy Week with me. Z. is inexpressibly interesting in his deep, reverent interest, almost excitement."

We are probably quite incapable of measuring the religious receptivity of children. Nevertheless, their fitness to apprehend the deep things of God is a fact with which we are called to 'deal prudently,' and to deal reverently. And that, because, as none can appreciate more fully than the 'Darwinian,' the attitude of thought and feeling in which you place a child is the vital factor in his education.

Should know the Bible Text.—Children between the ages of six and nine should get a considerable knowledge of the Bible text. By nine they should have read the simple (and suitable) narrative portions of the Old Testament, and, say, two of the gospels.

The Old Testament should, for various reasons, be read to the children. The gospel stories they might be read for themselves as soon as they can read them beautifully. It is a mistake to use paraphrases of the text; the fine roll of Bible English appeals to children with a compelling music, and they will probably retain through life their first conception of the Bible scenes, and, also, the very words in which these scenes are portrayed. This is a great possession. Half the clever talk we hear to-day, and half the uneasiness which underlies this talk, are due to a thorough and perfect ignorance of the Bible text. The points of assault are presented to men's minds naked and jagged, without atmosphere, perspective, proportion; until the Bible comes to mean for many, the speaking of Balaam's ass or the standing still of the sun at Joshua's bidding.

But let the imaginations of children be stored with the pictures, their minds nourished upon the words, of the gradually unfolding story of the Scriptures, and they will come to look out upon a wide horizon within which persons and events take shape in their due place and due proportion. By degrees, they will see that the world is a stage whereon the goodness of God is continually striving with the wilfulness of man; that some heroic men take sides with God; and that others, foolish and headstrong, oppose themselves to Him. The fire of enthusiasm will kindle in their breast, and the children, too, will take their side, without much exhortation, or any thought or talk of spiritual experience.

Essential and Accidental Truth.—As for whether such and such a narrative be a myth, or a parable, or a circumstance that has actually occurred, such questions do not affect the sincere mind of a child, because they have nothing to do with the main issues. It is quite well to bring before children, in the course of their Bible readings, whatever new light modern research puts in our way; the more we can help them in this way, the more vivid and real will Bible teaching become to them. But this grace, at any rate, the children may claim at our hands, that they shall not be disturbed by questions of authenticity in their Bible reading any more than in their reading of English history. Let them hear the story of the Garden of Eden, for example, as it stands; just so, we might even let them have the story of the man who went fishing and found a goodly pearl; and this, because the thing that matters in both stories is the essential truths they embody, and not the mere accidents of time and place. It is conceivable that the 'pearl of great price' was matter of current talk at the time; a so-called 'fact' seized upon by upon our Lord to make of it the vehicle for essential truth. If we will believe it, the minds of children are, perhaps, more fit than our own to appropriate and deal with truth. By-and-by they will perceive and discard, if necessary, the accidental circumstances with which the truth is clothed upon; but let us be very chary of our own action. Let us remember that neither we nor the children can bear the white light of naked truth; that if, for example, we succeed in destroying the clothing that covers the story of the first fall—the tree and its fruit, the tempting serpent, the yielding woman—we have no other clothing at hand for the fundamental truths of responsibility, temptation, sin; and, once uncovered, with no vesture which we can lay hold upon, the truths themselves will assuredly slip from our grasp.

We need not be at the pains to discriminate, in teaching children Bible narratives, between essential and accidental truth—the truth which interprets our own lives, and that which concerns only the time, place, and circumstances proper to the narrative. The children themselves will discern and keep fast hold of the essential, while the merely accidental slips from their memory as from ours. Therefore, let the minds of young children be well stored with the beautiful narratives of the Old Testament and of the gospels; but, in order that these stories may be always fresh and delightful to them, care must be taken lest Bible teaching stale upon their minds. Children are more capable of being bored than even we ourselves and many a revolt has been brought about by the undue rubbing-in of the Bible, in season and out of season, even in nursery days. But we are considering, not the religious life of children, but their education by lessons; and their Bible lessons should help them to realise in early days that the knowledge of God is the principal knowledge, and, therefore, that their Bible lessons are their chief lessons.

Method of Bible Lessons.—The method of such lessons is very simple. Read aloud to the children a few verses covering if possible, an episode. Read reverently, carefully, and with just expression. Then require the children to narrate what they have listened to as nearly as possible in the words of the Bible. It is curious how readily they catch the rhythm of the majestic and simple Bible English. Then, talk the narrative over with them in the light of research and criticism. Let the teaching, moral and spiritual, reach them without much personal application. I know of no better help in the teaching of young children than we get in Canon Paterson Smyth's Bible for the Young. Mr. Smyth brings both modern criticism and research to bear, so that children taught from his little manuals will not be startled to be told that the world was not made in six days; and, at the same time, they will be very sure that the world was made by God. The moral and spiritual teaching in these manuals is on broad and convincing lines. It is rather a good plan occasionally to read aloud Mr. Smyth's lesson on the subject after the Bible passage has been narrated. Children are more ready to appropriate lessons that are not directly levelled at themselves; while the teacher makes the teaching her own by the interest with which she reads, the pictures and other illustrations she shows, and her conversational remarks. Click here for a Sample of one of Paterson Smyth's books

Picture Illustrations.—The pictures in the Illustrated New Testament are, at the same time, reverent and actual, an unusual combination, and children enjoy them greatly. It would be well for them to have only the penny gospel they are reading, but it should perhaps be protected (and honoured) by an embroidered cover. A tattered Bible is not a wholesome sight for children. The Holy Gospels with Illustrations from the Old Masters, published by the S.P.C.K., is admirable. The study of such pictures as are here reproduced should be a valuable part of a child's education; it is no slight thing to realise how the Nativity and the visit of the Wise Men filled the imagination of the early Masters, and with what exceeding reverence and delight they dwelt upon every detail of the sacred story. This sort of impression is not to be had from any up-to-date treatment, or up-to-date illustrations; and the child who gets it in early days, will have a substratum of reverent feeling upon which should rest his faith. But it is well to let the pictures tell their own tale. The children should study a subject quietly for a few minutes; and then, the picture being removed, say what they have seen in it. It will be found that they miss no little reverent or suggestive detail which the artist has thought well to include.

The various R.T.S. publications issued in the series of Bypaths of Bible Knowledge will be found very helpful by the teacher as illustrating modern research; notably, Professor Sayce's Fresh Light from Ancient Monuments, and Budge's Dwellers on the Nile.

Bible Recitations.—The learning by heart of Bible passages should begin while the children are quite young, six or seven. It is a delightful thing to have the memory stored with beautiful, comforting, and inspiring passages, and we cannot tell when and how this manner of seed may spring up, grow, and bear fruit; but the learning of the parable of the Prodigal son, for example, should not be laid on the children as a burden. The whole parable should be read to them in a way to bring out its beauty and tenderness; and then, day by day, the teacher should recite a short passage, perhaps two or three verses, saying it over some three or four times until the children think they know it. Then, but not before, let them recite the passage. Next day the children will recite what they have already learned, and so on, until they are able to say the whole parable.

XV.—Arithmetic

Educative Value of Arithmetic.—Of all his early studies, perhaps none is more important to the child as a means of education than that of arithmetic. That he should do sums is of comparatively small importance; but the use of those functions which 'summing' calls into play is a great part of education so much so, that the advocates of mathematics and of language as instruments of education have, until recently, divided the field pretty equally between them.

The practical value of arithmetic to persons in every class of life goes without remark. But the use of the study in practical life is the least of its uses. The chief value of arithmetic, like that of the higher mathematics, lies in the training it affords the reasoning powers, and in the habits of insight, readiness, accuracy, intellectual truthfulness it engenders. There is no one subject in which good teaching effects more, as there is none in which slovenly teaching has more mischievous results. Multiplication does not produce the 'right answer,' so the boy tries division; that again fails, but subtraction may get him out of the bog. There is no must be to him he does not see that one process, and one process only, can give the required result. Now, a child who does not know what rule to apply to a simple problem within his grasp, has been ill taught from the first, although he may produce slatefuls of quite right sums in multiplication or long division.

Problems within the Child's Grasp.—How is this insight, this exercise of the reasoning powers, to be secured? Engage the child upon little problems within his comprehension from the first, rather than upon set sums. The young governess delights to set a noble 'long division sum,'—, 953,783,465/873—which shall fill the child's slate, and keep him occupied for a good half-hour; and when it is finished, and the child is finished too, done up with the unprofitable labour, the sum is not right after all: the last two figures in the quotient are wrong, and the remainder is false. But he cannot do it again—he must not be discouraged by being told it is wrong; so, 'nearly right' is the verdict, a judgment inadmissible in arithmetic. Instead of this laborious task, which gives no scope for mental effort, and in which he goes to sea at last from sheer want of attention, say to him—

"Mr. Jones sent six hundred and seven, and Mr. Stevens eight hundred and nineteen, apples to be divided amongst the twenty-seven boys at school on Monday. How many apples apiece did they get?"

Here he must ask himself certain questions. 'How many apples altogether? How shall I find out? Then I must divide the apples into twenty-seven heaps to find out each boy's share.' That is to say, the child perceives what rules he must apply to get the required information. He is interested; the work goes on briskly; the sum is done in no time, and is probably right, because the attention of the child is concentrated on his work. Care must be taken to give the child such problems as he can work, but yet which are difficult enough to cause him some little mental effort.

Demonstrate.—The next point is to demonstrate everything demonstrable. The child may learn the multiplication-table and do a subtraction sum without any insight into the rationale of either. He may even become a good arithmetician, applying rules aptly, without seeing the reason of them; but arithmetic becomes an elementary mathematical training only in so far as the reason why of every process is clear to the child. 2+2=4, is a self-evident fact, admitting of little demonstration; but 4x7=28 may be proved.

He has a bag of beans; places four rows with seven beans in a row; adds the rows thus: 7 and 7 are 14, and 7 are 21, and 7 are 28; how many sevens in 28? 4. Therefore it is right to say 4x7=28; and the child sees that multiplication is only a short way of doing addition.

A bag of beans, counters, or buttons should be used in all the early arithmetic lessons, and the child should be able to work with these freely, and even to add, subtract, multiply, and divide mentally, without the aid of buttons or beans, before he is set to 'do sums' on his slate.

He may arrange an addition table with his beans, thus—

00 0 = 3 beans
00 00 = 4 beans
00 000 = 5 beans

and be exercised upon it until he can tell, first without counting, and then without looking at the beans, that 2+7=9, etc.

Thus with 3, 4, 5,—each of the digits: as he learns each line of his addition table he is exercised upon imaginary objects, '4 apples and 9 apples,' '4 nuts and 6 nuts' etc.; and lastly, with abstract numbers—6+5, 6+8.

A subtraction table is worked out simultaneously with the addition table. As he works out each line of additions, he goes over the same ground, only taking away one bean, or two beans, instead of adding, until he is able to answer quite readily, 2 from 7? 2 from 5? After working out each line of addition or subtraction, he may put it on his slate with the proper signs, that is, if he have learned to make figures. It will be found that it requires a much greater mental effort on the child's part to grasp the idea of subtraction than that of addition, and the teacher must be content to go slowly—one finger from four fingers, one nut from three nuts, and so forth, until he knows what he is about.

When the child can add and subtract numbers pretty freely up to twenty, the multiplication and division tables may be worked out with beans, as far as 6x12; that is, 'twice six are 12' will be ascertained by means of two rows of beans, six beans in a row.

When the child can say readily, without even a glance at his beans, 2x8=16, 2x7=14, etc., he will take 4, 6, 8, 10, 12 beans, and divide them into groups of two: then, how many twos in 10, in 12, in 20? And so on, with each line of the multiplication table that he works out.

Problems—Now he is ready for more ambitious problems: thus, 'A boy had twice ten apples; how many heaps of 4 could he make?' He will be able to work with promiscuous numbers, as 7+5-3. If he must use beans to get his answer, let him; but encourage him to work with imaginary beans, as a step towards working with abstract numbers. Carefully graduated teaching and daily mental effort on the child's part at this early stage may be the means of developing real mathematical power, and will certainly promote the habits of concentration and effort of mind.

Notation—When the child is able to work pretty freely with small numbers, a serious difficulty must be faced, upon his thorough mastery of which will depend his appreciation of arithmetic as a science; in other words, will depend the educational value of all the sums he may henceforth do. He must be made to understand our system of notation. Here, as before, it is best to begin with the concrete: let the child get the idea of ten units in one ten after he has mastered the more easily demonstrable idea of twelve pence in one shilling.

Let him have a heap of pennies, say fifty: point out the inconvenience of carrying such weighty money to shops. Lighter money is used—shillings. How many pennies is a shilling worth? How many shillings, then, might he have for his fifty pennies? He divides them into heaps of twelve, and finds that he has four such heaps, and two pennies over; that is to say, fifty pence are (or are worth) four shillings and two pence. I buy ten pounds of biscuits at fivepence a pound; they cost fifty pence, but the shopman gives me a bill for 4s. 2d.; show the child how to put down: the pennies, which are worth least, to the right; the shillings, which are worth more, to the left.

When the child is able to work freely with shillings and pence, and to understand that 2 in the right-hand column of figures is pence, 2 in the left-hand column, shillings, introduce him to the notion of tens and units, being content to work very gradually. Tell him of uncivilized peoples who can only count so far as five—who say 'five-five beasts in the forest,' 'five-five fish in the river,' when they wish to express an immense number. We can count so far that we might count all day long for years without coming to the end of the numbers we might name; but after all, we have very few numbers to count with, and very few figures to express them by. We have but nine figures and a nought: we take the first figure and the nought to express another number, ten; but after that we must begin again until we get two tens, then, again, till we reach three tens, and so on. We call two tens, twenty, three tens, thirty, because 'ty' (tig) means ten. But if I see figure 4, how am I to know whether it means four tens or four ones? By a very simple plan. The tens have a place of their own; if you see figure 6 in the ten-place, you know it means sixty. The tens are always put behind the units: when you see two figures standing side by side, thus, '55,' the left-hand figure stands for so many tens; that is, the second 5 stands for ten times as many as the first.

Let the child work with tens and units only until he has mastered the idea of the tenfold value of the second figure to the left, and would laugh at the folly of writing 7 in the second column of figures, knowing that thereby it becomes seventy. Then he is ready for the same sort of drill in hundreds, and picks up the new idea readily if the principle have been made clear to him, that each remove to the left means a tenfold increase in the value of a number. Meantime, 'set' him no sums. Let him never work with figures the notation of which is beyond him, and when he comes to 'carry' in an addition or multiplication sum, let him not say he carries 'two,' or 'three,' but 'two tens,' or 'three hundreds,' as the case may be.

Weighing and Measuring.—If the child do not get the ground under his feet at this stage, he works arithmetic ever after by rule of thumb. On the same principle, let him learn 'weights and measures' by measuring and weighing; let him have scales and weights, sand or rice, paper and twine, and weigh, and do up, in perfectly made parcels, ounces, pounds, etc. The parcels, though they are not arithmetic, are educative, and afford considerable exercise of judgment as well as of neatness, deftness, and quickness. In like manner, let him work with foot-rule and yard measure, and draw up his tables for himself. Let him not only measure and weigh everything about him that admits of such treatment, but let him use his judgment on questions of measure and weight. How many yards long is the tablecloth? How many feet long and broad a map, or picture? What does he suppose a book weighs that is to go by parcel post? The sort of readiness to be gained thus is valuable in the affairs of life, and, if only for that reason, should be cultivated in the child. While engaged in measuring and weighing concrete quantities, the scholar is prepared to take in his first idea of a 'fraction,' half a pound, a quarter of a yard, etc.

Arithmetic a Means of Training.—Arithmetic is valuable as a means of training children in habits of strict accuracy, but the ingenuity which makes this exact science tend to foster slipshod habits of mind, a disregard of truth and common honesty, is worthy of admiration! The copying, prompting, telling, helping over difficulties, working with an eye to the answer which he knows, that are allowed in the arithmetic lesson, under an inferior teacher, are enough to vitiate any child; and quite as bad as these is the habit of allowing that a sum is nearly right, two figures wrong, and so on, and letting the child work it over again. Pronounce a sum wrong, or right—it cannot be something between the two. That which is wrong must remain wrong: the child must not be let run away with the notion that wrong can be mended into right. The future is before him: he may get the next sum right, and the wise teacher will make it her business to see that he does, and that he starts with new hope. But the wrong sum must just be let alone. Therefore his progress must be carefully graduated; but there is no subject in which the teacher has a more delightful consciousness of drawing out from day to day new power in the child. Do not offer him a crutch: it is in his own power he must go. Give him short sums, in words rather than in figures, and excite him in the enthusiasm which produces concentrated attention and rapid work. Let his arithmetic lesson be to the child a daily exercise in clear thinking and rapid, careful execution, and his mental growth will be as obvious as the sprouting of seedlings in the spring.

The A B C Arithmetic—Instead of entering further into the subject of teaching elementary arithmetic, I should like to refer the reader to the A B C Arithmetic by Messrs Sonnenschein & Nesbit. The authors found their method upon the following passage from Mill's Logic:

"The fundamental truths of the science of Number all rest on the evidence of sense; they are proved by showing to our eyes and our fingers that any given number of objects, ten balls for example, may by separation and re-arrangement exhibit to our sense all the different sets of numbers the sum of which is equal to ten. All the improved methods of teaching arithmetic to children proceed on a knowledge of this fact. All who wish to carry the child's mind along with them in learning arithmetic, all who wish to teach numbers and not mere ciphers, now teach it through the evidence of the senses in the manner we have described."

Here we may, I think, trace the solitary source of weakness in a surpassingly excellent manual. It is quite true that the fundamental truths of the science of number all rest on the evidence of sense but, having used eyes and fingers upon ten balls or twenty balls, upon ten nuts, or leaves, or sheep, or what not, the child has formed the association of a given number with objects, and is able to conceive of the association of various other numbers with objects. In fact, he begins to think in numbers and not in objects, that is, he begins mathematics. Therefore I incline to think that an elaborate system of staves, cubes, etc., instead of tens, hundreds, thousands, errs by embarrassing the child's mind with too much teaching, and by making the illustration occupy a more prominent place than the thing illustrated.

Dominoes, beans, graphic figures drawn on the blackboard, and the like, are, on the other hand, aids to the child when it is necessary of him to conceive of a great number with the material of a small one; but to see a symbol of the great numbers and to work with such a symbol are quite different matters.

With the above trifling exception, which does not interfere at all with the use of the books, nothing can be more delightful than the careful analysis of numbers and the beautiful graduation of the work, "only one difficulty at a time being presented to the mind." The examples and the little problems could only have been invented by writers in sympathy with children. I advise the reader who is interested in the teaching of arithmetic to turn to Mr Sonnenschein's paper on 'The Teaching of Arithmetic in Elementary Schools,' in one of the volumes published by the Board of Education.

Preparation for Mathematics.—In the 'forties' and 'fifties' it was currently held that the continual sight of the outward and visible signs (geometrical forms and figures) should beget the inward and spiritual grace of mathematical genius, or, at any rate, of an inclination to mathematics. But the educationalists of those days forgot, when they gave children boxes of 'form' and stuck up cubes, hexagons, pentagons, and what not, in every available schoolroom space, the immense capacity for being bored which is common to us all, and is far more strongly developed in children than in grown-up people. The objects which bore us, or the persons who bore us, appear to wear a bland place in the mind, and thought turns from them with sick aversion. Dickens showed us the pathos of it in the schoolroom of the little Gradgrinds, which was bountifully supplied with objects of uncompromising outline. Ruskin, more genially, exposes the fallacy. No doubt geometric forms abound,—the skeletons of which living beauty, in contour and gesture, in hill and plant, is the covering; and the skeleton is beautiful and wonderful to the mind which has already entered within the portals of geometry. But children should not be presented with the skeleton, but with the living forms which clothe it. Besides, is it not an inverse method to familiarise the child's eye with patterns made by his compasses, or stitched upon his card, in the hope that the form will beget the idea? For the novice, it is probably the rule that the idea must beget the form, and any suggestion of an idea from a form comes only to the initiated. I do not think that any direct preparation for mathematics is desirable. The child, who has been allowed to think and not compelled to cram, hails the new study with delight when the due time for it arrives. The reason why mathematics are a great study is because there exists in the normal mind an affinity and capacity for this study; and too great an elaboration, whether of teaching or of preparation, has, I think, a tendency to take the edge off this manner of intellectual interest.

XVI.—Natural Philosophy

A Basis of Facts.—Of the teaching of Natural Philosophy, I will only remind the reader of what was said in an earlier chapter—that there is no part of a child's education more important than that he should lay, by his own observation, a wide basis of facts towards scientific knowledge in the future. He must live hours daily in the open air, and, as far as possible, in the country; must look and touch and listen; must be quick to note, consciously, every peculiarity of habit or structure, in beast, bird, or insect; the manner of growth and fructification of every plant. He must be accustomed to ask why—Why does the wind blow? Why does the river flow? Why is a leaf-bud sticky? And do not hurry to answer his questions for him; let him think his difficulties out so far as his small experience will carry him. Above all, when you come to the rescue, let it not be in the 'cut and dried' formula of some miserable little text-book; let him have all the insight available and you will find that on many scientific questions the child may be brought at once to the level of modern thought. Do not embarrass him with too much scientific nomenclature. If he discover for himself (helped, perhaps, by a leading question or two), by comparing an oyster and his cat, that some animals have backbones and some have not, it is less important that he should learn the terms vertebrate and invertebrate than that he should class the animals he meets with according to this difference.

Eyes and No-eyes.—The method of this sort of instruction is shown in Evenings at Home, where 'Eyes and No-eyes' go for a walk. No-eyes come home bored; he has seen nothing, been interested in nothing: while Eyes is all agog to discuss a hundred things that have interested him. As I have already tried to point out, to get this sort of instruction for himself is simply the nature of a child: the business of the parent is to afford him abundant and varied opportunities, and to direct his observations, so that, knowing little of the principles of scientific classification, he is, unconsciously, furnishing himself with the materials for such classification. It is needless to repeat what has already been said on this subject; but, indeed, the future of the man or woman depends very largely on the store of real knowledge gathered, and the habits of intelligent observation acquired, by the child. "Think you," says Mr. Herbert Spencer, "that the rounded rock marked with parallel scratches calls up as much poetry in an ignorant mind as in the mind of the geologist, who knows that over this rock a glacier slid a million of years ago? The truth is, that those who have never entered on scientific pursuits are blind to most of the poetry by which they are surrounded. Whoever has not in youth collected plants and insects, knows not half the halo of interest which lanes and hedgerows can assume."

Principles.—In this connection I should like to recommend The Sciences, by Mr. Holden. America comes to the fore with a schoolbook after my own heart. The Sciences is a forbidding title, but since the era of Joyce's Scientific Dialogues I have met with nothing on the same lines which makes so fit an approach to the sensible and intelligent mind of a child. This is what we may call a 'first-hand' book. The knowledge has of course all been acquired; but then it has been assimilated, and Mr. Holden writes freely out of his own knowledge both of his subject-matter and of his readers. The book has been thrown into the form of conversations between children—simple conversations without padding. About three hundred topics are treated of: Sand-dunes, Back-ice, Herculaneum, Dredging, Hurricanes, Echoes, the Prism, the Diving-bell, the Milky Way, and, shall I say, everything else? But the amazing skill of the author is shown in the fact that there is nothing scrappy and nothing hurried in the treatment of any topic, but each falls naturally and easily under the head of some principle which it elucidates. Many simple experiments are included, which the author insists shall be performed by the children themselves. I venture to quote from the singularly wise preface, a vade mecum for teachers:—

"The object of the present volume is to present chapters to be read in school or at home that shall materially widen the outlook of American schoolchildren in the domain of science, and of the applications of science to the arts and to daily life. It is in no sense a text-book, although the fundamental principles underlying the sciences treated are here laid down. Its main object is to help the child to understand the material world about him.

To be Comprehended by Children.—"All natural phenomena are orderly; they are governed by law; they are not magical. They are comprehended by someone; why not by the child himself? It is not possible to explain every detail of a locomotive to a young pupil, but it is perfectly practicable to explain its principles so that this machine, like others, becomes a mere special case of certain well-understood general laws. The general plan of the book is to awaken the imagination; to convey useful knowledge; to open the doors towards wisdom. Its special aim is to stimulate observation and to excite a living and lasting interest in the world that lies about us.

"The sciences of astronomy, physics, chemistry, meteorology, and physiography are treated as fully and as deeply as the conditions permit; and the lessons that they teach are enforced by examples taken from familiar and important things. In astronomy, for example, emphasis is laid upon phenomena that the child himself can observe, and he is instructed how to go about it. The rising and setting of the stars, the phases of the moon, the uses of the telescope, are explained in simple words. The mystery of these and other matters is not magical, as the child at first supposes. It is to deeper mysteries that his attention is here directed. Mere phenomena are treated as special cases of very general laws. The same process is followed in the exposition of the other sciences.

"Familiar phenomena, like those of steam, of shadows, of reflected light, of musical instruments, of echoes, etc., are referred to their fundamental causes. Whenever it is desirable, simple experiments are described and fully illustrated, and all such experiments can very well be repeated in the schoolroom. . . . The volume is the result of a sincere belief that much can be done to aid young children to comprehend the material world in which they live, and of a desire to have a part in a work so very well worth doing."

I cannot help quoting also in this connection from an article (Parents' Review, April 1904) by the Rev. H. H. Moore dealing with a forgotten pioneer of a rational education and his experiment. This pioneer was the Rev. Richard Dawes, at one time Rector of Kings Somborne parish, Hampshire, who, in 1841, worked out the problem of rational education in an agricultural village, in which he found the population unusually ignorant and debased. The whole story is of great interest, but our concern is with the question of Natural Philosophy, the staple of the teaching given in this school.

As taught in a Village School.—Mr. Dawes thus explained his object:—"I aimed at teaching what would be profitable and interesting to persons in the position in life which the children were likely to occupy. I aimed at their being taught what may be called the philosophy of common things of everyday life. They were shown how much there is that is interesting, and which it is advantageous for them to know, in connection with the natural objects with which they are familiar; they had explained to them, and were made acquainted with, the principles of a variety of natural phenomena, as well as the principles and construction of various instruments of a useful kind. A practical turn was given to everything the uses and fruits of the knowledge they were acquiring were never lost sight of." A list of some of the subjects included in this kind of teaching will be the best commentary on Mr. Dawes' scheme:—

"Some of the properties of air, explaining how its pressure enables them to pump up water, to amuse themselves with squirts and popguns, to suck up water through a straw; explaining also the principles and construction of a barometer, the common pump, the diving-bell, a pair of bellows. That air expands by heat, shown by placing a half-blown bladder near the fire, when the wrinkles disappear. Why the chimney-smoke sometimes rises easily in the air, sometimes not; why there is a draught up the chimney, and under the door, and towards the fire. Air as a vehicle of sound, and why the flash of a distant gun fired is seen before the report is heard; how to calculate the distance of a thunderstorm; the difference in the speeds at which different materials conduct sound. Water and its properties, its solid, fluid, and vaporous state; why water-pipes are burst by frost; why ice forms and floats on the surface of ponds, and not at the bottom; why the kettle-lid jumps up when the water is boiling on the fire; the uses to which the power of steam is applied; the gradual evolution of the steam-engine, shown by models and diagrams; how their clothes are dried, and why they feel cold sitting in damp clothes; why a damp bed is so dangerous; why one body floats in water, and another sinks;

the different densities of sea and fresh water; why, on going into the school on a cold morning, they sometimes see a quantity of water on the glass, and why on the inside and not on the outside; why, on a frosty day, their breath is visible as vapour; the substances water holds in solution, and how their drinking water is affected by the kind of soil through which it has passed. Dew, its value, and the conditions necessary for its formation; placing equal portions of dry wool on gravel, glass, and the grass, and weighing them the next morning. Heat and its properties; how it is that the blacksmith can fit iron hoops so firmly on the wheels of carts and barrows; what precautions have to be taken in laying the iron rails of railways and in building iron bridges, etc.; what materials are good, and what bad, conductors of heat; why at the same temperature some feel colder to our touch than others; why a glass sometimes breaks when hot water is poured into it, and whether thick or thin glass would be more liable to crack; why water can be made to boil in a paper kettle or an eggshell without its being burned. The metals, their sources, properties, and uses; mode of separating from the ores. Light and its properties, illustrated by prisms, etc; adaptation of the eye; causes of long and short-sightedness. The mechanical principles of the tools more commonly used, the spade, the plough, the axe, the lever, etc."

"It may surprise some who read carefully the above list that such subjects should have been taught to the children of a rural elementary school. But it is an undeniable fact that they were taught in Kings Somborne School, and so successfully that the children were both interested and benefited by the teaching. Mr. Dawes, in answer to the objection that such subjects are above the comprehension of the young, said:—'The distinguishing mark of Nature's laws is their extreme simplicity. It may doubtless require intellect of a high order to make the discovery of these laws; yet, once evolved, they are within the capacity of a child,—in short, the principles of natural philosophy are the principles of common sense, and if taught in a simple and common-sense way, they will be speedily understood and eagerly attended to by children; and it will be found that with pupils of even from ten to twelve years of age much may be done towards forming habits of observation and inquiry.' Such a fact, I think, suggests some valuable practical lessons for those who have the responsibility of deciding what subjects to include in an educational system for children."

In reading of this remarkable experiment, we feel that we must at once secure a man, all-informed like the late Dean Dawes, to teach our own Jack and Elsie; but it is something to realise what these young persons should know, and Mr. Holden has done a great deal for us. Some of the chapters in The Sciences may be beyond children under nine, but they will be able to master a good deal. One thing is to be borne in mind: nothing should be done without its due experiment. By the way, our old friend, Joyce's Scientific Dialogues, if it is still to be had, describes a vast number of easy and interesting experiments which children can work for themselves.

XVII.—Geography

Geography is, to my mind, a subject of high educational value; though not because it affords the means of scientific training. Geography does present its problems, and these of the most interesting, and does afford materials for classification; but it is physical geography only which falls within the definition of a science, and even that is rather a compendium of the results of several sciences than a science itself. But the peculiar value of geography lies in its fitness to nourish the mind with ideas, and to furnish the imagination with pictures. Herein lies the educational value of geography.

As commonly Taught.—Now, how is the subject commonly taught? The child learns the names of the capital cities of Europe, or of the rivers of England, or of the mountain-summits of Scotland, from some miserable text-book, with length in miles, and height in feet, and population, finding the names on his map or not, according as his teacher is more or less up to her work. Poor little fellow! the lesson is hard work to him; but as far as education goes—that is, the developing of power, the furnishing of the mind—he would be better employed in watching the progress of a fly across the window-pane. But, you will say, geography has a further use than this strictly educative one; everybody wants the sort of information which the geography lesson should afford. That is true, and is to be borne in mind in the schoolroom; the child's geography lesson should furnish just the sort of information which grown-up people care to possess. Now, do think how unreasonable we are in this matter; nothing will persuade us to read a book of travel unless it be interesting, graphic, with a spice of personal adventure. Even when we are going about with Murray in hand, we skip the dry facts and figures, and read the suggestive pictorial scraps; these are the sorts of things we like to know, and remember with ease. But none of this pleasant padding for the poor child, if you please; do not let him have little pictorial sentences that he may dream over; facts and names and figures—these are the pabulum for him!

Geography should be Interesting.—But, you say, this sort of knowledge, though it may be a labour to the child to acquire it, is useful in after life. Not a bit of it; and for this reason—it has never been really received by the brain at all; has never got further than the floating nebulae of mere verbal memory of which I have already had occasion to speak. Most of us have gone through a good deal of drudgery in the way of 'geography' lessons, but how much do we remember? Just the pleasant bits we heard from travelled friends, about the Rhine, or Paris, or Venice, or bits from The Voyages of Captain Cook, or other pleasant tales of travel and adventure. We begin to see the lines we must go upon in teaching geography: for educative purposes, the child must learn such geography, and in such a way, that his mind shall thereby be stored with ideas, his imagination with images; for practical purposes he must learn such geography only as, the nature of his mind considered, he will be able to remember; in other words, he must learn what interests him. The educative and the practical run in one groove, and the geography lesson becomes the most charming occupation of the child's day.

How to begin.—But, how to begin? In the first place, the child gets his rudimentary notions of geography as he gets his first notions of natural science, in those long hours out of doors of which we have already seen the importance. A pool fed by a mere cutting in the fields will explain the nature of a lake, will carry the child to the lovely lakes of the Alps, to Livingstone's great African lake, in which he delighted to see his children 'paidling'—"his own children 'paidling' in his own lake." In this connection will come in a great deal of pleasant talk about places, 'pictorial geography,' until the child knows by name and nature the great rivers and mountains, deserts and plains, the cities and countries of the world. At the same time, he gets his first notions of a map from a rude sketch, a mere few lines and dots, done with pencil and paper, or, better still, with a stick in the sand or gravel. 'This crooked line is the Rhine; but you must imagine the rafts, and the island with the Mouse Tower, and the Nuns' Island, and the rest. Here are the hills, with their ruined castles—now on this side, now on that. This dot is Cologne,' etc. Especially, let these talks cover all the home scenery and interests you are acquainted with, so that, by-and-by, when he looks at the map of England, he finds a score of familiar names which suggest landscapes to him—places where 'mother has been,'—the woody, flowery islets of the Thames; the smooth Sussex downs, delightful to run and roll upon, with soft carpet of turf and nodding harebells; the York or Devon moors, with bilberries and heather:—and always give him a rough sketch-map of the route you took in a given journey.

What next?—Give him next intimate knowledge, with the fullest details, of any country or region of the world, any county or district of his own country. It is not necessary that he should learn at this stage what is called the 'geography' of the countries of Europe, the continents of the world—mere strings of names for the most part: he may learn these, but it is tolerably certain that he will not remember them. But let him be at home in any single region; let him see, with the mind's eye, the people at their work and at their play, the flowers and fruits in their seasons, the beasts, each in its habitat; and let him see all sympathetically, that is, let him follow the adventures of a traveller; and he knows more, is better furnished with ideas, than if he had learnt all the names on all the maps. The 'way' of this kind of teaching is very simple and obvious; read to him, or read for him, that is, read bit by bit, and tell as you read, Hartwig's Tropical World, the same author's Polar World, Livingstone's missionary travels, Mrs. Bishop's Unbeaten Tracks in Japan—in fact, any interesting, well-written book of travel. It may be necessary to leave out a good deal, but every illustrative anecdote, every bit of description, is so much towards the child's education. Here, as elsewhere, the question is, not how many things does he know, but how much does he know about each thing.

Maps.—Maps must be carefully used in this type of work,—a sketch-map following the traveller's progress, to be compared finally with a complete map of the region; and the teacher will exact a description of such and such a town, and such and such a district, marked on the map, by way of testing and confirming the child's exact knowledge. In this way, too, he gets intelligent notions of physical geography; in the course of his readings he falls in with a description of a volcano, a glacier, a cañon, a hurricane; he hears all about, and asks and learns the how and the why, of such phenomena at the moment when his interest is excited. In other words, he learns as his elders elect to learn for themselves, though they rarely allow the children to tread in paths so pleasant.

What General Knowledge a Child of Nine should have.—Supposing that between the child's sixth and his ninth year half a dozen well-chosen standard books of travel have been read with him in this way, he has gained distinct ideas of the contours, the productions, and the manners of the people, of every great region of the world; has laid up a store of reliable, valuable knowledge, that will last his lifetime; and besides, has done something to acquire a taste for books and the habit of reading. Such books as Lady Brassey's Voyage in the 'Sunbeam' should be avoided, as covering too much ground, and likely to breed some confusion of ideas.

Particular Knowledge.—But we are considering lessons as 'Instruments of Education;' and the sort of knowledge of the world I have indicated will be conveyed rather by readings in the 'Children's Hour' and at other times than by way of lessons. I know of nothing so good as the old-fashioned World at Home by Mary and Elizabeth Kirby (for lessons) for children between six and seven. As they hear, they wonder, admire, imagine, and can even 'play at' a hundred situations. The first ideas of geography, the lessons on place, which should make a child observant of local geography, of the features of his own neighbourhood, its heights and hollows, and level lands, its streams and ponds, should be gained, as we have seen, out of doors, and should prepare him for a certain amount of generalisation—that is, he should be able to discover definitions of river, island, lake, and so on, and should make these for himself in a tray of sand, or draw them on the blackboard.

Definitions.—But definitions should come in the way of recording his experiences. Before he is taught what a river is, he must have watched a stream and observed that it flows; and so on with the rest.

Children easily simulate knowledge, and at this point the teacher will have to be careful that nothing which the child receives is mere verbiage, but that every generalisation is worked out somewhat in this way:—The child observes a fact, as, for example, a wide stretch of flat ground; the teacher amplifies. He reads in his book about Pampas, the flat countries of the north-west of Europe, the Holland of our own eastern coast, and, by degrees, he is prepared to receive the idea of a plain, and to show it on his tray of sand.

Fundamental Ideas.—By the time he is seven, or before, he finds himself in need of further knowledge. He has read of hot countries and cold countries, has observed the seasons and the rising and setting of the sun, has said to himself—

"Twinkle, twinkle, little star,
How I wonder what you are!"—

Knows something of ocean and sea, has watched the tide come in and go out, has seen many rough sketch-maps made and has made some for himself, and has, no doubt, noticed the criss-cross lines on a 'proper' map; that is to say, his mind is prepared for knowledge in various directions; there are a number of things concerned with geography which he really wants to know.

The shape and motions of the earth are fundamental ideas, however difficult to grasp, but the difficulty is of a kind which increases with years.

The principle in each case is simple enough, and a child does not concern himself, as do his elders, with the enormous magnitude of the scale upon which operations in space are carried on. It is probable that a child's vivid imagination puts him on a level with the mathematician in dealing with the planetary system, with the behaviour and character of Earth, with the causes of the seasons, and much besides.

Meaning of a Map.—Then, again, geography should be learned chiefly from maps. Pictorial readings and talks introduce him to the subject, but so soon as his geography lessons become definite they are to be learned, in the first place, from the map. This is an important principle to bear in mind. The child who gets no ideas from considering the map, say of Italy or of Russia, has no knowledge of geography, however many facts about places he may be able to produce. Therefore he should begin this study by learning the meaning of a map and how to use it. He must learn to draw a plan of his schoolroom, etc., according to scale, go on to the plan of a field, consider how to make the plan of his town, and be carried gradually from the idea of a plan to that of a map; always beginning with the notion of an explorer who finds the land and measures it, and by means of sun and stars, is able to record just where it is on the earth's surface, east or west, north or south.

Now he will arrive at the meaning of the lines of latitude and longitude. He will learn how sea and land are shown on a map, how rivers and mountains are represented; and having learned his points of direction and the use of his compass, and knowing that maps are always made as if the beholder were looking to the north, he will be able to tell a good deal about situation, direction, and the like, in very early days. The fundamental ideas of geography and the meaning of a map are subjects well fitted to form an attractive introduction to the study. Some of them should awaken the delightful interest which attaches in a child's mind to that which is wonderful, incomprehensible, while the map lessons should lead to mechanical efforts equally delightful. It is only when presented to the child for the first time in the form of stale knowledge and foregone conclusions that the facts taught in such lessons appear dry and repulsive to him. An effort should be made to treat the subject with the sort of sympathetic interest and freshness which attracts children to a new study.

XVIII.—History

A Storehouse of Ideas.—Much that has been said about the teaching of geography applies equally to that of history. Here, too, is a subject which should be to the child an inexhaustible storehouse of ideas, should enrich the chambers of his House Beautiful with a thousand tableaux, pathetic and heroic, and should form in him, insensibly, principles whereby he will hereafter judge of the behaviour of nations, and will rule his own conduct as one of a nation. This is what the study of history should do for the child; but what is he to get out of the miserable little chronicle of feuds, battles, and death which is presented to him by way of 'a reign'—all the more repellent because it bristles with dates? As for the dates, they never come right; the tens and units he can get, but the centuries will go astray; and how is he to put the right events in the right reign, when, to him, one king differs from another only in number, one period from another only in date? But he blunders through with it; reads in his pleasant, chatty little history book all the reigns of all the kings, from William the Conqueror to William IV., and back to the dim days of British rule. And with what result? This: that, possibly, no way of warping the judgment of the child, of filling him with crude notions, narrow prejudices, is more successful than that of carrying him through some such course of English history; and all the more so if his little text-book be moral or religious in tone, and undertake to point the moral as well as to record the fact. Moral teaching falls, no doubt, within the province of history; but the one small volume which the child uses affords no scope for the fair and reasonable discussion upon which moral decisions should be based, nor is the child old enough to be put into the judicial attitude which such a decision supposes.

'Outlines' Mischievous—The fatal mistake is in the notion that he must learn 'outlines,' or a baby edition of the whole history of England, or of Rome, just as he must cover the geography of all the world. Let him, on the contrary, linger pleasantly over the history of a single man, a short period, until he thinks the thoughts of that man, is at home in the ways of that period. Though he is reading and thinking of the lifetime of a single man, he is really getting intimately acquainted with the history of a whole nation for a whole age. Let him spend a year of happy intimacy with Alfred, 'the truth-teller,' with the Conqueror, with Richard and Saladin, or with Henry V.—Shakespeare's Henry V.—and his victorious army. Let him know the great people and the common people, the ways of the court and of the crowd. Let him know what other nations were doing while we at home were doing thus and thus. If he come to think that the people of another age were truer, larger-hearted, simpler-minded than ourselves, that the people of some other land were, at one time, at any rate, better than we, why, so much the better for him.

So are most History Books written for Children—For the matter for this intelligent teaching of history, eschew, in the first place, nearly all history books written expressly for children; and in the next place, all compendiums, outlines, abstracts whatsoever. For the abstracts, considering what part the study of history is fitted to play in the education of the child, there is not a word to be said in their favour; and as for what are called children's books, the children of educated parents are able to understand history written with literary power, and are not attracted by the twaddle of reading-made-easy little history books. Given judicious skipping, and a good deal of the free paraphrasing mothers are so ready at, and the children may be taken through the first few volumes of a well-written, illustrated, popular history of England, say as far as the Tudors. In the course of such reading a good deal of questioning into them, and questioning out of them, will be necessary, both to secure their attention and to fix the facts. This is the least that should be done; but better than this would be fuller information, more graphic details about two or three early epochs.

Early History of a Nation best fitted for Children.—The early history of a nation is far better fitted than its later records for the study of children, because the story moves on a few broad, simple lines; while statesmanship, so far as it exists, is no more than the efforts of a resourceful mind to cope with circumstances. Mr. Freeman has provided interesting early English history for children; but is it not on the whole better to take them straight to the fountainhead, where possible? In these early years, while there are no examinations ahead, and the children may yet go leisurely, let them get the spirit of history into them by reading, at least, one old Chronicle written by a man who saw and knew something of what he wrote about, and did not get it at second-hand. These old books are easier and pleasanter reading than most modern works on history, because the writers know little of the 'dignity of history'; they purl along pleasantly as a forest brook, tell you 'all about it,' stir your heart with the story of a great event, amuse you with pageants and shows, make you intimate with the great people, and friendly with the lowly. They are just the right thing for the children whose eager souls want to get at the living people behind the words of the history book, caring nothing at all about progress, or statutes, or about anything but the persons, for whose action history is, to the child's mind, no more than a convenient stage. A child who has been carried through a single old chronicler in this way has a better foundation for all historical training than if he knew all the dates and names and facts that ever were crammed for examination.

Some old Chronicles.—First in order of time, and full of the most captivating reading, is the Ecclesiastical History of England (see Appendix) of the Venerable Bede, who, writing of himself so early as the seventh century, says, "It was always sweet to me to learn, to teach, and to write." "He has left us," says Professor Morley, "a history of the early years of England, succinct, yet often warm with life; business-like, and yet childlike in its tone; at once practical and spiritual, simply just, and the work of a true scholar, breathing love to God and man. We owe to Bede alone the knowledge of much that is most interesting in our early history." William of Malmesbury (twelfth century) says of Bede, "That almost all knowledge of past events was buried in the same grave with him"; and he is no bad judge, for in his Chronicles of the Kings of England he himself is considered to have carried to perfection the art of chronicle-making. He is especially vivid and graphic about contemporary events—the story of the dreary civil war of Stephen and Matilda. Meantime, there is Asser, who writes the life of Alfred, whose friend and fellow-worker he is. "It seems to me right," he says, "to explain a little more fully what I have heard from my lord Alfred." He tells us how, "When I had come into his presence at the royal vill, called Leonaford, I was honourably received by him, and remained that time with him at his court about eight months, during which I read to him whatever books he liked, and such as he had at hand; for this is his most usual custom, both night and day, amid his many other occupations of mind and body, either himself to read books or to listen whilst others read them." When he was not present to see for himself, as at the battle of Ashdown, Asser takes pains to get the testimony of eyewitnesses. "But Alfred, as we have been told by those who were present and would not tell an untruth, marched up promptly, with his men to give them battle; for King Ethelred remained a long time in his tent in prayer." Then there are Chronicles of the Crusades, contemporary narratives of the crusades of Richard Coeur de Lion, by Richard of Devizes, and Geoffrey de Vinsany, and of the crusade of St. Louis, by Lord John de Joinville.

It is needless to extend the list; one such old chronicle in a year, or the suitable bits of one such chronicle, and the child's imagination is aglow, his mind is teeming with ideas; he has had speech of those who have themselves seen and heard; and the matter-of-fact way in which the old monks tell their tales is exactly what children prefer. Afterwards, you may put any dull outlines into their hands, and they will make history for themselves.

Age of Myths.—But every nation has its heroic age before authentic history begins: these were giants in the land in those days, and the child wants to know about them. He has every right to revel in such classic myths as we possess as a nation; and to land him in a company of painted savages, by way of giving him his first introduction to his people, is a little hard; it is to make his vision of the past harsh and bald as a Chinese painting. But what is to be done? If we ever had an Homeric age, have we not, being a practical people, lost all record thereof? Here is another debt that we owe to those old monkish chroniclers: the echoes of some dim, rich past had come down to, at any rate, the twelfth century: they fell upon the ear of a Welsh priest, one Geoffrey of Monmouth; and while William of Malmesbury was writing his admirable History of the Kings of England, what does Geoffrey do but weave the traditions of the people into an orderly History of the British Kings, reaching back all the way to King Brut, the grandson of Aeneas. How he came to know about kings, that no other historian had heard of, is a matter that he is a little roguish about; he got it all, he says, out of "that book in the British language which Walter, Archdeacon of Oxford, brought out of Britainy." Be that as it may, here we read of Gorboduc, King Lear, Merlin, Uther Pendragon, and, best of all, of King Arthur, the writer making 'the little finger of his Arthur stouter than the back of Alexander the Great.' Here is, indeed, a treasure-trove which the children should be made free of ten years before they come to read the

Idylls of the King. Some caution must, however, be exercised in reading Geoffrey of Monmouth. His tales of marvel are delightful; but when he quits the marvellous and romances freely about historical facts and personages, he becomes a bewildering guide. Many of these 'chronicles,' written in Latin by the monks, are to be had in readable English; the only caution to be observed is, that the mother should run her eye over the pages before she reads them aloud. (Bohn's Antiquarian Library [5s. a volume] includes Bede, William of Malmesbury, Dr. Giles's Six Old English Chronicles—Asser and Geoffrey of Monmouth being two of them—Chronicles of the Crusaders, etc.)

Froissart, again, most delightful of chroniclers, himself 'tame' about the court of Queen Phillippa, when he chose to be in England—from whom else should the child get the story of the French wars? And so of as much else as there is time for; the principle being, that, whenever practicable, the child should get his first notions of a given period, not from the modern historian, the commentator and reviewer, but from the original sources of history, the writings of contemporaries. The mother must, however, exercise discrimination in her choice of early 'Chronicles,' as all are not equally reliable.

Plutarch's 'Lives.'—In the same way, readings from Plutarch's Lives will afford the best preparation for the study of Grecian or of Roman history. Alexander the Great is something more than a name to the child who reads this sort of thing:—

"When the horse Bucephalus was offered in sale to Philip, at the price of thirteen talents (= £2518, 15s.), the king, with the prince and many others, went into the field to see some trial made of him. The horse appeared very vicious and unmanageable, and was so far from suffering himself to be mounted, that he would not bear to be spoken to, but turned fiercely upon all the grooms. Philip was displeased at their bringing him so wild and ungovernable a horse, and bade them take him away. But Alexander, who had observed him well, said, 'What a horse they are losing for want of skill and spirit to manage him!'

"Philip at first took no notice of this; but upon the prince's often repeating the same expression, and showing great uneasiness, he said, 'Young man, you find fault with your elders as if you knew more than they, or could manage the horse better.'

"'And I certainly could,' answered the prince.

"'If you should not be able to ride him, what forfeiture will you submit for your rashness?'

"'I will pay the price of the horse.'"

"Upon this all the company laughed; but the king and prince agreeing as to the forfeiture, Alexander ran to the horse, and laying hold on the bridle, turned him to the sun, for he had observed, it seems, that the shadow which fell before the horse, and continually moved as he moved, greatly disturbed him. While his fierceness and fury lasted, he kept speaking to him softly and stroking him; after which he gently let fall his mantle, leaped lightly upon his back, and got his seat very safe. Then, without pulling the reins too hard, or using either whip or spur, he set him agoing. As soon as he perceived his uneasiness abated, and that he wanted only to run, he put him in a full gallop, and pushed him on both with the voice and spur.

"Philip and all his court were in great distress for him at first, and a profound silence took place; but when the prince had turned him and brought him safe back, they all received him with loud exclamations, except his father, who wept for joy, and kissing him, said 'Seek another kingdom, my son, that may be worthy of thy abilities, for Macedonia is too small for thee.'"

Here, again, in North's inimitable translation, we get the sort of vivid graphic presentation which makes 'History' as real to the child as are the adventures of Robinson Crusoe.

To sum up, to know as much as they may about even one short period, is far better for the children than to know the 'outlines' of all history. And in the second place, children are quite able to take in intelligent ideas in intelligent language, and should by no means be excluded from the best that is written on the period they are about.

History Books—It is not at all easy to choose the right history books for children. Mere summaries of facts must, as we have seen, be eschewed; and we must be equally careful to avoid generalisations.

The natural function of the mind, in the early years of life, is to gather the material of knowledge with a view to that very labour of generalisation which is proper to the adult mind; a labour which we should all carry on to some extent for ourselves.

As it is, our minds are so poorly furnished that we accept the conclusions presented to us without demur; but we can, at any rate, avoid giving children cut-and-dried opinions upon the course of history while they are yet young. What they want is graphic details concerning events and persons upon which imagination goes to work; and opinions tend to form themselves by slow degrees as knowledge grows.

Mr York Powell has, perhaps more than others, hit upon the right teaching for the young children I have in view. In the preface to his Old Stories from British History, he says:—"The writer has chosen such stories as he thought would amuse and please his readers, and give them at the same time some knowledge of the lives and thoughts of their forefathers. To this end he has not written solely of great folk—kings and queens and generals—but also of plain people and children, ay, and birds and beasts too"; and we get the tale of King Lear and of Cuculain, and of King Canute and the poet Otter, of Havelock and Ubba, and many more, all brave and glorious stories; indeed, Mr York Powell gives us a perfect treasure-trove in his two little volumes of Old Stories and Sketches from British History, which are the better for our purpose, because children can read them for themselves so soon as they are able to read at all. These tales, written in good and simple English, and with a certain charm of style, lend themselves admirably to narration.

Indeed, it is most interesting to hear children of seven or eight go through a long story without missing a detail, putting every event in its right order. These narrations are never a slavish reproduction of the original. A child's individuality plays about what he enjoys, and the story comes from his lips, not precisely as the author tells it, but with a certain spirit and colouring which express the narrator. By the way, it is very important that children should be allowed to narrate in their own way, and should not be pulled up or helped with words and expressions from the text.

A narration should be original as it comes from the child—that is, his own mind should have acted upon the matter it has received.

Narrations which are mere feats of memory are quite valueless.

I have already spoken of the sorts of old chronicles upon which children should be nourished; but these are often too diffuse to offer good matter for narration, and it is well to have quite fitting short tales for this purpose.

I should like to mention two other little volumes in which children delight, which feed patriotic sentiment and lay a broad basis for historical knowledge. I mean Mrs Frewen Lord's Tales from St Paul's and Tales from Westminister Abbey. It is a beautiful and delightful thing to take children informed by these tales to the Abbey or St Paul's, and let them identify for themselves the spots consecrated to their heroes. They know so much and are so full of vivid interest that their elders stand by instructed and inspired. There are, no doubt, multitudes of historical tales and sketches for children, and some of them, like Miss Brooke Hunt's Prisoners of the Tower, are very good; but let the mother beware: there is nothing which calls for more delicate tact and understanding sympathy with the children than this apparently simple matter of choosing their lesson-books, and especially, perhaps, their lesson-books in history.

Many children of eight or nine will be quite ready to read with pleasure A History of England, by H.O. Arnold Forster, who has long since won his spurs in the field of educational literature. In this, as in matters of more immediate statecraft, Mr Arnold Forster has the gift to see a defect and a remedy, an omission and the means of supplying it. He saw that English children grew up without any knowledge of the conditions under which they live, and of the laws which govern them; but since the appearance of The Citizen Reader and The Laws of Every-day Life, we have changed all that.

The History of England, or, as the children call it, History, ignoring the fact that there is any other history than that of England, has hitherto been presented to young people as "outlines of dates and facts, or as collections of romantic stories, with little coherence and less result on the fortunes of the country." Mr Arnold Forster says in his preface that he "is reluctant to introduce his book by any such repellent title as 'A Summary,' or 'An Outline of English History.'

Such titles seem on the face of them to imply that the element of interest and the romance inseparable from the life and doings of individuals are excluded, and that an amplified chronological table has been made to do duty for history. But to read English history and fail to realise that it is replete with interest, sparkling with episode, and full of dramatic incident, is to miss all the pleasure and most of the instruction which its study, if properly pursued, can give." The author fulfills his implied promise, and his work is, I venture to say, as "replete with interest, sparkling with episode, and full of dramatic incident" as is possible, considering the limitations imposed upon him by the facts that he writes for uneducated readers, and gives us a survey of the whole of English History in a pleasant, copiously and wisely illustrated volume of some eight hundred pages.

How telling and lucid this is, for example, and how we all wish we had come across such a paragraph in our early studies of architecture:—"On page 23 we have pictures of two windows. One of them is what is called a Pointed window. All the arches in it go up to a point. It was built a long time before the Tudor period. The other was built in the time of Queen Elizabeth. In it the upright shaft, or mullion, of the window goes straight up to the top without forming an arch. This style of building a window is called the Perpendicular Style, because the mullions of the window are 'perpendicular.' Some of the most famous buildings in England built in Tudor times, and in the perpendicular style, are the Chapel of King's College, Cambridge, and Hatfield House, the residence of the Marquis of Salisbury, in Hertfordshire." Mr Arnold Forster has done in this volume for children and the illiterate, what Professor Green did in his Shorter History of England for somewhat more advanced students, awakening many to the fact that history is an entrancing subject of study. This is a real introduction to real history. The portraits are an especially valuable feature of the work.

Dates.—In order to give definiteness to what may soon become a pretty wide knowledge of history—mount a sheet of cartridge-paper and divide it into twenty columns, letting the first century of the Christian era come in the middle, and let each remaining column represent a century B.C. or A.D., as the case may be.

Then let the child himself write, or print, as he is able, the names of the people he comes upon in due order, in their proper century.

We need not trouble ourselves at present with more exact dates, but this simple table of the centuries will suggest a graphic panorama to the child's mind, and he will see events in their time-order.

Illustrations by the Children—History readings afford admirable material for narration, and children enjoy narrating what they have read or heard. They love, too, to make illustrations. Children who had been reading Julius Caesar (and also, Plutarch's Life), were asked to make a picture of their favourite scene, and the results showed the extraordinary power of visualising which the little people possess. Of course that which they visualise, or imagine clearly, they know; it is a life possession.

The drawings of the children in question are psychologically interesting as showing what various and sometimes obscure points appeal to the mind of a child; and also, that children have the same intellectual pleasure as persons of cultivated mind in working out new hints and suggestions. The drawings, be it said, leave much to be desired, but they have this in common with the art of primitive peoples: they tell the tale directly and vividly. A girl of nine and a half pictures Julius Caesar conquering Britain. He rides in a chariot mounted on scythes, he is robed in blue, and bits of blue sky here and there give the complementary colour. In the distance, a soldier plants the ensign bearing the Roman eagle, black on a pink ground.

In the foreground, is a hand-to-hand combat between Roman and Briton, each having a sword of enormous length. Other figures are variously employed.

Another, gives us Antony 'making his speech after the death of Caesar.' This girl, who is older, gives us architecture; you look through an arch, which leads into a side street, and, in the foreground, Antony stands on a platform at the head of a flight of marble steps. Antony's attitude expresses indignation and scorn. Below, is a crowd of Romans wearing the toga, whose attitudes show various shades of consternation and dismay. Behind, is Antony's servant in uniform, holding his master's horse; and on the platform, in the rear of Antony, lies Caesar, with the royal purple thrown over him. The chief value of the drawing, as a drawing, is that it tells the tale.

Another girl draws Calpurnia begging Caesar not to go to the Senate. Caesar stands armed and perturbed, while Carpurnia holds his outstretched hand with both of hers as she kneels before him, her face raised in entreaty; her loose blue night-robe and long golden hair give colour to the picture. This artist is fourteen, and the drawing is better done.

Another artist presents Brutus and Portia in the orchard with a 'south-wall' of red brick, espaliers, and two dignified figures which hardly tell their tale.

Another child gives us the scene in the forum, Caesar seated in royal purple, Brutus kneeling before him, and Casca standing behind his chair with out-stretched hand holding a dagger, saying "Speak, hands, for me," while Caesar says, "Doth not Brutus bootless kneel?"

Again, we get Lucius playing to Brutus in the tent. Brutus, armed cap-a-pie, seated on a stool, is vainly trying to read, while Lucius, a pretty figure, seated before him, plays the harp. The two sentries, also fully armed, are stretched on the floor sound asleep.

Another, gives us Claudius dressed as a woman at the women's festival—the ladies with remarkable eyes, and each carrying a flaming torch.

Another pictures, with great spirit, Caesar reading his history to the conquered Gauls, who stand in rows on the hillside listening to the great man with exemplary patience.

In these original illustrations (several of them by older children than those we have in view here), we get an example of the various images that present themselves to the minds of children during the reading of a great work; and a single such glimpse into a child's mind convinces us of the importance of sustaining that mind upon strong meat. Imagination does not stir at the suggestion of the feeble, much-diluted stuff that is too often put into children's hands.

'Playing at' History—Children have other ways of expressing the conceptions that fill them when they are duly fed. They play at history lessons, dress up, make tableaux, act scenes; or they have a stage, and their dolls act, while they paint the scenery and speak the speeches. There is no end to the modes of expression children find when there is anything in them to express.

The mistake we make is to suppose that imagination is fed by nature, or that it works on the insipid diet of children's storybooks.

Let a child have the meat he requires in his history readings, and in the literature which naturally gathers round this history, and imagination will bestir itself without any help of ours; the child will live out in detail a thousand scenes of which he only gets the merest hint.

XIX.—Grammar

Grammar a Difficult Study.—Of grammar, Latin and English, I shall say very little here. In the first place, grammar, being a study of words and not of things, is by no means attractive to the child, nor should he be hurried into it. English grammar, again, depending as it does on the position and logical connection of words, is peculiarly hard for him to grasp. In this respect the Latin grammar is easier; a change in the form, the shape of the word, to denote case, is what a child can see with his bodily eye, and therefore is plainer to him than the abstract ideas of nominative and objective case as we have them in English. Therefore, if he learns no more at this early stage than the declensions and a verb or two, it is well he should learn thus much, if only to help him to see what English grammar would be at when it speaks of a change in case or mood, yet shows no change in the form of a word.

Latin Grammar.—Of the teaching of Latin grammar, I think I cannot do better than mention a book for beginners that really answers. Children of eight and nine take to this First Latin Course (Scott and Jones) very kindly, and it is a great thing to begin a study with pleasure. It is an open question, however, whether it is desirable to begin Latin at so early an age.

English Grammar a Logical Study.—Because English grammar is a logical study, and deals with sentences and the positions that words occupy in them, rather than with words, and what they are in their own right, it is better that the child should begin with the sentence, and not with the parts of speech; that is, that he should learn a little of what is called analysis of sentences before he learns to parse; should learn to divide simple sentences into the thing we speak of, and what we say about it—'The cat-sits on the hearth'—before he is lost in the fog of person, mood, and part of speech.

"So then I took up the next book. It was about grammar. It said extraordinary things about nouns and verbs and particles and pronouns, and past participles and objective cases and subjunctive moods. 'What are all these things?' asked the King. 'I don't know, your Majesty,' and the Queen did not know, but she said it would be very suitable for children to learn. 'It would keep them quiet.'" (2)

It is so important that children should not be puzzled as were this bewildered King and Queen, that I add a couple of introductory grammar lessons; as a single example is often more useful than many precepts.

Lesson I

Words put together so as to make sense form what is called a sentence.

'Barley oats chair really good and cherry' is not a sentence, because it makes no(n)sense.

'Tom has said his lesson' is a sentence.

It is a sentence because it tells us something about Tom.

Every sentence speaks of someone or of something, and tells us something about that of which it speaks.

So a sentence has two parts: (1) The thing we speak of; (2) What we say about it.

In our sentence we speak of 'Tom.'

We say about him that he 'has learned his lesson.'

The thing we speak of is often called the *subject*, which just means that which we talk about.

People sometimes say 'the subject of conversation was so and so,' which is another way of saying 'the thing we were speaking about was so and so.'

To be learnt—

Words put together so as to make sense form a sentence. A sentence has two parts: that which we speak of, and what we say about it. That which we speak of is the *subject*.

Exercises on Lesson I

1. Put the first part to—
—has a long mane.
—is broken.
—cannot do his sums.
—played for an hour;
etc., etc.

2. Put the second part to—
That poor boy—.
My brother Tom—.
The broken flowerpot—.
Bread and jam—.
Brown's tool-basket—;
etc., etc.

3. Put six different subjects to each half sentence in 1.

4. Make six different sentences with each subject in 2.

5. Say which part of the sentence is wanting, and supply it in—
Has been mended
Tom's knife
That little dog
Cut his finger
Ate too much fruit
My new book
The snowdrops in our garden, etc., etc.

N.B.—Be careful to call the first part of each sentence the subject.

Draw a line under the subject of each sentence in all the exercises.

Lesson II

We may make a sentence with only two words—the name of the thing we speak of, and what we say about it:—

John writes.
Birds sing.
Mary sews.

We speak about 'John.' We say about him that he 'writes.' We speak about 'birds.' We say about them that they 'sing.'

These words, writes, sing, sews, all come out of the same group of words, and the words in that group are the chief words of all, for this reason—we cannot make sense, and therefore cannot make a sentence, without using at least one of them.

They are called *verbs*, which means words, because they are the chief words of all.

A verb always tells one of two things about the subject. Either it tells what the subject is, as—

I am hungry.

The chair is broken.
The birds are merry;

or it tells what the subject does, as—

Alice writes.
The cat mews.
He calls.

To be learnt—

We cannot make a sentence without a verb. Verb means word. Verbs are the chief words. Verbs show that the subject is something—

He is sleepy;
or does something—

He runs.

Exercises on Lesson II

1. Put in a verb of being:—
Mary—sleepy.
Boys—rough.
Girls—quiet.
He—first yesterday.
I—a little boy.
Tom and George—swinging before dinner.
We—busy to-morrow.
He—punished;
etc., etc.
2. Make three sentences with each of the following verbs:—
Is, are, should be, was, am, were, shall be, will be.
3. Make six sentences with verbs of being in each.
4. Put a verb of doing to—
Tigers—.
The boy with the pony—.
My cousins—;
etc., etc.
5. Make twenty sentences about—
That boy in kilts,
with verbs showing what he does.
6. Find the verbs, and say whether of being or doing, in—
The bright sun rises over the hill.
We went away.
You are my cousin.
George goes to school.
He took his slate.
We are seven.
7. Count how many verbs you use in your talk for the next ten minutes.
8. Write every verb you can find in these exercises, and draw a line under it.

XX.—French

French should be acquired as English is, not as a grammar, but as a living speech. To train the ear to distinguish and the lips to produce the French vocables is a valuable part of the education of the senses, and one which can hardly be undertaken too soon. Again, all educated persons should be able to speak French. Sir Lyon Playfair, once speaking a conference of French masters, lamented feelingly our degeneracy in this respect, and instanced the grammar school of Perth to show that in a Scotch school in the sixteenth century the boys were required to speak Latin during school hours, and French at all other times. There is hardly another civilised nation so dull in acquiring foreign tongues as we English of the present time; but, probably, the fault lies rather in the way we set about the study than in any natural incapacity for languages.

As regards French, for instance, our difficulties are twofold—the want of a vocabulary, and a certain awkwardness in producing unfamiliar sounds. It is evident that both these hindrances should be removed in early childhood. The child should never see French words in print until he has learned to say them with as much ease and readiness as if they were English. The desire to give printed combinations of letters the sounds they would bear in English words is the real cause of our national difficulty in pronouncing French. Again, the child's vocabulary should increase steadily, say, at the rate of half a dozen words a day. Think of fifteen hundred words in a year! The child who has that number of words, and knows how to apply them, can speak French. Of course, his teacher, will take care that, in giving words, she gives idioms also, and that as he learns new words, they are put into sentences and kept in use from day to day. A note-book in which she enters the child's new words and sentences will easily enable the teacher to do this. The young child has no foolish shame about saying French words—he pronounces them as simply as if they were English.

But it is very important that he should acquire a pure accent from the first. It is not often advisable that young English children should be put into the hands of a French governess or nurse; but would it not be possible for half a dozen families, say, to engage a French lady, who would give half an hour daily to each family?

M. Gouin's Method—A serious effort is being made to approach the study of foreign languages rationally and scientifically. I have no hesitation in saying that M. [Monsieur Francois] Gouin's work (The Art of Teaching and Studying Languages) is the most important attempt that has yet been made to bring the study of languages within the sphere of practical education. Indeed, the great reform in our methods of teaching modern languages owe their origin to this remarkable work. The initial idea, that we must acquire a new language as a child acquires his mother tongue, is absolutely right, whether the attempt to follow this idea out by analysing a language into a certain number, say fifteen, exhaustive 'series,' be right or not. Again, it is incontestable that the ear, and not the eye, is the physical organ for apprehending a language, just as truly as it is by the mouth, and not the ear, we appropriate food. If M. Gouin's book establish these two points only, it will be a valuable contribution to educational thought. Equally important is his third position, that the verb is the key to the sentence, and more, is the living bridge between thought and act. He maintains, too, that the child thinks in sentences, not in words; that his sentences have a logical sequence; that this sequence is one of time —the order of the operations in, for example, the growth of a plant, or the grinding of corn in a mill; that, as the child perceives the operations, he has an absolute need to express them; that his ear solicits, his memory cherishes, his tongue reproduces, the words which say the thing he thinks.

No doubt M. Gouin's method should be more successful than any other in steeping the student (child or man) in German or French thought. If you are all day long trying to work out a 'series' in French, say, you come to think in French, to dream in French, to speak French. Moreover, one has a delightful sense that at last the way is made clear to us to conduct all teaching in the language under study. You have the 'Art Series' and the 'Bee Series' and the 'River' and the 'Character Series' and the 'Poet Series,' and any series you like. You think the thing out in the order of time and natural sequence; you get the right verbs, nouns, and such epithets as are necessary, follow suit, and in amazingly few sentences, very short sentences too, connected by 'and,' you have said all that is essential to the subject. The whole thing is a constant surprise, like the children's game which unearths the most extraordinary and out-of-the-way thing you can think of by means of a dozen or so questions.

The 'Series.'—Thus, a language learned by M. Gouin's method is 'a liberal education in itself.' One learns how few and simple are, after all, the conceptions of which the human mind is cognisant, and how few and simple, putting mere verbiage aside, are the words necessary to express these.

You really learn to think in the new language, because you have no more than vague impressions about these acts or facts in your mother tongue.

You order your thoughts in the new language, and, having done so, the words which express these are an inalienable possession.

Here is an example of an elementary 'Series,' showing how 'the servant lights the fire':

"The servant takes a box of matches, (takes.)
She opens the match-box, (opens.)
She takes out a match, (takes out.)
She shuts up the match-box, (shuts up.)
She strikes the match on the cover, (strikes.)
The match takes fire, (takes fire.)
The match smokes, (smokes.)
The match flames, (flames.)
The match burns, (burns.)
And spreads a smell of burning over the kitchen, (spreads.)
The servant bends down to the hearth, (bends down.)
Puts out her hand, (puts out.)
Puts the match under the shavings, (puts.)
Holds the match under the shavings, (holds.)
The shavings take fire, (take fire.)
The servant leaves go of the match, (leave go.)
Stands up again, (stands up.)
Looks at her fire burning, (looks.)
And puts back the box of matches in its place, (puts back.)

But any attempt to quote gives an uncertain and unsatisfactory idea of this important work.

How does the Child learn?—Whatever may be said of M. Gouin's methods, the steps by which he arrives at them are undoubtedly scientific. He learns from a child:

"Unhappily the child has remained up to the present a hackneyed riddle, which we have never taken sufficient trouble to decipher or examine...."

The little child, which at the age of two years utters nothing but meaningless exclamations, at the age of three finds itself in possession of a complete language. How does it accomplish this? Does this miracle admit of explanation or not? Is it a problem of which there is a possiblity of finding the unknown quantity? . . . The organ of language—ask the little child—is not the eye: it is the ear. The eye is made for colours, and not for sounds and words . . . This tension, continuous and contrary to nature, of the organ of sight, the forced precipitancy of the visual act, produced what it was bound to produce, a disease of the eyesight."

This refers to M. Gouin's herculean labours in the attempt to learn German. He knew everybody's 'Method,' learned the whole dictionary through, and found at the end that he did not know one word of German 'as she is spoke.'

He returned to France, after a ten months' absence, and found that his little nephew—whom he had left a child of two and a half, not yet able to talk—had in the interval done what his uncle had signally failed to do. "'What!' I thought; 'this child and I have been working for the same time, each at a language. He, playing round his mother, running after flowers, butterflies and birds, without weariness, without apparent effort, without even being conscious of his work, is able to say all he thinks, express all he sees, understand all he hears; and when he began his work, his intelligence was yet a futurity, a glimmer, a hope. And I, versed in the sciences, versed in philosophy, armed with a powerful will, gifted with a powerful memory . . . have arrived at nothing, or at practically nothing!'"

"The linguistic science of the college has deceived me, has misguided me. The classical method, with its grammar, its dictionary, and its translations, is a delusion." "To surprise Nature's secret, I must watch this child."

M. Gouin watches the child—the work in question is the result of his observations.

The method of teaching may be varied, partly because that recommended by M. Gouin requires a perfect command of the French tongue, and teachers who are diffident find a conversational method founded on book and picture easier to work and perhaps as effectual—more so, some people think; but, be this as it may, it is to M. Gouin we owe the fundamental idea.

It is satisfactory to find principles, which we have urged continually, enunciated in this most thoughtful work. For example: "If one learns French without being able to read it—as the child does—there will be no longer much greater difficulty in pronouncing it than in pronouncing words in English. 'How about the spelling?' you will ask. The spelling? You would learn it as the young French children learn it, as you yourself have learnt the English spelling, ten times more difficult than the French; and this without letting the study of the spelling spoil your already acquired pronunciation. Besides, the spelling is a thing that can be reformed—the pronunciation hardly at all. We must choose between the two evils." M. Gouin speaks of the possiblity of a child's picking up another tongue—even Chinese from a Chinese nurse; and his words remind me of an extraordinary instance of a child's facility in picking up languages, which once came before me. Having occasion to speak in public of three little children, all aged three, belonging to different families, where one parent was English, the other German, I said that these three children of my acquaintance could each say everything they had to say, express the whole range of their ideas, with equal ease and fluency in the two languages. At the close of the meeting, a gentleman present came forward and endorsed my remarks. He said he had a son whose wife was a German lady, and who was now a missionary in Bagdad. They have a child of three, and their child speaks three languages with perfect fluency—English, German, and Arabic! No doubt the child will forget two of the three, and this is no argument for teaching foreign tongues to babies, but surely it does prove that the acquisition of a foreign tongue need not present insuperable difficulties to any of us.

XXI.—Pictorial Art

Study of Pictures.—The art training of children should proceed on two lines. The six-year-old child should begin both to express himself and to appreciate, and his appreciation should be well in advance of his power to express what he sees or imagines. Therefore it is a lamentable thing when the appreciation of children is exercised only upon the coloured lithographs of their picture-books or of the 'Christmas number.' But the reader will say, 'A young child cannot appreciate art; it is only the colour and sentiment of a picture that reach him. A vividly coloured presentation of Bobbie's Birthday, or of Barbara's Broken Doll, will find its way straight to his "business and bosom."' 'Therefore,' says the reader, 'Nature indicates the sort of art proper for the children!' But, as a matter of fact, the minds of children and of their elders alike accommodate themselves to what is put in their way; and if children appreciate the vulgar and sentimental in art, it is because that is the manner of art to which they become habituated. A little boy of about nine was (with many others) given reproductions of some half dozen of the pictures of Jean Francois Millet to study during a school term. At the end, the children were asked to describe the one of these pictures which they liked best. Of course they did it, and did it well. This is what a little boy I mentioned makes of it:—"I liked the Sower best. The sower is sowing seeds; the picture is all dark except high up on the right-hand side where there is a man ploughing the field. While he is ploughing the field the sower sows. The sower has got a bag in his left hand and is sowing with this right hand. He has wooden clogs on. He is sowing at about six o'clock in the morning. You can see his head better than his legs and body, because it is against the light."

A little girl of seven prefers the 'Angelus', and says:—"The picture is about people in the fields, man and a woman. By the woman is a basket with something in it; behind her is a wheelbarrow. They are praying; the man has his hat off in his hand. You can tell that it is evening, because the wheelbarrow and the basket are loaded."

Should be Regular.—When children have begun regular lessons (that is, as soon as they are six), this sort of study of pictures should not be left to chance, but they should take one artist after another, term by term, and study quietly some half-dozen reproductions of his work in the course of the term.

The little memory outlines I have quoted show his studies; but this is the least of the gains. We cannot measure the influence that one or another artist has upon the child's sense of beauty, upon his power of seeing, as in a picture, the common sights of life; he is enriched more than we know in having really looked at even a single picture. It is a mistake to think that colour is quite necessary to children in their art studies. They find colour in many places, and are content, for the time, with form and feeling in their pictures. By the way, for schoolroom decorations, I know of nothing better than the Fitzroy Pictures [see Appendix.], especially those of the Four Seasons, where you get beauty, both of line and colour, and poetic feeling. I should like, too, to quote Ruskin's counsel that English children should be brought up on Jean Richter's picture-books for children, the Unser Vater, Sontag [see Appendix], and the rest.

I subjoin notes of a lesson on a Picture-talk [by a student of the House of Education] given to children of eight and nine, to show how this sort of lesson may be given.

Picture-Talk

"Objects

"1. To continue the series of Landseer's pictures the children are taking in school. "2. To increase their interest in Landseer's works. "3. To show the importance of his acquaintance with animals. "4. To help them to read a picture truly. "5. To increase their powers of attention and observation.

"Step I.—Ask the children if they remember what their last picture-talk was about, and what artist was famous for animal-painting. Tell them Landseer was acquainted with animals when he was quite young: he had dogs for pets, and because he loved them he studied them and their habits—so was able to paint them.

"Step II.—Give them the picture 'Alexander and the Diogenes' to look at, and ask them to find out all they can about it themselves, and to think what idea the artist had in his mind, and what idea or ideas he meant his picture to convey to us.

"Step III.—After three or four minutes, take the picture away and see what the children have noticed. Then ask them what the different dogs suggest to them; the strength of the mastiff representing Alexander; the dignity and stateliness of the bloodhounds in his rear; the look of the wise counselor on the face of the setter; the rather contemptuous look of the rough-haired terrier in the tub. Ask the children if they have noticed anything in the picture which shows the time of day: for example, the tools thrown down by the side of the workman's basket suggesting the mid-day meal; and the bright sunshine on the dogs who cast a shadow on the tub shows it must be somewhere about noon.

"Step IV.—Let them read the title, and tell any facts they know about Alexander and Diogenes; then tell them Alexander was a great conqueror who lived B.C. 356-323, famous for the battles he won against Persia, India, and along the coast of the Mediterranean He was very proud, strong, and boastful. Diogenes was a cynic philosopher. Explain cynic, illustrating by the legend of Alexander and Diogenes; and from it find out which dog represents Alexander and which Diogenes.

"Step V.—Let the children draw the chief lines of the picture, in five minutes, with a pencil and paper."

Original Illustrations.—I have spoken, from time to time, of original illustrations drawn by the children. It may be of use to subjoin notes of a lesson [By a student of the House of Education] showing the sort of occasional help a teacher may give in this kind of work; but in a general way it is best to leave children to themselves.

"Objects

"1. To help the children to make clear mental pictures from description, and to reproduce the same in painting. "2. To increase their power of imagination. "3. To help them in their ideas of form and colour. "4. To increase their interest in the story of Beowulf by letting them illustrate a scene from the book they are reading. "5. To bring out their idea of an unknown creature (Grendel).

Steps

"Step I.—To draw from the children what they know of the poem 'Beowulf', and of the hero himself. "Step II.—To tell them any points they may miss in the story, as far as they have read (i.e. to the death of Grendel).

"Step III.—To read the description of the dress at that time, and the account of Grendel's death (including three possible pictures).

"Step IV.—To draw from the children what mental pictures they have made—and to re-read the passage.

"Step V.—To let them produce their mental picture with brush and paint.

"Step VI.—To show them George Harrow's 'original illustration' of Beowulf in "Heroes of Chivalry and Romance."

Drawing Lessons.—But 'for their actual drawing lessons,' says the reader, 'I suppose you use "blobs"?'—i.e. splashes of paint made with the flat of the brush, which take an oval form. I think blobs have one use—they give certain freedom in using colour. Otherwise 'blobs' seem to me a sort of apparatus of art which a child acquires with a good deal of labour, and which, by proper combinations into flowers, and so on he can produce effects beyond his legitimate power as an artist, while all the time he can do this without a particle of the feeling for the natural object which is the very soul of the art. The power of effective creation by a sort of clever trick maims those delicate feelers of a child's nature by which he apprehends art.

"Let the eye (says Ruskin) "but rest on rough piece of branch for curious form during a conversation with a friend, rest, however unconsciously, and though the conversation be forgotten, though every circumstance connected with it be as utterly lost to the memory as though it had not been, yet the eye will, through the whole life after, take a certain pleasure in such boughs which it had not before, a pleasure so slight, a trace of feeling so delicate, as to leave us utterly unconscious of its peculiar power, but undestroyable by any reasoning, a part thence-forward of our constitution."

This is what we wish to do for children in teaching them to draw—to cause the eye to rest, not unconsciously, but consciously, on some object of beauty which will leave in their minds an image of delight for all their lives to come. Children of six and seven draw budding twigs of oak and ash, beech and larch, with such tender fidelity to colour, tone, and gesture, that the crude little drawings are in themselves things of beauty.

Children have 'Art' in them.—With art, as with so many other things in a child, we must believe that it is there, or we shall never find it. Once again, here is a delicate Ariel whom it is our part to deliver from his bonds. Therefore we set twig or growing flower before a child and let him deal with it as he chooses. He will find his own way to form and colour, and our help may very well be limited at first to such technical matters as the mixing of colours and the like. In order that we may not impede the child's freedom or hinder the deliverance of the art that is in him, we must be careful not to offer any aids in the way of guiding lines, points, and such other crutches; and, also, he should work in the easiest medium, that is, with paint brush or with charcoal, and not with a black-lead pencil. Boxes of cheap colours are to be avoided. Children are worthy of the best, and some half-dozen tubes of really good colours will last a long time, and will satisfy the eye of the little artists.

Clay-modelling.—While speaking of the art training of children, it may be as well to give a word to clay-modelling. Neat little birds-nests, baskets of eggs, etc., are of no use in the way of art development, and soon cease to be amusing. The chief thing the teacher has to do is to show the child how to prepare his clay so as to expel air-bubbles, and to give him the idea of making a little platform for his work, so that it may from the first have an artistic effect. Then put before him an apple, a banana, a Brazil nut, or the like; let him, not take a lump of clay and squeeze it into shape, but build up the shape he desires morsel by morsel. His own artistic perception seizes on the dint in the apple, the crease in the child's shoe, the little notes of expression in the objects which break uniformity and make for art.

The Piano and Singing.—I must close, with the disappointing sense that subjects of importance in the child's education have been left out of count, and that no one matter has been adequately treated.

Certain subjects of peculiar educational value, music, for instance, I have said nothing about, partly for want of space, and partly because if the mother have not Sir Joshua Reynold's 'that!' in her, hints from an outsider will not produce the art-feeling which is the condition of success in this sort of teaching. If possible, let the children learn from the first under artists, lovers of their work: it is a serious mistake to let the child lay the foundation of whatever he may do in the future under ill-qualified mechanical teachers, who kindle in him none of the enthusiasm which is the life of art. I should like, in connection with singing, to mention the admirable educational effects of the Tonic Sol-fa method. [See Appendix] Children learn by it in a magical way to produce sign for sound and sound for sign, that is, they can not only read music, but can write the notes for, or make the proper hand signs for, the notes of a passage sung to them. Ear and Voice are simultaneously and equally cultivated.

Mrs. Curwen's Child Pianist [See Appendix] method is worked out, with minute care, upon the same lines; that is, the child's knowledge of the theory of music and his ear training keep pace with his power of execution, and seem to do away with the deadly dreariness of 'practising.'

Handicrafts and Drills.—It is not possible to do more than mention two more important subjects—the Handicrafts and Drills—which should form a regular part of a child's daily life. For physical training nothing is so good as Ling's Swedish Drill, and a few of the early exercises are the reach of children under nine. Dancing, and the various musical drills, lend themselves to grace of movement, and give more pleasure, if less scientific training, to the little people.

The Handicrafts best fitted for children under nine seem to me to be chair-caning, carton-work, basket-work, Smyrna rugs, Japanese curtains, carving in cork, samplers on coarse canvas showing a variety of stitches, easy needlework, knitting (big needles and wool), etc. The points to be borne in mind in children's handicrafts are: (a) that they should not be employed in making futilities such as pea and stick work, paper mats, and the like; (b) that they should be taught slowly and carefully what they are to do; (c) that slipshod work should not allowed; (d) and that, therefore, the children's work should be kept well within their compass.

May I hope, in concluding this short review of the subjects proper for a child's intellectual education, that enough has been said to show the necessity of grave consideration on the mother's part before she allows promiscuous little lesson-books to be put into the hands of her children, or trust ill-qualified persons to strike out methods of teaching for themselves?

Part VI
The Will—The Conscience—The Divine Life in the Child

I.—The Will

Government of Mansoul.—We have now to consider a subject of unspeakable importance to every being called upon to sustain a reasonable life here, with the hope of the fuller life hereafter; I mean, the government of the kingdom of Mansoul. Every child who lives long enough in the world is invested, by degrees, with this high function, and it is the part of his parents to instruct him in his duties, and to practise him in his tasks. Now, the government of this kingdom of Mansoul is, like that of some well-ordered states, carried on in three chambers, each chamber with its own functions, exercised, not by a multitude of counsellors, but by a single minister.

Executive Power vested in the Will.—In the outer of the three chambers sits the Will. Like that Roman centurion, he has soldiers under him: he says to this man, Go, and he Goeth; to another, Come, and he cometh; to a third, Do this, and he doeth it. In other words, the executive power is vested in the will. If the will have the habit of authority, if it deliver its mandates in the tone that constrains obedience, the kingdom is, at any rate, at unity with itself. If the will be feeble, of uncertain counsels, poor Mansoul is torn with disorder and rebellion.

What is the Will?—I do not know what the will is; it would appear to be an ultimate fact, not admitting of definition: but there are few subjects on which those who have the education of children in their hands make more injurious mistakes; and therefore it is worth while to consider, as we may, what are the functions of the will, and what are its limitation.

Persons may go through life without deliberate act of Will.—In the first place, the will does not necessarily come into play in any of the aspects in which we have hitherto considered the child. He may reflect and imagine; be stirred by the desire of knowledge, of power, of distinction; may love and esteem; may form habits of attention, obedience, diligence, sloth, involuntarily—that is, without ever intending, purposing, willing these things for himself. So far is this true, that there are people who live through their lives without an act of deliberate will: amiable, easy-going people, on the one hand, hedged in by favouring circumstances; and poor souls, on the other, whom circumstances have not saved, who have drifted from their moorings, and are hardly to be named by those to whom they belong. Great intellectual powers by no means imply a controlling will. We read how Coleridge had to be taken care of, because he had so little power of willing. His thoughts were as little under his own volition as his actions, and the fine talk people went to hear was no more than an endless pouring forth of ideas connected by no other link than that of association; though so fine was his mind, that his ideas flowed methodically—of their own accord, so to speak.

Character the Result of Conduct regulated by Will.—It is not necessary to say a word about the dignity and force of character which a confirmed will gives to its possessors. In fact, character is the result of conduct regulated by will. We say, So-and-so has a great deal of character, such another is without character; and we might express the fact equally by saying, So-and-so has a vigorous will, such another has no force of will. We all know of lives, rich in gifts and graces, which have been wrecked for the lack of a determining will.

Three Functions of the Will.—The will is the controller of the passions and emotions, the director of the desires, the ruler of the appetites. But observe, the passions, the desires, the appetites, are there already, and the will gathers force and vigour only as it is exercised in the repression and direction of these; for though the will appears to be of purely spiritual nature, yet it behaves like any member of the body in this—that it becomes vigorous and capable in proportion as it is duly nourished and fitly employed.

A Limitation of the Will disregarded by some Novelists.—The villain of a novel, it is true, is, or rather used to be, an interesting person, because he was always endowed with a powerful will, which acted, not in controlling his violent passions, but in aiding and abetting them: the result was a diabolical being out of the common way of nature. And no wonder, for, according to natural law, the member which does not fulfil its own functions is punished by loss of power; if it does not cease to be, it becomes as though it were not; and the will, being placed in the seat of authority, is not able to carry its forces over to the mob—the disorder would be too fearful; just as when the executive powers of a state are seized upon by a riotous mob, and there are shootings in the highways and hangings from the lanterns, infinite confusion everywhere.

Parents fall into this Metaphysical Blunder.—I am anxious to bring before you this limitation of the will to its own proper functions, because parents often enough fall into the very metaphysical blunder we have seen in the novel-writer. They admire a vigorous will, and rightly. They know that if their child is to make his mark in the world, it must be by force of will. What follows? The baby screams himself into fits for a forbidden plaything, and the mother says, 'He has such a strong will.' The little fellow of three stands roaring in the street, and will neither go hither or thither with his nurse, because 'he has such a strong will.' He will rule the sports of the nursery, will monopolise his sisters' playthings, all because of this 'strong will.' Now we come to a divergence of opinion: on the one hand, the parents decide that, whatever the consequence, the child's will is not to be broken, so all his vagaries must go unchecked; on the other, the decision is, that the child's will must be broken at all hazards, and the poor little being is subjected to a dreary round of punishment and repression.

Wilfulness indicates want of Will Power.—But, all the time, nobody perceives that it is the mere want of will that is the matter with the child. He is in a state of absolute 'wilfulness,'—the rather unfortunate word we use to describe the state in which the will has no controlling power; willessness, if there were such a word, would describe this state more truly. Now, this confusion, in the minds of many persons, between the state of wilfulness and that of being dominated by will, leads to mischievous results even where wilfulness is not fostered nor the child unduly repressed: it leads to the neglect of the due cultivation and training of the will, that almost divine possession, upon the employment of which every other gift, be it beauty or genius, strength or skill, depends for its value.

What is Wilfulness?—What, then, is wilfulness, if it be not an exercise of will? Simply this: remove bit and bridle—that is, the control of the will—from the appetites, the desires, the emotions, and the child who has mounted his hobby, be it resentment, jealousy, desire of power, desire of property, is another Mazeppa, borne along with the speed of the swift and the strength of the strong, and with no power at all to help himself. Appetite, passion, there is no limit to their power and their persistence if the appointed check be removed; and it is this impetus of appetite or of passion, this apparent determination to go in one way and no other, which is called wilfulness and mistaken for an exercise of will. Whereas the determination is only apparent; the child is, in fact, hurried along without resistance, because that opposing force which should give balance to his character is undeveloped and untrained.

The Will has Superior and Inferior Functions.—The will has its superior and its inferior, what may be called its moral and its mechanical, functions; and that will which, for want of practice, has grown flaccid and feeble in the exercise of it higher functions, may yet be able for the ordering of such matters as going or coming, sitting or standing, speaking or refraining from speech.

The Will not a Moral Faculty.—Again, though it is impossible to attain moral excellence of character without the agency of a vigorous will, the will itself is not a moral faculty, and a man may attain great strength of will in consequence of continued efforts in the repression or direction of his appetites or desires, and yet be an unworthy man; that is, he may be keeping himself in order from unworthy motives, for the sake of appearances, for his own interest, even for the injury of another.

A Disciplined Will necessary to Heroic Christian Character.—Once again, though a disciplined will is not a necessary condition of the Christian life, it is necessary to the development of the heroic Christian character. A Gordon, a Havelock, a Florence Nightingale, a St. Paul, could not be other than a person of vigorous will. In this respect, as in all others, Christianity reaches the feeblest souls. There is a wonderful Guido 'Magdalen' in the Louvre, with a mouth which has plainly never been set to any resolve for good or ill—a lower face moulded by the helpless following of the inclination of the moment; but you look up to the eyes, which are raised to meet the gaze of eyes not shown in the picture, and the countenance is transfigured, the whole face is aglow with a passion of service, love, and self-surrender. All this the divine grace may accomplish in weak unwilling souls, and then they will do what they can; but their power of service is limited by their past. Not so the child of the Christian mother, whose highest desire is to train him for the Christian life. When he wakes to the consciousness of whose he is and whom he serves, she would have him ready for that high service, with every faculty in training—a man of war from his youth; above all, with an effective will, to will and to do of His good pleasure.

The sole Practical Faculty of Man.—Before we consider how to train this 'sole practical faculty of man,' we must know how the will operates—how it manages the ordering of all that is done and thought in the kingdom of Mansoul. "Can't you make yourself do what you wish to do?" says Guy, in the Heir of Redclyffe [by Mary Charlotte Yonge], to poor Charlie Edmonston, who has never been in the habit of making himself do anything. There are those, no doubt, who have not even arrived at wishing, but most of us desire to do well; what we want to know is, how to make ourselves do what we desire. And here is the line which divides the effective from the non-effective people, the great from the small, the good from the well-intentioned and respectable; it is in proportion as a man has self-controlling, self-compelling power that he his able to do, even of his own pleasure; that he can depend upon himself, and be sure of his own action in emergencies.

How the Will operates.—Now, how does this autocrat of the bosom behave? Is it with a stern 'Thou shalt,' 'Thou shalt not,' that the subject man is coerced into obedience? By no means. Is it by a plausible show of reasons, mustering of motives? Not this either. Since Mr. John Stuart Mill taught us that "all that man does, or can do, with matter" is to "move one thing to or from another," we need not be surprised if great moral results are brought about by what seem inadequate means; and a little bit of nursery experience will show better than much talking what is possible to the will. A baby falls, gets a bad bump, and cries piteously. The experienced nurse does not "kiss the place to make it well," or show any pity for the child's trouble—that would make matters worse; the more she pities, the more he sobs. She hastens to 'change his thoughts,' so she says; she carries him to the window to see the horses, gives him his pet picture-book, his dearest toy, and the child pulls himself up in the middle of a sob, though he is really badly hurt. Now this, of the knowing nurse, is precisely the part the will plays towards the man. It is by force of will that a man can 'change his thoughts,' transfer his attention from one subject of thought to another, and that, with a shock of mental force of which he is indistinctly conscious. And this is enough to save a man and to make a man, this power of making himself think only of those things which he has beforehand decided that it is good to think upon.

The Way of the Will—Incentives.—His thoughts are wandering on forbidden pleasure, to the hindrance of his work; he pulls himself up, and deliberately fixes his attention on those incentives which have most power to make him work, the leisure and pleasure which follow honest labour, the duty which binds him to the fulfilling of his task. His thoughts run in the groove he wills them to run in, and work is no longer an effort.

Diversion.—Again, some slight affront has called up a flood of resentful feeling: So-and-so should not have done it, he had no right, it was mean, and so on, through all the hard things we are ready enough to say in our hearts of an offender against our amour propre. But the man under the control of his own will does not allow this to go on: he does not fight it out with himself, and say, 'This is very wrong in me. So-and-so is not so much to blame, after all.' He is not ready for that yet; but he just compels himself to think of something else—the last book he has read, the next letter he must write, anything interesting enough to divert his thoughts. When he allows himself to go back to the cause of offence, behold, all rancour is gone, and he is able to look at the matter with the coolness of a third person. And this is true, not only of the risings of resentment, but of every temptation that besets the flesh and spirit.

Change of Thought.—Again, the sameness of his duties, the weariness of doing the same thing over and over, fills him with disgust and despondency, and he relaxes his efforts;—but not if he be a man under the power of his own will, because he simply does not allow himself in idle discontent; it is always within his power to give himself something pleasant, something outside of himself, to think of, and he does so; and, given what we call a 'happy frame of mind,' no work is laborious.

The Way of the Will should be taught to Children.—It is something to know what to do with ourselves when we are beset, and the knowledge of this way of the will is so far the secret of a happy life, that it is well worth imparting to the children. Are you cross? Change your thoughts. Are you tired of trying? Change your thoughts. Are you craving for things you are not to have? Change your thoughts; there is a power within you, your own will, which will enable you to turn your attention from thoughts that make you unhappy and wrong, to thoughts that make you happy and right. And this is the exceedingly simple way in which the will acts; this is the sole secret of the power over himself which the strong man wields—he can compel himself to think of what he chooses, and will not allow himself in thoughts that breed mischief.

Power of Will implies Power of Attention.—But you perceive that, though the will is all-powerful within certain limits, these are but narrow limits after all. Much must go before and along with a vigorous will if it is to be a power in the ruling of conduct. For instance, the man must have acquired the habit of attention, the great importance of which we have already considered. There are bird-witted people, who have no power of thinking connectedly for five minutes under any pressure, from within or from without. If they have never been trained to apply the whole of their mental faculties to a given subject, why, no energy of will, supposing they had it, which is impossible, could make them think steadily thoughts of their own choosing or of anyone else's. Here is how the parts of the intellectual fabric dovetail: power of will implies power of attention; and before the parent can begin to train the will of the child, he must have begun to form in him the habit of attention.

Habit may Frustrate the Will.—Again, we have already considered the fatal facility in evil, the impulse towards good, which habit gives. Habit is either the ally or the opponent, too often the frustrator, of the will. The unhappy drunkard does will with what strength there is in him; he turns away the eyes of his mind from beholding his snare; he plies himself assiduously with other thoughts; but alas, his thoughts will only run in the accustomed groove of desire, and habit is too strong for his feeble will. We all know something of this struggle between habit and will in less vital matters. Who is without some dilatory, procrastinating, in some way tiresome, habit, which is in almost daily struggle with the rectified will? But I have already said so much about the duty of parents to ease the way of their children by laying down for them the lines of helpful habits, that it is unnecessary to say a word more here of habit as an ally or a hinderer of will.

Reasonable Use of so effective an Instrument.—And, once more, only the man of cultivated reason is capable of being ruled by a well-directed will. If his understanding does not show good cause why he should do some solid reading every day, why he should cling to the faith of his fathers, why he should take up his duties as a citizen,—the movement of his will will be feeble and fluctuating, and very barren of results. And, indeed, worse may happen: he may take up some wrong-headed, or even vicious, notion and work a great deal of mischief by what he feels to be a virtuous effort of will. The parent may venture to place the power of will in the hands of his child only in so far as he trains him to make a reasonable use of so effective an instrument.

How to Strengthen the Will.—One other limitation of the will we shall consider presently; but supposing the parent take pains that the child shall be in a fit state to use his will, how is he to strengthen that will, so that by and by the child may employ it to control his own life by? We have spoken already of the importance of training the child in the habit of obedience. Now, obedience is valuable only in so far as it helps the child towards making himself do that which he knows he ought to do. Every effort of obedience which does not give him a sense of conquest over his own inclinations, helps to enslave him, he will resent the loss of his liberty by running into license when he can. That is the secret of the miscarrying of many strictly brought-up children. But invite his co-operation, let him heartily intend and purpose to do the thing he is bidden, and then it is his own will that is compelling him, and not yours; he has begun the greatest effort, the highest accomplishment of human life—the making, the compelling of himself. Let him know what he is about, let him enjoy a sense of triumph, and of your congratulation, whenever he fetches his thoughts back to his tiresome sum, whenever he makes his hands finish what they have begun, whenever he throws the black dog off his back, and produces a smile from a clouded face.

Habit of Self-management.—Then, as was said before, let him know the secret of willing; let him know that, by an effort of will, he can turn his thoughts to the thing he wants to think of—his lessons, his prayers, his work, and away from the things he should not think of;—that, in fact, he can be such a brave strong little fellow, he can make himself think of what he likes; and let him try little experiments—that if he once get his thoughts right, the rest will take care of itself, he will be sure to do right then; that if he feels cross, naughty thoughts coming upon him, the plan is, to think hard about something else, something nice—his next birthday, what he means to do when he is a man. Not all this at once, of course; but line upon line, precept upon precept, here a little and there a little, as opportunity offers. Let him get into the habit of managing himself, controlling himself, and it is astonishing how much self-compelling power quite a young child will exhibit. "Restrain yourself, Tommy," I once heard a wise aunt say to a boy of four, and Tommy restrained himself, though he was making a terrible hullabaloo about some small trouble.

Education of the Will more important than that of the Intellect.—All this time, the will of the child is being both trained and strengthened; he is learning how and when to use his will, and it is becoming every day more vigorous and capable. Let me add one or two wise thoughts from Dr. Morell's Introduction to Mental Philosophy: "The education of the will is really of far greater importance, as shaping the destiny of the individual, than that of the intellect. . . . Theory and doctrine, and inculcation of laws and propositions, will never of themselves lead to the uniform habit of right action. It is by doing, that we learn to do; by overcoming, that we learn to overcome; and every right act which we cause to spring out of pure principles, whether by authority, precept, or example, will have a greater weight in the formation of character than all the theory in the world."

II.—The Conscience

Conscience is Judge and Lawgiver.—But the will by no means carries on the government of the kingdom of Mansoul single-handed. True, the will wields the executive power; it is only by willing we are enabled to do; but there is a higher power behind, whose mandate the will does no more than express. Conscience sits supreme in the inner chamber. Conscience is the lawgiver, and utters the 'Thou shalt' and the 'Thou shalt not' whereon the will takes action; the judge, too, before whom the offending soul is summoned; and from the 'Thou art the man' of conscience, there is no appeal.

'I am, I ought, I can, I will.'—'I am, I ought, I can, I will'—these are the steps of that ladder of St. Augustine, whereby we

"rise on stepping stones
Of our dead selves to higher things."

'I am'—we have the power of knowing ourselves. "I ought'—we have within us a moral judge, to whom we feel ourselves subject, and who points out and requires of us our duty. 'I can'—we are conscious of power to do that which we perceive we ought to do. 'I will'—we determine to exercise that power with a volition which is in itself a step in the execution of that which we will. Here is a beautiful and perfect chain, and the wonder is that, so exquisitely constituted as he is for right-doing, error should be even possible to man. But of the sorrowful mysteries of sin and temptation it is not my place to speak here; you will see that it is because of the possibilities of ruin and loss which lie about every human life that I am pressing upon parents the duty of saving their children by the means put into their hands. Perhaps it is not too much to say, that ninety-nine out of a hundred lost lives lie at the door of parents who took no pains to deliver them from sloth, from sensual appetites, from willfulness, no pains to fortify them with the habits of a good life.

Inertness of Parents not supplemented by Divine Grace.—We live in a redeemed world, and infinite grace and help from above attend every rightly directed effort in the training of the children; but I do not see much ground for hoping that divine grace will step in as a substitute for any and every power we choose to leave unused or misdirected. In the physical world, we do not expect miracles to make up for our neglect of the use of means; the rickety body, the misshapen limb, for which the child has to thank his parents, remain with him through life, however much else he may have to thank God for; and a feeble will, bad habits, an uninstructed conscience, stick by many a Christian man through his life, because his parents failed in their duty to him, and he has not had force enough in himself to supply their omission.

Conscience not an Infallible Guide.—In this matter of conscience, for instance, the laissez-faire habit of his parents is the cause of real wrong and injury to many a child. The parents are thankful to believe that their child is born with a conscience; they hope his conduct may be ruled thereby: and the rest they leave; the child and his conscience may settle it between them. Now this is to suppose, either that a fully-informed conscience is born into an infant body, or that it grows, like the hair and the limbs, with the growth of the body, and is not subject to conditions of spiritual progress proper to itself. In other words, it is to suppose that conscience is an infallible guide, a delusion people cling to in spite of common sense and of everyday experience of the wrong-headed things men do from conscientious motives. The vagaries of the uninstructed conscience are so familiar as to have given rise to popular proverbs: 'Honour among thieves,' 'To strain out the gnat and swallow the camel,' point to cases of misguided conscience; while 'The wish is father to the thought,' 'None is so blind as he who won't see,' point to the still more common cases, in which a man knowingly tricks his conscience into acquiescence.

But a real Power.—Then, if conscience be not an infallible guide—if it pass blindfold by heinous offences, and come down heavily upon some mere quibble, tithing mint, rue, and all manner of herbs, and neglecting the weightier matters of the law—if conscience be liable to be bamboozled, persuaded into calling evil good and good evil, when Desire is the special pleader before the bar, where is its use, this broken reed? Is this stern lawgiver of the breast no more, after all, than a fiction of the brain? Is your conscience no more than what you happen to think about your own actions and those of other people? On the contrary, these aberrations of conscience are perhaps the strongest proof that it exists as a real power. As Adam Smith has well said, "The supreme authority of conscience is felt and tacitly acknowledged by the worst, no less than by the best, of men; for even they who have thrown off all hypocrisy with the world, are at pains to conceal their real character from their own eyes."

That Spiritual Sense whereby we know Good and Evil.—What conscience is, how far it lies in the feelings, how far in the reason, how far it is independent of both, are obscure questions which it is not necessary for practical purposes to settle; but this much is evident—that conscience is as essential a part of human nature as are the affections and the reason, and that conscience is that spiritual sense whereby we have knowledge of good and evil. The six-months-old child who cannot yet speak exhibits the workings of conscience; a reproving look will make him drop his eyes and hide his face. But, observe, the mother may thus cover him with confusion by way of an experiment when the child is all sweetness, and the poor little untutored conscience rises all the same, and condemns him on the word of another.

Facts like this afford a glimpse of the appalling responsibility that lies upon parents. The child comes into the world with a moral faculty, a delicate organ whereby he discerns the flavour of good and evil, and at the same time has a perception of delight in the good—in himself or others,—of loathing and abhorrence of the evil. But, poor little child, he is like a navigator who does not know how to box his compass. He is born to love the good, and to hate the evil, but he has no real knowledge of what is good and what is evil; what intuitions he has, he puts no faith in, but yields himself in simplicity to the steering of others. The wonder that Almighty God can endure so far to leave the very making of an immortal being in the hands of human parents is only matched by the wonder that human parents can accept this divine trust with hardly a thought of its significance.

A Child's Conscience Undeveloped Capability rather than a Supreme Authority.—Looking, then, upon conscience in the child rather as an undeveloped capability than as a supreme authority, the question is, how is this nascent lord of the life to be educated up to its high functions of informing the will and decreeing the conduct? For though the ill-taught conscience may make fatal blunders, and a man may carry slaughter amongst the faithful because his conscience bids; yet, on the other hand, no man ever attained a godly, righteous, and sober life except as he was ruled by a good conscience—a conscience with not only the capacity to discern good and evil, but trained to perceive the qualities of the two. Many man may have the great delicacy of taste which should qualify him for a tea-taster, but it is only as he has trained experience in the qualities of teas that his nice taste is valuable to his employers, and a source of income to himself.

The Uninstructed Conscience.—As with that of the will, so with the education of the conscience; it depends upon much that has gone before. Refinement of conscience cannot coexist with ignorance. The untutored savage has his scruples that we cannot enter into; we cannot understand to this day how it was that the horrors of the Indian Mutiny arose from the mere suspicion that mixture of hog's lard and beef fat had been used to grease the cartridges dealt out to the Sepoys. Those scruples which are beyond the range of our ideas we call superstitions and prejudices, and are unwilling to look upon conduct as conscientious, even when prompted by the uninstructed conscience, unless in so far as it is reasonable and right in itself.

The Processes implied in a 'Conscientious' Decision.—Therefore, it is plain that before conscience is in a position to pronounce its verdict on the facts of a given case, the cultivated reason must review the pros and cons; the practiced judgment must balance these, deciding which have the greater weight. Attention must bring all the powers of the mind to bear on the question; habits of right action must carry the feelings, must make right-doing seem the easier and the pleasanter. In the meantime, desire is clamorous; but conscience, the unbiased judge, duly informed in full court of the merits of the case, decides for the right. The will carries out the verdict of conscience; upon the verdicts of conscience is the conscientious man, of whose actions and opinions you may be sure beforehand, and then what becomes of these elaborate proceedings? That is just the advantage of an instructed conscience backed by a trained intelligence; the judge is always sitting, the counsel always on the spot.

The Instructed Conscience nearly always right.—Here is, indeed, a high motive for the all-round training of the child's intelligence; he wants the highest culture you can give him, backed by carefully formed habits, in order that he may have a conscience always alert, supported by every power of the mind; and such a conscience is the very flower of a noble life. The instructed conscience may claim to be, if not infallible, at any rate nearly always right. It is not generally mature until the man is mature; young people, however right-minded and earnest, are apt to err, chiefly because they fix their attention too much upon some one duty, some one theory of life, at the expense of much besides.

The Good Conscience of a Child.—But even the child, with the growing conscience and the growing powers, is able to say, 'No, I can't; it would not be right'; 'Yes, I will; for it is right.' And once able to give either of these answers to the solicitations that assail him, the child is able to live; for the rest, the development, and what may be called the adjustment, of conscience will keep pace with his intellectual growth. But allowing that a great deal of various discipline must go to secure that final efflorescence of a good conscience, what is to be done by way of training the conscience itself, quickening the spiritual taste so that the least soupçon [suspicion] of evil is detected and rejected?

Children play with Moral Questions.—There is no part of education more nice and delicate than this, nor any in which grown-up people are more apt to blunder. Everyone knows how tiresome it is to discuss any nice moral question with children; how they quibble, suggest a hundred ingenious explanations or evasions, fail to be shocked or to admire in the right place—in fact, play with the whole question; or, what is more tiresome still, are severe and righteous overmuch, and 'deal damnation round' with much heartiness and goodwill. Sensible parents are often distressed at this want of conscience in the children; but they are not greatly in fault; the mature conscience demands to be backed up by the mature intellect, and the children have neither the one nor the other. Discussions of the kind should be put down; the children should not be encouraged to give their opinions on questions of right and wrong, and little books should not be put into their hands which pronounce authoritatively upon conduct.

The Bible the Chief Source of Moral Ideas.—It would be well if the reticence of the Bible in this respect were observed by the writers of children's books, whether of story or history. The child hears the history of Joseph (with reservations) read from the Bible, which rarely offers comment or explanation. He does not need to be told what was 'naughty' and what was 'good'; there is no need to press home the teaching, or the Bible were written in vain, and good and bad actions carry no witness with them. Let all the circumstances of the daily Bible reading—the consecutive reading, from the first chapter of Genesis onwards, with necessary omissions—be delightful to the child; let him be in his mother's room, in his mother's arms; let that quarter of an hour be one of sweet leisure and sober gladness, the child's whole interest being allowed to go to the story without distracting moral considerations; and then, the less talk the better; the story will sink in, and bring its own teaching, a little now, and more every year as he is able to bear it. Once such story will be in him a constantly growing, fructifying moral idea.

Tales fix attention upon Conduct.—The Bible (the fitting parts of it, that is) first and supreme; but any true picture of life, whether a tale of golden deeds or of faulty and struggling human life, brings aliment to the growing conscience. The child gets into the habit of fixing his attention on conduct; actions are weighed by him, at first, by their consequences, but by degrees his conscience acquires discriminating power, and such and such behavior is bad or good to him whatever its consequences. And this silent growth of the moral faculty takes place all the more surely if the distraction of chatter on the subject is avoided; for a thousand small movements of vanity and curiosity and mere love of talk are easily called into play, and these take off the attention from the moral idea which should be conveyed to the conscience. It is very important, again, that the child should not be allowed to condemn the conduct of the people about him. Whether he is right or wrong in him verdict, is not the question; the habit of bestowing blame will certainly blunt his conscience, deaden his sensibility to the injunction, "Judge not, that ye be not judged."

Ignorance of a Child's Conscience.—But the child's own conduct: surely he may be called upon to look into that? His conduct, including his words, yes; but his motives, no; nothing must be done to induce the evil habit of introspection. Also, in setting the child to consider his ways, regard must be had to the extreme ignorance of the childish conscience, a degree of ignorance puzzling to grown-up people when they chance to discover it, which is not often, for the children, notwithstanding their endless chatter and their friendly, loving ways, live very much to themselves. They commit serious offences against truth, modesty, love, and do not know that they have done wrong, while some absurd featherweight of transgression oppresses their souls. Children will bite and hurt one another viciously, commit petty thefts, do such shocking things that their parents fear they must have very bad natures: it is not necessarily so; it is simply that the untaught conscience sees no clear boundary line between right and wrong, and is as apt to err on the one side as the other. I once saw a dying child of twelve who was wearing herself out with her great distress because she feared she had committed 'the unpardonable sin,' so she said (how she picked up the phrase nobody knew); and that was—that she had been saying her prayers without even kneeling up in bed! The ignorance of children about the commonest matters of right and wrong is really pathetic; and yet they are too often treated as if they knew all about it, because 'they have consciences,' as if conscience were any more than a spiritual organ waiting for direction!

Instructing the Conscience—Kindness.—That the children do wrong knowingly is another matter, and requires, alas, no proving; all I am pressing for is the real need there exists to instruct them in their duty; and this, not at all haphazard, but regularly and progressively. Kindness, for instance, is, let us say, the subject of instruction this week. There is one of the talks with their mother that the children love—a short talk is best—about kindness. Kindness is love, showing itself in act and word, look and manner. A well of love, shut up and hidden in a little boy's heart, does not do anybody much good; the love must bubble up as a spring, flow out in a stream, and then it is kindness. Then will follow short daily talks about kind ways, to brothers and sisters, to playmates, to parents, to grown-up friends, to servants, to people in pain and trouble, to dumb creatures, to people we do not see but yet can think about—all in distress, the heathen. Give the children one thought at a time, and every time some lovely example of loving-kindness that will fire their hearts with the desire to do likewise.

Take our Lord's parable of the 'Good Samaritan' for a model of instruction in morals. Let tale and talk make the children emulous of virtue, and then give them the "Go and do likewise," the law. Having presented to them the idea of kindness in many aspects, end with the law: Be kind, or, "Be kindly affectioned one to another." Let them know that this is the law of God for children and for grown-up people. Now, conscience is instructed, the feelings are enlisted on the side of duty, and if the child is brought up, it is for breaking the law of kindness, a law that he knows of, that his conscience convicts him in the breaking. Do not give children deterrent examples of error, because of the sad proclivities of human nature, but always tell them of beautiful 'Golden Deeds,' small and great, that shall stir them as trumpet-calls to the battle of life.

The Conscience made effective by Discipline.—Be courteous, be candid, be grateful, be considerate, be true; there are aspects of duty enough to occupy the attention of mother and child for every day of the child-life; and all the time, the idea of duty is being formed, and conscience is being educated and developed. At the same time, the mother exercises the friendly vigilance of a guardian angel, being watchful, not to catch the child tripping, but to guide him into the acting out of the duty she has already made lovely in his eyes; for it is only as we do that we learn to do, and become strong in the doing. As she instructs her child in duty, she teaches him to listen to the voice of conscience as to the voice of God, a 'Do this,' or 'Do it not,' within the breast, to be obeyed with full assurance. It is objected that we are making infallible, not the divinely implanted conscience, but that same conscience made effective by discipline. It is even so; in every department of life, physical or spiritual, human effort appears to be the condition of the Divine energizing; there must be a stretching forth of the withered arm before it receives strength; and we have every reason to believe that the instructedconscience, being faithfully followed, is divinely illuminated.

III. The Divine Life In The Child

"The very Pulse of the Machine."—It is evident we have not yet reached

"The very pulse of the machine."

Habits, feeling, reason, conscience—we have followed these into the inmost recesses of the child's life; each acts upon the other, but what acts upon the last: what acts upon them all? "It is," says a writer who has searched into the deep things of God—"it is a King that our spirits cry for, to guide them, discipline them, unite them to each other; to give them a victory over themselves, a victory over the world. It is a Priest that our spirits cry out for, to lift them above themselves to their God and Father,—to make them partakers of his nature, fellow-workers in one authentic testimony that He is both the Priest and King of Men." [Maurice, Sermons on Sacrifice.] [Possibly The Doctrine of Sacrifice by John Frederick Denison Maurice, (1805–1872), whom Charles Kingsley called 'the most beautiful human soul whom God has ever allowed me to meet with.']

Parents have some Power to Enthrone the King.—Conscience, we have seen, is effective only as it is moved from within, from that innermost chamber of Mansoul, that Holy of Holies, the secrets of which are only known to the High-Priest, who "needed not that any man should tell Him, for He knew what was in man." It is necessary, however, that we should gather up crumbs of fact and inference and set in order such knowledge as we have; for the keys even of this innermost chamber are placed in the hands of parents, and it is a great deal in their power to enthrone the King, to induct the Priest, that every human cries for.

The Functions and Life of the Soul.—We take it for granted in common speech that every soul is a 'living soul,' a fully developed, full-grown soul; but the language of the Bible and that of general experience seem to point to startling conclusions. It has been said of a great poet—with how much justice is not the question here—that if we could suppose any human being to be made without a soul, he was such an abortive attempt; for while he had reason, imagination, passions, all the appetites and desires of an intelligent being, he appeared to exercise not one of the functions of the soul. Now, what are these functions, the suspension of which calls the very existence of a man's soul in question? We must go back to the axiom of Augustine—"The soul of man is for God, as God is for the soul." The soul has one appetite, for the things of God; breathes one air, the breath, the Spirit of God; has one desire, for the knowledge of God; one only joy, in the face of God. "I want to live in the Light of a Countenance which never ceases to smile upon me," [Christmas Day, and other Sermons] is the language of the soul. The direct action of the soul is all Godward, with a reflex action towards men. The speech of the soul is prayer and praise, the right hand of the soul is faith, the light of the soul is love, the love of God shed abroad upon it. Observe, these are the functions, this, the life of the soul, the only functions, the only life it can have: if it have not these, it has no power to turn aside and find the "life of its hand" elsewhere. As the conscience, the will, the reason, is ineffective till it be nourished with its proper food, exercised in its proper functions, so of the soul; and its chamber is dull, with cobwebbed doors and clouded windows, until it awake to its proper life; not quite empty, though, for there is the nascent soul; and the awakening into life takes place, sometimes with the sudden shock, the gracious miracle, which we call conversion; sometimes, when the parents so will, the soul of the child expands with a gentle, sweet growth and gradual unfolding as of a flower. There are torpid souls, which are yet alive; there are feeble, sickly souls, which are yet alive; and there are souls which no movement Godward ever quickens.

What is the Life of the Soul?—This life of the soul, what is it? Communicated life, as when one lights a torch at the fire? Perhaps; but it is something more intimate, more unspeakable: "I am the Life"; "In Him was life, and the life was the light of men"; "Abide in Me and I in you." The truth is too ineffable to be uttered in any words but those given to us. But it means this, at least, that the living soul does not abide alone in its place; that place becomes the temple of the living God. "Surely the Lord is in this place, and I knew it not. How dreadful is this place!"

The Parent must present the idea of God to the Soul of the Child.—But this holy mystery, this union and communion of God and the soul, how may human parents presume to meddle with it? What can they do? How can they promote it? and is there not every risk that they may lay rude hands upon the ark? In the first place, it does not rest with the parent to choose whether he will or will not attempt to quicken and nourish this divine life in his child. To do so this is his bounden duty and service. If he neglect or fail in this, I am not sure how much it matters that he has fulfilled his duties in the physical, moral and mental culture of his child, except in so far as the child is the fitter for the divine service should the divine life be awakened in him. But what can the parent do? Just this, and no more: he can present the idea of God to the soul of the child. Here, as throughout his universe, Almighty God works by apparently inadequate means. Who would say that a bee can produce apple trees? Yet a bee flies from an apple tree laden with the pollen of its flowers: this it unwittingly deposits on the stigmas of the flowers of the next tree it comes to. The bee goes, but the pollen remains, but with all the length of the style between it and the immature ovule below. That does not matter; the ovule has no power to reach the pollen grain, but the latter sends forth a slender tube, within the tube of the style; the ovule is reached; behold, then, the fruit, with its seed, and, if you like, future apple trees! Accept the parable: the parent is little better in this matter than the witless bee; it is his part to deposit, so to speak, within reach of the soul of the child some fruitful idea of God; the immature soul makes no effort towards that idea, but the living Word reaches down, touches the soul,—and there is life; growth and beauty, flower and fruit.

Must not make Blundering Efforts.—I venture to ask you to look, for once, at these divine mysteries from the same philosophical standpoint we have taken up in regarding all the capabilities and functions of the child, partly, because it is instructive to see how the mysteries of the religious life appear when it is looked at from without its own sphere; partly, because I wish to rise by unbroken steps to the supreme function of the parent in the education of his child. For here the similitude of the bee and the apple tree fails. The parent must not make blundering, witless efforts: as this is the highest duty imposed upon him, it is also the most delicate; and he will have infinite need of faith and prayer, tact and discretion, humility, gentleness, love, and sound judgement, if he would present his child to God, and the thought of God to the soul of his child.

God presented to Children as an Exactor and a Punisher.—"If we think of God as an exactor and not a giver," it has been well said, "exactors and not givers shall we become." Yet is not this the light in which God is most commonly set before the children—a Pharoah demanding his tale of bricks, bricks of good behaviour and right-doing? Do not parents deliberately present God as an exactor, to back up the feebleness of their own government; and do they not freely utter, on the part of God, threats they would be unwilling to utter on their own part? Again, what child has not heard from his nurse this, delivered with much energy, 'God does not love you, you naughty boy! He will send you to the bad place!' And these two thoughts of God, as an exactor and a punisher, make up, often enough, all the idea the poor child gets of his Father in heaven. What fruit can come of this but aversion, the turning away of the child from the face of his Father? What if, instead, were given to him the thought well expressed in the words, "The all-forgiving gentleness of God"?

Parents must select Inspiring Ideas.—These are but two of many deterrent thoughts of God commonly presented to the tender soul; and the mother, who realises that the heart of her child may be irrevocabley turned against God by the ideas of Him imbibed in the nursery, will feel the necessity for grave and careful thought, and definite resolve, as to what teaching her child shall receive on this momentous subject. She will most likely forbid any mention of the Divine Name to the children, except by their parents, explaining at the same time that she does so because she cares so much that her children should get none but right thoughts on this great matter. It is better that children should receive a few vital ideas that their souls may grow than a great deal of indefinite teaching.

We must Teach only what we Know.—How to select these few quickening thoughts of the infinite God? The selection is not so difficult to make as would appear at first sight. In the first place, we must teach that which we know, know by the life of the soul, not with any mere knowledge of the mind. Now, of the vast mass of the doctrines and the precepts of religion, we shall find that there are only a few vital truths that we have so taken into our being that we live upon them—this person, these; that person, those; some of us, not more than a single one. One or more, these are the truths we must teach the children, because these will come straight out of our hearts with the enthusiasm of conviction which rarely fails to carry its own idea into the spiritual life of another. There is no more fruitful source of what it is hardly too much to call infant infidelity than the unreal dead words which are poured upon children about the best things, with an artificial solemnity of tone and manner intended to make up for the want of living meaning in the words. Let the parent who only knows one thing from above teach his child that one; more will come to him by the time the child is ready for more.

Fitting and Vital Ideas.—Again, there are some ideas of the spiritual life more proper than others to the life and needs of the child. Thus, Christ the Joy-giver is more to him than Christ the Consoler.

And there are some few ideas which are as the daily bread of the soul, without which life and growth are impossible. All other teaching may be deferred until the child's needs bring him to it; but whoever sends his child out into life without these vital ideas of the spiritual life, sends him forth with a dormant soul, however well-instructed he may be in theology.

The Knowledge of God distinct from Morality.—Again, the knowledge of God is distinct from morality, or what the children call 'being good', though 'being good' follows from that knowledge. But let these come in their right order. Do not bepreach the child to weariness about 'being good' as what he owes to God, without letting in upon him first a little of that knowledge which shall make him good.

We are no longer suffering from an embarrassment of riches; these limitations shut out so much of the ordinary teaching about divine things that the question becomes rather, What shall we teach? than, How shall we choose?

The Times and the Manner of Religious Instruction.—The next considerations that will press upon the mother are of the times, and the manner, of this teaching in the things of God. It is better that these teachings be rare and precious, than too frequent and slighty valued; better not at all, than that the child should be surfeited with the mere sight of spiritual food, rudely served. At the same time, he must be built up in the faith, and his lessons must be regular and progressive; and here everything depends upon the tact of the mother. Spiritual teaching, like the wafted odour of flowers, should depend on which way the wind blows. Every now and then there occurs a holy moment, felt to be holy by mother and child, when the two are together—that is the moment for some deeply felt and softly spoken word about God, such as the occasion gives rise to. Few words need be said, no exhortation at all; just the flash of conviction from the soul of the mother to the soul of the child. Is 'Our Father' the thought thus laid upon the child's soul? there will be, perhaps, no more than a sympathetic meeting of eyes hereafter, between mother and child, over thousand showings forth of 'Our Father's' love; but the idea is growing, becoming part of the child's spiritual life. This is all: no routine of spiritual teaching; a dread of many words, which are apt to smother the fire of the sacred life; much self-restraint shown in the allowing of seeming opportunities to pass; and all the time, earnest purpose of heart, and a definite scheme for the building up of the child in the faith. It need not be added that, to make another use of our Lord's words, "this kind cometh forth only by prayer." It is as the mother gets wisdom liberally from above, that she will be enabled for this divine task.

The Reading of the Bible.—A word about the reading of the Bible. I think we make a mistake in burying the text under our endless comments and applications. Also, I doubt if the picking out of individual verses, and grinding these into the child until they cease to have any meaning for him, is anything but a hindrance to the spiritual life. The Word is full of vital force, capable of applying itself. A seed, light as thistledown, wafted into the child's soul will take root downwards and bear fruit upwards. What is required of us is, that we should implant a love of the Word; that the most delightful moments of the child's day should be those in which his mother reads for him, with sweet sympathy and holy gladness in voice and eyes, the beautiful stories of the Bible; and now and then in the reading will occur one of those convictions, passing from the soul of the mother to the soul of the child, in which is the life of the Spirit. Let the child grow, so that,

"New thoughts of God, new hopes of heaven,"

are a joy to him, too; things to be counted first amongst the blessings of a day. Above all, do not read the Bible at the child: do not let any words of the Scriptures be occasions for gibbeting his faults. It is the office of the Holy Ghost to convince of sin; and He is able to use the Word for this purpose, without risk of that hardening of the heart in which our clumsy dealings too often result.

The matter for this teaching of divine things will come out of every mother's own convictions. I will attempt to speak of only one or two of those vital truths on which the spiritual life must sustain itself.

Father and Giver.—"Our Father, who is in heaven," is perhaps the first idea of God which the mother will present to her child—Father and Giver, straight from whom comes all the gladness of every day. 'What a happy birthday our Father has given to my little boy!' 'The flowers are coming again; our Father has taken care of the life of the plants all through the winter cold!' 'Listen to the skylark! It is a wonder how our Father can put so much joy into the heart of one little bird.' 'Thank God for making my little girl so happy and merry!' Out of this thought comes prayer, the free utterance of the child's heart, more often in thanks for the little joys of the day counted up than in desire, just yet. The words do not matter; any simple form the child can understand will do; the rising Godward of the child-heart is the true prayer. Out of this thought , too, comes duty—the glad acknowledgement of the debt of service and obedience to a Parent so gracious and benign—not One who exacts service at the sword's point, as it were, but One whom His children run to obey.

The Essence of Christianity is Loyalty to a Person.—Christ, our King. Here is a thought to unseal the fountains of love and loyalty, the treasures of faith and imagination, bound up in the child. The very essence of Christianity is personal loyalty, passionate loyalty to our adorable Chief. We have laid other foundations—regeneration, sacraments, justification, works, faith, the Bible—any one of which, however necessary to salvation in its due place and proportion may become a religion about Christ and without Christ. And now a time of sifting has come upon us, and thoughtful people decline to know anything about our religious systems; they write down all our orthodox beliefs as things not knowable. Perhaps this may be because, in thinking much of our salvation, we have put out of sight our King, the divine fact which no soul of man to whom it is presented can ignore. In the idea of Christ is life; let the thought of Him once get touch of the soul, and it rises up, a living power, independent of all formularies of the brain. Let us save Christianity for our children by bringing them into allegiance to Christ, the King. How? How did the old Cavaliers bring up sons and daughters, in passionate loyalty and reverence for not too worthy princes? Their own hearts were full of it; their lips spake it; their acts proclaimed it; the style of their clothes, the ring of their voices, the carriage of their heads—all was one proclamation of boundless devotion to their king and his cause. That civil war, whatever else it did, or missed doing, left a parable for Christian people. If a Stuart prince could command such measure of loyalty, what shall we say of "the Chief amongst ten thousand, the altogether lovely"?

Jesus, our Saviour. Here is a thought to be brought tenderly before the child in the moments of misery that follow wrong-doing. 'My poor little boy, you have been very naughty to-day! Could you not help it?' 'No, mother,' with sobs. 'No, I suppose not; but there is a way of help.' And then the mother tells her child how the Lord Jesus is our Saviour, because He saves us from our sins. It is a matter of question when the child should first learn the 'Story of the Cross.' One thinks it would be very delightful to begin with Moses and the prophets: to go through the Old Testament history, tracing the gradual unfolding of the work and character of the Messiah; and then, when their minds are full of the expectation of the Jews, to bring before them the mystery of the Birth in Bethlehem, the humiliation of the Cross. But perhaps no gain in freshness of presentation would make up to the children for not having grown up with the associations of Calvary and Bethlehem always present to their minds. One thing in this connection: it is not well to allow the children in a careless familiarity with the Name of Jesus, or in the use of hymns whose tone is not reverent. "Ye call Me Master and Lord; and ye say well, for so I am."

The Indwelling of Christ is a thought particularly fit for the children, because their large faith does not stumble at the mystery, their imagination leaps readily to the marvel, that the King Himself should inhabit a little child's heart. 'How am I to know He is come, mother?' 'When you are quite gentle, sweet, and happy, it is because Christ is within,—

"And when He comes, He makes your face so fair,
Your friends are glad, and say, 'The King is there.'"

I will not attempt to indicate any more of the vital truths which the Christian mother will present to her child; having patience until they blossom and bear, and his soul is as a very fruitful garden which the Lord hath blessed. But, once more, "This kind cometh forth only by prayer."

Appendix

Questions for the Use of Students

Part I: Some Preliminary Considerations

1. Show that children are a public trust. What follows? 2. What questions does Pestalozzi put to mothers? 3. What is Mr Herbert Spencer's argument for the study of education? 4. How do parents usually proceed? 5. What is the strenuous part of a parent's work?

I. A Method of Education

1. Contrast four or five older theories with later and perhaps sounder notions. 2. Point out the opposite characters of a system and a method. 3. Why is a system tempting to parents?

II. The Child's Estate

1. What do the Gospel sayings about children indicate? 2. What are the three commandments of the Gospel code of education?

III. Offending the Children

1. Distinguish between 'offending' and 'despising' children. 2. What is to be said of parents whose children have 'no sense of ought'? 3. Trace the steps by which a mother's 'no' comes to be disregarded. 4. Why must parents themselves be law-compelled? 5. Show that parents may offend their children by disregarding the laws of health. 6. By disregarding the laws of the intellectual life. 7. Of the moral life.

IV. Despising the Children

1. Show that children may be despised in the choice of a nurse. 2. By taking their faults too lightly.

V. Hindering the Children

1. In what ways may parents hinder their children's access to God?

VI. Conditions of Healthy Brain Activity

1. What is the first condition of successful education? 2. Show that daily efforts, intellectual, moral, and physical, are necessary for children. 3. On what principle is the blood-supply regulated? 4. Show the importance of rest after meals. 5. What is the best time for lessons? Why? 6. On what principle should a time-table be arranged? 7. Show that brain activity is affected by nourishment. 8. Under what conditions does food increase the vital quality of the blood? 9. Why must food be varied? 10. Show that children are spendthrifts of vitality. 11. Give a few useful hints concerning meals. 12. Why should there be talk at meals? 13. Give some rules to secure variety. 14. Show fully that air is as important as food. 15. What have you to say of the children's daily walk ? 16. What is meant by the oxygenation of the blood? 17. Show that oxygen has its limitations. 18. What are the dangers of unchanged air in spacious rooms? 19. 'I feed Alice on beef-tea.' Why? 20. What of Alice's mind? 21. What are the joys of Wordsworth's 'Lucy'? 22. Show the danger of stuffy rooms. 23. What principle must regulate ventilation? 24. Why is night air wholesome? 25. Upon what physical facts does the need of sunshine depend? 26. Show that the skin does much scavenger's work. 27. Why do persons die of external scalds or burns? 28. Why is a daily bath necessary? 29. Give some instructions for clothing children.

VII. 'The Reign of Law' in Education

1. What should be the method of all education? 2. Why are common sense and good intentions not sufficient? 3. How may we meet the danger to religion arising from the blameless lives of some non-religious persons? 4. Account for the superior morality of such nonbelievers. 5. Show that all observance of law brings its reward. 6. Show that parents should not lay up crucial difficulties for their children. 7. Why should parents study mental and moral science?

Part II Out-of-door Life for the Children

I. A Growing Time

1. Why is out-of-door life for young children especially important in these days? 2. What are the gains of meals out of doors? 3. What might be accomplished by dwellers in towns and suburbs? 4. What five or six

points should be remembered in a day in the open? 5. What of story-books or tale-telling on such occasions? 6. What of 'the baby'?

II. 'Sight-seeing'

1. Give an example of 'sight-seeing.' 2. What five or six educational uses may be made of 'sight-seeing'? 3. Show the value of discriminating observation.

III. 'Picture Painting'

1. What is meant by 'picture painting'? 2. Give an example. 3. Show the value of this exercise. 4. What caution must be borne in mind? 5. What invaluable habit should this play tend to form? 6. What is the mother's part in the play? 7. What is the after-reward for taking pains in the act of seeing?

IV. Flowers and Trees

1. With what field crops may children become acquainted in your neighbourhood? 2. What should a child know about any wild flower of his neighbourhood? 3. How should children take up the study of trees? 4. Show how the seasons should be followed in this study. 5. What does Leigh Hunt say about flowers? 6. What use should be made of calendars and notebooks? 7. What of the child who says, 'I can't stop thinking'?

V. 'Living Creatures'

1. What part of the pleasure in living creatures may be secured for town dwellers? 2. Of what 'creatures' may children observe the habits? 3. What points about an insect should children observe? 4. How did White of Selborne and Audubon get their bent towards nature? 5. What can town children do in getting a knowledge of 'living creatures'? 6. Show that nature-knowledge is the most important knowledge for young children. 7. What intellectual powers are trained in the child naturalist? 8. Show that nature-work is especially valuable for girls.

VI. Field Lore and Naturalists' Books

1. Should young children be taught the elements of natural science? 2. Show the value of rough classifications. 3. Contrast with classifications learnt from books. 4. What are the uses of Naturalists' books? 5. Name a few. 6. Why should mothers and teachers have some knowledge of nature?

VII. The Child Gets Knowledge by Means of His Senses

1. Show, from the behaviour of a baby, that a child gets knowledge by means of his senses. 2. Characterise Nature's teaching. 3. Wherein lies the danger of over-pressure? 4. Why are object lessons inefficient? 5. Why does a child learn most from things? 6. Give some examples showing that a sense of beauty comes from early contact with nature. 7. What does Dickens say on the subject of a child's observing powers ?

VIII. The Child Should Be Made Familiar with Natural Objects

1. Compare town and country as to things worth observing. 2. How does the fact that every natural object is a member of a series affect education? 3. 'Power win pass more and more into the hands of scientific men'—how should this influence parents and teachers? 4. In what ways does intimacy with nature make for personal well-being?

IX. Out-of-Door Geography

1. Show that small things may suggest great in pictorial geography. 2. What should children be taught to observe about the position of the sun? 3. What, of clouds, rain, snow, and hail? 4. Show how, by pacing, a child should get the idea of distance. 5. What is the first step towards a knowledge of direction? 6. What practice should a child have in finding direction? 7. What compass-drill would you give him? 8. How should

a child get the notion of boundaries? 9. When should he begin to make 'plans'? 10. What geographical ideas should he get from his own neighbourhood?

X. the Child and Mother Nature

1. Why must the mother refrain from much talk? 2. How is a new acquaintance begun? 3. What are the two things permissible to the mother?

XI. Out-of-door Games, Etc.

1. Why should not the French lesson be omitted? 2. Why should children indulge in cries and shouts out of doors? 3. Why should rondes be preserved? 4. What are the best ways of using skipping-rope and shuttlecock? 5. What is to be said for climbing? 6. What, for woollen garments?

XII. Walks in Bad Weather

1. Why are winter walks as necessary as summer walks? 2. What pleasures are connected with frost and snow? 3. How may children be kept alert on dull days? 4. How does winter lend itself to observation? 5. Why are wet weather tramps wholesome and necessary? 6. What sort of garments are necessary? Why? 7. What precautions should be borne in mind?

XIII. 'Red Indian' Life

1. What do you understand by 'scouting'? Show the value of scouting. 2. Describe a 'bird-stalking' expedition. 3. In what ways should these things afford training?

XIV. The Children Require Country Air

1. How may the essential proportion of oxygen be diminished? 2. How is excess of carbonic acid gas produced? 3. Why do children, especially, need unvitiated, unimpoverished air? 4. Show that children require solar light. 5. Describe a physical ideal for a child, and show the use of having such an ideal.

Part III 'Habit Is Ten Natures'

I. Education Based upon Natural Law

1. Show that a healthy brain and outdoor life are conditions of education. 2. Show that habit is the instrument by which parents work.

II. The Children Have No Self-compelling Power

1. Show that education is commonly a cul-de-sac. 2. Name three great educational forces. 3. Why are not these forces sufficient? 4. Why are children incapable of steady effort? 5. Why should young children be, to some extent, saved the effort of decision?

III. What Is 'Nature'?

1. What may we state of the child as a human being? 2. Show that all persons are born with the same primary desires. 3. And affections. 4. Name affections common to us all. 5. What does the most elemental notion of human nature include? 6. What have you to say of the strength of nature plus heredity? 7. What manner of differences may physical conditions bring about? 8. Of what is human nature the sum? 9. Why must not the child be left to his human nature? 10. What is the problem before the educator? 11. Show that divine grace works on the lines of human effort. 12.. Why must not the trust of parents be supine?

IV. Habit May Supplant 'Nature'

1. Show that habit runs on the lines of nature. 2. How must habit work to be a lever? 3. Show that a mother forms her children's habits involuntarily. 4. Illustrate the fact that habit may force nature into new channels. 5. To what end must parents and teachers lay down the lines of habit?

V. the Laying down of Lines of Habit

1. Show that parents initiate their children's habits of thought and feeling by their own behaviour. 2. Does education in habit interfere with free-will? 3. Show how good it is that habit should rule our thoughts. 4. Show that habit is powerful even when the will decides.

VI. The Physiology of Habit

1. Illustrate the fact that growing tissues form themselves to the modes of action required of them. 2. Show fully and exactly why children should learn dancing, swimming, etc., at an early age. 3. To what fact is the strength of moral habits probably due? 4. Show the danger of persistent trains of thought. 5. What does the incessant regeneration of brain tissue imply to the educator? 6. Show that to acquire artificial reflex action in certain directions is a great part of education. 7. What are the aims of intellectual and moral education? 8. Show that character is affected by the acquired modification of brain tissue. 9. Show the need for care with regard to outside influences.

VII. The Forming of a Habit—'Shut the Door after You'

1. What remains to be tried when neither time, reward, nor punishment is effective in curing a bad habit? 2. Show that habit is a delight in itself. 3. Show that misguided sympathy is a hindrance in the formation of habits. 4. What are the qualities necessary in the mother who would form habits in her children? 5. What are the stages in the formation of a habit? 6. Which is the dangerous stage?

VIII. Infant Habits

1. Show the necessity for cleanliness in the nursery. 2. How do cleanliness, order, etc., educate a child? 3. Why is the training of a sensitive nose an important part of education? 4. Why should nurses know that the baby is ubiquitous? 5. Show that personal cleanliness should be made an early habit. 6. How may parents approach the subjects of modesty and purity? 7. Show how the habit of obedience and the sense of honour are safeguards. 8. What manner of life is the best safeguard? 9. Give some suggestions with regard to 'order' in the nursery. 10. Show how and why the child of two should put away his playthings. 11. Distinguish between neatness and order. 12. What occasions are there for regularity with an incant? 13. Show that irregularity leads to self-indulgence.

IX. Physical Exercises

1. Show the importance of daily physical exercises. 2. What moral qualities appear in alert movements? 3. Suggest a drill of good manners. 4. How would you train the ear and voice? 5. How may the habit of music be cultivated? 6. Show that the mother who trains habits can let her children alone.

Part IV Some Habits of Mind—Some Moral Habits

1. What can a knowledge of the science of education effect? 2. Show that education in habit favours an easy life. 3. Show how the mother's labours are eased by the fact that training in habits becomes a habit. 4. Instance some habits inspired with the home atmosphere.

I. The Habit of Attention

1. Why is the habit of attention of supreme importance? 2. Instance minds at the mercy of associations. 3. Give instances from literature of the habit of wandering attention. 4. Where is the harm of wandering attention? 5. How may the habit of attention be cultivated in the infant? 6. How would you cultivate attention to lessons? 7. What principles should help the teacher to. make lessons attractive? 8. Show the value of definite work in a given time. 9. On what principle must a time-table be drawn up? 10. What is the natural reward of attention at lessons? 11. What is to be said for and against emulation? 12. What is the risk in employing affection as a motive? 13. Show that the attractiveness of knowledge is a sufficient motive to the learner. 14. What is attention? 15. How would you induce self-compelled attention? 16. What is the secret

of over-pressure? 17. How may parents be of use in the home-work of the day-schoolboy? 18. Describe a wholesome home-treatment for 'mooning.' 19. What have you to say of the discipline of consequences? 20. Show that rewards and punishments should be relative, rather than natural, consequences of conduct. 21. Distinguish between natural and educative consequences.

II. The Habits of Application, Etc.

1. How may rapid mental effort be secured? 2. How may zeal be stimulated?

III. The Habit of Thinking

1. Give the example of thinking cited. 2. What operations are included in 'thinking'?

IV. The Habit of Imagining

1. What is the double danger of many books ministering to the sense of the incongruous? 2. Show that commonplace tales leave nothing to the imagination. 3. In what way do tales of the imagination afford children a second life? 4. Show that we can have great conceptions only as we have imagination. 5. Upon what does imagination grow? 6. What lessons should feed imagination? 7. Why? 8. Show the educative value of the right story-books. 9. How would you promote the habit of thinking?

V. The Habit of Remembering

1. Distinguish between remembering and recollecting. 2. Describe what is here called a 'spurious' memory. 3. What results from the fact that memory is a record on the brain substance? 4. Made under what conditions? 5. Show that recollection depends upon the law or association of ideas. 6. What is the condition for recollecting a course of lessons? 7. Given what conditions may we say there is no limit to the recording power of the brain? 8. Show that links of association are a condition of recollection. Where are these to be discovered?

VI. The Habit of Perfect Execution

1. What national error hinders us from the effort to throw perfection into all we do? 2. Show the danger of the habit of turning out imperfect work. 3. How may a child be taught to execute perfectly?

VII. Some Moral Habits—Obedience

1. What is the whole duty of a child? 2. What is the state opposed to obedience? 3. Show that a parent has no right to forego obedience. 4. What is the true motive for obedience? 5. Account for the fact that strictly brought up children are often failures. 6. Why may parents and teachers expect obedience? 7. How may children be brought up to 'do as they choose'? 8. What manner of obedience is of lasting value to the child? 9. How may children be trained towards liberty?

VIII. Truthfulness, Etc.

1. What are the causes of lying? 2. Show that all kinds of lying are vicious. 3. How is it that only one kind is visited on children? 4. How would you train a child in accuracy of statement? 5. How would you deal with exaggeration? 6. With ludicrous embellishments? 7. Show that reverence, consideration, etc., claim special attention in these days. 8. Is temper born in a child? 9. Show that, not temper, but tendency is 'born.' 10. How must parents correct such tendency? 11. Show fully the efficacy of changing the child's thoughts. 12. Distinguish between changing a child's thoughts and conveying to him the thought you intend him to think.

Part V Lessons as Instruments of Education

I. The Matter and Method of Lessons

1. Discuss the statement, This is 'an age of pedagogy.' 2. Why must parents reflect on the subject-matter of instruction? 3. Show that home is the best growing ground for young children. 4. Why must a mother have

definite views? 5. What are the three questions for the mother? 6. Show that children learn, to grow. 7. Show that any doctoring of the material of knowledge is unnecessary for a healthy child. 8. What is an idea? 9. Show that an idea feeds, grows, and produces. 10. What did Sir Walter Scott and George Stephenson each do with an idea? 11. Show the value of dominant ideas. 12. Why must lessons furnish ideas? 13. What quality of knowledge should children get? 14. What is the evil of 'diluted knowledge'? 15. Illustrate a child's power of getting knowledge (Dr Arnold). 16. What is the harm of lesson-books with pretty pictures and easy talk? 17. What are the four tests which should be applied to children's lessons? 18. Give a resume of six points already considered.

II. The Kindergarten as a Place of Education

1. Show that the mother is the best Kindergartnerin, 2. How may the child get education out of his daily nursery life? 3. Show that the children's pursuit of real knowledge may be hindered by the kindergarten. 4. Show that a just eye and a faithful hand may be trained at home. 5. In what respects does the kindergarten give a hint of the discipline proper for the nursery. 6. What temper should be cultivated in the nursery? 7. What general conclusion may we come to as to the principles and practices of the kindergarten?

III. Further Consideration of the Kindergarten

1. What anecdote of a child is quoted from Tolstoi's Childhood, Boyhood, and Youth? 2. Why are such tales as Miss Deland's The Story of a Child valuable? 3. What do we owe to Froebel? 4. What may we learn from the true Kindergartnerin? 5. Comment upon, 'Persons do not grow in a garden.' 6. Show that we must leave opportunity for the work of nature in education. 7. Give instances showing the intelligence of children. 8. Account for the pleasure children take in kindergarten games. 9. In what ways do teachers mediate too much? 10. Show the danger of personal magnetism in the teacher. 11. Show fully that the name 'kindergarten' implies a false analogy. 12. What might be said concerning the Froebel 'mothergames'? 13. Is the society of a large number of his equals in age the best for a young child? 14. Show the dangers of supplanting nature. 15. What would you say regarding the importance of personal initiative? 16. In what ways must parents and teachers sow opportunities? 17. Do 'only' children profit by the kindergarten? 18. In what ways should children be allowed some ordering of their lives? 19. Give a few of the lessons we may learn from the autobiography of Helen Keller. 20. What conclusions does Miss Sullivan, Helen Keller's teacher, arrive at with regard to systems of education? 21. Account for the success of the kindergarten in the United States. 22. What changes does Mr Thistleton Mark observe? 23. Give some of the comments of Dr Stanley Hall.

IV. Reading

1. Discuss the question of the age at which children should learn to read. 2. How did Mrs Westey teach her children to read? 3. Give a few hints for teaching the alphabet. 4. How would you introduce a child to word-making? 5. Describe a lesson in word-making with long vowels, etc. 6. How should the child's first reading lessons help him to spell? 7. Give the steps of a reading lesson on 'Twinkle, twinkle, little star.' 8. Why is prose better in some ways than verse for early lessons? 9. Describe a second reading lesson on 'Twinkle, twinkle, little star.' 10. Show that slow and steady progress tends to careful enunciation. 11. Show how much a child might gain in a year's work on these lines.. 12. Contrast this steady progress with the casual way in which children generally learn to read.

V. First Reading Lesson

(Two Mothers Confer) [No questions]

VI. Reading by Sight and by Sound

1. Why is learning to read hard work? 2. What are the symbols children must learn ? 3. What do we definitely propose in teaching a child to read? 4. Can the symbols he learns be interesting? 5. Describe the stages of a lesson on 'I like little Pussy.' 6. How does Tommy learn to read sentences? 7. Describe Tommy's

first spelling lesson. 8. How would you deal with the fact that like combinations have different sounds? 9. Show that his reading lesson should afford moral training to a child.

VII. Recitation 'The Children's Art'

1. What should we aim at in teaching children to recite? 2. How should we proceed? 3. What should we avoid? 4. Why may we expect success? 5. Distinguish between reciting and memorising. 6. Show that children have a, natural capacity for memorising. 7. How would you teach them to memorise a poem?

VIII. Reading for Older Children

1. To what two points must the teacher attend? 2. What is the most common and the monstrous defect in the education of the day? 3. How may we correct this defect? 4. What points require attention when the child is reading aloud? 5. What must the teacher be careful to avoid? 6. What is to be said for and against reading to children? 7. Should children be questioned about the meaning of what they read? 8. Why not? 9. Suggest a better test of their intelligence. 10. Why is the selection of a child's early lesson-books a matter of great importance? 11. What general rule should help in the choice of these? 12. How may the attention of children be secured during a reading lesson? 13. Give two or three hints with regard to careful pronunciation.

IX. The Art of Narration

1. Prove from your own observation that children narrate by nature. 2. How should this power be used in their education? 3. What points must be borne in mind with regard to a child's narrations? 4. Describe the method of a lesson.

X. Writing

1. How would you avoid the habit of careless work? 2. What printing should a. child do before he comes to write? 3. What stages should be followed in teaching writing? 4. What is to be said about copperplate headlines? 5. Why should children practise in text-hand? 6. What arguments are advanced in favour of a beautiful handwriting? 7. What is to be said for a beautiful basis for characteristic handwriting? 8. Suggest a way of using A New Handwriting.

XI. Transcription

1. Show the use of transcription before children write dictation. 2. What should children transcribe? 3. How should transcription help children to spell? 4. Why should text-hand and double-ruled lines be used? 5. Describe the proper position in writing. 6. How should children hold their pens? 7. What are the points of a good desk? 8. Describe a school-table for little children.

XII. Spelling and Dictation

1. Show how dictation may be made a cause of bad spelling. 2. What is the rationale of spelling? 3. What are the steps of a dictation lesson as it should be? 4. Show clearly what principle is involved. 5. What are the two causes of illiterate spelling?

XIII. Composition

1. Show that the exaction of original composition from school-boys and school-girls is a futility. 2. And a moral injury to the children. 3. Illustrate the sort of teaching that should be regarded as a public danger. 4. Upon what condition does composition 'come by nature'?

XIV. Bible Lessons

1. Illustrate the religious receptivity of children. 2. What Bible knowledge should children of nine have? 3. What would you say with regard to Bible narratives done into modern English? 4. Show fully why children should be made familiar with the text. 5. What conception should gradually unfold itself to them? 6.

Distinguish between essential and accidental truth. 7. In what event may it be said that' the truths themselves will assuredly slip from our grasp'? 8. Why should care be taken lest Bible teaching stale upon the minds of children? 9. Describe the method of a Bible lesson. 10. What use would you make of illustrations? 11. What is to be said as to the learning by heart of Bible passages ?

XV. Arithmetic

1. Why is arithmetic important as a means of education? 2. How would you test a child's knowledge of principles? 3. Why are long sums mischievous? 4. What mental exercise should a problem offer? 5. What caution must be observed? 6. How may arithmetic become an elementary training in mathematics? 7. How should a child demonstrate 4 x 7 = 28? 8. How would you use buttons, beans, etc.? 9. Show how you would teach a child to work out an addition and subtraction table with each of the digits. 10. When would you introduce multiplication and division tables? 11. How would you teach division? 12. What is the step between working with things and with abstract numbers? 13. How would you introduce our system of notation? 14. Why? 15. Show fully how you would deal with 'tens.' 16. How long should a child work with 'tens' and units only? 17. What should follow? 18. What rule must be observed throughout? 19. How would you apply the same principle to weights and measures? 20. What part should parcels play at this stage, and why? 21. Show how the child should use a foot-rule. 22. How would you exercise his judgment as to measures and weights. 23. How does the idea of a fraction occur in this work with concrete quantities? 24. What should be the moral value of the study of arithmetic? 25. How does the inferior teacher instill a disregard of truth and common honesty in this study? 26. How would you deal with a 'wrong' sum? 27. What should the daily arithmetic lesson be to the children? 28. Discuss the ABC Arithmetic. 29. What is to be said against accustoming young children to the sight of geometrical forms and figures?

XVI. Natural Philosophy

1. Show that childhood is the time for gathering materials for classification. 2. What does Mr Herbert Spencer say as to the value of scientific pursuits? 3. Show that children are able to comprehend principles. 4. Mention some of the phenomena they might readily understand. 5. From the subjects taught successfully in a village school, write a list of questions which intelligent children should be able to answer. 6. 'The principles of natural philosophy are the principles of common sense.' Show how this statement should be a key to our educational practice.

XVII. Geography

1. Wherein lies the peculiar educational value of geography? 2. How is geography commonly taught? 3. What sort of information about places do children and grown-up people enjoy? 4. Why is the geography learnt at school of little use in after life? 5. What should a child learn in geography? 6. How should he get his rudimentary notions? 7. How should children be introduced to maps? 8. Why should a child be made 'at home' in some one region? 9. Why is it well to follow the steps of a traveller? 10. Mention a few books useful in this connection. 11. How should maps be used in this kind of work? 12. How should a child get his first notion of a glacier, a canon, etc.? 13. What course of reading might parents aim at between a child's fifth and his tenth year? 14. How should young children get their lessons on Place? 15. How should they arrive at definitions? 16. What fundamental ideas should a child receive? 17. How should he be introduced to the meaning of a map?

XVIII. History

1. What is the intellectual and what the moral worth of history as an educational subject? 2. What is to be said of the usual ways of teaching English history? 3. What, if the little text-book be moral or religious in tone? 4. What is the fatal mistake as regards the early teaching of history? 5. What is the better way? 6. What should a child know of the period in which any person, about whom he is reading, lived? 7. What moral gain may he get from such intimate knowledge? 8. What manner of books must be eschewed? 9. What is the least that should be done to introduce children to the history of England? 10. Why is the early history of a nation better fitted for children than its later records? 11. Why are the old Chronicles profitable reading for them? 12. Name and comment upon a few of the Chronicles upon which children's knowledge of history should rest.

13. What effect on a child should the reading of such old Chronicles have? 14. Show that children should know something of the heroic age of their own nation. 15. What use may be made of Geoffrey of Monmouth's History of the British Kings? 16. From what authority should a child get the story of the French wars? 17. Why do Plutarch's Lives afford the best preparation for the study of Grecian and Roman history? 18. Give two counsels which should regulate the teaching of history. 19. Upon what principles should history books for children be selected? 20. Mention one or two books that lend themselves to narrating. 21. Comment upon Mr Arnold Forster's History of England. 22. How would you help children to clearness with regard to dates? 23. Mention two or three ways in which children's minds work if their history books are of the proper quality.

XIX. Grammar

1. Why is grammar uninteresting to a child? 2. Why is English grammar peculiarly hard? 3. Show that the Latin grammar is easier. 4. Show that the Latin, affords some help in the learning of English grammar. 5. Why should a child begin with a sentence and not with the parts of speech? 6. Write notes of one or two introductory lessons.

XX. French

1. How should French be acquired? 2. Show that the learning of French is an education of the senses. 3. What are our two difficulties in speaking French? 4. Show that these hindrances should be removed in childhood. 5. How? 6. How might the difficulty of accent be dealt with? 7. What half-dozen principles has M. Gouin made plain to us? 8. Show that the Series method enables a child to think in the new language 9. Trace fully the steps by which the author worked out his theory. 10. How does he treat the difficulty of spelling? 11. Illustrate the facility with which a child learns a new language.

XXI. Pictorial Art, Etc.

1. Upon what two lines should the art training of children proceed? 2. How should picture-talks be regulated? 3. What gains may we hope for from this kind of teaching? 4. Discuss the use of blobs in early drawing lessons. 5. What should be our aim in these lessons? 6. Children have 'art' in them. How should this fact affect our teaching? 7. What should we bear in mind in teaching clay-modelling to children? 8. Name methods of teaching singing and the piano which are to be commended. 9. What physical exercises would you recommend? 10. Name some handicrafts suitable for young children.

Part VI the Will—The Conscience—The Divine Life in the Child

I. The Will

1. How is the government of Mansoul carried on? 2. Show that the executive power is vested in the will. 3. What is the will? 4. In what respects may persons go through life without a deliberate act of will ? 5. Show that character is the result of conduct regulated by will. 6. What are the three functions of the will? 7. What limitation of the will is disregarded by certain novelists? 8. Show that parents blunder into this metaphysical error. 9. Show that wilfulness indicates want of will-power. 10. What is wilfulness? 11. What are the superior and inferior functions of the will? 12. Show that the will does not always act for good. 13. Show that a disciplined wilt is necessary to heroic Christian character. 14. How would you distinguish between effective and non-effective persons? 15. How does the will operate? 16. Show how incentives, diversion, change of thought are severally aids to the will. 17. What should be taught to children as to the 'way of the will'? 18. Show that power of will implies power of attention. 19. Show that habit may frustrate the will. 20. Show the necessity for the reasonable use of so effective an instrument. 21. By what line of conduct should parents strengthen the wills of their children? 22. How may children be taught to manage themselves? 23. Show that the education of the will is more important than that of the intellect.

II. Conscience

1. What are the functions of conscience? 2. What is implied in 'I am, I ought, I can, I will'? 3. What mistake is made by the inert parent with regard to the divine grace? 4. Show that conscience is not an infallible guide.

5. How does Adam Smith illustrate the fact that conscience is a real power? 6. What do we know of conscience? 7. Distinguish between a nascent and a trained conscience. 8. Show that refinement of conscience cannot coexist with ignorance. 9. What are the processes implied in a 'conscientious' decision? 10. What may be said of the instructed conscience? 11. What may be expected of the good conscience of a child? 12. Show that children play with moral questions. 13. How would you impart any of the moral ideas contained in the Bible to a child? 14. Show the use of tales in the training of conscience. 15. Show the extreme ignorance of a child's conscience. 16. How would you instruct children in the duty of 'kindness,' for example? 17. What is to be said of the conscience made effective by discipline?

III. The Divine Life in the Child

1. What is the 'very pulse of the machine'? 2. Show that parents have some power to enthrone the King. 3. Define as far as you can the functions of the soul. 4. What is the life of the soul? 5. Show by the illustration of the bee and the apple-tree what is the parent's part in quickening the Divine life in his child. 6. Show where the similitude of the bee and the apple tree fails. 7. By what two deterrent ideas is God most often presented to children? 8. What precautions must a mother take to secure that her children get inspiring ideas of God? 9. What considerations should help us to select the quickening thoughts proper for children? 10. How would you select fitting and vital ideas? 11. Show the danger of confounding 'being good' with knowing God. 12. What cautions will the mother observe as to the times and the manner of religious instruction? 13. Make some suggestions for the reading of the Bible. 14. How might a mother give her child the idea of God as Father and Giver? 15. How may children be brought up in allegiance to Christ? 16. How would you bring the thought of their Saviour home to children? 17. Show that the indwelling of Christ is a thought fit for children.

Parents And Children
Table of Contents

Preface to the Home Education Series

The educational outlook is rather misty and depressing both at home and abroad. That science should be a staple of education, that the teaching of Latin, of modern languages, of mathematics, must be reformed, that nature and handicrafts should be pressed into service for the training of the eye and hand, that boys and girls must learn to write English and therefore must know something of history and literature; and, on the other hand, that education must be made more technical and utilitarian—these, and such as these, are the cries of expedience with which we take the field. But we have no unifying principle, no definite aim; in fact, no philosophy of education. As a stream can rise no higher than its source, so it is probable that no educational effort can rise above the whole scheme of thought which gives it birth; and perhaps this is the reason of all the fallings from us, vanishings, failures, and disappointments which mark our educational records.

Those of us, who have spent many years in pursuing the benign and elusive vision of Education, perceive her approaches are regulated by a law, and that this law has yet to be evoked. We can discern its outlines, but no more. We know that it is pervasive; there is no part of a child's home life or school work which the law does not penetrate. It is illuminating, too, showing the value, or lack of value, of a thousand systems and expedients. It is not only a light, but a measure, providing a standard whereby all things, small and great, belonging to educational work must be tested. The law is liberal, taking in whatsoever things are true, honest, and of good report, and offering no limitation or hindrance save where excess should injure. And the path indicated by the law is continuous and progressive, with no transition stage from the cradle to the grave, except that maturity takes up the regular self direction to which immaturity has been trained. We shall doubtless find, when we apprehend the law, that certain German thinkers—Kant, Herbart, Lotze, Froebel—are justified; that, as they say, it is necessary to believe in God; that, therefore, the knowledge of God is the principal knowledge, and the chief end of education. By one more character shall we be able to recognise this perfect law of educational liberty when it shall be made evident. It has been said that The best idea which we can form of absolute truth is that it is viable to meet every condition by which it can be tested. This we shall expect of our law—that it shall meet every test of experiment and every test of rational investigation.

Not having received the tables of our law, we fall back upon Froebel or upon Herbart; or, if we belong to another School, upon Locke or Spencer; but we are not satisfied. A discontent, is it a divine discontent? Is upon us; and assuredly we should hail a workable, effectual philosophy of education as a deliverance from much perplexity. Before this great deliverance comes to us it is probable that many tentative efforts will be put forth, having more or less of the characters of a philosophy; notably, having a central idea, a body of thought with various members working in vital harmony.

Such a theory of education, which need not be careful to call itself a system of psychology, must be in harmony with the thought movements of the age; must regard education, not as a shut off compartment, but as being as much a part of life as birth or growth, marriage or work; and it must leave the pupil attached to the world at many points of contact. It is true that educationalists are already eager to establish such contact in several directions, but their efforts rest upon an axiom here and an idea there, and there is no broad unifying basis of thought to support the whole.

Fools rush in where angels fear to tread; and the hope that there may be tentative efforts towards a philosophy of education, and that all of them will bring us nearer to the magnum opus, encourages me to launch one such attempt. The central thought, or rather body of thought, upon which I found, is the somewhat obvious fact that the child is a person with all the possibilities and powers included in personality. Some of members which develop from this nucleus have been exploited from time to time by educational thinkers, and exist vaguely in the general common sense, a notion here, another there. One thesis, which is, perhaps, new, that Education is the Science of Relations, appears to me to solve the question of curricula, as showing that the object of education is to put a child in living touch as much as may be of the life of Nature and of thought. Add to this one or two keys to self knowledge, and the educated youth goes forth with some idea of self management, with some pursuits, and many vital interests. My excuse for venturing to offer a solution, however tentative and passing, to the problem of education is twofold. For between thirty and forty years I have laboured without pause to establish a working and philosophic theory of education; and in the next place, each article of the educational faith I offer has been arrived at by inductive processes; and has, I think, been verified by a long and wide series of experiments. It is, however, with sincere diffidence that I

venture to offer the results of this long labour; because I know that in this field there are many labourers far more able and expert than I—the angels who fear to tread, so precarious is the footing!

But, if only pour encourager les autres, I append a short synopsis of education theory advanced in the volumes of the Home Education Series.

The treatment is not methodic, but incidental; here a little, there a little, as seemed to me most likely to meet the occasions of parents and teachers. I should add that in the course of a number of years the various essays have been prepared for the use of the Parents National Education Union in the hope that that Society might witness for a more or less coherent body of educational thought.

"The consequence of truth is great; therefore the judgment of it must not be negligent."—Whichcote

1. Children are born persons.

2. They are not born either good or bad, but with possibilities for either good or evil.

3. The principles of authority on the one hand and obedience on the other, are natural, necessary and fundamental; but

4. These principles are limited by the respect due to the personality of children, which must not be encroached upon, whether by fear or love, suggestion or influence, or undue play upon any one natural desire.

5. Therefore we are limited to three educational instruments—the atmosphere of environment, the discipline of habit, and the presentation of living ideas.

6. By the saying, Education is an atmosphere, it is not meant that a child should be isolated in what may be called a 'child environment,' especially adapted and prepared; but that we should take into account the educational value of his natural home atmosphere, both as regards persons and things, and should let him live freely among his proper conditions. It stultifies a child to bring down his world to a 'child's' level.

7. By Education is a discipline, is meant the discipline of habits formed definitely and thoughtfully, whether habits of mind or body. Physiologists tell us of the adaptation of brain structure to habitual lines of thought—i.e. to our habits.

8. In the saying that Education is a life, the need of intellectual and moral as well as of physical sustenance is implied. The mind feeds on ideas, and therefore children should have a generous curriculum.

9. But the mind is not a receptacle into which ideas must be dropped, each idea adding to an 'apperception mass' of its like, the theory upon which the Herbartian doctrine of interest rests.

10. On the contrary, a child's mind is no mere sac to hold ideas; but is rather, if the figure may be allowed, a spiritual organism, with an appetite for all knowledge. This is its proper diet, with which it is prepared to deal, and which it can digest and assimilate as the body does foodstuffs.

11. This difference is not a verbal quibble. The Herbartian doctrine lays the stress of education—the preparation of knowledge in enticing morsels, presented in due order—upon the teacher. Children taught upon this principle are in danger of receiving much teaching with little knowledge; and the teacher's axiom is, 'What a child learns matters less than how he learns it.'

12. But, believing that the normal child has powers of mind that fit him to deal with all knowledge proper to him, we must give him a full and generous curriculum; taking care, only, that the knowledge offered to him is vital—that is, the facts are not presented without their informing ideas. Out of this conception comes the principle that,

13. Education is the Science of Relations; that is, that a child has natural relations with a vast number of things and thoughts: so we must train him upon physical exercises, nature, handicrafts, science and art, and upon many living books; for we know that our business is, not to teach him all about anything, but to help him make valid, as many as may be of

'Those first born affinities,
'That fit our new existence to existing things.'

14. There are also two secrets of moral and intellectual self management which should be offered to children; these we may call the Way of the Will and the Way of the Reason.

15. The Way of the Will.—Children should be taught

(a) To distinguish between 'I want' and 'I will.'

(b) That the way to will effectively is to turn our thoughts from that which we desire but do not will.

(c) That the best way to turn our thoughts is to think of or do some quite different thing, entertaining or interesting.

(d) That, after a little rest in this way, the will returns to its work with new vigour.

(This adjunct of the will is familiar to us as diversion, whose office is to ease us for a time from will effort, that we may 'will' again with added power. The use of suggestion—even self suggestion—as an aid to the will, is to be deprecated, as tending to stultify and stereotype character. It would seem that spontaneity is a condition of development, and that human nature needs the discipline of failure as well as of success.)

16. The Way of the Reason.—We should teach children, too, not to 'lean' (too confidently) 'unto their own understanding,' because of the function of reason is, to give logical demonstration (a) of mathematical truth; and (b) of an initial idea, accepted by the will. In the former case reason is, perhaps, an infallible guide, but in the second it is not always a safe one, for whether that initial idea be right or wrong, reason will confirm it by irrefragable proofs.

17. Therefore children should be taught, as they become mature enough to understand such teaching that the chief responsibility which rests on them as persons is the acceptance or rejection of initial ideas. To help them in this choice we should give them principles of conduct and a wide range of the knowledge fitted for them.

These three principles (15, 16 and 17) should save children from some of the loose thinking and heedless action which cause most of us to live at a lower level than we need.

18. We should allow no separation to grow up between the intellectual and 'spiritual' life of children; but should teach them that the divine Spirit has constant access to their spirits, and is their continual helper in all the interests, duties and joys of life.

The 'Home Education' Series is so called from the title of the first volume, and not as dealing, wholly or principally with 'Home' as opposed to 'School" education.

Preface to the Third Edition

Our conduct is the outcome of our principles, even if these be only such as—'It does not matter'; 'What's the good?'

Every office implies the observance of certain fundamental principles in its discharge.

These two considerations lead me to think that a careful examination of the principles which naturally and necessarily underlie the office of parents may be of some little use to those who take their great work seriously.

Believing that the individuality of parents is a great possession for their children, and knowing that when an idea possesses the mind, ways of applying it suggest themselves, I have tried not to weight these pages with many directions, practical suggestions, and other such crutches, likely to interfere with the free relations of parent and child. Our greatness as a nation depends upon how far parents take liberal and enlightened views of their high office and of the means to discharge it which are placed in their hands.

The following essays have appeared in the Parents' Review, and were addressed, from time to time, to a body of parents who are making a practical study of the principles of education—the 'Parents' National Educational Union.' The Parents' Union exists to advance, with more or less method and with more or less steadfastness, a definite school of educational thought of which the two main principles are—the recognition of the physical basis of habit, i.e., of the material side of education; and of the inspiring and formative power of ideas, i.e., of the immaterial, or spiritual, side of education. These two guiding principles, covering as they do the whole field of human nature, should enable us to deal rationally with all the complex problems of education; and the object of the following essays is, not to give an exhaustive application of these principles—the British Museum itself would hardly contain all the volumes needful for such an undertaking—but to give an example or a suggestion, here and there, as to how such and such a habit may be formed, such and such a formative idea be implanted and fostered. The intention of the volume will account to the reader for the iteration of the same principles in various connections. The author ventures to hope that the following hints and suggestions will not prove the less practically useful to busy parents, because they rest on profound educational principles; and also, that they may prove in some degree, suggestive and inspiring to teachers.

Ambleside,
May 1904.

Chapter 1 The Family

'The family is the unit of the nation.'—F. D. Maurice.

Rousseau succeeded in awaking Parents—It is probable that no other educational thinker has succeeded in affecting parents so profoundly as did Rousseau. Emile is little read now, but how many current theories of the regimen proper for children have there their unsuspected source? Everybody knows—and his contemporaries knew it better than we—that Jean Jacques Rousseau had not enough sterling character to warrant him to pose as an authority on any subject, least of all on that of education. He sets himself down a poor thing, and we see no cause to reject the evidence of his Confessions. We are not carried away by the charm of his style; his 'forcible feebleness' does not dazzle us. No man can say beyond that which he is, and there is a want of grit in his philosophic theories that removes most of them from the category of available thought.

But Rousseau had the insight to perceive one of those patent truths which, somehow, it takes a genius discover; and, because truth is indeed prized above rubies, the perception of that truth gave him rank as a great teacher. Is Jean Jacques also among the prophets? people asked, and ask still; and that he had thousands of fervent disciples amongst the educated parents of Europe, together with the fact that teaching has filtered into many a secluded home our own day, is answer enough. Indeed, no other educationalist has had a tithe of the influence exerted by Rousseau. Under the spell of his teaching, people in the fashionable world, like that Russian Princess Galitzin, forsook society, and went off with their children to some quiet corner where they could devote every hour of the day, and every power they had, to the fulfilment of the duties which devolve on parents. Courtly mothers retired from the world, sometimes even left their husbands, to work hard at the classics, mathematics, sciences, that they might with their own lips instruct their children. 'What else am I for?' they asked; and the feeling spread that the bringing-up of their children was the one work of primary importance for men and women.

Whatever extravagance he had seen fit to advance, Rousseau would still have found a following, because he had chanced to touch a spring that opened many hearts. He was one of the few educationalists who made his appeal to the parental instincts. He did not say, 'We have no hope of the parents, let us work for the children!' Such are the faint-hearted and pessimistic things we say today. What he said was, in effect, "Fathers and mothers, this is your work, and you only can do it. It rests with you, parents of young children, to be the saviours of society unto a thousand generations. Nothing else matters. The avocations about which people weary themselves are as foolish child's play compared with this one serious business of bringing up our children in advance of ourselves."

People listened, as we have seen; the response to his teaching was such a letting out of the waters of parental enthusiasm as has never been known before nor since. And Rousseau, weak and little worthy, was a preacher of righteousness in this, that he turned the hearts of the fathers to the children, and so far made ready a people prepared for the Lord. But alas! having secured the foundation, he had little better than wood, hay, and stubble to offer to the builders.

Rousseau succeeded, as he deserved to succeed, in awakening many parents to the binding character, the vast range, the profound seriousness of parental obligations. He failed, and deserved to fail, as he offered his own crude conceits by way of an educational code. But his success is very cheering. He perceived that God placed the training of every child in the hands of two, a father and a mother; and the response to his teaching proved that, as the waters answer to the drawing of the moon, so do the hearts of parents rise to the idea of the great work committed to them.

Though it is true, no doubt, that every parent is conscious of unwritten laws, more or less definite and noble according to his own status, yet an attempt, however slight, to codify these laws may be interesting to parents.

The Family a Commune—'The family is the unit of the nation.' This pregnant saying suggests some aspects of the parents' calling. From time to time, in all ages of the world, communistic societies have arisen, sometimes for the sake of co-operation in a great work, social or religious, more recently by way of protest against inequalities of condition; but, in every case, the fundamental rule of such societies is, that the members shall have all things in common. We are apt to think, in our careless way, that such attempts at communistic association are foredoomed to failure. But that is not the case. In the United States, perhaps because hired labour is less easy to obtain than it is with us, they appear to have found a congenial soil, and there many well-regulated communistic bodies flourish. There are failures, too, many and disastrous, and it appears that these may usually be traced to one cause, a government enfeebled by the attempt to combine democratic and communistic principles; that is, to dwell together in a common life, while each does what is right in his own eyes. A communistic body can thrive only under a vigorous and absolute rule.

A favourite dream of socialism is—or was until the idea of collectivism obtained—that each State of Europe should be divided into an infinite number of small self-contained communes. Now, it sometimes happens that the thing we desire is already realised had we eyes to see. The family is, practically, a commune. In the family the undivided property is enjoyed by all the members in common, and in the family there is equality of social condition, with diversity of duties. In lands where patriarchal practices still obtain, the family merges into the tribe, and the head of the family is the chief of the tribe—a very absolute sovereign indeed. In our own country, families are usually small, parents and their immediate with the attendants and belongings which gather to a household, and, let it not be forgotten, form part of the family. The smallness of the family tends to obscure its character, and we see no force in the phrase at the head of this chapter; we do not perceive that, if the unit of the nation is the natural commune, the family; then, is the family pledged to carry on within itself all the functions of the State, with the delicacy, precision, and fulness of detail proper to work done on a small scale.

The Family must be Social—It by no means follows from this communistic view of the family that the domestic policy should be a policy of isolation; the contrary, it is not too much to say a nation is civilised in proportion as it is able to establish close and friendly relations with other nations; and that, not with one or two, but with many and, conversely, that a nation is barbarous in proportion to its isolation; and does not a family decline in intelligence and virtue when from generation to generation it 'keeps itself to itself'?

The Family must serve Neighbours—Again, it is probable that a nation is healthy in proportion as it has its own proper outlets, its colonies and dependencies, which it is ever solicitous to include in the national life. So of the nation in miniature, the family: the struggling families at 'the back,' the orphanage, the mission, the necessitous of our acquaintance, are they not for the sustenance of the family in the higher life?

The Family must serve the Nation—But it is not enough that the family commune maintain neighbourly relations with other such communes, and towards the stranger within the gates. The family is the unit of the nation; and the nation is an organic whole, a living body, built up, like the natural body, of an infinite number of living organisms. It is only as it contributes its quota towards the national life that the life of the family is complete. Public interests must be shared, public work taken up, the public welfare cherished—in a word, its integrity with the nation must be preserved, or the family ceases to be part of a living whole, and becomes positively injurious, as decayed tissue in the animal organism.

The Divine Order for the Family as regards other Nations—Nor are the interests of the family limited to those of the nation. As it is the part of the nation to maintain wider relations, to be in touch with all the world, to be ever in advance in the great march of human progress, so is this the attitude which is incumbent on each unit of the nation, each family, as an integral part of the whole. Here is the simple and natural realisation of the noble dream of Fraternity: each individual attached to a family by ties of love where not of blood; the families united in a federal bond to form the nation; the nations confederate in love and emulous in virtue, and all, nations and their families, playing their several parts as little children about the feet and under the smile of the Almighty Father. Here is the divine order which every family is called upon to fulfil: a little leaven leaveneth the whole lump, and, therefore, it matters infinitely that every family should realise the nature and the obligations of the family bond, for as water cannot rise above its source, neither can we live at a higher level than that of the conception we form of our place and use in life.

The Family should (a) learn Languages; (b) show Courtesy abroad.—Let us ask the question: Has this, of regarding all education and all civil and social relations from the standpoint of the family, any practical outcome? So much so, that perhaps there is hardly a problem of life for which it does not contain the solution. For example: What shall we teach our children? Is there one subject that claims our attention more than another? Yes, there is a subject or class of subjects which has an imperative moral claim upon us. It is the duty of the nation to maintain relations of brotherly kindness with other nations; therefore it is the duty of every family, as an integral part of the nation, to be able to hold brotherly speech with the families of other nations as opportunities arise; therefore to acquire the speech of neighbouring nations is not only to secure an inlet of knowledge and a means of culture, but is a duty of that higher morality (the morality of the family) which aims at universal brotherhood; therefore every family would do well to cultivate two languages besides the mother tongue, even in the nursery.

Again; a fair young Englishwoman was staying with her mother at a German Kurhaus. They were the only English people present, and probably forgot that the Germans are better linguists than we. The young lady sat through the long meals with her book, hardly interrupting her reading to eat, and addressing no more than one or two remarks to her mother, as 'I wonder what that mess is!' or, 'How much longer shall we have to sit with these tiresome people?' Had she remembered that no family can live to itself, that she and her mother represented England, were England for that little German community, she would have imitated the courteous greetings which the German ladies bestowed on their neighbours.

The Restoration of the Family—But we must leave further consideration of this great subject, and conclude with a striking passage from Mr. Morley's Appreciation of Emile. "Education slowly came to be thought of in connection with the family. The improvement of ideas upon education was only one phase of the great general movement towards the restoration of the family, which was so striking a spectacle in France after the middle of the century. Education now came to comprehend the whole system of the relations between parents and their children, from earliest infancy to maturity. The direction of such wider feeling about those relations tended strongly towards an increased closeness in them, more intimacy, and a more continuous suffusion of tenderness and long attachment."

His labours in this great cause, 'the restoration of the family,' give Rousseau a claim upon the gratitude and respect of mankind. It has proved a lasting, solid work. To this day, family relations in France are more gracious, more tender, more close and more inclusive, than they are with us. They are more expansive too, leading to generally benign and friendly behaviour; and so strong and satisfying is the family bond, that the young people find little necessity to 'fall in love.' The mother lays herself out for the friendship of her young daughters, who respond with entire loyalty and devotion; and, Zola notwithstanding, French maidens are wonderfully pure, simple, and sweet, because their affections are abundantly satisfied.

Possibly 'the restoration of the family' is a labour that invites us here in England, each within the radius of our own hearth; for there is little doubt that the family bond is more lax amongst us than it was two or three generations ago. Perhaps nowhere is family life of more idyllic loveliness than where we see it at its best in English homes. But the wise ever find some new thing to learn. Though a nation, as an individual, must act on the lines of its own character, and we are, on the whole, well content with our English homes, yet we might learn something from the inclusiveness of the French family, where mother-in-law and father-in-law, aunt and cousins, widow and spinster, are cherished; and a hundred small offices devised for dependants who would be in the way in an English home. The result is that the children have a wider range for the practice of the thousand sweet attentions and self-restraints which make home life lovely. No doubt the medal has its obverse; there is probably much in French home life which we should shrink from; nevertheless, it offers object-lessons which we should do well to study. Again, where family life is most beauteous with us, is not the family a little apt to become self-centred and self-sufficient, rather than to cultivate that expansiveness towards other families which is part of the family code of our neighbors?

Chapter 2 Parents As Rulers

The Family Government an Absolute Monarchy—Let us continue our consideration of the family as the nation in miniature, with the responsibilities, the rights, and the requirements of the nation. The parents represent the 'Government'; but, here, the government is ever an absolute monarchy, conditioned very loosely by the law of the land, but very closely by that law more or less of which every parent bears engraved on his conscience. Some attain the levels of high thinking, and come down from the Mount with beaming countenance and the tables of the law intact; others fail to reach the difficult heights, and are content with such fragments of the broken tables as they pick up below. But be his knowledge of the law little or much, no parent escapes the call to rule.

The Rule of Parents cannot be Deputed—Now, the first thing we ask for in a ruler is, 'Is he able to rule? Does he know how to maintain his authority?' A ruler who fails to govern is like an unjust judge, an impious priest, an ignorant teacher; that is, he fails in the essential attribute of his office. This is even more true in the family than in the State; the king may rule by deputy; but, here we see the exigeant nature of the parent's functions; he can have no deputy. Helpers he may have, but the moment he makes over his functions and authority to another, the rights of parenthood belong to that other, and not to him. Who does not know of the heart-burnings that arise when Anglo-Indian parents come home, to find their children's affections given to others, their duty owing to others; and they, the parents, sources of pleasure like the godmother of the fairy tale, but having no authority over their children? And all this, nobody's fault, for the guardians at home have done their best to keep the children loyal to the parents abroad.

Causes which lead to the Abdication of Parents—Here is indicated a rock upon which the heads of families sometimes make shipwreck. They regard parental authority as inherent in them, a property which may lie dormant, but is not to be separated from the state of parenthood. They may allow their children from infancy upwards to do what is right in their own eyes; and then, Lear turns and makes his plaint to the winds, and cries—

'sharper than a serpent's tooth it is
To have a thankless child!'

But Lear has been all the time divesting himself of the honour and authority that belong to him, and giving his rights to his children. Here he tells us why; the biting anguish is the 'thankless' child. He has been laying himself out for the thanks of his children. That they should think him a fond father has been more to him than the duty he owes them; and in proportion as he omits his duty are they oblivious of theirs. Possibly the unregulated love of approbation in devoted parents has more share in the undoing of families than any other single cause. A writer of today represents a mother as saying—

"'But you are not afraid of me, Bessie?"

'No indeed; who could be afraid of a dear, sweet, soft, little mother like you?'"

And such praise is sweet in the ears of many a fond mother hungering for the love and liking of her children, and not perceiving that words like these in the mouth of a child are as treasonable as words of defiance.

Authority is laid down at other shrines than that of popularity. Prospero describes himself as,

'all dedicate
To study, and the bettering of my mind'

And, meantime, the exercise of authority devolves upon Antonio; is it any wonder that the habit of authority fits the usurper like a glove, and that Prospero finds himself ousted from the office he failed to fill? Even so, the busy parent, occupied with many cares, awakes to find the authority he has failed to wield has dropped out of his hands; perhaps has been picked up by others less fit, and a daughter is given over to the charge of a neighbouring family, while father and mother hunt for rare prints.

In other cases, the love of an easy life tempts parents to let things take their course; the children are good children, and won't go far wrong, we are told; and very likely it is true. But however good the children be, the parents owe it to society to make them better than they are, and to bless the world with people, not merely good-natured and well-disposed, but good of set purpose and endeavour.

The love of ease, the love of favour, the claims of other work, are only some of the causes which lead to a result disastrous to society—the abdication of parent. When we come to consider the nature and uses of the parents' authority, we shall see that such abdication is as immoral as it is mischievous. Meantime, it is well worth while to notice that the causes which lead parents to resign the position of domestic rulers are resolvable into one—the office is too troublesome, too laborious. The temptation which assails parents is the same which has led many a crowned head to seek ease in the cloister—

'Uneasy lies the head that wears a crown,'

even if it be the natural crown of parenthood.

The Majesty of Parenthood—The apostolic counsel of 'diligence' in ruling throws light upon the nature and aim of authority; it is no longer a matter of personal honour and dignity; authority is for use and service, and the honour that goes with it is only for the better service of those under authority. The arbitrary parent, the exacting parent, who claims this and that of deference and duty because he is a parent, all for his own honour and glory, is more hopelessly in the wrong than the parent who practically abdicates; the majesty of parenthood is hedged round with observances only because it is good for the children to 'faithfully serve, honour, and humbly obey' their natural rulers. Only at home can children be trained in the chivalrous temper of 'proud submission and dignified obedience'; and if the parents do not inspire and foster deference, reverence, and loyalty, how shall these crowning graces of character thrive in a hard and emulous world?

It is perhaps a little difficult to maintain an attitude of authority in these democratic days, when even educationists counsel that children be treated on equal terms from the very beginning; but the children themselves come to our aid; the sweet humility and dependence natural to them fosters the gentle dignity, the soupçon of reserve, which is becoming in parents. It is not open to parents either to lay aside or to sink under the burden of the honour laid upon them; and, no doubt, we have all seen the fullest, freest flow of confidence, sympathy, and love between parent and child where the mother sits as a queen among her children and the father is honoured as a crowned head. The fact that there are two parents, each to lend honour to the other, yet free from restraint in each other's presence, makes it the easier to maintain the impalpable 'state' of parenthood. And the presence of the slight, sweet, undefined feeling of dignity in the household is the very first condition for the bringing-up of loyal, honourable men and women, capable of reverence and apt to win respect.

Children are a Public Trust and a Divine Trust—The foundation of parental authority lies in the fact that parents hold office as deputies; and that in a two-fold sense. In the first place, they are the immediate and personally appointed deputies of the Almighty King, the sole Ruler of men; they have not only to fulfil his counsels regarding the children, but to represent his Person; his parents are as God to the little child; and, yet more constraining thought, God is to him what his parents are; he has no power to conceive a greater and lovelier personality than that of the royal heads of his own home; he makes his first approach to the Infinite through them; they are measure for the highest; if the measure be easily his small compass, how shall he grow up with the reverent temper which is the condition of spiritual growth?

More; parents hold their children in trust for society. 'My own child' can only be true in a sense; the children are held as a public trust to be trained as is best for the welfare of the community and in this sense also the parents are persons in authority with the dignity of their office to support; and are even liable to deposition. The one State whose name has passed into a proverb, standing for a group of virtues which we have no other word to describe, is a State which practically deprived parents of the functions which they failed to fulfil to the furtherance of public virtue. No doubt the State reserves to itself virtually the power to bring up its own children in its own way, with the least possible co-operation of parents. Even today, a neighbouring nation has elected to charge itself with the training of its infants. So soon as they can crawl, or sooner, before ever they run or speak, they are to be brought to the 'Maternal School,' and carefully nurtured as with mother's milk, in the virtues proper for a citizen. The scheme is as yet but in the experimental stage, but will doubtless be carried through, because the nation in question has long ago discovered—and acted consistently upon the discovery—that what you would have the man become, you must train the child to be.

Perhaps such public deposition of parents is the last calamity that can befall a nation. These poor little ones are to grow up in a world where the name of God is not to be named; to grow up, too, without the training in filial duty and brotherly love and neighbourly kindness which falls to the children of all but the few unnatural parents. They may be returned to their parents at certain hours or after certain years; but once alienation has been set up, once the strongest and sweetest tie has been loosened and the parents have been publicly delivered from their duty, the desecration of the home is complete, and we shall have the spectacle of a people growing up orphaned almost from their birth. This is a new thing in the world's history, for even Lycurgus left the children to the parents for the first half-dozen years of life. Certain newspapers commend the example for our imitation, but God forbid that we should ever lose faith in the blessedness of family life. Parents who hold their children as at the same time a public trust and a divine trust, and who recognise the authority they hold as deputed authority, not to be trifled with, laid aside, or abused—such parents preserve for the nation the immunities of home, and safeguard the privileges of their order.

The Limitations and Scope of Parental Authority—Having seen that it does not rest with the parents to use, or to forego the use of, the authority they hold, let us examine the limitations and the scope of this authority. In the first place, it is to be maintained and exercised solely for the advantage of the children, whether in mind, body, or estate. And here is room for the nice discrimination, the delicate intuitions, with which parents are blessed. The mother who makes her growing-up daughter take the out-of-door exercise she needs, is acting within her powers. The father of quiet habits, who discourages society for his young people, is considering his own tastes, and not their needs, and is making unlawful use of his authority.

Again, the authority of parents, though the deference it begets remains to grace the relations of parents and child, is itself a provisional function, and is only successful as it encourages the autonomy, if we may call it so, of the child. A single decision made by the parents which the child is, or should be, capable of making for itself, is an encroachment on the rights of the child, and a transgression on the part of the parents.

Once more, the authority of parents rests on a secure foundation only as they keep well before the children that it is deputed authority; the child who knows that he is being brought up for the service of the nation, that his parents are acting under a Divine commission, will not turn out a rebellious son.

Further, though the emancipation of the children is gradual, they acquiring day by day more of the art and science of self-government, yet there comes a day when the parents' right to rule is over; there is nothing left for them but to abdicate gracefully, and leave their grown-up sons and daughters free agents, even though these still live at home; and although, in the eyes of their parents, they are not fit to be trusted with the ordering of themselves: if they fail in such self-ordering, whether as regards time, occupations, money, friends, most likely their parents are to blame for not having introduced them by degrees to the full liberty which is their right as men and women. Anyway, it is too late now to keep them in training; fit or unfit, they must hold the rudder for themselves.

As for the employment of authority, the highest art lies in ruling without seeming to do so. The law is a terror to evil-doers, but for the praise of them that do well; and in the family, as in the State, the best government is that in which peace and happiness, truth and justice, religion and piety, are maintained without the intervention of the law. Happy is the household that has few rules, and where 'Mother does not like this,' and, 'Father wishes that,' are all-constraining.

Chapter 3 Parents as Inspirers

Children must be born again into the Life of Intelligence

Parents owe a Second Birth to their Children—M. Adolf Monod claims that the child must owe his mother a second birth—the first into the natural, the second into the spiritual life of the intelligence—and moral sense. Had he not been writing of women and for women, no doubt he would have affirmed that the long travail of this second birth must be undergone equally by both parents. Do we ask how he arrives at this rather startling theory? He observes that great men have great mothers; mothers, that is, blest with an infinite capacity of taking pains with their work of bringing up children. He likens this labour to a second bearing which launches the child into a higher life; and as this higher life is a more blessed life, he contends that every child has a right to this birth into completer being at the hands of his parents. Did his conclusions rest solely upon the deductive methods he pursues, we might afford to let them pass, and trouble ourselves little about this second birth, which parents may and ofttimes do, withhold from their natural offspring. We, too, could bring forward our contrary instances of good parents with bad sons, and indifferent parents with earnest children; and, pat to our lips, would come the Cui bono? which absolves us from endeavour.

Science supports this Contention—Be a good mother to your son because great men have had good mothers, is inspiring, stimulating; but is not to be received as a final word. For an appeal of irresistible urgency, we look to natural science with her inductive methods; though we are still waiting her last word, what she has already said is law and gospel for the believing parent. The parable of Pandora's box is true today; and a woman may in her heedlessness let fly upon her offspring a thousand ills. But is there not also 'a glass of blessings standing by,' into which parents may dip, and bring forth for their children health and vigour, justice and mercy, truth and beauty?

'Surely,' it may be objected, 'every good and perfect gift comes from God above, and the human parent sins presumptuously who thinks to bestow gifts divine.' Now this lingering superstition has no part nor lot with true religion, but, on the contrary, brings upon it the scandal of many an ill-ordered home and ill-regulated family. When we perceive that God uses men and women, parents above all others, as vehicles for the transmission of his gifts, and that it is in the keeping of his law He is honoured—rather than in the attitude of the courtier waiting for exceptional favours—then we shall take the trouble to comprehend the law written not only upon tables of stone and rolls of parchment, but upon the fleshly tablets of the living organisms of the children; and, understanding the law, we shall see with thanksgiving and enlargement of heart in what natural ways God does indeed show mercy unto thousands of them that love Him and keep his commandments.

But his commandment is exceeding broad; becomes broader year by year with every revelation of science; and we had need gird up the loins of our mind to keep pace with this current revelation. We shall be at pains, too, to keep ourselves in that attitude of expectant attention wherein we shall be enabled to perceive the unity and continuity of this revelation with that of the written word of God. For perhaps it is only as we are able to receive the two, and harmonise the two in a willing and obedient heart, that we shall enter on the heritage of glad and holy living which is the will of God for us.

Processes and Methods of this Second Birth—Let us, for example, consider, in the light of current scientific thought, the processes and the methods of this second birth, which the child claims at the hands of his parents. 'Train up a child in the way he should go, and when he is old he will not depart from it,' is not only a pledge, but is a statement of a result arrived at by deductive processes. The writer had great opportunities for collecting data; he had watched many children grow up, and his experience taught him to divide them into two classes—the well-brought-up who turned out well; and the ill-brought-up who turned ill. No doubt, then, as now, there were startling exceptions, and—the exception proves the rule.

But, here as elsewhere, the promises and threatenings of Bible will bear the searching light of inductive methods. We may ask, Why should this be so?

and not content ourselves with a general answer, that this is natural and right; we may search until we discover that this result is inevitable, and no other result conceivable (except for alien influences), and our obedience will be in exact proportion to our perception of the inevitableness of the law.

Dr Maudsley on Heredity—The vast sum of what we understand by heredity is not to be taken into account in the consideration of this second birth; by the first natural birth it is, that "his father and mother, his grandfather and grandmother, are latent or declare themselves in the child; and it is on the lines thus laid down in his nature that his development will proceed. It is not by virtue of education so much as by virtue of inheritance that he is brave or timid, generous or selfish, prudent or reckless, boastful or modest, quick or placid in temper; the ground tone of his character is original in him, and it colours all the subsequently formed emotions and their sympathetic ideas... The influence of systematic culture upon anyone is no doubt great, but that which determines the limit, and even in some degree the nature, of the effects of culture, that which forms the foundations upon which all the modifications of art must rest, is the inherited nature."

Disposition and Character—If heredity means so much—if; as would seem at the first glance, the child comes into the world with his character ready-made—what remains for the parents to do but to enable him to work out his own salvation without let or hindrance of their making, upon the lines of his individuality? The strong naturalism, shall we call it, of our day, inclines us to take this view of the objects and limitations of education; and without doubt it is a gospel; it is the truth; but it is not the whole truth. The child brings with him into the world, not character, but disposition. He has tendencies which may need only to be strengthened, or, again, to be diverted or even repressed. His character—the efflorescence of the man wherein the fruit of his life is a-preparing—is original disposition, modified, directed, expanded by education; by circumstances; later, by self-control and self-culture; above all, by the supreme agency of the Holy Ghost, even where that agency is little suspected, and as little solicited.

How is this great work of character-making, the single effectual labour possible to human beings, to be carried on? We shall rest our inquiries on a physiological basis; the lowest, doubtless, but therefore the foundation of the rest. The first-floor chambers of the psychologist are pleasant places, but who would begin to build with the first floor? What would he rear it upon? Surely the arbitrary distinction between the grey matter of the brain and the 'mind' which plays upon it—even as the song upon the vocal chords of the singer—is more truly materialistic than is the recognition of the pregnant truth that the brain is the mere organ of the spiritual part; registering and effecting every movement of thought and feeling, whether conscious or unconscious, by appreciable molecular movement; and sustaining the infinite activities of mind by corresponding enormous activity and enormous waste; that it is the organ of mind which, under present conditions, is absolutely inseparable from, and indispensable to, the quickening spirit. Once we recognise that in the thinking of a thought there is as distinct motion set up in some tract of the brain as there is in the muscles of the hand employed in writing a sentence, we shall see that the behaviour of the grey nerve-substance of the cerebrum should afford the one possible key to certitude and system in our attempts at education, using the word in the most worthy sense—as its concern is the formation of character.

Having heard Dr Maudsley on the subject of heredity, let us hear him again on this other subject, which practically enables us to define the possibilities of education.

Dr Maudsley on the Structural Effects of 'Particular Life Experiences.'—"That which has existed with any completeness in consciousness leaves behind it, after its disappearance therefrom, in the mind or brain, a functional disposition to its reproduction or reappearance in consciousness at some future time. Of no mental act can we say that it is 'writ in water'; something remains from it, whereby its recurrence is facilitated. Every impression of sense upon the brain, every current of molecular activity from one to another part of the brain, every cerebral action which passes into muscular movement, leaves behind it some modification of the nerve elements concerned in its function, some after-effect, or, so to speak, memory of itself in them which renders its reproduction an easier matter, the more easy the more often it has been repeated, and makes it impossible to say that, however trivial, it shall not under some circumstances recur. Let the excitation take place in one of two nerve cells lying side by side, and between which there was not any original specific difference, there will be ever afterwards a difference between them. This physiological process, whatever be its nature, is the physical basis of memory, and it is the foundation of the development of all our mental functions.

"That modification which persists, or is retained, in structure after functions, has been differently described as a residuum, or relic, or trace, or disposition, or vestige; or again as potential, latent, or dormant idea. Not only definite ideas, but all affections of the nervous system, feelings of pleasure and pain, desire, and even its outward reactions, thus leave behind them their structural effects, and lay the foundation of modes of thought, feeling, and action. Particular talents are sometimes formed quite, or almost quite, involuntarily; and complex actions, which were first consciously performed by dint of great application, become automatic by repetition; ideas which were at first consciously associated, ultimately coalesce and call one another up without any consciousness, as we see in the quick perception or intuition of the man of large worldly experience; and feelings, once active, leave behind them their large unconscious residua, thus affecting the generation of the character, so that, apart from the original or inborn nature of the individual, contentment, melancholy, cowardice, bravery, and even moral feeling, are generated as the results of particular life-experiences."

Our Age has acquired a great Educational Charter—Here we have sketched out a magnificent educational charter. It is as well, perhaps, that we do not realise the extent of our liberties; if we did, it may be, such a fervour of educational enthusiasm would seize us that we should behave as did those early Christians who every day expected the coming of the Lord. How should a man have patience to buy and sell and get gain had it been revealed to him that he was able to paint the greatest picture ever painted? And we, with the enthralling vision of what our little child might become under our hands, how should we have patience for common toils? That science should have revealed the rationale of education in our day is possibly the Divine recognition that we have become more fit for the task, because we have come to an increasing sense of moral responsibility. What would it be for an immoral people to discern fully the possibilities of education? But how slow we are! how—

'Custom lies upon us with a weight,
Heavy as frost, and deep almost as life!'

A generation has passed away since these words of Dr Maudsley, and many of like force by other physiologists, were published to the world. We have purposely chosen words that have stood the test of time; for today a hundred eminent scientific men, at home and abroad, are proclaiming the same truths. Every scientist believes them! And we? We go on after our use and wont, as if nothing had been said; dropping, hour by hour, out of careless hands, seeds of corn and hemlock, of bramble and rose.

Let us run over the charter of our liberties, as Dr Maudsley has summed them up in the passage quoted above.

Some Articles of this Charter—We may lay the physical basis of memory: while the wide-eyed babe stretches his little person with aimless kickings on his rug, he is receiving unconsciously those first impressions which form his earliest memories; and we can order those memories for him: we can see that the earliest sights he sees are sights of order, neatness, beauty; that the sounds his ear drinks in are musical and soft, tender and joyous; that the baby's nostrils sniff only delicate purity and sweetness. These memories remain through life, engraved on the unthinking brain. As we shall see later, memories have a certain power of accretion—where there are some, others of a like kind gather, and all the life is ordered on the lines of these first pure and tender memories.

We may lay the foundation for the development of all the mental functions. Are there children who do not wonder, or revere, or care for fairy tales, or think wise child-thoughts? Perhaps there are not; but if there are, it is because the fertilising pollen grain has never been conveyed to the ovule waiting for it in the child's soul.

These are some of the things that—according to the citations we have given from Dr Maudsley's Physiology of Mind—his parents may settle for the future man, even in his early childhood:—

His definite ideas upon particular subjects, as, for example, his relations with other people.
His habits, of neatness or disorder, of punctuality, of moderation.
His general modes of thought, as affected by altruism or egoism.
His consequent modes of feeling and action.
His objects of thought—the small affairs of daily life, the natural world, the operations or the productions of the human mind, the ways of God with men.
His distinguishing talent—music, eloquence, invention.
His disposition or tone of character, as it shows itself in and affects his family and other close relations in life—reserved or frank, morose or genial, melancholy or cheerful, cowardly or brave.

Chapter 4 Parents As Inspirers

The Life of the Mind grows upon Ideas

'Sow an act, reap a habit; sow a habit, reap a character; a character, reap a destiny.'

Summary of the Preceeding Chapter—The last chapter closed with an imperfect summary of what we may call the educational functions of parents. We found that it rests with the parents of the child to settle for the future man his ways of thinking, behaving, feeling, acting; his disposition, his particular talent; the manner of things upon which his thoughts shall run. Who shall fix limitations to the power of parents? The destiny of the child is ruled by his parents, because they have the virgin soil all to themselves. The first sowing must be at their hands, or at the hands of such as they choose to depute.

Educational Conceptions of the Past—What do parents sow? Ideas. We cannot too soon recognize what is the sole educational seed in our hands, or how this seed is to be distributed. But how radically wrong is all our thought upon education! We cannot use the fit words because we do not think the right thing. We have perhaps got over the educational misconception of the tabula rasa. No one now looks on the child's white soul as a tablet prepared for the exercise of the educator's supreme art. But the conception which has succeeded this time-honoured heresy rests on the same false bases of the august office and the infallible wisdom of the educator. Here it is in its cruder form:

Pestalozzi's Theory—'Pestalozzi aimed more at harmoniously developing the faculties than at making use of them for the acquirement of knowledge; he sought to prepare the vase rather than to fill it.'

Froebel's Theory—In the hands of Froebel the figure gains in boldness and beauty; it is no longer a mere vase to be shaped under the potter's fingers; but a flower, say, a perfect rose, to be delicately and consciously and methodically moulded, petal by petal, curve and curl; for the perfume and living glory of the flower, why, these will come; do you your part and mould the several petals; wait, too, upon sunshine and shower, give space and place for your blossom to expand. And so we go to work with a touch to 'imagination' here, and to 'judgment' there; now, to the 'perceptive faculties,' now, to the 'conceptive'; in this, aiming at the moral, and in this, at the intellectual nature of the child; touching into being, petal by petal, the flower of a perfect life under the genial influences of sunny looks and happy moods.

The Kindergarten a Vital Conception—This reading of the meaning of education and of the work of the educator is very fascinating, and it calls forth singular zeal and self-devotion on the part of those gardeners whose plants are the children. Perhaps, indeed, this of the Kindergarten is the one vital conception of education we have had hitherto.

But Science is changing Front—But in these days of revolutionary thought, when all along the line—in geology and anthropology, chemistry, philology and biology—science is changing front, it is necessary that we should reconsider our conception of Education.

As to Heredity—We are taught, for example, that 'heredity' is by no means the simple and direct transmission, from parent or remote ancestor, to child of power and proclivity, virtue and defect; and we breathe freer, because we had begun to suspect that if this were so, it would mean to most of us an inheritance of exaggerated defects: imbecility, insanity, congenital disease—are they utterly removed from any one of us?

Is Education Formative?—So of education, we begin to ask, Is its work so purely formative as we thought? Is it directly formative at all? How much is there in this pleasing and easy doctrine, that the drawing forth and strengthening and directing of the several 'faculties' is education? Parents are very jealous over the individuality of their children; they mistrust the tendency to develop all on the same plan; and this instinctive jealousy is right; supposing that education really did consist in systematised efforts to draw out every power that is in us, why, we should all develop on the same lines, be as like as 'two peas,' and (should we not?) die of weariness of one another. Some of us have an uneasy sense that things are tending towards this deadly sameness; but, indeed, the fear is groundless.

We may believe that the personality, the individuality of each of us, is too dear to God, and too necessary to a complete humanity, to be left at the mercy of empirics. We are absolutely safe, and the tenderest child is fortified against a battering-ram of educational forces.

'Education' an inadequate Word—The problem of education is more complex than it seems at first sight, and well for us and the world that it is so. 'Education is a life'; you may stunt and starve and kill, or you may cherish and sustain; but the beating of the heart, the movement of the lungs, and the development of the faculties (are there any 'faculties'?) are only indirectly our care. The poverty of our thought on the subject of education is shown by the fact that we have no word which at all implies the sustaining of a life: education (e, out, and ducere, to lead, to draw) is very inadequate; it covers no more than those occasional gymnastics of the mind which correspond with those by which the limbs are trained: training (trahere) is almost synonymous, and upon these two words rests the misconception that the development and the exercise of the 'faculties' is the object of education (we must needs use the word for want of a better).

'Bringing-up'?—Our homely Saxon 'bringing-up' is nearer the truth, perhaps because of its very vagueness; any way, 'up' implies an aim, and 'bringing' an effort.

The happy phrase of Mr. Matthew Arnold [The writer has not been able to trace the phrase in question, but this attribution persists in her memory.]—'Education is an atmosphere, a discipline, a life'—is perhaps the most complete and adequate definition of education we possess. It is a great thing to have said it; and our wiser posterity may see in that 'profound and exquisite remark' the fruition of a lifetime of critical effort.

An Adequate Definition—Observe how it covers the question from the three conceivable points of view. Subjectively, in the child, education is a life; objectively, as affecting the child, education is a discipline; relatively, if we may introduce a third term, as regards the environment of the child, education is an atmosphere.

We shall examine each of these postulates later; at present we shall attempt no more than to clear the ground a little, with a view to the subject of this chapter, 'Parents as Inspirers'—not 'modellers,' but 'inspirers.'

Method, a Way to an End—It is only as we recognise our limitations that our work becomes effective: when we see definitely what we are to do, what we can do, and what we cannot do, we set to work with confidence and courage; we have an end in view, and we make our way intelligently towards that end, and a way to an end is method. It rests with parents not only to give their children birth into the life of intelligence and moral power, but to sustain the higher life which they have borne.

The Life of the Mind grows upon Ideas—Now that life, which we call education, receives only one kind of sustenance; it grows upon ideas. You may go through years of so-called 'education' without getting a single vital idea; and that is why many a well-fed body carries about a feeble, starved intelligence; and no society for the prevention of cruelty to children cries shame on the parents. Some years ago I heard of a girl of fifteen who had spent two years at a school without taking part in a single lesson, and this by the express desire of her mother, who wished all her time and all her pains to be given to 'fancy needlework.' This, no doubt, is a survival (not of the fittest), but it is possible to pass even the Universities Local Examinations with credit, without ever having experienced that vital stir which marks the inception of an idea; and, if we have succeeded in escaping this disturbing influence, why, we have 'finished our education' when we leave school; we shut up our books and our minds, and remain pigmies in the dark forest of our own dim world of thought and feeling.

What is an Idea?—A live thing of the mind, according to the older philosophers, from Plato to Bacon, from Bacon to Coleridge. We say of an idea that it strikes us, impresses us, seizes us, takes possession of us, rules us; and our common speech is, as usual, truer to fact than the conscious thought which it expresses. We do not in the least exaggerate in ascribing this sort of action and power to an idea. We form an ideal—a, so to speak, embodied idea—and our ideal exercises the very strongest formative influence upon us. Why do you devote yourself to this pursuit, that cause? 'Because twenty years ago such and such an idea struck me,' is the sort of history which might be given of every purposeful life—every life devoted to the working out of an idea. Now is it not marvellous that, recognising as we do the potency of ideas, both the word and the conception it covers enter so little into our thought of education? Coleridge brings the conception of an 'idea' within the sphere of the scientific thought of today; not as that thought is expressed in Psychology—a term which he himself launched upon the world with an apology for it as an insolens verbum, [We beg pardon for the use of this insolens verbum, but it is one of which our language stands in great need. (Method—S. T. Coleridge)] but in that science of the correlation and interaction of mind and brain, which is at present rather clumsily expressed in such terms as 'mental physiology' and 'psycho-physiology.'

In his Method Coleridge gives us the following illustration of the rise and progress of an idea:—

Rise and Progress of an Idea—"We can recall no incident of human history that impresses the imagination more deeply than the moment when Columbus, on an unknown ocean, first perceived that startling fact, the change of the magnetic needle. How many such instances occur in history when the ideas of Nature (presented to chosen minds by a Higher Power than Nature herself) suddenly unfold, it were, in prophetic succession, systematic views destined to produce the most important revolutions in the state of man! The clear spirit of Columbus was doubtless eminently methodical. He saw distinctly that great leading idea which authorised the poor pilot to become a 'promiser of kingdoms.'"

Genesis of an Idea—Notice the genesis of such ideas—'presented to chosen minds by a Higher Power than Nature'; notice how accurately this history of an idea fits in with what we know of the history of great inventions and discoveries, with that of the ideas which rule our own lives; and how well does it correspond with that key to the origin of 'practical' ideas which we find elsewhere:—

"Doth the plowman plow continually to . . . open and break the clods of his ground? When he hath made plain the face thereof, doth he not cast abroad the fitches, and scatter the cummin, and put in the wheat in rows, and the barley in the appointed place, and the spelt in the border thereof? For his God doth instruct him aright, and doth teach him . . .

"Bread corn is ground; for he will not ever be threshing it . . . This also cometh forth from the Lord of hosts, which is wonderful in counsel and excellent in wisdom." [Isaiah xxviii]

An Idea may exist as an 'Appetency.'—Ideas may invest as an atmosphere, rather than strike as a weapon. 'The idea may exist in a clear, distinct, definite form, as that of a circle in the mind of a geometrician; or it may be a mere instinct, a vague appetency towards something, . . . like the impulse which fills the young poet's eyes with tears, he knows not why: To excite this 'appetency towards something'—towards things lovely, honest, and or good report, is the earliest and most important ministry of the educator. How shall these indefinite ideas which manifest themselves in appetency be imparted? They are not to be given of set purpose, nor taken at set times. They are held in that thought-environment which surrounds the child as an atmosphere, which he breathes as his breath of life; and this atmosphere in which the child inspires his unconscious ideas of right living emanates from his parents. Every look of gentleness and tone of reverence, every word of kindness and act of help, passes into the thought-environment, the very atmosphere which the child breathes; he does not think of these things, may never think of them, but all his life long they excite that 'vague appetency towards something' out of which most of his actions spring. Oh, wonderful and dreadful presence of the little child in the midst!

A Child draws Inspiration from the Casual Life around him—That he should take direction and inspiration from all the casual life about him, should make our poor words and ways the starting-point from which, and in the direction of which, he develops—this is a thought which makes the best of us hold our breath. There is no way of escape for parents; they must needs be as 'inspirers' to their children, because about them hangs, as its atmosphere about a planet the thought-environment of the child, from which he derives those enduring ideas which express themselves as a life-long 'appetency' towards things sordid or things lovely, things earthly or divine.

Order and Progress of Definite Ideas—Let us now hear Coleridge on the subject of those definite ideas which are not inhaled as air; but conveyed as meat to the mind:—[Method—S. T. Coleridge.]

"From the first, or initiative idea, as from a seed, successive ideas germinate."

"Events and images, the lively and spirit-stirring machinery of the external world, are like light and air and moisture to the seed of the mind, which would else rot and perish"

"The paths in which we may pursue a methodical course are manifold, and at the head of each stands its peculiar and guiding idea."

"Those ideas are as regularly subordinate in dignity as the paths to which they point are various and eccentric in direction. The world has suffered much, in modern times, from a subversion of the natural and necessary order of Science . . . from summoning reason and faith to the bar of that limited physical experience to which, by the true laws or method, they owe no obedience."

"Progress follows the path of the idea from which it sets out; requiring, however, a constant wakefulness of mind to keep it within the due limits of its course. Hence the orbits of thought, so to speak, must differ among themselves as the initiative ideas differ."

Platonic Doctrine of Ideas—Have we not here the corollary to, and the explanation of that law of unconscious cerebration which results in our 'ways of thinking,' which shapes our character, rules our destiny? Thoughtful minds consider that the new light which biology is throwing upon the laws of mind is bringing to the front once more the Platonic doctrine, that "An idea is a distinguishable power, self-affirmed, and seen in its unity with the Eternal Essence."

Ideas alone matter in Education—The whole subject is profound, but as practical as it is profound. We must disabuse our minds of the theory that the functions of education are, in the main, gymnastic. In the early years of the child's life it makes, perhaps, little apparent difference whether his parents start with the notion that to educate is to fill a receptacle, inscribe a tablet, mould plastic matter, or nourish a life; but in the end we shall find that only those ideas which have fed his life are taken into the being of the child; all the rest is thrown away, or worse, is like sawdust in the system, an impediment and an injury to the vital processes.

How the Educational Formula should run—This is, perhaps, how the educational formula should run: Education is a life; that life is sustained on ideas; ideas are of spiritual origin; and,

'God has made us so'

that we get them chiefly as we convey them to one another. The duty of parents is to sustain a child's inner life with ideas as they sustain his body with food. The child is an eclectic; he may choose this or that; therefore, in the morning sow thy seed, and in the evening withhold not thy hand, for thou knowest not which shall prosper, whether this or that, or whether they both shall be alike good.

The child has affinities with evil as well as with good; therefore, hedge him about from any chance lodgment of evil ideas.

The initial idea begets subsequent ideas; therefore, take care that children get right primary ideas on the great relations and duties of life.

Every study, every line of thought, has its 'guiding idea'; therefore, the study of a child makes for living education in proportion as it is quickened by the guiding idea 'which stands at the head.'

'Infallible Reason'; what is it?—In a word, our much boasted 'infallible reason'—is it not the involuntary thought which follows the initial idea upon necessary logical lines? Given, the starting idea, and the conclusion may be predicated almost to a certainty. We get into the way of thinking such and such manner of thoughts, and of coming to such and such conclusions, ever further and further removed from the starting-point, but on the same lines. There is structural adaptation in the brain tissue to the manner of thoughts we think—a place and a way for them to run in. Thus we see how the destiny of a life is shaped in the nursery, by the reverent naming of the Divine Name; by the light scoff at holy things; by the thought of duty the little child gets who is made to finish conscientiously his little task; by the hardness of heart that comes to the child who hears the faults or sorrows of others spoken of lightly.

Chapter 5 Parents as Inspirers

The Things of the Spirit

Parents, Revealers of God to their Children—It is probable that parents as a class feel more than ever before the responsibility of their prophetic office. It is as revealers of God to their children that parents touch their highest limitations; perhaps it is only as they succeed in this part of their work that they fulfil the Divine intention in giving them children to bring up—in the nurture and admonition of the Lord.

How to Fortify them against Doubt—How to fortify the children against the doubts of which the air is full, is an anxious question. Three courses are open: to teach as we of an older generation have been taught, and to let them bide their time and their chance; to attempt to deal with the doubts and difficulties which have turned up, or are likely to turn up; or, to give children such hold upon vital truth, and at the same time such an outlook upon current thought, that they shall be landed on the safe side of the controversies of their day, open to truth, in however new a light presented, and safeguarded against mortal error.

Three Ways: the First Unfair—The first course is unfair to the young: when the attack comes, they find themselves at a disadvantage; they have nothing to reply; their pride is in arms; they jump to the conclusion that there is no defence possible of that which they have received as truth; had there been, would they not have been instructed to make it? They resent being made out in the wrong, being on the weaker side—so it seems to them,—being behind their times; and they go over without a struggle to the side of the most aggressive thinkers of their day.

'Evidences' are not Proof—Let us suppose that, on the other hand, they have been fortified with 'Christian evidences,' defended by bulwarks of sound dogmatic teaching. Religion without definite dogmatic teaching degenerates into sentiment, but dogma, as dogma, offers no defence against the assaults of unbelief. As for 'evidences,' the rôle of the Christian apologist is open to the imputation conveyed in the keen proverb, qui s'excuse, s'accuse ['he who excuses himself, accuses himself; a guilty conscience needs no accuser']; the truth by which we live must needs be self-evidenced, admitting of neither proof nor disproof. Children should be taught Bible history with every elucidation which modern research makes possible. But they should not be taught to think of the inscriptions on Assyrian monuments, for example, as proofs of the truth of the Bible records, but rather as illustrations of those records; though they are, and cannot but be, subsidiary proofs.

The Outlook upon Current Thought—Let us look at the third course: and first, as regards the outlook upon current thought. Contemporary opinion is the fetish of the young mind. Young people are eager to know what to think on all the serious questions of religion and life. They ask what is the opinion of this and that leading thinker of their day. They by no means confine themselves to such leaders of thought as their parents have elected to follow; on the contrary, the 'other side' of every question is the attractive side for them, and they do not choose to be behind the foremost in the race of thought.

Free-will In Thought—Now, that their young people should thus take to the water need not come upon parents as a surprise. The whole training from babyhood upward should be in view of this plunge. When the time comes, there is nothing to be done; openly it may be, secretly if the home rule is rigid, the young folk think their own thoughts, that is, they follow the leader they have elected; for they are truly modest and humble at heart, and do not yet venture to think for themselves; only they have transferred their allegiance. Nor is this transfer of allegiance to be resented by parents; we all claim this kind of 'suffrage' in our turn when we feel ourselves included in larger interests than those of the family.

Preparation—But there is much to be done beforehand, though nothing when the time comes. The notion that any contemporary authority is infallible may be steadily undermined from infancy onwards, though at some sacrifice or ease and glory to the parents. 'I don't know' must take the place of the vague wise-sounding answer, the random shot which children's pertinacious questionings too often provoke. And 'I don't know' should be followed by the effort to know, the research necessary to find out. Even then, the possibility of error in a 'printed book' must occasionally be faced. The results of this kind of training in the way of mental balance and repose are invaluable.

Reservation as regards Science—Another safeguard is in the attitude of reservation, shall we say? which it may be well to preserve towards 'science.' It is well that the enthusiasm of children should be kindled, that they should see how glorious it is to devote a lifetime to patient research, how great to find out a single secret of Nature, a key to many riddles. The heroes of science should be their heroes; the great names, especially of those who are amongst us, should be household words. But here, again, nice discrimination should be exercised; two points should be kept well to the front—the absolute silence of the oracle on all ultimate questions of origin and life, and the fact that, all along the line, scientific truth comes in like the tide, with steady advance, but with ebb and flow of every wavelet of truth; so much so, that, at the present moment, the teaching of the last twenty years is discredited in at least a dozen departments of science. Indeed, it would seem to be the part of wisdom to wait half a century before fitting the discovery of today into the general scheme of things. And this, not because the latest discovery is not absolutely true, but because we are not yet able so to adjust it—according to the 'science of the proportion of things'—that it shall be relatively true.

Knowledge is Progressive—But all this is surely beyond children? By no means; every walk should quicken their enthusiasm for the things of Nature, and their reverence for the priests of that temple; but occasion should be taken to mark the progressive advances of science, and the fact that the teaching of to-day may be the error of tomorrow, because new light may lead to new conclusions even from the facts already known. 'Until quite lately, geologists thought . . . they now think . . . but they may find reason to think otherwise in the Future.' To perceive that knowledge is progressive, and that the next 'find' may always alter the bearings of what went before; that we are waiting, and may have very long to wait, for the last word—; that science also is 'revelation,' though we are not yet able fully to interpret what we know; and that 'science' herself contains the promise of great impetus to the spiritual life—to perceive these things is to be able to rejoice in all truth and to wait for final certainty.

Children should learn some Laws of Thought—In another way we may endeavour to secure for the children that stability of mind which comes of self-knowledge. It is well that they should know, so early that they will seem to themselves always to have known, some of the laws of thought which govern their own minds. Let them know that, once an idea takes possession of them, it will pursue, so to speak, its own course, will establish its own place in the very substance of the brain, will draw its own train of ideas after it. One of the most fertile sources of youthful infidelity is the fact that thoughtful boys and girls are infinitely surprised when they come to notice the course of their own thoughts. They read a book or listen to talk with a tendency to what is to them 'free-thought.' And then, the 'fearful joy' of finding that their own thoughts begin with the thought they have heard, and go on and on to new and startling conclusions on the same lines! The mental stir of all this gives a delightful sense of power, and a sense of inevitableness and certainty too; for they do not intend or try to think this or that. It comes of itself; their reason, they believe, is acting independently of them, and how can they help assuming that what comes to them of itself with an air of absolute certainty, must of necessity be right?

To look at Thoughts as they come—But what if from childhood they had been warned, 'Take care of your thoughts, and the rest will take care of itself; let a thought in, and it will stay; will come again tomorrow and the next day, will make a place for itself in your brain, and will bring many other thoughts like itself. Your business is to look at the thoughts as they come, to keep out the wrong thoughts, and let in the right. See that ye enter not into temptation.' This sort of teaching is not so hard to understand as the rules for the English nominative, and is of infinitely more profit in the conduct of life. It is a great safeguard to know that your 'reason' is capable of proving any theory you allow yourself to entertain.

The Appeal of the Children—We have touched here only on the negative side of the parent's work as prophet, inspirer. There are perhaps few parents to whom the innocence of the babe in its mother's arms does not appeal with pathetic force. 'Open me the gates of righteousness, that I may go in unto them,' is the voice of the little unworldly child; and a wish, anyway, that he may be kept unspotted from the world, is breathed in every kiss of his mother, in the light of his father's eyes. But how ready we are to conclude that children cannot be expected to understand spiritual things. Our own grasp of the things of the Spirit is all too lax, and how can we expect that the child's feeble intelligence can apprehend the highest mysteries of our being? But here we are altogether wrong. It is with the advance of years that a materialistic temper settles upon us. But the children live in the light of the morning-land. The spirit-world has no mysteries for them; that parable and travesty of the spirit-world, the fairy-world, where all things are possible, is it not their favourite dwelling-place? And fairy-tales are so dear to children because their spirits fret against the hard and narrow limitations of time and place and substance; they cannot breathe freely in a material world. Think what the vision of God should be to the little child already peering wistfully through the bars of his prison-house. Not a far-off God, a cold abstraction, but a warm, breathing, spiritual Presence about his path and about his bed—a Presence in which he recognises protection and tenderness in darkness and danger, towards which he rushes as the timid child to hide his face in his mother's skirts.

'My Hiding-place.'—A friend tells me the following story of her girlhood. It so happened that extra lessons detained her at school until dark every day during the winter. She was extremely timid, but, with the unconscious reserve of youth, never thought of mentioning her fear of 'something.' Her way home lay by a river-side, a solitary path under trees—big trees, with masses of shadow. The black shadows, in which 'something' might lie hid—the swsh-sh, swsh-sh of the river, which might be whisperings or the rustle of garments filled her night by night with unabated terror. She fled along that river-side path with beating heart; but, quick as flying steps and beating heart, these words beat in her brain, over, and over, and over, the whole length of the way, evening by evening, winter after winter: 'Thou art my hiding-place; Thou shalt preserve me from trouble; Thou shalt compass me about with songs of deliverance.' Years after, when the woman might be supposed to have outgrown girlish terrors, she found herself again walking alone in the early darkness of a winter's evening under trees by the swsh-sh of another river. The old terror returned, and with it the old words came to her, and kept time the whole length of the way with her hasty steps. Such a place to hide him in should be the thought of God to every child.

The Mind of the Child is 'Good Ground.'—Their keen sensitiveness to spiritual influences is not due to ignorance on the part of the children. It is we, not they, who are in error. The whole tendency of modern biological thought is to confirm the teaching of the Bible: the ideas which quicken come from above; the mind of the little child is an open field, surely 'good ground,' where, morning by morning, the sower goes forth to sow, and the seed is the Word. All our teaching of children should be given reverently, with the humble sense that we are invited in this matter to co-operate with the Holy Spirit; but it should be given dutifully and diligently, with the awful sense that our co-operation would appear to be made a condition of the Divine action; that the Saviour of the world pleads with us to 'suffer the little children to come unto Me,' as if we had the power to hinder, as we know that we have.

Children suffer from a deep-seated discontent—This thought of the Saviour of the world implies another conception which we sometimes leave out of sight in dealing with children. Young faces are not always sunny and lovely; even the brightest children in the happiest circumstances have their clouded hours. We rightly put the cloud down to some little disorder, or to the weather, but these are the secondary causes which reveal a deep-seated discontent. Children have a sense of sin, acute in proportion to their sensitiveness. We are in danger of trusting too much to a rose-water treatment; we do not take children seriously enough; brought face to face with a child, we find he is a very real person, but in our educational theories we take him as 'something between a wax doll and an angel.' He sins; he is guilty of greediness, falsehood, malice, cruelty, a hundred faults that would be hateful in a grown-up person; we say he will know better by-and-by. He will never know better; he is keenly aware of his own odiousness. How many of us would say about our childhood, if we told the whole truth, 'Oh, I was an odious little thing!' and that not because we recollect our faults, but because we recollect our childish estimate of ourselves. Many a bright and merry child is odious in his own eyes; and the 'peace, peace, where there is no peace,' of fond parents and friends is little comfort. It is well that we 'ask for the old paths, where is the good way'; it is not well that, in the name of the old paths, we lead our children into blind alleys; nor that we let them follow the new into bewildering mazes.

Chapter 6 Parents as Inspirers

Primal Ideas Derived from Parents

'One of the little boys gazing upon the terrible desolation of the scene, so unlike in its savage and inhuman aspects anything be had ever seen at home, nestled close to his mother, and asked with bated breath, "Mither; is there a God here?"'—John Burroughs.

The Chief Thing we have to do—The last chapter introduced the thought of parents in their highest function—as revealers of God to their children. To bring the human race, family by family, child by child, out of the savage and inhuman desolation where He is not, into the light and warmth and comfort of the presence of God, is, no doubt, the chief thing we have to do in the world. And this individual work with each child, being the most momentous work in the world, is put into the hands of the wisest, most loving, disciplined, and divinely instructed of human beings. Be ye perfect as your Father is perfect, is the perfection of parenthood, perhaps to be attained in its fulness only through parenthood. There are mistaken parents, ignorant parents, a few indifferent parents; even, as one in a thousand, callous parents; but the good that is done upon the earth is done, under God, by parents, whether directly or indirectly.

Ideas of God fitting for Children—Parents who recognise that their great work is to be done by the instrumentality of the ideas they are able to introduce into the minds of their children, will take anxious thought as to those ideas of God which are most fitting for children, and as to how those ideas may best be conveyed. Let us consider an idea which is just now causing some stir in people's thoughts.

'We ought to work slowly up through the Human Side'—why not?—'We read some of the Old Testament history as "history of the Jews," and Job and Isaiah and the Psalms as poetry—and I am glad to say he is very fond of them; and parts of the Gospels in Greek, as the life and character of a hero. It is the greatest mistake to impose them upon children as authoritative and divine all at once. It at once diminishes their interest: we ought to work slowly up through the human side.' (Memoirs of Arthur Hamilton. Messrs Kegan Paul & Co.)

Here is a theory which commends itself to many persons because it is 'so reasonable.' But it goes upon the assumption that we are ruled by Reason, in infallible entity, which is certain, give it fair play, to bring us to just conclusions. Now the exercise of that function of the mind which we call reasoning—we must decline to speak of 'the Reason'—does indeed bring us to inevitable conclusions; the process is definite, the result convincing; but whether that result be right or wrong depends altogether upon the initial idea which, when we wish to discredit it, we call a prejudice; when we wish to exalt, we call an intuition, even an inspiration. It would be idle to illustrate this position; the whole history of Error is the history of the logical outcome of what we happily call misconceptions. The history of Persecution is the tale of how the inevitable conclusions arrived at by reasoning pass themselves off for truth. The Event of Calvary was due to no hasty, mad outburst of popular feeling. It was a triumph of reasoning: the inevitable issue of more than one logical sequence; the Crucifixion was not criminal, but altogether laudable, if that is right which is reasonable. And this is why the hearts of religious Jews were hardened and their understanding darkened; they were truly doing what was right in their own eyes. It is a marvellous thing to perceive the thoughts within us driving us forward to an inevitable conclusion, even against our will. How can that conclusion which presents itself to us in spite of ourselves fail to be right?

Logical Certainty and Moral Right—the Conscientious Jew and the Crucifixion—Let us place ourselves for one instant in the position of the logical and conscientious Jew. '"Jehovah" is a name of awe, unapproachable in thought or act except in ways Himself has specified. To attempt unlawful approach is to blaspheme. As Jehovah is infinitely great, presumptuous offence is infinitely heinous, is criminal, is the last crime as committed against Him who is the First. The blasphemer is worthy of death. This man makes himself equal with God, the unapproachable. He is a blasphemer, arrogant as Beelzebub. He is doubly worthy of death. To the people of the Jews is committed in trust the honoured Name; upon them it is incumbent to exterminate the blasphemer. The man must die.' Here is the secret of the virulent hatred which dogged steps of the blameless Life. These men were following the dictates of reason, and knew, so they would say, that they were doing right. Here we have the invincible ignorance which the Light of the world failed to illumine; and He,

'who knows us as we are,

Yet loves us better than He knows,'

offers for them the true plea, 'They know not what they do.' The steps of the argument are incontrovertible; the error lies in the initial idea—such a conception of Jehovah as made the conception of Christ inadmissible, impossible.

The Patriotic Jew and the Crucifixion—Thus reasoned the Jew upon whom his religion had the first claim. The patriotic Jew, to whom religion itself was subservient to the hopes of his nation, arrived by quite another chain of spontaneous arguments at the same Inevitable conclusion:—'The Jews are the chosen people. The first duty of a Jew is towards his nation. These are critical times. A great hope is before us, but we are in the grip of the Romans; they may crush out the national life before our hope is realised. Nothing must be done to alarm their suspicions. This Man? By all accounts He is harmless, perhaps righteous. But He stirs up the people. It is rumoured that they call Him King of the Jews. He must not be permitted to ruin the hopes of the nation. He must die. It is expedient that one man die for the people, and that the whole nation perish not.' Thus the Consummate crime that has been done upon the earth was done probably without any consciousness of criminality; on the contrary, with the acquittal of that spurious moral sense which supports with its approval all reasonable action. The Crucifixion was the logical and necessary outcome of ideas imbibed from their cradles by the persecuting Jews. So of every persecution; none is born of the occasion and the hour, but comes out of the habit of thought of a lifetime.

Primal Ideas derived from Parents—It is the primal impulse to habits of thought which children must owe to their parents; and, as a man's thought and action Godward, is

'The very pulse of the machine,'

the introduction of such primal ideas as shall impel the soul to God is the first duty and the highest privilege of parents. Whatever sin of unbelief a man is guilty of, are his parents wholly without blame?

First Approaches to God—Let us consider what is commonly done in the nursery in this respect. No sooner can the little being lisp than he is taught to kneel up in his mother's lap, and say 'God bless . . .' and then follows a list of the near and dear, and 'God bless . . . and make him a good boy, for Jesus' sake. Amen.' It is very touching and beautiful. I once peeped in at an open cottage door in a moorland village, and saw a little child in its nightgown kneeling in its mother's lap and saying its evening prayer. The spot has ever since remained to me a sort of shrine. There is no sight more touching and tender. By-and-by, so soon as he can speak the words,

'Gentle Jesus, meek and mild,'

is added to the little one's prayer, and later, 'Our Father.' Nothing could be more suitable and more beautiful than these morning and evening approaches to God, the little children brought to Him by their mothers. And most of us can 'think back' to the hallowing influence of these early prayers. But might not more be done? How many times a day does a mother lift up her heart to God as she goes in and out amongst her children, and they never know! 'Today I talked to them' (a boy and girl of four and five) 'about Rebekah at the well. They were very much interested, especially about Eliezer praying in his heart and the answer coming at once. They said, "How did he pray?" I said, "I often pray in my heart when you know nothing about it. Sometimes you begin to show a naughty spirit, and I pray for you in my heart, and almost directly I find the good spirit comes, and your faces show my prayer is answered." O. stroked my hand and said, "Dear mother, I shall think of that!" Boy looked thoughtful, but didn't speak; but when they were in bed I knelt down to pray for them before leaving them, and when I got up, Boy said, "Mother, God filled my heart with goodness while you prayed for us; and, mother, I will try to-morrow."'

Communing out loud before the Children—Is it possible that the mother could, when alone with her children, occasionally hold this communing out loud, so that the children might grow up in the sense of the presence of God? It would probably be difficult for many mothers to break down the barrier of spiritual reserve in the presence of even their own children. But, could it be done, would it not lead to glad and natural living in the recognised presence of God?

A Child's Gratitude—A mother, who remembered a little penny scent-bottle as an early joy of her own, took three such small bottles home to her three little girls. They got them next morning at the family breakfast, and enjoyed them all through the meal. Before it ended the mother was called away, and little M. was sitting rather solitary with her scent-bottle and the remains of her breakfast. And out of the pure well of the little girl's heart came this, intended for nobody's ear, 'Dear mother, you are too good!' Think of the joy of the mother who should overhear her little child murmuring over the first primrose of the year, 'Dear God, you are too good!' Children are so imitative, that if they hear their parents speak out continually their joys and fears, their thanks and wishes, they, too, will have many things to say.

Another point in this connection; the little German child hears and speaks many times a day of der liebe Gott; to be sure he addresses Him as 'Du,' but du is part of his every-day speech; the circle of the very dear and intimate is hedged in by the magic du. So with the little French child, whose thought and word are ever of le bon Dieu; he also says Tu, but that is how he speaks to those most endeared to him.

Archaic Forms in Children's Prayers—But the little English child is thrust out in the cold by an archaic mode of address, reverent in the ears of us older people, but forbidding, we may be sure, to the child. Then, for the Lord's Prayer, what a boon would be a truly reverent translation of it into the English of to-day! To us, who have learned to spell it out, the present form is dear, almost sacred; but we must not forget that it is after all only a translation, and is, perhaps, the most archaic piece of English in modern use: 'which art,' [Catholics say 'who art'] commonly rendered 'chart,' means nothing for a child. 'Hallowed' is the speech of a strange tongue to him—not much more to us; 'trespasses' is a semi-legal term, never likely to come into his every-day talk; and no explanation will make 'Thy' have the same force for him as 'your'. To make a child utter his prayers in a strange speech is to put up a barrier between him and his 'Almighty Lover.' Again, might we not venture to teach our children to say 'Dear God'? A parent, surely, can believe that no austerely reverential style can be so sweet in the Divine Father's ears as the appeal to 'dear God' for sympathy in joy and help in trouble, which flows naturally from the little child who is 'used to God.' Let children grow up aware of the constant, immediate, joy-giving, joy-taking Presence in the midst of them, and you may laugh at all assaults of 'infidelity,' which is foolishness to him who knows his God as—only far better than—he knows father or mother, wife or child.

'The Shout of a King.'—Let them grow up, too, with the shout of a King in their midst. There are, in this poor stuff we call human nature, founts of loyalty, worship, passionate devotion, glad service, which have, alas! to be unsealed in the earth-laden older heart, but only ask place to flow from the child's. There is no safeguard and no joy like that of being under orders, being possessed, controlled, continually in the service of One whom it is gladness to obey.

We lose sight of the fact in our modern civilisation, but a king, a leader, implies warfare, a foe, victory—possible defeat and disgrace. And this is the conception of life which cannot too soon be brought be before children.

The Fight of Christ against the Devil—"After thinking the matter over with some care, I resolved that I cannot do better than give you my view of what it was that the average boy carried away from our Rugby of half a century ago which stood him in the best stead—was of the highest value to him—in after life . . . I have been in some doubt as to what to put first and am by no means sure that the few who are left of my old schoolfellows would agree with me; but, speaking for myself, I think this was our most marked characteristic, the feeling that in school and close we were in training for a big fight—were, in fact, already engaged in it—a fight which would last all our lives, and try all our powers, physical, intellectual, and moral, to the utmost. I need not say that this fight was the world-old one of good with evil, of light and truth against darkness and sin, of Christ against the devil."

So said the author of Tom Brown's School Days [Thomas Hughes] in an address to Rugby School delivered on a recent Quinquagesima Sunday. This is plain speaking; education is only worthy of the name as it teaches this lesson; and it is a lesson which should be learnt in the home or ever the child sets foot in any other school of life. It is an insult to children to say they are too young to understand this for which we are sent into the world.

'Oh dear, it's very hard to do God's Work!'—A boy of five, a great-grandson of Dr Arnold, was sitting at the piano with his mother, choosing his Sunday hymn; he chose 'Thy will be done,' and, as his special favourite, the verse beginning 'Renew my will from day to day.' The choice of hymn and verse rather puzzled his mother, who had a further glimpse into the world of child-thought when the little fellow said wistfully, 'Oh, dear, it's very hard to do God's work!' The difference between doing and bearing was not plain to him, but the battle and struggle and strain of life already pressed on the spirit of the 'careless, happy child.' That an evil spiritual personality can get at their thoughts, and incite them to 'be naughty,' children learn all too soon and understand, perhaps, better than we do. Then, they are cross, 'naughty,' separate, sinful, needing to be healed as truly as the hoary sinner, and much more aware of their need, because the tender soul of the child, like an infant's skin, is fretted by spiritual soreness. 'It's very good of God to forgive me so often; I've been naughty so many times today,' said a sad little sinner of six, not at all because any one else had been at the pains to convince her of naughtiness. Even 'Pet Marjorie's' [Marjorie Fleming] buoyancy is not proof against this sad sense of shortcoming:—

'Yesterday I behaved extremely ill in God's most holy church, for I would never attend myself nor let Isabella attend, . . . and it was the very same Devil that tempted Job that tempted me, I am sure; but he resisted Satan, though he had boils and many other misfortunes which I have escaped.'—(At six!)

We must needs smile at the little 'crimes,' but we must not smile too much, and let children be depressed with much 'naughtiness' when they should live in the instant healing, in the dear Name, of the Saviour of the world.

Chapter 7 The Parent as Schoolmaster

'The Schoolmaster will make him sit up!'—'sit up,' that is, 'come when he's called,' apparently, for the remark concerned a young person who went on spinning his top with nonchalance, ignoring an intermittent stream of objurgations from his mother, whose view was that bedtime had arrived. Circumstances alter cases, but is it unheard of in higher ranks of life to trust to the schoolmaster to make a child 'sit up' after a good deal of mental and moral sprawling about at home?

Reasons why this task is left to the Schoolmaster—'Oh, he's a little fellow yet; he will know better by-and-by.'

'My view is, let children have a delightful childhood. Time enough for restraint and contradiction when they go to school.'

'We do not hold with punishing children; love your children, and let them alone, is our principle.'

'They will meet with hardness enough in the world. Childhood shall have no harsh memories for them.'

'School will break them in. Let them grow like young colts till the time comes to break them. All young things should be free to kick about.'

'What's bred in the bone must come out in the flesh. I do not care much for all this clipping and shaping of children. Destroys individuality.'

'When he's older, he will know better. Time cures many faults.'

And so on; we might fill pages with the wise things people say, who, for one excellent reason or another, prefer to leave it to the schoolmaster to make a child 'sit up.' And does the schoolmaster live up to his reputation? how far does he succeed with the child who comes to him with no self-management? His real and proud successes are with the children who have been trained to 'sit up' at home. His pleasure in such children is unbounded; the pains he takes with them unlimited; the successful careers he is able to launch them upon exceed the ambition of those most wildly ambitious of human beings (dare we say it?)—parents, quiet, sensible, matter-of-fact parents. But the schoolmaster takes little credit to himself for these happy results. Schoolmasters and schoolmistresses are modest people, though they are not always credited with their virtues.

His Successes are with Children who have been trained at Home—'You can do anything with So-and-so; his parents have turned him out so well.' Observe, the master takes little credit to himself (by no means so much as he deserves); and why? Experience makes fools wise; and what then of those who add experience to wisdom? 'People send us their cubs to lick into shape, and what can we do?' Now the answer to this query concerns parents rather closely: what and how much can the schoolmaster do to make the boy 'sit up' who has not been to the manner bred?

No suasion will make you 'sit up' if you are an oyster; no, nor even if you are a cod. You must have a backbone, and your backbone must have learned its work before sitting up is possible to you. No doubt the human oyster may grow a backbone, and the human cod may get into the way of sitting up, and some day, perhaps, we shall know of the heroic endeavours made by schoolmaster and mistress to prop up, and haul up, and draw up, and anyhow keep alert and sitting up, creatures whose way it is to sprawl. Sometimes the result is surprising; they sit up in a row with the rest and look all right; even when the props are removed they keep to the trick of sitting up for a while. The schoolmaster begins to rub his hands, and the parents say, 'I told you so. Didn't I always say Jack would come right in the end?' Wait a bit. The end is not yet.

The Habits of School Life are Mechanical—The habits of school, as of military life, are more or less mechanical. The early habits are vital; reversion to these takes place, and Jack sprawls as a man just as he sprawled as a child, only more so. Various social props keep him up; he has the wit to seem to 'sit up'; he is lovable and his life is respectable; and no one suspects that this easy-going Mr. John Brown is a failure: a man who had the elements of greatness in him, and might have been of use in the world had he been put under discipline from his infancy.

Mental 'sprawling' exemplified in 'Edward Waverley.'—Sprawling is an ugly word, but the attitude we are thinking of is by no means always inelegant. Scott gives a delightful illustration of one kind of mental sprawling in Waverly:—

"Edward Waverley's powers of apprehension were quick as almost to resemble intuition, and the care of his preceptor was to prevent him, as a sportsman would phrase it, from overrunning his game; that is, from acquiring his knowledge in a slight, flimsy, and inadequate manner. And here the instructor had to combat another propensity too often united with brilliancy of fancy and vivacity of talent—the indolence, namely, which can only be stirred by some strong motive of gratification, and which renounces study as soon as curiosity is gratified, the pleasure of conquering the first difficulties exhausted, the novelty of pursuit at an end." And the story goes on to show, without laborious pointing of the moral, how Waverly by name was wavering by nature, was ever the sport of circumstances because he had not learned in youth to direct his course. He blunders into many (most interesting) misadventures because he had failed to get, through his studies, the alertness of mind and the self-restraint which should make a man of him. Many pleasant things befall him, but not one of them, unless we except Rose Bradwardine's love—and when did woman study justice in the bestowal of her favours?—not one did he earn by his own wit or prowess; each advantage and success which came to him was the earnings of another man. The elder Waverley had not only fortune but force of character to make friends, so we are not made sad for the amiable young man for whom we must needs feel affection; he does nothing to carve out a way for himself; and he does everything to his own hindrance out of pure want of the power of self-direction, but his uncle has fortune and friends, and all ends well. For the sake, no doubt, of young persons less happily situated, and of parents who are not able to play the part of bountiful Providence to sons and daughters whom they have failed to fit for the conduct of their own lives, the great novelist takes care to point out that Edward Waverly's personal failure in life was the fault of his education. His abilities were even brilliant, but 'I ought' had waited upon 'I like' from his earliest days, and he had never learned to make himself do the thing he would.

Parents are apt to leave training in Self-compelling Power to the schoolmaster—Now it is this sort of 'bringing under' that parents are apt to leave to the schoolmaster. They do not give their children the discipline which results in self-compelling power; and by-and-by, when they make over the task to another, the time for training in the art of self-mastery has gone by, and a fine character is spoiled through indolence and wilfulness.

'But why will it not do to leave it to the schoolmaster to make a child "sit up"? It is natural for a child to be left free as a bird in matters of no moral significance. We would not let him tell lies, but if he hate his lessons, that may be Nature's way of showing he had better let them alone.'

We are not meant to grow up in a state of Nature—We must face the facts. We are not meant to grow up in a state of nature. There is something simple, conclusive, even idyllic, in the statement that So-and-so is 'natural.' What more would you have? Jean Jacques Rousseau preached the doctrine of natural education, and no reformer has had a greater following. 'It's human nature,' we say, when stormy Harry snatches his drum from Jack; when baby Marjorie, who is not two, screams for Susie's doll. So it is, and for that very reason it must be dealt with early. Even Marjorie must be taught better. 'I always finish teaching my children obedience before they are one year old,' said a wise mother; and any who know the nature of children, and the possibilities open to the educator, will say, Why not? Obedience in the first year, and all the virtues of the good life as the years go on; every year with its own definite work to show in the training of character. Is Edward a selfish child when his fifth birthday comes? The fact is noted in his parents' year-book, with the resolve that by his sixth birthday he shall, please God, be a generous child. Here, the reader who has not realised that to exercise discipline is one of the chief functions of parenthood, smiles and talks about 'human nature' with all the air of an unanswerable argument.

The First Function of the Parent is that of Disciple—But we live in a redeemed world, and one of the meanings which that unfathomable phrase bears is, that it is the duty of those who have the care of childhood to eradicate each vulgar and hateful trait, to plant and foster the fruits of that kingdom in the children who have been delivered from the kingdom of nature into the kingdom of grace; that is to say, all children born into this redeemed world. The parent who believes that the possibilities of virtuous training are unlimited will set to work with cheerful confidence, will forego the twaddle about 'Nature,' whether as lovely in itself or as an irresistible force, and will perceive that the first function of the parent is that function of discipline which is so cheerfully made over to the schoolmaster.

Education is a Discipline—Discipline does not mean a birch-rod, nor a corner, nor a slipper, nor a bed, nor any such last resort of the feeble. The sooner we cease to believe in merely penal suffering as part of the divine plan, the sooner will a spasmodic resort to the birch-rod die out in families. We do not say the rod is never useful; we do say it should never be necessary. The fact is, many of us do not believe in education, except as it means the acquirement of a certain amount of knowledge; but education which shall deal curatively and methodically with every flaw in character does not enter into our scheme of things possible. No less than this is what we mean when we say, Education is a Discipline. Where his parents fail, the poor soul has one further chance in the discipline of life; but we must remember that, while it is the nature of the child to submit to discipline, it is the nature of the undisciplined man to run his head in passionate wilfulness against the circumstances that are for his training; so that the parent who wilfully chooses to leave his child to be 'broken in' by the schoolmaster or by life leaves him to a fight in which all the odds are against him. The physique, the temper, the disposition, the career, the affections, the aspirations of a man are all, more or less, the outcome of the discipline his parents have brought him under, or of the lawlessness they have allowed.

Discipline is not Punishment—What is discipline? Look at the word; there is no hint of punishment in it. A disciple is a follower, and discipline is the state of the follower; the learner, imitator. Mothers and fathers do not well to forget that their children are, by the very order of Nature, their disciples. Now no man sets himself up for a following of disciples who does not wish to indoctrinate these with certain principles, or at the least, maxims, rules of life. So should the parent have at heart notions of life and duty which he labours without pause to instill into his children.

How Disciples are Lured—He who would draw disciples does not trust to force; but to these three things—to the attraction of his doctrine, to the persuasion of his presentation, to the enthusiasm of his disciples; so the parent has teachings of the perfect life which he knows how to present continually with winning force until the children are quickened with such zeal for virtue and holiness as carries them forward with leaps and bounds.

Steady Progress on a Careful Plan—Again, the teacher does not indoctrinate his pupils all at once, but here a little and there a little, steady progress on a careful plan; so the parent who would have his child a partaker of the Divine nature has a scheme, an ascending scale of virtues, in which he is diligent to practise his young disciple. He adds to the faith with which the child is so richly dowered, virtue; and to virtue, knowledge; and to knowledge, self-control. Having practised his child in self-control, he trains him in patience; and to patience he adds godliness; and to godliness, kindness; and to kindness, love. These, and such as these, wise parents cultivate as systematically and with as definite results as if they were teaching the 'three R's.'

But how? The answer covers so wide a field that we must leave it for another chapter. Only this here—every quality has its defect, every defect has its quality. Examine your child; he has qualities, he is generous;

Vol 2 pg 68

see to it that the lovable little fellow, who would give away his soul, is not also rash, impetuous, self-willed, passionate, 'nobody's enemy but his own.' It rests with parents to make low the high places and exalt the valleys, to make straight paths for the feet of their little son.

Chapter 8 The Culture Of Character

Parents as Trainers

"What get I from my father?
Lusty life and vigorous will:
What from my gentle mother?
Cheerful days and poet's skill,"

("Vom Vater hab' ich die Statur,
Des Lebens ernstes Führen;
Vom Mütterchen die Frohnatur,
Und Lustzu fabuliren.")

says Goethe; for poets, like the rest of us, are born, not made, and get the most of what they are from their parents. But it did not take poet or modern scientist to discover this; people have known it time out of mind. Like father, like child, they said, and were satisfied; for it was not the way in earlier days to thresh out the great facts of life.

How far does Heredity count?—Not so now; we talk about it and about it; call it heredity, and take it into count in our notions, at any rate, if not in our practice. Nobody writes a biography now without attempting to produce progenitors and early surroundings that shall account for his man or his woman. This fact of heredity is very much before the public, and by-and-by will have its bearing on the loose notions people hold about education. In this sort of way—'Harold is a bright little boy, but he hasn't the least power of attention.'

'Oh, I know he hasn't; but then, poor child, he can't help it! "What's bred in the bone," you know; and we are feather-brained on both sides of the house.'

Now the practical educational question of our day is just this, Can he help it? or, Can his parents help it? or, Must the child sit down for life with whatever twist he has inherited? The fact is, many of us, professional teachers, have been taking aim rather beside the mark; we talk as if the development of certain faculties were the chief object of education; and we point to our results, intellectual, moral, æsthetic, physical, with a—'See there, what culture can effect!'

For their Education, Children want chiefly Opportunity—But we forget that the child has inborn cravings after all we have given him. Just as the healthy child must have his dinner and his bed, so too does he crave for knowledge, perfection, beauty, power, society; and all he wants is opportunity. Give him opportunities of loving and learning, and he will love and learn, for 'tis his nature to.' Whoever has taken note of the sweet reasonableness, the quick intelligence, the bright imaginings of a child, will think the fuss we make about the right studies for developing these is like asking, How shall we get a hungry man to eat his dinner?

Many a man got his turn for natural science because as a boy he lived in the country, and had a chance to observe living things and their ways. Nobody took pains to develop his faculty; all he had was opportunity. If the boy's mind is crammed with other matters, he has no opportunity; and you may meet men of culture who have lived most of their lives in the country, and don't know a thrush from a blackbird. I know of a woman who has developed both a metaphysical and a literary turn, because as a girl of ten she was allowed to browse on old volumes of the Spectator, the most telling part of her education, she thinks.

An Experiment in Art Education—Again, I watched quite lately an extraordinary educational result of opportunity. A friend, interested in a Working Boys' Club, undertook to teach a class to model in clay. There was no selection made; the boys were mill-boys, taken as they came in, with no qualifications, except that, as their teacher said, they had not been spoilt—that is, they had not been taught to draw in the ordinary way. She gave them clay, a model, one or two modelling tools, and also, being an artist, the feeling of the object to be copied. After half a dozen lessons, the things they produced cannot be called less than works of art; and delightful it was to see the vigour and spirit they worked with, the artistic instinct which caught the sentiment of the object, as the creases made by a little foot which make a child's shoe a thing to kiss. This lady maintains that she only let out what was in the boys; but she did more—her own art enthusiasm forced out artistic effort. Even taking into account the enthusiasm of the teacher—I wish we might always count on that factor—this remains a fair case to prove our point, which is, give them opportunity and direction, and children will do the greater part of their own education, intellectual, æsthetic, even moral, by reason of the wonderfully balanced desires, powers, and affections which go to make up human nature. A cheerful doctrine this, which should help to swell the ranks of the unemployed. Outlets for their energies, a little direction, a little control, and then we may sit by with folded hands and see them do it. But, in fact, there are two things to be done: powers to be developed—where a little of our help goes a long way; and character to be formed—and here children are as clay in the hands of the potter, absolutely dependent on their parents.

But Character is an Achievement—Disposition, intellect, genius, come pretty much by nature; but character is an achievement, the one practical achievement possible to us for ourselves and for our children; and all real advance in family or individual is along the lines of character. Our great people are great simply by reason of their force of character. For this, more than for their literary successes, Carlyle and Johnson are great. Boswell's Life is, and perhaps deserves to be, more of a literary success than anything of his master's; but what figure does he make after all?

Two Ways of Preserving Sanity—Greatness and littleness belong to character, and life would be dull were we all cast in one mould; but how come we to differ? Surely by reason of our inherited qualities. It is hereditary tendencies which result in character. The man who is generous, obstinate, hot-tempered, devout, is so, on the whole, because that strain of character runs in his family. Some progenitor got a bent from his circumstances towards fault or virtue, and that bent will go on repeating itself to the end of the chapter. To save that single quality from the exaggeration which would destroy the balance of qualities we call sanity, two counter-forces are provided: marriage into alien families, and education.

The Development of Character the Main Work of Education—We come round now to the point we started from. If the development of character rather than of faculty is the main work of education, and if people are born, so to speak, ready-made, with all the elements of their after-character in them certain to be developed by time and circumstances, what is left for education to do?

Plausible Reasons for Doing Nothing—Very commonly, the vote is, do nothing; though there are three or four ways of arriving at that conclusion.

As, What's the good? The fathers have eaten sour grapes; the children's teeth must be set on edge. Tommy is obstinate as a little mule—but what would you have? So is his father. So have been all the Joneses, time out of mind; and Tommy's obstinacy is taken as a fact, not to be helped nor hindered.

Or, Mary is a butterfly of a child, never constant for five minutes to anything she has in hand. 'That child is just like me!' says her mother; 'but time will steady her.' Fanny, again, sings herself to sleep with the Sicilian Vesper Hymn (her nurse's lullaby) before she is able to speak. 'It's strange how an ear for music runs in our family!' is the comment, but no particular pains are taken to develop the talent.

Another child asks odd questions, is inclined to make little jokes about sacred things, to call his father 'Tom,' and, generally, to show a want of reverence. His parents are earnest-minded people—think with pain of the loose opinions of Uncle Harry, and decide on a policy of repression. 'Do as you're bid, and make no remarks,' becomes the child's rule of life, until he finds outlets little suspected at home.

In another case, common thought is much more on a level with the science of the day; there is a tendency to lung-trouble: the doctors undertake to deal with the tendency so long as the habit of delicacy is not set up. The necessary precautions are taken, and there is no reason why the child should not die at a good old age.

Once more—there are parents who are aware of the advances science has made in education, but doubt the lawfulness of looking to science for aid in the making of character. They see hereditary defects in their children, but set them down as of 'the natural fault and corruption of the nature of every man which naturally is engendered of the offspring of Adam.' This, they believe, it is not their part to remedy; that is, unless the boy's fault be of a disturbing kind—a violent temper, for example—when the mother thinks no harm to whip the offending Adam out of him.

But the Laws by which Body, Mind, and Moral Nature flourish have been Revealed by Science—But so surely as we believe the laws of the spiritual life to have been revealed to us, so, not less surely, though without the same sanctity, have been revealed the laws by which body, mind and moral nature flourish or decay. These it behoves us to make ourselves acquainted with; and the Christian parent who is shy of science, and prefers to bring up his children by the light of Nature when that of authoritative revelation fails, does so to his children's irreparable loss.

The Race is Advancing—If the race is advancing, it is along the lines of character; for each new generation inherits and adds to the best that has gone before it. We should have to-day the very flower and fruit that has been a-preparing through long lines of progenitors. Children have always been lovely, so far back as that day when a little child in the streets of Jerusalem was picked up and set in the midst to show of what sort are the princes in the Kingdom to come:

'In the Kingdom are the children—
You may read it in their eyes;
All the freedom of the Kingdom
In their careless humour lies.'

And what mother has not bowed before the princely heart of innocence in her own little child? But apart from this, of their glad living in the sunshine of the Divine countenance, surely our children are 'more so' than those of earlier days. Never before was a 'Jackanapes' written, or the 'Story of a Short Life' [both by Juliana Horatia Gatty Ewing] Shakespeare never made a child, nor Scott, hardly Dickens, often as he tried; either we are waking up to what is in them, or the children are indeed advancing in the van of the times, holding in light grasp the gains of the past, the possibilities of the future. It is the age of child-worship; and very lovely are the well-brought-up children of Christian and cultured parents. But alas, how many of us degrade the thing we love! Think of the multitude of innocents to be launched on the world, already mutilated, spiritually and morally, at the hands of doting parents.

The duty of cherishing certain Family Traits—The duteous father and mother, on the contrary, who discern any lovely family trait in one of their children, set themselves to nourish and cherish it as a gardener the peaches he means to show. We know how 'that kiss made me a painter,' that is, warmed into life whatever art faculty the child [Benjamin West] had. The choicer the plant, the gardener tells us, the greater the pains must he take with the rearing of it: and here is the secret of the loss and waste of some of the most beauteous and lovable natures the world has seen; they have not had the pains taken with their rearing that their delicate, sensitive organisations demanded. Think how Shelley was left to himself! We live in embarrassing days. It is well to cry, 'Give us light—more light and fuller'; but what if the new light discover to us a maze of obligations, intricate and tedious?

Distinctive Qualities ask for Culture—It is, at first sight, bewildering to perceive that for whatever distinctive quality, moral or intellectual, we discern in the children, special culture is demanded; but, after all, our obligation towards each such quality resolves itself into providing for it these four things: nourishment, exercise, change, and rest.

Four Conditions of Culture—Exercise—A child has a great turn for languages (his grandfather was the master of nine); the little fellow 'lisps in Latin,' learns his 'mensa' from his nurse, knows his declensions before he is five. What line is open to the mother who sees such an endowment in her child? First, let him use it; let him learn his declensions, and whatever else he takes to without the least sign of effort. Probably the Latin case-endings come as easily and pleasantly to his ear as does 'see-saw, Margery Daw,' to the ordinary child, though no doubt 'Margery Daw' is the wholesomer kind of thing.

Nourishment—Let him do just so much as he takes to of his own accord; but never urge, never applaud, never show him off. Next let words convey ideas as he is able to bear them. Buttercup, primrose, dandelion, magpie, each tells its own tale; Daisy is day's-eye, opening with the sun, and closing when he sets—

'That well by reason it men callen may
The daisie, or else the eye of day.'

Let him feel that the common words we use without a thought are beautiful, full of story and interest. It is a great thing that the child should get the ideas proper to the qualities inherent in him. An idea fitly put is taken in without effort, and, once in, ideas behave like living creatures—they feed, grow, and multiply.

Change—Next, provide him with some one delightful change of thought, that is, with work and ideas altogether apart from his bent for languages. Let him know, with friendly intimacy, the out-of-door objects that come in his way—the redstart, the rosechaffer, the ways of the caddis-worm, forest trees, field flowers—all natural objects, common and curious, near his home. No other knowledge is so delightful as this common acquaintance with natural objects.

Or again, some one remarks that all our great inventors have in their youth handled material—clay, wood, iron, brass, pigments. Let him work in material. To provide a child with delightful resources on lines opposed to his natural bent is the one way of keeping a quite sane mind in the presence of an absorbing pursuit.

Rest—At the same time, change of occupation is not rest: if a man ply a machine, now with his foot, and now with his hand, the foot or the hand rests, but the man does not. A game of romps (better, so far as mere rest goes, than games with laws and competitions), nonsense talk, a fairy tale, or to lie on his back in the sunshine, should rest the child, and of such as these he should have his fill.

Work and Waste of Brain Tissue Necessary—This, speaking broadly, is the rationale of the matter: just as actually as we sew or write through the instrumentality of the hand, so the child learns, thinks, feels, by means of a material organ—the very delicate nervous tissue of the cerebrum. Now this tissue is constantly and rapidly wearing away. The more it is used, whether in the way of mental effort or emotional excitement, the more it wears away. Happily, rapid new growth replaces the waste, wherefore work and consequent waste of tissue are necessary. But let the waste get ahead of the gain, and lasting mischief happens. Therefore never let the child's brain-work exceed his chances of reparation, whether such work come in the way of too hard lessons, or of the excitement attending childish dissipations. Another plea for abundant rest is that one thing at a time, and that done well, appears to be Nature's rule; and his hours of rest and play are the hours of the child's physical growth; witness the stunted appearance of children who are allowed to live in a whirl of small excitements.

A word more as to the necessity of change of thought for the child who has a distinct bent. The brain tissue not only wastes with work, but, so to speak, wastes locally. We all know how done up we are after giving our minds for a few hours or days to any one subject whether anxious or joyous: we are glad at last to escape from the engrossing thought, and find it a weariness when it returns upon us. It would appear that, set up the continuous working of certain ideas, and a certain tract of the brain substance is, as it were, worn out and weakened with the constant traffic in these ideas. And this is of more consequence when the ideas are moral than when they are merely intellectual. Hamlet's thoughts play continuously round a few distressing facts; he becomes morbid, not entirely sane; in a word, he is eccentric.

Danger of Eccentricity—Possibly, eccentricity is a danger against which the parents of well-descended children must be on the watch. These are born with strong tendencies to certain qualities and ways of thinking. Their bringing-up tends to accentuate their qualities; the balance between these and other qualities is lost, and they become eccentric persons. Mr. Matthew Arnold writes down the life and the work of a great poet as ineffectual; and this is often enough, the verdict passed upon the eccentric. Whatever force of genius and of character, whatever lovely moral traits they may have, the world will not take them as guides for good unless they do as others do in things lawful and expedient; and truly there is a broad margin for originality in declining to hunt with the hounds in things neither lawful nor expedient.

Causes of Oddity in Children—What is the mother's course who notices in her most promising child little traits of oddity? He does not care much for games, does not get on well with the rest, has some little den of his own where he ruminates—Poor little fellow! he wants a confidante badly; most likely he has tried nurse and brothers and sisters, to no purpose. If this go on, he will grow up with the idea that nobody wants him, nobody understands him, will take his slice of life and eat it (with a snarl) all by himself. But if his mother have tact enough to get at him, she will preserve for the world one of its saving characters. Depend upon it, there is something at work in the child—genius, humanity, poetry, ambition, pride of family; it is that he wants outlet and exercise for an inherited trait almost too big for his childish soul. Rosa Bonheur was observed to be a restless child whose little shoes of life were a misfit: lessons did not please her, and play did not please her; and her artist father hit on the notion of soothing the child's divine discontent by—apprenticing her to a needlewoman! Happily she broke her bonds, and we have her pictures. In the case of pride of birth, it is well that the child should be brought face to face and heart to heart with the 'great humility' of our Pattern. But that being done, this sense or family distinction is a wonderful lever to raise the little world of the child's nature. Noblesse oblige. He must needs add honour and not dishonour to a distinguished family. I know of a little boy who bears two distinguished family names—Browning-Newton, let us say. He goes to a preparatory school, where it is the custom to put the names of defaulters on the blackboard. By-and-by, his little brother went to school too, and the bigger boy's exordium was: 'We'll never let two such names as ours be stuck up on the blackboard!'

The Dreariness of a Motiveless Life—Amongst the immediate causes of eccentricity is the dreariness of daily living, the sense of which falls upon us all at times, and often with deadly weight upon the more finely strung and highly gifted. 'Oh, dear, I wish I was in Jupiter!' sighed a small urchin who had already used up this planet. It rests with parents to see that the dreariness of a motiveless life does not settle, sooner or later, on any one of their children. We are made with a yearning for the 'fearful joy' of passion; and if this do not come to is in lawful ways, we look for it in eccentric, or worse, in illegitimate courses. The mother, to whom her child is as an open book, must find a vent for the restless workings of his nature, the more apt to be troubled by—

'The burden of the mystery,
The heavy and the weary weight
Of all this unintelligible world'—

the more finely he is himself organised. Fill him with the enthusiasm of humanity. Whatever gifts he has, let them be cultivated as 'gifts for men.' "The thing best worth living for is to be of use," was well said lately by a thinker who has left us; and the child into whose notion of life that idea is fitted will not grow up to find time heavy on his hands. The life blessed with an enthusiasm will not be dull; but a weight must go into the opposite scale to balance even the noblest enthusiasm. As we have said, open for him some door of natural science, some way of mechanical skill; in a word, give the child an absorbing pursuit and a fascinating hobby, and you need not fear eccentric or unworthy developments.

We must Save our 'splendid Failures'—It seems well to dwell at length on this subject of eccentricity, because the world loses a great deal by its splendid failures, the beautiful human beings who, through one sort of eccentricity or another, become ineffectual for the raising of the rest of us.

Chapter 9 The Culture Of Character

The Treatment of Defects

The Ultimate Object of Education—Suppose the parent see that the formation of character is the ultimate object of education; see, too, that character is, in the rough, the inherited tendencies of the child, modified by his surroundings, but that character may be debased or ennobled by education; that it is the parents' part to distinguish the first faint budding of family traits; to greet every fine trait as the highest sort of family possession to be nourished and tended with care; to keep up at the same time the balance of qualities by bringing forward that which is of little account—the more so when they must deliver their child from eccentricity, pitfall to the original and forceful nature;—suppose they have taken all this into the role of their duties, there yet remains much for parents to do.

The Defects of our Qualities—We are open to what the French call the defects of our qualities; and as ill weeds grow apace, the defects of a fine character may well choke out the graces. A little maiden loves with the passion and devotion of a woman, but she is exacting of return, and jealous of intrusion, even with her mother. A boy is ambitious; he will be leader in the nursery, and his lead is wholesome for the rest; but there is the pugnacious little brother who will not 'follow my leader' and the two can hardly live in the same rooms; the able boy is a tyrant when his will is crossed. There is the timid, affectionate little maid who will even tell a fib to shield her sister; and there is the high-spirited girl who never lies, but who does, now and then, bully; and so on without end. What is the parents' part here? To magnify the quality; make the child feel that he or she has a virtue to guard—a family possession, and, at the same time, a gift from above. A little simple reasonable teaching may help; but let us beware of much talk. 'Have you quite finished, mother?' said a bright little girl of five in the most polite way in the world. She had listened long to her mother's sermonising, and had many things on hand. A wise word here and there may be of use, but much more may be done by carefully hindering each 'defect of its quality' from coming into play. Give the ill weeds no room to grow. Then, again, the defect may often be reclaimed and turned back to feed the quality itself. The ambitious boy's love of power may be worked into a desire to win by love his restive little brother. The passion of the loving girl may be made to include all whom her mother loves.

Children with Defects—There is another aspect of the subject of heredity and the duties it entails. As the child of long lineage may well inherit much of what was best in his ancestors—fine physique, clear intellect, high moral worth—so also he has his risks. As some one puts it, not all the women have been brave, nor all the men chaste. We know how the tendency to certain forms of disease runs in families; temper and temperament, moral and physical nature alike, may come down with a taint. An unhappy child may, by some odd of nature, appear to have left out the good and taken into him only the unworthy. What can parents do in such a case? They may, not reform him—perhaps that is beyond human skill and care, once he has become all that is possible to his nature—but transform him, so that the being he was calculated to become never develops at all; but another being comes to light blest with every grace of which he had only the defect. This brings us to a beneficent law of Nature, which underlies the whole subject of early training, and especially so this case of the child whose mother must bring him forth a second time into a life of beauty and harmony. To put it in an old form of words—the words of Thomas à Kempis—what seems to me the fundamental law of education is no more than this: 'Habit is driven out by habit.' People have always known that 'Use is second nature,' but the reason why, and the scope of the saying, these are discoveries of recent days.

A Malicious Child—A child has an odious custom, so constant, that it is his quality, will be character, if you let him alone; he is spiteful, he is sly, he is sullen. No one is to blame for it; it was born in him. What are you to do with such inveterate habit of nature? Just this; treat it as a bad habit, and set up the opposite good habit. Henry is more than mischievous; he is a malicious little boy. There are always tears in the nursery, because, with 'pinches, nips, and bobs,' he is making some child wretched. Even his pets are not safe; he has done his canary to death by poking at it with a stick through the bars of its cage; howls from his dog, screeches from his cat, betray him in some vicious trick. He makes fearful faces at his timid little sister; sets traps with string for the housemaid with her water-cans to fall over; there is no end to the malicious tricks, beyond the mere savagery of untrained boyhood, which come to his mother's ear. What is to be done? 'Oh, he will grow out of it!' say the more hopeful who pin their faith to time. But many an experienced mother will say, 'You can't cure him; what is in will out, and he will be a pest to society all his life.' Yet the child may be cured in a month if the mother will set herself to the task with both hands and of set purpose; at any rate, the cure may be well begun, and that is half done.

Special Treatment—Let the month of treatment be a deliciously happy month to him, be living all the time in the sunshine of his mother's smile. Let him not be left to himself to meditate or carry out ugly pranks. Let him feel himself always under a watchful, loving, and approving eye. Keep him happily occupied, well amused. All this, to break the old custom which is assuredly broken when a certain length of time goes by without its repetition. But one habit drives out another. Lay new lines in the old place. Open avenues of kindness for him. Let him enjoy, daily, hourly, the pleasure of pleasing. Get him into the way of making little plots for the pleasure of the rest—a plaything of his contriving, a dish of strawberries of his gathering, shadow rabbits to amuse the baby; take him on kind errands to poor neighbours, carrying and giving of his own. For a whole month the child's whole heart is flowing out in deeds and schemes and thoughts of lovingkindness, and the ingenuity which spent itself in malicious tricks becomes an acquisition to his family when his devices are benevolent. Yes; but where is his mother to get time in these encroaching days to put Henry under special treatment? She has other children and other duties, and simply cannot give herself up for a month or a week to one child. If the boy were ill, in danger, would she find time for him then? Would not other duties go to the wall, and leave her little son, for the time, her chief object in life?

Moral Ailments need Prompt Attention—Now here is a point all parents are not enough awake to—that serious mental and moral ailments require prompt purposeful, curative treatment, to which the parents must devote themselves for a short time, just as they would to a sick child. Neither punishing him nor letting him alone—the two lines of treatment most in favour—ever cured a child of any moral evil. If parents recognised the efficacy and the immediate effect of treatment, they would never allow the spread of ill weeds. For let this be borne in mind, whatever ugly quality disfigures the child, he is but as a garden overgrown with weeds: the more prolific the weeds, more fertile the soil; he has within him every possibility of beauty of life and character. Get rid of the weeds and foster the flowers. It is hardly too much to say that most of the failures in life or character made by man or woman are due to the happy-go-lucky philosophy of the parents. They say, 'The child is so young; he does not know any better; but all that will come right as he grows up.' Now, a fault of character left to itself can do no other than strengthen.

An objection may be raised to this counsel of short and determined curative treatment. The good results do not last, it is said; a week or two of neglect, and you lose the ground gained: Henry is as likely as ever to grow up of the 'tiger' order, a Steerforth or a Grandcourt. But here science comes to help us to cheerful certainty.

There is no more interesting subject of inquiry open just now than that of the interaction between the thoughts of the mind and the configuration of the brain. The fair conclusion appears to be that each is greatly the cause of the other; that the character of the persistent thoughts actually shapes the cerebrum, while on the configuration of this organ depends in turn the manner of thoughts we think.

Automatic Brain Action—Thought is, for the most part, automatic. We think, without intention or effort, as we have been accustomed to think, just as we walk or write without any conscious arrangement of muscles. Mozart could write an overture, laughing all the time at the little jokes his wife made to keep him awake; to be sure he had thought it out before, and there it was, ready to be written; but he did not consciously try for these musical thoughts, they simply came to him in proper succession. Coleridge thought 'Kubla Khan' in his sleep, and wrote it when he awoke; and, indeed, he might as well have been asleep all the time for all he had to do with the production of most of his thoughts.

'Over the buttons she falls asleep
And stitches them on in a dream,'

—is very possible and likely. For one thing which we consciously set ourselves to think about, a thousand words and acts come from us every day of their own accord; we don't think of them at all. But all the same, only a poet or a musician could thus give forth poetry or music, and it is the words and acts which come from us without conscious thought which afford the true measure of what we are. Perhaps this is why such serious weight is attached to our every 'idle word'—words spoken without intention or volition.

We are getting, by degrees, to Henry and his bad habits. Somehow or other, the nervous tissue of the cerebrum 'grows to' the thoughts that are allowed free course in the mind. How, science hardly ventures to guess as yet; but, for the sake of illustration, let us imagine that certain thoughts of the mind run to and fro in the nervous substance of the cerebrum until they have made a way there: busy traffic in same order of thoughts will always be kept up, there is the easy way for them to run in. Take a child with an inherited tendency to a resentful temper: he has begun to think resentful thoughts; finds them easy and gratifying; he goes on; evermore the ugly traffic becomes more easy and natural, and resentfulness is rapidly becoming himself, that trait in his character which people couple with his name.

One Custom Overcomes Another—But one custom overcomes another. The watchful mother sets up new tracks in other directions; and she sees to it, that while she is leading new thoughts through the new way, the old, deeply worn 'way of thinking' is quite disused. Now, the cerebrum is in a state of rapid waste and rapid growth. The new growth takes shape from the new thought: the old is lost in the steady waste, and the child is reformed, physically as well as morally and mentally. That the nervous tissue of the cerebrum should be thus the instrument of the mind need not surprise us when we think how the muscles and joints of the tumbler, the vocal organs of the singer, the finger-ends of the watchmaker; the palate of the tea-taster, grow to the uses they are steadily put to; and, much more, both in the case of the brain and all other organs, grow to the uses they are earliest put to.

This meets in a wonderful way the case of the parent who sets himself to cure a moral failing. He sets up the course of new thoughts, and hinders those of the past, until the new thoughts shall have become automatic and run of their own accord. All the time a sort of disintegration is going on in the place that held the disused thoughts; and here is the parent's advantage. If the boy return (as, from inherited tendency, he still may do) to his old habits of thought, behold, there is no more place for them in his physical being; to make a new place is a work of time, and in this work the parent can overtake and hinder him without much effort

A Material Register of Educational Efforts—Here, indeed, more than anywhere, 'Except the Lord build the house, they labour but in vain that build it'; but surely intelligent co-operation in this divine work is our bounden duty and service. The training of the will, the instruction of the conscience, and, so far as it lies with us, the development of the divine life in the child, are carried on simultaneously with this training in the habits of a good life; and these last will carry the child safely over the season of infirm will, immature conscience, until he is able to take, under direction from above, the conduct of his life, the moulding of his character, into his own hands.

It is a comfort to believe that there is even a material register of our educational labours being made in the very substance of the child's brain; and, certainly, here we have a note of warning as to the danger of letting ill ways alone in the hope that all will come right by-and-by.

Mother-love is not Sufficient for Child-training—Some parents may consider all this as heavy hearing; that even to 'think on these things' is enough to take the joy and spontaneousness out of their sweet relationship; and that, after all, parents' love and the grace of God should be sufficient for the bringing-up of children. No one can feel on this subject more sincere humility than those who have not the honour to be parents; the insight and love with which parents—mothers most so—are blest is a divine gift which fills lookers-on with reverence, even in many a cottage home; but we have only to observe how many fond parents make foolish children to be assured that something more is wanted. There are appointed ways, not always the old paths, but new ones, opened up step by step as we go. The labour of the mother who sets herself to understand her work is not increased, but infinitely lightened; as for life being made heavy with the thought of these things, once make them our own, and we act upon them as naturally as upon such knowledge—scientific also—as, loose your hold of a cup, and it falls. A little painstaking thought and effort in the first place, and all comes easy.

Chapter 10 Bible Lessons

Parents as Instructors in Religion

"The history of England is now reduced to a game at cards,—the problems of mathematics to puzzles and riddles. There wants but one step further, and the Creed and Ten Commandments may be taught in the same manner, without the necessity of the grave face, deliberate tone of recital, and devout attention hitherto exacted from the well-governed childhood of this realm"—Waverly.

Sunday Schools are Necessary—That parents should make over the religious education of their children to a Sunday School is, no doubt, as indefensible as if they sent them for their meals to a table maintained by the public bounty. We 'at home' plead not guilty to this particular count. Our Sunday Schools are used by those toil-worn and little-learned parents who are willing to accept at the hands of the more leisured classes this service of the religious teaching of their children. That is, the Sunday School is, at present, a necessary evil, an acknowledgment that there are parents so hard pressed that they are unable for their first duty. Here we have the theory of the Sunday School—the parents who can, teach their children at home on Sunday, and substitutes step in to act for those who can not.

But Educated Parents should Instruct their Children in Religion—An Australian Outcome of the Parents' Union—It is upon this delightful theory of the Sunday School that a clergyman (The Rev. E. Jackson, sometime of Sydney.) at Antipodes has taken action. Never does it appear to occur to him that the members of the upper and middle classes do not need to be definitely and regularly instructed in religion—'from a child.' His contention is, only that such children should not be taught at Sunday School, but at home, and by their parents; and the main object of his parochial 'Parents' Union' is to help parents in this work. These are some of the rules:—

1. The object of the Union shall be to unite, strengthen, and assist fathers and mothers in the discharge of their parental duties.
2. Members shall be pledged, by the fact of their joining, to supervise the education of their own children, and to urge the responsibility of the parental relationship upon other parents.
3. Lesson sketches shall be furnished monthly to each family in connection with the Union.
4. Members shall bring their children to the monthly catechising, and sit with them, etc., etc.

Probably the 'lesson-sketches' are to secure that the children do just such Bible-lessons at home with their parents on Sunday as they have hitherto done at the Sunday School with teachers.

It seems to be contemplated that parents of every class will undertake their proper duties in this matter, and that the Sunday School may be allowed to drop, the clergyman undertaking instead to ascertain, by means of catechising, that certain work is done month by month.

The scheme seems full of promise. Nothing should do more to strengthen the bonds of family life than that the children should learn religion at the lips of their parents; and to grow up in a Church which takes constant heed of you from baptism or infancy, until, we will not say confirmation, but through manhood and womanhood, until the end, should give the right tone to corporate life.

Parents are the Fit Instructors—No doubt we have parishes, and even whole denominations, in which the young people are taken hold of from first to last; but then it is by the clergy, teachers, class leaders, and so on; and all parents do not regard it as an unmixed blessing that the most serious part of their children's training should be undertaken by outsiders. The thing that seems most worthy of imitation in this Australian movement is, that parents themselves are recognised as the fit instructors of their children in the best things, and that they are led to acknowledge some responsibility to the Church with regard to the instruction they give.

Report of a Committee on the Religious Education of the Upper and Middle Classes—But do we manage these things so well 'at home' that we have no occasion to look about us for hints? It may be in the memories of some of us, that in May 1889 a Committee of the House of Laymen for the Province of Canterbury was appointed to examine into the religious education of the upper and middle classes. [See "Report of the Committee of the House of Laymen for the Province of Canterbury on the Duty of the church with regard to the Religious Education of the Upper and Middle Classes."—Nat. Soc. Depository, Westminster.] The Committee considered that they might obtain a good basis for their investigations by examining into the religious knowledge of boys entering school. They sent a paper of inquiries to sixty-two headmasters, most of whom sent replies; and from these replies the Committee were led to conclude that "for the most part, the standard of religious education attained by boys before going to school is far below what might be hoped or expected; and that even this standard, thus ascertained to be far low, is deteriorating; and further, that the chief cause of deterioration is considered to be the want of home-teaching and religion."

Why do Parents Neglect this Duty?—Here is matter of grave consideration for us all—for, though the investigation was conducted by Churchmen, it naturally covered boys of various denominations attending public and middle-class schools; the distinctive character of the religious education was the subject of separate inquiry. No doubt there are many beautiful exceptions; families brought up in quiet homes in the nurture and admonition of the Lord; but if it is, as some of us fear, a fact that there is a tendency among parents of the middle and upper classes to let the religious education of their children take care of itself, it is worth while to ask, What is the reason? and, What is the remedy? Many reasons are assigned for this alleged failure in parental duty—social claims, the restive temper of the young people and their impatience of religious teaching, and much else. But these reasons are inadequate. Parents are, on the whole, very much alive to their responsibilities; perhaps there has never been a generation more earnest and conscientious than the young parents of these days. All the same, these thoughtful young parents do not lay themselves out to teach their children religion, before all things.

Discredit thrown upon the Bible—The fact is, our religious life has suffered, and by-and-by our national character will suffer, through the discredit thrown upon the Bible by adverse critics. We rightly regard the Bible as the entire collection of our Sacred Books. We have absolutely nothing to teach but what we find written therein. But we no longer go to the Bible with the old confidence: our religion is fading into a sentiment not easy to impart; we wait until the young people shall conceive it for themselves. Meantime, we give them such æsthetic culture as should tend to develop those needs of the soul that find their satisfaction in worship. The whole superstructure of 'liberal' religious thought is miserably shaky and no wonder there is some shrinking from exposing it to the Ithuriel's spear of the definite and searching young mind. For we love this flimsy habitation we have builded. It bears a shadowy resemblance to the old home of our souls, and we cling to it with a tender sentiment which the younger generation might not understand.

'Miracles do not Happen.'—Are we then unhoused? Undoubtedly we are, upon one assumption—that assumption which it takes a brilliant novelist to put forth in its naked asperity—'Miracles do not happen.' The educated mind is more essentially logical than we are apt to suppose. Remove the keystone of miracle and the arch tumbles about our ears. The ostentatious veneration for the Person of Christ, as separated from the 'mythical' miraculous element, is, alas, no more than a spurious sentiment toward a self-evolved conception. Eliminate the 'miraculous' and the whole fabric of Christianity disappears; and not only so, what have we to do with that older revelation of 'the Lord, the Lord, a God full of compassion and gracious'? Do we say, Nay, we keep this; here is no miracle; and, of Christ have we not the inimitable Sermon on the Mount—sufficient claim on our allegiance? No, we have not; therein we are taught to pray, to consider lilies or the field, the fowls of the air, and to remember that the very hairs of our head are all numbered. Here we have the doctrine of the personal dealing, the particular providence of God, which is of the very essence of miracles. If 'miracles do not happen,' it is folly and presumption to expect in providence and invite in prayer the faintest disturbance of that course of events which is fixed by inevitable law. The educated mind is severely logical, though an effort of the will may keep us from following out our conclusions to the bitter end. What have we left? A God who, of necessity, can have no personal dealings with you or me, for such dealings would be of the nature of a miracle; a God, prayer to whom, in the face of such certainty, becomes blasphemous. How dare we approach the Highest with requests which, in the nature of things (as we conceive), it is impossible He should grant?

Our Conception of God depends upon Miracles—We cannot pray, and we cannot trust, may be yet we are not utterly godless; we can admire, adore, worship, in uttermost humility. But how? what shall we adore? The Divine Being can be known to us only through His attributes; He is a God of love and a God of justice; full of compassion and gracious, slow to anger, and plenteous in mercy. But these are attributes which can only be conceived of as in action, from Person to person. How be gracious and merciful unless to a being in need of grace and mercy? Grant that grace and mercy may modify the slightest circumstance in a man's existence, spiritual or temporal, and you grant the whole question of 'miracles'; grant, that is, that it is possible to God to act otherwise than through such inevitable laws as we are able to recognise. Refuse to concede 'the miraculous element' and the Shepherd of Israel has departed from our midst; we left are orphaned in a world undone.

Such and so great are the issues of that question of 'miracle' with which we are fond of dallying, with a smile here and a shrug there, and a special sneer for that story of the swine that ran violently down a steep place, because we know so much about the dim thoughts of the brute creation—living under our eyes indeed, but curiously out of our ken. Grant the possibility of miracles, that is, of the voluntary action of a Personal God, and who will venture to assign limits of less or more?

Natural Law and Miracles—How long halt we betwixt two opinions?—to the law and to the testimony. Let us boldly accept the alternative which Hume proposes, however superciliously. Let it be that 'No testimony is sufficient to establish a miracle unless the testimony be of such a kind that its falsehood would be more miraculous than the fact which it endeavours to establish.' Even so. We believe that Christ rose again the third day and ascended into heaven; or we accept the far more incredible hypothesis that 'there is no God'; or, anyway, the God of Revelation, in his adorable Personality, has ceased to be for us. There is no middle way. Natural law, as we understand it, has nothing to do with these issues; not that the Supreme abrogates his laws, but that our knowledge of 'natural law' is so agonisingly limited and superficial that we are incompetent to decide whether a break in the narrow circle within which our knowledge is hemmed, is or is not an opening into a wider circle, where what appears to us as an extraordinary exception does but exemplify the general rule. ["What are the laws of Nature? To me perhaps the rising of one from the dead were no violation of these laws, but a confirmation; even some far deeper law, now first penetrated into, and by spiritual force (even as the rest have been) brought to bear on us with its material force."—Carlyle]

We would not undervalue the solid fruits of Biblical criticism, even the most adverse. This should be a great gain in the spiritual life; that henceforth a miracle is accredited, not merely by the fact that it is recorded in the sacred history, but by its essential fitness with the divine Character; just as, if we may reverently compare human things with divine, we say of a friend, 'Oh, he would never do that!' or, 'That is just like him.' Tried by this test, how unostentatious, simple, meekly serviceable are the miracles of Christ; how utterly divine it is

"To have all power, and be as having none!"

How fit are the Miracles of Christ—The mind which is saturated with the Gospel story in all its sweet reasonableness, which has absorbed the more confused and broken rays wherein the Light of the World is manifested in Old Testament story, will perhaps be the least tempted to the disloyalty of 'honest doubt'; for disloyalty to the most close and sacred of all relationships it is, though we must freely concede that such doubt is the infirmity of noble minds. Believing that faith comes by hearing, and hearing by the word of God, that the man is established in the Christian faith according as the child has been instructed, the question of questions for us, is, how to secure that the children shall be well grounded in the Scriptures by their parents, and shall pursue the study with intelligence, reverence, and delight.

Chapter 11 Faith and Duty (Reviews) Parents as Teachers of Morals

Laws of Nature and Ways of Man—Education, properly understood, is the science of life and every attempt to formulate this science is to be hailed with interest, and with a measure of gratitude in proportion to its success. Thinking minds everywhere are engaged in furnishing their quota towards this great work in one or another of its aspects, physical, social, religious. We see at once the importance of every attempt to solve scientific and social problems, or problems of faith as helping us to understand those 'laws of nature' and 'ways of men,' the love and dutiful attitude or the will towards which, Mr. Huxley considers to be the sole practical outcome of education. Let us consider three important works [The Moral Instruction of Children. 6s. By Felix Adler. Published by Edward Arnold. Education from a National Standpoint. By Alfred Fouillée. Translated and edited by W.J. Greenstreet, M.A. Published by Edward Arnold Faith. Eleven Sermons with a Preface, by Rev. H.C. Beeching. Published by Percival and Co.] on these lines. One deals with the problems of 'secular' morality from an American point of view; the second with the whole problem of national education from a French and 'scientific' standpoint. The third is not professedly an educational work. It deals with 'the ways of men,' but with the ways of men as they are concerned with the ways and will of God. That is, it deals with the deep-seated springs out of which are the issues of life. As the true educationalist works from within outwards, he will probably find much aid in a work whose outlook on life is from the standpoint of faith.

The Moral Instruction of Children—Mr. Felix Adler; in The Moral Instruction of Children undertakes a by no means easy task in setting himself to solve the problem of unsectarian moral instruction. He brings unusual qualifications to the work—a wide outlook, philosophic training, and that catholic love of literature and knowledge of books which is essential to the teacher of morals. The work before us is one which should find a place on the educated parent's bookshelves, not perhaps to be swallowed whole as a 'complete guide;' but to be studied with careful attention and some freedom of choice as to which counsel of perfection is worthy to be acted upon, and which other counsel may be rejected as not fitting in with that scheme of educational thought which the parent has already made for himself. Mr. Adler is most seriously handicapped at the outset. He writes for American schools; in which the first condition of moral instruction is that it must be unsectarian. This he, rightly or wrongly, interprets to exclude all theistic teaching whatever; that is to say, the child he writes for has no sanctions beyond those he finds in his own breast. For example: 'It is the business of the moral instructor in the school to deliver to his pupils the subject matter of morality, but not to deal with the sanctions of it. He says to the pupil, "Thou shalt not lie." He takes it for granted that the pupil feels the force of this commandment and acknowledges that he ought to yield obedience to it. For my part, I should suspect of quibbling and dishonest intention any boy or girl who would ask me, Why ought I not to lie? I should hold up before such a child the ought in all its awful majesty. The right to reason about these matters cannot be conceded until after the mind has attained a certain maturity.'

No Infallible Sense of 'Ought'—Where does the ought get its awful Majesty? That there is in the human breast an infallible sense of 'ought' is an error prolific of much evil. It is a common idea today that is right to do that which the doer holds to be right; as it is popularly expressed, a man does all can be expected of him when he acts according his 'light.' Now, a very slight acquaintance with history demonstrates that every persecution and most outrages, from the Inquisition to Thuggee, are the outcome of that same majesty of 'ought' as it makes its voice heard in the breast or an individual or of a community. To attempt to treat of morals without dealing with the sanctions of morality is to work from the circumference instead of from the center.

Moses, Moses, und immer Moses! says a German pedagogue of the modern school, who writes in hot disdain of the old-school system, in which ten or twelve, and in some of the German States, fifteen or sixteen hours a week were devoted to Bible-teaching. We in England, and they in America, rebel against the Bible as a class-book. Educationalists say there is so much else to be learned, that this prolonged study of sacred literature is a grievous waste of time and many religious persons, on the other hand, object on the ground that it is not good to make the Bible common as a class-book.

The Bible a Classic Literature—But it is singular that so few educationalists recongnise that the Bible is not a single book, but a classic literature of wonderful beauty and interest; that, apart from its Divine sanctions and religious teaching, from all that we understand by 'Revelation,' the Bible, as a mere instrument of education, is, at the very least, as valuable as the classics of Greece or Rome. Here is poetry, the rhythm of which soothes even the jaded brain past taking pleasure in any other. Here is history, based on such broad, clear lines, such dealing of slow and sure and even-handed justice to the nations, such stories of national sins and national repentences, that the student realises, as from no other history, the solidarity of the race, the brotherhood, and, if we may call it so, the individuality of the nations. Here is philosophy which of all the philosophies which have been propounded, is alone adequate to the interpretation of human life. We say not a word here of that which is the raison d'être of the Bible, its teaching of religion, its revelation of God to man; but to urge only one point more, all the literatures of the world put together utterly fail to give us a system of ethics, in precept and example, motive and sanction, complete as that to which we have been born as our common inheritance in the Bible.

The Bible Tabooed In Education—For 1700 years, roughly speaking, the Bible has been the school-book of modern Europe; its teaching, conveyed directly or indirectly, more or less pure, has been the basis upon which the whole superstructure of not only religious but ethical and, to some extent, literary training rested. Now, the Bible as a lesson-book is tabooed; and educationalists are called upon to produce what shall take its place in the origination of ideas and the formation of character. This is the task to which Mr. Adler sets himself; and that he is at all successful is obviously due to the fact that his own mind is impregnated with the Bible lore and the sacred law which he does not feel himself at liberty to propound to his students. But this prepossession of the author's makes his work very helpful and suggestive to parents who desire to take the Bible as the groundwork and the sanction of that moral teaching which they are glad to supplement from other sources.

May we recommend the following suggestion to Parents?—

A Mother's Diary—"Parents and teachers should endeavour to answer such questions as these: When do the first stirrings of the moral sense appear in the child? How do they manifest themselves? What are the emotional and the intellectual equipments of the child at different periods, and how do these respond with its moral outfit? At what time does conscience enter on the scene? To what acts or omissions does the child apply the terms right or wrong? If observations of this kind were made with care and duly recorded, the science of education would have at its disposal a considerable quantity of material from which, no doubt, valuable generalisations might be deduced. Every mother, especially, should keep a diary in which to note the successive phases of her child's physical, mental, and moral growth, with particular attention to the moral; so that parents may be enabled to make a timely forecast of their children's character; to foster in them every germ of good, and by prompt precautions to suppress, or at least restrain, what is bad."

Fairy Tales and how to Use them—We are glad to find that Mr. Adler reinstates fairy tales. He says, justly, that much of the selfishness of the world is due, not to actual hard-heartedness, but to a lack of imaginative power; and adds: 'I hold that something, nay, much, has been gained if a child has learned to take the wishes out of its heart, as it were, and to project them on the screen of fancy.' The German Märchen hold the first place in his regard. He says they represent the childhood of mankind, and it is for this reason that they never cease to appeal to children.

"But how shall we handle these Märchen? and what method shall we employ in putting them to account for our special purpose? My first counsel is, Tell the story. Do not give it to the child to read. The child, as it listens to the Märchen, looks up with wide-opened eyes to the face of the person who tells the story, and thrills responsive to the touch of the earlier life of the race, which thus falls upon its own." That is, our author feels, and rightly so, that traditions should be orally delivered. This is well worth noting. His second counsel is equally important. 'Do not,' he says, 'take the moral plum out of the fairy-tale pudding, but let the child enjoy it as a whole . . . Treat the moral element as an incident, emphasise it indeed, but incidentally. Pluck it as a wayside flower.'

Mr. Felix Adler's third counsel is, to eliminate from the stories whatever is merely superstitious, merely a relic of ancient animism, and, again, whatever is objectionable on moral grounds. In this connection he discusses the vexed question of how far we should acquaint children with the existence of evil in the world.

'My own view,' he says, 'is that we should speak in the child's hearing only of those lesser forms of evil, physical or moral, with which it is already acquainted.' On this ground he would rule out all the cruel stepmother stories, the unnatural father stories, and so on; though probably most of us would make an exception in favour of Cinderella, and its charming German rendering Aschenbrödel. I am inclined to think, too, that fairy tales suffer in vigour and charm when they are prepared for the children; and that Wordsworth is right in considering that the very knowledge of evil conveyed in fairy tales under a certain glamour is of use in saving children from painful and injurious shocks in real life.

Fables—Fables, according to our author, should in the basis of moral instruction at the second stage; probably when children emerge from the nursery., We have all grown up on 'Aesop's Fables'; and 'The Dog in the Manger,' 'King Log,' 'The Frog and the Stork,' have passed into the current coinage of our thought. But it is interesting to be reminded that the so-called Aesop's fables are infinitely older than the famous Greek story-teller, and are, for the most part, of Asiatic origin. We are reminded that it is important to keep this origin of the fable before us, and to exercise discrimination in our choice of those which we use to convey moral ideas to our children.

Such fables as 'The Oak and the Reed,' 'The Brazen and the Earthen Pot,' 'The Kite and the Wolf,' Mr. Adler would reject, as breathing of Eastern subserviency and fear. But possibly for the very reason that the British backbone is little disposed to bow before man or circumstances, the lessons of life culled by peoples of other, habits and other thoughts may be quite specially useful to the English child. Any way, we should lose some of the most charming fables if we cut out all that savours of the wisdom of the East. The fables Mr. Felix Adler specially commends are those which hold up virtue for our praise or evil for our censure; such as Cowardice, the fable of 'The Stag and the Fawn'; Vanity, 'The Peacock and the Crane'; Greediness, 'The Dog and the Shadow.'

"In the third part of our primary course," he says, "we shall use selected stories from the classical literature of the Hebrews, and later on from that of Greece, particularly the 'Odyssey' and the 'Iliad.'"

Bible Stories—Here we begin to be at issue with our author. We should not present Bible stories as carrying only the same moral sanction as the myths of ancient Greece; neither should we defer their introduction until the child has gone through a moral course of fairy tales and a moral course of fables. He should not be able to recall a time before the sweet stories of old filled his imagination; he should have heard the voice of the Lord God in the garden in the cool of the evening; should have been an awed spectator where the angels ascended and descended upon Jacob's stony pillow; should have followed Christ through the cornfield on the Sabbath-day, and sat in the rows of the hungry multitudes—so long ago that such sacred scenes form the unconscious background of his thoughts. All things are possible to the little child, and the touch of the spiritual upon our material world, the difficult problems, the bard sayings, which are offence, in the Bible sense of the word, to elders, present no difficulties to the child's all-embracing faith. We should not say, far otherwise, that every Bible story is fit for children because it is a Bible story; neither would we analyse too carefully, nor draw hard and fast lines to distinguish what we should call history from that of which it may be said, 'Without a parable spake He not unto them.'

The child is not an exegetical student. The moral teaching, the spiritual revelations, the lovely imagery of the Bible, are the things with which he is concerned, and of these he cannot have too much. As Adler says: 'The narrative of the Bible is saturated with the moral spirit, the moral issues are everywhere to the forefront. Duty, guilt and its punishment, the conflict of conscience with inclination, are the leading themes. The Hebrew people seem to have been endowed with what may be called a moral genius and especially did they emphasise the filial and paternal duties. Now, it is precisely these duties that must be impressed on young children.'

Let us see how our author would use the Bible narratives. We have only space for a fragmentary sentence here and there: 'Once upon a time there two children, Adam and Eve. Adam was a fine and noble-looking lad.' . . . 'It was so warm that the children never needed to go indoors.' . . . 'And the snake kept on whispering, "Just take one bite of it; nobody sees you."' . . . 'You, Adam, must learn to labour, and you, Eve, to be patient and self-denying for others,' etc.

We leave it to our readers to decide whether 'treatment' improves the Bible narrative, or whether this is the sort of thing to lay hold of a child's imagination.

The Cadence of Biblical phraseology Charming to a Child—Mr. Ruskin tells us that his incomparable style is due entirely to his early familiarity with the Bible classics. It is a mistake to translate Bible stories into slipshod English, even when the narrator keeps close to the facts of the narrative. The rhythm and cadence of Biblical phraseology is as charming to a child as to his elders, if not more so. Read your Bible story to the child, bit by bit; get him to tell you in his own words (keeping as close as he can to the Bible words) what you have read, and then, if you like, talk about it; but not much. Above all, do not let us attempt a 'practical commentary on every verse in Genesis' to quote the title of a work lately published. Two points it seems worth while to dwell upon here.

Shall the stories of Miracles be used in Moral Instruction?—Is it advisable to tell children the stories of the Bible miracles in an age when the possibility of miracles is so hotly discussed? In the first place, all that the most advanced scientists have to urge against 'miracles' is that precisely such phenomena have not come under their personal notice; but they, before all people, are open to admit that nothing is impossible and that no experience is final. In the second place, as for the moral and spiritual instruction which the story of the miracle affords, it is immaterial whether, in the particular case in question, a historical fact is recorded; or whether, in this case also, it is true that 'without a parable spake He not unto them.' It is the essential, not the historical, truth of the story which matters to the child. As for the latter, he is a bold critic, and well in advance of the scientific knowledge of the day, who ventures to 'This is possible; that other is impossible.'

Should the whole Bible be put into the hands of a Child?—The second point worthy of our attention in regard to Bible-teaching is, Is the Bible to be taken whole and undivided, or to be dealt out to children as they are able to bear it? There are recitals in the Bible which we certainly should not put into the hands of children in any other book. We should do well to ask ourselves gravely, if we have any warrant for supposing that our children will be shielded from the suggestions of evil which we deliberately lay before them; or if there is any Divine law requiring that the whole Bible—which is not only the Word of God, but is also a collection of the legal, literary, historical, poetical, philosophical, ethical, and polemical writings of a nation—should be placed altogether and at once in the hands of a curious child, as soon as he is able to read? When will our superstitious reverence for the mere letter of the Scriptures allow to break the Bible up, to be read, as all other literature is, in separate books; and, for the children anyway, those passages 'expunged' which are not fit for their reading; and even those which are perfectly uninteresting, as, for example, long genealogies? How delightful it would be that each birthday should bring with it a gift of a new book of the Bible, progressing in difficulty from year to year, beautifully bound and illustrated, and printed in clear, inviting type and on good paper. One can imagine the Christian child collecting his library of sacred books with great joy and interest, and making a diligent and delighted study of the volume for the year in its appointed time. The next best thing, perhaps, is to read bit by bit (of the Old Testament anyway) to the children, as beautifully as may be, requiring them to tell the story, after listening, as nearly in the Bible words as they can.

Moral Rules from the Pentateuch—But to return to Mr. Adler: here is a valuable suggestion: "Children should be taught to observe moral pictures before any attempt is made to deduce moral principles. But certain simple rules should be given to the very young—must, indeed, be given them—for their guidance. Now, in the legislation ascribed to Moses we find a number of rules fit for children, and a collection of these rules might be made for the use of schools, such as: Ye shall not lie; ye shall not deceive one another; ye shall take no bribe; thou shalt not go about as a tale-bearer among thy fellows;" and so on—a very useful collection of sixteen rules by way of specimen.

Further on we read: "The story of David's life is replete with dramatic interest. It may be arranged in a series of pictures. First picture, David and Goliath—i.e., skill pitted against brute strength, or the deserved punishment of a bully." Conceive the barren, common, self-complete and self-complacent product of 'moral' teaching on this level!

The 'Odyssey' and the 'Iliad.'—In his treatment of the 'Odyssey' and the 'Iliad," Mr. Adler makes some good points: 'My father, anxious that I should become a good man, made me learn all the poems of Homer,' Xenophon makes one of his characters say; and here we have suggestive lines as to how the great epics may be used for example of life and instruction in manners.

What so inspiring as the story of Ulysses to the boy in search of adventures? And what greater stimulus to courage, prudence, presence of mind, than in the escapes of the hero? 'Ulysses is the type of sagacity as well as of bravery; his mind teems with inventions.' The ethical elements of the 'Odyssey' are said to be conjugal affection, filial conduct (Telemachus), presence of mind, and veneration shown to grandparents (Laertes). Friendly relations with dependents might have been added, as illustrated by the lovely story of the nurse Eurycleia recognising Ulysses when his wife sat by with stony face. Friendship, again, in the story of Achilles' grief for Patroclus.

The initial Weakness of 'secular Morality.'—Mr. Adler treats the Homeric stories with more grace and sympathy, and with less ruthless violation, than he metes out to those of the Bible; but here again we trace the initial weakness of 'secular' morality. The 'Odyssey' and the 'Iliad' are religious poems or they are nothing. The whole motive is religious; every incident is supernaturally directed. The heroic inspiration is entirely wanting if we fail to bear in mind that the characters do and suffer with superlative courage and fortitude, only because they willed to do and suffer, in all things, the will of the gods. The acquiescence of the will with that which they guessed, however darkly, of the divine will, is the truly inspiring quality of the Homeric heroes; and here, as much as in the teaching of Bible morality, 'secular' ethics are at fault.

Lessons on Duty—The third section of Mr. Adler's work consists of lessons on duty. Here again we have excellent counsels and delightful illustrations. 'The teacher should always take the moral habit for granted. He should never give his pupils to understand that he and they are about to examine whether, for instance, it is wrong or not wrong to hit. The commandment against lying is assumed, and its obligation acknowledged at the outset.' This we heartily agree with, and especially we like the apparently inadvertent use of the word 'commandment,' which concedes the whole question at issue—that is, that the idea of duty is a relative one depending on an Authority supreme and intimate, which embraces the thoughts of the heart and the issues of the life.

A Child's Inducements to Learn—The story of Hillel, as illustrating the duty of acquiring knowledge, is very charming, and is deeply interesting to the psychologist, as illustrating that a naturally implanted desire for knowledge is one of the springs of action in the human breast. The motives proposed for seeking knowledge are poor and inadequate: to succeed in life, to gain esteem, to satisfy yourself, and even to be able, possibly, to benefit others, are by no means soul-compelling motives. The child, who is encouraged to learn, because to learn is his particular duty in that state or life to which it has pleased God to call him, has the strongest of conceivable motives, in the sense that he is rendering that which is required of him by the Supreme Authority.

This one note of feebleness runs through the whole treatment of the subject. The drowning man is supposed to counsel himself to 'be brave, because as a human being you are superior to the forces of Nature, because there is something in you—your moral self—over which the forces of Nature have no power, because what happens to you in your private character is not important; but it is important that you assert dignity of humanity to the last breath.' This reads rather well; but how much finer is the attitude the man who struggles manfully to save the life that God has given him!

Moral Value of Manual Training—The chapter on the influence of manual training is well worthy of consideration. The concluding sentence runs: 'It is a cheering and encouraging thought that technical labour, which is the source of our material aggrandisement, may also become, when employed in the education of the young, the means of enlarging their manhood, quickening their intellect, and strengthening their character.'

I have taken up Mr. Adler's work so fully because is one of the most serious and successful attempts with which I am acquainted to present a graduated course of ethics suitable for children of all ages. Though I am at issue with the author on the all-important point of moral sanctions, I commend the work to the perusal of parents. The Christian parent will assuredly present the thought of Law in connection with a Law-giver, and will supplement the thousand valuable suggestions he will find here with his own strong conviction that 'Ought' is of the Lord God.

Slipshod Moral Teachings—But even the Christian child suffers from what may be called slipshod moral teaching. The failings of the good are a source of sorrow and surprise to the moralist as well as to the much-endeavouring and often-failing Christian soul. That temptation and sin are inseparable from our present condition may be allowed; but that an earnest and sincere Christian should be habitually guilty of failing in candour, frankness, justice to the characters and opinions of others, should be intemperate in censure, and—dare we say it—spiteful in criticism, is possibly to be traced, not to fallible human nature, but to defective education.

Importance of Ethical Instruction—The ethical idea has never been fairly and fully presented to the mind on these vulnerable points. The man is unable to give due weight to the opinions of another, because the child has not been instructed in the duty of candour. There is little doubt that careful, methodical, ethical instruction, with abundant illustration—and, we need not add—inspired by the thought, 'God wills it,' should, if such instruction could be made general, have an appreciable effect in elevating the national character. Therefore we hail with gratitude such a contribution to the practical ethics of the nursery and school-room as Mr. Adler's work on the moral instruction of children.

Chapter 12 Faith and Duty

Claims of Philosophy as an Instrument of Education

English Educational Thought tends towards Naturalism—Since Locke established a school of educational thought, based on English philosophy, our tendency has been exclusively towards naturalism, if not materialism; to the exclusion of an element in education—the force of the idea.

Madame de Staël has a remarkable passage concerning this tendency in English philosophy which, though we may not be disposed to admit her conclusions en bloc, should certainly give us pause, and lead us to consider whether we should not wisely modify the tendencies of our national thought by laying ourselves open to foreign influences:—

Madame de Staël upon Locke—'Hobbes prit à la lettre la philosophie qui fait dériver toutes nos idées des impressions des sens; il n'en craignit point les conséquences, et il a dit hardiment que l'âme était, soumise à la nécessité comme la société au despotisme. Le culte des tous les sentiments éléves et purs est tellement consolidé en Angleterre par les institutions politiques et religieuses, que les spéculations de l'esprit tournent autour de ces imposantes colonnes sans jamais les ébranler. Hobbes eut donc peu de partisans dans son pays; mais l'influence de Locke fut plus universelle. Comme son caractère était morale et religieuse, il ne se permit aucun des raisonnements corrupteurs qui derivaient nécessairement de sa métaphysique; et la plupart de ses compatriotes, en l'adoptant, ont eu comme lui la noble inconséquence de séparer les résultats des principes, tandis que Hume et les philosophes français, après avoir admis le système, l'ont appliqué d'une manière beaucoup plus logique.

'La métaphysique de Locke n'a en d'autre effet sur les esprits, en Angleterre, que de ternir un peu leur originalité naturelle; quand même elle dessé cherait la source des grandes pensées philosophiques, elle ne saurait detruire le sentiment religieux, qui sait si bien y suppléer; mais cette métaphysique reçue dans le reste de l'Europe, l'Allemagne exceptée, a été l'une des principales causes de l'immoralité' dont on s'est fait une théorie pour en mieux assurer la pratique.' [See Appendix.]

Our Educational Efforts lack Definite Aim—It is well that we should recognise the continuity of English educational thought, and perceive that we have in Spencer and Bain the lineal descendants of the earlier philosophers. Probably the chief source of weakness in our attempt to formulate a science of education is that we do not perceive that education is the outcome of philosophy. We deal with the issue and ignore the source. Hence our efforts lack continuity and definite aim. We are content to pick up a suggestion here, a practical hint there, without even troubling ourselves to consider what is that scheme of life of which such hints and suggestions are the output.

We are on the Verge of Chaos—Mr. Greenstreet's translation of M. Fouillée's remarkable work [Education from a National Standpoint] should not be without its effect upon the burning questions of the hour. As the translator well says in his preface: 'The spirit of reform is in the air; the question of the retention of Greek at the Universities is but a ripple of the great wave that seems ready to burst upon us and to obliterate the characteristic features of our national system of education . . . A glance at the various forms of the educational Systems obtaining in Europe and America is sufficient to betray to the observant eye how near to the verge of chaos we are standing.'

But also in the Throes of an Educational Revolution—These are words of insight and wisdom, but let us not therefore despair as though the end of all things were at hand. The truth is, we are in the throes of an educational revolution; we are emerging from chaos rather than about to plunge into it; we are beginning to recognise that education is the applied science of life, and that we really have existing material in the philosophy of the ages and the science of the day to formulate an educational code whereby we may order the lives of our children and regulate our own. We need not aspire to a complete and exhaustive code of educational laws. This will come us duly when humanity has, so to speak, fulfilled itself. Meantime, we have enough to go on with if we would believe it. What we have to do is to gather together and order our resources; to put the first thing foremost and all things in sequence, and see that education is neither more nor less than the practical application of our philosophy. Hence, if our educational thought is to be sound and effectual we must look to the philosophy which underlies it, and must be in a condition to trace every counsel of perfection for the bringing-up of children to one or other of the two schools of philosophy of which it must needs be the outcome.

Is our System of Education to be the Issue of Naturalism or Idealism?—Is our system of education to be the issue of naturalism or of idealism, or is there indeed a media via? This is practically the question which M. Fouillée sets himself to answer in the spirit of a philosophical educationalist. He examines his premises and draws his deductions with a candour, culture, and philosophic insight which carry the confidence of the reader. No doubt he is of a mind with that umpire in a cricket-match who lays down the dictum that one must be quite fair to both sides with a little leaning to one's own. M. Fouillée takes sides with classical as preferred to scientific culture. But he is not a mere partisan; he has philosophic reasons for the faith that is in him, and his examination of the question of national education is full of instruction and inspiration for the thoughtful parent as well as for the schoolmaster.

The Ethical View in Education—M. Fouillée gives in his preamble a key to his treatment of the subject. He says,

"On this as on all great questions of practical philosophy Guyau has left his mark. . . . He has treated the question from the highest standpoint, and has treated it in a strictly scientific form. 'Given the hereditary merits and faults of a race, how far can we modify existing heredity by means of education for a new heredity?' For the problem is nothing less than this. It is not merely a matter of the instruction of individuals, but of the preservation and improvement of the race. Education must therefore be based upon the physiological and moral laws of the culture of races . . . The ethnical is the true point of view. By means of education we must create such hereditary tendencies as will be useful to the race both physically and intellectually."

M. Fouillée begins at the beginning. He examines the principle of selection, and shows that it is a working principle, not only in animal, but in intellectual, æsthetic, and moral life. He demonstrates that there is what may be called psychological selection, according to whose laws those ideas which are the fittest rule the world; and it is in the light of this truth, of the natural selection of ideas and of their enormous force, that he would examine the vexed question of the subjects and methods of education.

No Attempt has been made to Unify Education—M.Fouillée complains with justice that no attempt has been made to harmonise or unify education as a whole in any one civilised nation. Controversy rages round quite secondary questions—whether education shall be literary or scientific? and, again, whether the ancient or the modem languages shall be taught? But science and literature do not exhaust the field. Our author introduces a new candidate. He says,

"In this volume we shall inquire if the link between science and literature is not to be found in the knowledge of man, of society, of the great laws of the universe—i.e. in morals and social science and æsthetics—in a word, in philosophy."

Claims of Philosophy as an Educational Agent—Now this is the gist of the teaching which we have laboured to advance in the Parents' Union and its various agencies. 'The proper study of mankind is man,' is one of those 'thoughts beyond their thought' which poets light upon; and I am able to add my personal testimony to the fact that under no other study with which I am acquainted is it possible to trace such almost visible expansion of mind and soul in the young student as in this of philosophy.

A peculiarly interesting and original line of thought, worked out very fully in this volume, is, that just as the child with an individual bent should have that bent encouraged and 'educated,' so of a nation:—

'If social science rejects every mystical interpretation of the common spirit animating a nation, it by no means rejects the reflected consciousness or spontaneous divination, possessed by every nation, of the functions which have devolved upon it.'

A Nation should be Educated for its Proper Functions—Here is a most fruitful suggestion. Think of the fitness of a scheme of physical, intellectual, and moral training, based upon our ideal of the English character and of the destiny of the English nation.

The chapter on 'Power of Education and of Idea-Forces—Suggestions—Heredity' is very valuable, as utilising a floating nebulæ of intuitions, which are coming upon us in connection with the hundred and one hypnotic marvels of the day. M. Fouillée maintains that—

'The power of instruction and education, denied by some and exaggerated by others, being nothing but the power of ideas and sentiments, it is impossible to be too exact in determining at the outset the extent and limits of this force. This psychological problem is the foundation of pedagogy.'

M. Fouillée Neglects the Physiological Basis of Education—In a word, M. Fouillée returns boldly to the Platonic philosophy; the idea is to him all in all, in philosophy and education. But he returns empty-handed. The wave of naturalism, now perhaps on the ebb, has left neither flotsam nor jetsam for him save for stranded fragments of the Darwinian theory. Now, it is to this wave of thought, materialistic, what you will, that we owe the discovery of the physiological basis of education.

While we believed that thought was purely volatile, incapable of impact upon matter, or of being acted by matter, our theories of education were necessarily vague. We could not catch our Ariel; how, then, could we school him? But now, the physiologists have taught us that our wilful sprite rests with the tips of his toes, at any rate, upon solid ground; nay more, his foothold is none so slight but that it leaves footmarks behind, an impress on that domain of the physical in which we are somewhat at home. The impalpable thoughts that we think leave their mark upon the quite palpable substance of the brain; set up, so the physiologists tell us, connections between the nerve-cells of which that organ is composed, in fact, to make a long story short, the cerebrum 'grows to the uses it is earliest and most constantly put to.' This fact opens up a function of education upon which M. Fouillée hardly touches, that most important function of the formation of habits—physical, intellectual, moral. As has been well said, 'Sow an act, reap a habit; sow a habit, reap a character; sow a character, reap a destiny.' And a great function of the educator is to secure that acts shall be so regularly, purposefully, and methodically sown that the child shall reap the habits of the good life, in thinking and doing, with the minimum of conscious effort.

The Minor Moralities become Matters of Habit—We are only now beginning to discover how beneficial are the laws which govern our being. Educate the child in right habits and the man's life will run in them, without the constant wear and tear of the moral effort of decision. Once, twice, three times in a day, he will still, no doubt, have to choose between the highest and the less high, the best and the less good course. But all the minor moralities of life may be made habitual to him. He has been brought up to be courteous, prompt, punctual, neat, considerate; and he practises these virtues without conscious effort. It is much easier to behave in the way he is used to, than to originate a new line of conduct. And this is so, because it is graciously and mercifully ordered that there shall be a physical record and adaptation as the result of our educational efforts, and that the enormous strain of moral endeavour shall come upon us only occasionally. 'Sow a habit, reap a character'; that is, the formation of habits is one of the chief means whereby we modify the original hereditary disposition of the child until it becomes the character of the man.

The Idea which Initiates a Habit—But even in this physiological work, the spiritual force of the idea has its part to play. For a habit is set up by following out an initial idea with a long sequence of corresponding acts. You tell a child that the Great Duke slept in so narrow a bed that he could not turn over, because, said he, 'When you want to turn over it's time to get up.' The boy does not wish to get up in the morning, but he does wish to be like the hero of Waterloo. You stimulate him to act upon this idea day after day for a month or so, until the habit is formed, and it is just as easy as not to get up in good time.

Can Spirit act upon Matter?—The functions of education may be roughly defined as twofold: (a) the formation of habits; (b) the presentation of ideas. The first depends far more largely than we recognise on physiological processes. The second is purely spiritual in origin, method, and result. Is it not possible that here we have the meeting point of the two philosophies which have divided mankind since men began to think about their thoughts and ways? Both are right; both are necessary; both have their full activity in the development of a human being at his best. The crux of modern thought, as indeed of all profound thought, is, Is it conceivable that the spiritual should have any manner of impact upon the material? Every problem, from the education of a little child to the doctrine of the Incarnation, turns upon this point. Conceive this possibility and all is plain, from the unlawful marvels resulting from hypnotic suggestion to the miracles of our faith. It becomes possible, though not easy, to believe what we are told, that, by an effort of passionate concentration of thought and feeling the devout have arrived at the figure of the stigmata upon hands and feet. With this key nothing is impossible to our faith; all we ask for is precedent. And, after all, this interaction of forces is the most common and everyday of our experiences. What is it but the impact of spirit upon matter which writes upon the face of flesh that record of character and conduct which we call countenance? And not only upon the face; he is a dull scholar in the lore of human nature who cannot read a man fairly well from a back view. The sculptor knows the trick of it. There is a statue of the late Prince Consort in Edinburgh in which representative groups pay homage to the Prince. Stand so as to get the back view of any one of them and the shoulders of scholar, soldier, peasant, artisan, tell unmistakably the tale of their several lives. What is this but the impress of spirit upon matter?

There is no Middle Way Open—Anyway we are on the horns of a dilemma. There is no middle course open to us. The physiologists have made it absolutely plain that the brain is concerned with thinking. Nay, more, that thought may go on without any volition on the part of the thinker. Further, that much of our best work in art and literature is the result of what is called unconscious cerebration. Now, we must admit one of two things. Either thought is a process of the material brain, one more 'mode of motion,' as the materialists contend, or the material brain is the agent of the spiritual thought, which acts upon it, let us say, as the fingers of a player upon the keys of his instrument. Grant this and the whole question is conceded. The impact of the spiritual upon the material is an accepted fact.

The Individuality of Children is Safeguarded—As we have had occasion to say before, in this great work of education parents and teachers are permitted to play only a subordinate part after all. You may bring your horse to the water, but you can't make him drink; and you may present ideas of the fittest to the mind of the child; but you do not know in the least which he will take, and which he will reject. And very well for us it is that this safeguard to his individuality is implanted in every child's breast. Our part is to see that his educational plat is constantly replenished with fit and inspiring ideas, and then we must needs leave it to the child's own appetite to take which he will have, and as much as he requires. Of one thing we must beware. The least symptom of satiety, especially when the ideas we present are moral and religious, should be taken as a serious warning. Persistence on our part just then may end with the child's never willingly sitting down to that dish any more.

Importance of Salient Ideas—The very limitations we see to our own powers in this matter of presenting ideas should make us the more anxiously careful as to the nature of the ideas set before our children. We shall not be content that they learn geography, history, Latin, what not,—we shall ask what salient ideas are presented in each such study, and how will these ideas affect the intellectual and moral development of the child. We shall be in a mood, that is, to go calmly and earnestly into the question of education as presented by M. Fouillée. We shall probably differ from him in many matters of detail, but we shall most likely be inclined to agree with his conclusion that, not some subject of mere utility, but moral and social science conveyed by means of history, literature, or otherwise, is the one subject which we are not at liberty to leave out from the curriculum of 'a being breathing thoughtful breath.'

The tables of studies given in the Appendix are of extreme value. Every subject is treated from what may be called the ideal point of view.

A Scientific Spirit—"Two things are necessary. First, we must introduce into the study of each science the philosophic spirit and method, general views, the search for the most general principles and conclusions. We must then reduce the different sciences to unity by a sound training in philosophy, which will be as obligatory to students in science as to students in literature . . . Scientific truths, said Descartes, are battles won; describe to the young the principal and most heroic of these battles; you will thus interest them in the results of science, and you will develop in them a scientific spirit by means of the enthusiasm for the conquest of truth; you will make them see the power of the reasoning which has led to discoveries in the past, and which will do so again in the future. How interesting arithmetic and geometry might be if we gave a short history of their principal theorems; if the child were mentally present at the labours of a Pythagoras, a Plato, a Euclid, or in modern times of a Viète, a Descartes, a Pascal, or a Leibnitz. Great theories, instead of being lifeless and anonymous abstractions, would become human, living truths, each with its own history, like a statue by Michael Angelo, or like a painting by Raphael."

Chapter 13 Faith and Duty

Man lives by Faith, Godward and Manward

Things 'Sacred' and Things 'Secular' an Irreligious Classification—There is a little involuntary resistance in our minds to any teaching which shall draw the deep things of our faith within the sphere of the laws which govern our development as human beings. We prefer that the commerce between God and the soul, in which is our life, should be altogether 'supernatural'; apart from the common laws of life, arbitrary, inexplicable, opposed to reason. If we err in this, it is in reverence we err. Our thought may be poor and crude, but all our desire is to hallow the divine Name, and we know no other way in which to set it apart. But though we err in reverence, we do err, and in the spiritual, as in the natural world, the motive does not atone for the act. We lose through this misconception of our relations with God the sense of unity in our lives. We become aware of an altogether unnatural and irreligious classification into things sacred and things secular. We are not in all things at one with God. There are beautiful lives in which there is no trace of this separation, whose aims are confined to the things we call sacred. But many thoughtful, earnest persons feel sorely the need of a conception of the divine relation which shall embrace the whole of human life which shall make art, science, politics, all those cares and thoughts of men which are not rebellious, sacred also as being all engaged in the great evolution, the evolution of the Kingdom of God.

Every Man develops his own Philosophy—Our religious thought, as our educational thought is, far more than we imagine, the outcome of our philosophy. And do not let us imagine that philosophy is not for the general run of men, but only for the few. On the contrary, there is no living soul who does not develop his own philosophy of life—that which he appropriates of the current thought of his time, modified by his own experiences.

It would be interesting to trace the effect upon religious thought of the two great schools of philosophy—the Idealistic and the Naturalistic; but that is beyond the writer's power, and beyond our purpose here; we must confine ourselves to what is immediately practical. The present day crux is, that naturalistic philosophy being in the ascendant, and the things of our religion being altogether idealistic, many noble natures are in revolt, feeling that they cannot honestly accept as truth that which is opposed to human reason. Others, to whom their religious faith is the first thing, but who are yet in touch with the thought and discovery of the day, affect an only half honest compromise with themselves, and say that there are certain questions which they will not examine; matters secular alone being open to searching scrutiny. Now, it is not, as we so often hear, that the times are out of joint, that Christianity is effete, that there is any inherent antagonism between the facts of natural and the facts of spiritual life. It is our own philosophy which needs to be adjusted. We have somehow managed to get life out of focus; we have begun with false initial ideas, and have taken the logical inferences from these for essential truth. We have not perceived that the concern of the reasoning powers is not with moral or spiritual truth, or even with what we call facts, but is, simply, with the logical inferences from any premises whatever accepted by the mind.

All Intercourse of Thought belongs to the Realm of Ideas—In our examination of M. Fouillée's Education from a National Standpoint, we made some attempt to show that the two schemes of philosophy, which have hitherto divided the world, have done so because both are right, and neither is exclusively right. Matter and Spirit, force and idea, work together in the evolution of character. The brain, somehow, makes material record of those ideas which inspire the life. But the brain does not originate those ideas, They are spiritual in their nature, and are spiritually conveyed, whether by means of the printed page, the glance of an eye, the touch of a hand, or in that holy mystery of the inbreathing of the Divine Spirit, of which we cannot tell whence it comes nor whither it goes. Once we recognise that all thoughts that breathe and words that burn are of their nature spiritual, and appeal to the Spiritual within us—that, in fact, all intercourse of thought and feeling belongs to the realm of ideas, spiritually conveyed, the great mysteries of our religion cease to be hedged off from our common experiences. If the friend who sits beside us deals with us, spirit with spirit, by means of quick interchange of ideas, is it hard to believe that just so is the intercourse between the Spirit of God and the spirit of man? The more perfect the sympathy between human souls, the less the need for spoken words. How easy to go on from this to the thought of that most intimate and blissful of all intercourse, the converse between the devout soul and its God.

It is Obvious and Natural that the Father of Spirits should keep Open Access to the Spirits of Men—Nothing can be more obvious, real, natural, necessary, than that the Father of spirits should graciously keep open such intimate access to, and converse with, the spirits of men.

'I would that one would grant me,
O my Lord,
To find Thee only.

That Thou alone wouldst speak to me, and I to Thee,
As a lover talking to his loved one,
A friend at table with his friend,'
["The Imitation of Christ" (rhythmic translation).]

is ever the aspiration of the devout soul. This continuous aspiration towards closest communion is, spoken or unspoken, the prayer of faith. A vain and fond imagination, says the sceptic, begotten of the heart, as when Narcissus became enamoured of his reflected image! What have we to say in reply? Nothing. He who does not perceive that he loves in his brother, not the material form, but the spiritual being of which this form is one expression, how can he understand that the Spirit of God should draw with irresistible drawings the spirit of man, which is indeed the whole man? For, after all, what is the body but the garment which the spirit shapes to its uses?

Easy Tolerance Commends itself to many Minds—To accept the outward seeming, to ignore the spiritual reality, is the easier way. To say that prayer is flung, as a child flings his kite, into the air, only to come down again; to say that men are the creatures of circumstances, with no power to determine their own fate; that this belief and that are equal verities, and that the worship of Christ or of Buddha is a mere affair of climate and conditions; this easy tolerance commends itself to many minds in these days.

Thackeray on the Easy and Sceptical Attitude—'And to what does this easy and sceptical life lead a man? . . . To what, we say, does this scepticism lead? It leads a man to shameful loneliness and selfishness, the more shameful because it is so good-humoured and conscienceless and serene. Conscience! What is conscience? Why accept remorse? What is public or private faith? Mythuses alike enveloped in enormous tradition. If, seeing and acknowledging the lies of the world, Arthur, as see them you can with only too fatal a clearness, you submit to them without any protest further than a laugh; if, plunged yourself in easy sensuality, you allow the whole wretched world to go past groaning by you unmoved; if the fight for the truth is taking place, and all men of honour are on the ground armed on the one side or the other, and you alone are to lie on your balcony and smoke your pipe out of the noise and the danger, you had better have died, or never have been at all, than be such a sensual coward.' [Pendennis—Thackeray.]

Man lives by Faith, Godward and Manward— Canon Beeching's Eleven Sermons on Faith are in refreshing contrast with this sort of modern Sadduceeism. In his view, faith is not mystic, supernatural, an exceptional development; it is the common basis of our dealings with each other. Credit, trust, confidence—the framework of society rests upon these. 'I can not trust you'—what worse thing can we say to one another? The law recognises every man's right to the confidence of his fellowmen, and will have a man accounted innocent until he is proven guilty. Our whole commercial and banking systems, what are they but enormous systems of credit, and only one in a hundred, or one in a thousand, fails to sustain this credit. Family and social life rest upon credit of another sort, let us call it moral credit; and only one in a hundred or one in a thousand forfeit the trust. If one here and there give occasion for jealousy, mistrust, suspicion, why, the exception proves the rule. In his dealings with men man lives by credit; in his dealings with God, man lives by faith. Let us use the same word in both cases and say that man is a spiritual being, and in all his relations,

Godward or manward, he lives by faith. How simple and easy a thing faith becomes! How especially easy to the children who trust everybody and offer a confiding hand to any guide. Could we only rid ourselves of the materialistic notion that spiritual things are not to be understood by us and that to believe in God is altogether a different thing from to trust a friend, how easy we should find the questions which we allow to stagger our faith.

Faith is the Simple Trust of Persons in a Person—But the Kingdom of God is coming upon us with power. Let us only break down this foolish barrier of the flesh; let us perceive that our relations with each other are the relations of spirit with spirit, and that spoken and written words are no more than the outward and visible signs of ideas spiritually conveyed, and how inevitable, incessant, all encompassing, becomes the presence of God about us. Faith is, then, the simple trust of person in Person. We realise with fearful joy that He is about our path, and about our bed, and spieth out all our ways—not with the austere eye of a judge, but with the caressing, if critical, glance of a parent. How easy, then, to understand the never-ceasing, ever-inspiring intercourse of the Divine Spirit with the Spirit of man—how, morning by morning, He awakeneth our ear, also; how His inspiration and instruction come in the direction and in the degree, in which the man is capable of receiving them. It is no longer a puzzle to us that the uninstructed savage shows sweet traits of pity and generosity, 'for his God doth instruct him and doth teach him.' We are not confounded when we hear of a righteous man who lifts up his face to Heaven, and says, 'There is no God'; because we know He maketh His sun to shine upon the evil and upon the good, and that just that measure of moral light and leading which a man lays himself open to receive is freely given to him. He may shut his eyes and say, 'There is no sun,' but none the less is he warmed and fed and comforted by the light he denies. This is the faith in which we would bring up our children, this strong, passionate sense of the dear nearness of our God; firm in this conviction, the controversies of the day will interest but not exercise us, for we are on the other side of all doubt once we know Him in whom we have believed.

Faith, a Lore of the Soul which demands Study—Faith comes by hearing, and hearing by the Word of God. We advance in this lore of the soul only in proportion as we make it our study; and all of us who have the bringing-up of children must needs be thankful for every word of help and insight which shall open our eyes to the realities which are spiritually discerned. In this view parents will be glad to read and ponder the Sermons before us. Profound thought is conveyed in language of very great simplicity and purity. The sermons are written from the standpoint of present-day thought, are not at all emotional, nor even hortatory, but they are very strengthening and refreshing. You read and go on your way rejoicing in a strong sense of the reality of things unseen. Perhaps this result is due to Mr. Beeching's presentation of the naturalness of faith.

The Naturalness of Faith—"It is noticeable that while our Lord is always demanding Faith, He offers no definition of the Faith He requires; so that there is a presumption that He meant by Faith just what men ordinarily mean by it. And the presumption is increased when it is remembered that Faith in our Lord began with being faith in human qualities before those qualities were seen to be divine. The faith of the Apostles increased under our Lord's careful training, both in depth and breadth; but between the first attraction that drew (say) Peter from his nets, and the last declaration of his worship upon the shores of Gennesaret, there was no breach of continuity. Indeed, as if to assure us that the Apostle's human faith had not after the Resurrection 'changed to something else,' and become an indefinite theological virtue, we find the word used to express it which, of all the words which labour to express faith, is the one most deeply tinged with human feeling: "Simon, son of Jonas, lovest thou me more than these?" We must ask, therefore, what, as between man and man, is commonly meant by Faith, and then we can examine whether our explanation fits the several groups of passages in the Gospels."

Faith is no Self-originated Impulse—The above extract from the very thoughtful and instructive preface illustrates what we mean by the naturalness of faith; not that which comes of itself and by itself, but that which is acceptable, fit, and proper to our nature whenever and whencesoever it arrive. 'For,' as Mr. Beeching says, 'as faith is itself no self-originated impulse, but the springing up of a man's heart in response to the encircling pressure of the 'Everlasting Arms,' so its reward is to feel more deeply and ever more deeply their divine support.'

The eleven sermons are upon The Object of Faith, The Worship of Faith, The Righteousness of Faith, The Food of Faith, National Faith, The Eye of Faith, The Ear of Faith, The Activity of Faith, The Gentleness of Faith, The Discipline of Faith, Faith in Man.

The Compassion of Christ—In his examination of 'The Object of Faith,' Mr. Beeching asks: What, then, is He like; what kind of countenance is it that shines out upon us from the Gospel pages? Let us turn to them and see.' And we read the story of how Jesus, being moved with compassion, touched the eyes of the two blind men by the wayside going out from Jericho. How Christ had compassion on other things besides bodily sickness. 'Christ has compassion also on ignorance; on the aimless wandering of men after their own desires, without a Master to follow; on the weariness of spirit that such a life brings about.' Again, 'Christ has compassion not only on sickness and ignorance, but on sin—on the sinner who repents.' And we read the story of the woman whose sins which were many, were forgiven, for she loved much. Again we see the countenance of Christ as it is turned upon that young man of whom it is said, 'Then Jesus, looking upon him, loved him.' 'Compassion then, for suffering and ignorance, and sin that repents, love for enthusiasm, this we have seen in the face of Christ.' One more divine regard we are invited to contemplate; how the Lord turned and looked upon Peter. 'Can you imagine with what a face our Lord looked upon Peter, who had thrice denied Him, after confidently affirming that he would go with Him to death? Would that that face would shine upon us with whatever reproach when we in word or deed deny Him, that so we too may remember and weep.' How the heart rises to such teaching as this—the simple presentation of Christ as He walked among men. Well did our Lord say, 'I, if I be lifted up, will draw all men unto Me.' The pity of it is that He, the altogether lovely, is so seldom lifted up to our adoring gaze. Perhaps, when our teachers invite us to behold the face of Christ, we shall learn the full interpretation of that profound word. He will draw all men, because it is not possible for any human soul to resist the divine loveliness once it is fairly and fully presented to his vision.

The Worship of Faith—The sermon on the 'Worship of Faith' sets forth that 'To worship Christ is to bow down with love and wonder and thankfulness, before the most perfect goodness that the world has ever seen, and to believe that that goodness was the express image of God the Father.' All aims and all ideals that are not the aims and ideals of Christ, are distinctly opposed to such worship, and the man who entertains these alien ideals may not call himself a Christian. After examining that attitude of the spirit towards Christ which belongs to the worship of faith, the rest of the sermon is very practical. 'Work is Worship,' is the keynote: one longs that a writer who knows so well how to touch the secret springs had taken this opportunity to move us to that 'heart's adoration,' which is dearer to God; but, indeed, the whole volume has this tendency. It is well to be reminded that 'the thorough and willing performance of any duty, however humble or however exalted, is like the offering of incense to Christ, well-pleasing and acceptable.'

The sermon on the 'Righteousness of Faith' is extremely important and instructive. The writer dwells on the 'deplorable cant' with which we pronounce ourselves 'miserable sinners,' combining the 'sentiments of the Pharisees in the parable with the expressions of the publican.'

Righteousness is a certain Disposition of the Spirit of Man to the Spirit of God—"Christ's language about man's sinfulness is altogether free from vagueness and hyperbole; when He blames He blames for definite faults which we can appreciate, and He is so far from declaring that men can do no good thing, that He assumes always that man in his proper state of dependence upon God has the power to do righteousness. 'Whosoever shall do the will of My Father, which is in heaven, the same is My brother, and sister, and mother.' But the question remains, How, considering our actual shortcomings, can any of us be spoken of by Christ as righteous here and now? This is the question in answer to which St Paul wrote two of his greatest Epistles. His answer was, that according to Christ, a man is accounted righteous, not from a consideration of his works, but from a consideration of his faith in God. Human righteousness is not a verdict upon the summing up of a life, but it is reckoned to a man at any moment from a certain disposition of his spirit to the Spirit of God; a disposition of trust, love, reverence, the disposition of a dutiful son to a good father . . . Righteousness, in the only sense in which it is possible for men, means believing and trusting God."

The Teaching of these Sermons should be Helpful to Parents—I have not space to take up in detail all the teaching of this inspiring little volume; but I commend it to parents. Who, as they, have need to nourish the spiritual life in themselves? Who, as they, have need to examine themselves as to with how firm a grasp they hold the mysteries of our faith? Who, as they, need to have their ideas as to the supreme relationship so clear that they can be translated into baby speech? Besides, we have seen that it is the duty of the educator to put the first thing foremost, and all things in sequence; only one thing is needful—that we 'have faith in God'; let us deliver our thoughts from vagueness and our ways from variableness, if we would help the children towards this higher life. To this end we gladly welcome teaching which is rather nourishing than stimulating, and which should afford real help towards 'sober walking in pure Gospel ways.'

Chapter 14 Parents are Concerned to Give the Heroic Impulse

[History of Early English Literature. By Stopford A. Brooke. 2 vols. Macmillan & Co.]

Heroic Poetry Inspires to Noble Living—"To set forth, as only art can, the beauty and the joy of living, the beauty and the blessedness of death, the glory of battle and adventure, the nobility of devotion—to a cause, an ideal, a passion even—the dignity of resistance, the sacred quality of patriotism, that is my ambition here," says the editor of Lyra Heroica in his preface. We all feel that some such expression of the 'simpler sentiments, more elemental emotions' should be freely used in the education of children—that, in fact, heroic poetry contains such inspiration to noble living as is hardly to be found elsewhere; and also we are aware that it is only in the youth of peoples that these elemental emotions find free expression in song. We look at our own ballad literature and find plenty of the right material, but it is too occasional and too little connected; and so, though we would prefer that the children should imbibe patriotism and heroism at the one fountain-head, we think it cannot be done.

We have no truly English material, so we say, for education in this kind, and we fall back on the Homeric myths in one or other of the graceful and spirited renderings which have been made specially for children.

Beowulf, our English Ulysses—But what if it should turn out that we have our own Homer, our own Ulysses? Mr. Stopford Brooke has made a great discovery for us, who look at all things from the child standpoint. Possibly he would not be gratified to know that his History of Early English Literature, invaluable addition as it is to the library of the student and the man of letters, should be appropriated as food for babes. All the same, here is what we have long wanted. The elemental emotions and heroic adventures of the early English put into verse and tale, strange and eerie as the wildest fairy tale, yet breathing in every line the English temper and the English virtue that go to the making of heroes. Not that Beowulf, the hero of the great poem, was precisely English, but where the English came from, there dwelt he, and Beowulf was early adopted as the national hero, whose achievements were sung in every hall.

Beowulf is Prudent and Patient—The poem, says Mr. Stopford Brooke, consisting of three thousand one hundred and eighty-three lines, is divided into two parts by an interval of fifty years; the first, containing Beowulf's great deeds against the monster Grendel and his dam; the second, Beowulf's conquest of the Fire-drake and his death and burial. We are told that we may fairly claim the poem as English, that it is in our tongue and in our country alone that it is preserved. The hero Beowulf comes of brave and noble parents, and mildness and more than mortal daring meet in him. When he comes to Hrothgar to conquer Grendel, it is of his wise counsel as much as of his strength that we hear. The queen begs him to be friendly in council to her sons, saying to him, 'Thou holdest thy faith with patience and thy might with prudence of mind. Thou shalt be a comfort to thy people and a help to heroes.' None, it is said, could order matters more wisely than he. When he is dying he looks back on his life, and that which he thinks of the most is not his great war deeds, but his patience, his prudence, his power of holding his own well and of avoiding new enmities.

'Have Patience of thy Woes.'—'Each of us must await the close of life,' says he; 'let him who can, gain honour before he die. That is best for a warrior when he is dead. But do thou throughout this day have patience of thy woes; I look for that from thee.' Such the philosophy of this hero, legendary or otherwise, of some early century after Christ, before His religion had found its way among those northern tribes.

'I Swore no False Oaths.'—Gentle, like Nelson, he had Nelson's iron resolution. What he undertook to do he went through without a thought, save of getting to the end of it. Fear is wholly unknown to him, and he seems, like Nelson, to have inspired his captains with his own courage. 'I swore no false oaths,' he said when dying; so also he kept his honour in faithfulness to his lord. On foot, alone, in front, while life lasted, he was his king's defence. He kept it in equal faithfulness when his lord was dead, and that to his own loss, for when the kingdom was offered to him he refused, and trained Heardreg, the king's son, to war and learning, guarded him kindly with honour, and avenged him when he was slain. He kept it in generosity, for he gave away all the gifts that he received; in courtesy, for he gave even to those who had been rude to him; and he is always gentle and grave with women. Above all, he kept it in war, for these things are said of him: 'so shall a man do when he thinks to gain praise that shall never end, and cares not for his life in battle.' 'Let us have fame or death,' he cries, and when Wiglaf comes to help him against the dragon, and Beowulf is wrapped in the flame, Wiglaf recalls to him the aim of his whole life:—

'Bear thyself Well.'—'Beowulf, beloved, bear thyself well. Thou wert wont to say in youth that thou wouldst never let honour go. Now, strong in deeds, ward thy life, firm-souled prince, with all thy might, I will be thy helper.' 'These,' adds Mr. Stopford Brooke, 'are the qualities of the man and the hero, and I have thought it worth while to dwell on them, because they represent the ancient English ideal, the manhood which pleased the English folk even before they came to Britain, and because in all our histories since Beowulf's time, for twelve hundred years or so, they have been repeated in the lives of the English warriors by land and sea whom we chiefly honour.'

The English Ideal—'But it is not only the idea of a hero which we have in Beowulf, it is also the idea of a king, the just governor, the wise politician, the builder of peace, the defender of his own folk at the price of his life, "the good king, the folk king, the beloved king, the war ward of his land, the winner of treasure for the need of his people, the hero who thinks in death of those who sail the sea, the gentle and terrible warrior, who is buried amid the tears of his people."'

We owe Mr. Stopford Brooke much gratitude for bringing this heroic ideal of the youth of our nation within reach of the unlearned. But what have we been about to let a thousand years and more go by without ever drawing on the inspiration of this noble ideal in giving impulse to our children's lives? We have many English heroes, it may be objected: we have no need of this resuscitated great one from a long-buried past. We have indeed heroes galore to be proud of, but somehow they have not often been put into song in such wise as to reach the hearts of the children and the unlearned.

Children should be in Touch with Beowulf—We have to thank Tennyson for our Arthur, and Shakespeare for our Henry the Fifth, but we imagine that parents will find their children's souls more in touch with Beowulf than with either of these, no doubt because the legends of a nation's youth are the pages of history which most easily reach a child; and Beowulf belongs to a younger stage of civilisation than even Arthur. We hope the author of Early English Literature will sometime give us the whole of the poem translated with a special view to children, and interspersed with his own luminous teaching as we have it here. The quaintness of the metre employed gives a feeling of eld which carries the reader back, very successfully, to the long ago of the poem.

We have already quoted largely from this History of Early English Literature but perhaps a fuller extract will give a better idea of the work and of its real helpfulness to parents. The cost of the two rather expensive volumes should be well repaid if a single child were to be fired with emulation of the heroic qualities therein sung:—

Action of the Poem—'The action of the poem now begins with the voyage of Beowulf to the Danish coast. The hero has heard that Hrothgar, the chief of the Danes, is tormented by Grendel, a man-devouring monster. If Hrothgar's warriors sleep in Heorot—the great hall he has built—they are seized, torn to pieces, and devoured. "I will deliver the king," thought Beowulf, when he heard the tale from the roving seamen. Over the swan road I will seek Hrothgar; he has need of men.' His comrades urged him to the adventure, and fifteen of them were willing to fight it out with him. Among the rest was a sea-crafty man who knew the ocean-paths. Their ship lay drawn up on the beach, under the high cliff. Then—

'There the well-geared heroes
Stepped upon the stem, while the stream of ocean
Whirled the sea against the sand. To the ship, to its breast.
Bright and carved things of cost carried then the heroes
And the armour well-arrayed. So the men outpushed,
On desired adventure, their tight ocean wood
Swiftly went above the waves, with a wind well-fitted,
Likest to a fowl, the Floater, foam around its neck,
Till about the same time, on the second day,

The up-curvéd prow had come on so far,
That at last the seamen saw the land ahead;
Shining sea-cliffs, soaring headlands,
Broad sea-nesses. So the Sailor of the Sea
Reached the sea-way's end.'
Beowulf, I. 211

'This was the voyage, ending in a fiord with two high sea-capes at its entrance. The same kind of scenery belongs to the land whence they had set out. When Beowulf returns over the sea the boat groans as it is pushed forth. It is heavily laden; the hollow, under the single mast with the single sail, holds eight horses, swords and treasure and rich armours. The sail is hoisted, the wind drives the foam-throated bark over the waves, until they see the Geats' Cliffs—the well-known sea-nesses. The keel is pressed up by the wind on the sand, and the "harbour-guard who had looked forth afar o'er the sea with longing for their return"—one of the many human touches of the poem—"fastens the wide-bosomed ship with anchoring chains to the strand, lest the violence of the waves should sweep away the winsome boat." . . . At the end of the bay into which Beowulf sails is a low shore, on which he drives his ship, stem on. Planks are pushed out on either side of the prow; the Weder folk slipped down on the shore, tied up their sea-wood; their battle sarks clanged on them as they moved. Then they thanked the gods that the war-paths had been easy to them . . . On the ridge of the hill above the landing-place the ward of the coast of the Scyldings sat on his horse, and saw the strangers bear their bright shields over the bulwarks of the ship to the shore. He rode down, wondering, to the sea, and shook mightily in his hands his heavy spear, and called to the men—

'Who are ye of men, having arms in hand,
Covered with your coats of mail. Who your keel afoaming
O'er the ocean street thus have urged along.
Hither on the high sea!'

'Never saw I greater
Earl upon this earth than is one of you;
Hero in his harness. He is no home-stayer,
'Less his looks belie him, lovely with his weapons.
Noble is his air!'
Beowulf, II. 237-247.

'Beowulf replies that he is Hrothgar's friend, and comes to free him from "Grendel, the secret foe on the dark nights." He pities Hrothgar, old and good. Yet, as he speaks, the Teutonic sense of the inevitable Wyrd passes by in his mind, and he knows not if Hrothgar can ever escape sorrow. "If ever," he says, "sorrow should cease from him, release ever come, and the welter of care become cooler." The coastguard shows them the path, and promises to watch over their ship. The ground rises from the shore, and they pass on to the hilly ridge, behind which lies Heorot.'

Our Gentle Forefathers—Old English Riddles—The History of the Early English Literature takes us into other pleasant places. Here are two or three specimens of the riddles of the old bards, and in riddle and saga we get most vivid pictures of the life and thoughts, the ways and words of the forefathers whom we are too ready to think of as 'rude,' but who are here portrayed to us as gentle, mild, and large of soul; men and women whom we, their posterity, may well delight to honour.

I. Here is Cynewulf's Riddle of the Sword.
'I'm a wondrous wight for warstrife shapen;
By my Lord beloved, lovelily adorned:
Many coloured is my corslet, and a clasping wire
Glitters round the gem of death which my wielder gave to me:
He who whiles doth urge me, wide-wanderer that I am,

With him to conquest.

Then I carry treasure,
Cold above the garths, through the glittering day;
I of smiths the handiwork! Often do I quell
Breathing men with battle edges! Me bedecks a king
With his hoard and silver; honours me in hall,
Doth withhold no word of praise! Of my ways he boasts
'Fore the many heroes, where the mead they drink.
In restraint he lulls me, then he lets me loose again,
Far and wide to rush along; me the weary with wayfarings,
Cursed of all weapons.'
Riddle xxi.

II. The helmet speaks:—
"Wretchedness I bear;
Wheresoe'er he carries me, he who clasps the spear!
On me, still upstanding, smite the streams (of rain);
Hail, the hard grain (helms me), and the hoar-frost covers me
And the (flying) snow (in flakes) falls all over me."
Riddle lxxix., 6-10.

It is unnecessary to say a word about the literary value and importance of Mr. Stopford Brooke's great work. 'There is nothing like leather,' and to parents all things present themselves as they may tell on education. Here is a very treasure-trove.

Chapter 15 Is It Possible?

The Attitude of Parents toward Social Questions

A Moral Crisis—The economic aspects of the great philanthropic scheme [Issue of Darkest England] which brought timely relief to the national conscience before the setting in of the hard winter of 1891, are, perhaps, outside our province; but it has educational aspects which we are, in some measure, bound to discuss. In the first place, the children in many homes hear 'I do not believe that' it is possible for the leopard to change his spots. General Booth's scheme brought this issue before us with startling directness; and what the children hear said to-day at the table and by the fireside about all such philanthropic efforts will probably influence for their lives their attitude towards all philanthropic and all missionary endeavour. Not only so, but we ourselves, who stand in some measure in loco parentis to the distressed in mind, body, or estate, are compelled to examine our own position. How far do we give, and work, for the ease of our own conscience, and how far do we believe in the possibility of the instant and utter restoration of the morally degraded, questions which, to-day, force themselves upon us. We must be ready with a yea or a nay; we must take sides, for or against such possibilities as should exalt philanthropic effort into a burning passion. The fact is, that great scheme forced a sort of moral crisis upon us whose effects are continually in evidence.

[William Booth's book 'In Darkest England and the Way Out' urged people to give money to help the unemployed start their own communities as a way out of poverty.]

We, too, Love our Brother—Whether or no the scheme commends itself to us for its fitness, seasonableness, and promise, one thing it assuredly did: it revealed us to ourselves, and that in an agreeable light. It discovered to us that we, too, love our brother; that we, too, yearn over 'the bruised' with something, however little, of the tenderness of Christ. The brotherhood of man is no fancy bred in the brain; and we have loved our brother all the time—the sick, the poor, the captive, and the sinner, too; but the fearful, and unbelieving, and slothful amongst us—that is, the most of us—have turned away our eyes from beholding evils for which we saw no help. But when a promise of deliverance was offered, more adequate, conceivably, than any heretofore proposed, why, the solidarity of humanity asserts itself; our brother who is bruised is not merely near and dear; he is our very self, and whoso will ease and revive him is our deliverer too.

The 'Idol of Size.'—The first flush of enthusiasm subsided, we ask, Are we not, after all, led away by what Coleridge calls the 'Idol of Size'?

Wherein does this scheme differ from ten thousand others, except in the colossal scale on which the experiment is to be tried? And perhaps we should concede at the outset that this hope of deliverance is 'the same, only more so,' as is being already worked out effectually in many an otherwise sunless corner of the great vineyard. Indeed, the great project has its great risks—risks which the quieter work escapes. All the same, there are aspects in which the remedy, because of its vastness and inclusiveness, is new.

Hitherto we have helped the wretched in impossible circumstances, not out of them. Our help has been as a drop in the bucket, reaching to hundreds or thousands only of the lost millions. Even so, we cannot keep it up; we give to-day, and withhold to-morrow; worse than all, our very giving is an injury, reducing the power and the inclination for self-help. Or, do we start some small amateur industry by way of making our people independent? This pet industry may sometimes be a transparent mask for almsgiving, and an encroachment upon regular industries and the rights of other workers.

Cui Bono?—Now and then is a gleam of hope, now and then a soul and body snatched into safety; but the hardest workers are glad of the noise of the wheels to keep the eternal Cui bono? out of their ears. There is so much to be done, and so little means of doing it. But this scheme—what with the amplitude of its provisions, what with the organisation and regimentation it promises, the strong and righteous government, the moral compulsion to well-doing—considering these, and the enormous staff of workers already prepared to carry it out, the dreariest pessimist amongst us concedes that General Booth's scheme may be worth trying. 'But,' he says, 'but—

Do We Believe in Conversion?'

Can Character be Changed?—Everything turns on the condition the originator wisely puts first. There is the crux. Given money enough, land enough, men enough, fully equip and officer this teeming horde of incapables, and some sort of mechanical drill may be got through somehow. But, 'when a man's own character and defects constitute the reasons for his fall, that character must be changed and that conduct altered if any permanent beneficial results are to be obtained.' The drunkard must be made sober; the criminal, honest; the impure, clean. Can this be done? is the crucial question.

The Question of the Age—Is it possible that a man can emerge altogether out of his old self and become a new creature, with new aims, new thoughts, even new habits? That such renovation is possible is the old contention of Christianity. Here, and not on the ground of the inspiration of the sacred text, must the battle be fought out. The answer to the one urgent question of the age, What think ye of Christ? depends upon the power of the idea of Christ to attract and compel attention, and of the indwelling of Christ to vivify and elevate a single debased and torpid human soul.

Many of us believe exultingly that the 'all power' which is given into the hands of our Master includes the power of upright standing, strength, and beauty, for every bruised human reed. That this is so, we have evidence in plenty, beginning with ourselves. But many others of us, and those not the less noble, consider, with Robert Elsmere [Ward's novel about a man who lost his faith], that 'miracles do not happen.'

The Essential Miracle—The recorded miracles serve as pegs for the discussion; the essential miracle is the utter and immediate renovation of a human being. Upon this possibility the saving of the world must hang; and this many cannot receive, not because they are stiff-necked and perverse, but because it is dead against natural law as they know it. Proofs? Cases without end? The whole history of the Christian Church in evidence? Yes; but the history of the Church is a chequered one; and for individual cases, we do not doubt the veracity of the details; only, nobody knows the whole truth; some preparation in the past, some motive in the present inadvertently kept out of sight, may alter the bearing of any such case.

The Honest Sceptic—This is, roughly, the position of the honest sceptic, who would, if he could believe heartily in General Booth's scheme, and by consequence, in the convertibility of the entire race. To improve the circumstances, even of millions is only a question of the magnitude of the measures taken, the wisdom of the administration. But human nature itself, depraved human nature, is, to him the impossible quantity. Can the leopard change his spots?

The Law Against Us—Heredity.

The Vicious by Inheritance—Who are these whom General Booth cheerfully undertakes to fashion and make amenable to the conditions of godly and righteous and sober living? Let us hear the life history of many of them in his own words:—

'The rakings of the human cesspool.'
'Little ones, whose parents are habitually drunk.
. . . Whose ideas of merriment are gained from the familiar spectacle of the nightly debauch.'
'The obscenity of the talk of many of the children of some of our public schools could hardly be outdone even in Sodom and Gomorrah.'

And the childhood—save the word!—of the children of today reproduces the childhood of their parents, their grandparents, who knows? their great grand parents. These are, no doubt, the worst; but the worst must be reckoned with first, for if these slip through the meshes of the remedial net, the masses more inert than vicious slide out through the breaks. In the first place, then, the scheme embraces the vicious by inheritance; proposes to mix up with the rest a class whose sole heritage is an inconceivable and incalculable accumulation of vicious inclinations and propensities. And this, in the face of that conception of heredity which is quietly taking possession of the public mind, and causing many thoughtful parents to abstain from very active efforts to mould the characters of their children.

Those of us whose attention has been fixed upon the working of the law of heredity until it appears to us to run its course, unmodified and unlimited by other laws, may well be pardoned for regarding with doubtful eye a scheme which has, for its very first condition, the regeneration of the vicious; of the Vicious by inherited propensity.

The Law Against Us—Habit.

The Vicious by Inveterate Habit—Use is second nature, we say. Habit is ten natures; habit begins as a cobweb, and ends as a cable. 'Oh, you'll get used to it,' whatever it is. Dare we face the habits in which these people have their being? It is not only the obscene speech, the unholy acts; that which signifies is the manner of thoughts we think; speech, act, are the mere outcome; it is the habitual thought of a man which shapes that which we call his character. And these, can we reasonably doubt that every imagination of their heart is only evil continually? We say, use is second nature, but let us consider what we mean by the phrase; what is the philosophy of habit so far as it has been discovered to us. The seat of habit is the brain; the actual grey nervous matter of the cerebrum. And the history of a habit is shortly this: 'The cerebrum of man grows to those modes of thought in which it is habitually exercised.' That 'immaterial' thought should mould the 'material' brain need not surprise nor scandalise us, for do we not see with our eyes that immaterial thought moulds the face, forms what we call countenance, lovely or loathsome according to the manner of thought it registers? The how of this brain growth is not yet in evidence, nor is this the time and place to discuss it; but, bearing in mind this structural adaptation to confirmed habit, what chance, again, we say, has a scheme which has for its first condition the regeneration of the vicious, vicious not only by inherited propensity, but by unbroken inveterate habit?

The Law Against Us—Unconscious Cerebration.

Thoughts Think Themselves—Those who are accustomed to write know what it is to sit down and 'reel off' sheet after sheet of matter without plan or premeditation, clear, coherent, ready for press, hardly needing revision. We are told of a lawyer who wrote in his sleep a lucid opinion throwing light on a most difficult case; of a mathematician who worked out in his sleep a computation which baffled him when awake. We know that Coleridge dreamed 'Kubla Khan' in an after-dinner nap, line by line, and wrote it down when he awoke. What do these cases and a thousand like them point to? To no less than this: that, though the all-important ego must, no doubt, 'assist' at the thinking of the initial thought on a given subject, yet, after that first thought or two, 'brain' and 'mind' manage the matter between them, and the thoughts, so to speak, think themselves;

not after the fashion of a pendulum which moves to and fro, to and fro, in the same interval of space, but in that of a carriage rolling along the same road, but into ever new developments of the landscape. An amazing thought—but have we not abundant internal evidence of the fact? We all know that there are times when we cannot get rid of the thoughts that will think themselves within us, though they drive away sleep and peace and joy. In the face of this law, benign as it eases us of the labour of original thought and decision about the everyday affairs of life, terrible when it gets beyond our power of control and diversion, what hope for those in whose debauched brain vile thoughts, involuntary, automatic, are for ever running with frightful rapidity in the one well-worn track? Truly, the in-look is appalling. What hope for these?

Vicious Imaginations—And what of a scheme whose first condition is the regeneration of the vicious—vicious, not only by inherited propensity, and by unbroken inveterate habit, but reduced to that state of, shall we say, inevitable viciousness—when 'unconscious cerebration,' with untiring activity, goes to the emanation of vicious imaginations? All these things are against us.

The Law for Us—Limitations to the Doctrine of Heredity

But the last word of Science, and she has more and better words in store, is full of hope. The fathers have eaten sour grapes, but it is not inevitable that the children's teeth be set on edge. The soul that sinneth it shall die, said the prophet of old and Science is hurrying up with her 'Even so.'

Acquired Modification not Transmitted—The necessary corollary to the latest presentation of the theory of evolution is—acquired modifications of structure are not transmitted. All hail to the good news; to realise it, is like waking up from a hideous nightmare. This, definitely, is our gain; the man who by the continuous thinking of criminal thoughts has modified the structure of his brain so as to adapt it to the current of such thoughts, does not necessarily pass on this modification to his child. There is no necessary adaptation in the cerebrum of the new-born child to make place for evil thoughts. In a word, the child of the vicious may be born as fit and able for good living as the child of the righteous. Inherent modifications are, it is true transmitted, and the line between inherent and acquired modifications may not be easy to define. But anyway, there is hope to go on with. The child of the wicked may have as good a start in life, so far as his birthright goes, as the child of the just.

Education Stronger than Nature—The child's future depends not upon his lineage so much as upon his bringing-up, for education is stronger than nature, and no human being need be given over to despair. We need not abate our hope of the regeneration of the vicious for the bugbear of an inheritance of irresistible propensity to evil.

The Law for Us—'One Custom Overcometh Another.'

But habit! It is bad enough to know that use is second nature, and that man is a bundle of habits; but how much more hopeless to look into the rationale of habit, and perceive that the enormous strength of the habit that binds us connotes a structural modification, a shaping of the brain tissues to the thought of which the habit is the outward and visible sign and expression. Once such growth has taken place, is not the thing done, so that it can't be undone—has not the man taken shape for life when his ways of thinking are registered in the substance of his brain?

Not so; because one habit has been formed and registered in the brain is no reason at all why another and contrary habit should not be formed and registered in its turn. To-day is the day of salvation, physically speaking, because a habit is a thing of now; it may be begun in a moment, formed in a month, confirmed in three months, become the character, the very man, in a year.

Natural Preparation for Salvation—There is growth to the new thoughts in a new tract of the brain, and, 'One custom overcometh another'; here is the natural preparation for salvation. The words are very old, the words of Thomas a' Kempis, but the perception that they have a literal physical meaning has been reserved for us to-day. Only one train of ideas can be active at one time; the old cell connections are broken, and benign Nature is busy building up the waste places, even be they the waste places of many generations. *No road* is set up in the track where unholy thoughts carried on their busy traffic. New tissue is formed; the wound is healed, and, save, perhaps, for a scar, some little tenderness, that place is whole and sound as the rest.

This is how one custom overcometh another: there is no conflict, no contention, no persuasion. Secure for the new idea a weighty introduction, and it will accomplish all the rest for itself. It will feed and grow; it will increase and multiply; it will run its course of its own accord; will issue in that current of automatic unconscious involuntary thought of the man which shapes his character. Behold, a new man! Ye must be born again, we are told; and we say, with a sense of superior knowledge of the laws of Nature, How can a man be born again? Can he enter the second time into his mother's womb and be born? This would be a miracle, and we have satisfied ourselves that 'miracles do not happen.'

Conversion no Miracle—And now, at last, the miracle of conversion is made plain to our dull understanding. We perceive that conversion, however sudden, is no miracle at all—using the word miracle to describe that which takes place in opposition to natural law. On the contrary, we find that every man carries in his physical substance the gospel of perpetual, or of always possible, renovation; and we find how, from the beginning, Nature was prepared with her response to the demand of Grace. Is conversion possible? we ask; and the answer is, that it is, so to speak, a function for which there is latent provision in our physical constitution, to be called forth by the touch of a potent idea. Truly His commandment is exceeding broad, and grows broader day by day with each new revelation of Science.

Many Conversions in a Lifetime—A man may, most men do, undergo this process of renovation many times in their lives; whenever an idea strong enough to divert his thoughts (as we most correctly say) from all that went before is introduced, the man becomes a new creature; when he is 'in love,' for example; when the fascinations of art or of nature take hold of him; an access of responsibility may bring about a sudden and complete conversion:—

The breath no sooner left his father's body
But that his wildness, mortified in him,
Seem'd to die too; yea, at that very moment,
Consideration, like an angel came
And whipped the offending Adam out of him;
Leaving his body as a paradise
To envelop and contain celestial spirits.

Here is a picture—psychologically true, anyway; Shakespeare makes no mistakes in psychology—of an immediate absolute conversion. The conversion may be to the worse, alas, and not to the better, and the value of the conversion must depend upon the intrinsic worthiness of the idea by whose instrumentality it is brought about. The point worth securing is, that man carries in his physical structure the conditions of renovation; conditions, so far as we can conceive, always in working order, always ready to be put in force.

'Conversion' is not Contrary to Natural Law—Wherefore 'conversion' in the Biblical sense, in the sense in which the promoters of this scheme depend upon its efficacy, though a miracle of divine grace in so far as it is a sign and a marvel, is no miracle in the popular sense of that which is outside of and opposed to the workings of 'natural law.' Conversion is entirely within the divine scheme of things, even if we choose to limit our vision of that scheme to the 'few, faint, and feeble' flashes which Science is as yet able to throw upon the mysteries of being. But is this all? Ah, no; this is no more than the dim vestibule of Nature to the temple of grace; we are not concerned, however, to say one word here of how 'great is the mystery of godliness'; of the cherishing of the Father, the saving and the indwelling of the Son, the sanctifying of the Spirit; neither need we speak of 'spiritual wickedness in high places.' The aim of this slight essay is to examine the assertion that what we call conversion is contrary to natural law; and we do this with a view, not to General Booth's scheme only, but to all efforts of help.

Hope shows an ever stronger case for the regeneration of the vicious. Not only need we be no more oppressed by the fear of an inheritance of invincible propensities to evil, but the strength of lifelong habit may be vanquished by the power of an idea, new habits of thought may be set up on the instant, and these may be fostered and encouraged until that habit which is ten natures is the habit of the new life, and the thoughts which, so to speak, think themselves all day long are thoughts of purity and goodness.

The Law for Us—Potency of an Idea

'Hath not a Jew eyes? hath not a Jew hands, organs, dimensions, senses, affections, passions?'

Conditions of the Potency of an Idea—In effecting the renovation of a man the external agent is ever an idea, of such potency as to be seized upon with avidity by the mind, and, therefore, to make an impression upon the nervous substance of the cerebrum. The potency of an idea depends upon the fact of its being complementary to some desire or affection within the man. Man wants knowledge, for example, and power, and esteem, and love, and company; also he has within him capacities for love, esteem, gratitude, reverence, kindness. He has an unrecognised craving for an object on which to spend the good that is in him.

Fitness of the Ideas included in Christianity—The idea which makes a strong appeal to any one of his primal desires and affections must needs meet with a response. Such idea and such capacity are made for one another; apart, they are meaningless as ball and socket; together, they are a joint, effective in a thousand ways. But the man who is utterly depraved has no capacity for gratitude, for example? Yes, he has; depravity is a disease, a morbid condition; beneath is the man, capable of recovery. This is hardly the place to consider them, but think for a moment of the fitness of the ideas which are summed up in the thought of Christ to be presented to the poor degraded soul: divine aid and compassion for his neglected body; divine love for his loneliness; divine forgiveness in lieu of the shame of his sin; divine esteem for his self-contempt; divine goodness and beauty to call forth the passion of love and loyalty that is in him; the Story of the Cross, the lifting up, which perhaps no human soul is able to resist if it be fitly done. The divine idea once received, the divine life is imparted also, grows, is fostered and cherished by the Holy Ghost. The man is a new creature, with other aims, and other thoughts, and a life out of himself. The old things have passed away, and all things have become new—the physical being embodying, so to speak, the new life of the spirit.

We may well believe, indeed, that 'conversion' is so proper to the physical and spiritual constitution of man that it is inevitable to all of us if only the ideas summed up in Christ be fitly introduced to the soul.

The question then turns, not upon the possibility of converting the most depraved, nor upon the potency of the ideas to be presented, but altogether upon the power of putting these ideas so that a man shall recognise and seize upon the fulness of Christ as the necessary complement to the emptiness of which he is aware.

The Habits of the Good Life.

Curative Treatment Necessary—The man converted, the work is not done. These sinners exceedingly are not only sinful, but diseased; morbid conditions of brain have been set up, and every one of them needs individual treatment, like any other sick man, for disease slow of cure. For a month, three months, six months, it will not do to let one of them alone. Curative treatment is an absolute condition of success, and here is where human co-operation is invited in what is primarily and ultimately the work of God. There are places in the brain where ill thoughts have of old run their course; and these sore places must have time, blessed time, wherein to heal. That is to say, all traffic in the old thoughts must be absolutely stopped at whatever cost.

Think of the Army of Vigilance which must be ever on the alert to turn away the eyes of the patients from beholding evil; for, a single suggestion, of drink, of uncleanness, and, presto, the old thoughts run riot, and the work of healing must begin anew. There is no way to keep out the old, but by administering the thoughts of the new life watchfully, one by one, as they are needed, and can be taken; offering them with engaging freshness, with comforting fitness, until at last the period of anxious nursing is over, the habits of the good life are set up, and the patient is able to stand on his own feet and labour for his own meat. This is no work to be undertaken wholesale. The spiritual care of a multitude diseased, even physically diseased, of sin, is no light thing. And if it be not undertaken systematically, and carried out efficiently, the whole scheme must of necessity fall through. Who is sufficient for these things? No one perhaps; but a following of a great corps of nurses trained to minister to minds diseased, and with the experience and the method belonging to a professional calling, is surely a fitting qualification for the Herculean task.

The Ease of Discipline.

How readily we can understand how, in the days when monarchs were more despotic than they are now, one and another would take refuge in a convent for the ease of doing the will of another rather than his own! Is not this the attraction of conventual life to-day, and is not this why the idea of the Salvation Army is powerfully attractive to some of us who know, all the same, that we (individually) should be wrong to lay down our proper function of ordering and acting out our own lives?

The Relief of Inclusion In a Strong Organisation—But for these, strong of impulse and weak of will, who have no power at all to do the good they vaguely and feebly desire, oh, the ease of being taken up into a strong and beneficent organisation, of having their comings and goings, their doings and havings, ordered for them! Organisation, regimentation, we are reminded, make a hero of Tommy Atkins. And these all have it in them to be heroes, because restlessness, rebellion, once subdued, they will rejoice more than any others in the ease of simply doing as they are bidden. Here is a great secret of power, to treat these, lapsed and restored, like children; for what is the object of family discipline, of that obedience which has been described as the whole duty of a child? Is it not to ease the way of the child, while will is weak and conscience immature, by getting it on the habits of the good life where it is as easy to go right as for a locomotive to run on its lines? Just such present relief from responsibility, such an interval for development, do these poor children of larger growth demand for their needs; and any existing possibility of ordering and disciplining this mixed multitude must needs appear to us a surpassing adaptation of 'supply' to 'demand.'

Work and Fresh Air are Powerful Agents—The saving grace of work, and the healing power of the fresh air, again, should do their part in the restoration of the 'submerged.' But it is not our part to examine the methods proposed by General Booth, or to adumbrate his chances of success. Our concern is solely with the children. The attitude of thought towards all good work which children will henceforth take may depend very much upon how far the underlying principles are made clear to them in one typical instance. Whatever the agency, let children be assured that the work is the work of God, to be accomplished in the strength of God, according to the laws of God that it is our part to make ourselves acquainted with the laws we would work out, and that, having done all, we wait for the inspiration of the divine life, even as the diligent farmer waits upon sunshine and shower.

Chapter 16 Discipline

A Serious Study for Parents

Discipline is not Punishment—'What part does Discipline play in your system of education?' We should hail the query as manifesting a cheering degree of interest if we were not quite sure that our interlocutor uses discipline as a euphuism for punishment. That conviction puts one's mind into the attitude of protest. In the first place, we have no system of education. We hold that great things, such as nature, life, education, are 'cabined, cribbed, confined,' in proportion as they are systematised. We have a method of education, it is true, but method is no more than a way to an end, and is free, yielding, adaptive as Nature herself. Method has a few comprehensive laws according to which details shape themselves, as one naturally shapes one's behaviour to the acknowledged law that fire burns. System, on the contrary, has an infinity of rules and instructions as to what you are to do and how you are to do it. Method in education follows Nature humbly; stands aside and gives her fair play.

A Method is not a System—System leads Nature: assists, supplements, rushes in to undertake those very tasks which Nature has made her own since the world was. Does Nature endow every young thing, child or kitten, with a wonderful capacity for inventive play? Nay, but, says System, I can help here; I will invent games for the child and help his plays, and make more use of this power of his than unaided Nature knows how. So Dame System teaches the child to play, and he enjoys it; but, alas, there is no play in him, no initiative, when he is left to himself; and so on, all along the lines. System is fussy and zealous and produces enormous results—in the teacher!

A Wise Passiveness—Method pursues a 'wise passiveness.' You watch the teacher and are hardly aware that he is doing anything. The children take the initiative, but, somehow, the result here is in these and not in the teacher. They develop, become daily more and more of persons, with

'The reason firm, the temperate will,
Endurance, foresight, strength, and skill.'

Such as these are the golden fruits which ripen under the eyes of the parent, who is wise to discriminate between the role of Nature and that of the educator, who follows sympathetically and dutifully the lead of the great mother.

'Oh, then you have no discipline. I thought not. I daresay it would answer very well to leave children to themselves and make them happy. Children are always good when they are happy, are they not?' Not so fast, dear reader. He who would follow a great leader must needs endeavour himself, Ohne hast ohne Rast [without haste, without rest]; and the divine lead which we call Nature is infinitely blessed in the following, but the way is steep to tread and hard to find, and this uphill work is by no means to be confounded with leisurely strolling in ways of our own devising.

The parent who would educate his children, in any large sense of the word, must lay himself out for high thinking and lowly living; the highest thinking indeed possible to the human mind and the simplest, directest living.

This thought of discipline, for example, is one of the large comprehensive ideas which must inform and direct the life, rather than be gathered up into a rule, easy to remember and easy to apply, now and then. If Tommy is naughty, whip him and send him to bed—is a ready-reckoner kind of rule, handy to have about one, and is the sort of thing which many people mean by discipline. Now we would not say that punishment is never to be used, very much otherwise. Neither would we say that physic is never to be taken. But punishment, like physic, is a casualty only of occasional occurrence at the worst, and punishment and physic alike are reduced to a minimum in proportion as we secure healthy conditions of body and mind. We are not anxious to lay down canons for punishment. Mr. Herbert Spencer has not perhaps said the last word, but he has given us a quite convenient rule to go on with.

Punishment by Consequences—A child should be punished by the natural consequences of his offence. To carry this suggestion out au pied de la lettre would often enough mean lasting, even fatal, injury to the child, bodily and mental. You cannot let the indolent child be punished by ignorance, or the wilful and adventurous child break a limb; but, so far as punishments have been allowed to become necessary, the nature of the offence gives one a clue to a suitable punishment. The child who does not eat his porridge goes without his plum. This is, anyway, a punishment in kind, perhaps the nearest approach to natural consequences which it is advisable to try.

Children rather Enjoy Punishments—But parents should face the fact that children rather enjoy punishments. In these they find the opportunities, so frequent in story-books, so rare in real life, for showing a fine pluck. The child who is in punishment is very commonly enjoying himself immensely, because he is respecting himself intensely.

Heroism in Bearing Penalties—There is a bit of heroism in the bearing of a penalty which is very apt to do away with any sense of contrition for the offence; and the plucky little fellow, who takes his punishment with an air, is by no means a bad and hardened young offender; but is an economist of opportunities, making the best of what comes to hand for his own real education. His mother's distress, his father's disapproval, these are quite different matters, and carry no compensating sense of hardihood. Reflections like these lead one to spare the rod, not at all out of over-sensibility to the child's physical suffering, for we must have him endure hardness if we mean to make a man of him, but purely because it is not easy to find a punishment that does not defeat its own ends.

Wrongdoing followed by its own Penalties—The light smart slap with which the mother visits the little child when he is naughty, is often both effective and educative. It changes the current of baby's thoughts, and he no longer wishes to pull his sister's hair. But should not the slap be a last resort when no other way is left of changing his thoughts? With the older child a theory of punishment rests less upon the necessity to change the culprit's thoughts than upon the hope of forming a new association of ideas, that is, of certain pains and penalties inevitably attached to certain forms of wrongdoing. This, we know too well, is a teaching of life, and is not to be overlooked in education. The experience of each of us goes to prove that every breach of law, in thought, or deed, is attended by its own penalties, immediate or remote, and the child who is not brought up to know that 'due follows deed, in course,' is sent out to his first campaign undrilled and untrained, a raw recruit.

Our contention is twofold: (a), that the need for punishment is mostly preventable; and (b), that the fear of punishment is hardly ever so strong a motive as the delight of the particular wrongdoing in view.

Punishment is not Reformative—If punishment were necessarily reformative, and able to cure us all of those 'sins we have a mind to,' why, the world would be a very good world; for no manner of sin escapes its present punishment. The fact is, not that punishment is unnecessary or that it is useless, but that it is inadequate and barely touches our aim; which is, not visitation for the offence, but the correction of that fault of character of which the offence is the outcome. Jemmy tells lies and we punish him; and by so doing we mark our sense of the offence; but, probably, no punishment could be invented drastic enough to cure Jemmy of telling lies in the future; and this is the thing to be aimed at. No, we must look deeper; we must find out what weak place in character, what false habit of thinking, leads Jemmy to tell lies, and we must deal with this false habit in the only possible way, by forming the contrary habit of true thinking, which will make Jemmy grow up a true man. 'I think I have never told a lie since,' said a lady, describing the single conversation in which her father cured her, when she was a child, of lying by setting up an altogether new train of thought.

Good Habits the best Schoolmasters.—Not mere spurts of occasional punishment, but the incessant watchfulness and endeavour which go to the forming and preserving of the habits of the good life, is what we mean by discipline; and, from this point of view, never were there such disciplinarians as the parents who labour on the lines we would indicate. Every habit of courtesy, consideration, order, neatness, punctuality, truthfulness, is itself a schoolmaster, and orders life with the most unfailing diligence.

A habit is so easily formed, so strong to compel. There are few parents who would not labour diligently if for every month's labour they were able to endow one of their children with a large sum of money. But, in a month, a parent may begin to form a habit in his child of such value that money is a bagatelle by comparison. We have often urged that the great discovery which modern science has brought to the aid of the educator is, that every habit of the life sets up, as it were, a material record in the brain tissues. We all know that we think as we are used to think and act as we are used to act. Ever since man began to notice the ways of his own mind, this law of habit has been matter of common knowledge, and has been more or less acted upon by parents and other trainers of children. The well-brought-up child has always been a child carefully trained in good habits. But it is only within our own day that it has been possible to lay down definite laws for the formation of habits. Until now, the mother who wished to train her children in such and such a good habit has found herself hindered by a certain sense of casualty.

Always Telling—'I'm sure I am always telling her'—to keep her drawers neat, or to hold up her head and speak nicely, or to be quick and careful about an errand, says the poor mother, with tears in her eyes; and indeed this, of 'always telling' him or her is a weary process for the mother; dull, because hopeless. She goes on 'telling' to deliver her own soul, for she has long since ceased to expect any result: and we know how dreary is work without hope. But, perhaps, even his mother does not know how unutterably dreary is this always 'telling,' which produces nothing, to the child. At first he is fretful and impatient under the patter of idle words; then he puts up with the inevitable; and comes at last hardly to be aware that the thing is being said. As for any impression on his character, any habit really formed, all this labour is without result; the child does the thing when he cannot help it, and evades as often as he can. And the poor disappointed mother says,' I'm sure I've tried as much as any mother to train my children in good habits, but I have failed.' She is not altogether dispirited, however. The children have not the habits she wished to train them in; but they grow up warm-hearted, good-natured, bright young people, by no means children to be ashamed of. All the same, the mother's sense of failure is a monition to be trusted.

Our failures in life are, perhaps, due, for the most part, to the defects of our qualities; and, therefore, it is not enough to send children into the world with just the inheritance of character they get from their parents.

Some Practical Counsels—Let me offer a few definite practical counsels to a parent who wishes to deal seriously with a bad habit. First—Let us remember that this bad habit has made its record in the brain. Second—There is only one way of obliterating such record; the absolute cessation of the habit for a considerable space of time, say some six or eight weeks. Third—During this interval new growth, new cell connections, are somehow or other taking place, and the physical seat of the evil is undergoing a natural healing. Fourth—But the only way to secure this pause is to introduce some new habit as attractive to the child as is the wrong habit you set yourself to cure. Fifth—As the bad habit usually arises from the defect of some quality in the child it should not be difficult for the parent who knows his child's character to introduce the contrary good habit. Sixth—Take a moment of happy confidence between parent and child; introduce, by tale or example, the stimulating idea; get the child's will with you. Seventh—Do not tell him to do the new thing, but quietly and cheerfully see that he does it on all possible occasions, for weeks if need be, all the time stimulating the new idea, until it takes great hold of the child's imagination. Eighth—Watch most carefully against any recurrence of the bad habit. Ninth—Should the old fault recur, do not condone it. Let the punishment, chiefly the sense of your estrangenient, be acutely felt. Let the child feel the shame not only of having done wrong, but of having done wrong when it was perfectly easy to avoid the wrong and do the right. Above all, 'watch unto prayer' and teach your child dependence upon divine aid in this warfare of the spirit; but, also, the absolute necessity for his own efforts.

An Inquisitive Child—Susie is an inquisitive little girl. Her mother is surprised and not always delighted to find that the little maid is constantly on voyages of discovery, of which the servants speak to each other as prying and poking. Is her mother engaged in talk with a visitor or the nurse—behold, Susie is at her side, sprung from nobody knows where. Is a confidential letter being read aloud—Susie is within earshot. Does the mother think she has put away a certain book where the children cannot find it—Susie volunteers to produce it. Does she tell her husband that cook has asked for two days' leave of absence—up jumps Susie, with all the ins and outs of the case. 'I really don't know what to do with the child. It is difficult to put down one's foot and say you ought not to know this or that or the other. Each thing in itself is harmless enough; but it is a little distressing to have a child who is always peering about for gossipy information.' Yes it is tiresome, but is not a case for despair, nor for thinking hard things of Susie, certainly not for accepting the inevitable.

The Defect of her Quality—Regarding this tiresome curiosity as the defect of its quality, the mother casts about for the quality, and, behold, Susie is reinstated. What ails the child is an inordinate desire for knowledge, run to seed, and allowed to spend itself on unworthy objects. When the right moment comes, introduce Susie to some delightful study, of Nature, for example, which will employ all her prying proclivities. Once the new idea has taken possession of the little girl, a little talk should follow about the unworthiness of filling one's thoughts with trifling matters so that nothing really interesting can get in. For weeks together see that Susie's mind is too full of large matters to entertain the small ones; and, once the inquisitive habit has been checked, encourage the child's active mind to definite progressive work on things worth while. Susie's unworthy curiosity will soon cease to be a trial to her parents.

Chapter 17 Sensations And Feelings

Sensations Educable by Parents

Common-sense—Children whose parents have little theoretic knowledge of the values of the various food-stuffs are often thoroughly nourished; their parents rely on what they call common-sense; and the result is, on the whole, better than if scientific consideration were given to the family dietary. But this common-sense has usually scientific opinion for its basis, though the fact may be forgotten, and when scientific opinion has become the groundwork of habit it is of more value, and works in a more simple way, than while it is still in the stage of experiment. In the same way it is a good thing to have such an acquaintance with the functions of human nature that we act on our knowledge unconsciously, and do not even know that we possess it. But if we have no such floating capital of cognisance we must study the subject, even if we have to make experiments. Most people suppose that the sensations, feelings, and emotions of a child are matters that take care of themselves. Indeed, we are apt to use the three terms indiscriminately, without attaching very clear ideas to them. But they cover, collectively, a very important educational field; and though common-sense, that is to say, judgments formed upon inherited knowledge, often helps us to act wisely without knowing why, we shall probably act more wisely if we act reasonably.

Origin of Sensations—Let us consider, first, the subject of sensations. We speak of sensations of cold, and sensations of heat, and sensations of pain, and we are quite right. We also speak of sensations of fear and sensations of pleasure, and we are commonly wrong. The sensations have their origin in impressions received by the several organs of sense—eye, tongue, nostrils, ear, and the surface of the external skin—and are conveyed by the sensory nerves, some to the spinal cord and some to the lower region of the brain. Many sensations we know nothing about; when we become aware of our sensations, it is because communications are sent by nerve fibres, acting as telegraph wires, from the sensorium to the thinking brain; and this happens when we give our attention to any one of the multitudinous messages carried by the sensory nerves. The physiology of the senses is too complicated a subject to touch upon here, but it is deeply interesting, and perhaps no better introduction exists than Professor Clifford's little book, Seeing and Thinking (Macmillan). Now, the senses are the Five Gateways of Knowledge, to quote the title of a little book which many of us have used in early days; and an intelligent person should be aware of, and capable of forming judgments upon, the sensations he receives.

Sensations should be treated as of Objective Interest—We all recognise that the training of the senses is an important part of education. One caution is necessary: from the very first a child's sensations should be treated as matters of objective and not of subjective interest. Marmalade, for example, is interesting, not because it is 'nice'—a fact not to be dwelt upon at all—but because one can discern in it different flavours and the modifying effect of the oil secreted in the rind of the orange. We shall have occasion to speak more of this subject later; but a useful piece of education is this of causing a child's interest to centre in the objects which produce his sensations and not in himself as the receiver of those sensations.

Object-Lessons in Disfavour—The purpose of so-called object-lessons is to assist a child, by careful examination of a given object, to find out all he can about it through the use of his several senses. General information about the object is thrown in, and lodges only because the child's senses have been exercised and his interest aroused. Object-lessons are a little in disfavour just now, for two reasons. In the first place, miserable fragments are presented to the children which have little of the character of the object in situ, and are apt to convey inadequate, if not wrong, ideas. In the next place, object-lessons are commonly used as a means to introduce children to hard words, such as opaque and translucent, which never become part of their living thought until they pick them up for themselves incidentally as they have need of them. But the abuse of this kind of teaching should not cause us to overlook its use. No child can grow up without daily object teaching, whether casual or of set purpose; and the more thorough this is, the more intelligent and observant will he become. It is singular how few people are capable of developing an intelligent curiosity about the most attractive objects, except as their interest is stimulated from without.

A Baby's Object-Lesson—The baby is a wonderful teacher in this matter of object-lessons. To be sure, his single pupil is his own small self; but his progress is amazing. At first he does not see any difference between a picture of a cow and the living animal; big and little, far and near, hard and soft, hot and cold, are all alike to him; he wishes to hold the moon in his pinafore, to sit on the pond, to poke his finger into the candle, not because he is a foolish little person, but because he is profoundly ignorant of the nature of the contents of this unintelligible world. But how he works! he bangs his spoon to try if it produces sound; he sucks it to try its flavour; he fumbles it all over and no doubt finds out whether it is hard or soft, hot or cold, rough or smooth; he gazes at it with the long gaze of infancy, so that he may learn the look of it; it is an old friend and an object of desire when he sees it again, for he has found out that there is much joy in a spoon. This goes on with great diligence for a couple of years, at the end of which time baby has acquired enough knowledge of the world to conduct himself in a very dignified and rational way.

Nature's Teaching—This is what happens under nature's teaching; and for the first five or six years of his life, everything, especially everything in action, is an object of intelligent curiosity to the child—the street or the field is a panorama of delight, the shepherd's dog, the baker's cart, the man with the barrow, are full of vivid interest. He has a thousand questions to ask, he wants to know about everything; he has, in fact, an inordinate appetite for knowledge. We soon cure all that: we occupy him with books instead of things; we evoke other desires in place of the desire to know; and we succeed in bringing up the unobservant man (and more unobservant woman) who discerns no difference between an elm, a poplar and a lime tree, and misses very much of the joy of living. By the way, why is it that the baby does not exercise with purpose his organ of smell? He screws up a funny little nose when he is taught to sniff at a flower, but this is a mere trick; he does not naturally make experiments as to whether things are odorous, while each of his other senses affords him keen joy. No doubt the little nose is, involuntarily, very active; but can his inertness in this matter be a hereditary failing? It may be that we all allow ourselves to go about with obtuse nostrils. If so, this is a matter for the attention of mothers, who should bring up their children not only to receive, which is involuntary and vague, but to perceive odours from the first.

Education of the Senses—Two points call for our attention in the education of the senses; we must assist the child to educate himself on Nature's lines, and we must take care not to supplant and crowd out Nature and her methods with that which we call education. Object-lessons should be incidental; and this is where the family enjoys so great an advantage over the school. It is almost impossible that the school should give any but set lessons; but this sort of teaching in the family falls in with the occurrence of the object. The child who finds that wonderful and beautiful object, a 'paper' wasp's nest, attached to a larch-twig, has his object-lesson on the spot from father or mother. The grey colour, the round symmetrical shape, the sort of cup-and-ball arrangement, the papery texture, the comparative size, the comparative smoothness, the odour or lack of odour, the extreme lightness, the fact that it is not cold to the touch—these and fifty other particulars the child finds out unaided, or with no more than a word, here and there, to direct his observation. One does not find a wasp's nest every day, but much can be got out of every common object, and the commoner the better, which falls naturally under the child's observation, a piece of bread, a lump of coal, a sponge.

Advantages of Home Teaching—In the first place, it is unnecessary in the family to give an exhaustive examination to every object; one quality might be discussed in this, another quality in that. We eat our bread and milk, and notice that bread is absorbent; and we overhaul our experience to discover other things which we know to be absorbent also; and we do what we can to compare these things as to whether they are less absorbent or more absorbent than bread. This is exceedingly important: the unobservant person states that an object is light, and considers that he has stated an ultimate fact: the observant person makes the same statement, but has in his mind a relative scale, and his judgment is of the more value because he compares, silently, with a series of substances to which this is relatively light.

Positive and Comparative Terms—It is important that children should learn to recognise that high, sweet, bitter, long, short, agreeable, etc., etc., are comparative terms; while square, round, black, white, are positive terms, the application of which is not affected by comparison with other objects.

Indiscriminate Use of Epithets—Care in this matter makes for higher moral, as well as intellectual development: half the dissensions in the world arise from an indiscriminate use of epithets. 'Would you say your bread (at dinner) was light or heavy?' The child would probably answer, 'Rather light' 'Yes, we can only say that a thing is light by comparing it with others; what is bread light compared with?' 'A stone, a piece of coal, of cheese, of butter of the same size.' 'But it is heavy compared with?' 'A piece of sponge cake, a piece of sponge, of cork, of pumice,' and so on. 'What do you think it weighs?' 'An ounce,' 'an ounce and a half?' 'We'll try after dinner; you had better have another piece and save it,' and the weighing after dinner is a delightful operation. The power of judging of weight is worth cultivating. We heard the other day of a gentleman who was required at a bazaar to guess the weight of a monster cake; he poised it and said it weighed eighteen pounds fourteen ounces, and it did exactly. Caeteris paribus [all other things being equal],one has a greater respect for the man who made this accurate judgment than for the vague person who suggested that the cake might weigh ten pounds.

Judgment as to Weight—Letters, book parcels, an apple, an orange, a vegetable marrow, fifty things in the course of the day, give opportunities for this kind of object teaching; i.e. the practice of forcing judgments as to the relative and absolute weight of objects by the irresistance, that is their opposition to our muscular force, perceived by our sense of touch. By degrees the children are trained to observe that the relative weights of objects depend upon their relative density, and are introduced to the fact that we have a standard of weight.

Judgment as to Size—In the same way children should be taught to measure objects by the eye. How high is that candlestick? How long and broad that picture-frame? and so on—verifying their statements. What is the circumference of that bowl? of the clock-face? of that flower-bed? How tall is So-and-so, and So-and-so? How many hands high are the horses of their acquaintance? Divide a slip of wood, a sheet of paper into halves, thirds, quarters by the eye, lay a walking-stick at right angles with another; detect when a picture, curtain, etc., hangs out of the perpendicular. This sort of practice will secure for children what is called a correct, or true, eye.

Discrimination of Sounds—A quick and true ear is another possession that does not come by Nature, or anyway, if it does, it is too often lost. How many sounds can you distinguish in a sudden silence out of doors? Let these be named in order from the less to the more acute. Let the notes of the birds be distinguished, both call-notes and song-notes; the four or five distinct sounds to be heard in the flow of a brook. Cultivate accuracy in distinguishing footfalls and voices; in discerning, with their eyes shut, the direction from which a sound proceeds, in which footsteps are moving. Distinguish passing vehicles by the sounds; as lorry, brougham, dog-cart. Music is, no doubt, the means par excellence for this kind of ear culture. Mrs.Curwen's

'Child Pianist' puts carefully graduated work of this kind into the hands of parents; and, if a child never become a performer, to have acquired a cultivated and correct ear is no small part of a musical education.

Discrimination of Odours—We do not attach enough importance to the discrimination of odours, whether as a safeguard to health or as a source of pleasure. Half the people one knows have nostrils which register no difference between the atmosphere of a large, and so-called 'airy,' room, whose windows are never opened, and that of a room in which a through current of air is arranged for at frequent intervals: and yet health depends largely on delicate perception as regards the purity of the atmosphere. The odours which result in diphtheria or typhoid are perceptible, however slight, and a nose trained to detect the faintest malodorous particles in food, clothing, or dwelling, is to the possessor a safeguard from disease.

Then, odours enter more readily than other sense perceptions into those—

'sensations sweet,
Felt in the blood, and felt along the heart,'

which add so much to the sum of our happiness, because they unite themselves readily with our purely incorporeal joys by links of association. 'I never smell woodruff without being reminded—' is the sort of thing we hear and say continually, but we do not trouble ourselves to realise that we owe a double joy to the odour of the woodruff (or it may be, alas! a reflected sorrow)—the joy of the pleasant influences about us when we pluck the flower, and the possibly more personal joy of that other time with which we associate it. Every new odour perceived is a source, if not of warning, of recurrent satisfaction or interest. We are acquainted with too few of the odours which the spring-time offers. Only this spring the present writer learned two peculiarly delightful odours quite new to her, that of young larch twigs, which have much the same kind and degree of fragrance as the flower of the syringe, and the pleasant musky aroma of a box-hedge. Children should be trained to shut eyes, for example, when they come into the drawing-room, and discover by their nostrils what odorous flowers are present; should discriminate the garden odours let loose by a shower of rain:--

'Houses and rooms are full of perfumes, the shelves are crowded with perfumes,
I breathe the fragrance myself and know it and like it.

'The atmosphere is not a perfume, it has no taste of the distillation, it is odourless,
It is for my mouth for ever, I am in love with it.

'The sniff of green leaves, and dry leaves, and of the shore, and dark-coloured sea-rocks, and of hay in the barn.'

The American poet has, perhaps, done more than any other to express the pleasure to be found in odours. This is one direction in which much remains to be done; we have not yet arrived even at a scale of odours, as of sound and of colour.

Discrimination of Flavour—Flavour, again, offers a wide range for delicate discrimination. At first sight it would appear difficult to cultivate the sense of flavour without making a child more or less of a gourmand; but the fact is, that the strong flavours which titillate the palate destroy the power of perception. The young child who lives upon milk-foods has, probably, more pleasure in flavour than the diner-out who is familiar with the confections of a cordon bleu. At the same time, one would prefer to make flavour a source of interest rather than of sensuous pleasure to children: it is better that they should try to discern a flavour with their eyes shut, than that they should be allowed to think or say that things are 'nice' or 'nasty.' This sort of fastidiousness should be cried down. It is not well to make a child eat what he does not like, as that would only make him dislike that particular dish always; but to let him feel that he shows a want of self-control and manliness, when he expresses distaste for wholesome food, is likely to have a lasting effect.

Sensory Gymnastics—We have barely touched on the sorts of object-lessons, appealing now to one sense and now to another, which should come incidentally every day in the family. We are apt to regard an American Indian as a quite uneducated person; he is, on the contrary, highly educated in so far as that he is able to discriminate sensory impressions, and to take action upon these, in a way which is bewildering to the book-learned European. It would be well for parents to educate a child, for the first half-dozen years of his life, at any rate, on 'Red Indian' lines. Besides the few points we have mentioned, he should be able to discriminate colours and shades of colour; relative degrees of heat in woollen, wood, iron, marble, ice; should learn the use of the thermometer; should discriminate objects according to their degrees of hardness; should have a cultivated eye and touch for texture; should, in fact, be able to get as much information about an object from a few minutes' study as to its form, colour, texture, size, weight, qualities, parts, characteristics, as he could learn out of many pages of a printed book. We approach the subject by the avenue of the child's senses rather than by that of the objects to be studied, because just now we have in view the occasional test exercises, the purpose of which is to give thorough culture to the several senses. An acquaintance with Nature and natural objects is another thing, and is to be approached in a slightly different way. A boy who is observing a beetle does not consciously apply his several senses to the beetle, but lets the beetle take the initiative, which the boy reverently follows: but the boy who is in the habit of doing sensory daily gymnastics will learn a great deal more about the beetle than he who is not so trained.

Sensory Games—Definite object-lessons differ from these incidental exercises in that an object is in a manner exhausted by each of the senses in turn, and every atom of information it will yield got out of it. A good plan is to make this sort of a lesson a game. Pass your object round—a piece of bread, for example—and let each child tell some fact that he discovers by touch; another round, by smell; again, taste; and again, by sight. Children are most ingenious in this kind of game, and it affords opportunities to give them new words, as friable, elastic, when they really ask to be helped to express in a word some discovery they have made. Children learn in this way to think with exactitude, to distinguish between friable and brittle; and any common information that is offered to them in the course of these exercises a possession for ever. A good game in the nature of an object-lesson, suitable for a birthday party, is to have a hundred objects arranged on a table, unknown to the children; then lead the little party into the room, allow them three minutes to look round the table; afterwards, when they have left the room, let them write or tell in a corner, the names of all the objects they recollect. Some children will easily get fifty or sixty.

No doubt the best and happiest exercise of the senses springs out of a loving familiarity with the world of nature, but the sorts of gymnastics we have indicated render the perceptions more acute, and are greatly enjoyed by children. That the sensations should not be permitted to minister unduly to the subjective consciousness of the child is the great point to be borne in mind.

Chapter 18 Sensations And Feelings

Feelings Educable by Parents

'These beauteous forms
Through a long absence, have not been to me
As is a landscape to a blind man's eye;
But oft, in lonely rooms, and 'mid the din
Of towns and cities, I have owed to them,
In hours of weariness, sensations sweet
Felt in the blood, and felt along the heart;
And passing even into my purer mind,
With tranquil restoration:—feelings, too,
Of unremembered pleasure: such, perhaps,
As have no slight or trivial influence
On that best portion of a good man's life,
His little, nameless, unremembered acts
Of kindness and of love.'
W. Wordsworth, Tintern Abbey.

Reflected Sensations—Insight—the, so to speak, scientific grip of a great poet—is amongst those 'more things' in heaven and earth than our philosophy has dreamed of: Wordsworth tells us that, after the lapse of years, those beauteous forms (of Tintern Abbey) gave him sensations. Now we are apt to think that sensations can only be immediate, perceived on the instant that the object is present to the senses; but the poet is, as usual, absolutely right: we may have, so to speak, reflected sensations, as well as those that are immediate; because a conscious sensation depends upon the recognition of an impression in the sensory centres, and this recognition may be evoked, not only by an immediate sensation, but by an association which recalls the image once permanently impressed by the original sensation. Wordsworth is exquisitely right when he speaks of the repeated enjoyment of sensations sweet. 'In lonely rooms and 'mid the din of towns and cities,' some sudden touch of the chords of association has brought to him the soothing joy of a picture—'Forms' with every grace of symmetry, harmony, venerable antiquity, in the ever fresh and gracious setting of a beautiful landscape. The eye of his mind is infinitely gladdened; the ear of his mind, no longer conscious of the din of cities, hears the chord struck by the Wye in its flow, and the notes of the birds and the lowing of the cattle and the acuter notes of the insect world. Again he perceives the odour of the meadowsweet, he touches the coolness of the grass; and all these are as absolutely sensations as when they were for the first time conveyed to his consciousness by the sensory organs.

Open-air Memories should be Stored—We have in these few lines a volume of reasons why we should fill for children the storehouse of memory with many open-air images, capable of giving them reflected sensations of extreme delight. Our constant care must be to secure that they do look, and listen, touch, and smell; and the way to this is by sympathetic action on our part: what we look at they will look at; the odours we perceive, they, too, will get. We heard, the other day, of a little girl who traveled in Italy with her parents in the days of dignified family travelling-carriages. The child's parents were conscientious, and time was precious, not by any means to be wasted on the mere idleness of travelling; so the governess and the little girl had the coupé to themselves, and in it were packed all the paraphernalia of the schoolroom; and the little girl did her sums, learned her geography, probably the counties of England, and all the rest of it, with the least possible waste of time in idle curiosity as to what the 'faire londes' through which she was passing might be like. A story like this shows that we are making advances, but we are still far from fully recognising that our part in the education of children should be thoughtfully subordinated to that played by Nature herself.

Memories of Delight a Source of Physical Well-being and of Mental Restoration—To continue our study of this amazingly accurate, as well as exquisitely beautiful, psychological record:—the poet goes on to tell us that these sensations sweet are 'felt in the blood and felt along the heart,' a statement curiously true to fact; for a pleasurable sensation causes the relaxation of the infinitesimal nerve fibres netted around the capillaries; the blood flows freely, the heart beats quicker, the sense of well-being is increased; gaiety, gladness, supervene; and the gloom of the dull day, and the din of the busy city, exist for us no more; that is to say, memories of delight are, as it were, an elixir of life, capable, when they present themselves, of restoring us at any moment to a condition of physical well-being.

But even this is not the whole. Wordsworth speaks of these memories as 'passing into my purer mind with tranquil restoration'—purer, because less corporeal, less affected by physical conditions, but all the same so intimately related to the physical brain, that the condition of the one must rule the other. Mind and brain, perhaps, have been alike fagged by the insistent recurrence of some one line of thought; when, suddenly, there flashes into the 'purer mind' the cognition of images of delight, presented in consequence of a touch to some spring of association: the current of thought is diverted into new and delightful channels; and weariness and brain fag give place to 'tranquil restoration.'

If mere sensations are capable of doing so much for our happiness, our mental refreshment, and our physical well-being, both at the time of their reception and for an indefinite number of times afterwards, it follows that it is no small part of our work as educators to preserve the acuteness of the children's perceptions, and to store their memories with images of delight.

Sensations and Feelings Distinguished—The poet pursues the investigation and makes a pointed distinction; he not only recovers 'sensations sweet,' but 'feelings, too, of unremembered pleasure.' Very few persons are capable of discriminating between the sensations and the feelings produced by an image recovered by some train of association. Wordsworth's psychology is not only delicately nice, but very just, and the distinction he draws is important to the educator. The truth is, 'the feelings' are out of fashion at present: The Man of Feeling is a person of no account; if he still exists he keeps in the shade, being aware, through a certain quickness of perception which belongs to him, that any little efflorescence proper to his character would be promptly reduced to pulp by some wielder of a sledge hammer. The Man of Feeling has himself to thank for this; he allowed his feelings to become fantastic; his sweet sensibilities ran away with him; he meant pathos and talked bathos; he became an exaggerated type, and, in self-preservation, Society always cuts off the offending limb, so The Man of Feeling is no more.

The Feelings should be Objective, not Subjective—Nor is this the only charge that 'the feelings' have to sustain. So long as the feelings remain objective, they are, like the bloom to the peach, the last perfection of a beautiful character; but when they become subjective, when every feeling concerns itself with the ego, we have, as in the case of sensations, morbid conditions set up; the person begins by being 'over sensitive,' hysteria supervenes, perhaps melancholia, an utterly spoilt life. George Eliot has a fine figure which aptly illustrates this subjective condition of the feelings. She tells us that a philosophic friend had pointed out to her that whereas the surface of a mirror or of a steel plate be covered with minute scratches going in every direction, if you hold a lighted candle to the surface these random scratches appear to arrange themselves and radiate from the central flame; just so with the person whose feelings have been permitted to minister to his egoistic consciousness: all things in heaven and earth are 'felt' as they affect his own personality.

What the Feelings are and are not—What are the feelings? Perhaps they are best expressed in Coleridge's phrase of 'a vague appetency of the mind'; and we may do something to clear our thoughts by a negative examination. The feelings are not sensations, because they have no necessary connection with the senses; they are to be distinguished from the two great affections (of love and justice) because they are not actively exercised upon any objects; they are distinct from the desires because they demand no gratification; and they are distinguishable from the intellectual operations which we call thought, because while thought proceeds from an idea, is active, and arrives at a result, the feelings arrive from perceptions, are passive, and not definitely progressive.

Every Feeling has its Positive and its Negative—Every feeling has its positive and its negative, and these in almost infinitely varying degrees: pleasure, displeasure; appreciation, depreciation; anticipation, foreboding; admiration, contempt; assurance, hesitancy; diffidence, complacency; and so on, through many more delicate nuances of feeling that are nameable, and yet more, so delicate that language is too rough an instrument for their expression.

The Feelings not Moral or Immoral—It will be observed that all these feelings have certain conditions in common; none are distinctly moral or immoral; they have not arrived at the stage of definite thought; they exist vaguely in what would appear to be a semi-conscious intellectual region. Why, then, need we concern ourselves about this little known tract of that terra incognita which we call human nature? This 'why' is the question of the prose-philosopher—our poet sees deeper. In one of the most exquisitely discriminating passages in the whole field of poetry, he speaks of feelings of unremembered pleasure as having no slight or trivial influence on a good man's life, as the sources of 'little nameless unremembered acts of kindness and of love.'

Connection between Unremembered Feelings and Acts—Even the feeling of 'unremembered pleasure'—for it is possible to have the spring of association touched so lightly that one recovers the feeling of former pleasure without recovering the sensation, or the image which produced the sensation, but only just the vague feeling of the pleasure, as when one hears the word 'Lohengrin' and does not wait, as it were, to recover the sensation of musical delight, but just catches a waft of the pleasure which the sensation brought—the feeling of unremembered pleasure, intangible, indefinite, as it is, produces that glow of the heart which warms a good man to 'acts of kindness and of love,' as little, as nameless, and as unremembered as the feelings out of which they spring.

These Trifling Acts the Best Portion of a Good Man's Life—Nameless as they are, the poet does not hesitate to rank these trifling acts as the 'best portion of a good man's life.' But it is only out of the good man's heart that these good issues come, because, as we have said, the feelings are not in themselves moral; they act upon that which is there, and the point brought before us is, that the influence of the feelings is, at the same time, powerful and indirect. Why should the recollection of Tintern Abbey cause a good man to do some little kind thing? We can only give the ultimate answer that 'God has made us so,' that a feeling of even unremembered pleasure prompts the good man to give forth out of the good treasure of his heart in kindness and in love. We have but to think of the outcome of feelings at the negative pole to convince us of the nice exactitude of the poet's psychology. Suppose, that we are not exactly displeased, but unpleased, dull, not quickened by any feeling of pleasure: let us ask ourselves if; in this condition of our feelings, we are prompted to any outpouring of love and kindness upon our neighbours.

The Perception of Character one of our Finest Feelings—Here is another aspect of the feelings, of very great importance to us who have the education of children.

'I do not like you, Doctor Fell,
The reason why I cannot tell,'

is a feeling we all know well enough, and is, in fact, that intuitive perception of character—one of our finest feelings and best guides in life—which is too apt to be hammered out of us by the constant effort to beat down our sensibilities to the explicit and definite. One wonders why people complain of faithless friends, untrustworthy servants, and disappointed affections. If the feelings were retained in truth and simplicity, there is little doubt that they would afford for each of us such a touchstone of character in the persons we come in contact with, that we should be saved from making exigeant demands on the one hand, and from suffering disappointment on the other.

The Orator Plays upon Feelings—The orator plays, by preference, upon the gamut of the feelings. He throws in arguments by the way; brightens his discourse with graphic word-picture, metaphor, simile; for his final effect he relies upon the impression has been able to make upon the feelings of audience, and the event proves him to be right.

Enthusiasm—Not only our little nameless acts, but the great purposes of our lives, arise out of our feelings. Enthusiasm itself is not thought, though it arises when we are

'stung with the rapture of a sudden thought';

it is a glowing, malleable condition of the forces of our nature, during which all things are possible to us, and we only wait for a lead. Enthusiasm in its earliest stage is inconsequent, incoherent, devoid of purpose, and yet is the state out of which all the great purposes of life shape themselves. We feel, we think, we say, we do; this is the genesis of most of our activities.

In Educating the Feelings we Modify the Character—But our feelings, as our thoughts, depend upon what we are; we feel in all things as 'tis our nature to,' and the point to be noticed is that our feelings are educable, and that in educating the feelings we modify the character. A pressing danger our day is that the delicate task of educating shall be exchanged for the much simpler one of blunting the feelings. This is the almost inevitable result of a system where training is given en masse; but not the necessary result, because the tone of feeling of a headmaster or mistress is almost with certainty conveyed, more or less, to a whole school. Still, perhaps, the perfect bloom of the feelings can only be preserved under quite judicious individual culture, and, therefore, necessarily devolves upon parents!

The Sixth Sense of Tact—The instrument to be employed in this culture is always the same—the blessed sixth sense of Tact. It is possible to call up the feeling one desires by a look, a gesture; to dissipate it entirely by the rudeness of a spoken word. Our silence, our sympathy, our perception, give place and play to fit feelings, and, equally, discourage and cause to slink away ashamed the feeling which should not have place.

Beware of Words—But let us beware of words; let us use our eyes and our imagination in dealing with the young; let us see what they are feeling and help them by the flow of our responsive feeling. But words, even words of praise and tenderness, touch this delicate bloom of nature as with a hot finger, and behold! it is gone. Let us consider carefully what feelings we wish to stimulate, and what feelings we wish to repress in our children, and then, having made up our minds, let us say nothing. We all know the shrinking, as of a sore place, with which children receive some well-meant word from a tactless friend.

A Feeling is Communicated by Sympathy—The sense of spiritual touch is our only guide in this region of the feelings, but with this alone we may tune the spirits of the children to great issues, believing that they are capable of all things great. We wish them to revere. Now, reverence is a feeling before it becomes a thought or an act, and it is a communicable feeling, but communicable, like the light of a torch, only by contact. The sentiment of reverence fills our own souls when we see a bird on its nest, an old man at his cottage door, a church in which have centred the aspirations of a village for many an age; we feel, and the children feel our feeling, and they feel too; a feeling is communicated by sympathy, but perhaps in no other way. The ignoble habit of depreciation is in the first place a feeling. It is quite easy to put the children into that other attitude of feeling called forth by the fitness and goodness of the thing regarded, and we all know that it is easy to appreciate or depreciate the same thing. These two feelings alone illustrate the importance of the delicate culture we have in view, for among the minor notes of character none tend more to differentiate persons than this of perceiving cause of satisfaction in an object or a person, or of perceiving cause of dissatisfaction in the same object or person.

Persons are Differentiated by their Powers of Appreciation or Depreciation—An appreciative habit of feeling is a cause of tranquil joy to its possessor, and of ease and contentment to the people connected with him. A depreciative habit, on the contrary, though it affords a little pleasurable excitement because it ministers to the vanity of the ego (I dislike this person or this thing, therefore I know better or am better than others), disturbs tranquillity and puts the person out of harmony with himself and with his surroundings; no stable joy comes of depreciation. But even in dealing with feelings of class we must remember that tact, sympathy and communicable feeling are our only implements; feelings are not thoughts to be reasoned down; they are neither moral nor immoral to challenge our praise or our blame; we cannot be too reticent in our dealings with them in children, nor too watchfully aware that the least inadvertence may bruise some tender blossom of feeling.

Some Danger in Persiflage—This is the risk which attends the habit of persiflage and banter in family talk; a little is thoroughly good and whole some, but this kind of play should be used with very great tact, especially by the elders. Children understand each other so well that there is far less risk of hurt feelings from the tormenting schoolboy than from the more considerate elder.

To Deal with the Feelings of the Young a Delicate Task—There is only one case in which the feelings may not have free play, and that is when they reflect the consciousness of the ego. What are commonly called sensitive feelings—that is, susceptibility for oneself and about oneself, readiness to perceive neglect or slight, condemnation or approbation—through belonging to a fine and delicate character, are in themselves of less worthy order, and require very careful direction lest morbid conditions should be set up. To ignore wisely is an art, and the girl who craves to know what you thought of her when she said this or did the other, need not be told brutally that you did not think of her at all; it is quite enough for her to perceive that your regard is fixed upon something impersonal both to her and you; she takes the hint and looks away from herself, and nothing is said to cause her pain. It appears to be an immutable law that our feelings, as our sensations, must find their occupation in things without; the moment they are turned in upon themselves harm is done. The task of dealing with the susceptibilities of young people is one of the most delicate that falls to us elders, whether we be parents or friends. Undiscriminating sympathy is very perilous, and bluntness of perception is very damaging; we are between Scylla and Charybdis, and must needs walk humbly and warily in this delicate work of dealing with the feelings of children and young people. Our only safeguard is to cherish in ourselves 'the soft, meek, tender soul,' sensitive to the touch of God, and able to deal in soft, meek, tender ways with children, beings of fine and delicate mould as they are.

Chapter 19 'What Is Truth?'

Moral Discrimination required by Parents

We are as a Nation Losing and Gaining in Truthfulness—It is said that we English are no longer to be characterised as a truth-speaking people. This is a distressing charge, and yet we cannot put it away from us with a high hand. Possibly we are in a stage of civilisation which does not tend to produce the fine courage of absolute truthfulness. He who is without fear is commonly without falsehood; and a nation brought up amid the chivalries of war dares to be true. But we live in times of peace; we are no longer called on to defend the truth of our word by the strength of our hand. We speak with very little sense of responsibility, because no one calls us to account; and, so far as we are truth-tellers, we are so out of pure truth of heart and uprightness of life. That is, we may be, as a nation, losing the habit of truth to which the nation's childhood was trained, in ways however rough and ready; but we are growing up, and the truth that is among us is perhaps of a higher quality than the more general truthfulness of earlier days. Now, truth is indeed the white flower of a blameless life, and not the mere result of a fearless habit. The work before us is to bring up our children to this higher manner of truth. We no longer treat this or that particular lie or bit of deceit as a local ailment, for which we have only to apply the proper lotion or plaster; we treat it as symptomatic, as denoting a radical defect of character which we set ourselves to correct.

Opinion without knowledge, says Darwin, has no value, and to treat the tendency to untruthfulness that children often show, one should have a great deal of knowledge of a special kind. To treat a child de novo, place him under a moral microscope, record our observations, and formulate opinions based upon that child, and as many more as we can get into focus, is, it may be, useful and important public work. But it is work for the trained expert, rather than for the busy parent or teacher.

The Child a Human Being, perhaps at his Best—It is not sufficient to bring unaided common-sense and good intentions to this most delicate art of child-study. We cannot afford to discard the wisdom of the past and begin anew with the effort to collect and systematise, hoping to accomplish as much and more in our short span than the centuries have brought us. For, indeed, the child is a human being, immature, but yet, perhaps, a human being at his best. Who amongst us has such gifts of seeing, knowing, comprehending, imagining, such capacities for loving, giving, believing as the little child in the midst! We have no higher praise for our wisest and best than that they are fresh and keen as little children in their interests and loves.

In the Matter of Lying: Two Theories—In this matter of lying, for example, unaided common-sense is likely to start on one of two theses: either the child is born true and you must keep him so; or the child is born false, and you must cure him of it. Popular opinion leans strongly to the first theory in these days; and as we perceive only that which we believe, the tendency is, perhaps, to take the absolute truthfulness and honour of children a little too much for granted. If you would have children true, you must, of course, treat them as if they were true and believe them to be true. But, all the same, wisdom may not play the ostrich. In the last generation, people accepted their children as born false, and what more likely to make them so than this foregone conclusion? Possibly some falling off in truthfulness in our day is traceable to the dogmatic teaching upon which our forebears were brought up.

A Child is Born without Virtue or Vice—The wisdom of the ages—i.e. philosophy, and the science of the present, especially physiology, and more particularly what we may call psycho-physiology—show us that both these positions are wrong, and that all theories founded upon either position, or upon any midway point between the two, must needs be wrong too. A child is born neither true nor false. He is absolutely without either virtue or vice when he comes into the world. He has tendencies, indeed, but these are no more either virtuous or vicious than is the colour of his eyes. Even the child of a liar is not necessarily born a liar, because we are assured acquired tendencies are not transmitted. But there is this to be said. The child born of a family which has from generation to generation been in a subject position may have less predisposition to truthfulness than the child of a family which has belonged for generations to the ruling class. As in the natural world all substances must be reduced to their elements before they can be chemically dealt with, so in the moral world, if we wish to treat an offence, it is best to trace it to that elemental property of human nature of which it is the probable outcome.

Lying is not Elemental, but Secondary and Symptomatic—Now, lying, even in its worst forms, is by no means elemental. Ambition is elemental, avarice, vanity, gratitude, love and hate. But lying arises from secondary causes. The treatment is all the more difficult. It is no longer a case of—the child has lied, punish him; but, where is the weak place in his character, or what is the defect in his education, which has induced this lying habit, if it be a habit? How shall we, not punish the lie, but treat the failing of which it is symptomatic? From this point of view let us consider the extremely interesting classification of lies presented to us by an American educationalist. [Professor G. Stanley Hall, in an article which appeared in the American Journal of Psychology, Jan. 1891. The headings are from Professor Stanley Hall's classification.]

1. Pseudophobia—Treatment—Janet thinks she may have glanced at Mary's slate and seen the answer to her sum. A comparison of the two slates shows that she has not done so, and that Janet, in the effort to save herself from a lie, has actually told one. This sort of morbid conscientiousness is Argus-eyed for other forms of sin. I knew a sick girl of fourteen who was terribly unhappy because she was not able to kneel up in bed when she said her prayers. Was this the 'unpardonable sin'? she asked in unaffected terror. I agree with the writer in question, as to the frequent occurrence of this form of distress, and also in tracing it, not to moral but to physical causes. I should say, too, it is more common in girls than in boys, and in the home-taught than

in the school-taught child. Healthy interests, out-of-door life, engrossing and delightful handiworks, general occupation with things rather than with thoughts, and avoidance of any word or hint that may lead to self-consciousness or the habit of introspection, will probably do much to carry the young sufferer through a difficult stage of life.

2. The Lie Heroic—The lie heroic is, par excellence, the schoolboy's lie, and has its rise, not in any love for lying, but in a want of moral balance; that is to say, the boy has been left to form his own code of ethics. 'Who spilled the ink?' little Tom Brown is asked. I did,' he says, because Jack Spender, the real culprit, is his particular hero at the moment. Faithfulness to a friend is a far higher virtue in Tom's eyes than mere barren truthfulness. And how is Tom to know, if he has not been taught, that it is unlawful to cherish one virtue at the expense of another? Considering how little clear, definite, authoritative teaching children receive on ethical questions, the wonder is that most persons do elaborate some kind of moral code, or code of honour, for themselves.

3. Truth for Friends, Lies for Enemies—A lie under this head differs from the lie heroic chiefly in that it need not bring any risk to the speaker. This class of lies, again, points to the moral ignorance which we are slow to recognise in children because we confound innocence with virtue. It is quite natural for a child to believe that truth is relative, and not absolute, and that whether a lie is a lie or not depends on whom you are speaking to. The children are in the position of 'jesting Pilate.' What is truth? they unconsciously ask.

4. Lies inspired by Selfishness—This is a form of lying for which superficial treatment is quite idle. The lie and the vice of which it is the instrument are so allied that those two cannot be put asunder. Professor Stanley Hall well points out that school is a fertile field for this kind of lying. But it is the selfishness and not the lying that must be dealt with. Cure the first, and the second disappears, having no further occasion. How? This is a hard question. Nothing but a strong impulse to the heroism of unselfishness, initiated and sustained by the grace of God, will deliver boy or girl from the vice of selfishness of which lying is the ready handmaid. But let us not despair; every boy and girl is open to such impulse, is capable of heroic effort. Prayer and patience, and watchfulness for opportunities to convey the stimulating idea—these will not be in vain. Every boy and girl is a hero in posse. There is no worse infidelity than that which gives up the hope of mending any flaw of character, however bad, in a young creature. All the same, happy those parents who have not allowed selfishness and virtue (whether in the form of truthfulness, or under some other name) to come to hand to hand conflict. It is easy to give direction to the tendencies of a child; it is agonisingly difficult to alter the set of character in a man.

5. Deceptions of Imagination and Play—Due to an Unfed Imagination—Lessons in Truth Telling—I passed little Muriel in the park one day; the child was not looking; her companion was unknown to me. I was engaged with my companion, and believed that Muriel had not noticed me. The little girl went home and told her mother that I had kissed her and asked various questions about the family health. What could be the child's motive? She had none. Her active imagination rehearsed the little dialogue which most naturally would have taken place; and this was so real to her that it obscured the fact. The reality, the truth, to Muriel, was what she imagined had taken place. She had probably no recollection whatever of the actual facts. This sort of failure in verbal truthfulness is excessively common in imaginative children, and calls for prompt attention and treatment; but not on the lines a hasty and righteous parent might be inclined to adopt. Here is no call for moral indignation. The parents and not the child are in fault. The probability is that the child's ravenous imagination is not duly and daily supplied with its proper meat, of fairy tale in early days, of romance, later. Let us believe of the children that trailing clouds of glory do they come from the place where all things are possible, where any delightful thing may happen. Let us believe that our miserable limitations of time and space and the laws of matter irk them inconceivably, imprison the free soul as a wild bird in a cage. If we refuse to give the child outlets into the realms of fancy, where everything is possible, the delicate Ariel of his imagination will still work within our narrow limits upon our poor tasks, and every bit of our narrow living is played over with a thousand variations, apt to be more vivid and interesting than the poor facts, therefore, more likely to remain with the child as the facts which he will produce when required to speak the truth. What is the cure? Give the child free entrance into, abundant joyous living in, the kingdom of make-believe. Let him people every glen with fairies, every island with Crusoes. Let him gift every bird and beast with human interests, which he will share when the dear fairy godmother arrives with an introduction. Let us be glad and rejoice that all things are possible to the children, recognising, in this condition of theirs, their fitness to receive and

believe and understand, as, alas! we cannot do, the things of the kingdom of God. The age of faith is a great sowing time, doubtless designed, in the Divine scheme of things, especially that parents may make their children at home in the things of the Spirit before contact with the world shall have materialised them.

At the same time the more imaginative the child, the more essential is it that the boundaries of the kingdom of make-believe should be clearly defined, and exact truthfulness insisted upon in all that concerns the narrower world where the grown-ups live. It is simply a matter of careful education; daily lessons in exact statement, without any horror or righteous indignation about misstatements, but warm, loving encouragement to the child who gives a long message quite accurately, who tells you just what Miss Brown said and no more, just what happened at Harry's party without any garnish. Every day affords scope for a dozen little lessons at least, and, gradually, the more severe beauty of truth will dawn upon the child whose soul is already possessed by the grace of fiction.

6. Pseudomania—We have little to say on this score, except to counsel parents to keep watch at the place of the letting out of waters. No doubt the condition is pathological, and calls for curative treatment rather than punishment. But we believe it is a condition which need never be set up. The girl who has been able to win esteem for what she really is and really does, is not tempted to 'pose,' and the boy who has found full outlet for his energies, physical and mental, has no part of himself left to spend upon 'humbugging.' This is one of the cases which show how important it is for parents to acquaint themselves with that delicate borderland of human nature which touches the material and the spiritual. How spiritual thought and material brain interact; how brain and nerves are inter-dependent; how fresh air and wholesome food affect the condition of the blood which nourishes the nerves; how the nerves again may bear tyrannous sway over all that we include under 'bodily health'; these are matters that the parent should know who would avoid the possibility of the degradation described as Pseudomania from being set up in any one of his children.

Signs of Pseudomania—It is as well that those who have to do with young people should be familiar with one or two marked signs of this mentally diseased condition; as, the furtive glance from under half-closed lids, shot up to see how you are taking it all; the flowing recital, accompanied by a slightly absent preoccupied look, which denotes that the speaker is in the act of inventing the facts he relates.

It is not necessary to enlarge upon palliatives, lies of terror, or one or two more classes of lies which seem to be of frequent occurrence, as lies of display (boasting), lies of carelessness (inaccuracy), and, worst of all, lies of malice (false witness).

Children must be Trained to Truthfulness—It is well, however, to commend the subject to the attention of parents; for, though one child may have more aptitude than another, neither truthfulness nor the multiplication table come by nature. The child who appears to be perfectly truthful is so because he has been carefully trained to truthfulness, however indirectly and unconsciously. It is more important to cultivate the habit of truth than to deal with the accident of lying.

Moral teaching must be as simple, direct and definite as the teaching which appeals to the intellect; presented with religious sanctions, quickened by religious impulses, but not limited to the prohibitions of the law nor to the penalties which overtake the transgressor.

Chapter 20 Show Cause Why

Parents responsible for Competitive Examinations

We have been asking, Why?—We have been asking, Why? like Mr. Ward Fowler's Wagtail, for a long time. We asked, Why? about linen underclothing, and behold it is discarded. We asked, Why? about numberless petticoats, and they are going. We are asking—Why? about carpets and easy chairs, and all manner of luxurious living; and probably the year 1910 will see of these things only the survivals. It is well we should go about with this practical Why? rather than with the 'Why does a wagtail wag its tail?' manner of problem. The latter issues in vain guesses, and the pseudo-knowledge which puffeth up. But if; Why? leads us to—'Because we should not; then let us do the thing we should.' This manner of Why? is like a poker to a dying fire.

Tom goes to School to get a good place in Class—Why is Tom Jones sent to school? That he may be educated, of course, say his parents. And Tom is dismissed with a fervent hope that he may take a good place.

But never a word about the delights of learning, or of the glorious worlds of Nature and of thought to which his school studies will presumably prove an open sesame. 'Mind you be a good boy and get a good place in your class,' is Tom's valediction; and his little soul quickens with purpose. He won't disappoint father, and mother shall be proud of him. He'll be the top boy in his class. Why, he'll be the top boy in the whole school, and get prizes and things, and won't that be jolly! Tommy says nothing of this, but his mother sees it in his eyes and blesses the manly little fellow. So Tommy goes to school, happy boy, freighted with his father's hopes and his mother's blessings.

Tom passes his 'Exams.'—By-and-by comes a report the main delight of which is, that Tommy has gained six places; more places are gained, prizes, removes—by-and-by scholarships. Before he is twelve Tommy is able to earn the whole of his future schooling by his skill in that industry of the young popularly known as Exams. Now he aims at larger game; 'exams' still, but 'exams' big with possibilities, 'exams' which will carry him through his University career. His success is pretty certain, because you get into the trick of 'exams' as of other crafts. His parents are congratulated, Tom is more or less of a hero in his own eyes and in those of his compeers. Examinations forever! Hip, hip! Never was a more facile way for a youth to distinguish himself; that is, if his parents have sent him into the world blessed with any inheritance of brains. For the boy not so blessed—why, he may go to the Colonies and that will make a man of him.

So do the Girls—The girls come in a close second. The 'Junior,' the 'Senior,' the 'Higher,' the 'Intermediate,' the 'B.A.,' and what else you will, mark the epochs in most girls' lives. Better, say you, than having no epochs at all. Unquestionably, yes. But the fact that a successful examination of one sort or another is the goal towards which most of our young people are labouring with feverish haste and with undue anxiety, is one which possibly calls for the scrutiny of the investigating Why?

In the first place, people rarely accomplish beyond their own aims. Their aim is a pass, not knowledge; 'they cram to pass and not to know; they do pass and they don't know,' says Mr. Ruskin; and most of us who know the 'candidate' will admit that there is some truth in the epigram. There are, doubtless, people who pass and who also know, but, even so, it is open to question, whether passing is the most direct, simple, natural and efficacious way of securing knowledge, or whether the persons who pass and know are not those keen and original minds which would get blood out of a stone,—anyway, sap out of sawdust.

The Tendency of Grind—Again—except for the fine power of resistance possessed by the human mind, which secures that most persons who go through examination grind come out as they went in, absolutely unbiassed towards any intellectual pursuits whatever—except for this, the tendency of the grind is to imperil that individuality which is the one incomparably precious birthright of each of us. The very fact of a public examination compels that all who go in for it must study on the same lines.

No Choice as to the Matter or Manner of Studies—It will be urged that there is no necessary limitation to studies outside the examination syllabus, nor any restrictions whatever as to the direction of study even upon the syllabus; but this is a mistake.

Whatever public examinations a given school takes, the whole momentum of pupils and staff urges towards the great issue. As to the manner of study, this is ruled by the style of questions set in a given subject; and Dry-as-dust wins the day because it is easier and fairer to give marks upon definite facts than upon mere ebullitions of fancy or genius. So it comes to pass that there is absolutely no choice as to the matter or manner of their studies for most boys and girls who go to school, nor for many of those who work at home. For so great is the convenience of a set syllabus that parents and teachers are equally glad to avail themselves of it

Tyranny of Competitive Examination Supported by Parents—It appears, then, that the boy is in bondage to the schoolmaster, and the schoolmaster to the examiner, and the parents do no more than acquiesce. Would parents be astounded if they found themselves in this matter a little like the man who had talked prose all his life without knowing it? The tyranny of the competitive examination is supported for the most part by parents. We do not say altogether. Teachers do their part manfully; but, in the first place, teachers unsupported by parents have no power at all in the matter; not a single candidate could they present beyond their own sons and daughters; in the next place, we do not hesitate to say that the whole system is forced upon teachers (though, perhaps, by no means against their will) by certain ugly qualities of human nature as manifested in parents. Ignorance, idleness, vanity, avarice, do not carry a pleasant sound; and if we, who believe in parents, have the temerity to suggest such shadows to the father basking in the sunshine of his boy's success, we would add that the rest of us who are not parents are still more to blame; that it is terribly hard to run counter to the current of the hour; and that 'harm is wrought through want of thought.'

The Evil Lies in the Competition—Ignorance is excusable, but wilful ignorance is culpable, and the time has come for the thoughtful parent to examine himself and see whether or no it be his duty to make a stand against the competitive examination system. Observe, the evil lies in the competition, not in the examination. If the old axiom be true, that the mind can know nothing but what it can produce in the form of an answer to a question put by the mind itself; it is relatively true that knowledge conveyed from without must needs be tested from without. Probably, work on a given syllabus tested by a final examination is the condition of definite knowledge and steady progress. All we contend for is that the examination shall not be competitive.

Examination Necessary—but should Include the whole School—It will be urged that it is unfair to rank such public examinations as the Universities' Local—which have done infinitely much to raise the standard of middle-class education, especially amongst girls, and upon which neither prize nor place depends—as competitive examinations. They are rarely competitive, it is true, in the sense of any extraneous reward to the fortunate candidate; but, happily, we are not so far gone from original righteousness but that Distinction is its own reward. The pupil is willing to labour, and rightly so, for the honour of a pass which distinguishes him among the élite of his school. The schools themselves compete (con+petere = to seek with) as to which shall send in the greatest number of candidates and come out with the greatest number of Honours, Scholarships, and what not. These distinctions are well advertised, and the parent who is on the look-out for a school for his boy is all too ready to send him where the chances of distinction are greatest. Examinations which include the whole school, and where every boy has his place on the list, higher or lower, are another thing, though these also appeal to the emulous principle, they do not do so in excess, the point to be noted.

The Primary Desires—But why should so useful an incentive to work as a competitive examination be called in question? There are certain facts which may be predicated of every human being who is not, as the country folk say, 'wanting.' Everyone wants to get on; whatever place we occupy we aim at the next above it. Everyone wants to get rich, or, anyway, richer; whether the wealth he chooses to acquire be money or autographs. Everyone wants the society of his fellows; if he does not, we call him a misanthrope and say, to use another popular and telling phrase, 'He's not quite right.' We all want to excel, to do better than the rest, whether in a tennis-match or an examination. We all want to know, though some of us are content to know our neighbours' affairs, while others would fain know about the stars in their courses. We all, from the sergeant in his stripes to the much-decorated commanding officer, want people to think well of us. Now the several desires, of power, of wealth, of society, of excelling, of knowledge, of esteem, are primary springs of action in every human being. Touch any one of them, in savage or in savant, and you cannot fail of a response. The Russian moujik besieges a passing traveller with questions about the lands he has seen, because he wants to know. The small boy gambles with his marbles because he wants to get. The dairymaid dons a new bow because she wants to be admired, the only form of esteem to which she is awake. Tom drives when the children play horses because he wants to rule. Maud works herself into a fever for her examination because she wants to excel and 'to pass' is the hall-mark of excellence, that is, of those who excel.

Neither Virtuous nor Vicious—Now these desires are neither virtuous nor vicious. They are common to us all and necessary to us all, and appear to play the same part towards our spiritual being that the appetites do to our material existence; that is, they stimulate us to the constant effort which is the condition of progress, and at the same time the condition of health. We know how that soul stagnates which thinks nothing worth an effort

They Stimulate to Effort—He is a poor thing who is content to be beaten on all hands. We do not quarrel with the principle of emulation any more than we do with that of respiration. The one is as natural and as necessary as the other, and as little to be brought before a moral tribunal. But it is the part of the educator to recognise that a child does not come into the world a harp with one string; and that the perpetual play upon this one chord through all the years of adolescence is an evil, not because emulation is a vicious principle, but because the balance of character is destroyed by the constant stimulation of this one desire at the expense of the rest.

Curiosity as Active as Emulation—Equally strong, equally natural, equally sure of awakening a responsive stir in the young soul, is the divinely implanted principle of curiosity. The child wants to know; wants to know incessantly, desperately; asks all manner of questions about everything he comes across, plagues his elders and betters, and is told not to bother, and to be a good boy and not ask questions. But this only sometimes. For the most part we lay ourselves out to answer Tommy's questions so far as we are able, and are sadly ashamed that we are so soon floored by his insatiable curiosity about natural objects and phenomena. Tommy has his reward.

Extent of a Child's Knowledge—The most surprising educational feat accomplished amongst us is the amount of knowledge, about everything within his range, which Tommy has acquired by the end of his sixth year. 'Why, he knows as much as I do, about'—this, and that, and the other, says his astonished and admiring father. Take him to the seaside, and in a week he will tell you all about trawling and mackerel fishing, the ways of the fisherfolk, and all that his inquisitive mind can find out unaided. He would tell all about sand, and shells, and tides, and waves, only, poor little boy, he must have help towards this manner of knowledge, and there is no one to give it to him. However, he finds out all that he can about all that he sees and hears, and does amass a surprising amount of exact knowledge about things and their properties.

Why the Schoolboy is no longer Curious—When Tommy goes to school, his parents find themselves relieved of the inconvenience of his incessant Why? They are probably so well pleased to be let off that it does not occur to them to ask themselves, Why Tommy no longer wonders Why? Up to this period Nature has been active. She has been allowed to stimulate that one of his desires most proper to minister to his mental growth, just as, if let alone, she would give him that hearty appetite which should promote his physical growth. She has it all her own way. The desire of knowledge is that spring of action most operative in Tommy's childhood. But he goes to school. Knowledge is a pure delight to Tommy. Let his lessons approach him on the lines of his nature—not on the lines proper for certain subjects of instruction—and the little boy has no choice. He cannot help learning and loving to learn, ''cos 'tis his nature to.'

This, of presenting knowledge to Tommy on the lines of his nature, is, however, a difficult and delicate task. Not every schoolmaster, any more than every parent, is keen to give Tommy what he wants in this matter of needful knowledge. So, once upon a time, let us suppose, there arose a pedagogue to whom was discovered a new and easier way. The morning had seen the poor man badly baffled by the queries of boys who wanted to know. How was a man, who had pretty well done with fresh studies for his own part, to keep up with these eager intelligences? In a vision of the night it is disclosed to Cognitus that there is another and an easier way. The desire of knowledge is not the only desire active in the young bosom.

Every Boy Wants to Excel—Just as much as he wants to know, he wants to excel, to do better than the rest. 'Every soul of them wants to be first in one way or another—first in games, if not in class.'

Now, Cognitus was a philosopher; he knew that, as a rule, but one desire is supremely active at one time in the breast of boy or man. Kindle their emulation, and all must needs do the same thing in the same way to see who can do it best. The boys will no longer want to know; they will get their due share of learning in regular ways, and really get on better than if they were moved by the restless spirit of inquiry. Eureka! A discovery; honour and renown for master and boys—no need for cane or imposition, for emulation is the best of all disciplinarians—and steady-going, quiet work, without any of the fatiguing excursions into new fields to which the craving for knowledge leads. 'How pleased the parents will be, too,' says Cognitus, for he knows that paternal love, now and then, looks for a little sustenance from paternal vanity, that the child who does well is dear.

Emulation an Easier Spring to Work than Curiosity—Nay, who knows but the far-seeing Cognitus beheld, as in a vision, the scholarships and money awards which should help to fill the pocket of Paternus, or should, any way, lessen the drain there upon. Here, indeed, is a better way, upon which Paternus and Cognitus may well consent to walk together. Every one is happy, everyone content, nobody worried, a great deal of learning got in. What would you have more? Just one thing, honoured Cognitus—that keen desire for knowledge, that same incessant Why? with which Tommy went to school, and which should have kept him inquisitive about all things good and great and wise throughout the years given to him wherein to lay the groundwork of character, the years of his youth.

But the Boy no longer Wants to Know—We cannot put our finger upon Cognitus, and are pretty sure that he arrived by a consensus of opinion, and through considerable urgency on the part of parents. No one is to blame for a condition of things which is an enormous advance upon much of what went before. Only, knowledge is advancing, and it is full time that we reconsider our educational principles and recast our methods. We absolutely must get rid of the competitive examination system if we would not be reduced to the appalling mediocrity which we see, in China, for example, to have befallen an examination-ridden empire.

An Examination-ridden Empire—Probably the world has never seen a finer body of educationalists than those who at the present moment man our schools, both Boys' and Girls'. But the originality, the fine initiative, of these most able men and women is practically lost. The schools are examination-ridden, and the heads can strike out no important new lines. Let us begin our efforts by believing in one another, parents in teachers and teachers in parents. Both parents and teachers have the one desire, the advance of the child along the lines of character. Both groan equally under the limitations of the present system. Let us have courage, and united and concerted action will overthrow this Juggernaut that we have made.

Chapter 21 A Scheme of Educational Theory Proposed to Parents

Each Class in Society should have its Ideal—One of Mr. Matthew Arnold's discriminating utterances may help us in the effort to define anew the scope and the methods of education. In A French Eton (page 61) he says:—'The education of each class in society has, or ought to have, its ideal, determined by the wants of that class, and by its destination. Society may be imagined so uniform that one education shall be suitable for all its members; we have not a society of that kind, nor has any European country . . . Looking at English society at this moment one may say that the ideal for the education of each of its classes to follow, the aim which the education of each should particularly endeavour to reach, is different.'

This remark, to which we can give only a doubtful assent, helps us, nevertheless, to define our position. In this matter of class differentiation we believe we have scientific grounds for a line of our own. The Fathers (why should we not have Fathers in education as well as in theology?) worked out, for the most part, their educational thought with an immediate view to the children of the poor.

Poor Children need a Vocabulary—Because the children that he had to deal with had a limited vocabulary, and untrained observing powers, Pestalozzi taught them to see and then to say: 'I see a hole in the carpet. I see a small hole in the carpet. I see a small round hole in the carpet. I see a small round hole with a black edge in the carpet,' and so on; and such training may be good for such children. But what is the case with the children we have to deal with? We believe to-day on scientific grounds in the doctrine of heredity, and certainly in this matter experience supports our faith.

Children of Educated Parents do not—Punch has hit off the state of the case. 'Come and see the puff-puff, dear.' 'Do you mean the locomotive, Grandmamma?' As a matter of fact, the child of four and five has a wider, more exact vocabulary in everyday use than that employed by his elders and betters, and is constantly adding to this vocabulary with surprising quickness; ergo, to give a child of this class a vocabulary is no part of direct education. Again, we know that nothing escapes the keen scrutiny of the little people. It is not their perceptive powers we have to train, but the habit of methodical observation and accurate record.

Generations of physical toil do not tend to foster imagination. It may be good, then, for the children of the working classes to have games initiated for them, to be carried through little dramatic plays until, perhaps, in the end they will be able to invent such little dramas for themselves!

This, true of Imagination—But the children of the cultured classes—why, surely their danger is rather to live too much in realms of fancy. A single sentence in lesson or talk, the slightest sketch of a historical character, and they will play at it for a week, inventing endless incidents. Like Tennyson, when he was a child, they will carry on a story of the siege and defence of a castle (represented by a mound, with sticks for its garrison) for weeks together; and a child engrossed with these larger interests feels a sensible loss of dignity when he flaps his wings as a pigeon or skips about as a lamb, though, no doubt, he will do these things with pleasure for the teacher he loves. Imagination is ravenous for food, not pining for culture, in the children of educated parents, and education need not concern herself directly, for them, with the development of the conceptive powers. Then with regard to the child's reasoning powers, most parents have had experiences of this kind. Tommy is five. His mother had occasion to talk to him about the Atlantic Cable, and said she did not know how it was insulated; Tommy remarked next morning that he had been thinking about it, and perhaps the water itself was an insulator. So far from needing to develop their children's reasoning powers, most parents say—'Oh, wad the gods the giftie gie us'—to answer the everlasting 'why' of the intelligent child.

The Development of Faculties Important for Ignorant and Deficient Children—In a word, to develop the child's so-called faculties is the main work of education when ignorant or otherwise deficient children are concerned; but the children of educated parents are never ignorant in this sense. They awake to the world all agog for knowledge, and with keen-edged faculties; therefore the principle of heredity causes us to re-cast our idea of the office of education, and to recognise that the child of intelligent parents is born with an inheritance of self-developing faculties.

But not for Children of Educated Parents—Thus education naturally divides itself into education for the children of lettered, and education for the children of unlettered parents. In fact, this class question, which we are all anxious to evade in common life, comes practically into force in education. It is necessary to individualise and say, this part of education is the most important for this child, or this class, but may be relegated into a lower place for another child or another class.

The Educator should form Habits—If science limits our range of work as regards the development of so-called faculties, it extends it in equal measure with regard to habit. Here we have no new doctrine to proclaim. 'One custom overcometh another,' said Thomas a' Kempis, and that is all we have to say; only, physiologists have made clear to us the rationale of this law of habit. We know that to form in his child right habits of thinking and behaving is a parent's chief duty, and that this can be done for every child definitely and within given limits of time. But this question has been already dealt with, and we need do no more than remind parents of what they already know.

Should Nourish with Ideas—To nourish a child daily with loving, right, and noble ideas we believe to be the parent's next duty. The child having once received the Idea will assimilate it in his own way, and work it into the fabric of his life; and a single sentence from his mother's lips may give him a bent that will make him, or may tend to make him, painter or poet, statesman or philanthropist. The object of lessons should be in the main twofold: to train a child in certain mental habits, as attention, accuracy, promptness, etc., and to nourish him with ideas which may bear fruit in his life.

Our Main Objects—There are other educational principles which we bear in mind and work out, but for the moment it is worth while for us to concentrate our thought upon the fact that one of our objects is to accentuate the importance of education under the two heads of the formation of habits and the presentation of ideas; and, as a corollary, to recognise that the development of faculties is not a supreme object with the cultivated classes, because this is work which has been done for their children in a former generation.

We recognise Material and Spiritual Principles of Human Nature—But how does all this work? Is it practical? Is it the question of to-day? It must needs be practical because it gives the fullest recognition to the two principles of human nature, the material and the spiritual. We are ready to concede all that the most advanced biologist would ask of us. Does he say, 'Thought is only a mode of motion?' If so, we are not dismayed. We know that ninety-nine out of a hundred thoughts that pass through our minds are involuntary, the inevitable result of those modifications of the brain tissue which habit has set up. The mean man thinks mean thoughts, the magnanimous man great thoughts, because we all think as we are accustomed to think, and Physiology shows us why. On the other hand, we recognise that greater is the spirit within us than the matter which it governs. Every habit has its beginning. The beginning is the idea which comes with a stir and takes possession of us.

We recognise the Supreme Educator—The idea is the motive power of life, and it is because we recognise the spiritual potency of the idea that we are able to bow reverently before the fact that God the Holy Spirit is Himself the Supreme Educator, dealing with each of us severally in the things we call sacred and those we call secular. We lay ourselves open to the spiritual impact of ideas, whether these be conveyed by the printed page, the human voice, or whether they reach us without visible sign.

Studies are Valued as they present Fruitful Ideas—But ideas may be evil or may be good; and to choose between the ideas that present themselves is, as we have been taught, the one responsible work of a human being. It is the power of choice that we would give our children. We ask ourselves, 'Is there any fruitful idea underlying this or that study that the children are engaged in?' We divest ourselves of the notion that to develop the faculties is the chief thing; and a 'subject' which does not rise out of some great thought of life we usually reject as not nourishing, not fruitful; while we usually, but not invariably, retain those studies which give exercise in habits of clear and orderly thinking. We have some gymnastics of the mind whose object is to exercise what we call faculties as well as to train in the habit of clear and ordered thinking. Mathematics, grammar, logic, etc., are not purely disciplinary; they do develop, if a bull may be allowed intellectual muscle. We by no means reject the familiar staples of education, in the school sense, but we prize them even more for the record of intellectual habits they leave in the brain tissue than for their distinct value in developing certain 'faculties.'

Nature-Knowledge—Thus our first thought with regard to Nature-knowledge is that the child should have a living personal acquaintance with the things he sees. It concerns us more that he should know bistort from persicaria, hawkweed from dandelion, and where to find this and that, and how it looks, living and growing, than that he should talk about epigynous and hypogynous. All this is well in its place, but should come quite late, after the child has seen and studied the living growing thing in situ, and has copied colour and gesture as best he can.

Object-Lessons—So of object-lessons; we are not anxious to develop his observing powers on little bits of everything, which he shall describe as opaque, brittle, malleable, and so on. We would prefer not to take the edge off his curiosity in this way; we should rather leave him receptive and respectful for one of those opportunities for asking questions and engaging in talk with his parents about the lock in the river, the mowing machine, the ploughed field, which offer real seed to the mind of a child, and do not make him a priggish little person able to tell all about it.

We trust much to Good Books—Once more, we know that there is a storehouse of thought wherein we may find all the great ideas that have moved the world. We are above all things anxious to give the child the key to this storehouse. The education of the day, it is said, does not produce reading people. We are determined that the children shall love books, therefore we do not interpose ourselves between the book and the child. We read him his Tanglewood Tales, and when he is a little older his Plutarch, not trying to break up or water down, but leaving the child's mind to deal with the matter as it can.

We do not recognise 'Child-Nature.'—We endeavour that all our teaching and treatment of children shall be on the lines of nature, their nature and ours, for we do not recognise what is called 'Child-nature.' We believe that children are human beings at their best and sweetest, but also at their weakest and least wise. We are careful not to dilute life for them, but to present such portions to them in such quantities as they can readily receive.

We are Tenacious of Individuality: we consider Proportion—In a word, we are very tenacious of the dignity and individuality of our children. We recognise steady, regular growth with no transition stage. This teaching is up to date, but it is as old as common sense. Our claim is that our common sense rests on a basis of Physiology, that we show a reason for all that we do, and that we recognise 'the science of the proportion of things,' put the first thing foremost, do not take too much upon ourselves, but leave time and scope for the workings of Nature and of a higher Power than Nature herself.

We think that Children have a Right to Knowledge—Much guidance and stimulation are afforded by another principle. We are not anxious to contend with Kant that the mind possesses certain a priori knowledge; nor with Hume that it holds innate ideas. The more satisfying proposition seems to be that the mind has, as it were, prehensile adaptations to each department of universal knowledge. We find that children lay hold of all knowledge which is fitly presented to them with avidity, and therefore we maintain that a wide and generous curriculum is due to them.

Chapter 22 A Catechism Of Educational Theory

Character an Achievement—As the philosophy which underlies any educational or social scheme is really the vital part of that scheme, it may be well to set forth, however meagrely, some fragments of the thought on which we found our teaching. We believe—

That disposition, intellect, genius, come pretty much by nature.

That character is an achievement, the one practical achievement possible to us for ourselves and for our children.

That all real advance, in family or individual or nation, is along the lines of character.

That, therefore, to direct and assist the evolution of character is the chief office of education.

But perhaps we shall clear the ground better by throwing a little of the teaching of the Union ['The Parents' National Educational Union.'] into categorical form:—

Character and Disposition.

Origin of Conduct—What is character?

The resultant or residuum of conduct. That is to say, a man is what he has made himself by the thoughts which he has allowed himself, the words he has spoken, the deeds he has done.

How does conduct itself originate?

Commonly, in our habitual modes of thought. We think as we are accustomed to think, and, therefore, act as we are accustomed to act.

What, again, is the origin of these habits of thought and act?

Commonly, inherited disposition. The man who is generous, obstinate, hot-tempered, devout, is so, on the whole, because that strain of character runs in his family.

Means of Modifying Disposition—Are there any means of modifying inherited dispositions?

Yes; marriage, for the race; education, for the individual.

Life-History of a Habit.

How may a bad habit which has its rise in an inherited disposition be corrected?

By the contrary good habit: as Thomas à Kempis has said, 'One custom overcometh another.'

Genesis of a Habit—Trace the genesis of a habit.

Every act proceeds from a thought. Every thought modifies somewhat the material structure of the brain. That is, the nerve substance of the brain forms itself to the manner of thoughts we think. The habit of act rises from the habit of thought. The person who thinks, 'Oh, it will do'; 'Oh, it doesn't matter,' forms a habit of negligent and imperfect work.

Correction of Bad Habit—How may such habit be corrected?

By introducing the contrary line of thought, which will lead to contrary action. 'This must be done well, because—'

Is it enough to think such thought once?

No, the stimulus of the new idea must be applied until it is, so to speak, at home in the brain, and arises involuntarily.

Involuntary Thought.

What do you mean by involuntary thought?

The brain is at work unceasingly, is always thinking, or rather is always being acted upon by thought, as the keys of an instrument by the fingers of a player.

Is the person aware of all the thoughts that the brain elaborates?

No; only of those which are new and 'striking.' The old familiar 'way of thinking' beats in the brain without the consciousness of the thinker.

Conduct depends on Unconscious Cerebration—What name is given to this unconscious thought?

Unconscious (or involuntary) cerebration.

Why is it important to the educator?

Because most of our actions spring from thoughts of which we are not conscious, or, anyway, which are involuntary.

Is there any means of altering the trend of unconscious cerebration?

Yes, by diverting it into a new channel.

The 'unconscious cerebration' of the greedy child runs upon cakes and sweetmeats: how may this be corrected?

By introducing a new idea—the pleasure of giving pleasure with these good things, for example.

Springs of Action.

Is the greedy child capable of receiving such new idea?

Most certainly; because benevolence, the desire of benefiting others, is one of those springs of action in every human being that need only to be touched to make them act.

Give an example of this fact.

Benevolence—Mungo Park, dying of thirst, hunger, and weariness in an African desert, found himself in the vicinity of a cannibal tribe. He gave himself up for lost, but a woman of the tribe found him, took compassion on him, brought him milk, hid him, and nourished him until he was restored and could take care of himself.

Are there any other springs of action which may be touched with effect in every human being?

Yes, such as the desire of knowledge, of society, of distinction, of wealth; friendship, gratitude, and many more. Indeed, it is not possible to incite a human being to any sort of good and noble conduct but you touch a responsive spring.

How, then, can human beings do amiss?

Malevolence—Because the good feelings have their opposite bad feelings, springs which also await a touch. Malevolence is opposed to benevolence. It is easy to imagine that the unstable savage woman might have been amongst the first to devour the man she cherished, had one of her tribe given an impulse to the springs of hatred within her.

In view of these internal impulses, what is the duty of the educator?

To make himself acquainted with the springs of action in a human being, and to touch them with such wisdom, tenderness and moderation that the child is insensibly led into the habits of the good life.

Habits of the Good Life

Habits of 'Well-brought-up' Persons—Name some of these habits.

Diligence, reverence, gentleness, truthfulness, promptness, neatness, courtesy; in fact, the virtues and graces which belong to persons who have been 'well brought up.'

Is it enough to stimulate a spring of action—say, curiosity, or the desire of knowledge, once, in order to secure a habit?

No; the stimulus must be repeated, and action upon it secured over and over many times before a habit is formed.

What common error do people make about the formation of habits?

They allow lapses; they train a child to 'shut the door after him' twenty times, and allow him to leave it open the twenty-first.

With what result?

That the work has to be done over again, because the growth of brain tissue to the new habit (the forming of cell-connections) has been disturbed. The result would appear to be much the same as when the flesh-forming process which knits up a wound is disturbed.

Time should be given to the Forming of Habit—Then the educator should 'time' himself in forming habits? How long may it take to cure a bad habit, and form the contrary good one?

Perhaps a month or six weeks of careful incessant treatment may be enough.

But such treatment requires an impossible amount of care and watchfulness on the part of the educator?

Yes; but not more than is given to the cure of some bodily diseases—measles, or scarlet fever, for example.

Then the thoughts and actions of a human being may be regulated mechanically, so to speak, by setting up the right nerve currents in the brain?

This is true only so far as it is true to say that the keys of a piano produce music.

Thoughts Follow in Sequence—But the thoughts, which may be represented by the fingers of the player, do they not also run their course without the consciousness of the thinker?

They do; not merely vague, inconsequent musings, but thoughts which follow each other with more or less logical sequence, according to the previous training of the thinker.

Would you illustrate this?

Mathematicians have been known to think out abstruse problems in their sleep; the bard improvises, authors 'reel off' without premeditation, without any deliberate intention to write such and such things. The thoughts follow each other according to the habit of thinking previously set up in the brain of the thinker.

Into new Developments—Is it that the thoughts go round and round a subject like a horse in a mill?

No; the horse is rather drawing a carriage along the same high road, but into ever new development of the landscape.

The Initial Thought—In this light, the important thing is how you begin to think on any subject?

Precisely so; the initial thought or suggestion touches as it were the spring which sets in motion a possibly endless succession, or train, of ideas; thoughts which are, so to speak, elaborated in the brain almost without the consciousness of the thinker

Are these thoughts, or successive ideas, random, or do they make for any conclusion?

They make for the logical conclusion which should follow the initial idea.

Then the reasoning power may be set to work involuntarily?

Yes; the sole concern of this power is, apparently, to work out the rational conclusion from any idea presented to it.

Makes for Logical Conclusions—But surely this power of arriving at logical rational conclusions almost unconsciously is the result of education, most likely of generations of culture?

It exists in greater or less degree according as it is disciplined and exercised; but it is by no means the result of education as the word is commonly understood: witness the following anecdote: [From Thompson's Laws of Thought]

'When Captain Head was travelling across the Pampas of South America, his guide one day suddenly stopped him, and, pointing high into the air, cried out, "A lion!" Surprised at such an exclamation, accompanied with such an act, he turned up his eyes, and with difficulty perceived, at an immeasurable height, a flight of condors soaring in circles in a particular spot. Beneath this spot, far out of sight of himself or guide, lay the carcass of a horse, and over this carcass stood, as the guide well knew, a lion, whom the condors were eyeing with envy from their airy height. The sight of the birds was to him what the sight of the lion alone would have been to the traveller, a full assurance of its existence. Here was an act of thought which cost the thinker no trouble, which was as easy to him as to cast his eyes upward, yet which from us, unaccustomed to the subject, would require many steps and some labour.'

'Reason' Acts without Volition—Then is what is called the reason innate in human beings?

Yes, it is innate, and is exercised without volition by all, but gains in power and precision in proportion as it is cultivated.

Not an Infallible Guide to Conduct—If the reason, especially the trained reason, arrives at the right conclusion without any effort of volition on the part of the thinker, it is practically an infallible guide to conduct?

On the contrary, the reason is pledged to pursue a suggestion to its logical conclusion only. Much of the history of religious persecutions and of family and international feuds turns on the confusion which exists in most minds between that which is logically inevitable and that which is morally right.

But according to this doctrine any theory whatever may be shown to be logically inevitable?

Exactly so; the initial idea once received, the difficulty is, not to prove that it is tenable, but to restrain the mind from proving that it is so.

Can you illustrate this point?

The child who lets himself be jealous of his brother is almost startled by the flood of convincing proofs, that he does well to be angry, which rush in upon him. Beginning with a mere flash of suspicion in the morning, the little Cain finds himself in the evening possessed of irrefragable proofs that his brother is unjustly preferred to him: and,

'All seems infected that the infected spy,
As all looks yellow to the jaundiced eye.'

But supposing it is true that the child has cause for jealousy?

Given the starting idea, and his reason is equally capable of proving a logical certainty, whether it is true or whether it is not true.

Is there any historical proof of this startling theory?

Confusion as to Logical and Moral Right—Perhaps every failure in conduct, in individuals, and in nations, is due to the confusion which exists as to that which is logically right, as established by the reason, and that which is morally right, as established by external law.

Is any such distinction recognised in the Bible?

Distinctly so; the transgressors of the Bible are those who do that which is right in their own eyes that is, that of which their reason approves. Modern thought considers, on the contrary, that all men are justified in doing that which is right in their own eyes, acting 'up to their lights,' 'obeying the dictates of their reason.'

For example?

A mother whose cruel usage had caused the death of her child was morally exonerated some time ago in a court of justice because she acted 'from a mistaken sense of duty.'

Error from Mistaken Sense of Duty—But is it not possible to err from a mistaken sense of duty?

Not only possible, but inevitable, if a man accept his 'own reason' as his lawgiver and judge. Take a test case, the case of the superlative crime that has been done upon the earth. There can be no doubt that the persons who caused the death of our Lord and Saviour Jesus Christ acted under a mistaken sense of duty. 'It is expedient that one man die for the people, and that the whole nation perish not,' said, most reasonably, those patriotic leaders of the Jews; and they relentlessly hunted to death this Man whose ascendency over the common people and whose whispered claims to kingship were full of elements of danger to the subject race. 'They know not what they do,' He said, who is the Truth.

Children should be taught Self-knowledge.

All this may be of importance to philosophers; but what has it to do with the bringing-up of children?

A Child should know what he is as a Human Being—It is time we reverted to the teaching of Socrates. 'Know thyself,' exhorted the wise man, in season and out of season; and it will be well with us when we understand that to acquaint a child with himself—what he is as a human being—is a great part of education.

It is difficult to see why; surely much harm comes of morbid introspection?

Introspection is morbid or diseased when the person imagines that all which he finds within him is peculiar to him as an individual. To know what is common to all men is a sound cure for unhealthy self-contemplation.

How does it work?

This Knowledge a Safeguard—To recognise the limitations of the reason is a safeguard in all the duties and relations of life. The man who knows that loyalty is his first duty in every relation, and that if he admit doubting, grudging, unlovely thoughts, he cannot possibly be loyal, because such thoughts once admitted will prove themselves to be right and fill the whole field of thought, why, he is on his guard and writes up 'no admittance' to every manner of mistrustful fancy.

That rule of life should affect the Supreme relationship?

Truly, yes; if a man will admit no beginning of mistrustful surmise concerning his father and mother, his child and his wife, shall he do so of Him who is more than they, and more than all, the 'Lord of his heart'? 'Loyalty forbids' is the answer to every questioning of His truth that would intrude.

Against 'Honest Doubt.'—But when others whom you must needs revere, question and tell you of their 'honest doubt'?

You know the history of their doubt, and can take it for what it is worth—its origin in the suggestion, which, once admitted, must needs reach a logical conclusion even to the bitter end. 'Take heed that ye enter not into temptation,' He said, who needed not that any should tell Him, for He knew what was in men.

Man as Free Agent.

If man is the creature of those habits he forms with care or allows in negligence, if his very thoughts are involuntary and his conclusions inevitable, he ceases to be a free agent. One might as well concede at once that 'thought is a mode of motion,' and cease to regard man as a spiritual being capable of self-regulation. Is not this the case?

It is hardly possible to concede too wide a field to biological research, if we keep well to the front the fact that man is a spiritual being whose material organs act in obedience to non-material ideas; that, for example, as the hand writes, so the brain thinks, in obedience to stimulating ideas.

Life Sustained upon Ideas—Is the idea self originated?

Probably not; it would appear that, as the material life is sustained upon its appropriate food from without, so the immaterial life is sustained upon its food,—ideas spiritually conveyed.

May the words 'idea' and 'suggestion' be used as synonymous terms?

Only in so far as that ideas convey suggestions to be effected in acts.

What part does the man himself play in the reception of this immaterial food?

It is as though one stood on the threshold to admit or reject the viands which should sustain the family.

Volition in the Reception of Ideas—Is this free-will in the reception or rejection of ideas the limit of man's responsibility in the conduct of his life?

Probably it is; for an idea once received must run its course, unless it be superseded by another idea, in the reception of which volition is again exercised.

Origin of Ideas.

How do ideas originate?

They appear to be spiritual emanations from spiritual beings; thus, one man conveys to another the idea which is a very part of himself.

How Ideas are Conveyed—Is the intervention of a bodily presence necessary for the transmission of an idea?

By no means; ideas may be conveyed through picture or printed page; natural objects convey ideas, but, perhaps, the initial idea in this case may always be traced to another mind.

The Supreme Educator—Then the spiritual sustenance of ideas is derived directly or indirectly from other human beings?

No; and here is the great recognition which the educator is called upon to make. God, the Holy Spirit, is Himself the supreme Educator of mankind.

How?

He openeth man's ear morning by morning, to hear so much of the best as the man is able to hear.

In things Natural and Spiritual—Are the ideas suggested by the Holy Spirit confined to the sphere of the religious life?

No; Coleridge, speaking of Columbus and the discovery of America, ascribes the origin of great inventions and discoveries to the fact that 'certain

Vol 2 pg 246

ideas of the natural world are presented to minds already prepared to receive them by a higher Power than Nature herself.'

Is there any teaching in the Bible to support this view?

Yes; very much. Isaiah, for example, says that the ploughman knows how to carry on the successive operations of husbandry, 'for his God doth instruct him and doth teach him.'

Are all ideas which have a purely spiritual origin ideas of good?

Unhappily, no; it is the sad experience of mankind that ideas of evil also are spiritually conveyed.

What is the part of the man?

To choose the good and refuse the evil.

This View throws Light on Christian Doctrine—Does this doctrine of ideas as the spiritual food needful to sustain the immaterial life throw any light on the doctrines of the Christian religion?

Yes; the Bread of Life, the Water of Life, the Word by which man lives, the 'meat to eat which ye know not of,' and much more, cease to be figurative expressions, except that we must use the same words to name the corporeal and the incorporeal sustenance of man. We understand, moreover, how ideas emanating from our Lord and Saviour, which are of His essence, are the spiritual meat and drink of His believing people. We find it no longer a 'hard saying,' nor a dark saying, that we must sustain our spiritual selves upon Him, even as our bodies upon bread.

Divine Co-operation in Education—What practical bearing upon the educator has this doctrine of ideas?

He knows that it is his part to place before the child daily nourishment of ideas; that he may give the child the right initial idea in every study, and respecting each relation and duty of life; above all, he recognises the divine co-operation in the direction, teaching, and training of the child.

The Functions of Education.

How would you summarise the functions of education?

Education is a discipline—that is, the discipline of the good habits in which the child is trained. Education is a life, nourished upon ideas; and education is an atmosphere—that is, the child breathes the atmosphere emanating from his parents; that of the ideas which rule their own lives.

Part of Lessons in Education—What part do lessons and the general work of the schoolroom play in education thus regarded?

They should afford opportunity for the discipline of many good habits, and should convey to the child such initial ideas of interest in his various studies as to make the pursuit of knowledge on those lines an object in life and a delight to him.

A Curriculum—Has a child any natural fitness for knowledge?

Yes; it would appear that he has a natural affinity for all knowledge, and has a right to a generous curriculum of studies.

What duty lies upon parents and others who regard education thus seriously, as a lever by means of which character may be elevated, almost indefinitely?

Perhaps it is incumbent upon them to make conscientious endeavours to further all means used to spread the views they hold; believing that there is such 'progress in character and virtue' possible to the redeemed human race as has not yet been realised or even imagined. 'Education is an atmosphere, a discipline, a life.'

Chapter 23 Whence And Whither

A *Question for Parents—I. Whence?*

Progress of the Parents' National Educational Union—'The Union goes on,' an observer writes, 'without puff or fuss, by its own inherent force'; and it is making singularly rapid progress. At the present moment thousands of children of thinking, educated parents, are being brought up, more or less consciously and definitely, upon the lines of the Union. Parents who read the Parents' Review or other literature of the Society, parents who belong to our various branches, or our other agencies, parents who are influenced by these parents are becoming multitudinous; and all have one note in common—the ardour of persons working out inspiring ideas.

Its Importance—It is hardly possible to overestimate the force of this league of educated parents. When we think of the part that the children being brought up under these influences will one day play in the leading and ruling of the land, we are solemnised with the sense of a great responsibility, and it behoves us to put to ourselves, once again, the two searching queries by which every movement should from time to time be adjudged—Whence? and Whither?

Whence? The man who is satisfied with his dwelling-place has no wish to move, and the mere fact of a 'movement' is a declaration that we are not satisfied, and that we are definitely on our way to some other ends than those commonly accepted. In one respect only we venture boldly to hark back.

The Legacy of the Past—Exceedingly fine men and women were brought up by our grandfathers and grandmothers, even by our mother's and fathers; and the wise and old amongst us, though they look on with great sympathy, yet have an unexpressed feeling that men and women were made on the old lines of a stamp which we shall find it hard to improve upon. This was no mere chance result, nor did it come out of the spelling-book or the Pinnock's Catechisms which we have long ago consigned to the limbo they deserve.

Children Responsible Persons—The teaching of the old days was as bad as it could be, the training was haphazard work, reckless alike of physiology and psychology; but our grandfathers and grandmothers had one saving principle, which, for the last two or three decades, we have been, of set purpose, labouring to lose. They, of the older generation, recognised children as reasonable beings, persons of mind and conscience like themselves, but needing their guidance and control, as having neither knowledge nor experience. Witness the queer old children's books which have come down to us; before all things, these addressed children as reasonable, intelligent and responsible (terribly responsible!) persons. This fairly represents the note of home-life in the last generation. So soon as the baby realised his surroundings, he found himself a morally and intellectually responsible person. Now one of the secrets of power in dealing with our fellow-beings is, to understand that human nature does that which it is expected to do and is that which it is expected to be. We do not mean believed to do and to be, with the fond and foolish faith which Mrs. Hardcastle bestowed on her dear Tony Lumpkin. Expectation strikes another chord, the chord of 'I am, I can, I ought' which must vibrate in every human breast, for 'tis our nature to.' The capable, dependable men and women whom we all know were reared upon this principle.

Now, we are not Sure—But now? Now, many children in many homes are still brought up on the old lines, but not with quite the unfaltering certitude of the old times. Other thoughts are in the air. A baby is a huge oyster (says one eminent psychologist) whose business is to feed, and to sleep, and to grow. Even Professor Sully, in his most delightful book, [Studies of Children, by Professor Sully—Longmans, 10s, 6d] is torn in two. The children have conquered him, have convinced him beyond doubt that they are as ourselves, only more so. But then he is an evolutionist, and feels himself pledged to accommodate the child to the principles of evolution. Therefore the little person is supposed to go through a thousand stages of moral and intellectual development, leading him from the condition of the savage or ape to that of the intelligent and cultivated human being. If children will not accommodate themselves pleasantly to this theory, why, that is their fault, and Professor Sully is too true a child-lover not to give us the children as they are, with little interludes of the theory upon which they ought to evolve. Now I have absolutely no theory to advance, and am, on scientific grounds, disposed to accept the theories of the evolutionary psychologists. But facts are too strong for me.

Intellectual Labour of the Child's First Year—When we consider the enormous intellectual labour the infant goes through during his first year in accommodating himself to the conditions of a new world, in learning to discern between far and near, solid and flat, large and small, and a thousand other qualifications and limitations of this perplexing world, why, we are not surprised that John Stuart Mill should be well on in his Greek at five; that Arnold at three should know all the Kings and Queens of England by their portraits; or that a musical baby should have an extensive repertoire of the musical classics.

Intelligence of Children—I was once emphasising the fact that every child could learn to speak two languages at once with equal facility, when a gentleman present stated that he had a son who was a missionary in Bagdad, married to a German lady, and their little son of three expressed all he had to say with equal fluency in three languages—German, English, and Arabic, using each in speaking to those persons whose language it was. 'Nana, which does God love best, little girls or little boys?' said a meditative little girl of four. 'Oh, little girls, to be sure,' said Nana, with a good-natured wish to please. 'Then if God loves little girls best, why was not God Himself a little girl?' Which of us who have reached the later stages of evolution would have hit upon a more conclusive argument? If the same little girl asked on another occasion, watching the blackbirds at the cherries: 'Nana, if the bees make honey, do the birds make jam?' it was by no means an inane question, and only proves that we older persons are dull and inappreciative of such mysteries of Nature as that bees should make honey.

Children highly Endowed but Ignorant—This is how we find children—with intelligence more acute, logic more keen, observing powers more alert, moral sensibilities more quick, love and faith and hope more abounding; in fact, in all points like as we are, only much more so; but absolutely ignorant of the world and its belongings, of us and our ways, and, above all, of how to control and direct and manifest the infinite possibilities with which they are born.

Happy and Good, or Good and Happy—Our conception of a child rules our relations towards him. Pour s'amuser is the rule of child-life proper for the 'oyster' theory, and most of our children's books and many of our theories of child-education are based upon this rule. 'Oh! he's so happy,' we say, and are content, believing that if he is happy he will be good; and it is so to a great extent; but in the older days the theory was, if you are good you will be happy; and this is a principle which strikes the keynote of endeavour, and holds good, not only through the childish 'stage of evolution,' but for the whole of life, here and hereafter. The child who has learned to 'endeavour himself' (as the Prayer Book has it) has learned to live.

Our Conception of the Child is Old, of Education New—If our conception of Whence? regards the child, as of

'A Being, breathing thoughtful breath,
A traveller betwixt life and death,'—

is old, that of our grandfathers, our conception of the aims and methods of education is new, only made possible within the late decades of the last century; because it rests one foot upon the latest advances in the science of Biology and the other upon the potent secret of these latter days, that matter is the all-serviceable agent of spirit, and that spirit forms, moulds, is absolute lord, over matter, as capable of affecting the material convolutions of the brain as of influencing what used to be called the heart.

Knowing that the brain is the physical seat of habit, and that conduct and character alike are the outcome of the habits we allow: knowing, too, that an inspiring idea initiates a new habit of thought, and, hence a new habit of life, we perceive that the great work of education is to inspire children with vitalising ideas as to the relations of life, departments of knowledge, subjects of thought: and to give deliberate care to the formation of those habits of the good life which are the outcome of vitalising ideas.

Divine Co-operation—In this great work we seek and assuredly find the co-operation of the Divine Spirit, whom we recognise, in a sense rather new to modern thought, as the Supreme Educator of mankind in things that have been called secular, fully as much as in those that have been called sacred.

Two Educational Labours—We are free to give our whole force to these two great educational labours, of the inspiration of ideas and the formation of habits, because, except in the case of children somewhat mentally deficient, we do not consider that the 'development of faculties' is any part of our work; seeing that the children's so-called faculties are already greatly more acute than our own.

Test for Systems—We have, too, in our possession, a test for Systems that are brought under our notice, and can pronounce upon their educational value. For example, some time ago the London Board Schools held an exhibition of work; and great interest was excited by an exhibit which came from New York representing a week's work (on 'Herbartian' lines) in a school. The children worked for a week upon 'an apple.' They modelled it in clay, they painted it in brushwork, they stitched the outline on cardboard, they pricked it, they laid it in sticks (the pentagonal form of the seed vessel.) Older boys and girls modelled an apple-tree and made a little ladder on which to run up the apple tree and gather the apples, and a wheel-barrow to carry the apples away, and a great deal more of the same kind. Everybody said, 'How pretty, how ingenious, what a good idea!' and went away with the notion that here, at last, was education. But we ask 'What was the informing idea?' The external shape, the internal contents of an apple,—matters with which the children were already exceedingly well acquainted. What mental habitudes were gained by this week's work? They certainly learned to look at the apple, but think how many things they might have got familiar acquaintance with in the time. Probably the children were not consciously bored because theimpulse of the teachers' enthusiasm carried them on, But, think of it—

'Rabbits hot and rabbits cold,
Rabbits young and rabbits old
Rabbits tender and rabbits tough'—

no doubt those children had enough of apples anyway. This 'apple' course is most instructive to us as emphasising the tendency in the human mind to accept and rejoice in any neat system which will produce immediate results, rather than to bring every such little course to the test of whether it does or does not further either or both of our great educational principles.

Advance with the Tide—Whither? Our 'whence' opens to us a 'whither' of infinitely delightful possibilities. Seeing that each of us is labouring for the advance of the human race through the individual child we are educating, we consider carefully in what directions this advance is due, and indicated, and we proceed of set purpose and endeavour to educate our children so that they shall advance with the tide. 'Can ye not discern the signs of the times?' A new Renaissance is coming upon us, of unspeakably higher import than the last; and we are bringing up our children to lead and guide, and by every means help in the progress—progress by leaps and bounds—which the world is about to make. But 'whither' is too large a question for the close of a chapter.

Chapter 24 Whence And Whither

2. Whither?

Physical and Psychical Evolutions—The biologists leave thinking persons without hesitation in following the great bouleversement of thought, summed up in the term evolution. They are no longer able to believe otherwise than that man is the issue of processes, ages long in their development; and what is more, and even more curious, that each individual child, from the moment of his conception to that of his birth, appears in his own person to mark an incredible number of the stages of this evolutionary process. The realisation of this truth has made a great impression on the minds of men. We feel ourselves to be part of a process, and to be called upon, at the same time, to assist in the process, not for ourselves exactly, but for any part of the world upon which our influence bears; especially for the children who are so peculiarly given over to us. But there comes, as we have seen, a point where we must arise and make our protest. The physical evolution of man admits of no doubt; the psychical evolution, on the other hand, is not only not proven, but the whole weight of existing evidence appears to go into the opposite scale.

The Greatness of Children—The age of materialism has run its course; we recognise matter as force, but as altogether subject force, and that it is the spirit of a man which shapes and uses his material substance in its own ways to its own ends. Who can tell the way of the spirit? Perhaps this is one of the ultimate questions upon which man has not yet been able to speculate to any purpose; but when we consider the almost unlimited powers of loving and trusting, of discriminating and of apprehending, of perceiving and of knowing, which a child possesses, and compare these with the blunted sensibilities and slower apprehension of the grown man or woman of the same calibre, we are certainly not inclined to think that growth from less to more, and from small to great, is the condition of the spiritual life: that is, of that part of us which loves and worships, reasons and thinks, learns and applies knowledge. Rather would it seem to be true of every child in his degree, as of the divine and typical Child, that He giveth not the Spirit by measure to him.

Wisdom, the Recognition of Relations—It is curious how the philosophy of the Bible is always well in advance of our latest thought. 'He grew in wisdom and in stature,' we are told. Now what is wisdom, philosophy? Is it not the recognition of relations? First, we have to understand relations of time and space and matter, the natural philosophy which made up so much of the wisdom of Solomon; then, by slow degrees, and more and more, we learn that moral philosophy which determines our relations of love and justice and duty to each other: later, perhaps, we investigate the profound and puzzling subject of the inter-relations of our own most composite being, mental philosophy. And in all these and beyond all these we apprehend, slowly and feebly, the highest relation of all, the relation to God, which we call religion. In this science of the relations of things consists what we call wisdom, and wisdom is not born in any man,—apparently not even in the Son of man Himself.

Wisdom increases; Intelligence does not—He grew in wisdom, in the sweet gradual apprehension of all the relations of life: but the power of apprehending, the strong, subtle, discerning spirit, whose function it is to grasp and understand, appropriate and use, all the relations which bind all things to all other things—this was not given to Him by measure; nor, we may reverently believe, is it so given to us.

Differences in Men—That there are differences in the measures of men, in their intellectual and moral stature, is evident enough; but it is well that we should realise the nature of these differences, that they are differences in kind and not in degree; and depend upon what we glibly call the laws of heredity, which bring it to pass that man in his various aspects shall make up that conceivably perfect whole possible to mankind. This is a quite different thing from the notion of a small and feeble measure of heart and intellect in the child, to grow by degrees into the robust and noble spiritual development which, according to the psychical evolutionist, should distinguish the adult human being.

Ignorance is not Impotence—These are quite practical and simple considerations for every one entrusted with the bringing up of a child, and are not to be set aside as abstract principles, the discussion of which should serve little purpose beyond that of sharpening the wits of the schoolmen. As a matter of fact, we do not realise children, we under-estimate them; in the divine words, we 'despise' them, with the best intentions in the world, because we confound the maturity of their frames, and their absolute ignorance as to the relations of things, with spiritual impotence: whereas the fact probably is, that never is intellectual power so keen, the moral sense so strong, spiritual perception so piercing, as in those days of childhood which we regard with a supercilious, if kindly, smile.

All Possibilities Present in a Child—A child is a person in whom all possibilities are present—present now at this very moment—not to be educed after years and efforts manifold on the part of the educator; but indeed it is a greater thing to direct and use this wealth of spiritual power than to develop the so-called faculties of the child. It cannot be too strongly urged that our education of children will depend, nolens volens, upon the conception we form of them. If we regard them as instruments fit and capable for the carrying out of the Divine purpose in the progress of the world, we shall endeavour to discern the signs of the times, perceive in what directions we are being led, and prepare the children to carry forward the work of the world, by giving them vitalising ideas, concerning, at any rate, some departments of that work.

We Live for the Advancement of the Race—Having settled it with ourselves that we and the children alike live for the advancement of the race, that our work is immediately with them, and, through them immediately for all, and that they are perfectly fitted to receive those ideas which are for the inspiration of life, we must next consider in what directions we shall try to set up spiritual activities in the children.

Our Whence in the Potency of the Child, our Whither in the Thought of the Day—We have sought to establish our whence in the potency of the child, we will look for our whither in the living thought of the day, which probably indicates the directions in which the race is making progress. We find that all men everywhere are keenly interested in science, that the world waits and watches for great discoveries; we, too, wait and watch, believing that, as Coleridge said long ago, great ideas of Nature are imparted to minds already prepared to receive them by a higher Power than Nature herself.

All Men are Interested in Science—At a former meeting of the British Association, the President lamented that the progress of science was greatly hindered by the fact that we no longer have field naturalists—close observers of Nature as she is. A literary journal made a lamentable remark there-upon. It is all written in books, said this journal, so we have no longer any need to go to Nature herself. Now the knowledge of Nature which we get out of books is not real knowledge; the use of books is, to help the young student to verify facts he has already seen for himself. Let us, before all things, be Nature-lovers; intimate acquaintance with every natural object within his reach is the first, and, possibly, the best part of a child's education. For himself, all his life long, he will be soothed by—

'The breathing balm,
The silence and the calm,
Of mute, insensate things.'

Children Trained to Observe—And for science, he is in a position to do just the work which is most needed; he will be a close, loving observer of Nature at first hand, storing facts, and free from all impatient greed for inferences.

A new Conception of Art; great Ideas demand great Art—Looking out on the realm of Art again, we think we discern the signs of the times. Some of us begin to learn the lesson which a prophet has been raised up to deliver to this, or the last, generation. We begin to understand that mere technique, however perfect—whether in the rendering of flesh tints, or marbles, or of a musical composition of extreme difficulty is not necessarily high Art. It is beginning to dawn upon us that Art is great only in proportion to the greatness of the idea that it expresses; while what we ask of the execution, the technique, is that it shall be adequate to the inspiring idea. But surely these high themes have nothing to do with the bringing up of children? Yes, they have; everything. In the first place, we shall permit no pseudo Art to be in the same house with our children; next, we shall bring our own facile tastes and opinions to some such searching test as we have indicated, knowing that the children imbibe the thoughts that are in us, whether we will or no; and lastly, we shall inspire our children with those great ideas which shall create a demand, anyway, for great Art.

Children should Learn to Care for Books—In literature, we have definite ends in view, both for our own children and for the world through them. We wish the children to grow up to find joy and refreshment in the taste, the flavour of a book. We do not mean by a book any printed matter in a binding, but a work possessing certain literary qualities able to bring that sensible delight to the reader which belongs to a literary word fitly spoken. It is a sad fact that we are losing our joy in literary form. We are in such haste to be instructed by facts or titillated by theories, that we have no leisure to linger over the mere putting of a thought. But this is our error, for words are mighty both to delight and to inspire. If we were not as blind as bats, we should long ago have discovered a truth very fully indicated in the Bible—that that which is once said with perfect fitness can never be said again, and becomes ever thereafter a living power in the world. But in literature, as in art, we require more than mere form. Great ideas are brooding over the chaos of our thought; and it is he who shall say the thing we are all dumbly thinking, who shall be to us as a teacher sent from God.

Children must be Nurtured on the Best—For the children? They must grow up upon the best. There must never be a period in their lives when they are allowed to read or listen to twaddle or reading-made-easy. There is never a time when they are unequal to worthy thoughts, well put; inspiring tales, well told. Let Blake's 'Songs of Innocence' represent their standard in poetry; De Foe and Stevenson, in prose; and we shall train a race of readers who will demand literature—that is, the fit and beautiful expression of inspiring ideas and pictures of life. Perhaps a printed form to the effect that gifts of books to the children will not be welcome in such and such a family, would greatly assist in this endeavour.

The Solidarity of the Race—To instance one more point—there is a reaching out in all directions after the conception expressed in the words 'solidarity of the race.' We have probably never before felt as now in absolute relation with all men everywhere; everything human is precious to us, the past belongs to us as the present, and we linger tenderly over evidences of the personality of men and women who lived ages ago. An American poet expresses this feeling with Western intensity, but he does not exaggerate when he tells us that he is the soldier wounded in battle, he is the galley slave, and he is the hero come to the rescue, that every human pulse is his pulse, every fall his fall, and every moral victory his triumph. The present writer recollects the moment when the conviction of the common sisterhood of women was brought home to her in a way never to be forgotten. She was driving from station to station in London, and saw a drunken woman carried on a door. She knew by the shock of pain and the tears the sight brought that the woman was not outside of her, but was in some mysterious way part of her—her very self. This was a new perception to a girl, and one never again to be lost sight of. Such shocks of recognition probably come to most of us, and when they come to the Greathearts of the world we get our Elizabeth Frys, our Wilberforces, our Florence Nightingales. Deeds of pity have been done through all the Christian ages, and, indeed, wherever the human heart has had free play; but to feel pity for another and to be aware, however dimly, that that other is, part and lot, indissolubly bound up with ourselves—these are two things. We venture to believe that this is the stage which the education of mankind, as divinely conducted, has reached in our day. In other days, men did good for the love of God, or to save their own souls; they acted uprightly, because it behoved themselves to be just in all their dealings; but the motives which stir us in our relation to each other now are more intimate, tender, indefinable, soul-compelling. What the issues will be when we have learned to con understandingly this new page in the Book of Life we cannot foretell, but we may hope that the Kingdom of God is coming upon us.

Children should be Brought up to Live for All Men—Studying reverently these signs of the times, what indications do we find for our guidance in the bringing up of children? The tender sympathy of the child must be allowed to flow in ways of help and kindness towards all life that anyway touches his. I knew a little girl of five, who came in from her walk under an obvious cloud of distress. 'What is the matter, H—?' she was asked. A quick little 'Nothing,' with the reticence of her family, was all that could be got out of her for some minutes; but a caress broke her down, and, in a passion of pity, she sobbed out, 'A poor man, no home, no food, no bed to lie upon!' Young as she was, the revelation of the common life in humanity had come upon her; she was one with the beggar and suffered with him. Children must, of course, be shielded from intense suffering, but woe to mother or nurse who would shield, by systematically hardening, the child's heart. This little girl had the relief of helping, and then the pain of sympathy ceased to be too much for her.

Children should not hear of 'Impostors'—Whatever our own opinion of the world and of human nature, let us be careful how we breathe the word 'impostor' into the ear of a child, until he is old enough to understand that if the man is an impostor, that does but make him the object of a deeper pity and a wiser help—a help whose object is not to relieve but to reform.

To Serve is Promotion—Again, children are open to vanity as to all other evil dispositions possible to human nature. They must be educated to give and to help without any notion that to do so is goodness on their part. It is very easy to keep them in the attitude of mind natural to a child, that to serve is promotion to the person who serves for indeed he has no absolute claim to be in a position to pour benefits upon another. The child's range of sympathy must be widened, his love must go out to far and near, rich and poor; distress abroad and distress at home should appeal to him equally; and always he should give some manner of help at real cost to himself. When he is old enough, the object-lessons of the newspapers should be brought before him.

No Considerations of Expediency—He should know that atrocities in Armenia, for instance, are the cause of real heart-trouble in English homes; that there are cases of abstract right and wrong for nations as for individuals, which admit of no considerations of expediency; that to succour our neighbour in mortal distress is such an occasion, and that he who has fallen among thieves is therefore our neighbour, whether as a nation or as an individual. Do not let us bring up our children in glass houses, for fear of the ravages of pity upon their tender hearts. Let them know of any distress which would naturally come before them, and let them ease their own pain by alleviating in some way the sufferings they sorrow for. Children were not given to us with infinite possibilities of love and pity that we might choke the springs of pity and train them into hardness of heart. It is our part, on the contrary, to prepare these little ministers of grace for the larger and fuller revelation of the kingdom of heaven that is coming upon us.

Chapter 25 The Great Recognition Required Of Parents

Ruskin on the 'Vaulted Book.'—Mr. Ruskin has done a great service to modern thought in interpreting for us the harmonious and ennobling scheme of education and philosophy recorded upon one quarter of what he calls the 'Vaulted Book,' that is, the Spanish Chapel attached to the Church of St. Maria Novella, in Florence.

Many of my readers have probably studied under Mr. Ruskin's guidance the illuminating teaching of the frescoes which cover roof and walls; but all will like to be reminded of the lessons they have pondered, with reverence and wonder. "The descent of the Holy Ghost is on the left hand (of the roof) as you enter. The Madonna and Disciples are gathered in an upper chamber: underneath are the Parthians, Medes, Elamites, etc., who hear them speak in their own tongues. Three dogs are in the foreground—their mythic purpose, to mark the share of the lower animals in the gentleness given by the outpouring of the Spirit of Christ . . . On this and the opposite side of the Chapel are represented by Simon Memmi's hand, the teaching power of the Spirit of God and the saving power of the Christ of God in the world, according to the understanding of Florence in his time.

"We will take the side of intellect first. Beneath the pouring forth of the Holy Spirit in the point of the arch beneath are the three Evangelical Virtues. Without these, says Florence, you can have no science. Without Love, Faith, and Hope—no intelligence. Under these are the four Cardinal Virtues . . . Temperance, Prudence, Justice, Fortitude. Under these are the great Prophets and Apostles . . . Under the line of Prophets, as powers summoned by their voices, are the mythic figures of the seven theological or spiritual and the seven geological or natural sciences; and under the feet of each of them the figure of its Captain-teacher to the World."

The Seven Natural Sciences—I hope the reader will continue to study Mr. Ruskin's exposition of the 'Vaulted Book' in Mornings in Florence: it is wonderfully full of teaching and suggestions. Our immediate concern is with the seven mythic figures representing the natural sciences, and with the figure of the Captain-teacher of each. First we have Grammar, a gracious figure teaching three Florentine children; and, beneath, Priscian. Next, Rhetoric, strong, calm, and cool; and below, the figure of Cicero with a quite beautiful face. Next, Logic, with perfect pose of figure and lovely countenance; and beneath her, Aristotle—intense keenness of search in his half-closed eyes. Next, Music, with head inclined in intent listening to the sweet and solemn strains she is producing from her antique instrument; and underneath, Tubal Cain, not Jubal, as the inventor of harmony—perhaps the most marvellous record that Art has produced of the impact of a great idea upon the soul of a man but semi-civilised. Astronomy succeeds, with majestic brow and upraised hand, and below her, Zoroaster, exceedingly beautiful—'the delicate Persian head made softer still by the elaborately wreathed silken hair.' Next, Geometry, looking down, considering some practical problem, with her carpenter's square in her hand, and below her, Euclid. And lastly, Arithmetic, holding two fingers up in the act of calculating, and under her, Pythagoras wrapped in the science of number.

'The thoughts of God are broader than the measures of man's mind,' but here we have the breadth of minds so wide in the sweep of their intelligence, so profound in their insight, that we are almost startled by the perception that, pictured on these walls, we have indeed a true measure of the thoughts of God. Let us glance for a moment at the conception of education in our own century.

Education not Religious and Secular—In the first place, we divide education into religious and secular. The more devout among us insist upon religious education as well as secular. Many of us are content to do without religious education altogether; and are satisfied with what we not only call secular but make secular, in the sense in which we understand the word, i.e. entirely limited to the uses of this visible world.

The Great Recognition—Many Christian people rise a little higher; they conceive that even grammar and arithmetic may in some not very clear way be used for God; but the great recognition, that God the Holy Spirit is Himself, personally, the Imparter of knowledge, the Instructor of youth, the Inspirer of genius, is a conception so far lost to us that we should think it distinctly irreverent to conceive of the divine teaching as co-operating with ours in a child's arithmetic lesson, for example. But the Florentine mind of the Middle Ages went further than this: it believed, not only that the seven Liberal Arts were fully under the direct outpouring of the Holy Ghost, but that every fruitful idea, every original conception, whether in Euclid, or grammar, or music, was a direct inspiration from the Holy Spirit, without any thought at all as to whether the person so inspired named himself by the name of God, or recognised whence his inspiration came. All of these seven figures are those of persons whom we should roughly class as pagans, and whom we might be lightly inclined to consider as outside the pale of the divine inspiration. It is truly difficult to grasp the amazing boldness of this scheme of the education of the world which Florence accepted in simple faith.

Knowledge, like Virtue, Divine—But we must not accept even an inspiring idea blindly. Were these people of the Middle Ages right in this plan and conception of theirs? Plato hints at some such thought in his contention that knowledge and virtue are fundamentally identical, and that if virtue be divine in its origin, so must knowledge be also. Ancient Egypt, too, was not in the dark in this matter. 'Pharaoh said unto his servants, can we find such a one as this, a man in whom the Spirit of God is?' Practical discernment and knowledge of everyday matters, and of how to deal with emergencies, were not held by this king of Egypt to be teachings unworthy of the Spirit of God. 'The Spirit of God came upon him and he prophesied among them,' we are told of Saul, and we may believe that this is the history of every great invention and every great discovery of the secrets of Nature. 'Then David gave to Solomon his son . . . . the pattern of all that he had by the spirit, of the courts of the house of the Lord.' We have here a suggestion of the source of every conception of beauty to be expressed in forms of art.

Science, Art and Poetry 'by the Spirit.'—But it is not only with high themes of science, art and poetry that the divine Spirit concerns Himself. It sometimes occurs to one to wonder who invented, in the first place, the way of using the most elemental necessaries of life. Who first discovered the means of producing fire, of joining wood, of smelting ores, of sowing seed, of grinding corn?

Ideas of Common Things—We cannot think of ourselves as living without knowing these things; and yet each one must have been a great idea when it first made a stir in the mind of the man who conceived it. Where did he get his first idea? Happily, we are told, in a case so typical that it is a key to all the rest:—

'Doth the plowman plow all day to sow? doth he open and break the clods of his ground? When he hath made plain the face thereof, doth he not cast abroad the fitches and scatter the cummin, and cast in the principal wheat and the appointed barley and the rie in their place? For his God doth instruct him to discretion, and doth teach him. For the fitches are not threshed with a threshing instrument, neither is a cart wheel turned about upon the cummin; but the fitches are beaten out with a staff, and the cummin with a rod. Bread corn is bruised; because he will not ever be threshing it, nor break it with the wheel of his cart, nor bruise it with his horsemen. This also cometh forth from the Lord of Hosts, which is wonderful in counsel, and excellent in working.'—Isa. xxviii. 24, etc.

'God doth Instruct.'—In the things of science, in the things of art, in the things of practical everyday life, his God doth instruct him and doth teach him, her God doth instruct her and doth teach her. Let this be the mother's key to the whole of the education of each boy and each girl; not of her children; the Divine Spirit does not work with nouns of multitude, but with each single child. Because He is infinite, the whole world is not too great a school for this indefatigable Teacher, and because He is infinite, He is able to give the whole of his infinite attention for the whole time to each one of his multitudinous pupils. We do not sufficiently rejoice in the wealth that the infinite nature of our God brings to each of us.

Subjects Divinely Taught—And what subjects are under the direction of this Divine Teacher? The child's faith and hope and charity—that we already knew; his temperance, justice, prudence and fortitude—that we might have guessed; his grammar, rhetoric, logic, music, astronomy, geometry, arithmetic—this we might have forgotten, if these Florentine teachers had not reminded us; his practical skill in the use of tools and instruments, from a knife and fork to a microscope, and in the sensible management of all the affairs of life—these also come from the Lord, which is wonderful in counsel and excellent in working. His God doth instruct him and doth teach him. Let the mother visualise the thought as an illuminated scroll about her newborn child, and let her never contemplate any kind of instruction for her child, except under the sense of the divine co-operation. But we must remember that here as everywhere the infinite and almighty Spirit of God works under limitations.

Our Co-operation Indispensable—Our co-operation appears to be the indispensable condition of all the divine workings. We recognise this in what we call spiritual things, meaning the things that have to do more especially with our approaches to God; but the new thing to us is, that grammar, for example, may be taught in such a way as to invite and obtain the co-operation of the Divine Teacher, or in such a way as to exclude His illuminating presence from the schoolroom. We do not mean that spiritual virtues may be exhibited by the teacher, and encouraged in the child in the course of a grammar lesson; this is no doubt true, and is to be remembered; but perhaps the immediate point is that the teaching of grammar by its guiding ideas and simple principles, the true, direct, and humble teaching of grammar; without pedantry and without verbiage, is, we may venture to believe, accompanied by the illuminating power of the Holy Spirit, of whom is all knowledge.

Teaching that Invites and that Repels Divine Co-operation—The contrary is equally true. Such teaching as enwraps a child's mind in folds of many words that his thought is unable to penetrate, which gives him rules and definitions, and tables, in lieu of ideas—this is teaching which excludes and renders impossible the divine co-operation.

Discord in our Lives Resolved—This great recognition resolves that discord in our lives of which most of us are, more or less, aware. The things of sense we are willing to subordinate to the things of spirit; at any rate we are willing to endeavour ourselves in this direction. We mourn over our failures and try again, and recognise that here lies the Armageddon for every soul of man. But there is a debateable land. Is it not a fact that the spiritual life is exigeant, demands our sole interest and concentrated energies? Yet the claims of intellect—mind, of the æsthetic sense—taste, press upon us urgently. We must think, we must know, we must rejoice in and create the beautiful. And if all the burning thoughts that stir in the minds of men, all the beautiful conceptions they give birth to, are things apart from God, then we too must have a separate life, a life apart from God, a division of ourselves into secular and religious—discord and unrest. We believe that this is the fertile source of the unfaith of the day, especially in young and ardent minds. The claims of intellect are urgent; the intellectual life is a necessity not to be foregone at any hazard. It is impossible for these to recognise in themselves a dual nature; a dual spirituality, so to speak; and, if there are claims which definitely oppose themselves to the claims of intellect, those other claims must go to the wall; and the young man or woman, full of promise and power, becomes a free-thinker, an agnostic, what you will. But once the intimate relation, the relation of Teacher and taught in all things of the mind and spirit, be fully recognised, our feet are set in a large room; there is space for free development in all directions, and this free and joyous development, whether of intellect or heart, is recognised as a Godward movement.

We are Safeguarded from Intellectual as from Moral Sin—Various activities, with unity of aim, bring harmony and peace into our lives; more, this perception of the intimate dealings of the divine Spirit with our spirit in the things of the intellect, as well as in those of the moral nature, makes us as keenly alive in the one case as in the other to the insidious promptings of the spirit of evil; we become aware of the possibility of intellectual sin as of moral sin; we perceive that in the region of pure reason, also, it behoves us to see that we enter not into temptation. We rejoice in the expansion of intellect and the expansion of heart and the ease and freedom of him who is always in touch with the inspiring Teacher, with whom are infinite stores of learning, wisdom, and virtue, graciously placed at our disposal.

Harmony in our Efforts—Such a recognition of the work of the Holy Spirit as the Educator of mankind, in things intellectual as well as in things moral and spiritual, gives us 'new thoughts of God, new hopes of Heaven,' a sense of harmony in our efforts and of acceptance of all that we are. What stands between us and the realisation of this more blessed life? This; that we do not realise ourselves as spiritual beings invested with bodies, living, emotional, a snare to us and a joy to us, but which are, after all, the mere organs and interpreters of our spiritual intention. Once we see that we are dealing spirit with spirit with the friend at whose side we are sitting, with the people who attend to our needs, we shall be able to realise how incessant is the commerce between the divine Spirit and our human spirit. It will be to us as when one stops one's talk and one's thoughts in the springtime, to find the world full of bird-music unheard the instant before. In like manner we shall learn to make pause in our thoughts, and shall hear in our intellectual perplexities, as well as in our moral, the clear, sweet, cheering and inspiring tones of our spiritual Guide. We are not speaking here of what is commonly called the religious life, or of our definite approaches to God in prayer and praise; these things all Christian people comprehend more or less fully; we are speaking only of the intellectual life, the development of which in children is the aim of our subjects and methods of instruction.

Conditions of Divine Co-operation—Supposing we are willing to make this great recognition, to engage ourselves to accept and invite the daily, hourly, incessant co-operation of the divine Spirit, in, to put it definitely and plainly, the schoolroom work of our children, how must we shape our own conduct to make this co-operation active, or even possible? We are told that the Spirit is life; therefore, that which is dead, dry as dust, mere bare bones, can have no affinity with Him, can do no other than smother and deaden his vitalising influences. A first condition of this vitalising teaching is that all the thought we offer to our children shall be living thought; no mere dry summaries of facts will do; given the vitalising idea, children will readily hang the mere facts upon the idea as upon a peg capable of sustaining all that it is needful to retain. We begin by believing in the children as spiritual beings of unmeasured powers—intellectual, moral, spiritual—capable of receiving and constantly enjoying intuitions from the intimate converse of the Divine Spirit.

Teaching must be Fresh and Living—With this thought of a child to begin with, we shall perceive that whatever is stale and flat and dull to us must needs be stale and flat and dull to him, and also that there is no subject which has not a fresh and living way of approach. Are we teaching geography? The child discovers with the explorer, journeys with the traveller, receives impressions new and vivid from some other mind which is immediately receiving these impressions; not after they have been made stale and dull by a process of filtering through many intermediate minds, and have found at last their way into a little text-book. Is he learning history? his concern is not with strings of names and of dates, nor with nice little reading-made-easy stories, brought down, as we mistakenly say, to the level of his comprehension; we recognise that his power of comprehension is at least equal to our own, and that it is only his ignorance of the attendant circumstances we have to deal with as luminously as we can.

Books must be Living—We recognise that history for him is, to live in the lives of those strong personalities which at any given time impress themselves most upon their age and country. This is not the sort of thing to be got out of nice little history books for children, whether 'Little Arthur's,' or somebody's 'Outlines.' We take the child to the living sources of history—a child of seven is fully able to comprehend Plutarch, in Plutarch's own words (translated), without any diluting and with little explanation. Give him living thought in this kind, and you make possible the co-operation of the living Teacher. The child's progress is by leaps and bounds, and you wonder why. In teaching music, again, let him once perceive the beautiful laws of harmony, the personality, so to speak, of Music, looking out upon him from among the queer little black notes, and the piano lesson has ceased to be drudgery.

No Neat System is of Use—It is unnecessary to go further into details; every subject has its living way, with what Coleridge calls 'its guiding idea' at the head, and it is only as we discover this living way in each case that a subject of instruction makes for the education of a child. No neat system is of any use; it is the very nature of a system to grow stale in the using; every subject, every division of a subject, every lesson, in fact, must be brought up for examination before it is offered to the child as to whether it is living, vital, of a nature to invite the living Intellect of the universe.

Children must have the Best Books—One more thing is of vital importance; children must have books, living books; the best are not too good for them; anything less than the best is not good enough; and if it is needful to exercise economy, let go everything that belongs to soft and luxurious living before letting go the duty of supplying the books, and the frequent changes of books, which are necessary for the constant stimulation of the child's intellectual life. We need not say one word about the necessity for living thought in the teacher; it is only so far as he is intellectually alive that he can be effective in the wonderful process which we glibly call 'education.'

Chapter 26 The Eternal Child

The Highest Counsel of Perfection to Parents

The Waits!
Slowly they play, poor careful Souls,
With wistful thoughts of Christmas cheer,
Unwitting how their music rolls
Away the burden of the year.
And with the charm, the homely rune,
Our thoughts like childhood's thoughts are given,
When all our pulses beat in tune
With all the stars of heaven.'
—John Davidson.

Children necessary to Christmas Joy—In these levelling days we like to think that everybody has quite equal opportunities in some direction; but Christmas joy, for example, is not for every one in like measure. It is not only that those who are in need, sorrow, or any other adversity do not sit down to the Christmas feast of joy and thanksgiving; for, indeed, a Benjamin's portion is often served to the sorrowful. But it takes the presence of children to help us to realise the idea of the Eternal Child. The Dayspring is with the children, and we think their thoughts and are glad in their joy; and every mother knows out of her own heart's fulness what the Birth at Bethlehem means. Those of us who have not children catch echoes. We hear the wondrous story read in church, the waits chant the tale, the church-bells echo it, the years that are no more come back to us, and our hearts are meek and mild, glad and gay, loving and tender, as those of little children; but, alas, only for the little while occupied by the passing thought. Too soon the dreariness of daily living settles down upon us again, and we become a little impatient, do we not, of the Christmas demand of joyousness.

But it is not so where there are children. The old, old story has all its first freshness as we tell it to the eager listeners; as we listen to it ourselves with their vivid interest it becomes as real and fresh to us as it is to them. Hard thoughts drop away like scales from our eyes; we are young once more with the children's young life, which, we are mysteriously made aware, is the life eternal. What a mystery it is! Does not every mother, made wise unto salvation, who holds a babe in her arms, feel with tremulous awe that, that deep saying is true for her also, 'The same is my mother'?

Every Babe bears an Evangel—For the little child is the true St Christopher: in him is the light and life of Christ; and every birth is a message of salvation, and a reminder that we, too, must humble ourselves and become as little children. This is, perhaps, the real secret of the world's progress—that every babe comes into the world with an evangel, which witnesses of necessity to his parents' hearts. That we, too, are children, the children of God, that He would have us be as children, is the message that the newborn child never fails to bear, however little we heed, or however soon we forget. It is well that parents should ponder these things, for the child's estate is a holy one, and it is given to his parents to safeguard the little heir of blessedness.

A Child is Humble—It is not possible to enter fully into so large a subject, but it may be worth while to characterise two or three of the landmarks of this child's estate; for how shall we safeguard that which we do not recognise, and how recognise that to which we have failed to give deliberate attention? The note of childhood is, before all things, humility. What we call innocence is probably resolvable into grace—repellent to the nature of man until he shall embrace it, and then disclosing itself to him as divine. An old and saintly writer has a luminous thought on this subject of humility.

'There never was nor ever will be, but one humility in the whole world, and that is the humility of Christ, which never any man, since the fall of Adam has the least degree of but from Christ. Humility is one, in the same sense and truth that Christ is one, the Mediator is one, Redemption is one . . . There are not two Lambs of God that take away the sins of the world. But if there was any humility besides that of Christ, there would be something else besides him that could take away the sins of the world.' [William Law.] Now, if there be but one humility in the whole world, and that humility be the humility of Christ, and if our Lord pronounced the little child also to be humble is it not because of the indwelling divinity, the glory in the child which we call innocence?

Humility not Relative, but Absolute—Our common notion of humility is inaccurate. We regard it as a relative quality. We humble ourselves to this one and that, bow to the prince and lord it over the peasant. This is why the grace of humility does not commend itself even to ourselves in our most sincere moods. We feel that this relative humility is hardly consistent with self-respect and due independence of character. We have been taught to recognise humility as a Christian grace, and therefore do not utter our protest; but this misconception confuses our thought on an important subject. For humility is absolute, not relative. It is by no means a taking of our place among our fellows according to a given scale, some being above us by many grades and others as far below. There is no reference to above or below in the humble soul, which is equally humble before an infant, a primrose, a worm, a beggar, a prince.

This, if we think of it, is the state natural to children. Every person and thing commands their interest; but the person or thing in action is deeply interesting. 'May I go and make mud-pies with the boy in the gutter?' prays the little prince, discerning no difference at all; and the little boy in the gutter would meet him with equal frankness.

Children do not make Self-depreciatory Remarks—What is the secret of this absolute humility, humble alike towards higher or lower, and unaware of distinctions? Our notion of a humble person is one who thinks rather slightingly of himself, who says, deprecatingly, 'Oh, I can't do this or that, you know, I'm not clever'; 'I'm not cut out for public work of any sort, I've no power or influence'; 'Ah! well, I hope he'll be a better man than his father, I don't think much of myself anyway'; 'Your children have great advantages; I wish mine had such a mother, but I'm not a bit wise.' Such things are often said, in all sincerity, without the least soupçon of the 'Uriah Heep' sentiment. The thing we quarrel with is, that the speakers are apt to feel that they have, anyway, the saving grace of humility. It is worth while to reflect that there are no such self-depreciatory utterances ascribed to the Example of that 'great humility' which we are bound to follow; and if there is not the slightest evidence of humility in this kind in the divine life, which was all humility, we must re-cast our notions. Children, too, never make self-depreciatory remarks; that is because they are humble, and with the divine Example before us, and the example of our children, we may receive it that humility does not consist in thinking little of ourselves. It is a higher principle, a blessed state, only now and then attained by us elders, but in which the children perpetually dwell, and in which it is the will of God that we should keep them.

Humility Unconscious of Self.—Humility does not think much or little of itself; it does not think of itself at all. It is a negative rather than a positive quality, being an absence of self-consciousness rather than the presence of any distinctive virtue. The person who is unaware of himself is capable of all lowly service, of all suffering for others, of bright cheerfulness under all the small crosses and worries of everyday life. This is the quality that makes heroes, and this is the quality that makes saints. We are able to pray, but we are hardly able to worship or to praise, to say, 'My soul doth magnify the Lord' so long as in the innermost chamber of our hearts we are self-occupied.

The Christian Religion Objective—The Christian religion is, in its very nature, objective. It offers for our worship, reverence, service, adoration and delight, a Divine Person, the Desire of the world. Simplicity, happiness and expansion come from the outpouring of a human heart upon that which is altogether worthy. But we mistake our own needs, are occupied with our own falls and our own repentances, our manifold states of consciousness. Our religion is subjective first, and after that, so far as we are able, objective. The order should rather be objective first and after that, so far as we have any time or care to think about ourselves, subjective.

Children are Objective in Tendency—Now, the tendency of children is to be altogether objective, not at all subjective, and perhaps that is why they are said to be first in the kingdom of heaven. This philosophic distinction is not one which we can put aside as having no bearing on everyday life. It strikes the keynote for the training of children. In proportion as our training tends to develop the subjective principle, it tends to place our children on a lower level of purpose, character, and usefulness throughout their lives; while so far as we develop the objective principle, with which the children are born, we make them capable of love, service, heroism, worship.

Every Function may have its Subjective or Objective Development—It is curious to observe how every function of our most complex nature may have its subjective or its objective development. The child may eat and drink and rest with most absolute disregard of what he is about, his parents taking care that these things are happily arranged for him, but taking equal care that his attention shall not be turned to the pleasures of appetite. But this is a point that we hardly need to dwell upon, as thoughtful parents are agreed that children's meals should be so regularly pleasant and various that the child naturally eats with satisfaction and thinks little or nothing of what he is eating; that is, parents are careful that, in the matter of food, children shall not be self-regardful.

Fortitude—Perhaps parents are less fully awake to the importance of regulating a child's sensations. We still kiss the place to make it well, make an obvious fuss if a string is uncomfortable or a crumpled rose-leaf is irritating the child's tender skin. We have forgotten the seven Christian virtues and the seven deadly sins of earlier ages, and do not much consider in the bringing up of our children whether the grace of fortitude is developing under our training. Now fortitude has its higher and its lower offices. It concerns itself with things of the mind and with things of the body, and, perhaps, it is safe to argue that fortitude on the higher plane is only possible when it has become the habit of the nature on the lower. A baby may be trained in fortitude, and is much the happier for such training. A child should be taught that it is beneath him to take any notice of cold or heat, pain or discomfort. We do not perceive the sensations to which we do not attend, and it is quite possible to forget even a bad toothache in some new and vivid interest. Health and happiness depend largely upon the disregard of sensations, and the child who is encouraged to say, 'I am so cold,' 'I am so tired,' 'My vest pricks me,' and so on, is likely to develop into the hysterical girl or the hypochondriac man; for it is an immutable law, that, as with our appetites, so with our sensations, in proportion as we attend to them will they dominate us until a single sensation of slight pain or discomfort may occupy our whole field of vision, making us unaware that there is any joy in living, any beauty in the earth.

The Self-regarding Child no longer Humble—But these are the least of the reasons why a child should be trained to put up with little discomforts and take no notice. The child who has been allowed to become self-regardful in the matter of sensations, as of appetites, has lost his child's estate, he is no longer humble; he is in the condition of thinking about himself; instead of that infinitely blessed condition of not being aware of himself at all. Nor must we permit ourselves to make an exception to this rule in the case of the poor little invalid. For him, far more than for the healthy child, it is important that he should be trained to take no account of his sensations; and many a brave little hero suffers anguish without conscious thought, and therefore, of course, suffers infinitely less than if he had been induced to dwell upon his pains. We say, induced, because, though a child may cry with sudden distress, he does not really think about his aches and pains unless his thoughts be turned to his ailments by those about him.

No Spartan Regimen—I am not advising any Spartan regimen. It is not permitted to us to inflict hardness in order that the children may learn to endure. Our care is simply to direct their consciousness from their own sensations. The well-known anecdote of the man who, before the days of chloroform, had his leg cut off without any conscious sensations of pain, because he determinedly kept his mind occupied with other things, is an extreme but instructive instance of what may be done in this direction. At the same time, though the child himself be taught to disregard them, his sensations should be carefully watched by his elders, for they must consider and act upon the danger signals which the child himself must be taught to disregard. But it is usually possible to attend to a child's sensations without letting him know they have been observed.

The Altruistic or Egoistic Direction—This, of the sensations, is only one example of the altruistic or egoistic direction which the various operations of a child's complex nature may receive. His affections, again, are capable of receiving a subjective or objective direction, according to the suggestions which reach him from without. Every child comes into the world richly endowed with a well of love, a fountain of justice; but whether the stream of love shall flow to the right or the left, whether it shall be egoistic or altruistic, depends on the child's earliest training. A child who is taught from the first the delights of giving and sharing, of loving and bearing, will always spend himself freely on others, will love and serve, seeking for nothing again; but the child who recognises that he is the object of constant attention, consideration, love and service, becomes self-regardful, self-seeking, selfish, almost without his fault, so strongly is he influenced by the direction his thoughts receive from those about him. So, too, of that other fountain, of justice, with which every child is born. There, again, the stream may flow forth in either, but not in both, of the channels, the egoistic or the altruistic. The child's demand for justice may be all for himself, or, from the very first, the rights of others may be kept before his eyes.

'It's not Fair!'—He may be taught to occupy himself with his own rights and other people's duties, and, if he is, his state of mind is easily discernible by the catchwords often on his lips, 'It's a shame!' 'It's not fair!' or he may, on the other hand, be so filled with the notion of his own duties and other people's rights, that the claims of self slip quietly into the background. This kind cometh forth only by prayer, but it is well to clear our thoughts and know definitely what we desire for our children, because only so can we work intelligently towards the fulfilment of our desire. It is sad to pray, and frustrate the answer by our own action; but this is, alas, too possible.

During each coming festival of the Eternal Child, may parents ponder how best to keep their own children in the blessed child-estate, recollecting that the humility which Christ commends in the children is what may be described, philosophically, as the objective principle as opposed to the subjective, and that, in proportion as a child becomes self-regardful in any function of his being, he loses the grace of humility. This is the broad principle; the practical application will need constant watchfulness and constant efforts, especially in holiday seasons, to keep friends and visitors from showing their love for the children in any way that shall tend to develop self-consciousness.

Humility the Highest Counsel of Perfection—This, of humility, is not only a counsel of perfection, but is, perhaps, the highest counsel of perfection and when we put it to parents, we offer it to those for whom no endeavour is too difficult, no aim too lofty; to those who are doing the most to advance the Kingdom of Christ.

Appendix

Questions for the use of Students

Chapter I — The Family

1. How and to what did Rousseau succeed in awaking parents?
2. In what respects is the family a commune?
3. Why, and in what ways, must the family be social?
4. Show some ways in which the family must serve poorer neighbours.
5. In what way is it open to the family to serve the nation?
6. What is the divine order for the family as regards other nations?
7. Mention ways of securing fellowship with other nations.
8. What is meant by the phrase 'the restoration of the family'?
9. Add hints from your own experience on each of the points taken up in this chapter.

Chapter II — Parents as Rulers

1. In what respects is the family an absolute monarchy?
2. Show that the rule of parents cannot be deputed.
3. Give some causes which lead to the abdication of parents.
4. In what does the majesty of parents consist?
5. Show that children are a public trust and a divine trust.
6. Define the scope and state the limitation of parental authority.
7. Comment and enlarge upon any of the above points from your knowledge and experience.

Chapter III — Parents as Inspirers

Children must be born again to the Life of Intelligence

1. Explain and verify the statement that parents owe a second birth to their children.
2. Show exactly how science supports this contention.
3. What are the processes and methods of this second birth?
4. Summarise Dr Maudsley's views on heredity.
5. Distinguish between disposition and character.

6. What does Dr Maudsley say regarding the structural effects of 'particular life experiences'?
7. Enumerate the articles of the educational charter which our age may be said to have acquired.
8. Make further comments on any of the above points.

Chapter IV — Parents as Inspirers

The Life of the Mind grows upon Ideas

1. Summarise the preceding chapter.
2. Why are not the educational conceptions of the past necessarily valid now?
3. Explain and illustrate Pestalozzi's theory.
4. And Froebel's theory.
5. In what way is the kindergarten a vital conception?
6. But science is changing front. How does this fact affect educational thought?
7. What bearing has 'heredity' upon education?
8. Is education formative? Discuss the question.
9. Prove that the individual is not at the mercy of empirics. Is this a gain?
10. Why is 'education' an inadequate word?
11. What is the force of 'bringing up'?
12. Give an adequate definition, and show why it is adequate.
13. Show the importance of method as a way to an end.
14. Illustrate the fact that the life of the mind grows upon ideas.
15. What is an idea?
16. Trace the rise and progress of an idea.
17. Illustrate the genesis of an idea.
18. An idea may exist as an 'appetency.' Give examples.
19. Show that a child draws inspiration from the casual life around him.
20. Describe and illustrate the order and progress of definite ideas.
21. What is the Platonic doctrine of ideas?
22. Show that ideas only are important in education.
23. How should the educational formula run?
24. The 'infallible reason'—what is it?

Chapter V — Parents as Inspirers

The Things of The Spirit

1. Show that parents are necessarily the revealers of God to their children.
2. Show that they must fortify children against doubt.
3. In what three ways may this be attempted?
4. Why is the first unfair?
5. Show that 'evidences' are not proofs.
6. How does their outlook upon current thought affect young people?
7. Show that children have a right to 'freewill' in thought.
8. What may be done in the way of preparation?
9. In what ways should children be taught to wait upon science?
10. Knowledge is progressive. How should this affect our mental attitude?
11. Show that children should learn some laws of thought.
12. Should look at thoughts as they come.
13. Upon what does the appeal of the children rest?
14. Show that children should have the thought of God as a 'hiding-place.'
15. Prove and illustrate from your own experience that the mind of the child is good ground.
16. Is it true that children suffer from a deep-seated discontent? If so, why? Illustrate.

Chapter VI — Parents as Inspirers

Primal Ideas derived from Parents

1. What is the chief thing we have to do in the world?
2. Name two ideas of God specially fit for children.
3. 'We ought to move slowly up through the human side.' Why not?
4. Distinguish between logical certainty and moral right.
5. How might the Crucifixion have appeared to a conscientious Jew? How, to a patriotic Jew?
6. Show what primal ideas children get from their parents.
7. What have you to say as to the first approaches to God made by a little child?
8. Discuss the question of archaic forms in children's prayers.
9. Show how fit for a child is 'the shout of a King.'
10. Also the notion of the 'fight for Christ against the devil.'
11. "How very hard it is to be a Christian." Is this a child's experience?

Chapter VII — The Parent as Schoolmaster

1. What is a schoolmaster supposed to do for a boy?
2. For what various reasons is this task left to the schoolmaster?
3. With what class of children does he succeed?
4. Why does not the discipline of school always affect the life?
5. Discuss 'Edward Waverley' as an example of mental 'sprawling.'
6. Show that we are not meant to grow up in a state of Nature.
7. Prove that the first function of the parent is that of discipline.
8. Show that education is a discipline.
9. Distinguish between discipline and punishment.
10. How are disciples lured?
11. Show that discipline means steady progress on a careful plan.

Chapter VIII — The Culture of Character

Parents as Trainers

1. How far does heredity count?
2. Show the value of opportunity to children.
3. Describe a curious experiment in education.
4. Show that character is an achievement.
5. What two ways have we of preserving sanity?
6. Show that the development of character is the chief work of education.
7. Give some plausible reasons for doing nothing towards character training.
8. How does the advance of science affect the question?
9. What is a parent's duty towards a lovely family trait?
10. Towards distinctive qualities?
11. What are the four conditions of culture?
12. Exemplify in the case of a child with an inherited turn for languages.
13. Show that work and waste of brain tissue are necessary.
14. Point out the danger of eccentricity.
15. Name some causes of oddity in children.
16. How shall we save our 'splendid failures'?

Chapter IX — The Culture of Character

The Treatment of Defects

1. What is the ultimate object of education?
2. How are parents concerned with 'the defects of their qualities' in their children?
3. Give some cases of children thus 'defective.'

4. Indicate the special treatment in each case.
5. Show that moral ailments need prompt attention.
6. Show that 'one custom overcometh another' is a gospel for parents.
7. In what way is there a material register of educational efforts ?
8. Prove that mother-love is not sufficient in itself for child-training.

Chapter X — Bible Lessons

Parents as Instructors in Religion

1. Why are Sunday Schools necessary?
2. Show that parents should instruct their own children in religion.
3. Describe an Australian outcome of the Parents' Union.
4. What is the gist of the report of the Committee on the Religious Education of the Upper and Middle Classes?
5. Give a few of the reasons why parents fail to instruct their children in religion.
6. Discuss the discredit thrown upon the Bible.
7. Discuss, 'miracles do not happen.'
8. Show that our conception of God depends upon miracles.
9. Discuss miracles as contrary to natural law.
10. Show how fitting are the miracles of Christ.

Chapter XI — Faith and Duty

Parents as Teachers of Morals

1. What does Mr Huxley consider to be the sole practical outcome of education?
2. Have we an infallible sense of 'ought' ?
3. Show the educational value of the Bible as a classic literature.
4. How should a mother's diary be useful?
5. Show the use of fairy tales in moral instruction.
6. Of fables.
7. Of Bible stories.
8. Why should the language of the Bible be used in teaching?
9. Should the stories of miracles be used in moral instruction?
10. Should the whole Bible be put into the hands of a child?
11. Give some moral rules to be gleaned from the Pentateuch.
12. Show the value of the 'Odyssey' and the 'Iliad' in moral teaching.
13. What is the initial weakness of 'secular' morality?
14. What is to be said in favour of lessons on duty?
15. Show the moral value of manual training.
16. Show the danger of slipshod moral teaching.
17. Show the importance of methodical ethical instruction.

Chapter XII — Faith and Duty

Claims of Philosophy as an Instrument of Education

1. Show that English educational thought tends towards naturalism.
2. What is Madame de Staël's verdict upon 'Locke'?
3. Show that our educational efforts lack aim.
4. That we are on the verge of chaos.
5. But also on the verge of an educational revolution.
6. Is our system of education to be the issue of naturalism or idealism?
7. What is to be said of the ethical view of education?
8. Show that no attempt has been made to unify education.
9. What are the claims of philosophy as an educational agent?

10. Show that a nation should be educated for its proper functions.
11. How do the minor moralities become easy?
12. How is a habit initiated?
13. Can spirit act upon matter?
14. How is the individuality of children safeguarded?

Chapter XIII — Faith and Duty

Man lives by Faith, Godward and Manward
1. Show that 'sacred' and 'secular' is an irreligious classification.
2. How is all intercourse of thought maintained?
3. Why is it obvious and natural that the Father of spirits should deal with the spirits of men?
4. Why is easy tolerance mischievous?
5. Show that man lives by faith in his fellows and in God.
6. Describe faith in God.
7. Show that faith is natural.
8. Is not a self-originated impulse.
9. What have you to say of the worship of faith?
10. How is 'righteousness' defined by the author in question?

Chapter XIV — The Heroic Impulse

Parents are concerned to give this impulse
1. Of what value is heroic poetry in education?
2. Show that Beowulf is our English Ulysses.
3. Show that he represents the English ideal.
4. Illustrate the gentleness of our forefathers.
5. Can you give any old English riddles?

Chapter XV — Is it Possible?

The Attitude of Parents towards Social Questions
1. Show that we are facing a moral crisis.
2. How does this crisis show that we love our brother?
3. How does the 'idol of size' affect us?
4. Cui bono? Show the paralysing effect of.
5. Can character be changed?
6. What is the question of the age?
7. What is the essential miracle?
8. Why should hope fail for the vicious by inheritance?
9. For the vicious by inveterate habit?
10. For the vicious in thought?
11. What hope is there in the received doctrine of heredity?
12. Show that education is stronger than nature.
13. That there is natural preparation for salvation.
14. That 'conversion' is no miracle.
15. That 'conversion' is not contrary to natural law.
16. That there may be many 'conversions' in a lifetime.
17. Under what conditions is an idea potent?
18. Show the potency and fitness of the ideas included in Christianity.
19. Why is curative treatment necessary?
20. Show that a strong organisation may afford relief.
21. Show that work and fresh air are powerful agents.

Chapter XVI — Discipline

A Consideration for Parents

1. What do people commonly mean by discipline?
2. Distinguish between a method and a system.
3. What is to be said for a 'wise passiveness'?
4. Discuss the question of punishment by consequences.
5. Show that children may rather enjoy punishment.
6. Show that wrongdoing is necessarily followed by penalties.
7. Is punishment reformative?
8. What are the best disciplinarians?
9. Comment on the mother who is 'always telling' her children to do so and so.
10. Give nine practical counsels for a parent who wishes to deal seriously with a bad habit.
11. How would you treat an inquisitive child, for instance?

Chapter XVII — Sensations and Feelings

Sensations Educable by Parents

1. Show that 'common sense' has usually scientific opinion for its basis.
2. What is the origin of sensations?
3. Show that sensations should be treated as interesting on account of the thing perceived, not of the person who perceives.
4. Why are object-lessons in disfavour?
5. Show that a baby works at object-lessons.
6. What is the effect of Nature's early teaching?
7. What two points must we bear in mind in the education of the senses?
8. Show that object-lessons, to be of value, should be incidental.
9. What advantages has the home in this sort of teaching?
10. How should children be taught care in the use of positive and comparative terms?
11. How would you correct the indiscriminate use of epithets?
12. How would you teach children to form judgments as to weight?
13. As to size?
14. To discriminate sounds?
15. To discriminate odours?
16. To discriminate flavours?
17. Can you suggest some sensory gymnastics?
18. Some sensory games?

Chapter XVIII — Sensations and Feelings

Feelings Educable by Parents

1. What do you understand by reflected sensations?
2. Show that we have here a reason why open-air memories should be stored.
3. Show that delightful memories are a source of bodily well-being.
4. And of mental restoration.
5. Distinguish between sensations and feelings.
6. Show that feelings should be objective, not subjective.
7. Show what the feelings are and are not.
8. Show that every feeling has its positive and its negative mode.
9. Are the feelings moral or immoral?
10. Show the connection between unremembered feelings and acts.
11. Certain trifling acts may be 'the best portion of a good man's life.' Why so?
12. Is perception of character a feeling?

13. Show its delicacy and importance.
14. Show how feelings influence conduct.
15. Discuss enthusiasm.
16. Give the genesis of our activities.
17. Show that in educating the feelings we modify the character.
18. What is to be said of the sixth sense of tact?
19. Why must we beware of words?
20. How is a feeling communicated?
21. What feelings especially differentiate persons?
22. Show that to deal with the feelings of the young is a delicate task.

Chapter XIX — What Is Truth?

Moral Discrimination required by Parents

1. Show that, as a nation, we are both losing and gaining in truthfulness.
2. What two theories are held with regard to lying?
3. Is lying an elemental or a secondary symptom?
4. How would you treat 'pseudophobia'?
5. 'The lie heroic.'
6. 'Truth for friends, lies for enemies.'
7. 'Lies inspired by selfishness.'
8. 'The deceptions of imagination and play.'
9. 'Pseudomania.'
10. How must children be trained to truthfulness?

Chapter XX — Show Cause Why

Parents Responsible for Competive Examinations

1. Mention some points we have gained by asking 'Why?'
2. Why does Tom go to school?
3. Show that the same impulse carries him through school and university.
4. What is the tendency of 'grind'?
5. Show that the tyranny of competitive examinations is supported by parents.
6. Are examinations themselves an evil?
7. Under what conditions should they be held?
8. What are the primary desires?
9. Are they virtuous or vicious?
10. What end do they serve?
11. Show that throughout the schoolboy's life one natural desire takes the place which properly belongs to another.
12. Why does he no longer want to know?
13. How is this a loss to the boy?
14. Show that emulation is an easier spring to work than curiosity.
15. Show that an examination-ridden empire would be a calamity.

Chapter XXI — A Theory of Education Proposed to Parents

1. How far should the ideal of education be a class ideal?
2. What difference is there between the children of educated and those of ignorant parents as regards vocabulary, imagination, etc.?
3. When is the development of 'faculties' an important part of education, and when is it not so?
4. What are the chief things the educator has to do ?
5. Show that it is necessary to recognise the material and spiritual principles of human nature.
6. How does this lead us to recognise the supreme Educator?

7. By what test may the value of studies be judged?
8. Show that 'Nature' knowledge educates a child.
9. What is to be said for the use of good books in education?
10. Discuss the question of 'child-nature.'
11. Why are we tenacious of the individuality of children?
12. Why must we consider proportion in our scheme of education?
13. Show that children have a right to knowledge.

Chapter XXII — A Catechism of Educational Theory

1. Show that character is an achievement.
2. What gives rise to conduct?
3. What means have we of modifying disposition?
4. Give the history of a habit.
5. How may a bad habit be corrected?
6. Show that our conduct is generally directed by unconscious, or sub-conscious cerebration.
7. How far do the habits of a 'well-brought-up' person make life easy for him?
8. Why does the forming of a habit demand time?
9. Trace the logical development of a notion.
10. Show that reason is not an infallible guide to conduct.
11. Show how confusion as to logical and moral right works in the history of the world.
12. Why, then, should a child know what he is as a human being?
13. Show how far such knowledge is a safeguard.
14. What is the part of the will in the reception of ideas?
15. How are ideas conveyed?
16. What may we believe is the part of the divine Educator in things natural and spiritual?
17. What part do lessons play in education?
18. What principle as regards a curriculum do we find in a child's natural aptitude for knowledge?

Chapter XXIII — Whence and Whither

A Question for Parents: Whence?
1. What was the leading thought about children in the past generation?
2. What intellectual labour does a child go through in his first year?
3. Remark on the intelligence of children.
4. Show that they are highly endowed but ignorant.
5. Choose between 'happy and good' and 'good and happy' as an educational maxim.
6. By what test would you try various systems of education?
7. Show the duty of advancing with the tide.

Chapter XXIV — Whence and Whither

A Question for Parents: Whither?
1. How are children great?
2. What is wisdom?
3. Show that children grow in wisdom rather than in intelligence.
4. Show that all possibilities are present in a child.
5. Show that we all live for the advancement of the race.
6. Show that we find our 'whence' in the potency of the child.
7. Our 'whither' in the thought of the day.
8. How should the thought of the day affect education with regard to science?
9. With regard to art?
10. With regard to books?
11. How should the idea of the solidarity of the race affect education?

12. How may we teach children that to serve is promotion?
13. How shall we guard them from considerations of expediency?

Chapter XXV — The Great Recognition Required of Parents

1. Show that education is not religious and secular.
2. Show that knowledge, like virtue, is from above.
3. Have we any authority for thinking that science, art and poetry are 'by the Spirit'?
4. Have we any teaching as to the origin of the first ideas of common things?
5. Show that divine teaching waits upon our co-operation.
6. What manner of teaching invites and what repels divine co-operation?
7. Show that this 'recognition' resolves certain discords in our lives.
8. How does it safeguard us from intellectual sin?
9. How does it lead to harmony in our efforts?
10. Why must teaching be fresh and living?
11. Why must books be living?
12. Why can we not get rid of our responsibility by using some neat system?
13. Why must children read the best books?

Chapter XXVI — The Eternal Child

The Highest Counsel of Perfection for Parents

1. Show that every babe bears an evangel.
2. Show that a child is humble.
3. That humility is not relative but absolute.
4. Show that the Christian religion is objective.
5. That children are objective in tendency.
6. Show that our care must be to give every function an objective and not a subjective employment.
7. What part should fortitude play in education?
8. Show that the self-regardful child is no longer humble.
9. Show that the tendencies of children may receive an altruistic or an egoistic direction.
10. How does this apply to the cry,—'It's not fair'?
11. Show that humility is the highest counsel of perfection.

School Education
Table of Contents

Preface to the Home Education Series

The educational outlook is rather misty and depressing both at home and abroad. That science should be a staple of education, that the teaching of Latin, of modern languages, of mathematics, must be reformed, that nature and handicrafts should be pressed into service for the training of the eye and hand, that boys and girls must learn to write English and therefore must know something of history and literature; and, on the other hand, that education must be made more technical and utilitarian—these, and such as these, are the cries of expedience with which we take the field. But we have no unifying principle, no definite aim; in fact, no philosophy of education. As a stream can rise no higher than its source, so it is probable that no educational effort can rise above the whole scheme of thought which gives it birth; and perhaps this is the reason of all the fallings from us, vanishings, failures, and disappointments which mark our educational records.

Those of us, who have spent many years in pursuing the benign and elusive vision of Education, perceive her approaches are regulated by a law, and that this law has yet to be evoked. We can discern its outlines, but no more. We know that it is pervasive; there is no part of a child's home life or school work which the law does not penetrate. It is illuminating, too, showing the value, or lack of value, of a thousand systems and expedients. It is not only a light, but a measure, providing a standard whereby all things, small and great, belonging to educational work must be tested. The law is liberal, taking in whatsoever things are true, honest, and of good report, and offering no limitation or hindrance save where excess should injure. And the path indicated by the law is continuous and progressive, with no transition stage from the cradle to the grave, except that maturity takes up the regular self direction to which immaturity has been trained. We shall doubtless find, when we apprehend the law, that certain German thinkers—Kant, Herbart, Lotze, Froebel—are justified; that, as they say, it is necessary to believe in God; that, therefore, the knowledge of God is the principal knowledge, and the chief end of education. By one more character shall we be able to recognise this perfect law of educational liberty when it shall be made evident. It has been said that The best idea which we can form of absolute truth is that it is viable to meet every condition by which it can be tested. This we shall expect of our law—that it shall meet every test of experiment and every test of rational investigation.

Not having received the tables of our law, we fall back upon Froebel or upon Herbart; or, if we belong to another School, upon Locke or Spencer; but we are not satisfied. A discontent, is it a divine discontent? Is upon us; and assuredly we should hail a workable, effectual philosophy of education as a deliverance from much perplexity. Before this great deliverance comes to us it is probable that many tentative efforts will be put forth, having more or less of the characters of a philosophy; notably, having a central idea, a body of thought with various members working in vital harmony.

Such a theory of education, which need not be careful to call itself a system of psychology, must be in harmony with the thought movements of the age; must regard education, not as a shut off compartment, but as being as much a part of life as birth or growth, marriage or work; and it must leave the pupil attached to the world at many points of contact. It is true that educationalists are already eager to establish such contact in several directions, but their efforts rest upon an axiom here and an idea there, and there is no broad unifying basis of thought to support the whole.

Fools rush in where angels fear to tread; and the hope that there may be tentative efforts towards a philosophy of education, and that all of them will bring us nearer to the magnum opus, encourages me to launch one such attempt. The central thought, or rather body of thought, upon which I found, is the somewhat obvious fact that the child is a person with all the possibilities and powers included in personality. Some of members which develop from this nucleus have been exploited from time to time by educational thinkers, and exist vaguely in the general common sense, a notion here, another there. One thesis, which is, perhaps, new, that Education is the Science of Relations, appears to me to solve the question of curricula, as showing that the object of education is to put a child in living touch as much as may be of the life of Nature and of thought. Add to this one or two keys to self knowledge, and the educated youth goes forth with some idea of self management, with some pursuits, and many vital interests. My excuse for venturing to offer a solution, however tentative and passing, to the problem of education is twofold. For between thirty and forty years I have laboured without pause to establish a working and philosophic theory of education; and in the next place, each article of the educational faith I offer has been arrived at by inductive processes; and has, I think, been verified by a long and wide series of experiments. It is, however, with sincere diffidence that I

venture to offer the results of this long labour; because I know that in this field there are many labourers far more able and expert than I—the angels who fear to tread, so precarious is the footing!

But, if only pour encourager les autres, I append a short synopsis of education theory advanced in the volumes of the Home Education Series.

The treatment is not methodic, but incidental; here a little, there a little, as seemed to me most likely to meet the occasions of parents and teachers. I should add that in the course of a number of years the various essays have been prepared for the use of the Parents National Education Union in the hope that that Society might witness for a more or less coherent body of educational thought.

"The consequence of truth is great; therefore the judgment of it must not be negligent."—Whichcote

1. Children are born persons.

2. They are not born either good or bad, but with possibilities for either good or evil.

3. The principles of authority on the one hand and obedience on the other, are natural, necessary and fundamental; but

4. These principles are limited by the respect due to the personality of children, which must not be encroached upon, whether by fear or love, suggestion or influence, or undue play upon any one natural desire.

5. Therefore we are limited to three educational instruments—the atmosphere of environment, the discipline of habit, and the presentation of living ideas.

6. By the saying, Education is an atmosphere, it is not meant that a child should be isolated in what may be called a 'child environment,' especially adapted and prepared; but that we should take into account the educational value of his natural home atmosphere, both as regards persons and things, and should let him live freely among his proper conditions. It stultifies a child to bring down his world to a 'child's' level.

7. By Education is a discipline, is meant the discipline of habits formed definitely and thoughtfully, whether habits of mind or body. Physiologists tell us of the adaptation of brain structure to habitual lines of thought—i.e. to our habits.

8. In the saying that Education is a life, the need of intellectual and moral as well as of physical sustenance is implied. The mind feeds on ideas, and therefore children should have a generous curriculum.

9. But the mind is not a receptacle into which ideas must be dropped, each idea adding to an 'apperception mass' of its like, the theory upon which the Herbartian doctrine of interest rests.

10. On the contrary, a child's mind is no mere sac to hold ideas; but is rather, if the figure may be allowed, a spiritual organism, with an appetite for all knowledge. This is its proper diet, with which it is prepared to deal, and which it can digest and assimilate as the body does foodstuffs.

11. This difference is not a verbal quibble. The Herbartian doctrine lays the stress of education—the preparation of knowledge in enticing morsels, presented in due order—upon the teacher. Children taught upon this principle are in danger of receiving much teaching with little knowledge; and the teacher's axiom is, 'What a child learns matters less than how he learns it.'

12. But, believing that the normal child has powers of mind that fit him to deal with all knowledge proper to him, we must give him a full and generous curriculum; taking care, only, that the knowledge offered to him is vital—that is, the facts are not presented without their informing ideas. Out of this conception comes the principle that,

13. Education is the Science of Relations; that is, that a child has natural relations with a vast number of things and thoughts: so we must train him upon physical exercises, nature, handicrafts, science and art, and upon many living books; for we know that our business is, not to teach him all about anything, but to help him make valid, as many as may be of

'Those first born affinities,
'That fit our new existence to existing things.'

14. There are also two secrets of moral and intellectual self management which should be offered to children; these we may call the Way of the Will and the Way of the Reason.

15. The Way of the Will.—Children should be taught

(a) To distinguish between 'I want' and 'I will.'

(b) That the way to will effectively is to turn our thoughts from that which we desire but do not will.

(c) That the best way to turn our thoughts is to think of or do some quite different thing, entertaining or interesting.

(d) That, after a little rest in this way, the will returns to its work with new vigour.

(This adjunct of the will is familiar to us as diversion, whose office is to ease us for a time from will effort, that we may 'will' again with added power. The use of suggestion—even self suggestion—as an aid to the will, is to be deprecated, as tending to stultify and stereotype character. It would seem that spontaneity is a condition of development, and that human nature needs the discipline of failure as well as of success.)

16. The Way of the Reason.—We should teach children, too, not to 'lean' (too confidently) 'unto their own understanding,' because of the function of reason is, to give logical demonstration (a) of mathematical truth; and (b) of an initial idea, accepted by the will. In the former case reason is, perhaps, an infallible guide, but in the second it is not always a safe one, for whether that initial idea be right or wrong, reason will confirm it by irrefragable proofs.

17. Therefore children should be taught, as they become mature enough to understand such teaching that the chief responsibility which rests on them as persons is the acceptance or rejection of initial ideas. To help them in this choice we should give them principles of conduct and a wide range of the knowledge fitted for them.

These three principles (15, 16 and 17) should save children from some of the loose thinking and heedless action which cause most of us to live at a lower level than we need.

18. We should allow no separation to grow up between the intellectual and 'spiritual' life of children; but should teach them that the divine Spirit has constant access to their spirits, and is their continual helper in all the interests, duties and joys of life.

The 'Home Education' Series is so called from the title of the first volume, and not as dealing, wholly or principally with 'Home' as opposed to 'School" education.

Preface

The intention of the following volume is to offer some suggestions towards a curriculum for boys and girls under twelve. A curriculum, however, is not an independent product, but is linked to much else by chains of cause and consequence; and the manner of curriculum I am anxious to indicate is the outcome of a scheme of educational thought, the adoption of which might, I believe, place educational work generally upon a sounder footing.

The fundamental principles of docility and authority have been considered in the first place because they are fundamental; but, for that very reason, they should be present but not in evidence: we do not expose the foundations of our house. Not only so, but these principles must be conditioned by respect for the personality of children; and, in order to give the children room for free development on the lines proper to them, it is well that parents and teachers should adopt an attitude of 'masterly inactivity.'

Having considered the relations of teachers and taught, I have touched upon those between education and current thought. Education should be in the flow, as it were, and not shut up in a watertight compartment. Perhaps, reverence for personality as such, a sense of the solidarity of the race, and a profound consciousness of evolutionary progress, are among the elements of current thought which should help us towards an educational ideal.

In considering the training of children under the convenient divisions of physical, mental, moral, and religious, I have not thought it necessary to enlarge upon matters of common knowledge and general acceptance, but have dwelt upon aspects of training under each heading which are likely to be overlooked. Under the phrase, 'Education is a life,' I have tried to show how necessary it is to sustain the intellectual life upon ideas, and, as a corollary, that a school-book should be a medium for ideas, and not merely a receptacle for facts. That normal children have a natural desire for, and a right of admission to, all fitting knowledge, appears to me to be suggested by the phrase, 'Education is the science of relations.'

These considerations clear the ground towards that of a curriculum.

The sort of curriculum I have in view should educate children upon Things and Books. Current thought upon the subject of education by Things is so sound and practical, and so thoroughly carried into effect, that I have not thought it necessary to dwell much here upon this part of education. Our great failure seems to me to be caused by the fact that we do not form the habit of reading books that are worth while in children while they are at school and are under twelve years of age. The free use of books implies correct spelling and easy and vigorous composition without direct teaching of these subjects.

The Appendices show, I think, that such use of books in education works out well in practice, and is a great saving of time and labour to both teacher and pupils, especially relieving both of the deadly dull labour wasted on 'corrections.'

The much-diluted, or over-condensed, teaching of the oral lesson, or the lecture, gives place to the well thought out, consecutive treatment of the right book, a living book in which facts are presented as the outcome of ideas.

Children taught in this way are remarkable for their keenness after knowledge, and do well afterwards in any examination for which they may have to prepare; and, what is of much more consequence, are prepared to take their full share of all that life offers of intellectual and practical interests.

Ambleside,

Novemberber 1904.

Chapter 1 Docility and Authority in the Home and the School

Better Relations between Children and their Elders.—All of us who have accepted education as our métier are keenly alive to the signs of the times as they are to be read in the conduct and manners of children. Upon one thing, anyway, we may congratulate ourselves with unmixed satisfaction: the relations between children and parents, and indeed between children and their grown-up friends generally, are far more intimate, frank and friendly than such relations used to be. There does not seem to be any longer that great gulf fixed between child thought and grown-up thought, which the older among us once tried to cross with frantic but vain efforts. The heads of the house, when we were little, were autocratic as the Czars of all the Russias. We received everything at their hands, from bread and milk to mother's love, with more or less gratitude, but with invariable docility. If they had stubborn questionings as to whether was better for us, this or that, they kept them to themselves. For us, everything was decreed, and all decrees were final. There were rebellious children, perhaps, as one in a score, or one in a hundred, but then these were rebellious with the fine courage of Milton's Satan: they dared everything and set themselves up in bold opposition. These were the open rebels who would, sooner or late; come to a bad end; so we were told and so we secretly believed. For the others, there was no middle course. They were brought under rule, and that rule was arbitrary and without appeal.

The Elder Generation of Parents, Autocratic.—This is how children were brought up some forty or fifty years ago, and even young parents of today have, in many cases, grown up under a régime, happy, loving and wise very likely, but, before all things, arbitrary. There were what the Scotch would call 'ill-guided' homes, where the children did what was right in their own eyes. These will always exist so long as there are weak and indolent parents, unconcerned about their responsibilities. But the exceptions went to prove the rule; and the rule and tradition, in most middle-class homes, was that of well-ordered and governed childhood. Every biography, that issues from the press, of the men and women who made their mark during the first half of the century, is a case in point. John Stuart Mill, Ruskin, the Lawrences, Tennyson, almost everyone who has made for himself a distinguished name, grew up under a martinet rule. Only the other day we heard of an instance, the recollection of which had survived for seventy years. A boy of twelve or thirteen had been out shooting rabbits. He came home in the early darkness of a bitterly cold winter evening. His father asked him by which gate he had entered the park. 'By (such a) gate.' 'Did you shut it?' 'I don't recollect.' 'Go and see'; and the boy went, though he was already tired out, and the gate in question was more than a mile from the house. Such an incident would scarcely happen to-day; the boy would protest, plead his own benumbed fatigue, and suggest that a man should be sent to shut the gate, if, as did not appear from the story, it was important that it should be shut at all. Yet this was a kind father, whom his children both loved and honoured; but arbitrary rule and unquestioning obedience were the habits of the household. Nor is this notion of domestic government quite obsolete yet. I heard the other day of a Scotch father who confined his daughter of eighteen to her room for a week on account of some, by no means serious, breach of discipline. The difference is, that where you find an arbitrary parent now, he is a little out of touch with the thought and culture of the day; while, a few decades ago, parents were arbitrary of set principle and in proportion as they were cultivated and intelligent.

Arbitrary Rule not always a Failure.—It cannot be said that this arbitrary rule was entirely a failure. It turned out steadfast, capable, able, self-governed, gentle-mannered men and women. In our less hopeful moments, we wonder as we watch the children of our day whether they will prove as good stuff as their grandfathers and their fathers. But we need not fear. The evolution of educational thought is like the incoming of the tide. The wave comes and the wave goes and you hardly know whether you are watching ebb or flow; but let an hour elapse and then judge.

But truer Educational Thought results in Worthier Character.—After all allowances for ebb and flow, for failure here and mistake there, truer educational thought must of necessity result in an output of more worthy character. For one thing, this very arbitrariness arose from limitations. Parents knew that they must govern. Righteous Abraham, who ruled his house, was their ensample; and it is far easier to govern from a height, as it were, than from the intimacy of close personal contact. But you cannot be quite frank and easy with beings who are obviously of a higher and of another order than yourself; at least, you cannot when you are a little boy. And here we have one cause of the inscrutable reticence of children. At the best of times they carry on the busy traffic of their own thoughts all to themselves. We can all recollect the pathetic misgivings of our childish days which a word would have removed, but which yet formed the secret history of years of our lives. Mrs. Charles, in her autobiography, tells us how her childhood was haunted by a distressing dream. She dreamed that she had lost her mother and hunted for her in vain for hours in the rooms and endless corridors of a building unknown to her. Her distress was put down to fear of 'the dark,' and she never told her tender mother of this trouble of the night. Probably no degree of loving intimacy will throw the closed doors of the child's nature permanently ajar, because, we may believe, the burden of the mystery of all this unintelligible world falls early upon the conscious soul, and each of us must beat out his conception of life for himself. But it is much to a child to know that he may question, may talk of the thing that perplexes him, and that there is comprehension for his perplexities. Effusive sympathy is a mistake, and bores a child when it does not make him silly. But just to know that you can ask and tell is a great outlet, and means, to the parent, the power of direction, and to the child, free and natural development.

Doctrine of the Infallible Reason.—With the advance of one line of educational insight, we have, alas, to note the receding of another and a most important principle. Early in the century, authority was everything in the government of the home, and the docility of the children went without saying, that is, always excepting the few rebellious spirits. However little we may be aware of the fact, the direction of philosophic thought in England has had a great deal to do with the relations of parents and children in every home. Two centuries ago Locke promulgated the doctrine of the infallible reason. That doctrine accepted, individual reason becomes the ultimate authority, and every man is free to do that which is right in his own eyes. Provided, Locke would have added, that the reason be fully trained, and the mind instructed as to the merits of the particular case; but such proviso was readily lost sight of; and the broad principle remained. The old Puritanic faith and the elder traditions for the bringing up of children, as well as Locke's own religious feelings and dutiful instincts, were too strong for the new philosophy in England; but in France there was a soil prepared for the seed. Locke was eagerly read because his opinions jumped with the thought of the hour. His principles were put into practice, his conclusions worked out to the bitter end, and thoughtful writers consider that this religious and cultivated English gentleman cannot be exonerated from a share of the guilt of the atrocities of the French Revolution.

Leads to the Dethronement of Authority.—We in the twentieth century have lost some of the safeguards that held good in the seventeenth, and we have our own, perhaps greater, philosopher, who carries the teaching of Locke to the inevitable conclusions which the earlier thinker shirked. Mr. Herbert Spencer proclaims, as they did in France, the apotheosis of Reason. He sees, as they saw in France, that the principle of the infallible reason is directly antagonistic to the idea of authority. He traces this last idea to its final source and justification. So long as men acknowledge a God, they of necessity acknowledge authority, supreme and deputed. But, says Mr. Spencer, in effect, every man finds his own final authority in his own reason. This philosopher has the courage of his convictions; he perceives, as they did in France, that the enthronement of the human reason is the dethronement of Almighty God. He teaches, by processes of exhaustive reasoning, that—

"We sit unowned upon our burial sod,
And know not whence we come nor whose we be."

From the dethronement of the divine, follows the dethronement of all human authority, whether it be of kings and their deputies over nations, or of parents over families. Every act of authority is, we are taught, an infringement of the rights of man or of child. Children are to be brought up from the first self-directed, doing that which is right in their own eyes, governed by the reason which is to be trained, by experience of right and wrong, in the choosing of the right course. Life has its penalties for those who transgress the laws of reason, and the child should be permitted to learn these laws through the intervention of these penalties. But 'thou shalt' and 'thou shalt not' are to be eliminated from the vocabulary of parents. So complete and detailed is Mr. Spencer's scheme for the emancipation of children from rule, that he objects to the study of languages on the ground that the rules of grammar are a transgression of the principle of liberty.

Authority not Inherent, but Deputed.—Mr. Spencer's work on education is so valuable a contribution to educational thought that many parents read it and embrace it, as a whole, without perceiving that it is a part, and a carefully worked out part, of a scheme of philosophy with which perhaps they are little in sympathy. They accept the philosopher's teaching when he bids them bring up children without authority in order to give them free room for self-development; without perceiving, or perhaps knowing, that it is the labour of the author's life to eliminate the idea of authority from the universe, that he repudiates the authority of parents because it is a link in the chain which binds the universe to God. For it is indeed true that none of us has a right to exercise authority, in things great or small, except as we are, and acknowledge ourselves to be, deputed by the one supreme and ultimate Authority. When we take up this volume on education, small as it is, easy reading as it is, we must bear in mind that we have put ourselves under the lead of a philosopher who overlooks nothing, who regards the least important things from the standpoint of their final issue, and who would not have the little child do as he is bid lest he should learn, as a man, to obey that authority, other than himself, which we believe to be Divine.

'Quick as Thought.'—The influence of his rationalistic philosophy is by no means confined to those who read this author's great works, or even to those who read his manual on education. 'Quick as thought' is a common phrase, but it would be interesting to know how quick thought is, to have any measure for the intensity, vitality, and velocity of an idea, for the rate of its progress in the world. One would like to know how soon an idea, conceived in the study, becomes the common property of the man in the street, who regards it as his own possession, and knows nothing of its source. We have no such measures; but there is hardly a home, of even the lowest stage of culture, where this theory of education has not been either consciously adopted or rejected, though the particular parents in question may never have heard of the philosopher. An idea, once launched, is 'in the air,' so we say. As is said of the Holy Spirit, we know not whence it comes, nor whither it goes.

The Notion of the Finality of Human Reason Intolerable.—But, because philosophic thought is so subtle and permeating an influence, it is our part to scrutinise every principle that presents itself. Once we are able to safeguard ourselves in this way, we are able to profit by the wisdom of works which yet rest upon what we regard as radical errors. It seems not improbable that the early years of this very century may thus see the advent of England's truly great philosopher, who shall not be confined by the limitations of rationalistic or of materialistic thought. Men have become weary of themselves. The notion of the finality of human reason has grown an intolerable limitation. Nothing less than the Infinite will satisfy the spirit of a man. We again recognise that we are made for God, and have no rest until we find Him; and philosophic thought, at home and abroad, has, to some degree, left these channels high and dry, and is running in other courses, towards the Infinite and the Divine.

Authority and Docility, Fundamental principles.—One of the first efforts of this reconstructive thought, which is building us once more a temple for our spirits, a house not made with hands, is to restore Authority to its ancient place as an ultimate fact, no more to be accounted for than is the principle of gravitation, and as binding and universal in the moral world as is that other principle in the natural. Fitting in to that of authority, as the ball fits the socket to make a working joint, is the other universal and elemental principle of Docility, and upon these two hang all possibilities of law and order, government and progress, among men. Mr. Benjamin Kidd, in his Social Evolution, has done much for the recognition of these two fundamental principles. Why a football team should obey its captain, an army its commanding officer; why a street crowd should stand in awe of two or three policemen; why property should be respected, when it is the many who want and the few who have; why, in a word, there should be rule and not anarchy in the world—these are the sorts of questions Mr. Kidd sets himself to answer. He turns to Reason for her reply, and she has none to give. Her favourite argument is that the appeal to self-interest is final; that we do, individually and collectively, whatever is shown to be for our advantage. But when that company went down in the 'Royal George,' standing at 'Attention!' because that was the word of command; when the Six Hundred rode 'into the valley of death' because

"Theirs not to make reply,
Theirs not to reason why,
Theirs but to do and die,"

— the subtlest reasoning can find no other motive than the single and simple one of authority acting upon docility. These men had been told to do these things, and, therefore, they did them. That is all. And that they did well, we know; our own heart is the witness. We speak of such deeds as acts of heroism, but it is well to notice that these splendid displays of human nature at its best resolve themselves for the most part into acts of obedience to the word of authority. The abuse of authority gives us the slave and the despot, but slavery and despotism could not exist except that they are founded upon elemental principles in human nature. We all have it in us to serve or to rule as occasion demands. To dream of liberty, in the sense of every man his own sole governor, is as futile as to dream of a world in which apples do not necessarily drop from the tree, but may fly off at a tangent in any direction.

Work of Rationalistic Philosophers, Inevitable.—What is Authority? The question shows us how inevitable in the evolution of thought has been the work of the rationalistic philosophers. It is to them we owe our deliverance from the autocrat, whether on the throne or in the family.

Their work has been to assert and prove that every human soul is born free, that liberty is his inalienable right, and that an offence against the liberty of a human being is a capital offence. This also is true. Parents and teachers, because their subjects are so docile and so feeble, are tempted more than others to the arbitrary temper, to say—Do thus and thus because I bid you. Therefore they, more than others, owe a debt of gratitude to the rationalistic school for holding, as they do, a brief for human freedom, including the freedom of children in a family. It would seem to be thus that God educates the world. It is not only one good custom, but one infallible principle, which may 'corrupt a world.' Some such principle stands out luminous in the vision of a philosopher; he sees it is truth; it takes possession of him and he believes it to be the whole truth, and urges it to the point of reductio ad absurdum. Then the principle at the opposite pole of thought is similarly illuminated and glorified by a succeeding school of thought; and, later, it is discerned that it is not by either principle, but by both, that men live.

Authority, vested in the Office.—It is by these countercurrents, so to speak, of mind forces that we have been taught to rectify our notion of authority. Easily within living memory we were upon dangerous ground. We believed that authority was vested in persons, that arbitrary action became such persons, that slavish obedience was good for the others. This theory of government we derived from our religion; we believed in the 'divine right' of kings and of parents because we believed that the very will of God was an arbitrary will. But we have been taught better; we know now that authority is vested in the office and not in the person; that the moment it is treated as a personal attribute it is forfeited. We know that a person in authority is a person authorised; and that he who is authorised is under authority. The person under authority holds and fulfils a trust; in so far as he asserts himself; governs upon the impulse of his own will, he ceases to be authoritative and authorised, and becomes arbitrary and autocratic. It is autocracy and arbitrary rule which must be enforced, at all points, by a penal code; hence the confusion of thought which exists as to the connection between authority and punishment. The despot rules by terror; he punishes right and left to uphold his unauthorised sway. The person who is vested with authority, on the contrary, requires no rigours of the law to bolster him up, because authority is behind him; and, before him, the corresponding principle of docility.

Chapter 2 Docility and Authority in the Home and the School

Part II.—How Authority Behaves

Mistakes made on Principle.—Mr. Augustus Hare has, apparently, what somebody calls a bad memory, i.e. one which keeps a faithful record of every slight and offence that had been done to him since the day he was born! For this reason The Story of My Life (by Augustus Hare—George Allen.) is not quite pleasant reading, though it is full of interesting details. But all is fish that comes to our net. We have seldom had a more instructive record of childhood, even if we must allow that the instruction comes to us on the lines of what not to do. The fine character and beautiful nature of Mrs. Augustus Hare have been known to the world since the Memorials of a Quiet Life were published by this very son; and when we find how this lady misinterpreted the part of mother to her adopted and dearly beloved son, we know that we are not reading of the mistakes of an unworthy or even of a commonplace woman. Mrs. Hare always acted upon principle, and when she erred, the principle was in fault. She confounded the two principles of authority and autocracy. She believed that there was some occult virtue in arbitrary action on the part of a parent, and that a child must be the better in proportion as he does as he is bidden—the more outrageous the bidding the better the training. Here is an example of what a loving mother may force herself to do:—"Hitherto, I had never been allowed anything but roast mutton and rice pudding for dinner. Now all was changed. The most delicious puddings were talked of—dilated on—until I became, not greedy, but exceedingly curious about them. At length le grand moment arrived. They were put on the table just before me, and then, just as I was going to eat some of them, they were snatched away, and I was told to get up and carry them off to some poor person in the village. I remember that, though I did not really in the least care about the dainties, I cared excessively about Lea's wrath at the fate of her nice puddings, of which, after all, I was most innocent." Here is another arbitrary ruling:—"Even the pleasures of this home-Sunday, however, were marred in the summer, when my mother gave in to a suggestion of Aunt Esther that I should be locked in the vestry of the church between the services. Miserable, indeed, were the three hours which—provided with a sandwich for dinner—I had weekly to spend there; and, though I did not expect to see ghosts, the utter isolation of Hurstmonceaux church, far away from all haunts of men, gave my imprisonment an unusual eeriness. Sometimes I used to clamber over the tomb of the Lords Dacre, which rises like a screen against one side of the vestry, and be sticken with vague terrors by the two grim white figures lying upon it in the silent desolation, in which the scamper of a rat across the floor seemed to make a noise like a whirlwind. . . . It was a sort of comfort to me, in the real church-time, to repeat vigorously all the worst curses in the Psalms, those in which David showed his most appalling degree of malice, and apply them to Aunt Esther & Co. As all the Psalms were extolled as beatific, and the Church of England used them constantly for edification, their sentiments were all right, I supposed."

And yet how wise this good mother is when she trusts to her own instinct and insight rather than to a fallacious principle:—"I find in giving any order to a child, it is always better not to look to see if he obeys, but to take it for granted that it will be done. If one appears to doubt the obedience, there is given for the child to hesitate, 'Shall I do it or no?' If you seem not to question the possibility of non-compliance, he feels a trust committed to him to keep and fulfils it. It is best never to repeat a command, never to answer the oft-asked question 'Why?'"

Authority distinguished from Autocracy.—Mrs. Hare, like many another ruler, would appear to have erred, not from indolence, and certainly not harshness, but because she failed to define to herself the nature of the authority she was bound to exercise. Autocracy is defined as independent or self-derived power. Authority, on the other hand, may qualify as not being self-derived and not independent. The centurion in the Gospels says: "I also am a man set under authority, having under me soldiers, and I say unto one, 'Go,' and he goeth; another, 'Come,' and he cometh; and to my servant, 'Do this,' and he doeth it."

Here we have the powers and the limitations of authority. The centurion is set under authority, or, as we say, authorised, and, for that reason, he is able to say to one, 'go,' to another, 'come,' and to a third, 'do this,' in the calm certainty that all will be done as he says, because he holds his position for this very purpose—to secure that such and such things shall be accomplished. He himself is a servant with definite tasks, though they are the tasks of authority. This, too, is the position that our Lord assumes; He says: "I came not to do mine own will, but the will of Him that sent me." That is His commission and the standing order of His life, and for this reason He spake as one having authority, knowing Himself to be commissioned and supported.

Behaviour of Autocracy.—Authority is not uneasy; captious, harsh and indulgent by turns. This is the action of autocracy, which is self-sustained as it is self-derived, and is impatient and resentful, on the watch for transgressions, and swift to take offence. Autocracy has ever a drastic penal code, whether in the kingdom, the school, or the family. It has, too, many commandments. 'Thou shalt' and 'thou shalt not,' are chevaux de frise about the would-be awful majesty of the autocrat. The tendency to assume self-derived power is common to us all, even the meekest of us, and calls for special watchfulness; the more so, because it shows itself fully as often in remitting duties and in granting indulgences as in inflicting punishments. It is flattering when a child comes up in the winning, coaxing way the monkeys know how to assume, and says, 'Please let me stay at home this morning, only this once!' The next stage is, 'I don't want to go out,' and the next, 'I won't!' and the home or school ruler, who has no principle behind his own will, soon learns that a child can be autocratic too—autocratic and belligerent to an alarming extent.

Behaviour of Authority.—Authority is neither harsh nor indulgent. She is gentle and easy to be entreated in all matters immaterial, just because she is immovable in matters of real importance; for these, there is always a fixed principle. It does not, for example, rest with parents and teachers to dally with questions affecting either the health or the duty of their children. They have no authority to allow to children in indulgences—in too many sweetmeats, for example—or in habits which are prejudicial to health; nor to let them off from any plain duty of obedience, courtesy, reverence, or work. Authority is alert; she knows all that is going on and is aware of tendencies. She fulfils the apostolic precept—"He that ruleth (let him do it), with diligence." But she is strong enough to fulfil that other precept also, "He that showeth mercy (let him do it), with cheerfulness"; timely clemency, timely yielding, is a great secret of strong government It sometimes happens that children, and not their parents, have right on their side: a claim may be made or an injunction resisted, and the children are in opposition to parent or teacher. It is well for the latter to get the habit of swiftly and imperceptibly reviewing the situation; possibly, the children may be in the right, and the parent may gather up his wits in time to yield the point graciously and send the little rebels away in a glow of love and loyalty.

Qualities proper to a Ruler.—Nobody understood this better than Queen Elizabeth, who contrived to make a curious division of her personality and be, at the same time, a model ruler and, as a woman, full of the weaknesses of her sex. It has been well said that she knew when to yield and how to yield. Her adroitness in getting over many a dangerous crisis has been much praised by historians; but, possibly, this saving grace was not adroitness so much as the tact born of qualities proper to all who are set in authority—the meekness of one who has been given an appointed work, the readiness to take counsel with herself and with others, the perception that she herself was not the be-all and the end-all of her functions as a queen, but that she existed for her people, and the quick and tender open-minded sympathy which enabled her to see their side of every question as well as her own—indeed, in preference to her own. These are the qualities proper to every ruler of a household, a school, or a kingdom. With these, parents will be able to order and control a fiery young brood full of energy and vitality, as Elizabeth was, to manage the kingdom when the minds of men were in a ferment of new thought, and life was intoxicating in the delightfulness of the possibilities it offered.

Mechanical and Reasonable Obedience.—It is a little difficult to draw the line between mechanical and reasonable obedience. 'I teach my children obedience by the time they are one year old,' the writer heard a very successful mother remark; and, indeed, that is the age at which to begin to give children the ease and comfort of the habit of obeying lawful authority. We know Mr. Huxley's story of the retired private who was carrying home his Sunday's dinner from the bakehouse. A sergeant passed by who recognised the man's soldierly gait and was bent on a practical joke. 'Attention!' he cried, and the man stood at attention while his mutton and potatoes rolled in the gutter. Now, this kind of obedience is a mere question of nerves and muscles, a habit of the brain tissue with which the moral consciousness has nothing to do. It is a little the fashion to undervalue any but reasonable obedience, as if we were creatures altogether of mind and spirit, or creatures whose bodies answer as readily to the ruling of the spirit as does the ship to the helm. But, alas for our weakness! this description fits us only in proportion as our bodies have been trained to the of unthinking mechanical obedience. We know the child who is fully willing to do the right thing so far as mind is concerned, but with whom bodily vis inertiae is strong enough to resist a very torrent of good intentions and good resolutions; and if we wish children to be able, when they grow up, to keep under their bodies and bring them into subjection we must do this for them in their earlier years.

Response of Docility to Authority, a Natural Function.—So far as the daily routine of small obediences goes, we help them thus to fulfil a natural function—the response of docility to authority. It may be said that a child who has acquired the habit of involuntary obedience has proportionately lost power as a free moral agent; but, as the acts of obedience in question are very commonly connected some physical effort, as, 'Make haste back,' 'Sit straight,' 'Button your boots quickly,'—they belong to the same educational province as gymnastic exercises, the object of which is the masterly use of the body as a machine capable of many operations.

Now, to work a machine such as a typewriter or a bicycle, one must, before all things, have practice; one must have got into the way of working it involuntarily, without giving any thought to the matter: and to give a child this power over himself—first in response to the will of another, later, in response to his own, is to make a man of him.

The Habit of Prompt Obedience.—It is an old story that the failures in life are not the people who lack good intentions; they are those whose physical nature has not acquired the habit of prompt and involuntary obedience. The man who can make himself do what he wills has the world before him, and it rests with parents to give their children this self-compelling power as a mere matter of habit. But is it not better and higher, it may be asked, to train children to act always in response to the divine mandate as it makes itself heard through the voice of conscience? The answer is, that in doing this we must not leave the other undone. There are few earnest parents who do not bring the power of conscience to bear on their children, and there are emergencies enough in the lives of young and old when we have to make a spiritual decision upon spiritual grounds—when it rests with us to choose the good and refuse the evil, consciously and voluntarily, because it is God's will that we should.

The Effort of Decision.—But it has been well said by a celebrated preacher that the effort of decision is the greatest effort of life. We find it so ourselves; shall we take this line of action or the other, shall we choose this or the other quality of carpet, send our boy to this or the other school? We all know that such questions are difficult to settle, and the wear and tear of nervous tissue the decision costs is evidenced often enough by the nervous headache it leaves behind. For this reason it is, we may reverently believe, that we are so marvellously and mercifully made that most of our decisions arrive, so to speak, of themselves: that is, ninety-nine out of a hundred things we do, are done, well or ill, as mere matters of habit. With this wonderful provision in our tissues for recording repeated actions and reproducing them upon given stimuli—a means provided for easing the burden of life, and for helping us to realise the gay happiness which appears to be the divine intention for us so far as we become like little children—it is startling and shocking that there are many children of thoughtful parents whose lives are spent in day-long efforts of decision upon matters which it is their parents' business to settle for them. Maud is nervous, excitable, has an over-active brain, is too highly organised, grows pale, acquires nervous tricks. The doctor is consulted, and, not knowing much about the economy of the home, decides that it is a case of over-pressure. Maud must do no lessons for six months; change of air is advised, and milk diet. Somehow the prescription does not answer, the child's condition does not improve; but the parents are slow to perceive that it is not the soothing routine of lessons which is exhausting the little girl, but the fact that she goes through the labour of decision twenty times a day, and not only that, but the added fatigue of a contest to get her own way. Every point in the day's routine is discussed, nothing comes with the comforting ease of a matter of course; the child always prefers to do something else, and commonly does it. No wonder the poor little girl is worn out.

Authority avoids Cause of Offence.—On the other hand, children are before all things reasonable beings, and to some children of acute and powerful intelligence, an arbitrary and apparently unreasonable command is cruelly irritating. It is not advisable to answer children categorically when they want to know the why for every command, but wise parents steer a middle course. They are careful to form habits upon which the routine of life runs easily, and, when the exceptional event requires a new regulation, they may make casual mention of their reasons for having so and so done; or, if this is not convenient and the case is a trying one, they give the children the reason for all obedience—"for this is right." In a word, authority avoids, so far as may be, giving cause of offence.

Authority is Alert.—Another hint as to the fit use of authority may be gleaned from the methods employed in a well-governed state. The importance of prevention is fully recognised: police, army, navy, are largely preventive forces; and the home authority, too, does well to place its forces on the Alert Service. It is well to prepare for trying efforts: 'We shall have time to finish this chapter before the clock strikes seven'; or, 'we shall be able to get in one more round before bedtime.' Nobody knows better than the wise mother the importance of giving a child time to collect himself for a decisive moment. This time should be spent in finishing some delightful occupation; every minute of idleness at these critical junctures goes to the setting up of the vis inertiae, most difficult to overcome because the child's will power is in abeyance. A little forethought is necessary to arrange that occupations do come to an end at the right moment; that bedtime does not arrive in the middle of a chapter, or at the most exciting moment of a game. In such an event authority, which looks before and after, might see its way to allow five minutes' grace, but would not feel itself empowered to allow a child to dawdle about indefinitely before saying good-night.

Who gave thee this Authority?—We need not add that authority is just and faithful in all matters of promise-keeping; it is also considerate, and that is why a good mother is the best home-ruler; she is in touch with the children, knows their unspoken schemes and half-formed desires, and where she cannot yield, she diverts; she does not crush with a sledge-hammer, an instrument of rule with which a child is somehow never very sympathetic.

We all know how important this, of changing children's thoughts, diverting, is in the formation of habit. Let us not despise the day of small things nor grow weary in well-doing; if we have trained our children from their earliest years to prompt mechanical obedience, well and good; we reap our reward. If we have not, we must be content to lead by slow degrees, by ever-watchful efforts, by authority never in abeyance and never aggressive, to 'the joy of self-control,' the delight of proud chivalric obedience which will hail a command as an opportunity for service. It is a happy thing that the 'difficult' children who are the readiest to resist a direct command are often the quickest to respond to the stimulus of an idea. The presentation of quickening ideas is itself a delicate art, which I have, however, considered elsewhere.

I am not proposing a one-sided arrangement, all authority on the one part and all the docility on the other; for never was there a child who did not wield authority, if only over dolls or tin soldiers. And we of the ruling class, so far as the nursery and schoolroom go, are we not fatally docile in yielding obedience to anyone who will take the trouble to tell us we had better do this or that? We need not be jealous for the independence of children: that will take care of itself.

To conclude: authority is not only a gift, but a grace; and,

"As every rainbow hue is light,
So every grace is love."

Authority is that aspect of love which parents present to their children; parents know it is love, because to them it means continual self-denial, self-repression, self-sacrifice: children recognise it as love, because to them it means quiet rest and gaiety of heart. Perhaps the best aid to the maintenance of authority in the home is for those in authority to ask themselves daily that question which was presumptuously put to our Lord—"Who gave Thee this authority?"

Chapter 3 'Masterly Inactivity'

Increased Sense of Responsibility.—It would be an interesting task for a literary expert to trace the stages of ethical thought marked by the uses, within living memory, of the word responsibility. People, and even children, were highly responsible in the fifties and sixties, but then it was for their own character, conduct, and demeanour. It is not at all certain that we hold ourselves responsible in this matter to the same degree. We are inclined to accept ourselves as inevitable, to make kindly allowance for our own little ways and peccadilloes, and are, perhaps, wanting in that wholesome sense of humour, 'the giftie' which should "gie us

"To see oursels as ithers see us."

A Sign of Moral Progress.—If we take ourselves more easily, however, we take other people more seriously. The sense of responsibility still rests upon us with a weight 'heavy as frost'; we have only shifted it to the other shoulder. The more serious of us are quite worn with the sense of what we owe to those about us, near and far off. Men carry the weight more easily than women, because, for most of them, each day brings work that must be done, and they have less time than women to think anxiously about their relations with, and duties to, others. By the way, it is rather a note of the time that the translators of the Revised Version have given us 'Be not anxious for your life;' instead of the older rendering. But, if women feel the wear of responsibility for others more constantly, let but a burning question arise—the condition of East London, Home Rule, massacres in Armenia—and men feel it more intensely and passionately. This sharpened sense is not a malady of the age, but a sign of the times.

To those of us who believe we are all at school and have our lessons set as we are fit to take them in, this general sense of responsibility for others is an encouraging sign that we are being taught from above, and are, on the whole, getting on.

Parental Responsibility—If we all feel ourselves responsible for the distressed, the suffering, the sick, the feeble in body or mind, the deficient, the ignorant, and—would that we all felt this particular burden more—for the heathen, there is one kind of responsibility which is felt by thoughtful people with almost undue acuteness. Parental responsibility is, no doubt, the educational note of the day. People feel that they can bring up their children to be something more than themselves, that they ought to do so, and that they must; and it is to this keen sense of higher parental duty that the Parents' Union owes its successful activity.

Anxiety the Note of a Transition Stage—Every new power, whether mechanical or spiritual, requires adjustment before it can be used to the full. In the scientific world there is always a long pause between the first dawn of a great discovery—as the Röntgen rays, for example—and the moment when it is applied to the affairs of everyday life with full effect and without the displacement of other powers whose functions are just as important and as necessary. We should regard with suspicion any attempt to make the Röntgen rays supply the place of stethoscope, thermometer, and all other clinical apparatus. Just so is it in the moral sphere. Our keener sense of responsibility arises from a new development of altruistic feeling—we have greater power of loving and wider scope for our love; we are more leavened by the Spirit of Christ, even when we do not recognise the source of our fuller life. But to perceive that there is much which we ought to do and not to know exactly what it is, nor how to do it, does not add to the pleasure of life or to ease in living. We become worried, restless, anxious; and in the transition stage between the development of this new power and the adjustment which comes with time and experience, the fuller life, which is certainly ours, fails to make us either happier or more useful.

A Fussy and Restless Habit—It is by way of an effort towards this adjustment of power that I wish to bring before parents and teachers the subject of 'masterly inactivity.' We ought to do so much for our children, and are able to do so much for them, that we begin to think everything rests with us and that we should never intermit for a moment our conscious action on the young minds and hearts about us. Our endeavours become fussy and restless. We are too much with our children, 'late and soon.' We try to dominate them too much, even when we fail to govern, and we are unable to perceive that wise and purposeful letting alone is the best part of education. But this form of error arises from a defect of our qualities. We may take heart. We have the qualities, and all that is wanted is adjustment; to this we must give our time and attention.

'Masterly Inactivity.'—A blessed thing in our mental constitution is, that once we receive an idea, it will work itself out, in thought and act, without much after-effort on our part; and, if we admit the idea of 'masterly inactivity' as a factor in education, we shall find ourselves framing our dealings with children from this standpoint, without much conscious effort. But we must get clearly into our heads what we mean by masterly inactivity. Carlyle's happy phrase has nothing in common with the laisser allez attitude that comes of thinking 'what's the good?' and still further is it removed from the sheer indolence of mind that lets things go their way rather than take the trouble to lead them to any issue. It indicates a fine healthy moral pose which it is worth while for us to analyse. Perhaps the idea is nearly that conveyed in Wordsworth's even more happy phrase, 'wise passiveness'. It indicates the power to act, the desire to act, and the insight and self-restraint which forbid action. But there is, from our point of view at any rate, a further idea conveyed in 'masterly inactivity.' The mastery is not over ourselves only; there is also a sense of authority, which our children should be as much aware of when it is inactive as when they are doing our bidding. The sense of authority is the sine quâ non of the parental relationship, and I am not sure that without that our activities or our inactivity will produce any great results. This element of strength is the backbone of our position. 'We could an' if we would' and the children know it—They are free under authority, which is liberty; to be free without authority is license.

The Element of Good Humour.—The next element in the attitude of masterly inactivity is good humour—frank, cordial, natural, good humour. This is quite a different thing from overmuch complacency, and a general giving-in to all the children's whims. The one is the outcome of strength, the other of weakness, and children are very quick to see the difference. 'Oh, mother, may we go blackberrying this afternoon, instead of lessons?' The masterly and the abject 'yes' are quite different notes. The first makes the holiday doubly a delight; the second produces a restless desire to gain some other easy victory.

Self-confidence.—The next element is confidence. Parents should trust themselves more. Everything is not done by restless endeavour. The mere blessed fact of the parental relationship and of that authority which belongs to it, by right and by nature, acts upon the children as do sunshine and shower on a seed in good soil. But the fussy parent, the anxious parent, the parent who explains overmuch, who commands overmuch, who excuses overmuch, who restrains overmuch, who interferes overmuch, even the parent who is with the children overmuch, does away with dignity and simplicity of that relationship which, like all the best and most delicate things in life, suffer by being asserted or defended.

The fine, easy way of Fathers.—Fathers are, sometimes, more happy than mothers in assuming fine easy way with their children which belongs of right to their relationship, but this is only because the father is occupied with many things, and the mother is apt to be too much engrossed with her children. It is a little humiliating to the best of us to see a careless, rather a selfish mother, whose children are her born slaves and run to do her bidding with delight. The moral is, not that all mothers should be careless and selfish, but that they should give their children the ease of a good deal of letting alone, and should not oppress the young people with their own anxious care. The small person of ten who wishes to know if her attainments are up to the average for her age, or he who discusses his bad habits with you and the best way of curing them, is displeasing, because one feels instinctively that the child is occupied with cares which belong to the parent only. The burden of their children's training must be borne by the parents alone. But let them bear it with easy grace and an erect carriage, as the Spanish peasant bears her water-jar.

Confidence in the Children—Not only confidence in themselves, but confidence in their children, is an element of the masterly inactivity, which I venture to propose to parents as a 'blue teapot' for them 'to live up to'. Believe in the relation of parent and child, and trust the children to believe in it and fulfil it on their part. They will do so if they are not worried.

Omniscience of Parents and Teachers.—Parents and teachers must, of course, be omniscient; their children expect this of them, and a mother or father who can be hoodwinked is a person easy to reckon with in the mind of even the best child. For children are always playing a game—half of chance, half of skill; they are trying how far they can go, how much of the management of their own lives they can get for the taking, and how much they must leave in the hands of the stronger powers. Therefore the mother who is not up to children is at their mercy, and need expect no quarter. But she must see without watching, know without telling, be on the alert always, yet never obviously, fussily, so. This open-eyed attitude must be sphinx-like in its repose. The children must know themselves to be let alone, whether to do their own duty or to seek their own pleasure. The constraining power should be present, but passive, so that the child may not feel himself hemmed in without choice. That free-will of man, which has for ages exercised faithful souls who would prefer to be compelled into all righteousness and obedience, is after all a pattern for parents. The child who is good because he must be so, loses in power of initiative more than he gains in seemly behaviour. Every time a child feels that he chooses to obey of his own accord, his power of initiative is strengthened. The bearing-rein may not be used. When it occurs to a child to reflect on his behaviour, he should have that sense of liberty which makes good behaviour appear to him a matter of his preference and choice.

'Fate' and 'Freewill'—This is the freedom which a child enjoys who has the confidence of his parents as to his comings and goings and childish doings, and who is all the time aware of their authority. He is brought up in the school proper for a being whose life is conditioned by 'fate' and 'freewill.' He has liberty, that is, with a sense of must behind it to relieve him of that unrest which comes with the constant effort of decision. He is free to do as he ought, but knows quite well in his secret heart that he is not free to do that which he ought not. The child who, on the contrary, grows up with no strong sense of authority behind all his actions, but who receives many exhortations to be good and obedient and what not, is aware that he may choose either good or evil, he may obey or not obey, he may tell the truth or tell a lie; and, even when he chooses aright, he does so at the cost of a great deal of nervous wear and tear. His parents have removed from him the support of their authority in the difficult choice of right-doing, and he is left alone to make that most trying of all efforts, the effort of decision. Is the distinction between being free to choose the right at one's own option, and not free to do the wrong, too subtle to be grasped, too elusive to be practical? It may be so, but it is precisely the distinction which we are aware of in our own lives so far as we keep ourselves consciously under the divine governance. We are free to go in the ways of right living, and have the happy sense of liberty of choice, but the ways of transgressors are hard. We are aware of a restraining hand in the present, and of sure and certain retribution in the future. Just this delicate poise is to be aimed at for the child. He must be treated with full confidence, and must feel that right-doing is his own free choice, which his parents trust him to make; but he must also be very well aware of the deterrent force in the background, watchful to hinder him when he would do wrong.

The Component Parts of Masterly Inactivity.—We have seen that authority, good humour, confidence, both self-confidence and confidence in the children, are all contained in masterly inactivity, but these are not all the parts of that whole. A sound mind in a sound body is another factor. If the sound body is unattainable, anyway, get the sound mind. Let not the nervous, anxious, worried mother think this easy, happy relation with her children is for her. She may be the best mother in the world, but the thing that her children will get from her in these moods is a touch of her nervousness—most catching of complaints. She will find them fractious, rebellious, unmanageable, and will be slow to realise that it is her fault; not the fault of her act but of her state.

Serenity of a Madonna.—It is not for nothing that the old painters, however diverse their ideas in other matters, all fixed upon one quality as proper to the pattern Mother. The Madonna, no matter out of whose canvas she looks at you, is always serene. This is a great truth, and we should do well to hang our walls with the Madonnas of all the early Masters if the lesson, taught through the eye, would reach with calming influence to the heart. Is this a hard saying for mothers in these anxious and troubled days? It may be hard, but it is not unsympathetic. If mothers could learn to do for themselves what they do for their children when these are overdone, we should have happier households. Let the mother go out to play! If she would only have courage to let everything go when life becomes too tense, and just take a day, or half a day, out in the fields, or with a favourite book, or in a picture gallery looking long and well at just two or three pictures, or in bed, without the children, life would go on far more happily for both children and parents. The mother would be able to hold herself in 'wise passiveness,' and would not fret her children by continual interference, even of hand or eye—she would let them be.

Leisure.—Another element is leisure. Sometimes events hurry us, and sometimes—is it not true?—we like the little excitement of a rush. The children like it, too, at first—Father's birthday is coming, and Nellie must recite a poem for him; the little fête has only been thought of a week in advance, and Nellie is seized at all sorts of odd moments to have some lines of the recitation crammed into her. At first she is pleased and important, and goes joyously to the task; but by-and-by it irks her; she is cross and naughty, is reproached for want of love for father, sheds tears over her verses, and, though finally the little performance may be got through very well, Nellie has suffered physically and morally in doing what, if it had been thought of a month beforehand, would have been altogether wholesome and delightful. Still worse for the children is it when mother or teacher has a 'busy' day. Friends are coming, or the family wardrobe for the summer must be seen to, or drawers and cupboards must be turned out, or an examination is at hand. Anyway, it is one of those fussy, busy days which we women rather delight in. We do more than we can ourselves, our nerves are 'on end,' what with the fatigue and what with the little excitement, and everybody in the house or the school is uncomfortable. Again, the children take advantage, so we say; the real fact being that they have caught their mother's mood and are fretful and tiresome. Nerve storms in the nursery are the probable result of the mother's little ebullition of nervous energy.

Leisure for themselves and a sense of leisure in those about them is as necessary to children's well being, as it is to the strong and benign parental attitude of which I am speaking.

Faith.—Other ingredients go to the making of the delectable compound we call 'masterly inactivity,' but space will allow me to speak of only one more. That highest form of confidence, known to us as faith, is necessary to full repose of mind and manner. When we recognise that God does not make over the bringing up of children absolutely even to their parents, but that He works Himself, in ways which it must be our care not to hinder, in the training of every child, then we shall learn passiveness, humble and wise. We shall give children space to develop on the lines of their own characters in all right ways, and shall know how to intervene effectually to prevent those errors which, also, are proper to their individual characters.

Let us next consider a few of the various phases of children's lives in which parents and teachers would do well to preserve an attitude of 'masterly inactivity.'

Chapter 4 Some of the Rights of Children as Persons

Children should be Free in their Play—We have considered the wisdom and duty of 'a wise passiveness,' 'a masterly inactivity,' in the bringing up of children. It remains to glance in detail at the various points in a child's life, where this principle should govern us. And, first, as regards children's play. There is a little danger in these days of much educational effort that children's play should be crowded out, or, what is from our present point of view the same thing, should be prescribed for and arranged until there is no more freedom of choice about play than that about work. We do not say a word against the educational value of games. We know that many things are learned in the playing-fields; that the qualities which we associate with the name of Englishman are largely the product of the laws of the games; and there is a pretty steady effort being made to bring these same forces to bear upon girls, that they, too, may grow up with the law-abiding principle, the moral stamina, and the resourcefulness, which are more or less the outcome of the education carried on in the playing-fields.

Organised Games are not Play—But organised games are not play in the sense we have in view. Boys and girls must have time to invent episodes, carry on adventures, live heroic lives, lay sieges and carry forts, even if the fortress be an old armchair; and in these affairs the elders must neither meddle nor make. They must be content to know that they do not understand, and, what is more, that they carry with them a chill breath of reality which sweeps away illusions. Think what it must mean to a general in command of his forces to be told by some intruder into the play-world to tie his shoe-strings! There is an idea afloat that children require to be taught to play—to play at being little fishes and lambs and butterflies. No doubt they enjoy these games which are made for them, but there is a serious danger. In this matter the child who goes too much on crutches never learns to walk; he who is most played with by his elders has little power of inventing plays for himself; and so he misses that education which comes to him when allowed to go his own way and act,

"As if his whole vocation
Were endless imitation."

Personal Initiative in Work.—In their work, too, we are too apt to interfere with children. We all know the delight with which any scope for personal initiative is hailed, the pleasure children take in doing anything which they may do their own way; anything, in fact, which allows room for skill of hand, play of fancy, or development of thought. With our present theories of education it seems that we cannot give much scope for personal initiative. There is so much task-work to be done, so many things that must be, not learned, but learned about, that it is only now and then a child gets the chance to produce himself in his work. But let us use such opportunities as come in our way. A very interesting and instructive educational experiment on these lines has lately been tried at the School Field, Hackney, where Mr. Sargent got together some eighty boys and girls under the conditions of an ordinary elementary school, except that the school was supported, not by the Education Department nor by the rates, but by the founder. The results seem to have been purely delightful; the children developed an amazing capacity for drawing, perhaps because so soon as they were familiar with the outlines of the flower and foliage of a given plant, for example, they were encouraged to form designs with these elements. The really beautiful floral designs produced by these girls and boys, after quite a short art training, would surprise parents whose children have been taught drawing for years with no evident result. These School Field children developed themselves a great deal on their school magazine also, for which they wrote tales and poems, and essays, not prescribed work, but self-chosen. The children's thought was stimulated, and they felt they had it in them to say much about a doll's ball, Peter, the school cat, or whatever other subject struck their fancy. 'They felt their feet' as the nurses say of children when they begin to walk; and our non-success in education is a good deal due to the fact that we carry children through their school work and do not let them feel their feet.

Children must Stand or Fall by their own Efforts.—In another way, more within our present control, we do not let children alone enough in their work. We prod them continually and do not let them stand or fall by their own efforts. One of the features, and one of the disastrous features, of modern society, is that, in our laziness, we depend upon prodders and encourage a vast system of prodding. We are prodded to our social duties, to our charitable duties, and to our religious duties. If we pay a subscription to a charity, we expect the secretary to prod us when it becomes due. If we attend a meeting, do we often do so of our own spontaneous will, or because somebody asks us to go and reminds us half a dozen times of the day and the hour? Perhaps it is a result of the hurry of the age that there is a curious division of labour, and society falls into those who prod and those who are prodded. Not that anybody prods in all directions, nor that anybody else offers himself entirely as a pincushion. It is more true, perhaps, to say that we all prod, and that we are all prodded. Now, an occasional prick is stimulating and wholesome, but the vis inertiae of human nature is such that we would rather lean up against a wall of spikes than not lean at all. What we must guard against in the training of children is the danger of their getting into the habit of being prodded to every duty and every effort. Our whole system of school policy is largely a system of prods. Marks, prizes, exhibitions, are all prods; and a system of prodding is apt to obscure the meaning of must and ought for the boy or girl who gets into the habit of mental and moral lolling up against his prods.

Boys and Girls are generally Dutiful—It would be better for boys and girls to suffer the consequences of not doing their work, now and then, than to do it because they are so urged and prodded on all hands they have no volition in the matter. The more we are prodded the lazier we get, and the less capable of the effort of will which should carry us to, and nearly carry us through, our tasks. Boys and girls are, on the whole, good, and desirous to do their duty. If we expect the tale of bricks to be delivered at the due moment without urging or entreating, rewarding or punishing, in nine cases out of ten we shall get what we look for. Where many of us err is in leaning too much to our own understanding and our own efforts, and not trusting sufficiently to the dutiful impulse which will carry children through the work they are expected to do.

Children should Choose their own Friends.—With regard to the choice of friends and companions, again, we should train children so that we should be able to honour them with a generous confidence; and if we give them such confidence we shall find that they justify it. If Fred has made a companion of Harry Jones, and Harry is not a nice boy, Fred will find the fact out as soon as his mother if he is let alone, and will probably come for advice and help as to the best way of getting out of an intimacy which does not really please him. But if Harry is boycotted by the home authorities and made the object of various prohibitions and exclusions, why Fred, if he be a generous boy, will feel in honour bound to take his comrade's part, and an intimacy which might have been easily dropped becomes cemented. Ethel will not see the reason why she, as the daughter of a professional man, may not make a friend of Maud, who sits beside her at school and is the daughter of a tradesman. But these minor matters must be left to circumstances, and the mother who brings forward questions of class, appearance, etc., as affecting her children's choice of friends, does her best to create obtuseness as to vital points of character which is the cause of most shipwrecked lives. In this matter, as in all others, the parent's inactivity must be masterly; that is, the young people should read approval or disapproval very easily, and should be able to trace one or the other to general principles of character and conduct, though nothing be said or done or even looked in disparagement of the ally of the hour.

Should be free to Spend their own Pocket-Money—In the spending of pocket-money is another opportunity for initiative on the children's part and for self-restraint on that of the parents. No doubt the father who doles out the weekly pocket-money and has never given his children any large thoughts about money—as to how the smallest income is divisible into the share that we give, and the share that we keep, and the share that we save for some object worth possessing, to be had, perhaps, after weeks or months of saving; as to the futility of buying that we may eat, an indulgence, that we should rarely allow ourselves, and never except for the pleasure of sharing with others; as to how it is worth while to think twice before making a purchase, with the lesson before us of Rosamund and the Purple Jar—such a father cannot expect his children to think of money in any light but as a means to self-indulgence. But talks like these should have no obvious and immediate bearing on the weekly pocket-money; that should be spent as the children like, they having been instructed as to how they should like to spend it. By degrees pocket-money should include the cost of gloves, handkerchiefs, etc., until, finally, the girl who is well on in her teens should be fit to be trusted with her own allowance for dress and personal expenses. The parents who do not trust their young people in this matter, after having trained them, are hardly qualifying them to take their place in a world in which the wise, just, and generous spending of money is a great test of character.

Should form their own Opinions—We have only room to mention one more point in which all of us, who have the care of young people, would do well to practise a wise 'letting alone.' There are burning questions in the air, seething opinions in men's minds: as to religion, politics, science, literature, art, as regards every kind of social effort, we are all disposed to hold strenuous opinions. The person who has not kept himself in touch with the movement of the thought of the world in all these matters has little cause to pride himself. It is our duty to form opinions carefully, and to hold them tenaciously in so far as the original grounds of our conclusions remain unshaken. But what we have no right to do, is to pass these opinions on to our children. We all know that nothing is easier than to make vehement partisans of young people, in any cause heartily adopted by their elders. But a reaction comes, and the swinging of the pendulum is apt to carry them to a point of thought painfully remote from our own. The mother of the Newmans was a devoted Evangelical, and in their early years passed her opinions over to her sons, ready-made; believing, perhaps, that the line of thought they received from her was what they had come to by their own thinking. But when they are released from the domination of their mother's opinions, one seeks anchorage in the Church of Rome, and another will have no restriction as to his freedom of thought and will, and chooses to shape for himself his own creed or negation of a creed. Perhaps this pious mother would have been saved some anguish if she had given her children the living principles of the Christian faith, which are not matters of opinion, and allowed them to accept her particular practice in their youth without requiring them to take their stand on Evangelical opinions as offering practically the one way of salvation.

In politics, again, let children be fired with patriotism and instructed in the duties of citizenship, but, if they can be kept out of the party strife of an election, well for them. Children are far more likely to embrace the views of their parents, when they are ripe to form opinions, if these have not been forced upon them in early youth when their lack of knowledge and experience makes it impossible for them to form opinions at first hand. Only by masterly inactivity,' 'wise passiveness,' able 'letting alone,' can a child be trained—

"To reverence his conscience as his king."

Spontaneity.—We all admire spontaneity, but this grace, even in children, is not an indigenous wild-flower. In so far as it is a grace, it is the result of training,—of pleasant talks upon the general principles of conduct, and wise 'letting alone' as to the practice of these principles. To parents, who have in their hands the making of family customs, it belongs especially to beware—

"Lest one good custom should corrupt the world."

Chapter 5 Psychology in Relation to Current Thought

Educational Thought in the Eighteenth Century.—If the end of the eighteenth and the end of the nineteenth centuries have one feature in common more than another, it is, that in both education comes to the front as among the chief ends of man. The eighteenth-century people had the best of it. They had clear oracles in their Locke and their Rousseau. They knew what they wanted to do, and they did it with charming enthusiasm. The period teems with memoirs; and it is very pleasant to read about the philosophically and consistently brought up children of the more thoughtful families. They had convictions, and they had the courage of their convictions. We are less happy. A few decades ago we too were in a furore of joyous excitement about education. Educational 'movements,' schools, colleges, lectures, higher education for women, 'public' day schools for girls, examination tests which should give assurance on every point, were multiplied all over the country and all over the world. It was a forward movement which has brought us incalculable gains; and not the least of these gains is the fact that today we are dissatisfied and depressed, and inclined to wonder whether we are not on the wrong tack. If educational work of the best kind had not been going on amongst us for the last two or three decades, we should not have arrived at this 'divine discontent.' All the same, it is pretty evident that the time has come when we must change our front. Now, elementary schools, now, girls' high schools, now, public schools, now, women's colleges, are pronounced to be, on the whole, 'a failure.' They do a great deal, it is said, but is what they do worth doing? Is it, in fact, education? The bolder sceptics go so far as to attack our two ancient universities; but they, very likely, will weather the storm because of the very inertness, the 'masterly inactivity,' let us call it, which their opponents abuse; the universities do a great deal of 'letting-alone.'

General Dissatisfaction with Education.—Our pretty general dissatisfaction with education, as it is, is a wholesome symptom, and probably means that sounder theory and happier practice are on their way to us. One thing we begin to see clearly, that the stream can rise no higher than its source, that sound theory must underlie successful work. We begin to suspect that we took up schemes and methods of education a little hastily, without considering what philosophy or, let us say, psychology, underlies those schemes and methods; now, we see that our results cannot be in advance of our principles. To-day the psychologist is abroad, as, twenty or thirty years ago, the schoolmaster was abroad.

Psychologies are many.—But, alas, psychologies are many, and educational denominations are bitterly opposed to one another. We must feel our way to some test by which we can discern a working psychology for our own age; for, like all science, psychology is progressive. What worked even fifty years ago will not work to-day, and what fulfils our needs to-day will not serve fifty years hence; there is no last word to be said upon education; it evolves with the evolution of the race. At the same time, that there should be at least half a dozen systems in the field, no one of them entirely satisfactory even to the persons who adopt it, shows that we, who practise education, should at any rate attempt to know what are the requirements of a sound system of psychology.

Conditions of an Adequate System.—That system which shall be of use to practical people in giving purpose, unity and continuity to education, must satisfy the following demands:—It must be adequate, covering the whole nature of man and his relations with all that is other than himself. It must be necessary, that is, no other equally adequate psychology should present itself; and it must touch at all points the living thought of the age; that is, it must not be a by-issue to be discussed by specialists at their leisure, but the intelligent man in the street should feel its movement to be in step with the two or three great ideas by which the world is just now being educated.

Sacredness of the Person—Among the thoughts which the mysterious Zeitgeist is employing to bring us up, I think we may put first the sacredness of the person. Every person is interesting to us to-day. The interviewer does more than satisfy vulgar curiosity; what he has to tell is equally welcome to us all, whether he interviews the London 'step-girl,' the costermonger, the man of the book-barrow, 'Arry and 'Arriet out for a holiday, an ambassador, an author, an artist, a royal personage; every detail that will help us to realise the personality of one or other is more than welcome. So, too, of what is called the 'Kailyard' literature; it rests on a sound basis. Literary merit it may or may not have, but it tells us what we want to know—everyday details about the people, any people, of any county, or of any country. Slang dictionaries, collections of folk-lore, big biographies which tell us minutely how a man dines and breakfasts, walks and sleeps, all is grist to our mill. We set an enormous and, I think, an increasing value upon persons, simply, per se; and any system of psychology which is to appeal to us must bring the person to the fore. He may be influenced by this and that; but he, himself, the indefinable person, of whom we are sensible while he is yet in arms, and of whom we never finally lose sight, however he be marred by vice and misery, must play for himself the game of life, and shape for himself those influences of environment, education, and what not, that do their part to make him what he is. A system of psychology which gives us man in this sort of relation to educational forces should become common property at once, because this is what every mother of a family and teacher of a school, every sort of director of men and women, knows about.

The Evolution of the Individual.—Next we demand of education that it should make for the evolution of the individual; should not only put the person in the first place, but should have for its sole aim the making the very most of that person, intellectually, morally, physically. We do not desire any dead accretions of mere knowledge, or externals of mere accomplishment We desire an education that shall be assimilated; shall become part and parcel of the person; and the psychology which shall show us how to educate our children in this vital way will meet our demands. The doctrine of evolution has brought about a greater bouleversement in philosophy than perhaps we are aware of, and we shall find by-and-by that 'education' means nothing less than the evolution of the human being at all points; and that the acquisition of mere learning is not necessarily education at all.

The Solidarity of the Race.—One other idea that appears to be at work in the world for the elevation of mankind is that of the solidarity of the race. The American poet, Walt Whitman, expresses one side of this intuition when he tells us how he conquers with every triumphant general, bleeds with every wounded soldier, shares the spring morning and the open road and the pride of the horses with every jolly waggoner—in fact, lives in all other lives that touch him anywhere, even in imagination. This is something more than the brotherhood of man; that belongs to the present; but our sense of the oneness of humanity reaches into the remotest past, making us regard with tender reverence every relic of the antiquity of our own people or of any other; and, with a sort of jubilant hope, every prognostic of science or philanthropy which appears to us to be the promise of the centuries to come. Is it too much to expect that psychology shall take cognisance of this great educational force as well as of the two others I have indicated? I do not say that these three are the only, so to speak, motor ideas of our age; but I think they are the three of which we are all most aware, and I think, too, that any system of psychology which takes no cognisance of either, or of all of them, does not afford that basis for our educational theory and practice of which we are in search.

The Best Thought is Common Thought—Let us consider now some three or four of the psychologies which have the most widespread influence to-day. But we do not presume to do this as critics, rather as inheritors of other men's labour, who take stock of our possessions in order that we may use them to the most advantage. For the best thought of any age is common thought; the men who write it down do but give expression to what is working in the minds of the rest. But we must bear in mind that truth behaves like a country gate allowed to 'swing to' after a push. Now it swings a long way to this side and now a long way to that, and at last after shorter and shorter oscillations the latch settles. The reformer, the investigator, works towards one aspect of truth, which is the whole truth to him, and which he advances out of line with the rest. The next reformer works at a tangent, apparently in opposition, but he is bringing up another front of truth. Then there is work for us, the people of average mind. We consider all sides, balance what has been done, and find truth, perhaps in the mean, perhaps as a side issue which did not make itself plain to original thinkers of either school. But we do not scorn the bridge that has borne us.

Locke's 'States of Consciousness.'—We need not go further back than Locke, who represents the traditional educational notions in the homes of the upper middle classes. People who bring up their children by 'common sense,' according to 'the way of our family,' do so more often than they know because their great-great-grandfathers read Locke. He did not concern himself with the mind, or soul of man, but with 'states of consciousness.' Ideas, images, were for him to be got only through the senses; and a man could know nothing but what he got hold of through his own senses and assimilated by his own understanding. As for choice and selection in these ideas and images, Locke gives a comprehensive counsel—'What it becomes a gentleman to know' is the proper subject-matter for education. The mind (i.e. the man?) appears to have little colour or character of its own, but has certain powers and activities for the employment of the ideas it receives; and to account for these, Locke invented the pestilent fallacy which has, perhaps, been more injurious than any other to the cause of education—the fallacy of the 'faculties of the mind.'

Does not provide for the Evolution of the Person.—Now let us bring Locke up to the standard which we have erected, remembering always that our power to raise a higher standard is due to him and such as he. There is no unity of an inspiring idea, no natural progress and continuity, no ennobling aim, in an education which stops at the knowledge a gentleman should acquire and the accomplishments a gentleman should possess. The person hardly appears except in the way of the semi-mechanical activities of his so-called faculties; he is practically the resultant of the images conveyed through his senses. The evolution, the expansion of the individual in the directions proper to him, has no place here; every man is shut tight, as it were, in his own skin, but is taught to behave himself becomingly within that limit. That intellectual commerce of ideas whereby the dead yet speak their living thoughts in the work they have left us, and by which as by links of an endless chain all men are bound to each and all men influence each, has no place in a philosophy which teaches that a man can know only through his own understanding working upon the images he receives through his senses. In so far as we wish to attain to the possibilities of the hour we must take farewell of Locke, though we do so with gratitude, and even with affection.

Modern Physiological Psychology.—The modern school, which regards psychology strictly as a 'natural science,' works more or less on the basis of Locke, plus an illuminating knowledge of biology. Here, as with Locke, the 'mind' is apprehended only as 'states of consciousness'; the senses are the sole avenues of knowledge, which reaches the brain in the form of ideas or images. But I shall represent this 'rational psychology' best by citing a few sentences from Professor James (Harvard University), whose wise and temperate treatment of the subject commands the respect and attention of even those who differ from him. He opens with a limiting definition of psychology as the 'description and explanation of states of consciousness as such.' He treats psychology as a 'natural science.' After bringing forward facts familiar to most of us, showing the intimate connection between acts of thought and the cerebral hemisphere, he says: "Taking all such facts together, the simple and radical conception dawns upon the mind that mental action may be uniformly and absolutely a function of brain action varying as the latter varies, and being to the brain action as effect to cause. This conception is the working hypothesis which underlies all the physiological-psychology of recent years." This is not far removed from the announcement of the Frenchman that the brain secretes thought as the liver secretes bile, both processes being purely material and mechanical, and doing away with any requirement for the profoundest thinking beyond that of a well-nourished brain.

Unjustifiable Materialism.—No wonder the author finds himself compelled to admit that to some readers "such an assumption will seem like the most unjustifiable à priori materialism." The discussion of 'the self' might be supposed to present insuperable difficulties, but they are disposed of, and, says our author, "The logical conclusion seems to be that the states of consciousness are all that psychology needs to do her work with. Metaphysics or theology may prove the soul to exist, but for psychology the hypothesis of such a substantial principle of unity is superfluous." That is to say, the important personage which I call I, myself, need be no more than perpetually shifting states of consciousness effected by the brain; and the sameness or identity of person, which seems at first sight the one bit of solid ground in a shifting morass, rests upon no more than the fact that the brain may be conscious of the same objects to-day that it was conscious of years ago.

Psychology, 'A Phrase of Diffidence.'—But, after proving with great clearness and power through a considerable volume (Outlines of Psychology) that all the phenomena of intelligent life may have their sole source in the physical brain, Professor James concludes—"When, then, we talk of psychology as a natural science we must not assume that that means a sort of psychology that stands at last on solid ground. It means just the reverse; it means a psychology particularly fragile and into which the waters of metaphysical criticism leak at every joint, a psychology all of whose elementary assumptions and data must be reconsidered in wider connections and translated into other terms It is, in short, a phrase of diffidence and not of arrogance, and it is indeed strange to hear people talk triumphantly of the 'New Psychology' and write 'Histories of Psychology' when into the real elements and forces, which the word covers, not the first glimpse of clear insight exists. A string of raw facts, a little gossip and wrangle about opinions, a little classification and generalisation on the mere descriptive level . . . but not a single law . . . . not a single proposition from which any consequence can causally be deduced." This is soothing, and we close Professor James's book with satisfaction; but the pity of it is that all the 'new' psychologists are not so modest as the Professor, some of them are, may we venture to say so, not a little arrogant: what is more, the student who goes carefully through this text-book of psychology is only too likely to consider that the author has proved his case—that psychology is a 'natural science,' 'and it is,' like Peter Bell's primrose, 'nothing more'—up to the hilt, and he is not likely to go through a process of reconversion at the last page.

We become Devitalised.—It is dreary to suppose that one may not be anybody after all, but only a momentary state of consciousness. Hope goes out of life, for there is nothing pleasant to look forward to. If something agreeable should happen next year, there is no I, myself, to enjoy it; only the 'state of consciousness' of some moment to come. Faith goes where all is fortuitous; when other people and ourselves are, so to speak, the circumstances of the moment. Where there are no persons, there is no possibility of that divine afflatus which we call enthusiasm; for that recognition of another on a higher plane which we mean when we say 'I believe in so and so,' for that recognition of the divine Being which we call Faith. We become devitalised; life is flat and grey; we throw desperate, if dull, energy into the task of the hour because we shall so, any way, get rid of that hour; we are glad to be amused, but still more glad of the stimulus of feverish work; but the work, like ourselves, is devitalised, without living idea, without consecrating aim. Our manner becomes impassive, our speech caustic, our countenance dreary and impenetrable. This is the change that is passing over large numbers of the teaching profession, men and women of keen intelligence, who might well have been inspired by high ideals, quickened by noble enthusiasms, had they not imbibed an educational faith which meets all aspirations with a Cui bono? We give what we have, and only what we have. What have these to pass on to the children under their care?

This System Inadequate, Unnecessary, Inharmonious.—But we need not sit down under this blighting system of thought. It is inadequate, as the best of their own prophets—Mr. James, for example—freely allow; there is more in man than this philosophy has ever dreamt of. It is unnecessary, for, as we shall presently see, more than one other psychology accounts with greater, though never with complete, success for the phenomena which a human being presents. It is inharmonious with the movement of the age. It effaces that personality which the age tends to exalt and magnify, and to regard with tender interest, under even sordid conditions. The principle of solidarity is lost, and those of social and family life loosened; for what binding tie can there be between beings whose entity may be no more than a state of consciousness?

Evolution is checked.—Again, the evolution of the individual is checked at the point of mechanical perfection. Good mathematicians, clear-headed scientists, may be turned out; but what place is there for the higher forces of humanity, aspiration, speculation, devotion? We have reason to keep watch at the place of the letting out of waters, that is, the psychology upon which our educational thought and action rest. There is delightful certitude in the results of anthropometrical research. You may predicate with certainty given facts about a child from the way in which he stretches out his arm. Good pathological work is being done, and many a child's hidden weakness is revealed and consequently brought under curative treatment by the tests which it is now possible to apply. The danger is that we should take a part for the whole and allow this 'new psychology' to usurp the whole field of education.

Chapter 6 Some Educational Theories Examined

Theories of Pestalozzi and Froebel—It is refreshing to turn to that school of German educational thought which has produced the two great apostles, Pestalozzi and Froebel. What we may call the enthusiasm of childhood, joyous teaching, loving and lovable teachers and happy school hours for the little people, are among the general gains from this source. To look a gift horse in the mouth is unworthy, and it would seem pure captiousness to detect any source of weakness in a system of psychology to which our indebtedness is so great. But no stream can rise higher than its source, and it is questionable whether the conception of children as cherished plants in a cultured garden has not in it an element of weakness. Are the children too carefully tended? Is Nature too sedulously assisted? Is the environment too perfectly tempered? Is it conceivable that the rough-and-tumble of a nursery should lend itself more to the dignity and self-dependence of the person and to the evolution of individual character, than that delightful place, a child-garden? I suppose we have all noticed that children show more keen intelligence and more independent thought in home-play and home-talk than one expects of the angelic little beings one sees at school. I daresay the reader will know Fra Angelico's picture of 'The Last Judgement,' one of the scenes in which gives us a circle of little monks (become as little children) dancing round, hand-in-hand, with gracious angels on their way to Paradise. The little monks are obviously very happy and very good; but somehow one misses the force of personality; they do not look as if they were capable of striking out a line for themselves; and this may be a danger in the Kindergarten.

Lack the Element of Personality.—'Make children happy and they will be good,' is absolutely true, but does it develop that strenuousness, the first condition of virtue, which comes of the contrary axiom—'Be good and you will be happy'? Kindergarten teachers are doing beautiful work; but many of them are hampered by the original metaphor of the plant, which is exactly lacking in that element of personality, the cherishing and developing of which is a sacred and important part of education. The philosophic German mind beheld in man a part of the Cosmos, which, like the rest, needed only to be placed in fit conditions to develop according to its nature.

The Struggle for Existence, a Part of Life.—The weak point in the argument is that man would appear to fall under the laws of two universes, the material and the spiritual; and that to energise and resist and repel is the law of his being. It will be said that this need not apply to the child; that the struggle for existence may well begin after a happy childhood has been secured; but probably any sort of transition violates the principles of unity and continuity which should rule education. No doubt all thoughtful Kindergarten teachers recognise in what direction the limitations—all men have their limitations—of their Founder lay, and their practices are levelled up to modern thought. The general substitution of free brush-drawing, in which the children have some initiative, for the cramped pencil drawing in chequers of the old Kindergarten, is an illustration of the modern spirit; but it is well for us all to remember our origins and our tendencies, that we may recognise and avoid our dangers.

Herbartian Psychology.—I have only space to glance at one more 'psychology,' that which is, curiously enough, dividing the American mind with the school which regards psychology as a 'natural science,' and at which English teachers are beginning to snatch as a drowning man snatches at a straw. This is the psychology of Herbart, another German philosopher of the beginning of the last century, contemporary with both Pestalozzi and Froebel during the best years of his life. His theory of man is wide as the poles apart from either of those we have already considered; and there is no denying that it affords a tempting working basis for education. It is only when we come to examine the Herbartian psychology in connection with the two or three great thoughts upon which, as we have seen, the world is being educated, that it is found wanting. Herbart begins to account for man minus what I have called the person. (Person is used in the common-sense, everyday acceptance of the word.) He allows a soul, but he says, "The soul has no capacity nor faculty whatever either to receive or to produce anything. It has originally neither ideas nor feelings nor desires. It knows nothing of itself and nothing of other things. Further, within it lie no forms of intuition or thought, no laws of willing and acting, nor any sort of predisposition, however remote, to all this." (Lehrbuch zur Psychologie, Part III, sects.152—See Herbatian Psychology, by J. Adams) There remain two possibilities for the soul: an effective vis inertiae and what Herbart describes as the power of reacting on an idea; that is to say, the soul itself is no longer quite as it was after it has thus reacted.

The Person, an Effect and not a Cause.—The problem is simplified anyway. All our complex notions of intellect, will, feeling and so on, disappear. The soul is thrown open to ideas—a fair field and no favour; and ideas, each of them a living entity, according to the familiar Platonic notion, crowd and jostle one another for admission, and for the best places, and for the most important and valuable coalitions, once they have entered. They lie below the 'threshold' watching a chance to slip in. They hurry to join their friends and allies upon admission, they 'vault' and they 'taper,' they form themselves into powerful 'appreception masses' which occupy a more or less permanent place in the soul; and the soul—what does it do? It is not evident otherwise than as it affords a stage for this drama of ideas; and the self, the soul or the person, however we choose to call him, is an effect and not a cause, a result, and not an original fact.

A philosopher who emphasises. the potency of ideas does good work in the cause of education. We get glimpses of a perfect theory—how our function shall be, to supply the child always with fit ideas, and with the best ideas; how we shall take care so to select and arrange these ideas that they shall naturally fly to one another and make strong 'apperception masses' once they have got beyond the 'threshold' in the child's soul.

A Tempting Vista.—A fascinating vista is open before us; education has all things made plain and easy for her use; she has nothing to do but to select her ideas and turn out a man to her mind. Here is a tempting scheme of unity and continuity! One might occupy all the classes in a school for a whole month upon all the ideas that combine in one 'apperception mass' with the idea 'book.' We might have object-lessons on the colours, shapes, and sizes of books; more advanced object-lessons on paper-making and book-binding; practical lessons in book-sewing and book-binding; lessons, according to the class, on the contents of books, from A B C and little Bo-Peep to philosophy and poetry. A month! why, a whole school education might be arranged in groups of ideas which should combine into one vast 'apperception mass,' all clustering about 'book.' The sort of thing was done publicly some time ago, in London, apple being the idea round which the 'apperception mass' gathered.

Eliminates Personality.—If one is to find the principles of unity and continuity in the ideas presented to the soul, this is all good and well. But if, as we believe, these principles must emanate from the soul, or person, himself, this tempting unity may result in the collection of a mass of heterogeneous and unassimilated information.

Turns out Duplicates—Again, given two souls supplied with precisely the same ideas, in precisely the same order, and with no other ideas whatsoever, and we get duplicates of the same person, a possibility which would demolish once and for ever that great conception, the solidarity of the race. Once more, what does the Herbartian theory of man minister to our interest in personality, our sense of the sacredness of the person? The person is non est, or is the mere sport of the ideas which take possession of him. He has not so much as a special fitness for one class of ideas rather than for another; all is casual; and, as for the evolution of the individual it is not he, but this or that mass of ideas which possesses him, that expands. The man appears to be no more than a sort of vessel of transport to carry ideas into their proper sphere of action. Herbartian psychology is rich in suggestion, but we cannot take it up as it stands without losing the educational value of the two or three leading principles which are, as we say, 'in the air' for the teaching of mankind.

Each System fails to meet our Tests—I have now examined briefly the three or four psychologies which hold, more or less, the field of educational thought. We see that each advances truth, but that neither expresses the whole truth even so far as to afford a working basis for educators. So people either work on by rule of thumb, or they borrow a fragment here and a fragment there as the case appears to demand; like children with a hard sum whose answer they know, and who try now division, now multiplication, now subtraction, to make it come right. No doubt there are also many able psychologists who may not have written books, but who work out the problems of education, not with a view to the answer, but according to a code of inherent principles which they have discerned for themselves.

A Psychology that meets the Demands upon it—What have we to bring forward in the way of a working psychology which shall meet the demands I have indicated? We do not claim to be philosophers; we are modest and practical people looking out for a secure basis for education. It is just possible that bringing unbiased minds and a few guiding principles to the task, we have, not joined the parts of the puzzle, but perceived dimly how an outline here and an outline there indicate, not so many separate psychologies, but shadowings forth of a coherent, living, educational principle destined to assume more and more clearness and fulness until it is revealed to us at last as the educational gospel, the discovery of which may be the destined reward and triumph of our age. Let me try to set forth, though with diffidence, what we have done, knowing that no man and no society can say of educational truth, 'This is mine and that is thine,' for all is common, and none of us can know how much he gives and how much he takes.

Educational Truth a Common Possession.—For years we have worked definitely and consistently upon a psychology which appears to me fairly adequate, necessary, and in touch with the thought of our age. (The references here and after are to the distinctive thought and work of the Parents' National Educational Union.) Children brought up on this theory of education, wherever we come across them, have certain qualities in common. They are curiously vitalised; not bored, not all alive in the playing-field and dull and inert in the schoolroom—even when it is that place, proverbial for dulness, a home school-room taught by a governess. There is unity in their lives; they are not two persons, one with their play-fellows and quite other with their teachers and elders; but frank, fresh, showing keen interest in whatever comes in their way Then, too, there is continuity in their education. Little children are always eager to know; but the desire for knowledge seldom survives two or three years of school-life. But these children begin on lines that go on from the first baby lessons, through boyhood, girlhood, womanhood, motherhood; there is no transition stage, but simple, natural, living progress. The claims I venture to make for these children must rest, not only on the evidence of the few, but on the principles upon which we work.

We take Children as Persons.—In the first place, we take children seriously as persons like ourselves, only more so; the first question that comes before us is—What do we understand by a person? We believe the thinking, invisible soul and acting, visible body to be one in so intimate a union that—

"Nor soul helps flesh more now than flesh helps soul."

If the doctrine of the Resurrection had not been revealed to us, it would be a necessity, in however unimagined a form, to our conception of a person. The countenance of our friend with the thousand delicate changes which express every nuance of feeling; the refinement, purpose, perception, power, revealed in his hand, the dear familiar carriage, these are all inseparable from our conception of the person. Whatever is advanced by the physiologist and the rational psychologist as to the functions of that most marvellous brain cortex, the seat of consciousness, as furnishing us with images and impulses, of the motor nerves as originating action, of the brain as the seat of habit; of the possibility of educating a child in all becoming habits of act, in all sweet habits of thought, by taking measures to secure that these habits become, as it were, a memory of the brain to be awakened by due stimuli,—all these things we believe and receive; and we believe further that the possibility of a rational education rests upon this physiological basis, only fully discovered to us within the present generation.

The Person Wills, and Thinks, and Feels.—But then, we believe the assumption that all this delicate mechanism is automatic to be gratuitous and inadequate; it is to be assumed that the person should possess such vehicle of expression and medium of relation to the outer world. For the rest, we believe that the person wills and thinks and feels; is always present, though not always aware of himself; is without parts or faculties; whatever he does, he does, all of him, whether he take a walk or write a book. It is so much the habit to think of the person as a dual being, flesh and spirit, when he is, in truth, one, that it is necessary to clear our minds on this subject The person is one and not several, and he is no more compact of ideas on the one hand than he is of nervous and muscular tissues on the other. That he requires nutriment of two kinds is no proof that he is two individuals. Pleasant and well-cooked food makes man of a cheerful countenance, and wine gladdens the heart of man, and we all know the spiritual refreshment of a needed meal. On the other hand, we all know the lack-lustre eye and pallid countenance of the well-fed who receive none of that other nutriment which we call ideas; quick and living thought is as necessary for the full and happy development of the body as it is for that of the soul.

An Adequate Doctrine.—Holding this view, we believe that our educational doctrine is adequate, while following the progress of biological psychology with avidity, and making use of every gain presents itself, and while following with equal care the advance of philosophic thought, we recognise that each of these sees the chameleon in a different light, that the person includes both and is more than both; and, if our educational creed is by no means conclusive, we think it is not narrow, because we have come across no problem of life or mind the solution of which is shut out from us by any dogma of ours. We cannot say that our doctrine is necessary, but we do say that some educational theory which shall include the whole nature of man and the results of scientific research, in the same or a greater degree, is necessary. We find ourselves, too, in touch with those three great ideas which seem to me to be the schoolmasters of the world at the present moment. The person of the child is sacred to us; we do not swamp his individuality in his intelligence, in his conscience, or even in his soul; perhaps one should add to-day, or even in his physical development. The person is all these and more. We safeguard the initiative of the child and we realise that, in educational work, we must take a back seat; the teacher, even when the teacher is the parent, is not to be too much to the front. There is no more facile way of swamping character and individuality than by that idol of the 'fifties'—personal influence.

Education the Science of Relations.—We consider that education is the science of relations, or, more fully, that education considers what relations are proper to a human being, and in what ways these several relations can best be established; that a human being comes into the world with capacity for many relations; and that we, for our part, have two chief concerns—first, to put him in the way of forming these relations by presenting the right idea at the right time, and by forming the right habit upon the right idea; and, secondly, by not getting in the way and so preventing the establishment of the very relations we seek to form:

Teaching must not be Obtrusive.—Half the teaching one hears and sees is more or less obtrusive. The oral lesson and the lecture, with their accompanying notes, give very little scope for the establishment of relations with great minds and various minds. The child who learns his science from a text-book, though he go to Nature for illustrations, and he who gets his information from object-lessons, has no chance of forming relations with things as they are, because his kindly obtrusive teacher makes him believe that to know about things is the same thing as knowing them personally; though every child knows that to know about Prince Edward is by no means the same thing as knowing the boy-prince. We study in many ways the art of standing aside. People sometimes write that the books set in our school constitute much of its usefulness; they do not always see that the choice of books, which implies the play of various able minds directly on the mind of the child, is a great part of that education which consists in the establishment of relations.

The Art of Standing Aside.—I have even known of teachers who have thought well to compose the songs and poems which their children use. Think of it! not even our poets are allowed to interpose between the poor child and the probably mediocre mind of the teacher. The art of standing aside to let a child develop the relations proper to him is the fine art of education, when the educator perceives the two things he must do and how to do these two things. The evolution of the individual is a natural sequence of the opening up of relations.

How we labour towards the solidarity of the race I hope to show more fully, later. But, for example, we do not endeavour to give children outlines of ancient history, but to put them in living touch with a thinker who lived in those ancient days. We are not content that they should learn the history of their own country alone; some living idea of contemporaneous European history, anyway, we try to get in; that the history we teach may be the more living, we work in, pari passu, some of the literature of the period and some of the best historical novels and poems that treat of the period; and so on with other subjects.

There is nothing new in all this; what we venture to claim is that our work is unified and vitalised by a comprehensive theory of education and a sound basis of psychology.

Chapter 7 An Adequate Theory Of Education

A Human Being—I have laid before the reader, as a working hypothesis,—that man is homogeneous, a spiritual being invested with a body—capable of responding to spiritual impulses, the organ by which he expresses himself, the vehicle by which he receives impressions, and the medium by which he establishes relations with what we call the material world;—that will, conscience, affection, reason, are not the various parts of a composite whole, but are different modes of action of the person.

His Capacities—That he is capable of many relations and consequently of many modes of action; that, given the due relations, his power of expansion in these relations appears to be, not illimitable, but, so far as we know, as yet unlimited.

His Limitations—But that, deprived of any or all of the relations proper to him, a human being has no power of self-development in these directions; though he would appear not to lose any of his capacity for these relations.

His Education.—Again, that any relation once initiated leaves, so to speak, an organic memory of itself in the nervous tissue of the brain; that in this physical registration of an experience or a thought, or of the memory of an experience or a thought, lies the possibility of habit; that some nine-tenths of our life run upon lines of habit; and that, therefore, in order to educate, we must know something of both the psychological and physiological history of a habit, how to initiate it and how to develop it; and, finally, that a human being under education has two functions the formation of habits and the assimilation of ideas.

The Behaviour of Ideas.—Physiologists and 'rational psychologists' have made the basis of habit pretty plain to us. All who run may read. The nature, functions, and behaviour of ideas, and how ideas have power in their impact upon the cerebral hemisphere to make some sort of sensible impression—all this is matter as to which we are able only to make 'guesses at truth.' But this need not dismay us, for such other ultimate facts as sleep and life and death are equally unexplained. In every department of science we are brought up before facts which we have to assume as the bases of our so-called science. Where a working hypothesis is necessary, all we can do is to assume those bases that seem to us the most adequate and the most fruitful. Let us say with Plato that an idea is an entity, a live thing of the mind.

No one can Beget an Idea by Himself—Apparently no one has power to beget an idea by himself; it appears to be the progeny of two minds. So-and-so 'put it in my head,' we say, and that is the history of all ideas—the most simple and the most profound. But, once begotten, the idea seems to survive indefinitely. It is painted in a picture, written in a book, carved into a chair, or only spoken to someone who speaks it again, who speaks it again, who speaks it again, so that it goes on being spoken, for how long? Who knows! Nothing so strikes the student of history as the persistent way in which ideas recur, except the way in which they elude observation until occasion calls them forth. Our natural progeny may indeed die and be buried; but of this spiritual progeny of ideas, who may forecast the history or foretell the end?

Certain Persons attract Certain Ideas.—Perhaps we may be allowed this further hypothesis—that, as an idea comes of the contact of two minds, the idea of another is no more than a notion to us until it has undergone a process of generation within us; and for that reason different ideas appeal to different minds—not at all because the ideas themselves have an independent desire to club into 'apperception masses,' but because certain persons have in themselves, by inheritance, may we assume, that which is proper to attract certain ideas. To illustrate invisible things by visible, let us suppose that the relation is something like that between the pollen and the ovule it is to fertilise. The ways of carrying the pollen are various, not to say promiscuous, but there is nothing haphazard in the result. The right pollen goes to the right ovule and the plant bears seed after its kind; even so, the person brings forth ideas after his kind.

The Idea that 'Strikes' Us—The crux of the situation is: how can an emanation so purely spiritual as an idea make an impression upon even the most delicate material substance? We do not know. We have some little demonstration that it is so in the fact of the score of reflex actions by which we visibly respond to an idea that 'strikes' us. The eye brightens, the pulse quickens, the colour rises, the whole person becomes vitalised, capable, strenuous, no longer weighed down by this clog of flesh. Every habit we have formed has had its initial idea, and every idea we receive is able to initiate a habit of thought and of action. Every human being has the power of communicating notions to other human beings; and, after he is dead, this power survives him in the work he has done and the words he has said. How illimitable is life! That the divine Spirit has like intimate power of corresponding with the human spirit, needs not to be urged, once we recognise ourselves as spiritual beings at all.

Expansion and Activity of the Person—Nor does this teeming population of ideas arise to us without order and without purpose beyond the scope of our busy efforts and intentions. It would seem as if a new human being came into the world with unlimited capacity for manifold relations, with a tendency to certain relations in preference to certain others, but with no degree of adaptation to these relations. To secure that adaptation and the expansion and activity of the person, along the lines of the relations most proper to him, is the work of education; to be accomplished by the two factors of ideas and habits. Every relation must be initiated by its own 'captain' (Cf. Coleridge's Method) idea, sustained upon fitting ideas; and wrought into the material substance of the person by its proper habits. This is the field before us.

Story of Kaspar Hauser.—To make my meaning plainer, let me run over the story of Kaspar Hauser, that 'child of Nuremberg,' upon whom an unique experiment was said to have been tried, criminal in its character, and therefore not to be repeated. The story is as well accredited as most of our data, but we will assume its truth in so far only as the experience of this boy tallies with what we know of the experience of an infant; or, as regards the use of his senses, with the experience of an adult person who has for the first time attained to, sight, let us say. On 28th May 1828, the attention of a cobbler in Nuremberg was excited by a strange figure leaning, as if unable to support itself, against a wall and uttering a moaning sound. The figure was that of a young man of about seventeen, who, when the cobbler approached, moaned some incoherent sounds. He had fair hair and blue eyes, and the lower part of his face projected a little like a monkey's. Everyone who watched him came to the same conclusion, that his mind was that of a child of two or three, while his body was nearly grown up; and yet he was not half-witted, because he immediately began to pick up words and phrases, had a wonderful memory, and never forgot a face he had once seen or the name which belonged to it. At first, he was placed in the guard-house for safety, and the children of the gaoler taught him to walk and to talk as they did their own baby-sister. He was not afraid of anything. After six or seven weeks the townspeople decided to adopt him as the 'child of Nuremberg.' He was placed under the charge of Professor Daumer, whose interest led him to undertake the difficult task of developing his mind so that it might fit his body. Later, Dr Daumer gleaned a short account of his previous life from Hauser by careful questioning. It was to this effect. 'He neither knows who he is nor where he came from. He always lived in a hole where he sat on straw on the ground. He never heard a sound nor saw any vivid light. He awoke and he slept and awoke again. When he awoke he found a loaf of bread and a pitcher of water beside him. Sometimes the water tasted nasty, and then he fell asleep again. He never saw the face of the man who came to him. At last the man taught him to stand and to walk, and finally carried him out of his hole.' For several months after he came to Nuremberg he refused to eat anything but bread and water, and was, in fact, made quite ill by the smell of meat, beer, wine or milk. For the first four months of his stay with Daumer, his senses of sight, taste, hearing and smell were very acute. He could see much further than most people by day, without, however, losing his power of seeing in the dark. At the same time he could not distinguish between a thing and a picture of that thing, and could not for a long time judge distances at all, for he saw everything flat. He thought a ball rolled because it wished to do so, and could not see why animals should not behave, at table for instance, like human beings. His sense of smell was very keen, painfully so, in fact, for he was made quite ill by the smell of the dye in his clothes, the smell of paper, etc. On the other hand, he could distinguish the leaves of trees by their smell. In about three months Dr Daumer was able to teach him other things besides the use of his senses. He was encouraged to write letters and essays, to use his hands in every way, to dig in the garden, etc. For the next eleven months he lived a happy, simple life with his friend and tutor, who mentions, however, that the intense acuteness of his senses was gradually passing away, but that he had still the charming, obedient, child-like nature which had won all hearts.

What Nature does for a Child.—Here we have an instance (more or less credible), and the only instance on record, of what Nature, absolutely unaided and unhindered, has done for a child. Kaspar Hauser came out of his long retirement, unusually intelligent, with his senses intensely acute, and 'sweet and docile' in disposition. This is an object-lesson which cannot lawfully be repeated, and we may not take a single instance as proving any position. But certainly this illuminating story—coupled with the fact that Kaspar Hauser, on his emergence, was in some respects in the condition of an infant in arms—that is, he knew nothing of round, or flat, or far, or near, or hot, or cold, he had no experience; and in some respects in that of a child of two years old with quick intelligence, keen perceptive powers, capital memory, and child-like sweetness—Kaspar Hauser's story and our common experience go to prove that the labour we spend on developing the 'faculties,' or in cultivating the senses, is largely thrown away. Nature has no need of our endeavours in these directions. Under the most adverse conceivable conditions she can work wonders if let alone. What she cannot away with is our misdirected efforts, which hinder and impede her beneficent work. Nature left to herself hands over every child to its parents and other educators in this condition of acute perceptive powers, keen intelligence, and moral teachableness and sweetness. This solitary instance goes to show that she is even capable of maintaining a human being in this child-like condition until he reaches the verge of manhood.

The Child has every Power that will serve Him. — What, then, have we to do for the child? Plainly we have not to develop the person; he is there already, with, possibly, every power that will serve him in his passage through life. Some day we shall be told that the very word education is a misnomer belonging to the stage of thought when the drawing forth of 'faculties' was supposed to be a teacher's business. We shall have some fit new word meaning, perhaps, 'applied wisdom,' for wisdom is the science of relations and the thing we have to do for a young human being is to put him in touch, so far as we can, with all the relations proper to him.

Fulness of Living depends on the Establishment of Relations.—We begin to see light, both as to the lines upon which we should form habits and as to that much-vexed question—the subjects of instruction proper for children. We are no longer divided between the claims of the classical and the modern side. We no longer ask ourselves whether it is better to learn a few subjects 'thoroughly,' so we say, or to get a 'smattering' of many. These questions are beside the mark. In considering the relationships which we may initiate for a child, I will begin with what we shall probably be inclined to call the lowest rung of the ladder. We may believe that a person—I have a 'baby person' in view—is put into this most delightful world for the express purpose of forming ties of intimacy, joy, association, and knowledge with the living and moving things that are therein, with what St Francis would have called his brother the mountain and his brother the ant and his brothers in the starry heavens. Fulness of living, joy in life, depend, far more than we know, upon the establishment of these relations. What do we do? We consider the matter carefully; we say the boy will make a jumble of it if he is taught more than one or two sciences. We ask our friends—'What sciences will tell best in examinations?' and, 'Which are most easily learned?' We discover which are the best text-books in the smallest compass. The boy learns up his text, listens to lectures, makes diagrams, watches demonstrations. Behold! he has learned a science and is able to produce facts and figures, for a time any way, in connection with some one class of natural phenomena; but of tender intimacy with Nature herself he has acquired none. Let me sketch what seems to me the better way for the child.

The Power of Recognition.—His parents know that the first step in intimacy is recognition; and they will measure his education, not solely by his progress in the 'three R's,' but by the number of living and growing things he knows by look, name, and habitat. A child of six will note with eager interest the order of time in which the trees put on their leaves; will tell you whether to look in hedge, or meadow, or copse, for eyebright, wood-sorrel, ground-ivy; will not think that flowers were made to be plucked, for—

'Tis (his) faith that every flower
Enjoys the air it breathes"—

but will take his friends to see where the milk-wort grows, or the bog-bean, or the sweet-gale. The birds of the air are no longer casual; he soon knows when and where to expect the redstart and the meadow pipit. The water-skater and the dragon-fly are interesting and admired acquaintances. His eyes have sparkled at the beauty of crystals, and, though he may not have been able to find them in situ, he knows the look of the crystals of lime and quartz, and the lovely pink of felspar, and many more.

Aesthetic Appreciation.—Aesthetic appreciation follows close upon recognition, for does he not try from very early days to catch the flower in its beauty of colour and grace of gesture with his own paintbrush? The wise mother is careful to open her child's eyes to another kind of appreciation. She makes him look from a distance at a wild cherry-tree, or at a willow with its soft catkins, and she shows him that the picture on a Japanese screen has caught the very look of the thing, though when he comes to compare a single catkin or a single cherry blossom with those on the screen, there is no portraiture; and so he begins to learn at a very early age that to paint that which we see and that which we know to be there, are two different things, and that the former art is the more gratifying.

First-hand Knowledge.—By-and-by he passes from acquaintance, the pleasant recognition of friendly faces, to knowledge, the sort of knowledge we call science. He begins to notice that there are resemblances between wild-rose and apple blossom, between buttercup and wood-anemone, between the large rhododendron blossom and the tiny heath floret. A suggestion will make him find out accurately what these resemblances are, and he gets the new and delightful idea of families of plants. His little bit of knowledge is real science, because he gets it at first-hand; in his small way he is another Linnæus.

Appreciative Knowledge and Exact Knowledge.—All the time he is storing up associations of delight which will come back for his refreshment when he is an old man. With this sort of appreciative knowledge of things to begin with, the superstructure of exact knowledge, living science, no mere affair of text-books and examinations, is easily raised, because a natural desire is implanted. We might say the same of art, so far, any way, as the appreciation of art goes. The child who has been taught to see, appreciates pictures with discrimination.

How a Child Sets up a New Relation.—This is how a child goes to work to set up a new relation: a little girl of seven was handling an oar for the first time and remarked—'What a lot of crab-water there is to-day!' Then the next day—'There's not near so much crab-water to-day.' She was asked—'How do you know when it's crab-water?' 'Oh! it's so tough and you can't get your oar through, and it knocks you off your seat!' The child was all wrong, of course, but she was getting a scrap of real science and would soon get on the right track. How much better this than to learn out of a text-book, 'the particles which constitute water have no cohesion, and may be readily separated by a solid substance.'

When we consider that the setting up of relations, moral and intellectual, is our chief concern in life, and that the function of education is to put the child in the way of relations proper to him, and to offer the inspiring idea which commonly initiates a relation, we perceive that a little incident like the above may be of more importance than the passing of an examination.

Chapter 8 Certain Relations Proper to a Child

Geology, mineralogy, physical geography, botany, natural history, biology, astronomy—the whole circle of the sciences is, as it were, set with gates ajar in order that a child may go forth furnished, not with scientific knowledge, but with, what Huxley calls, common information, so that he may feel for objects on the earth and in the heavens the sort of proprietary interest which the son of an old house has in its heirlooms.

We are more exacting than the Jesuits. They are content to have a child till he is seven; but we want him till he is twelve or fourteen, if we may not have him longer. You may do what you like with him afterwards. Given this period for the establishing of relations, we may undertake to prepare for the world a man, vital and vigorous, full of living interests, available and serviceable. I think we may warrant him even to pass examinations, because he will know how to put living interest into the dullest tasks.

Dynamic Relations.—But we have not yet done with his relations with mother earth. There are, what I may call, dynamic relations to be established. He must stand and walk and run and jump with ease and grace. He must skate and swim and ride and drive, dance and row and sail a boat. He should be able to make free with his mother earth and to do whatever the principle of gravitation will allow. This is an elemental relationship for the lack of which nothing compensates.

Power over Material—Another elemental relationship, which every child should be taught and encouraged to set up, is that of power over material. Every child makes sand castles, mud-pies, paper boats, and he or she should go on to work in clay, wood, brass, iron, leather, dress-stuffs, food-stuffs, furnishing-stuffs. He should be able to make with his hands and should take delight in making.

Intimacy with Animals.—A fourth relation is to the dumb creation; a relation of intelligent comprehension as well as of kindness. Why should not each of us be on friendly terms with the 'inmates of his house and garden'? Every child longs for intimacy with the creatures about him; and—

"He prayeth best, who loveth best
All things both great and small;
For the dear God who loveth us,
He made and loveth all"

The Great Human Relationships.—Perhaps the main part of a child's education should be concerned with the great human relationships, relationships of love and service, of authority and obedience, of reverence and pity and neighbourly kindness; relationships to kin and friend and neighbour, to 'cause' and country and kind, to the past and the present. History, literature, archeology, art, languages, whether ancient or modern, travel and tales of travel; all of these are in one way or other the record or the expression of persons; and we who are persons are interested in all persons, for we are all one flesh, we are all of one spirit, and whatever any of us does or suffers is interesting to the rest. If we will approach them with living thought, living books, if we will only awaken in them the sense of personal relation, there are thousands of boys and girls to-day capable of becoming apostles, saviours, great orientalists who will draw the East and the West together, great archeologists who will make the past alive for us and make us aware in our souls of men who lived thousands of years ago.

The Awakening Idea.—It rests with us to give the awakening idea and then to form the habit of thought and of life. Here is an example of what a youth could do. "Young Rawlinson had" (I quote from the Academy) "from the outset of his career, a taste for the history and antiquities of Persia, a leaning which he himself attributed to his conversations with Sir John Malcolm on his first passage to India; and when with the Shah's army he chanced to be quartered at Kirmanshah, in Persian Kurdistan. Close to this stands the Rock of Behistun, bearing on its face a trilingual inscription which we now know to be due to Darius Hystaspes, the restorer of Cyrus' Empire. The cuneiform or wedge-shaped letters in which it is written had long baffled all attempts to decipher them. Rawlinson contrived, at the risk of life and limb, to climb the almost inaccessible face of the rock and to copy the easiest of the three versions of the inscription. A prolonged study of it enabled him to pronounce it to be in the Persian language, and, two years later, he succeeded in discovering the system by which the Persian words were reproduced in cuneiform characters." What is the result? "We can now produce the chronicles of empires, more highly-organised than was ever any Greek state, going back to dates millennia before that which our fathers used to assign to the earliest appearance of man upon the earth. The changes of thought consequent upon these discoveries are incalculable;" and all are more or less due to Rawlinson's climb up the face of the Behistun Rock, which again was due to the awakening of an idea by his conversation with Sir John Malcolm.

Human Intelligence limited to Human Interests.—We are not all Henry Rawlinsons, but there seems good reason to believe that the limit to human intelligence arises largely from the limit to human interests, that is, from the failure to establish personal relations on a wide scale with the persons who make up humanity,—relations of love, duty, responsibility, and, above all, of interest, living interest, with the near and the far-off, in time and in place. We hammer away for a dozen years at one or two languages, ancient or modern, and rarely know them very well at the end of that time, but directly they become to us the languages of persons whom we are aching to get at and can only do so through the medium of their own tongues, there seems no reason why many of us should not be like the late Sir Richard Burton, able to talk in almost any known tongue.

The Full Human Life.—I think we should have a great educational revolution once we ceased to regard ourselves as assortments of so-called faculties and realised ourselves as persons whose great business it is to get in touch with other persons of all sorts and conditions, of all countries and climes, of all times, past and present. History would become entrancing, literature, a magic mirror for the discovery of other minds, the study of sociology, a duty and a delight. We should tend to become responsive and wise, humble and reverent, recognising the duties and the joys of the full human life. We cannot, of course, overtake such a programme of work, but we can keep it in view; and, I suppose, every life is moulded upon its ideal. We talk of lost ideals, but perhaps they are not lost, only changed; when our ideal for ourselves and for our children becomes limited to prosperity and comfort, we get these, very likely, for ourselves and for them, but we get no more.

Duty not within the Scope of Present-day Psychology.—The psychology of the hour has had a curious effect upon the sense of duty. Persons who are no more than a 'state of consciousness' cannot be expected to take up moral responsibilities, except such as appeal to them at the moment. Duty, in the sense of relations imposed by authority and due to our fellows, does not fall within the scope of present-day psychology. It would be interesting to know how many children of about ten years of age can say the Ten Commandments, and those most clear interpretations of them which children are taught to call 'my duty towards God and my duty towards my neighbour'; or, if they are not members of the Church of England, whatever explanation their own Church offers of the law containing the whole duty of man. With the Ten Commandments as a basis, children used to get a fairly thorough ethical teaching from the Bible. They knew St Paul's mandates 'Love the brethren,' 'Fear God,' 'Honour the King,'

'Honour all men,' 'Study to be quiet.' They knew that thoughts of hatred and contempt were of the nature of murder. They knew what King Solomon said of the virtuous woman, of the sluggard, of the fool. Their knowledge was not confined to precepts; from history, sacred and profane, they were able to illustrate every text. We in England have not the wealth of moral teaching carved in wood and stone—so that the unlettered may read and learn—which some neighbouring countries rejoice in, but our teaching, until the present generation, has been systematic and thorough.

Casual Ethical Teaching.—I appeal to common experience as to whether this is now the case. We eschew for our children (and we often eschew wisely) all stories with a moral; their books must be amusing, and we ask little more; next after that, they must be literary, and then, perhaps, a little instructive. But we do not look for a moral impulse fitly given. It is not that we give no ethical teaching, but our teaching is casual. If we happen on a story of heroism or self-denial, we are glad to point the moral. But children rarely get now a distinct ethical system resting on the broad basis of the brotherhood of man. It is something for a child only to recite—'My duty towards my neighbour is to love him as myself,' and 'to do unto all men as I would that they should do unto me.' A great many fine things are said to-day about the brotherhood of man and the solidarity of the race, but I think we shall look in vain in modern writings for a sentence which goes to the root of the matter as does this authoritative code of duty.

The Moral Relation of Person to Person.—If we receive it, that the whole of education consists in the establishment of relations, then, the relations with our fellow-beings must be of the first importance; and all associations formed upon any basis except that of 'my duty towards my neighbour,'—as upon sympathy in art or literature, for example,—are apt to degenerate into sentimental bonds; and the power of original thought appears curiously to depart with that of moral insight. If you ask, 'But how are we to get a scheme of ethical teaching for our children?' I really do not know, if we choose to forego the Ten Commandments and the old-fashioned teaching of exposition and example founded upon them. There are a thousand supplementary ways of giving such teaching; but these are apt to be casual and little binding if they do not rest upon the solid foundation of duty imposed upon us by God, and due to each other, whether we will or no. This moral relation of person to person underlies all other relations. We owe it to the past to use its gains worthily and to advance from the point at which it left off: We owe it to the future to prepare a generation better than ourselves. We owe it to the present to live, to live with all expansion of heart and soul, all reaching out of our personality towards those relations appointed for us.

The sense of what is due from us does not come by Nature.—We owe knowledge to the ignorant, comfort to the distressed, healing to the sick, reverence, courtesy and kindness to all men, especially to those with whom we are connected by ties of family or neighbourhood; and the sense of these dues does not come by nature. We all know the vapid young man and the vapid young woman who care for none of these things; but do we always ask ourselves—why? and whether there are not many children to-day growing up in good homes as untrained in their moral relations as are these young people whom we despise and blame, perhaps more than they deserve, for have they not been neglected children?

Relations of Oneself with Oneself.—Another preparation for his relations in life which we owe to a young person is, that he should be made familiar with such a working system of psychology or philosophy, whichever one likes to call it, as shall help him to conduct his relations with himself and with other people. The world is not ripe, perhaps, for a bonâ fide science of life, but we are unhappily more modest than the ancients, who made good use of what they had, and turned out a Marcus Aurelius, an Epictetus, a Socrates. Neither did they think that their youth were furnished for life without instruction in philosophy. Modern scientists have added a great deal to the sum of available knowledge which should bear on the conduct of those relations of oneself with oneself which are implied in the terms, self-management, self-control, self-respect, self-love, self-help, self-abnegation, and so on. This knowledge is the more important because our power to conduct our relations with other people depends upon our power of conducting our relations with ourselves. Every man carries in his own person the key to human nature, and, in proportion as we are able to use this key, we shall be tolerant, gentle, helpful, wise and reverent. The person who has 'given up expecting anything' of servants or of dependents, of employees, or of working people, proclaims his ignorance of those springs of conduct common to us all.

I think we may really take a little credit to ourselves as a Society (The Parents' National Education Union) for an advance in this direction. Most people associated with us know something of the treatment of sensations, the direction of the will, the treatment of temper, the psychology of attention, the desires and affections which are the springs of conduct, and other practical matters concerned with the management of one's life. We hear people who use that fine old nursery plan expressed 'change your thoughts' with method and success the case of cross, or even delirious, or morbid patients. We (of the Parents' Union) feel as if we had a tool in our hands and knew how to set to work. The principle, anyhow, we perceive to be right, and, if we blunder in its application, we try again, whether for ourselves or for our children. We know that 'one custom overcometh another,' and that one idea supplants another. We do not give up a child to be selfish, or greedy, or lazy. These are cases for treatment; and a child who has been cured by his mother of some such blemish will not be slow to believe when he grows up in the possibility of reform for others, and in the use of simple, practical means.

Intimacy with Persons of All Classes.—Sociology is a long word, but it implies a practical relation with other people which children should begin to get, and it is a kind of knowledge they are very ready for. The carpenter, the gardener, the baker, the candlestick make; are all delightful persons; and it is surprising how much a child at the seaside will get to know about boats and sails and fishermen's lives that will pass by his unobservant elders. Most working men are on their honour with children, and every craftsman is a valuable acquaintance to a child. Later, when his working neighbours come before him in the shape of 'causes' and 'questions,' he will see the men and their crafts behind the veil of words; and in his 'Book of Trades,' a Who's Who for the million, he will look out for the heading Recreation, for shoemaker, tailor, factory-hand, as well as for the distinguished author and the member of Parliament. There is nothing like early intimacy for helping one to know people. That is why what the tuborator calls 'the bloated aristocrat' knows how to get on with everybody; he has been intimate with all sorts and conditions of men since his babyhood.

Fitness as Citizens.—The value of self-managed clubs and committees, debating societies, etc., for young people, is becoming more and more fully recognised. Organising capacity, business habits, and some power of public speaking, should be a part of our fitness as citizens. To secure the power of speaking, I think it would be well if the habit of narration were more encouraged, in place of written composition. On the whole, it is more useful to be able to speak than to write, and the man or woman who is able to do the former can generally do the latter.

Relations with each other as Human Beings.—But the subject of our relations with each other as human beings is inexhaustible, and I can do no more than indicate a point here and there, and state again my conviction that a system of education should have for its aim, not the mastery of certain 'subjects,' but the establishment of these relations in as many directions as circumstances will allow.

Relation to Almighty God.—I have set before the reader the proposition that a human being comes into the world, not to develop his faculties nor to acquire knowledge, nor even to earn his living, but to establish certain relations; which relations are to him the means of immeasurable expansion and fulness of living. We have touched upon two groups of these relations—his relations to the universe of matter and to the world of men. To complete his education, I think there is but one more relation to be considered—his relation to Almighty God. How many children are to-day taught to say at their mother's knee, to learn from day to day and from hour to hour, in all its fulness of meaning—'My duty towards God is to believe in Him, to fear Him, and to love Him with all my heart, with all my mind, with all my soul, and with all my strength; to worship Him, to give Him thanks, to put my whole trust in Him, to call upon Him, to honour His holy name and His word, and to serve Him truly all the days of my life'? Whether children are taught their duty towards God in these or other words matters little; but few of us will venture to say that, in this short summary, more is demanded than it is our bounden duty and service to yield. But I fear that many children grow up untaught in these matters. The idea of duty is not wrought into the very texture of their souls; and duty to Him who is invisible, which should be the very foundation of life, is least taught of all. I do not say that children are allowed to grow up without religious sentiments and religious emotions, and that they do not say quaint and surprising things, showing that they have an insight of their own into the higher life.

Sentiment is not Duty.—But duty and sentiment are two things. Sentiment is optional; and young people grow up to think that they may believe in God, may fear God, may love God in a measure—but that they must do these things, that there is no choice at all about the love and service of God, that it is their duty, that which they owe, to love Him 'with all their heart, with all their mind, with all their soul, with all their strength,' these things are seldom taught and understood as they should be. Even where our sentiment is warm, our religious notions are lax; and children, the children of good, religious parents, grow up without that intimate, ever-open, ever-cordial, ever-corresponding relation with Almighty God, which is the very fulfilment of life; which, whoso hath, hath eternal life; which, whoso hath not, is, like Coleridge's 'lovely Lady Geraldine,' ice-cold and dead at heart, however much he may labour for the free course of all other relations.

"I want,— am made for,—and must have a God,
Ere I can be aught, do aught;—no mere Name
Want,—but the True Thing, with what proves its truth,
To wit, a relation from that Thing to me,
Touching from head to foot—which Touch I feel,
And with it take the rest, this Life of ours!
— Browning.

Chapter 9 A Great Educationalist

(A Review)

We look to Germany for Educational Reform.—We in England require, every now and then, to pull ourselves together, and to ask what they are doing on the Continent in the way of education. We still hark back to the older German educational reformers. We may not know much of Comenius, Basedow, Ratich; we do know something of Pestalozzi and Froebel; but how much do we know of the thought of Johann Friedrich Herbart, the lineal successor of these, who has largely displaced his predecessors in the field of Pedagogics?

Herbartian Thought the most advanced on the Continent.—How entirely German educators work upon Herbart, and Herbart only, is proved by the existence of a Herbartian educational literature greatly more extensive than the whole of our English educational literature put together. A little volume on the Outlines of Pedagogics, (Sonnenschein & Co.;3s) by Professor W. Rein, of the University of Jena, is offered to us by the translators, C. C. and Ida J. Van Liew, as a brief introduction to the study of Herbart and his school, the author making due allowance for the advances that have been made in the decades that have elapsed since Herbart's death.

As Herbart and his interpreters represent the most advanced school of educational thought on the Continent, it will, perhaps, be interesting to the reader to make a slight comparison between the educational philosophy I am trying to set forth, and tile school of thought which exercises such immense influence in Germany.

Comparison with P.N.E.U. Thought.—One of the most characteristic features of Herbart's thinking, and that feature of it which constitutes a new school of educational thought, is, that he rejects the notion of separate mental faculties. The earlier reformers, notably Pestalozzi and Froebel, divide the faculties up with something of the precision of a phrenologist, and a chief business of education is, according to them, 'to develop the faculties.'

The Development of the Faculties.—There is a certain pleasing neatness in this idea which is very attractive. We want to know, definitely, what we have to do. Why, develop the perceptive faculties here, with the conceptive there, the judgment in this lesson, the affections in the other, until you have covered the whole ground, giving each so-called faculty its due share of developmental exercise! But, say the followers of Herbart, we have changed all that. The mind, like Wordsworth's cloud, moves altogether when it moves at all.

We, like Herbart, discard the 'Faculties.'—Now this appears to be but a slight fundamental difference, but it is one upon the recognition of which education changes front. The whole system of beautifully organised lessons, whose object is to develop this or that faculty, is called in question; for the raison d'être of specialised intellectual gymnastics is gone when we no longer recognise particular 'muscles' of the mind to be developed. The aim of education must be something quite other, and, if the aim is other, the methods must be altered, for what is method but a way to an end? So far we are entirely with Herbart; we do not believe in the 'faculties'; therefore we do not believe in the 'development of the faculties therefore we do not regard lessons as instruments for this 'development': in fact, our whole method of procedure is altered.

Pervasiveness of Dominant Ideas.—Again, we are with the philosopher in his recognition of the force of an idea, and especially of those ideas which are, as we phrase it, in the air at any given moment. "Both the circle of the family and that of social intercourse are subjected to forces that are active in the entire social body, and that penetrate the entire atmosphere of human life in invisible channels. No one knows whence these currents, these ideas arise; but they are there. They influence the moods, the aspirations, and the inclinations of humanity, and no one, however powerful, can withdraw himself from their effects; no sovereign's command makes its way into their depths. They are often born of a genius to be seized upon by the multitude that soon forgets their author; then the power of the thought that has thus become active in the masses again impels the individual to energetic resolutions: in this manner it is constantly describing a remarkable circle. Originating with those that are highly gifted, these thoughts permeate all society, reaching, in fact, not only its adult members, but also through these its youth, and appearing again in other highly gifted individuals in whom they will perhaps have been elevated to a definite form.

"Whether the power of these dominant ideas is greater in the individual, or in the body of individuals as a whole, is a matter of indifference here. Be that as it may, it cannot be denied that their effect upon the one is manifested in a reciprocal action upon the other, and that their influence upon the younger generation is indisputable."

The Zeitgeist.—We entirely agree that no one can escape the influence of this Zeitgeist, and that the Zeitgeist is, in fact, one of the most powerful of the occult educational influences, and one which parents and all who have the training of children will do well to reckon with in the adjustment of their work.

The Child's Schoolmasters.—Nature, family, social intercourse, this Zeitgeist, the Church and the State, thus Professor Rein, as interpreting Herbart, sums up the schoolmasters under whose influences every child grows up; a suggestive enumeration we should do well to consider. 'Erziehung ist Sache der Familien; von da geht sie aus und dahin kehrt sie grössenteils zurück,' says Herbart. He considers, as do we, that by far the most valuable part of education is carried on in the family, because of the union of all the members under a common parentage, of the feeling of dependence upon a head, of the very intimate knowledge to be gained of the younger members.

A Noble Piety.—The members of the family look confidently to the head; and this sense of dependence favours, at the same time, the proper reception of that which is dearest to mankind, namely, the religious feeling. If the life of the family is permeated by a noble piety, a sincere religious faith take root in the hearts of the children. Faithful devotion to the guide of the youth also calls forth faithful devotion to Him who controls human destinies—a thought which Herbart expresses so beautifully the words—'To the child, the family should be the symbol of the order in the world; from the parents one should derive by idealisation the characteristics of the deity.'"

A Medieval Conception of Education—This idea of all education springing from and resting upon our relation to Almighty God is one which we have ever laboured to enforce. We take a very distinct stand upon this point. We do not merely give a religious education, because that would seem to imply the possibility of some other education, a secular education, for example. But we hold that all education is divine, that every good gift of knowledge and insight comes from above, that the Lord the Holy Spirit is the supreme educator of mankind, and that the culmination of all education (which may, at the same time, be reached by a little child) is that personal knowledge of and intimacy with God in which our being finds its fullest perfection. We hold, in fact, that great conception of education held by the medieval Church, as pictured upon the walls of the Spanish chapel in Florence. Here we have represented the descent of the Holy Ghost upon the Twelve, and directly under them, fully under the Illuminating rays, are the noble figures of the seven liberal arts, Grammar, Rhetoric, Logic, Music, Astronomy, Geometry, Arithmetic, and under these again the men who received and expressed, so far as the artist knew, the initial idea in each of these subjects; such men as Pythagoras, Zoroaster, Euclid, whom we might call pagans, but whom the earlier Church recognised as divinely taught and illuminated.

The Family Principle.—Here follows a passage which we do more than endorse, for it contains the very raison d'être of our society. "The education of the children will always remain the holiest and highest of all family duties. The welfare, civilisation, and culture of a people depend essentially upon the degree of success that attends the education in the homes. The family principle is the point at which both the religious and educational life of a people centres, and about which it revolves. It is a force in comparison with which every sovereign's command appears powerless."

By the way, we are inclined to think that Dr Rein's mention of Rousseau is a little misleading. It is true that in Emil the parents are supplanted, but, notwithstanding that fact, perhaps no other educationalist has done so much to awaken parents to their great work as educators. After investigating the conditions of home training, Dr Rein proceeds to a discussion of schools (a) as they exist in Germany; (b) as they exist in his own ideal, a discussion which should be most interesting to parents.

Uncertainty as to the Purpose of Education.—Teleology, i.e. the theory of the purpose of education, falls next under discussion in an extremely instructive chapter. It is well we should know the vast uncertainty which exists on this fundamental point. As a matter of fact, few of us know definitely what we propose to ourselves in the education of our children. We do not know what it is possible to effect, and, as a man does not usually compass more than he aims at, the results of our education are very inadequate unsatisfactory.

Some Attempts to fix the Purpose of Education.—"Shall the educator follow Rousseau and educate a man of nature in the midst of civilised men? In so doing, as Herbart has shown, we should simply repeat from the beginning the entire series of evils that have already been surmounted. Or shall we turn to Locke and prepare the pupil for the world which is customarily in league with worldlings? We should then arrive at the standpoint of Basedow, and aim to educate the pupil so that he would become a truly useful member of human society. Of course we should always be harassed with the secret doubt as to whether this is ideal purpose after all, and whether we are not at times directly enjoined to place the pupil at variance with the usage and customary dealings of the world. If we reflect that an endless career is open to man for his improvement, we realise that only that education, whose aims are always the highest, can hope to reach the lofty goals that mark this career.

"Therefore an ideal aim must be present in the mind of the educator. Possibly he can obtain information and help from Pestalozzi, whose nature evinced such ideal tendencies. Pestalozzi wished the welfare of mankind to be sought in the harmonious cultivation of all powers. If one only knew what is to be understood by a multiplicity of mental powers, and what meant by the harmony of various powers. These phrases sound very attractive, but give little satisfaction. The purely formal aims of education will appeal as little to the educator: 'Educate the pupil to independence'; or, 'Educate the pupil to be his own educator'; or,'Educate the pupil so that "it" will become better than "its" educator.' (Hermann and Dorothea, Hector and Astyanax in the Iliad.) Such and similar attempts to fix the purpose of education are abundant in the history of pedagogy; but they do not bring us nearer the goal. In their formal character they do not say, for example, of what kind the independence shall be, what content it shall have, what aims it shall have in view, or in what directions its course shall lie. For the pupil that has become independent can use his freedom rightly for good just as well as misuse it for evil."

Herbart's Theory, Ethical—Herbart's own theory of education, so far as we may venture to formulate it, is strictly ethical as opposed to intellectual, that is, the development and sustenance of the intellect is of secondary importance to the educator for two reasons: character building is the matter of first importance to human beings; and this because, (a) train character and intellectual 'development' largely takes care of itself, and (b) the lessons designed for intellectual culture have high ethical value, whether stimulating or disciplinary. This is familiar ground to us: we too have taught, in season and out of season, that the formation of character is the aim of the educator. So far, we are at one with the philosopher; but, may we venture to say it? we have arrived, through the study of Physiology, at the definiteness of aim which he desires but does not reach.

Obscurity of Psychology.—We must appeal, he says, to Psychology, but then, he adds, "of course we cannot expect a concordant answer from all psychologists; and in view of the obscurity which still prevails in this sphere, the different views as to the nature of the human soul and the extraordinary difficulty with which the empirical method of investigation meets, an absolutely indubitable explanation can hardly be expected."

Two Luminous Principles.—This is doubtless true of Psychology alone, but of Psychology illuminated by Physiology we have another tale to tell. It is the study of that border-land betwixt mind and matter, the brain, which yields the richest results to the educator. For the brain is the seat of habit: the culture of habit is, to a certain extent, physical culture: the discipline of habit is at least a third part of the great whole which we call education, and here we feel that the physical science of to-day has placed us in advance of the philosopher of fifty years ago. We hold with him entirely as to the importance of great formative ideas in the education of children, but we add to our ideas, habits, and we labour to form habits upon a physical basis. Character is the result not merely of the great ideas which are given to us, but of the habits which we labour to form upon those ideas. We recognise both principles, and the result is a wide range of possibilities in education, practical methods, and a definite aim. We labour to produce a human being at his best physically, mentally, morally, and spiritually, with the enthusiasms of religion, of the good life, of nature, knowledge, art, and manual work; and we do not labour in the dark.

I have ventured to indicate in a former chapter what appears to me the root-defect of the educational philosophy of this great thinker—that it tends to eliminate personality, and therefore leads to curious futilities in teaching. It is therefore the more gratifying to observe that certain fundamental ideas, long the property of the world, which we have embraced in our scheme of thought, appealed with equal force to so great an original a thinker as Herbart.

Chapter 10 Some Unconsidered Aspects of Physical Training

Perhaps never since the days of the Olympian games has more attention been paid to physical culture than it receives in England to-day. But possibly this physical cult suffers from the want of unity and sanctity of purpose which nullifies to a considerable extent most of our educational efforts.

Does our Physical Culture make Heroes?—We want to turn out 'a fine animal,' a man or woman with a fine physique and in good condition, and we get what we lay ourselves out for. The development, in women especially, within the last twenty years, is amazing. I heard it remarked the other day that the stiff little brocaded dresses of our great-grandmothers, which are kept here and there, appear to have belonged to little women, while the grandmothers we are rearing to-day promise to be daughters of Anak. So far, so good. All the same, it is questionable whether we are making heroes; and this was the object of physical culture among the early Greeks, anyway. Men must be heroes, or how could they fulfil the heavy tasks laid upon them by the gods? Heroes are not made in a day; therefore, the boy was trained from his infancy in heroic exercises, and the girl brought up to be the mother of heroes. Flashes of the heroic temper seem to remain to this day in that little country with a great history. 'Your son has behaved like a hero,' was said to the mother of a soldier who fell some years ago. 'That's what I bore him for,' was the reply. Englishmen, too, can die, but it is not so certain that they can live, like heroes. The object of the fine physical culture that English youths and maidens receive is, too often, the poor and narrow one that they may get the most, especially the most of physical enjoyment, out of life; and so young people train their bodies to hardships, and pamper them with ease and self-indulgence, by turns, the one and the other being for their own pleasure; the pampering being the more delightful after the period of training, the training itself rather a pleasant change from the softness of pampering.

A Serviceable Body, the End of Physical Culture.—Some of our young people prefer to endure hardness all the time, and go off in the Berserker spirit to find adventures; but even this is not the best that might be done. The object of athletics and gymnastics should be kept steadily to the front; enjoyment is good by the way, but is not the end; the end is the preparation of a body, available from crown to toe, for whatever behest 'the gods' may lay upon us. It is a curious thing that we, in the full light of Revelation, have a less idea of vocation and of preparation for that vocation than had nations of the Old World with their 'few, faint and feeble' rays of illumination as to the meaning and purpose of life. 'Ye are your own,' is perhaps the unspoken thought of most young persons—your own, and free to do what you like with your own. Therefore, excess in sports, excess in easy-going pleasure, excess in study, excess in desultory reading, excess of carelessness in regard to health, any excess that we have a mind to, is lawful to us if only it is expedient. This loose morality with regard to our physical debts, without touching actual vice, which is probably on the decline, is the reason why the world does not get all that it should out of such splendid material.

Ye Are not Your Own.—But if children are brought up from the first with this magnet—'Ye are not your own'; the divine Author of your being has given you life, and a body finely adapted for His service; He gives you the work of preserving this body in health, nourishing it in strength, and training it in fitness for whatever special work He may give you to do in His world,—why, young people themselves would readily embrace a more Spartan regimen; they would desire to be available, and physical transgressions and excesses, however innocent they seem, would be self-condemned by the person who felt that he was trifling with a trust.

It would be good work to keep to the front this idea of living under authority, training under authority, serving under authority, a discipline of life readily self-embraced by children, in whom the heroic impulse is always strong. We would not reduce the pleasures of childhood and youth by an iota; rather we would increase them, for the disciplined life has more power of fresh enjoyment than is given to the unrestrained. Neither is it lawful for parents to impose any unnecessary rigours upon their children; this was the error of the eighteenth century and of the early decades of our own age, when hunger, cold, and denial, which was by no means self-denial, were supposed wholesome for children. All we claim is that every young person shall be brought up under the sense of authority in the government, management, and training of his body. The sense that health is a duty, and that any trifling with health, whether vicious or careless, is really of the nature of suicide, springs from this view—that life is held in trust from a supreme Authority.

Direct teaching or reading on such subjects as the following might be profitable to parents and teachers on the one hand and to boys and girls on the other:—

Greek games and Greek heroes.
How a child may be trained to his physical responsibilities.
The vocation of the body.
'Innocent' excesses.
Unlawful and lawful home discipline.
The heroic impulse.
The training afforded by games.
Athletics, their use and abuse.
Parental authority in physical matters.
The right uses of self-denial.
The government, management, and training of the body.
The duty of health.

Use of Habit in Physical Training.—It is well that a child should be taught to keep under his body and bring it into subjection, first, to the authority of his parents and, later, to the authority of his own will; and always, because no less than this is due, to the divine Authority in whom he has his being. But to bring ourselves under authority at all times would require a constantly repeated effort of thought and which would make life too laborious. Authority must be sustained by habit We all know something of the genesis of a habit, and most of us recognise its physical basis, i.e. that frequently-repeated thoughts or acts leave some sort of register in the brain tissue which tends to make the repetition of such thoughts, at first easy, and at last automatic. In all matters physical exercise it is obvious to us that—do a thing a hundred times and it becomes easy, do a thing a thousand times and it becomes mechanical, as easy to do as not. This principle is abundantly applied in cricket, boating, golf, cycling, all the labours we delight in. But there is an outfit of half-physical, half-moral habits of life which the playing-field tends to form, but which are apt to be put on and off with the flannels if they are not steadily and regularly practised in the home life also. These are the habitudes which it is the part of parents to give their children, and, indeed, they do form part of the training of all well brought-up young people; but it is well not to lose sight of this part of our work.

Self-restraint.—Self-restraint in indulgences is a habit which most educated mothers form with care. Children are well and agreeably fed, and they do not hanker after a bit of this and a taste of the other. Whether one or two sweetmeats a day are allowed, or whether they go without any, well brought-up children do not seem to mind. It is the children of cottage homes who, even when they are comfortably fed and clothed, keep the animal instinct of basking in the heat of the fire. But there is perhaps danger lest the habits of the nursery and schoolroom should lapse in the case of older boys and girls. It is easy to get into the way of lounging in an arm-chair with a novel in the intervals between engagements which are, in fact, amusements. This sort of thing was a matter of conscience with an older generation; lethargic, self-indulgent intervals were not allowed. When people were not amusing themselves healthfully, they were occupying themselves profitably; and, little as we may think of the crewel-work our grandmothers have left behind, it was better for them morally and physically than the relaxed muscles and mind of the novel and the lounge. No doubt the bodily fatigue which follows our more active exercises has something to say in the matter, but it is a grave question whether bodily exercises of any kind should be so frequent and so excessive as to leave us without mental and moral vigour in the intervals.

Self-control.—Self-control in emergencies is another habit of the disciplined life in which a child should be trained from the first; it is the outcome of a general habit of self-control. We all see how ice accidents, boat accidents, disasters by fire (like a late melancholy event in Paris), might be minimised in their effects if only one person present were under perfect self-control, which implies the power of organising and controlling others. But the habit of holding oneself well in hand, the being impervious to small annoyances, cheerful under small inconveniences, ready for action with what is called 'presence of mind' in all the little casualties of the hour—this is a habit which should be trained in the nursery. If children were sent into the world with this part of their panoply complete, we should no longer have the spectacle of the choleric Briton and of the nervous and fussy British lady at every foreign doûane; people would not jostle for the best places at a public function; the mistresses of houses would not be fretted and worn out by the misdoings of their maids; the thousand little sorenesses of social life would be soothed, if children were trained to bear little hurts body and mind without sign. 'If you are vexed, don't show it,' is usually quite safe teaching, because every kind of fretfulness, impatience, resentfulness, nervous irritability generally, grows with expression and passes away under self-control. It is worth while to remember that the physical signs promote mental state just as much as the mental state causes the physical signs.

Self-discipline.—The discipline of habit is never complete until it becomes self-discipline in habits. It is not a trifle that even the nursery child messes his feeder, spills his milk, breaks his playthings, dawdles about his small efforts. The well-trained child delights to bring himself into good habits in these respects. He knows that to be cleanly, neat, prompt, orderly, is so much towards making a man of him, and man and hero are in his thought synonymous terms. Supposing that good habits have not been set up at home, parents look to school life to supply the omission; but the habits practised in school and relaxed at home, because 'it's holidays now, you know,' do not really become habits of the life.

Local Habits.—The fact that habits have a tendency to become local, that in one house a child will be neat, prompt, diligent; in another untidy, dawdling, and idle, points to the necessity for self- discipline on the part of even a young child.

"Self-reverence, self-knowledge, self-control,
These three alone lead life to sovereign power."

This subject of training in becoming habits is so well understood amongst us that I need only add that such habits are not fully formed so long as supervision is necessary. At first, a child wants the support of constant supervision, but, by degrees, he is left to do the thing he ought of his own accord. Habits of behaviour; habits of deportment, habits of address, tones of voice, etc., all the habits of a gentleman-like bearing and a kind and courteous manner, fall under this head of self-discipline in bodily habits.

"When first thou camest—such a courtesy
Spake through the limbs and in the voice—I knew
For one of those who eat in Arthur's hall."

Alertness.—Many a good man and woman thinks regretfully of the opportunities in life they have let slip through a certain physical inertness. They missed the chance of doing some little service, or some piece of courtesy, because they did not see in time. It is well to bring up children to think it is rather a sad failure if they miss a chance of going a message, opening a door, carrying a parcel, any small act of service that presents itself. They should be taught to be equally alert to seize opportunities of getting knowledge; it is the nature of children to regard each grown-up person they meet as a fount of knowledge on some particular subject; let their training keep up the habit of eager inquiry. Success in life depends largely upon the cultivation of alertness to seize opportunities, and this is largely a physical habit. We all know how opportunity is imaged—a figure flying past so rapidly that there is no means of catching him but, in advance, by the forelock which overhangs his brow.

Quick Perception.—Closely connected with that alertness is the habit of quick perception as to all that is to be seen, heard, felt, tasted, smelt in a world gives illimitable information through our five gateways of knowledge. Mr. Grant, in his most interesting studies of Neapolitan character, describes the training of a young Camorrist (the Camorra is dangerous political faction; and, ill as we may of the ends of such training, the means are worth recording). "The great object of this of his training was to teach him to observe habitually with minuteness and accuracy, and it was conducted in something like the following manner. When walking through the city the Camorrist would suddenly pause and ask, 'How was the woman dressed who sat at the door of the fourth house in last street?' or, 'What were the two men talking about whom we met at the corner of the last street but three?' or, 'Where was cab 234 ordered to drive to?' or perhaps it would be, 'What is the height of that house and the breadth of its upper window?' or 'Where does that man live?'" This habit, again largely a physical habit, of quick perception has been dwelt upon in other aspects. All that now need be urged is that the quickness of observation natural to a child should not be relied upon; in time, and especially as school studies press upon him, his early quickness deserts the boy, but the trained habit of seeing all that is to be seen, hearing all that is to be heard, remains through life. I have not space to go further into these habitudes of body, which become also, mental and moral habitudes, but perhaps reading and reflection and direct teaching on such subjects as the following would be useful

Self-control in emergencies.
Self-restraint in indulgences.
Self-discipline in habits.
Alertness to seize opportunities.
Promptness and vigour in bodily exercises.
Quick perception as to that which is to be seen, heard, felt, tasted, smelt.

Stimulating Ideas.—A habit becomes morally binding in proportion to the inspiring power of the idea which underlies it. When I was a child I used to have a book full of moral aphorisms from the Greek and Latin classics, translated. These fine rolling sentences, full of matter, made, I recollect, a great impression on me; and one can understand that the Greek or Roman boy, brought up on this strong meat, developed virtues in regard to which we are a little slack. In like manner the early Church personified and typified in a thousand ways the three evangelical and four cardinal virtues and the opposing seven deadly sins. We shall have to revive this kind of teaching if we would have children undertake the labour of the discipline of habit, a discipline that we can do no more than initiate.

Fortitude.—Touch the right spring and children are capable of an amazing amount of steady effort. I know a little boy of ten who set himself the task of a solitary race of three miles every day in the hot summer holidays because he was to compete in a race when he went back to school; and this, not because he cared much about sports, but because his eldest brother had always distinguished himself in them, and he must do the same. When we think how little power we have to do the tiresome things we set ourselves to do every day, we appreciate the compelling power a child can use, given a strong enough impulse. The long name, Fortitude, would have its effect on the little boy in the dentist's hands. It is good to know that it is a manly and knightly virtue to be strong to bear pain and inconvenience without making any sign. The story of the Spartan boy and the fox will still wake an echo; and the girl who finds it a fine thing to endure hardness will not make a fuss about her physical sensations. She will be pained for the want of fortitude which called the reproof, 'Could ye not watch with me one hour?' and will brace herself to bear, that she may able to serve. Portia, the wife of Brutus, gave a fair test of her quality when she wounded her tender flesh to prove that she was fit to share her husband's counsels.

Service.—Service is another knightly quality which a child should be nerved for by heroic examples until he grudges to let slip an opportunity.

Courage.—Courage, too, should be something more than the impulse of the moment; it is a natural fire to be fed by heroic example and by the teaching that the thing to be done is always of more consequence than the doer.

Prudence.—Prudence, too, is a condition of knightly service, whether to our kind or to our kin, and courage without prudence is recklessness; but, in this connection of bodily service, prudence is largely concerned with the duty of health, I have heard of a boy at a school where a good deal of hygienic teaching was given, getting quite anxious and overcharged with the care of his own health. This meaner kind of caution is not worthy to be called prudence, which should regard every physical power as a means of service and of conflict, and should think it a shame by any fool-hardiness to make any part of the body unable for its due service.

Chastity—For Chastity we can have no impulse higher than 'Your bodies are the temples of the Holy Ghost'; but how inadequately do we present the thought! The inspiring ideas which should sustain all physical culture and training are very numerous, and teaching on such subjects as Chastity, Fortitude, Courage, Constancy, Prudence, Temperance, with the consideration of heroic examples, should strengthen the hands of parents and teachers for the better physical culture of their charges. Parents would do well to see to it that they turn out their children fit for service, not only by observing the necessary hygienic conditions, but by bringing their bodies under rule, training them in habits and inspiring them with the ideas of knightly service.

Chapter 11 Some Unconsidered Aspects of Intellectual Training

We are Law-abiding in Matters Physical and Moral.—We all recognise that we are under the reign of law so far as our bodies go. We know that 'put your finger in the fire and it will be burnt,' 'sit in a draught and you will catch cold,' 'live a vigorous and temperate life and health will be your reward.' That law attends our steps with its penalties and rewards in all matters physical we know very well. Some of us go further and have a personal sense of the Lawgiver in matters of sickness and health. In sickness especially we feel that God is dealing with us, and we endeavour to lay ourselves open to the lesson of the hour. In moral matters, too, we live under the law. We may forget ourselves, but we have compunctions and are aware of penalties.

Not so in Matters Intellectual.—But in matters intellectual we are disposed to stand upon our rights. Here we recognise no authority, abide by no law. Every man is free to his own opinion, however casually formed. Every man kindles his own 'lights,' and thinks that no more is expected of him than to live up to those lights. In fact our attitude with regard to our own intellectual processes leads to that disturbing sense of duality which causes the shipwreck of many lives, the distressing unrest of others, and the easy drifting of many more. Our thinking is not a separate thing from our conduct and our prayers, or even from our bodily well-being. Man is not several entities. He is one spirit (visibly expressed in bodily form), with many powers. He can work and love and pray and live righteously, but all these are the outcome of the manner of thoughts he thinks.

Three Ultimate Facts—Not open to Question.—There are two directions in which we commit intellectual offences against the law, and oppose ourselves to authority. In the first place we are disposed to regard everything by turns as an open question. We forget that there are three ultimate postulates which the thought of man can neither prove nor disprove, though in every age it has played uneasily about one or the other. God, Self, and the World, are the three fixed points of thought. The active Western mind, with each new evolution of scientific thought, finds again and again that there is no place for God in the world; nay, so active and pleasant is the conception of self that an important school of philosophy has demonstrated that the real world is no more than a simulacrum, a mirage, as it were, projected from the conscious self. The more passive Eastern mind, is, on the contrary, inclined to regard selfhood as a passing phase in a state of absorption or reabsorption by deity. But when we learn to realise that—God is, Self is, the World is, with all that these existences imply, quite untouched by any thinking of ours, unprovable, and self-proven,—why, we are at once put into a more humble attitude of mind. We recognise that above us, about us, within us, there are "more things . . . than are dreamt of in our philosophy." We realise ourselves as persons, we have a local habitation, and we live and move and have our being in and under a supreme authority. It is not well we should take it for granted that everybody knows these things. Perhaps we all have a hearsay acquaintance with, but very few of us have a realising knowledge of, these ultimate facts.

Limitations of Reason.—A second direction in which it is well that we should recognise our limitations is with regard to the nature and function of what we call our reason, and should, perhaps, describe more accurately as our power of reasoning. We all know how often we go to bed with a difficult question to settle. We say we will sleep upon it, and, in the morning, behold, the whole question has worked itself into shape: we see all its bearings and know just how to act. We are so accustomed to take wonders as matters of course, mere everyday events, that it does not occur to us to be surprised. We even say, the mind is clearer after sleep, regardless of the fact that we have no labour of thinking at all in the morning; all comes straight of itself. When we come to think of it, most of our decisions arrive in this unlaborious way. We really cannot say that we have thought such and such a matter out: the decision comes to us in a flash, by an intuition, what you will. The subject is a large one, but all I care to stipulate for here is that children should be taught to know that much of our reasoning and so-called thinking is involuntary,—is as much a natural function as is the circulation of our blood, and that this very fact points to the limitations of reason.

Reason brings Logical Proof of any Idea we Entertain.—We, personally, might or might not be trusted to come to a morally right conclusion from any premise we entertain. But the reasoning power, acting in a more or less mechanical and involuntary manner, does not necessarily work towards the morally right conclusion. All that reason does for us is to prove, logically, any idea we choose to entertain. For example, as we have said, important schools (Eastern and Western) of philosophy entertain the idea that there is no actual real world independent of man's conception thereof. The logical proofs of this premise pour in upon their minds in such volume that a considerable literature exists to prove an idea which on the face of it appears absurd. We all know that, entertain a notion that a servant is dishonest, that a friend is false, that a dress is unbecoming, and some power within us, unconsciously to us, sets to work to collect evidence and bring irrefragable proof of the position we have chosen to take up. This is the history of wars and persecutions and family feuds all over the world. How necessary then that a child should be instructed to understand the limitations of his own reason, so that he will not confound logical demonstration with eternal truth, and will know that the important thing to him is the ideas he permits himself to entertain, and not by any means the conclusions he draws from these ideas, because these latter are self-evolved.

A Third Fallacy—Intellect Man's Peculiar Sphere, Knowledge his Proper Discovery.—A third fallacy which lies at the root of our thinking, and therefore, of our education, is, that while nature, morals, and theology may be more or less divine in their origin and relations, not only is intellect man's proper and peculiar sphere, but knowledge,—the knowledge of witty inventions, of man and nature, of art and literature, of the heavens above and the earth beneath,—all this knowledge is man's proper discovery. He has found it out himself, thought it out for himself, observed, reasoned, collected, laboured, gathered his forces, altogether of his own will and for own ends and as an independent agent. Now, this pride of intellect also comes of the arrogance of man; not only in our age, which, I venture to think, is the very best age the world has ever seen, but in all time, it is our nature to lift up our heads and say, 'We are the people; before us there were none like unto us, neither shall there be any more after us.' But when we come to ourselves we realise that our Author and Father has not in this way made over any single vast realm of our lives into our own hands.

Great Eras come from Time to Time.—The knowledge that comes to us is given us in repasts, so to speak. Great eras of scientific discovery or literary activity or poetic insight or artistic interpretation come to the world from time to time; and then there is a long interval for the assimilation of the new knowledge or the new thought. After that, the world is taken by storm by the rise of another constellation of its great intellects; and yet we do not discern the signs of the times nor realise that thus our God is bringing us up in knowledge, which is also divine, just as much as in the nurture and admonition of the Lord. The mediæval Church recognised this great truth—as Mr. Ruskin has eloquently pointed out, showing how the 'Captain Figures,' the inventors, as it were, of grammar and music, astronomy and geometry, arithmetic and logic, all spake that which was in them under the direct outpouring of the Holy Spirit, even though none of them had any such revelation of the true God as we recognise. What a revolution should we have in our methods of education if we could once conceive that dry-as-dust subjects like grammar and arithmetic should come to children, living with the life of the Holy Spirit, who, we are told, 'shall teach you all things.'

Nothing so Practical as Great Ideas.—It may occur to some readers to consider that such lines of thought as I have suggested are perhaps interesting but not practical. Believe me, nothing is so practical as a great idea, because nothing produces such an abundant outcome of practical effort We must not turn the cold shoulder to philosophy. Education is no more than applied philosophy—our effort to train children according to the wisdom that is in us; and not according to the last novelty in educational ideas.

'Man, know thyself,' is a counsel which we might render, 'Child, know thyself, and thy relations to God and man and nature'; and to give their children this sort of preparation for life it is necessary that parents should know something of the laws of mind and of the source of knowledge.

The Formation of Intellectual Habits.—The second part of our subject—the formation of intellectual habits—need not occupy us long. We know that the possession of some half-dozen such habits makes up what is well called ability. They make a man able to do that which he desires to do with his mental powers, and to labour at the cost of not a tenth part of the waste of tissue which the same work would exact of a person of undisciplined mental habits. We know, too, that the habits in question are acquired through training and are not bestowed as a gift. Genius itself, we have been told, is an infinite capacity for taking pains; we would rather say, is the habit of taking infinite pains, for every child is born with the capacity.

We trust blindly to Disciplinary Subjects.—We trust perhaps a little blindly to the training which certain subjects give in certain mental habits. The classics, we consider, cultivate in one direction, the mathematics, in another, science, in a third. So they do, undoubtedly, so far as each of these subjects is concerned; but possibly not in forming the general habits of intellectual life which we expect to result. Remove the mathematician from his own field and he is not more exact or more on the spot than other men; indeed he is rather given to make a big hole for the cat and a little hole for the kitten! The humanities do not always make a man humane, that is, liberal, tolerant, gentle, and candid, as regards the opinions and status of other men. The fault does not lie in any one of these or in any other of the disciplinary subjects, but in our indolent habit of using each of these as a sort of mechanical contrivance for turning up the soil and sowing the seed. There is no reprieve for parents. It rests with them, even more than with the schoolmaster and his curriculum, to form those mental habits which shall give intellectual distinction to their children throughout their lives.

Some Intellectual Habits.—I need not refer again to the genesis of a habit; but perhaps most of us set ourselves more definitely to form physical and moral than we do to form intellectual habit. I will only mention a few such, which should be matters of careful training during the period of childhood:—Attention, the power of turning the whole force of the mind upon the subject brought before it: Concentration, which differs from attention in that the mind is actively engaged on some given problem rather than passively receptive: Thoroughness, the habit of dissatisfaction with a slipshod, imperfect grasp of a subject, and of mental uneasiness until a satisfying measure of knowledge is obtained;—this habit is greatly encouraged by a reference to an encyclopædia, to clear up any doubtful point, when it turns up: Intellectual Volition, the power, that is, of making ourselves think of a given subject at a given time;—most of us know how trying our refractory minds are in this matter, but, if the child is accustomed to take pleasure in the effort as effort, the man will find it easy to make himself think of what he will: Accuracy, which is to be taught, not only through arithmetic, but through all the small statements, messages, and affairs of daily life: Reflection, the ruminating power which is so strongly developed in children and is somehow lost with much besides of the precious cargo they bring with them into the world. There is nothing sadder than the way we allow intellectual impressions to pass over the surface of our minds, without any effort to retain or assimilate.

Meditation—I can mention only one more invaluable habit. Mr. Romanes consulted Darwin about the conduct of his intellectual life. 'Meditate,' was the answer, and we are told that the younger scientist set great store on this advice. Meditation is also a habit to be acquired, or rather preserved, for we believe that children are born to meditate, as they are to reflect; indeed, the two are closely allied. In reflecting we ruminate on what we have received. In meditating we are not content to go over the past, we allow our minds to follow out our subject to all its issues. It has long been known that progress in the Christian life depends much upon meditation; intellectual progress, too, depends, not on mere reading or the laborious getting up of a subject which we call study, but on that active surrender of all the powers of the mind to the occupation of the subject in hand, which is intended by the word meditation. It would be easy for any of us to suggest to himself a dozen more important intellectual habits, the consideration of which should be profitable and stimulating.

The Sustenance of Living Ideas.—The intellectual life, like every manner of spiritual life, has but one food whereby it lives and grows—the sustenance of living ideas. It is not possible to repeat this too often or too emphatically, for perhaps we err more in this respect than any other in bringing up children. We feed them upon the white ashes out of which the last spark of the fire of original thought has long since died. We give them second-rate story books, with stale phrases, stale situations, shreds of other people's thoughts, stalest of stale sentiments. They complain that they know how the story will end! But that is not all; they know how every dreary page will unwind itself. I saw it stated the other day that children do not care for poetry, that a stirring narrative in verse is much more to their taste. They do like the tale, no doubt, but poetry appeals to them on other grounds, and Shelley's Skylark will hold a child entranced sooner than any moving anecdote. As for children's art, we hang the nursery with 'Christmas Number' pictures, and their books are illustrated on a lower level still. In regard to book illustrations, we are improving a little, but still there is room.

Children's Literature.—The subject of 'Children's Literature' has been well threshed out, and only one thing remains to be said,—children have no natural appetite for twaddle, and a special literature for children is probably far less necessary than the book sellers would have us suppose. Out of any list of 'the hundred best books,' I believe that seventy-five would be well within the range of children of eight or nine. They would delight in Rasselas, Eöthen would fascinate them as much as Robinson Crusoe, the Faëry Queen, with its allegory and knightly adventures and sense of free moving in woodland scenery, would exactly fall in with their humour. What they want is to be brought into touch with living thought of the best, and their intellectual life feeds upon it with little meddling on our part.

Independent intellectual Development of Children.—We do not sufficiently recognise the independent intellectual development of children which it is our business to initiate and direct, but not to control or dominate. I know a little girl of nine who pined every day because the poems of Tennyson which she loved best were not to be found in the volumes of the larger works, which were all the house she was visiting at afforded. She literally missed her favourite poems as a child would miss a meal; and why not? The intellectual appetite is just as actual and just as exigeant as bodily hunger; more so, alas, in some cases. Miss Martineau has a charming story (Quoted by Mr. Lewis in The Child and Its Spiritual Nature) of the intellectual awakening of "a schoolboy of ten who laid himself down, back uppermost, with Southey's Thalaba before him, on the first day of the Easter holidays, and turned over the leaves, notwithstanding his inconvenient position, as fast as if he were looking for something, till in a few hours it was done, and be was off with it to the public library, bringing back the Curse of Keharna. Thus he went on with all Southey's poems and some others through his short holidays, scarcely moving voluntarily all those days except to run to the library. He came out of the process so changed that none of his family could help being struck by it. The expression of his eye, the cast of his countenance, his use of words, and his very gait were changed. In ten days he had advanced years in intelligence; and I have always thought that this was the turning-point of his life. His parents wisely and kindly let him alone, aware that school would presently put an end to all excess in the new indulgence."

As there is no religious conversion for the child who has always been brought up in the conscious presence of God, so parents who have always satisfied the intellectual craving of their children must needs forego the delight of watching a literary awakening. A little girl brought up on temperance principles, who said, 'I am so sorry my father isn't a drunkard,' that she might rejoice in his reformation, put the case for us very plainly.

Self-selection and Self-appropriation.—Given a bountiful repast of ideas, the process of natural selection soon begins. Tennyson with his—

"Our elm tree's ruddy-hearted blossom-flake is fluttering down,"
"Ruby-budded lime,"
"Black as ash-buds in the front of March,"

has done more to make field botanists than ever the Science and Art Department was able to undo with its whole apparatus of lectures and examinations.

Here, again, Browning gives us a poet's impulse to a nature student:—

"By boulder stones where lichens mock
The marks on a moth, and small ferns fit
Their teeth to the polished block."

Ideas of nature, of life, love, duty, heroism,—these children find and choose for themselves from the authors they read, who do more for their education than any deliberate teaching; just for this reason, that these vital ideas are self-selected and self-appropriated.

I shall touch later upon the burning question of a curriculum which shall furnish children, not with dry bones of fact, but with fact clothed upon with the living flesh, breathed into by the vital spirit of quickening ideas. A teacher objected the other day that it was difficult to teach from Freeman's Old English History, because there were so many stories; not perceiving that the stories were the living history, while all the rest was dead.

Inherited Parsimony in Lesson-books.—I should like to say here that a sort of unconscious, inherited parsimony, coming down to us from the days when incomes were smaller and books were fewer, sometimes causes parents to restrict their children unduly in the matter of lesson-books—living books, varied from time to time, and not thumbed over from one schoolroom generation to another until the very sight of them is a weariness to the flesh. But the subject of the intellectual sustenance of children upon ideas is so large and important that I must content myself with bald suggestions. Further considered, such subjects as the following might be useful

(1) Children's tastes in Fiction, in Poetry, in books of Travel and Adventure, in History, in Biography (most stimulating subject).

(2) Ideas of life and conduct that children assimilate from their reading.

(3) Ideas of duty assimilated in the same way.

(4) Ideas of nature that children seize.

(5) The leading, vitalising ideas in subjects of school study, as geography, grammar, history, astronomy, Ceasar's Commentaries, etc., etc.

Let me again refer the reader to Mr. Ruskin's description of the 'Captain Figures' at the head of each of the Liberal Arts, in his account of the Spanish Chapel; and conclude with a wise sentence of Coleridge's concerning the method of Plato, which should be always present to the minds of persons engaged in the training of children:—

Plato's Educational Aim.—"He desired not to assist in storing the passive mind with the various sorts of knowledge most in request, as if the human soul were a mere repository or banqueting room, but to place it in such relations of circumstance as should gradually excite its vegetating and germinating powers to produce new fruits of thought, new conceptions and imaginations and ideas."

Chapter 12 Some Unconsidered Aspects of Moral Training

Three Foundation Principles.—Three principles which underlie the educational thought of the Union, (The Parents' National Educational Union) and the furtherance of which some of us have deeply at heart, are:—(a) The recognition of authority as a fundamental principle, as universal and as inevitable in the moral world as is that of gravitation in the physical; (b) the recognition of the physical basis of habits and of the important part which the formation of habits plays in education; (c) the recognition of the vital character and inspiring power of ideas.

Authority, the Basis of Moral Teaching.—First let us consider the principle of authority, which is the basis of moral as it is of religious teaching. 'Ought' is part of the verb 'to owe,' and that which we owe is a personal debt to a Lawgiver and Ruler, however men name the final authority. If they choose to speak of Buddha or Humanity, they do not escape from the sense of a moral authority. They know that that which they ought is that which they owe to do, a debt to some power or personality external to themselves. God has made us so that, however much we may be in the dark as to the divine Name, we can never for a minute escape from the sense 'Ought,' the law, which becomes flesh-torturing and spirit-quelling in proportion as we are removed from the light of Revelation. To us, who know the name of God and have the revelation of the Scriptures, authority carries no vague terror. We know what is required of us, and that the requirements are never arbitrary, but necessary in the nature of things, both for the moral government of the world and to gratify the unquenchable desire of every human soul to rise into a higher state of being. Perhaps parents, great as they are and should be in the eyes of their children, should always keep well to the front the fact that their authority is derived.

Principles, not Rules.—'God does not allow' us to do thus and thus should be a rarely expressed but often present thought to parents who study the nature of the divine authority where it is most fully revealed, that is, in the Gospels. They see there that authority works by principles and not by rules, and as they themselves are the deputy authorities set over every household, it becomes them to consider the divine method of government. They should discern the signs of the times too; the tendency is to think that a man can only act according to his 'lights,' and, therefore, that it is right for him to do that which is right in his own eyes; in other words, that every man is his own final authority in questions of right and wrong. It is extremely important that parents should keep in view, and counteract if need be, this tendency of the day.

Limitations of Authority.—On the other hand, it is well that they should understand the limitations of authority. Even the divine authority does not compel. It indicates the way and protects the wayfarer, and strengthens and directs self-compelling power. It permits a man to make free choice of obedience rather than compels him to obey. In the moral training of children arbitrary action almost always produces revolt. Parents believe that they are doing well to rule their households, without considering the pattern, the principles, and the limitations of parental authority.

Duty can exist only as that which we owe.—An American writer on the moral instruction of children states that 'it is the business of the moral instructor in the school to deliver to his pupils the subject-matter of morality, but not to deal with the sanctions of it.' Here we have a contention at least two thousand years old. Socrates combated it as expressed in the formula:—'Man is the measure of all things'; 'Just as each thing appears to each man, so it is to him'; 'All truth is relative.' We say to-day that a man can but live up to his 'lights'; in other words, there is no authority, no truth, and no law beyond what every man carries in his own bosom. The necessary issue of this teaching is the doctrine of the unknowable God—the God who, if He exists, does not exist for us, because we have no relations with Him. It is in their early years at home that children should be taught to realise that duty can exist only as that which we owe to God; that the law of God is exceeding broad and encompasses us as the air we breathe, only more so, for it reaches to our secret thoughts; and this is not a hardship but a delight. That mothers should love their little children and make them happy all day long—this is part of the law of God: that children are glad when they are good, and sad when they are naughty—this, too, is the law of God: that, if Tommy drops his spoon, it falls to the ground, is a law of God too, of a different kind. Mother or teacher cannot give children a better inheritance than the constant sense of being ruled and encompassed by law, and that law is another name for the will of God.

Morals do not come by Nature.—No doubt every child is born with a conscience, that is, with a sense that he ought to choose the right and refuse wrong; but he is not born with the power to discern good and evil. An educated conscience is a far rarer possession than we imagine; we are all startled now and then by the laxities of right-minded neighbours in matters the right and wrong of which is patent to ourselves; but probably our own moral eccentricities are equally startling to our friends. The blame rests on our faulty moral education, which has hardly made us aware of fallacious thought and insincere speech; we believe that Latin and Greek must be taught, but that morals come by nature. A certain rough-and-ready kind of morality, varying with our conditions, does come by heredity and environment; but that most delicate and beautiful of human possessions, an educated conscience, comes only by teaching with authority and adorning by example.

Children born neither Moral nor Immoral.—It is curious how educated people are still at sea as regards the moral status of children. Some time ago I was present at an interesting discussion, among the members of an educational society, on the subject of children's lies. It was interesting to notice that the meeting, consisting of able, educated people, divided itself into those who held that children were born true and those who held that they were born false; it did not occur to anybody to recall his own childhood, or even to reflect on his own condition at the present moment. The question lay between children being born moral and born immoral. Nobody reflected that every human being comes into the world with infinite possibilities for good; and, alas! infinite possibilities for evil; possibly with evil hereditary tendencies which may be rectified by education, or with good tendencies which his bringing-up may nullify.

Moral Teaching.—We need go no further than the Ten Commandments and our Lord's exposition of the moral law to find corrective teaching for the spasmodic, impulsive moral efforts which tend to make up our notion of what the children call 'being good,' and nowhere shall we find a more lucid and practical commentary on the moral law than is set forth in the Church Catechism. It was the practice of a venerable Father of the Church, Bishop Ken, to recite the 'duty towards God,' and the 'duty towards my neighbour' every day. It is a practice worth imitating, and it would not be amiss to let all children of whatever communion learn these short abstracts of the whole duty of man.

Of the Poets.—The poets give us the best help in this kind of teaching; as, for example, Wordsworth's Ode to Duty:—

"Stern lawgiver I yet thou dost wear
The Godhead's most benignant grace;
Nor know we anything so fair
As is the smile upon thy face;
Flowers laugh before thee on their beds;

And fragrance in thy footing treads;
Thou dost preserve the stars from wrong;
And the most ancient heavens, through thee, are
fresh and strong."

Or Matthew Arnold's lines on Rugby Chapel—

"Servants of God! or sons
Shall I not call you? because
Not as servants ye knew
Your Father's innermost mind,
His, who unwillingly sees
One of His little ones lost
Yours is the praise, if mankind
Hath not as yet in its march
Fainted, and fallen, and died!"

Or this, again, of Tennyson—

'Not once or twice in our fair island story
The path of duty was the way to glory:

He, that ever following her commands,
On with toil of heart and knees and hands,
Thro' the long gorge to the far light, has won
His path upward and prevail'd,—
Shall find the toppling crags of duty, scaled,
Are close upon the shining tablelands
To which our God Himself is moon and sun."

Or Matthew Arnold's Morality—

How, "Tasks in hours of insight willed
Can be through hours of gloom fulfilled."

Possibly we could hardly do better than lead children to reflect on some high poetic teaching, adding love to law and devotion to duty, so that children shall know themselves, by duty as by prayer,

"Bound by gold chains about the feet of God."

In the matter of the ideas that inspire the virtuous life, we miss much by our way of taking things for granted.

Ethical Teaching of the Middle Ages.—The medieval Church preserved classical traditions. It endeavoured to answer the Socratic inquiry: "What ought we to do and what do we mean by the words 'ought' and 'doing' or 'acting'?" and it answered, as far as might be by way of object-lessons, visible signs of spiritual things signified. In the Arena Chapel at Padua, we have Giotto's Faith and Infidelity, Love and Envy, Charity and Avarice, Justice and Injustice, Temperance and Gluttony, Hope and Despair, pictured forth in unmistakable characters for the reading of the unlearned and ignorant. We have the same theme, treated with a difference, in what Mr. Ruskin calls the 'Bible of Amiens,' where we may study Humility and Pride, Temperance and Gluttony, Chastity and Lust, Charity and Avarice, Hope and Despair, Faith and Idolatry, Perseverance and Atheism, Love and Discord, Obedience and Rebellion, Courage and Cowardice, Patience and Anger, Gentleness and Churlishness,—in pairs of quatrefoils, an upper and a lower, each under the feet of an Apostle, who was held to personify the special virtue. But we know nothing about cardinal virtues and deadly sins.

We have no Authoritative Teaching.—We have no teaching by authoritative utterance strong in the majesty of virtue. We work out no schemes of ethical teaching in marble; we paint no scale of virtues on our walls, and no repellent vices. Our poets speak for us, it is true; but the moral aphorisms, set like jewels though they be on the forefinger of time, are scattered here and there, and we leave it serenely to happy chance whether our children shall or shall not light upon the couple of lines which should fire them with the impulse to virtuous living. It may be said that we neglect all additional ethical teaching because we have the Bible; but how far and how do we use it? Here we have indeed the most perfect ethical system, the most inspiring and heart-enthralling, that the world has ever possessed; but it is questionable whether we attempt to set a noble child's heart beating with the thought that he is required to be perfect as his Father which is in Heaven is perfect.

High Ideals.—It is time we set ourselves seriously to this work of moral education which is to be done, most of all, by presenting the children with high ideals. 'Lives of great men all remind us we can make our lives sublime,' and the study of the lives of great men and of the great moments in the lives of smaller men is most wonderfully inspiring to children, especially when they perceive the strenuousness of the childhood out of which a noble manhood has evolved itself. As one grows older no truth strikes one more than that 'the child is father to the man.' It is amazing how many people of one's own acquaintance have fulfilled the dreams of their childhood and early youth, and have had their days indeed bound each to each in natural piety.'

Value of Biography.—The Bible is, of course, a storehouse of most inspiring biographies; but it would be well if we could manage our teaching so as to bring out in each character the master-thought of all his thinking. The late Queen has done this with singular tact and power in the Albert Memorial Chapel, where, as we know, Prophets and Patriarchs are presented, each showing in action that special virtue or form of endeavour which seemed to her the keynote of his character. This is a happy effort to revive the mediaeval object teaching of which I have already spoken. The same thing occurs again in the School of Song of the Edinburgh Cathedral, where Mrs. Traquair has frescoed the walls to illustrate the Benedicite, where 'holy and humble men of heart,' for example, is illustrated by three men of our own day of different schools of thought—Cardinal Newman is the only one I recollect. The force of this kind of master-idea, and the unity it gives to life, cannot be better illustrated than by the perhaps apocryphal 'I will be good' of our late beloved Queen. There are few children in the kingdom whose hearts have not thrilled to the phrase. Perhaps she will one day know how much was done to give moral impulse to this great Empire by that simple child-like promise so abundantly fulfilled.

Of Patriotic Poems.—Next in value to biographies from the point of view of inspiration are the burning words of the poets,—Tennyson's Ode to the Iron Duke, for example. Perhaps no poet has done more to stir the fire of patriotism amongst us than Mr. Rudyard Kipling: "We learn from our wistful mothers to call Old England 'home,'" opens the door to a flood of patriotic feeling; as indeed do the whole of the poems,

The Native-born and The Flag of England:—

"Never was isle so little,
Never were seas so lone,
But over the scud and the palm trees
The English flag has flown."

From another point of view, how this (of Browning's) makes the heart quick with patriotic emotions!—

"Buy my English posies,
Kent and Surrey may,
Violets of the undercliff
Wet with Channel spray,
Cowslips of the Devon combe,
Midland furze afire;

Buy my English posies
And I'll sell you heart's desire."

Mottoes.—In the reading of the Bible, of poetry, of the best prose, the culling of mottoes is a delightful and most stimulating occupation, especially if a motto book be kept, perhaps under headings, perhaps not. It would not be a bad idea for children to make their own year-book, with a motto for every day in the year culled from their own reading. What an incentive to a good day it would be to read in the morning as a motto of our very own choice and selection, and not the voice of an outside mentor: 'Keep ye the law; be swift in all obedience'! The theme suggests endless subjects for consideration and direct teaching: for example, lives with a keynote; Bible heroes; Greek heroes; poems of moral inspiration; poems of patriotism, duty, or any single moral quality; moral object-lessons; mottoes and where to find them, etc.

The Habit of Sweet Thoughts.—Moral habits, the way to form them and the bounden duty of every parent to send children into the world with a good outfit of moral habits, is a subject so much to the front in our thoughts, that I need not dwell further upon it here. The moral impulse having been given by means of some such inspiring idea as we have considered, the parent's or teacher's next business is to keep the idea well to the front, with tact and delicacy, and without insistence, and to afford apparently casual opportunities for moral effort on the lines of the first impulse. Again, let us keep before the children that it is the manner of thoughts we think which matters; and, in the early days, when a child's face is an open book to his parents, the habit of sweet thoughts must be kept up, and every selfish, resentful, unamiable movement of children's minds observed in the countenance must be changed before consciousness sets in.

Virtues in which Children should be Trained.—One more point: parents should take pains to have their own thoughts clear as to the manner of virtues they want their children to develop. Candour, fortitude, temperance, patience, meekness, courage, generosity, indeed the whole role of the virtues, would be stimulating subjects for thought and teaching, offering ample illustrations. One caution I should like to offer. A child's whole notion of religion is 'being good.' It is well that he should know that being good is not his whole duty to God, although it is so much of it; that the relationship of love and personal service, which he owes as a child to his Father, as a subject to his King, is even more than the 'being good' which gives our Almighty Father such pleasure in His children.

Chapter 13 Some Unconsidered Aspects of Religious Training

Authority in Religious Education.—I should like to preface my remarks on Religious Education by saying that there is not the slightest pretence that they are exhaustive. My treatment has for its object indication of practical lines for religious education, and I very earnestly hope that the reader will find I have left out things I ought to have said, or said things I ought not to have said.

Let us first consider how the principle of authority bears on religious teaching. The sense of duty, more or less illuminated, or more or less benighted, is always relative to a ruler with whom it rests to say 'Thou shalt' or 'Thou shalt not.' It is brought home, to most of us who are set in authority, that we ourselves are acting under a higher, and finally, under the highest rule. A child cannot have a lasting sense of duty until he is brought into contact with a Supreme Authority, who is the source of law, and the pleasing of whom converts duty into joy. In these rather latitudinarian days, there is perhaps no part of religious teaching more important than to train children in the sense of the immediate presence and continual going forth of the supreme Authority.

'Thou art about my path and about my bed and spiest out all my ways,' should be a thought, not of fear, but of very great comfort to every child. This constant recognition of authority excites the twofold response of docility and of reverence. It is said that the children of our day are marked by wilfulness and a certain flippancy and want of reverence; if this is so, and in so far as it is so, it is because children are brought up without the consciousness of their relation to God, whom we are taught to call 'Our Father.' This divine name reminds us that authority is lodged in the Author of our being, and is tender, pitiful, preventive, strong to care for and wise to govern; as we see it feebly shown forth even in the best of human fathers.

Questions in the Air.—But there are questions in the air about the authenticity of the Scriptures and what not, and we are all more or less at the mercy of words; and, because the so-called higher criticism finds much to question as to the verbal accuracy of passages of the Scriptures, we get a dim idea that the divine authority itself is in question. One part of the work of this Union (The Parents' Union) is, no doubt, to strengthen the hands of parents by comforting them with the sense of the higher Power behind theirs and always supporting them in the exercise of the deputed powers they hold as heads of families. There is another notion in the air which tells against the recognition of authority, and that is, the greatly increased respect for individual personality and for the right of each individual to develop on the lines of his own character. But it is a mistake to suppose that the exercise of authority runs counter to any individual development that is not on morally wrong lines.

How Authority Works.—The supreme authority (and all deputed authority) works precisely as does a good and just national government, whose business it Is to defend the liberties of the subject at all points, even by checking, repressing, and punishing the licence which interferes with the rights of others and with the true liberty of the transgressor. The law (that is, the utterance of authority) is for the punishment of evil-doers, but for the praise of them that do well; and the association of harshness, punishment, force, arbitrary dealings, with the idea of authority, and divine, is an example of the confusion of thought to which most of our errors in conduct are traceable. It is not authority which punishes: the penalties which follow us through life, of which those the family are a faint foretaste, are the inevitable consequences of broken law, whether moral or physical, and from which authority, strong and benign, exists to save us by prevention, and, if needs be, by lesser and corrective penalties.

It seems to me that reading and teaching on the following subjects, for example, might help to focus thought on a subject of vital importance—our relation to the supreme authority, not a relation of choice, but as inevitable as the family relationships into which we are born; the duty of loyalty and the shame of infidelity; the duty of reverence; the duty of docility to indications of the divine will; scriptural revelations of God as the ruler of men, as saying to Abraham, 'Go, and he goeth'; to Cyrus, 'Do this, and he doeth it'; revelations which history affords of God as the ruler of nations, and as the benign ruler of men who prospers the ways of His servants; how the sense of the divine authority may be imparted in the home; how reverence for holy things may be taught; definite Bible teaching on this head.—Indeed, the subject is capable of great amplification, and suggests trains of thought very important in these days.

The Habits of the Religious Life.—The next point we must set ourselves to consider is the laying down of lines of habit in the religious life. We need not enter again into the physiological reasons for the compelling power of habit. My present purpose is to consider how far this power can be employed in the religious development of a child. Let us consider the subject as it bears upon habits of thought and of attitude, of life and of speech; though indeed all these are one, for every act and attitude is begotten of a thought, however unaware we be of thinking.

Habit of the Thought of God.—It is said of the wicked that 'God is not in all their thoughts.' Of the child it should be said that God is in all his thoughts; happy-making, joyous thoughts, restful and dutiful thoughts, thoughts of loving and giving and serving, the wealth of beautiful thoughts with which every child's heart overflows. We are inclined to think that a child is a little morbid and precocious when he asks questions and has imaginings about things divine, and we do our best to divert him. What he needs is to be guided into true, happy thinking; every day should bring him 'new thoughts of God, new hopes of heaven.' He understands things divine better than we do, because his ideas have not been shaped to a conventional standard; and thoughts of God are to him an escape into the infinite from the worrying limitations, the perception of the prison bars which are among the bitter pangs of childhood. To keep a child in this habit of the thought of God—so that to lose it, for even a little while, is like coming home after an absence and finding his mother out—is a very delicate part of a parent's work.

Reverent Attitudes.—The importance of reverent attitudes is a little apt to be overlooked in these days. We are, before all things, sincere, and are afraid to insist upon 'mere forms,' feeling it best to leave the child to the natural expression of his own emotions. Here perhaps we are wrong, as it is just as true to say that the form gives birth to the feeling as that the feeling should give birth to the form. Children should be taught to take time, to be reverent at grace before meals, at family prayers, at their own prayers, in church, when they are old enough to attend. Perhaps some of us may remember standing daily by our mother's knee in reverent attitude to recite the Apostles' Creed, and the recollection of the reverence expressed in that early act remains with one through a lifetime. 'Because of the angels' should be a thought to repress unbecoming behaviour in children. It is a mistake to suppose that the forms of reverence need be tiresome to them. They love little ceremonies, and to be taught to kneel nicely while saying their short prayers would help them to a feeling of reverence in after life. In connection with children's behaviour in church, the sentiment and forms of reverence cannot be expected if they are taken to church too young, or to too long services or are expected to maintain their attention throughout. If children must be taken to long services, they should be allowed the resource of a Sunday picture-book, and told that the hymns and the 'Our Father,' for example, are the parts of the service for them. But in these days of bright short services especially adapted for children the difficulty need not arise.

Regularity in Devotions.—The habit of regularity in children's devotions is very important. The mother cannot always be present, but I have known children far more punctual in their devotions when away from their mother, because they know it to be her wish, than if she were there to remind them. They may say, like a little friend of mine, aged four, 'Mother, I always worship idols.' 'Do you indeed, Margaret? when?' 'Why, when I say my prayers to the chair.' But it is a great thing for all of us to get the habit of 'saying our prayers' at a given time and in a given place, which comes to be to us as a holy place. The chair, or the bedside, or the little prayer-table, or, best of all, the mother's knee, plays no small part in framing the soul to a habit of devotion. In this connection it is worth while to remark that the evening prayers of children and of school girls and boys should not be left until the children are tired and drop asleep over their evening exercises. After tea is a very good set time for prayers when it can be managed.

The Habit of Reading the Bible.—The habit of hearing, and later, of reading the Bible, is one to establish at an early age. We are met with a difficulty—that the Bible is, in fact, a library containing passages and, indeed, whole books which are not for the edification of children; and many parents fall back upon little collections of texts for morning and evening use. But I doubt the wisdom of this plan. We may believe that the narrative teaching of the Scriptures is far more helpful to children, anyway, than the stimulating moral and spiritual texts picked out for them in little devotional books. The twopenny single books of the Bible, published by the Bible Society, should be a resource for parents. A child old enough to take pleasure in reading for himself would greatly enjoy reading through the Gospel of St Mark, bit by bit, for example, in a nice little book, as part of his morning's devotions.

Children Formalists by Nature.—But while pressing the importance of habits of prayer and devotional reading, it should be remembered that children are little formalists by nature, and that they should not be encouraged in long readings or long prayers with a notion of any merit in such exercises.

The Habit of Praise.—Perhaps we do not attach enough importance to the habit of praise in our children's devotion. Praise and thanksgiving come freely from the young heart; gladness is natural and holy, and music is a delight. The singing of hymns at home and of the hymns and canticles in church should be a special delight; and the habit of soft and reverent singing, of offering our very best in praise, should be carefully formed. Hymns with a story, such as: 'A little ship was on the sea,' 'I think when I read that sweet story of old,' 'Hushed was the evening hymn,' are perhaps the best for little children. Children should be trained in the habits of attention and real devotion during short services or parts of services. The habit of finding their places in the prayer-book and following the service is interesting and aids attention, but perhaps it would be well to tell children, of even ten or eleven, that during the litany, for example, they might occupy themselves by saying over silently hymns that they know.

The Habit of Sunday-keeping.—The habit of Sunday observances, not rigid, not dull, and yet peculiar to the day, is especially important. Sunday stories, Sunday hymns, Sunday walks, Sunday talks, Sunday painting, Sunday knitting even, Sunday card-games, should all be special to the day,—quiet, glad, serene. The people who clamour for a Sunday that shall be as other days little know how healing to the jaded brain is the change of thought and occupation the seventh day brings with it. There is hardly a more precious inheritance to be handed on than that of the traditional English Sunday, stripped of its austerities, we hope, but keeping its character of quiet gladness and communion with Nature as well as with God. But I cannot pursue the subject further. The field of the habits of the religious life should afford many valuable matters for reflection and teaching; as, for example, the habitual thought of God in a family; the habit of reverence in thought, attitude, act, and speech; the habit of prayer as regards time, place, manner, matter; the habit of praise and thanksgiving; the habits of attention and devotion during a service (or part of a service); aids to devout habits; the habit of devotional reading.

Inspiring Ideas of the Religious Life.—The most important part of our subject remains to be considered—the inspiring ideas we propose to give children in the things of the divine life. This is a matter we are a little apt to leave to chance; but when we consider the vitalising power of an idea, and how a single great idea changes the current of a life, it becomes us to consider very carefully what ideas of the things of God we may most fitly offer children, and how these may be most invitingly presented. It is a very sad fact that many children get their first ideas of God in the nursery, and that these are of a Being on the watch for their transgressions and always ready to chastise. It is hard to estimate the alienation which these first ideas of the divine Father set in the hearts of His little children. Another danger is, lest the things of the divine life should be made too familiar and hackneyed, that the name of our blessed Lord should be used without reverence; and that children should get the notion that the Lord God exists for their uses, and not they, for His service.

The Fatherhood of God.—Perhaps the first vitalising idea to give children is that of the tender fatherhood of God; that they live and move and have their being within the divine embrace. Let children grow up in this joyful assurance, and, in the days to come, infidelity to this closest of all relationships will be as shameful a thing in their eyes as it was in the eyes of the Christian Church during the age of faith.

The Kingship of Christ.—Next, perhaps, the idea of Christ their King is fitted to touch springs of conduct and to rouse the enthusiasm of loyalty in children, who have it in them, as we all know, to bestow heroic devotion on that which they find heroic. Perhaps we do not make enough of this principle of hero-worship in human nature in our teaching of religion. We are inclined to make our religious aims subjective rather than objective. We are tempted to look upon Christianity as a 'scheme of salvation' designed and carried out for our benefit; whereas the very essence of Christianity is passionate devotion to an altogether adorable Person.

Our Saviour.—But, recognising this, there is still a danger in these days of adopting a rose-water treatment in our dealings with children. Few grown up people, alas! have so keen and vivid a sense of sin as a little transgressor say of six or seven. Many a naughty, passionate, or sulky and generally hardened little offender is so, simply because he does not know, with any personal knowledge, that there is a Saviour of the world, who has for him instant forgiveness and waiting love. But here again, the thoughts of a child should be turned outwards to Jesus, our Saviour, and not inward to his own thoughts and feelings towards our blessed Saviour.

The Indwelling of the Holy Ghost.—One more salient truth of the Christian verity I have space to touch upon. Most Christian parents teach their children to recognise the indwelling of the Holy Ghost, the Comforter; they expand the ideas expressed in—

"Enable with perpetual light
The dulness of our blinded sight."

"Anoint and cheer our soiled face
With the abundance of Thy grace."

But it would be well if we could hinder in our children's minds the rise of a wall of separation between things sacred and things so-called secular, by making them feel that all 'sound learning,' as well as all 'religious instruction,' falls within the office of God, the Holy Spirit, the supreme educator of mankind.

Many other inspiring ideas concerning the religious life will occur to every parent and teacher, ideas of more value than any I can suggest. Teaching, reading, and meditation, for example, on any one of the several clauses of the Lord's Prayer and of the Apostles' Creed, or; again, on the clauses of that Duty towards God in the Church Catechism which all who receive the Old and the New Testament Scriptures must accept, should be profitable.

I have touched very inadequately, not upon all that is necessary to bring up children in 'the nurture and admonition of the Lord,' but on a few of the principles which seem to me essential.

Chapter 14 A Master-Thought

A Motto.—Some of my readers will know the Parents' Union motto, 'Education is an atmosphere, a discipline, a life,' especially well in the neat diagrammatic form in which it appears on the covers of our Library books. I am told that we, as a society, are destined to live by our motto. A notable educationalist writes to me, in connection with public education: 'There is more need than ever for such a view of education as that embodied in the memorable words which are the motto of the Parents' Review.' An inspiring motto must always be a power, but to live upon the good repute of our motto, and to live up to it and in it, are two different things, and I am afraid the Parents' Union has much and continual thinking and strenuous living to face, if it proposes to stand before the world as interpreting and illustrating these 'memorable words.' But we are not a faint-hearted body; we mean, and mean intensely; and to those who purpose the best, and endeavour after the best, the best arrive.

Nineteenth-Century Formula, Education is an Atmosphere.—Meantime, we sometimes err, I think, in taking a part for the whole, and a part of a part for the whole of that part. Of the three clauses of our definition, that which declares that 'education is an atmosphere' pleases us most, perhaps, because it is the most inviting to the laissez aller principle of human nature. By the way, we lose something by substituting 'environment' (that blessed word, Mesopotamia!) for atmosphere. The latter word is symbolic, it is true, but a symbol means more to us all than the name of the thing signified. We think of fresh air, pure, bracing, tonic,—of the definite act of breathing which must be fully accomplished; and we are incited to do more and mean more in the matter of our children's surroundings if we regard the whole as an atmosphere, than if we accept the more literal 'environment.'

Results in Inanition.—But, supposing that 'Education is an atmosphere' brings a fresh and vigorous thought to our minds, suppose that it means to us, for our children, sunshine and green fields, pleasant rooms and good pictures, schools where learning is taken in by the gentle act of inspiration, followed by the expiration of all that which is not wanted, where charming teachers compose the children by a half-mesmeric effluence which inclines them to do as others do, be as others are,—suppose that all this is included in our notion of 'Education is an atmosphere,' may we not sit at our ease and believe that all is well, and that the whole of education has been accomplished? No; because though we cannot live without air, neither can we live upon air, and children brought up upon 'environment' soon begin to show signs of inanition; they have little or no healthy curiosity, power of attention, or of effort; what is worse, they lose spontaneity and initiative; they expect life to drop into them like drops into a rain-tub, without effort or intention on their part

And Ennui.—This notion, that education is included in environment, or, at the best, in atmosphere, has held the ground for a generation or two, and it seems to me that it has left its mark upon our public and our private lives. We are more ready to be done unto than to do; we do not care for the labour of ordering our own lives in this direction or in that; they must be conducted for us; a press of engagements must compel us into what next, and what next after. We crave for spectacular entertainment, whether in the way of pageants in the streets, or spectacles on the boards. Even Shakespeare has come to be so much the occasion for gorgeous spectacles that what the poet says is of little moment compared with the show a play affords. There is nothing intentionally vicious in all this; it is simply our effort to escape from the ennui that results from a one-sided view of education,—that education is an atmosphere only.

Eighteenth-Century Formula, Education is a Life, results in Intellectual Exhaustion—A still more consuming ennui set in at the end of the eighteenth century, and that also was the result of a partial view of education. 'Education is a life' was the (unconscious) formula then; and a feverish chase after ideas was the outcome. It is pathetic to read how Madame de Staël and her coterie, or that 'blue-stocking' coterie which met at the Hôtel Rambouillet, for example, went little to bed, because they could not sleep; and spent long nights in making character sketches of each other, enigmas, anagrams, and other futilities of the intellect, and met again (some of them) at early breakfast to compose and sing little airs, upon little themes. We may be as much inclined to yawn in each other's faces as they were, but, anyway, if we sin as they did by excess in one direction, there is less wear and tear in a succession of shows than in their restless pursuit of inviting notions. Still, the beginning of the nineteenth century has its lessons for the beginning of the twentieth. They erred, as we do, because they did not understand the science of the proportion of things. We are inclined to say,

'Education is environment'; they would say, 'Education is ideas.' The truth includes both of these, and a third definition introducing another side, a third aspect, of education.

Education is the Cultivation of Faculties, leads to Abnormal Developments.—The third conceivable view, 'Education is a discipline,' has always had its votaries, and has them still. That the discipline of the habits of the good life, both intellectual and moral, forms a good third of education, we all believe. The excess occurs when we imagine that certain qualities of character and conduct run out, a prepared product like carded wool, from this or that educational machine, mathematics or classics, science or athletics; that is, when the notion of the development of the so-called faculties takes the place of the more physiologically true notion of the formation of intellectual habits. The difference does not seem to be great; but two streams that rise within a foot of one another may water different countries and fall into different seas, and a broad divergence in practice often arises from what appears to be a small difference in conception, in matters educational. The father of Plutarch had him learn his Horner that he might get heroic ideas of life. Had the boy been put through his Homer as a classical grind, as a machine for the development of faculty, a pedant would have come out, and not a man of the world in touch with life at many points, capable of bringing men and affairs to the touchstone of a sane and generous mind. It seems to me that this notion of the discipline which should develop 'faculty' has tended to produce rather one-sided men, with the limitations which belong to abnormal development. An artist told me the other day that the condition of successful art is absorption in art, that the painter must think pictures, paint pictures, nothing but pictures. But when art was great, men were not mere artists. Quentin Matsys wrought in iron and painted pictures and did many things besides. Michael Angelo wrote sonnets, designed buildings, painted pictures; marble was by no means his only vehicle of expression. Leonardo wrote treatises, planned canals, played instruments of music, did a hundred things, and all exquisitely. But then, the idea of the development of faculty, and the consequent discipline, had not occurred to these great men or their guardians.

Education has Three Faces.—Having safe-guarded ourselves from the notion that education has only one face, we may go on to consider how 'education is a life,' without the risk of thinking that we are viewing more than one side of the subject.

Education is a Life, one of these.—It has been said that 'man doth not live by bread alone, but by every word that proceedeth out of the mouth of God'; and the augustness of the occasion on which the words were spoken has caused us to confine their meaning to what we call the life of the soul; when, indeed, they include a great educational principle which was better understood by the mediæval Church than by ourselves. May I be allowed once again to describe a painting in which the educational creed of many of us is visibly expressed? The reader is, probably, familiar with the frescoes on the walls of the so-called Spanish Chapel of the church of S. Maria Novella. The philosophy of the Middle Ages dealt, as we know, with theology as its subject-matter; and, while there is much ecclesiastical polity with which we have little sympathy pictured on the remaining walls, on one compartment of wall and roof we have a singularly satisfying scheme of educational thought. At the highest point of the picture we see the Holy Ghost descending in the likeness of a dove; immediately below, in the upper chamber are the disciples who first received His inspiration; below, again, is the promiscuous crowd of all nationalities who are brought indirectly under the influence of that first outpouring; and in the foreground are two or three dogs, showing that the dumb creation was not excluded from benefiting by the new grace. In the lower compartment of the great design are angelic figures of the cardinal virtues, which we all trace more or less to divine inspiration, floating above the seated figures of apostles and prophets, of whom we know that they 'spake as they were moved by the Holy Ghost.' So far, this mediæval scheme of philosophy reveals no new thought to persons instructed in the elements of Christian truth. But below the prophets and apostles are a series of pictured niches, those to the right being occupied by the captain figures, the ideal representations, of the seven Liberal Arts, figures of singular grace and beauty, representing such familiar matters as grammar, rhetoric, logic, music, astronomy, geometry, and arithmetic, all of them under the outpouring of the Spirit of God. Still more liberal is the philosophy which places at the foot of each of these figures him who was then accepted as the leader and representative of each several science,—Priscian, Cicero, Aristotle, Tubal Cain, Zoroaster, Euclid, Pythagoras; men whom a narrower and later theology would have placed beyond the pale of the Christian religion, and therefore of the teaching of the Spirit of God. But here all are represented as under the same divine outpouring which illuminated the disciples in the upper chamber.

A Creed which unifies Life.—Our nature craves after unity. The travail of thought, which is going on to-day and has gone on as long as we have any record of men's thoughts, has been with a view to establishing some principle for the unification of life. Here we have the scheme of a magnificent unity. We are apt to think that piety is one thing, that our intellectual and artistic yearnings are quite another matter, and that our moral virtues are pretty much matters of inheritance and environment, and have not much to do with our conscious religion. Hence, there come discords into our lives, discords especially trying to young and ardent souls who want to be good and religious, but who cannot escape from the overpowering drawings of art and intellect and mere physical enjoyment; they have been taught to consider that these things are, for the most part, alien to the religious life, and that they must choose one or the other; they do choose, and the choice does not always fall upon those things which, in our unscriptural and unphilosophical narrowness, we call the things of God. Let us bless Taddeo Gaddi and Simone Memmi for placing before our eyes a creed (copies ['La Discessa dello Spirot Santo' and Allegoria filosofica della Religione Cattolica' to be had from Mr. G. Cole, 1 Via Torna Buoni, Forence—shilling size, Nos. 4077 and 4093] of which we might all hang upon our walls), which shows that our piety, our virtue, our intellectual activities, and, let us add, our physical perfections, are all fed from the same source, God Himself; are all inspired by the same Spirit, the Spirit of God. The ages which held this creed were ages of mighty production in every kind; the princely commerce of Venice was dignified and sobered by this thought of the divine inspiration of ideas—ideas of trade, ideas of justice and fair balance and of utility; Columbus went out to discover a new world, informed by the divine idea, as our own philosopher, Coleridge, points out, adding that 'great inventions and Ideas of Nature presented to chosen minds by a higher power than nature herself, suddenly unfold as it were in prophetic succession systematic views destined to produce the most important revolutions in the state of man.' When Columbus came back, his new world discovered, people and princes took it as from God and sang Te Deum.

The Diet of Great Ideas.—Michael Angelo writes to his friend Vittoria Colonna, that 'good Christians always make good and beautiful figures. In order to represent the adored image of our Lord, it is not enough that a master should be great and able. I maintain that he must also be a man of good morals and conduct, if possible a saint, in order that the Holy Ghost may give him inspiration.' In truth, a nation or a man becomes great upon one diet only, the diet of great ideas communicated to those already prepared to receive them by a higher Power than Nature herself.

Science, the Teaching vouchsafed to Men to-day.—I think we (of 'The Parents' Union') hold amongst us the little leaven which is able to leaven the whole lump. Let us set ourselves to labour with purpose and passion to restore to the world, enriched by the additions of later knowledge, that great scheme of unity of life which produced great men and great work in the past. Nor need we fear that in endeavouring after some such doctrine of ideas as may help us in the work of education, we are running counter to science. Many of us feel, and, I think, rightly, that the teaching of science is the new teaching which is being vouchsafed to mankind in our age. Some of us are triumphant, and believe that the elements of moral and religious struggle are about to be eliminated from life, which shall run henceforth, whether happy or disastrous, on the easy plane of the inevitable; others are bewildered and look in vain for a middle way, a place of reconciliation for science and religion; while others of us, again, take refuge in repudiating 'evolution' and all its works and nailing our colours to religion, interpreted on our own narrow lines. Whichever of these lines we take, we probably err through want of faith.

Let us first of all settle it with ourselves that science and religion cannot, to the believer in God, by any possibility be antagonistic. Having assured ourselves of this, we shall probably go on to perceive that the evolution of science is in fact a process of revelation, being brought about in every case, so far as I am aware, by the process which Coleridge has so justly described; that is, "that the Ideas of Nature, presented to chosen minds by a higher power than Nature herself, suddenly unfold as it were in prophetic succession systematic views destined to produce the must important revolutions in the state of man." Huxley defines the utility of Biology "as helping to give right ideas in this world, which is, after all," he goes on to say, "absolutely governed by ideas, and very often by the wildest and most hypothetical ideas." Again, he writes, "those who refuse to go beyond the fact rarely get as far as the fact; and anyone who has studied the history of science knows that almost every great step therein has been made by the 'anticipation of nature,' that is, by the invention of hypotheses." One cannot help thinking that scientific men would find the unifying principle they are in search of in the fine saying of Coleridge's which I have quoted more than once or twice; so would they stand revealed to themselves as the mouthpieces, not merely of the truth, for which they are so ready to combat and suffer, but also as the chosen and prepared servants of Him who is the Truth.

Evolution, the Master-thought of the Age.—Few of us can forget Carlyle's incomparable picture of the Tiers état waiting for organisation: "Wise as serpents; harmless as doves: what a spectacle for France! Six hundred inorganic individuals, essential for its regeneration and salvation, sit there, on their elliptic benches, longing passionately towards life." Less picturesque, but otherwise very much on a par with this, is Coleridge's description of Botany, as that science existed in his own day, waiting for the unifying idea which should give it organisation. "What," he says, "is Botany at this present hour? Little more than an enormous nomenclature; a huge catalogue, bien arrangé, yearly and monthly augmented, in various editions, each with its own scheme of technical memory and its own conveniences of reference! The innocent amusement, the healthful occupation, the ornamental accomplishment of amateurs; it has yet to expect the devotion and energies of the philosopher." The keyword for the interpretation of life, both animal and vegetable, has been presented to our generation, and we cannot make too much of it.

The Ages have sought for a Unifying Principle.—We cannot overrate the enormous repose and satisfaction to the human mind contained in the idea of evolution. But it is well to remember that for three thousand years thinkers have been occupied with attempts to explain the world by means of a single principle, which should also furnish an explanation of reason and the human soul. Herakleitos and his age thought they had laid hold of the informing idea in the phrase, 'The true Being is an eternal Becoming': the 'universal flux of things' explained all. Demokritos and his age cried—Eureka! solved the riddle of the universe, with the saying that 'nothing exists except atoms moving in vacancy.' Many times since, with each epoch-making discovery, has science cried—Eureka! over the one principle which should explain all things and eliminate Personality.

But Personality Remains.—But some little knowledge of history and philosophy will give us pause. We shall see that each great discovery, each luminous idea of nature that the world has received hitherto, is like a bend in a tortuous lake which appears final until your boat approaches it, and then—behold an opening into further and still further reaches beyond! And the knowledge of God will give us something more than the wider outlook which comes of a knowledge of history—the knowledge that there is what Wordsworth calls the 'stream of tendency,' a stream of immeasurable force in shaping character and events; but there is also Personality, a power able to turn the 'stream of tendency' to its uses, if also liable to be carried away in its current

Attitude of Parents and Teachers towards Evolution.—If I appear to dwell on a subject which at first sight appears to have little to do with the bringing up of children, it is because I think that his attitude towards the great idea, great lesson, set for his age to grasp, is a vital part of a parent's preparation. If parents take no heed of the great thoughts which move their age, they cannot expect to retain influence over the minds of their children. If they fear and distrust the revelations of science, they introduce an element of distrust and discord into their children's lives. If, with the mere neophyte of science, they rush to the conclusion that the last revelation is final, accounts for all that is in man, and, to say the least, makes God unnecessary and unknowable, or negligible, they may lower the level of their children's living to that struggle for existence—without aspiration, consecration, and sacrifice—of which we hear so much. If, lastly, parents recognise every great idea of nature as a new page in the progressive revelation made by God to men already prepared to receive such idea; if they realise that the new idea, however comprehensive, is not final nor all-inclusive, nor to be set in opposition with that personal knowledge of God which is the greatest knowledge, why, then, their children will grow up in that attitude of reverence for science, reverence for God, and openness of mind, which befits us for whom life is a probation and a continual education. So much for the nutriment of ideas laid on the table of the world during this particular course of its history.

Education is a World Business.—Next, we may have poetry, or art, or philosophy; we cannot tell; but two things are incumbent upon us,—to keep ourselves and our children in touch with the great thoughts by which the world has been educated in the past, and to keep ourselves and them in the right attitude towards the great ideas of the present. It is our temptation to make too personal a matter of education, to lose sight of the fact that education is a world business, that the lessons of the ages have been duly set, and that each age is concerned, not only with its own particular page, but with every preceding page. For who feels that he has mastered a book if he is familiar with only the last page of it? This brings me to a point I am anxious to bring forward.

We do not sufficiently realise the need for unity of principle in education. We have no Captain Idea which shall marshal for us the fighting host of educational ideas which throng the air; so, in default of a guiding principle, a leading idea, we feel ourselves at liberty to pick and choose. This man thinks he is free to make science the sum of his son's education, the other chooses the classics, a third prefers a mechanical, a fourth, a commercial programme, a fifth makes bodily health his cult, and chooses a school which makes the care of health a special feature of its programme (not that we must allow health to be neglected, but that, given good general conditions, the less obvious attention their health receives the better for the boys and girls); and everyone feels himself at liberty to do that which is right in his own eyes with regard to the education of his children.

Let it be our negative purpose to discourage in every way we can the educational faddist, that is, the person who accepts a one-sided notion in place of a universal idea as his educational guide. Our positive purpose is to present, in season and out of season, one such universal idea; that is, that education is the science of relations.

A Captain Idea for us,—Education is the Science of Relations.—A child should be brought up to have relations of force with earth and water, should run and ride, swim and skate, lift and carry; should know texture, and work in material; should know by name, and where and how they live at any rate, the things of the earth about him, its birds and beasts and creeping things, its herbs and trees; should be in touch with the literature, art and thought of the past and the present I do not mean that he should know all these things; but he should feel, when he reads of it in the newspapers, the thrill which stirred the Cretan peasants when the frescoes in the palace of King Minos were disclosed to the labour of their spades. He should feel the thrill, not from mere contiguity, but because he has with the past the relationship of living pulsing thought; and, if blood be thicker than water, thought is more quickening than blood. He must have a living relationship with the present, its historic movement, its science, literature, art, social needs and aspirations. In fact, he must have a wide outlook, intimate relations all round; and force, virtue, must pass out of him, whether of hand, will, or sympathy, wherever he touches. This is no impossible programme. Indeed it can be pretty well filled in by the time an intelligent boy or girl has reached the age of thirteen or fourteen; for it depends, not upon how much is learned, but upon how things are learned.

A Wider Curriculum.—Give children a wide range of subjects, with the end in view of establishing in each case some one or more of the relations I have indicated. Let them learn from first-hand sources of information—really good books, the best going, on the subject they are engaged upon. Let them get at the books themselves, and do not let them be flooded with a warm diluent at the lips of their teacher. The teacher's business is to indicate, stimulate, direct and constrain to the acquirement of knowledge, but by no means to be the fountain-head and source of all knowledge in his or her own person. The less parents and teachers talk-in and expound their rations of knowledge and thought to the children they are educating, the better for the children. Peptonised food for a healthy stomach does not tend to a vigorous digestion. Children must be allowed to ruminate, must be left alone with their own thoughts. They will ask for help if they want it.

We may not Choose or Reject Subjects.—You will see at a glance, with this Captain Idea of establishing relationships as a guide, the unwisdom of choosing or rejecting this or that subject, as being more or less useful or necessary in view of a child's future. We decide, for example, that Tommy, who is eight, need not waste his time over the Latin Grammar. We intend him for commercial or scientific pursuits,—what good will it be to him? But we do not know how much we are shutting out from Tommy's range of thought besides the Latin Grammar. He has to translate, for example,—'Pueri formosos equos vident.' He is a ruminant animal, and has been told something about that strong Roman people whose speech is now brought before him. How their boys catch hold of him! How he gloats over their horses! The Latin Grammar is not mere words to Tommy, or rather Tommy knows, as we have forgotten, that the epithet 'mere' is the very last to apply to words. Of course it is only now and then that a notion catches the small boy, but when it does catch, it works wonders, and does more for his education than years of grind.

Let us try, however imperfectly, to make education a science of relationships—in other words, try in one subject or another to let the children work upon living ideas. In this field small efforts are honoured with great rewards, and we perceive that the education we are giving exceeds all that we intended or imagined.

Chapter 15 School-Books and How They Make for Education

Line upon Line.—The theme of 'School-books' is not a new one, and I daresay the reader will find that I have said before what I shall say now. But we are not like those men of Athens who met to hear and to tell some new thing; and he will, I know, bear with me because he will recognise how necessary it is to repeat again and again counsels which are like waves beating against the rock of an accepted system of things. But, in time, the waves prevail and the rock wears away; so we go to work with good hope. Let me introduce what I have to say about school-books by a little story from an antiquated source.

An Incident of School-Girl Life.—Frederika Bremer, in her novel of The Neighbours (published 1837), tells an incident of school-girl life (possibly a bit of autobiography), with great spirit. Though it is rather long, I think the reader will thank me for it—the little episode advances what I have to say better than could any duller arguments of my own.

The heroine says:—"I was then sixteen, and, fortunately for my restless character, my right shoulder began to project at the time. Gymnastics were then in fashion as remedies against all manner of defects, and my parents determined to let me try gymnastics. Arrayed in trimmed pantaloons, a Bonjour coat of green cloth and a little morning cap with pink ribbon, I made my appearance one day in an assemblage of from thirty to forty figures dressed almost the same as myself, who were merrily swarming about a large saloon, over ropes, ladders, and poles. It was a strange and novel scene. I kept myself in the background the first day, and learned from my governess the 'bending of the back' and the 'exercises of the arms and legs.' The second day I began to be intimate with some of the girls, the third I vied with them on ropes and ladders, and ere the close of the second week I was the leader of the second class, and began to encourage them to all manner of tricks.

"At that time I was studying Greek history; their heroes and their heroic deeds filled my imagination even in the gymnastic school. I proposed to my band to assume masculine and antique names and, in this place, to answer to no other than such as Agamemnon, Epaminondas, etc. For myself I chose the name of Orestes, and called my best friend in the class, Pylades. There was a tall thin girl, with a Finlandish accent, whom I greatly disliked, chiefly on account of the disrespect for me and my ideas which she manifested without reserve; .... from this arose fresh cause for quarrels.

"Although in love with the Greek history, I was no less taken with the Swedish. Charles XII. was my idol, and I often entertained my friends in my class with narration of his deeds till my own soul was on fire with the most glowing enthusiasm. Like a shower of cold water, Darius (the tall girl, whose name was Britsa) one day came into the midst of us, and opposed me with the assertion that the Czar Peter I. was a much greater man than Charles XII. I accepted the challenge with blind zeal and suppressed rage. My opponent brought forward a number of facts with coolness and skill, in support of her opinion, and when I, confuting all her positions, thought to exalt my victorious hero to the clouds, she was perpetually throwing Bender and Pultawa in my way. O Pultawa! Pultawa! many tears have fallen over thy bloody battlefield, but none more bitter than those which I shed in secret when I, like Charles himself, suffered a defeat there. Fuel was added to the flame until—'I challenge you, I demand satisfaction,' cried I to Darius, who only laughed and said, 'Bravo, bravo!' . . . I exclaimed, 'You have insulted me shamefully, and I request that you ask my pardon in the presence of the whole class, and acknowledge that Charles XII. was a greater man than Czar Peter, or else you shall fight with me, if you have any honour in your breast and are not a coward.' Britsa Kaijsa blushed, but said with detestable coolness: 'Ask pardon indeed? I should never dream of such a thing. Fight? O, yes, I have no objection! but where and with what? With pins, think you, or'—'With the sword if you are not afraid, and on this very spot. We can meet here half an hour before the rest; arms I shall bring with me; Pylades is my second and you shall appoint your own!' .... Next morning when I had entered the spacious saloon, I found my enemy already there with her second. Darius and I saluted each other proudly and distantly. I gave her the first choice of the swords. She took one and flourished it about quite dexterously, as if she had been accustomed to the use of it. I saw myself (in imagination) already stabbed to the heart. . . 'Czar Peter was a great man,' cried Darius. 'Down with him! long life to Charles XII!' I cried, bursting into a furious rage. I placed myself in an attitude of defence. Darius did the same..... Our swords clashed one against the other, and in the next moment I was disarmed and thrown on the ground. Darius stood over me and I believed my last hour had arrived. How astonished was I, however, when my enemy threw her sword away from her, took me by the hand and lifted me up, whilst she cheerfully cried: 'Well, now you have satisfaction; let us be good friends again; you are a brave little body!' At this moment a tremendous noise was heard at the door and in rushed the fencing master and three teachers. My senses now forsook me."

I hope the reader is not among the naughty children who read the fable and skip the moral; for, whatever is to follow, is, in fact, the moral of this pretty incident.

How did the Girls get their Enthusiasm?—What was it, we wonder, in their school-books that these Swedish maidens found so exciting? There is no hint of other than school reading. In the first place we may conclude it was books. The oral lesson for young children, the lecture for older, had not been invented in the earlier years of the last century. We use books in our schoolrooms; but one does not hear of wild enthusiasm, ungovernable excitement, over the tabulated events of the history books, the tabulated facts of the science primers. Those Swedish girls must have used books of another sort; and it is to our interest to find out of what sort. As records would be hard to come by, we must look for information to the girls themselves; not that we can summon them to give a direct answer, but if we can get at what they were, we shall be able to make a good guess at what should fire their souls.

What manner of Book sustains the Life of Thought?—The story discloses no more than that they were intelligent girls, probably the children of intelligent parents. But that is enough for our purpose. The question resolves itself into—What manner of book will find its way with upheaving effect into the mind of an intelligent boy or girl? We need not ask what the girl or boy likes. She very often likes the twaddle of goody-goody story books, he likes condiments, highly-spiced tales of adventure. We are all capable of liking mental food of a poor quality and a titillating nature; and possibly such food is good for us when our minds are in need of an elbow-chair; but our spiritual life is sustained on other stuff, whether we be boys or girls, men or women. By spiritual I mean that which is not corporeal; and which, for convenience sake, we call by various names—the life of thought, the life of feeling, the life of the soul.

It is curious how every inquiry, superficial as it may seem to begin with, leads us to fundamental principles. This simple-seeming question—what manner of school-books should our boys and girls use?—leads us straight to one of the two great principles which bottom educational thought.

The School-books of the Publishers.—I believe that spiritual life, using spiritual in the sense I have indicated, is sustained upon only one manner of diet—the diet of ideas—the living progeny of living minds. Now, if we send to any publisher for his catalogue of school books, we find that it is accepted as the nature of a school-book that it be drained dry of living thought It may bear the name of a thinker, but then it is the abridgment of an abridgment, and all that is left for the unhappy scholar is the dry bones of his subject denuded of soft flesh and living colour, of the stir of life and power of moving. Nothing is left but what Oliver Wendell Holmes calls the 'mere brute fact.'

It cannot be too often said that information is not education. You may answer an examination question about the position of the Seychelles and the Comoro Islands without having been anywise nourished by the fact of these island groups existing in such and such latitudes and longitudes; but if you follow Bullen in The Cruise of the Cachelot the names excite that little mental stir which indicates the reception of real knowledge.

Reason for Oral Teaching.—Intelligent teachers are well aware of the dry-as-dust character of school books, so they fall back upon the 'oral' lesson, one of whose qualities must be that it is not bookish. Living ideas can be derived only from living minds, and so it occasionally happens that a vital spark is flashed from teacher to pupil. But this occurs only when the subject is one to which the teacher has given original thought. In most cases the oral lesson, or the more advanced lecture, consists of information got up by the teacher from various books, and imparted in language, a little pedantic, or a little commonplace, or a little reading-made-easy in style. At the best, the teacher is not likely to have vital interest in, and, consequently, original thought upon, a wide range of subjects.

Limitations of Teachers.—We wish to place before the child open doors to many avenues of instruction and delight, in each one of which he should find quickening thoughts. We cannot expect a school to be manned by a dozen master-minds, and even if it were, and the scholar were taught by each in turn, it would be much to his disadvantage. What he wants of his teacher is moral and mental discipline, sympathy and direction; and it is better, on the whole, that the training of the pupil should be undertaken by one wise teacher than that he should be passed from hand to hand for this subject and that.

Our aim in Education is to give a Full Life.—We begin to see what we want. Children make large demands upon us. We owe it to them to initiate an immense number of interests. Thou hast set my feet in a large room; should be the glad cry of every intelligent soul. Life should be all living, and not merely a tedious passing of time; not all doing or all feeling or all thinking—the strain would be too great—but, all living; that is to say, we should be in touch wherever we go, whatever we hear, whatever we see, with some manner of vital interest. We cannot give the children these interests; we prefer that they should never say they have learned botany or conchology, geology or astronomy. The question is not,—how much does the youth know? when he has finished his education—but how much does he care? and about how many orders of things does he care? In fact, how large is the room in which he finds his feet set? and, therefore, how full is the life he has before him? I know you may bring a horse to the water, but you cannot make him drink. What I complain of is that we do not bring our horse to the water. We give him miserable little text-books, mere compendiums of facts, which he is to learn off and say and produce at an examination; or we give him various knowledge in the form of warm diluents, prepared by his teacher with perhaps some grains of living thought to the gallon. And all the time we have books, books teeming with ideas fresh from the minds of thinkers upon every subject to which we can wish to introduce children.

We undervalue Children.—The fact is, we undervalue children. The notion that an infant is a huge oyster, who by slow degrees, and more and more, develops into that splendid intellectual and moral being, a full-grown man or woman, has been impressed upon us so much of late years that we believe intellectual spoon-meat to be the only food for what we are pleased to call 'little minds.' It is nothing to us that William Morris read his first Waverley Novel when he was four and had read the whole series by the time he was seven. He did not die of it, but lived and prospered; unlike that little Richard, son of John Evelyn, who died when he was five years and three days old, a thing not to be wondered at when we read that he had 'a strong passion for Greek, could turn English into Latin and vice versa with the greatest ease,' had 'a wonderful disposition to Mathematics, having by heart divers propositions of Euclid'; but I quote little Richard (nobody could ever have called him Dick) by way of warning and not of example. Macaulay seems to have begun life as a great reader. We know the delightful story of how, when Hannah More called on his parents, he, a little boy of four, came forward with pretty hospitality to say that if she 'would be good enough to come in' he would bring her 'a glass of old spirits.' He explained afterwards that 'Robinson Crusoe often had some.'

Children of the Last Generation.—But we may dismiss these precocious or exceptional children. All we ask of them is to remind us that our grandfathers and grandmothers recognised children as reasonable beings, persons of mind and conscience like themselves; but, needing their guidance and control, as having neither knowledge nor experience. Witness the queer old children's books which have come down to us; these addressed children as, before all things, reasonable, intelligent, and responsible persons. This is the note of home-life in the last generation. So soon as the baby realised his surroundings, he found himself morally and intellectually responsible.

Children as they are.—And children have not altered. This is how we find them—with intelligence more acute, logic more keen, observing powers more alert, moral sensibilities more quick, love and faith and hope more abounding; in fact, in all points like as we are, only more so; but absolutely ignorant of the world and its belongings, of us and our ways, and, above all, of how to control and direct and manifest the infinite possibilities with which they are born.

Our Work, to give vitalising Ideas.—Knowing that the brain is the physical seat of habit and that conduct and character, alike, are the outcome of the habits we allow; knowing, too, that an inspiring idea initiates a new habit of thought, and hence, a new habit of life; we perceive that the great work of education is to inspire children with vitalising ideas as to every relation of life, every department of knowledge, every subject of thought; and to give deliberate care to the formation of those habits of the good life which are the outcome of vitalising ideas. In this great work we seek and assuredly find the co-operation of the Divine Spirit, whom we recognise, in a sense rather new to modern thought, as the supreme Educator of mankind in things that have been called secular, fully as much as in those that have been called sacred.

Chapter 16 How to Use School-Books

Disciplinary Subjects of Instruction.—Having cleared our minds as to the end we have in view, we ask ourselves—'Is there any fruitful idea underlying this or that study that the children are engaged in?' We divest ourselves of the notion that to develop the faculties is the chief thing, and a 'subject' which does not rise out of some great thought of life we usually reject as not nourishing, not fruitful; while we retain those studies which give exercise in habits of clear and orderly thinking. Mathematics, grammar, logic, etc., are not purely disciplinary, they do develop (if a bull may be allowed) intellectual muscle. We by no means reject the familiar staples of education in the school sense, but we prize them even more for the record of intellectual habits they leave in the brain tissue, than for their distinct value in developing certain 'faculties.'

'Open, Sesame.'—I think we should have a great educational revolution once we ceased to regard ourselves as assortments of so-called faculties, and realised ourselves as persons whose great business it is to get in touch with other persons of all sorts and condition; of all countries and climes, of all times, past and present. History would become entrancing, literature a magic mirror for the discovery of other minds, the study of sociology a duty and a delight. We should tend to become responsive and wise, humble and reverent, recognising the duties and the joys of the full human life. We cannot of course overtake such a programme of work, but we can keep it in view; and I suppose every life is moulded upon its ideal.

The Bible, the great Storehouse of Moral Impression.—Valuable as are some compendiums of its moral teaching, it is to the Bible itself we must go as to the great storehouse of moral impressions. Let us hear De Quincey on this subject:—

"It had happened, that among our vast nursery collection of books was the Bible, illustrated with many pictures. And in long dark evenings, as my three sisters with myself sat by the firelight round the guard of our nursery, no book was so much in request amongst us. It ruled us and swayed us as mysteriously as music. Our younger nurse, whom we all loved, would sometimes, according to her simple powers, endeavour to explain what we found obscure. We, the children, were all constitutionally touched with pensiveness; the fitful gloom and sudden lambencies of the room by firelight suited our evening state of feelings; and they suited also, the divine revelations of power and mysterious beauty which awed us. Above all, the story of a just man—man and yet not man, real above all things, and yet shadowy above all things—who had suffered the passion of death in Palestine, slept upon our minds like early dawn upon the waters. The nurse knew and explained to us the chief differences in oriental climates; and all these differences (as it happens) express themselves, more or less, in varying relation to the great accidents and powers of summer. The cloudless sunlights of Syria—these seemed to argue everlasting summer; the disciples plucking the ears of corn—that must be summer; but, above all, the very name of Palm Sunday (a festival in the English Church) troubled me like an anthem."

Effect of our Liturgy on a Child.—I cannot refrain from adding De Quincey's beautiful words describing the effect of our liturgy upon him as a child. "On Sunday mornings I went with the rest of my family to church: it was a church on the ancient model of England, having aisles, galleries, organ, all things ancient and venerable, and the proportions majestic. Here, whilst the congregation knelt through the long litany, as often as we came to that passage, so beautiful amongst many that are so, where God is supplicated on behalf of 'all sick persons and young children,' and that He would 'show His pity upon all prisoners and captives,' I wept in secret; and raising my streaming eyes to the upper windows of the galleries, saw, on days when the sun was shining, a spectacle as affecting as ever prophet can have beheld. The sides of the windows were rich with stained glass; through the deep purples and crimsons streamed the golden light; emblazonries of heavenly illumination (from the sun) mingling with the earthly emblazonries (from art and its gorgeous colouring) of what is grandest in man. There were the apostles that had trampled upon earth, and the glories of earth, out of celestial love to man. There were the martyrs that had borne witness to the truth through flames, through torments, and through armies of fierce, insulting faces. There were the saints who, under intolerable pangs, had glorified God by meek submission to His will." "God speaks to children, also, in dreams and by the oracles that lurk in darkness. But in solitude, above all things, when made vocal to the meditative heart by the truths and services of a national church, God holds with children 'communion undisturbed.' Solitude, though it may be silent as light, is, like light, the mightiest of agencies; for solitude is essential to man. All men come into this world alone; all leave it alone."

Principles on which to select School-books.—In their power of giving impulse and stirring emotion is another use of books, the right books; but that is just the question—which are the right books?—a point upon which I should not wish to play Sir Oracle. The 'hundred best books for the schoolroom' may be put down on a list, but not by me. I venture to propose one or two principles in the matter of school-books, and shall leave the far more difficult part, the application of those principles, to the reader. For example, I think we owe it to children to let them dig their knowledge, of whatever subject, for themselves out of the fit book; and this for two reasons: What a child digs for is his own possession; what is poured into his ear, like the idle song of a pleasant singer, floats out as lightly as it came in, and is rarely assimilated. I do not mean to say that the lecture and the oral lesson are without their uses; but these uses are, to give impulse and to order knowledge; and not to convey knowledge, or to afford us that part of our education which comes of fit knowledge, fitly given.

Again, as I have already said, ideas must reach us directly from the mind of the thinker, and it is chiefly by means of the books they have written that we get into touch with the best minds.

Marks of a Fit Book.—As to the distinguishing marks of a book for the school-room, a word or two may be said. A fit book is not necessarily a big book. John Quincy Adams, aged nine, wrote to his father for the fourth volume of Smollett for his private reading, though, as he owned up, his thoughts were running on birds' eggs; and perhaps some of us remember going religiously through the many volumes of Alison's History of Europe with a private feeling that the bigness of the book swelled the virtue of the reader. But, now, big men write little books, to be used with discretion; because sometimes the little books are no more than abstracts, the dry bones of the subjects; and sometimes the little books are fresh and living. Again, we need not always insist that a book should be written by the original thinker. It sometimes happens that second-rate minds have assimilated the matter in hand, and are able to give out what is their own thought (only because they have made it their own) in a form more suitable for our purpose than that of the first-hand thinkers. We cannot make any hard and fast rule—a big book or a little book, a book at first-hand or at second-hand; either may be right provided we have it in us to discern a living book, quick, and informed with the ideas proper to the subject of which it treats.

How to use the Right Books.—So much for the right books; the right use of them is another matter. The children must enjoy the book. The ideas it holds must each make that sudden, delightful impact upon their minds, must cause that intellectual stir, which mark the inception of an idea. The teacher's part in this regard is to see and feel for himself, and then to rouse his pupils by an appreciative look or word; but to beware how he deadens the impression by a flood of talk. Intellectual sympathy is very stimulating; but we have all been in the case of the little girl who said, "Mother, I think I could understand if you did not explain quite so much." A teacher said of her pupil, "I find it so hard to tell whether she has really grasped a thing or whether she has only got the mechanical hang of it" Children are imitative monkeys, and it is the 'mechanical hang' that is apt to arrive after a douche of explanation.

Children must Labour.—This, of getting ideas out of them, is by no means all we must do with books. 'In all labour there is profit,' at any rate in some labour; and the labour of thought is what his book must induce in the child. He must generalise, classify, infer, judge, visualise, discriminate, labour in one way or another, with that capable mind of his, until the substance of his book is assimilated or rejected, according as he shall determine; for the determination rests with him and not with his teacher.

Value of Narration.—The simplest way of dealing with a paragraph or a chapter is to require the child to narrate its contents after a single attentive reading,—one reading, however slow, should be made a condition; for we are all too apt to make sure we shall have another opportunity of finding out 'what 'tis all about' There is the weekly review if we fail to get a clear grasp of the news of the day; and, if we fail a second time, there is a monthly or a quarterly review or an annual summing up: in fact, many of us let present-day history pass by us with easy minds, feeling sure that, in the end, we shall be compelled to see the bearings of events. This is a bad habit to get into; and we should do well to save our children by not giving them the vague expectation of second and third and tenth opportunities to do that which should have been done at first.

A Single Careful Reading.—There is much difference between intelligent reading, which the pupil should do in silence, and a mere parrot-like cramming up of contents; and it is not a bad test of education to be able to give the points of a description, the sequence of a series of incidents, the links in a chain of argument, correctly, after a single careful reading. This is a power which a barrister, a publisher, a scholar, labours to acquire; and it is a power which children can acquire with great ease, and once acquired, the gulf is bridged which divides the reading from the non-reading community.

Other Ways of using Books.—But this is only one way to use books: others are to enumerate the statements in a given paragraph or chapter; to analyse a chapter, to divide it into paragraphs under proper headings, to tabulate and classify series; to trace cause to consequence and consequence to cause; to discern character and perceive how character and circumstance interact; to get lessons of life and conduct, or the living knowledge which makes for science, out of books; all this is possible for school boys and girls, and until they have begun to use books for themselves in such ways, they can hardly be said to have begun their education.

The Teacher's Part.—The teacher's part is, in the first place, to see what is to be done, to look over the of the day in advance and see what mental discipline, as well as what vital knowledge, this and that lesson afford; and then to set such questions and such tasks as shall give full scope to his pupils' mental activity. Let marginal notes be freely made, as neatly and beautifully as may be, for books should be handled with reverence. Let numbers, letters, underlining be used to help the eye and to save the needless fag of writing abstracts. Let the pupil write for himself half a dozen questions which cover the passage studied; he need not write the answers if he be taught that the mind can know nothing but what it can produce in the form of an answer to a question put by the mind to itself.

Disciplinary Devices must not come between Children and the Soul of the Book.—These few hints by no means cover the disciplinary uses of a good school-book; but let us be careful that our disciplinary devices, and our mechanical devices to secure and tabulate the substance of knowledge, do not come between the children and that which is the soul of the book, the living thought it contains. Science is doing so much for us in these days, nature is drawing so close to us, art is unfolding so much meaning to us, the world is becoming so rich for us, that we are a little in danger of neglecting the art of deriving sustenance from books. Let us not in such wise impoverish our lives and the lives of our children; for, to quote the golden words of Milton: "Books are not absolutely dead things, but do contain a potency of life in them to be as active as that soul was, whose progeny they are; nay, they do preserve, as in a vial, the purest efficacy and extraction of that living intellect that bred them. As good almost kill a man, as kill a good book; who kills a man kills a good reasonable creature, God's image; but he who destroys a good book, kills reason itself—kills the image of God, as it were, in the eye."

Chapter 17 Education, the Science of Relations: We are Educated by Our Intimacies: The Prelude and Præterita

"But who shall parcel out
His intellect by geometric rules,
Split like a province into round and square?
Who knows the individual hour in which
His habits were first sown, even as a seed?
Who that shall point as with a wand and say
'This portion of the river of my mind
Came from yon fountain'? "—Prelude.

I need not again insist upon the nature of our educational tools. We know well that "Education is an atmosphere, a discipline, a life." In other words, we know that parents and teachers should know how to make sensible use of a child's circumstances (atmosphere) to forward his sound education; should train him in the discipline of the habits of the good life; and should nourish his life with ideas, the food upon which personality waxes strong.

Only Three Educational Instruments.—These three we believe to be the only instruments of which we may make lawful use in the upbringing of children; and any short cut we take by trading on their sensibilities emotions, desires, passions, will bring us and our children to grief. The reason is plain; habits, ideas, and circumstances are external, and we may all help each other to get the best that is to be had of these; but we may not meddle directly with the personality of child or man. We may not work upon his vanity, his fears, his love, his emulation, or any thing that is his by very right, anything that goes to make him a person.

Our Limitations.—Most thinking people are in earnest about the bringing up of children; but we are in danger of taking too much upon us, and of not recognising the limitations which confine us to the outworks of personality. Children and grown-up persons are the same, with a difference; and a thoughtful writer has done us good service by carefully tracing the method of our Lord's education of the Twelve.

"Our Lord," says this author, "reverenced whatever the learner had in him of his own, and was tender in fostering this native growth—. . . . Men, in His eyes, were not mere clay in the hands of the potter, matter to be moulded to shape. They were organic beings, each growing from within, with a life of his own—a personal life which was exceedingly precious in His and His Father's eyes—and He would foster this growth so that it might take after the highest type." (Pastor Pastorum, by H. Latham, M.A., page 6.)

We temper Life too much for Children.—I am not sure that we let life and its circumstances have free play about children. We temper the wind too much to the lambs; pain and sin, want and suffering, disease and death—we shield them from the knowledge of these at all hazards. I do not say that we should wantonly expose the tender souls to distress, but that we should recognise that life has a ministry for them also; and that Nature provides them with a subtle screen, like that of its odour to a violet, from damaging shocks. Some of us will not even let children read fairy tales because these bring the ugly facts of life too suddenly before them. It is worth while to consider Wordsworth's experience on this point. Indeed I do not think we make enough use of two such priceless boons to parents and teachers as the educational autobiographies we possess of the two great philosophers, Wordsworth and Ruskin.

Fairy Lore a Screen and Shelter—The former tells us how, no sooner had he gone to school at Hawkshead, than the body of a suicide was recovered from Esthwaite Lake; a ghastly tale, but full of comfort as showing how children are protected from shock. The little boy was there and saw it all

"Yet no soul-debasing fear,
Young as I was, a child not nine years old,
Possessed me, for my inner eye had seen
Such sights before, among the shining streams
Of fairyland, the forests of romance:
Their spirit hallowed the sad spectacle
With decoration of ideal grace;
A dignity, a smoothness, like the works
Of Grecian art, and purest poesy."

It is delightful to know, on the evidence of a child who went through it, that a terrible scene was separated from him by an atmosphere of poetry—a curtain woven of fairy lore by his etherealising imagination.

But we may run no needless risks, and must keep a quiet, matter-of-fact tone in speaking of fire, shipwreck, or any terror. There are children to whom the thought of Joseph in the pit is a nightmare; and many of us elders are unable to endure a ghastly tale in newspaper or novel. All I would urge is a natural treatment of children, and that they be allowed their fair share of life, such as it is; prudence and not panic should rule our conduct towards them.

Spontaneous Living.—The laws of habit are, we know, laws of God, and the forming of good and the hindering of evil habits are among the primary duties of a parent. But it is just as well to be reminded that habits, whether helpful or hindering, only come into play occasionally, while a great deal of spontaneous living is always going on towards which we can do no more than drop in vital ideas as opportunity occurs. All this is old matter, and I must beg the reader to forgive me for reminding him again that our educational instruments remain the same. We may not leave off the attempt to form good habits with tact and care, to suggest fruitful ideas, without too much insistence, and to make wise use of circumstances.

On what does Fulness of Living depend?—What is education after all? An answer lies in the phrase—Education is the Science of Relations. I do not use this phrase, let me say once more, in the

Herbartian sense—that things are related to each other, and we must be careful to pack the right things in together, so that, having got into the brain of a boy, each thing may fasten on its cousins, and together they may make a strong clique or 'apperception mass.' What we are concerned with is the fact that we personally have relations with all that there is in the present, all that there has been in the past, and all that there will be in the future—with all above us and all about us—and that fulness of living, expansion, expression, and serviceableness, for each of us, depend upon how far we apprehend these relationships and how many of them we lay hold of.

George Herbert says something of what I mean

"Man is all symmetry,
Full of proportions, one limb to another,
And all to all the world besides;
Each part may call the farthest brother,
For head with foot hath private amity,
And both with moons and tides. (The italics are mine.)

Every child is heir to an enormous patrimony, heir to all the ages, inheritor of all the present. The question is, what are the formalities (educational, not legal) necessary to put him in possession of that which is his? You perceive the point of view is shifted, and is no longer subjective, but objective, as regards the child.

The Child a Person.—We do not talk about developing his faculties, training his moral nature, guiding his religious feelings, educating him with a view to his social standing or his future calling. The joys of 'child-study' are not for us. We take the child for granted, or rather, we take him as we find him—a person with an enormous number of healthy affinities, embryo attachments; and we think it is our chief business to give him a chance to make the largest possible number of these attachments valid.

An Infant's Self-Education.—An infant comes into the world with a thousand such embryonic feelers, which he sets to work to fix with amazing energy:—

"The Babe,
Nursed in his Mother's arms, who sinks to sleep
Rocked on his Mother's breast; who with his soul
Drinks in the feelings of his Mother's eye!
For him, in one dear Presence, there exists
A virtue which irradiates and exalts
Objects through widest intercourse of sense.
No outcast he, bewildered and depressed:
Along his infant veins are interfused
The gravitation and the filial bond
Of nature that connects him with the world." (The Prelude)

He attaches his being to mother, father, sister, brother, 'nanna,' the man in the street whom he calls 'dada,' cat and dog, spider and fly; earth, air, fire, and water attract him perilously; his eyes covet light and colour, his ears sound, his limbs movement; everything concerns him, and out of everything he gets—

"That calm delight
Which, if I err not, surely must belong
To those first-born affinities that fit
Our new existence to existing things,
And, in our dawn of being, constitute
The bond of union between life and joy."(The Prelude)

He gets also, when left to himself, the real knowledge about each thing which establishes his relation with that particular thing.

Our Part, to remove Obstructions and to give Stimulus.—Later, we step in to educate him. In proportion to the range of living relationships we put in his way, will he have wide and vital interests, fulness of joy in living. In proportion as he is made aware of the laws which rule every relationship, will his life be dutiful and serviceable: as he learns that no relation with persons or with things, animate or inanimate, can be maintained without strenuous effort, will he learn the laws of work and the joys of work. Our part is to remove obstructions and to give stimulus and guidance to the child who is trying to get into touch with the universe of things and thoughts which belongs to him.

Our Error.—Our deadly error is to suppose that we are his showman to the universe; and, not only so, but that there is no community at all between child and universe unless such as we choose to set up. We are the people! and if we choose that a village child's education should be confined to the 'three R's,' why, what right has he to ask for more? If life means for him his Saturday night in the ale-house, surely that is not our fault! If our own boys go through school and college and come out without quickening interests, without links to the things that are worth while, we are not sure that it is our fault either. We resent that they should be called 'muddied oafs' because we know them to be fine fellows. So they are, splendid stuff which has not yet arrived at the making!

Business and Desire.—Quoth Hamlet,—

"Every man hath business and desire."

Doubtless that was true in the spacious days of great Elizabeth; for us, we have business, but have we desire? Are there many keen interests soliciting us outside of our necessary work? Perhaps not, or we should be less enslaved by the vapid joys of Ping-Pong, Patience, Bridge, and their like. The fact is that 'interests' are not to be taken up on the spur of the moment; they spring out of affinities we have found and laid hold of. Or, in the words of an old writer: "In worldly and material things, what is Used is spent; in intellectual and spiritual things, what is not Used is not Had."

Supposing we have realised that we must make provision for the future of our children otherwise than by safe investments, the question remains, how to set about it.

The Setting-up of Dynamic Relations.—We say a child should have what we will call Dynamic Relations with earth and water, must run and leap and dance, must ride and swim. This is how not to do it, as set forth in Præterita:—

"And so on to Lianberis and up Snowdon . . . And if only then my father and mother had seen the real strengths and weaknesses of their little John; if they had given me but a shaggy scrap of a Welsh pony, and left me in charge of a good Welsh guide, and of his wife, if I needed any coddling, they would have made a man of me there and then . . . If only! But they could no more have done it than thrown me like my cousin Charles into Croydon Canal, trusting me to find my way out by the laws of nature. Instead, they took me back to London; my father spared time from his business hours, once or twice a week, to take me to a four-square, sky-lighted, saw-dust floored prison of a riding school in Moorfields, the smell of which, as we turned in at the gate of it, was a terror and horror and abomination to me: and there I was put on big horses that jumped and reared, and circled, and sidled, and fell off them regularly whenever they did any of these things; and was a disgrace to my family, and a burning shame and misery to myself, till at last the riding school was given up on my spraining my right hand fore-finger (it has never come straight again since); and a well-broken Shetland pony bought for me, and the two of us led about the Norwood roads by a riding master with a leading string.

"I used to do pretty well as long as we went straight, and then get thinking of something and fall off as we turned a corner. I might have got some inkling of a seat in heaven's good time, if no fuss had been made about me, nor inquiries instituted whether I had been off or on; but as my mother the moment I got home made searching scrutiny into the day's disgraces, I merely got more nervous and helpless after every tumble; and this branch of my education was at last abandoned, my parents consoling themselves as best they might, in the conclusion that my not being able to learn to ride was the sign of my being a singular genius."

Ruskin's Indictment of the Limitations of His Condition.—Ruskin suffered from the malady of his condition. He was of the suburban dwellers of the rich middle class who think, not wisely but too much, about the bringing up of their children, who choke a good deal of life with care and coddling, and are apt to be persuaded that their children want no outlets but such as it occurs to them to provide. Suburban life is a necessity, but it is also a misfortune, because, in a rich suburb, people live too much with their own sort. They are cut off from the small and the great, from labour, adventure, and privation. Let me recommend all rich educated parents who live in suburbs to read Præterita. With all his chivalrous loyalty to his parents, Ruskin has left here a grave indictment, not of them, but of the limitations of his condition. One hears the cry of the child, like that of Laurence Sterne's caged starling—'I can't get out, I can't get out'—repeated from page to page.

You will say, whatever were the faults of his education, Ruskin emerged from it, such as it was; and we look for no more. But it is not for us to say how much greater an apostle among men even Ruskin would have become had he been allowed his right of free living as a child. And it may be, on the other hand, safe to admit that not every child, born and bred in a villa, will certainly be another Ruskin! We cannot follow Mr. Ruskin further in the setting up of the dynamic relations proper to him, because his parents forbade, and nothing happened. His mother, he says, 'never allowed me to go to the edge of a pond or be in the same field with a pony.' But he notes 'with thankfulness the good I got out of the tadpole-haunted ditch in Croxted Lane.' Camberwell Green had a pond, and, he says, 'it was one of the most valued privileges of my early life to be permitted by my nurse to contemplate this judicial pond with awe from the other side of the way.'

Wordsworth's Recognition of his Opportunities.—Wordsworth tells us of a much more rough-and-tumble bringing up. When he was nine, he was sent to the Grammar School in the little village of Hawkshead and lodged with Dame Tyson in the cottage many of us know; and found most things, at home and abroad, congenial to his soul. He had no lessons in riding and skating, hockey and tennis; but no doubt the other boys made it plain to the little chap that he must do as they did or be thought a fool. But then he went to school a hardy youngster; his mother had let her little boy live:—

"Oh, many a time have I, a five years' child,
In a small mill-race severed from his stream,
Made one long bathing of a summer's day;
Basked in the sun, and plunged, and basked again."

Of his childhood, he says:—

"Fair seed-time had my soul, and I grew up
Fostered alike by beauty and by fear."

Ere he had told ten birthdays, he was transplanted to that 'beloved Vale' of which he says:—

"There were we let loose
For sports of wider range."

What was there those Hawkshead boys did not do! He tells us of times,—

"When I have hung
Above the raven's nest, by knots of grass
And half-inch fissures in the slippery rock
But ill-sustained, and almost (so it seemed)
Suspended by the blast that blew amain,
Shouldering the naked crag."

The boys skated:—

"All shod with steel,
We hissed along the polished ice in games
Confederate, imitative of the chase
And woodland pleasures,—the resounding horn,

The pack loud chiming, and the hunted hare."

They played:—

"From week to week, from month to month, we lived
A round of tumult. Duly were our games
Prolonged in summer till the daylight failed."

They boated:—

"When summer came,
Our pastime was, on bright half-holidays,
To sweep along the plain of Windermere
With rival oars . . .
In such a race
So ended disappointment could be none,
Uneasiness, or pain, or jealousy:
We rested in the shade, all pleased alike,
Conquered and conqueror."

The young Wordsworth, too, had his essays on horseback when he and his schoolmates came back rich from the half-yearly holidays and hired horses from 'the courteous innkeeper,' and off they went, 'proud to curb, and eager to spur on, the galloping steed'; and then, the home-coming:—

"Through the walls we flew
And down the valley, and, a circuit made
In wantonness of heart, through rough and smooth
We scampered homewards."

Chapter 18 We are Educated by Our Intimacies Part II.—Further Affinities

Affinity for Material: Ruskins's Opportunities.—Of the Affinity for Material, the joy of handling and making, Wordsworth says little, but Ruskin sent out feelers in this direction which began with 'two boxes of well-cut wooden bricks' and culminated, perhaps, in the road-making of the Oxford days:—

"I was afterwards," he says, "gifted with a two-arched bridge, admirable in fittings of voussoir and keystone, and adjustment of the level courses of masonry with bevelled edges, into which they dovetailed in the style of Waterloo Bridge. Well-made centrings, and a course of inlaid steps down to the water, made this model largely, as accurately, instructive: and I was never weary of building, un-building—(it was too strong to be thrown down, but had always to be taken down)—and re-building it."

We know how he busied himself with making a small dam and reservoir at both the Herne Hill and Denmark Hill homes; and how, while still a boy, he scrubbed down, with pail of water and broom, the dirty steps of an Alpine hotel, because they offended his mother. We feel that in this direction, again, his nature cried aloud for opportunities.

Intimacy with Natural Objects.—We do not hear much of the intimacy of either boy with Natural Objects, such as birds and flowers; but here, again, we feel that Ruskin was deprived of opportunity. His flower friends were garden dwellers; and could anything be more pathetic than this: "My chief prayer for the kindness of heaven, in its flowerful seasons, was that the frost might not touch the almond blossom." (Students of Love's Meinie and Proserpine will know what rich compensations later life brought for the child's disadvantages.)

Wordsworth appears to have waited for his intimacy with wild-flowers until he could say of his sister Dorothy, "She gave me eyes, she gave me ears." Birds, as we have seen, he knew through the wicked joy of birdsnesting; but not only so, that day when the wild cavalcade rode to Furness Abbey, he marked—

"That simple wren
Which one day sang so sweetly in the nave
Of the old church, that. . .
I could have made
My dwelling-place, and lived for ever there
To hear such music."

Ruskin's Flower Studies.—If Ruskin had not, as a child, a wide acquaintance with the flowers of the field, he made up, perhaps, by the enormous attention he gave to such as came in his way; and, just as his toy bricks and his bridge gave him his initiation in the principles of architecture, so, perhaps, his early flower studies resulted in his power of seeing and expressing detail. He says of flowers: "My whole time passed in staring at them or into them. In no morbid curiosity, but in admiring wonder, I pulled every flower to pieces till I knew all that could be seen of it with a child's eyes; and used to lay up little treasures of seeds, by way of pearls and beads,—never with any thought of sowing them." He complains that books on Botany were harder than the Latin Grammar.

His Pebble Studies.—"Had there been anybody then to teach me anything about plants or pebbles," he says, "it had been good for me." He loved the pebbles of the Tay, and followed up his acquaintance with pebbles at Matlock. "In the glittering white broken spar, speckled with galena, by which the walks of the hotel garden were made bright, and in the slopes of the pretty village, and in many a happy walk along its cliffs, I pursued my mineralogical studies on fluor, calcite, and the ores of lead, and with indescribable rapture when I was allowed to go into a cave."

A Life-shaping Intimacy.—Later we find him going up Snowdon, "of which ascent I remember, as the most exciting event, the finding for the first time in my life a real 'mineral' for myself, a piece of copper pyrites!" This eagerly sought acquaintance with pebbles resulted in the life-shaping intimacy with minerals to which we owe The Ethics of the Dust.

Insatiate Delight in a Book—Ruskin's.—As for Books, we are told how Ruskin grew up upon the Waverley Novels, on Pope's Homer's Iliad, many of Shakespeare's plays, and much else that is delightful; but he does not give us an instance of the sort of thing we are looking for—the sudden keen, insatiate delight in a book which means kinship—until he is introduced to Byron. His first acquaintance with Byron he puts "about the beginning of the teen period ":—

"But very certainly, by the end of this year 1834, I knew my Byron pretty well all through, all but Cain, Werner, the Deformed Transformed, and Vision of Judgment, none of which I could understand, nor did papa and mamma think it would be well I should try to. . . . So far as I could understand it, I rejoiced in all the sarcasm of Don Juan. But my firm decision, as soon as I got well into the later cantos of it, that Byron was to be my master in verse, as Turner in colour, was made of course in that gosling (or say cygnet) epoch of existence, without consciousness of the deeper instincts that prompted it: only two things I consciously recognised, that his truth of observation was the most exact, and his chosen expression the most concentrated, that I had yet found in literature. . . But the thing wholly new and precious to me in Byron was his measured and living truth—measured, as compared with Homer; and living, as compared with everybody else . . . He taught me the meaning of Chillon and of Meillerie, and bade me seek first in Venice—the ruined homes of Foscari and Falieri Byron told me of, and reanimated for me, the real people whose feet had worn the marble I trod on."

Wordsworth's.—This is how Wordsworth took to his books:—

"A precious treasure had I long possessed,
A little yellow canvas-covered book,
A slender abstract of the Arabian tales;
And, from companions in a new abode,
When first I learnt, that this dear prize of mine
Was but a block hewn from a mighty quarry—
That there were four large volumes, laden all
With kindred matter, 'twas to me, in truth,

A promise scarcely earthly
And when thereafter to my father's house
The holidays returned me, there to find
That golden store of books which I had left,
What joy was mine! How often . . .
  have I lain
Down by thy side, O Derwent I murmuring stream,
On the hot stones, and in the glaring sun,
And there have read, devouring as I read,
Defrauding the day's glory, desperate!"

"They must have their Food" of Romance.—Nor can I omit the counsel that follows:—

"A gracious spirit o'er this earth presides,
And o'er the heart of man: invisibly
It comes, to works of unreproved delight,
And tendency benign, directing those
Who care not, know not, think not what they do.
The tales that charm away the wakeful night
In Araby romances; legends penned
For solace by dim light of monkish lamps;
Fictions, for ladies of their love, devised
By youthful squires; adventures endless, spun
By the dismantled warrior in old age,
Out of the bowels of those very schemes
In which his youth did first extravagate;
These spread like day, and something in the shape
Of these will live till man shall he no more.
Dumb yearnings, hidden appetites, are ours,
And they must have their food. Our childhood sits,
Our simple childhood, sits upon a throne
That hath more power than all the elements."

Children must range at will among Books—And this other counsel:—

"Rarely and with reluctance would I stoop
To transitory themes; yet I rejoice,
And, by these thoughts admonished, will pour out
Thanks with uplifted heart, that I was reared
Safe from an evil which these days have laid
Upon the children of the land, a pest
That might have dried me up, body and soul
Where had we been, we two, belovèd Friend:
If in the season of unperilous choice,
In lieu of wandering, as we did, though vales
Rich with indigenous produce, open ground
Of fancy, happy pastures ranged at will,
We had been followed, hourly watched, and noosed
Each in his several melancholy walk."

Words, 'a Passion and a Power.'—Later, follows the story of his first enthralment by poetry:—

"Twice five years
Or less I might have seen, when first my mind
With conscious pleasure opened to the charm
Of words in timeful order, found them sweet
For their own sakes, a passion and a power;
And phrases pleased me chosen for delight,
For pomp, or love. Oft, in the public roads
Yet unfrequented, while the morning light
Was yellowing the hill tops, I went abroad
With a dear friend, and for the better part
Of two delightful hours we strolled along
By the still borders of the misty lake,
Repeating favourite verses with one voice,
Or conning more, as happy as the birds
That round us chaunted.'

Ruskin's Local Historic Sense.—The awakening of the Historic Sense in Ruskin appears to be always, and here is a great lesson for us, connected with places: that historic interest and æsthetic delight are one with him, is another thing to take note of. We have seen how Byron served him in this way. Again, he tells us of the "three centres of my life's thought, Rouen, Geneva, and Pisa, which have been tutoresses of all I know and were mistresses of all I did from the first moments I entered their gates." These came later, but Abbeville "was entrance for me into immediately healthy labour and joy. . . My most intense happinesses have of course been among mountains. But for cheerful, unalloyed, unwearying pleasure, the getting sight of Abbeville on a fine summer afternoon, jumping out in the courtyard of the Hotel de l'Europe and rushing down the street to see St. Wulfran again before the sun was off the towers, are things to cherish the past for—to the end."

Having Touch with the Past necessary.—But Ruskin's want of living touch with the past, except as such touch was given by the newly discovered history of a place he happened to be in, is shown in his first impressions of Rome:—

My stock of Latin learning, with which to begin my studies of the city, consisted of the two first books of Livy, never well known, and the names of places remembered without ever looking where they were on a map; Juvenal, a page or two of Tacitus, and in Virgil the burning of Troy, the story of Dido, the episode of Euryalus, and the last battle. Of course, I had nominally read the whole Aeneid, but thought most of it nonsense. Of later Roman history, I had read English abstracts of the imperial vices, and supposed the malaria in the Campagna to be the consequence of the Papacy. I had never heard of a good Roman Emperor, or a good Pope; was not quite sure whether Trajan lived before Christ or after, and would have thanked, with a sense of relieved satisfaction, anybody who might have told me that Marcus Antoninus was a Roman philosopher contemporary with Socrates . . . We of course drove about the town, and saw the Forum, Coliseum, and so on. I had no distinct idea what the Forum was or ever had been, or how the three pillars, or the seven, were connected with it, or the Arch of Severus. . . What the Forum or Capitol had been, I did not in the least care; the pillars of the Forum I saw were on a small scale, and their capitals rudely carved, and the houses above them nothing like so interesting as the side of any close in the 'auld toun' of Edinburgh."

Wordsworth and Ruskin, aloof from the Past.—Wordsworth, too, stood aloof. He was aware of

"Old, unhappy, far-off things
And battles long ago;"

but the past of nations did not enthral him; even the throes of the French Revolution, to judge by what he tells us in the Prelude, hardly shook him to his foundation, though he took a walking tour on the Continent at the moment when, as he himself says—

"As if awaked from sleep, the nations hailed
Their great expectancy."

But for him—

"I looked upon these things
As from a distance; heard and saw and felt,
Was touched, but with no intimate concern."

Knowledge learned in Schools.—As for the Knowledge learned in Schools, Ruskin gives us rather dry details of his experiences in Euclid, the Latin grammar, and the like, but neither boy appears to have been 'stung with the rapture of a sudden thought' in the course of his lessons, unless Hawkshead Grammar School can take this to itself:—

"Many are our joys
In youth, but oh! what happiness to live
When every hour brings palpable access
Of knowledge, when all knowledge is delight,
And sorrow is not there!"

But the praise of the unfolding of the seasons follows, and I am afraid it is the lore they brought with them that the poet had in his mind's eye.

Comradeship.—We have all been interested in the late Mr. Rhodes's illuminating will, and I suppose most mothers and most masters have pondered the four groups of qualifications for scholarships. In (3) we have 'fellowship,' in (4) 'instincts to lead and take an interest in his schoolmates.' It is well that a talent for Comradeship should be brought before us in this prominent way as a sine quâ non. Here is the rock upon which Ruskin's education split, as he was sadly aware; he never knew the joys of comradeship. Having spoken of 'peace, obedience, faith; these three for chief good; next to these the habit of fixed attention with both eyes and mind,' as the main blessings of his childhood, he goes on to enumerate 'the equally dominant calamities':—

"First, that I had nothing to love. My parents were—in a sort—visible powers of nature to me, no more loved than the sun and the moon: only I should have been annoyed and puzzled if either of them had gone out; (how much, now, when both are darkened!)—still less did I love God; not that I had any quarrel with Him, or fear of Him; but simply found what people told me was His service, disagreeable; and what people told me was His book, not entertaining. I had no companions to quarrel with neither; nobody to assist, and nobody to thank. Not a servant was ever allowed to do anything for me, but what it was their duty to do; and why should I have been grateful to the cook for cooking, or the gardener for gardening? . . . . My present verdict, therefore, on the general tenor of my education at that time, must be, that it was at once too formal and too luxurious; leaving my character at the most important moment for its construction, cramped indeed, but not disciplined; and only by protection innocent, instead of by practice virtuous."

Wordsworth, on the contrary, as we have seen, lived the life of his school-fellows with entire abandon. He was with a crowd of his mates or he was with a friend, and was only alone in those moments of deeper intimacy which we shall speak of presently. The simple life of his 'beloved Vale' took such hold on his tenacious northern nature that not Cambridge, nor London, nor (as we have seen) Europe in its time of convulsion, could displace the earlier images or give new direction to his profoundest thought. Scott laid claim to 'intimacy with all ranks of my countrymen from the Scottish peer to the Scottish ploughman,' and—we get the Waverley Novels. Wordsworth was satisfied to know the fine-natured peasant folk of his own dales, and poet-souls like his own. Perhaps such limitations went to the making of the poet of plain living and high thinking; but limitations are hazardous.

Chapter 19 We are Educated by Our Intimacies Part III.—Vocation

I might trace the consummation of various other affinities in these two illustrious subjects, but space fails; I can only indicate the joy of pursuing the acquaintanceship, followed by the endless occupation for mind and heart, in that high intimacy which we call the Vocation of each of these men of genius.

Turner's Call to Ruskin.—Ruskin's 'career,' to use our own common and expressive figure, began when,—

"On my thirteenth (?) birthday, 8th February 1832, my father's partner, Mr. Henry Telford, gave me Rogers's Italy, and determined the main tenor of my life..... I had no sooner cast my eyes on the Turner vignettes than I took them for my only masters, and set myself to imitate them as far as I possibly could by fine pen shading. . . .

"My father at last gave me, not for a beginning of a Turner collection, but for a specimen of Turner's work, which was all—as it was supposed—I should ever need or aspire to possess, the 'Richmond Bridge, Surrey.'"

Again, anent his purchase of Turner's 'Harlech'

"Whatever germs of better things remained in me, were then all centred in this love of Turner. It was not a piece of painted paper, but a Welsh castle and village, and Snowdon in blue cloud, that I bought for my seventy pounds."

Sincere Work.—Not until he is twenty-two does he produce what he considers his first sincere drawing:—

"One day on the road to Norwood, I noticed a bit of ivy round a thorn stem, which seemed, even to my critical judgment, not 'ill-composed,' and proceeded to make a light and shade pencil study of it in my grey paper pocketbook, carefully, as if it had been a bit of sculpture, liking it more and more as I drew. When it was done, I saw that I had virtually lost all my time since I was twelve years old, because no one had ever told me to draw what was really there!"

Initiation.—Later, follows the story of his true initiation:—

"I took out my book and began to draw a little aspen tree, on the other side of the cart road, carefully. . . . Languidly, but not idly, I began to draw it; and as I drew, the langour passed away, the beautiful lines insisted on being traced, without weariness. More and more beautiful they became as each rose out of the rest and took its place in the air. With wonder increasing every instant, I saw that they composed themselves by finer laws than any known of men. At last the tree was there, and everything that I had thought before about trees nowhere. . .'He hath made everything beautiful in His time' became for me thenceforward the interpretation of the bond the human mind and all visible things."

Nature a Passion.—Let us intrude into the consummation of one more intimacy. Already the boy has made acquaintance with mountains; he is now to have his first sight of the Alps. He, his father, his mother, and his cousin Mary, went out to walk the first Sunday evening after their arrival on the garden terrace of Schaffhausen, and—

"Suddenly—behold—beyond! There was no thought in any of us for a moment of their being clouds. They were clear as crystal, sharp on the pure horizon sky, and already tinged with rose by the setting sun. Infinitely beyond all that we had ever thought or dreamed—the seen walls of lost Eden could not have been more beautiful to us; not more awful, round heaven, the walls of sacred death. It is not possible to imagine, in any time of the world, a more blessed entrance into life, for a child of such temperament as mine."

How shall we venture to trace the growth of that austere, most gracious and enthralling intimacy with Nature which was to Wordsworth the master-light of all his seeing? He unfolds to us—

"The simple ways in which my childhood walked;
Those chiefly that first led me to the love
Of rivers, woods, and fields. The passion yet
Was in its birth, sustained as might befall
By nourishment that came unsought."

We cannot trace every step of the growth of this ethereal passion, but only take a phase of it here and there. The boy and some of his schoolfellows were boating on Windermere in the late evening, and they left one of their number, 'the Minstrel of the Troop,' on a small island:—

"And rowed off gently, while he blew his flute
Alone upon the rock—oh, then, the calm
And dead still water lay upon my mind
Even with a weight of pleasure, and the sky,
Never before so beautiful, sank down
Into my heart, and held me like a dream!
Thus were my sympathies enlarged, and thus
Daily the common range of visible things
Grew dear to me: already I began
To love the sun; a boy, I loved the sun,
Not as I since have loved him, as a pledge
And surety of our earthly life, a light
Which we behold and feel we are alive;
Not for his bounty to so many worlds—
But for this cause, that I had seen him lay
His beauty on the morning hills, had seen
The western mountain touch his setting orb."

The Calling of a Poet.—We may take one more look at this marvellous boy, who, become a man, held that every child, as he, is born a poet:—

"My seventeenth year was come,
. . . I, at this time,
Saw blessings spread around me like a sea.
Thus while the days flew by, and years passed on,
From nature and her overflowing soul
I had received so much, that all my thoughts
Were steeped in feeling; I was only then
Contented, when with bliss ineffable
I felt the sentiment of Being spread
O'er all that moves and all that seemeth still;
O'er all that, lost beyond the reach of thought
And human knowledge, to the human eye
Invisible, yet liveth to the heart;
O'er all that leaps and runs, and shouts and sings,
Or beats the gladsome air; o'er all that glides
Beneath the wave, yea, in the wave itself,
And mighty depth of waters.
. . . If I should fail with grateful voice
To speak of you, ye mountains, and ye lakes
And sounding cataracts, ye mists and winds
That dwell among the hills where I was born.
If in my youth I have been pure in heart,
If, mingling with the world, I am content
With my own modest pleasures, and have lived
With God and nature communing, removed
From little enmities and low desires,
The gift is yours."

The Education of the Little Prig.—Before taking of the Prelude, may I introduce Wordsworth's sketch of the 'child-studied' little prig of his days—days of much searching of heart and of many theories the subject of education?—

"That common sense
May try this common system by its fruits,
Leave let me take to place before her sight
A specimen pourtrayed with faithful band.
Full early trained to worship seemliness,
This model of a child is never known
To mix in quarrels; that were far beneath
Its dignity; with gifts he bubbles o'er
As generous as a fountain; selfishness
May not come near him, nor the little throng
Of flitting pleasures tempt him from his path;
The wandering beggars propagate his name,
Dumb creatures find him tender as a nun,
And natural or supernatural fear,
Unless it leaps upon him in a dream,
Touches him not. To enhance the wonder, see
How arch his notices, how nice his sense
Of the ridiculous; . . . . he can read
The inside of the earth, and spell the stars;
He knows the policies of foreign lands;
Can string you names of districts, cities, towns,
The whole world over, tight as beads of dew
Upon a gossamer thread; he sifts, he weighs;
All things are put to question; he must live
Knowing that he grows wiser every day,
Or else not live at all, and seeing too
Each little drop of wisdom as it falls
Into the dimpling cistern of his heart:
For this unnatural growth the trainer blame,
Pity the tree...
Meanwhile old grandame earth is grieved to find
The playthings, which her love designed for him,
Unthought of: in their woodland beds the flowers
Weep, and the river sides are all forlorn.
Oh! give us once again the wishing-cap
Of Fortunatus, and the invisible coat
Of Jack the Giant-killer, Robin Hood,
And Sabra in the forest with St George!
The child, whose love is here, at least, doth reap
One precious gain, that he forgets himself.'"

Children have Affinities and should have Relations.—I cannot stop here to gather any more of the instruction and edification contained in those two great educational books, The Prelude and Præterita. It is enough for the present if they have shown us in what manner children attach themselves to their proper affinities, given opportunity and liberty. Our part is to drop occasion freely in the way, whether in school or at home. Children should have relations with earth and water, should run and leap, ride and swim, should establish the relation of maker to material in as many kinds as may be; should have dear and intimate relations with persons, through present intercourse, through tale or poem, picture or statue; through flint arrow-head or modern motor-car: beast and bird, herb and tree, they must have familiar acquaintance with. Other peoples and their languages must not be strange to them. Above all they should find that most intimate and highest of all Relationships,—the fulfilment of their being.

This is not a bewildering programme, because, in all these and more directions, children have affinities; and a human being does not fill his place in the universe without putting out tendrils of attachment in the directions proper to him. We must get rid of the notion that to learn the 'three R's' or the Latin grammar well, a child should learn these and nothing else. It is as true for children as for ourselves that, the wider the range of interests, the more intelligent is the apprehension of each.

Education not Desultory.—But I am not preaching a gospel for the indolent and proclaiming that education is a casual and desultory matter. Many great authors have written at least one book devoted to education; and Waverley seems to me to be Scott's special contribution to our science.

Edward Waverley, we are told, 'was permitted in a great measure to learn as he pleased, when he pleased, and what he pleased.' That he did please to learn and that his powers of apprehension were uncommonly quick, would appear to justify this sort of education. But wavering he was allowed to grow up, and 'Waverley' he remained; instability and ineffectiveness marked his course. The manner of his education and its results are thus shortly set forth:—

"Edward would throw himself with spirit upon any classical author of which his preceptor proposed the perusal, make himself master of the style so far as to understand the story, and, if that pleased or interested him, he finished the volume. But It was in vain to attempt fixing his attention on critical distinctions of philology, upon the difference of idiom, the beauty of felicitous expression, or the artificial combinations of syntax. 'I can read and understand a Latin author,' said young Edward, with the self-confidence and rash reasoning of fifteen, 'and Scaliger or Bentley could not do much more.' Alas while he was thus permitted to read only for the gratification of his amusement, he foresaw not that he was losing for ever the opportunity of acquiring habits of firm and assiduous application, of gaining the art of controlling, directing, and concentrating the powers of his mind for earnest investigation—an art far more essential than even that intimate acquaintance with classical learning which is the primary object of study."

Waverley but illustrates, what Mr. Ruskin says in plain words; that our youth—whatever we make of it—abides with us to the end:—

"But so stubborn and chemically inalterable the laws of the prescription were, that now, looking back from 1886 to that brook shore of 1837, whence I could see the whole of my youth, I find myself in nothing whatsoever changed. Some of me is dead, more of me is stronger. I have learned a few things, forgotten many. In the total of me, I am but the same youth, disappointed and rheumatic."

Strenuous Effort and Reverence.—We have seen in Ruskin and Wordsworth the strenuous attention condition of receptiveness—which made each of them a producer after his kind; and whosoever will play the game, whether it be cricket or portrait painting, must learn the rules with all diligence and get skill by his labour. It is true, 'the labour we delight in physics pain,' but it is also true that we cannot catch hold of any one of the affinities that are in waiting for us without strenuous effort and without reverence. A bird-lover, one would say, has chosen for himself an easy joy; but no: your true bird-lover is out of doors by four in the morning to assist at the levée of the birds; nay, is he not in Hyde Park by 2.30 a.m. to see—the kingfisher, no less! He lies in wait in secret places to watch the goings on of the feathered peoples, travels far afield to make a new acquaintance in the bird-world; in fact, gives to the study of birds attention, labour, love, and reverence. He gets joy in return, so is perhaps little conscious of effort; but the effort is made all the same.

Comradeship has Duties.—To take one more instance of an affinity—comradeship. Most of us have serious thoughts about friendship; but we are apt to take comradeship, fellowship, very casually, and to think it is sufficiently maintained if we meet for parties, games, picnics, or what not. Public school boys generally learn better; they know that comradeship means much cheerful give-and-take, chaff, help, unsparing criticism; if need be, the taking or giving of serious reproof; loyalty each to each, plucky and faithful leading, staunch following, truth-speaking; the power to see others put first without chagrin, and to bear advancement without conceit, Here, too, are calls for attention, labour, love and reverence; but, again, labour is swallowed up in delight

The Angel troubles the still Pool—One more point. We are steadfast to the affinities we take hold of, till death do us part, or longer. And here let me say a word as to the 'advantages' (?) which London offers in the way of masters and special classes. I think it is most often the still pool which the angel comes down to trouble: a steady unruffled course of work without so-called advantages lends itself best to that 'troubling' of the angel—the striking upon us of what Coleridge calls 'the Captain Idea,' which initiates a tie of affinity.

The Highest Relationship.—Neither The Prelude nor Præterita lends itself to the study of the highest Relationship, the profoundest Intimacy, which awaits the soul of man. I think I cannot do better than close with an extract from a little book (The Secret of the Presence of God, Masters) which tells the spiritual history of Brother Lawrence, a lay Brother among the barefooted Carmelites, at Paris, in the seventeenth century.

"The first time I saw Brother Lawrence was upon the 3rd of August, 1666. He told me that God had done him a singular favour in his conversion at the age of eighteen. That in the winter, seeing a tree stripped of its leaves, and considering that within a little time the leaves would be renewed, and after that the flower and fruit appear, he received a high view of the Providence and Power of God, which has never since been effaced from his soul. That this view had perfectly set him loose from the world, and kindled in him such a love for God, that he could not tell whether it had increased in about forty years that he had lived since. That he had been footman to M. Fieubert, the treasurer, and that he was a great awkward fellow who broke everything. That he had desired to be received into a monastery, thinking he would there be made to smart for his awkwardness and the faults he should commit, and so he should sacrifice to God his life, with its pleasures: but that God had disappointed him, he having met with nothing but satisfaction in that state. . . . That with him the set times of prayer were not different from other times; that he retired to pray according to the directions of his Superior, but that he did not want such retirement, nor ask for it, because his greatest business did not divert him from God . . . . That the greatest pains or pleasures of this world were not to be compared with what he had experienced of both kinds in a spiritual state; so that he was careful for nothing and feared nothing, desiring but one only thing of God, viz., that he might not offend Him . . . That he had so often experienced the ready succours of Divine Grace upon all occasions, that from the same experience, when he had business to do, he did not think of it beforehand; but when it was time to do it he found in God, as in a clear mirror, all that was fit for him to do. That of late he had acted thus, anticipating care; but before the experience above mentioned he had used it in his affairs. When outward business diverted him a little from the thought of God, a fresh remembrance coming from God invested his soul, and so inflamed and transported him that it was difficult for him to contain himself, that he was more united to God in his outward employments than when he left them for devotion in retirement."

"I want,—am made for,—and must have a God,
Ere I can be aught, do aught;—no mere Name
Want, but the True Thing, with what proves its truth,—
To wit, a relation from that Thing to me
Touching from head to foot—which Touch I feel,
And with it take the rest, this Life of Ours!,'
—Browning.

An Educational Manifesto

"Studies serve for Delight, for Ornament, and for Ability."

Every child has a right of entry to several fields of knowledge.
Every normal child has an appetite for such knowledge.
This appetite or desire for knowledge is a sufficient stimulus for all school work, if the knowledge be fitly given.

There are four means of destroying the desire for knowledge:—

(a) Too many oral lessons, which offer knowledge in a diluted form, and do not leave the child free to deal with it.

(b) Lectures, for which the teacher collects, arranges, and illustrates matter from various sources; these often offer knowledge in too condensed and ready prepared a form.

(c) Text-books compressed and recompressed from the big book of the big man.

(d) The use of emulation and ambition as incentives to learning in place of the adequate desire for, and delight in, knowledge.

Children can be most fitly educated on Things and Books. Things, e.g.—

i. Natural obstacles for physical contention, climbing, swimming, walking, etc.
ii. Material to work in—wood, leather, clay, etc.
iii. Natural objects in situ—birds, plants, streams, stones, etc,
iv. Objects of art.
v. Scientific apparatus, etc.

The value of this education by Things is receiving wide recognition, but intellectual education to be derived from Books is still for the most part to seek.

Every scholar of six years old and upwards should study with 'delight' his own, living, books on every subject in a pretty wide curriculum. children between six and eight must for the most part have their books read to them.

This plan has been tried with happy results for the last twelve years in many home schoolrooms, and some other schools.

By means of the free use of books the mechanical difficulties of education—reading, spelling, composition, etc.—disappear, and studies prove themselves to be 'for delight, for ornament, and for ability.'

There is reason to believe that these principles are workable in all schools, Elementary and Secondary; that they tend in the working to simplification, economy, and discipline.

Chapter 20 Suggestions Toward a Curriculum

(For children under 14)

Part 1

Summary of Preceding Chapters.—I have left the consideration of a curriculum, which is, practically, the subject of this volume, till the final chapters; because a curriculum is not an independent product, but is linked to much else by chains of cause and consequence. The fundamental principles of docility and authority have been considered in the first place because they are fundamental; but, for that very reason, they should be present but not in evidence; we do not expose the foundations of our house. Not only so, but these principles must be conditioned by respect for the personality of children; and, in order to give children room for free development on the lines proper to them, it is well that parents and teachers should adopt an attitude of masterly inactivity.

Having considered the relations of teachers and taught, I have touched upon those between education and current thought. Education should be in the flow, as it were, and not shut up in a watertight compartment. Perhaps reverence for personality as such, a sense of the solidarity of the race, and a profound consciousness of evolutionary progress, are among the elements of current thought which should help us towards an educational ideal.

In considering the training of children under the convenient divisions of physical, mental, moral, and religious, I have not thought it necessary to give counsels upon matters of common knowledge and general acceptance, but have dwelt upon aspects of training under each heading which are rather likely to be overlooked. Under the phrase 'Education is a life,' I have tried to show how necessary it is to sustain the intellectual life upon ideas, and, as a corollary, that a school-book should be a medium for ideas and not merely a receptacle for facts. That normal children have a natural desire for, and a right of admission to, all knowledge, appears to me to be covered by the phrase, 'Education is the science of relations.'

These considerations clear the ground for the consideration of a curriculum, which occupies the remaining chapters; these are, in fact, a summary of what has gone before; and therefore I beg the reader's patience with such repetitions as seem to me necessary in bringing the argument to a point.

Some Preliminary Considerations.—As the following suggestions have been worked out in connection with the Parents' National Educational Union, it may perhaps be desirable to repeat here that the first effort of this society, continued through ten years of its existence, was to impress upon its members the definition of Education contained in our motto, 'Education is an Atmosphere, a Discipline, a Life.' By this we mean that parents and teachers should know how to make sensible use of a child's circumstances (atmosphere), should train him in habits of good living (discipline), and should nourish his mind with ideas, the food of the intellectual life. These three we believe to be the only instruments of which we may make lawful use in bringing up children. An easier way may be found by trading on their sensibilities, emotions, desires, passions; but the result must be disastrous. And for this reason, that bits, ideas, and circumstances are external, and we may help each other to get the best that is to be had of them; we may not, however, meddle directly with personality of child or man; we may not work upon his vanity, his fears, his love, his emulation, or anything that goes to make him a person. Most people are in earnest about the bringing up of children; but we are in danger of taking too much upon us, and of not recognising the limitations which confine us to the outworks of personality.

A Definite Aim.—The Parents' Union, having devoted as I have said, ten years of its existence to learning how to use the three instruments of education (circumstances, habits, and ideas), took a new departure some few years ago, and asked what should be the end in view as the result of a wise use of due means. What is education? The answer we accept is that Education is the Science of Relations.

We do not use this phrase in the Herbartian sense, that things or thoughts are related to each other and that teachers must be careful to pack the right things, in together, so that, having got into the pupil's brain, each may fasten on its kind, and, together, make a strong clique or apperception mass.

What concerns us personally is the fact that we have relations with what there is in the present and with what there has been in the past, with what is above us, and about us; and that fulness of living and serviceableness depend for each of us upon how far we apprehend these relationships and how many of them we lay hold of. Every child is heir to an enormous patrimony. The question is, what are the formalities necessary to put him in possession of that which is his?

Education Objective, not Subjective—The point of view is shifted; it is no longer subjective as regards the child, but objective. We do not talk about developing his faculties, training his moral nature, guiding his religious feelings, educating him with a view to his social standing or his future calling. We take the child as we find him, a person with many healthy affinities and embryonic attachments, and we try to give him a chance to make the largest possible number of these attachments valid.

An infant comes into the world with a thousand feelers which he at once begins to fix with great energy; and out of everything about him he gets—

"That calm delight which, if I err not, surely must belong,
To those first-born affinities that fit
Our new existence to existing things,
And in our dawn of being, constitute
The bond of union between life and joy."
(The Prelude)

He gets also when left to himself that real knowledge about each thing he comes across which establishes his relations with that thing. Later, we step in to educate him. In proportion to the range of living relationships we put in his way will he have wide and vital interests and joy in living. His life will be dutiful and serviceable if he is made aware of the laws which rule each relationship; he will learn the laws of work and the joys of work as he perceives that no relation with persons or with things can be kept up without effort.

Our part is to remove obstructions, to give stimulus and guidance to the child who is trying to get into touch with the universe of things and thoughts. Our error is to suppose that we must act as his showman to the universe, and that there is no community between child and universe except such as we choose to set up.

Interests—Have we many keen Interests soliciting us outside of our necessary work? If we have, we shall not be enslaved by vapid joys.

Interests are not to be taken up on the spur of the moment; they spring out of the affinities which we have found and laid hold of: And the object of education is, I take it, to give children the use of as much of the world as may be.

Influenced by such considerations as these, the phrase, 'Education is the Science of Relations,' gives us the advantage of a definite aim in our work.

Educational Unrest.—We have been made familiar with the phrase 'educational unrest,' and we all feel its fitness. Never were there more able and devoted teachers, whether as the heads or on the staffs of schools of all classes. Money, labour, and research are freely spent on education, theory is widely studied, and pains are taken to learn what is done elsewhere; yet there is something amiss beyond that 'divine discontent' which leads to effort. We know that a change of front is necessary; and we are rea*dy, provided that the change be something more than an experiment. Headmasters and mistresses are, I believe, amongst the persons most ready to fall in with a sound reform; but, because these are persons with wide experience and highly-trained intellects, they are unwilling to launch changes which have not a philosophic basis as well as a utilitarian end.

A Unifying Principle.—Hitherto we, of the Parents' Union, have pressed on the public rather our views on home-training than those on school-teaching, but this is because we have been unwilling to disturb the existing order. We have, however, during the last twelve years worked out in our training college and school a unifying principle and adequate methods with happy results. We exist because we have a definite aim, and to carry out that aim. I need not now speak of the few principles which form a guide to us in the upbringing of children; but that principle which guides us in what is commonly called education—the teaching of knowledge—may be found to indicate the cause of many educational failures and may point the way to reform.

Education should give Knowledge touched with Emotion.—To adapt a phrase of Matthew Arnold's concerning religion,—education should aim at giving knowledge 'touched with emotion.' I have already quoted the charming episode in Frederika Bremer's Neighbours, where two school-girls fight a duel on behalf of their heroes—Charles XII. and Peter the Great. Parents maybe glad that we have no girl-duels to-day! The school-girl does not care for heroes, she cares for marks. Knowledge for her is not 'touched with emotion,' unless it be those of personal acquisitiveness and emulation. The boys and girls have it in them to be generous and enthusiastic; that they leave school without interests, beyond that of preparing for further examinations or the absorbing interest of games, is no doubt the fault of the schools. Perhaps the 'unrest' of the public mind at home and abroad about secondary education is due to the fact that young people are turned out from excellent schools devitalised so far as their minds go. No 'large draughts of intellectual day' have been offered to their thirst; and yet the thirst was there to begin with.

Mr. Benson ("The Schoolmaster," by H. C. Benson, of Eton College.—Nineteenth Century, December 1902.) speaks very frankly. He says: "I honestly believe that the masters of public schools have two strong ambitions—to make boys good and to make them healthy; but I do not think they care about making them intellectual: intellectual life is left to take care of itself. My belief is that a great many masters look upon the boys' work as a question of duty—that is, they consider it from the moral standpoint and not from the intellectual. . .It must frankly admitted that the intellectual standard maintained at the English public schools is low; and, what is more serious, I do not see any evidence that it is tending to become higher."

Professor Sadler, with a perhaps wider outlook, says, practically, the same thing—our secondary schools have capital points, but intellectually they are behindhand, compared even with those of some continental nations. Mr. Benson speaks no doubt from personal knowledge; but is it a fact that so intellectual a body as our headmasters deliberately forego intellectual distinction in their schools? Or is it not rather that examinations throw them back on the pseudo-intellectual work known as 'cram'? It is because cram is deadening that some of us deprecate the registration of teachers as a backward movement. Hundreds of mediocre young women set themselves to cram for a course of examinations, often a long course, to end at last in registration; and already headmistresses feel the evil and inquire diligently for assistants who are 'not the usual sort.' Women are apt to be over-strenuous and over-conscientious, and the strain of moral effort carried on through years of preparation for successive examinations often leaves a certain dulness of apprehension. There are brilliant exceptions, but the average young woman who has undergone such an experience has little initiative, is slow of perception, not readily adaptable, not quick in the uptake; is, in fact, a little devitalised. I speak of moral effort, because the labour of preparing for examinations, of going through steady long-sustained grind, is apt to be rather a moral than an intellectual effort. With young men it is otherwise; they are commonly less strenuous, less absorbed, and therefore, perhaps, more receptive to the ideas that beset the way of their studies.

Education is the Science of Relations.—The idea that vivifies teaching in the Parents' Union is that Education is the Science of Relations; by which phrase we mean that children come into the world with a natural 'appetency,' to use Coleridge's word, for, and affinity with, all the material of knowledge; for interest in the heroic past and in the age of myths; for a desire to know about everything that moves and lives, about strange places and strange peoples; for a wish to handle material and to make; a desire to run and ride and row and do whatever the law of gravitation permits. Therefore we do not feel it is lawful in the early days of a child's life to select certain subjects for his education to the exclusion of others; to say he shall not learn Latin, for example, or shall not learn Science; but we endeavour that he shall have relations of pleasure and intimacy established with as many as possible of the interests proper to him; not learning a slight or incomplete smattering about this or that subject, but plunging into vital knowledge, with a great field before him which in all his life he will not be able to explore. In this conception we get that 'touch of emotion' which vivifies knowledge, for it is probable that we feel only as we are brought into our proper vital relations.

Is there such a thing as the 'Child-Mind'?—We get courage to attack so wide a programme through a few working ideas or principles: one of these is, there is no such thing as the 'child-mind'; we believe that the ignorance of children is illimitable, but that, on the other hand, their intelligence is hardly to be reckoned with by our slower wits. In practical working we find this idea a great power; the teachers do not talk down to the children; they are careful not to explain every word that is used, or to ascertain if children understand every detail. As a girl of twelve or so the writer browsed a good deal on Cowper's poems and somehow took an interest in Mrs. Montague's Feather Hangings. Only the other day did the ball to fit that socket arrive in the shape of an article in The Quarterly on 'The Queen of the Bluestockings.' Behold, there was Mrs. Montague with her feather hangings! The pleasure of meeting with her after all these years was extraordinary; for in no way is knowledge more enriching than in this of leaving behind it a, so to speak, dormant appetite for more of the kind. The recent finds at Knossos are only to be appreciated by those who recollect how Ulysses told Penelope about Crete with its ninety cities, and Knossos, and King Minos. Not what we have learned, but what we are waiting to know is the delectable part of knowledge. Nor should knowledge be peptonised or diluted, but offered to the children with some substance in it and some vitality. We find that children can cover a large and various field with delight and intelligence in the time that is usually wasted over 'the three R's,' object-lessons, and other much-diluted matter in which the teaching is more than the knowledge.

Knowledge versus Information.—The distinction between knowledge and information is, I think, fundamental. Information is the record of facts, experiences, appearances, etc., whether in books or in the verbal memory of the individual; knowledge, it seems to me, implies the result of the voluntary and delightful action of the mind upon the material presented to it. Great minds, a Darwin or a Plato, are able to deal at first hand with appearances or experiences; the ordinary mind gets a little of its knowledge by such direct dealing, but for the most part it is set in action by the vivifying knowledge of others, which is at the same time a stimulus and a point of departure. The information acquired in the course of education is only by chance, and here and there, of practical value. Knowledge, on the other hand, that is, the product of the vital action of the mind on the material presented to it, is power; as it implies an increase of intellectual aptitude in new directions, and an always new point of departure.

Perhaps the chief function of a teacher is to distinguish information from knowledge in the acquisitions of his pupils. Because knowledge is power, the child who has got knowledge will certainly show power in dealing with it. He will recast, condense, illustrate, or narrate with vividness and with freedom the arrangement of his words. The child who has got only information will write and speak in the stereotyped phrases of his text-book, or will mangle in his notes the words of his teacher.

Children have a Natural Craving for Knowledge.—It is the easier for us to deal in this direct fashion with knowledge because we are not embarrassed by the necessity of cultivating faculties; for working purposes the so-called faculties are sufficiently described as mind; and the normal mind is, we find, as able to deal with knowledge as are the normal digestive organs with food. Our concern is give a child such knowledge as shall open up for him as large a share as may be of the world he lives for his use and enjoyment. As there are gymnastics for the body, so for the mind there are certain subjects whose use is chiefly disciplinary, and of these we avail ourselves. Again, as our various organs labour without our consciousness in the assimilation food, so judgment, imagination, and what not, deal their own accord with knowledge, that it may be incorporated, which is not the same thing as 'remembered.' A further analogy—as the digestive organs are incited by appetite, so children come into the world with a few inherent desires, some with more, some less, to incite them to their proper activities. These are, roughly speaking, the desire for power, for praise, for wealth, for distinction, for society, and for knowledge.

It seems to me that education, which appeals to the desire for wealth (marks, prizes, scholarships, or the like), or to the desire of excelling (as in the taking of places, etc.), or to any other of the natural desires, except that for knowledge, destroys the balance of character; and, what is even more fatal, destroys by inanition that desire for and delight in knowledge which is meant for our joy and enrichment through the whole of life. "A desire for knowledge," says Dr. Johnson, "is the natural feeling of mankind, and every human being whose mind is not debauched will be willing to give all that he has to get knowledge." Is it possible that what has been called 'mark-hunger' is a debauchery of the mind? The undebauched mind takes knowledge with avidity; and we find their studies are so interesting to children that they need no other stimulus.

Children must be Educated on Books.—A corollary of the principle that education is the science of relations, is, that no education seems to be worth the name which has not made children at home in the world of books, and so related them, mind to mind, with thinkers who have dealt with knowledge. We reject epitomes, compilations, and their like, and put into children's hands books which, long or short, are living. Thus it becomes a large part of the teacher's work to help children to deal with their books; so that the oral lesson and lecture are but small matters in education, and are used chiefly to summarise or to expand or illustrate.

Too much faith is commonly placed in oral lessons and lectures; "to be poured into like a bucket," as says Carlyle, "is not exhilarating to any soul"; neither is it exhilarating to have every difficulty explained to weariness, or to have the explanation teased out of one by questions. "I will not be put to the question. Don't you consider, sir, that these are not the manners of a gentleman? I will not be baited with what and why; what is this? what is that? why is a cow's tail long? why is a fox's tail bushy?" said Dr Johnson. This is what children think, though they say nothing. Oral lessons have their occasional use, and when they are fitly given it is the children who ask the questions. Perhaps it is not wholesome or quite honest for a teacher to pose as a source of all knowledge and to give 'lovely' lessons. Such lessons are titillating for the moment, but they give children the minimum of mental labour, and the result is much the same as that left on older persons by the reading of a magazine. We find, on the other hand, that in working through a considerable book, which may take two or three years to master, the interest of boys and girls is well sustained to the end; they develop an intelligent curiosity as to causes and consequences, and are in fact educating themselves.

Chapter 21 Suggestions Toward a Curriculum

(For Children under Twelve)

Part II.—School-Books

Books that supply the Sustenance of Ideas.—Mr. H. G. Wells has put his finger on the place when he says that the selection of the right schoolbooks is a great function of the educator. I am not at all sure that his remedy is the right one—or that a body of experts and a hundred thousand pounds would, in truth, provide the manner of schoolbooks that reach children. They are kittle cattle, and, though they will plod on obediently over any of the hundreds of dry-as-dust volumes issued by the publishers under the heading of 'School Books,' or of 'Education,' they keep all such books in the outer court, and allow them no access to their minds. A book may be long or short, old or new, easy or hard, written by a great man or a lesser man, and yet be the living book which finds its way to the mind of a young reader. The expert is not the person to choose; the children themselves are the experts in this case. A single page will elicit a verdict; but the unhappy thing is, this verdict is not betrayed; it is acted upon in the opening or closing of the door of the mind. Many excellent and admirable school- books appreciated by masters are on the Index Expurgatorius of the school-boy; and that is why he takes nothing in and gives nothing out. The master must have it in him to distinguish between twaddle and simplicity, and between vivacity and life. For the rest, he must experiment or test the experiments of others, being assured of one thing—that a book serves the ends of education only as it is vital. But this subject has been treated at some length in an earlier chapter.

Books and Oral Teaching.—Having found the right book, let the master give the book the lead and be content himself with a second place. The lecture must be subordinated to the book. The business of the teacher is to put his class in the right attitude towards their book by a word or two of his own interest in the matter contained, of his own delight in the manner of the author. But boys get knowledge only as they dig for it. Labour prepares the way for assimilation, that mental process which converts information into knowledge; and the effort of taking in the sequence of thought of his author is worth to the boy a great deal of oral teaching.

Do teachers always realise the paralysing and stupefying effect that a flood of talk has upon the mind? The inspired talk of an orator no doubt wakens a response and is listened to with tense attention; but few of us claim to be inspired, and we are sometimes aware of the difficulty of holding the attention of a class. We blame ourselves, whereas the blame lies in the instrument we employ—the more or less diluted oral lesson or lecture, in place of the living and arresting book. We cannot do without the oral lesson—to introduce, to illustrate, to amplify, to sum up. My stipulation is that oral lessons should be few and far between, and that the child who has to walk through life,—and has to find his intellectual life in books or go without,—shall not be first taught to go upon crutches.

The Use of Appliances.—For the same reason, that is, that we may not paralyse the mental vigour of children, we are very chary in the use of appliances (except such as the microscope, telescope, magic lantern, etc.). I once heard a schoolmaster, who had a school in a shipbuilding town, say that he had demanded and got from his committee a complete sectional model of a man-of-war. Such a model would be of use to his boys when they begin to work in the Yards, but during their school years I believe the effect would be stultifying, because the mind is not able to conceive with an elaborate model as basis. I recently visited M. Bloch's admirable 'Peace and War' show at Lucerne. Torpedoes were very fully illustrated by models, sectional diagrams, and what not, but I was not enlightened. I asked my neighbour at dinner to explain the principle; he took up his spectacle case as an illustration, and after a few sentences my intelligence had grasped what was distinctive in a torpedo. This gentleman turned out to have been in the War Office and to have had much concern with torpedoes. The power in the teacher of illustrating by inkpot and ruler or any object at hand, or by a few lines on the blackboard, appears to me to be of more use than the most elaborate equipment of models and diagrams; these things stale on the senses and produce a torpor of thought the moment they are presented.

The Co-ordination of Studies.—Another point, the co-ordination of studies is carefully regulated without any reference to the clash of ideas on the threshold or their combination into apperception masses; but solely with reference to the natural and inevitable co-ordination of certain subjects. Thus, in readings on the period of the Armada, we should not devote the contemporary arithmetic lessons to calculations as to the amount of food necessary to sustain the Spanish fleet, because this is an arbitrary and not an inherent connection; but we should read such history, travels, and literature as would make the Spanish Armada live in the mind.

Our Aim in Education.—Our aim in education is to give children vital interests in as many directions as possible—to set their feet in a large room—because the crying evil of the day is, it seems to me, intellectual inanition.

Believing that he is in the world to lay hold of all he can of those possessions which endure; that full, happy living, expansion, expression, resourcefulness, power of initiative, serviceableness—in a word, character, for him, depends upon how far he apprehends the relationships proper to him and how many of them he seizes, we should be gravely uneasy when his education leaves a young person with prejudices and caring for 'events' (in the sporting sense) rather than with interests and pursuits. Principles, we believe, the best of our young people have and bring away from their schools fully as much as from their homes. Our educational shortcomings seem to be intellectual rather than moral.

Education by Things.—Education should be by Things and by Books. Ten years ago education by Things was little thought of except in the games of public schools. To-day, a great reform has taken place, and the worth of education by Things is recognised everywhere. Disciplinary exercises, artistic handicrafts, are seen to make for education as truly as do geography and Latin. 'Nature study' has come in later, but has come with a rush. If that Sikh quoted by Cornelia Sorabji (Spectator, 2nd August 1902) should visit us again ten years hence, it is to be hoped he would not then say of us, "The very thoughts of the people are merchandise; they have not learned the common language of Nature." The teaching of Science is receiving enormous attention; and the importance of education in this kind need not be enforced here. Works of art are, here and there, allowed their chance with boys and girls, and we shall look more and more to this means of education. What everyone knows it is unnecessary to repeat; and such general attention is given to education by Things, and this is carried on so far on right lines, that I have nothing to add to the general knowledge of this subject.

Education by Books.—The great educational failure we have still to deal with is in the matter of Books. We know that Books store the knowledge and thought of the world; but the mass of knowledge, the multitude of books, overpower us, and we think we may select here and there, from this book and that, fragments and facts of knowledge, to be dealt out, whether in the little cram book or the oral lesson.

Sir Philip Magnus, in a recent address on Headwork and Handwork in Elementary Schools, says some things worth pondering. Perhaps he gives his workshop too big a place in the school of the future, but certainly he puts his finger on the weak point in the work of both elementary and secondary schools—the 'getting by heart scraps of knowledge, fragments of so-called science.' And we are with him in the emphasis he lays upon reading and writing; it is through these that even school 'studies' shall become 'for delight.' Writing, of course, comes of reading, and nobody can write well who does not read much. Sir Philip Magnus says, (Education, 16th April 1903) speaking of the schools of the future:—"We shall no longer require children to learn by constant repetition, scraps of history, geography, and grammar, nor try to teach them fragments of so-called science. The daily hours devoted to these tasks will be applicable to the creation of mental aptitudes, and will be utilised in showing the children how to obtain knowledge for themselves . . . In future the main function of education will be to train our hands and our sense organs and intellectual faculties, so that we may be placed in a position of advantage for seeking knowledge. . . The scope of the lessons will be enlarged. Children will be taught to read in order that they may desire to read, and to write that they may be able to write. It will be the teacher's aim to create in his pupils a desire for knowledge, and consequently a love of reading, and to cultivate in them, by a proper selection of lessons, the pleasure which reading may be made to yield. The main feature of the reading lesson will be to show the use books, how they may be consulted to ascertain what other people have said or done, and how they be read for the pleasure they afford. The storing of the memory with facts is no part of elementary school work. . . It is not enough that a child should learn how to write, he must know what to write. He must learn to describe clearly what he has heard or seen, to transfer to written language his sense-impressions, and to express concisely his own thoughts."

We should like to add a word to Sir Philip Magnus's conception, emphasising the habit of reading as a chief acquirement of school life. It is only those who have read who do read.

The Question of a Curriculum.—In regard to a curriculum, may I enforce what I have said in an earlier chapter? Perhaps the main part of a child's education should be concerned with the great human relationships. History, literature, art, languages (whether ancient or modern), travel—all of these are the record or expression of persons; so is science, so far as it is the history of discoveries, the record of observations, that is, so far as it is to be got out of books. Essentially, however, science falls under the head of Education by Things, and is too large a subject to be dealt with, by the way. Before all these ranks Religion, including our relations of worship, loyalty, love and service to God; and next in order, perhaps, the intimate interpersonal relations implied in such terms as self-knowledge, self-control. Knowledge in these several kinds is due to children; for there seems reason to believe that the limit to human intelligence coincides with the limit to human interests; that is, that a normal person of poor and narrow intelligence is so because the interests proper to him have not been called into play. The curriculum which should give children their due falls into some six or eight groups—Religion, Philosophy (?), History, Languages, Mathematics, Science, Art, Physical Exercises, and Manual Crafts.

Religion.—For Religion it is, no doubt, to the Bible itself we must go, as the great storehouse of spiritual truth and moral impressions. A child might, in fact, receive a liberal education from the Bible alone, for The Book contains within itself a great literature.

There was a time when 'National Schools' brought up their scholars on one of the three great bodies of ancient classical literature which the Western world possesses, and which we include under the one name, Bible; and, perhaps, there has been some falling off both in national intelligence and character since the Bible has been practically deposed for the miscellaneous 'Reader.' It is not possible or desirable to revert to old ways in this matter; but we should see to it that children derive as much intellectual, as well as moral and religious, nutriment from books as they did when their studies ranged from the story of Joseph to the Epistles of St Paul.

History.—In History, boys and girls of twelve to fourteen should have a fairly intimate knowledge of English history, of contemporary French history, and of Greek and Roman history—the last, by way of biography;—perhaps nothing outside of the Bible has the educational value of Plutarch's Lives. The wasteful mistake often made in teaching English history is to carry children of; say, between nine and fourteen through several small compendiums, beginning with Little Arthur; whereas their intelligence between those ages is equal to steady work on one considerable book.

Language.—In Language, by twelve, they should have a fair knowledge of English grammar, and should have read some literature. They should have more or less power in speaking and understanding French, and should be able to read a fairly easy French book; the same with German, but considerably less progress; and in Latin, they should be reading 'Fables,' if not 'Caesar,' and perhaps 'Virgil.'

Mathematics.—I need not touch upon the subject of Mathematics. It is receiving ample attention, and is rapidly becoming an instrument for living teaching in our schools.

'Practical Instruction.'—To turn to the question of practical instruction, under the heads of 'Science, Drawing, Manual and Physical Training,' etc., I can do no more here than repeat our convictions. We believe that education under these four heads is due to every child of whatever class; and, for boys and girls under twelve, probably the same general curriculum would be suitable for all. I have nothing to add to the sound ideas as to the teaching of each of these subjects which are now common property.

Science.—In Science, or rather, nature study, we attach great importance to recognition, believing that the power to recognise and name a plant or stone or constellation involves classification and includes a good deal of knowledge. To know a plant by its gesture and habitat, its time and its way of flowering and fruiting; a bird by its flight and song and its times of coming and going; to know when, year after year, you may come upon the redstart and the pied fly-catcher, means a good deal of interested observation, and of; at any rate, the material for science. The children keep a dated record of what they see in their nature note-books, which are left to their own management and are not corrected. These note-books are a source of pride and joy, and are freely illustrated by drawings (brushwork) of twig, flower, insect, etc. The knowledge necessary for these records is not given in the way of teaching. On one afternoon in the week, the children (of the Practising School) go for a 'nature walk' with their teachers. They notice for themselves, and the teacher gives a name or other information as it is asked for, and it is surprising what a range of knowledge a child of nine or ten acquires. The teachers are careful not to make these nature walks an opportunity for scientific instruction, as we wish the children's attention to be given to observation with very little direction. In this way they lay up that store of 'common information' which Huxley considered should precede science teaching; and, what is much more important, they learn to know and delight in natural objects as in the familiar faces of friends. The nature-walk should not be made the occasion to impart a sort of Tit-Bits miscellany of scientific information. The study of science should be pursued in an ordered sequence, which is not possible or desirable in a walk. It seems to me a sine quâ non of a living education that all school children of whatever grade should have one half-day in the week, throughout the year, in the fields. There are few towns where country of some sort is not accessible, and every child should have the opportunity of watching from week to week, the procession of the seasons.

Geography, geology, the course of the sun, the behaviour of the clouds, weather signs, all that the 'open' has to offer, are made use of in these walks; but all is incidental, easy, and things are noticed as they occur. It is probable that in most neighbourhoods there are naturalists who would be willing to give their help in the 'nature walks' of a given school.

We supplement this direct 'nature walk' by occasional object-lessons, as, on the hairs of plants, on diversity of wings, on the sorts of matters taken up in Professor Miall's capital books; but our main dependence is on books as an adjunct to out-of-door work—Mrs. Fisher's, Mrs. Brightwen's, Professor Lloyd Morgan's, Professor Geikie's, Professors Geddes' and Thomson's (the two last for children over fourteen), etc., etc. In the books of these and some other authors the children are put in the position of the original observer of biological and other phenomena. They learn what to observe, and make discoveries for themselves, original so far as they are concerned. They are put in the right attitude of mind for scientific observations and deductions, and their keen interest is awakened. We are extremely careful not to burden the verbal memory with scientific nomenclature. Children learn of pollen, antennae, and what not, incidentally, when the thing is present and they require a name for it. The children who are curious about it, and they only, should have the opportunity of seeing with the microscope any minute wonder of structure that has come up in their reading or their walks; but a good lens is a capital and almost an indispensable companion in field work. I think there is danger in giving too prominent a place to education by Things, enormous as is its value; a certain want of atmosphere is apt to result, and a deplorable absence of a standard of comparison and of the principle of veneration. 'We are the people!' seems to be the note of an education which is not largely sustained on books as well as on things.

Drawing.—In pictorial art we eschew mechanical aids such as chequers, lines of direction, etc., nor do we use the blacklead pencil, which lends itself rather to the copying of linear work than to the free rendering of objects. The children work always from the round, whether in charcoal or brushwork. They produce, also, illustrations of tales or poems, which leave much to seek in the matter of drawing, and are of little value as art instruction, but are useful imaginative exercises.

Picture Talks.—We attach a good deal of value to what we call picture talks, that is:—a reproduction of a suitable picture, by Millet, for example, is put into the children's hands, and they study it by themselves. Then, children of from six to nine describe the picture, giving all the details and showing by a few lines on the blackboard where is such a tree or such a house; judging if they can the time of day; discovering the story if there be one. The older children add to this some study of the lines of composition, light and shade, the particular style of the master; and reproduce from memory certain details. The object of these lessons is that the pupils should learn how to appreciate rather than how to produce.

But there is no space for further details of a curriculum which is more fully illustrated in an appendix.

Chapter 22 Suggestions Toward a Curriculum

(For Children under Twelve)

Part III.—The Love of Knowledge

The Use of Books makes for Short Hours.—Considering that under the head of 'Education by Books' some half-dozen groups of subjects are included, with several subjects in each group, the practical teacher will be inclined to laugh at what will seem to him Education in Utopia. In practice, however, we find that the use of books makes for short hours. No book-work or writing, no preparation or report, is done in the Parents' Review School, except between the hours of 9 and 11.30 for the lowest class, to 9 and 1 for the highest, with half an hour's interval for drill, etc.

From one to two hours, according to age and class, are given in the afternoons to handicrafts, field-work, drawing, etc.; and the evenings are absolutely free, so that the children have leisure for hobbies, family reading, and the like. We are able to get through a greater variety of subjects, and through more work in each subject, in a shorter time than is usually allowed, because children taught in this way get the habit of close attention and are carried on by steady interest.

'Utilitarian' Education.—I should be inclined to say of education, as Mr. Lecky says of morals, that "the Utilitarian theory is profoundly immoral." To educate children for any immediate end—towards commercial or manufacturing aptitude, for example—is to put a premium upon general ignorance with a view to such special aptitude. The greater includes the less, but the less does not include the greater. Excellent work of whatever kind is produced by a person of character and intelligence, and we who teach cannot do better for the nation than to prepare such persons for its uses. He who has intelligent relations with life will produce good work.

Relations and Interests.—I have throughout spoken of 'Relations,' and not of 'Interests,' because interests may be casual, unworthy, and passing. Everyone, even the most ignorant, has interests of a sort; while to make valid any one relation, implies that knowledge has begun in, at any rate, that one direction. But the defect in our educational thought is that we have ceased to realise that knowledge is vital; and, as children and adults, we suffer from underfed minds. This intellectual inanition is, no doubt, partly due to the fact that educational theorists systematically depreciate knowledge. Such theorists are, I think, inclined to attach more importance to the working of the intellectual machinery than to the output of the product; that is, they feel it to be more important that a child should think than that he should know. My contention is rather that he cannot know without having thought; and also that he cannot think without an abundant, varied, and regular supply of the material of knowledge. We all know how the reading of a passage may stimulate in us thought, inquiry, inference, and thus get for us in the end some added knowledge.

The depreciation of which I speak is by no means of set purpose, nor is it even realised; but the more education presents itself as a series of psychological problems, the greater will be the tendency to doctor, modify, and practically eliminate knowledge;—that knowledge, which is as the air, and the food, and the exercise, the whole life of the mind of man. In giving 'education' without abundant knowledge, we are as persons who should aim at physical development by giving the maximum of exercise with the minimum of food. The getting of knowledge and the getting of delight in knowledge are the ends of a child's education; and well has said one of our prophets, "that there should one man die ignorant who had capacity for knowledge, this I call a tragedy."

To sum up, I believe that our efforts at intellectual education commonly fail from six causes:

Causes of Failure.—(a) The oral lesson, which at its worst is very poor twaddle, and at its best is far below the ordered treatment of the same subject by an original mind in the right book. (The right books exist, old and new, in countless numbers, but very great care is necessary in the choice, as well as much experience of the rather whimsical tastes and distastes of children.)

(b) The lecture, commonly gathered from various books in rapid notes by the teacher; and issuing in hasty notes, afterwards written out, and finally crammed up by the pupils. The lecture is often careful, thorough, and well-illustrated; but is it ever equal in educational value to direct contact with the original mind of one able thinker who has written his book on the subject? Arnold, Thring, Bowen, we know, lectured with great effect, but then each of them lectured on only a few subjects, and each lecture was as the breaking out of a spring of slowly gathered knowledge. We are not all Arnolds or even Bowens.

(c) The text-book, compressed and re-compressed from one or many big books. These handbooks are of two kinds—the frankly dry and uninteresting, which enumerate facts and details; and the easy and beguiling. I think we are safe in saying that there is no educational value in either sort of text-book.

(d) The debauchery of the mind which comes of exciting other desires to do the work of the inherent and fully adequate desire of knowledge.

(e) In elementary schools, the dependence upon apparatus and illustrative appliances which have a paralysing effect on the mind.

(f) Again in elementary schools, the use of 'Readers,' which, however well selected, cannot have the value of consecutive works.

Education by Books.—For the last twelve years we have tried the plan of bringing children up on Books and Things, and, on the whole, the results are pleasing. The average child studies with 'delight.' We do not say he will remember all he knows, but, to use a phrase of Jane Austen's, he will have had his 'imagination warmed' in many regions of knowledge.

Blind Alleys.—May I digress for a moment to raise a warning note against the following of blind alleys, whether in our educational thought or our methods. We do not, in the sphere of education, find hidden treasure by casual digging in the common roadways. Believing in evolution, we perceive that ideas also have their pedigree and their progeny and follow their own laws of generation. A learned and thoughtful Chinese will abstract himself from the outer world, separate himself from the ideas of others, and, when he has arrived at a due state of vacuity, take his writing-brushes and produce out of his inner consciousness—not anything that he has ever seen or heard of; or even imagined—but some hieroglyph of curves, rather pleasing and presentable if he happen to be an artist. This disconnected production he arbitrarily invests with the character of a symbol, and his fellows are willing to receive it as such, and it is duly hung in his Hall of Tablets. (See 'Through a Hidden Shensi,' by F. Nichols) Some of us perhaps know the flowing curves which stand for 'happiness' in this language of symbols.

Now, all this is very engaging, and the Western mind is ready enough to succumb to the charm of such fancies. But does it not offer a key to that baffling problem we call China? Here we have a vast people with some high moral qualities, of astute and sometimes profound intelligence, whose civilisation has for thousands of years remained to all appearance stationary. Is the cause, perhaps, a tendency to follow intellectual futilities, blind alleys, in every direction? These people do not realise that method implies an end perceived, a way to that end, and step by step progress in the way; nor do they perceive that a notion becomes a fruitful idea only upon the impact of an idea from without. A fine Celestial arrogance assures them of their right to casual finds; hence, they do not progress, but remain in all things as they were.

Now, here is the danger that besets us in education. We seize upon ambidexterity, upon figures drawn with the compasses without intention, upon 'child study' as applied to mind, upon terrible agglutinations which we call 'apperception masses,' upon intellectual futilities in a hundred directions, each of which will, we hope, give us the key to education. We may perceive the futility of such notions by applying the test of progress. Are they the way to anything, and, if so, to what? Let us, out of reverence for the children, be modest; let us not stake their interests on the hope that this or that new way would lead to great results if people had only the courage to follow it. It is exciting to become a pioneer; but, for the children's sake, it may be well to constrain ourselves to follow those roads only by which we know that persons have arrived, or those newer roads which offer evident and assured means of progress towards a desired end. Self-will is not permitted to the educationalist; and he may not take up fads.

An Educated Child.—Knowledge is, no doubt, a comparative term, and the knowledge of a subject possessed by a child would be the ignorance of a student. All the same, there is such a thing as an educated child—a child who possesses a sound and wide knowledge of a number of subjects, all of which serve to interest him; such a child studies with 'delight.'

Children delight In School, but not for Love of Knowledge.—It will be said with truth that most children delight in school; they delight in the stimulus of school life, in the social stir of companionship; they are emulous, eager for reward and praise; they enjoy the thousand lawful interests of school life, including the attractive personality of such and such a teacher; but it seems doubtful whether the love of knowledge, in itself and for itself; is usually a powerful motive with the young scholar. The matter is important, because, of all the joyous motives of school life, the love of knowledge is the only abiding one; the only one which determines the scale, so to speak, upon which the person will hereafter live. My contention is, to repeat what has been said, that all children have a capacity for and a latent love of knowledge; and, that knowledge concerning persons and States can best be derived from books, and should be got by the children out of their own books.

In a hundred biographies there are hints of boys and girls who have grown up on books; and there is no doubt that in many schools the study of books is the staple of the work. This probably is the principle which keeps our great public schools perennially alive; they live, so far as they do live, upon books. The best public schoolboy is a fine product; and perhaps the worst has had his imagination touched by ideas; yet most of us recognise that the public school often fails, in that it launches the average and dull boy ignorant upon the world because the curriculum has been too narrow to make any appeal to him. And we must remember, that if a young person leave school at seventeen or eighteen without having become a diligent and delighted reader, it is tolerably certain that he will never become a reader, it may be, however, that the essential step in any reform of public schools should come in the shape of due preparation upon a wide curriculum, dealt with intelligently, between the ages of six and twelve.

An Educational Revolution.—I add appendices to show, (a) how a wide curriculum and the use of many books work in the Parents' Review School; (b) what progress a pupil of twelve should have made under such conditions; and (c) what use is made of oral lessons. Should the reader consider that the children in question prove their right of entry to several fields of knowledge, that they show a distinct appetite for such knowledge, that thought and power of mind develop upon the books we read, as they do not and cannot upon the lectures we hear; should he indeed be convinced of the truth of what I have advanced, I think he will see that, not an educational reform here and there, but an *educational revolution* is before us to which every one of us is bound to put his hand.

The Children's Magna Carta.—My plea is, and I think I have justified it by experience, that many doors shall be opened to boys and girls until they are at least twelve or fourteen, and always the doors of good houses, ('Education,' says Taine, 'is but a card of invitation to noble and privileged salons'); that they shall be introduced to no subject whatever through compendiums, abstracts, or selections; that the young people shall learn what history is, what literature is, what life is, from the living books of those who know. I know it can be done, because it is being done on a considerable scale.

If conviction has indeed reached us, the Magna Carta of children's intellectual liberty is before us. The need is immediate, the means are evident. This, least, I think we ought to claim, that, up to the age of twelve, all boys and girls shall be educated on some such curriculum, with some such habit of Books as we have been considering. (It is highly encouraging that the new regulations of the Board of Education both for primary and secondary schools lend themselves to the lines of work advocated in these pages.)

Appendix I

Questions for the Use of readers 1

Chapter I: Docility and Authority in the Home and School

I. In what points are there better relations between children and their elders than there were a generation or two ago?
2. Characterise the elder generation of parents.
3. What of 'ill-guided' homes?
4. Give an example of martinet rule. Name some notable men who grew up under such rule.
5. Compare the arbitrary parent now with the arbitrary parent of the past.
6. Was arbitrary rule a failure?
7. What thought should encourage our own efforts?
8. Show that arbitrariness arose from limitations.
9. That it is one cause of the reticence of children.
10. In what way has the direction of philosophic thought altered the relations of parents and children?
11. What effect has the doctrine of the 'Infallible Reason' upon authority?
12. Show that English thought again proclaims the apotheosis of Reason.
13. What is the final justification of the idea of authority?
14. Why is the enthronement of the human reason the dethronement of the highest authority?
15. Show that the spread of an idea is 'quick as thought.'
16. Why has the notion of the finality of human reason become intolerable?
17. On what grounds would you say that authority and docility are fundamental principles?
18. Show that self-interest does not account for the response of docility to authority.
19. Show that the work of the rationalistic philosophers was necessary.
20. Show that they hold a brief for human freedom.
21. Describe the way in which the education of the world seems to be carried on.
22. Show the danger of the notion that authority is vested in persons.
23. Show that a person in authority is under authority.

Chapter II: Docility and Authority in the Home and School

Part II—How Authority Behaves

I. Show, by example, that it is easy to go wrong on principle.
2. Distinguish between authority and autocracy.
3. How does autocracy behave?
4. Show that it is the autocrat who remits duties and grants indulgences.
5. How does authority behave?
6. Give half-a-dozen features by which we may distinguish the rule of authority.
7. What are the qualities proper to a ruler?
8. Distinguish between mechanical and reasonable obedience.
9. Show the use of the former.
10. Show how acts of mechanical obedience help a child to the masterly use of his body.
11. How is the man, who can make himself do what he wills, trained?
12. Why is the effort of decision the greatest effort of life?
13. Show how habit spares us much of this labour.
14. Show how the habit of obedience eases the lives of children.
15. How does authority avoid cause of offence?
16. Show that alert authority in the home is a preventive force.
17. Show how important the changing of the thoughts, diverting, is in the formation of habit.
18. Show that children, too, exercise authority.
19. What question might parents put to themselves daily as an aid to the maintenance of authority?

Chapter III: 'Masterly Inactivity'

I. Contrast our sense of responsibility with that held in the fifties and sixties.
2. Show that the change in our point of view indicates moral progress.
3. What kind of responsibility presses heavily at present upon thoughtful people?
4. Show that anxiety is the note of a transition stage.
5. Why does a sense of responsibility produce a fussy and restless habit?
6. Why should we do well to admit the idea of 'masterly inactivity, as a factor in education?
7. What four or five ideas are contained in this of 'masterly inactivity'?
8. What is Wordsworth's phrase?
9. What is the first element in this attitude of mind?
10. Show that good-humour is the second element.
11 That self-confidence also is necessary.
12. What may mothers learn from the fine, easy, way of some fathers?
13. Show that confidence in children, also, is an element of 'masterly inactivity.'
14. Why must parents and teachers be omniscient?
15. Show why 'masterly inactivity' is necessary to the bringing up of a child whose life is conditioned by 'fate and free-will.'
16. What delicate poise between fate and free-will is to be aimed at for the child?
17. Show the importance of a sound mind in a sound body to the parent.
18. What may we learn from the quality which all the early painters have bestowed upon the pattern Mother?
19. Give one or two practical hints for tired mothers.
20. Why is leisure necessary to children's well-being?
21. What is the foundation of the 'masterly inactivity' we have in view?

Chapter IV: Some of the Rights of Children as Persons

I. Why should children be free in their play?
2. In what respect are organised games not play?
3. Why should we beware of interfering with children's work?
4. Show that children must stand or fall by their own efforts.
5. Show the danger of a system of prodding.
6. How far may we count upon the dutifulness of boys and girls?
7. How far should children be free to choose their friends?
8. To spend their pocket-money?
9. To form their opinions?
10. Show that spontaneity is not an indigenous wildflower.

Chapter V: Psychology in Relation to Current Thought

I. Characterise the educational thought of the eighteenth century.
2. Show that we, too, have had a period of certainty.
3. Account for the general dissatisfaction we labour under now.
4. By what tests may we discern a working psychology for our own age?
5. Illustrate the fact that the sacredness of the person is among the living thoughts of the age upon which we are being brought up.
6. On what grounds do we demand of education that it should make the most of the person?
7. How is 'the solidarity of the race' to be reckoned with in education?
8. Show that the best thought of any age is common thought.
9. Discuss Locke's States of Consciousness.
10. Show that this theory does not provide for the evolution of the person.
11. How does modern physiological-psychology compare with Locke's theory?
12. How does Professor James define this psychology?

13. Show that this definition makes the production of thought, etc., purely mechanical.
14. How far is this assumption 'unjustifiable materialism'?
15. What is Professor James' pronouncement about what is called the 'new psychology'?
16. Illustrate the fact that a psychology which eliminates personality is dreary and devitalising.
17. By what signs may we recognise the fact when the 'new psychology' becomes part of our faith?
18. Show that this system is inadequate, unnecessary, and inharmonious.
19. At what point does it check the evolution of the individual?

Chapter VI: Some Educational Theories Examined

I. What do we owe to the Schools of Pestalozzi and Froebel?
2. What is the source of weakness in their conceptions?
3. Compare 'make children happy and they will be good' with 'be good and you will be happy.'
4. Show the fundamental error of regarding man merely as part of the Cosmos.
5. Show that the struggle for existence is a part of life even to a child.
6. That any sort of transition violates the principles of unity and continuity.
7. Why is the Herbartian theory tempting?
8. Show that this theory treats the person as an effect and not a cause.
9. Show that the functions of education are overrated by it.
10. Show that this system of psychology is not in harmony with current thought in three particulars.
11. Show that educational truth is a common possession.
12. What are the characteristics of a child who is being adequately educated?
13. What, roughly speaking, is expressed in the word person?
14. Show how a person is like Wordsworth's 'cloud.'
15. Describe an adequate doctrine of education.
16. Show how it is in touch with the three great ideas which are now moving in men's minds.
17. What would you say of personal influence in education?
i8. What is implied in saying, Education is the science of relations?
19. Why must teaching not be obtrusive?
20. What attitude on the teacher's part arises from the recognition of a child as a person?

Chapter VII: an Adequate Theory of Education

I. Give, roughly, a definition of a human being.
2. What would you say of his capacities?
3. What of his limitations?
4. What are the two functions of a human being under education?
5. Upon what physical process does education depend?
6. What do we know, or guess, of the behaviour of ideas?
7. What appears to be the law of the generation of ideas?
8. Why do different ideas appeal to different minds? Illustrate by a figure.
9. Have we any reason for believing that an idea is able to make an impression upon matter?
10. Mention some of the reflex actions by which we respond to an idea which strikes us.
II. How does spirit correspond with spirit, human or divine?
12. Is a child born equipped with ideas?
13. What is the field open to the educationalist?
14. What may we learn from the fairly well accredited story of the 'Child of Nuremberg'?
15. What does nature, unassisted, do for a child?
16. Show that the normal child has every power that will serve him.
17. In how far does fulness of living depend on the establishment of relations?
18. Show that in our common way of treating science, for instance, we maim a natural affinity.
19. Why should a child be taught to recognise the natural things about him?
20. How may he be helped to appreciate beauty?

21. Why should he begin with a first-hand knowledge of science?
22. Show that appreciation and exact knowledge each has its season.

Chapter VIII: Certain Relations Proper to a Child

I. How long would you give a child to initiate the range relationships proper to him?
2. What dynamic relations should he have?
3. What power over material?
4. Show that he should have intimacy with animals.
5. What range of studies belong to the human relationships?
6. Give example of the awakening idea and its outcome.
7. Show that intelligence is limited by interests.
8. What should be the effect if children were fully realised persons?
9. What effect has the psychology of the hour had upon the sense of duty?
10. Show that children used to get a fairly sound ethical training.
11. What is the case now?
12. Show that 'my duty towards my neighbour' is the only sound basis for moral relations.
13. Does the sense of what is due from us come by nature?
14. Why should a child be taught something of self-management?
15. Why should children have intimacy with persons of all classes?
16. How may their fitness as citizens be promoted?
17. What are the three great groups of relations a child has to establish?
18. Which is the most important of these?
19. Show that religious sentiments or emotions do not fulfil 'duty towards God.'
20. Distinguish between sentiment and duty.

Chapter IX: A Great Educationalist

1. Illustrate the fact that Herbartian thought has more influence than any other on the Continent.
2. Show that we, like Herbart, discard the 'faculties.'
3. What does Herbart say of the pervasiveness of dominant ideas?
4. In what ways do we, too, recognise the influence of the Zeitgeist?
5. How does Herbart enumerate the child's schoolmasters?
6. Show that we are one with him in realising the place of the family.
7. What does Herbart say of the child in the family?
8. Show that we, too, hold that all education springs from and rests upon our relation to Almighty God.
9. Why should we not divide education into religious and secular?
10. What doctrine of the medieval Church do we hold with regard to 'secular subjects '?
11. Upon what, according to Herbart, does the welfare, civilisation, and culture of a people depend?
12. Discuss the vast uncertainty that exists as to the purpose of education.
13. Shall we follow Rousseau, Basedow, Locke, Pestalozzi, Froebel, in our attempts to fix the purpose of education?
14. Show, according to Dr Rein, why not, in each case?
15. Show that Herbart's theory is ethical, as is ours.
16. Quote this author on the obscurity of psychology.
17. But we have two luminous principles. What are they?
18. What is probably the root defect of the educational philosophy of this great thinker?

Chapter X: Some Unconsidered Aspects of Physical Training

I. Why does not our physical culture tend to make heroes?
2. What is the end of physical culture?
3. Show that this implies the idea of vocation.
4. What principle should check excess, whether in labour or pleasure?

5. Should parents bring up their children with rigour? Why not?
6. Write a short theme on each of the points suggested for consideration.
7. Show how large a part habit plays in physical training.
8. Prove that self-restraint is a habit.
9. Show the evil of the excessive exercises that lead to indulgence.
10. How may self-control in emergencies become a trained
11. What have you to say of the physical signs of mental states?
12. Show that discipline must become self-discipline.
13. What is the part of parents in the holidays as regards school discipline?
14. How do 'local habits' point to the necessity for self-discipline in even a young child?
15. Show how alertness must be trained as a physical habit.
16. That 'quick perception' is less a gift than a habit.
17. Write short themes on each of the subjects here suggested for consideration.
18. Show the value of inspiring ideas in initiating habits.
19. How could you use the idea of 'fortitude' in education?
20. Of 'service'?
21. Of 'courage'?
22. Of 'prudence' as concerned with the duty of health?
23. What is the highest impulse towards chastity we can have?
24 Write short themes on the subjects suggested.

Chapter XI: Some Unconsidered Aspects of Intellectual Training

1. Show that we are somewhat law-abiding in matters physical and moral.
2. That we are not so in matters intellectual.
3. What are the three ultimate facts which are not open to question?
4. Show that one or other of the three is always matter of debate.
5. What three fixed points of thought do we attain when we realise that God is, self is, and the world is?
6. Why is it necessary to recognise the limitations of reason?
7. Describe the involuntary action of reason.
8. Show, by examples, (a) what the function of reason is, and (b) what the function of reason is not.
9. Show, by examples, that wars, persecutions, and family feuds are due to the notion that, what reason demonstrates is right and true.
10. Why should a child be taught the limitations of his own reason?
11. What mistake is commonly made regarding intellect and knowledge?
12. Show that the world is educated by knowledge given 'in repasts.'
13. How would you characterise our own era as regards the knowledge given to us?
14. How did the medieval Church recognise the divine origin of knowledge?
15. Why is nothing so practical as a great idea?
16. Show the importance of forming intellectual habits.
17. Show that we trust blindly to disciplinary studies for the formation of such habits.
18. Name and describe half-a-dozen intellectual habits in which a child should be trained.
19. Show that progress in the intellectual as in the Christian life depends upon meditation.
20. Show that a child must have daily sustenance of living ideas. How do we err in this respect?
21. Make some remarks upon the literature proper for children.
22. Illustrate the fact that the intellectual development of children is independent.
23. By what law do children appropriate nourishing ideas?
24. What, then, is the part of parents and teachers?
25. What failing on the part of parents is often fatal to growth?
26. Write a few remarks on each of the subjects suggested in connection with the intellectual life of children.
27. What was the educational aim of Plato?

Chapter XII: Some Unconsidered Aspects of Moral Training

I. What are the three principles which underlie the educational thought proposed in these volumes?
2. What principle is universally acknowledged as the basis of moral teaching?
3. How does authority work?
4 'A man can but act up to his lights' discuss this fallacy.
5. Define the limits of authority.
6. What is the consequence of arbitrary action?
7. What old contention as to the sanctions of morality is exercising men now?
8. Show that Socrates had to contend with the popular doctrine of to-day in other forms.
9. What is the necessary issue of this teaching?
10. How should children be taught that duty can exist only as that which we owe to God?
11. Show that morals do not come by nature.
12. That a certain rough and rea*dy morality does come by heredity and environment.
13. How do we get an educated conscience?
14. Show that children are born neither moral nor immoral.
15. Show the danger of spasmodic moral efforts.
16. Where shall we look for the basis of our moral teaching?
17. What do we owe to the poets in this regard?
18. How did the medieval Church provide moral object lessons?
19 Illustrate our failure in this respect.
20. Why should children have the inspiration of high ideals?
21. Show the value of biography in this Connection.
22. Name any virtues with which the poets inspire us.
23. Make a suggestion with regard to the culling of mottoes.
24. How may parents and teachers help children to the habit of sweet thoughts?
25. Enumerate and discuss some of the virtues which children should be trained to develop.
26. Distinguish between 'being good' and loving God.

Chapter XIII: Some Unconsidered Aspects of Religious Education

I. Show how the principle of authority bears on religious teaching.
2. In what ideas do the children of our day need especially to be brought up?
3. How do certain questions 'in the air' militate against the sense of authority?
4. In what respects does authority work like a good and just national government?
5. Discuss authority in connection with punishment.
6. Discuss each of the various themes suggested in connection with the subject of authority in the religious life.
7. Show that lines of habit are as important for the religious as for the physical, moral, and intellectual life.
8. How would you endeavour to keep a child in the habit of the thought of God?
9. Discuss the question of reverent attitudes.
10. How would you use 'because of the angels' in this connection?
11. Show the importance of regularity in time and place in children's prayers.
12. Why should not their evening prayers be left till bed-time?
13. What is to be said of little text-books?
14. Show the danger of losing the narrative teaching of the Scriptures.
15. Why should not children be encouraged in long readings or long prayers?
16. How should the habit of praise be fostered?
17. Show the value of the habit of Sunday-keeping, and describe a child's Sunday.
18. Write your reflections on each of the themes suggested in connection with the habits of the religious life.

19. Show the importance of selecting the inspiring ideas we propose to give children in the things of the Divine life.
20. What other point demands our care?
21. What vitalising idea is of first importance in the teaching of children?
22. How should children be taught that the essence of Christianity is devotion to a Person?
23. Why is it necessary to teach children that there is a Saviour of the world?
24. What teaching would you give them about the work of the Holy Spirit?

Chapter XIV: A Master-Thought

I. What is the motto of the Parents' Union?
2. Show that this motto is a master-thought.
3. Why is 'education is an atmosphere' the clause of the motto that pleases us most?
4. What is the result if this part be taken for the whole?
5. What defect in education leads to ennui and the desire to be amused by shows.
6. What was the unconscious formula of the eighteenth century?
7. What was the result of this one-sided view of education?
8. Show that the idea of the development of the faculties also rests upon a one-sided notion.
9. What is the tendency of an education grounded upon the development of faculties?
10. Should it be our aim to produce specialists? Why not?
11. Show what manner of education results in a sound and well-balanced mind.
12. Show that the medieval Church understood, better than we, that 'education is a life.'
13. Sketch the scheme of educational philosophy to be found on the walls of the 'Spanish Chapel' of S. Maria Novella.
14. Show how this educational creed unifies life.
15. What does Coleridge say of the origin of great ideas of nature?
16. What does Michael Angelo write to his friend of the need for a diet of great ideas?
17. What is the special teaching vouchsafed to men today?
18. What views are people apt to take with regard to this teaching?
19. What does Huxley say about ideas in science?
20. How does the teaching of Simone Memmi and Coleridge relieve us from anxiety and make clear our perplexities?
21. How does Coleridge describe Botany, as that science existed in his day?
22. What has evolution, the key-word of our age, done for this and other perplexities?
23. But what has been the object of pursuit among philosophers for three thousand years?
24 How did Heraklitos attempt to solve the problem?
25. How did Demokritos?
26. Show that some knowledge of history and philosophy should give us pause in using the key of evolution.
27. Show that personality remains, and is not resolvable by this key.
28. Why is it necessary for parents and teachers to consider their attitude towards this question?
29. What are the four attitudes which it is possible to take up?
30. What gains will the children derive if their teachers adopt the last-mentioned of these?
31. What two things are incumbent upon us with regard to the great ideas by which the world is being taught?
32. Show the danger of making too personal a matter of education.
33. If education is a world-business, show that we must have a guiding idea about it.
34 What ideas should regulate the curriculum of a boy or girl under fourteen?
35. Show the importance of good books and many books for the use of children.
36. Why may we not choose or reject certain 'subjects' arbitrarily?

Chapter XV: School-Books, and How They Make for Education

I. What ideas do we get from the incident quoted from The Neighbours?
2. What manner of books sustains the life of thought?
3. What have you to say of the 'school-books, of the publishers?
4. Why do intelligent teachers fall back upon oral lessons?
5. Mention some of the disadvantages of these.
6. What questions should we ask about a youth who has finished his education?
7. Wherein lies the error of our educational system?
8. Show that we undervalue children, and therefore educate them amiss.
9. What was the note of home-life in the last generation?
10. How would you describe children as they are?
11. Show that our great work is to give them vitalising ideas.

Chapter XVI: How to Use School-Books

I. What question must we ask concerning a subject of instruction?
2. What do you understand by disciplinary subjects?
3. What danger attends the blind use of these?
4. What idea should prove an 'open sesame' to many vitalising studies?
5. Illustrate the fact that the Bible is the great source of moral impressions.
6. What impressions were made on De Quincey by his nursery Bible readings?
7. In what ways did the liturgy appeal to him?
8. Why should a child dig for his own knowledge?
9. What are the uses of the oral lesson and the lecture?
10. Why should children use living books for themselves?
11. What is the mark of a fit book?
12. How shall we know if children enjoy a book?
13. What should the teacher do towards the teaching by the book?
14. In what ways must children labour over their books?
15. What is the simplest way of dealing with a paragraph or chapter?
16. Why should preparation consist of a single careful reading?
17. Mention some other ways of using books.
18. What mechanical devices might children use in their studies?
19. What does the teacher do towards the preparation of a lesson?
20. What is the danger of too many disciplinary devices?
21. Why are we in some danger of neglecting books?

Chapter XVII: Education Is the Science of Relations: We Are Educated by Our Intimacies

I. What are our three educational instruments, and why are we confined to these?
2. Why may we not encroach upon the personality of children?
3. In what ways may we temper life too much for children?
4. What example of fairy-lore serving as a screen and shelter does Wordsworth give us in The Prelude?
5. What have you to say of the spontaneous living of children?
6. On what does fulness of living depend?
7. Distinguish between the relation of ideas to ideas and the relation of persons to the ideas proper for them.
8. Show that the object of education is not to make something of the child, but to put the child in touch with all that concerns him.
9. Describe the self-education of an infant. What does Wordsworth tell us on this point?
10. What is our part in his education?
11. What is our common error; what are its results?

12. Distinguish between business and desire.
13. What attempts were made to teach Ruskin to ride, and what does he think of those attempts?
14. What indictment does he bring against the limitations of his condition?
15. Why should those parents especially who are villa-dwellers learn much from Præterita?
16. Enumerate Wordsworth's opportunities for forming dynamic relations.
17. Show that these came naturally in the course of things.

Chapter XVIII: We Are Educated by Our Intimacies

Part II—Further Affinities

I. What chances had Ruskin to learn the use of material?
2. What do we hear of the intimacy of either boy with natural objects?
3. Describe Ruskin's flower studies.
4. His pebble studies.
5. Show that these became a life-shaping intimacy.
6. Upon what books did Ruskin grow up?
7. What is the first mention we get of his insatiate delight in a book?
8. What qualities in Byron delighted him?
9. Describe Wordsworth's delight in the Arabian Nights.
10. What is Wordsworth's plea for 'romance' in education?
Ii. What does he say in favour of liberty to range among books?
12. Describe his first enthralment by poetry.
13. Show that Ruskin's historic sense appears to be always connected with places.
14 How does he betray some want of living touch with the past?
15. Show that Wordsworth, too, was aloof
16. Show that the knowledge 'learned in schools' laid little hold of either boy.
17. Compare the experiences of the two boys with regard to chances of comradeship.

Chapter XIX: We Are Educated by Our Intimacies

Part III—Vocation

i. Describe Turner's 'call' to Ruskin.
2. What does Ruskin consider his first sincere drawing?
3. What account does he give of his true initiation?
4. What is the first hint we get of nature as a passion?
5. How does Wordsworth trace the beginnings of this passion?
6. Describe the 'calling' of the poet.
7. How does Wordsworth describe the education of the little prig of his day?
8. Show that the child prig is the child who is the end and aim of his own education.
9. Mention a few of the directions in which children have affinities.
10. Show from the example of Waverley the danger of a desultory education.
11. How does Mr. Ruskin express that 'the child is father to the man'?
12. Show that strenuous effort and reverence are conditions of education.
13. Show that comradeship has its duties.
14. Why should children have a steady, unruffled course of work?
15. Describe from Brother Lawrence one way in which the highest relationship may be initiated.
16. What does Browning say about this relation?

Chapter XX: Suggestions Towards a Curriculum

1. Give a short summary of the preceding chapters.
2. Comment upon the educational methods of the day.
3. What two conditions are necessary to any sound reform?
4. Why do many boys and girls leave school intellectually vitalised?

5. How does Mr. Benson characterise the aims of Masters of public schools?
6. How may we characterise the minds of children?
7. Show the practical working of this view.
8. Distinguish between knowledge and information.
9. In what ways will the child show power in dealing knowledge?
10. To what do stereotyped phrases and mangled notes children's work point?
11. Work out an analogy between knowledge and food.
12. Why may we call 'mark-hunger' a debauchery of mind?
13. Why should not epitomes and compilations be allowed for children's use?
14. What are the advantages of working through a considerable book?

Chapter XXI: Suggestions Towards a Curriculum

Part II-School-Books

I. Who must, in the end, decide upon the right school-books?
2. What are the relative places of lecture and book?
3. Show the danger of elaborate appliances.
4. Upon what principle should studies be co-ordinated?
5. What results of education should we look for in a young person leaving school?
6. Show that the worth of education by things is now fully recognised.
7. What habit should we look for as a chief acquirement of school-life?
8. Give a rough classification of the subjects in which knowledge is due to children.
9. Show the importance of the Bible as a means of education.
10. What knowledge of history should boys and girls of twelve to fourteen have?
ii. What mistake is commonly made in teaching this subject?
12. What knowledge of languages should they have?
13. What should we aim at in the early teaching of science?
14. What least amount of time in the open is a sine quâ non of a living education?
15. What is the use of books in nature-teaching?
16. Name a few useful books.
17. What do you understand by 'picture-talks'?

Chapter XXII: Suggestions Towards a Curriculum

Part III—The Love of Knowledge

1. Why does the use of books make for short hours?
2. What is the evil of a utilitarian education?
3. Distinguish between relations and interests.
4. Show that the tendency of present-day education is to depreciate knowledge.
5. Enumerate some causes of the failure of our efforts at intellectual education.
6. Show the danger, which besets teachers, of pursuing intellectual futilities.
7. By what test may we distinguish a fad from an educational method?
8. Our end is to produce an educated child. How is he to be recognised?
9. Children delight in school for many reasons. Which of these is the only abiding motive?
10. What change in our educational methods should secure the children's educational Magna Carta?

APPENDIX II

Some Specimens of Examination Work Done in the 'Parents' Review' School, in Which the Pupils Are Educated upon Books and Things

The Parents' Review School, an output of the Parents Union, was, in the first place, designed to bring home schools, taught by governesses, up to the standard of other schools. A Training College for governesses, with Practising School, etc., was established later. Children may not enter the School under six; because we think the first six years of life are wanted for physical growth and the self-education which children carry on with little ordered aid. The Parents' Review School is conducted by means of programmes of work, in five classes, sent out, term by term, to each of the home schools (and to some other schools); and the same programmes are used in the Practising School.

Examination papers are set at the end of each term.

The work is arranged on the principles which have been set forth in this volume; a wide curriculum, a considerable number of books for each child in the severnl classes, and, besides, a couple of hours' work daily, not with Books but with Things. Many of the pupils in the school have absorbed, in a way, the culture of their parents; but the children of uncultured parents take with equal readiness and comparable results to this sort of work, which is, I think, fitted, not only for the clever, but for the average and even the dull child.

Class Ia.—The child of six goes into Class Ia.; he works for 2 1/2 hours a day, but half an hour of this time is spent in drill and games. Including drill, he has thirteen 'subjects' of study, for which about sixteen books are used.

He recites hymns, poems, and Bible verses; works from Messrs Sonnenschein and Nesbitt's ABC Arithmetic; sings French and English songs; begins Mrs Curwen's Child Pianist, learns to write and to print, learns to read, learns French orally, does brush-drawing and various handicrafts.

All these things are done with joy, but cannot be illustrated here. Bible lessons, read from the Bible; tales, natural history, and geography are taught from appointed books, helped by the child's own observation.

Our plan in each of these subjects is to read him the passage for the lesson (a good long passage), talk about it a little, avoiding much explanation, and then let him narrate what has been read. This he does very well and with pleasure, and is often happy in catching the style as well as the words of the author.

Certain pages, say 40 or 50, from each of the children's books are appointed for a term's reading. At the end of the term an examination paper is sent out containing one or two questions on each book. Here are a few of the answers. The children in the first two classes narrate their answers, which someone writes from their dictation.

Q. Tell the story of Naaman.

A. (aged 6 3/4) :—

"Naaman had something the matter with him, and his master sent a letter to the King of Israel, and the king was very unhappy and did not know what to do because he thought that he wanted to come and fight against him, and he rent his clothes. And he said, 'I can't cure him,' so he sent him to Elisha, and he told him to take a lot of presents and a lot of things with him. And when Naaman came to Elisha's door, Elisha sent Gehazi to tell him to dip himself seven times in the waters of Jordan, and he said to himself, 'I surely thought he would have come out, and I thought a lot of people would come out and make a fuss'; and he went back in a rage. And his servant said to him, 'Why didn't you go?' And he said, 'My rivers are much the best.' So his servants said, 'If he had asked you to do some great thing, wouldst thou have done it?' So he went and dipped himself seven times in the water, and when he came out he was quite all right again. And when he was coming home they saw Gehazi coming, so Naaman told them to stop the horses, and so they stopped, and Gehazi said, 'There are some people come to see me, please give me some money and some cloaks,' and they were very heavy, so Naaman sent some of his men to carry them, and when he came near the house he said to his servants, 'You can go now.' Elisha said, 'Because you have done this you shall have the leprosy that Naaman had.'"

Q. Tell a fairy story.

B. (aged 6 3/4):—

"When Ulysses was coming back from Troy he passed the Sirens. He could hear them, but he couldn't get to them, because he was bound. He wanted to get to them so as he could listen to them a long time, because a lot of people had come and listened to them, and they found it so beautiful that they wanted to stay there, and they stayed till they died. His companions couldn't hear them because they stopped up their ears with wax and cotton-wooL And this was the song they sang:—

Hither, come hither and hearken awhile,
Odysseus far-famed king,

No sailor has ever passed this way
But has paused to hear us sing.
Our song is sweeter than honey,
And he that hears it knows
What he never learnt from another,
And his joy before he goes.

We know what the heroes bore at Troy
In the ten long years of strife,
We know what happened in all the world,
And the secret things of life.'

And then they rowed on till at last the song faded away, and they rowed on and on for a long time, and then when they could not hear them nor see them, the wax was taken out of their ears, and then they unbound Ulysses."

Q. What have you noticed (yourself) about a spider?

C. (aged 7 3/4):—

"We have found out the name of one spider, and often have seen spiders under the microscope—they were all very hairy.

We have often noticed a lot of spiders running about the ground—quantities. Last term we saw a spider's web up in the corner of the window with a spider sucking out the juice of a fly; and we have often touched a web to try and make the spider come out, and we never could, because she saw it wasn't a fly, before she came out.

"I saw the claw of a spider under the microscope, with its little teeth; we saw her spinnerets and her great eyes. There were the two big eyes in one row, four little ones in the next row, and two little ones in the next row. We have often found eggs of the spiders; we have some now that we have got in a little box, and we want to hatch them out, so we have put them on the mantelpiece to force them.

"Once we saw a spider on a leaf, and we tried to catch it, but we couldn't; he immediately let himself down on to the ground with a thread.

"We saw the circulation in the leg of another spider under the microscope; it looked like a little line going up and down."

Q. Gather three sorts of tree leaf-buds and two sorts of catkin, and tell all you can about them.

D. (aged 6):—

(1) "The chestnut bud is brown and sticky, it is a sort of cotton-woolly with the leaves inside. It splits open and sends out two leaves, and the leaves split open.

(2) "The oak twig bas always a lot of buds on the top, and one bud always dies. Where the bud starts there is a little bit of knot-wood. The oak-bud is very tiny.

(3) "The lime bud has a green side and a red side, and then it bursts open and several little leaves come out and all the little things that shut up the leaves die away.

(4) "Golden catkins and silver pussy palms' of a willow tree. The golden catkins have stamens with all the pollen on them. They grow upwards, and two never grow opposite to each other.

The silver pussy palms have seed boxes, with a little tube growing out, and a little sticky knob on the top. The bees rub the pollen off their backs on to the sticky knob."

Q. Tell about the North-West Passage. (Book studied, The World at Home.)

E. (aged 7):—

"People in England are very fond of finding things out, and they wanted to find out the North-West Passage. If people wanted to go to the Pacific Ocean, they had to go round Africa, by the Cape of Good Hope, or else round South America by Cape Horn. This was a very long way. They thought they might find out a shorter way by going along the North Coast by America, and they would come out in the Pacific Ocean. They would call this way the North-West Passage. First one man and then another tried to find a way. They found a lot of straits and bays which they called after themselves. The enemy they met which made them turn back was the cold. It was in the frozen zone, and the sea was all ice, and the ice lumps were as big as mountains, and when they came against a ship they crashed it to pieces. Once a man named Captain Franklin tried over and over again to find the North-West Passage, and once he went and never came back again, for he got stuck fast in the ice, and the ice did not break, and he had not much food with him, and what he had was soon eaten up, and he could not get any more, for all the animals in that country had gone away, for it was winter, and he could not wait for the summer, when they would return. A ship went out from England called the Fox to look for him, but all they found was a boat, a Bible, a watch, and a pair of slippers near each other. After looking a lot they found the North-West Passage, but because there is so much ice there the ships can't use it."

Class lb.—In Class lb., the children are usually between seven and eight, but may be nine. They have fifteen 'subjects' (perhaps twenty-three books). The subjects which do not lend themselves to illustration are a continuation of the work in Class la. But by this time the children can usually read, and read for themselves some, at any rate, of their books for History, Geography, and Tales. In Class lb. the children narrate their lessons as in la., and, also, their answers to the examination questions. They appear to enjoy doing this; indeed, the examinations which come at the end of each term are a pleasure; the only difficulty is that small children want to go on 'telling.' Their words are taken down literally. One is struck by the correctness and copiousness of the language used; but young children delight in words, and often surprise their elders by their free and correct use of 'dictionary words.' One notices the verve with which the children tell the tale, the orderly sequence of events, the correctness and fulness of detail, the accuracy of names. These things are natural to children until they are schooled out of them.

Q. Tell all you know about St Patrick. (Book studied, Old Tales from British History.)

A. (aged 7):—

"St Patrick was the son of a Scotch farming clergyman, and one day some Irish pirates came and took Patrick with them to make him a slave; and they sold him to an Irish nobleman. And the Irish nobleman made him a shepherd to take care of his flocks, and shepherds have a lot of time to think when they are out guarding their flocks by night. And Patrick was very sorry that the poor Irish were heathens. One day he slipped off and got into a boat with some sailors, and after a great adventure, for their food ran short, they arrived safely in Scotland. And Patrick was still thinking about the Irish, so he went off in a boat of his own, with a few followers, to Ireland. A shepherd saw them coming, and told his master the pirates were coming. So he armed his servants and went down to meet the pirates, but when he heard the errand they were on, he offered them to come into his house. Now Patrick settled in Ireland, but some heathen priests rose up against him, and a wise man said, 'What is the good of killing him? Other Irish people are now Christians, and they will teach too.' So he saved his life. And Patrick gave him the book of Psalms written by his own hand. One day Patrick asked a rich man if he might have a little plot of land on the top of a hill, but the rich man refused him, but gave him a little plot of land at the bottom of the hill. And there Patrick built a church, and a house for himself and servants to live in. Then the rich man got ill, and was just about to die, but got better, but as he thought Patrick was like a wizard, who could foretell his fortune, he thought he'd better try to please him. So he sent him a brass cauldron, enough to hold one whole sheep, and Patrick said 'I thank you, master.' The rich man was angry, and sent for the cauldron back again, and Patrick said, 'I thank you, master.' So the rich man was ashamed, and brought back the cauldron, and said he could have the little plot of land on the top of the hill. So they went up to measure it. Then a roe-deer dashed out of the thicket, but left her fawn behind her, and the men were going to kill the fawn, but Patrick took it up and carried it down the hill; the mother followed, for she saw he was doing no harm to it. On that place he built a fine church, which is still standing. And Patrick died on a journey, and was buried at a place called Downpatrick after him."

Q. Tell what you know about Alfred Tennyson. (Book studied, Mrs Frewen Lord's Tales from Westminster Abbey.)

B. (aged 7 1/2):—

"Alfred Tennyson was born in 1809, and he loved the country very much. One Sunday when they were going out to chapel, except Lord Tennyson as he was very young, his brother Charles gave him his slate to write about birds and flowers, and when they came back he had filled his slate with his first poem. He and his brother used to make up stories that sometimes lasted a month. He was very shortsighted, and when he was looking at anything it looked as if he were smelling it. He had. good ears, for he could hear the shriek of a bat. Alfred Tennyson wrote The Revenge and The Siege of Lucknow, and Sir John Franklin's poem:—

'Not here; the white North hath thy bones,
And thou, heroic sailor soul,
Art passing on thy happier voyage now,
Toward no earthly pole.'

And he also wrote the May Queen and Cradle Song. Because his poetry was so good the Queen gave him a name and knighted him. He says that if you tread on a daisy it will turn up and get red. He was 83 years old when he died—the year he died in was 1892. He was buried in Westminster Abbey, in Poets' Corner.'

Q. What is a hero? What heroes have you heard of? Tell about one.

C. (aged 7):—

(1) A hero is a brave man. (2) Count Roland, Huon at Bordeaux, the Horatii and Curatii. (3) Once there was a brave Emperor called Charlemagne, and he was fighting with the neathen King of Saragossa. Just a wee bit of land was left to the heathen king, so he sent a messenger to speak about peace.

They pretended that they would have peace, so they went back to Charlemagne and asked him to leave Roland behind to take charge of the mountain passes. So Charlemagne said that he would leave Roland behind because there was none so brave as him, so that when Charlemagne had turned his army they should come in great numbers to fight against Roland. And Roland stayed behind with twenty thousand men, and Oliver heard a great noise by the side of Spain, and then Oliver climbed on a pine tree, and he saw the arms glimmering and the spears shining, and then he said to Roland that there were a full hundred thousand, and that they just had so few, and that it was much better to sound his horn and Charlemagne will turn his army. Roland said he would be mad if he did that. Oliver said again to sound his horn, and Roland said he would lose his fame in France if he did it. Then Oliver said again, 'Friend Roland, sound thy horn and Charles will hear it, and turn his army.' Then all the mountain passes were full of the enemies, and when they came nearer they fought, and they fought, and they fought, and at last the Christians were falling too, and when there were only sixty left he blew his horn, Charlemagne heard it and said he must go, and Ganelon said he was just pretending, but then Charlemagne heard it fainter, and knew that it was true that he must go, and then fainter again, but Charlemagne was nearer and so heard it better. And Roland said, 'Ride as fast as you can for many men have been killed, and there are few left.' Then Charlemagne bade his men sound their horns, so that they knew that help was near and then the heathen fled away. There were just the two left, Roland and the Archbishop, and Roland said to the Archbishop that he would try to fetch the dead bodies of the braver soldiers. Then the Archbishop said to Roland, 'Quick, before I die.' Then Roland went and brought them before the Archbishop and laid them down there. Then he went and searched the field again, and under a pine tree he found Oliver's body, then he brought it too and laid it in front of the Archbishop. Then Roland fainted to the ground, then the Archbishop tried to bring some water for Roland, and he fell down and died. Then Roland put the hands over the chest of the Archbishop, then he prayed to God to give him a place in Paradise, and then he said that the field was his. Before he died he put his sword and his ivory horn under him, and laid himself down on the ground, so that Charlemagne, when he came, would know that he was the conqueror. And God sent St Michael and another saint to fetch his soul up to heaven."

Q. Gather three sorts of tree leaf-bud and two sorts of catkin and tell all you can about them.

E. (a cottage child aged 9):—

"Beech Twig.—It has rather a woody stalk, and it is a very light grey-browny stalk, and it is very thin, and the little branches that grow out are light brown and it is thicker where the buds are and it is a lighter brown up at the top than it is at the bottom, and the buds are a light reddy-brown and very pointed, and they are scaly. The bark is rather rough and there is a lot of little kind of brown spots on it.

"Lime Twig.—It is called Ruby-budded Lime because the buds are red, and they are fat rather, and they have got some green in as well, and they come rather to a point at the top, they grow alternately and the little stalk that they grow out of is reddy-green, and the top part of the stalk is green, and it is woody, and it is rough, and it is a reddy-green at the bottom.

Where the buds come out it is swelled out, the bark has come off and it has left it white and woody. At the top of one of the stalks the bud has come off.

"Sycamore Twig.—Well, the back is very woody, and it is a brown stalk and it is rough and there is a little weeny bud growing out of the side, and the buds grow out two and two, and there. are a lot of little buds.

"Willow.—Well, the stalk is a dark brown, and is very smooth and it will bend very easily, and the buds when they first come on the stalk are little brown ones, and then a silvery-green comes out and there is a scale at the bottom, and then they get greyer and bigger with little green leaves at the bottom, and then it comes yellow, and there is a lot of pollen on it. If you touch it the pollen comes on your finger.

"Hazel.—Well, the stalk is a dark brown, something the colour of the willow, and it bends easily, and the buds are green and there is little scales, and then the catkins come and they grow very long, and there is a lot of little flowers in one, and there is pollen in that, and the stalk is rather rough, and there are some big buds at the top just bursting, and the leaves are coming out, and the buds are very soft and glossy, and the scales are at the bottom."

Q. What have you noticed about a thrush? Tell all you know about it.

F. (aged 8):—

"Thrushes are browny birds. They eat snails, and they take the snail in their mouths and knock it against a stone to break the shell and eat the snail. I found a stone with a lot of bits of shell round it, so knew that a thrush had been there. Where we used to live a thrush used to sing every morning on the same tree. The song of the thrush is like a nightingale. We often see a lot of thrushes on the lawn before breakfast or after a shower. They have yellow beaks and their breasts are specked with lovely yellow and brown. Once we found a thrush asleep on a sponge in a bedroom and we carried it out and put it on a tree. Thrushes eat worms as well as snails, and on the lawn they listen with their heads on one side and go along as the worm gets under the ground, and presently, perhaps, the worm comes up and they gobble it up, or they put their beaks in and get it. Thrushes build their nests with sticks at the bottom and line them with little bits of wool they pick up, or feathers, and they like to get down very much."

Class II.—In Class II. the children are between nine and twelve, occasionally over twelve. They have twentyone 'subjects,' and about twenty-five books are used. They work from 9 to 12 each day, with half an hour's interval for games and drill. Some Latin and German (optional) are added to the curriculum. In music we continue Mrs Curwen's (Child Pianist) method and Tonic Sol-fa, and learn French, German (optional), and English songs. But I cannot here give details of our work, and must confine myself to illustrations from seven of the subjects on the programme. Children in Class II. write or dictate, or write a part and dictate a part of their examination answers according to their age. The examination lasts a week, and to write the whole of their work would be fatiguing at this stage. The plan followed is, that the examination in each subject shall be done in the time for that subject on the time-table.

I should like to say a word about the Greek and Roman History. Plutarch's Lives are read in Classes II. and Ill, and as children are usually five years in these two classes, they may read some fifteen of these Lives, which I think stand alone in literature as teaching that a man is part of the State, that his business is to be of service to the State, but that the value of his service depends upon his personal character. The Lives are read to the children almost without comment, but with necessary omissions.. Proper names are written on the blackboard; and, at the end, children narrate the substance of the lesson. The English History book used in Classes II. and III. is extremely popular; it is Mr Arnold-Forster's (of about 800 pages), and is well known as a serious, manly, and statesmanlike treatment of English History; in no case is there any writing down to the children.

Mrs Creighton's First History of France is also a favorite, though I should have thought there was hardly enough detail to make it so. Contemporary periods of English and French History are studied term by term. For Natural History, Miss Arabella Buckley's Fairyland of Science and Lift and Her Children, Mrs Brightwen's books, etc., give scientific information and excite intelligent curiosity, while out-of-door nature-study lays the foundation for science. The handiworks of Class II. are such as cardboard Sloyd, clay modelling, needlework, gardening, etc. These, field-work, piano practice, etc., are done in the afternoons or after tea.

Q. "Ah! Pericles, those that have need of a lamp, take care to supply it with oil." Who said this? Tell the story. (Book studied, Plutarch's Lives: Pericles.)

D. (aged 11 1/2), answer dictated:—

"Anaxagoras, the philosopher, said these words to Pericles.

"Pericles was the ruler of Athens, and Anaxagoras had taught him when a boy. Being ruler of Athens, he led a very busy life, attending to the affairs of State, and so was not able to give much time to his household affairs. Once a year he collected his money, and could only manage his income by giving out an allowance to each member of his family and household every day: this was done by Evangelus, his steward.

Anaxagoras thought this a very wrong way of arranging matters, and said that Pericles paid too much heed to bodily affairs, because he thought you ought to mind only about philosophy and spiritual doings, and not about the affairs of the world. To give an example to Pericles he gave up all his household and tried to live entirely on philosophy. But he soon found his mistake when he found himself starving and penniless, with no house. So he covered his head up and prepared to die. Pericles, hearing of this, went immediately to his rescue and begged him to live; not because he thought death a misfortune, but that he said, 'What shall I do without your help in the affairs of State!' And then Anaxagoras uttered the words which are above, meaning, of course (though putting it in a clever way), that Pericles was to keep him. On the other hand, he might have meant that he had been mistaken in his philosophy."

Q. Tell the history of 'F.D.' on a penny. (Book studied, Arnold-Forster's History of England.)

C. (aged 10), answer written by child:—

"The letters 'F.D.' stand for the Latin words Fidei Defensor, meaning 'The Defender of the Faith.' Henry VIII. had a little while ago written a book on the Pope (who was Clement VII.) saying that the Pope was the true head of the Church, and everyone ought to obey him. The Pope was so pleased that he made Henry Fedei Defensor. It must be remembered that the king had married his brother Arthur's 1 widow, a Spanish princess, namely, Catherine of Aragon (sic), and as they had no son Henry wished to divorce her, but the Pope would not anow him to, as he had given Henry special leaf (sic) to marry her. At this Henry was furious, and began to think about the Pope's words, 'Defender of the Faith.' He would not act as he thought till someone suggested it. So two men, called Cromwell and Cranmer, came forward, telling the king to take the Pope's words, not as he meant them, but as they really were, as they stood. The king was delighted, and made Cranmer a bishop and Cromwell his wisest counsellor. 1 In 1534 Parliament 1 was called upon to declare Henry head of the Church. All said he was, except two men, Sir Thomas More and Fisher, bishop of Rochester; these would not agree, and were executed in 1535.

If we look on a penny we see the letters 'F.D.,' which shows from the reign of Henry VIII. till now the Pope has not been allowed to interfere with England. In order to spite the Pope, Henry allowed the Lutherans and learned men to come into England."

Q. What did you see in the Seagull sailing up the Firth of Forth? (Book studied, Geographical Reader, Book II.)

G. (aged 9), answer dictated:—

"In sailing up the Forth we first of all see Leith, which is the seaport town of Edinburgh. Then we come to Edinburgh. The old and new Edinburghs are built on opposite hills, the valley in between is laid out in lovely gardens. One thing very odd about Edinburgh is that the streets look as if they are built one on top of the other. At one end of the town there is a castle which looks so like the rocks and mountains it is built on, one can hardly distinguish it. At the other end of the town there is Holyrood, where the ancient kings used to live. We do not see many merchantmen because there are no good harbours, there are a good many fishing smacks and pleasure boats. As we go along we see women with big baskets with a strap across their foreheads, and they are calling out 'caller herrings.'"

1 The writers have been in two minds about the spelling of words marked (1).

Q. "And Jonathan loved him as his own soul." Of whom was this said? Tell a story of Jonathan's love.

E. (aged 9), answer dictated:—

"This was said of David. Saul's anger was kindled against David; and Jonathan and David were talking together, and Jonathan had been telling David that he would do anything for him, and David said, 'To-morrow is the feast of a new moon, and Saul will expect me to sit with him at the table; therefore say, 'David earnestly asked leave of me to go to Bethlehem, his city, where there is a sacrifice of his family.' If Saul is angry, then I shall know that he would kill me, but if he is not angry, it will be all right.' Jonathan said, 'So shall it be, but it will not be safe for anybody to know anything about it; come into the field, and I will tell you what to do. Thou shalt remain hidden by the stone, and I will bring a lad and my arrows and bow, and I will shoot an arrow as if firing at a target; and if I say 'Run,' to the lad, is not the arrow beyond thee? go fetch it,' then thou shalt know that thou must flee from Saul.' David's seat was empty at the feast that night, but Saul said nothing. But the next day his seat was empty, and when Saul asked why, Jonathan told him what David had asked him to say. And. Saul's anger was kindled, so much so that Jonathan feasted not that day, for he was grieved; and next morning he went out with his bow and arrows, and the lad, and shot an arrow as if at a mark. Then Jonathan said to the lad, 'Run, is not the arrow beyond thee? haste.' Then Jonathan gave his artillery unto the lad and sent him back to the city ; and David came out of his hiding-place, and they made a covenant together, for Jonathan loved him as his own soul. Then David had to flee to Naioth in Ramah and Jonathan went back to the city."

Q. What do you know of Richelieu? (Book studied, Mrs Creighton's First History of France.)

E. (aged 10), answer partly written, partly dictated:—

"Cardinal Richeleu (sic) was brought to the French Court by the Queen mother, who thought he would do as she wished, but she was mistaken, for he no sooner was there than he turned against her, for Louse (sic) took him into his favour and made him Prime Minister after he had been there a few weeks.

Richeleu (sic) was a devoted Catholic, and was determined to put down the Hugenots (sic), or Protestants as we call them, so he laid siege to La Rochelle, the chief town of the Hugenots (sic), who applied to the English for help. Charles sent a fleet to La ROchelle under pretence of helping the Hugenots (sic) [After this the answer was dictated.] but Admiral Pennington, who was in command of the ships, received orders when half way down the channel to take in French soldiers and sailors at Calais and to go to the French side.

When Admiral Pennington ordered the ships to take in the soldiers, his men mutinied and he had to go back. Richelieu had thrown up earthworks across the harbour so that it was impossible to get in. Now Rochelle held out bravely, but at last it had to surrender, and out of 40,000, 140 crawled out, too weak to bury the dead in the streets. La Rochelle was razed to the ground, and never recovered its prosperity. One by one the Huguenot towns surrendered, and thus the Huguenots were destroyed. When Richelieu was made Prime Minister, the nobles did not like him, because they thought he had too much power, and now when Louis was ill, the Queen mother came to him, and in a stormy passion of tears begged Louis to send away his ungrateful servant. Louis promised he would do so, and Richelieu's fall seemed certain. Now all the nobles crowded to the Queen mother to pay their respects to her, as they thought she would now be the most important person in the Government.

But one noble, who was wiser than the rest, went to Richelieu and begged to plead his cause before the King. The King promised he would keep him if he would serve him as he had done before.

The Queen mother was foiled, and returned to Brussels, where she died."

Q. What towns, rivers, and castles would you see in travelling about Warwickshire? (Book studied, Geographical Reader, Book III.)

B. (aged 9 1/2), answer dictated:—

"Warwick, Kenilworth, Coventry, Stratford, Leamington, and Birmingham are all towns which you would see if you travelled through Warwick.

"The Avon stretches from north to south of Warwickshire.

It has its tributary the Learn, upon which Leamington is situated.

"There is a castle of Warwick and Coventry and Kenilworth.

"Warwick is the capital of the county. It has a famous castle, whose high and lofty towers stand upon the bank of the river Avon.

"Coventry is a very old town. It also has a beautiful castle, where the fair Lady Godiva and her father used to live, about whom I suppose you have read.

"Stratford is called 'The Swan on the Avon,' because that is where Shakespeare, the great poet, was born and died, and this is a little piece of poetry about him;—

'Where his first infant lays, sweet Shakespeare sung,
Where the last accents faltered on his tongue.'

"The river Avon takes its rise in the vale of Evesham, then winds through pleasant fields and meadows till it comes to the south of Warwickshire, and then it becomes broad and stately and flows on up to Coventry, where the Leam branches off from it (!), and then it becomes narrower and narrower until it gets out of Warwickshire and stops altogether at Naseby (!)"

Q. How many kinds of bees are there in a hive? What work does each do? Tell how they build the comb. (Book studied, Fairyland of Science.)

F. (aged 10), answer dictated:—

"Three kinds. The drones or males, the workers or females, and the queen bee. The drone is fat, the queen is long and thin, the workers are small and slim. The queen bee lays the eggs, the worker bee brings the honey in and makes the cell, and the drones wait to be fed. On a summer's day you see something hanging on a tree like a plum pudding, this is a swarm of bees. You will soon see someone come up with a hive, turn it upside down, shake the bough gently, and they will fall in. They will put some clean calico quickly over the bottom of the hive, and turn it back over on a bench. The bees first close up every little hole in the hive with wax, then they hang on to the roof, clinging on to one another by their legs. Then one comes away and scrapes some wax from under its body, and bites it in its mouth until it is pulled out like ribbon, this she plasters on the roof of the hive, then she flies out to get honey, and comes home to digest it, hanging from the roof, and in 24 hours this digested honey turns to wax, then she goes through the same process again. Next, the nursing bees come and poke their heads into this wax, bite the wax away (20 bees do this before one hole is ready to make a cell). Other bees are working on the other side at the same time. Each cell is made six-sided, so as to take up the least wax and the smallest space. When the cells are made the bees come in with honey in their honey-bag or first stomach; they can easily pass the honey back though their mouths into the cells. It takes many bees to fill one cell, so they are hard at work."

G. (aged 9), written by child:Composition on 'The Opening of Parliament.'

"The opening of Parliament by King Edward VII and Queen Alexander (sic) was rather grand. First, they drove to the Houses of Parliament in a grand state carriage which had been used by George III, and then when they got there they had to robe in a certain room in great big robes, all edged with ermine fur, and with huge trains. Queen Alexandra had an evening dress on, and King Edward a very nice kingly sort of suit (which was nearly covered up by his robes), and then they walked along to the real Houses of Parliament, where the members really sit. Then the king made a speech to open Parliment (sic), and other people made speeches too, and everything was done with grandeur and stateliness such as would befit a king. May Parliament long be his!"

Class III.—In Class III. the range of age is from eleven or twelve to fifteen. The 'subjects': Bible Lessons and Recitations (Poetry and Bible passages); English Grammar, French, German, and Latin; Italian (optional); English, French, and Ancient History (Plutarch's Lives); Singing (French, English, and German Songs); Writing, Dictation, Drill; Drawing in Brush and Charcoal; Natural History, Botany, Physiology, Geography; Arithmetic; Geo,metry, and Reading.' About thirty-five books are used. Time, 3 1/2 hours a day; half an hour out of this time, as before, for drill and games. There is no preparation or home work in any of the classes. The reader will notice from the subjoined specimens that the papers are still written con amore, and show an intelligent grasp of the several subjects. Though there are errors in many of the papers, they are not often the mistakes of ignorance or stupidity, nor are they those of a person who has never understood what he is writing about. 'Composition' is never taught as a subject; well-taught children compose as well-bred children behave-by the light of nature. It is probable that no considerable writer was ever taught the art of 'composition.' The same remark may be made about spelling: excepting for an occasional 'inveterate' case, the habit of reading teaches spelling. All the pupils of the Parents' Review School do not take all the subjects set in the programmes of the several classes.. Sometimes, parents have the mistaken notion that the greater the number of subjects the heavier the work; though, in reality, the contrary is the case, unless the hours of study are increased. Sometimes, outside lessons in languages, music, etc., interfere; some times, health will not allow of more than an hour or two of work in the day. The children in the practising school do all the work set, and their work compares satisfactorily with the rest, though the classes have the disadvantage of changing teachers every week. Children in Class III. write the whole of their examination work.

Q. Describe the founding of Christ's Kingdom. What are the laws of His Kingdom?

A. (aged 13):—

"Christ came to found His kingdom. He preached the laws to His people. He taught them to pray for it: 'Thy kingdom come.' And He told His chosen few to 'go and preach the Gospel of the kingdom.' He founded His kingdom in their hearts, and He reigned there. He will still found His kingdom in our hearts. He will come and reign as King.. The kingdom was first founded by the sea of Galilee. 'Follow Me,' said our Lord to Andrew, and from that moment the kingdom was founded in Andrew's heart. Then there were Peter, James, John, Phillip (sic), Nathaniel (sic), and the kingdom grew. From that moment Christ never stopped

His work for the. kingdom—preaching and teaching, healing and comforting, proclaiming the laws of the kingdom. 'Think not that I am come to destroy the law or the prophets. I am not come to destroy, but to fulfil.' 'One jot or one tittle shall in no wise pass from the law.' ' Whosoever shall break one of these least commandments, and shall teach men so, the same shall be called the least in the kingdom.' No commandment was to pass from the law, but there was a new commandment, a new law, and that was' love.' 'Love your enemies.' The Pharisees could not understand it. 'Love your friends, and hate your enemies,' was their law. But Jesus said, 'Bless them that curse you, and pray for them that despitefully use you.' 'Give, hoping for nothing in return'; and, 'Whosoever shall smite thee on one cheek turn to him the other also.' Christ's law is the love which' suffereth long and is kind. . . . seeketh not her own. . . . never faileth . . . . hopeth all things, endureth all things'; and' now abideth faith, hope, and charity, these three, but the greatest of these is—love.'"

Q. Explain 'English Funds, Consols 2 3/4 per cent, 113.

And give an account of the South Sea Bubble. (Book studied, Arnold-Forster's History of England.)

B. (aged 14 1/2):—

"This means that when the South Sea Company first appeared, the Government gave them (L)II3 on condition that the Company should give 2 3/4 per cent, which means (L)2 15s. on every (L)100 lent, for a certain number of years. In the reign of George I. the money matters of the country were in a very bad state. The Government was very much in debt, especially to those people who had purchased annuities, and had a right to receive a certain sum of money from the Government every year as long as they lived. Sir Robert Walpole, who was then Prime Minister, was most anxious to pay off part of this debt. He heard of a Company which had just been started, called the South Sea Company, whose object was to trade in the South Seas. This was what Walpole wished for. He suggested to them that they should payoff the debt due to the people who had bought annuities, and in return the Government would give them some priveleges (sic) and charts which would be useful to them. This the Company agreed to do,but instead of paying the people in money they gave them what were called' shares' .in the South Sea Company. These shares were supposed to be very valuable; and it was thought that the South Sea Company was really prosperous, and that those who had shares in it would have most enormous profit in the end. Thousands of people came to buy shares, and some of them were so anxious to get them that they spent enormous sums of money on these worthless pieces of paper. All was well for a time, but at last the people began to wish for their money instead of the shares, and claimed it loudly from the Company. It was then that the bubble burst.

It was discovered then that the Company was quite unable to pay what was due, and that all this time they had been deluding the nation by promises and giving them shares, and that they had never been the rich and prosperous Company they made themselves out to be. Naturally, the most dreadful distress prevailed everywhere, and many were absolutely ruined, so that the Government had to help those who. were most distressed.

At this point Sir Robert Walpole came to the rescue. He made the Bank of England pay some of the debts, and behaved with such cleverness that he saved the country almost from ruin."

Q. What do you know of the States General? (Book studied, Mrs Creighton's First History of France.)

C. (aged 12):—

"The States General met in May, 1789. The people had long wanted reforms, and been talking about them, and now on the 5th of May, 1789, the States General met again for the first time since 1614. If the nobles sat in one bouse, and the people in another, as was the custom, they could never get tbe changes made. So the people with their leader, the Marquis of Mirabeau, declared that they would not leave the tennis court on which they were standing till it was agreed that they could sit together with the nobles. When Louis XVI. came down in State, and told them they were to sit apart, tbey said they would not leave their place except at the bayonets (sic) point. When he heard this he said, 'Very well, leave them alone.' So they sat together."

Q. Show fully how Aristides acquired the title of 'The Just.' Why was it a strange title for a man in those days? (Book studied, Plutarch's Lives: Anstitles.)

D. (aged 13 1/4):—

"Aristides acquired the title of 'The Just' by his justice, and because he never did anything unjust in order to become rich or powerful. While many of the judges and chief men in Athens took bribes, he alone always refused to do so, and he also never spent the public money on himself. When, after having defeated the

Persians, at Platae, the Greek States decided to have a standing army, it was Aristides who was sent round to settle how much each town should contribute. And he did this so fairly and well, that ail the Greek States blessed and praised his arrangement. It is said that Aristides could not only resiste (sic) the unjust claims of those whom he loved, but also those of his enemies. Once when he was judging a quarrel between two men, one of them remarked that the other had often injured Aristides. 'Tell me not that,' was the reply of Aristides, 'but what he has done to thee, for it is thy cause I am judging, not my own.' Another time when he had gone to law himself, and when, after having heard what he had to say, his judges were going to pass sentence on his adversary without having heard him, Aristides rose and entreated his judges to hear what his enemy could say. in his own defence. In all that he did Aristides was inflexibly Just, and many stories were told of his justice. Though he loved his country well, he would never do anything wrong to gain for Athens some advantage, and in all he did his one aim was justice, and his only ambition to be called' The Just.' He was so just and good, that he was called the 'most just man in Greece.' In the times in which Aristides lived, men used to care more to be called great, rich, or powerful than just. Themistocles, the great rival of Aristides, used to do all he could to become the first man in Athens, and rich as well as powerful. He did not besitate to take bribes, and all he did for the Athenians was done with a view to making himself the head of the people, and the first man in the State. He used often to do unjust as well as cruel things in order to get his own ends. It was the same with most other men who lived at this time, they prefered (sic) being rich, powerful or great, to being distinguished by the title of 'The Just.'"

Q, Describe a journey in Northern Italy. (Book studied, Geographical Reader, Book IV.).

E. (aged I2):—

"I am about to go for a tour round the northern part of Italy, and after I have taken a train to Savoy, which is about the south-east of France, I enter into Italy by the Cenis pass, which is very lofty, about 7,000 feet above sea level.

"On arriving in Italy, I come'into the province of Piedmont, which has three mountain torrents or streams running through it. These streams join at Turin, the capital of Piedmont, and form the Po river, which flows out on the east coast of France into the Gulf of Venice, On the banks of the three mountain streams are some Protestants by the name of Waldenses, who say they are followers of the disciples, but if you ask any outsider, they will say, 'Oh I the Waldenses are followers of a good man, by the name of Waldo, who fled out of France in the 12th century!

"We will now go and see Turin, and the first thing we say is, 'What a clean town,' and so it certainly is, for it is quite the cleanest town in Italy, as the people have only to turn on the fountain taps to clean their paved streets. And after we have looked at Alessandria, where Napoleon gained his great victory, we leave Piedmont and follow up the river Po, until we come to its next tributary, the river Ticino, which runs up north into the Lake Maggiore, which is five to six miles wide and about sixty miles in length, This lake has four islands, which are named after Count Borromeo and so called the Borromean Islands, which are cultivated like gardens with terrases (sic) for resting places.

"Now let us go to Milan, which is so well known by its beautiful cathedral of white and black marble which have (sic) no less than 4000 sculptures of white marble, with pillars of Egyptian granite. Milan is famous for silks and lace to provide for the numerous palaces.

"We will now go back to the next lake, Lake Como, which is surrounded by mountains, and supposed to be the most beautiful of all lakes. At the south it goes out in a fork, and between the fork is a beautiful piece of land called Bellagia (sic).

"The next lake we come to is the Garda, the largest of all the lakes, and then we go on to the smallest of lakes called Lugano.

"We now having visited all the lakes, take a look at Lodi, the famous cheese market in Italy; after which we visit Verona, where Pliny the naturalist was born, also Paul Veronese. Shakespeare lays the scene of his play 'Romeo and Juliet' in Verona. The short time we have we spend at Venice, the queen of the Italian citys (sic) with its wonderful canals and the marvellous cathedral of St Mark's, also the dark, gloomy palace of the Doge."

Q. How are the following seeds dispersed :—Birch, Pine, Dandelion, Balsam, Broom? Give diagrams and observations. (Book studied, Mrs Brightwen's Glimpses info Plant Life.)

F. (aged 13):—

"The seeds of the Birch are very small, with two wings, one on each side, so that in a high wind numbers of them are blown on to high places, such as crevises (sic) on the face of a rock, or clevises (sic) on a church tower, or the tower of an old ruin.

They are so light that they are carried a long way.

"The seeds of the Pine are very small, and the veins in the seed are wriggly, so that the seed is curly, which makes it whirl rapidly in the air, and the whirling motion carries it along a little way before it rests on the ground. It has two small wings.

"The seeds of the Dandilion (sic) are large, with a kind of silky parashute (sic) attached, so that when they fall off they do not fall to the ground, but are carried a little way because the wind catches the under part of the parashute (sic). The seed has a little hook at the top of it which prevents'lt from being pulled out of the ground by the parashute (sic) after it is once in.

"The Balsam seed case splits when the seeds are ripe and sends them flying in all directions, so they are far enough dispersed, and need no wings or parashutes (sic) to help them.

"The Broom seed case is a carpel, more like that of the sweet pea. When the seeds are ripe the two sides of the carpel split open and curl up like springs and send the seeds flying out, so they are dispersed without needing wings or parachutes."

Q. Describe the tissue of a potato and of a piece of rhubarb. (Book studied, Oliver's Elementary Botany.)

G. (aged 13):—

"The tissue of Rhubarb is very fibrous indeed. In fact, it is almost entirely made up of vessels. These are cells which have become tubes by the dividing cell-wall being absorbed. These vessels are very beautiful when seen under a microscope, for their walls are all thickened in some way, in order to make them strong enough to bear the weight of the leaf. Some are thickened by a spiral cord, which goes round and round the wall of the vessel In some vessels this is quite tightly twisted round the wall, that is to say, the rings do not come far apart; in others it is quite loose and far apart. Another kind of thickening is by rings, which just go round the tube and are not joined to each other. Other vessels, again, have little knots in them like what there are in birch bark.

"The Potato tissue is mainly made up of starch, as it is one of the plant's storehouses, and starch is one of the plant's principal

Q. Give a diagram of the eye, and explain how we see everything. (Book studied, Dr Schofield's Physiology for schools.)

H. (aged 13):—

"The eye can be likened to a camera, and the brain to the man behind the camera. The image enters at the hole, passes through the lens, is reflected on the plate, but the camera does not see, it is the man behind the camera who sees. In the same way, the image passes. in at the pupil and through the lens, both sides of which are curved, and can be tightened or slackened according to the distance of the image. Then the image passes along the nerve of sight to the two bulbs in the brain which see.

If you hold a rounded glass between a sheet of paper and the image at the right distance (for the glass cannot tighten or slacken like our lens), you will see the image reflected upside-down on the paper. This is the way the lens acts. There is a small yellow spot a little below the middle of the back of the eye; here the sight is more acute, and so, though we can see lots of things at one time, we can only look at one thing at a time. There is a blind spot where the nerve enters the eye (which shows that the nerve of sight itself is blind) so that some part of every image is lost, like a black dot punched in it. But we are so used to it that we cannot see it.

Q. Describe your favourite scene in Waverley.

I. (aged 12 1/2):—

"A Highland Stag Hunt.-The Highland Cheifs (sic) were in various postures: some reclining lazily on their plaids, others stalking up and down conversing with one another, and a few were already seated in position for the sport. MacIvor was talking with another Cheif (sic) as to what the sport would be; but as they talked in Gaelic, Edward had no part in the conversation, but sat looking at the scene before him. They were seated on a low hill at the head of a broad valley which narrowed into a small opening or cleft in the hills at the extreme end. It was hemmed in on all sides by hills of various heights. It was through this opening that the beaters were to drive the deer.

Already Waverly (sic) could hear the distant shouts of the men calling to each other coming nearer and nearer. Soon he could distinguish the antlers of the deer moving towards the opening like a forest of trees stiped (sic) of their leaves. The sportsmen prepared themselves to give them a warm reception, and all were ready as the deer entered the valley.

"They looked very ferocious, as they advanced towards where Edward and the cheifs (sic) were standing and seemed as if they were determined to fight; the roes and weaker ones in the centre, and the bulls standing as if on defence. As soon as they came within range, some of the cheifs (sic) fired, and two or three deer came down. Waverly (sic) also had the good fortune (and also the skill) to bring down a couple and gain the aplause (sic) of the other sportsmen. But the herd was now charging furiously up the valley towards them. The order was given to lie down, as it was impossible to stem the coming wave of deer; but as it was given in Gaelic it conveyed no meaning to Edward's mind, and he remained standing.

"The heard (sic) was now not fifty yards from him; and in another minute he would have been trampled to death; but MacIvor at his own risk, jumped up and literaly (sic) dragged him to the ground just as the deer reached them. Edward had a sensation as if he was out in a severe hail storm, but this did not last long.

"When they had passed, and Edward attempted to rise, he found that besides a number of bruises he had also severely sprained his ancle (sic), and was unable to walk, or even stand. A shelter was soon made for him out of a plaid in which he was laid; and then MacIvor called the Highland doctor or herbalist, to attend him. The doctor approached Edward with every sign of humiliation, but before attending to his ancle (sic), he insisted upon walking slowly round him several times, in the direction in which the sun goes, muttering at the same time a spell over him as he went, and though Waverly (sic) was in great pain he bad to submit to his foolery. Waverly (sic) saw to his great astonishment that MacIvor believed or seemed to believe in the old man's cantations (sic). At last, when he bad finished his spells, which he seemed to think more necessary than the dressing, he drew from his pocket a little packet of herbs, some of which he applied to the sprained ancle (sic) and after it had been bound up, Edward felt much relieved. He rewarded the doctor with some money, the value of which seemed to exceed his wildest imaginations, for he heaped so many blessings upon the head of Waverly (sic) that MacIvor said, ' A hundred thousand curses on you,' whereupon he stopped."

Class IV.—Girls are usually in Class IV. for two or three years, from fourteen or fifteen to seventeen, after which they are ready to specialise and usually do well. The programme for Class IV. is especially interesting; it adds Geology and Astronomy to the sciences studied, more advanced Algebra to the Mathematics, and sets the history of Modern Europe instead of French history. The literature, to illustrate the history, includes the reading of a good many books, and the German and French books when possible illustrate the history studied. All the books (about forty) are of a different calibre from those used in the lower classes; they are books for intelligent students.

I think the reader will observe that due growth has taken place in the minds of the girls, both as regards judgment and power of appreciation. Not, I think, in intelligence,—

"Love has no nonage, nor the mind."

But as our concern is with boys and girls under twelve, it will be enough to show by two or three papers that this sort of education by books results in intelligence.

Q. For what purpose were priests instituted? (Book studied, Dr Abbot's Bible Lessons.) A. (aged 15 1/2):—

"The system of the Jewish priesthood was almost entirely symbolical. God ordained it, we believe, to lead the primitive mind of his chosen people onwards and upwards, to the true belief and earthly comprehension of that great sacrifice, by the grace of which we are all now honoured to become 'kings and priests unto God.' In the earliest times of the patriarchs, there was in every holy and honourable Jewish family some voluntary priest to offer up the burnt offerings and yearly sacrifices. We have an example of this in Job the patriarch, who, we read, ministered to his family in the capacity of priest of their offerings. In the wilderness, however, God commanded through Moses the foundation of a separate and holy priesthood to minister in His Tabernacle and offer His appointed sacrifices. The tribe of Levi and the family of Aaron were set apart for this purpose, and in the building of the tabernacle, and the annointing (sic) of Aaron and his four sons, the cornerstone was laid to that great building which became a fit dwelling for the presence of God and the heart of Israel, until Christ came to change and lighten the world; and the symbol and the shadow became the truth."

Q. "His power was to assert itself in deeds, not words."

Write a short sketch of the character of Cromwell, discussing the above statement. (Book studied, Green's Shorter History of the English. People.)

B. (aged 15):—

"Cromwell was no orator. It has been said that if all his speeches were taken and made into a book, it would seem simply a pack of nonsense. In Parliament though, the earnestness with which he spoke attracted attention. His deeds proved his innate power, which could not express itself in words. He may be called the inarticulate man. In his mind, everything was clear, and his various actions proved his purposes and determinations, but in speaking, he simply brought out a hurried volume of words, in the mazes of which one entirely lost the point meant to be implied. Cromwell also was more of an administrator than a statesman, unspeculative and conservative. He was subject to fits of hypocondria (sic), which naturally had some effect on his character. He considered himself a servant of God, and acted accordingly. Undoubtedly he was under the conviction that he was carrying out the Lord's will in all he did. He was not in calm moods a bloody man, but when his anger was kindled he would spare no one. At times be would be filled with remorse for the part he had taken in the martyrdom of the king; then, again be would say it was the just punishment of heaven on Charles. In giving orders his words were curt and to the point, but in making speeches he adopted the phraseology of the Bible, which added to their ambiguity. One would think he was ambitious, for at one time he asked Whitelock: 'What if a man should take upon himself to be king?' evidently having in view the regal power, and yet according to his own assertion he would rather have returned to his occupation as a farmer, than have undertaken the government of Britain. But in this, as in other acts, he recognised the call of God, (as he thought) and obeyed it."

Q. What do you know of the Girondins? (Book studied, Lord's Modern Europe.)

C. (aged I7):—

"The Girondins were the perhaps most tolerant and reasonable of the revolutionary parties. They were a body of men who found the government of France under the king more than they could stand, and who were the first to welcome any changes, but were shocked and horrified at the dreadful riots and massacres which followed the fall of the throne. Such a party, representing justice and reform, could not be popular with the more violent Jacobins and like clubs. The day came when these latter were in power, and all the Girondins were thrown into prison.

"They were all taken from prison before the Court of Justice for trial, and placed before the judge, where they sat quitb silently; they were one by one condemned to execution, receiving the sentence of death with perfect calmness. Only their leader was seen to fall down; one of his companions leant over him and said: 'What, are you afraid?' , Non,' was the answer, 'Je mours,' he had stabbed himself with his dagger.

"As the Girondins marched back to their cells, condemned to die the next morning, they all sang the 'Marseillaise,' as they had arranged, to tell their fellow-prisoners what the sentence had been. When they reached the prison a splendid supper was placed for them, and they all sat down with great cheerfulness to eat it, none of them showing the least signs of breaking down. Towards morning priests were sent to them, and very early in the day they all marched to the foot of the guillotine, singing as they went. They kept on singing a solemn chant when the executions commenced, which became fainter and fainter as one by one they were beheaded, until all were gone."

Q. Distinguish between arrogant and presumptuous, interference and interposition, genuine and authentic, hate and detest, loathe and abhor, education and instruction, apprehend and comprehend, using each word in a sentence. (Book studied, Trench's Study of Words.)

E. (aged 15):—

"A man who is 'arrogant' is a man who has right to what he wants, but who is harsh and exacting in taking it. A 'presumptuous' man is a man who expects more than is due and takes it. 'Judge Jeffries was an arrogant old man.' 'Charles II. was a presumptuous king, he thought he could have absolute power.' " 'Interference,' is not minding your own business, and meddling with other people's when we are not wanted. 'Interposition' is more the' doing good by interfering' as protecting a little boy from a bully. 'But for the interference of James all would have gone well.' 'Thanks to the interposition of Mary a quuarrel was averted.'

"Genuine' means real, true, what it seems to be a—'a real genuine ruby.' 'Authentic,' in speaking of a book, means really written by the author to which it is ascribed. 'Dickens' Oliver Twist is certainly authentic!

"You would 'hate' a man who killed your father. 'Charles II. hated Cromwell.' You would' detest' a man who had not done you any personal injury, but who (sic) you knew to be a murderer. 'Yeo detested the Spaniards.'

"You would 'loathe' a poisonous snake or a hypocrite. 'David Copperfield loathed Uriah Heep! You would abhor a man inferior to you in intellect or principles, as a great king would 'abhor' a cringing coward, leave him behind, go on without him, refuse to listen to him. 'Napoleon abhorred the traitor.'

"'Education' is the lessons you receive as a matter of course, as French, writing, grammar. 'Instruction' is this, but more also, it includes moral teaching, the teaching of honesty, and the teaching of gentleness. 'Henry had a good education.' 'No well-instructed Britain (sic) is a coward.'"

'Apprehend' is to see, or hear, and notice. 'Comprehend' is to understand, without seeing or hearing perhaps. 'Phillip apprehended that danger was near, but he did not comprehend it.'"

Q. Give shortly Carlyle's estimate of Burns, showing what he did for Scotland, and what was the cause of his personal failure in life. (Book studied, Carlyle's Essay on Burns.)

F. (aged 17):—

"Carlyle looked upon Burns as one of the nicest of men and greatest of poets; rather a weak man, perhaps, but covering all his faults with his genius and kindness of heart, clever and persevering, and basely neglected and shunned by his contemporaries. It is quite extraordinary to read the worldfamous poems of this poet, and to remember that he was a ploughman, and surrounded only by the most uneducated peasants and fellow-labourers, though, of course, the life of a ploughman in the hills of Scotland is far more likely to encourage poetry and reflection than the life of many a London dentist or hair-dresser far higher in rank; but it is easy to believe in fact, that Burns would have found inspirations for his genius in a flat sandy waste or a grocer's shop, and, as Carlyle says, a man or woman is not a genius unless they are extraordinary, not really inspired if such a person could have been imagined before. Robert Burns has provided Scotland for centuries at least, with plenty of national poetry, his poems are such as can be enjoyed, like flowers and trees and all things really beautiful, by old and young, stupid and clever, fishermen and prime ministers—surely that is a work of which any man would be proud!

"Burns (sic) chief fault, if fault it can be called, and the cause of his failure in life, seems to have been a sort of bitterness against people more fortunate than himself without the art of hiding it. This, real or affected, seems very common in poets, and such an inspired man, a man with a mind greater than kings, must have felt very deeply, almost without knowing it, the 'unrefinedness' of the people he loved best, and his own distance from the admirers who clustered round him later in life.

"All his life, it seems, he was in a place by himself, now spending his time with his own family, acting a part all day, trying to make his relations feel him an equal, pretending to take a great interest in what he did not care for—the pigs, and cows, and porridge, seeing his own dearest friends looking at him with awe, and feeling him something above them, thinking of his 'great' friends, and feeling embarrassed when he came, and more at ease without his presence.

"Now, on the other hand, associating with people, high in rank and education, enjoying their friendship and praise, but feeling, be they ever so kind and familiar, that he was not their equal by birth, and that they could not treat him quite as such, however hard they might try, turning familiarity in his mind into slights, and kindness into condescension. This to a proud man must have been misery, and Burns must have been very lonely in a crowd of companions, thronged with admirers, but without a friend.

"Nobody understood Burns; he shared his opinions with no one he knew. When, at the beginning of the French Revolution he expressed his delight and approval, the people who admired him were shocked, refused to speak to him, and regarded him either as mad or terribly wicked. His poems were not admired as much as they deserved to be, he had hardly any money, was never likely to get on in the world, was shunned and disgraced, and began, as a last resource, 1 to drink too much. Ill health was one of his misfortunes, and this intemperance killed him.

"Thus died at the age of thirty-seven, poor, friendless, despised, the man who has given pleasure to thousands, and an undying collection of poems and songs to his country."

Q. Give some account, as far as you can in the style of Carlyle, of the Procession of May 4th. (Book studied, Carlyle's Frenen Revolution.)

1 The writers have been in two minds about the spelling of words muked (1).

G. (aged I4 1/2):—

"See the doors of Notre Dame open wide, the Procession issuing 1 forth, a sea of human faces that are to reform France. First come the nobles in their gayly (sic) tinted robes, next the clergy, and then the commons, the Tiers Etats in their slouched hats firm and resolute, and lastly the king, and the OEuil-de-boeuf, these are greeted by a tremendous storm of vivats. Vive Ie roi! Vive la nation! Let us suppose we can take up some coigne (sic) of vantage from which we can watch the procession, but with eyes different from other eyes, namely with prophetic eyes. See a man coming, striding at the head of the Tiers Etats, tall and with thick lips and black hair, whose father and brother walk among the nobles. Close beside walks Doctor Guillotin, 1 learned Doctor Guillotin, 1 who said, 'My friends (mes amis), I have a machine that wiIl whisk off your heads in a second, and cause you no pain,' now doomed for two years to see and hear nothing but guillotin, and for more than two centuries after yonder a desolate ghost on this (sic) of the Styx. Mark, too, a small mean man, a sea-green man with sea-green eyes, Robespierre by name, a small underhand secretary walking beside one Dantun (sic) tall and massive, cruelty and vengeance on their faces. We may not linger longer, but one other we must note, one tall and active with a cunning air, namely, Camille Desmouellins (sic), one day to rise to fame and the next to be forgotten.

"Many more walk in that procession one day to become famous, Bailli, future president of a New Republick (sic), and Marat, with Broglie the War. God and others.

"The Tiers Etats with Mayor Bailli march to the rooms where they are to sit, but the doors are shut: there is sound of hammering within.

"Mayor Bailli knocks, and wants to know why they are shut out? It is the king's orders. He wants his papers. He may come in and get them, and with this they must be content.

"They swarm to Versailles, the king steps out on the balconny (sic) and speaks. He says the room is being prepared for his own august presence; a platform is being erected, he says he is sorry to inconvience (sic) them; but he is afraid they must wait, and with that he retires. Meanwhile patriotism consults as to what had best be done. Shall they meet on the palace steps? or even in the streets? At length they adjourn to the tennis court, and there patriotism swears one by one to be faithful to the New National Assembly, as they now name themselves This is known as the Oath of the Tennis Court."

1 The writers have been in two minds about the spelling of words marked (1), I have placed before the reader examples of a portion of some thirty pupils' work to illustrate their education by books. It is not necessary to speak of their education by Things: that is thorough and systematic; but may I point out that what has been cited is average work. I do not know if the reader considers that I have proved my point, that is, that 'studies'—schoolroom studies—'are for delight, for ornament, and for ability.'

APPENDIX III

What a Child Should Know at Twelve

In order to induce the heads of schools (private schools, preparatory schools, girls' schools, and' Lower' schools) to consider seriously whether it is not possible to introduce some such method of Education by Books, let me put forward a few considerations :—

1. The cost of the books per pupil for the six years—from six to twelve—does not average more than (L) 1 a year. A scheme of work for elementary schools might be arranged at a much less annual cost for books.

2. Two and a half, for Class I., to three and a half hours a day, for Class III., is ample time for this book education.

3. Much writing is unnecessary, because the pupils have the matter in their books and know where to find it.

4. Classes II. and III. are able to occupy themselves in study with pleasure and profit.

5. Teachers are relieved of the exhausting drudgery of many corrections.

6. The pupils have the afternoons for handicrafts, nature-work, walks, games, etc.

7. The evenings are free, whether at school or at home, for reading aloud, choral singing, hobbies, etc.

8. The pupils get many intelligent interests, beget hobbies, and have leisure for them.

9. There is no distressing cramming for the term's examination. The pupils know their work, and find it easy to answer questions set to find out what they know, rather than what they do not know.

10. Children of any age, however taught hitherto, take up this sort of work with a avidity.

11. Boys and girls taught in this way take up ordinary school work, preparation for examinations, etc., with intelligence, zeal, and success.

The six years' work—from six to twelve—which I suggest, should and does result in the power of the pupils—

(a) To grasp the sense of a passage of some length at a single reading: and to narrate the substance of what they have read or heard.

(b) To spell, and express themselves in writing with ease and fair correctness.

(c) To give an orderly and detailed account of any subject they have studied.

(d) To describe in writing what they have seen, or heard from the newspapers.

(e) They should have a familiar acquaintance with the common objects of the country, with power to reproduce some of these in brushwork.

(f) Should have skill in various handicrafts, as cardboard Sloyd, basket-making, clay-modelling, etc.

(g) In Arithmetic, they should have some knowledge of vulgar and decimal fractions, percentage, household accounts, etc.

(h) Should have a knowledge of Elementary Algebra, and should have done practical exercises in Geometry.

(i) Of Elementary Latin Grammar; should read fables and easy tales, and, say, one or two books of 'Caesar.'

(j) They should have some power of understanding spoken French, and be able to speak a little; and to read an easy French book without a dictionary.

(k) In German, much the same as in French, but less progress.

(l) In History, they will have gone through a rather detailed study of English, French, and Classical (Plutarch) History.

(m) In Geography they will have studied in detail the map of the world, and have been at one time able to fill in the landscape, industries, etc., from their studies, of each division of the map.

(n) They will have learned the elements of Physical Geography, Botany, Human Physiology, and Natural History, and will have read interesting books on some of these subjects.

(o) They should have some knowledge of English Grammar.

(p) They should have a considerable knowledge of Scripture History and the Bible text.

(q) They should have learned a good deal of Scripture and of Poetry, and should have read some Literature.

(r) They should have learned to sing on the Tonic Sol-fa method, and should know a number of English, French, and German Songs.

(s) They should have learned Swedish Drill and various drills and calisthenic exercises.

(t) In Drawing they should be able to represent common objects of the house and field with brush or charcoal; should be able to give rudimentary expression to ideas; and should be acquainted with the works of some artists through reproductions.

(u) In Music their knowledge of theory and their ear-training should keep pace with their powers of execution.

This is the degree of progress an average pupil of twelve should have made under a teacher of knowledge and ability. Progress in the disdplinary subjects, languages and mathematics, for example, must depend entirely on the knowledge and ability of the teacher.

APPENDIX IV

Examination of a Child of Twelve, in the 'Parents' Review' School, on the Work of a Term

Possibl a complete set of answers to an examination paper may be of use as showing the all-round standing of a scholar educated on the principles I have advanced. This paper is not exceptional, and some weakness will be noticed in what I have called the disciplinary subjects.

Programme of the Term's Work on which the Examination Queslions are sel.

Bible Lessons.

The Bible for the Young; by the Rev. J. Paterson Smyth (Sampson, Low, 2S.), Genesis, Lessons xvii.-xxiv., S. Matthew, Lessons xvi.-xxiv., and the Lesson on Christmas. Teacher to prepare lesson beforehand, and to use the Bible passages in teaching. Answers to Catechism with explanations from the beginning to the Lord's Prayer (optional).

Recitations.

Learn two passages of 20 verses each from chapters in Bible Lessons. Learn The Death of the Duke of Wellington; The Charge of the Light Brigade; You ask me Why.

French. [Where the Gouin Series are not taken, French, German, and Italian should be taught orally, teacher repeating aloud, pupil reciting after her.]

The Gouin Series; A Study of French, by Eugene & Duriaux (Edition 1898, Macmillan & Co., 3s. 6d.), pages 184, 194, 196, 198; teacher study preface. Premiere Annee Grammaire, par P. Larousse, Rules 61, 63, 64, 66, 70, 74, Exercises 55, 58, 61, 63. Read the first half of Le General Dourakine, par Mdme. de Segur (Hachette, lS.), parse two pages. Learn a poem from Recueil de Poesies, par Mdme. de Witt (Hachette, 2S.).

German. [Where the Gouin Series are not taken, French, German, and Italian should be taught orally, teacher repeating aloud, pupil reciting after her.]

Eight sections of the Gouin Series; (or, translate into English and retranslate into German pages 1-8 from Niebuhr's Heroengeschichten (Clarendon Press, IS. 6d.). Book of Ballads on German History (University Press, 2S.); two ballads to be learnt by heart. First German Book, by A. L. Becker (Hachette, IS.), Lessons xxvii-xxxv. Use the words, from the lists of useful words, in sentences. Beginners read from Part II., reading lessons, (ss) 16-23. Practise letters on pages xiii.-xvi.

Italian.

Ex-Students of House of Education, six of the Gouin Series. Twelve grammar rules exemplified in Series. Teachers use Perini's Italian Conversation Grammar (Hachette, 4s.).

Latin.

Young Beginners' Third Latin Book (Murray, 2S.), pages 9-15. Revise back work by means of exercises.

Young Beginners' Second Latin BooR (Murray, 2S.), pages 60-71.

Beginners.—Hall's Child's First Latin Book (Murray, 2S.), 15-32; or, better, A First Latin Book, by E. H. Scott and F. Jones (Blackie, IS. 6d.), pages 1-32.

English History.

A History oj England, by H. O. Arnold-Forster (Cassell, 5s.), pages 719-758 (1820-1897). Read Scott's Lady of the Lake, and, if possible, Henry Kingsley's Valentin (Ward, Lock & Co.).

French History.

Creighton's First History oj France (Longmans, 3s. 6d.), pages 279-293, to be contemporary with English history.

Roman History.

Plutarch's Romulus, teacher omitting unsuitable parts (Cassell's National Library, 3d.).

Geography.

Geikie's Physical Geography (Macmillan, IS.), pages 108-131, (ss) 224-270. London Geographical Readers (Stanford), Book V. (2S. 6d.), pages 238-267, with special reference to recent events; map questions to be answered from map and then from memory, and then in filling up blank map from memory before each Lesson. Know something about foreign places coming into notice in the current newspapers. Ten minutes' exercise on the map of the world every week. The School Atlas, edited by H. O. Arnold-Forster (37 Bedford Street, London, IS. 6d or 3s.). Read also Arnold-Forster's History of England, chapters lxxv. and lxxvi.

English Grammar.

Morris's English Grammar (Macmillan, IS.), pages 100-108, 98-99 (inclusive). Parse and analyse, using pages 109-125. Work from Morris's English Grammar Exercises (Macmillan, IS.).

Singing.

Three French songs, La Lyre ties Ecoles (Curwen & Son).

Three German songs, Erk's Deutsclter Liederschatz (Peters, Leipsic). Three English songs, Novello's School Songs, Vol. xx. (8eL). Stainer's Primer of Tonic Solfa (Curwen & Son).

Writing.

Choose and transcribe ten poems or passages from Wordsworth. German Copybook, No. I. (Nutt, 4d.). A New Handwriting for Teachers, by M. M. Bridges (Mrs Bridges, Yattenden, Newbury, 2s. 9g); work to page 6, following instructions.

Drill.

Grecian Exercises and Marching Drills from Musical Drills for the Standards (Philip & Son, 2S. 6eL).. Ex-Students, House of Education Drills.

Dictation.

Growth and Greatness of our World-wide Empire, pages 32-77 (four or five pages a week) to be prepared, a passage dictated, or, occasionally, written from memory.

Drawing.

Pour Dessiner Simplement, par V. Jacquot et P. Ravoux (3S. 6d.), cahier ii., iii., for occasional use. Twelve wild fruits on their branches, with background, in brushwork; illustrations in brush-drawing from The Lady of the Lake. Study and be able to describe the pictures in The Holy Gospels, Part II. (S.P.C.K., IS. 8d.) (optional); or, Join the Portfolio of Paintings (see The Children's Quarterly); or, Follow the Fisole Club Papers.

Natural History.

Keep a Nature Note-Book. Geikie's Geology (Macmillan, IS.), pages 125-144 (mountains), with questions.

Refer to in holidays, and study in term, Lowly Water Animals, Lessons 1-21, inclusive.

Botany.

Oliver's Elementary Botany (Macmillan, 45. 6d.), chapter vii., pages 63-87. Glimpses into Plant Life, Brightwen (Fisher Unwin, 2S.), chapters v. and ix. Record the finding of and describe twenty wild fruits (see Oliver).

Specimens must be used in all botanical work. Observe all you can about the structure of various fruits (not edible), and about the dispersion of seeds. Plant Lift in Field and Garden, by A. Buckley, pages 40-80.

Physiology.

Schofield's Physiology for Schools (Cassell, IS. 9d.), pages 43-64.

Arithmetic.

Mail's Mental Arithmetic (Sonnenschein, 9d.). Long. man's Junior School Arithmetic (IS.), chapters xxi. and xxii., Practice and Bills. Miscellaneous examples from pages 192 and 193.

Beginners, chapters xvii., xviii., and xix., (ss) 74-81.

Euclid.

A First Step in Euclid, by J. G. Bradshaw (Macmillan, IS. 6d.), pages 63-81.

Beginners. - Inductdive Geometry, by H. A. Nesbitt, M.A. (Sonnenschein, IS. 6d.), chapters iv., v., vi. Members who have Hamblin Smith's Euclid may continue to use it. The books now set are more modern and lead to more intelligent work.

Reading.

Geography, English history, French history, and tales should afford exercise in careful reading. Poetry should be read daily.

Composition.

Read on Thursdays and write from memory on Tuesdays (a) a passage from Ecce Homo, Ecce Rex, Part II., chapters ii. and iit, by Mrs R. Charles (S.P.C.K., 3S. 6d.); (b) Amold-Forster's History of England, chapter Ixxvii.

Work.

Attend to garden. Bent Iron Work, by F. J. Erskine (Upcott Gill, IS.). Make six models. Self-Teaching Needlework Manual, edited by S. Loch (Longmans, IS.), pages 25-54. Make a baby's crochet petticoat with body part. Make a linen book cover, with design drawn and worked by yourself.

N.B.—For illustrations for History, Geography, etc., see the catalogue of the Perry Pictures (Art for Schools Association, 46 Great Ormond Street, London, 3d.).

Children who are beginners or who have just been moved up from Class II., or who find the work difficult, may omit three subjects.

Questions on Preceding Programme.

Bible Lessons.

I. 1. Show how God trained Joseph for his work. What lessons may we learn from Joseph (a) in prison, (b) in a palace?

2. (a)" I am Joseph," (b) "Bless the lads," (c) "Until Shiloh come." Give the context in each case, and describe the occasions on which these words were used.

II. 1. Tell the parable (a) of the Fig-tree, (b) of the Two Sons. What lessons may we learn from each?

2. (a) "Shall I crucify your King?" (b) "He.... wept bitterly," (c) "He is risen." Give the context (in the Bible words if possible) of each of these quotations.

Recitations.

Father to choose two passages, of ten verses each, from the Bible Lessons, and a poem.

French.

1. Write down in French the names of things that a huntsman uses for the chase.

2. Recite the poem learned.

3. Write in French a short resume of the chapters read in Le General Dourakine.

4. Make sentences to show the use of cette, ces, ce, cet, leurs, ses, tel, chaque, meme, nul.

German.

1. Say three sections of a Gouin Series, and translate into English and retranslate into German page 6, lines 14-24, from Heroengeschichten.

2. Translate into German :—(a) Which of these flowers is the finest? (b) I have been once in Berlin and three times in Paris.

3. Make sentences with other adjectives, using the German for 6, 15, 17, 9, 4, 18.

Italian.

Recite two Series, and give two rules exemplified.

Latin.

1. Translate into English and retranslate into Latin Fable V., page 61, and parse each word in the first sentence.

2. Translate into Latin :—(a) We dream whole nights; (b) I will teach you music; (c) The Roman people elected Numa king; (d) The Gauls dwell on this side the Rhine; (e) The master sees that many boys play. What rule is illustrated in each sentence?

Beginners— Translate into Latin :—(a) Where is the shield? (b) A narrow shield is bad; (c) The hen is small.

2. Make sentences using the words hic, porta, augusta, duo, capita, dux, quattuor, qui, sumus, murum, vident.

English History.

1. What do you know of the Anti-Corn Law League, and what have you heard or read about a similar agitation in this country to-day?

2. What reasons induced each of the five countries engaged to enter on the Crimean War? Give some account of the war.

3. "It was felt by all .. . that the government of India. . . . could not be left in the hands of the East India Company." Why? Give some account of the events which led up to this.

French History.

1. Write shortly the history of the war with Prussia.

2. Describe the new constitution of 1875.

Roman History.

1. "Sardians to be sold." Who said this? Tell the story.

2. How did Romulus unite the Romans and the Sabines?

Geography.

1. Describe, with a map, a visit to the West Indies. What recent event in these islands do you know of?

2. Write a short description of (a) Mexico, and (b) a Brazilian forest.

3. What is meant by saying, "The gates of the pathways of the sea are in the hands of the British race"? Illustrate with a map.

4. How are coral reefs formed? Give a diagram of one. Describe, with diagrams, a volcano.

English Grammar.

1. Analyse, parsing the words in italics:—

One by one the flowers close,
Lily and dewy rose
Shutting their tender petals from the moon.
The grasshoppers are still; but not so soon
Are still the noisy crows.

2. Make sentences, showing the different ways in which the following may be used :—dying, making, t tell, but.

3. Give some words with each of the following prefixes :—eft, hypo, cata, di, syn.

Singing. 1

Father to choose an English, a French, and a German song, and three Tonic Sol-fa exercises.

Writing.

Write ten lines of Tennyson's from memory.

1 Subjects thus indicated to be marked by the parents according to Regulations.

Drill.

Drill, before parents.

Dictation.

Growth and Greatness of our World-Wide Empire, page 43, "Not. . . home."

Reading. 1

Father to choose unseen poem.

Drawing.

(a) Paint a carrot, an onion, and a potato grouped together, (b) an illustration in brushdrawing of a scene from The Lady of the Lake, (c) a glove, a trowel, and a rake in charcoal.

Natural History.

1. Describe (a) six sea (or pond) creatures you found this last summer, (b) the Foraminiferae. How do sponges grow? Give a diagram.

2. What do we know of the origin of mountains? Describe any formation you have examined this term -- in cliff, river basin, or quarry.

Botany.

1. Give rough diagrams showing the manner of growth, with leaf buds, of the twigs of the following trees:—oak, ash, horse-chestnut, beech, sycamore.

2. Compare the fruits of the raspberry, strawberry, and blackberry, with diagrams.

3. What are some of the ways in which plants store food? Give examples.

Physiology.

1. What are the functions of the skin? Give a diagram of the skin cells.

Arithmetic.

1. Find, by Practice, the cost of I ton 2 cwt. 2 qrs. and 20 lbs. at (L)1, 13S. 10d. per cwt.

2. Find the cost of 4959 balls at 11 3/4d. each.

3. How much property tax should I pay on (L)5238, IOS. od. at 8 1/2d. in the (L)?

4. Make out an invoice for 5 pairs of stockings at IS. 3 1/2d. per pair; 40 needles at 13 1/2d. per score; 96 buttons at 6 1/2d. a dozen; 6 3/4 yds. silk at 5s. IOd. a yard.

Beginners

1. Find the G.C.M. of 12321 and 54345, and the L.C.M. of 12, 18, 30, 48, and 60.

2. Reduce: 11385/16335, 96679/119427.

3. Find the sum of the quotient and remainder when 36789241 is divided by 365.

Euclid.

1. To bisect a given finite straight line.

2. To draw a straight line perpendicular to a given straight line of unlimited length from a given point without it.

3. Divide a given angle into four equal parts.

or,

1. Prove that the two angles of a triangle are always less than two right angles.

2. Draw a kite consisting of an equilateral triangle and an isosceles triangle twice the height.

3. The latitude of London is 51 1/2 degrees N. How far is it from the South Pole?

Compostition.

Write some account of (a) Recent events with regard to Korea and Macedonia;

or, (b) (a) Scott, or (b) Burns, and his work. (c) Write twenty lines on "An Autumn Evening" in the metre of The Lady of The Lake.

Work 1

Outside friend to examine.

P.Q., aged 12. CLASS III.

List of Subjects taken.

Bible Lessons.

French.

German.

Latin.

English History.

French do.

Roman do.

Geography.

English Grammar.

Writing.

Dictation.

Natural History.

Botany

Physiology.

Arithmetic.

Euclid.

Composition.

All the answers, in the subjects taken, have been attempted; a few of these are omitted here for reasons of space. The maps and diagrams are rather well done, but cannot be reproduced. The writer's spelling, pointing, etc. have been carefully preserved.

Bible Lessons.

1. 2. (a) "I am Joseph, your brother, whom ye sold into Egypt." These words were spoken by Joseph when he was revealing himself to his brethren. His brothers had come down into Egypt a second time to buy food, and had persuaded their father Jacob to let them take Benjamin down with them, because Joseph had told them that they must. So Jacob reluctantly let Benjamin go. And now they had bought their com, and actually been asked to dine with Joseph, and were on their homeward way, when some officers of Joseph's household come galloping after them, and angrily ask whether the way to return hospitality is to steal Joseph's cup, his favourite silver cup. Then when the cup is found in Benjamin's sack, Judah, who has promised to be surety for him, begs that he may be a slave to Joseph instead of Benjamin, as he promised Jacob his father to bring him back safe. Then they are all taken in to see Joseph, and he cannot stand it any longer, and bursts into tears, and says "I am Joseph; doth my father yet live?" 'And his brethren could not answer him for they were troubled at his presence. And Joseph said unto his brethren "Come near to me, I pray you." And they came

near. And he said "I am Joseph your brother whom ye sold into Egypt."' So then of course they believed him, and everything was made all right.

(c) Jacob lay on his death-bed with his sons around him, listening to his words which seemed to come straight from God. But instead of Reuben, as the first-born getting the best or most wonderful blessing, he seems to have been put below Judah, who is told that he shall be "a fruitful bough," and shall remain "Until Shiloh' come." This seems to be a wonderful inspiration in Jacob that someone should come from the descendants of his son Judah who "should save His people from their sins." Of course, now, we see in it a prophecy of the coming of our Lord Jesus Christ, though then it was most likely an undefined thought.

II. 1. (b) "There was a man that had two sons; and he went to one, and said "Son, go to work to-day in my vineyard." And he answered and said "I will not"; but afterwards he repented, and went. And the father went to the other son and said "Son, go to work to-day in my vineyard." And he answered and said "I go, sir," but went not at all to the work. Whether of the twain did the will of their father?" They (the priests) say unto him "the first." "From this we see that the parable was aimed at the chief priests, scribes, and Pharisees, who had been trying to trap him in his talk. The man was God, the two sons, those that did his will, and those that did not, and the vineyard was the world. The scribes and Pharisees were those who made a lot of show, and were very particular about all the little outside observances of religion, but did not really work, like the son in the parable who said "I go, sir" and did not go at all, Thus they were made to condemn themselves by saying that the first did the will of God, and not the second,

2, (a) Pilate had been cross-examining Jesus, and had "found no fault in him," When he asked the people what he should do with him, they cried out, saying "Crucify him, crucify him." But Pilate answered and said "Shall I crucify your King?" But they cried out yet the more, saying "Crucify him, crucify him." Then Pilate took a bason, and washed his hands before the multitude saying "I have nothing to do with this righteous man; see ye to it," And the people cried out, saying "His blood be upon us and upon our children," Then Jesus was led away,

French.

1. Un fusil, une bandouliere, des cartouches, une gibeciere, un permis de chasse, et une meute de chiens,

2 (recited),

"Savez-vous son nom?"—La nature
Reunit en vain ces cent voix.
L'etoile a l'etoile murmure
"Quel Dieu nous imposa nos lois?"
La vague a la vague demande
"Quel est celui qui nous gourmande?"
La foudre dit a l'aquilon
"Sais-tu comment ton Dieu se nomme?"
Et les astres, la terre, et l'homme
Ne peuvent achever son nom,
Que tes temples, Seigneur, sent etroits pour mon ame!
Tombez, murs impuissants, tombez!
Laissez-moi voir ce ciel que vous me derobez!
Architecte divin, tes domes sont de flammes !
Que tes temples, Seigneur, sont etroits pour mon ame!
Tombez, murs impuissants, tombez!

4. Cette aiguille est tres aigue. Ces animaux soot de trois familles. Ce mouvement est tres facile; un pas avec ce pied, et il faut qu'un bras faire ce tour. Cet homme etait bien fait de sa personne. Ils etaient tres sages; ils mettaient leurs livres dans l'armoire, pas sur la table. Ses filles etaient tres mechantes. Il fit un tel pas, que je pensais qu'il tomberait. Chaque personne fit une gran de reverence, quand Ie roi venait.

German.

1 (Heroengeschichten has not been taken, so "Kaiser Karl am Luther's Grab" is recited, from page 24 of A Book of German Ballads, Cambridge University Press.)

In Wittenberg, der starken Luther's Feste
Ist Kaiser Karl, der Sieger, eingedrungen;

Wohl ist den Stamm, zu fallen, ihm gelungen
Doch neue W urzeln schlagen rings die Aeste.
In Luther's Feste hausen fremde Geste
Doch Luthers Geist der bleibet unbezwungen
Da, wo des Geistes Schwert er hat geschwungen
Da ruhen billig auch des Leibes Reste.
Am Grabe steht der Kaiser, tier geriihret.
"Auf denn, und rache dich an dem Gebeinen
Den Flammen gib sic preis, wie sich's gebuhret."
So hort man aus der Diener Tross den Einen.
Der Kaiser spricht "Den Krieg hab' ich gefiihret
Mit Lebenden; um Todte lasst uns weinen."

2. Welche dieses Blumen ist den schonsten? Ich war einmal in Berlin und dreimal in Paris.

3. Ich babe sechs gute Bucher. Er ist funfzehnmal gestraft worden. Wir sind siebzehn edtele Knaben. Neun Knaben sind in dieses Spiel. Vier Bucher waren gross-Achtzehn-hundert schlecht Knauen.

Composition.

(a) Sir Walter Scott was a well-known writer in the early part of the 19th century. His novels are read by almost everyone; and, though, perhaps, his poetry is not quite so well-known, still at most places one finds people who have read or heard of the "Lady of the Lake" or "Marmion." The first of his novels was "Waverly" (sic), and so they are often called the "Waverley Novels." —The historical tales are very good, giving the reader a splendid idea of life in the 12th or 13th centuries; "Ivanhoe," "Betrothed," "The Talisman" and "Kenilworth" (this latter is about the 16th century, in Queen Elizabeth's reign). "The Heart of Midlothian " is also very interesting, and "Peveril of the Peak" tells about the fighting between the Cavaliers and Roundheads in the time of Charles I., and Oliver Cromwell. The "Lady of the Lake" is about the longest poem Sir Walter Scott ever wrote; it is very beautiful, and many pieces in it are most interesting. "Marmion" tell (sic) of a battle, and how a Lord Marmion was killed there.

Latin.

1. Alexander once upon a time asked a pirate whom he had taken by what right he infested the seas? At that,

"The same," said he "by which you do (infest) the world. But because I do it with a small ship, I am called a robber; you, because you do it with a great fleet and army are called a general." Alexander dismissed the man unhurt. Did he do rightly?

Alexander olim comprehensum piratam interrogavit, quo jure maria infestaret? me "Eodem," inquit "quo tu orbem terrarum. Sed quia ego parvo navigio facio, latro vocor; tu, quia magna classe et exercitu, imperator." Alexander inviolatum hominem dimisit. Num juste fecit?

Alexantkr, noun proper, masc., sing., nominative case.
Olim, adv. modifies verb" interrogavit."
Compreltensum, participle used as adj., modifying " piratam."
Piratam, n. common, masc., sing., objective case, governed by "interrogavit." .
Interrogavit, verb, transitive, 3rd pers. sing. Past Tense.
Quo, relative pron., ablative case, antecedent" jure."
Jure, n. common, neuter, sing., ablative case.
Maria, n. common, neuter singular, objective case to " infestaret."
Infestaret, intransitive verb, 3rd person singular Present Subjunctive Tense. .

2. (a) Somnimus totus noctes.
(b) Docebo te musicam.
(c) Romani Numam regem elexerunt.
(d) Galli cis Rhenum habitaverunt.
(e) Magister videt multos pueros ludere.
(a) illustrates that the object is in the accusative in Latin.
(b) the double object is in the accusative.
(c) the double object is in the accusative.

(d) illustrates that all prepositions as "cis" take the acc. case.

(e) "with a sentence like" The master sees that many boys play" you prefix with" Master sees" leave out" that" turn" many boys" into accusative, and turn "play" into the infinitive.

English History.

1. The Anti-Corn-law League was formed early in the reign of Queen Victoria. Its name shews that its object was to get the Corn Laws repealed or rather to have the taxes on corn taken off, as they were causing distress in the country. Eloquent men went about the country, speaking to the people, and telling them how much better it would he not to have them, until they were convinced that it was so, and made rather a fuss over it, so that one Prime Minister, Lord Russell, resigned, and Lord Melbourne came in, and took off some of the taxes. People now seem to be thinking that it would be a good thing to put on some of these corn taxes again, and the country is again rather agitated about it, and Mr Chamberlain, Mr Balfour, and many other gentlemen go about making speeches either for, or against it, according to their different views, just as people did then, when Sir Robert Peel did take them off.

2. England joined in the Crimean war, because they were afraid that if Russia got hold of Turkey, they might prevent the English going to and from India, and that thus the command we had over India might be loosened and India might once more become an independent country. France entered because Napoleon III. wished to show that he had some power, and was not afraid of war. Sardinia entered in because the King of Sardinia's minister, Count Cavour, wished to shew that Sardinia had some power, and he also thought that by making powerful friends such as England and France, his master, King Victor Emmanuel might one day become king of Italy. Russia wanted to put down Turkey, and Turkey of course went against Russia. It was a very sad war, mostly because of the bad management. The charges of the Light and Heavy Brigades, the battles of Inkerman, Balaclava, and last of all, the long siege of Sebastopol, which might have been prevented, had we charged the day before at the Russians, so as to prevent them get (sic) hold of, and fortifying the chief tower, all tells (sic) of suffering from the intense cold, and death of the soldiers by scores.

French History.

1. The Prussians advanced into France, meeting with resistance everywhere, but still they went steadily on; till at last they reached Paris, which they besieged for a long time, so that the people were obliged to eats cats dogs, horses and even rats and mice, so that they had to give in. Then there was a treaty made, and Prussia made France give up the two provinces of Alsace and Lorraine, and also made them pay an immense sum of money, which was only paid off about 10 years ago. France cannot rest with Alsace and Lorraine in the hands of the Emperor of Germany, and keeps up large armies in the hopes of winning them back some day. Germany also keeps up large armies, in readiness for resistance, and these two countries make Europe like an armed camp.

2. In 1875 people thought that they would like a king again, but after all a new Constitution was made and passed by the Assembly. This government still lasts. There is a Chamber of Deputies, something like our English Parliament. There is also another Chamber called the Senate, like the House of Lords in England. A President is chosen, and after seven years, gives up his post, and someone else is chosen. Ministers carry on the government so as to please the National Assembly. New people must be chosen if they are not liked by the Assembly.

Roman History.

1. The Veintes, one of the Tuscan nations, declared that Romulus ill-treated the Fidenre, who belonged to them.

This was absurd, as the Veintes had not tried to help the Fidenre when Romulus took them, and therefore they had a war, in which Romulus was victorious and on the anniversary for some years after the Romans celebrated their victory by having a herald who called through the town "Sardians to be sold" (the Veientes were called Sardians, because the Tuscans were descended from the Sardians, and several young boys in ropes represent (sic) the Veientes.

2. The Romans imagined that there were not enough women for them all to have a wife, so they attacked the Sabines and carried off several women. These were treated with courtesy and respect, but the Sabine men did not like it, and declared war. But while they were fighting the women ran in between, and beseeching, on one side their fathers, and on the other their husbands, to stop, they did stop, and made up the quarrel.

Geography.

1. The West Indies are a set of islands enclosing the Gulf of Mexico and the Caribbean Sea. They form two large groups, the Greater Antilles and the Lesser Antilles. The largest island in the Greater Antilles is Cuba, which belongs to Spain. It is a lovely place, with palm-trees cocoa and coffee plantations, and sugar and tobacco are largely exported. The capital is Havana, where the best cigars in the world are made; and it also has a good harbour from whence is exported the sugar, coffee, cocoa and rum made in the island. The island next in size in our first group is Hayti or St Domingo. Part of this island belongs to Spain, and the other part once belonged to France, but is now a little negro kingdom. Its capital is Port au Prince. Jamaica is the next island; this belongs to Britain, and is the chief place from which we get our sugar, cocoa and coffee. The capital is Kingston, a nice bright town, with churches and a Town Hall, and a governor's residence. Porto Rico is a Spanish island of not very much importance. Its capital is Don Juan, named after the Spanish sailor who first discovered it. Then comes a little group of islands called the Virgin Islands, of which the most important is Santa Cruz, which belongs to Denmark. They are between the Greater and Lesser Antilles. The largest island in the Lesser Antilles is Guadeloupe, which belongs to France. It is a pleasant island, with a lovely bay on which stands the capital, Grande Terre. Dominica (British), Barbuda, Anguilla, Antigua, and St John's (also British) are some of the most important British islands. The other French islands are Martinique, and Marie Galante. St Vincent, and Barbadoes (capital Bridgetown) are also important British islands. After passing the Lesser Antilles, we come to the beautiful island of Trinidad, with its capital, Port of Spain, on the lovely blue Gulf of Paria, which separates it from Venezuela.

4. Coral reefs are formed by tiny animals called "coral polypes" which, almost as soon as they are born, begin to separate part of their food to build up their houses. They often stick to one another and build in companies. We will imagine 10 of these little animals have started building at the bottom of the sea. Two or three of them may have stuck to each other, and soon a little pillar appears of red, white or (very rarely) black coral. New little polypes are born, and they build on and round their parents' work. So it get (sic) broader and higher, and more and more little ones come to enlarge the work, till one day a point of red or white coral appears above the surface of the sea. More and more of it appears, till there is quite a little island. Then the wind often blows seeds, and the birds bring them, and the sea washes up sand into the nooks and crannies, till palm-trees grow, and other plants, and birds build their nests there, and maybe have tiny birds themselves, and so there is an island fit for man's use, and it all started from two or three little coral polypes about 1 of an inch long.

Volcanos are apparently openings in the earth's crust down to (sic) very centre of the earth, where many people believe that there is a great fire, the remains of the days when the earth was a seething mass of fiery vapour. When eruptions break forth, flames and smoke reaching to an enormous height come out of the crater, and fiery lava runs in streams down the sides of the mountain, burning everything in its course, and stones and ashes are thrown out ever so far. , In the sad eruption of Mont Pelee in 1901 ashes fell on steamers more than 100 miles away, and the noise of the eruption was heard for miles, and the city of St Pierre (the capital of Martinique) was entirely buried in ashes and lava; only a few church walls or street corners are remaining now to show that St Pierre was once a flourishing city. This shews that volcanoes are evidently openings through which the inside of the earth seems sometimes to "let off steam."

English Grammar.

One, numeral adj., modifying "flowers." By, preposition, joining "one" to "one." Close, transitive verb, 3rd pers. plur., Present Tense. Shutting, present participle, governing "petals." Their, pels. poss. pron., 3rd pers. phil. From, preposition, governing "moon." Still, adj., modifying "grasshoppers." So, adv., modifying "soon." Soon, adv. of time, modifying "are still." Noisy, adj., qualifying "crows."

2. Go quickly; he is dying. A dying man lies there. Making a dress is difficult. I am making a box. To tell tales is mean. I was to tell you that. But for him, I should not be here. Had you but a knife, we should be safe. Yes, but he is stupid, so I cannot make him hear.

3. Episode, epi-tome. Hypo-crite, hypo-thesis. Cataract, cat-astrophe, cat-hedral. Di-phong (sic). Syn-tax, syl-lable, sym-pathy.

Natural History.

I. (b) Foraminiferre are in the Rhizopoda, or root-footed family. They have a little opening in their shells, through which they send out hairs to catch very tiny water creatures and suck them in. Their shells are made from something they swallow. They are all sorts of shapes, and can be seen without a microscope, though their lovely coloured shells and tiny bodies can be seen better with it They increase by self-division, but they generally grow from tiny buds on the bodies of their mothers.

Sponges are cousins to the Foraminiferre, but are slightly higher up in the Rhizopoda family. They are full of tiny holes, with sometimes a bigger opening. These little holes lead into little passages, which are continually leading into one another, and the bigger holes lead into bigger passages. They are made of some sort of fine tissue, which the sponge animal makes out of some part of its food after it has been digested. In these passages tiny, soft slimy creatures live, which are able to throw out hairs from themselves, with which they sweep water in and out of their house. Their children are born from buds, by self-division, and also from eggs. Some sponges increase in all these different ways at once, so that one sponge often becomes the father of several families. Little hard things called Sponge spicules grow round the eggs to protect them. They are made from the lime the Sponge finds in the water, and often have beautiful shapes.

2. It has been found, that though people speak of the "everlasting hills" yet they cannot have been always where they are now. Mountains that are formed of rocks of any kind, either sedimentary, or organic, must have been laid down at the sea-bottom and something must have pushed them up; either earthquakes, or volcanic eruptions. If, for example, several different kinds of Sedimentary Rocks were laid down flat at the sea-bottom (fig.1) till they were hundreds, perhaps thousands of feet thick, and they also happened to lie on some weak part of the earth's crust, where earthquakes sometimes happen, they may be squeezed or pushed up above the surface of the sea, and round them may be deposited more rocks, and they may be pushed up, and so land may be formed, with some parts higher than the rest, and these parts are called mountains.

Botany.

2. The raspberry, strawberry and blackberry are all of the Rose family. But there are little differences between them; they are not all alike. The raspberry is like the strawberry in that its seed boxes grow on a mound. But when you look at the ripe fruit, you will see that the seed boxes themselves grow bigger, softer and rounder, and also they shrink away from the white mound, so that a ripe raspberry comes off without a little stalk, etc., hanging on. The Blackberry is just the same as the raspberry, only it is black, and the round juicy seed boxes do not shrink away from the mound quite so much. The construction of the strawberry fruit, however, is slightly different. Here it is the little mound that swells, and becomes a bright red, and the seed boxes (generally wrongly called "seeds") remain hard and small, looking something like little yellow apple pips.

Euclid (first set).

APPENDIX V

How Oral Lessons Are Used

Though the part of the teacher should, in a general way, be that of the University tutor who "reads with" his men, the oral lesson, also, is indispensable, whether in introducing a course of reading or as bringing certain readings to a point. Oral lessons, too, give the teacher opportunities for the reading of passages from various books bearing on the subject in hand, a sure way to increase the desire of the children for extended knowledge. Some subjects, again, as Languages, Mathematics, Science, depend very largely upon oral teaching and demonstrations. It might be well if the lecture, with its accompaniments of note-taking and reports, were cut out of the ordinary curriculum, and the oral lesson made a channel for free intellectual sympathy between teacher and taught, and a means of widening the intellectual horizon of children. I add a few sets of notes of criticism lessons which have been given by various students of the House of Education to the children in the Practising School. These lessons are always expansions or illustrations or summaries of some part of the scholars' current book-work.

Oral Lessons

Some Notes of Bible Lessons

Subject: Old Testament History.

Group: History. Class lb. Average age: 8.

Time: 20 minutes.

Objects.

1. To so interest the children in the story of Jacob's death, that they may not forget it.

2. To give a new idea of God as drawn from the story of Jacob's deathbed :—God's abiding presence.
3. To give them an admiration for Joseph as one who honoured his father and mother.

Lesson.

Step I. Recapitulate the former lesson, and follow Jacob's journeying with his family from Canaan to Egypt, on a map.

Step 2. Show the children how Joseph was the first of Jacob's sons to visit him when he was ill. Draw their attention to the particular trait of Joseph's character shown in this story.

Step 3. Describe in a few words the surroundings in which the events of the story take place.

Step 4. Read carefully to the children suitable parts of Genesis xlviii., reminding them to pay special attention to the words of the Bible, as they so beautifully express the scene.

Step 5. While the children are narrating in the words of the Bible, help them by questions to bring out the important points of the story.

Step 6. Help the children to realise how Joseph's love of his father affected his life, and how they should let their parents feel their love.

Step 7. Let the children see that this family realised God's abiding presence, and show them how any family can realise it in the same way, if it will.

Subject: New Testament Story—The Stilling of the Tempest.

Group: History.

Class II. Average age of children: 10.
Time: 30 minutes.

Objects.

1. To try to give to the children some new spiritual thought and a practical idea of faith.
2. To bring the story of the Stilling of the Tempest vividly before their minds.
3. To interest them in the geography of the Holy Land.
4. By means of careful, graphic reading, to help them to feel the wonderful directness, beauty, and simplicity of the Bible language: in short, to make them feel the poetry of the Bible.

Apparatus Required.

1. Bibles for the children.
2. A map of Palestine.
3. Thomson's Land and Book.
4. Pictures of:—(1) A storm on a lake; (2) Galilean boats; (3) The Sea of Galilee.

Lesson.

Step 1. Ask the children to find St Matt. viii. 23 in their Bibles. Tell the story of the Stilling of the Tempest, keeping as closely as possible to the language of the Bible.

(a) Let the children find the Sea of Galilee on the map, gathering from the map some notion of the surrounding country; compare with Lake Windermere.

Show course of journey by reference to verses 5 and 28 in the same chapter.

Show pictures of ships used in the East and on the Sea of Galilee.

(b) Describe the tempest graphically, drawing from the children the reason for the sudden storms (caused by the ravines, down which the winds rush); get from them their idea of a storm at sea or on a lake.

Show photograph of a storm on Lake Windermere.

(c) Try to make the children understand the twofold nature of our Lord :

(1) His Humanity—He was evidently weary.

(2) His Divinity—His power over Nature

(d) Try to make the children feel the simplicity of the Bible language and the forceful way in which it brings pictures before the mind.

There arose a great tempest—His disciples came to Him—He arose—there was a great calm—Refer to Psalm cvii.

(e) "The men marvelled." Try to show the children that faith is just another word for understanding, knowing how, the better we know a person, the more we can trust him. Draw from the children how faith is shown in nearly every verse of this story, but, as far as the disciples were concerned, it did not go far enough.

Draw from them that it is not necessary to be with a person always in order to have faith in him. Ask them how people show faith in all the actions of their daily lives.

Step 2. Read the story from the Bible; read it carefully, so that the children will appreciate its literary value and see the vivid pictures which it brings before the mind.

Step 3. Let the children narrate the story, keeping as much as possible to the Bible words.

Subject: Reading.

Group: English. Class III. Average age: 13.

Time: 25 minutes.

Objects.

1. To try to improve the children's reading by drilling them in clear and pure pronunciation.
2. To show them that by their reading a series of mental pictures should be presented to the listener.

Lesson.

Step 1. Breathing exercises. Ask reason for the same.

Step 2. Practise the children in consonant and vowel sounds, by giving them sentences in which difficulties in pronunciation occur.

m, en, n. A stricken maiden musing on a mountain was given from heaven man in mortal form.

final t. A just knight felt a weight on his heart, and yet a sweet quiet rest was present when he went to meet the light.

p, b. A path of prickly brambles, bordered by pure pale poppies, breathed peace between the broken beams.

d. Touched by the hand that appeared from the cloud under which nodded the dead leaves. (Notice final d is sometimes pronounced like t.)

Step 3. Read the passage chosen, from Tennyson's 'Sir Galahad,' asking the girls afterwards to describe the mental pictures they have drawn.

"A maiden knight to me is given
Such hope, I know not fear;
I yearn to breathe the airs of heaven
That often meet me here.
I muse on joy that will not cease,
Pure spaces clothed in living beams,
Pure lilies of eternal peace,
Whose odours haunt my dreams;
And, stricken by an angel's hand,
This mortal armour that I wear,
This weight and size, this heart and eyes
Are touched, are turned to finest air.
The clouds are broken in the sky,
And through the mountain walls
A rolling organ-harmony
Swells up, and shakes and falls.
Then move the trees, the copses nod,
Wings flutter, voices hover clear:
'O just and faithful knight of God!
Ride on! the prize is near.'
So pass I hostel, hall and grange;
By bridge and ford, by park and pale,
All-armed I ride, whate'er betide,
Until I find the Holy Grail."

Step 4. Show the girls a reproduction of Watts' conception of the idea, asking them in what points the poet's and artist's ideas coincide.

Step 5. Let the children read the passage.

Subject: Narration (Plutarch's life of Alexander-part of the term's work).
Group: Language. Class II. Average age: 10.
Time: 20 minutes.
Objects.
1. To improve the children's power of narration by impressing on them Plutarch's style (as translated by North), and making them narrate as much as possible in his words.
2 To rouse in the children admiration of Alexander's love of simplicity, generosity, and kindness to his men.
Lesson.
Step 1. Connect with the last lesson by questioning the children. They read last time stories illustrating Alexander's graciousness and tact. .
Step 2. Tell the children shortly the substance of what I am going to read to them, letting them find any places mentioned, in their maps.
Step 3. Read to the children about three pages, dealing with the luxury of the Macedonians, Alexander's march to Bactria, and the death of Darius. Read this slowly and distinctly, and into the children as much as possible.
Step 4. Ask the children in turn to narrate, each narrating a part of what was read.
SubJect: From Plutarch's 'Greek Lives.'
Alexander the Great.
(An Introductory Lesson.)
Group: History. Class II. Age: 8 and 9.
Time: 30 minutes.
Objects.
1. To establish relations with the past.
2. To introduce the boys to a fresh hero.
3. To stir them to admiration of the wisdom, valour, and self-reliance of Alexander the Great.
4. To increase the boys' power of narration.
Lesson.
Step 1. Begin by connecting Alexander the Great with the time of Demosthenes, of whom the boys have been learning recently.
Step 2. Draw from them some account of the times in which Alcxander lived and of Philip of Macedon.
Step 3. Arouse the boys' interest in Alexander by the story of the taming of Bucephalus, which must be read, discussed, and then narrated by the boys.
Step 4. Ask the boys what they mean by a hero. The old meaning was demi-god, the Anglo-Saxon meaning, a man. Both really meant a man who was brave and true in every circumstance.
Ask them, 'What are the qualities which go to make a hero?' Draw from them how far we can trace these qualities in Alexander. We notice:—
Wisdom.—'What a horse are they losing for want of skill to manage him!'
Perseverance.—He kept repeating the same expression
Self-reliance.—'And I certainly could.' This was justified by the fact that he could.
Obseroation.—He noticed that the horse was afraid of Its shadow.
Courage.—Seeing his opportunity, he leaped upon its back.
Prudence.—He went very gently till he could feel that he had perfect control of the animal.
These are not all the qualities one looks for in a hero, but as the boys will be learning all about Alexander next term, they will be able to find out for themselves what others he had. They will see, for instance, how he never imagined a defeat but went on, conquering as he went (Hope).
The name of Alexander has never been forgotten, because he was so great a hero. Owing to him, the language and civilisation of Greece were carried over a great part of Asia. Show map illustrating his campaigns. He tried to improve the land wherever he went. Owing to his travels, people began to know more than they had ever known of geography and natural history.
Himself a hero, Alexander reverenced heroes, keeping 'the casket copy' of The Iliad.
Step 5. Recapitulate Step 4 by means of questions.

Subjed: The Godwins.

Group: History. Class III. Average age: 13.

Time: 30 minutes.

Objects.

1. To recapitulate and enlarge on the period of history taken during the term (A.D. 871-1066).

2. To increase the children's interest in it by giving as much as possible in detail the history of one of the prominent families of the period.

3. To exemplify patriotism in the character of the Godwins.

Lesson.

Step 1. Recapitulate what the girls know of the period briefly by questioning about the Saxon and the Danish kings and leading men, making a chart on the blackboard.

Step 2. Begin with the reign of Canute. Enlarge upon their present knowledge as to his character and deeds whilst king of England, and let a girl read the account of his pilgrimage to Rome (Freeman's OM English History, p. 242).

Step 3. Give an account of the early history of Earl Godwin—his apparently humble origin—his love of his country—his character. He rose by his valour and wisdom -was loved by both Saxons and Danes—was merciful to his foes. He married Gytha, sister of Earl Ulf—was made Earl by King Canute—and had Wessex given him as his kingdom. Put on the blackboard the names of the three divisions of England, with their earls or rulers.

Step 4. The period between the death of Canute and Edward the Confessor's coming to the throne. Under Harold and Hartha—Canute Danish rule became distasteful, and the English longed for an English king. Let a girl read the account of Hartha -- Canute's treatment of the people of Worcester and the conduct of Godwin and the other earls on that occasion (p. 250).

Step 5. Edward the Confessor. Ask them questions about his early life and education, and how these affected his character and ideas. Was he a suitable man for a king? Not powerful enough to rule—Godwin became his supporter and adviser. Marriage of Godwin's daughter, Edith, to the king. Godwin's eloquence and influence over the people. (Read from Knight's History, p. 162.)

Step 6. Godwin's patriotism is put to the test. Speak of his banishment with his wife and six sons, and its consequences. William of Normandy invited over to England—great dissatisfaction at misrule in. England—the people resent the Normans being put in office. Let G-- read (p. 262).

Step 7. Godwin's return—he and his family again received into favour—his death—the crime which had been laid to his charge—Harold a worthy successor.

Show from a map the divisions of England at the death of the 'Confessor.' Read from Lord Lytton's Harold (p. 63).

Subjed: History.

Group: History. Class IV. Age: 16.

Time: 40 minutes.

The State of France in 1789.

Objects.

1. To establish relations with the past.

2. To show how closely literature and history are linked together and how the one influences the other.

3. To try to give yet a clearer idea of the social ant{ political state of France before the Revolution thar the girls have now, and to draw from them the causes which brought about the Revolution in France and at this time (1789).

Lesson.

Step 1. Begin by noticing the state of France generally. Feudalism was still in existence, without its usefulness and with most of its abuses, and it led to the great division oj Classes—the Privileged and the Unprivileged. In both Army and Church it was impossible for the unprivileged to rise by merit; all offices were filled by the privileged classes. These were exempt from many taxes. Draw from G-- and S-- the chief taxes—Taille, levied on property, and the Gabelle, which forced everyone to buy a certain amount of salt from the Government at an enormous rate.

Step 2. Speak of the state of France in the country, showing what was the relation of the peasant to his lord. The land he lived on generally belonged to him; in return for which he had to grind his com at his lord's mill, etc., had to give his work free on certain days in the year, and help to make the roads in his lord's land (corole). Tell them something of the Game Laws and the 'Intendants.'

Step 3. Notice the state of France in the towns, showing how impossible it was for a poor man to set up in a trade, owing to the guilds and monopolies. The merchants, together with men who held certain offices under Government, formed a separate class, far removed from both the peasants and the nobles.

Step 4. The state of the Church. For the most part the higher ecclesiastics were hated and despised. This was not the case with the 'cures,' for they were of the peasantry, and shared their troubles. But the higher ecclesiastics were generally younger sons of nobles, who drew the salaries of their offices and lived a gay life at Court. The Church also imposed heavy dues.

Step 5. Show that these evils might have been remedied gradually (as in England) had there been a representative assembly regularly called, or any true justice. But as justice could be bought and sold, the poor man always lost his cause, and the pleadings of the peasants could in no way make themselves heard. They had risen just before this time, but unsuccessfully.

Step 6. Draw from G-- and S-- the reason why the Revolution broke out in France rather than in any other Continental country. Because, though the evils in France were no worse than those borne by the German peasants, the French people had been awakened to the knowledge of their misery and of their right to liberty by many great writers. Such were Voltaire, Rousseau, Diderot, d' Alembert, and Montesquieu. Get from G-- and S-- all I can about these men and their influence on history.

Step 7. Draw from G-- and S-- why the Revolution broke out just in 1789. Rousseau had written his works since about 1730, and Voltaire since 1718.

The French had borne their lot under Louis XIV.'s strong government. Louis XV. was very different. The evils of a despotic government were clearly shown by him. He it was who said, 'Apres nous Ie deluge!' Then came Louis XVI., conscientious and full of good intentions.

Get from the girls something of Louis' character. But the great opportunity of the people came in the calling of the States General, in order to raise money.

Step 8. A short recapitulation of the principal points.

Subject: Literature.

Group: English. Class IV. Age: 16 Time: 45 minutes.

Charles Lamb.

Objects.

1. To give some main principles to guide the choice of reading.
2. To give a short sketch of the life of Charles Lamb.
3. To show how the writer's character is reflected in The Essays of Elia.
4, To emphasise the fact that very thoughtful reading is necessary in order to get full pleasure and benefit from a book.

Lesson.

Step 1. Decide with the pupils as to some principles which should guide us in the choice of books, such as the following :

Never waste time on valueless books.

Have respect for the books themselves.

Try to cultivate taste by noticing the best passages in any book that is being read.

Time is too short to read much; there is a necessity, therefore, for judicious selection.

The best literature can only be appreciated by those who have fitted themselves for it.

It is more important to read well than to read much.

The gain of reading some of the most beautiful literature while we are young is that we shall then have beautiful thoughts and images to carry with us through life.

To get at the full significance of a book it is necessary to dig for it.

Thus The Essays oj Elia are not only pleasant reading, but they are the reflection of the writer's character. All that Lamb was can be gathered from his works, and to rightly understand these one must know something of the grand though obscure life of Charles Lamb.

Step 2. Try to draw from the girls, who are already familiar with some of the essays, what they tell us of Charles Lamb.

Charles Lamb was born 1775. His father was in the service of Mr Salt, whose portrait is found in The Old Benclzer of tlze Inner Temple. 1782, Charles received a presentation from Mr Salt to Christ's Hospital (see Essay).

The result of his education is summed up in The Schoolmaster. From fifteen to twenty he was a clerk in the South Sea House (Essay).

In 1795 he was transferred to the India House. He lived near Holbom with his parents and his sister Mary. Here took place the calamity occasioned by Mary's insanity.

Charles' heroic resolution. One learns something of the dream he renounced in Dream Children. His work at the India House was uninteresting, but such as left him leisure for intellectual pursuits. This distribution of occupation was a means of conserving his mental balance. His literary work was all done in the evening: 'Candle Light' in Popular Fallacies.

The girls will then read Talfourd's estimate of Lamb.

Letters to Robert Lloyd show Lamb's persistent cheerfulness. This cheerful tone is also noticeable in many of his essays: Mrs Battle, All Fool's Day, My Relations (portrait of John Lamb), Mackery End (portrait of Mary Lamb) Poor Relations, and Captain Jackson. C. Lamb died 1834.

Step 3. Summarise by questions.

Subjed: English Grammar.

Group: Language. Class II. Average age: 10.

Time: 20 minutes.

Objects.

1. To increase the children's power of reasoning and attention.
2. To increase their knowledge of English Grammar.
3. To introduce a new part of speech—preposition.

Lesson.

Step 1. Draw from the children the names of the two kinds of verbs and the difference between them, by putting up sentences on the board. Thus in the sentence 'Father slept,' 'slept,' as they know, is intransitive; therefore he could not 'slept' anything, as 'slept' cannot have an object.

Step 2. Put on the board the sentence 'Mary went,' and ask the children to try and make it more complete by adding an object. 'Mary went school' would not be sense, but' Mary went to school' would. Ask for other phrases saying where Mary went, as, for a walk, into the town, with mother, on her bicycle, by train, etc.

Step 3. Tell the children that these little words, on, in, by, for, with, etc., belong to a class of words which are very much used with intransitive verbs; they have not much meaning when used alone, yet in a sentence they cannot stand without an object. You cannot say 'Mary went in,' without saying what she went in.

Step 4. Introduce the word 'preposition,' giving its derivation. Because these little words always take objects after them, and because their place is before the object, they are called prepositions, 'pre' being the Latin word for 'before,' and 'position' another word for 'place.'

Step 5. Write on the board the definition:—'A pre-position always has an object after it.'

Step 6. Let the children work through the following exercises :

(1) Put three objects after each of the following prepositions:—in, on, over, by, with, and from.

(2) Put three prepositions and their objects after the following:—Mary plays, Mother sits, John runs.

(3) Supply three prepositions in each of the following sentences:— The book is __ the table. The chair is the door. I stood __ the window.

(4) Supply three subjects and verbs to each of the following prepositions and objects: __ in the garden, __ on the Boor, __ by the fire.

(5) Make three sentences about each of the following, each sentence to contain an intransitive verb, a preposition and its object:—The white pony, My little brother, That pretty flower.

Subject: German Grammar.

Group: Languages. Class III. Average age: 13.

Time: 30 minutes.

Objects.

1. To show the pupil that although the German construction of sentences may seem very much complicated, yet with the help of a few simple rules it can be made much clearer.

2. To draw these rules from the pupil by means of examples.

3. To teach two or three of these elementary rules.

4. To strengthen the relationship with the foreign language.

Lesson.

Step 1. Begin by finding out what the pupils know of compound sentences in English, i.e. that they consist of two or more clauses depending on each other, etc., and let them give one or two examples. Connect this lesson with a former one on the arrangement of words in German sentences by letting the pupils put one or two compound clauses on the board in German, and then giving the rule they illustrate.

Rule. Dependent clauses take the verb at the end of the clause.

These sentences the pupils can probably give themselves.

Step 2. Get the old rule that the past participle comes at the end of the sentence, with a few examples, one or two of which the pupils may write upon the board to compare with those illustrating the new rule.

Let the pupils put several sentences on the board illustrating the new rule.

Rule. In dependent clauses the auxiliary follows the past participle.

Sentences.—'Ich kehre zuruck, wenn sie angekommen ist' ,

'Das Kind, welches verloren war, ist gefunden.'

Let the pupils translate these literally into English, and with the simple German clauses already on the board and the translation let them find the rule. Let them translate a few sentences into German to show that they thoroughly understand the rule.

Step 3. Treat the next rule almost in the same way, but have each sentence put on the board twice in different order, and find the rule by comparing these.

Rule. If the subordinate clause comes first the principal clause takes its verb at the beginning.

Sentences:—

(1) 'Sie gab den Armen viel, weil sie gut war!

(2) 'Wiel sie gut war, gab sie den Armen viel.'

(1) 'Er ging immer fort, obwohl er mude war.'

(2) 'Obwohl er mude war, ging er immer fort.'

Step 5. Recapitulate.

Subject French Narration.

Group: Languages. Class III. Average age: 13.

Time: 30 minutes.

Objects.

1. To give the children more facility in understanding French when they hear it spoken, and also in expressing themselves in it.

2. To teach them some new words and expressions.

3. To improve their pronunciation.

4. To strengthen the habit of attention.

5. To introduce a new branch of the study of French and thus increase their interest in it.

6. To have the following passage narrated by the children.

Lesson.

Passage chosen: Le Corbeau.

"Auguste etant de retour a Rome, apres la bataille d'Actium, un artisan lui presenta un corbeau auquel il avait appris a. dire ces mots: Je te salue, Cesar vainquer!

Auguste charme, acheta cet oiseau pour six mille ecus. Un perroquet tit a. Auguste Ie meme compliment et fut achete fort chef. Une pie vint ensuite; Auguste l'acheta encore.

Entin un pauvre cordonnier voulut aussi apprendre a un cor beau cette salutation; il eut bien de la peine a. y parvenir, it se desesperait souvent et disait en enrageant:

Je perds mon temps et ma peine. Enfin il y reussit. Il alla aussitot attendre Auguste sur son passage, et lui presenta Ie corbeau, qui repeta fort bien sa lec;on: mais Auguste se contenta de dire: J'ai assez de ces complimenteurs la dans moo palais. Alors Ie corbeau, se ressouvenant de ce qu'il avait souvent entendu dire a son maitre, repeta: J'ai perdu mon temps et ma peine. Auguste se mit a. rire et acheta cet oiseau plus cher que tous les autres,"

Step 1. Read the passage slowly and distinctly, stopping frequently to make sure that the children understand. Write the new words and expressions on the board and give their meanings.

Step 2. Let the children repeat the story in English.

Step 3. Read the passage straight through.

Step 4. Let the children read the passage, paying special attention to the pronunciation.

Step 5. Have the passage narrated in French, helping the children when necessary with questions.

Speak as much French as possible throughout, but always make sure that the pupils understand.

Subject: Italian Gouin.

Group: Language. Class IV. Average age: 16.

Time: 30 minutes.

Objects.

1. To increase the girls' interest in foreign languages.
2. To enlarge their Italian vocabulary.
3. To give the girls more facility in understanding Italian when they hear it spoken, and also power to express themselves in it.

Lesson.

Step 1. Tell the children in a few words what the series is about.

Step 2. Explain the verbs in the infinitive, by doing the actions when possible.

Step 3. Let the children say the verbs in the infinitive.

Step 4. Let them write the verbs on the board.

Step 5. Explain, by actions, when possible, the rest of the series.

Step 6. Repeat each sentence several times slowly and carefully.

Step 7. Let the children repeat the sentences.

Step 8. Let them write the series on the board.

Verbs.

Volere esercitarse Aprire Suonare Studiare Volere imparare

Italian.

Luigia vuol esercitarsi sul piano.
Aprire il piano.
Suona una scala e degli arpeggio
Poi studia una Sonata. di Beethoven.
Che vuol imparare a mente.

English.

Louise wishes to practise.
She opens the piano.
She Plays a scale and some arpeggio
Then she studies a Sonata by Beethoven,
Which she wants to learn by heart.

Suubject: Geograplry.

Group: Science. Class III. Average Age: 13.

Time: 30 minutes.

Scandinavia—Norway in Particular.

Objects.

1. To introduce the children to Scandinavia.
2. To foster interest in foreign countries.
3. To teach the children how to learn the map of a country by means of map questions.
4. To implant mental pictures of the characteristic scenery of Norway in the children's minds.
5. To show, by means of comparison, the great difference in the physical features of the two countries which are included in Scandinavia, although they form only one peninsula.

Lesson.

Step 1. Let the children learn the map of Scandinavia, Norway in particular, by means of the map questions previously written on the blackboard, writing down their answers.

Step 2. Ask for a general description of Scandinavia.

Step 3. Let the children fill in the blank map on the blackboard.

Step 4. Require the children to give the answers to the questions, and, as they answer, give information, in order that they may become acquainted with each place as it is mentioned, and be able to picture it in their minds.

Map Questions.

From the Geographical Readers, Book IV.

1. What waters bound the Scandinavian peninsula? To what land is it attached? What' countries does it include?

Note.

Describe the government of Scandinavia briefly, showing that, although Sweden and Norway have a common sovereign, each country has an independent parliament, elected in very much the same way, as our English Parliament.

2. Through how many degrees of latitude does this peninsula stretch? What other countries of the world lie partly in the same latitude?

3. Describe the coast of Norway. Compare it with that of Sweden. Name the four largest fiords or openings, beginning at the extreme north.

Note.

Give the idea of the extraordinary way in which the coast is cut up, and the immense number of islands which fringe it. Girls to notice how these islands form an effective breakwater to the force of the Atlantic breakers, so that within their boundary the water is as calm and still as a lake.

Describe the rocky, almost perpendicular sides of the fiords, over which the rivers fall in roaring torrents. Mention the fact that many ships of the Spanish Armada were driven as far north as Stadtland, and wrecked around this dangerous headland.

The Sogne is the largest and most important fiord. It is like a long sea channel running into the country for a distance of 100 miles, with branches right and left, over which wonderful torrents fall. The sides are very steep, and the water is very deep at the entrance. At the Sulen Islands, at the mouth of the fiord, Harold Hardrada collected his force for his expedition against England.

4. Name a group of islands north of the Arctic Circle. The most northerly island. The cape on this island. The most northerly cape on the mainland. The most southerly cape.

Note.

The Lofoden Islands are granite rocks, rising from the water in hundreds of peaks, with jagged and fantastic outlines. The cod fisheries of these islands are very important, and employ a great number of people.

Nordkin, which means 'north chin,' is the most northerly point on the mainland of Europe. Incessant storms rage round the island of Mageroe, so that it is extremely difficult for anyone to land there.

Lindesnaes means 'Lime nose.'

5. Name five towns on the west, and three on the southeast coast of Norway.

Note.

Stavanger is the fourth largest city in Norway. Its chief trade is in herrings. It has a very ancient Cathedral.

At Bergen the houses are built on the slopes of the hills which run out into the deep sea. It was formerly the capital, and is now a great fish port.

Trondhjem is the oldest capital. The name means . home of the throne,' and in the Cathedral the kings of Norway are crowned.

Hammerfest is the most northerly town in Europe.

Tourists go there to see the midnight sun. Read Charles H. Wood's description of the midnight sun, from the GeograPhical Reader.

Christiania, the capital of Norway, is not a big town, but has a most beautiful situation. It is at the head of the Christiania Fiord, which is studded with countless grassy and wooded islands. Most of the hguses are of wood, painted white, with green blinds. The fiord, which used to be very much frequented by the old Vikings, is blocked by ice for four months of the year.

6. The Scandinavian mountains nearly fill Norway-by what name is the range known in the north, south, and centre? Name three or four of the highest peaks.

Note.

There is no continuous range in the Scandinavian mountains; the whole is a high table-land, which increases in height as we go south, with here and there groups of peaks which appear like huge rocks dotted over the surface.

These plateaux are topped with moors or snowfields from which glaciers descend right down into the sea.

7. How does the position of the mountains affect the rivers? Compare the rivers of Norway with those of Sweden.

Note.

Describe how, in Norway, the rivers rush in torrents over their rocky beds, while those in Sweden flow more gently down the gradual slope of the land. Give the threefold reason—great rainfall, small evaporation owing to the coldness of the climate, and small waste owing to the hardness of the rocks—for the great volume of water in the short, quick, Norwegian rivers.

8. Recapitulate with blank map, the girls adding descriptive notes as they answer the map questions.

Subject: Astronomy.

Group: Science. Class IV. Age: 16 Time: 30 minutes.

1. To interest the pupils in studying the heavens for themselves.
2. To show where the planets may be looked for and how they may be recognised.
3. To help the pupils to apply their theoretical knowledge of the planets to explain the movements they can observe with the naked eye.
4. To exercise the reasoning powers.

Lesson.

Step 1. Get the pupils to describe the changes to be seen in the sky at night, and, excluding the apparent motion caused by the earth's rotation, find out whether they have noticed and contrasted the constellations of fixt:d stars and the planets (wanderers).

let the pupils tell which of the planets are visible to the naked eye, and ask whether they have noticed when and where are to be seen, at the present date, Jupiter, Saturn, and Mars, which are in Capricorn us, Sagittarius, and Leo, respectively.

Step 2. Draw from the pupils, if possible, the marks by which planets can be distinguished from stars .

(a) Their steady light.

(b) Size (in the case of Venus and Jupiter).

(c) Colour (in the case of Mars).

(d) Position (relatively to known constellations).

(e) Motion (noticeable after successive observations).

Step 3. To enlarge on Point (d), let the pupils name the planets whose orbits are within that of the earth and those whose orbits are outside ours. By the help of a diagram (blackboard) of the solar system, get them to infer, from the nearness to the sun of Venus and Mercury, that these planets are never visible at midnight, but only just before sunrise and after sunset. .

Step 4. To appreciate Points (d) and (e), get the pupils to recognise the advantage of knowing the constellations by sight. Show Philip's Planisphere, and refer to the Zodiac, showing that, besides being the sun's apparent path, this is the region in which to seek the planets.

Let the pupils find the portion of the heavens visible at 6 p.m. to-day, and indicate, both in the heavens and with respect to our landscape, the positions of Jupiter and Saturn. Also show how Mars may be looked for in the south, too, about 6 o'clock in the morning.

Step 5. To enlarge on Point (e), show a diagram of the path of Venus among the constellations in 1868 (Lockyer's Elementary Lessons in Astronomy, p. 183), and get the pupils to notice how large a distance she travelled in one month, in order to induce them to make personal observations. Prepare them to see the planets sometimes move backwards and sometimes remain stationary. Explain this by letting one of the girls move round the table, while the other watches how, with respect to her background, she appears to move first from left to right, then to remain stationary, then to move from right to left, and again to remain stationary. The moving girl, observing the other with respect to her background, notices the same phenomena.

Then show the diagram in Lockyer, which illustrates these facts, p. 178, and also another in Reid's Elements of Astronomy, p. 137, which shows the apparent motion of one planet viewed from another in motion.

A Picture Talk.

Group: Art.

Class III.

Age: 13.

Time: 25 minutes.

Objects.

1. To give the girls some idea of composition, based on the work of the artist Jean Francsois Millet.

2. To inspire them with a desire to study the works of other artists, with a similar object in view.

3. To help them with their original illustrations, by giving them ideas, carried out in Millet's work, as to simplicity of treatment, breadth of tone, and use of lines.

Materials Needed.

See that the girls are provided with paint-boxes, brushes, water, pencils, rulers, india-rubber, and paper.

Photographs of some of Millet's pictures.

A picture-book by R. Caldecott.

Lesson.

Step 1. Introduce the subject by talking with the children about their original illustrations. Tell them how our great artists have drawn ideas and inspiration from the work of other artists; have studied their pictures, copied them, and tried to get at the spirit of them.

Tell them that to-day we are going to study some of the pictures of the great French artist, Millet, some of whose works Mr Yates has drawn for us on the walls of our Millet Room, considering them to be models of true art.

Step 2.-Tell the children a little about the life of Millet (giving them one or two pictures to look at meanwhile); give only a brief sketch, so that they will feel that he is not a stranger to them. ust talk to them a little about his early childhood, how he worked in the fields; how he had two great books—the Book of Nature and the Bible, from which he drew much inspiration; how later on he went to Paris and studied the pictures of great artists, Michael Angelo among them.

Step 3. Show the pictures to the girls, let them look well at them, and then draw from them their ideas as to the beauty and simplicity of the composition; call attention to the breadth of tone, and the dignity ofthe lines. Help them, sketching when necessary. to reduce a picture to its most simple form; half-closing their eyes to shut out detail, help them to get an idea of the masses of tone, etc.

Step 4. Let the children reproduce a detail of one of the pictures, working in water-colour with monochrome and making their washes simple and flat, reducing the tones to two or three.

Slep 5. Suggest to them to study the works of other artists in a similar way, and show them how the books of R. Caldecott will help them in making their figures look as if they were moving.

Subject: Fra Angelico.

Group: Art. Class IV. Average age: 16 1/2.

Time: 30 minutes.

Objects.

1. To show reproductions of some of Fra Angelico's pictures.

2. By means of them, to point out such distinguishing features as will enable my pupils to recognise Fra Angelico's work wherever they may see it.

3. To show in what degree his work holds a place in high art.

Lesson.

Step 1. Give a short sketch of the life of Fra Angelico.

Step 2. Allow time for my pupils to look at the pictures provided, namely, various reproductions of 'Christ in Glory,' 'Saints in Paradise,' 'Angels,' 'Christ as Pilgrim,' 'Annunciation,' 'Crucifixion,' 'Noll me tangere,' 'Descent from the Cross,' 'Transfiguration.'

Step 3. To notice what strikes us most in Fra Angelico's work—the exquisite jewel-like finish; the pure open skies and unpretending clouds; the winding and abundant landscapes; the angels; the touches of white light; the delicacy and grace of form; the colouring; the peace.

Step 4. If high art is to be seen 'in the selection of a subject and its treatment, and the expression of the thoughts of the persons represented,' how far does Fra Angelico come up to this standard?

He unites perfect unison of expression with full exertion of pictorial power. This will be illustrated by further reference to the pictures, and by reading some passages from Modern Painters. .

Step 5. Allow my pupils time to look again at the pictures, summarising meanwhile by a few questions.

Subject: Design.

Division: Art. Class IV. Average age: 16 1/2.

Time: 40 minutes.

Objects.

1. To give the girls an idea of how to fill a space decoratively, basing the design on a given plant.
2. To show them that good ornament is taken from nature, but a mere copy of nature to decorate an object is not necessarily ornamental.
3. To give them an appreciation of good ornament and help them to see what is bad.
4. To draw out their originality by letting them make designs for themselves.
5. If possible, to give them a taste for designing by giving them some ideas as to its use.

Lesson.

Step 1. Ask the girls what is meant by a design.

Step 2. After getting from them as much as possible, explain to them that a design is not a mere copy from nature, although it should be true to nature; make them see this by simply copying a plant in a required space to be designed (let this space be for a book cover). It will look meaningless and uninteresting, and does not fill the space, therefore it will not be ornamental. Then show the girls that a design requires thought and invention in arranging it to ornament the object. In the case of the book cover the flower must be designed to fill the space in some orderly pattern, and should be massed in good proportion. Give a few examples of this by illustrations on the board, and show them a book with a design upon it.

Step 3. Point out to them that the most beautiful designs and those that have had the most thought spent upon them are the most simple. Show examples of this in Greek Ornament—Greek Honeysuckle, Egg and Dart Moulding.

Step 4. Tell the pupils that you wish them to make a design for a linen book cover, 7 in. by 5 in., and if they have not time to finish to go on with it at home; if they like to carry the design out practically, to transfer it to linen and work it.

Step 5. Show the girls the flower from which they are to take their design, and point out its characteristics—the general growth of the plant, the curves which it makes, the form of the flower and leaves, and the way the leaves are joined to the central stem; these characteristics should not be lost sight of, but be made use of in giving character to the design, and treated as simply as possible.

Step 6. Let them begin their designs first of all by construction lines, and then clothe them with flowers and leaves, seeing that the masses are in good proportion. If time permits the design could be tinted in two colours, one for the background representing the linen, and the other for the pattern upon it.

Step 7. Suggest to them different ways in which they can make use of design in making simple patterns for their handicrafts, such as leather-work, wood-carving, and brass-work.

Subject: Leather.work (Embosset!).

Group: Handicrafts. Class IV. Age: I6 1/2.

Time: 40 minutes.

Objects.

1. To cultivate the artistic feeling in the pupils.
2. To train them in neatness and in manual dexterity.
3. To give training to the eye.
4. To introduce them to a new handicraft.
5. To work, as far as possible in the time, the top of a penwiper.

Lesson.

Step I. Show the pupils a shaded drawing of the design, also a partly finished penwiper top, with the same design on it. When they have compared the two, they will see that the effect of light and shade is obtained in the leather by raising the light parts and pressing back the dark ones.

Step 2. Let the pupils trace the design on the leather with a pointer. Remove the tracing-paper and accentuate the lines with a pointer. (This is best done with a wheel in a large design.)

Step 3. Damp the leather and with a moulder press the background away from the outline of the design, also the dark parts under the folds at the top of the petals and round the centre. From behind, raise up the light parts with a moulder, and fill the holes thus made with a mixture of sawdust and meal, wet enough to make a kind of rough thick paste. Press away the dark parts again, and make any ornamental lines, etc., while the stuffing is wet, as it soon dries very hard. For this reason a very little must be stuffed at once; in this design, about one petal at a time.

Step 4. Let the pupils punch their background or not as they prefer.

Work on my own half-finished piece of leather to avoid touching the pupils' work.

Subject. Cooking.

Division: Handicrafts. Class IV.

Time. 45 minutes.

Objects.

1. To teach the children to make little cakes.
2. To show them that cooking must have method in it.
3. To give them opportunity of thinking for themselves why certain things should be done.
4. To show them how they can alter a recipe to make it richer or plainer.
5. To interest them in cooking.

Age: 16 1/2.

Lesson

Step 1. Show the girls how to manage the stove for cooking.

Step 2. Show them all the utensils to be used, and let them arrange them on the table.

Step 3. Let them write out the recipe from dictation.

Step 4. Let them grease the tins first of all with melted butter. Then let them each weigh out the ingredients on pieces of kitchen paper, and let them work independently of each other, the teacher also doing the same thing, so that the pupils may be able to see how to set to work without having their own work interfered with. During the process ask them why certain things should be done—for instance, why baking powder should be used, why the patty-pans should be greased. Tell them that if they wished to make the cakes plainer they could use milk instead of eggs, or if richer, they could add raisins and currants and spice. When the mixture is sufficiently beaten and put into the patty-pans, let the girls put them into the oven.

Step 5. While the buns are cooking (they take about ten minutes), let the children and teacher wash up the things they have been using and put them away.

Step 6. Let the children see for themselves if the cakes are done; they should be a light brown. Then let them place them on a sieve to cool, and then arrange them on plates for the table.

Ourselves: Our Souls and Bodies

Table of Contents

Preface to the 'Home Education' Series

The educational outlook is rather misty and depressing both at home and abroad. That science should be a staple of education, that the teaching of Latin, of modern languages, of mathematics, must be reformed, that nature and handicrafts should be pressed into service for the training of the eye and hand, that boys and girls must learn to write English and therefore must know something of history and literature; and, on the other hand, that education must be made more technical and utilitarian—these, and such as these, are the cries of expedience with which we take the field. But we have no unifying principle, no definite aim; in fact, no philosophy of education. As a stream can rise no higher than its source, so it is probable that no educational effort can rise above the whole scheme of thought which gives it birth; and perhaps this is the reason of all the' fallings from us, vanishings,' failures, and disappointments which mark our educational records.

Those of us, who have spent many years in pursuing the benign and elusive vision of Education, perceive that her approaches are regulated by a law, and that this law has yet to be evoked. We can discern its outlines, but no more. We know that it is pervasive; there is no part of a child's home-life or school-work which the law does not penetrate. It is illuminating, too, showing the value, or lack of value, of a thousand systems and expedients. It is not only a light, but a measure, providing a standard whereby all things, small and great, belonging to educational work must be tested. The law is liberal, taking in whatsoever things are true, honest, and of good report, and offering no limitation or hindrance save where excess should injure. And the path indicated by the law is continuous and progressive, with no transition stage from the cradle to the grave, except that maturity takes up the regular self-direction to which immaturity has been trained. We shall doubtless find, when we apprehend the law, that certain German thinkers—Kant, Herbart, Lotze, Froebel—are justified; that, as they say, it is 'necessary' to believe in God; that, therefore, the knowledge of God is the principal knowledge, and the chief end of education. By one more character shall we be able to recognise this perfect law of educational liberty when it shall be made evident. It has been said that 'The best idea which we can form of absolute truth is that it is able to meet every condition by which it can be tested.' This we shall expect of our law—that it shall meet every test of experiment and every test of rational investigation.

Not having received the tables of our law, we fall back upon Froebel or upon Herbart; or, if we belong to another School, upon Locke or Spencer; but we are not satisfied. A discontent, is it a divine discontent? is upon us; and assuredly we should hail a workable, effectual philosophy of education as a deliverance from much perplexity. Before this great deliverance comes to us it is probable that many tentative efforts will be put forth, having more or less of the characters of a philosophy; notably, having a central idea, a body of thought with various members working in vital harmony.

Such a theory of education, which need not be careful to call itself a system of psychology, must be in harmony with the thought movements of the age; must regard education, not as a shut-off compartment, but as being as much a part of life as birth or growth, marriage or work; and it must leave the pupil attached to the world at many points of contact. It is true that educationalists are already eager to establish such contact in several directions, but their efforts rest upon an axiom here and an idea there, and there is no broad unifying basis of thought to support the whole.

Fools rush in where angels fear to tread; and the hope that there may be many tentative efforts towards a philosophy of education, and that all of them will bring us nearer to the magnum opus, encourages me to launch one such attempt. The central thought, or rather body of thought, upon which I found, is the somewhat obvious fact that the child is a person with all the possibilities and powers included in personality. Some of the members which develop from this nucleus have been exploited from time to time by educational thinkers, and exist vaguely in the general common sense, a notion here, another there. One thesis, which is, perhaps, new, that Education is the Science of Relations, appears to me to solve the question of a curriculum, as showing that the object of education is to put a child in living touch with as much as may be of the life of Nature and of thought. Add to this one or two keys to self-knowledge, and the educated youth goes forth with some idea of self-management, with some pursuits, and many vital interests. My excuse for venturing to offer a solution, however tentative and passing, to the problem of education is twofold. For between thirty and forty years I have laboured without pause to establish a working and philosophic theory of education; and in the next place, each article of the educational faith I offer has been arrived at by inductive processes; and has, I think, been verified by a long and wide series of experiments. It is, however, with sincere diffidence that I venture to offer the results of this long labour; because I know that in this field there are many labourers far more able and expert than I - the 'angels' who fear to tread, so precarious is the footing!

But, if only pour encourager les autres, I append a short synopsis of the educational theory advanced in the volumes of the 'Home Education Series.' The treatment is not methodic, but incidental; here a little, there a little, as seemed to me most likely to meet the occasions of parents and teachers. I should add that in the course of a number of years the various essays have been prepared for the use of the Parents' Educational Union in the hope that that Society might witness for a more or less coherent body of educational thought.

"The consequence of truth is great; therefore the judgment of it must not be negligent" —Whichcote.

1. Children are born persons.

2. They are not born either good or bad, but with possibilities for good and evil.

3. The principles of authority on the one hand and obedience on the other, are natural, necessary and fundamental; but—

4. These principles are limited by the respect due to the personality of children, which must not be encroached upon, whether by fear or love, suggestion or influence, or undue play upon anyone natural desire.

5. Therefore we are limited to three educational instruments—the atmosphere of environment, the discipline of habit, and the presentation of living ideas.

6. By the saying, *education is an atmosphere*, it is not meant that a child should be isolated in what may be called a 'child environment,' especially adapted and prepared; but that we should take into account the educational value of his natural home atmosphere, both as regards persons and things, and should let him live freely among his proper conditions. It stultifies a child to bring down his world to the 'child's' level.

7. By *education is a discipline*, is meant the discipline of habits formed definitely and thoughtfully, whether habits of mind or body. Physiologists tell us of the adaptation of brain structure to habitual lines of thought—i.e., to our habits.

8. In the saying that *education is a life*, the need of intellectual and moral as well as of physical sustenance is implied. The mind feeds on ideas, and therefore children should have a generous curriculum.

9. But the mind is not a receptacle into which ideas must be dropped, each idea adding to an 'apperception mass' of its like, the theory upon which the Herbartian doctrine of interest rests.

10. On the contrary, a child's mind is no mere sac to hold ideas; but is rather, if the figure may be allowed, a spiritual organism, with an appetite for all knowledge. This is its proper diet, with which it is prepared to deal, and which it can digest and assimilate as the body does foodstuffs.

11. This difference is not a verbal quibble. The Herbartian doctrine lays the stress of education—the preparation of knowledge in enticing morsels, presented in due order—upon the teacher. Children taught upon this principle are in danger of receiving much teaching with little knowledge; and the teacher's axiom is, 'What a child learns matters less than how he learns it.'

12. But, believing that the normal child has powers of mind that fit him to deal with all knowledge proper to him, we must give him a full and generous curriculum; taking care, only, that the knowledge offered to him is vital—that is, that facts are not presented without their informing ideas. Out of this conception comes the principle that,—

13. *Education is the science of relations*; that is, that a child has natural relations with a vast number of things and thoughts: so we must train him upon physical exercises, nature, handicrafts, science and art, and upon many living books; for we know that our business is, not to teach him all about anything, but to help him to make valid as many as may be of—

'Those first-born affinities
That fit our new existence to existing things.'

14. There are also two secrets of moral and intellectual self-management which should be offered to children; these we may call the Way of the Will and the Way of the Reason.

15. The Way of the Will.—Children should be taught—

(a) To distinguish between' I want' and 'I will.'

(b) That the way to will effectively is to turn our thoughts from that which we desire but do not will.

(c) That the best way to turn our thoughts is to think of or do some quite different thing, entertaining or interesting.
(d) That, after a little rest in this way, the will returns to its work with new vigour.
(This adjunct of the will is familiar to us as diversion, whose office it is to ease us for a time from will effort, that we may 'will' again with added power. The use of suggestion—even self-suggestion—as an aid to the will, is to be deprecated, as tending to stultify and stereotype character. It would seem that spontaneity is a condition of development, and that human nature needs the discipline of failure as well as of success.)

16. The Way of the Reason. - We should teach children, too, not to 'lean' (too confidently) 'unto their own understanding,' because the function of reason is, to give logical demonstration (a) of mathematical truth; and (b) of an initial idea, accepted by the will. In the former case reason is, perhaps, an infallible guide, but in the second it is not always a safe one; for whether that initial idea be right or wrong, reason will confirm it by irrefragable proofs.

17. Therefore children should be taught, as they become mature enough to understand such teaching, that the chief responsibility which rests on them as persons is the acceptance or rejection of initial ideas.

To help them in this choice we should give them principles of conduct and a wide range of the knowledge fitted for them.

These three principles (15, 16 and 17) should save children from some of the loose thinking and heedless action which cause most of us to live at a lower level than we need.

18. We should allow no separation to grow up between the intellectual and 'spiritual' life of children; but should teach them that the divine Spirit has constant access to their spirits, and is their continual helper in all the interests, duties and joys of life.

The 'Home Education' Series is so called from the title of the first volume, and not as dealing, wholly or principally, with 'Home' as opposed to 'School' education.

"Who was it that said 'Know thyself' came down from heaven? It is quite true—true as Gospel. It came straight to whoever said it first."—Life of Sir Edward Burne-Jones.

Possibly we fail to give 'effective moral training based upon Christian principles' to young people because our teaching is scrappy, and rests mainly upon appeals to the emotions through tale and song. Inspiring as these are, we may not depend upon them entirely, because emotional response is short-lived, and the appeal is deadened by repetition: the response of the intellect to coherent and consecutive teaching appears, on the contrary, to be continuous and enduring. Boys and girls, youths and maidens, have as much capacity to apprehend what is presented to their minds as have their elders; and, like their elders, they take great pleasure and interest in an appeal to their understanding which discovers to them the ground-plan of human nature—a common possession.

The point of view taken in this volume is, that all beautiful and noble possibilities are present in everyone; but that each person is subject to assault and hindrance in various ways, of which he should be aware in order that he may watch and pray. Hortatory teaching is apt to bore both young people and their elders; but an ordered presentation of the possibilities that lie in human nature, and of the risks that attend these, can hardly fail to have an enlightening and stimulating effect. This volume is intended as an appeal to the young to make the most of themselves, because of the vast possibilities that are in them and of the law of God which constrains them.

The teaching in Book I. is designed for boys and girls under sixteen. That in Book II. should, perhaps, appeal to young people of any age; possibly young men and women may welcome an attempt to thrash out some of the problems which must needs perplex. them. In the hands of the teachers of elementary schools, the book should give some help in the formation of character. If only half a dozen children in each such school got an idea of what is possible to them and what they should aim at, some elevation of character throughout the nation should be manifest in a single generation. In our moral as in our intellectual education, we work too entirely upon narrow utilitarian lines: we want the impulse of profounder conceptions. The middle and upper forms of a public school, and those indicated above, fairly represent the classes of readers the author has in view.

The two 'Books' are published separately in order that each may be put into the hands of the readers for whom it is designed; but, because parents and teachers should make a particular study of such moral teaching as they may offer to the young people for whom they are responsible, it seems desirable that the two volumes should form one of the 'Home Education Series.' Questions are appended for the use of more serious students. The more or less casual ordering of young people which falls to their elders might become more purposeful if it were laid down upon some such carefully considered ground-plan of human nature as this book attempts to offer. The scheme of thought rests upon intuitive morality, as sanctioned by the authority of Revelation.

The systems of morality formulated by authoritative writers upon ethics are, perhaps, expanded a little to include latent capacity for every kind of goodness in all normal human beings. Some attempt has been made to define certain limitations of reason, conscience, and the will, the disregard of which is a fertile cause of error in human conduct.

What is sometimes described as the 'immanence of God'; the capacity of man for relations with the divine; and the maimed and incomplete character of the life in which these relations are not fulfilled, are touched upon, because these matters belong to a knowledge which is 'the chief end of man.' The allusions and excerpts which illustrate the text have been carefully chosen from sources that fall within everybody's reading, because the object is rather to arrest the attention of the reader, and fix it, for example, upon the teaching of Scott and Plutarch, than to suggest unknown sources of edification. We are all too well content to let alone that of which we do not already know something.

Ambleside,
May 1905.

Introduction

"Self-reverence, self-knowledge, self-control—
These three alone lead life to sovereign power." Tennyson.

A Dual Self.—The whole question of self-management and self-perception implies a dual self. There is a self who reverences and a self who is reverenced, a self who knows and a self who is known, a self who controls and a self who is controlled. This, of a dual self, is perhaps our most intimate and our least-acknowledged consciousness. We are a little afraid of metaphysics, and are still more afraid of self-consciousness, and we do not take the trouble to analyse our fears.

It is well that we should fear to wander into regions of mind which we have no plummet to fathom, and from which we are incompetent to bring back any good thing. It is well, too, that we should dread that form of self-consciousness which makes us sensitively, or timorously, or proudly, aware of our individual peculiarities. But, for fear of Scylla and Charybdis, we have avoided unduly a channel which leads to a haven where we would be.

Our business at present is not to attempt any psychological explanation of the fact of the two selves of which each of us is aware; but, rather, to get some clear notions about that, let us call it, objective self, the conduct of which is the chief business of that other troublesome subjective self, of which we are all too much and too unpleasantly aware.

The 'Horrid' Self.—One of the miseries of thoughtful children and young people arises from their sense of the worthlessness of this poor, pushing, all too prominent self. They are aware that they are cross and clumsy, rude and 'horrid.' Nobody can like them. If even their mother does so, it must be because she does not quite see how disagreeable they are. Vanity, the laying of oneself out for the approbation of others, is very possible, even to children of generous temper. But I doubt if conceit is possible to any but the more commonplace minds, content to shape their opinions, even of themselves, upon what they suppose to be the opinions of those around them.

But for the uneasy young soul, whose chief business in life is the navigation of an unknown craft, some knowledge of the carrying and sailing powers of the vessel is not only beneficent in itself, but is a relief from the obsession of that tiresome other self—the subjective self, we have called it—of which we become aware in that day when we eat the fruit of the tree of knowledge, and leave the paradise of the unconscious child. This awakening must come to us all, and is not necessarily in our case of the nature of guilt, but it is the cause of uneasiness and self-depreciation.

The Great Self.—Any attempt to define the limits of each part of the dual self baffles us. We cannot tell where one begins and the other ends. But after every effort of thought which convinces us that we are but one, we become aware again of ourselves as two. Perhaps if we say that the one is the unsatisfactory self which we produce in our lives; the other, the self of great and beautiful possibilities, which we are aware of as an integral part of us, it is all we can do towards grasping this evasive condition of our being. It may help us to regard for a moment the human soul as a vast estate which it rests with us to realise. By soul, I mean all that we are, including even the visible presentment of us, all our powers of thinking, knowing, loving, judging, appreciating, willing, achieving. There is only one authoritative estimate of the greatness of the human soul. It is put into the balances with the whole world, and the whole world, glorious and beautiful as it is, weighs as nothing in the comparison. But we lose the value of this utterance of our Lord's because we choose to think that He is speaking of a relative and not an intrinsic value. That the soul of a man is infinitely great, beautiful, and precious in itself we do not venture to think; partly, because religion, for the most part, teaches a self-abasement and effacement contrary to the spirit and the teaching of Christ.

Emily Bronte.—We are indebted to the Belgian sage, M. Maeterlinck, for his vindication of the greatness of the soul, a vindication the more telling because he does not approach the subject from the religious standpoint, but brings, as it were, an outside witness. He has probably added nothing to the content of philosophy; but we have great need to be reminded, and reminded again, of the things that belong to our life; and to do this for us is a service. His contention, that in Emily Bronte we have an example of the immeasurable range of the soul, seems to me a just one: that a delicate girl, brought up almost in isolation in a remote parsonage, should be able to sound the depths of human passion, conceive of human tragedy, and gather the fruits of human wisdom, is a very fair illustration of the majesty of the soul; all the more so because she was not among the great as regards either virtue or achievement. When we turn from an obscure Emily Bronte to a Shakespeare, a Newton, a Rembrandt, a Dante, a Darwin, a Howard, we begin to discern the immensity of that soul which contains a measure for all things, capacity for all men; but we leave off too soon in our appreciation of our Great; we are too shamefaced to acknowledge to ourselves that it is in our own immensity we find some sort of measure for theirs.

Are there any little men? Perhaps not. It may be that all the properties of the soul are present in everyone, developed or undeveloped, in greater or lesser degree. So Christ seems to have taught; and many a poor and insignificant soul has been found to hold capacity for Him.

But here is a case in which the greater is blessed (or cursed?) of the less. The realised self of each of us is a distressfully poor thing, and yet upon its insight and its action depends the redemption of that greater self, whose limitations no man has discovered. It is, to use a figure, as the relation between a country and its government. The country is ever greater than the governing body; and yet, for its development, the former must depend upon the latter.

The Governing Powers.—What are these central governing powers, or officers, upon whose action the fulfilment of a human being depends? I cannot, as yet, go to Psychology for an answer, because she is still in the act of determining whether or no there be any spirit. Where I appear to abandon the dicta of our more ancient guide, Philosophy, it is only as I am led by common intuition. That which all men perceive to be true of themselves may be considered with a view to the conduct of the affairs of the inner life, just as it is wise to arrange our outward affairs on the belief that the sun rises at such an hour and sets at such an hour. The actual is of less immediate consequence than the apparent fact.

As I do not know of any book to recommend to parents which should help their children in the conduct of life in matters such as I have indicated, which are neither precisely ethical nor religious, I venture to offer an outline of the sort of teaching I have in view in the form in which it might be given to intelligent children and young people of any age, from eight or nine upwards.

How to use this Volume.—I think that in teaching children mothers should make their own of so much as they wish to give of such teaching, and speak it, a little at a time, perhaps by way of Sunday talks. This would help to impress children with the thought that our relations with God embrace the whole of our lives. Older students of life would probably prefer to read for themselves, or with their parents, and the more advanced teaching which is suitable for them will pass over the heads of their younger brothers and sisters.

Book 1—Self-Knowledge

"Self-reverence, self-knowledge, self-control,
These three alone lead life to sovereign power."
—Tennyson

Chapter 1 The Country of Mansoul

The Riches of Mansoul.—"Do ye not like fair londes?" says King Alfred; and he answers himself: "Why should I not like fair londes? They are the fairest part of God's creation." And of all the fair lands which God has made, there is no country more fair than the Kingdom of Mansoul.

The soil is, almost everywhere, very fertile, and where it is cultivated there are meadows, corn-fields, and orchards with all manner of fruit. There are, too, wild nooks, with rippling streams bordered by forget-me-nots and king-cups, places where the birds nest and sing. There are hazel copses where you may gather nuts, and there are forests with mighty trees. There are wildernesses, too, marshy and unlovely, but these only wait for good and industrious hands to reclaim them and make them as fertile as the rest of the country. Deep under the surface lie beds of fuel to be had for the working, so that in that land there need never be a cold hearth-stone. There are many other mines, too, where diligent workers find, not only useful and necessary metals like copper and iron, but also silver and gold and very precious stones. When the workers are weary they may rest for there are trees for shade and shelter, and pleasant playfields. And you may hear the laughter of the children, and see them at their sports.

The Rivers and Cities.—There are rivers, broad and deep, good to bathe in and to swim in, and also good to bear the ships which carry those things produced by Mansoul to other countries far and near. Upon these rivers, too, sail the ships of many lands, bringing passengers and goods. There are busy cities in Mansoul; and these, also, are pleasant places; because though there are factories where men work and make all manner of things for home use or to be sent abroad, there are also fair and beautiful buildings, palaces of delight, where are gathered the treasures of Mansoul—galleries of precious and beautiful pictures painted by the great artists of all countries, statues of the heroes that are had in reverence there, halls with organs of noble tone which can roar like the thunder and babble like a child, and all manner of musical instruments. To these halls great musicians come and play wonderful things that they have made; the people of Mansoul listen, and great thoughts swell in them, and everyone feels as if he could get up and go and be a hero.

Its Books and Playgrounds.—There are libraries, too—such libraries! containing every book of delight that ever was written. When anybody sits down to read, the author who made the book comes and leans over his shoulder and talks to him. I forgot to say that in the picture-galleries the old painters do the same thing; they come and say what they meant by it all.

There is no city in Mansoul so built up but there is plenty of space for parks and cricket-grounds, playing-fields and places where people meet and are merry, dance and sing. No body need be poor in Mansoul; and if anybody is poor, neglected, and stunted, it is for a reason which we shall consider by and by.

Its Churches and its Delectable Mountains.—The best treasures of the country are kept in the fairest of its buildings, in its churches, which are always open, so that people may go in and out many times a day to talk with God, and He comes and speaks with them. But, indeed, He walks about everywhere in the land, in the workshops, in the picture-galleries, and in the fields; people consult Him about everything, little things and great, and He advises about them all.

Much remains to be said about Mansoul, but I think I have left out the chief thing—the 'Delectable Mountains,' where people go that they may breathe mountain air, gather the lovely mountain flowers, and brace their limbs and their lungs with the toilsome delight of climbing. From the top, they get a view that makes them solemnly glad; they see a good deal of Mansoul, and they see the borders of the land that is very far off. They see a good deal of Mansoul, but they cannot see it all, for a curious thing is, that no map has been made of the country, because a great deal of it is unexplored, and men have not discovered its boundaries. This is exciting and delightful to the people, because, though here and there Mansoul is touched by another such country as itself, there are everywhere reaches which no man has seen, regions of country which may be rich and beautiful.

Chapter 2 The Perils Of Mansoul

The Government to Blame.—You are thinking, I daresay, what a rich and beautiful country Mansoul must be! But, like most other lands, it is subject to many perils. Unlike most other lands, however, Mansoul has means of escape from the perils that threaten it from time to time. In other countries, we hear the government blamed if poor people have not bread, and if rich people are annoyed by the crowing of a cock. This is usually great nonsense, but it is not nonsense to blame the government of Mansoul for the evils that occur in that country, for it has large power to prevent those evils. How the country is governed you shall hear later. Meantime, learn something of the perils which may overtake poor Mansoul and all that are in it.

Peril of Sloth.—Perhaps the most common evil is a sort of epidemic of sloth that spreads over the whole country. The scavengers sit with heavy eyes and folded arms, and let refuse and filth accumulate in the streets. The farmers and their labourers say, 'What's the good?' and fail to go out with the plough or to sow the seed. Fruit drops from the trees and rots because no one cares to pick it up.

The ships lie idle in the harbours because nobody wants anything from abroad. The librarians let their books be buried in dust and devoured by insects, and neglect their duty of gathering more. The pictures grow dim and tattered for want of care; and nobody in the whole country thinks it worth while to do anything at all. Sometimes the people still care to play; but play without work becomes dull after a time, and soon comes to a stop. And so the people, whatever be their business in Mansoul, sit or lounge about with dull eyes, folded arms, and hanging heads.

Peril of Fire.—Another risk that Mansoul runs is that of great conflagrations. Sometimes an incendiary will land at one of its ports from some foreign country, perhaps with the express purpose of setting fire to what is best in Mansoul; but perhaps a man sets fire to things by accident because he does not know how inflammable they are. The fire once begun, the wind carries the flames over many miles of country; noble buildings, precious works of art, farmsteads with stacks of corn, everything is consumed, and ruin follows the track of the fire. Sometimes these fires arise in Mansoul itself. I have told you that the country has great beds of underlying fuel. Here and there inflammable gases break out on the surface, and a spark, dropped in the region of these gases, is sufficient to cause a wide conflagration. But Mansoul ought to be as careful as people in Switzerland are when a hot wind called the Föhn blows, and orders are issued that everyone is to put out his fires and lights.

Perils of Plague, Flood, and Famine.—Some times there is a visitation of the plague, because dwelling-houses, streets, and out-buildings are not kept clean and wholesome, and the drains are allowed to get into disorder.

Sometimes the springs swell in the hills, the rivers overflow, and there is a flood; but this is not always a misfortune in the end, because much that is rotten and unclean is swept away, and lands washed by a flood are very fertile afterwards.

Again, it may happen that the crops fail, though the land has been diligently tilled and good seed sown. But neighbouring States are kind, and help Mansoul in these distressful times; and the crops of the following year are generally abundant

Peril of Discord.—Another cause of occasional misery in Mansoul is that a spirit of discord breaks out now and then among the members of the community, and becomes sometimes so violent as to lead to a devastating civil war. The servants and workmen will not obey the masters, and the masters will not consider their servants, and are at feud among themselves; one member of the ministry chooses to attend to the work of some other member; all useful employments are neglected, and the people are a prey to envy and discontent. I might tell you of some other causes of misery in Mansoul, but shall mention only one more, which is by far the worst that ever overtakes the State.

Peril of Darkness.—Lovely and smiling as the country is when it is well ordered, mists at times emanate from it, chilling, soaking mists, dense and black; not a ray of the sun can penetrate these mists, no light, no warmth; there is no seeing of one's way, so that the people say, 'There is no sun,' and some of the more foolish add, 'There never was a sun in heaven, and there never will be.' When they cannot see the sun, of course they cannot see each other, and blunder against one another in the darkness. You will say that many lands, especially low lands, are subject to blinding mists, but nowhere can they be so thick and heavy, and nowhere do they lie so long, as in the Kingdom of Mansoul. One quite exceptional thing about these mists is, that they also are largely under control of the government, especially of the Prime Minister. How this can be so I cannot fully explain here, but you will understand later.

Because all these things can happen to Mansoul, we must not run away with the idea that it is an unhappy country. On the contrary, it is radiant and lovely, busy and gay, full of many interests and of joyous life,—so long as the government attends to its duties.

Chapter 3 The Government of Mansoul

Each of us a Kingdom of Mansoul.—I must give up attempting to talk about Mansoul in parables. I daresay you have already found it difficult to make everything fit; but, never mind; what you do not understand now you may understand some day, or you may see a meaning better and truer than that which is intended. Every human being, child or man, is a Kingdom of Mansoul; and to be born a human being is like coming into a very great estate; so much in the way of goodness, greatness, heroism, wisdom, and knowledge, is possible to us all. Therefore I have said that no one has discovered the boundaries of the Kingdom of Mansoul; for nobody knows how much is possible to any one person. Many persons go through life without recognising this. They have no notion of how much they can do and feel, know and be; and so their lives turn out poor, narrow, and disappointing.

It is, indeed, true that Mansoul is like a great and rich country, with a more or less powerful and harmonious government; because there is a part of ourselves whose business it is to manage and make the best of the rest of ourselves, and that part of ourselves we shall call the Government.

Officers of State.—There are many Officers of State, each with his distinct work to do in the economy of this Kingdom of Mansoul; and, if each does his own work and if all work together, Mansoul is happy and prosperous. I will give a list of a few of the great Officers of State, and later we shall consider what each has to do. To begin with the lowest, there are the Esquires of the Body, commonly called the Appetites; then come the Lords of the Exchequer, known as the Desires; the Lords of the Treasury, that is, the Affections; then the Foreign Secretary, that is, the Intellect, with his colleagues, My Lord Chief Explorer (Imagination) and My Lord President of the Arts (the æsthetic Sense); the Lord Attorney-General, that is, the Reason; the Lords of the House of Heart: the Lord Chief Justice, that is, the Conscience; the Prime Minister, that is, the Will. There are various other Officers of State, whom we cannot name now, but these are the principal. Beyond and above all these is the King; for you remember that Mansoul is a Kingdom.

The Four Chambers.—These various Ministers we may conceive as sitting each in the House with the ordering of whose affairs he is concerned. These Houses are, the House of Body, the House of Mind, the House of Heart, and the House of Soul.

You must not understand that all these are different parts of a person; but that they are different powers which every person has, and which every person must exercise, in order to make the most of that great inheritance which he is born to as a human being.

PART I The House Of The Body

Chapter I The Esquires Of The Body: Hunger

The Work of the Appetites.—We will first consider the Esquires of the Body; not that they are the chief Officers of State, but in Mansoul, as in the world, a great deal depends upon the least important people; and the Esquires of the Body have it very much in their power to make all go right or all go wrong in Mansoul.

Their work is very necessary for the well-being of the State. They build up the Body, and they see to it that there shall be new Mansouls to take the place of the old when these shall pass away. If each would attend to his own business and nothing else, all would go well; but there is a great deal of rivalry in the government, and every member tries to make the Prime Minister believe that the happiness of Mansoul depends upon him. If any one of these gets things altogether into his hands, all is in disorder.

How Hunger Behaves.—Esquire Hunger is the first of the appetites that comes to our notice. He is a most useful fellow. If he do not come down to breakfast in the morning, a poor meal is eaten, and neither work nor play goes well in Mansoul that day. If, for weeks together, Hunger do not sit down to table, thin fingers and hollow cheeks will show you what a good servant has left his post. He is easily slighted. If people say, 'I hate' bread and milk, or eggs, or mutton, or what not, and think about it and think about it, Hunger is disgusted and goes. But if they sit down to their meals without thinking about what they eat, and think of something more interesting, Hunger helps them through, bit by bit, until their plates are emptied, and new material has been taken in to build up their bodies. Hunger is not at all fond of dainties. He likes things plain and nice; and directly a person begins to feed upon dainties, like pastry, rich cake, too many sweets, Hunger goes; or rather, he changes his character and becomes Gluttony.

Hunger a Servant, Gluttony a Ruler.—It is as Gluttony that he tries to get the ear of the Prime Minister, saying, 'Leave it all to me, and I will make Mansoul happy. He shall want nothing but what I can give him.' Then begins a fine time. As long as Hunger was his servant, Mansoul thought nothing about his meals till the time for them came, and then he ate them with a good appetite. But Gluttony behaves differently. Gluttony leads his victim to the confectioner's windows and makes him think how nice this or that would taste: all his pocket-money goes in tarts, sweets, and toffee. He thinks at breakfast what pudding he should like for dinner, and asks for it as a favour. Indeed, he is always begging for bits of cake, and spoonfuls of jam, and extra chocolates. He does not think much about his lessons, because he has a penny in his pocket and is considering what is the nicest thing he can buy for it; or, if he is older, perhaps he has a pound, but his thought is still the same, and Gluttony gets it all. The greedy person turns away from wholesome meals, and does not care for work or play, because Gluttony has got the ear of the Prime Minister, and almost every thought of Mansoul turns one way—'What shall I eat?' he says. Gluttony begins with the little boy and goes with him all through life, only that, instead of caring for chocolate creams when he is a man, he cares for great dinners two hours long.

How Gluttony affects the Body.—But, you will say, if Hunger builds up the body, surely Gluttony must do so a great deal faster. It is true that sometimes the greedy person becomes fat, but it is muscle and not fat which makes the body strong and useful. Gluttony does not make muscle, and does cause horrid illnesses.

How to avoid Greediness.—The way to keep this enemy out of Mansoul is to stick to the rules which Hunger lays down. The chief of them is—Never think of your meals till they come, and, while you are eating, talk and think of something more amusing than your food. As for nice things, of course we all want nice things now and then; but let us eat what is given to us of the chocolate or fruit at table, and not think any more about it. Sweets or fruits are seldom served at school, we know, and when at school it is quite fair for a boy to allow himself to spend a certain part of his pocket-money in this way, not only for himself, but that he may have something to give away. But the boy who spends the whole, or the greater part, of his week's money on things to eat, or who is always begging for hampers from home, is a poor fellow, the victim of Gluttony. The best plan is to want to spend your money upon something else—some sort of collection, perhaps; or to save up to buy a present or a fishing-rod or anything worth having. Gluttony lets you alone when you cease to think of him and his good things.

Chapter II The Esquires Of The Body: Thirst

Thirst likes Cold Water.—Another most serviceable Esquire of the Body is Thirst. How serviceable he is you will understand when you remember that by far the greater part of a man's weight is made up of water. This water is always wasting away in one way or another, and the business of Thirst is to make up for the loss. Thirst is a simple fellow; the beverage he likes best is pure cold water; and, indeed, he is quite right, for, when you come to think of it, there is only one thing to drink in the world, though we drink it mixed with many things. Sometimes the mixing is done by nature, as in milk or grapes; sometimes by man, as in tea or coffee.

Some of these mixed drinks are wholesome, because they contain food as well as drink, and by far the most wholesome of these is milk.

But Thirst himself does not care for or need anything in the water he drinks. He likes it best clear and cold, and if we lived in hot Eastern countries we should know how delicious cold water is. All little children like water, but bigger boys and girls sometimes like various things, such as lemon juice, in their water to give it a flavour. Though there is no harm in this, it is rather a pity, because they lose their taste for water itself.

Drunkenness craves for Alcohol.—You would think that so simple and useful an Esquire of the Body could never be a source of danger to Mansoul. But Thirst also gets the ear of the Prime Minister; he also says, 'Leave Mansoul to me, and he shall never more want anything in the world but what I can give him.' This saying of his is quite true, only, instead of calling him Thirst any longer, we must call him Drunkenness; and once Drunkenness has a man in his grip, that man wants nothing but drink, drink, from morning till night.

The chairs and tables out of his house, his children's bread, their mother's clothes, all go to buy drink. The man's time, health, and strength are spent in drink—he becomes homeless and friendless, sick and outcast, for the sake of drink. But he does not crave for home or friends; all he wants is more drink and more drink. By far the greater part of the sin, misery, and poverty in the world is caused by Drunkenness.

Why People Abstain.—As you know very well, it is not pure water that causes Drunkenness. Men long ago discovered how to prepare a substance called alcohol, and this it is that ruins thousands of men and women. Many good men and women, and children, too, make a solemn vow that they will never taste ale or wine or other strong drink, unless a doctor order it by way of medicine. They do this, not only for fear that they should themselves become drunkards—though indeed there is no knowing who may fall into that terrible temptation, or at what period of life such a fall may come,—but because every little good deed helps to stop the evil in the world by setting a good example to somebody; and perhaps there is never a good example set but someone follows it, though the person who set the example may never know.

This is one reason why it is well to keep one's taste for cold water, and to know how delicious it is.

Chapter III Esquires Of The Body: Restlessness And Rest

Restlessness makes the Body Strong.—I hardly know by what names to call the two Esquires of the Body whom I am now to introduce to you, but both are good body-servants. Perhaps Restlessness and Rest will do as well as any. You have noticed that a baby is seldom quite still when he is wide awake: he is kicking his legs about, or playing with his fingers or toes, or crawling, or clutching or throwing something down or picking it up, or laughing, or crowing, or crying. Little boys and girls, too, cannot bear to sit still long at lessons. They want to run into the garden and see what their pet frog is doing. When lessons are over a good romp is delightful, or a race, or a good deal of tumbling about head-over-heels. Later, people want to play cricket or football, or to ride bicycles, or climb mountains. They think they do all these things just because it is fun; but, really, good Esquire Restless will not let them alone, but gives them an uneasy feeling if they are not pretty often doing something which is rather hard to do and rather tiring. He is playing the part of a faithful body-servant. He is helping to make Mansoul a strong and wiry body, able to swim and ride, to jump and run; able to walk far and to hit true and to do every service that the Prime Minister may require. In fact, the business of Restlessness is to strengthen and harden the muscles which Hunger feeds.

But Restlessness may be a Hard Master.—Restlessness, from being a good servant, might become a hard master; indeed, he sometimes does become so, and people do things that are too hard for them in the way of rowing or climbing running or jumping. Worse still, the Dæmon of Restlessness possesses them, and they cannot settle to any kind of work or play because they always want to be doing something else. This is a very unfortunate state to get into, because it is only by going on doing one thing steadily that we learn to do it well, whether it be cricket or algebra; so it is well to be on the watch for the moment when Restlessness, the good servant, turns into Restlessness, the unquiet Dæmon who drives us about from post to pillar, and will not give us firm standing ground anywhere in life.

Rest, a Good Servant.—In a general way, his fellow-servant and brother, Rest, steps in with, 'It is my turn now,' and the tired person is glad to sit down and be quiet for a little, or lie on his face with a book, or, best of all, go to sleep soundly at night and wake up refreshed and ready for anything. Thus the muscles take such turns of work and rest as help them to grow and become strong.

Sloth, a Tyrant.—I daresay you are glad to hear of an Esquire of the Body who is not followed by a black shadow threatening Mansoul with ruin; but, alas! we cannot be let off. Rest, too, has his Dæmon, whose name is Sloth. 'A little more sleep, a little more slumber, a little folding of the hands to sleep,' is the petition with which he besieges the Prime Minister. Once Sloth is ruler in Mansoul, the person cannot wake up in the morning, dawdles over his dressing, comes down late for breakfast, hates a walk, can't bear games, dawdles over his preparation, does not want to make boats or whistles, or collect stamps, drops in all his lessons, is in the Third form when he ought to be in the Sixth, saunters about the corners of the playing-field with his hands in his pockets, never does anything for anybody, not because he is unkind or ill-natured, but because he will not take the trouble.

Poor fellow! he does not know that he is falling daily more and more under the power of a hard master. The less he exerts himself, the less he is able to exert himself, because the muscles, which Restlessness keeps firm and in good order, Sloth relaxes and weakens until it becomes a labour to raise the hand to the head or to drag one foot after another. People used to be very much afraid of Sloth and to call him one of the Seven Deadly Sins, but somehow he is less thought about now; perhaps because we find so many things to do that we cannot bear to be slothful. Still, if your friends call you idle about play or work, or, worse, indolent, or, worse still, lazy, pull yourself together without loss of time, for be sure the Dæmon, Sloth, is upon you, and once you get into his clutches you are in as bad a case, and your life is as much in danger of being ruined, as if Gluttony or Drunkenness had got hold of you. But take courage, the escape is easy: Restlessness is on the alert to save you from Sloth in the beginning. Up and be doing, whether at work or play.

Chapter IV The Esquires Of The Body: Chastity

How to Rule the Appetites.—We have seen how each of the Appetites—Hunger, Thirst, Restlessness, Rest—is a good body-servant, and how the work of each is to build up and refresh the body. We have seen, too, how a life may be ruined by each of these so innocent-seeming appetites if it be allowed to get the mastery. To save ourselves from this fate, we must eat, drink, sleep, at regular times, and then not allow ourselves to think of taking our ease, of dainty things to eat, of nice things to drink, in the intervals. We should always have something worth while to think about, that we may not let our minds dwell upon unworthy matters.

Each Appetite has its Time.—There is another Appetite which is subject to the same rules as those we have considered. It has its time like eating and sleeping, but its time is not until people are married. Just as eating, drinking, and sleeping are designed to help to make us strong, healthy, and beautiful bodies, so this other Appetite is meant to secure that people shall have children, so that there will always be people in the world, young people growing up as old people pass away. This Appetite is connected with a certain part of the body; and I should not speak about it now, only that one of the great duties we have in the world is to keep this part of the body pure. It is just like that tree of the Knowledge of Good and Evil planted in the Garden of Eden.

Uncleanness.—You remember that Adam and Eve were not to take thereof, or they should surely die; and then, you remember how the tempter came and told Eve that they should not die if they took of it, but should be like gods, knowing good and evil. Well, just in the same way, I fear, you may find tempters who will do their best to make you know about things you ought not to know about, to talk about and read about and do things you ought not to talk about, or read about, or do. I daresay they will tell you these things are quite right, that you would not have such parts of your body and such feelings about them unless you were meant to think and do these things. Now it will help you to know that this is the sin of Uncleanness, the most deadly and loathsome of all sins, the sin that all nice men and women hate and shrink from more than from any other.

Purity.—The opposite virtue is called Purity, and Christ has said, "Blessed are the pure in heart, for they shall see God." That does not mean, I think, 'shall see God' when they die, but 'shall see' Him with the eye of their soul, about them and beside them, and shall know, whenever temptation comes through this Appetite—'Thou, God, seest me.' That thought will come home to them, so that they will not be able to make themselves unclean by even a thought or a word. They will turn away their eyes from beholding evil; they will not allow themselves to read, or hear, or say a word that should cause impure thoughts.

Glorify God in your Bodies.—Thus they will glorify God in their bodies. Every boy or girl who realises this is a hero in the sight of God, is fighting a good fight, and is making the world better. When the pure marry, their children will be blessed, for they will be good, healthy, and happy, because they have pure parents. Remember that God puts before each of us in this matter the choice between good and evil, obedience and disobedience, which he put before Adam and Eve. They sinned, and death entered into the world. And so surely as you allow yourself in this sin of Uncleanness, even to think a thought which you could not go straight and tell your mother, death begins in you, death of body and soul. Fight the good fight, and do not let yourself, like our first parents, be the victim of unholy curiosity.

The Appetites our Servants, not our Masters.—Let each of the Appetites, so necessary to our bodies, be our servant and not our master, and remember, above all things, that sin and slavery to any Appetite begin in our thoughts. It is our thoughts that we must rule, and the way to rule them is very simple. We just have to think of something else when an evil thought comes, something really interesting and nice, with a prayer in our hearts to God to help us to do so.

Chapter V The Pages Of The Body: The Five Senses

The Esquires of the Body have in turn their attendants, their pages, let us call them; very useful persons in their way, but, like the Esquires, they require looking after—in the first place, to see that they do their work, in the next, to secure that they do not become tyrants. For even they, servants of servants as they are, aim, if they are indulged, at the sole rule and subjection of Mansoul. People sometimes call these pages feelings, but we will call them sensations, because it is through the five senses that they do their work.

Taste, Agreeable and Useful.—The sensation of Taste, one of these, is not only usually agreeable, but is most useful. When food tastes unpleasant, that is often a sign that it is not wholesome. Taste is an excellent servant, and people who know how to keep him in order find simple foods, such as milk and bread and butter, delicious.

But, Pampered, becomes our Master.—But people who pamper taste make themselves his servants. They say they do not like porridge; they do not like mutton, potatoes, eggs. They want things with strong flavours to please their Taste; the older they grow the more difficult it will be to gratify them, so that at last it will take a French cook to think of things quite nice enough for their dinners. The best rule is not to allow oneself in daintiness about food, but to eat what is set before one; indeed, a wise person is rather glad when something is served which he does not exactly like, or when he has to take disagreeable medicine, because this gives him an opportunity to keep Taste in his proper place, that of a servant and not of a master. It is a good plan not to talk about our likes or dislikes, not even to know which kind of jam we like best.

'Smell' is Lazy.—Smell is another of these pages, really a very good fellow, and I do not know that he tries much for mastery in Mansoul, unless as the ally of Taste. When he goes about sniffing savoury dishes and making Taste wish for them, he is very objectionable; excepting for that he is harmless enough, but he has a fault which is bad in a servant. He is lazy. As his work is very important, this lazy habit must be dealt with.

Should give Mansoul much Pleasure.—He might be the means of giving Mansoul a great deal of pleasure, because there are many faint, delightful odours in the world, like the odour of a box-hedge, of lime-trees in flower, of bog-myrtle, which he might carry, and thus add to the pleasure of life. But that is not his only use.

Should serve on the Board of Health.—He should be quick to detect when there is the least impurity in the air, when a room is close, when a drain is out of order, when there is any unpleasant, unwholesome odour about, however slight; because all odours are really atoms floating in the air, which, by breathing, we take into our bodies. As we breathe all day long and all night long, and only take food three or four times a day, it is perhaps more injurious to health to breathe evil odours than to eat food which is not quite fit, though both are bad. But there are people in whom Smell has become so inactive, that they will lean over an open drain without perceiving any bad smell. By and by we hear they are laid up with a fever, and nobody thinks of reproaching that lazy servant, Smell, who has been the cause of the whole mischief.

Practice in catching Odours.—It is a good rule to practise oneself in catching every sweet and delightful fragrance, and in learning to tell, with one's eyes shut, the leaves of various trees, various flowers, food-stuffs, materials for clothing, all by their odours. In this way Smell would be kept in good working order, and should be able to detect, when he goes into a room, whether the air is fresh or fusty.

Touch, most Pervasive.—There are five of these Pages classed together under the name of The Five Senses, but the three we have now to speak of are not so much pages to Esquires of the Body, as body-servants themselves. Touch is a most pervasive fellow. He is all over the body at once, and there are only one or two places, like the nails and the teeth, where he is not. He collects a great deal of useful information. It is he who discovers whether things be hard or soft, hot or cold, rough or smooth, whether they pierce or scratch, or prick or burn.

Most Useful.—You see at once how useful his work is, for without Touch one might accidentally put one's finger in the fire and not know it was burning.

Knives might cut, pins prick, frost bite, and fire burn, and we should be none the wiser, though our bodies might be receiving deadly injury. Some people have an exceedingly delicate sense of touch, especially in the finger-tips, and this enables them to work at making such delicate things as watch-springs and very fine lace.

The Touch of the Blind.—Blind people learn to find out through their finger-tips what their eyes no longer tell them. They learn even the faces of their friends by touch, and can tell whether they are well or ill, glad or sorry. You hear it sometimes said that a person has a nice touch in playing the piano, and it would really seem as if his finger-tips felt not only the keys of the instrument, but the music they are producing.

A Kind 'Touch.'—Some people, again, mothers especially, have so kind a touch that their hands seem to smooth away our troubles. But this sort of touch is only learned by loving. You remember Shakespeare thought that poor little Prince Arthur had it; certainly many loving children have comforting hands.

Practice in Touch.—Those persons whose senses are the most keen and delicate are the most alive and get most interest out of life; so it is worth while to practise our senses; to shut our eyes, for example, and learn the feel of different sorts of material, different sorts of wood, metal, leaves of trees, different sorts of hair and fur—in fact, whatever one comes across.

Touch tries for Mastery over Mansoul—it will surprise you to hear that Touch, simple and useful servant as he is, like the rest, watches for mastery over Mansoul. Have you ever found it hard to attend to lessons or other work because you have had a prick or a sting or a cut, which, as you, say, 'hurts'? When people let themselves think about these little things which can't be helped, they have no thoughts left for what is worth while; thus one of the least of the powers in their lives becomes master of all the rest. You remember the story of the Spartan boy and the fox? It is not necessary that we should be Spartans, because, if anything painful can be helped, it is right and necessary that we should speak about it, or do something to take away the cause of the pain.

Good to have Little Things to put up with.—But, on the other hand, I think we should be rather glad to have little things to put up with now and then—a scratch, a mustard poultice, or a vest that pricks—just that we may get into the way of not letting ourselves think about such matters. There is an instance of a man who was obliged to have his leg cut off, before Sir James Simpson had made the blessed discovery of the use of chloroform. This man was determined that he would not think about the pain, and he succeeded in so keeping his mind occupied with other things, that he was not aware of the operation. This would be too much for most of us, but we might all try to bear the prick of a pin, or even the sting of a wasp, without making a fuss.

Sight brings half our Joy.—The two senses that we have still to speak of are ministers of delight to Mansoul, and I do not know that they have any serious faults as servants, excepting those of laziness and inattention. Sight brings us half our joy. The faces of our friends, gay sunshine, flowers and green grass, and the flickering of the leaves, pretty clothes and little treasures and pictures, mountains and rivers, and the great sea—where would our joy in all these be if we could not see them? Kind friends might read to us, certainly, but it would not be the same thing always as to have our own book and read it in the apple-tree, or in the corner of the window seat. Let us pity the blind. But there are other people to be pitied, almost as much as they.

Eyes and No-Eyes.—Do you know how Eyes and No-Eyes went out for a walk? No-Eyes found it dull, and said there was nothing to see; but Eyes saw a hundred interesting things, and brought home his handkerchief full of treasures. The people I know are all either 'Eyes' or 'No-Eyes.' Do you wish to know which class you fall into? Let me ask you two or three questions. If you can answer them we shall call you, Eyes. If you cannot, why, learn to answer these and a thousand questions like them. Describe, from memory, one picture in your mother's drawing-room without leaving out a detail. Name a tree (not shrub) which has green leaf-buds? Do you know any birds with white feathers in their tails? If you do not know things such as these, set to work. The world is a great treasure-house full of things to be seen, and each new thing one sees is a new delight.

Hearing a Source of Joy.—There is a great deal of joy, again, to be had out of listening—joy which many people miss because Hearing is, in their case, an idle servant who does not attend to his business.

Have you ever been in the fields on a spring day, and heard nothing at all but your own voice and the voices of your companions, and then, perhaps, suddenly you have become silent, and you find a concert going on of which you had not heard a note? At first you hear the voices of the birds; then, by degrees, you perceive high voices, low voices, and middle voices, small notes and great notes, and you begin to wish you knew who sang each of the songs you can distinguish.

The more we Listen, the more we Hear.—Then, as you listen more, you hear more. The chirp of the grasshoppers becomes so noisy that you wonder you can hear yourself speak for it; then the bees have it all to themselves in your hearing; then you hear the hum or the trumpet of smaller insects, and perhaps the tinkle and gurgle of a stream. The quiet place is full of many sounds, and you ask yourself how you could have been there without hearing them. That just shows you how Hearing may sleep at his post. Keep him awake and alive; make him try to hear and know some new sound every day without any help from sight. It is rather a good plan to listen with shut eyes.

Some Nice Sounds.—Have you ever heard the beech-leaves fall one by one in the autumn? That is a very nice sound. Have you heard the tap, tap of the woodpecker, or have you heard a thrush breaking snail-shells on a stone? Of course you can tell the difference between one horse and a pair by sound. Can you tell one kind of carriage from another, or a grocer's cart from a carriage? Do you know the footfall of everybody in the house? Do you know the sound of every bell in the house? Do you listen to people's voices, and can you tell by the intonation whether the people are sad or glad, pleased or displeased?

Music, the Great Joy we owe to Hearing.—Hearing should tell us a great many interesting things, but the great and perfect joy which we owe to him is Music. Many great men have put their beautiful thoughts, not into books, or pictures, or buildings, but into musical score, to be sung with the voice or played on instruments, and so full are these musical compositions of the minds of their makers, that people who care for music can always tell who has composed the music they hear, even if they have never heard the particular movement before. Thus, in a manner, the composer speaks to them, and they are perfectly happy in listening to what he has to say. Quite little children can sometimes get a good deal of this power; indeed, I knew a boy of three years old who knew when his mother was playing 'Wagner,' for example. She played to him a great deal, and he listened. Some people have more power in this way than others, but we might all have far more than we possess if we listened.

How to get the Hearing Ear.—Use every chance you get of hearing music (I do not mean only tunes, though these are very nice), and ask whose music has been played, and, by degrees, you will find out that one composer has one sort of thing to say to you, and another speaks other things; these messages of the musicians cannot be put into words, so there is no way of hearing them if we do not train our ear to listen. A great help towards learning to hear music is to know the notes, to be able to tell with one's eyes shut any note or chord that is struck on the piano or sung with the voice. This is as entertaining as a puzzle, and if we find that we are rather dull of hearing at first we need not be discouraged. The hearing ear comes, like good batting, with much practice; and the time will come when in a whole chorus of birds you will be able to distinguish between the different voices, and say which is the thrush, which is the blackbird, which the white-throat, which the black-cap, which the wren, which the chaffinch. Think how happy the person must be for whom every bird's note is the voice of a friend whom he knows!

PART II—The House Of Mind

Chapter I Ourselves

'Ourselves,' a Vast Country not yet Explored.—When we think of our bodies and of the wonderful powers they possess, we say, under our breath, "Great and marvellous are Thy works, Lord God Almighty." Now, let us consider that still more wonderful Self which we cannot see and touch as we can our bodies, but which thinks and loves and prays to God; which is happy or sad, good or not good. This inner self is, as we have said, like a vast country much of which is not yet explored, or like a great house, built as a maze, in which you cannot find your way about. People usually talk of 'Ourselves' as made up of Body, Mind, Heart, and Soul; and we will do the same, because it is a convenient way to describe us. It is more convenient to say, 'The sun rises at six and sets at nine,' than to say, 'As the earth turns round daily before the sun, that part of the earth on which we live first gets within sight of the sun about six o'clock in the morning in March.' 'The sun rises and sets' is a better way of describing this, not only because it is easier to say, but because it is what we all appear to see and to know. In the same way, everybody appears to know about his own heart and soul and mind; though, perhaps, the truth is that there is no division into parts, but that the whole of each of us has many different powers and does many different things at different times.

Self-control, Self-knowledge, Self-reverence.—It would even seem as if we had two inside selves, one which wishes to do a wrong or unwise thing, and another which says, 'You must not.' And one of the great things we have to learn in life is how, where, and when to use this power, which we call Self-control. Before we can have true Self-control we must know a good deal about ourselves, that is, we must get Self-knowledge. Many persons think themselves quite different from everybody else, which is a mistake. Self-knowledge teaches that what is true of everybody else is true of us also; and when we come to know how wonderful are the powers and how immense are the possibilities of Mansoul, we are filled, not with pride, but with Self-reverence, which includes reverence and pity for the meanest and most debased, because each of these is also a great Mansoul, though it may be a Mansoul neglected, ruined, or decayed. The government of Mansoul is, as we know, the chief business of man; and we will go on to consider the Members of the Government.

Chapter II My Lord Intellect

Introduces Mansoul to Delightful Realms.—To begin with my Lord Intellect: he is the Foreign Secretary, because he conducts affairs and establishes relations with many foreign kingdoms. Through him Mansoul obtains the freedom of rich provinces and mighty states.

Science, a Vast and Joyous Region.—Science is one of these provinces. Here, the stars are measured, the ocean sounded, and the wind made the servant of man; here, every flower that blooms reveals the secret of its growth, and every grain of sand recounts its history. This is a vast and joyous realm; for the people who walk therein are always discovering new things, and each new thing is a delight, because the things are not a medley, but each is a part of the great whole. So immense is the realm of Science that one of the wisest and greatest travellers therein, who had discovered many things, said, when he was an old man, that he was only like a little child playing with pebbles on the beach. Do you, too, wish to walk in the pleasant ways of Science? My Lord Intellect will give you the necessary introductions, and do everything to make your progress easy.

Imagination cheers the Traveller here.—I should have mentioned that Intellect's colleague, my Lord Imagination, Chief Explorer (you recollect him?), usually journeys with travellers in the ways of Science, and cheers them by opening up fresh and delightful vistas before their eyes.

History, a Pleasant Place.—History is another glorious domain to which my Lord Intellect holds the key, and sends forth Imagination by way of courier and companion to the zealous traveller. Of all the pleasant places in the world of mind, I do not know that any are more delightful than those in the domain of History. Have you ever looked through a kinetoscope? Many figures are there, living and moving, dancing, walking in procession, whatever they happened to be doing at the time the picture was taken. History is a little like that, only much more interesting, because in these curious living photographs the figures are very small and rather dim, and most attentive gazing cannot make them clearer; now, History shows you its personages, clothed as they were clothed, moving, looking, speaking, as they looked, moved, and spoke, engaged in serious matters or in pleasures; and, the longer you look at any one person, the more clearly he stands out until at last he may become more real to you than the people who live in your own home.

The Shows of History.—Think of all the centuries and of every country full of a great procession of living, moving people. Think of the little byways of history where you see curious things that bring you very near to the people concerned, like that letter from a little boy in Egypt, some four thousand years ago, in which he tells his father that he won't be good or do his lessons unless his father takes him to the great festival that is coming on. Even little boys in Egypt four thousand years ago were not, it appears, all good. Here we see Alcibiades going about the streets of Athens, handsome, witty, and winning, reckless and haughty, and so far without principle that not even Socrates could make him good. Or we see the King, Henry VIII., walking arm-in-arm with Sir Thomas More in his garden at Chelsea, and his dear daughter Margaret hovering round and bringing her father sugar-plums when the King had gone.

We are making History.—We see, too, the working people, the smith at his forge, the ploughman in the field, the maypole on the village green, with the boys and girls dancing round it. Once Intellect admits us into the realms of History, we live in a great and stirring world, full of entertainment and sometimes of regret; and at last we begin to understand that we, too, are making History, and that we are all part of the whole; that the people who went before us were all very like ourselves, or else we should not be able to understand them. If some of them were worse than we, and in some things their times were worse than ours, yet we make acquaintance with many who were noble and great, and our hearts beat with a desire to be like them. That helps us to understand our own times. We see that we, too, live in a great age and a great country, in which there is plenty of room for heroes; and if these should be heroes in a quiet way, whom the world never hears of, that does not make much real difference. No one was ever the least heroic or good but an immense number of people were the better for it; indeed, it has been said that the whole world is the better for every dutiful life, and will be so until the end of time.

We cannot be at Home in History without Imagination.—But we must read History and think about it to understand how these things can be; and we owe a great debt of gratitude to the historians, of whom Herodotus has been called the 'father,' who called in Imagination to picture for them the men and events of the past (about which they had read and searched diligently), so that everything seemed to take place again before their eyes, and they were able to write of it for us. But their seeing and writing is not of much use to us unless, in our case, Lord Intellect invites Imagination to go forth with him, and we think of things and figure them to ourselves, until at last they are real and alive to us.

Mathematics, a Mountainous Land.—Another realm open to Intellect has an uninviting name, and travelling therein is difficult, what with steep faces of rock to climb and deep ravines to cross. The Principality of Mathematics is a mountainous land, but the air is very fine and health-giving, though some people find it too rare for their breathing. It differs from most mountainous countries in this, that you cannot lose your way, and that every step taken is on firm ground. People who seek their work or play in this principality find themselves braced by effort and satisfied with truth. Intellect now and then calls for the aid of Imagination as he travels here, but not often. My Lord Attorney-General Reason is his chosen comrade.

Philosophy explores Mansoul.—Another domain which opens interesting prospects to Intellect is that of fair Philosophy, a domain with which we are a little acquainted already, for it is that of Mansoul, with its mountain heights, its dark forests, its unexplored regions. Philosophy offers fascinating and delightful travelling, and the wayfarer here learns many lessons of life; but he does not find the same firm foothold as he whose way leads him through the Principality of Mathematics. Still, certainty is not the best thing in the world. To search, to endeavour, and to feel our way to a foothold from point to point is also exhilarating; and every step that is gained is a resting-place and a house of ease for Mansoul.

Literature, a very Rich and Glorious Kingdom.—Perhaps the least difficult of approach, and certainly one of the most joyous and satisfying of all those realms in which Intellect is invited to travel, is the very rich and glorious Kingdom of Literature. Intellect cannot walk here without Imagination, and, also, he does well to have, at his other side, that colleague of his, whom we will call the Beauty Sense. It is a great thing to be accustomed to good society, and, when Intellect walks abroad in this fair kingdom, he becomes intimate with the best of all ages and all countries. Poets and novelists paint pictures for him, while Imagination clears his eyes so that he is able to see those pictures: they fill the world, too, with deeply interesting and delightful people who live out their lives before his eyes. He has a multitude of acquaintances and some friends who tell him all their secrets. He knows Miranda and the melancholy Jaques and the terrible Lady Macbeth; Fenella and that Fair Maid of Perth, and a great many people, no two alike, live in his thoughts.

How to recognise Literature.—Observe, there is a poor place close at hand, where pictures are painted for you and where people are introduced; but you cannot see the pictures with your eyes shut, and the people do not live and act in your thoughts; there is as much difference between this region outside and that within the Kingdom of Literature as there is between a panorama and the real, beautiful country it is intended to portray. It is a horrible waste of time to wander about in this outside region, yet many people spend a large part of their lives there, and never once get within sight of the beauties and delights within the Kingdom of Literature.

There is another test, besides the two of scenes that you see and people that you know, which distinguishes Literature from the barren land on its borders; and if he is to apply this test, Intellect must keep his Beauty Sense always by his side. Read over, and see if you find a difference of flavour, shall I say, between the two passages that follow. Try if the first gives you a sense of delight in the words alone, without any thought of the meaning of them, if the very words seem to sing to you;

"That time of year thou mayst in me behold
When yellow leaves, or none, or few, do hang
Upon those boughs which shake against the cold,
Bare, ruined choirs, where late the sweet birds sang."

Now read the next passage;

"Household Deities!
Then only shall be happiness on earth
When man shall feel your sacred power and love
Your tranquil joys."

Can you perceive that, though the second passage is true, thoughtful, and well expressed, it just misses a certain charm in the wording which makes words go home to our heart with living power? If you cannot see any difference in value between these two passages, perhaps you will do so some day. The thing is, to keep your eye upon words and wait to feel their force and beauty; and, when words are so fit that no other words can be put in their places, so few that none can be left out without spoiling the sense, and so fresh and musical that they delight you, then you may be sure that you are reading Literature, whether in prose or poetry. A great deal of delightful literature can be recognised only by this test.

Our Beauty Sense.—There is another region open to Intellect, of very great beauty and delight. He must needs have Imagination with him to travel there, but still more must he have that companion of the nice ear and eye, who enabled him to recognise music and beauty in words and their arrangement. The æsthetic Sense, in truth, holds the key of this palace of delights. There are few joys in life greater and more constant than our joy in Beauty, though it is almost impossible to put into words what Beauty consists in; colour, form, proportion, harmony—these are some of its elements. Words give some idea of these things, and therefore some idea of Beauty, and that is why it is only through our Beauty Sense that we can take full pleasure in Literature.

Beauty in Nature.—But Beauty is everywhere—in white clouds against the blue, in the gray bole of the beech, the play of a kitten, the lovely flight and beautiful colouring of birds, in the hills and the valleys and the streams, in the wind-flower and the blossom of the broom. What we call Nature is all Beauty and delight, and the person who watches Nature closely and knows her well, like the poet Wordsworth, for example, has his Beauty Sense always active, always bringing him joy.

We cannot get away from Beauty, and we delight in it most perhaps in the faces and forms of many little children and of some grown-up people.

The Palace of Art.—We take pleasure, too, in the arrangement and colouring of a nice room, of a nice dress, in the cover of a book, in the iron fittings of a door, when these are what is called artistic. This brings us to another world of beauty created for us by those whose Beauty Sense enables them not only to see and take joy in all the Beauty there is, but whose souls become so filled with the Beauty they gather through eye and ear that they produce for us new forms of Beauty—in picture, statue, glorious cathedral, in delicate ornament, in fugue, sonata, simple melody. When we think for a moment, how we must admire the goodness of God in placing us in a world so exceedingly full of Beauty—whether it be of what we call Nature or of what we call Art—and in giving us that sense of Beauty which enables us to see and hear, and to be as it were suffused with pleasure at a single beautiful effect brought to our ear or our eye.

The Hall of Simulation.—But, like all the good gifts we have received, this too is capable of neglect and misuse. It is not enough that there should be a Beauty World always within reach; we must see to it that our Beauty Sense is on the alert and kept quick to discern. We may easily be all our lives like that man of whom the poet says:—

"A primrose by the river's brim
A yellow primrose was to him,
was that, and nothing more"

–that is, he missed the subtle sense of Beauty which lay, not so much in the primrose nor in the river, but, rather, in the fact of the primrose growing just there. Our great danger is that, as there is a barren country reaching up to the very borders of the Kingdom of Literature, so too is there a dull and dreary Hall of Simulation which we may enter and believe it to be the Palace of Art. Here people are busy painting, carving, modelling, and what not; the very sun labours here with his photographs, and he is as good an artist as the rest, and better, for the notion in this Hall is that the object of Art is to make things exactly like life. So the so-called artists labour away to get the colour and form of the things they see, and to paint these on canvas or shape them in marble or model them in wax (flowers), and all the time they miss, because they do not see, that subtle presence which we call Beauty in the objects they paint and mould. Many persons allow themselves to be deceived in this matter and go through life without ever entering the Palace of Art, and perceiving but little of the Beauty of Nature. We all have need to be trained to see, and to have our eyes opened before we can take in the joy that is meant for us in this beautiful life.

The Intellectual Life.—I cannot tell you more now of the delightful and illimitable sources of pleasure open to Intellect and his colleagues; but, if you realise at all what has been said, you will be surprised to know that many people live within narrow bounds, and rarely step into either of the great worlds we have been considering. The happiness of the intellectual life comes of knowing and thinking, imagining and perceiving or rather, comes of the range of things which we know and think about, imagine and perceive. Everybody's mind is occupied in these ways about something or other, but many people know and think about small matters. It is quite well to think of these for a little while, but they think about them always, and have no room for the great thoughts which great things bring to us.

Thus, a boy's head may be so full of his stamp collection or of the next cricket match that there is no room in it for bigger things. The stamps and the cricket are all right, but it is not all right by any means to miss the opportunities of great interests that come to us and pass unnoticed, while we think only of these small matters. Not only so: boys and girls may be so full of marks and places, prizes and scholarships, that they never see that their studies are meant to unlock the door for them into this or that region of intellectual joy and interest. School and college over, their books are shut for ever. When they become men and women, they still live among narrow interests, with hardly an outlook upon the wide world, past or present. This is to be the slaves of knowledge and not its joyful masters. Let it be said of us as it was of the late Bishop of London, "His was the rare gift of mastering knowledge as his splendid servant, not being himself mastered by it as its weary slave."

Chapter III The Daemons Of The Intellect

Inertia will not let us begin.—Like the Body, the Mind, too, has his Dæmons. The two which beset Intellect are, first, a sort of sloth or inertia which makes us unwilling to begin to think of anything but the small matters of everyday life. If we will only begin, Intellect bestirs himself, strong and eager for his work:—

"Are you in earnest? Seize this very minute;
What you can do, or dream you can, begin it;
Boldness has genius, power, and magic in it!
Only engage, and then the mind grows heated;
Begin it, and the work will be completed."
Marlowe's Faust.

We are delighted, and time flies; yet the next time we come to the same fence, Intellect jibs and we have to spur him to the leap; then all goes well. It is well to bear this in mind, because if we give way Intellect will again pull up before a little difficulty.

Habit goes always over the same Ground.—The other Dæmon of Intellect is Habit. Now Habit, as you know, is, whether for body or mind, a good servant and a bad master. It is when he is allowed to play the bad master and override Intellect that he spoils and narrows life. Under Habit, Intellect cannot be said to be slothful; he goes briskly enough, but he goes over the same ground, day after day, year in, year out. The course may be a good one and it may be quite necessary to follow it. The mistake is to keep always on the same beaten track. It may be the mechanical round of lessons, without a thought of what it is all about. It may be housekeeping, business, hunting, shooting, dress—things well enough in their way; but to confine Intellect to them is like harnessing a race-horse to a coster's barrow.

We may not stay in one Field of Thought.—Nor is it only the affairs and interests of daily life which deprive the Mind of its proper range of interests and occupations. It is possible for a person to go into any one of the great fields of thought we have considered, and to stay there with steady work and constant delight until he becomes incapable of finding his way into any other of these great fields. The greatest man of science of our age had this misfortune. He lost himself, so to speak, in Science, and in the end he could not read poetry, look at pictures, could not even think upon God, because he could not turn his mind out of the course he had exercised it in all his life. The people who lived when, perhaps, the greatest things were done, the greatest pictures painted, the greatest buildings raised, the greatest discoveries made, were very particular on this point. The same man was an architect and a painter, a sculptor and a poet, and a master of much knowledge besides; and all that he did, he did well; all that he knew was part of his daily thought and enjoyment.

Vasari, his biographer, says of Leonardo da Vinci the great painter:—"Possessed of a divine and marvellous intellect, and being an excellent geometrician, he not only worked at sculpture, . . . but also prepared many architectural plans of buildings, and he was the first, though so young, to propose to utilise the Arno to make a canal from Pisa to Florence. He made designs for mills and other engines to go by water, and as painting was to be his profession, he studied drawing from life."

A Magnanimous Mind.—It is a mistake, perhaps, to think that, to do one thing well, we must just do and think about that and nothing else all the time. It is our business to know all we can and to spend a part of our lives in increasing our knowledge of Nature and Art, of Literature and Man, of the Past and the Present. That is one way in which we become greater persons, and the more a person is, the better he will do whatever piece of special work falls to his share. Let us have, like Leonardo, a spirit 'invariably royal and magnanimous.'

Chapter IV My Lord Chief Explorer, Imagination

Living Pictures.—My Lord Chief Explorer, Imagination, deserves a more complete introduction than the by-the-way mention he has had as a colleague of Intellect. He is an amazing personage, with power to produce, as we have seen, a procession of living pictures in every region open to Intellect. Great artists, whether they be poets or painters, builders or musicians, have the power of expressing and showing to the rest of us some part, anyway, of the wonderful visions Imagination has revealed to them. But the reason why we enjoy their pictures, their poems, or their tales, is because Imagination does the same sort of thing for all of us, if in a less degree. We all have pictures and poems made for us on the inner curtains of our minds. Little children try to express their visions in their games: they play at events, and often in a very odd way, because they know so little that they make a jumble of facts, call a cow a hyæna, and expect to meet a lion and a tiger in every bit of spinney.

The Cultivated Imagination.—The more we know, the more ordered and the more rich should Imagination become in us. Have you read Feats on the Fjord? Miss Martineau, who wrote the book, never visited Norway, but no one could describe the life on the fjords more vividly than she has done; that is because her Imagination was at home in distant lands, as no doubt it was also in past ages. Have you thought how Sir Walter Scott must have lived, in Imagination, in the different times and scenes he gives us in his books? No wonder people called him a 'Wizard.' In order to have a richly-stored picture-gallery of the Imagination we must read much, and, as the French say, figure to ourselves, as we go on, that which we read.

Imagination must not make Pictures of Self.—Imagination, minister as it should be to the joy and breadth of life, has, alas! its two besetting Dæmons—Self and Sin. There is no one who does not imagine. You are a Princess with golden hair and blue eyes and a long, long train to your silken robe, and the Prince comes, and after great feats of valour which make the world wonder, he kneels before you and asks you to be his bride:—

"Little Ellie in her smile
Chooses—'I will have a lover,
Riding on a steed of steeds:
He shall love me without guile,
And to him I will discover
The swan's nest among the reeds.'

Or you are Prince Valorous himself, and you subdue the Paynim and conquer many lands, and the King places you at his right hand in war and at the feast. These are pretty dreams, and there is not much harm in them, except that, while one dreams, one forgets to do, and life is made up altogether of doing and not at all of dreaming. It is very nice to dream, when people have been finding fault with us, that we shall do wonderful and beautiful things—nurse the sick and build palaces for the poor and make gardens of delight for the mother or father who finds fault with us—and to think how everybody will admire us for all our beauty and goodness and cleverness especially those people who have laughed at us; to think, too, how kind we shall be to them and what presents we shall make them, and how sorry they will be that they have not always been polite and kind!

I do not think it is lawful to set Imagination to build us pleasure-houses in this way. In the first place, as I said before, while we are dreaming we are letting all our chances of doing slip by us. In the next place, when we have dreamed ourselves into being some high and mighty personage, ever so good and great, we are very easily affronted; and Imagination leaves off his building tasks to throw stones at our friends. Imagination tells us that 'Mother' does not understand us, does not know half what great persons we are; that 'Father' is not kind, that Lucy or Edward is more noticed than we are, that lessons are hateful, that going for a walk is a bother, that seeing people is a nuisance, that any book but a storybook is dull; and, by degrees, other people find us just what we, in our imagination, have pictured them.

Our best friends have to own that we are dull and disagreeable, peevish and resentful; they say there is no pleasing us, they complain that there is no getting us to join in games or to take any interest in plans. They say we do not try to be pleasant with, or helpful to, anybody. The little ones say we are cross, and do not woo us to play with them, and the big ones think us grumpy and let us alone. It is very provoking, because we know that all the time we have beautiful thoughts about what we shall do for every one of them, and the least they can do is to be kind meantime!

How to Exorcise the Dæmon.—But the others are right, and we are wrong. Just ask yourself, who is the chief person in all the pretty pictures you make, in all the plans you form? If you have to confess that you, yourself, are, why, Imagination has just been making pleasure-houses for Self instead of collecting pictures of the great rich world. See about it, in the future, and set this glorious servant to work in his rightful calling.

Then you will be a delight to your friends, because you will have much to tell, and will be interested about many things. You will not trouble them or yourself with that peevish, exacting, grudging Self, a tyrant in any home. In fact, you will find so much that is delightful to think about that you will hardly have a moment in which to think about yourself. Turn Self out the moment he intrudes upon any picture of the Imagination. A good plan is to take your Self by the shoulders, look him full in the face and laugh at him for a ridiculous fellow. This is what is called having 'the saving grace of humour,' and people who have it do not make themselves absurd by putting on airs and graces. It is nearly, though not quite, as good when your home people laugh at you and tease you. Learn from their laughing and bear their teasing with good humour.

Living Pictures of Sin.—The second Dæmon of Imagination is Sin. Have you ever heard people say, 'There seems to be quite an epidemic of burglaries' or 'of murders'? They are quite right.

There is an epidemic of these things. They are catching in a curious way. People read of a crime in the newspapers, they allow their Imagination to dwell upon all the details; the whole thing becomes a living picture which they cannot get rid of, and the end is that they attempt the same sort of crime themselves. That is why it is unwise for anyone to read newspaper accounts of those sorts of things, for even if you are not tempted to do the wickedness, the horrid picture of it remains, once you have allowed your Imagination to paint it for you.

Unclean Imaginings.—There is one kind of sins that we must be especially careful not to take impressions of; once we do so they will haunt us all our lives. These are sins of uncleanness. If people talk of such sins, do not listen; go away and do something. If you come across the mention of such sins in your reading—of the classics, of poetry, of history—learn, as it were, to shut the eyes of your Imagination, or your thoughts will become defiled. Never knowingly read anything or listen to anything which could suggest unclean imaginations. I once visited a young woman who was dying, a nice, good, married woman, and she told me this awful thing. She said her dying bed was made miserable and she could not say her prayers because horrible imaginations of uncleanness came to her. She said she never had thought of such things; but, I suppose, she must have allowed herself to think such thoughts at some time, perhaps many years before, and had forgotten it: but the evil spirit took this dreadful opportunity to remind her of them. Shun all such talk, all such readings, and all such imaginations, more than you would shun the plague.

Living Pictures of Horrors.—It is not of the nature of sin, but it is very foolish to allow Imagination to make living pictures of horrors, dreadful accidents, falls down precipices, ghosts, and what not. Once make a picture, and there it is, and it may show itself at any moment to torment.

I hear someone whose nature inclines her to such terrors say, 'But how can I help it?' That is really a foolish question about any of the evils we may fall into. Of course we can help them, and to do so is the battle of life. In this particular case the help lies in hurrying away from the thought to think of something else. If such terrors come at night, when you cannot do anything or read anything, you can always think of something else. The last story-book you have read, for instance,—go over the tale in your thoughts.

Chapter V The Beauty Sense

The Dæmon of Exclusiveness.—The Beauty Sense adds so much to the joy of life that it is not easy to see what danger attends it. But, perhaps, Exclusiveness is the Dæmon that waits on a too keen sense of the joy of Beauty, whether in music, painting, one's own surroundings, or even in natural scenery. Exclusiveness gets the ear of the Prime Minister and convinces him that the joys of Beauty are so full and satisfying that nothing else is necessary to complete the happiness of life. In vain does Intellect invite to new fields of research; in vain does good and necessary work present itself; in vain are duties clamorous. The person who is given up to the intoxication of Beauty conceives that Beauty and Goodness are one and the same thing, and that Duty is no more than seeking one's own pleasure in the ways one best likes. People, too, become excluded.

We may not Choose our Lives.—Instead of accepting the relations, friends, and neighbours that God sends us in the course of our lives, the devotee of Beauty chooses for himself, and cares to know only those people whose views of life are the same as his own. So with regard to places, he cannot tolerate for a moment things which are unsightly and unlovely, so he does not go where working people and poor people have to live. In the end, he misses the happiness to which the Beauty Sense was meant to minister. For happiness comes of effort, service, wide interests, and, last and least, of enjoyment; and when people put enjoyment, even of beautiful things, in the first place (and indeed in place of all else), they miss the very thing they seek, and become enfeebled in body and fretful and discontented in temper.

A Paradise of Pleasure.—But we need not let fear of evil keep us out of that paradise of pleasure which the Beauty Sense is meant to open for us all. Of two things we must take heed. In the first place, we must not let any better-than-my-neighbour notions get into our heads; and in the next, we must make it our business, as much as in us lies, to bring Beauty to places where it is not. Bearing these two cautions in mind, the Daemon of Exclusiveness need have no terror for us.

Chapter VI My Lord Chief Attorney-General, Reason

Reason, an Advocate.—I have spoken of my Lord Chief Attorney-General, Reason, as a mere colleague of Intellect; but, indeed, he is a person of great importance in the government of Mansoul—so much so, that he not infrequently gets the entire government into his hands. Reason is a personage of admirable powers and of independent character. If you should ever hear a great lawyer advocating a cause in court, bringing forward one argument after another to prove his point, with masterly clearness, until he brings his hearers to what seems an inevitable conclusion (until the other side pleads), you will have some idea of how Reason behaves. Have you ever watched yourself think? It seems as if another person, a K.C. [King's Counsel; a Barrister] of your own, were bringing forward point after point until you cannot help coming to one conclusion. Do you remember Prospero in Shakespeare's tale of The Tempest? You know how he neglected his duties as ruler, and how his brother, intending to take his life, was the means of his exile, with his child Miranda, on a desolate island.

How we Reason.—I suppose this is the sort of thing his Reason said to him: 'The thinking part of man is the most important part of him. It is better to live with thinkers than with everyday people. The greatest thinkers are to be found in books, not in my court. Everyday people can manage the affairs of everyday people. My brother Antonio can govern for me quite as well as I could do it myself, but he cannot read for me and think for me, and give his time to the bettering of his mind for me. These things a man must do for himself. Then there is my child; I should like her also to grow up a thinker. To that end I must prepare myself further to teach her. It is quite evident, considering all these things, that I must give up affairs and devote myself to my books."

Now, it is not that Prospero said all this to himself, but that his Reason said it to him and for him. Every argument is true, though it is not the whole truth; and Prospero's Reason would not have taken this line with him, only that he was already a student and a lover of books, and Reason usually begins with a notion which is already in a person's head.

Let us hear what Antonio's Reason would say to him: "The way my brother, the Duke, neglects his affairs is shameful; the state is going to ruin; everybody does what he likes. He expects me to act for him, but people know I am not the Duke, so I have no power. If he were to die, the dukedom would be mine, and I should do my best to bring things into order again. How his neglected subjects would bless me! Even to tamper with his life would hardly be a crime, because the sufferings of one would be for the good of all. Things get worse and worse every day. It must be done. There is no one to act in this matter but myself. I will do it." Antonio's Reason no doubt hastened thus to supply him with arguments to support the ambitious notion he had already secretly entertained.

The Good Man's Reason.—The good man's Reason makes speed to supply him with incontrovertible arguments for the good deed his good heart would incline him to. Thus Howard, the philanthropist, no doubt was convinced by many reasons that the arduous task he set himself was a quite simple, straightforward course. He saw the inside of one prison by chance, and the thought of its horrors worked upon him. Reason would say:—"People do not know that such things take place; someone must tell them. Whoever discovers this shame to the world must first investigate thoroughly. It will not do to speak upon a knowledge of one or two prisons. When the evil is fully known and talked about, and brought before Parliament, no doubt it will be redressed, new laws will be made, and prisoners will be treated like human beings instead of being kept in the state of filth, misery, sickness, and vice in which I find them. Why should not I be the man? The idea has first come to me: that may be my call. I am very delicate, it is true, but a man cannot die better than in doing his duty. I am under a great sorrow, but that sets me free from home ties; and I have money enough for the costs. I will do it. I will give up my life to the task."

Thus, doubtless, this good man's Reason argued for him. But if divine compassion had not put this notion of pity into his heart, you will see how very easily Reason could have adopted an opposite line of argument and brought him to the conclusion that this was not an affair for a single man to undertake, but was a matter for the governments of countries.

Reason's Part in Good Works and Great Inventions.—Every great work of benevolence for the sick and the helpless, the sorrowful and the ignorant, is the outcome of a chain of arguments which some man's Reason has furnished to him; and his Reason has taken this line because in each case a notion of pity has first come to the man. Every great work, every invention has been reasoned out. Have you ever seen in a museum the trunk of a tree hollowed out by burning, which early man has used for a canoe? It was an immense piece of reasoning, quite as intelligent as that by which Marconi arrived at his great discovery, that led the man, who had never seen a boat of any sort, to work out for himself this means of crossing the waters. You see, he had nothing to go upon: his was the first idea. Where and how he got it we shall consider presently; but his Reason worked the whole thing out for him.

What is Meant by Common Sense.—Most of the simple things we do every day, like cleaning our teeth and brushing our hair, behaving at table, and so on, were reasoned out in the first place—we do not in the least know by whom—and people no longer reason about them, but accept them by what is called Common Sense; that is to say, everybody, or nearly everybody, agrees that certain ways of doing certain things are the best ways. Every now and then a reformer appears who reasons out the old things afresh and comes to a different conclusion, perhaps a right one, perhaps a wrong one. For example, most people's Common Sense decides that we should wear boots or shoes; but a reformer arises and proves by a long chain of arguments that it is better to wear sandals; another will say and prove that it is better to go with bare feet; then people have to think again and to use their Reason about things they believed were long ago settled.

Everything we use has been Thought out by Someone.—It is very interesting to look about one in a room or in a street and try to recover for ourselves the chain of reasoning of the man who first made a chair, or a key, or a barrow. Things become much more to us when we remind ourselves that somebody has thought each thing out; and this sort of thinking-out is very delightful. You know this yourself. You say, 'Oh, I have thought of such a good plan; something uncle said put it into my head, and then the whole plan came out quite clear, one step after another.' It may be a plan for a new game, or for building a ship, or for getting plenty of house-room for poor people in towns; but, whatever the notion is, it is joyful and exciting to be quite still and listen, as it were, while Reason does his work and turns out the whole scheme complete before your mind.

It is no wonder many people think that there is nothing greater, in heaven or earth, than human Reason—more surprising in its workings, more searching in its conclusions!

You recollect that revolutionary France deified Reason—set up temples where the Goddess of Reason was worshipped; and the French nation believed that no man was called to do anything but what his own Reason commanded, and that whatever a man's Reason dictated, that he was bound to do. You remember, too, that things, fearful as a nightmare, were done under this reign of Reason, which is known in history as the Reign of Terror, though everything that was done was justified by the Reason of the men who did it. There is no longer an acknowledged reign of Reason, but many thoughtful and good people believe that there is no higher authority; that to act according to his own Reason is the best that can be expected of any man.

Good and Sensible Persons come to Opposite Conclusions.—It is quite true that good laws, benevolent enterprises, great inventions, are the outcome of Reason; but you will often be surprised when you hear good people talk and try to convince others of those things of which their own Reason has convinced them. On questions of war and peace and politics, of religion, of education, of public works, of clothing, of food, in fact, upon any and every point, you will find it possible that the Reason of equally good and equally intelligent people will bring them to quite opposite conclusions. That is the cause of all the controversy in the world. People think that they can convince each other by the arguments which their own Reason has accepted. So they could, if the other side were not already convinced by arguments exactly opposite; and upon which side a man is convinced, usually depends upon his own will:—

"Convince a man against his will,
He's of the same opinion still";

because we must remember that Reason is each man's own particular servant, and plays on his side, as it were, and convinces him of that which he is inclined to believe.

Reason is not Infallible.—You know it is said that the Pope is infallible—that is, that he cannot be mistaken, and that every decision he makes must be a right decision. This is what many people claim for Reason—that it is infallible. But you see at once that if two equally intelligent and equally good persons are intensely convinced by their Reason of two things exactly opposite to one another—as, for example, on the one side that a certain war is the duty of a nation, and, on the other, that this same war is a crime—Reason in both these good men cannot be infallible: one or the other, if not both, must be mistaken. Therefore, seeing that all men, who are not idiots or insane, are endowed with this same power of reasoning, we may conclude that Reason is not infallible, and that certain and fixed conclusions need not be right conclusions, but that all depends upon the notion from which the reasoning begins.

Anarchists.—We have all been saddened by the fact that there are certain men and women in the world who believe it to be their one duty to take the life of some royal person or ruler. These people are called anarchists. Though we all shrink with horror from their crimes, it is not difficult to see the chain of reasoning by which it comes about that they are doing that which is right in their own eyes, however wrong it may be in ours. The word anarchist means without rule; and the object of anarchists is to abolish national rule and government, whether of kingdom or republic. Why? you ask. Because, they say, every man is endowed with Reason; therefore, every man is able to rule himself; therefore, no man should have a ruler placed over him. You see, by this example, how an error of thought may lead to the most terror-striking crimes.

Reason in Mathematics.—Never are the operations of Reason more delightful and more perfect than in mathematics. Here men do not begin to reason with a notion which causes them to lean to this side or to that. By degrees, absolute truth unfolds itself. We are so made that truth, absolute and certain truth, is a perfect joy to us; and that is the joy that mathematics afford. Also, there is great joy in standing by, as it were, and watching our own thought work out an intricate problem. There is on record a case of a mathematician who had gone to bed perplexed by a problem, with pencil and paper beside him. He slept, as he believed, soundly all through the night; but, behold, beside him when he awoke, was the problem worked out in the clearest way. He must have done it his sleep.

Reason must be used to Good Purpose.—There are few things that prove the amazing greatness and power of man so much as this gift of Reason; but, like all gifts, this, of Reason, is also a trust to be used to true purpose, but not to be followed as an infallible guide. We may reason about things worthy and about things unworthy. An ill-tempered person goes through a long train of reasoning to prove to himself that he has been injured and has a right to be cross; so does the burglar, to carry out his designs; so does a mischievous and spiteful boy, to play a practical joke. Reason is so absolutely the servant of each of us that we may use him to what ends we please, noble or ignoble, great or small. Remembering that we have a great gift, let us use it in thinking out great matters; and then, some day, the opportunity to think out some great service for the world will be put in our way. The chance of doing nearly always comes when we are ready for it.

Reason works out a Notion received by the Will, and does not begin it.—"The kettle began it," Dickens says in one of his Christmas tales. Now, the point to be borne in mind is, that Reason does not begin it. Reason goes on with it, and Reason brings it to an end, but Reason does not begin. The beginning, that which sets Reason in motion, is almost always a notion admitted by the Prime Minister, Will. Once admitted, Reason seizes on the notion and runs it through his mill, and it comes out at the end of his processes a finished product. This, you will see, shifts the responsibility of our conclusions from Reason, who works them out, all the way back to Will, who takes in the first notion.

If Will is persuaded to let in a notion because it is an old one, or because it is a new one; because a man he respects thinks so-and-so, or because a man he dislikes thinks the other thing; because it is for his interest to think thus and thus, or because it is for his pleasure, or because it shows him to be a clever fellow, in advance of the rest of the world, to have such a notion; if, for any of these causes or for a hundred others, good or bad, Will is induced to admit a notion, he may tell in advance what his Reason will prove to him: because the business of Reason is rather to prove for us that what we think is right, than to bring us to conclusions which are right in themselves.

You see, therefore, that Reason has no right to speak the last word on most subjects; because to speak the first word does not rest with him, and the last word follows the lead of the first. Your arrival at a right destination does not depend upon your choice of a good road, or upon your journeying at a good pace, but entirely upon your starting in the right direction.

Why there are Different Schools of Philosophy.—Thinking of these things, and knowing that men cannot help trusting to Reason as one trusts to a skilful and learned advocate, you will not be surprised to know that philosophers, good and earnest men, have proved, conclusively to themselves, that there is no God. Others prove that there is nothing in man that you cannot see or investigate with instruments; in other words, they think that there is nothing but matter in the universe, and that there is no spirit either of God or man. This is less surprising, though perhaps not any more true, than the conclusion which another school of philosophers has worked out; these have been able to prove to themselves that there are no chairs nor tables, no trees, no people; but that what we think we see is really the thought of these things conceived in our minds.

Practice in Reasoning.—Perhaps we shall best use this wonderful power of reasoning, commonly called our Reason, by giving it plenty of work to do, by asking ourselves what is the cause of this and that; why do people and animals do certain things. Reason which is not worked grows sluggish; and there are persons who never wonder nor ask themselves questions about anything they see.

Chapter VII The Lords Of The Exchequer, The Desires (Part 1.)

Mind must be Fed.—We consider the Lords of the Exchequer, the Desires, after the Intellect, because their office is to do for Mind pretty much what the Appetites do for Body. It is as necessary that Mind should be fed, should grow and should produce, as that these things should happen to Body; and, just as Body would never take the trouble to feed itself if it never became hungry, so Mind would not take in what it needs, if it, also, had not certain Desires to satisfy. These gather the funds, as it were, for Mind, so we may amuse ourselves by calling them the Lords of the Exchequer.

The Desire of Approbation.—Have you ever watched a baby with his bricks? When he has managed to set one on end, he turns round to his mother for a smile. The little creature is not happy unless his mother or nurse approve of him. When he crawls up to the window, climbs up by the chairleg, says 'Mam-mam, dad-dad,' he wants a smile for all these things, and if his nurse looks grave and says 'Naughty!' the little face will fall and tears gather. No one has taught Baby to care that his friends should be pleased with him; it is born in him and is just a part of him as a human being, a little Mansoul.

This Desire of Approbation helps him later to conquer a sum, to climb a hill, to bring home a good report from school; and all the time he is bringing grist to the mill, knowledge to the mind, because the people whose Approbation is worth having care that we should learn and know, conquer our idleness and get habits of steady work, so that our minds may be duly nourished every day as are our bodies.

The Dæmon of Vanity.—This lawful and useful Desire of Approbation has his Dæmons; one of these is known as Vanity. We cannot live and be happy without Approbation, but some boys and girls, men and women, choose to have the approval of the worthless and silly rather than of the wise and good. Some boys would rather talk and show off in a way to make the stable-yard laugh, than work and play in a way to win the approval of their betters. People can be vain and can show off about almost anything—their rich relations, the parties they go to, their clothes, their pocket-knife, their cleverness. But when people show off, like a peacock spreading his tail, it is always in order that somebody whose good opinion is not worth having may think the better of them. Nice boys and girls, nice men and women, think well of us just for doing our best; we know that, and do not think of showing off before them. He is stupid who wants nobody's approval; he is vain who wants the approval of the unworthy.

Fame and Infamy.—Another danger is that a person may allow the desire of approval so to get possession of him that he thinks of nothing else. All his actions, good or bad, come to be done to win notice from other people. He would rather you spoke ill of him than that you did not speak of him at all. It is believed that robberies, murders, assassinations, take place at times for the mere sake of infamy, just as deeds of heroism may take place for the sake of fame. Both infamy and fame mean being talked and thought about by a large number of people, and if anyone should allow his natural Desire of Approbation so to possess him that he is always wondering what people will think of him and say of him, he loses that which is far more precious than the respect of others—self-respect, which one can only have when the desires, motives, powers of Mansoul are duly balanced.

The Desire of Excelling.—Another Desire which serves to feed the mind is that of Excelling. If we are learning to skate, we have no peace till we skate as well as a boy we know who learned last winter; then we want to outdo him; then, to skate as well as another better skater; then, to outdo him; and so on, and when we go to bed at night we dream of the day when we shall skate better than anyone in the neighbourhood; nay, we think how glorious it would be to be the very best skater in the whole world. It would seem as if some animals, horses anyway, have this Desire. Do you not know how another horse, in advance, puts yours on his mettle? It is as good as a prick of the spur to quicken his pace. And that is just what this Desire of Excelling does for us; it spurs us on to effort when we are lazy. If another boy read, we choose to read more. If he work at his lessons, we work more; and so, one way or another, the Mind is sustained by the food it needs.

Prizes and Places.—Emulation, or the Desire to Excel, has, like the Desire of Approbation, two Dæmons. One is, that people get so much taken up with the Desire of being ahead of some others that they have no time to think of anything else; they do not care two pins about what they learn, it does not interest them; they only want the marks, or prize, the place in class, or what not; and so it happens that his Mind is sometimes so starved by the boy who comes out first that it never afterwards recovers its appetite. History, Literature, Science, cease to interest and cease to be pursued. The whole object of life in such an one is to get ahead of somebody else. In this way Emulation, which was given to us, we may believe, for the nourishment of our Minds and the development of our Bodies, defeats its own ends, and is satisfied only to excel.

Excelling in Things Unworthy.—We may go wrong if we are unduly emulous about things that are right and good in themselves; but also, Emulation, like many another subordinate, may grasp at the whole rule of Mansoul through things unlawful and unworthy. In the old days of hard drinking, the excellence that men desired was, to excel in their power of drinking large quantities of wine at a sitting; to be a 'three-bottle man' was a distinction.

Distinctions as little worthy as this are still sought by boys and girls, men and women. We should each do well to think the matter over and see whether we are giving up our lives to the Desire of Excelling in an unworthy pursuit.

The Desire of Wealth.—The Desire of Wealth is another Desire that everybody has, more or less, and that does useful work in making us eager to acquire things useful and necessary for our lives, whether for our Bodies or our Minds. This same Desire moves a small boy to collect pocket-knives, buttons, string and marbles, and moves one rich man to get together a precious collection of great pictures, and another to become a millionaire, though he may not care to spend his money.

Dæmon of Selfishness.—As before, two Dæmons wait upon this natural Desire; one is the Dæmon of Selfishness: once a boy or man allows himself to be so far possessed by the Desire of getting and keeping, whether it be postage stamps or pictures, ornaments or money, that he thinks of nothing else—that this, of getting and keeping, becomes the ruling Desire of his life—why, he simply cannot part with that which has become his treasure; he cannot be generous, and his mind is so preoccupied that he has no time to be kind. His heart is set upon possessions for himself, and he becomes a selfish person. When the Desire of wealth fills the whole of life it becomes Avarice. The person who is always grasping after more wealth is avaricious; and he may come to such a pass that he cannot part with any of his wealth, even for his own bodily needs; such a man is a miser. On the other hand, he who takes pains to acquire as a part of his life, and not the chief part, may get for himself the means of being generous and helpful to other people.

Worthless Wealth.—Another risk is, that one may set oneself to acquire things of no real worth. In a charming French story a noble pair are introduced who spend their lives in hasty journeys. Now they rush off to Palermo—now, to Moscow—again, to Tokio; and what do you suppose for? Because they hear that in this country or that there is a match-box to be found of a kind they have not already got in their collection—a match-box covered with blue paper or with brown or yellow—a match-box three inches long or two and a quarter. They do not stop to ask what the distinction of the ugly little box may be, but it differs a little from the rest; so, at any cost of time and trouble, they hasten to possess it. The novelist is laughing at the craze people have for collections of any sort, worthy or unworthy; and this craze comes of the natural Desire of possessions implanted in Mansoul. But it rests with us that our possessions shall be worthy. Let us begin soon to collect a good library of books that we shall always value, of photographs of the works of the great masters; even of postage stamps, if we take the trouble to interest ourselves in the stamps—ask ourselves, for example, why the present German stamps bear the figure of Germania. No collection which has not an interest for the mind is worth possessing. Take this rule, and when you grow up you will not think that silver plate, for instance, is worth owning for its own sake, but for its antiquity, its associations, or for the beauty of its designs.

The Desire of Power.—Another Desire which stirs in all human breasts is the Desire of Power. All the children in the nursery have this Desire more or less, but the one who has the most of it rules the rest. They play his games, run his errands, let him lord it over them all day long. The people who love power most, get power; but if they are good-natured and kind; helpful and generous, clever and merry, they use their power to keep the rest happy, interested, and amused. Power is a good thing when it gives us many chances of serving; it is a bad thing when all we care about is to rule.

Ambition, the Desire for power, is not quite the same thing as Emulation, the Desire to excel. The emulous boy is content to be first; the ambitious boy wishes to lead the rest. I think the ambitious boy is of more use in the world than the emulous, because, if he wants to lead others, he must make himself worthy to take the lead. He must be best, whether he be captain of the school or of the cricket eleven. But let him remember that 'pride comes before a fall.' If he let himself be lifted up because he leads, let him beware! Others care to follow the lead of the dutiful and devoted, but not that of the proud and self-satisfied. The Desire for power, as each of the other Desires, may ruin a life that it is allowed to master. Once man or boy thinks of nothing but taking the lead, he will cease to care whether it be for worthy or unworthy objects. He will as soon head his fellows in riot and disorder as in noble effort in a good cause. Many lives have suffered shipwreck upon the rock of Ambition.

'Managing' People.—There is also a special danger attending the love of power—a danger to others rather than to ourselves. If we are bent upon taking the lead, we do not allow others fair play or a fair chance. We cheat our fellows out of a part of their lives, out of that fair share of power which belongs to them. We grow strong at their expense, and they wax feeble in proportion as we wax great. Few characters are more ignoble than those who are always trying to manage others, always manoeuvring to get power into their own hands. The best way of watching against this evil is to wait always until we have 'greatness thrust upon us.' Let us not take the lead, but wait until it is given to us, and then let us lead for the advancement and help of others rather than for our own.

Chapter VIII The Lords Of The Exchequer, The Desires (Part 2.)

The Desire of Society.—Another Desire common to all people is the Desire to be together. We all want company, neighbours, friends, acquaintances. Little children love to play with other little children in the street; you see half a dozen little creatures of two years old or so toddling about together, talking their baby talk, and taking much pleasure in one another. The great joy of going to school is to be with other boys and girls of about the same age and standing. Young men have their clubs, men and women have parties; men of little or no education will hang about together, if they seldom speak, and people of certain savage nations will sit in silent circles by the hour. The same reason is at work in them all; all have the Desire of Society. We want to see each other's faces, to hear each other's voices, to give pleasure to, and receive pleasure from, each other.

We learn from Society.—In this way we learn, for most people have things to say that it is good to hear; and we should have something to produce from our own stores that will interest others—something we have seen or heard, read or thought. When our late beloved Queen was a young girl, many interesting people were introduced to her that she might talk with them—great travellers, men of science, inventors, soldiers, sailors. She had already read and thought about the subject each was interested in, so she was able to converse with them with pleasure and profit both to herself and to them. If you know something of botany, a botanist will care to talk to you about his subject; something of history, a historian will do the same. If you know nothing of his subject, you may be in company with the greatest poet or adventurer or painter, and be able to talk only about the weather. This is well understood among royal and other great people, who, it is said, get most of their knowledge at first hand. They learn about recent discoveries in astronomy from the astronomer who is engaged upon them, about evolution from such an one as Darwin, and so on. We are sometimes inclined to envy the great their opportunities for first-hand information; but let us remember that to profit by the talk of even the most able persons implies a twofold preparation which princes and their like acquire at a cost of diligent labour that would surprise most young people. They bring two things as their share of the talk—cultivated and intelligent minds, and a pretty thorough knowledge of a great range of subjects. With the same equipment we, too, should make the most of our opportunities of talk, and it seems to me that people always get what they are really ready for. I am not sure that this is a rule of God's providence, but, so far as I can find out, it holds good. Anyway, it is worth while to be ready for the best in conversation as in other things, and then this natural Desire will do its devoir in collecting sustenance for the mind.

But it is not only from the best and ablest we may learn. I have seen ill-bred people in a room, and even at table, who had nothing to say because they did not think their neighbour worth talking to, whereas, if they could only get speech with So-and-so, whom they watch from a distance, how their words would flow! This is not only unmannerly and unkind, but is foolish, and a source of loss to themselves. Perhaps there is no one who has not some bit of knowledge or experience, or who has not had some thought, all his own. A good story is told of Sir Walter Scott, how he was travelling from London to Edinburgh by the stage-coach, and sharing the box-seat with him was a man who would not talk. He tried the weather, crops, politics, books, every subject he could think of—and we may be sure they were many. At last, in despair, he turned round with, "Well, what can you talk about, sir?" "Bent leather," said the man; and, added Sir Walter, "we had one of the most interesting conversations I remember." Everybody has his 'bent leather' to talk about, if we have the gift to get at it.

Dangers attending the Love of Society.—Two dangers attend the love of society: one belongs especially, as I said before, to the vain person who will, at all costs, be flattered, and therefore chooses his friends among those who are inferior to himself and who will make believe to look up to him and make much of him. The other danger attending the love of society is that which belongs to each of our natural desires. It is that this craving should take possession of our whole lives, and get the mastery over Mansoul. 'There is no harm in it,' says the woman at the cottage door, gossiping with her neighbour; so says the girl, who chances on her friends in the morning, plays tennis in the afternoon, and goes out in the evening—is, in fact, all day chattering here and there, with nothing to show for it. There are those who are so busy running hither and thither, seeing and being seen, talking and being talked to, that they are the veriest beggars as regards their own thoughts and resources. This is a sort of shipwreck of life which people do not lament over as they do when a man drinks or falls into some other flagrant vice; but the shipwreck is perhaps just as complete, though not so unpleasant to the person's friends.

Society, a Banquet, at which all Provide.—Society, if it be only a chat between two or three acquaintances, is a banquet to which each of the company must bring something. Young people often find this trying, because they feel they have nothing to say unless to one or two people with whom they are intimate. Let them take comfort; intelligent listening is a very good viand for this table, and, what is more, a viand to everybody's taste. There are more people who can talk than who can listen. I daresay you have been amused in watching groups of talkers to notice that everyone is talking at once and nobody listening. To listen with all one's mind is an act of delicate courtesy which draws their best out of even dull people.

People of little culture can talk only to their own set or to their own particular 'chums.' 'Horsey' men have nothing to say except to 'horsey' men; 'doggy' boys except to 'doggy' boys; school-boys to school-boys; school-girls to school-girls; soldiers to soldiers, and sailors to sailors. This is natural enough, for, says the proverb, 'birds of a feather flock together'; but it is not wise, for it is choosing to live in our own particular paddock instead of taking our share in the interests of the great world.

The Desire of Knowledge.—I have left till last the Desire which truly is to the Mind as Hunger is to the Body, that is, the Desire of Knowledge. Everybody wants to know, but some people wish to know things worthy, and others, things unworthy. The Desire of unworthy knowledge is commonly called Curiosity. 'Where did you buy it?' 'How much did it cost?' 'What did she say?' 'Who was there?' 'Why are they not on good terms?' and so on, are the sort of questions that Curiosity asks. It seems harmless enough to satisfy oneself with scraps of news about this notable person and the other, a murderer or a millionaire, a statesman or a soldier, a great lady or a dancing-girl—Curiosity is agape for news about any or all of them. Curiosity is eager, too, to know and to tell the latest news about wireless telegraphy, motor cars, and what not. The real, and not spurious, Desire for knowledge would lead a person from the marvels of wireless telegraphy to some serious study of electricity; but Curiosity is satisfied to know something about a matter, and not really to know it.

Curiosity and the Desire of Knowledge.—Just as sweets and tarts satisfy Hunger, while they do very little to sustain life, so Curiosity satisfies the mind with the tit-bits it gathers, and the person who allows himself to be curious has no Desire for real knowledge. This is a pitiable misfortune, because every human being has a natural Desire to explore those realms open to intellect of which I have already spoken. Upon the knowledge of these great matters—History, Literature, Nature, Science, Art—the Mind feeds and grows. It assimilates such knowledge as the body assimilates food, and the person becomes what is called magnanimous, that is, a person of great mind, wide interests, incapable of occupying himself much about petty, personal matters. What a pity to lose sight of such a possibility for the sake of miserable scraps of information about persons and things that have little connection with one another and little connection with ourselves!

Emulation and the Love of Knowledge.—The love of Knowledge, the noblest of our Desires, is in danger of being pushed out and deprived of its due share in the ordering of Mansoul if any one of the other Desires I have named gets the upper hand. This is especially the case when Emulation takes the place of the love of Knowledge. People employ themselves about Knowledge, about Mathematics, Poetry, History, in a feverish, eager way, not at all for the love of these things, but for the sake of prize or place, some reward bestowed on Emulation. But Knowledge has her own prizes, and these she reserves for her lovers. It is only in so far as Knowledge is dear to us and delights us for herself that she yields us lifelong joy and contentment. He who delights in her, not for the sake of showing off, and not for the sake of excelling others, but just because she is so worthy to be loved, cannot be unhappy. He says, 'My mind to me a kingdom is'—and, however unsatisfactory things are in his outer life, he retires into that kingdom and is entertained and delighted by the curious, beautiful, and wonderful things he has stored within.

'Marks' and Knowledge.—Many boys and girls take pleasure in going to school, not for the sake of what they learn there, but for the sake of the marks which give them places above certain of their classmates. They should understand that marks and places and the power to pass examinations is all they get. As Mr. Ruskin has said, "They cram to pass, and not to know; they do pass; and they don't know." Knowledge, as an abiding joy, comes only to those who love her for her own sake, and not to those who use her to get on in school or in life.

All Persons have Powers of Mind.—There is much more to be said about the House of Mind, but perhaps this is enough to go on with for the present. Probably you are aware, in hearing of Intellect, Imagination, the Beauty Sense, the Desires, and the rest, of a feeling of wondering interest and surprise to recognise that all these things are a part of you, your very self. Still more interesting and surprising it is to know that these amazing powers and possibilities belong, more or less, to every little urchin we meet in the street. I say, more or less, because the greater the powers and qualities of mind possessed by our parents, grandparents, and far-removed ancestors, the greater will our own probably, but by no means certainly, be. But, excepting in the sad case of idiots, there never was a child born into the world, of civilised or of savage parents, who did not come gifted with all these great possibilities in some degree. What a reason have we here for doing whatever in us lies towards giving every person in the world the chance of being all that he came into the world provided and intended to be!

The Ordering of our Thoughts.—We need not carry this little bit of knowledge about ourselves like a pack on our back. Once one knows a thing, it comes to mind when it is wanted, and is not a burden to think of all the time. You are not always thinking 'If I put my finger in the fire, it will be burnt,' but you know that is the case, and so do not do a foolish thing. In the same way, if you know the effect of caring for marks only, you endeavour to throw your mind and interest into your work for its own sake; so, far from being a burden, this knowledge will at once make work become delight. A king's palace is no more trouble to him than a labourer's cottage, to him, though the king knows of all the treasures his palace contains, and how they are to be safeguarded, used, and enjoyed; but the needful arrangements are made, and all goes on without further thought on his part. So with us in this matter of ordering our thoughts, for that is all it comes to. To know that we must order our thoughts; that we can do so; and how and when to interfere with the career of these same thoughts, is not the whole, but, I believe, it is half, the battle.

PART III—The House Of Heart

Lords Of The Heart: I. Love

Chapter I The Ways Of Love

The Lords of the House.—As Mansoul comes into the world with Rulers in his House of Mind, which are also powers of delight, so does he come with Rulers in his House of Heart, whose office is to bring him happiness; and, as no one was ever happy by himself, to cause him to bring happiness to others. The two great Lords and high officials of the House of Heart are Love and Justice.

Love.—Love, like a king, has his Lords in Waiting—Pity, Benevolence, Sympathy, Kindness, Generosity, Gratitude, Courage, Loyalty, Humility, Gladness. Have you ever thrown a stone into the water and watched the circles about it spread? As a matter of fact, they spread to the very shores of the pond or lake or sea into which you have thrown the stone; more, they affect the land on the further side. But those distant circles become so faint that they are imperceptible, while those nearest the point where you have thrown in the stone are clearly marked. So it is with our Love. It is as if, in the first place, our home were the stone thrown in to move our being; and from that central point the circle of our love widens until it embraces all men. No one, excepting our Lord Jesus Christ, ever knew how much he could love, or how much he could do for Love's sake; but the soldier who goes into the thick of the fight to rescue his comrade, at the risk of his own life; the mother who watches her sick child, and would give her life many times over to save it from suffering; the nurse who spends herself, body and soul, in ministering to the sick,—these know just a little of how much love there is in the human heart.

Counterfeit Loves—Self-Love.—There are many counterfeit loves going about ready to take possession of the House of our Heart and to expel the lawful lord. We know what it is to be exacting, selfish, jealous, with those dearest to us, even with our own mothers, and we call it love. So it is; but it is Self love, the poorest and lowest form of Love; but a Love which is lawful and necessary, or we should not take care of our own lives, property, or interests at all. We cannot do without Self-love, or we should become a burden and trouble to other people; but the person who loves himself only, looks only, or chiefly, after his own interests, pleasures and profits, is branded by the world as a selfish person, His mind is so full of his own feelings and affairs that he has little time to think about those of other persons. He gives little love, and he deserves to get as little; but the sad thing is, that perhaps he has a mother or sister, a wife or a friend, who pours great love out upon him and suffers at his hands. It is a comfort that the one who loves, in such a case, and not he who takes the love and makes no return, is really the happier; for it is they who love, rather than they who are beloved, who live every day in the kingdom of God. There is a kind of selfishness not so easily found out as that of the person who is always looking after his own interests and pleasures, that is, the selfishness of the person who is continually making claims on those who love him. He wants their time, their thoughts, all their attention, their company; and is irritable, offended, jealous, if he does not get the attention and affection he demands. He thinks it is because he loves this or that friend so dearly, but it is, in truth, because he loves himself that neither mother nor friend can give him all the love and consideration he seems to himself to deserve.

Philandering.—There is another counterfeit of Love whose satisfaction lies in kissing, caressing, touching, being always with the person beloved at the moment. I say, at the moment, because, though these expressions may belong, in their right measure and at their right time, to true Love, they do not in themselves constitute Love or necessarily belong to it, and some people go through life philandering, now with one person, now with another, in the indulgence of this spurious, rather animal affection, which is not sustained by any of the signs of true Love.

Love is a pearl of price which every heart holds; but, as many people pass counterfeits upon themselves and upon their friends, it is well that we should know how to recognise the jewel when we see it, and above all when we feel, or think we feel it.

Love delights in the Goodness of Another.—Love delights in the person who is beloved. Now it is natural to us to delight in that which is good; the hearts of the most savage and degraded have many times been conquered in this way. They have seen lives of goodness, unselfishness, and beauty lived before them from day to day; they have watched such lives with delight because ''tis their nature to,' and at last they have given their heart's love and reverence to the person whose goodness has been their joy. It is not merely that that person has been good to them; perhaps they have never had a word or look all to themselves, but they have watched, pondered, and loved. Some day, perhaps, we shall know the history of the soldier heroes, the missionary heroes, the saints, who have done good just because they were good. Now, we know only a few here and there,—St. Francis of Assisi, Elizabeth Fry, General Gordon; but, whenever we learn that people have been raised out of degradation, in countries savage or civilised, we may be sure that it is because someone has lived a blessed life before their eyes. Therefore, I say that Love delights before all things in the goodness of the person beloved, and would not, for any price, make his friend less loving to all, less dutiful, less serviceable. To influence his friend towards unworthy ways would seem to Love like burning his own house about his head.

Seeks the Happiness of his Friend.—Again, Love seeks the happiness of the beloved, and shrinks from causing uneasiness to his friend by fretful or sullen tempers, jealousy or mistrust.

Seeks to be Worthy.—Love seeks to be worthy of his friend; and as the goodness of his friend is his delight, so he will himself grow in goodness for the pleasure of his friend.

Desires to Serve.—Once more, Love desires to give and serve; the gifts and the service vary with the age and standing of the friends; the child will bring the gift of obedience, the parent may have to offer the service of rebuke, but the thought of service is always present to Love. "Love not in word, neither in tongue," says the Apostle, "but in deed and in truth"; that is, perhaps, "Do not rest content with the mere expression of love, whether in word or caress, but show your love in service and in confidence"; for the love that does not trust is either misplaced or unworthy. Love has other signs, no doubt, but these are true of all true love, whether between parent and child, friend and friend, married lovers, or between those who labour for the degraded and distressed and those for whom they labour. Let us notice the word degradation: it is literally to step from, to step down, and it is really a word of hope, for if it is possible to step down, it is also possible to step up again. All the great possibilities of Love are in every human heart, and to touch the spring, one must give Love.

Aversion.—But in every Mansoul, our own and all others, there are the opposed possibilities, what we have called the dæmons of the qualities. We are all capable of warmth, liking, friendliness, love; and we are all capable of coldness, dislike, aversion, hatred. Punch's old joke "'E's a stranger; let's 'eave 'arf a brick at 'im," gives us the key to a great deal of our coldness and aversion. It is commonly because we do not know people that we dislike them; and the way to get over such dislike is to think about the person disliked, to try to realise him from his own point of view; thus we shall find much in him that awakens friendly feelings. Hatred is an unusual feeling, and generally arises from the resentment of injuries. Let us remember that the one petition in the Lord's Prayer to which a condition is attached is, "Forgive us our trespasses, as we forgive them that trespass against us." We have it not in us in our own strength to forgive. It is only in the Love and the presence of God that we can forgive injuries, and when we forgive, we love.

Before we think of the particular manifestations of Love, we will consider the blessed presences whom we have called his Lords in Waiting.

Chapter II Love's Lords In Waiting: Pity

Knights and Ladies of Pity.—Have you seen a baby stroke the face of his nurse to cure her pain, or fondle his kitten and say 'Poor!' after treading on its tail? That is because there is a little well of Pity in every baby's heart. To be sure, baby will pull the kitten's tail to see what will happen, but that is only because he wants to know. Convince him of hurt, and he is sad and says 'Poor!' A little girl will come home and cry by herself about a strange dog she has seen beaten; Pity wells up into her eyes, and tears. I know a little girl who never could stand the story of Joseph in the pit. Little boys are sometimes too dignified to cry, but they will run away from a 'sorry' story or a 'sorry' sight because they know what would happen if they stayed. When people are older, they have too much self-control to cry; but, when they see suffering, sorrow and pain, they too have a pain in their hearts, the pain of Pity. The work of Pity in our hearts seems to be to stir us up to help those who suffer. Many tender hearts have been and are so consumed with Pity that they give up their whole lives to the comfort and help of sufferers. You know the story of that Knight of Pity, Father Damien, who gave up all that was pleasant in this life that he might take the comfort of God to the poor souls on that leper-island in the Pacific; or, of that Mr. E. J. Peck, 'the loneliest man in His Majesty's dominions,' who left his family that he might witness of the warm love of God to the Arctic dwellers of Greenland. Indeed, if one thinks long and much about any sufferers, until their distress becomes real to us, we have a sick pain at our hearts until we can give them help. It is because they have in this way taken thought of suffering that the noble army of martyrs, thousands and thousands of them all over the world, give up everything in life that they may serve the suffering. Sometimes such a Knight or Lady of Pity will work and watch day and night for one sufferer, and sometimes many will share the pitiful heart. Sometimes strangers, and sometimes one's own father or mother, sister or child, will require and will get the service of a lifetime. Many, very many, suffer in this happy yet sorrowful world; but, thank God, many also pity.

Idle Pity.—I have said that help is the office of Pity; but there are people who like to enjoy the luxury of Pity without taking the real pain and trouble of helping. They say, 'How sad!' and will even shed tears over a sorrowful tale, but will not exert themselves to do anything to help the sufferer. Indeed, on the whole, they would rather pity imaginary people who need no help, and it gives them pleasure to cry over a sad tale in a book or play. The tears of such people, who are rather pleased with themselves because they think they have 'feeling hearts' are like the water of certain springs in the limestone which have the property of coating soft substances with stone. Every movement of pity which does not lead to an effort to help goes to form a heart of stone. There are none so difficult to move to help as those who allow themselves the luxury of idle pity.

Self-Pity.—There is another class of persons in whom Pity is strong and ever-active; but all their pity is given to one object, and neither sorrow, pain, nor any other distress outside of that object has power to move them. These are the people who pity themselves. Any cause of pity is sufficient and all-absorbing. They are sorry for themselves because they have a headache, because they have a toothache, or because they have not golden hair; because they are lovely and unnoticed, or because they are lanky and unlovely; because they have to get up early, or because breakfast is not to their mind; because brother or sister has some pleasure which they have not, or because someone whose notice they crave does not speak to them, or, speaking, says, 'Make haste,' or 'Sit straight,' or some other form of 'Bo to a goose!' Such things are not to be borne, and the self-pitiful creature goes about all day with sullen countenance. As he or she grows older you hear of many injuries from friends, much neglect, much want of love, and, above all, want of comprehension, because the person who pities himself is never 'understood' by others. Even if he is a tolerably strong person he may become a hypochondriac, with a pain here, and a sensation there, which he will detail to his doctor by the hour. The doctor is sorry for his unhappy patient, and knows that he suffers from a worse malady than he himself imagines; but he has no drugs for Self-pity, though he may give bottles of coloured water and bread pills to humour his patient. You are inclined to laugh at what seems to be a morbid, that is, diseased, state of mind; but, indeed, the Dæmon of Pity, Self-pity, is an insidious foe. Many people, apparently strong and good, have been induced by him to give up their whole lives to brooding over some real or fancied injury. No tenant of the heart has alienated more friends or done more to banish the joys of life.

Our Defences.—Our defence is twofold. In the first place, we must never let our minds dwell upon any pain or bodily infirmity; we may be sick and pained in our bodies, but it rests with ourselves to be well and joyous in our minds; and, indeed, many great sufferers are the very hearth of their homes, so cheerful and comforting are they. Still more careful must we be never to go over in our minds for an instant any chance, hasty, or even intended word or look that might offend us. A spot no bigger than a halfpenny may blot out the sun of our friends' love and kindness, of the whole happiness of life, and shut us up in a cold and gloomy cell of shivering discontent. Never let us reflect upon small annoyances, and we shall be able to bear great ones sweetly. Never let us think over our small pains, and our great pains will be easily endurable.

The other and surer way of guarding ourselves from this evil possession is to think about others. Be quick to discern their pains and sufferings, and be ready to bring help. We cannot be absorbed in thinking of two things at the same time, and if our minds are occupied with others, far and near, at home and abroad, we shall have neither time nor inclination to be sorry for ourselves.

Chapter III Love's Lords In Waiting: Benevolence

"Reform the World, or bear with it."—It is usual to speak as if Benevolence meant nothing more than the giving of money or other help to persons in distress; but it is possible to give a great deal of such help without being benevolent, and to be benevolent without giving much material help. To be benevolent is to have goodwill towards all men. The wise emperor, Marcus Aurelius, described the lowest form of Benevolence when he said, "Men are born to be serviceable to one another; therefore either reform the world, or bear with it!" The very least we can do for the world is to bear with it; the world, in this case, being the people in it who are, for any reason, disagreeable to us. But Benevolence makes us able, not only to bear with the people who annoy us and irritate us, but to give them sincere and hearty liking. Perhaps there is nobody whom we should not be able to love if we really knew him, because all persons are born with the beautiful qualities of mind and heart we have spoken of, in a greater or less degree; and though the beauty of a person's nature may be like a gem buried under a dust-heap, it is always possible to remove the dust and recover the gem. A debased criminal has, possibly, a wife who loves him—not because she loves his baseness, but because she sees the possibilities of beauty in him.

His Faults are not the whole of a Person.—The benevolent perceive that obvious and unpleasant faults are no more compared with the whole human being than his spots are compared with the sun; so they have no difficulty in bearing with faults, or, what is better, trying to correct them; and at the same time giving just the same hearty liking or love to the person as if those faults were not present. This is the sort of Benevolence that parents show to their children, that brothers and sisters show to one another, that is due from friend to friend, from neighbour to neighbour, and, in a gradually widening circle, to all the people we come in contact with, or whose works and ways are brought before us. Benevolence does not use strong language about the joiner when he comes across a door that will not shut or a window that will not open. He knows that the joiner is at bottom a fine fellow, who has probably not been put in the way of making the best of himself, and so is content with slipshod work. Therefore the gaping door and immovable window stir Benevolence up to bring better thoughts before people generally, so that other joiners may turn out better work.

The Affairs of Goodwill.—You will observe that Benevolence is by no means a lazy Lord of the Bosom. He can put up with things done amiss, and with manners that displease him, but he cannot possibly let the people alone who behave amiss. He likes them too well to endure that they should spoil themselves by this or the other failing. He cannot endure either that people should grow up in ignorance, or that there should be sickness or suffering or friendlessness in the world; therefore his hands and heart are always busy with some labour of help.

Benevolence thus has many functions, but wherever his countenance turns he presents the same aspect. Benevolence is always gracious, simple, pleasant and accessible, because he so heartily likes all men and women, boys and girls. He is indefatigable too, because, with so many friends who have so many needs, there is much for him to do; but all that he does gives him pleasure, so it is easy for him to smile as he goes.

The Foes of Goodwill.—What a blessed world we should have if the spring of Benevolence had free play in every human heart! But a whole troop of dæmons obstruct every movement of this beneficent Lord. There is Fastidiousness, which finds offence in all ways which are not exactly our own ways. There is Exigeance, on the watch to resent slight or trespass, however small or unintentional. Censoriousness is at hand to blame without thought of improving. Selfishness is ready to occupy the whole field of the heart, so that no corner of space is left for all those concerns of other people with which Benevolence is engaged. Slothfulness is there to simulate Goodwill with that easy Good-nature which takes matters pleasantly so long as it is not required to take trouble about anything. Tolerance is that form of Good-nature which is as easy with regard to other people's opinions as Good-nature is with regard to their actions. To tolerate, or bear with, the principles and opinions which rule the lives of others is the part of Indifference and not of Goodwill. Candour, fair-mindedness to other people's thoughts, is what Benevolence offers.

The Peace of Good-will.—Benevolence has so many functions that we can only notice a few of them; but it is well we should know that it means at least an active and general Goodwill. When we realise this, the angelic message—"Peace on earth and Goodwill towards men of Goodwill"—will carry some meaning for us.

Chapter IV Love's Lords In Waiting: Sympathy

Sympathy with One, a Key to All.—Sympathy is a Lord of the Bosom who is rather unfairly treated. He is made to adopt a sentimental character and go about the world wiping tears and soothing distresses; and this is supposed to be the whole of his work. But Sympathy is comprehension; and he reaps harvests of joy for himself, though occasionally he must sorrow. For to understand one human being so completely that you feel his feelings and think his thoughts is really like gaining possession of a new world; it is gaining the power of living in another's life. It is as if the heart got room to expand, and one began to understand the large life of the angels of God. Occasionally we have an almost perfect sympathy with one person, and we allow it to become exclusive; we know that one to the exclusion of all others; but that is turning to selfish uses a gift meant for the general good. Each trait we know in one person should be to us as a key wherewith to open the natures of others. If we find that it is possible to wound one person with a word, beat one person with a look, let that knowledge make us tender and delicate in our dealings with all people; for how do we know how much power we have to hurt? If we know one person who grows pale at a lofty thought, whose tears come at the telling of a heroic action, let us learn, from that, that these are the thoughts and actions which have power to move us all; therefore, we must give freely of our best, without the supercilious notion that So-and-so would not understand. If music, poetry, art, give us joy, let us not hesitate to present these joys to others; for, indeed, those others are all made in all points like as we are, though with a different experience. The orator whose Sympathy is awake appeals to the generosity, delicacy, courage, loyalty of a mixed mob of people; and he never appeals in vain. His Sympathy, his comprehension, has discerned all these riches of the heart in the unpromising crowd before him; and, like Ariel released from his tree prison, a beautiful human being leaps out of many a human prison at the touch of this key.

A Lever to Raise.—Sympathy is an eye to discern, a lever to raise, an arm to sustain. The service to the world that has been done by the great thinkers—the poets and the artists—and by the great doers—the heroes—is, that they have put out feelers, as it were, for our Sympathy. A picture or poem, or the story of a noble deed, 'finds' us, we say. We, too, think that thought or live in that action, and, immediately, we are elevated and sustained. This is the sympathy we owe to our fellows, near and far off. If we have anything good to give, let us give it, knowing with certainty that they will respond. If we fail to give this Sympathy, if we regard the people about us as thinking small, unworthy thoughts, doing mean, unworthy actions, and incapable of better things, we reap our reward. We are really, though we are not aware of it, giving Sympathy to all that is base in others, and thus strengthening and increasing their baseness: at the same time we are shutting ourselves into habits of hard and narrow thinking and living.

Virtue goes out of us.—This greater office of Sympathy, this power to see, to elevate and to sustain, must not be lost sight of when it is the sorrow, anxiety, or suffering of another which calls it forth. We must see the calamity as the sufferer sees it, feel it as he feels it, if in less degree; we must suffer, also, or we have nothing to give. It was said of our Lord that 'virtue went out of Him' when He healed; and it is only as virtue—that is, our manhood, our strength, our life—goes out of us, that we have power to help and heal.

A Spurious Sympathy.—There is a spurious sympathy which is very popular with those who give and those who take; indeed, it is a bid for popularity. The sympathiser sees, but does not see deep enough. He sees that the egotism of the sufferer may be comforted in much the same way as an unwise nurse will comfort a child who has knocked his head against the table. 'Naughty table!' says nurse, and whips the table. Just so does the would-be sympathiser reproach the cause of suffering and enfeeble the sufferer by weak pity, leading him to pity himself. Self-pity is perhaps the last misfortune that can fall upon any man; and it is a degradation of sympathy when it goes to make the sufferer aware of himself, and not to raise him out of himself. The hardness which attempts to brace him without sharing his suffering is hardly worse than this spurious sympathy; and it does less harm, because the false ring of it is more easily discerned.

Tact.—'Tact' is almost another form of the word sympathy; both words employ the sense of touch to figure our perception of one another. Tact perceives where a word will grate, where a gesture would irritate, where words of sympathy are obtrusive, where a smile and a kindly look are better than a spoken word. Tact is commonly the result of good breeding; but the truest tact is an expression of sympathy which perceives what is going on in another mind. Perhaps, to Tact belong the lesser things of Sympathy, the active interest of co-operation in the pursuits and hobbies of the people we live with, the passive interest of a ready ear. An attentive and deferential listener performs some of the highest offices of Sympathy; he raises and sustains the person to whom he listens, increases the self-respect of him who has done something, or seen something, or suffered something, which he wishes to tell. This is true service, because we all, 'even the youngest,' think too little of ourselves; and for that reason have not the courage of that which is possible to us.

Dæmons attending this Lord of Virtue.—We cannot detail all the offices of Sympathy, but must consider a few of the Dæmons attending this Lord of Virtue. Chief of these, and entirely fatal, is the self-occupation born of egotism. He whose eye is fixed upon himself, his rights and his needs, his desires and his requirements, his powers or his weaknesses, his successes or his failures, his worth or his unworthiness, has no more room for sympathy within him than a full goblet has for wine. The passive manifestation of egotism is Indifference; among its active forms are credulous and solicitous Vanity, Dislike, Antipathy.

Chapter V Love's Lords In Waiting: Kindness

"That best portion of a good man's life,
His little, nameless, unremembered acts
Of kindness and of love."—
—Wordsworth.

It is interesting that a great poet should place little forgotten acts of kindness first in order of merit in the acts of a good man's life. Kindness, also, is a born Lord of the Bosom: I have known a little person, not old enough to talk, draw forward a chair and pat it for the visitor to sit down; the untutored savage has impulses of kindness.

Kindness makes Life Pleasant for Others.—The law of Kindness is universal. One would think at first sight that Pity, Benevolence, Sympathy, should cover the whole field; and that, with these present, the office of Kindness is but a sinecure in the House of Heart. But there is a curious principle in human nature, best described perhaps as vis inertiæ, which makes even the benevolent, pitiful, and sympathetic person slow to do the little everyday things about which Kindness concerns himself. The office of Kindness is simply to make everyday life pleasant and comfortable to others, whether the others be our pets which we feed and attend to, our dog which we play with and take for a scamper, our horse which we not only feed and care for, but cheer and encourage with friendly hand and friendly word, or our family and neighbours, rich and poor, who offer a large field for our Kindness. The kind person is described by various epithets: he is called courteous or thoughtful, obliging or considerate, according as he shows his kindness by refraining or speaking, by his manner, his regard, his words, his acts.

The Kindness of Courtesy.—We English people are rather ready to think that it does not much matter how we behave, so long as our hearts are all right; and some of us miss our chance of doing, the Kindness of Courtesy, and adopt a hail-fellow-well-met manner, which is a little painful and repellent, and therefore a little unkind. We miss, too, the courtesies of gesture; it is good in a German or Danish town to see one errand-boy raise his hat to another, or school-boy to school-boy, or porter to laundress, without any sense of awkwardness; but in these matters we have got into a national bad habit. In this field, perhaps, the rich and the poor meet together, because there is not in either an unconscious struggle after social status which does not belong to them, and so both can afford to be simple, considerate, gracious, and courteous to all who come in their way.

Simplicity.—Simplicity is the special quality of Kindness; people can be kind only when all their thoughts are given to the person or creature they are kind to, and when there is no backward glance to see how the matter affects self. A great deal has been said and written about Kindness, about slippers and footstools, and gifts of flowers, and much besides. There is even a movement to make children kind by counting up how many kind things they do in the course of each day; but that spoils all; the essence of acts of Kindness is that they should be unremembered. Of course, we never mention a kindness we have done, whether to the person concerned or to other people; but chiefly let us beware that we do not say to ourselves, 'I have done this and that for So-and-so, and now see how he serves me!' or think that, if we receive a kindness, we can blot it out, so to say, by conferring a favour. Worse still is the notion that having been kind to another gives us a right to expect great things from that other, and to be ungracious and disagreeable if the claims we set up do not seem to be recognised. But these pitfalls are escaped when Kindness is simple, and we do not even know that we are being kind; it is not only our gifts to the poor that are covered by our Lord's precept, "Let not thy right hand know what thy left hand doeth."

Everyone wants to be kind—

"Man is dear to man! the poorest poor
Long for some moments in a weary life,
When they can know and feel that they have been
Themselves, the fathers and the dealers-out
Of some small blessings; have been kind to such
As needed kindness."
—Wordsworth.

Kindness in Construction.—But the greatest, sweetest, most generous kindnesses perhaps that of which we take least thought; I mean kindness in construction. There are always two ways of understanding other people's words, acts, and motives; and human nature is so contradictory that both ways may be equally right; the difference is in the construction we put upon other people's thoughts. If we think kindly of another's thoughts—think, for example, that an ungentle action or word may arise from a little clumsiness and not from lack of kindness of heart—we shall probably be right and be no more than fair to the person concerned. But, supposing we are wrong, our kind construction will have a double effect. It will, quicker than any reproof, convict our neighbour of his unkindness, and it will stir up in him the pleasant feelings for which we have already given him credit. Of all the causes of unhappiness, perhaps few bring about more distress in the world than the habit, which even good people allow themselves in, of putting an ungentle construction upon the ways and words of the people they live with. This habit has another bad effect, especially upon young people, who are greatly influenced by the opinion of their fellows. They think So-and-so will laugh at them for doing a certain obliging action, so they refrain from following the good impulses of a good heart. Kindness which is simple thinks none of these things, nor does it put evil constructions upon the thoughts that others may think in the given circumstances. "Be ye kind one to another" is not an easy precept, but—

"All worldly joys go less
To the one joy of doing kindnesses."
—Herbert.

Chapter VI Love's Lords In Waiting: Generosity

Generous Impulses common to all the World—At first sight it seems as if Generosity were not a Lord in every bosom, but ruled only the noblest hearts; but this is not the fact. When all England goes mad with joy because little Mafeking is relieved, when everybody forgets private cares, schemes, worries, annoyances, even hunger and cold and bodily need, being warmed and fed, as it were, by a public joy, or softened and made tender by a public sorrow, it is because all are stirred by what is called a generous impulse, an impulse which causes them, if only for a moment, to live outside of their own lives. I once heard a generous lecture, upon a great poet, given to a crowded audience of some thousands of people of very varying culture and condition. It was interesting to listen to the remarks that were passing as we made our way out of the crowd. One man said, with a choke in his voice, "Why, why, that man could do anything with us, lead us on any crusade he liked!" and he was right. This is the history of the generous movements that have stirred the world, the Crusades, the Anti-Slavery War in America; a thought has been dropped which has stirred some Generous impulse common to all the world. The nature of Generosity is to bring forth, to give, always at the cost of personal suffering or deprivation, little or great. There is no generosity in giving what we shall never miss and do not want; this is mere good-nature, and is not even kindness, unless it springs out of a real thought about another person's needs.

Large Trustfulness.—Generosity at its highest level, and with a certain added tincture, becomes Enthusiasm, but of that we shall speak later. We may understand the nature of this ruler of men better if we consider that what Magnanimity is to the things of the mind, Generosity is to the things of the heart. Large and warm thoughts of life and of our relations with one another find place in the generous man. He is incapable of wholesale and bitter condemnation of classes or countries, parties or creeds. He is impatient of the cheap wit whose jokes are at the expense of the character for probity of some whole class of people, plumbers or plasterers or candlestick makers. He is equally impatient of the worldly wisdom which goes through life expecting to be defrauded here and cheated there; and he finds that, on the whole, it is he who possesses the wisdom of this world; for, by dint of fair and generous dealing, he may pass through a long life with hardly a record to show of the iniquity and cheating ways of his fellow-creatures. But then, if he has only sixpence to spend, he spends it in a liberal and trustful way. It is a certain large trustfulness in his dealings, rather than the largeness of his gifts, or the freedom of his outlay, that marks the generous man.

Generosity is Costly, but also Remunerative.—In like manner, in his commerce with his friends and neighbours, he harbours no grudges; that is, he is not on the watch that others should give him what he thinks his due of observance, consideration, service, or what not. He allows others to be the arbiters of their own conduct in all such matters; and those others respond, for the most part, to the trust reposed in them. This is not the easy attitude of mind which permits everything, because a want of self-respect creates a thirst for popularity. The generous man will have friends of widely different types, because he is able to give large entertainment to men of many minds, and to meet them upon many points. His interests are wide, his interpretations are liberal; and wherever his interest goes, it goes with a latent glow, ready to break forth in the heat of action upon occasion.

Generosity is costly, because it is always disbursing, be it the contents of the heart or of the purse; but it is also remunerative, for it has been said, "Give, and it shall be given unto you; good measure, pressed down, shaken together, and running over, shall men give into your bosom." Generosity is also a saving grace; for the generous man escapes a thousand small perplexities, worries, and annoys; he walks serene in a large room. There are so many great things to care about that he has no mind and no time for the small frettings of life; his concerns are indeed great, for what concerns man concerns him. But because his is a concern of the heart, warm and glowing, it is duly distributed. There are the equatorial and the polar regions of his care, neither of them quite unwarmed. He does not affect to love other countries as he loves his own, or his neighbour's children as his own family.

Fallacious Notions that restrain Generosity.—I have spoken of the generous man; but, indeed, this Lord of the Bosom is present in all of us, ready with the offer of large and warm living. But certain fallacious notions and small propensities are apt to keep him shut in narrow limits, unless some happy word or occasion let him loose. When this happens to the whole community, we become alarmed and fear that we are all going mad; but really it is that we have suddenly burst into large living without the restraints proper to an accustomed way of life.

'Let every man mind his own business' is one of the fallacies that come to a person with a sense of obligation, and of limitation to his own business only. The man not only shuts out the generous cares of a wider life, but he is consumed by the cares of his condition in all their petty details. Yet we must each mind our own business, or we are unworthy members of society, and throw so much of the world's work as is our own proper share upon the shoulders of other people. The secret is, to mind our business strenuously within its proper hours, whether these hours are ruled for us, or we rule them for ourselves. But the hours of work over, let us think it trespass so much as to turn our thoughts in that direction, and let us throw all our interest into outer and wider channels. That which seems to us our business in life, even that incessant business of being the mother of a family, will be far better done if we rule ourselves in this matter, because we shall be better, broader persons; and the more there is of a person, the more work will be done.

'Every man for himself, and Heaven for us all,' is another fallacy that shuts up lives in narrow rooms.

Man is not for himself, and to get out of ourselves and into the wide current of human life, of all sorts and conditions, is our wisdom and should be our care.

Another miserable and unspoken fallacy is 'Every person that I have dealings with is worse than myself.' This is startling, put into words; but why else should we suppose that this person means to slight us and the other to offend us, when we have no such intentions with regard to them; that we shall be cheated here and defrauded there, when we ourselves would not willingly cheat and defraud? It is generous to trust, to trust freely, to trust our tradespeople and our servants, our friends and neighbours, those in authority over us and those subordinate to us.

Be noble! and the nobleness that lies
In other men, sleeping, but never dead—
Will rise in majesty to meet thine own!"
—Lowell.

Chapter VII Love's Lords In Waiting: Gratitude

The Gladness of a Grateful Heart.—No other Lord of the Heart should do more to guide us into joyous and happy living than Gratitude. How good and glad it is to be grateful! The joy is not merely that we have received a favour or a little kindness which speaks of goodwill and love, but that a beautiful thing has come out of some other person's beautiful heart for us; and joy in that other's beauty of character gives more delight than any gain or pleasure which can come to us from favours. We lose this joy often enough because we are too self-absorbed to be aware of kindness, or are too self-complacent to think any kindness more than our desert. Young people are apt to take the abounding, overflowing kindnesses of their parents as matters of course; and so they come to miss the double joy they might have in a touch, a word, a look, a little arrangement for their pleasure, a thousand things over and above, so to speak, the love that is due from parent to child. A kindness is like a flower that has bloomed upon you unawares, and to be on the watch for such flowers adds very much to our joy in other people, as well as to the happy sense of being loved and cared for. You go into a shop, and the shopkeeper who knows you (I am not speaking of big stores) adds a pleasant something to your purchase which sends you cheerily on your way—some little kindness of look or word, some inquiry that shows his interest in you and yours, perhaps no more than a genial smile, but you have got into pleasant human relations with him because he has given you a kindness. There are two courses open to the receiver of this small kindness. One is to feel himself such an important person that it is to the interest of shopkeepers and the like to show him attention. The other is to go away with the springing gladness of a grateful heart, knowing that he takes with him more than he has bought.

A Grateful Heart makes a Full Return.—Life would be dull and bare of flowers if we were not continually getting more than we can pay for either by money or our own good offices; but a grateful heart makes a full return, because it rejoices not only in the gift but in the giver. Formal thanks are proper enough on occasions, but there are other ways of expressing gratitude, which, indeed, is like love and a fire, and cannot be hid. A glance, a smile, a word of appreciation and recognition straight from the heart, will fill the person who has done us a kindness with pleasure. But let us avoid all expressions of thanks which are not simple and sincere—simple in that we are really thinking of the kindness of the other person and not of ourselves; and sincere, in that we do not say a word more than we feel, or make believe to value a gift for its own sake when it is really not of value to us.

The Reproach of Ingratitude.—There is an ancient story of a city which decided that ingratitude was the blackest of crimes. The people of the city were practical, and set up a bell in an open but desolate spot to be rung by any who should experience ingratitude. Time passed by and the bell was forgotten, perhaps because people were on the watch against this offence. But one day the bell rang out, and the whole city rushed to see who had a complaint to make of an ungrateful fellow-citizen. An ass had caught the rope with his foot, and as he moved about in search of the miserable herbage that grew on the spot, the bell pealed out. At first people laughed; but when they looked at the poor ass and found him a wretched object, almost too feeble to stand, they looked at one another and said, "Whose ass is this?" Inquiry produced the owner, who was forced to confess that his ass, having served him well for many years, became at last too old for his work, so he turned the poor creature out to live as it could. The people decided that the ass had acted according to law in ringing the bell; and the mean man paid the penalty, which included the good keeping of the ass, with what grace he could. To make use of other people, to serve ourselves of them, is the sin of ingratitude. The grateful man has a good memory and a quick eye to see where those who have served need service in their turn. Especially does he cherish the memory of those who have served him in childhood and in youth, and he watches for opportunities to serve them.

Gratitude spreads his feast of joy and thanksgiving for gifts that come to him without any special thought of him on the part of the giver, who indeed may himself have gone from the world hundreds of years ago. Thus he says his grace for a delightful or helpful book, for a great picture, for a glorious day, for the face of a little child, for happy work, for pleasant places. According to the saying of Jeremy Taylor, he is quick to "taste the deliciousness of his employment." He is thankful for all the good that comes to him. The poor soul who believes that life yields him nothing beyond his deserts, that it would be, in fact, impossible to give him more than he pays for, whether in coin or merit, is to be pitied for all the joy he loses, as well as blamed for the pain and irritation his progress through life must cause. "Yea, a joyful and a pleasant thing it is to be thankful!"

Chapter VIII Love's Lords In Waiting: Courage

We all have Courage.—The word courage comes to us from the time when Norman French was the language of the court and when chivalry was the law of noble living. The Normans perceived that Courage was of the heart, as the word shows; Courage was the whole of character to a man; he who had not Courage, had no quality of manliness. We talk about it less in these days, but Courage is still a great Lord in the House of Heart, having his dwelling by right in every Mansoul, and, indeed, in even timid beasts.

The Courage of Attack.—The sheep has the Courage of Attack for the sake of her lamb; the bird will sit on her eggs in the face of that monster, man. A blue-tit once thought proper to nest in a letterbox; of course people went to see the sight, and the courage with which the little creature hissed at the gigantic intruders was very curious and admirable. The toddling child has courage to protect his pets. Many a tender mother has had the courage of an awful death to save her baby. If we would but believe it, we have all courage to face any calamity, any enemy, any death. But Courage, like the other Lords of our Life, is attended by his Dæmons, Fear, Cowardice, Pusillanimity, Nervousness.

The Courage of Endurance.—Fear, with his kin, Panic and Anxiety, is on the watch for those moments when Courage sleeps, lulled by security. When we consider the splendid valour that men of all sorts show in battle, we begin to see how universal Courage is; in our country it is those who choose that enlist in the army; but the Courage shown by men drawn by conscription is not less than that of our own army. Also, how possible it is for every man to be gripped by shameful Fear, and to act upon the panic born of Fear, is shown by the fact that a whole company, heretofore held as brave as the rest, has been known more than once to turn tail and fly before the enemy.

The Courage of Serenity.—Few of us are likely to be tried in a field of battle; but the battle-field has an advantage over the thousand battles we each have to fight in our lives, because the sympathy of numbers carries men forward. The Courage required to lose a leg at home through a fall or an injury on the cricket field is, perhaps, greater than that displayed by the soldier on the field; and the form of Courage which meets pain and misfortune with calm endurance is needed by us all. No one escapes the call for Fortitude, if it be only in the dentist's chair. It is well to be sure of ourselves, to know for certain that we have Courage for everything that may come, not because we are more plucky than others, but because all persons are born with this Lord and Captain of the Heart. Assured of our Courage, we must not let this courage sleep and allow ourselves to be betrayed into panic by a carriage accident or a wasp or a rat. It is unseemly, unbecoming, for any of us, even the youngest, to lose our presence of mind when we are hurt or in danger. We not only lose the chance of being of use to others, but we make ourselves a burden and a spectacle, Anxious fuss in the small emergencies of life, such as travelling, household mischances, pressure of work, is a form of panic fear, the fear that all may not go well, or that something may be forgotten and left undone. Let us possess ourselves and say: 'What does it matter? All undue concern about things and arrangements is unworthy of us.' It is only persons that matter; and the best thing we can do is to see that one person keeps a serene mind in unusual or fretting circumstances; then we shall be sure that one person is ready to be of use.

The Courage of our Affairs.—The form of fear that is inclined to fret and worry and become agitated under any slight stress of circumstances, darkens into anxiety in the face of some success we are striving after, some calamity that we fear. Anxiety obtains more sympathy than other forms of fear, because the person who is anxious suffers much, and the cause for anxiety is often sadly real. But we do ourselves injustice by being anxious. We have been sent into life fortified, some more so, some less, with a Courage which should enable us to take the present without any fearful looking forward. And, indeed, we do so, the feeblest of us, when we are kept fully employed by immediate things. That is how mothers and wives can go through months of the nursing of their nearest and dearest with cheerful countenance. They tell you they dare not look forward, and that they live from hour to hour, and so they are able to bring happiness and even gaiety into the sick-room, though a sorrowful end is before them. If this noble Courage is possible in the face of coming grief, it is also possible, if we would believe it, in the face of lesser matters—coming examinations, coming losses, coming distresses of every kind, even that worst distress, when those dear to us fail us and fall away from godly living. "Let not your heart be anxious" (R.V.) is the command of Christ. The command presupposes the power of obedience, and it is for this that heavy things are spoken of the 'fearful and the unbelieving.'

The Courage of our Opinions.—Besides the Courage of Attack, the Courage of Endurance, the Courage of Serenity, and the Courage of our Affairs, there are lesser forms of Courage which as truly belong to the courageous heart. There is the Courage of our opinions. By opinions I do not mean the loosely taken up catchwords of the moment, those things which 'everybody says,' and with which it is rather agreeable than otherwise to startle our less advanced friends; but those few opinions founded upon knowledge and principle which we really possess.

It is worth while to examine ourselves as to what our opinions are as to the questions discussed in conversation or otherwise. We may find that we have no distinct opinion. If so, let us not take up with the first that offers, but think, inquire, read, consider both sides, and then be ready with a gentle, clear, well-grounded expression of opinion, when someone remarks, for example—'I think missionaries are a mistake!' 'The religions people have are those best suited to their natures'; or, 'It is no use thinking about the multitude, it is the few who have intellect or art who are worth caring for'; and so on. We often allow other people's opinions to pass without protest, because we believe that they have been carefully thought out; but it is surprising how a word of simple conviction will arrest people who express the most outrageous opinions. At any rate this form of Courage is due from us.

The Courage of Frankness.—The Courage of Frankness is very charming. A certain degree of reticence is due to ourselves and to others: the person who pours out all his affairs indiscriminately is a bore; but, on the other hand, he who shows undue caution, discretion, distrust, is of a fearful and unbelieving spirit, and fails in the characters of the noble heart. Our motive is our best guide to the right mean in this matter. If we reserve our matters because we are unwilling to bore our friends with trivial things, it is well; but if we reserve them because we distrust the sympathy or the fairness, the kindness or the comprehension of the people we live amongst, we make a failure in Courage.

The Courage of Reproof—Many other forms of Courage will occur to each of us; we can only mention one or two more. The Courage of Reproof is to be exercised with delicacy and gentleness, but there can be no faithful friendship between equals in age without this Courage; the just and gentle reproofs given by the young to the young are perhaps more convincing and converting than the more natural and usual reproofs of elders.

The Courage of Confession.—To name one more form of Courage, the Courage of open, frank Confession of that which we have done amiss or left undone, in the small matters of daily life, to the person concerned, is very strengthening; but I am not sure that the habit of confessing feelings and thoughts always arises from Courage. Acts and omissions are safer ground.

The Courage of our Capacity.—Then there is what we may call the Courage of our Capacity—the courage which assures us that we can do the particular work which comes in our way, and will not lend an ear to the craven fear which reminds us of failures in the past and unfitness in the present. It is intellectual

Courage, too, which enables us to grapple with tasks of the mind with a sense of adequacy. Intellectual panic is responsible for many failures; for our failure to understand an argument, to follow an experiment, and very largely for our insular failure to speak and comprehend the vocables of foreign tongues. Intellectual panic is responsible, too, for the catchwords we pass as our opinions. We fear it is not in us to form an opinion worth the holding and worth the giving forth.

The Courage of Opportunity.—The Courage of Opportunity, of which Shakespeare says,

"There is a tide in the affairs of men,
Which, taken at the flood, leads on to fortune,"

is also connected with the Courage of Capacity, and is to be distinguished from the gambling spirit of Foolhardiness, which is ready to seek and try all hazards. One note of difference is perhaps that Courage is ready for that which comes, while Foolhardiness goes a-seeking. Courage waits for guidance,—

Holding as Creed,
That Circumstance, a sacred oracle,
Speaks with the voice of God to faithful souls.
(from Charlotte Mason's poem, Moses: A Study)

Chapter IX Love's Lords In Waiting: Loyalty

Loyalty of Youth.—Loyalty is the hall-mark of character; but that is a misguiding simile, for it is good to know that Loyalty is not a mark stamped upon us, but a Lord of the Bosom born within us. At different periods of history, or at different periods of life, people give the rule of their lives to one or another of these Powers of Heart. The age of Chivalry was the age of Loyalty; and youth ought to be especially the age of Chivalry and of Loyalty in each life. But perhaps this is not a loyal age. Our tendency is to believe that to think for ourselves and to serve ourselves in the way of advancement or pleasure is our chief business in life. We think that the world was made for us, and not we for the world, and that we are called upon to rule and not to serve. But such thoughts come to us only in our worst moods. Loyalty, whose note is service, asserts itself. We know that we are not our own, and that according to the Loyalty within us do we fulfil ourselves.

Our Loyalties prepared for us.—We are ready enough to give whimsical Loyalty to some poet or actor, soldier or priest, at whose feet we would gladly lay our service; but in this, as in the rest of our lives, we are not free to choose. Our Loyalties are all prepared for us, or come to us with our duties, and our choice is between being loyal and disloyal. In this regard, it is a happy thing for the nation which has a sovereign, a visible object-lesson in Loyalty, to be loyally loved and served for the sake of his office,

Loyalty to our King.—One of the best lessons history has to teach us is in the examples it holds of splendid loyalty and service, including unbounded honour and reverence to the person of the sovereign, and devotion of life and substance, children and followers, to his cause. Sir Henry Lee, in Woodstock, is an exquisite example of this fine Loyalty. As we read, we grudge that it should be spent on so little worthy a monarch; but in the end, let us remember, the knight gained more than the king, by this Loyalty, for it is better to "be" than to "receive." Our late beloved Queen commanded all our Loyalty, because she herself knew and lived for the Loyalty and service she owed to her people; and in that way she raised us to a higher level of living.

Loyalty due to our Own.—After our King, our country claims our Loyalty. Let us not make a mistake. Benevolence is due to the whole world, Loyalty is due to our own; and however greatly we may value or become attached to alien kings or alien countries, the debt of Loyalty is due, not to them, but to our own. Invidious comparisons, depreciating the land of our birth in favour of some land of our choice, whose laws and rulers, ways and weather, we may prefer, is of the nature of disloyalty.

Public Opinion responsible for Anarchy.—We older people are saddened, shocked, and greatly humbled by the fall of one ruler after another at the hands of the persons who call themselves anarchists. We are humbled and ashamed because we know that this manner of crime, which has no exact parallel in the history of the past, arises, in truth, from a failure in the spirit of Loyalty in what is called public opinion.

Therefore, the repeated crimes which shock us are brought home to us all, for we all help to form public opinion. There are always in every country men and women in whom the general wrong thinking about our duties to one another come, as it were, to a head and break out in crime; but it is from public opinion that these people get their original notions. We are told to speak no evil of the ruler of our people, and, if we allow ourselves to speak evil, others will take up our evil speech and turn it into criminal act. If we fret against rule others will rise against rulers, and kings everywhere will live in terror of the assault of the regicide. The way we are bound to one another and affect one another all over the world is a very solemn thought; but that we can help the whole world by keeping hold of our own Loyalty should be a cause of joy.

Loyalty to Country.—I am not sure but that people lose in moral fibre when they become voluntary exiles from their own country. Every tie that we are born to is necessary to our completion. Loyalty to country, Patriotism, is a noble passion. Revolutions come about when the character of a sovereign is such that right-thinking people can no longer be loyal to king and country; when unjust laws, undue taxes, the oppression of the poor, make men's hearts sore for their fatherland. Loyalty to country demands honour, service, and personal devotion.

The honour due to our country requires some intelligent knowledge of her history, laws, and institutions; of her great men and her people; of her weaknesses and her strength; and is not to be confounded with the ignorant and impertinent attitude of the Englishman or the Chinese who believes that to be born an Englishman or a Chinese puts him on a higher level than the people of all other countries; that his own country and his own government are right in all circumstances, and other countries and other governments always wrong. But, on the other hand, still more to be guarded against, is the caitiff spirit of him who holds his own country and his own government always in the wrong and always the worse, and exalts other nations unduly for the sake of depreciating his own.

The Service of Loyalty.—Our service to our country in these days may not mean more than that we should take a living interest in the questions that occupy the government and the social problems that occupy thinkers; and that, if we are not called upon to serve the country in general, in Parliament, for example, we should give time, labour, and means to advance whatever local administration we are connected with. Perhaps this kind of Loyalty has never been more nobly displayed than it is at the present time. Nor do we fail when our country claims our personal devotion. Recent events seem to show that every Briton, of the lesser and the greater Britain, is ready for the honour of laying down his life for his country.

Loyalty to a Chief—Perhaps the Loyalty in which we fall short, as compared with the Middle Ages, is that Loyalty which every man and woman owes to a chief. Again, Scott gives us the perfect expression in Torquil of the Oak—the Highland foster-father, who sacrificed himself and his nine stalwart sons to shield the honour of the young chief whom he knew to be a confessed coward. [The Fair Maid of Perth, Sir Walter Scott] The whole incident, told, as it is, with reserve and sympathy, offers one of the strongest situations in literature. But Loyalty in this kind lives amongst us still. Few subalterns in either service would allow themselves to discuss without reserve the action or character of their chief; and as for the men, they still accept it that—"Theirs not to make reply, theirs not to reason why; theirs but to do and die"; and, given that they do die because "someone has blundered," one supreme moment of unquestioning Loyalty to king, country, and commander is, probably, worth fifty years at the dead level of daily living; that is, supposing that the purpose of this life is our education for a fuller. It is told of certain elegant young diplomats, who serve their several chiefs as private secretaries, that one, more superb than the rest, grumbled because his chief summoned him by ringing a bell; but another, who had learned the secret of 'dignified obedience and proud submission,' asserted that, if his chief asked him to clean his shoes, he would do it of course. Instances of splendid Loyalty to the heads of family, party, cause, house, school, or what not, abound on every hand.

Loyalty to Personal Ties.—Loyalty to personal ties, relationships, friendships, dependents, is a due recognised by most people. We all know that these ties, whether they come by nature, as relationships, or by choice, as friendships and the lesser friendly relations,—servants, for example—must be loyally entertained. We know that the character and conduct of our friend is sacred from adverse criticism even in our private thoughts; that what we think and have to say of censure must be said to him and him only; that our time, our society, our sympathy and our service are at his disposal, so far as we can determine. Not only so, but we know that he should have the best of us, our deepest thoughts, our highest aspirations, so far as we are able to give these forth. This last is freely acknowledged in friendships of election; but in the natural friendships of relationship, which surround most of us, we are sometimes chary of our best, and give only our commonplace, surface thoughts; and to our dependents, those on a lower educational level than ourselves, we are apt to talk down, as we suppose, to that level. We are wrong here; our best is due in varying degrees to maintain all those relationships, natural, elected, or casual, which make up the sweetness and interest of our lives.

A Constant Mind.—Steadfastness is, of course, of the essence of all Loyalties. A man of sixty, who said he had always had his boots from the same bootmaker since he first wore boots, gives us a hint of the sort of Loyalty we owe all round. We miss a great deal of the grace of life by running hither and thither to serve ourselves of the best, so we think, in friends, acquaintances, religions, tradesmen, servants, preachers, prophets. Perhaps there is always more of the best to be had in sticking to that we have got than in looking out continually for a new shop for every sort of ware. The strength, grace, and dignity of a constant mind is the ingathering of Loyalty.

It is objected that some relations are impossible and insupportable; that a servant is lazy, a tradesman dishonest, a friend unworthy, a relative aggravating.

Some relations are not of our seeking and are for life; and that which must be continued, should be continued with Loyalty; but it is best, perhaps, to give up a chief or a dependent, for example, to whom we cannot any longer be loyal. But let the breach be with simplicity and dignity. Let us not indulge in previous gossiping and grumbling; and we should recognise that Loyalty forbids small personal resentment of offences to our amour propre. Many lives are shipwrecked upon this rock. In wronging our friends by a failure in Loyalty, we injure ourselves far more.

Thoroughness.—The same principles of Loyalty apply to Loyalty to our work and to any cause we have taken up. Thoroughness and unstinted effort belong to this manner of Loyalty; and, therefore, we have at times to figure as unamiable persons because we are unable to throw ourselves into every new cause that is brought before us. We can but do what we are able for; and Loyalty to that which we are doing will often forbid efforts in new directions.

Loyalty to our Principles.—A personal loyalty of a high order is that which we owe to our principles. At first, it is those principles upon which we are brought up to which our faithfulness is due; but, by and by, as character develops, convictions grow upon us which come to be bound up with our being. These, not catchwords caught up here and there from the newspapers or from common talk, are our principles—possessions that we have worked out with labour of thought and, perhaps, pain of feeling. He is true to himself who is true to these; and no other.

Loyalty is to be expected of him who is not true to himself. Perhaps highest amongst these principles is our religion—not our faith in God; that is another matter—but that form of religion which to us is the expression of such faith. A safe rule is, that Loyalty forbids our dallying with other forms and other ideas, lest we should cease to hold religious convictions of any sort, and become open to change and eager for the excitement of novelty.

The habit of unworthy and petty criticism of the clergy or the services to which we are accustomed is apt to end in this unstable habit; Loyalty forbids this manner of petty gossip, as it also forbids the habit of running hither and thither in search of novelties.

Tempers alien to Loyalty.—The Dæmons which labour for the destruction of Loyalty are, perhaps, Self-interest, Self-conceit, and Self-importance. Self-interest would lead us to better ourselves at the expense of any bond. Self-conceit keeps us in a ferment of small resentments which puts allegiance out of court; and Self-importance is unable to give the first place to another in things small or great, in affairs of country, parish, or home. These enemies be about us, but Loyalty is within us, strong and steadfast, and asking only to be recognised that he may put the alien to flight.

Chapter X Love's Lords In Waiting: Humility

Pride of Life.—The Apostle points out three causes of offence in men—the lust of the flesh, that is, the desire to satisfy the cravings of what we call 'human nature'; the lust of the eye, which makes the pursuit of the delight of beauty, not a part, but the whole of life; and, the pride of life. Of the three, perhaps, the last is the most deadly, because it is the most deceitful. People born in, and brought up upon, principles of self-control and self-restraint are on the watch against the lusts of the flesh. The lust of the eye does not make too fascinating an appeal to all of us; but who can be aware of the approaches of the pride of life? Still, Pride, mighty as he is, and manifold as are his forms, is but the Dæmon, the more or less subject Dæmon, of a mightier power than himself.

Humility is Born in us all.—Humility is born in us all, a Lord of the Bosom, gracious and beautiful, strong to subdue. That is why our Lord told the Jews that except they should humble themselves and become as a little child they could not enter into the Kingdom of Heaven, the state where humble souls have their dwelling. We think of little children as being innocent and simple rather than humble; and it is only by examining this quality of children that we shall find out what Humility is in the divine thought. We have but two types of Humility to guide us—Christ, for 'He humbled Himself,' and little children, for He pronounced them humble. An old writer who has pondered on this matter says that, as there is only one Sanctification and one Redemption, so also there is only one Humility.

Humility travestied.—But no grace of heart is so travestied in our thoughts as this of Humility. We call cowardice Humility. We say—'Oh, I can't bear pain, I am not as strong as you are'; 'I can't undertake this and that, I have not the ability that others have'; 'I am not one of your clever fellows, there is no use in my going in for reading'; 'Oh, I'm not good enough, I could not teach a class in the Sunday School,' or, 'care for the things of the spiritual life.' Again, what we call Humility is often a form of Hypocrisy. 'Oh! I wish I were as capable as you,' we say, 'or as good,' or 'as clever,' priding ourselves secretly on the very unfitness which seems to put us somehow, we hardly know how, out of the common run of people. The person who is loud in his protestations of Humility is commonly hugging himself upon compensations we do not know of, and which, to his own thinking, rank him before us after all.

This sort of thing has brought Humility into disrepute. People take these self-deceivers at their word, and believe that they are humble; so, while they acknowledge Humility to be a Christian grace, it is a grace little esteemed and rarely coveted. This error of conception opens the gate for pride who comes riding full tilt to take possession. We prefer to be proud, openly proud of some advantage in our circumstances or our parentage, proud of our prejudices, proud of an angry or resentful temper, proud of our easy-going ways, proud of idleness, carelessness, recklessness; nay, the very murderer is a proud man, proud of the skill with which he can elude suspicion or destroy his victim. "Thank God, I have always kept myself to myself," said a small London housekeeper who did not "hold with neighbouring." There is hardly a failing, a fault or a crime which men have not felt to be a distinction, a thing to be proud of. We can do few things simply, that is, without being aware that it is we who are doing them, and taking importance to ourselves for the fact.

Humility one with Simplicity.—Many who are sound of mind in other respects arrive at incipient megalomania, through a continual magnification of self. Their affairs, their dogs, their pictures, their opinions, their calling, their good works, their teaching, their religious convictions, fill the whole field of vision; and that, because they are theirs rather than for the sake of the things themselves. This pride of life is so insidious and importunate, the necessity of exalting self presses upon us so unceasingly, so spoils all our relations of friendship and neighbourliness by resentful tempers and exigeant demands, that we are fain to cry, "Oh, wretched man that I am, who shall deliver me?" when, for a moment, we face facts. But we need not despair, even about our hateful Pride. He is but an encroacher, an usurper; the Lord of the Heart whom he displaces is Humility; and a true conception of this true Lord, who is within us, is as the shepherd's stone against the giant. For it is not Humility to think ill of ourselves; that is faint-hearted when it is not false. Humility is perhaps one with Simplicity, and does not allow us to think of ourselves at all, ill or well. That is why a child is humble. The thought of self does not come to him at all; when it does, he falls from his child estate and becomes what we call self-conscious. In that wonderful first lesson of the Garden of Eden, the Fall consisted in our first parents becoming aware of themselves; and that is how we all fall—when we become aware.

It is good to be humble. Humble people are gay and good. They do not go about with a black dog on their shoulder or a thunder-cloud on their brow. We are all born humble. Humility sits within us all, waiting for pride to be silent that he may speak and be heard. What must we do to get rid of pride and give place to Humility?

The Way of Humility.—In the first place, we must not try to be humble. That is all make-believe, and a bad sort of pride. We do not wish to become like Uriah Heep, and that is what comes of trying to be humble. The thing is, not to think of ourselves at all, for if we only think how bad we are, we are playing at Uriah Heep.

There are many ways of getting away from the thought of ourselves; the love and knowledge of birds and flowers, of clouds and stones, of all that nature has to show us; pictures, books, people, anything outside of us, will help us to escape from the tyrant who attacks our hearts. One rather good plan is, when we are talking or writing to our friends, not to talk or write about 'thou and I.' There are so many interesting things in the world to discuss that it is a waste of time to talk about ourselves. All the same, it is well to be up to the ways of those tiresome selves, and that is why you are invited to read these chapters. It is very well, too, to know that Humility, who takes no thought of himself, is really at home in each of us:—

"If that in sight of God is great
Which counts itself for small,
We by that law humility
The chiefest grace must call;
Which being such, not knows itself
To be a grace at all."
—Trench.

Chapter XI Love's Lords In Waiting: Gladness

"It is a seemly fashion to be glad."
"The merry heart goes all the day."

Gladness enough in the World for all.—Yorkshire people say their bread is 'sad' when it is heavy, does not rise. It is just so with ourselves. We are like a 'sad' loaf when we are heavy—do not rise to the sunshine, to the voices of our friends, to interesting sights, to kindness, love, or any good thing. When we do rise to these things, when our hearts smile because a ray of sunshine creeps in through the window, because a bird sings, because a splash of sunlight falls on the trunk of a dark tree, because we have seen a little child's face—why, then we are glad. Carlyle, whom we do not think of as a very happy man, used to say that no one need be unhappy who could see a spring day or the face of a little child. Indeed, there is Gladness enough in the world for us all; or, to speak more exactly, there is a fountain of Gladness in everybody's heart only waiting to be unstopped. Grown-up people sometimes say that they envy little children when they hear the Gladness bubbling out of their hearts in laughter, just as it bubbles out of the birds in song; but there is no room for regret; it is simply a case of a choked spring: remove the rubbish, and Gladness will flow out of the weary heart as freely as out of the child's.

Gladness springs in Sorrow and Pain.—But, you will say, how can people be glad when they have to bear sorrow, anxiety, want and pain? It is not these things that stop up our Gladness. The sorrowful and anxious wife of a dying husband, the mother of a dying child, will often make the sick-room merry with quips and cranks, a place of hearty Gladness. It is not that the mother or wife tries to seem glad for the sake of the sufferer; there is no pretending about Gladness. No one can be taken in by smiles that are put on. The fact is that love teaches the nurse to unstop the fount of Gladness in her own heart for the sake of the sufferer dear to her, and out come lots of merry words and little jokes, smiles and gaiety, things better than any medicine for the sick. In pain, too, it is not impossible to be glad. Have we not all been touched by merry sayings that have come from suffering lips? I doubt if Margaret Roper could help a smile through her tears at the merry quips her father, Sir Thomas More, made on his way to the scaffold. We commonly make a mistake about Gladness. We think of it as a sort of ice-cream or chocolate—very good when it comes, but not to be expected every day. But, "Rejoice evermore," says the Apostle; that is, "Be glad all the time." We laugh now and then, we smile now and then, but the fountain of Gladness within us should rise always; and so it will if it be not hindered.

Gladness is Catching.—Before we consider the Dæmons of Gladness, let us make ourselves sure of one thing. We cannot be glad by ourselves, and we cannot be sad, that is, heavy, by ourselves. Our gladness rejoices the people we come across, as our heaviness depresses them.

A London mother once wrote to me of how she took her little golden-haired daughter of two out for her first walk, and the little girl smiled at the policeman, and he was glad, and kissed her hand to some French laundresses working in a cellar, and they were glad, and smiled at the crossing-sweeper, and generally went on her way like a little queen dispensing smiles and gladness. A still prettier story was told by a Bible-woman in a big town who went out of doors depressed by the sordid cares and offences of her neighbours; and a small child sitting in a gutter looked up at her and smiled, and in the gladness of that little child she went gaily for the rest of the day. There is nothing so catching as Gladness, and it is good for each of us to know that we carry joy for the needs of our neighbours. But this is treasure that we give without knowing it or being any the poorer for what we have given away.

Gladness is Perennial.—Now, if we have made it clear to ourselves that there is in each of us a fountain of Gladness, not an intermittent but a perennial spring, enough and to spare for every moment of every year of the longest life, not to be checked by sorrow, pain, or poverty, but often flowing with the greater force and brightness because of these obstructions; if we are quite sure that this golden Gladness is not our own private property, but is meant to enrich the people we pass in the street, or live with in the house, or work with or play with, we shall be interested to discover why it is that people go about with a black dog on their shoulder, the cloud of gloom on their brow; why there are people heavy in movement, pale of countenance, dull and irresponsive. You will wish to find out why it is that children may go to a delightful party, picnic, haymaking, or what not, and carry a sullen countenance through all the fun and frolic; why young people may be taken to visit here or travel there, and the most delightful scenes might be marked with a heavy black spot in the map of their memories, because they found no gladness in them; why middle-aged people sometimes go about with sad and unsmiling countenances; why the aged sometimes find their lot all crosses and no joys.

This question of gladness or sadness has little to do with our circumstances. It is true that we should do well to heed the advice of Marcus Aurelius.—"Do not let your head run upon that which is none of your own, but pick out some of the best of your circumstances, and consider how eagerly you would wish for them were they not in your possession."

We are Sad when we are Sorry for Ourselves.—Let us get the good out of our circumstances by all means, but as a matter of fact it is not our circumstances but ourselves that choke the spring. We are sad and not glad because we are sorry for ourselves. Somebody has trodden on our toe, somebody has said the wrong word, has somehow offended our sense of self-importance, and behold! the Dæmon of self-pity digs diligently at his rubbish-heap, and casts in all manner of poor and paltry things to check the flow of our spring of Gladness. Some people are sorry for themselves by moments, some for days together, and some carry all their life long a grudge against their circumstances, or burn with resentment against their friends.

Gladness a Duty.—We need only look this matter in the face to see how sad and wrong a thing it is not to be glad, and to say to ourselves, 'I can, because I ought!' Help comes to those who endeavour and who ask. We may have to pull ourselves up many times a day, but every time we give chase to the black dog, the easier we shall find it to be gay and good. The outward and visible sign of gladness is cheerfulness, for how can a dour face and sour speech keep company with bubbling gladness within? The inward and spiritual grace is contentment, for how can the person who is glad at heart put himself out and be dissatisfied about the little outside things of life? "Rejoice evermore, and again I say, rejoice."

Lords Of The Heart: II. Justice

Chapter XII Justice, Universal

We must know the Functions of Love and Justice.—We have said that two potent personages hold rule in the House of Heart—Love and Justice. The question occurs, do not the claims of the two clash? They do sometimes. Love leans to leniency, and injures where it should sustain. Justice leans to severity, and repels where it should win. Therefore it is necessary for us to think on these things and con the several parts of Love and Justice at least as carefully as we should con a Greek verb or a problem in Euclid. Indeed, these latter we can live without, but Love and Justice are inseparable from Mansoul; they are there, and we must take count of them. Not that they are as self-adjusting wheels, so to speak, which go right whether we will or no. On the contrary, these Lords of the Bosom require the continual supervision of the Prime Minister, himself ruled by the higher Power; and without such over-looking they produce tangles in the lives of men.

Everyone has Justice in his Heart.—We have already considered the ways of Love and the various offices of his Lords in Waiting. Let us now think upon Justice, and who they are surrounding his seat and carrying out his mandates. First let us realise our wealth. It is a great thing to know that there is not a Mansoul in the world, however mean or unconsidered, neglected or savage, who has not justice in his heart. A cry for fair-play will reach the most lawless mob. 'It's not fair,' goes home to everybody. Different nations have different notions as to the way of it, but fair-play for himself and others is the demand of every man's heart.

I must hurt nobody by Word or Deed.—Justice requires that we should take steady care every day to yield his rights to every person we come in contact with; that is, "to do unto others as we would that they should do unto us: to hurt nobody by word or deed"; therefore we must show gentleness to the persons of others, courtesy to their words, and deference to their opinions, because these things are due. We must be true and just in all our dealing. Veracity, fidelity, simplicity, and sincerity must therefore direct our words. Candour, appreciation, discrimination must guide our thoughts. Fair-dealing, honesty, integrity must govern our actions.

I must be Just to all other Persons.—This justice to the persons, property, words, thoughts, and actions of others, I must show to my parents, teachers, rulers, and all who are set in authority over me and over my country, because it is their right and my duty. In the same way, I must be just to the words, thoughts, and actions of my brothers, sisters, friends, and rieighbours, and all others who are my equals, in my own words, thoughts, and actions. I must be just, too, in word, thought and deed to servants, to all people who are employed by me or mine, to all who work for me, whether in my own home or in the world. I must be fair, that is, just, to all persons whose opinions and ways of life differ from my own, even to all who offend against the laws of God and man. It is my duty to be just in this way to the persons, the reputation, and the property of all other persons, so far as I have anything to do with them. Therefore, "I must bear no malice or hatred in my heart, must keep my hands from picking and stealing, my tongue from evil-speaking, lying, and slandering," and "I must not covet nor desire other men's goods, but must learn and labour truly to get mine own living and do my duty in that state of life to which it hath pleased God to call me."

We are able to pay the Dues of Justice.—It is quite plain that to think fairly, speak truly, and act justly towards all persons at all times and on all occasions, which is our duty, is a matter requiring earnest thought and consideration—is, in fact, the study of a lifetime. We might be a little discouraged by the thought of how much is due from us to all our neighbours everywhere, if it were not that justice is within us, ready to rule; that the Lords in waiting of his court wait upon his bidding. Candour, sincerity, simplicity, integrity, fidelity, and the rest are our servants at command, and what we have to do is to find our way about in the Circuit of justice, to recognise the dues of others as they come before us, and behold! we have in hand always that coin of the realm of justice wherewith to pay the dues of all our neighbours. It is a great thing to know this; to be able to walk about wealthy in the streets of our Mansoul, and to know that we have wherewith to pay our way on all hands. Many a poor soul goes a pauper; he has all the coinage of Justice, but does not know it, and therefore does not use it. He is blind because he fixes his eyes all the time on his own rights and other people's duties; therefore he cannot see other people's rights and his own duties; that is, he cannot be just.

Our own Rights.—You ask: Have we then no rights ourselves, and have other people no duties towards us? We have indeed rights, precisely the same rights as other people, and when we learn to think of ourselves as one of the rest, with just the same rights as other people and no more, to whom others owe just such duties as we owe to them and no more, we shall, as it were, get our lives in focus and see things as they are. There is a wonderful parable in the story of the man who first was blind and saw no man, and then had his eyes partially opened so that he saw men as trees walking, and at last was blessed with the full vision of other people as they are.

Chapter XIII Justice To The Persons Of Others

We begin to understand this Duty.—The reader may have heard sorrowfully the story of that young German officer who fell lately in a duel on the eve of his marriage-day. It is not so long ago since in England also men thought it right to wipe out a slight offence by the death of the offender or of the offended. Now, we understand that it is not lawful to hurt anybody by deed. Masters may not beat their apprentices, mistresses their maids; in fact, we try as a nation to make all persons treat the persons of others with respect. Children, too, have gained by this truer sense of justice to the persons of others. Their little bodies were at one time subject to many whippings, 'pinches, nips, and bobs,' from those in authority over them. It was thought quite wholesome for them to be fed on bread and water, or put in a dark closet when they were naughty. But now their persons receive much cherishing love, and they are rarely beaten. This is because people begin to see, and are eager to do, all that justice requires. There still are countries where people do not see the harm of hurting others. We have read lately of a bandit in Southern Italy, who owned to having killed twenty-seven persons—not that he wanted their money or goods, and not that they had injured him, but because a relative of theirs had, years before, killed his brother. This man believed that his vengeance was fair-play. He had a notion of justice, but a misguided one; and an incident like this shows how necessary it is that instruction should help us to think clearly upon the difficult question of what is fair. There are few things about which people make more mistakes.

To think fairly requires Knowledge and Consideration.—To think fairly about the personal rights of others requires a good deal of knowledge as well as judgment. But we can all arrive at some right conclusions by calling in the help of Imagination. That boy is none the less a good fellow who realises his mother's love for the beauty of neatness; who recollects that the maids have enough to do with their regular work; that enough work makes people happy, while too much spoils their lives; and, thinking upon these things, is careful about such little matters as to wipe his feet when he comes in, to confine his messes to his own den, to avoid leaving tracks of soil, tear and damage to show where he has been, because he knows that this sort of recklessness spoils the comfort and increases the labour of other people. The young lady who thinks of the persons of others will not hurry her dressmaker for a new party frock which must be ready by such a date, if the dressmaker's assistants have to sit up until midnight to get it done. She uses her Imagination, and sees, on the one hand, girls with pale faces and tired eyes; and, on the other, bright girls sewing with interest and pleasure at the pretty frock. Indeed, this sort of care not to do bodily hurt to other people should guide us in many of the affairs of life—should, for example, forbid us to buy at the cheapest shops; for most likely some class of work-people have been 'sweated' to produce the cheap article. A fair sense of the value of things helps us much in leading the just life.

Persons hurt in Mind suffer in Body—Gentleness.—But there are other ways of doing bodily hurt to the people we have to do with than by overworking, underfeeding, or directly misusing them. If you hurt people in mind they suffer in body, and it is for this reason that we should not push in a crowd to get the best place—should not jostle others to get the best share of what is going, even if it be a good sermon, should give place gently in walking the streets, should make room on public seats or in railway carriages for others who wish to sit. If we are ungentle in such small matters, we may not do such direct hurt to the persons of others as would make a surgeon necessary, but we produce a state of mental fret and discomfort which is really more wearing. We all know how soothing is the presence of a gentle person in a room; a person whose tone of voice and whose movements show that he has imagination, that he realises the presence of other people whose comfort he would not willingly destroy. The Dæmons at whose instigation we are unjust to the persons of others are usually Thoughtlessness, Selfishness, and Cruelty.

A Word may hurt as much as a Blow—Courtesy.—Bearing in mind how easy it is to hurt other people's bodies through their minds, we begin to see that a word may hurt as much as a blow, that a want of courtesy may do as much harm to another as want of food. Once we see this, we are courteous to the words of others; we listen, we do not contradict, we try to understand; and, when other persons express their opinions, however much they may differ from those in which we have been brought up, we keep ourselves from violence in thought and word, and listen with deference where we cannot agree. Then, when we state our own notions with gentleness and modesty, we shall find that they are gently received.

We are not free to think Hard Things about Others.—We may not 'run a-mock' in the world! To go, head down, feet foremost, for all we are worth, and run into whatever comes in our way, may be inviting, but it does not answer. Nobody is born a Hooligan; that lordly justice within our hearts is always down upon us for the claims of other people; and having considered the persons of these others, we awake to the fact that they, all of them, have claims upon us in regard to their character and reputation. Most of us know that we are not free to think what we like about our parents or other Heads, of our school household, or office. Some of us do not let ourselves think disagreeable things about our brothers and sisters, servants, or other inmates of our home. There are still a few more who are careful about thoughts regarding acquaintances and outside relations; but, having got thus far, most of us feel ourselves free to think what we please about the characters of outsiders, whether it be of the man who makes our shoes, or the statesman who helps to govern us, or an acquaintance in another set.

Justice to the Characters of Others.—Justice, holding court within, ordains that we shall think fair thoughts of everybody, near or far, above or below us. When we are minded to think fairly, he has his group of servitors at our command, whose business it is to attend to this very matter and to come at call when they are wanted.

Candour.—Candour is at our side, and presents us with glasses of unusual power, to bring far things near and make dim things clear. Wearing these, we can see round the corner, to the other side of the question. We see that Mr. Jones may be disagreeable, but that, all the same, he is trying to do his duty. That boy wore candid spectacles who (so the story goes) wrote home of his Master, "Temple is a beast, but he is a just beast." His candid schoolmate sees that Brown is not a sneak, but a timid boy anxious to get on. Candour points out that Miss Jenkins' annoying remark was not spiteful, but merely awkward; that even public men have a conscientious wish to do their best; that the parson probably tries to practise what he preaches; that very likely the much-abused plumber takes an interest in his work, and cares to make a good job of it; and that, even supposing the person in question has no right intention and makes no worthy effort, he is all the more to be pitied; and, if possible, helped, because in this case things must have been against him all his life. Candour shows us that a Frenchman, a German, a Russian, has qualities which John Bull would be the better for; that a Whig or a Tory, whichever it may be, has something to teach his opponent. But Candour does not take sides. He does not say to himself, 'My family, my country, my party, my school, is pretty sure to be in the right always, and is altogether the best going,' because he always sees that the other side, whether it be family, school, or country, may have something to say worth

Vol 4 pg 145

hearing. Fair-play all round is his watchword, and that makes him in the end the most staunch supporter of the side he belongs to.

Prejudice.—Opposed to Candour is Prejudice, who also hands you a pair of spectacles; but these are not clear and open to the light of day, but are rose-coloured or black, green or yellow, as the case may be. We cannot see persons as they are through these spectacles, but one person is black, another rosy as the dawn, another a sickly green or an evil yellow, according as affection, envy, hatred, or jealousy creates a prejudice in our minds, through which we cannot judge justly of the character of another. Persons cannot be candid who allow themselves to be prejudiced, either in favour of the persons they like, or against those they dislike. Indeed, dislike is itself Prejudice; and true love is quite clear-sighted and candid. There is enough beauty in the persons we love, enough right in the causes we care for, to enable us to let the light of day upon them and dispense with rose-coloured spectacles.

We shall not have our love for our country called 'Jingoism' if we love her with a candid love. She is great and glorious, able to bear the light of day. But what about the 'candid friend,' the person who sees that England is going to ruin; that we ourselves are poor things, made up on the whole of a single fault of character? England, like other countries, has need to go softly; we probably have that fault of character, we may be priggish or lazy, selfish, or what not; but where our 'candid friend' errs is in taking a part for the whole and magnifying one fault or weakness, so that there is nothing else to be seen. We have something to learn from him, though he is not agreeable; but, for ourselves we must use the spectacles of Candour, which bring the whole landscape out in due relief.

Respect.—Candour never acts alone; on his right is that other servitor of my Lord justice—Respect. No one can be just who does not follow the Apostolic precept, "Honour all men." We are inclined to object that we do honour those who are worthy of honour; but that is another way of saying that we single out people here and there of whom we shall think justly; but every man and every child calls for our honour, not only because of the common brotherhood that is between us, seeing that we are all the children of one Father, but because Love and Justice, Intellect, Reason, Imagination, all the lofty rulers of Mansoul, are present, however dormant, in every man we meet. It is by honouring all men that we find out how worthy they are of honour. We may see the faults of one another in the white light of candour, but that same white light will show us that a fault, however trying, is by no means the whole person, and that there are beautiful qualities in the poorest nature to call forth our reverence. There is seldom a daily paper but reveals the unsuspected glory in some human soul. Honour begets gentleness to the persons of others, courteous attention to their words, however dull and prosy they may seem to us, and deference towards their opinions, however foolish we may think them. The person whose rash opinions are received with deference is ready to hear the other side of the question and becomes open to conviction.

Conceit.—Why do we not all honour one another? Because our vision is blinded by a graven image of ourselves. We are so taken up with thinking about ourselves that we cannot see the beauty in those about us, though we may be able to admire people removed from us. Conceit and self-absorption are the Dæmons which hinder us from giving that honour to all men which is their due.

Discernment.—See, now, how the servitors of justice stand by one another! Candour, we have seen, is accompanied by Respect, and Respect is supported by Discernment. People talk about being deceived in this one and that, and we hear much of disappointed affection and of unworthy friends; but all this is quite unnecessary. In every House of Heart there stands that modest servitor of Justice whom we call Discernment. Give him free play, unhindered by Vanity or Prejudice, and he will bring you a pretty accurate report of the character of everyone with whom you come in contact. He will show you, alike, faults and virtues in another, the good and the evil. More, he will hold up his glass to your own Mansoul, and enable you to see that, though such an one has virtues as well as faults, yet the faults are of a kind that would be a snare and temptation to you, and that therefore that person is not fitted for your friendship. For lack of Discernment in character, many a person makes shipwreck of life and unites himself to another, not for goodness' sake, but because the two have the same failings. We owe honour to all men; but Discernment steps in to help us to do justice to ourselves, and choose for our intimacy, or service, those whose characters should be a strength to our own.

Appreciation.—Lest Discernment in his zeal should become too keen to see that which is amiss, another servitor of Justice, exquisite and delicate as Ariel, is at hand to stand or go with him. This is Appreciation, whose business it is to weigh and consider, duly and delicately, the merits, the fine qualities, of a person, a country, a cause, of a book or a picture. Appreciation is a delightful inmate of the House of Heart, and is continually bringing an ingathering of joy. It is so good and pleasant to notice a trait of unselfishness here, of delicacy there, of honour elsewhere; to observe and treasure the record of the beauty of perfectness in any man's work, whether the work be a great poem or the sweeping of a room. It is a happy thing to discriminate peculiar beauties in another country and find traits of character that differ from our own in people of another nationality. Life has no greater joy-giver than Appreciation, and though this Appreciation is the due of others, and our duty towards them, we get more than we give, for there is no purer pleasure than that of seeing the good in everything, the beauty in everyone.

Depreciation.—Depreciation is the sneering Dæmon who goes about to oust this genial servitor of justice. There are people for whom neither the weather nor their dinner, their abode nor their company, is ever quite good enough. You remark when they come down, 'What a beautiful morning!' They answer, 'Yes, it is fine to-day,' with a depreciatory reference to a day that is past. 'What a nice woman Mrs. Jones is!' 'Yes, if she did not wear such dreadful garments.' 'I enjoyed the Black Forest so much.' 'Oh, did you? there's always such a lot of Germans in the hotels.' And so goes on the depreciatory person, who moves through the world like a cuttlefish, ready at a touch to blacken the waters about him. It is well to remember that Depreciation is Injustice. The depreciative remark may be true in the letter, but it is false in spirit, because it takes a part for the whole, a single defect for many excellences. Depreciation may be inspired by the monster Envy, who is perpetually going about to put stumbling-blocks in the way of justice, and belittle the claims of others; or it may arise from Thoughtlessness, which is but a form of Self-occupation. Many of the crude and unworthy criticisms we hear of books, pictures, speeches, a song, a party, arise from the latter cause. We would not allow ourselves to depreciate if we recollected that Appreciation is one part of the Justice we owe to the characters and the works of others.

Chapter XIV Truth: Justice In Word

Truth is not Violent.—If our thoughts are not our own, if what we think of other people is a matter of justice or of Injustice, so also a certain manner of words is due from us to all other persons with whom we speak; and if we do not say these words we are unjust to our neighbours. If we say a false thing to another and are believed, our neighbour has a right to be angry with us; and, if he does not believe, he has a right to despise us. We have done him a hurt, not to his body perhaps, but to his mind and soul, which smart and are sore under such a hurt in much the same way as our flesh smarts and is sore after a blow. Very likely a professional 'champion' gets used to bruises; certainly, a person who puts himself in the way of hearing and reading what is false learns to think untruly, and must of necessity speak falsely, even if he does not intentionally tell lies. Truth is in every Mansoul, waiting upon justice; but Truth is never violent, and there be many clamorous ones at hand to drown her voice. It rests with us to choose whom we shall hear.

Botticelli's 'Calumny.'—There is a picture in the Uffizi painted by Sandro Botticelli—in a passion of grief and righteous anger at the martyrdom of his friend and teacher, Savonarola,—wherein you see the clamorous crew who drown the words of Truth. But the figures are surprising. You expect the painter to depict these Dæmons as wrinkled hags, ugly and forbidding. We should none of us offend if sin came to us looking hateful; and Botticelli, painting from an account of a picture by the old Greek painter, Apelles, puts in the foreground a lady young and fair, with a mantle of heavenly blue over a white robe of innocence, but which reveals through slashes the black garment below. She looks composed and drops her eyes as if in regret, whilst with her right hand she drags forward, by the hair of his head, the naked and prostrate fizure of Innocence. This is Calumny.

On either hand are two other beautiful maidens, clothed in fair robes, apparently dressing the hair of Calumny, in reality whispering in her ears. The one is Insidiousness, who by soft, persuasive words makes the lies of Calumny look like the Truth; and the other is Envy, fair also, for Envy of others always takes the guise of Fairness and justice to ourselves.

Holding the left wrist of Calumny is the dark, cowled figure of Treachery, who stretches out his hand to King Midas upon his throne in order to demand a hearing. His long ears show the character of this king, for Falsehood and all her crew, Calumny, Envy, and the rest, are, in the end, but Folly. Suspicion whispers into the one and Prejudice into the other of the long ears of Midas, and he leans his ear now to the one and now to the other, so that their words are the only sounds that can reach him. The action of the picture takes place in a beautiful loggia, richly decorated with sculpture, for it is not in places where men work hard and live simply that Calumny and her ministers prosper. Quite in the background stands the naked Truth, pure and beautiful, averting her eyes from the evil spectacle and raising her hand to heaven, sure of a hearing there; and between her and tortured Innocence stands the dark figure of Remorse. It would be well to keep a copy of this picture before our eyes, not only for the sake of its beauty, but because it should keep us in mind of many things—that the whole brood of Falsehood, Calumny, Envy, Folly, Prejudice, Suspicion come to us in pleasant places and by insidious ways,—that they torture the innocent and drive holy Truth away by the din of many voices in our ears.

Calumny.—Truth may be driven away, but she is there; and we must keep still hearts to hear her words and obedient tongues to speak them. Calumny, we all know, is the speaking of injurious words about other people. We must keep our tongues from evil-speaking, lying, and slandering; and Wesley says that to speak evil of another when it is true is to slander, and when it is false, is to lie. Most persons are careful to cherish Truth in all they say about the people in their own homes, but how many of us are equally careful in speaking of people who live next door or in the next street? It is so easy to say that Jones is a sneak and Brown is a cad, that Mrs. Jones does not feed her servants properly or that Mrs. Brown over-dresses her children; that Minna cribs from Maria's translation, that Harrison does not give full weight. Such things as these, about the people we have dealings with, are lightly said, often without intention; but two things have happened—our neighbour's character has received a wound; and Truth, perhaps the most beautiful inmate of the House of Heart, has also received a hurt at our hands.

Insidiousness and Envy.—But it is not always from thoughtlessness that we let Insidiousness persuade us of the untrue thing, which, by and by, we speak. Envy is an ever-present Dæmon, ready with a calumnious word for those who excel us. If they dance better, we do not care about dancing, and they must waste a great deal of time upon it. If they dress better, it is because they spend far too much money and thought on their clothes. If they speak better, Envy calls it affectation. If they are handsomer than we, Envy says that beauty is skin-deep, and there's not much in a handsome face if it goes with an empty head. In the Middle Ages people were afraid of Envy, and counted it one of the Seven Deadly Sins. Now, we forget that there is such a vice; and when we allow ourselves in grudging thoughts about the possessions or advantages of others, we say, 'It's not fair'; that is, we cover our injustice to others with a mantle of what we call justice and fairness to ourselves. But we deceive ourselves, and every sin of deceit disables us from uttering truth.

Calumnious Hearing and Calumnious Reading.—It is not only by calumnious talk that Truth is wounded. Calumnious hearing or calumnious reading may do her to death; and a simple rule will help us to discern what manner of speaking and reading is calumnious. Truth is never violent; and the newspaper or magazine or book, the party or the public speech, which makes strong and bitter charges against the other side, we may be sure is, for the moment, calumnious; and, if we steep ourselves in such speaking or reading, the punishment that will come upon us is that we shall become incapable of discerning Truth and shall rejoice in evil speaking.

Fanaticism.—This is what happens to people when they become fanatics. It is not that they will not believe what is said on the other side, but that they cannot; they have lost the power; and efforts to convince them are futile. A man may be a fanatic for peace or a fanatic for war, a fanatic for religion or a fanatic for atheism. In fact, it is sad that good as well as evil causes may have their fanatics, who injure what they would support by their incapacity to see more than one side of a question. A good cause may also have its martyrs; but a martyr is not a clamorous person; he suffers, but does not shout, for the cause he has at heart. It was good and refreshing, after the calumnious clamour of the press on both sides and in several countries, to come upon a book by a British officer wherein the courage and endurance of Boer and Briton alike were duly honoured, and the Boer women who followed their husbands into the trenches were spoken of with kindliness and reverence. There are few better equipments for a citizen than a mind capable of discerning the Truth, whether it lie on the side of our party or on that of our opponents. But this just mind can only be preserved by those who take heed what they hear, and how.

The Sovereign Good.—"But howsoever," as Bacon says, "these things are thus in men's depraved judgments and affections, yet truth, which only doth judge itself, teacheth that the inquiry of truth, which is the love-making, or wooing of it; the knowledge of truth, which is the presence of it; and the belief of truth, which is the enjoying of it; is the sovereign good of human nature."

Chapter XV Spoken Truth

We have not yet come to 'telling the truth,' because no one can tell the Truth who does not see it and know it in his heart, and who does not believe, with Sir Roger de Coverley, that "there is a great deal to be said on both sides" of most questions.

Veracity.—First among the handmaidens of Truth, that is, spoken Truth, is Veracity—the habit of letting our words express the exact fact so far as we know it. Having spoken what we believe to be the fact, let us avoid qualifications. Do not let us say, 'At least I think so,' 'At least I believe so,' 'Perhaps it was not so,' 'All the girls were there, at least some of them,' 'We walked ten miles, at any rate six'; such qualifications imply a want of Veracity; we are self-convicted of a loose statement, and try to set ourselves right with our conscience by an excess of scrupulousness which has the effect of making our hearers doubt the Truth of what we have spoken. But what are we to do, when, having said a thing, we begin to doubt if it is true? Words once spoken must be let alone: it is useless to unsay or qualify, explain or alter, or to appeal for confirmation or denial to another person. When we think how final words are, we shall be careful not to rush into statements without knowledge; we shall not come in with the cry, 'Mother! mother! there are a thousand cats in the garden.' 'Are there, George? Have you counted them?' 'Well, anyway, there's our cat and another!' We must be sure of our facts before we speak, and avoid speaking about matters concerning which we have only the vaguest knowledge. People are too apt to assume in conversation an intimate knowledge of matters of literature and art, for example, that they know very little about.

Scrupulosity is not Veracity.—At the same time it is well to remember that Scrupulosity is not Veracity, and that to put an end to talk by tiresome scrupulousness is not the behaviour of a truthful person. One can avoid a false assumption of knowledge without saying, 'I do not know'; a remark inconvenient to the other person.

Another kind of Scrupulosity is very tiresome in talk. Somebody says, 'I saw seven men in the lane,' and the scrupulous person corrects him with, 'Excuse me, I think it was six men and a youth.' 'I met Mr. Jones on Tuesday,' and the correction is, 'I think, if you recollect, it was on Wednesday.' 'It has been fine all the week': correction, 'No, I think not; there was a shower on Thursday'; and so on, to distraction; for there are few habits which more successfully put an end to conversation than the distinctly priggish one of looking after the Veracity of other people in matters of not the smallest moment. Common politeness requires us to assume the good faith of the speaker; and, that being assumed, it is not of the least consequence whether there were ten or twelve people in the hayfield, whether a flock of sheep, passed on the road, numbered eighty or a hundred. Veracity requires us to speak the fact so far as we know it, to take pains not to talk about what we do not know; but it by no means requires us to keep watch over the conversation of others and correct their information by means of our own, probably even less accurate.

Exaggeration.—Another more or less casual departure from Veracity comes of the habit of Exaggeration. We have 'a thousand things to do': perhaps we have four; 'everyone says so,' which means that our friends Mrs. Simpson and Mary Carter have said so, or perhaps only Mrs. Simpson. Few heads of a household do not know the tiresome tyranny of—'We always do so-and-so': probably we have done it once. In the case of sickness, war, calamity, people are eager to make the most and the worst of what has happened, and the headlines of the newspaper showing the biggest number of casualties are most often quoted and most readily believed, though to-morrow may show how false they are. We cannot keep a delicate sense of Truth if we let ourselves listen to and carry rumours. Let us use our Common Sense to sift what we hear, and still more what we read, and wait for facts to be ascertained before we help to spread reports. Men have been ruined, the good name of a family destroyed, through the thoughtless carrying on of an idle rumour.

Exaggeration in speech, even when it is more foolish than mischievous, is a failure in Veracity. One cannot be 'awfully sorry' not to go for a walk and 'awfully glad' to get a letter, and leave anything to say when we have lost our best friend or gained a great happiness.

The Habit of Generalising.—The habit of generalising, of stating something about a whole class of persons or things which we have noticed in only one or two cases, is one to be carefully guarded against by a person who would fain be, like our King Alfred, a truth-teller. 'All the cups are cracked,' when one is so. 'All the streets are up': perhaps two are. 'Oh, no, I can't bear Rossetti's pictures': the critic has seen but one. 'I love Schumann's songs': again, the critic has heard one. Let us stop generalisations of this kind before they escape our lips. They are not truthful, because they give the idea of a wider knowledge or experience than we possess; and, by the indulgence of this manner of loose statement, we incapacitate ourselves for the scientific habit of mind—accurate observation and exact record.

Of Making a Good Story.—Many persons are tempted to make a good story of a trifling incident. If a dog cock his tail at a whistle, they see enough fun in the situation to make you 'laugh consumedly.' All power to their elbow, as the Irishman would say. Humour, the power, of seeing and describing the ludicrous side of things, is a gift that, like mercy, blesses him that gives and him that takes. It is a dangerous gift, all the same. The temptations to Irreverence, Discourtesy, even to a touch of Malice, for the embellishment of a story, are hard to be resisted; and, if these pitfalls be escaped, the incessant making of fun, perpetration of small jokes, becomes a weariness to the flesh of those who have to listen. The jocose person has need of self-restraint, or he becomes a bore; and his embellishments must be of the sort which no one is expected to believe, like the golden leg of Miss Kilmansegg, or his Veracity is at stake and he perils Truth to win a laugh.

The Realm of Fiction—Essential and Accidental Truth.—What shall we say of fable, poetry, romance, the whole realm of fiction? There are two sorts of Truth. What we may call accidental Truth; that is, that such and such a thing came to pass in a certain place at a certain hour on a certain day; and this is the sort of Truth we have to observe in our general talk. The other, the Truth of Art, is what we may call essential Truth; that, for example, given, such and such a character, he must needs have thought and acted in such and such a way, with such and such consequences; given, a certain aspect of nature, and the poet will receive from it such and such ideas; or, certain things of common life, as a dog with a bone, for example, will present themselves to the thinker as fables, illustrating some of the happenings of life. This sort of fiction is of enormous value to us, whether we find it in poetry or romance; it teaches us morals and manners; what to do in given circumstances; what will happen if we behave in a certain way. It shows how, what seems a little venial fault is often followed by dreadful consequences, and our eyes are opened to see that it is not little or venial, but is a deep-seated fault of character; some selfishness, shallowness, or deceitfulness upon which a man or woman makes shipwreck. We cannot learn these things except through what is called fiction, or from the bitter experience of life, from the penalties of which our writers of fiction do their best to spare us.

The Value of Fiction depends on the Worth of the Writer.—But you will see at once that the value of fiction as a moral teacher depends upon the wisdom, insight, and goodness of the writer; that a shallow mind will give false and shallow teaching; and, therefore, that it is only the best fiction that is lawful reading, because in no other shall we find this sort of essential Truth.

Fiction affects our Enthusiasms.—Not only are morals and manners taught, but our enthusiasms, even our religion, are kindled by fiction, whether in prose or verse. Our Lord Himself gave some of his deepest teaching in the fabulous stories known to us as parables; and, when severely literal people (who do not realise that, as we have said, Truth is of two sorts, the merely accidental and the essential, the passing and the everlasting, the Truth for to-day and the Truth for all time), would fain throw scorn upon the Bible records by telling us that the Garden of Eden and the Serpent and the Apple, the Flood, and much besides, are mere fables or allegories, we are not staggered.

Essential Truth.—The thing that matters to us in the Bible stories is their essential Truth. All godly people have known the walls of Jericho to fall before their faith and the trumpet-blast of their prayers. They have known seas of difficulty, which threatened to overwhelm them, divide to let them go forward. They have heard the voice of the Lord in the cool of the evening speaking to quiet and obedient hearts; and they know out of the experience of their own lives that by means of song and story, psalm and prophecy, the Bible reveals the ways of God with man, and all that there is in the heart of man. These are the things that matter; so they are quite ready to wait the verdict of the critics as to whether a certain narrative records facts that took place in a given year; whether such a book was written by one man, or by two. All this is deeply interesting, but has nothing to do with the essential, permanent Truth, the revelation of the otherwise unknown about God and about man which stamps the several books of the Bible with the divine seal.

Chapter XVI Some Causes Of Lying

Malicious Lies.—Scrupulosity, rash generalisation, exaggeration, amusing representation, are, as it were, the light skirmishers which assault the defences of the fortress of Truth as chance offers; but there are also the sappers and miners who dig under its foundations, and these ask for our more serious attention. There are, as we have seen, Malice and Envy, which lead to Calumny; and of all lies none are more hateful than those told to lower another in the esteem of his friends. The law of the land steps in to save our reputation from hurt, as it does to save us from bodily harm, but many hurtful words may be lightly spoken without fear of the law against libel.

Cowardly Lies.—Cowardice, again, makes for Falsehood. We have done or said a thing that we are made ashamed of, and our first impulse is to deny it. We didn't drop the match which caused the fire, or forget to write the note which politeness required, or say the thing which offended Mrs. Foster. The lie is the refuge of the coward when he is found out in a fault. But let us rally our forces and own up; our friends love us the better, in spite of our fault, if we will only say we have done it; they like our courage and honour us for remembering that "all liars are an abomination unto the Lord."

"Dare to be true. Nothing can need a lie;
A fault which needs it most grows two thereby."

The Falsehood of Reserve.—Akin to the lie of Concealment is the habit of Reserve, which, though it does not tell a lie, fails to tell the truth. 'Where have you been to-day?' 'Oh! I went for a walk in the direction of Milton.' We have really been to the town and bought chocolate or shopped, let us say. Frank speech would have made all plain, and to be frank about our little affairs is of the nature of Truth, and is a duty we owe to the people we live with. As a matter of fact, most people know when a lie is being told them, or when something is being held back.

Boasting Lies.— Vain persons tell boasting lies; they think their friends will value them the more for what they have got or for the things they have seen or done, or for the fine people they know. Like all lying, this is foolish as well as wicked. If we gain, by boastful lies, the friendship of the foolish and the vain; that very friendship is an injury to our own character, and it is only the vain and foolish that we can deceive; good and sensible people are quite up to us, and the more we boast the less they think of us.

Romancing Lies.—There are people who live so constantly in castles in Spain of their own building that they romance in their talk. They will tell you they have been here and there, have talked with this and that grand person, or perhaps that they have been kidnapped and left on a desert island, or that they are not really the children of their parents, but changelings, the sons and daughters of a duke or of a rag-picker. This manner of lying comes of a very dangerous habit of mind. When people cannot discern between fact and fancy, and mix the two in their talk, they are gradually losing the use of their Reason, and are qualifying themselves to end in a madhouse. We may not allow ourselves to say things of which Reason and Conscience do not approve.

Lies for Friendship's Sake.—It is not easy to speak the truth when to do so will get a friend into trouble. 'Did you leave the gate open?' 'No.' 'Did Tom?' You know that Tom did, and that it is his fault that the sheep have eaten the carnations. What are you to say? No decent boy could own up another's fault, but neither may he tell a lie to screen his friend at his own expense. But if you say, 'Tom is my friend, I cannot tell of what he does or does not do,' most likely no more questions will be asked. One more caution: 'All's fair in love and war' is made to cover many lies. People think they must speak the truth on their own side, but a lie is good enough for their opponents. They forget that a lie is a two-edged sword, injuring those who speak more than those who hear, and that no one can wear 'the white flower of a blameless life' who is not known to friend and foe alike as one whose word is to be trusted.

Magna est Veritas (Truth is Great).—Let us take courage: Truth, the handmaid of justice, is a beautiful presence in every Mansoul, and with her are her attendant group, Veracity; Simplicity, whose part it is to secure that every spoken word means just what it appears to mean, and nothing more and nothing less: Sincerity, which secures that word of mouth tallies exactly with thought of heart, that we say exactly what we think: Fidelity, which makes us faithful to every promise at any cost—always excepting such promises as should never have been made; the only honourable thing that we can do is to break a promise which is wrong in itself. It is true that the Dæmons of the qualities are there also—Duplicity, with hints and innuendoes and double meanings; Deceit, trying to trip up Sincerity and pour out words of congratulation, sympathy, kindness, from the teeth outwards; Perfidiousness, which breaks through faith and makes promises of none effect. But, again, let us take courage; these are the aliens to be routed by every valiant Mansoul:

Magna est Veritas et Prævalebit. (Truth is great and will prevail)

Chapter XVII Integrity: Justice In Action

Integrity in Work—'Ca' Canny.—Some time ago the newspapers brought a serious charge against the 'British workman.' He was said to have taken 'Ca' canny' for his motto. That is to say, the man paid by the hour was pledged to do as little work as he decently could in the time. If he were a bricklayer, for example, he was limited to the laying of a certain number of bricks, perhaps half as many as might be laid in the time; and so on with other employments. This action was supposed to promote the interests of men out of work, because there would in this way be more work to go round.

Persons of understanding see that this is a fallacy. It is the man who does good and honest work, getting in as much as he can in a given time, who promotes the interests of his class; because he induces people with money to spend it in getting work well and honestly done, whether it be the building of houses or the making of shoes. The 'ca' canny' workman is a hindrance and cause of loss to his employer, puts other employers out of conceit with his trade, and gives a bad name both to his class and his country; and of all the complaints that men and nations suffer from, there is none which it takes so long to get over as that of a bad name. The man who does less work than he can, or worse work than he can, in a given time, may make fine pretences to himself about benefiting his fellows, but he will never deceive anyone.

A Standard.—You have probably noticed the standard yard measure cut in the granite at a corner of Trafalgar Square. Should there be a dispute as to the proper length of a yard, it could be finally settled by comparison with this standard measure. Now, everyone carries a similar standard measure in his own breast—a rule by which he judges of the integrity of a workman. He knows whether the work turned out by such and such a man is whole and complete, is what we call honest work. It is by this unwritten law of integrity that every true man, who is neither grasping nor lax, tries the work that is brought to him. Though his verdict may not be spoken, he classes the work either as honest or dishonest. The honest worker he considers a person of integrity, that is, a whole man.

We are all Paid Labourers.—We may not all be bricklayers or carpenters, but in some sense we are all paid labourers, and cannot escape the binding obligation of integrity.

The schoolboy, the young man at college, receives payment in two kinds—the cost of his education and the trust reposed in him by his parents and teachers. He has also another employer, who is apt to be lax while the work is being done, but visits the worker with heavy penalties in the long run. Every person owes integrity to himself as well as to others; and it is he, himself, who will suffer most in the end for every failure to produce honest work in a given time.

After the period of what we call education, whether the girl employ herself at home, or girl or boy go to work to Carve Out a place in the world, there are still employers to be counted with, and wages to be accounted for, though they be the unstinted and ungrudging wages given in the freedom of home life. We cannot escape the duty of integrity, however easy things may be for us. Certain obligations are due from us in return for what we receive; due from us to our parents and family, or to our employer or chief; and still more, due to ourselves and our own future—to the character we are continually making or marring. As a matter of fact, it is easier to do the definite work of school or profession than the easily evaded, indefinite work which belongs to the home daughter.

Integrity grows.—We know that an integer is a whole number; and a man of integrity is a whole man, complete and sound. Like Rome itself, such a man is not built in a day. From his youth up he has been aware of temptations to scamp, dawdle over, postpone, get out of his work—nay, even to crib his work, that is, get it done by another hand and pass it off as his own.

He has been tempted to say to himself, 'It doesn't matter,' 'Oh, that'll do,' 'It's as good as Jones's, anyway,' 'He'll never know the difference,' 'He won't notice,' 'I don't see the good of taking so much trouble,' 'This won't count in the exam.' (and pages of thoughtful writing are left unread). These, and a hundred other temptations to dally with his work, the man of integrity has put from him. He has said to himself, 'I owe it to my parents'—or my teachers, or my employers—'to do this thing as well and as quickly as I can; what is more, I owe it to myself.' He buckles to, and is not to be decoyed by a lazy comrade or inviting hobby until the particular task is done.

Everything he has undertaken has helped to make him a whole man; every bit of work, Latin hexameters, quadratics, a set of bookshelves, everything he has attempted, has been an honest job. I do not say he has never shirked a job that came his way for the sake of an engrossing hobby, but he has never played 'ca' canny' with his work. If he have shirked now and then, he has done it completely, and has had to own up; but the things he has done have been done honestly. That is the history of the man of integrity—who was not made in a day. 'Oh, I could not grind like that, whatever I should get by it!' Now, that is a mistake. The whole worker goes at his job with a will, does it completely and with pleasure, and has more leisure for his own diversions than the poor 'ca'-canny' creature whose jobs never get done.

It is a fine thing to look back upon even a single year in which the tasks that came to hand have been done, wholly done, in which we have kept our integrity—as son, in such small matters as exactness in messages; as pupil or student, by throwing our whole mind into our work. Even games want the whole of the player, they want Integrity.

'Do ye Nexte Thynge.'—We are all convinced that Integrity is a fine thing. Our hearts rise within us at the name of this grace. We say to ourselves, 'It shall be mine. I am determined that I shall be a man of integrity.' But in the Kingdom of Mansoul, as in the bigger world, everything depends upon other things, and no one can have this fine quality without putting his mind, as well as his heart, into the effort of getting it.

Now, the eager soul who gives attention and zeal to his work often spoils its completeness by chasing after many things when he should be doing the next thing in order.

He has to write a theme, and looks up 'Plassy' in the Encyclopaedia; but he finds 'Plato' on the way, and sets off on a course of investigation so interesting that time is up, and his theme unwritten, or scrambled through in a poor and meagre way. It is well to make up our mind that there is always a next thing to be done, whether in work or play; and that the next thing, be it ever so trifling, is the right thing; not so much for its own sake, perhaps, as because, each time we insist upon ourselves doing the next thing, we gain power in the management of that unruly filly, Inclination.

Do the Chief Thing.—But to find 'ye nexte thynge' is not, after all, so simple. It is often a matter of selection. There are twenty letters to write, a dozen commissions to do, a score of books you want to read, and much ordering and arranging of shelves and drawers that you would like to plunge into at once.

It has been amusingly said, "Never do to-day what you can put off till to-morrow." The dilatory, procrastinating person rejoices over a counsel he can follow! But not so fast, friend; this easy-going rule of life means "putting first things first." Now, the power of ordering, organising, one's work which this implies distinguishes between a person of intelligence and the unintelligent person who lets himself be swamped by details. The latter will grind steadily through the twenty letters, say, just as they come to hand.

He has to leave his correspondence unfinished; and the three or four letters which it was necessary to answer by return are left over for another day.

The power to distinguish what must be done at once, from what may be done, comes pretty much by habit. At first it requires attention and thought. But mind and body get into the way of doing most things; and the person, whose mind has the habit of singling out the important things and doing them first, saves much annoyance to himself and others, and has gained in Integrity.

The Habit of Finishing.—What is worth beginning is worth finishing, and what is worth doing is worth doing well. Do not let yourself begin to make a dozen things, all of them tumbling about unfinished in your box. Of course there are fifty reasons for doing the new thing; but here is another case where we must curb that filly, Inclination. It is worth while to make ourselves go on with the thing we are doing until it is finished. Even so, there is the temptation to scamp in order to get at the new thing; but let us do each bit of work as perfectly as we know how, remembering that each thing we turn out is a bit of ourselves, and we must leave it whole and complete; for this is Integrity.

The idle, the careless, and the volatile may be engaging enough as companions, but they do not turn out honest work, and are not building up for themselves integrity of character. This rests upon the foundations of diligence, attention, and perseverance. In the end, integrity makes for gaiety, because the person who is honest about his work has time to play, and is not secretly vexed by the remembrance of things left undone or ill done.

Integrity in Use of Time

Drifters and Dawdlers.—It is a bad thing to think that time is our own to do what we like with. We are all employed; we all have duties, and a certain share of our time must be given to those duties. It is astonishing how much time there is in a day, and how many things we can get in if we have a mind. It is also astonishing how a day, a week, or a year may slip through our fingers, and nothing done. We say we have done no harm, that we have not meant to do wrong. We have simply let ourselves drift. Boys or girls will drift through life at school, men or women through life in the world, effecting nothing, because they have not taken hold. They fail in examinations, in their professions, in the duty of providing for a family, in the duty of serving their town or their country, not because they are without brains, nor because they are vicious, but because they do not see that to use time is a duty.

They dawdle through the working day, hoping that some one will make them do the thing they ought. Now, this is a delusion. No one can make even a little child do things. If he is obedient, it is because he makes himself obey; if he is diligent, he makes himself work, and not all the king's Horses and all the king's men can make the dawdler diligent; he himself must make himself do the thing he ought at the right time. This power of making oneself work is a fine thing. Every effort makes the next easier, and, once we mount upon that easy nag, Habit, why, it is a real satisfaction to do the day's work in the day, and be free to enjoy the day's leisure.

Cribbing Time.—Some people dearly like to be going on with a little job of their own in the time which should have a fixed employment. The girl who is sewing has a story-book at hand. The youth tries chemical experiments when he should be 'reading.' The time may be used for quite a good end, but it is 'cribbed' from the occupation to which it belongs.

We cannot, as you will see presently, afford to have cracks in our character. Integrity forbids this sort of meanness. Every piece of work has its due time. The time which is due to an occupation belongs to that, and must not be used for any other purpose. Dick Swiveller is an amusing fellow enough as he entertains himself by poising the ruler on his chin, shooting pens at a mark, and bantering the 'Marchioness' during his office hours. But that is why Dick found himself where he was, and made such a poor thing of his life; he had not got it into his by no means stupid head that work and time have anything to do with each other.

Integrity in Material. Honesty.—"My duty towards my neighbour is—to keep my hands from picking and stealing"; so says the Church Catechism, and this is the common acceptation of the word honesty. We should, of course, all scorn to take what belongs to another person, and feel ourselves safe so far, anyway, as this charge goes.

Strange things come to light from time to time: we hear of a man, who has lived for sixty years; a respected and prosperous citizen, a gentleman, not only in position, but in the sense of being an honourable man; and when this man is sixty, he embezzles large sums of money, apparently for the first time. Now, people do not go down in this way the first time.

It is the vessel with a leak that sinks; and that leak, the breach in a man's integrity, may have existed since his boyhood without sinking him until he was in the rough sea of a great temptation.

We must be careful in our money dealings, all the more, the more we are trusted. Honest persons are scrupulous about giving a right account of change, for example.

One caution we must bear in mind.—we may not spend what we have not got. Our allowance may come at the end of the month, but we must wait to lay it out until it is actually in hand. Mr. Micawber was right in theory if not in practice, and who should know if not he? "Annual income twenty pounds, annual expenditure nineteen, nineteen six, result happiness. Annual income twenty pounds, annual expenditure twenty pounds ought and six, result misery."

The schoolboy who gets 'tick' or borrows from his schoolmates grows into the man who is behind-hand with his accounts, and that means, not only an injury to the persons who have supplied him with their goods, but a grave injury to himself. He becomes so harassed and worried with the pressure of debts here and debts there, that he has no room in his mind for thoughts that are worth while. His loss of integrity is a leak which sinks his whole character.

Small Debts.—In this connection we should bear in mind the duty of promptness in paying small debts. We commonly have the money for them, but do not take the trouble to pay. A tradesman, say, has sent in a bill for eighteenpence half a dozen times, he paying the postage. The debtor will not take the pains to transmit the small amount. Again, a girl will let herself be asked seven times for a sum of threepence. No person of integrity allows himself in this kind of negligence. That it is troublesome and annoying to other people is not the worst of the mischief. That beautiful whole which we call integrity is marred by sins of negligence.

Bargains.—There is another failure in integrity which people do not realise to be as debasing as debt, though probably its effects are as bad; and that is the bargain-hunting in which even right-minded persons allow themselves.

It arises from an error in thought. People set out with the idea that they must get the best that is to be had at the lowest possible price; and out of this idea arise the unseemly scramble to be seen at 'Sales'; the waste of time, temper, and health in going from shop to shop in search of the 'cheapest and best' article; the dishonest waste of the time of the assistants in all these shops—a waste for which, of course, the customers pay in the end: and to these is often added the fretful disappointment of a 'Purple jar'; a fine and showy thing is brought home which fails to bear the tests of close examination and calm judgment. The whole thing might be set right, and the ways of trade mended, by the exercise of clear judgment informed by integrity of purpose.

What we want is—not the best thing that can be had at the lowest possible price—but a thing suitable for our purpose, at a price which we can afford to pay and know to be just.

Looked at from this point of view, the whole matter is simplified; we are no longer perpetually running round, harassing ourselves and wearing out other people in the search after bargains. Every purchase becomes a simple, straightforward duty. We feel it to be a matter of integrity to deal with tradesmen of our own neighbourhood, so far as they can supply us. If they fail to do so, we are at liberty to go further afield; but in this case, we soon fix upon the distant tradesman who can supply our needs, and escape the snare of bargain-hunting.

There is a further risk in bargain-hunting of which we should be aware. Nothing is cheap that we do not want; and the temptation to buy a thing for which no need has yet arisen, because it is a bargain, leads to a waste of money wanted for other uses, and to the accumulation of meaningless objects in our rooms. It is worth while to remember that space is the most precious and also the most pleasing thing in a house or room; and that even a small room becomes spacious if it is not crowded with useless objects.

Our Neighbour's Property.—Another point of integrity is care for our neighbour's property. To love our neighbour as ourselves means that we shall be at least as careful in the use of his property as in that of our own. We all borrow books, whether from public libraries or from our friends, and it behoves us to take as much care of the books we borrow as of our own treasured possessions. We do not spot the covers by laying them in damp places, nor curl them before the fire, nor strain the binding by marking our place with some big object.

If we are walking in public gardens, we remember that it is not an easy thing to keep the grass nice in such places, and take heed not to walk on the edges. We are careful of the school property if we are at school, of the college property if at college; for these matters belong to integrity. Care in small matters makes us trustworthy in greater. When we come to be trusted with the property of others, whether in money or material, we are on our guard against wastefulness, carelessness, extravagance, because integrity requires that we should take care of and make the most of whatever property is put into our hands. We may not allow ourselves to waste even a stick of sealing-wax for amusement.

Borrowed Property.—The question of borrowing falls under the head of the care we owe to other people's property. From a black-lead pencil to an umbrella, young people borrow without stint; and there is so much community of property and good fellowship among them that the free use of each other's belongings is perhaps hardly to be objected to. One word, though, in the name of honesty! What we borrow we must return promptly, the thing being none the worse for our use of it. No degree of community of life excuses us from this duty. The friend we borrow from may take no heed of the fact that we do not return the object; but we suffer in our wholeness, our integrity, from all such lapses.

As we have seen, our work, our time, the material or property of which we have the handling, are all matters for the just and honest use of which we are accountable. We may be guilty of many lapses which no one notices, but every lapse makes an imperfection in our own character. We have less integrity after a lapse than before it; and the habit of permitting ourselves in small dishonesties, whether in the way of waste of time, slipshod work, or injured property, prepares the way for a ruinous downfall in afterlife. But we need fear no fall, for integrity is, with us, a part of 'ourselves,' and only asks of us a hearing.

Chapter XVIII Opinions: Justice In Thought

Three 'Opinions.—When we say, 'I think it will be fine to-morrow,' we express an opinion. When we say, 'Jones is first-rate; you should hear his lectures on the Anabasis,' again we express an opinion, though the 'I think' is left out. Even if we say,' Let us walk to Purley Woods.' what we really mean is, 'I think it would be pleasant to walk to Purley Woods.' We cannot escape from thinking, however much we try; and the thought we have about person or thing is our opinion. People often say 'I think' when they mean 'I wish'; for really to have an opinion about such a matter as the weather, for example, means that one has noticed weather signs and is able to judge. Therefore, when we want an opinion about the weather that is worth having, we consult the gardener, or a farmer, or sailor, for the business of these men has made them observant of weather signs.

When we say, 'Jones is first-rate,' it may mean that we have enjoyed the lectures of that master and like him personally; if so, our opinion is worth having; or it may only mean that we have caught up a catchword of the class. Everybody speaks well of Mr. Jones, and we only join in the cry. This sort of opinion is quite worthless, and would shift round like a weather-cock if some ill-natured boy raised a contrary opinion about Jones, as, 'What queer ties he wears!' The boy who lives upon chance opinions does not look at the relative importance of those he gets hold of. Jones's ties and Jones's lectures are all one to him, and poor Mr. Jones rises or sinks in his scales with every chance remark he hears about him.

If Mary says, 'Let's go to Purley Woods,' her opinion is sincere enough. She remembers the primroses of former years, and inclination influences her thoughts. We get a real opinion, his very own, from the person who wants something; but it is not a safe opinion, because our wishes drown our judgment, and we rush headlong after the thing we want. This is the history of the youth who falls into bad ways. His opinions are subservient to his wishes, and he thinks only that which it pleases him to believe.

An Opinion worth having.—We may gather three rules, then, as to an opinion that is worth the having. We must have thought about the subject and know something about it, as a gardener does about the weather; it must be our own opinion, and not caught up as a parrot catches up its phrases; and lastly, it must be disinterested, that is, it must not be influenced by our inclination.

But, 'Why need we have opinions at all,' you are inclined to ask, 'if they mean such a lot of trouble?' Just because we are persons. Every person has many opinions, either his own, honestly thought out, or picked up from his pet newspaper, or from his favourite companion. The person who thinks out his opinions modestly and carefully is doing his duty as truly as if he helped to save a life. There is no more or less about duty; and it is a great part of our work in life to do our duty in our thoughts and form just opinions.

Opinions on Trial.—As you know, we have a mentor within us, about which I shall have to speak more fully later; but, once we get into the habit of bringing our thoughts before Conscience, we shall soon be able to distinguish as to the right or wrong of an opinion before we utter it.

'Fads.'—'But such a fuss about what one thinks is a fad, and people with fads are a nuisance'; you say, adding, 'I hate fellows that have notions; they never let you alone.' It is quite true, fads are tiresome; and for one of two reasons—either the person with the fad thinks too much about it, and does not trouble himself to form opinions upon a hundred other matters of equal importance; or, he has taken up his opinion without full, all-round knowledge of the subject. 'Fads' are tiresome, but some men seem called to be faddists, in so far as they are persons ruled by one idea, because it is laid upon them to bring about a reform.

Thus were Wilberforce and Clarkson occupied with the question of the slave-trade; Plimsoll, with that of unseaworthy vessels; Howard, with the question of prison discipline. Every great missionary, every great reformer, has his mind so largely occupied with one subject that there is little room for others. Such men as these are not faddists: they do not take extreme or one-sided views, though one subject occupies them to the exclusion of others.

But only a few of us are called to give ourselves up to some work of reformation; and therefore the rest of us must not allow ourselves to be occupied too much with one set of ideas. The faddist is the person who talks and thinks about one subject; but if, instead of merely talking and thinking, he devotes his life to one good end, he becomes one of the world's workers, a reformer.

Matters upon which we must form Opinions.—We must all get opinions about our own country, about other countries, about occupations, amusements, about the books we read, the persons we hear of, the persons we meet, the pictures we see, the characters we read of, whether in fiction or history; in fact, there is nothing which passes before our minds about which it is not our business to form just and reasonable opinions. That we may be able to do this, we spend a good many years, while we are young, in getting the knowledge which should enable us to think. When we are grown-up, also, it is still necessary to spend time in getting knowledge, but few can give the chief part of the day to this labour, as we all have the chance of doing while we are young. This chance is, however, wasted upon young people who read to learn up facts towards an examination. The lectures we hear, the books we read, are of no use to us, except as they make us think.

When Numa was offered the kingship of Rome, he had thought about the subject. He said that he had no special gifts of education or birth to fit him for rule: but the Romans, too, thought, and expressed their opinion. Would he not take the crown, they asked, to save his country from misrule? That question contained an opinion which Numa had not considered. There were, no doubt, those who might wish to govern Rome for selfish ends; the opinion of the Romans was a just one, he would be guided by it, so he became king. Here we get a very good example of how opinion should rule us in life. We must think about things, about everything, for ourselves; think out the responsibility of judge and general, king and minister, so that, should we be suddenly asked to take any of these positions, we shall know what to answer.

Of course, we should say, as did Numa in the first place, that we have not had the experience or education to fit us for such high office; and, of course again, we shall not be asked! But it is a great thing to have realised what other people have to do and to think about; to have gone with Colonel Younghusband to Thibet, to have defended Port Arthur with General Stoessel. Thus we get opinions which are worth holding about war, patriotism, the duties of a public servant, and many other matters. What is more, we endeavour to figure to ourselves the responsibilities and purposes of parents, masters, or whatever chief is placed above us; and, when we give an opinion about their actions, it is likely to be a just one.

As for the clergyman and his teaching, it is, as in other cases, only as we care about the things of religion and think much about them, that we have the right to give opinions.

Opinions about Books.—In the same way, we must be just in what we think about books. Trashy books are not worth the trouble of thinking about, and therefore they are not worth reading; but a book that is worth reading, whether it be a novel or a homily, contains the best thought of the writer, and we can only get at his meaning by serious thinking.

As a fact, the books which make us think, the poems which we ponder, the lives of men which we consider, are of more use to us than volumes of good counsel. We read what boys call 'good books,' thinking how good they are, and how good we are to read them! Then it all goes, because the writer has put what he had to say so plainly that we have not had to think for ourselves; and it seems to be a law in the things of life and mind that we do not get anything for our own unless we work for it. It is a case of lightly come, lightly go. That is why we are told of our Lord that "without a parable spake He not unto them." He told the people stories which they might allow to pass lightly through their minds as an interest of the moment, or which they might think upon, form opinions upon, and find in them a guide to the meaning of their lives.

Your opinions about books and other things will very likely be wrong, and you will yourself correct them by and by when you have read more, thought more, know more. Indeed, no wise person, however old, is sure of his opinions. He holds them fast, but he holds them modestly; and, should he be like Numa, convinced that the opinion of others is more sound than his own, why, he has no shame in what we call 'changing his mind.' "We are none of us infallible, not even the youngest!" was said by a wise and witty man, who knew that young people are apt to be cocksure—that is, to take up opinions at second hand and stick to them obstinately. The word opinion literally means 'a thinking'; what I think, with modesty and hesitation, and not what I am certain-sure about.

Our Duty with regard to Opinion.—We begin to see what is our duty about opinions. In the first place, we must have 'a thinking' about an immense number of things. So we must read, mark, learn, and inwardly digest; must listen and consider, being sure that one of the purposes we are in the world for is, to form right opinions about all matters that come in our way.

Next, we must avoid the short road to opinions; we must not pick them up ready made at any street-corner; and next, we must learn—and this is truly difficult, a matter that takes us all our lives to recognise a fallacy, that is, an argument which appears sound but does not bear examination. For example, 'We are all born equal'; so we are, with equal right to the pure air, to the beauty of earth and sky, to the protection of the laws of our country, and much besides. But the sense in which men use the phrase is,—that we are all born with an equal right to the property that is in the world. That is absurd, as the very word 'property' shows us: property means ownership, it is the own possession of the persons who hold it. We are ashamed even of a cuckoo that appropriates the own nest of another bird. But the question of fallacies is a big one, and all we need bear in mind now is, that popular cries, whether in the school or the country, very often rest upon fallacies or false judgments. So we must look all round the notions we take up.

Next, before forming an opinion about anyone in place and power, we must try to realise and understand that person's position and all that belongs to it.

One more thing, when we have arrived at an opinion we must remember that it is only 'a thinking,' and must hold it with diffidence; but because it is our thinking, our very own property that has come to us through pondering, we must hold it firmly, unless, like Numa, we are convinced that another view is sounder than our own.

But, once again, we may not be sluggish in this matter of opinion. It is the chief part of justice to think just thoughts about the matters that come before us, and the best and wisest men are those who have brought their minds to bear upon the largest number of subjects, and have learned to think just thoughts about them all. It is a comfort to know that Justice, that lord of the heart, is always at hand to weigh the opinions we allow ourselves to take up.

Chapter XIX Principles: Justice In Motive

Principles, Bad and Good.—There is a certain class of opinions of which we must take special heed. Sometimes we get them from others, sometimes we think them out for ourselves; but, in either case, we make them our own because we act upon them. These opinions rule our conduct, and they are called Principles because they are princeps, first or chief in importance of all the opinions we hold. We speak of a well-principled boy, a man of principle, a young woman of high principles; but everyone has principles—that is, everyone has a few chief and leading opinions upon which every bit of his conduct is based. The boy who is late for roll-call, cribs his translation, shirks both games and work, may not know it, but he is acting upon principle. His principles may not even have found their way into words, but, if we fish for them, they come up something in this form: 'What's the good of doing more than you can help?' 'What's the good of hurrying a fellow? I'm not going to hustle!' 'It's all rot anyway, I shall never have to talk Latin.' These, and the like, are the principles on which his whole conduct is based. He has allowed himself in thinking the thoughts of the slothful and negligent until he cannot get away from them. People call him an unprincipled boy, but probably there are no unprincipled persons; he is a boy who has deliberately chosen bad principles upon which to build all his conduct.

Another fellow is punctual, prompt, and diligent in his work; he hardly knows why himself, but he has gathered, by degrees, certain principles upon which he cannot help acting. He remembers that he owes it to his parents and teachers to work; that what he owes, he ought to do; it is his duty. Again, he recognises that knowledge is delightful, and that his business while he is young is to get all he can of it. He sees, too, that his future career depends upon his present work; that he is making in the schoolroom the man that is to be. He may have heard such things as these said at home or at school, or they may have come into his head, he does not know how; but, anyway, he has taken them for his chief things, his principles, and he acts upon them always. In both cases the conduct of the boys is ruled by their principles; to account for the difference between the two we must go back to their choice of principles; and the choosing of these is a very important part of life.

How to Distinguish.—The traveller who arrives at a foreign station or port is often both amused and annoyed at the number of porters who clamour for his luggage, the number of hotel omnibuses which try to get possession of him. Just so clamorous and tiresome are the principles that are forced upon us by almost everyone we meet, by the very books and papers we read, the pictures we look at.

From the first we may detect a difference. Good principles are offered to us in an unobtrusive way, with little force and little urging. Bad principles are clamorous and urgent, drowning the voice of conscience by noisy talk, inviting us to go the way we are inclined and to do the thing we like.

Our Principles 'Writ Large.'—It is an interesting fact, that, though a person's principles of conduct are often not put into words, they are always written in characters of their own. Everyone carries his rules of conduct writ large upon his countenance, that he who runs may read. It is well to remember this, because, though we may like a boy who has slothfulness or self-indulgence, envy or malice, dishonesty, cruelty, or greed, written about his eyes and mouth, yet we like him with a difference. We are on our guard against the particular bad principle which he chooses to follow, and while we may enjoy his wit or cleverness, we do not admit him to intimacy, or allow him a voice in our own choice of principles of conduct.

'But what are my principles?' you say; 'I'm sure I don't know'; and, indeed, we need not trouble ourselves much to find out; this is a case where lookers-on see most of the game, and some of the youngest persons we know are better acquainted with our principles than we are ourselves. Our part is simply to take heed; to ask ourselves, now and then, why we are always running after Jones, for instance. Is it that he flatters us? puts false ideas of manliness, perhaps foul ideas of pleasure, into our heads? If so, our principles are in fault. We choose a friend who will minister to what is bad in us. Do we stick to Brown because 'he's an honest old chap,' and tells us straight when he thinks we are silly or lazy? Good for us if so. Do we join with other fellows in calling

Smith a sneak, a cad, or a muff, when he has distinguished himself in some school study? If so, we must be careful; envy is perhaps the principle which chooses that no one shall be better than ourselves.

We gather our principles unconsciously; but they are our masters; and it is our business every now and then to catch one of them, look it in the face, and question ourselves as to the manner of conduct such a principle must bring forth.

Chapter XX Justice To Ourselves: Self-Ordering

My Duty to Myself.—We know that we owe justice to our neighbour, that is, to those about us and those beneath us, and those on our own level; to our own family, our servants, the people we employ, and at whose shops we deal; and to all those whom we know as relations and friends; to a gradually widening circle of persons which comes at last to include all the world.

There remains one person to whom we owe a debt of justice, and many lives are wasted because this person is unjustly treated. The friend whom we are apt to neglect when we are dealing out justice is ourself "My duty toward my neighbour," says the Catechism, "is to keep my body in temperance, soberness, and chastity,"—and this, partly because, if we neglect this rule of life, we become injurious and offensive to our neighbours, and partly because we owe a first duty to that closest of all neighbours, our very self.

Some people do great things in the world—they save lives, write books, build hospitals; but the person who orders his own body properly also does a service to the world. In the first place, a good man or woman, whose body is kept under the threefold rule I have quoted, adorns the world, helps to make it beautiful, just by being there; and, in the next place, both evil and good are catching. One unchaste boy in a school will make many who think and speak of matters they should never allow their thoughts to touch; so a single chaste boy who puts all such talk away from him, will not listen to it or allow it, helps to make his whole school chaste. Few things are more sad than to see a beautiful body, made for health, strength, and happiness—made in the image of God—injured and destroyed by bad habits.

Temperance avoids every Excess.—Of the three rules of life by which our bodies should be ordered, perhaps temperance is least understood by young people. We think of Burne-Jones's stately figure of Temperantia pouring pure water out of her pitcher to quench the flames, of temperance societies, and so on; and thus we come to associate temperance with abstinence from drink. That certainly is one kind of temperance; but the boy who is greedy, the girl who is slothful, are also intemperate, as you may tell by watching them walk down the street. They have not the springing step, the alert look, which belong to Temperance.

One may even be intemperate in the matter of restlessness. We may carry games, cramming for an examination, novel-reading, bridge, any interest which absorbs us, to excess; and all excess is intemperance. It means that the person who indulges in excesses has lost control over himself, so that there is some one thing he must have or must do, at whatever loss to himself or inconvenience to others. Once we are aware of this danger of intemperance, even in things innocent in themselves, why, we keep watch. We don't go on to a fifth jam tart (!); we get up early; we brace ourselves with a cold bath and a vigorous walk; we use muscular movements, dumb-bells, or Indian clubs in our rooms. We are ashamed if we find ourselves running to fat and not to muscle, and knit ourselves up by means of more exercise, less lounging; we are careful, too, not to have a second or a third helping when we like the dish. By the way, that is rather a good rule. If one helping of cold mutton is enough, there is proof positive that one helping of roast lamb, let us say, is also enough. We must beware of becoming gross, because gross in body means slow of wits, dull in thought. We can all be temperate without putting ourselves under any particular course of diet, (we need not live upon apples and nuts and the like); indeed, perhaps temperance is best shown in eating temperately of that which is set before us, however nice it may be.

Soberness does not seek Excitement.—Soberness appears to mean in the first place, according to the derivation of the word, being removed from drunkenness. Never was it easier for young persons to remain sober by never tasting alcohol than it is to-day, when so many good and thoughtful people, men of affairs, people in what is called 'society,' drink water and not wine.

We have heard of that nation of ancient Greece, the custom of whose great men it was to give drink to their slaves, in order that their children might see how absurd and how disgusting a drunken man becomes; they did this, in order that their young people might grow up loathing drunkenness as the vice of slaves. Christian people may not cause others to offend; but, alas! we do not want for examples. Even children who live in towns see something of the horror of drunkenness, and they wonder at it. How can Jervis, such a nice man when he is sober, go on drinking until at last he falls, a horrid object, by the roadside? This is a question worth asking, because the whole history of drunkenness, and indeed of every vice that becomes a man's master, hangs upon the answer.

Self-Indulgence leads to Vice.—A man begins to drink for pretty much the same reason that takes a boy to the tuck-shop. He wants to indulge himself with something agreeable, and thinks there is 'no harm' in a glass of beer or wine. Now, 'no harm' is a dangerous sign-post to follow. It points to a broad road upon which there are many gay travellers; and the going is easy, because it is downhill all the way. This is the road of self-indulgence; and whenever we have to justify anything we do to ourselves by saying, 'There's no harm in it,' we may be pretty sure we are on the downward grade. Our only chance then is to struggle back by the uphill track of duty. The person who persists on the easy downgrade, amused by the song and laugh of gay comrades, and choosing to go the way that gives him no trouble, comes by and by to a parting of the ways; to the four cross-roads where the companions divide.

The Parting of the Ways.—At this point, they lose their gaiety, and hurry away by one or other cross-road with the eagerness of men engaged on a matter of life or death; so they are, on a matter of death but not of life.

They are engaged upon the gradual injuring, the slow killing, of their beautiful and noble body, that great gift of God to each of us; upon the soddening and weakening of the wonderful brain we use when we think and know, when we love and pray. The greatest master in the world cannot produce any but cracked and feeble tones out of an instrument whose cords are worn and injured; so, however brilliant the man who lets himself go down either of the four crossroads of vice, he loses all the promise and power of his genius once he has injured his brain by vicious habits; for we can do no thinking or acting that is worth while without a sound brain.

The Fate of the Drunkard.—The first of these cross-roads leads to drunkenness, and the man turns into it when he passes the stage of self-indulgence; that is, when he no longer drinks because it pleases him, but drinks because he must. That is the dreadful penalty man or woman pays for self-indulgence. A craving habit is set up which very few indeed are able to resist; conscience, the help of friends, even faint and feeble prayers, appear to be of no avail. The poor wretch drinks because he is miserable; for the moment, drink makes him happy because it stimulates him. It causes a quick current of blood to flow through his brain; his thoughts are brisk and life is pleasant. But, alas! a time of depression follows immediately. The man cannot think and cannot feel, is very sorry for himself, sheds maudlin tears, cannot endure the burden of existence, and flies again to the enemy. He tells you he must drink, that it is beyond flesh and blood to endure the maddening craving that consumes him.

He drinks his health and his wealth, his friends and his profession; he is a wreck in body and mind, and men wonder how he lives at all—if such manner of crawling about in obscure ways can be called life.

Is this a just return to God for the wonderful endowments of body and mind this man has received? Is it just to his family and neighbours to make himself a burden and an offence? Is it just to himself—that wonderful, beautiful self, with all its powers of heart, mind and soul, of which it is everyone's first business to make the most?

What would one say of a young man who received as a birthday gift a costly repeater, and immediately opened the case and poured vitriol into the works? You would say he was a fool or a madman to destroy what cost much money to buy, much thought and delicate labour to construct. What, then, of him who destroys that far more wonderful mechanism of brain and body, by means of which he thinks, lives, and feels?

You think it would be a merciful thing to place such offenders in a madhouse with other lunatics : but God does not allow us to escape the responsibility of choosing between right and wrong, even though we always choose the wrong, and continually offend against Him, ourselves, and our neighbour.

'En parole.'—That thought makes our responsibility for ordering our bodies very great. just because we can, if we like, do the wrong thing, we have to be all the more on honour to choose the right. The French have a pretty expression which we use in the case of prisoners of war. The prisoner is allowed a great deal of liberty en parole, that is, if he will give his word not to try to escape. So binding is the word of a gentleman, both in France, England, and elsewhere, that the prisoner of war, who may be clever enough to contrive ways to get out of the most strongly guarded cell, cannot escape from his own word. He may walk about the streets, go here and there, do what he likes; but there is an invisible wall, confining him which he cannot pass beyond, and this wall is no more than his word—he is en parole.

This is very much the way that God treats us in the matter of self-indulgence. The way is open to us down the Broad Road, but we are hindered by our parole. We may not have given our word out loud, but the word is only a sign, it means 'on my honour'; and we are all on our honour to safeguard ourselves from ruin, however easy and inviting may be the way thereto.

The difficulty is, that many young people go down the. Broad Road without knowing they are on it; they do not stop to think and look about them: they say, 'It does not matter'—this little pleasure or the other—and they have lost their honour before they know it.

Excitement.—There are some other ways of becoming intoxicated besides that of strong drink. Whatever produces an unnatural flow of blood to the brain has some of the qualities of intoxication, and is sure to be followed by depression when that extra flow of blood has left the brain, impoverished. We call this sort of intoxication excitement, and it is no harm as an occasional thing; but persons may come to want excitement every day, every hour, and may mope and be dull without it; they want excitement for the same reason that the drunkard wants drink, and for the same reason, too, the more they have the more they want.

They cannot enjoy the company of their friends without a great deal of wild laughing and talking. They want to be always with people who will 'make them laugh,' however unseemly the jest. They are uneasy if they cannot go to every party of pleasure within reach. They find no games sufficiently exciting unless they be games of chance; and, in the end, the gambling habit may settle upon them—a habit as ruinous, if not as disgusting, as the drink habit.

He who would keep his body in soberness must avoid all these excesses. I do not say he must never be excited, because whatever pleases or troubles us very much, excites us; but that is quite a different thing from going after excitement, being uneasy if something exciting is not happening all the time.

The Ways of the Glutton—Circe.—The other byways branching off the Broad Road lead to the quarters of Gluttony, Sloth, and Unchastity. Persons who break parole with regard to the ordering of their bodies find their way down one or other of the four. Some persons hover between the four cross-roads, now going down one, now another, and now another; but others—like the drunkard, the gourmand, the slothful person, and the unclean—choose their way and stick to it, letting themselves be lost, body and soul, in the pursuit of some lust of the body.

You remember how Circe turned the hardy seamen of Ulysses into swine. I cannot do better than quote the tale in the words of Nathaniel Hawthorne. Circe, you remember, met the wandering mariners who had been drawn into her palace by the sounds of pleasant singing. The beautiful lady of the island came forward, smiling and stretching out her hand, and bade the whole party welcome. "'You see,' she said, 'that I know all about your troubles; and you cannot doubt that I desire to make you happy for as long a time as you may remain with me. For this purpose, my honoured guests, I have ordered a banquet to be prepared. Fish, fowl and flesh, roasted and in luscious stews, and seasoned, I trust, to all your tastes, are ready to be served up. If your appetites tell you it is dinner-time, then come with me to the festal saloon.' At this kind invitation, the hungry mariners were quite overjoyed; and one of them . . . assured their hospitable hostess that any hour of the day was dinner-time with them . . .

"They entered a magnificent saloon . . . Each of the strangers was invited to sit down; and there they were . . . sitting on two-and-twenty cushioned and canopied thrones . . . Then you might have seen the guests nodding, winking with one eye, and leaning from one throne to another, to communicate their satisfaction in hoarse whispers. 'Our good hostess has made kings of us all,' said one. 'Ha, do you smell the feast?' . . . 'I hope,' said another, 'it will be mainly good substantial joints, sirloins, spare ribs, and hinder quarters, without too many kickshaws. If I thought the good lady would not take it amiss, I should call for a fat slice of fried bacon to begin with.' But the beautiful woman clapped her hands; and immediately there entered a train of two-and-twenty serving men, bringing dishes of the richest food, all hot from the kitchen fire, and sending up such a steam that it hung like a cloud below the crystal dome of the saloon. An equal number of attendants brought great flagons of wine of various kinds, some of which sparkled as it was poured out and went bubbling down the throat . . . Whatever little fault they might find with the dishes, they sat at dinner a prodigiously long while, and it would really have made you ashamed to see how they swilled down the liquor and gobbled up the food. They sat on golden thrones, to be sure, but they behaved like pigs in a sty . . . It brings a blush to my face to reckon up, in my own mind, what mountains of meat and pudding, what gallons of wine, these two-and-twenty gormandisers ate and drank. They forgot all about their homes . . . and everything else except this banquet at which they wanted to keep feasting forever. But at length they began to give over, from mere incapacity to hold any more. . .

"They all left off eating, and leaned back on their thrones, with such a stupid and helpless aspect as made them ridiculous to behold. When their hostess saw this, she laughed aloud; so did her four damsels; so did the two-and-twenty serving men that bore the dishes, and their two-and-twenty followers that poured out the wine. 'Wretches!' cried she, 'you have abused a lady's hospitality; and in this princely saloon your behaviour has been suited to a hog-pen. You are already swine in everything but the human form . . . Assume your proper shapes, gormandisers, and begone to the sty!' Uttering these last words, she waved her wand, stamping her foot imperiously; each of the guests was struck aghast at beholding, instead of his comrades in human shape, one-and-twenty hogs sitting on the same number of golden thrones . . . It looked so intolerably absurd to see hogs on cushioned thrones, that they made haste to wallow down upon all fours, like other swine. They tried to groan and beg for mercy, but forthwith emitted the most awful grunting and squealing that ever came out of swinish throats . . . Dear me! what pendulous ears they had! what little red eyes, half buried in fat! and what long snouts instead of Grecian noses!"

Interests in Life.—If we wish to do justice to 'ourselves,' by keeping our bodies in temperance, soberness, and chastity, we must begin with our thoughts, remembering that in this matter we can be heroes, though nobody knows. Of each of us it is true, that

"A charge to keep I have,
A God to glorify."

And what a splendid reason we have in this for taking care of our thoughts! People say, 'Take care of the pennies, and the pounds will take care of themselves'; but far more true it is, 'Take care of the thoughts, and the acts will take care of themselves.'

If we would keep in soberness, we must work, read, and think; more—we must be thankful. There is no person's life which would not be exceedingly interesting if he lived it fully; and he whose life is full of interests does not seek excitement, from drink or other sources.

The person who has interests gives them to everybody about him. The boy who sets up a picture post-card album sets a fashion which his school follows; and so with every interest in life—poetry, history, or any class of natural objects.

Have interests and give them to others, and you are fairly safe from the desire for excitement which leads to drunkenness. Interests, too, will shield us all from the degradation of gluttony. The child who watches his brother's plate, and longs for what he thinks is the better helping, is a child who has nothing better to think of.

Slothfulness.—The boy or girl who has interests is not a sluggard. Hockey, tennis, cricket, long walks, football, rowing, skating,—all these help to give him the vigorous body to which it would be a bore to lie abed or lounge about. By the way, one must not let oneself be the 'fat boy' in Pickwick, or anywhere else! When persons grow fat it is not always that they eat too much, though that may have something to do with it; but it is certainly because they do not take enough exercise, and therefore run to fat and not to muscle. Young men at college, boys at public schools, do not let themselves get fat; to do so would be 'bad form.' So, if we find this unpleasant symptom developing in ourselves, we had better consider whether slothfulness is not the cause—a horrid vice for which nobody would be content to wreck his life.

Uncleanness.—One Road to Ruin remains to be considered, the last and the worst of the four crossroads, that which leads to the deadly sin of uncleanness. Here, too, is a sin that is committed in thought: we have done the offence when we have thought it. We know the danger of allowing ourselves to be talked to by persons of unclean mind, and the dreadful danger of imaging ourselves things we may read. We cannot help coming across what may lead to evil imaginings; perhaps if we could there would be no battle to fight, and then we could not obey the command, "Glorify God with your bodies." Every one of us must get the power to draw down the blinds, as it were, not to let imagination picture the unclean thing. For once imagination behaves like Peeping Tom, it becomes a fight to keep out impure thoughts. "Watch and pray, that ye enter not into temptation," says our Lord and Master; watch, that is, look at the thoughts you let in, and shut the door upon intruders. Pray every day and every night with the confidence of a child speaking to his father,—"Our Father which art in Heaven, lead us not into temptation"; and then, think no more of the matter, but live all you can the beautiful, full life of body and mind, heart and soul, for which our Father has made provision.

PART IV—Vocation

Plans.—'I'm going to be a chimney sweep and wear a tall hat,' says the little Frankfort child (who rarely sees tall hats excepting on chimney sweeps), 'I'm going to be a cabby and drive a hansom,' 'I'm going to be a general and fight a great battle,' I'm going to be a nurse and mind a dear little baby,' 'I'm going to be "mother" and have little girls and boys of my own.' say the children; and they change their minds every week, because all sorts of trades and professions interest them, and they figure to themselves how nice it would be to belong to each.

The growing boy or girl leaves all that behind as one of the 'silly' ways of the little ones; but, by and by, wonder begins to stir in a boy's head as to what particular bit of the world's work he will be called to do. It is good and pleasant to think that the work, whatever it is, will be really his, and will also be world-work upon some task that is wanted. The girl's heart, too, reaches out wistfully: she wants a task, a bit of work for herself in the world that is wanted; that is the thing that both boy and girl desire. They understand the words of a great man, who said, "The thing worth living for is to be of use." The boy knows he must go out into the world and do something definite. For a girl, too, there are many careers, as they are called, opened in these days; and, if a girl is only called to the sweet place of a home daughter, all she need ask for herself is 'to be of use,' and, perhaps, no calling will offer her more chances of usefulness.

Preparation.—Some boys know, at an early age, that they are being brought up for the navy, for example. For others, both boys and girls, their calling does not come until, perhaps, they have left college.

All callings have one thing in common—they are of use; and, therefore, a person may prepare for his calling years before he knows what it is. What sort of person is of use in the world? You think of the most brilliant and handsome of your friends, and say to yourself, 'So-and-so, anyway, is a person the world could not do without'; but you may be quite wrong. The good looks, wit and cleverness, which give boy or girl the first place in school, often enough lead to a back seat in the world; because the person with these attractive qualities may be like a vessel without ballast, at the mercy of winds and waves. None need think small things of himself and of his chances of being serviceable because he is without the attractive qualities he admires in another. Everyone has immense 'chances,' as they are called; but the business of each is to be ready for his chance. The boy who got a medal from the Royal Humane Society for saving life, was ready for his chance; he had learned to swim; and, also, he had practised himself in the alert mind and generous temper which made him see the right thing to do and do it on the instant, without thought of the labour or danger of his action; without any thought, indeed, but of the struggling, sinking creature in the water.

This illustrates what I mean; boys and girls who would be ready for their chances in life must have well-trained, active bodies; alert, intelligent, and well-informed minds; and generous hearts, ready to dare and do all for any who may need their help. It is such persons as these the world wants, persons who have worked over every acre of that vast estate of theirs which we have called Mansoul; men and women ordered in nerve and trained in muscle, self-controlled and capable; with well-stored imagination, well-practised reason; loving, just, and true.

Possibilities.—There is nothing in the wide world so precious, so necessary for the world's uses, as a boy or girl prepared on these lines for the calling, that may come; and that is why I have tried to lay before you some of the great possibilities of the Kingdom of Mansoul. These possibilities belong to each of us; and the more we realise what we can be and what we can do, the more we shall labour to answer to our call when it comes. The boy who works only that he may pass, or be the head of his class, may get what he works for; but perhaps no one is of use unless he means to be of use. This is not a thing that comes to us casually, because it is the very best thing in life; and that fellow who means to have a good time, or to be first in any race, even the race for riches, may get the thing he aims at; but do not let him deceive himself; he does not also get the honour of being of use.

"Get leave to work
In this world!—'tis the best you get at all.

Get work! get work!
Be sure 'tis better than what you work to get."
E. B. Browning.
[from Aurora Leigh, Third Book, by Elizabeth Barrett Browning]

The Habit of being of Use.—'Hell is paved with good intentions' is a dreadful saying with which we are all familiar. I suppose it means that nothing is so easy to form as a good intention, and nothing so easy to break, and that lost and ruined souls have, no doubt, formed many good intentions. Therefore we must face the fact that the intention to be of use is not enough. We must get the habit, the trick, of usefulness.

In most families there is the brother who cuts whistles and makes paper boats for the little ones, who gallops like a war-horse with Billy on his back, whom his mother trusts with messages and his father with commissions of importance; or, there is the sister to whose skirts the babies cling, who has learnt Latin enough to help her young brothers in their tasks, who can cut a garment or trim a hat for one of the maids; who writes notes for her mother and helps to nurse the baby through measles.

The 'Neverheeds.'—The heedless members of the families—Jack, in whose pocket a note is found three days after it should have been delivered, Nellie, whose parcel comes to pieces in the post—say, 'Oh, that sort of thing's no trouble to Tom and Edith; they like it, you know.' It is quite true that they like it, because we all like to do what we do well; but—nobody can do well what he has not had a good deal of practice in doing; and you may depend upon it that the useful members of a family have had much practice in being of use, that is, they have looked out for their chances.

Servant or Master?—Each of us has in his possession an exceedingly good servant or a very bad master, known as Habit. The heedless, listless person is a servant of habit; the useful, alert person is the master of a valuable habit. The fact is, that the things we do a good many times over leave some sort of impression in the very substance of our brain; and this impression, the more often it is repeated, makes it the easier for us to do the thing the next time. We know this well enough as it applies to skating, hockey, and the like. We say we want practice, or, are out of practice, and must get some practice; but we do not realise that, in all the affairs of our life, the same thing holds good. What we have practice in doing we can do with ease, while we bungle over that in which we have little practice.

The Law of Habit.—This is the law of habit, which holds good as much in doing kindnesses as in playing the piano. Both habits come by practice; and that is why it is so important not to miss a chance of doing the thing we mean to do well. We must not amuse ourselves with the notion that we have done something when we have only formed a good resolution. Power comes by doing and not by resolving, and it is habit that serves us, whether it be the habit of Latin verse or of carving. Also, and this is a delightful thing to remember, every time we do a thing helps to form the habit of doing it; and to do a thing a hundred times without missing a chance, makes the rest easy.

Our Calling.—Of this thing I am quite sure, that his calling, or, if you like to name it so, his chance, comes to the person who is ready for it. That is why the all-round preparation of body, mind, soul, and heart is necessary for the young knight who is waiting to be called. He will want every bit of himself in the royal service that is appointed him; for it is a royal service. God, who fixes the bounds of our habitation, does not leave us blundering about in search of the right thing; if He find us waiting, ready and willing, He gives us a call. It may come in the advice of a friend, or in an opening that may present itself, or in the opinion of our parents, or in some other of the quiet guidings of life that come to those who watch for them, and who are not self-willed; or it may come in a strong wish on our own part for some particular work for which we show ourselves fit.

But this, I think, we may be sure of, that his call comes as truly to a ploughman as to a peer, to a dairymaid as to a duchess. And each person, in whatever station, requires preparation for his calling; first, the general preparation of being a person ready and fit; and next, a special preparation of training and teaching for the particular work in question.

But in the first stage of our apprenticeship, the time of general preparation, while we are yet at school or college, let us remember that it rests with us to fit ourselves for our vocation. The worth of any calling depends upon its being of use; and no day need go by without giving us practice in usefulness.

Each one is wanted for the special bit of work he is fit for; and, of each, it is true that —

"Thou cam'st not to thy place by accident:
It is the very place God meant for thee."

Ourselves—Book II. Self-Direction "Order my Goings."

In Book I. of Ourselves, which deals with Self-knowledge, I have tried to lay before the reader a panoramic view of the Kingdom of Mansoul. I shall continue to use the expression, Mansoul, which we owe to Bunyan, because I do not know any other that suggests a view from the outside, as if one surveyed a tract of country from an eminence. From our imaginary height, we have—supposing that the reader has been my fellow-student in the considerations that occupied the former volume—taken a bird's-eye view of the riches of Mansoul, of the wonderful capacities there are in every human being to enter upon the world as a great inheritance.

All its beauty and all its thought are open to everyone; everyone may take service for the world's uses; everyone may climb those delectable mountains in the recesses of his own nature from whence he gets the vision of the city of God. If Mansoul has infinite resources and glorious possibilities, it has also perils, any one of which may bring devastation and ruin. None of these perils is inevitable, because Mansoul is a kingdom under an established government. It is convenient to think of this government as carried on in four Chambers.

The House of Body is, we have seen, sustained by the Appetites; but ruined when any one of these appetites obtains sole control. The five Senses are, as it were, pages running between body and mind, and ministering to both.

The House of Mind is amazingly ordered with a view to the getting of knowledge. "Studies serve for delight, for ornament, and for ability," is writ large upon the portals, and within are the powers fitted to deal with all knowledge. There is Intellect, waiting to apprehend knowledge of many sorts; Imagination, taking impressions, living pictures of the glories of the past and the behaviour of the remote; there is the æsthetic Sense, whose motto is, "A thing of beauty is a joy for ever," ready to appropriate every thing of beauty, whether picture, poem, wind-flower, or starry heavens—a possession of joy for ever. Reason is there, eager to discern causes and consequences, to know the why and the wherefore of every fact that comes before the mind; and lest, with all these powers, Mind should become an uninhabited house, with rusty hinges and cobwebbed panes, there are certain Desires which bestir us to feed the mind, in much the same way as our Appetites clamour for the food of the body.

Just as each Appetite carries in itself the possibilities of excess and universal ruin to Mansoul, so each of these admirable functions of the mind has what we have called its dæmons; and each of these may not only paralyse that mind-power which it shadows, but may distort and enfeeble the whole of the powers of Mind.

The House of Heart is, we have seen, dominated, in every Mansoul, by two benign powers, Love and Justice. Pity, Benevolence, Sympathy, Kindness, Generosity, Gratitude, Courage, Loyalty, Humility, Gladness, are among the lords in waiting attendant upon Love; and Justice has its own attendant virtues—Gentleness, Courtesy, Candour, Respect, Discernment, Appreciation, Veracity, Integrity, and more.

Temperance, Soberness, and Chastity, too, are of the household of Justice; for these include that justice which we owe to ourselves; but, alas! upon every one of these waits its appropriate dæmon, and the safe-conduct of life depends, first, upon discerning, and then upon avoiding, the malevolent dispositions which are ready to devastate the House of Heart. We know how Cowardice, Meanness, Rudeness, Calumny, Envy, and a hundred other powers of evil beset us. The perils are so great, the risks so numerous, that many a goodly Mansoul perishes without ever realising the vast wealth which belongs to it—like a prince brought up in peasant's estate, and unaware of his birthright. Those who begin to realise how much is possible to Mansoul, and how many are the perils of the way, know that a certain duty of self-direction belongs to them; and that powers for this direction are lodged in them as truly as are intellect and imagination, hunger and thirst.

The governing powers lodged within us are the Conscience and the Will: but conscience (even the conscience of a good Christian person) is not capable of judging for us, in the various affairs of our life, without instruction, any more than the intellect of the ignorant hind can pronounce upon a problem of the differential calculus.

Therefore, Conscience must learn its lessons, regular and progressive lessons, upon the affairs of body, heart, and mind. One of the objects of this volume is to point out some of the courses of instruction proper for conscience, and some of the ends at which this instruction should aim. The affairs of the heart are so far interdependent with those of mind and body that the separate consideration we need give them at present is contained in the former volume of Ourselves.

Concerning the Will, too, the highest but one of all the powers of Mansoul, we need instruction. Persons commonly suppose that the action of the will is automatic; but no power of Mansoul acts by itself and of itself; and some little study of the 'way of the will'—which has the ordering of every other power—may help us to understand the functions of what we have called the prime minister in the kingdom of Mansoul.

It is well, too, that we should know something of the Soul, the name we give to that within us which has capacity for the knowledge and love of God, for prayer and praise and faith, for the enthronement of the King, whose right it is to reign over Mansoul. We may believe that the Creator is honoured by our attempt to know something of the powers and the perils belonging to that human nature with which He has endowed us.

PART I—Conscience

SECTION I—Conscience In The House Of Body

Chapter I The Court Of Appeal

Conscience, the Judge, always in Court.—The affairs of Mansoul do not by any means go right of themselves. We have seen how the powers that be, in body, mind, and heart, are in conflict with one another, each of them trying for sole rule in Mansoul; and again, how the best servants of the state are beset by certain dæmons. But all this conflict and rivalry is provided against. There is a Court of Appeal always open, and therein sits the Lord Chief justice whom we call Conscience. Let us consider for a moment what is the office of a judge in a court of law. He does not know, and is not expected to know, the rights and wrongs of every case brought before him. Advocates on both sides get up these and set them in order before the judge; but he is in authority; he knows the law, and gives the right decision upon what he knows.

Everyone has a Sense of Duty.—Just so, with Conscience. He proclaims the law, that is, Duty. No Mansoul is left without the sense of ought—everyone knows that certain behaviour is due from him, that he owes the ordering of his conduct to a higher Power. Duty, that which is due from us; ought, that which we owe, is the proclamation of Conscience. We are not our own; but God, who has given us life, and whose we are, has planted within us Conscience, to remind us continually that we owe ourselves to Him, and must order our ways to please Him, and that He is the judge who will visit every offence surely and directly, if not to-day, then to-morrow. Conscience informs us, too, of the reason of this judging of our God. Judging is saving. It is the continual calling of us back from wrong ways, which injure and ruin, into right ways of peace and happiness. All this Conscience testifies to us; morning by morning, hour by hour, he witnesses that we are not free to do what we like, but must do what we ought.

Conscience may give Wrong Judgments.—But if Conscience gives judgment in every Mansoul, how is it that people continually go wrong? As we have seen, there is apt to be anarchy in the State. Sloth or temper, pride or envy, betrays Mansoul.

I need not dwell upon the fate of those who will not listen to Conscience; but there is danger, too, for those who do listen. We hear it said that a man acts 'up to his lights,' or 'according to his lights.' However wrong he may be, there are some who excuse him because he knew no better. If the man has had no chance of knowing better, the excuse may be allowed; but it is not enough to act according to our lights, if we choose to carry a dim wick in a dirty lantern, when we might have good light.

Conscience may be tampered with.—We have seen that the judge is not familiar with the ins and outs of the case he tries. It is so with the judge of our bosom. He, too, listens to advocates; Inclination hires Reason to plead before Conscience; and Reason is so subtle and convincing that the judge gives the verdict for the defendant. 'Obey the law,' says Conscience; but, 'This that I choose to do is the law,' says Reason, on behalf of the defendant. 'Then, defendant' (i.e. Inclination), 'you may do the thing you choose.' This subtle misleading of Conscience is an art practised alike by little children and hardened criminals. It is possible that in this sense everyone acts up to his lights; he justifies himself; his reason proves that what he does is right in the circumstances, and Conscience lets him off—never ceasing to cry, 'Thou shalt do right,' but leaving each one free, to some extent, to decide as to what is right.

It is well we should know this limit to the power of Conscience, for many reasons; amongst others, it helps us to understand the histories of nations and individuals.

Conscience must be instructed.—It is necessary that we should all know something about the constitution of Mansoul, in order that we may recognise the voice of the speaker who instructs reason to put the case to conscience. Envy, for example, does not say, 'I hate Jones because he has a rich father,' or, 'because he scores, whether in lessons or games,' or 'because he is popular with the other fellows.' Envy pretends that all he wishes for is fair play. 'It's not fair that one fellow should have lots of pocket-money and another have to pinch and scrape.' 'Jones got up by a fluke in the Ovid.' 'He's always hunting for popularity: no decent fellow would lay himself out like that.' With arguments such as these does envy prompt reason, who makes out a good case before conscience, and the defendant gets off.

But the person who knows that any depreciation of another, by way of making much of ourselves, comes of envy, and not justice, is on his guard. He keeps his tongue from evil and his thoughts from malice, and submits to the condemnation of his unbiassed conscience.

This straight way of looking at things is what our Lord calls the single eye. Many people seem to have it by nature, and cannot easily be deceived into calling wrong, right. But evil is specious and ready; and it is well for each of us to take pains that we may recognise misrepresentations brought before conscience. An instructed conscience rarely makes mistakes.

Chapter II The Instruction Of Conscience

Instruction by Books.—The instructed conscience knows that Temperance, Chastity, Fortitude, Prudence must rule in the House of Body. But how is the conscience to become instructed? Life brings us many lessons—when we see others do well, conscience approves and learns; when others do ill, conscience condemns. But we want a wider range of knowledge than the life about us affords, and books are our best teachers.

There is no nice shade of conduct which is not described or exemplified in the vast treasure-house of literature. History and biography are full of instruction in righteousness; but what is properly called literature, that is, poetry, essays, the drama, and novels, is perhaps the most useful for our moral instruction, because the authors bring their insight to bear in a way they would hesitate to employ when writing about actual persons.

Autobiographies, again, often lift the veil, for the writer may make free with himself. In the Bible the lives of men and the history of a nation are told without the reticence which authors are apt to use in telling of the offences of the good or the vices of the bad.

Plutarch, perhaps alone among biographers, writes with comparable candour, if not always with equal justice.

The Poet and the Essayist are our Teachers.—A child gets moral notions from the fairy-tales he delights in, as do his elders from tale and verse. So nice a critic as Matthew Arnold tells us that poetry is a criticism of life; so it is, both a criticism and an inspiration; and most of us carry in our minds tags of verse which shape our conduct more than we know;

"Wisdom is ofttimes nearer when we stoop
Than when we soar." [Wordsworth.]

"The friends thou hast, and their adoption tried,
Grapple them to thy soul with hooks of steel." [Hamlet.]

A thousand thoughts that burn come to us on the wings of verse; and, conceive how our lives would be impoverished were we to awake one day and find that the Psalms had disappeared from the world and from the thoughts of men! Proverbs, too, the words of the wise king and the sayings of the common folk, come to us as if they were auguries; while the essayists deal with conduct and give much delicate instruction, which reaches us the more surely through the charm of their style.

So are the Novelists and the Dramatists.—Perhaps the dramatists and novelists have done the most for our teaching; but not the works of every playwright and novelist are good 'for example of life and instruction in manners.' We are safest with those which have lived long enough to become classics; and this, for two reasons. The fact that they have not been allowed to die proves in itself that the authors have that to say, and a way of saying it, which the world cannot do without. In the next place, the older novels and plays deal with conduct, and conduct is our chief concern in life. Modern works of the kind deal largely with emotions, a less wholesome subject of contemplation. Having found the book which has a message for us, let us not be guilty of the folly of saying we have read it. We might as well say we have breakfasted, as if breakfasting on one day should last us for every day! The book that helps us deserves many readings, for assimilation comes by slow degrees.

Literature is full of teaching, by precept and example, concerning the management of our physical nature. I shall offer a lesson here and there by way of sample, but no doubt the reader will think of many better teachings; and that is as it should be; the way such teaching should come to us is, here a little and there a little, incidentally, from books which we read for the interest of the story, the beauty of the poem, or the grace of the writing.

Chapter III The Rulings Of Conscience In The House Of The Body: Temperance

Temperance in Eating.—Who can forget how 'the fortunes of Nigel' turned upon that mess which Laurie Linklater prepared after the King's own heart? The telling is humorous; but not all the King's scholarship enables us to get over the supping of the cock-a-leekie! Thus Scott prepares us:—"But nobody among these brave English cooks can kittle up his Majesty's most sacred palate with our own gusty Scotch dishes. So I e'en betook myself to my craft and concocted a mess of friar's chicken for the soup, and a savoury hachis [i.e., haggis], that made the whole cabal coup the crans; and, instead of disgrace, I came by preferment." It was through these same gusty Scotch dishes that James was approached, and Laurie Linklater figures as a deus ex machina. Richie Moniplies "having reached the palace in safety demanded to see Master Linklater, the under-clerk of his Majesty's kitchen. The reply was that he was not to be spoken withal, being then employed in cooking a mess of cock-a-leekie for the King's own mouth. 'Tell him,' said Moniplies, 'that it is a dear countryman of his, who seeks to converse with him on matter of high import . . . I maun speak with the King.' 'The King? Ye are red wud,' said Linklater . . . 'I will have neither hand nor foot in the matter,' said the cautious clerk of the kitchen; 'but there is his Majesty's mess of cock-a-leekie just going to be served to him in his closet—I cannot prevent you from putting the letter between the gilt-bowl and the platter; his sacred Majesty will see it when he lifts the bowl, for he aye drinks out the broth.'"

And The Fortunes of Nigel closes with the King's last word—"And, my lords and lieges, let us all to our dinner, for the cock-a-leekie is cooling." [The Fortunes of Nigel, by Sir Walter Scott.]

Where's the harm? In this: King James's moral worth and intelligence are swamped, his dignity of character and title to respect forfeited, through ignominious failures in self-restraint in this and other matters. Did not the patriarch Isaac, too, lend himself to the deception which divided his family by his love for that savoury meat upon which so much turns? It is well and a sign of health that we should like and enjoy our 'meat,' but to love and long for any particular dish is of the nature of intemperance. So thought Plutarch when he tells us this tale [Preface to Plutarch's Lives.] of his bringing up:—

"Our master (says he) having one day observed that we had indulged ourselves too luxuriously at dinner, at his afternoon lecture ordered his freedman to give his own son the discipline of the whip in our presence; signifying at the same time that he suffered this punishment because he could not eat his victuals without sauce. The philosopher all the while had his eye upon us, and we knew well for whom this example of punishment was intended."

In Drinking.—That Le Balafré [Quentin Durward, by Sir Walter Scott.] should behave like a sot is what we expect of his lower nature; but it is painful that the generous and noble Lord Crawford should lose dignity and self-possession over the wine-cup. The occasion is the banquet given by the Mess to welcome the election of Quentin Durward. "At present, however, Lord Crawford declined occupying the seat prepared for him, and bidding them 'hold themselves merry,' stood looking on at the revel with a countenance which seemed greatly to enjoy it. 'Let him alone,' whispered Cunningham to Lindesay, as the latter offered wine to their noble Captain, 'let him alone—hurry no man's cattle—let him take it of his own accord.' In fact, the old Lord, who at first smiled, shook his head, and placed the untasted wine-cup before him, began presently, as if it were in absence of mind, to sip a little of the contents, and in doing so, fortunately recollected that it would be ill luck did he not drink a draught to the health of the gallant lad who had joined them this day . . . The good old Lord could not but in courtesy do reason to this pledge also, and gliding into the ready chair, as it were, without reflecting what he was doing he caused Quentin to come up beside him, and assailed him with many more questions concerning the state of Scotland, and the great families there, than he was well able to answer; while ever and anon, in the course of his queries, the good Lord kissed the wine-cup by way of parenthesis, remarking that sociality became Scottish gentlemen, but that young men, like Quentin, ought to practice it cautiously, lest it might degenerate into excess; upon which occasion he uttered many excellent things, until his own tongue, although employed in the praises of temperance, began to articulate something thicker than usual."

Times have changed since Quentin Durward played his part; and if men still drink, they are commonly not men of Lord Crawford's dignity of character. People begin to see that plain living and high thinking go together; self-restraint is practised both in eating and drinking, and the day is coming when excess in either will be regarded with general contempt.

In taking our Ease.—Miss Edgeworth's Lazy Lawrence has passed into a proverb; and many a more attractive hero is tarred with the same brush. Here is Harry Warrington, for example:—

"Harry's lace and linen were as fine as his aunt could desire. He purchased fine shaving-plate of the toyshop women, and a couple of magnificent brocade bedgowns, in which his worship lolled at ease and sipped his chocolate of a morning. He had swords and walking-canes and French watches with painted backs and diamond settings, and snuffboxes enamelled by artists of the same cunning nation. He had a levee of grooms, jockeys, tradesmen, daily waiting in his ante-room, and admitted one by one to him, and Parson Sampson, over his chocolate, by Gumbo, the groom of the chambers. We have no account of the men whom Mr. Gumbo had now under him. Certain it is that no single negro could have taken care of all the fine things which Mr. Warrington now possessed, let alone the horses and the post-chaise which his honour had bought. Also Harry instructed himself in the arts which became a gentleman in those days. A French fencing-master, and a dancing-master of the same nation, resided at Tunbridge during that season when Harry made his appearance: these men of science the young Virginian sedulously frequented, and acquired considerable skill and grace in the peaceful and warlike accomplishments which they taught. Ere many weeks were over he could handle the foils against his master or any frequenter of the fencing-school . . . As for riding, though Mr. Warrington took a few lessons on the great horse from a riding-master who came to Tunbridge, he declared that their own Virginian manner was well enough for him." [The Virginians, by W. M. Thackeray.]

Here we have the pursuits of busy idleness; for idleness is generally busy: Hogarth painted what Thackeray describes, this same luxury and abandon of idleness. Such another idler was Charles II.; while he was a great walker, he shirked every hint of the work proper to his condition. But history and fiction, and, alas, everyday life, afford many examples of men and women who never bestir themselves to catch the flying opportunity.

In Day-Dreaming.—There are other kinds of intemperance besides the grosser sorts of overeating, over-drinking, over-sleeping. Nathaniel Hawthorne [The House of the Seven Gables.] describes another type of idleness in Hepzibah Pyncheon, the solitary old maid who inhabited the House of the Seven Gables, and spent her days in the erection of curious castles in the air.

"All the while Hepzibah was perfecting the scheme of her little shop, she had cherished an unacknowledged idea that some harlequin trick of fortune would intervene in her favour. For example, an uncle—who had sailed for India fifty years before, and had never been heard of since—might yet return, and adopt her to be the comfort of his very extreme and decrepit age, and adorn her with pearls, diamonds, oriental shawls, and turbans, and make her the ultimate heiress of his unreckonable riches. Or the member of parliament, now at the head of the English branch of the family,—with which the elder stock, on this side of the Atlantic, had held little or no intercourse for the last two centuries,—this eminent gentleman might invite Hepzibah to quit the ruinous House of the Seven Gables, and come over to dwell with her kindred at Pyncheon Hall . . . But, for reasons the most imperative, she could not yield to his request."

But, indeed, there is little to be said for the slothful:

How comes it that of all
The lusts that could enthral
Yon Bible worthies to so hapless fall,
Sloth shows not first, Hell-frame acurst,
Where every pestilent root of ill is nursed?
Who slips must erst have stood,
Have made his foothold good,
Have risen and held him up, ere fall he could:
But who lies prone, Such toils unknown,
May comfort him, lapse for him is there none;
The sum of ill-doing is—leaving undone.

'Know thy Work and do it.'—Let us hear Carlyle, [Past and Present.] the apostle of work, upon idleness and work:—"And who art thou that braggest of thy life of idleness; complacently showest thy bright gilt equipages; sumptuous cushions; appliances for folding of the hands to mere sleep? . . . One monster there is in the world: the idle man . . . The latest gospel in this world is, Know thy work and do it: . . . know what thou canst work at; and work at it, like a Hercules! That will be thy better plan.

"It has been written, 'An endless significance lies in work'; a man perfects himself by working. Foul jungles are cleared away, fair seed-fields rise instead, and stately cities; and withal the man himself first ceases to be a jungle and foul unwholesome desert thereby. The man is now a man."

Principle underlying Temperance.—Conscience is not, in fact, so much concerned with the manner of our intemperance as with the underlying principle which St Paul sets forth when he condemns those who "worship and serve the creature more than the Creator." This is the principle according to which we shall be justified or condemned; and, in its light, we have reason to be suspicious of any system of diet or exercise which bespeaks excessive concern for the body, whether that concern be shown by a diet of nuts and apples, of peacocks' brains, or of cock-a-leekie. England is in serious danger of giving herself over to the worship of a deity whom we all honour as Hygeia. But never did men bow down before so elusive a goddess, for the more she is pursued, the more she flees; while she is ready with smiles and favours for him who never casts a thought her way. In truth and sober earnest, the pursuit of physical (and mental) well-being is taking its place amongst us as a religious cult; and the danger of such a cult is, lest we concentrate our minds, not upon Christ, but upon our own consciousness. We 'have faith' to produce in ourselves certain comfortable attitudes of mind and body; this serenity satisfies us, and we forget the danger of exalting the concerns of the creature above the worship of the Creator. The essence of Christianity is passionate love and loyalty towards a divine Person: and faith, the adoring regard of the soul, must needs make us like Him who is 'meek and lowly of heart.' A faith which raises us to a 'higher plane' should be suspect of the Christian conscience, as seeking to serve ourselves of the power of Christ, less to His glory than our own satisfaction.

Well said Carlyle that, whether you or I be in a state of well-being or not 'is not the central fact of the Universe.'

If undue attention to the physical nature be a kind of intemperance, still more so is the neglect of that nature through which every function we are enabled for is performed; and such neglect has its sources in the indifference of sloth and the excesses of greed. 'Take no thought for the life, what ye shall eat or what ye shall drink.' 'Eat that which is set before you.' These are the rules laid down by our Master, whereby we may 'keep our bodies in temperance, soberness, and chastity.' 'Take no thought,' for all offences against the body begin in the thoughts.

We Live in our Times.—I appear to have wandered wide of the mark, seeing that my subject is the dealings of Conscience with the House of Body in the matter of Temperance; but, indeed, it is necessary to keep a wide outlook upon the movements of the day, as well as upon those of our own appetites. We live with our times; and we must bear in mind that there is no freak of the moment,—whether it be that fruit-eating colony in the Pacific, or the living upon one meal a day, or the not permitting ourselves to drink anything at all, not even water,—for which Reason is not capable of being enlisted as special pleader. Only the instructed conscience is proof against persuasion. Let us hail Punch as our faithful mentor; whether we would be quadrumanous persons or nut-eaters, Punch laughs us into common sense!

Chapter IV The Rulings Of Conscience In The House Of The Body: Chastity (Part 1.)

Chastity of Soul.—In this field, also, the instructed Conscience takes a wide survey. The law forbids all sins of impurity, whether in imagination, word, or deed: of this we are aware, but do we recognise that the proportion of Love must be preserved as duly as the proportion of Faith? The instructed Conscience learns to regard all excessive affection, undue fondness, as sullying the chastity of the self-controlled soul. Any friendship, even if it be friendship between mother and child, which is over-fond and exclusive, making the one continually necessary to the other, and shutting out other claims of duty and affection, is suspect of the clear Conscience. To be 'all in all to each other' is not a quite pure desire, apart from the question of sex; for the chaste soul is, after the manner of Giotto's picture, walled within a tower. Noli me tangere is the law it chooses to obey, to the exclusion of all too close intimacies.

The Tragedy of 'Edward II.' [Marlowe.]—Perhaps nowhere is this law of the pure life more plainly indicated—by breach—than in the most sorrowful tragedy of Edward II., as set forth by Christopher Marlowe. Let us see how the tale goes, for one such lesson of life is worth many counsels and innumerable resolutions. Excess in affection is a weakness that besets generous natures, and King Edward is generous:

"My father is deceased! Come, Gaveston,
And share the kingdom with thy dearest friend."

Here indeed is friendship! eager to share all fortune to the utmost with a friend. And Gaveston is ready with love for love—

"Sweet prince, I come; these, these thy amorous lines
Might have enforced me to have swum from France."

The fond friendship is resented by the nobles, who have their own claims upon the King. They call a council and remonstrate, adding prayers and threats of rebellion. The King concludes the meeting with—

"I'll either die or live with Gaveston."
Gaveston. "I can no longer keep me from my lord."

Edward. "What, Gaveston! welcome!—kiss not my hand—
Embrace me, Gaveston, as I do thee.
Why should'st thou kneel? know'st thou not who I am?
Thy friend, thyself, another Gaveston!'

Edward pours titles, lands, and honours upon his friend with a free hand; nay, gives him his very seal—

"Save or condemn, and in our name command
Whatso thy mind affects, or fancy likes."

Again the nobles and great churchmen hold council as to how to dispose of 'that peevish Frenchman,'—a happy phrase, for the favourite or fondly beloved friend is ever peevish, ready to take offence, quick to resent.

"Thus arm in arm the King and he doth march," says Lancaster; and Warwick adds, "Thus leaning on the shoulder of the King he nods and scorns and smiles at those that pass."

The Queen herself complains,—

For now, my lord, the King regards me not,
But doats upon the love of Gaveston.
He claps his cheek, and hands about his neck,
Smiles in his face, and whispers in his ears;
And when I come he frowns, as who should say,
'Go whither thou wilt, seeing I have Gaveston.'"

The barons compass the exile of the favourite, and the King cries,—

"And long thou shalt not stay, or if thou dost,
I'll come to thee; my love shall ne'er decline."

They exchange pictures, and Edward says—

Here take my picture and let me wear thine;
O, might I keep thee here as I do this,
Happy were I! but now most miserable!
Kind words and mutual talk makes our grief greater:
Therefore, with dumb embracement, let us part—
Stay, Gaveston, I cannot leave thee thus."

Edward's threats and blandishments move Isabella; she, through the younger Mortimer, works upon the nobles, and Gaveston is recalled from his short exile in Ireland. The Queen brings the news to her lord, and is rewarded with momentary affection; Edward, in his elation, distributes rewards and praises amongst his nobles.

But the favourite, on his return, is as intolerable as ever, and the barons as intolerant. The King lives only in his 'minion,' and himself prepares for civil war, to 'abate these barons' pride.' One more attempt the barons make to convince the King of the ruin to the State brought about by his absorption in his favourite. The gifts and triumphs, masques and shows, 'bestowed on Gaveston have drained the treasury; rebellion threatens, deposition must follow; the King's garrisons are beaten out of France; the wild 'Oneyl' is making himself master of Ireland; the Scots make unresisted inroads in the north, the Dane commands the narrow seas;

"What foreign prince sends thee ambassadors?"
"Thy gentle queen, sole sister to Valois,
Complains that thou hast left her all forlorn."

The peers no longer attend the royal court. The people make ballads and rhymes of scorn.

Is the King moved? Not he. The remonstrances of the barons make them traitors in his eyes, and all the result is,

"Poor Gaveston, that he has no friend but me!
Do what they can, we'll live in Tynemouth here,
And, so I walk with him about the walls,
What care I though the Earls begirt us round?"

Things go from bad to worse, till, in the end, the exasperated barons behead Gaveston. But is the kingdom to have release from the intolerable yoke it has borne? No; for the news of the former favourite's death had not yet staled, when,

"And in this place of honour and of trust,
Spencer, sweet Spencer, I adopt thee here."

Spencer, too, had loved Gaveston; but the King only follows the rule. Our fond and absorbing friendships are succeeded by others as fond and absorbing, not precisely out of fickleness, but because the enervated, emasculated nature can no longer exist without the sweet philanderings to which it has accustomed itself.

The tragical tale continues through rebellion, insurrection, and civil war; the one gleam of brightness be in the young Prince Edward, who believes in his father through good report and ill,

"I warrant you, I'll win his highness quickly;
'A loves me better than a thousand Spencers."

And the King, when he learns how his wife dishonours him, his people desert him, he, too, has a thought for his child,—

"Ah, nothing grieves me, but my little boy
Is thus misled to countenance their ills."

All goes on as before. Spencer, by Isabella's order, is arrested in the presence of the King:

"Spencer, ah! sweet Spencer, thus then must we part."
Spencer. "Oh! is he gone? Is noble Edward gone?
Parted from hence? never to see us more?'—

for there seems to be no doubt that his friends gave love for love to the over-fond monarch.

The successive imprisonments follow; then, the final message:

"Commend me to my son, and bid him rule
Better than I. Yet how have I transgressed,
Unless it be with too much clemency?"

Each of us, King in his own Realm.—We need not follow the tragedy to the end; but this note—"Yet how have I transgressed?"—is full of profound instruction. His own ruined life, his devastated kingdom, dishonoured wife, loyal subjects converted into traitors and assassins—all these lay at the door of the King; and he asks at the end, "Yet how have I transgressed?" His uninstructed Conscience threw no light upon the fatal error of his life. He chose those duties which he would fulfil; and his code would appear to contain but one commandment,—'Be faithful to thy friend.' Never once did it dawn upon him that we may not choose amongst our duties, or that a self-elected duty may become a vice. You say, 'Ah, yes, if you are a king; but happily lesser people are free to please themselves.' Indeed we are not. Each of us stands king amongst a thousand relations, duties, interests, proper to us. If we choose to yield ourselves to the domination of another, so that our will is paralysed and we are unable to think or act except upon that other's initiative, are incapable of being happy and at ease except in his presence, then we too have sown disorder in a realm, less wide and great than that of the unhappy Edward, but our own realm, for which we are responsible.

We are not Free to give Ourselves without Reserve.—Men seem, on the whole, to have learnt restraint in their friendships since the Tudor days when Marlowe thought it well to offer this lesson to the world, perhaps because in his day men admired men with such fond and passionate intensity. But this is not strictly a question of sex; schoolboy and schoolboy, girl and girl, man and woman, and woman and woman, there are, for whom life means no more than this manner of doting fondness for the beloved object. This is the sort of thing:—

"'Our pension was full of mystery and romance,' said Coquette, brightening up, 'because of two German young ladies who were there. They introduced—what shall I call it?—exaltation. Do you know what it is? When one girl makes another exaltée, because of her goodness or her beauty, and worships her, and kisses her dress when she passes her, and serves her in all things, yet does not speak to her. And the girl who is exaltée—she must be proud and cold, and show scorn for her attendant—even although she has been her friend. It was these German young ladies from the Bohemian Wald who introduced it—and they were tall and dark, and very beautiful, and many would have wished to make them exaltées, but they were always the first to seek out someone whom they admired very much, and no one was so humble and obedient as they were. All the pension was filled with it—it was a religion, an enthusiasm—and you would see girls crying and kneeling on the floor, to show their love and admiration for their friend.'" [A Daughter of Heth, by William Black.]

Plutarch, [Life of Agesilaus.] of course, knows all about this matter. He (Agesilaus) had a private and more sensible cause of uneasiness in his attachment to the son of Spithridates; though, while he was with him, he had made a point to combat that attachment. One day Megabates approached to salute him, and Agesilaus declined that mark of his affection. The youth after this was more distant in his addresses. Then Agesilaus was sorry for the repulse he had given him, and pretended to wonder why Megabates kept at such a distance. His friends told him he must blame himself for rejecting his former application. 'He would still,' said they, 'be glad to pay his most obliging respects to you; but take care you do not reject them again.' Agesilaus was silent for some time; and when he had considered the thing, he said, 'Do not mention it to him, for this second victory over myself gives me more pleasure than I should have in turning all I look upon to gold.'"

So great an affection, doubtless, argues a generous Heart; but that is not enough; a magnanimous Mind and an instructed Conscience must go to the preservation of the soul's chastity. We are not our own to give ourselves away without reserve.

Chapter V The Rulings Of Conscience In The House Of The Body: Chastity (Part 2.) Ordered Friendship

A Sane and Generous Friendship.—But there are a thousand records of temperate, wholesome, and noble friendships for one of feeble excess. The classic friendships are too well known to be quoted. But here is a companionship of a healthy kind :

"Are you not my only friend? and have you not acquired a right to share my wealth? Answer me that, Alan Fairford. When I was brought from the solitude of my mother's dwelling into the tumult of the Gaits' class at the High School—when I was mocked for my English accent—salted with snow as a Southern—rolled in the gutter for a Saxon pock-pudding,—who with stout arguments, and stouter blows, stood forth my defender?—Why, Alan Fairford. Who beat me soundly when I brought the arrogance of an only son, and of course, a spoilt urchin, to the forms of the little republic?—Why, Alan . . . You taught me to keep my fingers off the weak, and to clench my fist against the strong—to carry no tales out of school—to stand forth like a true man—obey the stern order of a Pande manum, and endure my pawmies without wincing, like one that is determined not to be the better for them. In a word, before I knew thee I knew nothing. At college it was the same. When I was incorrigibly idle, your example and encouragement roused me to mental exertion and showed me the way to intellectual enjoyment. You made me an historian, a metaphysician (invita Minerva)—nay, by Heaven! you had almost made an advocate of me, as well as of yourself." [Redgauntlet, by Sir Walter Scott.]

Though a temperate friendship, that between Alan Fairford and Darsie Latimer was no alliance of the loose, commonplace sort. Friendship was subordinated to duty while things went well. Alan prepared earnestly for his career, and was a dutiful and affectionate son to a rather exacting father. But when his friend is in danger, this canny Alan throws up his chances and endangers his life with uncalculating ardour. The young advocate has made his first appearance with marked success in a difficult case. He is carrying the court with him when the strip of paper reaches him which tells of Darsie's danger. "He stopped short in his harangue—gazed on the paper with a look of surprise and horror—uttered an exclamation, and flinging down the brief which he had in his hand, hurried out of court without returning a single word of answer to the various questions, 'What was the matter?'—'Was he taken unwell?'—'Should not a chair be called?' etc., etc." He leaves the following lines for his father: "You will not, I trust, be surprised, nor perhaps very much displeased, to learn that I am on my way to Dumfriesshire, to learn, by my own personal investigation, the present state of my dear friend, and afford him such relief as may be in my power, and which, I trust, will be effectual . . . I can only say, in further apology, that if anything unhappy, which heaven forbid! shall have occurred to the person who, next to yourself, is dearest to me in this world, I shall have on my heart a subject of eternal regret."

A Friendship loyal in spite of Disillusion.—Mrs. Gaskell, [Wives and Daughters, by Mrs. Gaskell.] with the grace and sincerity which distinguish her style, tells us of the friendship between Molly Gibson and Cynthia Fitzgerald. Molly is a charming English girl, sound of heart and sound of head, to whom comes the vision of Cynthia, beautiful and bewitching. Of course she fell in love with her half-sister (it is a mistake to suppose that girls fall in love with men only); while Cynthia was equally attracted by Molly's freshness and simplicity. Pleasant hours are passed in Mrs. Gibson's drawing-room in chat and work. Both girls are kind, and each has a care for the interests of the other. There is the give-and-take of friendship between them; and, indeed, poor Molly is severely tried: Cynthia involves herself with men, and Molly endures many things to get her out of a dilemma. But she does endure them, without losing her own integrity; while Cynthia endures being obliged by her friend. But it is impossible to describe this natural friendship, not to be shattered by disillusion, in a few lines.

Friends brought to us by the Circumstances of Life.—It is a common error of youth to suppose that a friend must be a perfect person, and that the duty of loyalty ceases so soon as little failings show themselves. David Copperfield [David Copperfield, by Charles Dickens.] offers a fine study of the loyalties of life. David has a promiscuous collection of friends brought to him by the circumstances of his life; but how ready he is for the occasions of every one of them! With what simple good-humour he accepts Mr. Micawber's description of him as 'the friend of my youth,' and Mrs. Micawber's domestic confidences, when he himself was but a person of ten: how the Micawbers turn up at all sorts of inconvenient moments, and how they are always welcome to their friend: Traddles, too—what a nice person Traddles is; and what a sound and generous friendship exists between him and David! The list of friendships is a long one, the gradual ingathering of a life,—Peggotty, Mr. Dick, Ham, Dr Strong, Mrs. Peggotty, and the rest; in all he finds delight; all of them he honours, serves, and cherishes with entire loyalty. But not one of these friends dominates him or makes exclusive claims on his love. One friend he had with whom he lost his own individuality, who carried his heart by sheer fascination. Alas, this was Steerforth, and all the loyalty he could keep for him was that of a great sorrow over his friend's shame rather than over his death.

It is not the friends of our election who have exclusive claims upon us; the friends brought to us here and there by the circumstances of life all claim our loyalty, and from these we get, as did David Copperfield, kindness for kindness, service for service, loyalty for loyalty, full measure, heaped together and running over. One could hardly have a better guide in such matters than this charming tale of a life full of generous and loyal friendships, of fine chastity of soul, and containing, alas, the warning of a great unchastity!

Chapter VI The Rulings Of Conscience In The House Of The Body: Chastity (Part 3.) The Final Unchastity

It all begins so innocently, and the end is so irremediably disastrous both to the man and the woman! People say it is one of the crying injustices of society that the woman should suffer and the man go 'scot-free.' But does he?

The confirmed profligate, perhaps, is not capable of further degradation; but the man who falls for the first time loses his future as certainly as the woman, if less obviously. He may escape public disgrace, but he never gets over the loss of power, purpose, and integrity which accompanies the loss of purity. He is handicapped for life, though he may himself have forgotten why; and should he at last marry, his children too often repeat their father's sin.

It is worth while to follow the history of a seduction as Mrs. Gaskell gives it to us in Ruth. Ruth is a friendless orphan who is apprenticed to a milliner, and is distinguished among her fellow-apprentices by her quiet, lady-like manners and her beauty. "'I could not help knowing that I am pretty,' answered she simply, 'for many people have told me so.'"

She accompanies Mrs. Mason, her employer, to the shire ball, together with some other apprentices, that they might be at hand to mend rents in the ball dresses and the like; and a lady comes with her fiancé to have a tear mended. She is arrogant to the young apprentice, and "Mr. Bellingham looked grave," and, at the end picking up a camellia, he said: "Allow me, Miss Dunscombe, to give this in your name to this young lady as thanks for her dexterous help."

The reader admires Mr. Bellingham for his act of courtesy: and so, alas! does Ruth; the camellia becomes a treasure, and the girl's thoughts dwell on the courteous gentleman. Again she meets him, by accident, in romantic circumstances. She is trying to rescue a child from drowning, and he rides up and succeeds in saving the boy. This leads to further intercourse: he leaves his purse with Ruth to buy what is necessary for the child, and of course she has to see him again and account for what she has spent. Then there are accidental meetings at church—and still no wrong is intended. Next, the novelist introduces us to Mr. Bellingham at home:

"His thoughts had been far more occupied by Ruth than hers by him, although his appearance upon the scene of her life was more an event to her than to him . . . He did not analyse the nature of his feelings, but simply enjoyed them with the delight which youth takes in experiencing new and strong emotion . . . The fact of his being an only child had given him, as it does to many, a sort of inequality in those parts of the character which are usually formed by the number of years a person has lived. The unevenness of discipline to which only children are subjected: the thwarting resulting from over-anxiety: the indiscreet indulgence arising from a love centred in one object—had been exaggerated in his education." In these few words the author gives us a key to the situation, and we begin to suspect what is to follow. Steerforth, too, in David Copperfield, was the only son of a proud, indulgent, and wayward mother; and Arthur Donnithorne, in Adam Bede—he, too, is the only son of a fond and imperious father. It would seem as if only children had more need than others to walk circumspectly; perhaps this is a fact, because in a commonwealth of brothers and sisters it is not quite easy to follow devious ways; and the devious ways are the danger, whether to one of a large family or to the only child. Young Bellingham finds himself fascinated, he does not know why, and all the more so because "there was a spell in the shyness which made her avoid and shun all admiring approaches to acquaintance

. . . By no over-bold admiration or rash, passionate word would he startle her . . . In accordance with his determination, he resisted the strong temptation of walking by her side the whole distance home after church. He spoke a few words about the weather, bowed, and was gone. Ruth believed she should never see him again; and, in spite of sundry self-upbraidings for her folly, she could not help feeling as if a shadow had fallen on her life." Then comes a Sunday when Mr. Bellingham walks home from church with her through the fields.

"'How strange it is,' she thought that evening,' that I should feel as if this charming afternoon's walk were somehow, not exactly wrong, but yet as if it were not right!'" Other Sunday afternoon rambles follow.

The miseries she endures at Mrs. Mason's are fully confided; and then Bellingham wishes to see her old home, Milham Grange, only six miles off. A fine Sunday comes, and they go. He watched her with admiration as she "wound in and out in natural, graceful, wavy lines, between the luxuriant and overgrown shrubs." All goes merrily until Mrs. Mason, who is also out for a Sunday holiday, finds Ruth in the young man's company, and tells her she must never enter her doors again. Her lover, who had left Ruth for a few minutes, found her crying; and she told him what had happened in the interval.

"Her eyes were so blinded by the fast-falling tears, she did not see (nor, had she seen, would she have been able to interpret) the change in Mr. Bellingham's countenance, as he stood silently watching her. He was silent so long, that even in her sorrow she began to wonder that he did not speak, and to wish to hear his soothing words once more. 'It is very unfortunate,' he began, at last; and then he stopped; then he began again, 'It is very unfortunate; for, you see, I did not like to name it to you before, but I believe—I have business, in fact, which obliges me to go to town to-morrow—to London, I mean; and I don't know when I shall be able to return.'" Hitherto, perhaps, no more than dalliance had been intended; but such dalliance is like the play of a little child on the brink of a precipice. The novelist delicately marks the moment, that moment of silence, when lust awoke as a rage in the blood of the young man. Such a moment of lust in the fairly right-meaning Arthur Donnithorne led to the ruin of Hetty Sorrel and the tragedy that followed it. The particular moment of Steerforth's abandonment to his passions is not indicated; but it is well that every young man and young woman should know that there is for them, as well as for everyone else, the possibility of being at death-grapple with that monster of our nature which we know as Lust. Self-indulgence prepares the way, dalliance offers a flowery by-path, and then, behold, before a person is aware, lust is upon him, and two lives are ruined. Safety lies, not in any immunity we may claim because we are refined, superior to common temptations; but in the strenuous, vigorous life of one who can say with St Paul, "I keep under my body and bring it into subjection." The primrose path of dalliance has only one end.

They go to London; but we next meet with them in North Wales. "Indeed, and she's not his wife,' thought Jenny (the landlady of the inn); 'that's as clear as day.'" Still Ruth enjoyed the revelation, new to her, of mountain beauty, and "her admiration and her content made him angry"; she sighed a little "at her own want of power to amuse and occupy him she loved." The people at the inn comment upon the pair. "She's a very lovely creature," said one gentleman; "not above sixteen, I should think, very modest and innocent-looking in her white gown"; and his wife answered, "Well, I do think it's a shame such people should be allowed to come here." So thought others, and Ruth's lonely walks came to be annoyed by hostile notice. Next, Mr. Bellingham falls ill of a fever, and his mother is sent for to nurse him; poor Ruth is thrown upon the scant kindness of the busy landlady, and endures days and nights of terrible anxiety; and when he mends, there is a long discussion with his mother as to Ruth. He is weakly sorry, but chiefly sorry for himself; and without seeing Ruth, without a word of farewell, he says, "Could we not leave to-night? I should not be so haunted by this annoyance in another place. I dread seeing her again because I fear a scene; and yet I believe I ought to see her in order to explain." This was all he had to give for a ruined life and for the unbounded devotion of a loving heart. Ruth was so young and unsophisticated that we may believe the full meaning of her offence had hardly dawned upon her. The tale goes on, how mother and son depart in great state, and he never seeks to see her, or explain, or say a common farewell. A good and grievously deformed man finds her afterwards, crouching in a lonely place; "and she said low and mournfully, 'He has left me, sir!—sir, he has indeed!—he has gone and left me!' Before he could speak a word to comfort her, she had burst into the wildest, dreariest crying ever mortal cried. The settled form of the event, when put into words, went sharp to her heart; her moans and sobs wrung his soul; but, as no speech of his could be heard, if he had been able to decide what best to say, he stood by her in apparent calmness, while she, wretched, wailed and uttered her woe. But when she lay worn out, and stupefied into silence, she heard him say to himself in a low voice, 'Oh, my God! for Christ's sake, pity her!'" This good man and his sister nurse her through a perilous illness, and at last take the poor girl and her child with them to their home in Lancashire, where he is the minister of a small chapel. Ruth went through the bitter waters of repentance, and a life of penitence and humble service gave her the beauty of Christian character; all the more readily, no doubt, because her sin was rather the consequence of loneliness, despair and affliction than of lust.

David, we know, discovered that there was forgiveness even for sins of lust; but they would seem to leave ineradicable marks in the character. So we find it in Mr. Bellingham. Years after, when she was doing valued service in a subordinate position, Ruth met him again. "He was changed, she knew not how; in fact, the expression which had been only occasional formerly, when his worst self predominated, had become permanent. He looked restless and dissatisfied . . . He thought that Mrs. Denbigh" (the assumed name she went under) "was certainly like poor Ruth; but this woman was far handsomer . . . Poor Ruth! and for the first time for several years he wondered what had become of her, though of course there was but one thing that could have happened; and perhaps it was as well he did not know her end, for most likely it would have made him very uncomfortable." This is Mr. Bellingham as we get him after the lapse of years. Ruth, the sinned-against, was able to behave with Christian dignity and composure; while he, who was let off 'scot-free,' appears again in middle life—a man without aim, without conscience, and without heart, but a prey to consuming lust.

We need not follow the story to the end. It is well worth reading, the more so if the reader asks, with the Twelve, 'Lord, is it I?' Is this misery, or worse, this degradation of character, possible to me? Is there anything in me which could bring about so shameful a fall? Be assured there is.

Dark rumours reach our ears from time to time of white men in African wilds who have escaped from the restraints of civilisation and have broken out in acts of detestable cruelty. When we hear these things, too, let us say, 'Lord, is it I?' For it is true that, once we escape from the bonds of duty, our duty towards God and our duty towards our neighbour, lust and hate become rampant in us, and there is no fall of which we are not capable.

But let us take courage. No last fall can overtake him who keeps his soul from the first fall; who preserves his chastity as in that fabled tower of brass, and allows no image of uncleanness to sully his imagination; who keeps his mind, too, full of healthy interests and worthy employment; who keeps under his body, by self-compelled labours, and noble restraint as regards all laxity of eating and drinking, lounging and sleeping.

Such an one, knowing the perils that beset his way, prays steadfastly day by day, "Our Father which art in heaven, . . . lead us not into temptation, but deliver us from evil. Amen"; and, having prayed, he thinks no more of the matter, but goes on his way fearless and rejoicing in his life—

"So keep I fair through faith and prayer
A virgin heart in work and will."

Chapter VII The Rulings Of Conscience In The House Of The Body: Fortitude

Fortitude.—Botticelli's picture of Fortitude, and Ruskin's interpretation of it, are among the lessons which Conscience should get by heart. This 'Fortitude' is no colossal figure, standing stark, bristling with combative energy. Noble in stature, she yet sits, weary after long-sustained effort; wistful, too, as who should say, 'How long?' But, though resting, she is wary and alert, still grasping the unsheathed sword which lies across her knees. She is engaged in a warfare whose end is not within sight; but hers is not the joy of attack. She is weary indeed, yet neither sorry for herself nor pleased with herself; her regard is simple. She has the 'single eye' which looks upon the thing to be done, not upon herself as the doer—the thing to be borne, rather, for Fortitude suffers.

The Bible hardly commends Fortitude to us by name as a Christian grace, yet therein we shall find our best exemplars. Our Lord, who bore more than we are able to express, says of Himself, "I am meek and lowly of heart"; and this saying, perhaps, gives us a key to the meaning of Fortitude,—less a valiant than a patient grace, memorable more for what she suffers gladly than for what she does.

As St Paul would image the fulness of Christ in the characters of Charity, so Isaiah gives us an image of Fortitude in setting forth the humiliation and sufferings of Christ. Fortitude grows up within us, a tender plant, is without form or comeliness, bears griefs and carries sorrows, endures chastisement, suffers and is dumb, does no violence, nor speaks deceit, is put to grief, yet—divides the spoil with the strong. There is only one true Fortitude among men, the fortitude of Christ; and every little bit of cheerful bearing that we are able for, without self-pity or self-complacency, comes of that divine fortitude.

Moses was the meekest man that ever lived, and his meekness was Fortitude. For forty years in the wilderness he bore with the waywardness of Israel; and, when the offences of the people had, so he thought, exceeded the patience of God, he prayed, "Yet now, if Thou wilt forgive their sin; and if not, blot me also, I pray Thee, out of the Book of Life."

St Paul, too, after much bearing,—"in journeyings often; in perils of waters; in perils of robbers; in perils by mine own countrymen; in perils by the heathen; in perils in the city; in perils in the wilderness; in perils in the sea; in perils among false brethren; in weariness and painfulness; in watchings often; in hunger and thirst; in fastings often; in cold and nakedness:"—could wish that he, too, were accurst for his brethren.

Perhaps Fortitude has always an element of tenderness, and always means bearing for love's sake; if it be only the fortitude of a child who bears toothache cheerfully that he may not distress his mother. The tradition of Fortitude was carried on in the Middle Ages rather in the school of chivalry—a school wherein the teachers were manifold distresses—than in the discipline and self-mortification of the monastery. Roland and Oliver, and each of the 'champions of Christendom,' has a record of distresses comparable with that of the Apostle. "Endure hardness," says St Paul to Timothy; and to endure without wincing, and without resentment was a law of knightly bearing.

Sir Kenneth, in The Talisman, [By Sir Walter Scott.] brings home the notion of knightly Fortitude in a way possible for ourselves.

Fortitude in Poverty.—"'May I see your sick squire, fair sir?' The Scottish knight hesitated and coloured, yet answered at last, 'Willingly, my Lord of Gilsland; but you must remember, when you see my poor quarters, that the nobles and knights of Scotland feed not so high, sleep not so soft, and care not for the magnificence of lodgment, which is proper to their southern neighbours. I am poorly lodged, my Lord of Gilsland,' he added, with a haughty emphasis on the word, while, with some unwillingness, he led the way to his temporary place of abode. Sir Kenneth cast a melancholy look around him, but suppressing his feelings, entered the hut, making a sign to the Baron of Gilsland to follow . . . The interior of the hut was chiefly occupied by two beds. One was empty, but composed of collected leaves, and spread with an antelope's hide. It seemed, from the articles of armour laid beside it, and from a crucifix of silver, carefully and reverentially disposed at the head, to be the couch of the knight himself.

The other contained the invalid, of whom Sir Kenneth had spoken, a strong-built and harsh-featured man, past, as his looks betokened, the middle age of life. His couch was trimmed more softly than his master's, and it was plain, that the more courtly garments of the latter, the loose robe, in which the knights showed themselves on pacific occasions, and the other little spare articles of dress and adornment, had been applied by Sir Kenneth to the accommodation of his sick domestic."

Here we have an example of Fortitude under very difficult circumstances, where pity and tenderness for dependents, personal dignity and high courage, go along with extreme poverty. The man who shows this manner of fortitude is a hero. The knight it is, and not that strange hermit-monk of the Lebanon, his body scarred with penitential wounds, who braces us by an example of Christian fortitude.

Fortitude under Vexatious Provocations.—Indeed, we are grateful for high lessons fitted to homely occasions, and we can at least understand how it was nothing less than high fortitude that Mrs. Garth showed in the presence of an undeserved and vexatious calamity.

Mrs. Garth [Middlemarch, by George Eliot.] is at one and the same time making pies, superintending the baking and the washing, and teaching 'Lindley Murray' to her youngest boy and girl. Fred Vincy comes to see her husband, and, by and by, Caleb himself comes in.

"'Mr. Garth, I am come to tell something that I am afraid will give you a bad opinion of me. I am come to tell you and Mrs. Garth that I can't keep my word. I can't find the money to meet the bill after all. I have been unfortunate; I have only got these fifty pounds towards the hundred and sixty.'

"Mrs. Garth was mutely astonished, and looked at her husband for an explanation. Caleb blushed, and after a little pause said—

"'Oh, I didn't tell you, Susan: I put my name to a bill for Fred; it was for a hundred and sixty pounds. He made sure he could meet it himself.'

"There was an evident change in Mrs. Garth's face, but it was like a change below the surface of water which remains smooth. She fixed her eyes on Fred, saying—

"'I suppose you have asked your father for the rest of the money, and he has refused you.'

"'No,' said Fred, biting his lips, and speaking with more difficulty; 'but I know it will be of no use to ask him; and unless it were of use, I should not like to mention Mr. Garth's name in the matter.'

"'It has come at an unfortunate time,' said Caleb, in his hesitating way, looking down at the notes and nervously fingering the paper. 'Christmas upon us—I'm rather hard up just now. You see, I have to cut out everything like a tailor with short measure. What can we do, Susan? I shall want every farthing we have in the bank, It's a hundred and ten pounds, the deuce take it!'

"'I must give you the ninety-two pounds that I have put by for Alfred's premium,' said Mrs. Garth gravely and decisively, though a nice ear might have discerned a slight tremor in some of the words.

"'And I have no doubt that Mary has twenty pounds saved from her salary by this time. She will advance it.'

"Mrs. Garth had not again looked at Fred, and was not in the least calculating what words she should use to cut him the most effectively. Like the eccentric woman she was, she was at present absorbed in considering what was to be done, and did not fancy that the end would be better achieved by bitter remarks or explosions. But she had made Fred feel for the first time something like the tooth of remorse.

"'I shall certainly pay it all, Mrs. Garth—ultimately,' he stammered out.

"'Yes, ultimately,' said Mrs. Garth, who, having a special dislike to fine words on ugly occasions, could not now repress an epigram. 'But boys cannot well be apprenticed ultimately: they should be apprenticed at fifteen.' She had never been so little inclined to make excuses for Fred . . . Fred turned and hurried out of the room.

"'I was a fool, Susan.'

"'That you were,' said the wife, nodding and smiling. 'But I should not have gone to publish it in the market-place. Why should you keep such things from me? It is just so with your buttons; you let them burst off without telling me, and go out with your wristband hanging.'"

Mrs. Amos Barton, [Scenes of Clerical Life, by George Eliot.] too—what a record of gentle and dignified fortitude is the story of her life and death in that poor parsonage house!

Cheerful, Serviceable Fortitude.—We think of Mark Tapley [Martin Chuzzlewit, by Charles Dickens.] with relief; he found 'no credit in being jolly' when things went well; but for cheerful, serviceable Fortitude, can any bit of knight-errantry exceed the 'jolly' way in which he made the best of things in 'Eden'? The foes he fought were nothing more romantic than fever, famine, querulousness, helplessness in every member of that poor colony; and what a plucky, unostentatious fight it was! Mark Tapley deserves a place among our bosom friends; but he might think there was no credit in being jolly in so snug a niche.

Nor need we go to 'Eden' to find place for Fortitude. A birthday dinner cooked (!) by her loving family gave occasion to the 'old girl' (otherwise Mrs. Bagnet, who is to be found in Bleak House [By Charles Dickens.]) for much cheerful serenity.

What a contrast she is, by the way, to Mrs. Wilfer (Our Mutual Friend), who lets the world know she is enduring by tying a black ribbon round her face. How many of us do the like with the metaphorical black ribbon of a sullen temper and a falling countenance! Instead of gradually ascending, we have come down from the high ideal of Fortitude to commonplace, even absurd, examples; but these fit our occasions; and it would not be a bad plan to keep a note-book recording the persons and incidents that give a fillip to conscience in this matter of Fortitude.

The Roll of our Heroes.—Time fails to tell of Nansen, Gordon, Howard, Livingstone, Collingwood, Raleigh, Galileo, Florence Nightingale, Calpurnia, Mackay of Uganda, Grace Darling; for the roll of persons notable for their Fortitude is, in fact, the roll of our heroes, and our little 'Book of Fortitude' will come to be a book of heroes, whether in small things or great. The reader will perhaps object that Fortitude belongs to the mind and the heart rather than to the body; but, when the body is not kept in its proper place, trained to endure without murmur, Fortitude has no chance. It is in the body we must endure hardness, and the training comes in the cheerful bearing of small matters not worth mentioning.

The Song of the Lotos-Eaters has music for us all:—

All things have rest: why should we toil alone,
We only toil, who are the first of things,
And make perpetual moan,
Still from one sorrow to another thrown:
Nor ever fold our wings,
And cease from wanderings,
Nor steep our brows in slumber's holy balm;
Nor hearken what the inner spirit sings,
'There is no joy but calm!'
Why should we only toil, the roof and crown of things?" [Tennyson.]

therefore we have need of Fortitude, without which no man or woman has ever yet brought life to any purpose: "So fight I, not as one that beateth the air: but I keep under my body, and bring it into subjection."

Chapter VIII The Rulings Of Conscience In The House Of The Body: Prudence

Imprudence is Selfishness.—"I, wisdom, dwell with prudence, and find out knowledge of witty inventions." Here is a saying worth pondering in an age when Prudence is not a popular grace. Young people confound rashness with generosity, and therefore hold Prudence in disfavour; when, of all cunning and injurious forms of selfishness, Imprudence is perhaps the most disastrous. Prudence is to be ranked among the K.C.s who instruct conscience concerning the affairs of the House of Body, because this virtue is exhibited for the most part in connection with material matters, and these all affect the body, directly or indirectly.

Prudence in Affairs.—We know the description of the virtuous woman; and, for virtuous, we might read prudent. It is Prudence who seeketh wool and flax and worketh diligently with her hands, who bringeth her food from afar. It is she who riseth early and giveth meat to her household, who considereth a field and buyeth it, who girdeth her loins with strength and strengtheneth her arms, who stretcheth out her hands to the poor, who is able to enrich her household, and to keep her place in the world with peace and honour.

Joseph was prudent. He looked ahead, and took measures for the advancement of his adopted country and the service of Pharaoh. Our own King Alfred was eminently prudent. Every great commander wins his battles as much through his prudence as his courage.

Prudence in the Choice of a Friend.—There was a time when Alcibiades [Plutarch's Life of Alcibiades.] was prudent. "From the first he was surrounded with pleasures, and a multitude of admirers determined to say nothing but what they thought would please, and to keep him from all admonition and reproof; yet, by his native penetration, he distinguished the value of Socrates, and attached himself to him, rejecting the rich and great who sued for his regard. With Socrates he soon entered into the closest intimacy; and finding that he did not, like the rest of the unmanly crew, want improper favours, but that he studied to correct the errors of his heart, and to cure him of his empty and foolish arrogance,—

Then his crest fell, and all his pride was gone,
He droop'd the conquered wing.

In fact, he considered the discipline of Socrates as a provision from heaven for the preservation and benefit of youth. Thus, despising himself, admiring his friend, adoring his wisdom, and revering his virtue, he insensibly formed in his heart the image of love, or rather came under the influence of that power, who, as Plato says, secures his votaries from vicious love."

Here we have a fine example of prudence in the choice of a friend and mentor, and well had it been for Alcibiades had his constancy been equal to his prudence.

Prudence rejects Undue Influence.—Alexander, [Plutarch's Life of Alexander.] in his heroic days, showed admirable prudence. He was able to distinguish between things that differ, that is, he understood the relative importance of the matters that came before him. "As for his mother, he made her many magnificent presents, but he would not suffer her busy genius to exert itself in state affairs, or in the least to control the proceedings of government. She complained of this as a hardship, and he bore her ill-humour with great mildness. Antipater once wrote him a long letter full of heavy complaints against her, and when he had read it he said, 'Antipater knows not that one tear of a mother can blot out a thousand such complaints.'" Not even his mother might interfere with the duties of his office, and yet how tender was his love for her!

We know how a greater than Alexander said, "Wist ye not that I must be about my Father's business?" and it is eminently the part of Prudence to allow of no undue influence in any public capacity even from our nearest and dearest; because we are called upon to think, ourselves, for the good of all concerned, and not to be influenced by the private interests of any. There is something rotten in any state whose officers can be induced to act for the private good of themselves or their belongings.

Prudence chooses simplicity and eschews luxury, finds more honour in labours than in pleasures, trains the body to endure hardness. In all these respects we find in Alexander an example of gentle, heroic prudence.

Prudence Temperate in all Things.—"He found that his great officers set no bounds to their luxury, that they were most extravagantly delicate in their diet, and profuse in other respects; insomuch that Agnon of Teos wore silver nails in his shoes; Leonatus had many camel-loads of earth brought from Egypt to rub himself with when he went to the wrestling-ring; Philotas had hunting-nets that would enclose the space of a hundred furlongs; more made use of rich essences than oil after bathing, and had their grooms of the bath, as well as chamberlains who excelled in bed-making. This degeneracy he reproved with all the temper of a philosopher. He told them, 'It was very strange to him that, after having undergone so many glorious conflicts, they did not remember that those who come from labour and exercise always sleep more sweetly than the inactive and effeminate; and that, in comparing the Persian manners with the Macedonian, they did not perceive that nothing was more servile than the love of pleasure, or more princely than a life of toil. How will that man,' continued he, 'take care of his own horse, or furbish his lance and helmet, whose hands are too delicate to wait on his own dear person? Know you not that the end of conquest is, not to do what the conquered have done, but something greatly superior?'" [Plutarch's Life of Alexander.]

Prudent Citizens the Wealth of the State.—The laws of Lycurgus [Plutarch's Life of Lycurgus.] were the outcome of a noble and generous prudence. If Sparta were to hold its own in the long conflict with Athens, it must be through the fitness of its individual citizens. Lycurgus recognised that each citizen possessed in himself the wealth most valuable to the state, in a body fit for toil and endurance, and a mind capable of seeing 'the proportion of things.

"Desirous to complete the conquest of luxury and exterminate the love of riches, he introduced a third institution which was wisely enough and ingeniously contrived. This was the use of public tables where all were to eat in common of the same meat, and such kinds of it as were appointed by law. At the same time, they were forbidden to eat at home upon expensive couches and tables, to call in the assistance of butchers and cooks, or to fatten like voracious animals in private. For so not only their manners would be corrupted, but their bodies disordered; abandoned to all manner of sensuality and dissoluteness, they would require long sleep, warm baths, and the same indulgence as in perpetual sickness . . . Another ordinance, levelled against magnificence and expense, directed that the ceilings of the houses should be wrought with no tool but the axe, and the doors with nothing but the saw. For as Epaminondas is reported to have said afterwards, of his table, Treason lurks not under such a dinner, so Lycurgus perceived, before him, that such a house admits of no luxury and needless splendour. Indeed, no man could be so absurd as to bring into a dwelling so homely and simple, bedsteads with silver feet, purple coverlets, golden cups, and a train of expense that follows these;

but all would necessarily have the bed suitable to the room, the coverlet of the bed and the rest of their utensils and furniture to that."

There are many points in which a Christian commonwealth may not emulate the Spartan regimen; but wise men are feeling strongly that prudence requires of us, for the good of the state, to live simple lives, to avoid excesses, even if they come in the way of athletic or intellectual toils, and to eschew possessions more than are necessary for fit and simple living. Perhaps it is lawful for us to allow ourselves, in our furniture and implements, beauty of form and colour, and fitness for our uses; but it may be our duty not to accumulate unnecessary possessions, the care of which becomes a responsibility, and whose value lies in their costliness. These things interfere with that real wealth of a serviceable body and alert mind which we owe to the service of our country as well as that of our home.

"When the money was brought to Athens, Phocion [Plutarch's Life of Phocion.] asked the persons employed in that commission 'Why, among all the citizens of Athens, he should be singled out as the object of such bounty?' 'Because,' said they, 'Alexander looks upon you as the only honest and good man.' 'Then,' said Phocion, 'let him permit me always to retain that character, as well as really to be that man.' The envoys then went home with him, and, when they saw the frugality that reigned there, his wife baking bread, himself drawing water and afterwards washing his own feet, they urged him the more to receive the present. They told him, 'It gave them real uneasiness, and was indeed an intolerable thing, that the friend of so great a prince should live in such 'a wretched manner.' At that instant a poor old man happening to pass by, in a mean garment, Phocion asked the envoys, 'Whether they thought worse of him than of that man?' As they begged of him not to make such a comparison, he rejoined, 'Yet that man lives upon less than I do, and is contented. In one word, it will be to no purpose for me to have so much money if I do not use it; and if I was to live up to it, I should bring both myself and the king, your master, under the censure of the Athenians.' Thus the money was carried back from Athens, and the whole transaction was a good lesson to the Greeks, that the man who did not want such a sum of money was richer than he who could bestow it."

In the matter of Prudence, also, our Master shows us the better way. It was written of Christ, "My servant shall deal prudently"; and we should find great profit in studying the Gospel histories to see how our Lord dealt prudently with that possession of His personal life, the sole possession He allowed to Himself, and the sole possession of value to which any of us can attain. Thinking upon Christ, we shall walk soberly, and not run into any excess of riot.

SECTION II. Conscience In The House Of Mind

Chapter IX Opinions 'In The Air'

Everybody knows that the affairs of his body and those of his heart should be ordered by his conscience. Our acts and feelings towards other people, and our management of our own bodies, fall, we believe, properly under the judgment of Conscience; but we have a notion that thought is free; that, in the domain of intellect, every man is his own master, and that the opinions we form, the mental work we choose to do or to leave undone, are beyond the pale of duty. Thought is free, is our unconscious watchword.

Casual Opinions.—Now, of all the errors that have hindered men and nations, this is perhaps the most unfortunate. A man picks up a notion, calls it his opinion, spreads it here and there, until in the end that foolish notion becomes a danger to society and a bondage to the individual. "These be thy gods, O Israel!" is a cry that is constantly rising in our camp. We do not know in whose tent it began, but opinion flashed a lightning message over all the camp of Israel, and every man brought his precious things for the making of the golden calf. Why? Their leader was out of sight for the moment—with God, it is true, but, still, out of sight, and the tribes made haste to worship at a shrine of their own invention. This story typifies the sudden inroad of opinion by which nations and persons are apt to be carried away. The lawgiver fails to direct, and clamorous opinion fills the ear.

In the summer holidays, when people have not much to think about, the newspapers lend themselves to the discussion of such idle questions as, 'Is life worth living?' 'Is marriage a failure?'—the underlying opinion being that life is not worth living, and marriage is a failure. Sensible people laugh at these letters; but there are many who lie in wait for any chance notion that comes floating their way, take it up zealously, and make it their business in life to spread it.

When such minds get hold of the idea that marriage is a failure, for example, much immorality is the result. The notion has become the molten calf; the lawgiver, Conscience, is away or silenced; and people think it rather a fine thing to make sacrifices for the idea they cherish at the moment. Or, again, they go about asking, 'Is life worth living?' and though the results may seem less grave because less criminal, they are really as serious. That people should be sullen and ungrateful for rain and sunshine, food and raiment, the beauty of the world and the kindness of friends, is not a crime, because it is not one of the offences against society punishable by law; but it is a black sin, as catching as the plague, and he has caught it who allows himself to ask, 'Is life worth living?'

How Fallacies work.—We know, by hearsay, how the 'killing-no-murder' fallacy works; how apparently good men, who let in the notion, are convinced by their own Reason that the death of an offender against the liberties of the people is the only safety for the rest; that providence has called them to the great task, that they will be regarded thenceforth as the deliverers of their people. They kill the man, and are abhorred by all thinking persons as assassins. How has it come about?

Conscience, which thunders, '*thou shalt do no murder*,' had been silenced; Opinion played the part of director, Reason supported Opinion, and the shameful deed was done. The slightest waft of opinion is enough to mislead the open, or rather the empty, mind. The newspaper headings displayed day by day are enough. 'The Unreality of Sin,' figured in a local newspaper the other day (anent certain American teaching). Anyone who is aware of the hunger of the unoccupied mind for any chance deposit of ideas will realise how such a heading would be accepted by many minds, and cherished as a sanction for sin.

When I was a girl the darning of stockings was considered a great piece of domestic virtue; and, one day, I heard a Welsh lady of staidness and moral correctness say that she did not believe in darning stockings! I found out afterwards that the darning she meant was running the heels of new stockings; but I seized on the doctrine as applying to all manner of holes, with a great sense of emancipation. It is just so that chance sayings about more important matters are caught up and acted upon. There is ever some new fallacy in the air which allures its thousands, and no one is safe who is not cognisant of danger, and who does not know how to safeguard himself. Perhaps no rules for the right conduct of life are more important than the following: (a) that we may not play with chance opinions; (b) that our own Reason affords an insufficient test of the value of an opinion (because Reason, as we have seen, argues in behalf of Inclination); (c) that we must labour to get knowledge as the foundation of opinions; (d) that we must also labour to arrive at principles whereby to try our opinions.

Chapter X The Uninstructed Conscience

There is no end to the vagaries of the uninstructed conscience. It is continually straining out the gnat and swallowing the camel. The most hardened criminal has his conscience; and he justifies that which he does by specious reasons. 'Society is against' him, he says; he 'has never had a fair chance.' Why should he 'go about ragged and hungry when another man rides in his carriage and eats and drinks his fill?' 'If that man has so much, let him keep it if he can; if cleverer wits than his contrive to ease him of a little, that is only fair play.' Thus do reason and inclination support one another in the mind of the Ishmael whose hand is against every man; and, if every man's hand is against him, that is all the more reason, he urges, that he should get what he can take out of life.

Conscience Persistent upon some Points.—But there are points upon which the glib flow of reason does not silence his conscience. He must be true to his 'pals,' and to give up a pal to justice would probably be a greater crime in his eyes than to kill a man. Also, he will be fair in his dealings with his companions, and will share according to bargain. Perhaps he has a child whom he cherishes, or a friend whom he cares for. No man's conscience is silent on every point of duty; and perhaps there is no one, savage or civilised, who does not act up to his conscience in, at any rate, some few points. The first effort of the missionary or explorer is to find out in what matters the people he is amongst are dependable. Livingstone was able to live with the most degraded tribes of Africans, because his sympathy and knowledge helped him to discover safe ground,—the points on which the savage conscience was inflexible, as, for example, loyalty to a guest, gratitude to a benefactor. Indeed, Livingstone made some great discoveries in human nature amongst these barbarous tribes; for the good that is true of the worst must be true of those who are better. He found they all knew that they must not murder, nor steal, must be obedient to parents, kind to each other, and much besides; that is to say, they had the light of conscience. We know, too, from Captain Cook how the Otaheitans wept when they first saw a white man flogged. Cruelty was contrary to their savage code.

Moral Stability.—But the uninstructed conscience is open to every prompting of inclination, seconded, as it is sure to be, by a thousand good reasons. This is the cause of the instability of conduct shown by the savage, the criminal, the raw schoolboy, the rough yokel, and the ignorant and undisciplined of every class of life, even when such ignorance is credited by a university degree. It is only the instructed conscience which is stable.

There are persons of whom we say, 'We always know how so-and-so will act. We can depend upon him.' The reason is that he is not liable to be carried away by sudden inroads of outside opinion.

His knowledge affords him a standard by which he judges the worth of such opinion; his principles, a test of its moral rightness. Therefore the flashy new opinion, which history tells him has been tried and found wanting long ago, has no chance with him. He examines it in the light of his principles, finds it to be based on an error of thought, that it leads to further errors of thought and action; and it takes no hold upon his mind.

A Nation may be Unstable.—As for the rest—the persons who have taken no pains to instruct their conscience—the sudden rush of a community, a person, a nation after a new notion, the last crank, is extraordinary, and becomes a mania. Scott, who is a past master in moral philosophy, perhaps because of his legal habit of mind, gives us in Peveril of the Peak an historical example of the nation run mad with a notion. And a single example of the power of a notion on the uninstructed conscience, and of how such baseless notion may spread like an epidemic, is so instructive that I must quote part of a note relative to the Popish Plot appended to Peveril of the Peak:—"The infamous character of those who contrived and carried on the pretended Popish Plot, may be best estimated by the account given in North's Examen, who describes Oates himself with considerable power of colouring. 'He was now in his trine exaltation, his Plot in full force, efficacy and virtue; he walked about with his guards (assigned for fear of the Papists murdering him). He had lodgings in Whitehall, and £1200 per annum pension: and no wonder, after he had the impudence to say to the House of Lords, in plain terms, that, if they would not help him to more money, he must be forced to help himself. He put on an Episcopal garb (except the lawn sleeves), silk gown and cassock, great hat, satin hatband and rose, long scarf, and was called, or most blasphemously called himself, the Saviour of the nation; whoever he pointed at, was taken up and committed; so that many people got out of his way, as from a blast . . . The very breath of him was pestilential, and, if it brought not imprisonment or death over such on whom it fell, it surely poisoned reputation . . . The Queen herself was accused at the Commons' bar. The city, for fear of the Papists, put up their posts and chains: and the Chamberlain, Sir Thomas Player, in the Court of Aldermen, gave his reason for the city's using that caution, which was, that he did not know but the next morning they might all rise with their throats cut . . . Nothing ordinary or moderate was to be heard in people's communication; but every debate and action was high-flown and tumultuous. All freedom of speech was taken away; and not to believe the Plot, was worse than being Turk, Jew, or infidel.'"

A Besetting Idea.—This theme seems to have had some fascination for the mind of Scott. He presents it to us as the key to more than one historical character. In Balfour of Burley, [Old Mortality.] we have a monomaniac, a man possessed and impelled by a homicidal idea; and yet, when that idea had resulted in barbarous and sacrilegious crime, the man's native, uninstructed conscience wrestled with the 'reasonable' conclusion to which he had brought himself, and he suffered great mental anguish. This example of a besetting idea is even more instructive than that of Brutus, as Shakespeare interprets him, because Scott is at some pains to show that prejudice, credulousness, intolerance, superstition, lawless ambition, even homicidal crime, are the natural outcome of the dark mind of ignorance; the more so, when this ignorance is allied with mental power, and the mind is struck by a forcible idea. The belated action of conscience upon such a mind is portrayed in this case with wonderful vividness.

The same author brings again before us the perils of benighted ignorance, and its power of converting the purest teaching to the foulest uses, in the character of the Independent, Sergeant Tomkins [Woodstock] (or, as he calls himself, Honest Joe and Trusty Tomkins), who believed that he was saved, and therefore could do no sin; which he interpreted to mean that that which was foul sin in other men, he might commit and yet be void of offence.

Perils of Ignorance.—In our own days of enlightenment and progress, we seem to be less aware of the grossness, dulness and foulness of ignorance than were the more thoughtful minds of the Middle Ages. We do not understand that the uninstructed conscience is at the mercy of the darkened mind. Intelligent persons will be heard to remark, 'I don't see the good of missionaries,' 'Every nation and tribe has the religion best suited to it'; as though anything but evil can come out of the dark places of the earth, where passion, prejudice, and superstition extinguish the natural light of Conscience.

The ignorance at home, in our very schools and colleges, is a cause of alarm. It is because of our ignorance that we are like those seventy thousand Americans whom Emerson describes as "going about in search of a religion." The very 'tolerance' upon which we pride ourselves arises from the ignorance which does not know how to distinguish between things that differ. We are not so far gone, perhaps, as that nation which provides us with new notions and new religions, but our readiness to receive what comes in our way lays us open to the charge of an uninstructed conscience.

In political matters we trust to our newspaper, which is expressly the organ of our party, and do not look for the side-lights of other writings, or the illumination cast by history and literature. We get our education in this kind out of compendiums and lectures; and these, naturally, cannot afford the copious detail out of which conscience gathers instruction.

Scrupulosity.—We are in the way, too—like that young man of whom Mrs. Piozzi tells us in her Anecdotes of Johnson,—of erring by over-scrupulosity in one direction, as by laxity in another.

"A person," Johnson said, "had for these last five weeks often called at my door, but would not leave his name or any other message, but that he wished to speak with me. At last we met, and he told me that he was oppressed by scruples of conscience. I blamed him gently for not applying, as the rules of our Church direct, to his parish priest or other discreet clergyman; when, after some compliments on his part, be told me he was clerk to a very eminent trader, at whose warehouses much business consisted in packing goods in order to go abroad; that he was often tempted to take paper and packthread for his own use, and that he had indeed done so often, that be could recollect no time when he had ever bought any for himself. 'But probably,' said I, 'your master was wholly indifferent with regard to such trivial emoluments. You had better ask for it at once, and so take your trifles with content.' 'Oh, sir!' replies the visitor, 'my master bid me have as much as I pleased, and was half angry when I talked to him about it.' 'Then pray, sir,' said I, 'tease me no more about such airy nothings,' and was going on to be very angry, when I recollected that the fellow might be mad, perhaps; so I asked him, 'When he left the counting-house of an evening?' 'At seven o'clock, sir.' 'And when do you go to bed, sir?' ' At twelve o'clock.' 'Then,' replied I, 'I have at least learnt thus much by my new acquaintance—that five hours of the four-and-twenty unemployed are enough for a man to go mad in; so I would advise you, sir, to study algebra, if you are not already an adept in it. Your head would get less muddy and you will leave off tormenting your neighbours about paper and packthread, while we all live together in a world that is bursting with sin and sorrow.'"

Undue scrupulosity about small matters is a sure mark of the uninstructed conscience. The man should not have taken his master's packthread; but to occupy his own attention and that of others about so small a matter was a worse offence, and illustrates the fact that only the instructed conscience is capable of seeing things in due proportion, of distinguishing what really matters from that which is of no consequence. This is why a child makes such enormous mistakes in his valuation of life. He will be guilty of lying, unkindness, cruelty even, and not know that he has done wrong, while a trifling act, like the opening of a forbidden drawer, will fret his conscience for months. The schoolboy's moral code is marked by similar disproportion. To deceive his master is no offence, but to 'blab' on another boy puts him beyond the pale.

The subject of the uninstructed conscience is so wide, and covers so much of life, that I can only offer an illustration or a hint here and there; but let us be sure of this, that, though all men are endowed with conscience, its light is steady and certain only in proportion as it is informed by a cultivated intelligence; and of this, also, that the uninstructed conscience leaves its possessor open to bigotry, fanaticism, panic, envy, spite. His reason justifies every offence to a man who has little knowledge of persons and events whereby to correct his judgments. You will observe, I am not speaking of wilful sin; alas, the instructed conscience also is open to sin! But we shall consider this most anxious matter later: meantime, let us be well assured that more than half the errors and offences committed in the world are sins of ignorance; that is, people think and do amiss because they are at no pains to acquire an instructed conscience.

Chapter XI The Instructed Conscience

Sound Moral Judgment.—I do not say that the man with the instructed conscience is incapable of moral wrong. That is not the case. His advantage is that he can rarely do or think amiss without being aware of his offence; and the stability which this enlightenment gives to its possessor is a distinction. Emerson remarks upon the curious fact that many persons have a name, a force, in the world which exceeds their deeds or their recorded words. We are profoundly interested in Arnold Toynbee, John Sterling, Arthur Hallam, and other young men whose span of life did not by much exceed their university days. Emerson says that the secret of this sort of esteem which is not founded upon accomplishment is—character. Very likely he is right; but perhaps the particular development of character we reverence in such men is the sound moral judgment born of the instructed conscience. Goldsmith gives us a charming type of this manner of moral balance in Dr Primrose. [The Vicar of Wakefield.] How wise are his decisions, how just his resolutions, how gentle and how penetrating his reproofs. Can we ever forget that epitaph to which his wife should live up, or the way in which he allowed his family to have that portrait painted—too big for any room in the house—a reproof of vanity none of them could forget! How humble he is in prosperity, how equable in adversity! And all this has come to him through his books and his prayers—not through his books alone, and not through his prayers alone.

Dr Johnson, [Boswell's Life of Johnson.] too. We who are used to dictionaries are not impressed by 'the great lexicographer' as such. Indeed, his output, whether in action or in writing, was surprisingly small for a man of such vast power; and, as to the manner of his writing, why, Boswell himself had a style that we like better to-day; but there have been few men better qualified than he to arrive at the just judgments of an instructed conscience. That is why the Life is such inimitable reading. To be plied with Boswell's 'Sir?' on all manner of occasions must have been irritating, and we do not wonder that now and then Johnson whimsically chose to make the worse appear the better cause. But what a world of just and righteous judgments the wise man utters! No wonder his contemporaries waited on his words. We can all talk platitudes and air the moralities of others; but to say what he himself would call 'luminous' things about all the occasions of life, many of the personages in history—this is a distinction to which only the instructed conscience can enable a man to attain. It is probable that everyone who makes his mark beyond what we see of his accomplishment does so from the force, not of genius, but of moral judgment.

Moral Judgments and a Virtuous Life.—The power to form moral judgments and the power to live a virtuous life are not identical; but for persons whose living is not confined to a very narrow sphere the one is necessary to the other. Simple people may think duly about daily work and duties because their conscience is instructed by homely wisdom that has come down to them without their knowing it; but, if we mean to live in the wide world of thought and action, our first care must be to get, by slow degrees, the power of forming just opinions.

How are we to get such power? In the first place, we must observe and think for ourselves, not 'cute' and clever thoughts about our neighbours' doings, discovering a low motive here, a sharp practice there: persons who allow themselves in this habit of mind lose the power of interpreting life by the aid of an illuminated conscience. But, if we observe with gentle, large, and humble thoughts, we shall find much to instruct and improve us in the life of every family. We shall see good in the action of statesmen, at home and abroad; wisdom in the attitudes of nations.

But most of us have little chance of seeing men and things on a wide scale, and our way to an instructed conscience is to read, mark, learn, and inwardly digest. We must read novels, history, poetry, and whatever falls under the head of literature, not for our own 'culture.' Some of us begin to dislike the word 'culture,' and the idea of a 'cultivated' person; any effort which has self as an end is poor and narrow. But there is a better reason for an intimacy with literature as extensive and profound as we can secure. Herein we shall find the reflections of wise men upon the art of living, whether put in the way of record, fable, or precept, and this is the chief art for us all to attain.

Chapter XII Some Instructors Of Conscience: Poetry, Novels, Essays

Poetry.—Poetry is, perhaps, the most searching and intimate of our teachers. To know about such a poet and his works may be interesting, as it is to know about repoussé work; but in the latter case we must know how to use the tools before we get joy and service out of the art. Poetry, too, supplies us with tools for the modelling of our lives, and the use of these we must get at for ourselves. The line that strikes us as we read, that recurs, that we murmur over at odd moments—this is the line that influences our living, if it speak only—

"Of old, unhappy, far-off things,
And battles long ago."

A couplet such as this, though it appear to carry no moral weight, instructs our conscience more effectually than many wise saws. As we 'inwardly digest,' reverence comes to us unawares, gentleness, a wistful tenderness towards the past, a sense of continuance, and of a part to play that shall not be loud and discordant, but of a piece with the whole. This is one of the 'lessons never learned in schools' which comes to each of us only as we discover it for ourselves.

Many have a favourite poet for a year or two, to be discarded for another and another. Some are happy enough to find the poet of their lifetime in Spenser, Wordsworth, Browning, for example; but, whether it be for a year or a life, let us mark as we read, let us learn and inwardly digest. Note how good this last word is. What we digest we assimilate, take into ourselves, so that it is part and parcel of us, and no longer separable.

We probably read Shakespeare in the first place for his stories, afterwards for his characters, the multitude of delightful persons with whom he makes us so intimate that afterwards, in fiction or in fact, we say, 'She is another Jessica,' and 'That dear girl is a Miranda'; 'She is a Cordelia to her father,' and, such a figure in history, 'a base Iago.' To become intimate with Shakespeare in this way is a great enrichment of mind and instruction of conscience. Then, by degrees, as we go on reading this world-teacher, lines of insight and beauty take possession of us, and unconsciously mould our judgments of men and things and of the great issues of life.

Novels.—Novels, again, are as homilies to the wise; but not if we read them merely for the tale. It is a base waste of time to read a novel that you can skip, or that you look at the last page of to see how it ends. One must read to learn the meaning of life; and we should know in the end, who said what, and on what occasion! The characters in the books we know become our mentors or our warnings, our instructors always; but not if we let our mind behave as a sieve, through which the whole slips like water.

It would, of course, be a foolish waste of time to give this sort of careful reading to a novel that has neither literary nor moral worth, and therefore it is well to confine ourselves to the best—to novels that we can read over many times, each time with increased pleasure. The superficial way in which people read is illustrated by the fact that ninety-nine out of a hundred run away with the notion that Thackeray presents us with Amelia [Vanity Fair.] as an ideal woman; while few extract the solemn moral of the tale—that a man cannot give to a woman more than she is worth; and that Dobbin, the faithful Dobbin, found his life at last, not in Amelia, but in his books and his daughter. It is well that we should choose our authors with judgment, as we choose our friends, and then wait upon them respectfully to hear what they have to say to us.

Essays.—Of the ever-delightful essayists, I will not speak here. These, like the poets, we must find out for ourselves. They make a claim of special personal intimacy with their readers, and each apparently light phrase should give us pause: there may be more in it than meets the eye. Anyway, the essayist, to take him at his best, writes because he has something personal to say to you and me, because there is some fruit of the thought of his life he would have us taste; so let us read for edification.

Chapter XIII Some Instructors Of Conscience: History And Philosophy

History.—History, including the lives of historical personages, approaches us on other ground. The passion of patriotism, the bond of citizenship, are dominant in our age, perhaps because the new imperial idea has taken hold of us; but still more, perhaps, because we are in the rebound from the individualism of the preceding generation. Let us be thankful that we are moved by these strong forces; but their very strength may hurry us into presumptuous sins, unless we recognise our position with regard to country and city, and labour for the instructed conscience.

The Informed Patriot.—We must read our newspaper, of course—newspapers on both sides; but he who founds upon his newspaper is an ignorant patriot and an illiberal citizen. His opinions are no more than parrot-like repetitions of other men's sayings; whereas he who dwells with dutiful interest upon the history of his own country, distressed over her ignominies, proud when she has shown herself great; who has pondered the history of another great empire—admiring the temperate justice with which its distant colonies were administered, and scrutinising the causes of its fall—he gradually acquires some insight as to the meaning of national life. He is able to express an opinion which is not a mere echo, and gains convictions which will certainly be of use to his country, even if they are known only to the people about his own fireside.

He learns to esteem Xerxes as a great gardener, a planter, whose aim it was that every man should have his little 'paradise.' Lycurgus is to him more than a lawgiver, he is a hero able to keep the laws he made. Such a person regards, with half-envious interest, the records of those small yet great republics, distinguished in the arts of peace and of war, in whose open schools every man picked up philosophy, and the best men made it the study of a lifetime.

He who reads history in this way, not to pass examinations, nor to obtain culture, nor even for his own pleasure (delightful as such reading is), but because he knows it to be his duty to his country to have some intelligent knowledge of the past, of other lands as well as of his own, must add solid worth to the nation that owns him. It is something to prepare for the uses of the State a just, liberal, and enlightened patriotism in the breast of a single citizen.

Philosophy.—Philosophy lays her hand upon us, as upon the youth of Athens, with an absolute claim. We are remarkable among the civilised peoples for our ignorance of what has been already thought in the world, has been given up as futile, or has passed into common knowledge. For five thousand years, at least, philosophers have been in search of a single principle which shall cover, to put it crudely, matter and mind. We think, to-day, that we have found this principle in evolution. It may be so; but we allow ourselves to come to the conclusion without due knowledge of what has been already thought, without even taking in the fact that, if we accept the doctrine as including the evolution of mind, we give up the idea that there is any life here or hereafter excepting physical life, any existence beyond a physical existence. I do not propose to discuss this thesis; all I say is, that we should not lay ourselves open blindfold to such far-reaching conclusions, in the belief that things must be thus and thus because another man's reason has found them so; our own reason, taking his lead, finding them so too. Let us perceive and know with certainty that the function of reason is to bring us to the logical conclusion of any premises we think it well to receive.

Then we shall see that it rests with us to choose the notions which we are willing to admit to reasonable proof; and to make this choice, conscience must be instructed. The history of thought will bring us abundant evidence of the fallibility of reason; therefore, there is no certainty that what proves itself to us must be right. Approximate certainty lies in two directions—in a knowledge of the history of the thought of the past, and in a carefully calculated forecast of the issues. We must reach our convictions, not through our own reasoning, or another man's, however conclusive; but reason must work upon knowledge, and be instructed by a wide survey of all that is involved. The person who refuses to be influenced by what has gone before and what will follow, embraces what he calls ' the truth' in a spirit of ignorant partisanship.

Columbus, we know, received an idea that was, no doubt, floating in the air, the idea of a western passage to the Indies. After attempts in other quarters, he brought his idea to Ferdinand and Isabella; they gave it generous reception, and provided him with ships and money. But he would have been a mere adventurer had he come with no more than a notion that proved itself to his own understanding. He was armed with the history of the voyages of the past, which showed that his particular adventure had not been accomplished; with a knowledge of geographical principles, which proved his notion tenable; with a forecast of the results of his discovery, should he succeed; that is, he was able conscientiously to lay his scheme before the Spanish monarchs, and the result justified him.

We cannot escape from the necessity for knowledge, especially in this realm of ideas. The thousand quack philosophies of the day—as of all past days—have their birth in minds ignorant of the thought of the past, and unaware of the fact when they are offering a patched-up version of ideas and principles which have already been found wanting.

A 'Message.'—Many men believe that they have a message, become fanatics for their message, and make—nothing is so easy—innumerable converts. But not every notion is a message. Such indications come, as Coleridge has finely said, to minds "already prepared to receive them by a higher Power than Nature herself." As for the preparation,—knowledge, insight, foresight, and the meekness of wisdom, the gentleness of one under guidance,—these are signs by which we can discern, each for himself, if we, indeed, have a message, or (for this also is a mission) are prepared to take up and carry forward a message. The messages are manifold, the messengers are many; but few things hinder the progress of the world more than the wilful and fanatical adoption of notions because they appeal to us, and because our own reason proves them right. The secret of safety in matters of philosophy, as well as in all practical matters of life, is to know that we are capable of being convinced of anything, however wrong or foolish, unless we are able to bring an instructed conscience to the consideration of the acceptable notion.

Chapter XIV Some Instructors Of Conscience: Theology

Theology.—Theology, divinity, the knowledge of God, by whatever name we call it, is a sphere in which, more than any other, we must needs be ruled by the instructed conscience; and yet we are apt to think, as do the children, that God requires us to be good, and punishes us when we are bad; and this is all we care to know about religion: we leave out of count that knowledge of God which, we have it on the authority of Christ himself, 'is eternal life.'

Perhaps it is because the word 'eternal' casts our thoughts into the far future, about which we do not much concern ourselves. We do not realise that eternity is past, present, and to come. Life, in any real sense, is the knowledge of God now; and, without that knowledge, there cannot be the free and joyous activity of our powers, the glow of our feelings, the happy living, free from care, the open eye for all beauty, the open heart for all goodness, the responsive mind, the tender heart, the aspiring soul—which go to make up fulness of life. Most people live a poor maimed life, as though they carried about one or other mortified limb, dead in itself and a burden to the body. But they do not realise that their minds are slow and their hearts heavy for want of the knowledge which is life.

The Divine Method.—We think, too, that the knowledge of divine things comes by feeling, and chide ourselves because we do not feel more. If we examine the teaching of Christ, we shall find that exceedingly little is said about feeling, and a great deal about knowing: that our Lord's teaching appeals, not to the heart, but to the intelligence. "Without a parable spake he not unto them." Why? That, "hearing they should not hear, and seeing they should not see, neither should they understand."

Here we have a method exactly contrary to all usual methods of teaching. In a general way, the teacher labours to make what he has to say plain to the dullest; and, indeed, we are impatient and fretful under poem or apologue, the meaning of which is not clear at the first glance. That is, we choose that all labour shall be on the part of the teacher, and none upon that of the learner.

Whatever we get in this way is soon lost—'lightly come, lightly go'—for knowledge is only to be had at the cost of labour of mind. As regards the knowledge of our religion, above all, we must read, and inwardly digest; for it is only upon that which we take into us as part of ourselves that we grow. Our Lord knew this, and delivered no easy sayings for the instruction of the people. Even his disciples did not understand. Let us put ourselves in their place, and listen to the Master's 'hard' sayings—hard intellectually as well as morally—and see what we should get out of them on the first hearing. The involved arguments of St Paul are infinitely plainer; the dark sayings of the prophets, the Apocalypse itself, are easier to understand, so far as their meaning is decipherable at all, than the simple-sounding sayings of Christ. But this very fact evidences our Lord's way of teaching us that life comes of knowledge, the knowledge of God.

The Bible contains a Revelation of God.—Where shall we find our material?—for we can only think as we are supplied with the material for thought. First and last, in the Bible; for the knowledge of God comes by revelation. We can only know Him as he declares and manifests Himself to us. There are, no doubt, 'few, faint, and feeble' rays of revelation in books held sacred by various eastern nations; and this we should expect, because God is the God of all flesh, and does not leave Himself without a witness anywhere; but feeble rays in an immense void of darkness are not accepted even by the people who possess them as affording a knowledge of God. They do not aim at or conceive of such a knowledge. They sit in darkness as they have sat from the beginning, and must needs sit until they receive the light of revelation.

The Higher Criticism.—A serious danger threatens us who hold the means of knowledge in what is called the higher criticism. It is no doubt well that scholars should give critical attention to every jot and tittle of the Scriptures; and the danger to us does not lie in any possibility that in the Bible we have no word of God, but merely the literature of the Hebrew nation. So soon as men's eyes turn from minute literary criticism to the gradual revelation of our God in His beauty (the progressive revelation which we get in the Bible alone), the truth of the Book is confirmed to us; and we know, without proof

"Thou canst not prove the Nameless,
Nor canst thou prove the world thou movest in,
For nothing worthy proving can be proven,
Nor yet disproven."—[The Myths of Plato, Professor Stewart.]

Plato has said the last word on this matter for our day as well as his own. The danger I refer to is that, while occupying our minds about questions of criticism, we neglect the knowledge which cannot come without labour; that we forsake the earnest and devout study of the Bible, the one way of approach to the knowledge of God.

Already we begin to gather the fruits of our ignorance. Little books with Bible sayings, worked into specious arguments to prove a philosophy of life which the Bible does not sanction, come to us as a new and wonderful gospel. We talk of new developments of Christianity, when the Christianity of the Bible offers infinite scope for development in the beauty of holiness and in the knowledge of our illimitable God. We are offered on all hands religions about Christ and without Christ. We are taught to believe that, "God manifest in the flesh," means no more than the divine in ourselves, and that every power that was used by Christ is available to us.

A smug religiosity is upon us, a religion of which we ourselves are the measure; whether we call it 'Christianity on a Higher Plane,' or Buddhism, or Theosophy; or whether, like the Dukhobors, we decline to obey human law, because we choose to believe ourselves under the immediate direction of God,—saying, with that poor little community in Lancashire, 'There is no law but God's law,' and drawing the absurd inference that all human law is transgression:—all these things have the one interpretation; we are declining from the knowledge of God.

Indecision.—In another way still we are eating the fruit of our ignorance. A paralysing hesitancy and uncertainty are upon us. We are tolerant of all beliefs because we have none. 'We do not know,' we say; 'we are not sure.' 'What right have we to think that the creed of another man, or another people, is not as true as ours?' The very newspapers ask us, Is Christianity effete?—and we presume to discuss the question; or, at any rate, we are able to listen in calmness while men toss to and fro the one question which is vital to us. Let us believe it—What think ye of Christ? is the only question that matters. We cannot escape with the evasion, "We think not of Christ, but of the Father"—for the word is true, "No man cometh unto the Father but by me."

How are we to get this vital knowledge, without which we assuredly perish?—not in some unknown future state, but here and now, a slow paralysis creeps upon us. We have seen that there is but one source of illumination, the Bible itself. It is true that the divine Spirit is a light in every man's soul; but if a lamp is to be kindled, there must be the lamp; and it would seem as if the process followed by the Holy Spirit were to teach us by an arresting illumination, from time to time, of some phrase written in the Bible. Hence, our business is, before all things, to make ourselves acquainted with the text.

Study of the Bible.—How, then, shall we study our Bible, bearing in mind that our aim is not textual criticism, or even textual knowledge, but the knowledge of God?

The interpreter is too much with us. We lean on him—whether in commentary, essay, sermon, poem, critique—and are content that he should think for us. It is better that we should, in the first place, try our own efforts at interpretation; when we fail or are puzzled is the time to compare our thought with that of others, choosing as interpreters men of devout mind and scholarly accomplishment. Orderly study, with the occasional help of a sound commentary, is to be recommended. To use 'good books,' by way of a spiritual stimulus, deadens in the end the healthy appetite for truth. The same remark applies to little text-books, with remarks meant to stimulate certain virtues or states of mind. The error that underlies these aids to private devotion (public worship is another matter) is, that their tendency is to magnify ourselves and our occasions, while they create in us little or no desire for the best knowledge. It is probable that even our lame efforts at reading with understanding are more profitable than the best instruction. The preparedness we need is of the mind and heart; we must pray to be delivered from prejudices and prepossessions, and wait upon God as the thirsty earth waits for rain.

In the Old Testament it is well, for example, to read a life through, with such breaks as may be convenient, remembering that there has been no such constraint upon the author as to make him a recording machine. He writes as he is, a man with ignorances which have not been informed, with prejudices which have not been corrected. You discern the man in his book, as any author is discerned in his writings. The difference in the Scriptures is that the men who wrote the Bible books were charged with the revelation of God and of His dealings with men; revelations of men also, discovered with a certain childlike simplicity which shows us to each other—as we surely appear to our Father—without excuse or extenuation, but with a strong appeal in our simplicity. Men are, we may believe, shown to us in the Bible as we each appear before God. Good men offend, are chastised and forgiven, even as children in a family.

Thus, for example, we all leave our homes to seek our fortune, even as Abraham did; but, with Abraham, the veil is lifted, and we are shown that God called him forth, led him on his way, put him through the slow discipline of a life, the results of which belonged to a time that came after. The Bible lives are typical; they disclose to us the inner meaning of our own. That restraining touch of God of which we are all aware, that inspiring whisper in the ear which comes to us at great moments, that fixing of the bounds of our habitation which is part of our Father's plan for each of us,—these things are presented in the lives of holy men of old.

'Revelation' of the Bible Unique.—Do not let us make a mistake. Because we find little hints in many books, hints of the Lord God, merciful and gracious, who will by no means clear the guilty, let us not run away with the idea that the peculiar revelation of the Bible is, in truth, a universal revelation. Every hint we get of the Being of God is derived, consciously or unconsciously, from the Bible, even as that of a candle is derived from the light of the sun. Does the freethinker, who knows no God, proclaim the love of man? No hint of the brotherhood and sonship of men has escaped into the world except through the revelation which God has vouchsafed to us through certain chosen men. Thoughts already revealed are made luminous to us by the light that is vouchsafed to each, but that is a quite different thing from the first inception of a revealing thought.

When we have mastered all the knowledge of God that has been progressively revealed in the Bible, then perhaps further revelation will be granted to men in the same gradual way.

No Revelation is Repeated—It would appear, so far as we can discern the law, that God does not repeat a revelation which has been made; and, also, that as full a revelation as we are able to bear concerning our God has already been given, and recorded under divine authority. In this matter the present work of the Holy Spirit, who inspires, appears to be to illuminate a meaning here, another there, for each of us; so that our education in the knowledge of God is being gradually carried on, if we bring a hearing ear and an understanding heart.

In this way, our poets write and our painters paint under inspiration when they write and paint revealing truths. We may believe also, with the medieval Church, that a revelation is still going on of things not hitherto made known to men. Great secrets of nature, for example, would seem to be imparted to minds already prepared to receive them, as, for example, that of the 'ions' or 'electrons' of which that we call matter is said to consist. For this sort of knowledge also is of God, and is, I believe, a matter of revelation, given as the world is prepared to receive it.

But here the same two laws would appear to hold good. No revelation is repeated; the law of gravitation, the circulation of the blood, and the like, cannot twice be revealed to man; and, again, there is no overcrowding of such revelations. Not until we have mastered, digested and made our own, that which has already been presented, is a new revelation offered to us.

This, probably, is why the Bible is unique as containing original revelations of God. We know Him so little, we are so very far from attaining the Bible conception of the beauty and the goodness of our God, that we are not ready for more. Let us observe,—God's dealings with individuals in this matter of revelation would always seem to have reference to the world. No man is taught for himself alone; and that for which the world—as represented by its best and most thoughtful people—is unripe by reason of ignorance, that revelation is withheld until the world is prepared. Therefore, the instructed conscience does not allow us to give heed to the 'Lo, here!' and 'Lo, there!' continually sounding in our ears; and we are equally careful as to how we receive private interpretations of the Scriptures, which are put before us as having escaped the vigilance of the Church until to-day. In the matter of our great first duty, it behoves us to keep to 'sober walking in true gospel ways.' [from Ninth Sunday After Trinity by John Keble]

Interpretation.—As for distinguishing between the merely human and the inspired elements in the Bible, the way to this is not by critical study and destructive criticism, but by a gradual absorption of the idea of God as it is unfolded to us through the long preparation of the Old Testament, the glorious manifestation of the Gospels, and the application to the life of the Church which we find in the Acts and the Epistles. By long, slow study and by quick heart's love we shall learn to discern God, to know in an instant those words which are not of him; to know that 'break their teeth in their jaws,' for instance, is no word of God, but an utterance of the violent human heart, allowed to pass without comment, as are most of the ways and words of men recorded in the Bible.

We shall be able, as a reward of long study, to distinguish when a popular legend crops up, by the signs that it contains no revelation of God, no simple portrayal of man. But we shall not venture to say, that, because a story is not the sort of incident we may meet with any day in the street, it is therefore not of divine inspiration. The narration of such an incident (and there are many of them in the Bible) is merely one of accidental, outside truth, with little illuminating value. How the essential truth may be revealed to us, whether by parable or record, we cannot say; but we know that we have all heard the tempting voice in the garden, have all eaten the fruit, have all become miserably aware of ourselves, and have left, though not without hope, the paradise of innocent souls. Nay, that very story of the stopping of the sun in its course, an embedded myth, let us say, is recorded, we may believe, by the inspiration of God. We have all had times in our lives when the sun has not been permitted to go down upon us until we have wrought a deliverance, escaped a peril, done a work. It would seem as if the divine Spirit taught essential truths, the truths by which we live, by all means fitted to the understanding of men. But let us be extremely chary as to how we use this method of interpretation. No doubt God instructed his people by figures; but also, no doubt, he instructed them by facts; and when the simple fact carries its own interpretation, let us beware how we seek for another.

Sentimental Humanity.—Of another thing also let us beware. We may not endeavour to interpret the Scriptures in the spirit of sentimental humanity preached as the highest gospel to-day. That thousands should fall in the wilderness because they murmured or because they rebelled; that the earth should open and swallow certain haughty chieftains; that the punishment of death should fall upon men for an act of irreverence—such records as these by no means disprove the truth of the Bible. There may be inaccuracies of statement; for verbal inspiration, the use of the writer as an amanuensis, would destroy the human element which appears to be essential in all the communications of God with men. But let us not be in a hurry to cry, 'Away with all such fables!'

When a ship goes down with all hands, when flood and fire destroy their thousands, when famine and pestilence are abroad, an older piety would have called it the visitation of God; and that is precisely what the Bible statements amount to. If we say, bad drainage, unhealthy conditions, carelessness, errors in construction, flood or storm, we only put in the intermediate step. These are offences for which God visits men; and wind and storm are still fulfilling his word.

The mystery is one we find in life as well as in the chronicles of the Old Testament. Our Lord throws some light upon it in his remarks about that Galilean tower; but it is conceivable that the final answer may be that death is less momentous in the thought of God, who knows the hereafter, than to us, who are still in the dark. Christ wept, not for Lazarus: his sorrow was for the griefs that fall upon all men, as upon the two sisters. Perhaps He would have said, 'If they only knew!'

Superstition.—I have indicated some of the prejudices and misconceptions likely to obtrude themselves upon us in reading the Bible. These and such as these put away, we shall be prepared to read with open mind and willing heart, until we learn gradually the ways of God with men, and something of the divine purity, tenderness, love, and justice. If we are told that the story of the Flood, another tale like that of Joseph, laws like those of Moses, and much besides, appear in the records of nations that knew not God, here is no ground for surprise. God is the God of all flesh; and surely, there never was a nation with which he had no dealings. The distinction is in knowing. To the nation who knew God—and was favoured, on account of its peculiar spiritual insight, to transmit what it received to the rest of the world—was revealed something of the interpretation of those dealings of God with men about which the nations who knew not God were pathetically and cruelly in the dark. The mind that knows not God is of necessity a prey to superstition. Only the other day, in a plague-struck district of India, boxes containing stationery for a public examination came to hand. Soon the report was rife in the bazaar that plague was in the boxes, and that, as soon as the sahib opened them, he would let it loose in the town. Nay, did not Israel itself, for our warning, relapse into ignorance of God, and, like the nations, sacrifice its sons and daughters to Moloch—the people gave of the fruit of its body for the sins of its soul.

An Indulgent God.—An element of peril in the teaching of our day is the continual presentation of our God as an indulgent Parent; whereas the Bible presentation is of a Father "who chasteneth whom he loveth, and scourgeth every son whom he receiveth," and who most of all christened and scourged the only begotten Son of whom he said, "This is my beloved Son, in whom I am well pleased." Undue solicitude about our own pains and grievances may well interfere with the educative purposes of God.

Christ presented in the Gospels.—The main object of the Gospels is to hold up for our regard a presentation of the image of Christ; therein we may see him as he walked among men, as he looked upon men, as he spake, as he worked, as he died. There is no personage of history whom we have the means of knowing so completely as we may know our Lord; and the object in our gospel reading should be, less to find words of comfort and admonition for ourselves, than to perceive with our minds and receive upon our hearts the impress of Christ. To know him is life, and is the whole of life; and every thought of Him, walking in the cornfields, sitting weary by the well, moving among crowds or in solitary places, raising his eyes upon the multitude, taking by the hand that little maid,—every such living conception we get of Christ is life to us. Just as, from the apparently casual touches of the painter, the living likeness grows, so, by laying upon the canvas of our hearts every apparently casual and insignificant detail about our Master, we shall by degrees gather a living vision of the Son of Man; and dearer to us than any beauty on the earth or in the heavens will become the thought

"Of Jesus, sitting by Samaria's well,
Or teaching some poor fishers on the shore." [Trench's Sonnets.]

Miracles.—If we would see the vision, we must keep the single eye, unclouded by the breath of many words which wing from many mouths. Especially are men clamorous to prove that 'miracles do not happen,' except as it is within everyone's power to do miracles for himself!

The mist of words upon this subject is very apt to darken the mind; but, if we are careful to instruct our conscience on some two or three points, we shall not be blinded by this mote of destructive criticism. In the first place, perhaps miracles are no such great things as we make of them. St John calls those which he records not miracles, but signs. It is possible that in our day we have, or might have, the substance, the entire faith in Christ, which does away with the need of signs. As for the incredibility of the Gospel miracles, so fit and precious as evidences of the mind of Christ, all that scientists can say against them is that such a circumstance as the turning of water into wine, for example, has not come within their experience. They can no longer say that such acts are impossible, nor that they are contrary to the laws of nature. The amazing discoveries of recent years have made scientific men modest; they perceive that they do not know the laws of nature, and are only acquainted with few of the ways of nature; and therefore they know that nothing is impossible.

Again, people think they can effect a compromise. They think they can still believe in God and in Christ, may even call themselves Christians, and yet scoff at the possibility of miracles as at a notion belonging to a benighted age. But they lose sight of the proportion of faith. They fix their minds upon certain incidents, and lose sight of the fact that the Christian life is altogether of the nature of a miracle. That God should hold intercourse with man; that we may pray, knowing, with full assurance, that we are heard and shall be answered; that at our word the hearts of princes will surely be refrained; that the fit and right desires of our hearts will be fulfilled, though always in simple and seemingly natural ways—these things, which come to all of us as signs, are they not of the nature of miracles? Do they not imply the immediate and personal action of our God, not in your behalf or mine alone, but in behalf of each of the creatures of his infinite care?

The Words of Christ.—Next after the Death upon the Cross, the deepest amazement of the Gospel story is, not miracles, but words. "Never man spake like this man," said that servant of the Temple sent to apprehend Jesus; and it was given to him to declare the unique distinction of Christ. Dare any man stand up and offer himself to the world with such words as: "I am the bread of life," "I am the light of the world," "I am the truth," "Come unto me, all ye that are weary, and I will give you rest"? It is in verifying the truth of these and such like sayings of Christ that Christianity consists; and all Christians everywhere and at all times have known these things to be true, with the knowledge that comes of experience; and this is the knowledge which is life. When we begin to get this sort of knowledge, the miracles of Christ are important to us only as they manifest the mind of our Master, his kindness and his pity, the necessity that was upon him to do acts of mercy.

The Incarnation and the Resurrection.—Another tendency of thought in our day is to deny the Incarnation and the Resurrection of Christ, to suppose that He was born and died and remained in the grave as do other men; but that He was truly the best among men, and our great example.

None are more ready than scientific men to admit their profound ignorance of the causes of birth and life and death. They know the usual processes exactly; but causes, principles, elude them. We are hemmed in by mysteries as much in the domain of science as in that of religion. No one is prepared to say that the Incarnation could not be, nor the Resurrection; but, if these things were not as they are described, then are we indeed, as St Paul says, without hope. Christ is not. For, if He were a man like other men, then, indeed, would the charge brought against him by the Jews have been correct; and, "This man blasphemeth," would deprive us of all inspiration from the life of Christ, from the peace of his death, and from the hope of his resurrection.

Trivial Doubts.—It is necessary that conscience should be instructed as to the grave issues of doubts that are lightly handled in magazine or newspaper, and in books to be found in most houses, because our first duty is not possible to us while we have a divided mind. The first commandment is, we are told, "Thou shalt love the Lord thy God with all thy heart, and with all thy soul, and with all thy mind, and with all thy strength." How can we love Him whom we do not know, and how can we know Him concerning whom we are not sure? and, also, let us remember at our peril, that a doubt once entertained remains with us, is incorporated with us, and we are liable to its appearance at any moment. It recurs, as certain bodily ailments recur when they are, as we say, in the blood. We are inclined to think that there is a certain distinction in doubt, that a sceptical turn is a sign of intellectual power. The activity of a lesser mind may be shown by doubting in things divine as in things human; but the greater mind takes in all the bearings of the point at issue, and the darkness of doubt disappears before a luminous understanding. It has been well said that, "To the living and affirmative mind difficulties and unintelligibilities are as dross, which successively rises to the surface, and dims the splendour of ascertained and perceived truth, but which is cast away, time after time, until the molten silver remains unsullied; but the negative mind is lead, and, when all its formations of dross are skimmed away, nothing remains." [Coventry Patmore.]

The instructed conscience would pronounce, 'Loyalty forbids,' when we would entertain thoughts derogatory to Christ, dishonouring to God; because only such a conscience perceives how much is implied in this or that sceptical idea; knows, too, that the edifice of our faith is no dead structure of opinions and doctrines, but is a living body, liable to bleed to death through a wound.

The uninstructed conscience, on the contrary, is persuaded that 'Truth' is so all-important that it is our duty to consider, examine, and finally cherish every objection presented to the mind. It must be remembered that objections are negative and not affirmative; that Truth consists in affirmations and not in negations; that, the affirmation duly apprehended, the negation disappears as a cloud before the sun; that we have no right to tamper with the negations of doubt until we have got the assurance of knowledge

Chapter XV Some Instructors Of Conscience: Nature, Science, Art

Nature—The Debts of Recognition, Appreciation, and Preservation.—Conscience must brace itself under the instruction of other teachers besides those I have named. People are beginning to know that it is a shameful ignorance to live in this rich and beautiful world and not know the things about us even by name. The inheritors of precious collections recognise it as a duty to know, and to know about, the things they own: not to do so would be boorish ignorance. Here is a duty that lies upon us all; for we all enter on the inheritance of the heavens and the earth, the flowers of the field and the birds of the air. These are things to which we have right, no one can take them from us; but, until we get as much as a nodding and naming acquaintance with the things of Nature, they are a cause rather of irritation and depression than of joy.

Let us believe it, ignorance is a vice that never goes unpunished, and,

"The loud laugh that speaks the vacant mind,"

startling us in the midst of a quiet scene of natural beauty, speaks not only of vacuity, but of the resentment and soreness of ignorance. We owe debts to things as well as to persons—the debts of recognition, appreciation, and preservation.

The Schooling of Nature.—In this matter of instruction in the things of Nature, we owe yet more to ourselves: for,

"Nature never did betray the heart that loved her";—

and, in return for our discriminating and loving observation, she gives us the joy of a beautiful and delightful intimacy, a thrill of pleasure in the greeting of every old friend in field or hedgerow or starry sky, of delightful excitement in making a new acquaintance.

But Nature does more than this for us. She gives us certain dispositions of mind which we can get from no other source, and it is through these right dispositions that we get life into focus, as it were; learn to distinguish between small matters and great, to see that we ourselves are not of very great importance, that the world is wide, that things are sweet, that people are sweet, too; that, indeed, we are compassed about by an atmosphere of sweetness, airs of heaven coming from our God. Of all this we become aware in "the silence and the calm of mute, insensate things." Our hearts are inclined to love and worship; and we become prepared by the quiet schooling of Nature to walk softly and do our duty towards man and towards God.

In our Duty towards God.—In the chief duty of man, his duty towards God, Nature is an exquisite instructor. We know the story of that young footman [Brother Lawrence] who, oppressed by his clumsiness, was brought to a sudden standstill when upon an errand by the contemplation of a leafless tree; the surprising wonder of the fact that the tree would presently break out into leaves arrested him. All the fitness and beauty of God's ordering of the world was presented to his mind. The leafless tree converted him; and, almost from the moment, he became eminent as a saint of God, beautiful for his humility and simplicity of life.

As sweet a teacher was that 'small moss' of whose ministration to him Mungo Park tells us—

"I saw myself in the midst of a vast wilderness, in the depth of the rainy season—naked and alone, surrounded by savage animals, and men still more savage. I was five hundred miles from the nearest European settlement. All these circumstances crowded at once on my recollection, and I confess that my spirits began to fail me . . . At this moment, painful as my reflections were, the extraordinary beauty of a small moss in fructification irresistibly caught my eye. I mention this to show from what trifling circumstances the mind will sometimes derive consolation; for though the whole plant was not larger than the top of one of my fingers, I could not contemplate the delicate conformation of its roots, leaves, and capsula without admiration. Can that Being, thought I, who planted, watered, and brought to perfection, in this obscure part of the world, a thing which appears of so small importance, look with unconcern upon the situation and sufferings of creatures formed after His own image? Surely not! Reflections like these would not allow me to despair. I started up and, disregarding both hunger and fatigue, travelled forwards, assured that relief was at hand; and I was not disappointed."

Nature teaches us Gratitude.—But it is not only as she helps us in our own spiritual life that Nature instructs us in our duty to God. Some people have the grace to be tenderly and reverently thankful to the author of a great book, the painter of a great picture—thankful, if less reverently so, to the discoverer of a great invention. What daily and hourly thanks and praise, then, do we owe to the Maker and designer of the beauty, glory, and fitness above our heads and about our feet and surrounding us on every side! From the flower in the crannied wall to the glorious firmament on high, all the things of Nature proclaim without ceasing, "Great and marvellous are thy works, Lord God Almighty."

The advancement of Science in late years, and the preoccupation of men's minds with structural details of the various members of the natural world, have produced a thick mist to hide the Creator; and we have been content to receive the beauty that delights us and the fitness that astonishes us as self-produced and self-conceived. In this matter, Science has behaved like a child so much occupied with a new toy that to be reminded either of the maker or the giver of the toy is tiresome and vexatious. He does not deny either maker or giver, but the toy itself is all he cares about. This state of preoccupation, which has, no doubt, done good service to the cause of knowledge, is passing by, and the scientific mind is becoming more and more aware of that higher Power than Nature herself which is behind all the workings of Nature.

With this recognition will come gratitude; and the thankful heart is the glad heart. Truly, a joyful and a pleasant thing it is to be thankful!

Science.—Science herself, whose business it is to discover to us what we call the laws of Nature, is a teacher upon whom the conscience, seeking for instruction, must wait sedulously. The rash conclusions and reckless statements of the person who has had no scientific training make him mischievous in society—a source of superstition and prejudice.

Scientific training is not the same thing as information about certain scientific subjects. No one in these days can escape random information about radium, wireless telegraphy, heredity, and much else; but windfalls of this sort do not train the mind in exact observation, impartial record, great and humble expectation, patience, reverence, and humility, the sense that any minute natural object enfolds immense secrets—laws after which we are still only feeling our way.

Science distinguished from Information.—This scientific attitude of mind should fit us to behave ourselves quietly, think justly, and walk humbly with our God. But we may not confound a glib knowledge of scientific text-books with the patient investigation carried on by ourselves of some one order of natural objects; and it is this sort of investigation, in one direction or another, that is due from each of us. We can only cover a mere inch of the field of Science, it is true; but the attitude of mind we get in our own little bit of work helps us to the understanding of what is being done elsewhere, and we no longer conduct ourselves in this world of wonders like a gaping rustic at a fair.

Patient Observation.—Let me again say that this is due from us, and is not a thing we may take up or leave alone as we think fit. Let each of us undertake the patient, unflagging, day-by-day observation of the behaviour of sparrow, spider, teazel, of clouds or winds, recording what we ourselves have seen, correcting our records as we learn to be more accurate, and being very chary of conclusions. All we find out may be old knowledge, and is most likely already recorded in books; but, for us, it is new, our own discovery, our personal knowledge, a little bit of the world's real work which we have attempted and done. However little work we do in this kind, we gain by it some of the power to appreciate, not merely beauty, but fitness, adaptation, processes. Reverence and awe grow upon us, and we are brought into a truer relation with the Almighty Worker.

Art.—A great promise has been given to the world—that its teachers shall not any more be removed. There are always those present with us whom God whispers in the ear, through whom He sends a direct message to the rest. Among these messengers are the great painters who interpret to us some of the meanings of life. To read their messages aright is a thing due from us. But this, like other good gifts, does not come by nature. It is the reward of humble, patient study. It is not in a day or a year that Fra Angelico will tell us of the beauty of holiness, that Giotto will confide his interpretation of the meaning of life, that Millet will tell us of the simplicity and dignity that belong to labour on the soil, that Rembrandt will show us the sweetness of humanity in many a commonplace countenance.

The artist—

"Reaching, that heaven might so replenish him,
Above and through his art,"—

has indispensable lessons to give us, whether he convey them through the brush of the painter, the vast parables of the architect, or through such another cathedral built of sound as 'Abt Vogler' produced: the outward and visible sign is of less moment than the inward and spiritual grace.

We must learn to Appreciate and Discriminate.—That we may be in a condition to receive this grace of teaching from all great Art, we must learn to appreciate and to discriminate, to separate between the meretricious and the essential, between technique (the mere power of expression) and the thing to be expressed—though the thing be no more than the grace and majesty of a tree. Here, again, I would urge that appreciation is not a voluntary offering, but a debt we owe, and a debt we must acquire the means to pay by patient and humble study. In this, as in all the labours of the conscience seeking for instruction, we are enriched by our efforts; but self-culture should not be our object. Let us approach Art with the modest intention to pay a debt that we owe in learning to appreciate. So shall we escape the irritating ways of the connoisseur!

Chapter XVI Some Instructors Of Conscience: Sociology, Self-Knowledge

Sociology—How other People live.—"With all thy getting, get understanding," says the wise man; and we are never too young or too much engaged with work or pleasure to escape the duty of understanding how other people live. What are their needs? What things will do them good, and what things will do them harm? It behoves us all to think about the housing of the poor, the drink question, the care of the sick, the best way of dealing with crimes and offences, the teaching of the ignorant, whether they be persons or nations.

"I was an hungered," says Christ, "and ye fed me; naked, and ye clothed me; sick and in prison, and ye visited me." Perhaps no words spoken by our Master have come home with more intensity of meaning to every Christian soul, and few of us escape the sense of self-condemnation; and this, not so much because we are hard-hearted, unfeeling, and without pity—indeed, it is quite otherwise—an appeal in the newspapers brings an overwhelming and injurious amount of help. A beggar in the street grows rich on pennies. Any 'case' that we hear of we are very eager to help, as much to satisfy our conscience, because of those words of Christ's, as for the sake of the sufferer.

Conditions of Helpfulness.—But these casual efforts of ours are the despair of people who go to work steadily and conscientiously to help their brothers who are in need. These tell us of the evils of promiscuous charity, so we make up our minds that it is best not to 'give' at all; we are likely to do more harm than good, and so we content ourselves with a few subscriptions to certain public charities. In this matter, as in so many others, we err through the lack of an instructed conscience. It behoves each of us to lay ourselves out for instruction, to read, inquire, think, to look about us for a way of acting, believing

That Circumstance, a sacred oracle,
Speaks with the voice of God to faithful souls

and it is usually in our way, and not by going out of our way, that we shall find the particular piece of brotherly work appointed for us to do.

But we must keep our eyes open: the right thing is never obtrusive, and we may pass it by without observation. We must bear three things in mind. We must get a wide care and knowledge concerning the needs of men; we must devote ourselves, with understanding, to some particular effort for the needy; and, in all our endeavours, we must bear in mind our Master's way: What wouldst thou that I should do unto thee? he asked; and let us believe that charitable efforts, which go against the grain of the persons benefited, miss that principle of love which alone gives us a right to do service to others. It is particularly needful to bear this in mind in days when it is rather difficult to reach individuals, and we have to do our work through organisations. But organisations fail continually because they overlook this guiding principle, 'What wouldst thou?' It is not only self-relieving effort that is due from us, but discriminating and considerate love.

To know Ourselves is Wisdom.—It is difficult to find a name which covers what we are and what we may become, but let us call it philosophy; for to know ourselves is wisdom. We all like to get what we call knowledge of ourselves from phrenologists, readers of handwriting, and the like, and from the polite sayings of our acquaintances. But this is the knowledge that puffeth up, because it is usually flattering and, therefore, false. We may deserve praise for the thing we are praised for; but flattery fills us with the notion that we are made up of this or the other charming quality, and that those of our friends who see another side are unkind and unjust.

This is so plain to some people that they think the best plan is to leave self alone altogether, never thinking at all about what is in them, whether for good or ill, unless perhaps they are brought to book for some grave fault. Their course would be right enough if living were the easy, casual thing they make of it. But to be born a human being is to come into possession of a great estate—forest land here, copses there, cornfields, meadows, fisheries, what not: indeed, more than an estate, as I said before—a kingdom, the kingdom of Mansoul.

Self-Knowledge Impersonal.—Here, as in other estates, the casual proprietor ruins his land; field after field runs to waste and to weeds, and the land is hardly to be 'cleaned' in a generation.

All the same, it is a mistake to think about ourselves personally. Our Lord has said once, for all time, "If I bear witness of myself, my witness is not true." It is a wonderful saying, true even for our Master—how much more for us! We generally have too much taste to bear witness of ourselves out loud—to tell other people how plucky and generous, how clever or how sweet we are; but do we never bear witness to ourselves of ourselves—privately plume ourselves upon this or that good quality or fine action? When we do so, our witness is not true—the virtue for which we praise ourselves to ourselves is a virtue we do not possess. The fine action we admire ourselves for has ceased to be fine; our own praise of it has taken out all the virtue.

Greatness of Human Nature.—This would appear to prove them in the right who say it is best not to think of ourselves at all; but, ourselves may mean two things,—our own little sayings, doings and feelings—poor things at the best—or that glorious human nature, with its unmeasured capacities, which we share with heroes and sages, with Christ himself.

It is profanity to say of greed, sloth, sin, depravity of every kind, 'Oh, it's human nature'; for human nature is fitted for all godlike uses, and the Son of Man came to show us all that we may be when we do not reject the indwelling of our God. It is only as we realise the greatness of human nature that we understand what our Lord means when He says that one soul is worth more than the whole world. His words are always spoken in truth and soberness, and this is no fantastic valuation; nor does it mean, I think, that every single soul is so valuable to God; but that every single soul or person is so immeasurably great in itself; and this is the reason of the infinite divine solicitude that not one should perish. Therefore let us take stock, not of what is peculiar to us as individuals, but what is proper to each of us as human beings, remembering that we have no true ownership of the wealth of which we are ignorant.

Also, it is only a sense of the greatness of the poorest human soul that will awaken in us the passionate brotherhood which should help each of us to do our little share of the saving of the world; for we are called upon to work with our Master as well as for him. The object of this little book is to introduce to themselves any who are not yet acquainted with their own worth; so I need not here go over the reasons why, or the manner in which, we should know ourselves. Only one thing I should like to say on this point. Let us not put this sort of knowledge away from us as too troublesome and as making us too responsible. We have simply to know in the first place; and are not bound to be labouring all the time to feed imagination, exercise reason, instruct conscience, and the rest. In this sphere of self-knowledge, as in so much else, set things going, and they go

"Begin it, and the thing will be completed."

We are so mercifully made that the ordering of ourselves becomes unconscious to those of us who take it as a duty; it is the casual people who land in bogs or are brought up against stone walls.

SECTION II The Function Of Conscience

Chapter XVII Conviction Of Sin

Convicts of Sin.—Conscience would seem to have but a single office—to convince us of sin—that is, of transgression. The older divines used to speak much of an approving conscience; but this approval would appear to be no more than silence; for self-approbation, as we have seen, is, in itself, an offence. Then, when conscience says nothing we are all right? you ask. By no means, for the verdict of conscience depends upon what we know and what we habitually allow.

We gather from the reports of travellers among uncivilised tribes that the consciences of all men forbid them to murder, to steal, slander, dishonour their parents, and commit certain other offences. The consciences of all require them to be hospitable to strangers and faithful to friends, and in even the most debased there would seem to be a sense of the honour and worship due to God, however low a conception they may form of the divine. Even the baby, not able to run, knows that it is 'naughty' to disobey.

Each of us has a mentor within to condemn his misdeeds; but the judge of our bosom gives his verdict only upon the errors he knows; and conscience waits, as we have seen, for instruction in many directions.

Ignorance.—Not even religion is a substitute for the instructed conscience, any more than the love of God would teach an ignorant man to read. Conscience is given to us, but the due instruction of this power we must get for ourselves. It is very important to bear this in mind in our reading of history, in our judgment of current events, of public and of private persons; above all, in our judgment as to what we may and may not do and think ourselves.

This reflection, again, gives us a certain power of moral adjustment. We do not seek to justify hard things said or done by a good man; we perceive that on that point the good man's conscience has not been informed: we do not reverse our judgment of him and say, 'He is a bad man,' for this or that offence against gentleness or justice, but, 'He has done wrong in this, because he has not taken pains to inform himself.' Realising how liable the best and wisest are to err through moral ignorance, we are careful to keep ourselves open to instruction.

Allowance.—Not only may ignorance limit the action of conscience, but allowance may blind this inner judge. When we see offences in others, and do not call them by their right name; when we allow ourselves habitually to do that we ought not to do, or to think that we ought not to think, conscience stops speaking, as it were, and no longer testifies against the wrong.

Prejudice.—One more way of stultifying conscience we must watch against with jealous care, because this is an offence which has the appearance of righteousness: I mean the absorption of the mind by a single idea. Most wars and all persecutions, family quarrels, jealousies, envyings, resentment against friends, half the discords and unhappinesses of life, may be traced to this cause. The danger is, that good people may so fix their eyes upon one point of offence that they lose the sense of proportion. A spot the size of a penny piece hides the sun.

Bearing in mind that either ignorance, allowance, or prejudice makes conscience of little avail to its owner, we are not dismayed by even so appalling a vision of the Church in Alexandria as Kingsley gives us in Hypatia. Christianity itself does not suffer in our eyes. We perceive that the monks of Nitria, with Cyril at their head, sinned through moral ignorance, through the hardness that comes of allowance, and the madness wrought by a besetting idea; and that, through a conscience full of offence, they put shame on the Christianity they professed.

Considering these things, we do not miss the lessons of history, or of life, through the strife of contrary opinions about good men and great movements. We perceive the moral blind spot which might have been enlightened in many a great leader (and still we know him to be great and good); we discern the danger of the besetting idea in many a popular movement which is yet an advance.

There are few things more cheering to the student of history than the sense that the consciences of men and nations are under continually increasing enlightenment. From age to age and from year to year we become aware of more delicate offences, more subtle debts, because our God is dealing with us and instructing us; and the reward of men and nations who seek for that wisdom which cometh from above is a continual advance in moral enlightenment, an ever greater power of seeing the right in small things and great.

Sin.—"Conscience doth make cowards of us all," he said, who knew what was in men better than any save One. We put a gloss on the saying, and lose its force. We read: Conscience makes cowards of all wrong-doers; or, of us all, when we have done wrong, and, behold, a loophole through which we escape condemnation on most days in the year. We hear it stated that the sense of sin is no longer a general experience, that people can no longer confess with conviction that they "have left undone those things which they ought to have done, and done those things which they ought not to have done." In so far as this is true, it is because conscience is drugged or beguiled.

Uneasiness of Conscience.—That conscience makes us all cowards is still a luminous truth. We wake up in the morning with a sense of fear, uneasiness, anxiety—causeless, so far as we know, but there it is—the horrid fear that something is going to happen to us because we deserve it. 'Nerves,' says the man of science: very likely, though the hale and hearty know this fear as truly as do the ailing. But to say 'nerves' or 'hypochondria,' or 'the blues,' or the older 'megrims,' or 'vapours,' is only to name a symptom and not a cause. The cowardice of conscience drives us all, old and young, rich and poor, whether into what we call nervous ailments, or into the mad and lusty pursuit of business or pleasure. Either of these we know for a soporific, carrying us through the day, passing the time, as we say; and, if we only get tired enough, bringing sleep at night. But the busiest and gayest lives have their moments of blank fear when the terrors of conscience are sprung upon them. Men call reason to their aid. There is nothing in their lives of which they can convict themselves; they live as other men do, kindly, respectable, even religious lives. Why should they fear conscience? Why, indeed?

Sins of Omission.—At such moments that accusation, from which there is no escape, comes with startling force to the memory,—"I was an hungered, and ye fed me not," with those other charges summing up the casual omissions which seem to us at such moments to be the whole history of our lives. How can we ever overtake the little things we have not done? We are cast into the outer darkness of dismay, and are cowards, each of us, before his conscience. In a general way, we are content to confound sin with crime. Because we have not been guilty of lying or theft or any of the sins against society which the law punishes, we are like that young ruler, and say of the commandments, 'All these have I kept from my youth up.' Then, like him, we are shown the things we might do, and might have done, and go forth ashamed—aware of sin.

'There is no health in us,' we cry, with the sincerity of a broken heart; 'I am such a poor thing,' or, 'such a worthless fellow'; or, 'So foolish was I and ignorant, I was as a beast before Thee.' Such as these are the cries of the unsophisticated conscience, as it catches a glimpse, now and again, of the vastness of life, of the ten or ten thousand talents which it implies.

'Who is sufficient for these things?' And there is no rest for the uneasy conscience until we can say, 'My sufficiency is of God.'

The Chiding of Conscience.—It is the office, we are told, of the Holy Spirit to convince the world of sin, of righteousness, and of judgment; and, in the constant operation of the divine Spirit upon the spirits of men, we find the secret of how we become aware of sin when we have done nothing in particular to be ashamed of; how we crave after a righteousness greater than we know; and how the sense of a present judgment, to come upon us to-day or to-morrow, awakens with us many a morning and goes to bed with us many a night when no particular wrong-doing comes home to convict us.

Because these convictions are of God, we do not drive them away in the multiplicity of interests and amusements; neither do we sit down and pity ourselves, and encourage what are called nervous maladies. There is a more excellent way.

But when we count up our blessings, let us not fail to number this, of the continual chiding of conscience. A wise man has said that, were there no other evidence of the existence of God, the conscience of man is a final proof. Let us accept the strivings of conscience in this light, and rejoice.

Chapter XVIII Temptation

Sudden Temptation.—Though in placid moments they are what we are most aware of, our sins of omission are by no means the greatest trouble of our lives. Like St Christopher, we have to fight our way against the floods, however quiet our lives may seem. Some little peevishness or petulance about a trifle, some slight resentment against a friend, some entanglement in our circumstances,—and it is as though, like the cuttlefish, we had darkened all the waters about us. Suddenly, without an instant's warning, we are in a flood of rage, resentment, crooked contrivings, perhaps unclean imaginings. We are swept off our feet and cannot recover ourselves. We flounder and beat the waves, long and wearily, before we win our way back to righteousness and peace. We do not intend, will, or foresee these sudden falls; we become as persons possessed, and have no power in ourselves to struggle out of the flood of malice, pride, uncleanness, greed, envy, or whatever else of evil has overwhelmed us.

The fact that we have not foreseen these falls, points to a cause outside ourselves—to those powers and principalities in high places, whose struggle for dominion over us the Bible reveals; and the revelation is confirmed by our own sad and familiar experience.

Temptation comes from without and from within.—This is Temptation, reaching us sometimes plainly from without, but more often, it would seem, through the movement of some spirit of evil which has access to our own spirit. If we say there is no Holy Spirit, and no evil spirit, and no spirit of a man,—if, like the Sadducees of old and their kind to-day, we do not believe in any such thing—there is nothing more to be said. But if we are aware of the movements of our own spiritual life, and observant of that life in those about us, if we have taken cognisance of how good and evil come as a flood upon the world or upon an individual soul, we shall recognise that there is a source of temptation outside of ourselves, even as there is a source of strength and blessedness. We shall know that 'we wrestle not with flesh and blood,' but with spiritual wickedness in high places; and we shall lay ourselves out to understand the laws and conditions of temptation, and shall look eagerly for ways of escape.

Literature is full of tales of temptation, yielded to, struggled against, conquered. Sometimes temptation finds us ready and there is no struggle, as in the case of Tito Melema; [Romola.] sometimes there is a struggle, as in that of Maggie Tulliver; [The Mill on the Floss.] sometimes, a victory like that of Joseph.

It is in the Bible we find the most intimate records of temptations. We wonder to this day how Peter could, upon a sudden temptation, deny his Lord; how Judas should, after slow gathering of fretful and impatient thoughts, betray Him; how the disciples should, in a sudden panic of fear, forsake Him and flee. And, when we think of falls like these, we ask ourselves the awful question, 'Lord, is it I?' 'Should I have done the like in his place?' The very records of crimes and offences in the newspapers bring us the same awful fear; with like temptation, and in like conditions, perhaps we should have done the like. A sense of the inevitableness of temptation, the nearness of sin, comes upon us, now and then, like a terror; and it is well we should realise that temptation is a fact of life—a fact to be faced; and, also, that we are besieged in our weak places, tempted always to those sins we have a mind to. It is good and comforting to be assured, "There hath no temptation taken you but such as is common to men." It is good to know that, "He will with the temptation make a way of escape that ye may be able to bear it"; that, "Blessed is the man that endureth temptation"; that, "Resist the devil, and he will flee from you."

Enter not into Temptation.—But it is to our Master, "who was in all points tempted like as we are, yet without sin," that we go for the key of the whole matter. Because he knows what is in man, he has said to us, "See that ye enter not into temptation." This is the secret of heroic lives whose conflict is with circumstances and not with temptations: they do not enter into temptation. All our Lord's sayings come out of profound knowledge of the ways of the minds of men. He knew that an idea, an imagination, of envy or resentment, for example, once entertained, dallied with, takes possession of the mind; we cannot get rid of it, and we are hurried into action or speech upon that notion before ever we are aware. Here we have the line between temptation, and sin. That an offensive idea should be presented, is not of ourselves and is not sin. But, once we open the gates of our thought to let in the notion, why, we may conquer in the end, through the grace of Christ our Saviour, and after conflict, tears, and sore distress. But such a fight against temptation is a terror to the Christian soul. Upon this battlefield, he who fights and runs away lives to fight another day.

The Training of a Trusty Spirit.—Blessed are the souls that endure temptation from without; who endure grinding poverty without hardness or greed, uncongenial tempers without bitterness, contrary circumstances without petulance; who possess their souls in patience when all things are against them: these are temptations from which we cannot escape, and which are part of the education of a trusty spirit. But this education is accomplished by resisting the temptations that reach us from within—the offences in thought suggested by trying circumstances. For, let us not make a mistake, all sin, even all crime, is accomplished in thought. Word and act are but the fruit of which the received and permitted thought is the seed. The battle of life for each of us lies in the continual repetition of what seems a most trifling act—the rejection of certain thoughts which present themselves at the very moment when they come. This is how we shall keep our soul as a fortress; and therefore our Master, who is aware of us, who knows how the evil thought, once admitted, floods the soul and darkens the eye, bids us pray, day by day: "Our Father, which art in Heaven, lead us not into temptation, but deliver us from evil; for thine is the kingdom, the power, and the glory, for ever and ever. Amen."

We have a Father who cares and knows. We have a Saviour who saves his people from their sins. We are not left to ourselves; we have a King who governs us, whose power upholds us, and whom we glorify by every little effort of ours not to enter into temptation.

The way in the beginning is quite easy, before we enter, that is; we turn away our thoughts from beholding evil, the evil in another or the evil suggestion to ourselves; and we do so, not by reasoning the matter out, but just by thinking of something else, some other pleasant or interesting thing belonging for the moment to our lives. For we are so made that there is always with the temptation an easy and natural way of escape. It is well we should realise this, because, in things of the spirit, it is quite true that God helps those who help themselves; and, if we pray, "Lead us not into temptation," and do not take the simple provided way of escape by thinking of some other thing, we are asking to be treated as the men on a chessboard, and not as beings free to do as they will; who honour God by willing, to flee from temptation; who stretch out a hand for help to Him who saves us.

Penitence, Repentance, Restitution.—Many a life is spoiled by what the Church at one time set forth as a chief Christian grace. The penitent is a distressful figure in early Church history. Days, months, a life, of self-mortification, were appointed to the repentant sinner. Where there is no Church discipline of the sort, men and women of a sorrowful spirit go about, living in penitence for offences of the past or the present. We all know the people who will not forgive themselves, who weep and afflict themselves because they are guilty of some discovered wrong in word or deed, and they believe that this sorrowful gloom of theirs is due to God and man because of their offence.

The Forgiveness of Sins.—And yet these very people recite regularly, "I believe in the forgiveness of sins." They do not understand that forgiveness means instant, immediate, complete restoration to the joy of God's favour; that the forgiveness of Christian hearts is equally prompt, or it is not forgiveness; and that there are no tears to be shed, no dark remembrances to be cherished, after the one sore and sorrowful confession, made with many tears, "Father, I have sinned." Then, we hold up our heads as free men, and no longer drag the prisoner's chain. We repent—yes; that is, we turn away from the sin, we enter not into the temptation, we keep fast hold of the grace of our God; and we restore: "If I have taken anything from any man, I restore him fourfold:" fourfold love and gentleness and service the repentant soul brings to God and his brother; but this is because he is glad—out of the joy of his heart there is nothing he cannot do; and, above all, he will away with the proud and sullen tears and regrets of so-called penitence. Let that story of the Father who ran to meet his returning prodigal, who received him with honour and feasting, who fell upon his neck,—image too tender for a man to have dared to conceive it, but which is given us with the authority of Christ, let this amazing picture of the dealings of our God be with us always to light up the dark places in our own lives.

Chapter XIX Duty And Law

Right and Wrong.—Sin, temptation, repentance, throw us back upon something behind them all. Why is it wrong to do wrong? And, what is wrong? People have answered these questions in various ways. Some say it is wrong to neglect or offend other men, and that therefore to care for and consider our fellows is right; and right only because they choose to do it. Others say they have the right to do as they like: therefore they can do no wrong; but when other people injure them, these are ready enough to complain of suffering wrong. Others, again, say that whatever is natural is right; and on this ground they will justify greed, sloth, uncleanness, selfishness, saying, 'Oh, it's human nature.' By the way, let me again say, it is a grievous misrepresentation to put down what is low, lazy, and unworthy to human nature, and never to say of heroism, self denial, devotion, these are human nature too. For, indeed, what human nature is depends upon how we use it. This nature of ours is capable of base behaviour, as we know too well; but it is equally capable of magnanimity and generosity. But people usually mean the poor side of human nature when they say that what is natural is right.

We all know the Law.—These various gropings in the dark to find out the meaning and reasons of right and wrong are forms of self-deception.

We all know that sin is the transgression of the law. Every living soul is aware that there is a law. He is not able to put it into words, perhaps, and may make wild and dreadful errors in interpreting the law, but he is aware. The most ignorant savage knows as well as the Psalmist that, "Thy commandment is exceeding broad." But, because he is ignorant and base, he does not know that the law is beautiful and works for blessedness; that is, he has not an instructed conscience, but only a conscience dimly aware of a law, the meaning of which he gropes after in the dark.

He knows, too, that obedience to the undeciphered law is due from him. He is dimly conscious that law is everywhere; that—

Or act or say, or do but think a thought,
And such and such shall surely come to pass,
Fore-ordered sequent of such act or thought.

His uneasiness is appalling; he tries to appease his conscience by sacrifice; to explain the riddle of life by superstitions, making his god such an one as himself.

Contrast this restless uneasiness in the dark with the serenity of the enlightened Christian conscience. The Christian, too, is aware of the law which is about him, closer than the air he breathes, ordering his relations with all persons and all things, ordering his affections and his thoughts. But the law does not irk him. "Oh, how I love thy law!" he cries with the Psalmist; and he takes up gladly his share of the work of the world, so much of the fulfilling of the law as is due from him; he acknowledges his Duty.

As the planets revolve round the sun in obedience to their law, so he revolves in the orbit of his life, and his deepest joy is Duty. Not that he fulfils the law which is within his heart. Like the planet on which he lives, he is constantly pulling away from the law he owns; but he is as continually recovered, so that he does indeed finish his course.

Law and Will.—The reason why it is a joy to perceive the law, and an unspeakable gladness to fulfil even a little of that law, is, that we recognise law as the expression of the perfect will of God. Law, existing by itself and for itself, without any to will or desire, is a monstrous thought—a thought to chafe our spirits and take the heart out of all our strivings—because there is no comfort of love in it and no reasonable conviction. But how good and pleasant it is to know that at the heart of all things is our God, who wills the good and right behaviour of every creature in His universe, and who enables us all for right doing, for that fulfilling of His law in which all things work together for good! Our little lives are no longer small and poor when we think of the great things of the world. They are a necessary part of the great whole, ordered under law, fulfilling His will, and singing as the morning stars in the gladness of obedience.

Acquiescence.—The possibility of an erratic course, of breaking away into space—a glittering object, may be, for a time; to be, by and by, quenched in darkness—should make us the more fervent in our duty-doing. All sense of bondage ceases when we say, "I rejoice to do thy will, O my God; yea, thy law is within my heart." And, with this spring of glad obedience within us, we arise and shine, because every feeble, faltering step is sustained; when we fall we are raised, when we pause we are strengthened and cheered to go on; and, poor things as we know ourselves to be, our path is that of the just, shining more and more unto the perfect day.

"Stern Daughter of the Voice of God!
O Duty! if that name thou love,
Who art a light to guide, a rod
To check the erring, and reprove;
Thou, who art victory and law
Where empty terrors overawe;
From vain temptations dost set free;
And calm'st the weary strife of frail humanity!

"Through no disturbance of my soul,
Or strong compunction in me wrought,
I supplicate for thy control;
But in the quietness of thought.
Me this unchartered freedom tires,
I feel the weight of chance desires;
My hopes no more must change their name,
I long for a repose that ever is the same.

"Stern Lawgiver! yet thou dost wear
The Godhead's most benignant grace;
Nor know we anything so fair
As is the smile upon thy face:
Flowers laugh before thee on their beds,
And fragrance in thy footing treads;
Thou dost preserve the stars from wrong,
And the most ancient heavens, through thee, are fresh and strong.

"To humbler functions, awful Power,
I call thee: I myself commend
Unto thy guidance from this hour;
O let my weakness have an end!
Give unto me, made lowly wise,
The spirit of self-sacrifice;
The confidence of reason give;
And in the light of truth thy bondman let me live!"
—Wordsworth.

PART II—The Will

Chapter I The Will-Less Life

It perhaps occurs to the reader that man is indeed the Sphinx's riddle, and that the more we think of ourselves the more we are baffled. This is true enough; but the inference—'let the puzzle alone' is by no means safe. For this baffling problem of human nature must needs occupy us from the cradle to the grave. It is that of which we have to render account, whose content is, those talents, the use of which is our business in life.

Anarchy in Mansoul.—So far as we have considered the matter, Heart, with its affections of Love and Justice, Intellect, with its Reason and Imagination, even Conscience itself, behave pretty much as do the several organs of the body—brain, lungs, heart, and so on; give them proper food, exercise, rest, and air, and they do their work of themselves. It hardly seems to be we who imagine or who love. We may not all be consciously dominated by ideas; but every writer knows how he 'reels off' almost without intention. Everyone knows how the affections behave, how love, as lord of the bosom, plays unaccountable and vexatious pranks, and commonly gives the poor man a sorry time. The blind god with his mischievous tricks is more than a pretty fancy; it is a symbol which presents very truly the whimsical behaviour of love when left to itself.

Conscience, too, for all the dignity and sobriety we attach to his name, is, left to himself, as whimsical and aggravating as any blind god. We know the persons of morbid conscience who are fussy over some ridiculous bit of 'packthread, ' leaving their real relations and duties out of count.

Think, too, how heated and morbid the imagination becomes that is always feeding (commonly on poor trash), never working, never resting, and never coming into the fresh air of common day! We know the distorted views, sickly principles, and weak behaviour of the person who lets his imagination run away with him as a horse that has bolted runs away with his rider. Perhaps he takes to drugs, or drink, or trashy novels, to stimulate the tired jade; for go he must—he knows no other life. With a ménage full of unbroken horses, each minded to go his own way and each able to drag the poor man after him, what is he to do? Who is able to order his affairs?

Mansoul is saved from anarchy by the Will, that power within us which, we know not how, has the ordering of the rest.

An Easy Life.—It has been said that the Will is 'the sole practical faculty of man,' and we recognise this in our common speech. Whatever is done with the consent of the will we describe as voluntary; what is done without that consent is involuntary: and, as we have seen, we can reason, imagine, love, judge, without any action of the will. Indeed, life is made so easy for us, by conventions and class customs, that many poor souls live to man's estate, die in old age, and have never called upon Will to decide between this and that. They think as other people think, act as others act, feel what is commonly felt, and never fall back upon their true selves, wherein Will must act. Such lives are easy enough, but they are stunted and stinted in all directions. No power has been nourished and exercised or brought under the broad sky of God's dealings. Life is to such persons a series of casualties; things happen well or they happen ill, but they always happen; and the absence of purpose and resolution in themselves makes it impossible for them to understand that these exist in God; so their religion, also, comes to consist of conventional phrases and superstitions.

This is the most common development of the willless life, marked by a general inanition of powers and an absence of purpose,—beyond that of being as others are, and doing as others do. The inmate of the madhouse, who reasons with amazing cunning, has his affections and his conscience too (did not Mr. Dick make a valiant fight against that head of Charles I.?); but he is commonly lost for the want of will-power to order the inmates of his house of mind and his house of heart. So of the young man, who is nobody's enemy but his own, who is carried off his feet by every stray suggestion of pleasure or excitement.

It is well we should face the possibility of living without the exercise of will, in order that we may will and make our choice. Shall we live this aimless, drifting life, or shall we take upon us the responsibility of our lives, and will as we go?

Chapter II Will And Wilfulness

Wilful Persons are of Various Dispositions.—What of the person who always contrives to get his own way, whether he get it by means of stormy scenes, crafty management, sly evasion, or dogged persistence? The dogged and the blustering person are commonly supposed to have strong wills; the sly, and the managing person keep somehow out of our notice, we do not make up our minds about them. As a matter of fact, persons of these four classes may get each their own way, with as little action of the Will as is exercised by the casual person who lets things slide. When we have given ourselves to Greed or Vanity, Ambition or Lust, we pursue our way without restraint from Will, and get what we want by straight or devious ways, according to our nature. The robber baron of the Middle Ages, a turbulent man, without ruth or fear, whose action was commonly the outcome of stormy passions,—he and his like are supposed to be persons of strong will. Such a man was the Wild Boar of the Ardennes, [Quentin Durward, Scott.] such another, Charles of Burgundy

[Anne of Geierstein, Scott], and such another, indeed, our own reckless Coeur de Lion. [The Talisman, Scott.] These heroes of the 'strong will' are not without their qualities; they are generous and lavish, as ready to give as to take; and they will always have a following of the sort whose instinct it is to 'follow my leader.' The persons who compass their way by more subtle means are less attractive. King John [Shakespeare.] and Becky Sharp [Vanity Fair, Thackeray.] do not win a following; we prefer Joab to Achitophel; and Esau is a more winning person than Jacob.

In the last two, we get the contrast we want, between the man of Will and the creature of Wilfulness. This contrast is not, as it would seem at first, between the man who pursues his desires above board and generously, and his brother who wins his way, sometimes by prudence and sometimes by craft. The difference lies deeper.

The Wilful Person has one Aim.—The wilful person is at the mercy of his appetites and his chance desires. Esau must needs have that red pottage, he must needs hunt, or marry, or do whatever his desires move him towards at the moment. So must needs do the crafty gambler, the secret drunkard, the slothful soul, the inordinate novel-reader, the person for whom 'life' means 'pleasure.' Each of these is steady to only one thing, he must always have his way; but his way is a will-o'-the-wisp which leads him in many directions. Wherever gratification is to be found—for his vanity, his love of nice eating, his desire for gay company, or his ambition, his determination to be first,—there he goes. He is a wilful man, without power or desire to control the lead of his nature, having no end in view beyond the gratification of some one natural desire, appetite, or affection. Mr. J. M. Barrie's Sentimental Tommy is a valuable study of a wilful person. Tommy always attained his end, always found out a 'wy'; and his ends were often good enough in themselves. But Tommy is an ingrained poseur: he does many generous things, and is a bit of a genius; but all his efforts are prompted by the chance desires of his vanity. He must, at all hazards, impress an audience. He always gets his 'wy,' yet his life falls to pieces in the end because he is not dominated by Will, but by vanity.

Jacob, too, gets his way, often by subtle means, and every subtlety brings its chastisement; but he does not seek his way for its own sake. All his chance desires are subordinated to an end—in his case, the great end of founding the kingdom of promise. The means he uses are bad and good. "Few and evil are the days of my life," he complains at the end, so sore have been his chastisements; but, always, he has willed steadily towards an end outside of himself.

The career of the late Lord Beaconsfield is an interesting study, as showing the two phases of Wilfulness and Will. To begin with, he has only the rather dazzling wilfulness of a young man's ambition; he will shine, he will make himself heard in the House; and he does it. But there is nothing more; and the country feels him to be a creature of chance desires. But by and by Will manifests itself, the will of the great statesman. Personal desires are subjugated or disappear in the presence of the ruling will, and we get a man fit for the service of his country. We have no record of an era of wilfulness in Wellington; his was ever the iron will, iron to keep down not only those under him, but any turbulence of his own flesh or spirit. The 'Iron Chancellor' of Germany had this same steadfastness of will, always accomplishing towards an end.

A Brilliant Career does not demand Exercise of Will.—But it is even possible to make the world wonder without an exercise of Will. Napoleon, who came upon Europe as a portent, was but impelled along the lines of least resistance in his nature—his genius, high courage, vanity, and inordinate ambition,—but he never reached the elevation of a man with an impersonal aim. He willed nothing outside himself. He had the lavish generosity of a child, and a child's petulant wilfulness; a child's instability, too, or how could he have borne the shame of retreating from Russia in advance of his army?

It is not safe to take success in life as a criterion. His Will is the measure of the man; and many a man has become rich or famous without willing, on the easy lines of his nature, by the strength of his desires while many another of constant will lives unknown and yet it is the persons of constant will, which implies impersonal aims, who are the world's great possession, and are discerned to be such.

We distinguish, for example, between rich, successful men. There are those who are simply accepted as rich; and there are those—merchants, manufacturers, shopkeepers, it matters little what—who have become rich and successful by accident, as it were; these are not the things they have willed; but rather some manner of duty-doing, some sort of aim, outside of themselves; these are the men of weight recognised and valued by their neighbours.

Redgauntlet, [Redgauntlet, Scott.] as devoid as you please of amiable qualities, wins the reader's sympathy because he was a man of will. He had the power to project himself beyond himself and shape his life upon a purpose. We may draw upon Scott without reserve for instances in this kind. The great novelist had a certain legal acumen which never failed him in his discrimination of character. As for his historical accuracy, mere errors of detail are, perhaps, fewer than we imagine; for the man who could deal with the case of 'Poor Peter Peebles' [Redgauntlet, Scott.] knew well enough how to sift documentary evidence. I have already quoted two personages as figured by him, William de la Marck and Charles of Burgundy. Louis XI. [Quentin Durward.] again, mean and unlovely soul that he was, was yet concerned, if meanly concerned, with matters outside of himself. What a fine study, again, we get of Will and Wilfulness in that crusaders' camp in The Talisman! Each of the princes present was engaged in the wilful pursuit of personal ends, each fighting for his own hand. And Saladin looked on, magnanimous of mind and generous of heart, because he was a man of will, urged towards ends which were more than himself. I can hardly conceive a better moral education than is to be had out of Scott and Shakespeare. I put Scott first as so much the more easy and obvious; but both recognise that the Will is the man. As for Shakespeare, the time will come when our universities will own a Shakespeare 'faculty,' not for philological study, but for what is beginning to be known as 'ethology,' the study of man on the lines of character.

A Dividing Line.—Both Shakespeare and Scott use, as it were, a dividing line, putting on the one side the wilful, wayward, the weak and the strong; and on the other, persons who will.

Faust, Lady Macbeth, King Lear, Edward Waverley, Charles II., King John, Marlborough, all sorts of unlikely persons, fall to the side of the line where Will is not in command. On the other side, also, unlikely people find themselves in company—Wolsey, Sir Thomas More, Laud, Mahomet, Henry V. of England, and Henry IV. of France. The two Marys, of England and Scotland, fall to either side of the line.

To make even a suggestive list would be to range over all history and literature. Let me say again, however, that here is a line of study which should make our reading profitable, as making us intimate with persons, and the more able for life. The modern Psychical novel is rarely of use 'for example of life and instruction in manners.' It is too apt to accept persons as inevitable, to evade the question of Will, and to occupy itself with a thousand little traits which its characters manifest nolens volens. The way of the modern novel is to catch its characters and put them to disport themselves in a glass bowl, as it were, under observation.

A man standing in the ranks cannot drill the company, and the restless forces of Mansoul can only be ordered by a Will, projected, so to speak, from the man, thrown to the front, aiming at something without; and, from this point of vantage, able to order the movements of Mansoul, and to keep its forces under command.

'Will' may be a National Attribute.—We are at this moment (1904) contemplating a magnificent object-lesson presented by a nation of extraordinary will-power; for this power may belong to nations as well as individuals. It would seem that every Japanese has an impersonal aim. There is that which he wills to serve with the whole force of his nature, and in comparison with which his tastes and inclinations, his desires and deserts, matter not at all. Who can doubt that he loses his life to save it, when, with purpose, method, forethought, every reasonable device, and with unlimited skill, the Japanese gives himself for his country?

Nor is this the first time in their history that the Japanese have given an example of will-power unparalleled in the annals of any country. Thirty years ago they worked out such a revolution as the history of the world cannot match. The people did not rise in arms and wrest power from their rulers; but the rulers, who kept the state and held the authority of feudal princes, perceived of themselves that the people had not room to grow under this feudal dominion, and they, of their own free will, retired from ruling and owning the land, from vast wealth and dignity, and became as citizens with the rest, served in the rank and file of the army, manned the constabulary force. These, too, lost their life, a princely life, to find it in the regeneration of their country.

The neighbouring empire, China, presents a curious spectacle of incoherence and futile endeavour. Yet China, too, has taste, literature, ingenuity, an art of its own, morals perhaps of a higher order than we Westerns suspect, the prestige of a long, long history; and, with all this, China is a petulant, wayward, unstable child among the nations. Why? We of the West are apt to say superior things about race and colour; but perhaps recent events have taught us better. Great things have come out of the East in the past, and may in the future.

The truth probably is that China and Japan rank themselves on the two sides of our imaginary line.

In the meantime, we Western nations have become enfeebled by a philosophy whose first principle is that we must never under any circumstances lose our life. The greatest happiness of the greatest number is our avowed general aim; comfort at all hazards is our individual desire; and 'Every man for himself,' is the secret, or open, rule of life followed by many of us.

But we need not be alarmed, and talk of deterioration and the like; nor need we compare ourselves unfavourably with any great nation. What is in fault is the teaching we have allowed and fostered, teaching which urges men along those lines of least resistance proper to their nature.

With an aim outside ourselves, we are as capable of great things as any nation of the past or present. If we are able for no more than little Skepsey's cuckoo cry, of his 'England,' [One of our Conquerors, Meredith.] we shall be restored to the power of willing, which is only possible to us as we are moved from without ourselves. According as we will, we shall be able for effectual doing.

Our Lord's teaching appears to have been directed, in the first place, to awaken the Jews from the lethargy of national superstitions and personal aims; to give them the power of willing, again; because it is only as a man wills that he is, in any full sense, a man. "What wilt thou that I should do unto thee?" "O Jerusalem, Jerusalem! . . . how often would I have gathered thy children together, even as a hen gathereth her chickens under her wings, and ye would not!"

"If any man willeth to do His will, he shall know of the doctrine"

Chapter III Will Not Moral Or Immoral

To 'Will' is not to 'be Good'—Perhaps what has already been said about Will may lend itself to the children's definition of 'being good,' and our imaginary dividing line may appear to have all the good people on the one side, and all the not good on the other. But the man of will may act from mixed motives, and employ mixed means. Louis XI., for example, in all he did, intended France; he was loyal to his own notion of his kingly office; but, because he was a mean man, he employed low means, and his immediate motives were low and poor. An anarchist, a rebel, may propose things outside of himself, and steadfastly will himself to their accomplishment. The means he uses are immoral and often criminal, but he is not the less a man of steadfast will. Nay, there are persons whose business in life it is to further a propaganda designed to do away with social restraints and moral convictions. They deliberately purpose harm to society; but they call it good; liberty to do as he chooses is, they say, the best that can befall a man; and this object they further with a certain degree of self-less zeal. It is the fact of an aim outside of themselves which wins followers for such men; the looker-on confuses force of will with virtue, and becomes an easy convert to any and every development of 'free-thought.'

It is therefore well we should know that, while the turbulent, headstrong person is not ruled by will at all,—but by impulse, the movement of his passions or desires,—yet it is possible to have a constant will with unworthy and even evil ends. More, it is even possible to have a steady will towards a good end, and to compass that end by unworthy means. Rebecca had no desire but that the will of God should be done; indeed, she set herself to bring it about; the younger, the chosen son, should certainly inherit the blessing as God had appointed; and she sets herself to scheme the accomplishment of that which she is assured is good. What a type she offers of every age, especially of our own!

The simple, rectified Will, what our Lord calls 'the single eye,' would appear to be the one thing needful for straight living and serviceableness.

'Will' not the Same Thing as 'an Ideal.'—Another thought that may occur is, that 'Will' is synonymous with an ideal: that the ideal, whether high or low, is the compelling power which shapes conduct. This is a comfortable doctrine, for most of us have an ideal hidden away somewhere, if it be only that of the 'good fellow' or the 'nice girl.' We see for ourselves the enormous force of Bushido, apparently the ideal of chivalry in Japan; but the ideal owes its force to the will-power which gives it effect. Everybody knows that the nursing of sentimental dream-ideals, however perfect they be, is a source of weakness. We know, too, that there are persons who make a cult of great ideals, who enjoy exquisite emotions in the midst of elegant surroundings as they contemplate and idealise the life of St Francis! Self-culture is accepted as the pursuit of an ideal; but when we realise that it is an ideal accomplished in self, and with no aim beyond self, we perceive that the gentle youth with the lily in his fingers and his head a little posed, is not a man of will, because the first condition of will, good or evil, is an object outside of self. Browning raises the curious question whether it is not better to will amiss and do it, than to persist in a steady course of desiring, thinking, feeling amiss, without strength of will for the act. Most of us who read The Statue and the Bust will agree with the poet that the fall which fails of accomplishment through lack of will is as bad as such fall accomplished. If it be not goodness, the will is virtue, in the etymological sense of that word; it is manliness.

Another thing to be observed is, that even the constant will may have its times of rise and fall; and we shall consider later one of the secrets of living—how to tide over the times of fall in will-power.

As has been said, a great secret of the art of living is to be able to pass the tempting by-paths and strike ahead. The traveller who knows this art escapes many torments; and this way of the will I shall invite the reader to consider later.

There are few subjects of thought more evasive than this of the will; but it is the duty of everyone to understand something of the behaviour of the will-o'the-wisp who leads us. By degrees, we shall discover, that here is no ignis fatuus, but a power, working in co-ordination with the other powers of Mansoul, having its own functions and subject to its own laws.

Thus far we have seen, that, just as to reign is the distinctive quality of a king, so is to will the quality of a man. A king is not a king unless he reign; and a man is less than a man unless he will.

Further, we have seen that we have the choice of willing or not willing. It is even possible to go through life without an act of will. All that we do or think, in spite of ourselves, as it were, according to the impulses of our nature, is not willed. Will is neither virtuous nor vicious; but a constant will must have an object outside of self, whether good or bad. The will has, so to say, its times of high and low temperature; and the times of low temperature, of feeble will-power, are times of danger.

Chapter IV The Will And Its Peers

The Will subject to Solicitations.—It is rather easeful to think of Will standing before the forces of Mansoul, saying to this one, 'Go,' and to another, 'Come,' and to a third, 'Do this, and he doeth it.' The Will is subject to solicitations all round from 'the lust of the flesh, the lust of the eye, and the pride of life.' Every dæmon of Mansoul tries, as we have seen, [Cf. Book I., 'Self-Knowledge.'] to get the ear of the Prime Minister, and shows, with plausible reasoning, that he, alone and unaided, is able to satisfy all the wants of the State. From the mere greed of eating and drinking to ambition, that 'last infirmity of noble minds,' every single power of Mansoul will, if it be permitted, make for misrule. But, courage, my Lord Will! and the forces fall into place and obey the word of command.

We have already seen how the Reason firm, the enlightened Imagination, the ordered Affections, the instructed Conscience, are at hand with instant counsel towards every act of volition.

Will does not Act alone.—It takes the whole man to will, and a man wills wisely, justly, and strongly in proportion as all his powers are in training and under instruction. It is well to know this, to be quite sure that we may not leave any part of ourselves ignorant or untrained, with the notion that what there is of us will act for the best.

Living means more than the happenings of one day after another. We must understand in order to will. "How is it that ye will not understand?" said our Lord to the Jews, who would only see that which was obvious, and would not reflect or try to interpret the signs of the times; and that is the way with most of us, we will not understand. We think that in youth there is no particular matter to exercise our Will about, but that we shall certainly will when we get older and go into the world. But the same thing repeats itself: great occasions do not come to us at any time of our lives; or, if they do, they come in the guise of little matters of every day. Let us be aware of this. The 'great' sphere for our Will is in ourselves. Our concern with life is to be fit, and according to our fitness come the occasions and the uses we shall be put to. To preserve Mansoul from waste, to keep every province in order—that, and not efforts in the outside world, is the business of Will.

Chapter V The Function Of Will

There is, as we have seen, only one power in the Kingdom of Mansoul quite at its own disposal, a free agent, able to do what it likes, and that is the Will; and the one thing the Will has to do is to prefer. 'Choose ye this day' is the command that comes to each of us in every affair and on every day of our lives; and the business of the Will is to choose.

The Labour of Choice.—We are usually ready enough to choose between things, though some of us shirk even that responsibility. We gaze upon two stuffs for gowns, and cannot choose between them. Indeed, the whole success of advertisements depends upon the fact that we wish someone, if it be only the salesman, to make up our mind for us. Some one has a rather clever story of a girl with two lovers, who was quite unable to decide between them, and one of the two made things easy by a pretended decease. The girl had no longer the labour of choice.

We do as Others do.—There are many people who minimise the labour of life by following the fashion in their clothes, rooms, reading, amusements, in the pictures they admire and in the friends they select.

We are all glad of a little of this kind of help, because it is well to do as others do in some of the small things of life; but fashion herself is a broken reed, and we must sometimes choose. The Joneses put off the labour of choice till the last minute. They inquired of their friends and consulted guide-books and weighed many considerations; but the more information they got, the more difficult was the choice of where to go for the summer holidays. So they went to the station, and trusted to the inspiration of the last minute; but, after all, Margate was a choice!

This inability to choose appears to be growing upon us as a nation, perhaps as a race; and the reason may be, that, though we are slow to elect for ourselves, we are zealous propagandists on behalf of others. We choose their furniture, their careers, their tastes, for other people, and push them zealously into that which we are assured is for their good. The gown may be becoming or the career may be suitable; but, in so far as we have chosen for another, we have done that other person an injury. We have taken away a chance from him or her of fulfilling the chief function of life, that of choosing.

We do a worse hurt to ourselves when we dress our persons in ready-made garments and our minds in ready-made opinions; because, in so far as we do so, we lose the chance of using our Will; we act as an automaton and not as a person; and no more fulfil our function than do the sham plants used in tawdry decorations. Every man and woman who does not live in the continual thoughtful exercise of a temperate will, is more or less of a lay figure, pulled by the strings of other people's opinions.

Choice and Obedience.—But you will say, 'What about obedience, then—to the home authorities first; after that, to the State, to the Church, and always to the law of God? If a person be truly a person only as he acts upon the choice of his own will, surely,' you say, 'obedience must destroy personality.' On the contrary, obedience is the exquisite test, the sustainer of personality; but it must be the obedience of choice. Because choice is laborious, the young child must be saved the labour, and trained in the obedience of habit; but every gallant boy and girl has learned to choose to obey father and mother, pastor and master, and all who are set in authority over them. Such obedience is the essence of chivalry, and chivalry is that temper of mind opposed to self-seeking; the chivalrous person is a person of constant Will; for, as we have seen, Will cannot be exercised steadily for ends of personal gain. But obedience must be given only because it is right.

Life, you will say, becomes too laborious if every choice matters, and is to be made at first hand. That reminds one of the fable of the pendulum that 'struck,' thus stopping the clock, because it counted how many ticks it must give in a day, in a year, in many years. The sum was overwhelming, and the pendulum stopped. The clock-face inquired into the matter, and the pendulum presented his big sum. 'Oblige me,' said the face, 'by ticking once.' He did so. 'Did that fatigue you?'—'Not in the least,' said the pendulum; 'but it is not of one tick but of millions of ticks that I complain.' 'But,' said the face, 'you are only required to give one tick at once, and there is always a second of time to tick in.' The Will is precisely in the case of the discontented pendulum.

No doubt there are many choices to make, but they come one by one, and there is always the time to choose.

We choose between Ideas.—It is well, however, to know what it is that we choose between. Things are only signs which represent ideas. Several times a day we shall find two ideas presented to our minds; and we must make our choice upon right and reasonable grounds. The things themselves which stand for the ideas may not seem to matter much; but the choice matters. Every such exercise makes personality the stronger; while it grows the weaker for every choice we shirk.

Chapter VI The Scope Of Will

Allowance does Duty for Choice.—We have seen that the function of the Will is to choose, not between things, persons, and courses of action, but between the ideas which these represent. Every choice, of course, implies a rejection of one or many ideas opposed to the one we choose. If we keep the will in abeyance, things and affairs still present themselves, but we allow instead of choosing. We allow a suggestion from without, which runs with our nature, to decide for us. There would not seem to be much difference between the two courses; but most ruined lives and ruined families are the result of letting allowance do duty for will-choice.

It is not that a person need go through the labour of choice on all small occasions. A man goes to his tailor having made his choice; that is, he has long ago decided that the common sense and good taste of the class he belongs to are a sufficient guide in such matters. He remembers Lord Chesterfield's dictum; he will not be among the first to adopt a new fashion, nor among the last to follow an old one: therefore, his choice is limited enough, and his tailor sees to the rest. But, you will say, he has not chosen at all!

Yes, he has; he has chosen with modesty and good sense to follow the lead set by the common sense of his class.

A young man of more pretensions comes to his tailor and is shown the latest cut, a material that will be 'the thing' in a few months. He asks many questions, deliberates a good deal, or rather, invites his tailor to say, 'The very thing for you, sir! Lord Tom Foley ordered the very same thing last week.' That does it: the thing of a new cut or a striking pattern is sent home, and the young man considers that he has made his choice. Not at all: the tailor has played on his vanity, and his act, in ordering the garment, has been one of allowance, not of choice. He is but playing Malvolio after all! Another man visits his tailor, who takes his measure in more senses than one. This man is proud, not vain; he does not choose to set the fashion, but to be above it. 'I never wear' this, I 'prefer' the other, is the line he takes. The tradesman humours him, and the purchase, again, is not a matter of choice, but of allowance.

Or, again, there is the man whose conceit leads him to defy general usage and startle the world with checks and ties, feeling that he is a mighty independent fellow. He is merely obeying the good conceit he has formed of himself, and his daring ventures come of allowance and not of choice. We cannot follow the woman to her dressmaker's; the considerations are too complicated! But here, too, the decision arises either from choice made upon deliberate principles regulating taste and outlay, or upon allowance—the suggestion of a costume displayed in a shop window, or the insinuations of the tradeswoman as to what is worn and is becoming.

Once having arrived at principles of choice in such matters, the special occasions give very little trouble. A choice of will implies some previous action of judgment and conscience, some knowledge of the subject, and, generally, some exercise of taste and imagination. We do not choose a thing because we will to do so—that would be mere waywardness; but will acts upon information and reflection. The question of a lady's shopping is only a by-issue, but it is well worth considering; for, alas! the shopping scene at Madame Mantalini's is of too frequent occurrence, and is as damaging to the nerves and morale of the purchaser as to those of the weary shopwomen.

Cheap 'Notions.'—The dishonest fallacy, that it is our business to get the best that is to be had at the lowest price, is another cause of infinite waste of time, money, and nervous energy. The haunting of sales, the ransacking of shop after shop, the sending for patterns here, there, and everywhere, and various other immoralities, would be avoided if we began with the deliberate will-choice of a guiding principle; that, for example, we are not in search of the best and the cheapest, but, of what answers our purpose at the price we can afford to pay.

The mad hunt for the best, newest, most striking, and cheapest, is not confined to matters of dress and ornament, household use and decoration. We are apt to run after our opinions and ideas with the same restless uncertainty. Indeed, it is ideas we hunt all the time; even if we go to a sale with the dishonest and silly notion that we shall get such and such a thing—'a bargain,' that is, for less than its actual worth.

It is well to remember that in all our relations of life, our books and friends, our politics and our religion, the act of choice, the one possible act of the Will, has always to be performed between ideas. It is not that ideas stand for things; but things stand for ideas, and we have to ask ourselves what we really mean by allowing this and that, by choosing the one or the other. Are we going after the newest and cheapest things in morals and religion? are we picking up our notions from the penny press or from the chance talk of acquaintances? If we are, they are easily come by, but will prove in the end a dear bargain. We have expended the one thing that makes us of value, our personality, upon that which is worth nothing. For personality, the determination of the Will, is wasted,—not by use, but by disuse,—in proportion as it is not employed. We must bring wide reading, reflection, conscience, and judgment to bear upon our opinions, if it be only an opinion concerning a novel or a sermon—upon our principles, if they affect only the ordering of our day.

"Who sweeps a room as for Thy law
Makes that and the action fine,"
[The Elixir, George Herbert]

is a general principle; and no action is fine but as it reaches after a principle greater than itself. The ideas we admit become our opinions; the opinions upon which we take action become our principles; our principles and our opinions are ourselves, our character, the whole of us for which we are responsible.

One idea is free, one great will-choice is open to us all. We are inclined to wait upon circumstances and upon opportunities, but it is not necessary, nor, indeed, does it answer, for the person who waits for his opportunity is not ready for it when it comes. The great decision open to us all, the great will act of a life, is whether we shall make our particular Mansoul available for service by means of knowledge, love, and endeavour. Then, the opportunities that come are not our affair, any more than it is the affair of the soldier whether he has sentry duty or is called to the attack.

Chapter VII Self-Control —Self-Restraint —Self-Command —Self-Denial

Moral Self-culture.—The four types of behaviour now to be considered are not attractive. An instinct, perhaps a true instinct, repels us from all substantives compounded with 'self.' 'What's the good?' we say, when an ideal of self-culture is held up for our admiration, and the Will jibs. It is not to be moved to any constant action for self-centred ends. To be sure, as we have seen, a score of self-originated motives—self-esteem, self-respect, and the like—that come of vanity and pride move us to action, not against our will, but without our will. And the self-control and self-constraint to which we have been exhorted from infancy, and rightly so, even self-denial, may be practised and perfected, all for the sake of that dear Self which perceives that serenity is blessed, that self-approval is a happy state, that self-complacency is singularly agreeable to the one who has it; that, in fact, this sort of moral self-culture pays. Then, has not Self a right to be complacent on the score of such results; for, how they tend to the comfort of everyone else! How they make for peace and pleasantness!

Self-Absorption.—I am not sure. The moral self-culture which is practised for its own sake is apt to give a curious apartness to the self-cultured person. There is a loss of spontaneity, a suggestion of a 'higher plane,' which stops the flow of simple, natural sympathy, the only gift we have for one another. Any sort of absorption has this effect; no one expects much of a lover, or a poet, or of a student cramming for an examination; but the lover's case is, we know, only a phase, and so is the student's; and as for the poet, in so far as there is anything in him, he is working for the world. But nothing comes of self-absorption beyond that personal culture which is its aim. The rest of us are not very willing to be benefited by persons who are evidently on another plane: even Christ reached us where we are, for was He not in all points tempted like as we are?

I remember once meeting, amongst a large party, a lady who was rather a puzzle to me. She was striking-looking and very agreeable. She was a leader in whatever went on in the house—acting, reciting, games, talk—and excelled everyone else in whatever she did. She was very kind, too; wherever there was a little need or ailment, she was on the watch to give help. This lady was a puzzle to me, because, with so much that was charming, there was a certain aloofness about her that was repellent. I thought, perhaps she was a woman with a story; but, no, everybody knew all about her. At last her kind wish to help me disclosed the mystery. If I laid myself upon my bed in such and such a position, and said, 'I am very happy, there is nothing the matter with me,' etc., etc., for so long every day, the result would be perfect serenity of mind and health of body.

Then I saw what put this interesting woman out of touch with the people about her. She had a distinct personal cult, a cult of her own well-being, which, notwithstanding many kindnesses, proved like a wall topped with broken glass to the rest of us; we could not get at her, and though she practised every one of the behaviours at the head of this chapter, and more of the kind, I believe it was nothing to the rest of the party.

A Better Way.—Self-restraint, the ordering of our appetites; self-control, the keeping back the expression of our passions and emotions; self-command, which keeps our temper from running away with us; self-denial, which causes us to do without things that we want—all these may be excellent; but there is a better way.

When the Will aims at what is without self and more than self, the appetites are no longer ravenous, nor the emotions overpowering, nor the temper rebellious (except for a quick, impulsive instant, followed by regret and recovery). As for self-denial, it is impossible for love to go without what it wants, because it is not aware of personal wants. The mother who feeds her child with the last crust, covers it with her last rag, does not exercise self-denial, but love. Probably a great deal of harm to ourselves and others is done by what we call our self-denials. "I won't have you saving yer dirty sowl upon me," said an Irish woman to her district visitor; and it is just possible that she expressed a law of life,—that we are not allowed to be good to others, or even to be good in ourselves, just for the sake of being good. Love, and the service of love, are the only things that count.

Give the Will an object outside itself, and it will leap to service, even to that most difficult of all service, the control of the forces of Mansoul. It is not by one grand fiat, but by many ordered efforts of Will, that we overcome those failures in self-restraint, self-control, self-denial, which are the misery of our lives, and which we know to be sin by the wretchedness they bring upon ourselves and others, and the separateness from others which they set up in our hearts. It is not self-ordering, but an object outside of ourselves, leading to self-forgetfulness and a certain valiant rising of the will, to which we must look for a cure for the maladies that vex us.

But, you will say, our Lord Himself has bidden us to deny ourselves. Yes, but He asks of us the self-denial of a disciple who follows his Master and denies himself in the sense that he has no self, for the love that constrains him.

Chapter VIII The Effort Of Decision

We shirk Decisions.—I have attempted to show that the Will stirs at the touch of an uplifting thought. It may perhaps move in the train of vanity, greed, or the like; but, if it do so, it is a mere supernumerary; the forces of nature are strong enough to carry their ends without an effort of Will. They call, not for choice, but only for allowance. And, yet, there are many little wearing decisions to be made in the course of each day, to call upon the Will for which is like bringing a Nasmyth hammer to crack a nut. So we go on asking ourselves, 'What will Mrs. Jones say?' 'Will Mrs. Brown be there?' 'I wonder which side Holford will take?' and so on. We try to relieve ourselves of effort by imagining the decisions of our neighbours. This is a wearing process, because our neighbours are many and their decisions are various; and if we take any one man or woman for our guide, we are still thrown out, because circumstances are never the same for two persons. We are forced to act for ourselves, and so many minor considerations press upon us that, like the tired purchaser at the 'Stores,' we take, at last, the thing that is offered, for no better reason than that it is offered.

Indecision is perhaps a malady of the age, nor is it altogether a bad sign. It means a wider outlook on practices, opinions, creeds. Sir Roger de Coverley poses as our patron saint, invoked on all occasions:—there is so much to be said on both sides that we cannot make up our minds; and at last we make them up at a blind run, and find ourselves where we had never meant to be.

'Toleration'—We admire this attitude of mind in ourselves, and call it Toleration, a sort of creed that may be summed up in this wise. 'There is so much of good in everything and everybody, and so much of bad in everything and everybody; and nothing, and nobody, is better than anything else, or anybody else; so where are you?' 'What's the good?' follows—of going to church, of troubling oneself to vote for this measure or that, this man or that, of troubling oneself about public questions, of offering truth to the ignorant. "What is truth? as jesting Pilate said," and as we, with a lift of the brows, repeat. 'Everybody's creed or opinion is no doubt the best for him, and why should we meddle? We have enough to do to look after ourselves!'

Even about that we need not take much trouble. Some of us have 'luck,' and some of us, 'Providence,' to make for us all the decisions that matter. This is the sort of unformed thought that goes on in the minds of many people to-day; and they wear themselves out with petty decisions and walk blindfold into great ones.

'Providence' and Choice.—But surely, you will say, Providence does fix the bounds of our habitation and guide us in our undertakings. This is no doubt a blessed and restful truth upon which every Christian soul reposes; but Providence does not save us from the effort of decision, for upon this effort depends the education of character; and 'our Father which art in Heaven' brings up His children. As the wise parent sees that his children are invigorated by proper exercise, so we may venture to think that Providence strengthens the children of men by giving to each opportunities for effort, chiefly, perhaps, for this effort of decision. For the will grows strong by its efforts, and the will is the man.

Ludwig Richter has a charming picture to illustrate 'Give us this day our daily bread.' [Unser Vater.] A mother is spoon-feeding two dear round babies seated before her with open mouths; behind, is a big brother with his slice of schwarz brod; a sower has gone forth to sow in a neighbouring field, and a bird follows in his wake for private ends. Here we have the story of providential dealings. The sower sows, the mother feeds, and God giveth the increase. But these do not wait; they work with open eyes and busy hands, and the good that comes to them comes on the lines of their own efforts.

Opinions and Principles.—But, though the labour of decision is part of that sweat of our brow by which we earn our bread of every sort; yet, if our decisions mean worry, fuss, anxiety, and fatigue, whether it be about the buying of a yard of ribbon, or the furnishing of a house, or the choosing of a career, we may be quite sure we have got off the right lines; that Will is in abeyance, and we are being torn in pieces by conflicting desires or affections.

The decisions of Will are always simple, because they have, for good or ill, an end in view outside of Self. As we have seen, no part of us works alone in a watertight compartment. Throughout our lives, Will has been busy, taking counsel with Imagination, Reason, Conscience, Affection; and forming, by degrees, those great decisions on conduct which we call Principles, or those upon matters of thought which we call Opinions. The opinions and principles are at hand for little and great occasions. Our business is to see that we are not distracted by manifold little movements of Self. Then our decisions are prompt and final; we are not fretted by wondering if we have made a mistake, or, if we should have done better by deciding otherwise.

We have done the best that is in us, with prayer if it be a matter of any uncertainty; and then we are sure that we have Providence with us, as the sower has, whether the immediate harvest be rich or poor. We gain, at any rate; there is more of us for the next time of action, and we go our way with added strength and serenity.

You will say this is no ready-made way to a quiet life. No; but in all labour there is profit, and without labour there is no profit, whether in things of the heart or of the hand.

Chapter IX Intention —Purpose —Resolution

The History of a Resolution.—A gentleman was walking on the shore of a southern watering-place with his invalid wife. His attention was attracted by a greater black-backed gull which had fallen dead on the sands; other sea things attracted him, and by and by a little promiscuous collection began to form itself. This swelled and swelled, and, as the collection grew, his knowledge of the objects increased. At last he had so many objects, and so well arranged, that the idea of forming a big county museum presented itself. He embraced the idea, and formed a steady purpose, and the difficulties in the way only strengthened his resolution to face all the labours of collection and classification.

Here we have a sketch of the mental processes which all persons who do things go through. First, something strikes them: the man on the shore would not have called the gull an idea; but that which struck him was an idea all the same, the idea of interest and admiration roused, perhaps, by the dainty beauty of the gull's plumage seen close.

Then followed that arrest of the mind upon the natural objects offered by the sea which led to the intention of getting more knowledge about them. The intention was probably a little vague and general, but strong enough to move him to action; he found the things and got the knowledge. Then the intention became definite. He had an end in view which he meant to carry through, a purpose; and then, in the face of difficulties, came the strong resolution.

The Progress of an Idea.—Another man, perhaps, read, in his boyhood, a history of Drake. He got out of his reading a certain sense of spaciousness, and of the chivalry that adventures all for love of queen and country. His hero is not always to be admired for his goodness, but his manly devotion to a cause takes hold of the neophyte. He has found it good to be at home in "the spacious days of great Elizabeth," and his reading takes that direction for many years. He knows the Elizabethan dramatists, statesmen, 'sea-dogs,' poets. His thoughts become coloured. There is a certain largeness in his opinions and in his conduct of life. He has an uplifting effect upon his neighbours. He helps them to see matters from other than the personal or parochial standpoint. He himself may have followed no more adventurous career than that of a doctor or a squire, but he brings the breeze of the uplands about him, and all his neighbours are the healthier. Of his sons, too, one is in the navy, one in India, and a third has settled in South Africa; all carrying with them the spacious thoughts, the impersonal aims, they got from their father. We seem to leave this man at the inception of what we may call the 'Elizabethan idea, ' when he read his first story. The arrest of the mind and the intention came with the steady pursuit of Elizabethan literature. We cannot so well follow out the stages of purpose and resolution, but, no doubt, they were there, because the fruit of that first seed-thought perfected itself in his life, and it continued to bear in the lives of his sons.

Had the arresting idea come to him from the circumscribed, self-involved days of Queen Anne he might have become a dilettante on the look-out for Chelsea teapots and Chippendale tables. He, too, would have an influence on his neighbours, for we cannot spare anything that has been; but his influence would make rather for the small graces than for the larger issues of life.

Personal Influence must be Unconscious.—This question of influence is, by the way, very interesting. The old painters pictured the saints with a nimbus, a glory, coming out of them. The saint with a nimbus suggests what seems to be a universal truth, that each of us moves, surrounded by an emanation from his own personality; and this emanation is the influence which affects everyone who comes near him. Generosity emanates, so to speak, from the generous person; from the mean person, meanness. Those who come in contact with the generous become generous themselves; with the mean, mean.

This sort of influence we cannot help using; it is unconscious, and belongs to our nature. We have no business with the influence that comes out of ourselves, and have no right to try to influence other people.

We are, of course, called upon to give and receive reproof, counsel, instruction, as occasions arise; but these differ from what is known as 'influence,' in that they are above-board: the other person is aware of what is being done. Our business is to be good, and then our influence will take care of itself. What we must take heed of, however, is that we do not put ourselves in the way of the lowering influence of unworthy persons.

None of us can be proof against the influences that proceed from the persons he associates with. Wherefore, in books and men, let us look out for the best society, that which yields a bracing and wholesome influence. We all know the person for whose company we are the better, though the talk is only about fishing or embroidery. Probably no one is much the better for virtuous and pious conversation, what school-boys call 'pi-jaw'; but everyone is better for coming in contact with a sweet, wholesome, manly soul, whose nature is not only within him, but surrounds him, and is taken in as the air they breathe by all about him.

Sources of Ideas.—It is well to get the idea which leads to a resolution from such a source. It is possible that this idea may come as a seed-thought to some reader—may arrest his mind, form his intention, concentrate into purpose, strengthen into resolution—that, if he can do no more for the world, his shall, anyway, be a Mansoul from whom wholesome, and not unwholesome, influence will emanate. We may have other things to do; great philanthropic labours may come our way—indeed, all labours for the world are philanthropic if they are sincere; whether the writing of a book, the sitting on a parochial committee, the helping to make laws in the House of Commons. But no one need feel left out in the cold because his work seems to be for no greater a purpose than that of earning his living. That, too, is a great end, if he wills to do it with a single aim. He need not mourn that he has no influence; everyone has influence, not in the ratio of his opportunities, nor even of his exertions, but in that of his own personality. Mansoul is in truth a kingdom whose riches and opportunities are for whosoever will.

Will, the Instrument by which we appropriate Ideas.—But there are persons who never entertain the idea that presents itself, and who, therefore, form neither intention, purpose, nor resolution upon it—the persons who do not use their Will. And there are persons who deliberately will and choose to entertain harmful and injurious ideas; the thoughts of whose hearts are only evil continually, whose purposes, resolutions, are ever towards evil ends.

These several acts of the Will, intention, purpose, resolution, are not only possible to us, but are required of us. The Will is, in fact, the instrument by which we appropriate the good, uplifting thought that comes our way; and it is as we seize upon such thought with intention, act upon it with purpose, struggle, with resolution, against obstacles, that we attain to character and usefulness in the world.

Chapter X A Way Of The Will

The Way of the Will a Slow Way.—We have already seen something of the 'way of the Will.' We know that the Will acts upon ideas; that ideas are presented to the mind in many ways—by books, talk, spiritual influences; that, to let ourselves be moved by a mere suggestion is an act of allowance and not of will; that an act of will is not the act of a single power of Mansoul, but an impulse that gathers force from Reason, Conscience, Affection; that, having come to a head by degrees, its operations also are regular and successive, going through the stages of intention, purpose, resolution; and that, when we are called upon for acts of will about small matters, such as going here or there, buying this or that, we simply fall back upon the principles or the opinions which Will has slowly accumulated for our guidance.

We know that what we do or say matters less than what we will; for the Will is the man, and it is out of many acts of willing that our character, our personality, comes forth.

The Will is Opposed.—You will say, "This is all very well, and I should gladly choose to be among the men of good-will; but I know that sudden emergencies will overtake me, as they have always done before. Anger, greed, mean thoughts, the strong desire of favour here or friendship there, perplexity or fear, will come upon me with such force that I shall not be able to will or to do, but only to drift."

These sudden floods of the spirit—or the slow aggressions of outside influence—we are all sadly familiar with, and call them temptations; and we pray that we may not enter into temptation. But we forget that the mandate runs, 'Watch and pray'; and, perhaps, three-fourths of the falls of good men and women arise from the fact that they do not know or consider at what postern they must keep ward. They strive against what they call their besetting sin, occupying their minds about that sin, in order that they may strive against it; and they so surely prepare themselves for a fall by this very preoccupation, that their story has passed into a proverb, 'Hell is paved with good intentions.'

The Postern to be Guarded.—The place to keep watch at, is, not the way of our particular sin, but that very narrow way, that little portal, where ideas present themselves for examination. Our falls are invariably due to the sudden presentation of ideas opposed to those which judgment and conscience, the porters at the gate, have already accepted.

These foreign ideas get in with a rush. We know how that just man, Othello, was instantly submerged by the idea of jealousy which Iago cunningly presented. We know of a thousand times in our own lives when some lawless idea has forced an entrance, secured Reason as its advocate, thrown a sop to Conscience, and carried us headlong into some vain or violent course.

Seeing that neither Reason nor Conscience can be depended upon, once an idea has been admitted, though they offer infallible tests at the gateway, what we want to know is, how we are to treat insurgent ideas that press for an entrance. Fight them, say most Christian teachers; and the story of the mediaeval Church is a history of fights with thongs and lashes, hair shirts, fastings, and sore self-denials, shutting out all the sweetness of life. These terrific conflicts with evil, Martin Luther's inkpot, and the like, cannot, perhaps, be escaped when certain turbulent ideas have got in; but our Lord's merciful counsel of 'Watch and pray' saves us. Given, the good Will, there is a means at hand, simple and unpromising against our giant, as was David's sling and stone, and just as effectual. In the spiritual as well as in the natural world, great means are always simple.

When the new idea presents itself in a newspaper article or in the talk of our friends—or rises suddenly in our own hearts—by a rapid act of the trained Reason and instructed Conscience, we examine the newcomer. We do this unconsciously; it has become the habit of the trained will (and the way to train the will is to exercise it) to submit the chance ideas that come our way to this manner of inspection before we appropriate them—let them in, that is, and make them our own.

Supposing they fail to satisfy the two janitors which coalesce to form our judgment, what then? Here comes in the beautiful simplicity with which the will works. We do not struggle against, or argue down, or say bad things against the trespasser. By a conscious act of will, we simply and instantly think of something else—not something good and lofty, but something interesting, even something diverting; what we shall do on our next holiday, a story we are reading, a friend we mean to see, even a fly walking across the ceiling, is enough to think about; because any other occupation of the mind keeps out the insidious idea we would repel, and it has no power over us until it has been willingly admitted.

Whenever life becomes so strenuous that we are off guard, then is our hour of danger. Ideas that make for vanity, petulance, or what not, assault us, and our safety lies in an ejaculation of prayer,—'O God, make speed to save us! O Lord, make haste to help us!' and then, quick as thought, we must turn our eyes away from the aggravating circumstance and think of something diverting or interesting.—the weather, and the fitting garments for it, are always at hand!

We are all aware, more or less, that our moral Armageddon is to be fought against an army of insurgent ideas; but, perhaps, we are not all aware of the simple and effectual weapon put into our hands. Another thing that we are not all aware of is, that insurgent intellectual ideas have to be dealt with in precisely the same way as the moral insurgents within us. We are not free to think what we like, any more than to do what we like; indeed, the real act is the thought. Our opinions about God and man, Church and State, books and events, are as much the result of the operations of Will as are our moral judgments. They must be no more lightly entertained. Here is the need to watch and pray against the irresponsible flight of opinions for ever on the wing. Every such opinion must be examined at the postern, and, however attractive, if it fail to satisfy due tests, it must be pushed out of the way, diverted by some friendly and familiar thought waiting to occupy the mind. It is not that we must make up our minds beforehand to reject any class of intellectual ideas; but that it is our bounden duty to examine each as it presents itself, to submit it to the tests of Reason and Conscience; and, if it do not satisfy these, why—just to think of something else, really interesting and diverting!

An idea, once admitted, is our master and not our servant. There are ideas, both evil and good, both moral and intellectual, which strike us, possess us, carry us away, absorb all our powers of body and mind, so that we may come to live, for better for worse, as the instrument of a single idea. How necessary, then, that we should keep watch at the door of ideas, and that we should become adepts in the use of the simple means of repelling ideas we would not willingly entertain!

A careful study of the Gospels will show the vital importance of the ideas of the Intellect which we are apt to call merely a person's opinions—the opinions that 'every person has a right to form for himself.' Undoubtedly he has, both a right and a duty, but he should face his risks.

The Gospels are largely filled with the story of our Lord's controversies against fallacies,—that is, specious opinions proved by the Reason, and allowed to pass by the Conscience, because the Will permitted them unquestioned entrance. It is a perilous fact that Conscience and Reason themselves are at the mercy of an idea which they have not been summoned to examine before its admission.

Chapter XI Freewill

Summary of Points considered so far.—We have seen that the ordering of Mansoul, the due coordination of all its powers, belongs to Will; that the Will is neither moral nor immoral; that the function of the Will is to choose; that the choice lies, not between things, circumstances, or persons, but between ideas; that an act of the Will evolves from long preparation, under the guidance of the Intelligence, the Affections, and the Conscience; that the operations of the Will are also of slow evolution, going through, at least, the stages of intention, purpose, resolution; that immediate acts of Will, which do not seem to go through any process of evolution, either in preparation or operation, are really only the application of principles and opinions that have passed through their due stages and issue in acts of judgment: it is these, and not the immediate decision, which are acts of Will.

We have seen, too, that many persons shirk the exercise of Will, the proper work of a man, and drift into allowance instead of choice, or into the wayward impulses proper to their nature. Intellectual opinions, as well as moral principles, belong, it appears, to the sphere of the Will. We perceive that the good Will, which humbly undertakes its functions in Mansoul, finds itself continually beset with hazards, impulses here, suggestions there; but that the field of action for the Will is narrower than it seems: Will must watch at the postern where ideas enter. This is the more necessary because Reason, a dependable guide as to ideas which the Will has not admitted, becomes a special pleader for an idea that has once crossed the rubicon—so much so, that there is no conceivable act of crime or folly that the reason of men has not justified to themselves by logical arguments, not to be refuted. Conscience, too, that other judge of our actions, is able to be convinced by Reason. Therefore, if Mansoul is to be saved from anarchy, the Will must keep incessant watch at the door of ideas. We have seen, too, that the obstructions to the rule of Will, arising from strong impulses and powerful suggestions, may be met in a simple way. The Will asserts itself, not by struggle and insistence, but by a diversion of thought, to be repeated as often as the impulse or suggestion recurs; and each recurrence is fainter than the last: whilst the Will employs the pause secured by such diversion to gather force.

So much we have been able to gather, more or less vaguely, about the functions and behaviour of the Will; and it behoves us to know all we can about this one practical faculty of man, because the task set to us is to work out our own salvation from base habits of body, loose habits of mind, inordinate affections, from debased and conventional moral judgments; and the Will is the single instrument by which we are able to work.

Will and Conventionality.—Our Will must deliver us from the intellectual and moral fallacies of which the air is full. It is by our Will that we shall be saved from that commonplace respectability which never errs, because every act conforms to the standard of general custom; not by choice of will, but in lazy imitation. This habit of life, though it look like that of the man of good-will, is the despair of all who care profoundly for their kind; because the end of life—nay, life itself—is missed by all those excellent citizens who live to save their lives; to do well by themselves; to get on and prosper, that they may have the more, whether of luxury, culture, or pleasure. Life, circumscribed by self, its interests and advantages, falls under the condemnation,—"He that saveth his life shall lose it."

Therefore, Christ ate with publicans and sinners, and pronounced woes against the respectable classes because the sinners might still have a Will which might rise, however weakly, at the impact of a great thought, at the call to a life outside of themselves. The men at whom no one could point a finger were tied and bound in self, and were incapable of the great act of will implied in, "Choose ye this day whom ye will serve."

There are but two services open to men—that which has self as the end and centre, and that which has God (and, by consequence, man) for its object.

It is possible, indeed, to choose the service of God unconsciously, believing that we have only a passionate desire to help men; but it is not any way possible to drift into the service of God when our object is to do well by ourselves: no, not even if that doing well by ourselves reaches its ultimate aim—that of saving our own souls. It has been well said that selfishness is none the better for being eternal selfishness.

If Christ were to walk amongst us to-day, perhaps He would cry in our streets, 'Woe to the land which upholds the standard of his own well-being as the aim of every man!' We cannot live higher than our aims. Will must have an object outside of itself, whether for good or ill; and, therefore, perhaps there is more hope for some sinners than for certain respectable persons.

We seem able to discern something of the function of the Will and something of its behaviour. If we would look closer and know what the Will is, if we would enclose it in a definition, it eludes us, as do all the great mysteries of life, death, and personality. This much we discern—that, in the man of good-will, the Will is absolutely free; that, in fact, there can be no will but a free will. Wherefore, the conventional person who makes no choice is without freewill, because he is without will. Will, freewill, must have an object outside of self; and the poet has said the last word, so far as we yet know:

"Our wills are ours, we know not how;
Our wills are ours to make them Thine.'
Tennyson.

PART III—The Soul

Chapter I The Capacities Of The Soul

Step by step, we have tried to gather together the little knowledge that is open to us about Body, Mind and Heart, [See Book I., 'Self-Knowledge.'] Will and Conscience. We have seen that no clear definition of either of these is possible, and that there is no rigid boundary-line between any two. The powers of Mansoul are many, but they are one; and, by careful scrutiny, we gather hints enough from the behaviour of each to help us in discerning those laws of our being whereby we must order ourselves.

We leave now the outer courts of Mind and Body, the holy places of the Affections and the Will, and enter that holy of holies where man performs his priestly functions; for every man is of necessity a priest, bound to officiate in his most holy place.

In every Mansoul, the 'Soul' is the temple dedicate to the service of the living God. How wonderful is the Soul of man! We commonly speak of ourselves as finite beings; but whoever has experienced the rush of the Soul upon a great thought will wonder whether we are indeed finite creatures, or whether it is not because we have touch with the infinite that we have capacity for God.

What is there that baffles the understanding of a man, or that is out of the range of his thoughts, the reach of his aspirations? He is, it is true, baffled on all hands by his ignorance, the illimitable ignorance of the wisest: but ignorance is not incapacity; and the wings of a man's Soul beat with impatience against the bars of this ignorance; he would out, out, into the universe of infinite thought and infinite possibilities. How is the Soul of a man to be satisfied? Crowned kings have thrown up dominion because they want that which is greater than kingdoms. Profound scholars fret under the limitations which keep them playing upon the margin of the unsounded ocean of knowledge. No great love can satisfy itself in loving. There is no satisfaction for the Soul of a man, save one, because the things about him are finite, measurable, incomplete; and his reach is beyond his grasp; he has an urgent, incessant, irrepressible need of the infinite.

Even we lesser people, who are not kings or poets or scholars, are eager and content enough in pursuit; but we know well that when we have attained, be it place or power, love or wealth, the old insatiable hunger will be upon us: we shall still want—we know not what!

St Augustine knew, when he said that the Soul of man was made for God, and could never be satisfied until it found Him. But our religious thought has become so poor and commonplace, so self-concerned, that we interpret this saying of the sainted man's to mean, we shall not be satisfied till we find all the good we include in the name, salvation. We belie and belittle ourselves by this thought: it is not anything for ourselves we want; and the sops that we throw to our souls, in the way of one success after another, fail to keep us quiet.

'I want, am made for, and must have a God.' We have within us an infinite capacity for love, loyalty, and service; but we are deterred, checked on every hand, by limitations in the objects of our love and service. It is only to our God that we can give the whole, and only from Him can we get the love we exact; a love which is like the air, an element to live in, out of which we gasp and perish. Where, but in our God, the Maker of heaven and earth, shall we find the key to all knowledge? Where, but in Him, whose is the power, the secret of dominion? And, our search and demand for goodness and beauty baffled here, disappointed there—it is only in our God we find the whole. The Soul is for God, and God is for the Soul, as light is for the eye, and the eye is for light. And, seeing that the Soul of the poorest and most ignorant has capacity for God, and can find no way of content without Him, is it wholly true to say that man is a finite being? But words are baffling; we cannot tell what we mean by finite and infinite.

We say there is no royal road to learning; but this highest attainment of man is for the simple and needy; it is reached by the road in which the wayfaring man, though a fool, shall not err. In this fact, also, we get a glimpse of the infinite for which we hunger. How strange it is to our finite notions that ALL should be offered to the grasp of the simplest and the least!

Chapter II The Disabilities Of The Soul

The Soul, like the Mind and Heart, has its chronic disabilities, its deep-seated diseases. With an overpowering need of God, a great capacity to receive Him, common to all men, very few attain anything like a constant "fruition of Thy glorious Godhead." Many of us have fitful glimpses; and many, perhaps most of us, are 'unaware.' The causes of our deadness to things divine may be roughly classed under the three heads of inertia, preoccupation, and aversion.

Inertia.—We have seen how a certain lethargy of Mind withholds us from entering on the vast inheritance open to our intelligence. In like manner, the Soul is dead, and unaware of that hunger and thirst which God alone can satisfy. Conscience may be awake, may demand of us public worship, private prayers, the reading of good books; or, Conscience may be dulled, and we forgo these things; but, in either case, it is possible to have little or no apprehension of God—no wish, indeed, for such apprehension, for the lethargic Soul shrinks from that which must needs give it a great shaking out of its habits of ease. Such a Soul covets from others the praise that 'there is no harm in him'; from himself the praise that 'I do my duty' in all manner of proper observances.

The inner Soul is not dead; it could awake, if the Will of the man would respond to the approaches of the divine tenderness; but it is torpid—the cry, 'Awake! Awake!' does not penetrate the heavy ear.

The lethargic Soul is one with the wicked in this, that "God is not in all his thoughts." He is capable of living from hour to hour, nay, from day to day and from year to year, without that turning of the face of his soul towards God (as a flower to the sun) which is the sure indication of a living Soul. It is not that he never thinks upon God; perhaps there is not a man who never says in his need, 'God help me!' and perhaps not many who do not sometimes say, 'Thank God!' But this occasional and rare crying upon God is a widely different thing from having God in all his thoughts.

The hope for the inert Soul, whether he be a regular churchgoer or one of the 'careless ones,' is that some living idea of God may arrest his Mind and stir up his Will to desire, intend, resolve. This is what is called conversion, and is among the everyday dealings of the Almighty Father with His dull and callous children. We have all undergone such conversions, in a less degree, many times in our lives. And sometimes, to the generous heart or to the hardened sinner, a great conversion comes, which changes, from the moment, all the intents of his heart and the ways of his life.

Preoccupation.—As fatal as the lethargy of Soul which will not awake to the presence of God, is such preoccupation of Mind or Heart as leaves no room for the dominating and engrossing thought of God. "My duty towards God is to love Him with all my heart and all my mind," as well as "with all my soul and with all my strength." No power of Mansoul works alone in a compartment by itself, and Mind and Heart must unite in the worship of the Soul.

It is possible, and, alas! common enough, to be so preoccupied with one idea or with many that we are unaware of any need of God, practically unaware that He is. The preoccupation may be lawful enough in itself—praiseworthy ambition, family affection, or the passionate pursuit of knowledge; these are things for which we rightly give praise and honour; but any one of them may so absorb a man that he does not want God, that there is no room for God in all his thoughts, that the mere thought of God comes to be to him an encroachment upon thoughts he chooses to bestow elsewhere. He is not wicked, as men count wickedness, but he is living without God in the world. Though he does not know it, he is suffering a tremendous deprivation. He is crippled, mutilated in his best part, his highest function; and creeps through life like some poor wretch who spends his days and nights in a dark hole of a room, and never knows what it is to breathe in the open fields, under the broad sky. What joy for these, commonly generous, souls, to wake at last, here or hereafter, into the knowledge of God!

Involuntary Aversion.—But the Soul has another disability more puzzling and more astounding than either of those we have considered. There is in human nature an aversion to God. Whether it be, according to the Article, that "original sin which is the natural fault and corruption of the nature of every man that naturally is engendered of the offspring of Adam," or whether it is that jerk of the shoulder from the hand of authority which belongs to freewill, we need not stop to inquire. Anyway, there is in human nature, as well as a deep-seated craving for God, a natural and obstinate aversion to Him.

The baby does not want to say his prayers, and the ripe saint is aware of unwillingness, a turning away of his thoughts and affections; and this, though all his joy is in his God. This involuntary turning from God is the cross and discipline of the Godward Soul. But, from whatever cause it springs, it would seem to be allowed in the nature of things; for, if our hearts flew to God as inevitably as raindrops to the earth where would our election, our willing choice of God before all things, come in? Where would be the sense of victory in our allegiance?

Voluntary Aversion.—But there is a difference between this natural, involuntary aversion, for which we take shame; and the voluntary aversion, animosity, malignity, towards God, set up by the rebellious and sinful Soul; the Soul who, out of pride or open wickedness, cannot endure the thought of God, travesties His Word, defies His Laws, abjures His Will, and blasphemes His Name. When all this is done with violence, we are shocked; but, when it is done with an easy superiority and good-nature, and with power of intellect, we are all, alas, too apt to swerve from our allegiance, if it be only for an instant, and to believe that the scoffer has more knowledge than we. This is because there are in our own hearts the germs of that aversion which he has nourished into a seedbearing plant.

"Let him that standeth take heed lest he fall." Let us hold fast our loyalty, knowing that this, of making with our Will deliberate choice of God, is the only offering we can make Him; knowing, too, for our comfort, that involuntary aversion is not sin, and only gives us occasion for choice; but, when we choose to turn away, our sin does not put us without the limits of mercy, but it is immeasurably great.

Chapter III The Knowledge Of God

When we realise how the Soul of man is disabled by inertia, by preoccupation, even by aversion, from apprehending God, we discern, at the same time, what is the great thing which the Will has to do; and it rises to a noble effort, to the uplift of a great thought. So long as we think that the things of God which we sum up under the name, religion, may be taken or left according as we have a mind; so long as we wait passively for sufficient persuasion, for a strong enough impulse, towards our chief duty, Will cannot sustain us. But once we realise that we have not only the world, the flesh, and the devil, but alien tempers in our own soul to combat; when we see that, in desiring God, we have set before us a great aim, requiring all our courage and constancy, then the Will rises, chooses, ranks itself steadfastly on the side of God; and, though there be many failings away and repentings after this one great act of Will, yet, we may venture to hope, the Soul has chosen its side for good and all. The disorderly soldier is fined, imprisoned and worse—but he is not a rebel, and, when fighting comes, he does not desert.

We meet many people in the world whom we do not know; some are too high for us and some too low, some too good and some not good enough; with some we feel we could have perfect sympathy, but they are too far off, we cannot get at them; while the meannesses and limitations of the persons about as make them unworthy, so we think, of the outpouring of our mind and heart.

But there is one great, perfect and satisfying Intimacy open to us all,—whether we are lonely because we feel 'superior,' or because we know ourselves to be 'poor things,' unworthy of much notice. We are abashed when we think of the promotion open to every poor human soul. "This is eternal life," said our Lord, "to know Thee, the only true God, and Jesus Christ whom Thou hast sent"; and this knowledge, this exalted intimacy, is open to us all, on one condition only—if we choose. Feeling as we do that we ourselves are not good or clever enough for the friendship of some people, and are much too good and clever for that of some others, it is startling to know that this supreme friendship is to be had by each of us if he will, because every human soul has capacity for the knowledge of God; not for mathematics, perhaps, nor for science, nor for politics, but for that vast knowledge which floods the soul like a sea to swim in—the knowledge of God. The late Professor W. K. Clifford has told us of the agony with which, when he lost faith in God, he realised that "the great Companion was dead." The "great Companion" never dies. "He knoweth our downsitting and our uprising, and understandeth our thoughts long before," holds sweet counsel with us upon all we do and all we intend, cheers our dulness, rests our weariness, consoles our grief, gladdens our joy, chides, rebukes, chastises our sin, and gives us in ever-increasing measure that which all who have ever loved generously know to be the best and most perfect joy—the gradually disclosing vision of Himself. Like that blind man restored to sight, at first we see not at all; then we see men, as trees, walking; and then our eyes are fully opened to the vision of our God.

There are several ways by which the knowledge of God first comes to us; we may be struck by the words, acts, and looks of those who know—a very convincing lesson. A little plant of moss, the bareness of a tree in winter, may, as we have seen, awake us to the knowledge; or, dealings of strange intimacy with our own hearts, visitings of repentance and love, sweet answers to poor and selfish prayers, tokens of friendship that we can never tell, but most surely perceive, are all steps in this chief knowledge.

The Bible teaches the Knowledge of God.—But, as the friend listens to the voice, pores over the written word of his friend, so the lover of God searches the Bible for the fuller knowledge he craves. It matters very little to him that one manuscript should be superimposed upon another; that such and such passages should be ascribed to other authors than those whose name they bear; that not only the history, but the legends and myths, of the Jewish nation have found their way into the Book; that science disproves here, and history contradicts there: these things may be so, or may not be so. He is willing and thankful that science and scholarship should do their work, that the laws of textual criticism should be applied; at the same time, he sees a thousand reasons for caution and reserve in accepting the latest dicta of the critics. He reads in his newspaper how the King of Servia had twice to remove the crown during his coronation because he could not bear its weight, how the royal standard fell during the progress to the cathedral, and how uneasy these omens made the people; and he perceives that the future historian of Servia, reading of these incidents, pronounces them legendary, according to all the laws of criticism, and strikes them out of pages which shall only contain history scientifically treated.

Little things like these give the Bible student pause; he reveres truth and welcomes investigation, but he also perceives that the latest critic is not necessarily infallible. But all this is, for him, beside the mark. If errors of statement, false ascriptions, and the rest were found and proven beyond doubt upon every page of his sacred books, yet he believes that in these is to be found, and nowhere but in these, a revealed knowledge of God.

Greece, Rome, India, Persia, China, unwittingly affirm—alike through their poetry, history, and sacred books—that men cannot by searching find out God. A lovely gleam of the divine reaches one sage here, another there; but each attempt to combine these stray lineaments, and seize upon a complete idea of the Godhead, has produced a pantheon here, a monster there. And that, although the insight and wisdom of the past have given us all the philosophy of human life that we possess, every knowledge but the knowledge of God.

In what are we better than those great nations of antiquity who knew so much and did so much? Only in this, that we inherit a possession vouchsafed to the world by means of a nation whose spiritual insight fitted them to receive it. We have a revelation of God which satisfies and directs every aspiration of the Soul of man.

Think even of the one amazing revelation,—that God is love:—

"The very God! think, Abib: dost thou think?
So, the All-Great, were the All-Loving too—
So, through the thunder comes a human voice,
Saying, 'O heart I made, a heart beats here!
Face, my hands fashioned, see it in myself!
Thou hast no power, nor mayst conceive of mine,
But love I gave thee, with myself to love,
And thou must love me who have died for thee.' Browning.

Here is a knowledge that men had never dared to dream, except as it is revealed in the Bible; and, yet, there are those who behave as one who found a huge nugget, and discarded it because the gold lay in a matrix of ore, and he would not take the pains to separate, and had no eye to distinguish, the precious metal. Such behaviour seems puerile in the eyes of the diligent miner. This is how the matter lies. The Soul is able to apprehend God; in that apprehension is life, liberty, fruition. Knowing God, the Soul lives in its proper element, full, free, and joyous as a bird of the air. Without that knowledge, "the heavy and the weary weight of all this unintelligible world" crushes out life.

But, fit and necessary as it is to us to know our God, it is by no means inevitable; indeed, as we have seen, the Soul in very wilfulness tries to evade the knowledge which is its health. We must begin with an act of steadfast will, a deliberate choice; and then, we must labour to get our best good, knowing that, if we ask, we shall receive; if we seek, we shall find; if we knock, all shall be disclosed to us. But the seeking must be of single purpose; we must not be bent upon finding what we take for dross, whether in the Bible, in the ordering of the world, or in that of our own lives. Our search must be for the grains of gold, and, as we amass these, we shall live and walk in the continual intimacy of the divine Love, the constant worship of the divine Beauty, in the liberty of those whom the Truth makes free.

Chapter IV Prayer

Unconsidered Prayer.—It is hard to separate the functions of the Soul, because, indeed, all work together; but it is necessary to fulness of life that we should have continual speech with God, and also—though the soul is abashed before the greatness and sweetness of this hope—continual answering speech. These things are a necessity of that intimate union with our Father for which we are made. A hundred times a day our thoughts turn Godward in penitence, in desire, in fear, in aspiration, and—this is a truly delightful thought—in sympathy. Our hearts glow with delight at the blue of a gentian, the glory of a star, the grace of some goodness that we get news of: we lift up our hearts unto the Lord, though without a word; and the throb is one of sympathy, for we know that His delight, also, is in beauty and goodness.

Response.—These continual movements of the soul Godward hardly seem to us to be prayer, but they meet with response. We cry in fear, and hope is spoken to us; in penitence, and we breathe peace; in sympathy, and we expand in love. These are the answers of our 'Almighty Lover' to the dull, uncertain movements of our poor hearts. We all know how prayers for definite things have a thousand times brought answers which we have recognised; even the wilful prayer, which does not add, 'Thy will be done,' is not without its answer; the passionate heart is calmed; we learn to see God's way of looking at the matter, and are quiet.

Probably most persons who are seeking the knowledge of God would say, that, never once in the course of a long life has a prayer remained unanswered; but, that they have had in every case an answer which has reached their consciousness.

The walls of Jericho have fallen before them, the Jordan has been divided, their enemies have been smitten on the field of battle; and these things have come to pass in natural, unobvious ways, without any interference with what men call the laws of nature, but none the less supernatural, because they are over nature, above nature, ordered by Him who doth "refrain the spirit of princes," and "the hearts of kings are in whose rule and governance."

Habitual Prayer.—But, though there is this continual commerce between God and the Soul, the habit of prayer must be strengthened by set seasons, places, and purposes. We must give ourselves time to pray and times of prayer; rising early in the morning, we must seek our God and lay our day before Him, with its fears, hopes, and desires, in reverent attitude and with attentive mind. We must bring those who are dear to us for the blessing of our Father, and those in sorrow, need, sickness, or any other adversity, for His help. As the habit of prayer becomes confirmed, we shall be constrained to go abroad and help, while yet upon our knees.

Every record of war or famine, ignorance, crime, distress, will quicken our prayers. As we pray, our love for all men will increase, and ways of help will offer. We shall remember our Lord's caution against using many words, for our God is in heaven and we upon earth; and, therefore, before we kneel to pray we shall meditate.

"Ye are coming to a King;
Large petitions with you bring,"—

but they must be petitions thought out with purpose and winged with strong desire. Though

"Prayer is the breathing of a sigh,

The falling of a tear,
The upward glancing of an eye
When none but God is near,"—

yet, we must not neglect the ordered and purposeful approaches to our God wherein the soul stretches her wings.

"Watch and pray."

Chapter V Thanksgiving

The Nine.—"Whoso offereth Me thanks and praise, he honoureth Me," saith our God; and we are abashed when we realise that it rests with us to add honour to the Highest, and that we refrain our lips.

"Were there not ten cleansed, but where are the nine?" Alas, how often are we among the nine, the poor, pitiful souls who received everything and gave nothing, not even a word of thanks! It is worth noting that "the unthankful and the evil" go together in that list of lost souls which we find in the last book of the Bible. Even if we have our moments of thankfulness, when we cry,—

"When all Thy mercies, O my God,
My rising soul surveys,
Transported with the view I'm lost,
In wonder, love and praise";—

our fault, and our very great misfortune, is, that we fail to take at regular intervals that survey of our life which must indeed cause us transports of gratitude. We fail to give thanks, partly because we are inert partly because we are preoccupied with some fret or desire of the moment, and partly because of the petulant turning away of the shoulder from God which is our danger. But let us take time for the survey, if only on the Sundays, or, less frequently still, at the great seasons of the year.

'My Rising Soul surveys.'—How good is life, how joyous it is to go out of doors, even in the streets of a city! Surely a pleasant thing it is to see the sun! How good is health, even the small share of it allotted to the invalid! How good and congenial all the pleasant ways of home life, all family love and neighbourly kindness, and the love of friends! How good it is to belong to a great country and share in all her interests and concerns! How good to belong to the world of men, aware that whatever concerns men, concerns us! How good are books and pictures and music! How delightful is knowledge! How good is the food we eat! How pleasant are the clothes we wear! How sweet is sleep, and how joyful is awaking!

The Soul that surveys these and a thousand other good things of our common life is indeed a 'rising soul,' rising to the Father,—who knoweth that we have need of all these things,—with the gratitude and thanksgiving that are forced out of a heart overflowing with love. Even an occasional act of thanksgiving of this kind sweetens the rest of life for us; unconsidered thanks rise from us day by day and hour by hour. We say grace for a kind look, or a beautiful poem, or a delightful book, quite as truly as for a good dinner—more so, indeed; for it is true of us also that man doth not live by bread alone.

We honour God by thanking Him.—But we think so little of ourselves that it does not seem to us to matter much whether or no we thank God for all His surprising sweet benefits and mercies towards us. Indeed, we should not have known that it does matter, if, with the condescending grace that few earthly parents show, He had not told us that He is honoured by our thanks! How impossible it seems that we should add anything to God, much less that we should add to His honour! Here is our great opportunity: let us give thanks.

Perhaps most of us fall on our knees and give thanks for special mercies that we have begged of our Father's providing care—the restored health of one beloved, the removal of some cause of anxiety, the opening up of some opportunity that we have longed for. For such graces as these we give ungrudging thanks, and we do well; but the continual habit of thanksgiving is more;—

"Not thankful when it pleaseth me,
As if Thy blessings had spare days,
But such a heart whose pulse may be,
Thy praise."
Herbert.

Chapter VI Praise

Implies Discriminating Appreciation.—If our dull souls are slow to thank, perhaps they are still slower to praise, because praise implies discriminating appreciation and reflection as well as thankfulness.

We know how the painter, the musician, writhe under the compliments of people who do not understand, while a word of discriminating praise sends them on their way rejoicing: they are honoured. This is the honour that the divine condescension seeks at our hands.

'We praise Thee, O God,' has ever been the voice of the Church. Prophets, confessors, the noble army of martyrs have, we know, praised God in their lives and by their deaths. To-day, there are those who devote themselves to lives of pain and peril for the honour of God and the service of man; and these too, we can understand, praise God. There are poets to whom it is given to utter some vital word, painters who present us with 'The Light of the World,' or, like the Russian painter, Ivan Kramskoi, with a vision of Christ seated in the wilderness. Such as these praise God, we know, but they are few and far between. So, too, do honest, simple souls who bear affliction willingly, or who live their appointed lives with the sense that they are appointed. All of these ways of giving praise we recognise and bow before; but the duty would seem to pass us by as incompetent persons. We are not angels, we carry no harps.

But the duty of praise is not for occasional or rare seasons; it waits at our doors every day. If we had not been told otherwise, we should have thought it presuming to believe that the great Artificer, like every loving craftsman, delights in the recognition by others of the beauty, perfection, and fitness of the work He turns out. It is so good to know this of our God; it draws Him near to us with the cords of a man. The Psalmist knew that "the merciful and gracious Lord hath so done His marvellous works that they ought to be had in remembrance." He was never weary of telling how, "the heavens declare the glory of God, and the firmament showeth His handiwork," how, "He feedeth the young ravens when they call upon Him," how, "all the trees of the wood do clap their hands." We all see these things; but David not only saw them, but they gave voice in his heart to a continual hymn of praise. And he, who knew how to honour his God by giving praise, was, we are told, the man after God's own heart.

Discoverers give us Themes for Praise.—Every age would seem to have its prophets, be they painters, poets, or what else, whose function it is to lead in the praises of the choir. To-day, perhaps, scientific men are promoted to this high honour, and what multitudes of praises do they disclose to us! We call such men discoverers, and rightly so, because the thing discovered is there, they in no way produce it; but it is given to them to discover, to show to the rest of us. Every day there is still some new call upon us for wonder, admiration and praise, at the disclosure of some hitherto unknown and undiscovered great conception, mighty exhibition of the Power which every scientist to-day perceives to be behind all 'natural' operations.

Think of a ship in mid-Atlantic being able to communicate, without visible channel, with land a thousand miles away on either side; and that this possibility has been always hidden in the councils of the Almighty, and but now discovered to the man 'prepared'! What may there still be hidden in those councils, waiting till we are ready for disclosure? What amazing discoveries have been opened to us during the last few years! how the sense of the immanence of God presses upon us through all that which we call nature! "How excellent are Thy works, O Lord! in wisdom hast Thou made them all: the earth is full of Thy riches." "He that giveth thanks and praise, he honoureth Me." Let us not neglect to lift, day by day, our offering of praise to our God.

Chapter VII Faith In God

'Only Believe.'—"My duty towards God is to believe in Him," my first duty, the duty of my life, without which other duties would not appear to count much.

'Only believe,' the writer was told as a girl, to her great anger and soreness of heart. If 'only fly' had been said, she could not have flown, but anyway she would have known what definite thing was expected of her;

but 'only believe' carried no meaning. Of course she believed, as she believed that yesterday was Wednesday, the 5th of October, say; that there had been a Queen Elizabeth; that at least one Pharaoh had ruled in Egypt; these things, and thousands like them, she had never troubled herself to doubt, and believed as a matter of course; but—God?

Of course she believed in God in that way, but how could it matter? She was aware that such belief was no part of her life, and she knew of no other way of believing.

Some such perplexity, no doubt, tries many a soul to whom it is brought home as a duty that he must believe in God. My duty towards God, which I must fulfil for myself, which no one can do for me, and which others can give me little conscious help in fulfilling. No one can give me faith, but others can help me on the way to it; for, we are told, "faith cometh by hearing, and hearing, by the Word of God": that is, faith in God, just as faith in a friend, comes of knowledge. We trust our friend because we know him; because we know him, we believe in him. Faith, trust, confidence, belief—they are all one.

Faith in Persons.—To say that we believe in a person whom we hardly know even by hearsay—the Emperor of Korea, for example—would be to speak like a fool; but we do say we believe in this or that statesman, churchman, or what not. Indeed, the whole government and finance of the world are carried on upon a vast system of credit, that is, mutual belief. We say, 'safe as the Bank of England'; but the Bank of England itself is conducted upon credit. We send members to Parliament to represent us because we believe in them. The members of a family believe in each other; and, should jealousy or mistrust arise between parents and children, husband and wife, it is an exception, a shameful exception to the general rule of confidence.

So, too, of dishonesty and venality in common trade and public trusts. Such things occur, but they are shameful exceptions; the general rule is that we live by faith in one another, and this common trust comes of common knowledge. Experience of the world and of life teaches us faith; and it is only the sour and ill-conditioned person who judges by the exception, and says with the Psalmist in his black hour, "All men are liars."

As there are two sorts of faith which we give to our fellows,—one, the general faith we give to man and institutions, which comes of general knowledge and experience; and the other, the intimate and particular faith we give to those whom we believe we know perfectly—the faith which is love: so there are two sorts of faith in God,—one, the general faith that all is ordered for the best, that God will provide, and that God will have mercy upon us.

If we wish to trace the work of this sort of faith let us ask our hearts honestly if it means love. Does our soul spring at the thought of our God, crying, "I will arise and go to my Father," just as we have a heart-movement of springing and going at the thought of the person we love and believe in? If we do not love we do not believe, because faith does not come to us by accident, or even by nature. The faith we give to our friends is recognition of whatever nobleness and beauty of soul there is in them; and this is the manner of faith we owe to God, the recognition—born of knowledge—of Him who is Love and Light and Truth, Him to whom the heart cries, "Whom have I in heaven but Thee? and there is none upon earth that I desire in comparison of Thee." [Prayer Book version of the Psalms.]

Faith, an Act of Will.—We have already considered how we may attain the knowledge of God, and faith is the act of Will by which we choose Him whom we have learned to know. Out of faith comes love, out of love comes service, and it is hardly possible to distinguish under different names the outgoings of the Christian heart in desire after God. "Like as the hart desireth the water brooks, so longeth my soul after Thee, O God": [Prayer Book version of the Psalms.] there we have knowledge, faith, and love.

Not Optional.—The point I would urge is, that this attitude of Soul is not optional; it is a debt we owe, a duty required of us. To say that we do not know that which has been revealed to us, to say that we do not believe in a revelation the truth of which bears the ultimate test, in that it discloses to us the God whom our Souls demand, and in whom they find perfect satisfaction, "whose ways are ways of pleasantness, and all whose paths are peace": to say this is to commit an act of insubordination at the least, an act of infidelity in the simple meaning of the word, worse than infidelity to any human relationship, because our God is more and nearer to us than any.

Men satisfy their Conscience that they have done their whole duty when they do their duty towards their neighbour; but what right have we to choose a moiety of the law for our observance, the lesser moiety, and leave the greater,—our duties of personal knowledge, faith, love, and service towards our God, which are to be fulfilled directly; and not indirectly, through serving men. Both duties lie upon each of us—my duty; and my duty towards God is the first.

There is no space in a single short volume to consider the articles of the Christian faith, even in the concise form in which they are set forth in the Apostles' Creed.

We say 'The Creed' glibly enough, and think we understand it, until now one article and now another is challenged by the sceptic then, because we have nothing to reply, we secretly give up one clause after another, and think that we hold to the rest. It should help us to know that not a single article of our Creed appeals to our understanding. We know no more about the Creation than we do about the Incarnation, no more about the forgiveness of sins than about the resurrection of the body. All is mystery, being what the heart of man could not conceive of unless it had been revealed.

"Great is the mystery of Godliness: God manifest in the flesh, justified in the spirit, seen of angels, preached unto the Gentiles, believed on in the world, received up into glory." And what a barren and dry land should we dwell in if our spirits were narrowed to the limits of that which we can comprehend! Where we err is in supposing that mystery is confined to our religion, that everything else is obvious and open to our understanding. whereas the great things of life, birth, death, hope, love, patriotism, why a leaf is green, and why a bird is clothed in feathers—all such things as these are mysteries; and it is only as we can receive that which we cannot understand, and can discern the truth of that which we cannot prove, and can distinguish between a luminous mystery and a bewildering superstition, that we are able to live the full life for which we were made.

One thing we must hold fast—a clear conception of what is meant by Christianity. It is not 'being good' or serving our fellows: many who do not own the sovereignty of Christ are better than we who do. But the Christian is aware of Jesus as an ever-present Saviour, at hand in all his dangers and necessities; of Christ as the King whose he is and whom he serves, who rules his destinies and apportions his duties. It is a great thing to be owned, and Jesus Christ owns us. He is our Chief, whom we delight to honour and serve; and He is our Saviour, who delivers us, our Friend who cherishes us, our King who blesses us with His dominion. Christianity would only appear to be possible when there is a full recognition of the divinity of Christ.

Let us cry with St Augustine:—

"Take my heart! for I cannot give it thee:
Keep it! for I cannot keep it for Thee."

Appendix

Questions for the Use of Students

Book I

Chapter I The Country of Mansoul

No Questions

Chapter II The Perils of Mansoul

1. Who is to blame for these perils?
2. What effect has sloth upon Mansoul?
3. What are the causes of fire?
4. How may plague, flood, and famine be brought about?
5. What are the consequences of discord?
6. How does darkness arise in Mansoul?
7. Can it be prevented?
8. On what condition do things go well in Mansoul?

Chapter III The Government of Mansoul

1. Why is being born like coming into a great estate?

2. What do we mean by the government of Mansoul?
3. Name some of the officers of state.
4. Name the Chambers in which these 'sit.'
5. Are these parts of a person?

PART I THE HOUSE OF BODY

Chapter I The Esquires of the Body: Hunger

1. What is the work of the appetites?
2. When does an appetite become a danger?
3. How does hunger behave?
4. Distinguish between hunger and gluttony.
5. How is greediness to be avoided?

Chapter II The Esquires of the Body: Thirst

1. Why are we thirsty? What drink does thirst require?
2. What are some effects of drunkenness?
3. What is the principle on which persons abstain?

Chapter III The Esquires of the Body: Restlessness and Rest

1. What is the use of restlessness?
2. Wherein lies the danger?
3. Show that rest and work should alternate.
4. When does rest become sloth?

Chapter IV The Esquires of the Body: Chastity

1. How would you teach a child to rule his appetites?
2. How would you use the tree of knowledge of good and evil to give the idea of chastity?
3. How would you explain, "Blessed are the pure in heart"?
4. What heroic motive for purity would you give children?
5. Where does slavery to an appetite begin?
6. How would you rule the thoughts?

Chapter V The Pages of the Body: the Five Senses

1. What two errors are possible to each of the senses?
2. What are the uses and what the danger of the sense of taste?
3. Show that we fail to get full use and full pleasure out of the sense of smell.
4. What practice in catching odours would you give children?
5. What manner of knowledge do we obtain by touch?
6. Show by the 'touch of the blind,' a 'kind touch,' etc., that the sense of touch may be cultivated.
7. What practice would you recommend?
8. Why is it good to have little things to put up with?
9. Show that sight brings half our joy.
10. How may we learn to see more?
11. What joy and what knowledge should we get from a sense of hearing?
12. How may a good ear for music be acquired?

Part II The House of Mind

Chapter I

1. Show that our way of speaking of 'ourselves' is like saying 'the sun rises.'
2. Upon what does self-reverence depend?

3. Show that self-knowledge must go before self-reverence.
4. And that we must know ourselves before we can control ourselves.

Chapter II My Lord Intellect

1. What is the function of 'intellect' ?
2. Show that science is an immense and joyous realm.
3. How is imagination serviceable in science?
4. Compare history with the shows of a kinetoscope.
5. How does history enable us to live in a large world?
6. How are we making history?
7. Show that imagination is necessary to the realising of history.
8. What intellectual power is especially employed in mathematics?
9. Why are mathematics delightful?
10. Why is philosophy a necessary study?
11. What are some of the advantages of a knowledge of literature?
12. What powers of the mind go to the study of literature?
13. Give three tests by which literature may be discerned.
14. What are some of the uses of the aesthetic sense?
15. How may we distinguish between art and simulated art?
16. How may the intellectual life be promoted?
17. In what ways may it be extinguished?

Chapter III The Daemons of Intellect

1. What effect has inertia upon the intellectual life?
2. Why may we not stay in one field of thought?
3. What do you understand by a magnanimous mind?

Chapter IV My Lord Chief Explorer, Imagination

1. Describe the functions of imagination.
2. What effect has cultivation upon the imagination?
3. In what two regions is imagination forbidden to work?
4. How may self be exorcised from the imagination?
5. What imaginings are especially to be avoided?
6. How may wrong imaginings be hindered?

Chapter V The Beauty Sense

1. Show that exclusiveness is a temptation to persons who enjoy beauty.
2. What error does the devotee of beauty make?
3. Show that the beauty sense opens a paradise of pleasure.

Chapter VI My Lord Chief Attorney-General, Reason

1. Compare the behaviour of reason with that of an advocate.
2. Suggest the courses of reasoning which may have brought any two persons, Wycliffe and Wickham, for example, to different conclusions.
3. Trace the conceivable course of reasoning of any philanthropist.
4. Show the part of reason in all good works and great inventions.
5. What is meant by common sense?
6. Try to recover the train of reasoning of the man who first made a barrow.
7. How is it that men have come to deify reason?
8. Explain why equally good and sensible persons come to opposite conclusions.

9. How does this prove that reason may bring us to mistaken conclusions?
10. Show that an error of thought may lead to crime.
11. Why is reason almost infallible in mathematics?
12. Show that the power of reasoning is a trust to be used to good purpose.
13. Show that reason works out a notion received by the will.
14. Account for the fact that there are different schools of philosophy.
15. What practice in reasoning would you advise for children?

Chapter VII The Lords of the Exchequer, the Desires (Part I.)

1. Compare the work of the desires with that of the appetites.
2. How does the desire of approbation serve a man?
3. Show that vanity may play the part of a mischievous daemon in our lives.
4. Show that the desires of infamy and of fame come from the same source.
5. How does the desire of excelling work with a hockeyplayer, for example?
6. Show how this desire serves the man.
7. Show that emulation may have mischievous results in education.
8. Show the danger of emulation in things unworthy.
9. How does the desire of wealth serve mankind?
10. What are the risks attending this desire?
11. How may the desire for worthless possessions be counteracted?
12. Show that ambition is a serviceable desire.
13. What dangers attend the desire to rule?
14. Show that 'managing' people are injurious to those about them.

Chapter VIII The Lords of the Exchequer, the Desires (Part Ii.)

1. Show that the desire of society influences all sane persons.
2. What gain to the mind should come from society?
3. But upon what conditions?
4. Show that the society of every good person is an opportunity.
5. What two dangers attend the love of society?
6. Show that we lose by cultivating only the society of our own set or sort.
7. Which of the desires is to the mind as hunger is to the body?
8. Distinguish between the desire of knowledge and what is commonly called curiosity.
9. Show that it is upon the knowledge of great matters the mind feeds and grows.
10. Show that the love of knowledge may be extinguished by emulation.
11. What have you to say about 'marks' and 'places' in this connection?
12. How should we be influenced by the fact that all 'normal' persons have powers of mind?
13. Show that the duty of ordering our thoughts arises from the possession of these intellectual powers.

Part III the House of Heart
Lords of the Heart: I. Love
Chapter I the Ways of Love

1. What are the two affections?
2. Mention some of the ways in which love shows itself.
3. Have we any evidence of how much love is possible to a human being?
4. Why is self-love necessary?
5. When is love a counterfeit?
6. Describe another form of counterfeit love.
7. Name four tests by which love may be recognised.
8. What is the apostolic rule on this subject?
9. Of what feelings opposed to love are we capable?

10. Why?
11. What is the one petition in the Lord's Prayer to which a condition is attached?

Chapter II Love's Lords in Waiting: Pity

1. Show that there is pity in every heart.
2. Name a few knights and ladies of pity.
3. Show that 'a feeling heart' is a snare.
4. Name a few causes sufficient to excite self-pity.
5. Show the danger of this habit.
6. In what two ways may we defend ourselves from this danger?

Chapter III Love's Lords in Waiting: Benevolence

1. When is a person benevolent?
2. Why is hearty liking for all persons possible?
3. Show that his faults are not the whole of a person.
4. How does the recognition of this fact work?
5. Distinguish between goodwill and good-nature in dealing with other persons.
6. Characterise 'benevolence.'
7. Name half a dozen of the foes of goodwill, and show how they act.

Chapter IV Love's Lords in Waiting: Sympathy

1. Show that sympathy with one should be a key to all.
2. How should this fact affect our dealings with persons we suppose to be on a different intellectual level?
3. How is it that poets, painters, and the like raise the rest of the world?
4. On what condition is our sympathy helpful?
5. What are the mischievous effects of a spurious sympathy?
6. Show that tact is an expression of sympathy.
7. Show that egotism destroys sympathy.
8. What are the active and the passive manifestations of egotism?

Chapter V Love's Lords in Waiting: Kindness

1. What is the office of kindness?
2. Comment upon the kindness of courtesy.
3. Show that there can be no kindness without simplicity.
4. Comment upon a movement to make children kind.
5. What is the most generous kindness of all?
6. Show that the opposite behaviour is one of the chief causes of unhappiness in the world.

Chapter VI Love's Lords in Waiting: Generosity

1. Show that generous impulses are common to all the world.
2. Show that generosity is impatient of cheap cynicism and of worldly wisdom.
3. Show that generosity is costly but also remunerative.
4. Show that the interests of the generous heart are duly distributed.
5. Name a few fallacious notions that restrain generosity.
6. What is the rule of life of the generous person?

Chapter VII Love's Lords in Waiting: Gratitude

1. Why is gratitude a joy-giving emotion?
2. How do we come to miss the joy of being grateful?
3. What two courses are open to the receiver of small kindnesses?
4. Why does a grateful heart always make a full return ?

5. How may we escape the reproach of ingratitude?
6. Do we owe gratitude to those only who are present and living?

Chapter VIII Love's Lords in Waiting: Courage

1. Show that we all have the courage of attack.
2. What are the 'daemons' that suppress courage?
3. Show that we all have the courage of endurance.
4. That panic, anxiety, and shameful fear are possible to us all.
5. Show that the assurance of courage gives us the courage of serenity.
6. Show that we have the courage of our affairs, and need not be anxious.
7. Show that we fail if we have not the courage of our opinions.
8. How shall we make sure of our opinions?
9. Discuss the courage of frankness.
10. How far may we practise reticence?
11. Show that we are called upon for the courage of reproof.
12. And for the courage of confession.
13. What limits should we set to our confessions?
14. How does the courage of our capacity serve us?
15. Show that intellectual panic is responsible for many failures.
16. What do you understand by the courage of opportunity?

Chapter IX Love's Lords in Waiting: Loyalty

1. Why should youth be the age of loyalty?
2. What is the test of loyalty?
3. Show that our loyalties are prepared for us.
4. What have you to say of loyalty to our king?
5. Of loyalty to our own?
6. What would you say of persons who choose to bestow their loyalty upon aliens and the like?
7. Show that public opinion is responsible for anarchy.
8. What does loyalty to our country demand of us?
9. How shall we become ready to meet these demands?
10. What service of loyalty does our country ask of us?
11. Show that loyalty to a chief is the secret of "dignified obedience and proud submission."
12. Show what loyalty to personal ties demands of us.
13. Show that steadfastness is of the essence of all loyalty.
14. Are all our loyalties due for life?
15. When it is necessary to give up a chief or a dependent, how should the breach be made?
16. Show that thoroughness is of the nature of loyalty.
17. Describe the loyalty we owe to our principles.
18. What are the tempers alien to loyalty ?

Chapter X Love's Lords in Waiting: Humility

1. Show that 'pride of life' is the deadliest of our perils.
2. What are the two types of humility we have?
3. How do we travesty the grace of humility?
4. Why is humility rarely coveted as a Christian grace?
5. Show that resentful tempers are due to self-exaltation.
6. Show that humility is one with simplicity.
7. When do we fall from humility?
8. Why may we not try to be humble?

Chapter XI Love's Lords in Waiting: Gladness

1. Why is it inexcusable in us not to be glad?
2. Show that gladness springs in sorrow and pain.
3. Show that gladness is catching.
4. That gladness is perennial.
5, Why, then, are people gloomy and irresponsive?
6. Show that gladness is a duty.

Lords of the Heart: II. Justice

Chapter XII Justice, Universal

1. Show that we must know the functions of love and justice.
2. Why does a cry for fair play reach everybody?
3. What dispositions must we show (a) in word, (b) in thought, (c) in act, in order to be just?
4. In what respects do we owe justice to all other persons?
5. How may we ascertain the just dues of other persons?
6. What should encourage us in our efforts?
7. What is the demand of justice with regard to our own rights?

Chapter XIII Justice to the Persons of Others

1. Show that we begin to understand the duty of justice to the persons of others.
2. Show that to think fairly requires knowledge and consideration.
3. In what sense does ungentleness inflict bodily injury?
4. Why is courtesy a matter of justice?
5. Show that we are not free to think hard things about others.
6. Show that we must be just to the characters of others.
7. What quality enables us to be just in this sense?
8. How does prejudice interfere with justice?
9. Show that respect is justly due to all men.
10. What defect in ourselves interferes with the respect we owe?
11. Show that respect must be balanced by discernment.
12. How does appreciation fulfil the dues of justice?
13. Why is depreciation unjust?

Chapter XIV Truth: Justice in Word

1. Name a sign by which we may discern truth.
2. Describe Botticelli's 'Calumny.'
3. What instruction does the picture offer?
4. How does Wesley distinguish between lying and slandering?
5. How was envy regarded in the Middle Ages?
6. Show the danger of calumnious hearing and calumnious reading.
7. What misfortune has befallen the fanatic?
8. How does Bacon describe 'the sovereign good'?

Chapter XV Spoken Truth

1. What is veracity?
2. Show the error of qualified statements.
3. Show that scrupulosity is not veracity.
4. That exaggeration is mischievous as well as foolish.
5. Why is it not truthful to generalise upon one or two instances?
6. What temptations attend the desire to make a good story?

7. Distinguish between essential and accidental truth.
8. Show the value of fiction in this respect.
9. Show that fiction affects our enthusiasms, and even our religion.
10. Distinguish in some Bible stories between accidental and essential truth.
11. Which of the two is of vital consequence to us, and why?

Chapter XVI Some Causes of Lying

1. How would you characterise lies told to lower another in the esteem of his friends?
2. Comment upon cowardly lies.
3. Show that the habit of reserve is akin to the lie of concealment.
4. Show the folly of boastful lies.
5. Show the danger of indulging in romancing lies
6. Show that we owe truth to our opponents.
7. What four qualities sustain truth?

Chapter XVII Integrity: Justice in Action

1. Show that a 'ca' canny' policy is dishonest.
2. By what standard is the work of every person judged?
3. In what sense are we all paid labourers?
4. Show that integrity of character is of slow growth.
5. Why is 'Do ye nexte thynge' a part of integrity?
6. Why does it belong to integrity to do the chief thing first?
7. And also to finish that which we have begun?
8. Show that drifters and dawdlers fail in integrity.
9. That the person who cribs time also fails.
10. Show the importance of integrity in the use of material.
11. How does this principle apply to small debts?
12. And to bargains?
13. And to the care of our neighbours' property?

Chapter XVIII Opinions: Justice in Thought

1. Give examples of opinions that are of no value for three different reasons.
2. When is an opinion of value?
3. Why need we have opinions at all?
4. Distinguish between a faddist and a reformer.
5. Mention a few matters upon which we must form opinions.
6. Why should we be at pains to form opinions about books?
7. What sort of books are of lasting value to us, and why?
8. Give half a dozen counsels with regard to forming opinions.

Chapter XIX Principles: Justice in Motive

1. Why are our 'principles' so called?
2. Show that principles may be bad or good.
3. How are we to distinguish between bad and good principles?
4. 'Our principles are our masters.' What is our duty with regard to them?

Chapter XX Self-ordering: Justice to Ourselves

1. What is our duty towards our bodies?
2. Indicate several ways of being intemperate.
3. Show that soberness includes more than abstinence from drink.

4. What habit leads to the four kinds of physical vice?
5. What changes mark the parting of the ways?
6. Why does the drunkard drink?
7. Indicate his fate.
8. In what sense may we say that God puts us 'en parole' in the matter of self-indulgence?
9. Show that excitement is a kind of intoxication.
10. Show that gluttony is as offensive as drunkenness.
11. Show how interests in life are a safeguard against offences.
12. What is a common symptom of slothfulness, and what is the cure?
13. Of the four roads to ruin, which is the worst?
14. What caution and what command should help to safeguard us?

Part IV Vocation

1. What do boy and girl alike desire about the work they will have to do?
2. How is it possible to prepare for our calling when we do not know what it will be?
3. How may we get the habit of being of use?
4. Show how the law of habit may help us or hinder us.
5. Our calling comes to each of us. What must we do towards it?

Book II Introductory

1. How is the body sustained, and how ruined?
2. With what powers fitted to deal with knowledge is the mind endowed?
3. What functions serve the same purpose for the mind as do the appetites for the body?
4. Name some of the virtues which belong to love, and some of those which belong to justice.
5. What virtues include the justice we owe to our own bodies?
6. Why are body, heart, and mind in need of government?
7. What are the governing powers?

Part I Conscience
Section I. Conscience in the House of Body
Chapter I The Court of Appeal

1. In what ways may conscience be figured by a judge in a court of law?
2. To what two or three facts does conscience continually bear witness?
3. Why is it possible for conscience to give wrong judgments?
4. What advocate is employed to tamper with conscience?
5. Why is it necessary that conscience should be instructed?

Chapter II The Instruction of Conscience

1. Upon what teachers does conscience depend for instruction?
2. Account for the value of the teaching given by history and biography.
3. For the peculiar value of the Bible as our instructor in morals.
4. How does poetry teach us?
5. Why is the teaching of the older novelists and dramatists to be preferred?

Chapter III The Rulings of Conscience in the House of Body: Temperance

1. Give two or three examples from literature of intemperance in eating.
2. In drinking.
3. In taking our ease.
4. In day-dreaming.
5. What is Carlyle's counsel about work?

6. What principle underlies temperance?
7. Why may we not be solicitous about health?
8. Show that neglect, also, of the physical nature arises from intemperance.
9. Give a few rules for the ordering of our physical life.
10. Why is it necessary to have clear principles as to our duty in this matter?

Chapter IV The Rulings of Conscience in the House of Body: Chastity (Part I)

1. How do over-fond friendships affect chastity of soul?
2. 'Yet how have I transgressed?' What lesson for our own lives does this question of the King (Edward II.) bring home?
3. Why are we not free to give ourselves without reserve?

Chapter V The Rulings of Conscience in the House of Body: Chastity (Part Ii.)

1. Cite some examples of sane and generous friendships.
2. What rules for self-government may we deduce in each case?
3. What two classes of friends claim our loyalty?

Chapter VI The Rulings of Conscience in the House of Body: the Final Unchastity

1. Show the effect of dalliance in devious ways.
2. What habit prepares the way?
3. With what monster of our nature must we dread to be at death-grapple?
4. Where does safety lie?
5. How may we keep 'a virgin heart in work and will'?

Chapter VII the Rulings of Conscience in the House of Body: Fortitude

1. Describe Botticelli's 'Fortitude.'
2. Name some points in which Isaiah sets forth an image of fortitude.
3. From two or three examples show that there is an element of tenderness in fortitude.
4. Show that Sir Kenneth in The Talisman offers an example of fortitude.
5. Give an example of fortitude under vexatious provocations.
6. Of cheerful, serviceable fortitude.
7. What of the 'black ribbon' when things go wrong?
8. Show that fortitude belongs to the body.
9. What is the apostolic injunction as to fortitude?

Chapter VIII The Rulings of Conscience in the House of Body: Prudence

1. Illustrate the fact that 'imprudence is selfishness.'
2. Show that prudence is necessary in our affairs.
3. In the choice of our friends.
4. How does prudence act with regard to undue influence?
5. Show that prudence prefers simplicity to luxury.
6. That prudent citizens are the wealth of the state.
7. What does the simplicity of prudence allow us in our surroundings?
8. 'My servant shall deal prudently.' How was this fulfilled?

Section II. Conscience in the House of Mind

Chapter IX Opinions 'In the Air'

1. What part of our living do we emancipate from the judgment of conscience?
2. Show the danger of casual opinions.
3. How does a fallacy work?

4. Give four rules that should help us in this matter of opinions.

Chapter X The Uninstructed Conscience

1. Show that, in everyone, conscience is persistent upon some points.
2. How do you account for moral instability, and by whom is it shown?
3. Show, by example, that a nation may be unstable.
4. Illustrate the danger of a besetting idea.
5. Indicate some of the perils of moral ignorance.
6. Show that undue scrupulosity is an outcome of ignorance.
7. What moral advantage, exactly, has the instructed over the uninstructed conscience?

Chapter XI The Instructed Conscience

1. Show, by some examples, that sound moral judgment is a valuable asset.
2. Distinguish between the power to form moral judgments and the power to live a virtuous life.
3. How are we to get the former power?

Chapter XII Some Instructors of Conscience: Poetry, Novels, Essays

1. Show that the power of poetry to instruct conscience does not depend on its direct teaching.
2. Indicate the gradual way in which Shakespeare influences us.
3. To what purpose should we read novels, and what sort of novels should we read?
4. Why should essays be studied for instruction?

Chapter XIII Some Instructors of Conscience: History and Philosophy

1. Why does history make great claims upon us at the present time?
2. Distinguish between the informed and the ignorant patriot.
3. Illustrate the need there is for some study of philosophy.
4. By what means should we reach our convictions?
5. Illustrate, by the behaviour of Columbus.
6. How may we distinguish a 'message' from a fanatical notion?
7. Give one secret of safety in matters of philosophy.

Chapter XIV Some Instructors of Conscience: Theology

1. Most people 'live a poor, maimed life.' Why?
2. Contrast our Lord's method of teaching with all usual methods.
3. Account for the fact that our Lord's sayings are 'hard' intellectually as well as morally.
4. 'They sit in darkness.' Who sit thus, and wherefore?
5. Where is the harm of occupying our minds about questions of criticism?
6. Have we any indications that we are declining from the knowledge of God?
7. What is the one vital question for us all?
8. When are the little religious books we use unwholesome?
9. What should we bear in mind regarding the authors of the Scriptures?
10. What may we look for in the lives of men as told in the Bible?
11. Show that the revelation contained in the Bible is unique.
12. What two laws would appear to regulate the revelations given to the world?
13. What reflections should safeguard us from the 'Lo, here!' of each new religion?
14. What is our hope of distinguishing between the merely human and the inspired elements in the Bible?
15. How may we discern the essential truth in Bible narratives?
16. Show that the disregard of life which shocks us in some of these is paralleled in our own day.
17. Is there any key to the mystery?
18. Why is it necessary to put away prejudices and misconceptions regarding the Bible?

19. What is the penalty of ignorance about God?
20. Show that the common notion of God as an 'indulgent' Parent is unfounded.
21. Why is every slight record of Christ in the Gospels momentous to us?
22. Name any arguments that present themselves to the mind of a Christian in answer to the statement that 'miracles do not happen.'
23. Show that the words of Christ are more amazing than the miracles of the Gospels.
24. Why may we not accept the modern tendency to reservation on the doctrine of the Resurrection and the Incarnation?
25. What is the peril concealed in trivial doubts?
26. What would you say of the temper which examines, and finally cherishes, every objection presented to the mind?

Chapter XV Some Instructors of Conscience: Nature, Science, Art

1. Show that ignorance is a vice in regard to the things of nature.
2. In what two ways does nature approach us?
3. Show that nature is an instructor in our duty towards God.
4. That nature moves us to gratitude.
5. Show that preoccupation of mind has of late shut out this teaching from us.
6. What instruction has science for the conscience?
7. Distinguish between science and scientific information.
8. What duty is laid upon conscience with regard to science?
9. With regard to art?
10. In what spirit should we approach art?

Chapter XVI Some Instructors of Conscience: Sociology

1. Why is it necessary to understand how other people live?
2. Why is casual help usually a hindrance?
3. What are the conditions of helpfulness?
4. In what sense is it wisdom to know ourselves?
5. What have you to say of the greatness of human nature?

Section III. The Function of Conscience

Chapter XVII Conviction of Sin

1. What is the office of conscience?
2. What convictions appear to be common to all men?
3. Show that religion is not a substitute for the instructed conscience.
4. Name three habits of mind, either of which may stultify conscience.
5. Show that the uneasiness of conscience testifies to sin.
6. How do our sins of omission affect us ?
7. Show that the chiding of conscience is a thing to be thankful for.

Chapter XVIII Temptation

1. How does temptation come upon us?
2. Whence does temptation arise?
3. What is the secret of heroic lives?
4. How is a trusty spirit trained?
5. What is our part, that we may not enter into temptation?
6. Is it possible for penitence to become an error?
7. What is its due place?

8. What do you understand by, 'I believe in the forgiveness of sins'?

Chapter XIX Duty and Law

1. Why is it wrong to do 'wrong'?
2. What is 'wrong'?
3. In what various ways have people answered these questions?
4. May we excuse wrong-doing because it is 'human nature'?
5. Contrast the serenity of the enlightened Christian conscience with the uneasiness of superstition.
6. Why is it a delight to perceive and to fulfil the law?

Part II the Will

Chapter I the Will-less Life

1. Show that it is possible for conscience, love, intellect, reason, to behave whimsically and unworthily.
2. What power within us has the ordering of the rest?
3. Show that it is possible to live without the exercise of will.

Chapter II Will and Wilfulness

1. Show that wilful persons are of various dispositions.
2. What is the common characteristic of wilful persons? Give examples.
3. Contrast the behaviour of wilfulness and of will.
4. Give some examples of will-power and wilfulness from Scott.
5. Class a score or so of persons (in literature or history) on each side of a dividing line—on one side, the wilful; on the other, persons who will.
6. Instance nations that fall on either side of such a line. Why?
7. Describe the teaching which has weakened the will-power of Western nations.
8. What is our Lord's attitude in this matter?

Chapter III Will Not Moral or Immoral

1. Show that will may act towards good or evil ends.
2. That a person of will may use bad means towards good ends.
3. Distinguish between 'will' and 'an ideal.'
4. What curious question on this subject does Browning raise?
5. What is the distinctive quality of a man?
6. 'Thus far we have seen'—what six points concerning the will?

Chapter IV The Will and its Peers

1. Show that the will is subject to solicitations.
2. That the will does not act alone.
3. What is the business of will?
4. When exercised, and upon what?

Chapter V The Function of Will

1. What single power of man is a free agent?
2. What is the one act possible to the will?
3. Account for our increasing inability to choose.
4. Show the evil of ready-made garments and ready-made opinions.
5. Why may we choose for ourselves only, and not for others?
6. How would you reconcile the two duties of choice and obedience?
7. Distinguish between the obedience of habit and that of choice.
8. What is it that we are called upon to choose between?

Chapter VI The Scope of Will

1. Show how allowance may do duty for will-choice.
2. Contrast the behaviour of will and allowance at the tailor's, for example.
3. Is it necessary to make a choice of will, at first hand, on all small occasions?
4. How does the fallacy underlying the 'newest and cheapest' lead us astray?
5. What great will-choice is open to us all?

Chapter VII Self-Control — Self-Restraint — Self-Command — Self-Denial

1. What is to be said about moral self-culture for its own sake?
2. How does absorption of any kind affect others?
3. Show the difference between absorption as a phase, or for a purpose, and self-absorption.
4. Describe a better way than moral self-culture.
5. Show that what we call 'self-denial' is impossible to love.
6. In what sense does our Lord claim self-denial from us?

Chapter VIII The Effort of Decision

1. How do we try to escape the effort of decision?
2. Sum up the sort of creed held in the name of 'Toleration.'
3. Describe a picture of Ludwig Richter's showing how 'Providence' and 'freewill' co-operate.
4. How may we distinguish a decision of will from one of 'allowance'?
5. What two assets does the person who uses his will gather through his life?
6. Show how these serve him on small and great occasions.

Chapter IX Intention — Purpose — Resolution

1. Give two or three examples of the history of resolution.
2. What truth is figured by the nimbus of the pictured saint?
3. When does 'influence' become injurious?
4. From what sort of influence must we safeguard ourselves?
5. The influence of a person is in the ratio of—?
6. What several acts of the will are required of us ?

Chapter X A Way of the Will

1. Sum up the conclusions arrived at so far with regard to the will.
2. What is to be said to persons of good-will who dread temptation?
3. Particularise the postern to be guarded.
4. The porters on guard.
5. Shall we fight or run away?
6. In what 'way of the will' does our safety lie?
7. Show that the same rule (what rule?) applies to intellectual and moral insurgent ideas.
8. Show how our Lord's condemnation of fallacies proves that opinions are judged upon moral grounds.

Chapter XI Freewill

1. Why is it important to know all we can about the behaviour of the will?
2. Sum up (again) the sixteen, or so, points we have endeavoured to make, so far.
3. Distinguish between the man of good-will and the conventional person.
4. What two services are open to men?
5. What is the distinguishing mark of freewill?
6. 'The poet has said the last word'; what is it?

Part III the Soul

Chapter I the Capacities of the Soul

1. 'We wonder whether we are indeed finite creatures'; give four or five grounds for such wonder.
2. Show the limiting and deceptive nature of our ordinary religious thoughts.
3. Show in what respect the needs of the soul are satisfied by God alone.

Chapter II The Disabilities of the Soul

1. Name some of the chronic disabilities of the soul.
2. How may we discern in ourselves 'the inert soul'?
3. What is the cure of this soul-ailment?
4. How does preoccupation affect our relations with God?
5. Show how our 'involuntary aversion' to God may really be of service.
6. Distinguish between voluntary and involuntary aversion.
7. Show the supreme importance of will-choice.

Chapter III The Knowledge of God

1. What is the condition on which we may have the one satisfying intimacy?
2. What persons have capacity for this intimacy?
3. What tokens of the divine friendship may we look for?
4. Name some of the ways by which the knowledge of God may first come to us.
5. Show that the Bible is the immediate source of such knowledge.
6. In what respect does the Bible stand alone among the great writings of the past?
7. Show how fit and necessary the knowledge of God is to the soul of man.
8. Is this knowledge inevitable?

Chapter IV Prayer

1. Describe some of the movements of unconsidered prayer.
2. Some of the responses to these.
3. What two requirements of the soul are thus met?
4. What are some of the uses and occasions of habitual prayer?
5. How may we serve the world in our habitual prayers?

Chapter V Thanksgiving

1. What causes restrain us from the gratitude we owe?
2. 'My rising soul surveys'—what occasions for being thankful?
3. For what, besides our 'meat,' may we well 'say grace'?
4. Why does it matter that we should thank God?

Chapter VI Praise

1. Show that 'praise' implies more than thanksgiving.
2. Whom do we think of as being endowed with the right to praise God?
3. Show that 'praise' is our duty also.
4. Name some occasions of praise discovered by the Psalmist.
5. What persons, to-day, especially
afford us themes for praise?

Chapter VII Faith in God

1. Why do we find it perplexing to be told we must 'believe in God'?
2. How does faith come?
3. Show that we have faith in each other.

4. That there are two sorts of faith in persons.
5. Show that faith of both sorts is due to God.
6. How shall we know if we have the faith of recognition?
7. Show that faith is an act of will.
8. Show that to believe in God is a duty required of us.
9. Is this duty fulfilled in the service of men?
10. Show that no article of the Christian (or of the Apostles') Creed appeals to our understanding.
11. That all the great things of life also are mysteries.
12. Show that Christianity means the recognition of Christ.

Formation Of Character

Table of Contents

Preface to the 'Home Education' Series

The educational outlook is rather misty and depressing both at home and abroad. That science should be a staple of education, that the teaching of Latin, of modem languages, of mathematics, must be reformed, that nature and handicrafts should be pressed into service for the training of the eye and hand, that boys and girls must learn to write English and therefore must know something of history and literature; and, on the other hand, that education must be made more technical and utilitarian — these, and such as these, are the cries of expedience with which we take the field. But we have no unifying principle, no definite aim; in fact, no philosophy of education. As a stream can rise no higher than its source, so it is probable that no educational effort can rise above the whole scheme of thought which gives it birth; and perhaps this is the reason of all the 'fallings from us, vanishings,' failures, and disappointments which mark our educational records.

Those of us, who have spent many years in pursuing the benign and elusive vision of Education, perceive that her approaches are regulated by a law, and that this law has yet to be evoked. We can discern its outlines, but no more. We know that It is pervasive; there is no part of a child's home-life or school-work which the law does not penetrate. It is illuminating, too, showing the value, or lack of value, of a thousand systems and expedients. It is not only a light, but a measure, providing a standard whereby all things, small and great, belonging to educational work must be tested. The law is liberal, taking in whatsoever things are true, honest, and of good report, and offering no limitation or hindrance save where excess should injure. And the path indicated by the law is continuous and progressive, with no transition stage from the cradle to the grave, except that maturity takes up the regular self-direction to which immaturity has been trained. We shall doubtless find, when we apprehend the law, that certain German thinkers — Kant, Herbart, Lotze, Froebel — are justified; that, as they say, it is 'necessary' to believe in God; that, therefore, the knowledge of God is the principal knowledge, and the chief end of education. By one more character shall we be able to recognise this perfect law of educational liberty when it shall be made evident. It has been said that 'The best idea which we can form of absolute truth is that it is able to meet every condition by which it can be tested.' This we shall expect of our law — that it shall meet every test of experiment and every test of rational investigation.

Not having received the tables of our Law, we fall back upon Froebel or upon Herbart; or, if we belong to another School, upon Locke or Spencer; but we are not satisfied. A discontent, is it a divine discontent? is upon us; and assuredly we should hail a workable, effectual philosophy of education as a deliverance from much perplexity. Before this great deliverance comes to us it is probable that many tentative efforts will be put forth, having more or less of the characters of a philosophy; notably, having a central idea, a body of thought with various members working in vital harmony.

Such a theory of education, which need not be careful to call itself a system of psychology, must be in harmony with the thought movements of the age; must regard education, not as a shut-off compartment, but as being as much a part of life as birth or growth, marriage or work; and it must leave the pupil attached to the world at many points of contact; it is true that educationalists are already eager to establish such contact in several directions, but their efforts rest upon an axiom here and an idea there, and there is no broad unifying basis of thought to support the whole.

Fools rush in where angels fear to tread; and the hope that there may be many tentative efforts towards a philosophy of education, and that all of them will bring us nearer to the magnum opus, encourages me to launch one such attempt. The central thought, or rather body of thought, upon which I found, is the somewhat obvious fact that the child is a person with all the possibilities and powers included in personality. Some of the members which develop from this nucleus have been exploited from time to time by educational thinkers, and exist vaguely in the general common sense, a notion here. another there. One thesis, which is, perhaps, new; that Education is the Science of Relations, appears to me to solve the question of a curriculum, as showing that the object of education is to put a child in living touch with as much as may be of the life of Nature and of thought. Add to this one or two keys to self-knowledge. and the educated youth goes forth with some idea of self-management, with some pursuits, and many vital interests. My excuse for venturing to offer a solution. however tentative and passing, to the problem of education is twofold. For between thirty and forty years I have laboured without pause to establish a working and philosophic theory of education; and in the next place. each article of the educational faith I offer has been arrived at by inductive processes; and has, I think, been verified by a long and wide series of experiments. It is. however, with sincere diffidence that I

venture to offer the results of this long labour; because I know that in this field there are many labourers far more able and expert than I — the 'angels' who fear to tread, so precarious is the footing!
But,

if only pour encourager les autres, I append a short synopsis of the educational theory advanced to the volumes of the' Home Education Series.' The treatment is not methodic, but incidental; here a little, there a little, as seemed to me most likely to meet the occasions of parents and teachers. I should add that in the course of a number of years the various essays have been prepared for the use of the Parents' Educational Union in the hope that that Society might witness for a more or less coherent body of educational thought.

"The consequence of truth is great; therefore the judgment of it must not be negligent."—Whichcote.

1. Children are born persons.

2. They are not born either good or bad, but with possibilities for good and evil.

3. The principles of authority on the one hand and obedience on the other, are natural, necessary and fundamental; but —

4. These principles are limited by the respect due to the personality of children, which must not be encroached upon, whether by fear or love, suggestion or influence, or undue play upon anyone natural desire.

5. Therefore we are limited to three educational instruments — the atmosphere of environment, the discipline of habit, and the presentation of living ideas.

6. By the saying, *Education Is an Atmosphere*, it is not meant that a child should be isolated in what may be called a 'child environment,' especially adapted and prepared; but that we should take into account the educational value of his natural home atmosphere, both as regards persons and things, and should let him live freely among his proper conditions. It stultifies a child to bring down his world to the 'child's' level.

7. By *Education Is a Discipline*, is meant the discipline of habits formed definitely and thoughtfully, whether habits of mind or body. Physiologists tell us of the adaptation of brain structure to habitual lines of thought — i.e., to our habits.

8. In the saying that *Education Is a Life*, the need of intellectual and moral as well as of physical sustenance is implied. The mind feeds on ideas, and therefore children should have a generous curriculum.

9. But the mind is not a receptacle into which ideas must be dropped, each idea adding to an 'apperception mass' of its like, the theory upon which the Herbartian doctrine of interest rests.

10. On the contrary, a child's mind is no mere sac to hold ideas; but is rather, if the figure may be allowed, a spiritual organism, with an appetite for all knowledge. This is its proper diet, with which it is prepared to deal, and which it can digest and assimilate as the body does foodstuffs.

11. This difference is not a verbal quibble. The Herbartian doctrine lays the stress of education — the preparation of knowledge in enticing morsels, presented in due order — upon the teacher. Children taught upon this principle are in danger of receiving much teaching with little knowledge; and the teacher's axiom is, 'What a child learns matters less than how he learns it.'

12. But, believing that the normal child has powers of mind that fit him to deal with all knowledge proper to him, we must give him a full and generous curriculum; taking care, only, that the knowledge offered to him is vital — that is, that facts are not presented without their informing ideas. Out of this conception comes the principle that, —

13. *Education Is the Science of Relations;* that is, that a child has natural relations with a vast number of things and thoughts: so we must train him upon physical exercises, nature, handicrafts, science and art, and upon many living books; for we know that our business is, not to teach him all about anything, but to help him to make valid as many as may be of —

'Those first-born affinities
That fit our new existence to existing things!'

14. There are also two secrets of moral and intellectual self-management which should be offered to children; these we may call the Way of the Will and the Way of the Reason.

15. The Way of the Will. — Children should be taught — (a) To distinguish between 'I want' and 'I will.' (b) That the way to will effectively is to turn our thoughts from that which we desire but do not will. (c) That the best way to turn our thoughts is to think of or do some quite different thing, entertaining or interesting. (d) That, after a little rest in this way, the will returns to its work with new vigour. (This adjunct of the will is familiar to us as diversion, whose office it is to ease us for a time from will effort, that we may 'will' again with

added power. The use of suggestion — even self-suggestion — as an aid to the will, is to be deprecated, as tending to stultify and stereotype character. It would seem that spontaneity is a condition of development, and that human nature needs the discipline of failure as well as of success.)

16. The Way of the Reason. — We should teach children, too, not to 'lean' (too confidently) 'unto their own understanding,' because the function of reason is, to give logical demonstration (a) of mathmatical truth; and (b) of an initial idea, accepted by the will. In the former case reason is, perhaps, an infallible guide, but in the second it is not always a safe one; for whether that initial idea be right or wrong, reason will confirm it by irrefragable proofs.

17. Therefore children should be taught, as they become mature enough to understand such teaching, that the chief responsibility which rests on them as persons is the acceptance or rejection of initial ideas. To help them in this choice we should give them principles of conduct and a wide range of the knowledge fitted for them. These three principles (15, 16 and 17) should save children from some of the loose thinking and heedless action which cause most of us to live at a lower level than we need.

18. We should allow no separation to grow up between the intellectual and 'spiritual' life of children; but should teach them that the divine Spirit has constant access to their spirits, and is their continual helper. in all the interests, duties and joys of life.

The 'Home Education' Series is so called from the title of the first volume, and not as dealing, wholly or principally, with 'Home' as opposed to 'School' Education.

Preface

In editing Home Education and Parents and Chlldren for the 'Home Education' Series, the introduction of much new matter made it necessary to transfer a considerable part of the contents of those two members of the series to this volume, Some Studies In the Formation of Character.

I have used the current phrase 'formation of character' because it ls current, and therefore convenient; but, to show that I recognise the fallacy it contains, I venture to quote the following (very inadequate) definition: — "His character — the efflorescence of the man wherein the fruit of his life is a-preparing — character is original disposition,modified, directed, expanded by education, by circumstances; later, by self-control and self-culture; above all, by the supreme agency of the Holy Spirit, even when that agency is little suspected and as little solicited"; [Parents and Children.] that is to say, character is not the outcome of a formative educational process; but inherent tendencies are played upon, more or less incidentally, and the outcome is character.

I should like to urge that this incidental play of education and circumstances upon personality is our only legitimate course. We may not make character our conscious objective. Provide a child with what he needs in the way of instruction, opportunity, and wholesome occupation, and his character will take care of itself: for normal children are persons of good will, with honest desires toward right thinking and right living. All we can do further is to help a child to get rid of some hindrance — a bad temper, for example — likely to spoil his life. In our attempts to do this, our action should, I think, be most guarded. We may not interfere with his psychological development, because we recognise that children are persons, and personality should be far more inviolable in our eyes than property. We may use direct teaching and command, but not indirect suggestion, or even the old-fashioned 'influence.' Influence will act, of course, but it must not be consciously brought to bear.

But we may make use of certain physiological laws without encroaching on personality, because, in so doing, we should affect the instrument and not the agent. The laws of habit and, again, the tendency of will-power to rhythmic operation should be of use to us, because these are affected by brain-conditions and belong to the outworks of personality. The little studies in Part I. indicate ways of helping a child to cure himself of tiresome faults.

I am diffident about offering Part IV. of this volume, because, though the public is wonderfully patient with writers who 'adorn the tale,' — half the books we read are about other books, — I am not sure of equal forbearance towards an attempt to 'point the moral.' But, indeed, we read in such a hurry, are satisfied with such slight and general impressions, that the leisurely investigation of educational hints thrown out by great authors might well be of use to us. If, in the few following studies, the reader fail to find what Wordsworth calls the "authentic comment," why, he will be provoked into making the right comment for himself, and so the end will be gained.

I should like, in this fifth volume of the 'Home Education' Series, to acknowledge my indebtedness to Miss Elsie Kitching for the constant interest she has thrown into the work, and her always intelligent collaboration as amanuensis.

Charlotte M. Mason.

Ambleside, October 1906.

Part I

Some Studies in Treatment

(Weisall's Following)

Chapter 1. The Philosopher At Home

"He has such a temper, ma'am!'"'

And there, hot, flurried, and generally at her wits' end, stood the poor nurse at the door of her mistress's room. The terrific bellowing which filled the house was enough to account for the girl's distress. Mrs. Belmont looked worried. She went up wearily to what she well knew was a weary task. A quarter of an hour ago life had looked very bright—the sun shining, sparrows chirping, lilac and laburnum making a gay show in the suburban gardens about; she thought of her three nestlings in the nursery, and her heart was like a singing-bird giving out chirps of thanks and praise. But that was all changed. The outside world was as bright as ever, but she was under a cloud. She knew too well how those screams from the nursery would spoil her day.

There the boy lay, beating the ground with fists and feet; emitting one prodigious roar after another, features convulsed, eyes protruding, in the unrestrained rage of a wild creature, so transfigured by passion that even his mother doubted if the noble countenance and lovely smile of her son had any existence beyond her fond imagination. He eyed his mother askance through his tumbled, yellow hair, but her presence seemed only to aggravate the demon in possession. The screams became more violent; the beating of the ground more than ever like a maniac's rage.

"Get up, Guy."

Renewed screams; more violent action of the limbs!

"Did you hear me, Guy?" in tones of enforced calmness.

The uproar subsided a little; but when Mrs. Belmont laid her band on his shoulder to raise him, the boy sprang to his feet, ran into her head-foremost, like a young bull, kicked her, beat her with his fists, tore her dress with his teeth, and would no doubt have ended by overthrowing his delicate mother, but that Mr. Belmont, no longer able to endure the disturbance, came up in time to disengage the raging child and carry him off to his mother's room. Once in, the key was turned upon him, and Guy was left to "subside at his leisure'" said his father.

Breakfast was not a cheerful meal, either upstairs or down. Nurse was put out; snapped up little Flo, shook baby for being tiresome, until she had them both in tears. In the dining-room, Mr. Belmont read the Times with a frown which last night's debate did not warrant; sharp words were at his tongue's end, but, in turning the paper, he caught sight of his wife's pale face and untasted breakfast. He said nothing, but she knew and suffered under his thoughts fully as much as if they had been uttered. Meantime, two closed doors and the wide space between the rooms hardly served to dull the ear-torturing sounds that came from the prisoner.

All at once there was a lull, a sudden and complete cessation of sound. Was the child in a fit?

"Excuse me a minute, Edward;" and Mrs. Belmont flew upstairs, followed shortly by her husband. What was her surprise to see Guy with composed features contemplating himself in the glass! He held in his hand a proof of his own photograph which had just come from the photographers. The boy had been greatly interested in the process; and here was the picture arrived, and Guy was solemnly comparing it with that image of himself which the looking-glass presented.

Nothing more was said on the subject; Mr. Belmont went to the city, and his wife went about her household affairs with a lighter heart than she had expected to carry that day. Guy was released, and allowed to return to the nursery for his breakfast, which his mother found him eating in much content and with the sweetest face in the world; there was no more trace of passion than a June day bears when the sun comes out after a thunderstorm. Guy was, indeed, delightful; attentive and obedient to Harriet, full of charming play to amuse the two little ones, and very docile and sweet with his mother, saying from time to time the quaintest things. You would have thought he had been trying to make up for the morning's fracas, had he not looked quite unconscious of wrong-doing.

This sort of thing had gone on since the child's infancy. Now, a frantic outburst of passion, to be so instantly followed by a sweet April-day face and a sunshiny temper that the resolutions his parents made about punishing or endeavouring to reform him passed away like hoar-frost before the child's genial mood.

A sunshiny day followed this stormy morning; the next day passed in peace and gladness, but, the next, some hair astray, some crumpled rose-leaf under him, brought on another of Guy's furious outbursts. Once again the same dreary routine was gone through; and, once again, the tempestuous morning was forgotten in the sunshine of the child's day.

Not by the father, though—at last, Mr. Belmont was roused to give his full attention to the mischief which had been going on under his eyes for nearly the five years of Guy's short life. It dawned upon him—other people had seen it for years—that his wife's nervous headaches and general want of tone might well be due to this constantly recurring distress. He was a man of reading and intelligence, in touch with the scientific thought of the day, and especially interested in what may be called the physical basis of character—the interaction which is ever taking place between the material brain and the immaterial thought and feeling of which it is the organ. He had even made little observations and experiments, declared to be valuable by his friend and ally, Dr Weissall, the head physician of the county hospital.

For a whole month he spread crumbs on the window-sill every morning at five minutes to eight; the birds gathered as punctually, and by eight o'clock the "table" was cleared and not a crumb remained. So far, the experiment was a great delight to the children, Guy and Flo, who were all agog to know how the birds knew the time.

After a month of free breakfasts. "You shall see now whether or no the birds come because they see the crumbs." The prospect was delightful, but, alas, this stage of the experiment was very much otherwise to the pitiful childish hearts.

"Oh, father, please let us put out crumbs for the poor little birds, they are so hungry!" a prayer seconded by Mrs. Belmont, met with very ready acceptance. The best of us have our moments of weakness.

"Very interesting," said the two savants; "nothing could show more clearly the readiness with which a habit is formed in even the less intelligent of the creatures."

Yes, and more than that, it shows the automatic nature of the action once the habit is formed. Observe, the birds came punctually and regularly when there were no longer crumbs for them. They did not come, look for their breakfast, and take sudden flight when it was not there, but they settled as before, stayed as long as before, and then flew off without any sign of disappointment. That is, they came, as we set one foot before another in walking, just out of habit, without any looking for crumbs, or conscious intention of any sort—a mere automatic or machine-like action with which conscious thought has nothing to do."

Of another little experiment Mr. Belmont was especially proud, because it brought down, as it were, two quarries at a stroke; touched heredity and automatic action in one little series of observations. Rover, the family dog, appeared in the first place as a miserable puppy saved from drowning. He was of no breed to speak of, but care and good living agreed with him. He developed a handsome shaggy white coat, a quiet, well-featured face, and betrayed his low origin only by one inveterate habit; carts he took no notice of, but never a carriage, small or great, appeared in sight but he ran yelping at the heels of the horses in an intolerable way, contriving at the same time to dodge the whip like any street Arab. Oddly enough, it came out through the milkman that Rover came of a mother who met with her death through this very peccadillo.

Here was an opportunity. The point was, to prove not only that the barking was automatic, but that the most inveterate habit, even an inherited habit, is open to cure.

Mr. Belmont devoted himself to the experiment: he gave orders that, for a month, Rover should go out with no one but himself. Two pairs of ears were on the alert for wheels; two, distinguished between carriage and cart. Now Rover was the master of an accomplishment of which he and the family were proud. He could carry a newspaper in his mouth. Wheels in the distance, then, "Hi! Rover!" and Rover trotted along, the proud bearer of the Times. This went on daily for a month, until at last the association between wheels and newspaper was established, and a distant rumble would bring him up—a demand in his eyes. Rover was cured. By-and-by the paper was unnecessary, and "To heel! good dog!" was enough when an ominous falling of the jaw threatened a return of the old habit.

It is extraordinary how wide is the gap between theory and practice in most of our lives. "The man who knows the power of habit has a key wherewith to regulate his own life and the lives of his household, down to that of the cat sitting at his hearth." (Applause.) Thus, Mr. Belmont at a scientific gathering. But only this morning did it dawn upon him that, with this key between his fingers, he was letting his wife's health, his child's life, be ruined by a habit fatal alike to present peace, and to the hope of manly self-control in the future. Poor man! he had a bad half-hour that morning on his way Citywards. He was not given to introspection, but, when it was forced upon him, he dealt honestly.

"I must see Weissall to-night, and talk the whole thing out with him."

"Ah, so; the dear Guy! And how long is it, do you say, since the boy has thus out-broken?"

"All his life, for anything I know—certainly it began in his infancy."

"And do you think, my good friend"—here the Doctor laid a hand on his friend's arm, and peered at him with twinkling eyes and gravely set mouth—" do you think it possible that he has—er—inherited this little weakness? A grandfather, perhaps?"

"You mean me, I know; yes, it's a fact. And I got it from my father, and he, from his. We're not a good stock. I know I'm an irascible fellow, and it has stood in my way all through life."

"Fair and softly, my dear fellow! go not so fast. I cannot let you say bad things of my best friend. But this I allow; there are thorns, bristles all over; and they come out at a touch. How much better for you and for Science had the father cured all that!" "As I must for Guy! Yes, and how much happier for wife, children, and servants; how much pleasanter for friends. Well, Guy is the question now. What do you advise?"

The two sat far into the night discussing a problem on the solution of which depended the future of a noble boy, the happiness of a family. No wonder they found the subject so profoundly interesting that 'two' by the church clock startled them into a hasty separation. Both Mrs. Belmont and Mrs. Weissall resented this dereliction on the part of their several lords; but these ladies would have been meeker than Sarah herself had they known that, not science, not politics, but the bringing up of the children, was the engrossing topic.

Breakfast-time three days later. Scene, the dining room. *Nurse* in presence of *Master* and *Mistress*.

"You have been a faithful servant and good friend, both to us and the children, Harriet, but we blame you a little for Guy's passionate outbreaks. Do not be offended, we blame ourselves more. Your share of blame is that you have worshipped him from his babyhood, and have allowed him to have his own way in everything. Now, your part of the cure is, to do exactly as we desire. At present, I shall only ask you to remember that, Prevention is better than cure. The thing for all of us is to take precautions against even one more of these outbreaks.

"Keep your eye upon Guy; if you notice—no matter what the cause—flushed cheeks, pouting lips, flashing eye, frowning forehead, with two little upright lines between the eyebrows, limbs held stiffly, hands, perhaps, closed, head thrown slightly back; if you notice any or all of these signs, the boy is on the verge of an outbreak. Do not stop to ask questions, or soothe him, or make peace, or threaten. Change his thoughts. That is the one hope. Say quite naturally and pleasantly, as if you saw nothing, 'Your father wants you to garden with him,' or, 'for a game of dominoes'; or, 'Your mother wants you to help her in the store-room,' or,' to tidy her work-box.' Be ruled by the time of the day, and how you know we are employed. And be quite sure we do want the boy."

"But, sir, please excuse me, is it any good to save him from breaking out when the passion is there in his heart?"

"Yes, Harriet, all the good in the world. Your master thinks that Guy's passions have become a habit, and that the way to cure him is to keep him a long time, a month or two, without a single outbreak; if we can manage that, the trouble will be over. As for the passion in his heart, that comes with the outer signs, and both will be cured together. Do, Harriet, like a good woman, help us in this matter, and your master and I will always be grateful to you!"

"I'm sure, ma'am," with a sob (Harriet was a soft-hearted woman, and was very much touched to be taken thus into the confidence of her master and mistress), "I'm sure I'll do my best, especially as I've had a hand in it; but I'm sure I never meant to, and, if I forget, I hope you'll kindly forgive me."

"No, Harriet, you must not forget any more than you'd forget to snatch a sharp knife from the baby. This is almost a matter of life and death."

"Very well, sir, I'll remember; and thank you for telling me."

Breakfast time was unlucky; the very morning after the above talk, Nurse had her opportunity. Flo, for some inscrutable reason, preferred to eat her porridge with her brother's spoon. Behold, quick as a flash, flushed cheeks, puckered brow, rigid frame!

"Master Guy, dear," in a quite easy, friendly tone (Harriet had mastered her lesson), "run down to your father; he wants you to help him in the garden."

Instantly the flash in the eye became a sparkle of delight, the rigid limbs were all active and eager; out of his chair, out of the room, downstairs, by his father's side, in less time than it takes to tell. And the face—joyous, sparkling, full of eager expectation—surely Nurse had been mistaken this time? But no; both parents knew how quickly Guy emerged from the shadow of a cloud, and they trusted Harriet's discretion.

"Well, boy, so you've come to help me garden? But I've not done breakfast. Have you finished yours?"

"No, father," with a dropping lip.

"Well, I'll tell you what. You run up and eat your porridge and come down as soon as you're ready; I shall make haste, too, and we shall get a good half-hour in the garden before I go out." Up again went Guy with hasty, willing feet. "Nurse" (breathless hurry and importance), "I must make haste with my porridge. Father wants me directly to help him in the garden."

Nurse winked hard at the fact that the porridge was gobbled. The happy little boy trotted off to one of the greatest treats he knew, and that day passed without calamity.

"I can see it will answer, and life will be another thing without Guy's passions; but do you think, Edward, it's right to give the child pleasures when he's naughty—in fact, to put a premium upon naughtiness, for it amounts to that?"

"You're not quite right there. The child does not know he is naughty; the emotions of 'naughtiness' are there; he is in a physical tumult, but wilfulness has not set in; he does not yet mean to be naughty, and all is gained if we avert the set of the will towards wrong-doing. He has not had time to recognise that he is naughty, and his thoughts are changed so suddenly that he is not in the least aware of what was going on in him before. The new thing comes to him as naturally and graciously as do all the joys of the childish day. The question of desert does not occur."

For a week all went well. Nurse was on the alert, was quick to note the ruddy storm-signal in the fair little face; she never failed to despatch Guy instantly, and with a quiet unconscious manner, on some errand to father or mother; nay, she improved on her instructions; when father and mother were out of the way, she herself invented some pleasant errand to cook about the pudding for dinner; to get fresh water for Dickie, or to see if Rover had had his breakfast. Nurse was really clever in inventing expedients, in hitting instantly on something to be done novel and amusing enough to fill the child's fancy. A mistake in this direction would, experience told her, be fatal; propose what was stale, and not only would Guy decline to give up the immediate gratification of a passionate outbreak—for it is a gratification, that must be borne in mind—but he would begin to look suspiciously on the "something else" which so often came in the way of this gratification.

Security has its own risks. A morning came when Nurse was not on the alert. Baby was teething and fractious, Nurse was overdone, and the nursery was not a cheerful place. Guy, very sensitive to the moral atmosphere about him, got, in Nurse's phrase, out of sorts. He relieved himself by drumming on the table with a couple of ninepins, just as Nurse was getting baby off after a wakeful night.

"Stop that noise this minute, you naughty boy! Don't you see your poor little brother is going to sleep?" in a loud whisper. The noise was redoubled, and assisted by kicks on chair-rungs and table-legs. Sleep vanished and baby broke into a piteous wail. This was too much; the Nurse laid down the child, seized the young culprit, chair and all, carried him to the farthest corner, and, desiring him not to move till she gave him leave, set him down with a vigorous shaking. There were days when Guy would stand this style of treatment cheerfully, but this was not one. Before Harriet had even noted the danger signals, the storm had broken out. For half an hour the nursery was a scene of frantic uproar, baby assisting, and even little Flo. Half an hour is nothing to speak of; in pleasant chat, over an amusing book, the thirty minutes fly like five; but half an hour in struggle with a raging child is a day and a night in length. Mr. and Mrs. Belmont were out, so Harriet had it all to herself, and it was contrary to orders that she should attempt to place the child in confinement; solitude and locked doors involved risks that the parents would, rightly, allow no one but themselves to run. At last the tempest subsided, spent, apparently, by its own force.

A child cannot bear estrangement, disapproval; he must needs live in the light of a countenance smiling upon him. His passion over, Guy set himself laboriously to be good, keeping watch out of the corner of his eye to see how Nurse took it. She was too much vexed to respond in any way, even by a smile. But her heart was touched; and though, by-and-by when Mrs. Belmont came in, she did say 'Master Guy has been in one of his worst tempers again, ma'am: screaming for better than half an hour"—yet she did not tell her tale with the empressement necessary to show what a very bad half-hour they had had. His mother looked with grave reproof at the delinquent, but she was not proof against his coaxing ways.

After dinner she remarked to her husband, "You will be sorry to hear that Guy has had one of his worst bouts again. Nurse said he screamed steadily for more than half an hour."

"What did you do?"

"I was out at the time doing some shopping. But when I came back, after letting him know how grieved I was, I did as you say, changed his thoughts and did my best to give him a happy day.'

"How did you let him know you were grieved?"

"I looked at him in a way he quite understood, and you should have seen the deliciously coaxing, half-ashamed look he shot up at me. What eyes he has!"

"Yes, the little monkey! and no doubt he measured their effect on his mother; you must allow me to say that my theory certainly is not to give him a happy day after an outbreak of this sort."

"Why, I thought your whole plan was to change his thoughts, to keep him so well occupied with Pleasant things that he does not dwell on what agitated him."

"Yes, but did you not tell me the passion was over when you found him?"

"Quite over; he was as good as gold."

Well, the thing we settled on was to avert a threatened outbreak by a pleasant change of thought; and to do so in order that, at last, the habit of these outbreaks may be broken. Don't you see, that is a very different thing from pampering him with a pleasant day when he has already pampered himself with the full indulgence of his passion?"

"Pampered himself! Why, you surely don't think those terrible scenes give the poor child any pleasure. I always thought he was a deal more to be pitied than we."

"Indeed I do. Pleasure is perhaps hardly the word; but that the display of temper is a form of self-indulgence, there is no doubt at all. You, my dear, are too amiable to know what a relief it is to us irritable people to have a good storm and clear the air."

"Nonsense, Edward! But what should I have done? What is the best course after the child has given way?"

"I think we must, as you once suggested, consider how we ourselves are governed. Estrangement, isolation are the immediate consequences of sin, even of what may seem a small sin of harshness or selfishness."

"Oh, but don't you think that is our delusion? that God is loving us all the time, and it is we who estrange ourselves?'

"Without doubt; and we are aware of the love all the time, but, also, we are aware of a cloud between it and ourselves; we know we are out of favour."

We know, too, that there is only one way back, through the fire. It is common to speak of repentance as a light thing, rather pleasant than otherwise; but it is searching and bitter: so much so, that the Christian soul dreads to sin, even the sin of coldness, from an almost cowardly dread of the anguish of repentance, purging fire though it be."

Mrs. Belmont could not clear her throat to answer for a minute. She had never before had such a glimpse into her husband's soul. Here were deeper things in the spiritual life than any of which she yet knew.

"Well then, dear, about Guy; must he feel this estrangement, go through this fire?"

"I think so, in his small degree; but he must never doubt our love. He must see and feel that it is always there, though under a cloud of sorrow which he only can break through."

Guy's lapse prepared the way for further lapses. Not two days passed before he was again in a passion. The boy, his outbreak over, was ready at once to emerge into the sunshine. Not so his mother. His most bewitching arts met only with sad looks and silence.

He told his small scraps of nursery news, looking in vain for the customary answering smile and merry words. He sidled up to his mother, and stroked her cheek; that did not do, so he stroked her hand; then her gown; no answering touch, no smile, no word; nothing but sorrowful eyes when he ventured to raise his own. Poor little fellow! The iron was beginning to enter; he moved a step or two away from his mother, and raised to hers eyes full of piteous doubt and pleading. He saw love, which could not reach him, and sorrow, which he was just beginning to comprehend. But his mother could bear it no longer: she got up hastily and left the room. Then the little boy, keeping close to the wall, as if even that were something to interpose between him and this new sense of desolation, edged off to the farthest corner of the room, and sinking on the floor with a sad, new quietness, sobbed in his loneliness; Nurse had had her lesson, and although she too was crying for her boy, nobody went near him but Flo. A little arm was passed round his neck; a hot little cheek pressed against his curls:

"Don't cry, Guy!" two or three times, and when the sobs came all the thicker, there was nothing for it but that Flo must cry too; poor little outcasts!

At last bedtime came, and his mother; but her face had still that sad far-away look, and Guy could see she had been crying. How he longed to spring up and hug her and kiss her as he would have done yesterday. But somehow he dared not; and she never smiled nor spoke, and yet never before had Guy known how his mother loved him.

She sat in her accustomed chair by the little white bed, and beckoned the little boy in his nightgown to come and say his prayers. He knelt at his mother's knee as usual, and then she laid her hands upon his.

"Our Father—oh, mother, mo-o-ther, mother!" and a torrent of tears drowned the rest, and Guy was again in his mother's arms, and she was raining kisses upon him, and crying with him.

Next morning his father received him with open arms.

"So my poor little boy had a bad day yesterday!"

Guy hung his head and said nothing.

"Would you like me to tell you how you may help ever having quite such another bad day?"

"Oh yes, please, father; I thought I couldn't help."

"Can you tell when the 'Cross-man' is coming?"

Guy hesitated. "Sometimes, I think. I get all hot."

"Well, the minute you find he's coming, even if you have begun to cry, say, 'Please excuse me, Nurse,' and run downstairs, and then four times round the paddock as fast as you can, without stopping to take breath!"

"What a good way! Shall I try it now?"

"Why, the 'Cross-man' isn't there now. But I'll tell you a secret: he always goes away if you begin to do something else as hard as you can; and if you can remember to run away from him round the garden, you'll find he won't run after you; at the very worst, he won't run after you more than once round!"

"Oh, father, I'll try! What fun! See if I don't beat him! Won't I just give Mr. 'Cross-man' a race! He shall be quite out of breath before we get round the fourth time."

The vivid imagination of the boy personified the foe, and the father jumped with his humour. Guy was eager for the fray; the parents had found an ally in their boy; the final victory was surely within appreciable distance.

"This is glorious, Edward; and it's as interesting is painting a picture or writing a book! What a capital device the race with 'Mr. Cross-man' is! It's like 'Sintram.' He'll be so busy looking out for

'Cross-man' that he'll forget to be cross. The only danger I see is that of many false alarms. He'll try the race, in all good faith, when there is no foe in pursuit."

"That's very likely; but it will do no harm. He is getting the habit of running away from the evil, and may for that be the more ready to run when it's at his heels; this, of running away from temptation, is the right principle, and may be useful to him in a thousand ways."

"Indeed, it may be a safeguard to him through life. How did you get the idea?"

"Do you remember how Rover was cured of barking after carriages? There were two stages to the cure; the habit of barking was stopped, and a new habit was put in its place; I worked upon the recognised law of association of ideas, and got Rover to associate the rumble of wheels with a newspaper in his mouth. I tried at the time to explain how it was possible to act thus on the 'mind' of a dog."

"I recollect quite well; you said that the stuff—nervous tissue, you called it—of which the brain is made is shaped in the same sort of way—at least so I understood—by the thoughts that are in it, as the cover of a tart is shaped by the plums below. And then, when there's a place ready for them in the brain, the same sort of thoughts always come to fill it."

"I did not intend to say precisely that," said Mr. Belmont, laughing, "especially the plum part. However, it will do. Pray go on with your metaphor. It is decided that plums are not wholesome eating. You put in your thumb, and pick out a plum; and that the place may be filled, and well filled, you pop in a—a—figures fail me—a peach!"

"I see! I see! Guy's screaming fits are the unwholesome plum which we are picking out, and the running away from Cross-man the peach to be got instead. (I don't see why it should be a peach though, unpractical man!) His brain is to grow to the shape of the peach, and behold, the place is filled. No more room for the plum."

"You have it; you have put, in a light way, a most interesting law, and I take much blame to myself that I never thought until now of applying it to Guy's case. But now I think we are making way; we have made provision for dislodging the old habit and setting a new one in its place."

"Don't you think the child will be a hero in a very small way, when he makes himself run away from his temper?"

"Not in a small way at all; the child will be a hero. But we cannot be heroes all the time. In sudden gusts of temptation, God grant him grace to play the hero, if only through hasty flight; but in what are called besetting sins, there is nothing safe but the contrary besetting good habit. And here is where parents have immense power over the future of the children."

"Don't think me superstitious and stupid; but somehow this scientific training, good as I see it is, seems to me to undervalue the help we get from above in times of difficulty and temptation."

"Let me say that it is you who undervalue the virtue, and limit the scope of the Divine action. Whose are the laws Science labours to reveal? Whose are the works, body or brain, or what you like, upon which these laws act?"

"How foolish of me! But one gets into a way of thinking that God cares only for what we call spiritual things. Let me ask you one more question. I do see that all this watchful training is necessary, and do not wish to be idle or cowardly about it. But don't you think Guy would grow out of these violent tempers naturally, as he gets older?"

"Well, he would not, as youth or man, fling himself on the ground and roar; but no doubt he would grow up touchy, fiery, open at any minute to a sudden storm of rage. The man who has too much self-respect for an open exhibition may, as you know well enough, poor wife, indulge in continual irritability, suffer himself to be annoyed by trifling matters. No, there is nothing for it but to look upon an irate habit as one to be displaced by a contrary habit. Who knows what cheerful days we may yet have, and whether in curing Guy I may not cure myself? The thing can be done; only one is so lazy about one's own habits. Suppose you take me in hand?"

"Oh, I couldn't! and yet it's your only fault."

"Only fault! well, we'll see. In the meantime there's another thing I wish we could do for Guy—stop him in the midst of an outbreak. Do you remember the morning we found him admiring himself in the glass?"

"Yes, with the photograph in his hand."

"That was it; perhaps the Cross-man race will answer even in the middle of a tempest. If not, we must try something else."

"It won't work."

"Why not?"

"Guy will have no more rages; how then can he be stopped in mid-tempest?"

"Most hopeful of women! But don't deceive yourself. Our work is only well begun, but that, let us hope, is half done."

His father was right. Opportunities to check him in mid-career occurred; and Guy answered to the rein. Mr. Cross-man worked wonders. A record of outbreaks was kept; now a month intervened; two months; a year; two years; and at last his parents forgot their early troubles with their sweet-tempered, frank-natured boy.

Chapter 2. Inconstant Kitty

"But now for the real object of this letter—does it take your breath away to get four sheets? We want you to help us about Kitty. My husband and I are at our wits' end, and would most thankfully take your wise head and kind heart into counsel. I fear we have been laying up trouble for ourselves and for our little girl. The ways of nature are, there is no denying it, very attractive in all young creatures, and it is so delightful to see a child do as "tis its nature to,' that you forget that Nature, left to herself, produces a waste, be it never so lovely. Our little Kitty's might so easily become a wasted life.

"But not to prose any more, let me tell you the history of Kitty's yesterday—one of her days is like the rest, and you will be able to see where we want your help.

"Figure to yourself the three little heads bent over 'copy-books' in our cheery schoolroom. Before a line is done, up starts Kitty.

"'Oh, mother, may I write the next copy—s h e l l ? "Shell" is so much nicer than—k n o w, and I'm so tired of it.'

"'How much have you done?'

"'I have written it three whole times, mother, and I really can't do it any more! I think I could do—s h e l l. "Shell" is so pretty!'

"By-and-by we read; but Kitty cannot read—can't even spell the words (don't scold us, we know it is quite wrong to spell in a reading lesson), because all the time her eyes are on a smutty sparrow on the topmost twig of the poplar; so she reads, 'W i t h, birdie!' We do sums; a short line of addition is to poor Kitty a hopeless and an endless task. 'Five and three make—nineteen,' is her last effort, though she knows quite well how to add up figures. Half a scale on the piano, and then—eyes and ears for everybody's business but her own. Three stitches of hemming, and idle fingers plait up the hem or fold the duster in a dozen shapes. I am in the midst of a thrilling history talk: 'So the Black Prince—' 'Oh, mother, do you think we shall go to the sea this year? My pail is quite ready, all but the handle, but I can't find my spade anywhere!' "And thus we go on, pulling Kitty through her lessons somehow; but it is a weariness to herself and to all of us, and I doubt if the child learns anything except by bright flashes. But you have no notion how quick the little monkey is. After idling through a lesson she will overtake us at a bound at the last moment, and thus escape the wholesome shame of being shown up as the dunce of our little party.

"Kitty's dawdling ways, her restless desire for change of occupation, her always wandering thoughts, lead to a good deal of friction, and spoil our school-room party, which is a pity, for I want the children to enjoy their lessons from the very first. What do you think the child said to me yesterday in the most coaxing pretty way? 'There are so many things nicer than lessons! Don't you think so, mother?' Yes, dear aunt, I see you put your finger on those unlucky words 'coaxing pretty way,' and you look, if you do not say, that awful sentence of yours about sin being bred of allowance. Isn't that it? It is quite true; we are in fault. Those butterfly ways of Kitty's were delicious to behold until we thought it time to set her to work, and then we found that we should have been training her from babyhood. Well,

"'If you break your plaything yourself, dear,
Don't you cry for it all the same?
I don't think it is such a comfort
To have only oneself to blame.'

So, like a dear, kind aunt, don't scold us, but help us to do better. Is Kitty constant to anything? you ask. Does she stick to any of the 'many things so much nicer than lessons'? I am afraid that here, too, our little girl is 'unstable as water.' And the worst of it is, she is all agog to be at a thing, and then, when you think her settled to half an hour's pleasant play, off she is like any butterfly. She says her, 'How doth the little busy bee,' dutifully; but when I tell her she is not a bit like a busy bee, but rather like a foolish, flitting butterfly, I'm afraid she rather likes it, and makes up to the butterflies as if they were akin to her, and were having just the good time she would prefer. But you must come and see the child to understand how volatile she is.

"'Oh, mother, please let me have a good doll's wash this afternoon; I'm quite unhappy about poor Peggy! I really think she likes to be dirty!'

"Great preparations follow in the way of little tub, and soap, and big apron; the little laundress sits down, greatly pleased with herself, to undress her dirty Peggy; but hardly is the second arm out of its sleeve, than, presto! a new idea; off goes Kitty to clean out her doll's house, deaf to all Nurse's remonstrances about 'nice hot water,' and 'poor dirty Peggy.'

"I'm afraid the child is no more constant to her loves than to her play; she is a loving little soul, as you know, and is always adoring somebody. Now it's her father, now Juno, now me, now Hugh; and the rain of warm kisses, the soft clasping arms, the nestling head, are delicious, whether to dog or man. But, alas! Kitty's blandishments are a whistle you must pay for; tomorrow it is somebody else's turn, and the bad part is that she has only room for one at a time. If we could get a little visit from you, now, Kitty would be in your pocket all day long; and we, even Peggy, would be left out in the cold. But do not flatter yourself it would last; I think none of Kitty's attachments has been known to last longer than two days.

"If the chief business of parents is to train character in their children, we have done nothing for Kitty; at six years old the child has no more power of application, no more habit of attention, is no more able to make herself do the thing she ought to do, indeed, has no more desire to do the right thing than she had at six months old. We are getting very unhappy about it. My husband feels strongly that parents should labour at character as the Hindoo gold-beater labours at his vase; that character, is the one thing we are called upon to effect. And what have we done for Kitty? We have turned out a 'fine animal,' and are glad and thankful for that; but that is all; the child is as wayward, as unsteady, as a young colt. Do help us, dear aunt. Think our little girl's case over; if you can get at the source of the mischief, send us a few hints for our guidance, and we shall be yours gratefully evermore."

"And now for my poor little great-niece! Her mother piles up charges against her, but how interesting and amusing and like the free world of fairy-land it would all be were it not for the tendencies which, in these days, we talk much about and watch little against. We bring up our children in the easiest, happy-go-lucky way, and all the time talk solemnly in big words about the momentous importance of every influence brought to bear upon them. But it is true; these naughty, winsome ways of Kitty's will end in her growing up like half the 'girls!'—that is, young women—one meets. They talk glibly on many subjects; but test them, and they know nothing of any; they are ready to undertake anything, but they carry nothing through. This week, So-and-so is their most particular friend; next week, such another; even their amusements, their one real interest, fail and flag; but then, there is some useful thing to be learnt—how to set tiles or play the banjo! And, all the time, there is no denying, as you say, that this very fickleness has a charm, so long as the glamour of youth lasts, and the wayward girl has bright smiles and winning, graceful ways to disarm you with. But youth does not last; and the poor girl who began as a butterfly ends as a grub, tied to the earth by the duties she never learnt how to fulfil; that is, supposing she is a girl with a conscience; wanting that, she dances through life whatever befalls—children, husband, home, must take their chance. 'What a giddy old grandmother the Peterfields have!' remarked a pert young man of my acquaintance. But, indeed, the 'giddy old grandmother' is not an unknown quantity.

"Are you saying to yourself, a prosy old 'great-aunt' is as bad as a 'giddy old grandmother'? I really have prosed abominably, but Kitty has been on my mind all the time, and it is quite true, you must take her in hand.

"First, as to her lessons: you must help her to gain the power of attention; that should have been done long ago, but better late than never, and an aunt who has given her mind to these matters takes blame to herself for not having seen the want sooner. 'But,' I fancy you are saying,' if the child has no faculty of attention, how can we give it to her? It's just a natural defect.' Not a bit of it! Attention is not a faculty at all, though I believe it is worth more than all the so-called faculties put together; this, at any rate, is true, that no talent, no genius, is worth much without the power of attention; and this is the power which makes men or women successful in life. (I talk like a book without scruple, because you know my light is borrowed; Professor Weissall is our luminary.)

"Attention is no more than this—the power of giving your mind to what you are about—the bigger the better so far as the mind goes, and great minds do great things; but have you never known a person with a great mind, 'real genius,' his friends say, who goes through life without accomplishing anything? It is just because he wants the power to 'turn on,' so to speak, the whole of his great mind; he is unable to bring the whole of his power to bear on the subject in hand. 'But Kitty?' Yes, Kitty must get this power of 'turning on.' She must be taught to give her mind to sums and reading, and even to dusters. Go slowly; a little to-day and a little more tomorrow. In the first place, her lessons must be made interesting. Do not let her scramble through a page of 'reading,' for instance, spelling every third word and then waiting to be told what it spells, but let every day bring the complete mastery of a few new words, as well as the keeping up of the old ones.

"But do not let the lesson last more than ten minutes, and insist, with brisk, bright determination, on the child's full concentrated attention of eye and mind for the whole ten minutes. Do not allow a moment's dawdling at lessons.

"I should not give her rows of figures to add yet; use dominoes or the domino cards prepared for the purpose, the point being to add or subtract the dots on the two halves in a twinkling. You will find that the three can work together at this as at the reading, and the children will find it as exciting and delightful as 'old soldier.' Kitty will be all alive here, and will take her share of work merrily; and this is a point gained. Do not, if you can help it, single the little maid out from the rest and throw her on her own responsibility. 'Tis 'a heavy and a weary weight' for the bravest of us, and the little back will get a trick of bending under life if you do not train her to carry it lightly, as an Eastern woman her pitcher.

"Then, vary the lessons; now head, and now hands; now tripping feet and tuneful tongue; but in every lesson let Kitty and the other two carry away the joyous sense of—

"'Something attempted, something done.'

"Allow of no droning wearily over the old stale work—which must be kept up all the time, it is true, but rather by way of an exciting game than as the lesson of the day, which should always be a distinct step that the children can recognise.

"You have no notion, until you try, how the 'now-or-never' feeling about a lesson quickens the attention of even the most volatile child; what you can drone through all day, you will; what must be done, is done. Then, there is a by-the-way gain besides that of quickened attention. I once heard a wise man say that, if he must choose between the two, he would rather his child should learn the meaning of 'must' than inherit a fortune. And here you will be able to bring moral force to bear on wayward Kitty. Every lesson must have its own time, and no other time in this world is there for it. The sense of the preciousness of time, of the irreparable loss when a ten minutes' lesson is thrown away, must be brought home.

"Let your own unaffected distress at the loss of 'golden minutes' be felt by the children, and also be visited upon them by the loss of some small childish pleasure which the day should have held. It is a sad thing to let a child dawdle through a day and be let off scot-free. You see, I am talking of the children, and not of Kitty alone, because it is so much easier to be good in company; and what is good for her will be good for the trio.

"But there are other charges; poor Kitty is neither steady in play nor steadfast in love! May not the habit of attending to her lessons help her to stick to her play? Then, encourage her. 'What! The doll's tea-party over! That's not the way grown -up ladies have tea; they sit and talk for a long time. See if you can make your tea-party last twenty minutes by my watch!' This failing of Kitty's is just a case where a little gentle ridicule might do a great deal of good. It is a weapon to be handled warily, for one child may resent, and another take pleasure in being laughed at; but managed with tact I do believe it's good for children and grown-ups to see the comic side of their doings.

"I think we err in not enough holding up certain virtues for our children's admiration. Put a premium of praise on every finished thing, if it be only a house of cards. Steadiness in work is a step on the way towards steadfastness in love. Here, too, the praise of constancy might very well go with good-humoured family 'chaff,' not about the new loves, which are lawful, whether of kitten or playmate, but about the discarded old loves. Let Kitty and all of them grow up to glory in their constancy to every friend.

"There, I am sending you a notable preachment instead of the few delicate hints I meant to offer; but never mount a woman on her hobby—who knows when she will get off again?"

Chapter 3. Under A Cloud

You wish me to tell you the story of my little girl? Well, to begin at the beginning. In looking back through the pages of my journal I find many scattered notices of Agnes, and I always write of her I find, as to "poor Agnes." Now, I wonder why? The child is certainly neither unhealthy nor unhappy—at least, not with any reason; but again and again I find this sort of entry:—

"Agnes displeased with her porridge; says nothing, but looks black all day."

"Harry upset his sister's work-basket—by accident, I truly believe; but she can't get over it—speaks to no one, and looks as if under a cloud."

I need not go on; the fact is, the child is sensible of many injuries heaped upon her; I think there is no ground for the feeling, for she is really very sweet when she has not, as the children say, the black dog on her back. It is quite plain to me, and to others also, I think that we have let this sort of thing go on too long without dealing with it. We must take the matter in hand. Please God, our little Agnes must not grow up in this sullen habit, for all our sakes, but chiefly for her own, poor child. I felt that in this matter I might be of more use than Edward, who simply does not understand a temper less sunny and open than his own. I pondered and pondered, and, at last, some light broke in upon me. I thought I should get hold of one principle at a time, work that out thoroughly, and then take up the next, and so on, until all the springs of sullenness were exhausted, and all supplies from without stopped. I was beginning to suspect that the laws of habit worked here as elsewhere, and that, if I could get our dear child to pass, say, six weeks without a "fallen countenance," she might lose this distressing failing for life.

I meant at first to take most of the trouble of this experiment upon myself; but I think men have clearer heads than we women—that is, they can see both sides of a question and are not carried away by the one side presented to them. So I said—

"Well, Edward, our little Agnes does not get over her sulky fits; in fact, they last longer, and are harder to get out of than ever!"

"Poor little girl! It is unhappy for her and for all of us. But don't you think it is a sort of childish malaise she will soon grow out of?"

"Now, have you not said, again and again, that a childish fault, left to itself, can do no other than strengthen?"

"True; I suppose the fact is I am slow to realise the fault. But you are right. From the point of view of habit we are pledged to deal with it. Have you made any plans?"

"Yes; I have been trying to work the thing out on Professor Weissall's lines. We must watch the rise of the sullen cloud, and change her thoughts before she has time to realise that the black fit is coming."

"You are right; if we can keep the child for only a week without this settling of the cloud, the mere habit would be somewhat broken."

We had not to wait for our opportunity. At breakfast next day—whether Harry's porridge looked more inviting than her own, or whether he should not have been helped first, or whether the child had a little pain of which she was hardly aware—suddenly, her eyes fell, brows dropped, lips pouted, the whole face became slightly paler than before, the figure limp, limbs lax, hands nerveless—and our gentle child was transformed, become entirely unlovable. So far, her feelings were in the emotional stage; her injury, whatever it was, had not yet taken shape in her thoughts; she could not have told you what was the matter, because she did not know; but very soon the thinking brain would come to the aid of the quick emotions, and then she would be sulky of fixed purpose. Her father saw the symptoms rise and knew what they would lead to, and, with the promptness which has often saved us, he cried out—

"Agnes, come here, and hold up your pinafore!" and Agnes trotted up to his side, her pinafore held up very much to receive the morning dole of crumbs for the birds; presently, she came back radiant with the joy of having given the birds a good breakfast, and we had no more sulky fits that day. This went on for a fortnight or so with fair but not perfect success. Whenever her father or I was present, we caught the emotion before the child was conscious of it, and succeeded in turning her thoughts into some pleasant channel. But poor nurse has had bad hours with Agnes; there would sit the child, pale and silent, for hours together, doing nothing because she liked to do it, but only because she must. And, once the fit had settled down, thick and steady as a London fog, neither her father nor I could help in the least. Oh, the inconceivable settled cloudiness and irresponsiveness of that child face!

Our tactics were at fault. No doubt they helped so far as they went. We managed to secure bright days that might otherwise have been cloudy when we happened to be present at the first rise of the sullen mood. But it seemed impossible to bring about so long an abstinence from sullen fits as would nullify the habit. We pictured to ourselves the dreary life that lay before our pretty little girl; the distrust of her sweetness, to which even one such sullen fit would give rise; worse, the isolation which accompanies this sort of temper, and the anguish of repentance to follow. And then, I know, madness is often bred of this strong sense of injured personality.

It is not a pleasant thing to look an evil in the face. Whether or no "a little knowledge is a dangerous," certainly, it is a trying thing. If we could only have contented ourselves with, "Oh, she'll grow out of it by-and-by," we could have put up with even a daily cloud. But these forecasts of our little girl's future made the saving of the child at any cost our most anxious care.

"I'll tell you what, Helen; we must strike out a new line. In a general way, I do believe it's best to deal with a child's faults without making him aware that he has them. It fills the little beings with a ridiculous sense of importance to have anything belonging to them, even a fault. But in this case, I think, we shall have to strike home and deal with the cause at least as much as with the effects, and that, chiefly, because we have not effects entirely under our control."

"But, what if there is no cure? What if this odious temper were hereditary—our child's inheritance from those who should have brought her only good?"

"The question is not 'How has it come?' but 'How are we to deal with it?'—equally, you and I. Poor things! It's but a very half-and-half kind of matrimony if each is to pick out his or her own particular bundle of failings, and deal with it single-handed. This poor man finds the prospect too much for him! As a matter of fact, though, I believe that failings of mind, body, temper, and what not, are matters of inheritance, and that each parent's particular business in life is to pass his family forward freed from that particular vicious tendency which has been his own bane—or hers, if you prefer it."

"Well, do as you will; I can trust you. What it would be in these days of greater insight to be married to a man who would say, 'There, that boy may thank his mother' for this or the other failure! Of course, the thing is done now, but more often than not as a random guess."

"To return to Agnes. I think we shall have to show her to herself in this matter, to rake up the ugly feeling, however involuntary, and let her see how hateful it is. Yes, I do not wonder you shrink from this. So do I. It will destroy the child's unconsciousness."

"Oh, Edward, how I dread to poke into the little wounded heart, and bring up worse things to startle her!"

"I am sorry for you, but I think it must be done; and don't you think you are the person to do it? While they have a mother I don't think I could presume to pry too much into the secrets of the children's hearts."

"I'll try; but if I get into a mess you must help me through."

The opportunity came soon enough. It was pears this time. Harry would never have known whether he had the biggest or the least. But we had told Nurse to be especially careful in this matter. "Each of the children must have the biggest or best as often as one another, but there must be no fuss, no taking turns, about such trifles. Therefore, very rightly, you gave Harry the bigger and Agnes the smaller pear." Agnes's pear was not touched; there the child sat, without word or sob, but all gathered into herself, like a sea-anemone whose tentacles have been touched. The stillness, whiteness, and brooding sullenness of the face, the limp figure and desolate attitude, would have made me take the little girl in my arms if I had not too often failed to reach her in that way. This went on all day, all of us suffering; and in the evening, when I went to hear the children's prayers before bed, I meant to have it out.

We were both frozen up with sadness, and the weary child was ready to creep into her mother's arms again. But I must not let her yet.

"So my poor Agnes has had a very sad day?"

"Yes, mother," with a sob.

"And do you know we have all had a very sad day—father, mother, your little brother, Nurse—every one of us has felt as if a black curtain had been hung up to shut out the sunshine?"

The child was sympathetic, and shivered at the sight of the black curtain and the warm sunshine shut out.

"And do you know who has put us all out in the dark and the cold? Our little girl drew the curtain, because she would not speak to any of us, or be kind to any of us, or love any of us all the day long; so we could not get into the sunshine, and have been shivering and sad in the cold."

"Mother, mother!" with gasping sobs; "not you and father?"

"Ah! I thought my little girl would be sorry. Now let us try to find out how it all happened. Is it possible that Agnes noticed that her brother's pear was larger than her own?"

"Oh, mother, how could I?" The poor little face was hidden in her mother's breast, and the outbreak of sobs that followed was very painful. I feared it might mean actual illness for the sensitive child. I think it was the right thing to do; but I had barely courage enough to leave the results in more loving hands.

"Never mind; don't cry any more, darling, and we will ask 'Our Father' to forgive and forget all about it. Mother knows that her dear little Agnes will try not to love herself best any more. And then the black curtain will never fall, and we shall never again be a whole long day standing sadly out in the cold. Good-night from mother, and another good-night from father."

The treatment seems to answer. On the slightest return of the old sullen symptoms we show our little girl what they mean. The grief that follows is so painful that I'm afraid we could not go on with it for the sake of the child's health; but, happily, we very rarely see a sulky face now; and when we do we turn and look upon our child, and the look melts her into gentleness and penitence.

Chapter 4. Dorothy Elmore's Achievement

I

I know of no happier moment for parents than that when their eldest daughter returns from school to take her place finally by her mother's side. It was two years that very day since we had seen Dorothy, when her father set out for Lausanne to bring her home; and how the children and I got through the few days of his absence, I don't know. The last touches had been put many times over to her rooms—not the plain little room she had left, but a dainty bower for our young maiden, a little sitting-room opening into a pure nest of a bedroom. Our eyes met, her father's and mine, and moistened as we conjured up I don't know what visions of pure young life to be lived there, of the virginal prayers to be offered at the little prayer table, the gaiety of heart that should, from this nook, bubble over the house; and, who knows, by-and-by, the dreams of young love which should come to glorify the two little rooms.

Two or three times already had the children put fresh flowers into everything that would hold a flower. Pretty frocks and sweet faces, bright hair and bright eyes had been ready this long time to meet sister Dorothy.

At last, a telegram from Dover—"Home by five"—and our restlessness subsided into a hush of expectation.

Wheels sounded on the gravel, and we flew to the hall door and stood in two files, children and maids, Rover and Floss, waiting to welcome the child of the house. Then, a lovely face, glad to tears, looking out of a nest of furs; then, a light leap, almost before the carriage draw up, and I had her in my arms, my Dorothy, the child of my heart! The order of the day was "high tea," to which every one, down to baby May, sat up. We two, her father and I, gave her up to the children, only exchanging notes by the species of telegraphy married folk understand.

"Indubitably lovely!" said her father's eyes. "And what grace—what an elegant girl she is!" answered mine. "And do but see what tact she shows with the little ones—" "And notice the way she has with us, as if her heart were brimming with reverence and affection." Thus, we two with our eyes. For a week or more we could not settle down. As it was the Christmas holidays, we had not Miss Grimshaw to keep us in order, and so it happened that wherever Dorothy ran—no, she went with a quick noiseless step, but never ran—about the house to find out the old dear nooks, we all followed, a troop of children with their mother in the rear; their father too, if he happened to be in. Truly we were a ridiculous family, and did our best to turn the child's head. Every much has its more-so. Dorothy's two special partisans were Elsie, our girl of fifteen years, fast treading in her sister's steps, and Herbert, our eldest son, soon to go to college. Elsie would come to my room and discourse by the hour, her text being ever, "Dorothy says." And as for Herbs, it was pleasant to see his budding manhood express itself in all sorts of little attentions to his lovely sister.

For lovely she was; there could not be two opinions on that point. A lily maid, tall and graceful, without a trace of awkwardness or self-consciousness; the exquisite complexion of the Elmores (they are a Devonshire family), warm, lovely rose on creamy white, no hint of brunette colouring; a smile which meant spring and love and other good things; and deep blue eyes reflecting the light of her smile—this was Dorothy.

Never, not even during the raptures of early married life, have I known a month of such joyous exhilaration as that which followed Dorothy's return, and I think her father would own as much.

What a month it was! There was the pleasant earthly joy of going to town to get frocks for Dorothy; then, the bewilderment of not being able to find out what suited her best.

"Anything becomes her!" exclaims Mdme. la Modiste; "that figure, that complexion, may wear anything."

And then, how pleasant it was to enter a room where all eyes were bent upon us in kindliness—our dear old friends hurrying forward to make much of the child. The deference and gentleness of her manner to these, and the warmth with which she was received by her compeers, both maidens and men; her grace in the dance; her simplicity in conversation; the perfection of her manner, which was not manner at all but her own nature, in every situation—all these added to our delight. After all, she liked best to be at home, and was more amiable and lovely with father and mother, brothers and sisters, than with the most fascinating strangers. Our good child! We had grown a little shy of speaking to her about the best things, but we knew she said her prayers: how else this outflow of sweet maiden life upon us all?

I can imagine these ramblings of mine falling into the hands of a young pair whose life is in each other: "Oh, only the outpourings of a doting mother;" and they toss the pages aside. But never believe, young people, that yours are the only ecstatic moments, yours the only experiences worth recording; wait and see.

II

These happy days had lasted for a month or more, when, one bright day in February, I remember it well, a little cloud arose. This is how it was: Dorothy had promised Elsie that she would drive her in the pony-carriage to Banford to choose a doll for May's birthday. Now, it happened that I wanted the little carriage to take to my "Mothers" at Ditchling the clothing I had bought in London with their club money. My errand could not be deferred; it must be done that day or a week later. But I did not see why the children's commission would not do as well to-morrow; and so I said, in good faith, as I was stepping into the carriage, hardly noticing the silence with which my remark was received.

I came home tired, after a long afternoon, looking forward to the welcome of the girls. The two seniors were sitting in the firelight, bright enough just then to show me Dorothy, limp and pale, in a low chair, and Elsie watching her with a perplexed and anxious expression. Dorothy did look up to say, "Are you tired, mother?" but only her eyes looked, there was nothing behind them.

"You look tired and cold enough, my dear; what has been the matter?"

"Oh, I'm very well, thank you; but I am tired, I think I'll go to bed." And she held up a cold cheek for the mother's kiss for which she offered no return. Elsie and I gazed at one another in consternation; our fairy princess, our idol—was it indeed so?—what had come to her?

"What is the matter with Dorothy? Has she a headache?"

"Oh, mother, I don't know," said the poor child, on the verge of tears. "She has been like this ever since you went, saying 'Yes,' and 'No,' and 'No, thank you,' quite kindly, but never saying a word of herself. Has any one been grieving our Dorothy, or is she going to be ill? Oh, mother, mother!"

"Nay, child, don't cry. Dorothy is overdone; you know she has been out twice this week, and three times last, and late hours don't suit her. We must take better care of her, that's all."

Elsie was comforted, but not so her mother. I believed every word I had said to the child; but all the time there was a stir in my heart like the rustling of a snake in the grass. But I put it from me.

It was with a hidden fear that I came down to breakfast. Dorothy was in the room already, doing the little duties of the breakfast table. But she was pale and still; her hands moved, her figure hung, in the limp way I had noticed the night before, Her check, a cold "Good-morning, mother," and a smile on her lips that brought no light to her eyes, was all the morning salutation I got. Breakfast was an uncomfortable, constrained meal. The children wondered what was the matter, and nobody knew. Her father got on best with Dorothy, for he knew nothing of the evening's history, so he petted her as usual, making all the more of her for her pale looks.

For a whole week this went on, and never once was I allowed to meet Dorothy eye to eye. The children were hardly better served, for they, too, had noticed something amiss; only her father could win any of the old friendliness, because he treated her as the Dorothy who had come home to us, only a little done up.

"We must have the doctor for that child, wife. Don't you see she is beginning to lose flesh, and how the roses she brought home are fading! She has no appetite and no spirits. But, why, you surely don't think our dainty moth has singed her wings already? There's nobody here, unless it's young Gardiner, and she would never waste herself on a gawky lad like that!"

This was a new idea, and I stopped a moment to consider, for I knew of at least half-a-dozen young men who had been attentive to Dorothy, all to be preferred to this hobbledehoy young Gardiner. But, no! I could trace the change from the moment of my return from Ditchling. But I jumped at the notion of the doctor; it would, at any rate, take her out of herself, and—we should see.

The doctor came; said she wanted tone; advised, not physic, but fresh air, exercise, and early hours. So we all laid ourselves out to obey his directions that day, but with no success to speak of.

But the next was one of those glorious February days when every twig is holding itself stiffly in the pride of coming leafage, and the snowdrops in the garden beds lift dainty heads out of the brown earth. The joy of the spring did it. We found her in the breakfast-room, snowdrops at her throat, rosy, beaming, joyous; a greeting, sweet and tender, for each; and never had we known her talk so sparkling, her air so full of dainty freshness. There was no relapse after this sudden cure. Our good friend Dr. Evans called again, to find her in such flourishing health that ten minutes' raillery of "my poor patient" was the only attention he thought necessary. But, "H'm! Mighty sudden cure!" as he was going out, showed that he, too, found something odd in this sudden change.

In a day or two we had forgotten all about our bad week. All went well for awhile. At the end of five weeks, however, we were again pulled up—another attack of sudden indisposition, so outsiders thought. What did I think? Well, my thoughts were not enviable.

"Father, I wish you would call at Walker's and choose me some flowers for this evening." It was the evening of the Brisbanes' dance, and I had half an idea that Arthur Brisbane had made some impression on Dorothy. His state of mind was evident enough. But, without thinking twice, I interrupted with—

"Don't you think what we have in the 'house' will do, dear? Nothing could make up better than stephanotis and maidenhair."

Dorothy made no answer, and her father, thinking all was right, went off at once; he was already rather late. We thought no more of the matter for a minute or two, when, at the same moment, Elsie and I found our eyes fixed upon Dorothy. The former symptoms followed—days of pallor and indisposition, which were, at the same time, days of estrangement from us all. Again we had in Dr. Evans, "just to look at her," and this time I noticed—not without a foolish mother's resentment—that his greeting was other than cordial. "Well, young lady, and what's gone amiss this time?" he said, knitting his bushy brows, and gazing steadily at her out of the eyes which could be keen as well as kind. Dorothy flushed and fidgeted under his gaze, but gave only the cold unsatisfactory replies we had been favoured with. The prescription was as before; but again the recovery was sudden, and without apparent cause.

III

To make a long story short, this sort of thing went on, at longer or shorter intervals, through all that winter and summer and winter again. My husband, in the simplicity of his nature, could see nothing but—

"The child is out of sorts; we must take her abroad for a month or two; she wants change of air and scene."

The children were quicker-eyed; children are always quick to resent unevenness of temper in those about them. A single angry outbreak, harsh word, and you may lay yourself out to please them for months before they will believe in you again. George was the first to let the cat out of the bag.

"Dorothy is in a sulky fit again, mother; I wish she wouldn't!"

Elsie, who has her father's quick temper, was in the room.

"You naughty, ungrateful little boy, you! How can you say such a thing of Dorothy? Didn't she sit all yesterday morning making sails for your boat?"

"Yes," said George, a little mollified; "but why need she be sulky to-day? We all liked her yesterday, and I'm sure I want to, to-day!"

Now that the mask was fallen and even the children could see what was amiss, I felt that the task before me must not be put off. I had had great misgivings since the first exhibition of Dorothy's sullen temper; now I saw what must be done, and braced myself for a heavy task. But I could not act alone; I must take my husband into my confidence, and that was the worst of it.

"George, how do you account for Dorothy's fits of wretchedness?"

"Why, my dear, haven't I told you? The child is out of sorts, and must have change. We'll have a little trip up the Rhine, and perhaps into Switzerland, as soon as the weather is fit. It will be worth something to see her face light up at some things I mean to show her!"

"I doubt if there is anything the matter with her health; remember how perfectly well and happy she is between these fits of depression."

"What is it, then? You don't think she's in love, do you?"

"Not a bit of it; her heart is untouched, and her dearest loves are home loves."

My husband blew his nose, with a "Bless the little girl! I could find it in my heart to wish it might always be so with her. But what is your notion? I can see you have got to the bottom of the little mystery. Trust you women for seeing through a stone wall!"

"Each attack of what we have called 'poorliness' has been a fit of sullenness, lasting sometimes for days, sometimes for more than a week, and passing off as suddenly as it came."

My dear husband's face clouded with serious displeasure; never before had it worn such an expression for me. I had a sense of separation from him, as if we two, who had so long been one, were two once more.

"This is an extraordinary charge for a mother to bring against her child. How have you come to this conclusion?"

Already was my husband become my judge. He did not see that I was ill, agitated, still standing, and hardly able to keep my feet. And there was worse to come: how was I to go through with it?

"What causes for resentment can Dorothy conceivably have?' he repeated, in the same cold judicial tone.

"It is possible to feet resentment, it is possible to nurse resentment, to let it hang as a heavy cloud-curtain between you and all you love the best, without any adequate cause, without any cause, that you can see yourself when the fit is over!"

My voice sounded strange and distant in my own ears: I held by the back of a chair to steady myself, but I was not fainting; I was acutely alive to all that was passing in my husband's mind. He looked at me curiously, inquisitively, but not as if I belonged to him and were part and parcel of his life.

"You seem to be curiously familiar with a state of feeling which I should have judged to be the last a Christian lady would know anything about."

"Oh, husband, don't you see you are hurting me? I am not going through this anguish for nothing. I do know what it is. And if Dorothy, my poor child, suffers, it is all my fault! There is nothing bad in her but what she has got from me."

George was moved; he put his arm round me in time to save me. But I was not surprised, a few days later, to find my first grey hairs. If that hour were to be repeated, I think I could not bear it.

"Poor wife! I see; it is to yourself you have been savagely cruel, and not to our little girl. Forgive me, dear, that I did not understand at once; but we men are slow and dull. I suppose you are putting yourself (and me too) to all this pain because there is something to be gained by it. You see some way out of the difficulty, if there is one!"

"Don't say 'if there is one.' How could I go through this pain if I did not think some way of helping our daughter would come out of it?"

"Ah! appearances were against you, but I knew you loved the child all the time. Clumsy wretch that I am, how could I doubt it? But, to my mind, there are two difficulties: First, I cannot believe that you ever cherished a thought of resentment; and next, who could associate such a feeling with our child's angelic countenance? Believe me, you are suffering under a morbid fancy; it is you, and not Dorothy, who need entire change of scene and thought."

How should I convince him? And how again run the risk of his even momentary aversion? But if Dorothy were to be saved, the thing must be done. And, oh, how could he for a moment suppose that I should deal unlovingly with my firstborn?

"Be patient with me, George. I want to tell you everything from the beginning. Do you remember when you wooed me in the shady paths of our old rectory garden, how I tried hard to show you that I was not the loved and lovely home-daughter you pictured? I told you how I was cross about this and that; how little things put me out for days, so that I was under a cloud, and really couldn't speak to, or care about anybody; how, not I, but (forgive the word) my plain sister Esther, was the beloved child of the house, adored by the children, by my parents, by all the folk of the village, who must in one way or other have dealings with the parson's daughters. Do you recollect any of this?"

"Yes; but what of it? I have never for a moment rued my choice, nor wished that it had fallen on our good Esther, kindest of friends to us and ours."

"And you, dear heart, put all I said down to generosity and humility; every effort I made to show you the truth was put down to the count of some beautiful virtue, until at last I gave it up; you would only think the more of me, and think the less kindly of my dear home people, because, indeed, they didn't 'appreciate' me. How I hated the word. I'm not sure I was sorry to give up the effort to show you myself as I was. The fact is, your love made me all it believed me to be, and I thought the old things had passed away."

"Well, and wasn't I right? Have we had a single cloud upon our married life?"

"Ah, dear man, little you know what the first two years of married life were to me. If you read your newspaper, I resented it; if you spent half an hour in your smoking den, or an hour with a friend, if you admired another woman, I resented each and all, kept sulky silence for days, even for weeks. And you, all the time, thought no evil, but were sorry for your poor 'little wife,' made much of her, and loved her all the more, the more sullen and resentful she became. She was 'out of sorts,' you said, and planned a little foreign tour, as you are now doing for Dorothy. I do believe you loved me out of it at last. The time came when I felt myself hunted down by these sullen rages. I ran away, took immense walks, read voraciously, but could not help myself till our first child came; God's gift, our little Dorothy. Her baby fingers healed me as not even your love could do. But, oh, George, don't you see?"

"My poor Mary! Yes, I see; your healing was bought at the little child's expense, and the plague you felt within you was passed on to her. This, I see, is your idea; but I still believe it is a morbid fancy, and I still think my little trip will cure both mother and daughter."

"You say well, mother and daughter. The proverb should run, not, 'a burnt child dreads the fire,' but 'a burnt child will soonest catch fire!' I feel that all my old misery will come back upon me if I am to see the same thing repeated in Dorothy."

George sat musing for a minute or two, but my fear of him was gone; his face was full of tenderness for both of us.

"Do you know, Mary, I doubt if I'm right to treat this effort of yours with a high hand, and prescribe for evils I don't understand. Should you mind very much our calling our old friend, Dr. Evans, into council? I believe, after all, it will turn out to be an affair for him rather than for me."

This was worse than all. Were the miseries of this day to know no end? Should we, my Dorothy and her mother, end our days in a madhouse? I looked at my husband, and he understood.

"Nonsense, wife, not that! Now you really are absurd, and must allow me the relief of laughing at you. There, I feel better now, but I understand; a few years ago a doctor was never consulted about this kind of thing unless it was supposed to denote insanity. But we have changed all that, and you're as mad as a hatter to get the notion. You've no idea how interesting it is to hear Evans talk of the mutual relations between thought and brain, and on the other hand, between thought and character. Homely an air as he has, he is up to all that's going on. You know he went through a course of study at Leipsic, where they know more than we about the brain and its behaviour, and then, he runs across every year to keep himself abreast with the times. It isn't every country town that is blessed with such a man."

I thought I was being let down gently to the everyday level, and answered as we answer remarks about the weather, until George said—

"Well, when shall we send for Evans? The sooner we get more light on this matter, the better for all of us."

"Very well, send for him to-morrow; tell him all I have told you, and, if you like, I shall be here to answer further questions."

IV

"Mrs. Elmore is quite right; this is no morbid fancy of hers. I have observed your pretty Miss Dorothy, and had my own speculations. Now, the whole thing lies in a nutshell."

"Can you deal with our trouble, doctor?" I cried out.

"Deal with it, my dear madam? Of course I can. I am not a pupil of Weissall's for nothing. Your Dorothy is a good girl, and will yield herself to treatment. As to that, you don't want me. The doctor is only useful on the principle that lookers-on see most of the game. Once understand the thing, and it is with you the cure must lie."

"Please explain; you will find me very obedient."

"I'm not so sure of that; you know the whole of my mental property has not been gathered in Midlington. You ladies look very meek; but directly one begins to air one's theories—which are not theories, by the way, but fixed principles of belief and conduct—you scent all manner of heterodoxy, and because a valuable line of scientific thought and discovery is new to you, you take up arms, with the notion that it flies in the face of the Bible. When, as a matter of fact, every new advance in science is a further revelation, growing out, naturally, from that we already have."

"Try me, doctor; your 'doxy shall be my 'doxy if you will only take us in hand, and I shall be ready enough to believe that your science is by revelation."

"Well, here goes. In for a penny, in for a pound. In the first place, I want to do away with the sense of moral responsibility, both for yourself and Dorothy, which is wearing you out. Or, rather, I want to circumscribe its area and intensify its force. Dorothy has, perhaps, and conceivably her mother has also, inherited her peculiar temperament; but you are not immediately responsible for that. She, again, has fostered this inherited trait, but neither is she immediately responsible for the fact."

"How do you mean, doctor? That we can't help it, and must take our nature as we find it? But that is worse than ever. No; I cannot believe it. Certainly my husband has done a great deal to cure me."

"No doubt he has. And how he has done it—without intention, I dare say—I hope by-and-by to show you. Perhaps you now and then remark, What creatures of habit we are!"

"And what of that? No one can help being struck now and then with the fact; especially, no mother."

"Well, and what does this force of habit amount to ? and how do you account for it?"

"Why, I suppose it amounts to this, that you can do almost anything once you get into the way of it. Why, I don't know; I suppose it's the natural constitution of the mind."

"The 'natural constitution of the mind' is a conversational counter with whose value I am not acquainted. That you can get into the way of doing almost anything, is simple fact; but you must add, of thinking anything, of feeling anything, before you begin to limit the force of habit."

"I think I begin to see what you mean. We, my child and I, are not so much to blame now for our sullen and resentful feelings, because we have got the habit of them. But surely habits may be cured?"

"Ah, once we begin to see that, we are to blame for them. We must ask, How are we to set about the cure? What's to be done? What hopeless idiots we are, the best of us, not to see that the very existence of an evil is a demand for its cure, and that, in the moral world, there's a dock for every nettle!"

"And then, surely, the sins of the fathers visited upon the children, is a bitter law. How could Dorothy help what she inherited?"

"Dorothy could not help it, but you could; and what have you two excellent parents been about to defer until the child is budding into womanhood this cure which should have been achieved in her infancy? Surely, seventeen years ago at least, you must have seen indications of the failing which must needs be shown up now, to the poor girl's discredit."

I grew hot all over under this home thrust, while George looked half dubious, half repentant, not being quite sure where his offence lay.

"It is doubly my fault, doctor; I see it all now. When Dorothy was a child I would not face the fact. It was too awful to think my child would be as I still was. So we had many little fictions that both nurse and mother saw throug—the child was poorly, was getting her second teeth, was overdone. The same thing, only more so, went on during her schoolroom life. Dorothy was delicate, wanted stamina, must have a tonic. And this, though we had a governess who tried to convince me that it was temper and not delicacy that ailed my little girl. The worst of deceiving yourself is that you get to believe the lie. I saw much less of the schoolroom, than of the nursery party, and firmly believed in Dorothy's frequent attacks of indisposition."

"But, supposing you had faced the truth, what would you have done?"

"There is my excuse; I had no idea that anything could be done."

"Now, please, don't write me down a pagan if I try to show you what might have been done, and may yet be done."

"Doctor Evans!"

"Oh, yes, 'tis a fact; you good women are convinced that the setting of a broken limb is a work for human skill, but that the cure of a fault of disposition is for Providence alone to effect, and you say your prayers and do nothing, looking down from great heights upon us who believe that skill and knowledge come in here too, and are meant to do so in the divine scheme of things. It's startling when you come to think of it, that every pair of parents has so largely the making of their child!"

"But what of inherited failings—such cases as this of ours? "

"Precisely a case in point. Don't you see, such a case is just a problem set before parents with a, 'See, how will you work out this so as to pass your family on free from taint? '"

"That's a noble thought of yours, Evans. It gives every parent a share in working out the salvation of the world, even to thousands of generations.—Come, Mary, we're on our promotion! To pass on our children free from the blemishes they get from us is a thing worth living for."

"Indeed it is. But don't think me narrow-minded, doctor, nor that I should presume to think hard things of you men of science, if I confess that I still think the ills of the flesh fall within the province of man, but the evils of the spirit within the province of God."

"I'm not sure but that I'm of your mind; where we differ is as to the boundary-line between flesh and spirit. Now, every fault of disposition and temper, though it may have begun in error of the spirit in ourselves or in some ancestor, by the time it becomes a fault of character is a failing of the flesh, and is to be dealt with as such—that is, by appropriate treatment. Observe, I am not speaking of occasional and sudden temptations and falls, or of as sudden impulses towards good, and the reaching of heights undreamed of before. These things are of the spiritual world, and are to be spiritually discerned. But the failing or the virtue which has become habitual to us is flesh of our flesh, and must be treated on that basis whether it is to be uprooted or fostered."

"I confess I don't follow. this line of argument should make the work of redemption gratuitous. According to this theory, every parent can save his child, and every man can save himself."

"No, my dear; there you're wrong. I agree with Evans. It is we who lose the efficacy of the great Redemption by failing to see what it has accomplished. That we have still to engage in a spiritual warfare, enabled by spiritual aids, Dr Evans allows. His point is, as I understand it, why embarrass ourselves with these less material ills of the flesh which are open to treatment on the same lines, barring the drugs, as a broken limb or a disordered stomach. Don't you see how it works? We fall, and fret, and repent, and fall again; and are so over-busy with our own internal affairs, that we have no time to get that knowledge of God which is the life of the living soul?"

"All this is beyond me. I confess it is neither the creed nor the practice in which I was brought up. Meantime, how is it to affect Dorothy? That is the practical question."

Dr Evans threw a smiling "I told you so" glance at my husband, which was a little annoying; however, he went on:—

"To be sure; that is the point. Poor Dorothy is just now the occasional victim of a troop of sullen, resentful thoughts and feelings, which wear her out, shut out the sunshine, and are as a curtain between her and all she loves. Does she want these thoughts? No; she hates and deplores them on her knees, we need not doubt; resolves against them; goes through much spiritual conflict. She is a good girl, and we may be sure of all this. Now we must bring physical science to her aid. How those thoughts began we need not ask, but there they are; they go patter, patter, to and fro, to and fro, in the nervous tissue of the brain until—here is the curious point of contact between the material and the immaterial, we see by results that there is such point of contact, but how or why it is so we have not even a guess to offer—until the nervous tissue is modified under the continued traffic in the same order of thoughts. Now, these thoughts become automatic; they come of themselves, and spread and flow as a river makes and enlarges its bed. Such habit of thought is set up, and must go on indefinitely, in spite of struggles, unless—and here is the word of hope—a contrary habit is set up, diverting the thoughts into some quite new channel. Keep the thoughts running briskly in the new channel, and, behold, the old connections are broken, whilst a new growth of brain substance is perpetually taking place. The old thoughts return, and there is no place for them, and Dorothy has time to make herself think of other things before they can establish again the old links. There is, shortly, the philosophy of ordering our thoughts—the first duty of us all."

"That is deeply interesting, and should help us. Thank you very much; I had no idea that our thoughts were part and parcel, as it were, of any substance. But I am not sure yet how this is to apply to Dorothy. It seems to me that it will be very difficult for her, poor child, to bring all this to bear on herself. It will be like being put into trigonometry before you are out of subtraction."

"You are right, Mrs. Elmore, it will be a difficult piece of work, to which she will have to give herself up for two or three months. If I am not mistaken in my estimate of her, by that time we shall have a cure. But if you had done the work in her childhood, a month or two would have effected it, and the child herself would have been unconscious of effort."

"How sorry I am. Do tell me what I should have done."

"The tendency was there, we will allow; but you should never have allowed the habit of this sort of feeling to be set up. You should have been on the watch for the outward signs—the same then as now, some degree of pallor, with general limpness of attitude, and more or less dropping of the lips and eyes. The moment one such sign appeared, you should have been at hand to seize the child out of the cloud she was entering, and to let her bask for an hour or two in love and light, forcing her to meet you eye to eye, and to find love and gaiety in yours. Every sullen attack averted is so much against setting up the habit; and habit, as you know, is a chief factor in character."

"And can we do nothing for her now?"

"Certainly you can. Ignore the sullen humours let gay life go on as if she was not there, only drawing her into it now and then by an appeal for her opinion, or for her laugh at a joke. Above all, when good manners compel her to look up, let her meet unclouded eyes, full of pleasure in her; for, believe, whatever cause of offence she gives to you, she is far more deeply offensive to herself. And you should do this all the more because, poor girl, the brunt of the battle will fall upon her."

"I see you are right; all along, her sullenness has given away before her father's delight in her, and indeed it is in this way that my husband has so far cured me. I suppose you would say he had broken the habit. But won't you see her and talk to her? I know you can help her most."

"Well, to tell you the truth, I was going to ask you if I might; her sensitive nature must be gently handled; and, just because she has no such love for me as for her parents, I run less risk of wounding her. Besides, I have a secret to tell which should help her in the management of herself."

"Thank you, Evans; we are more grateful than I can say. Will you strike while the iron's hot? Shall we go away and send her to you, letting her suppose it is a mere medical call?"

V

"Good morning, Miss Dorothy; do you know I think it's quite time this state of things should come to an end. We are both tired of the humbug of treating you for want of health when you are quite strong and well."

Dorothy looked up with flushed face (I had it all later from both Dr Evans and Dorothy herself), and eyes half relieved, half doubtful, but not resentful, and stood quietly waiting.

"All the same, I think you are in a bad way, and are in great need of help. Will you bear with me while I tell you what is the matter, and how you may be cured?"

Dorothy was past speaking, and gave a silent assent.

"Don't be frightened, poor child; I don't speak to hurt you, but to help. A considerable part of a life which should be all innocent gaiety of heart, is spent in gloom and miserable isolation. Some one fails to dot his i's, and you resent it, not in words or manner, being too well brought up; but the light within you is darkened by a flight of black thoughts. He (or she) shouldn't have done it! It's too bad! They don't care how they hurt me!

I should never have done so to her!—and so on without end. Presently you find yourself swathed in a sort of invisible shroud; you cannot reach out a living hand to anybody, nor speak in living tones, nor meet your dear ones eye to eye with a living and loving glance. There you sit, like a dead man at the feast. By this time you have forgotten the first offence, and would give the world to get out of this death-in-life. You cry, you say your prayers, beg to be forgiven and restored, but your eyes are fixed upon yourself as a hateful person, and you are still wrapped in the cloud; until, suddenly (no doubt in answer to your prayers), a hug from little May, the first primrose of the year, a lark, filling the world with his gladness, and, presto! the key is turned, the enchanted princess liberated, glad as the lark, sweet as the flower, and gay as the bright child!"

No answer: Dorothy's arms were on the table, and her face hidden upon them. At last she said in a choked voice—"Please go on, doctor!"

"All this may be helped" (she looked up), "may, within two or three months, be completely cured, become a horrid memory and nothing more!"

Dorothy raised streaming eyes, where the light of hope was struggling with fear and shame.

"This is very trying for you, dear child! But I must get on with my task, and when I have done, it's my belief you'll forget the pain for joy. In the first place, you are not a very wicked girl because these ugly thoughts master you; I don't say, mind you, that you will be without offence once you get the key between your fingers; but as it is, you need not sit in judgment on yourself any more."

Then Dr Evans went on to make clear to Dorothy what he had already made clear to us of the interaction of thought and brain; how that Thought, Brain & Co. were such close allies that nobody could tell which of the two did what: that they even ran a business of their own, independently of Ego, who was supposed to be the active head of the firm, and so on.

Dorothy listened with absorbed intentness, as if every word were saving; but the light of hope died slowly out.

"I think I see what you mean; these black thoughts come and rampage even against the desire of the Ego, I, myself. but, oh doctor, don't you see, that's all the worse for me?"

"Stop a bit, stop a bit, my dear young lady, I have not done yet. Ego sees things are going wrong and asserts himself; sets up new thoughts in a new course, and stops the old traffic; and in course of time, and a very short time too, the old nerve connections are broken, and the old way under tillage; no more opening for traffic there. Have you got it?"

"I think so. I'm to think of something else, and soon there will be no room in the brain for the ugly thoughts which distress me. But that's just the thing I can't do!"

"But that is exactly the only thing you have power to do! Have you any idea what the will is, and what are its functions?"

"I don't know much about it. I suppose your will should make you able to do the right thing when you feel you can't! You should say, 'I will,' and go and do it. But you don't know how weak I am. It makes no difference to me to say, I will!"

"Well, now, to own up honestly, I don't think it ever made much difference to anybody outside of the story-books. All the same, Will is a mighty fellow in his own way, but he goes with a sling and a stone, and not with the sword of Goliath. He attacks the giant with what seems a child's plaything, and the giant is slain. This is how it works. When ill thoughts begin to molest you, turn away your mind with a vigorous turn, and think of something else. I don't mean think good forgiving thoughts, perhaps you are not ready for that yet; but think of something interesting and pleasant; the new dress you must plan, the friend you like best, the book you are reading; best of all, fill heart and mind suddenly with some capital plan for giving pleasure to some poor body whose days are dull. The more exciting the thing you think of, the safer you are. Never mind about fighting the evil thought. This is the one thing you have to do; for this is, perhaps, the sole power the will has. It enables you to change your thoughts; to turn yourself round from gloomy thoughts to cheerful ones. Then you will find that your prayers will be answered, for you will know what to ask for, and will not turn your back on the answer when it comes. There, child, I have told you the best secret I know—given to me by a man I revere—and have put into your hands the key of self-government and a happy life. Now you know how to be better than he that taketh a city."

"Thank you a thousand times for your precious secret. You have lifted my feet out of the slough. I will change my thoughts (may I say that?). You shall find that your key does not rust for want of use. I trust I may be helped never to enter that cloud again."

It is five years since Dorothy had that talk in the library with Dr Evans (he died within the year, to our exceeding regret). What battles she fought we never heard; never again was the subject alluded to. For two years she was our joyous home daughter; for three, she has been Arthur Brisbane's happy wife; and her little sunbeam of an Elsie—no fear that she will ever enter the cloud in which mother and grandmother were so nearly lost.

Chapter 5. Consequences

Have you ever played at "Consequences," dear reader? This is how it goes. He said to her, "It's a cold day." She said to him, "I like chocolates." The consequence was, they were both put to death, and the world said, "It serves them right."

Just so exquisitely inconsequent is the game of "consequences" in real life, at which many a child is an unwilling player, and just so arbitrary their distribution. We are all born heirs to all the Russias if a certain aptness at autocratic government can be construed into a title. Watch the children in the street play at keeping school; how the schoolmistress lavishes "handers," how she corners and canes her scholars! And the make-believe scholars enter into the game. They would do the same if they had the chance, and their turn will come.

How does it work in real life, this turn for autocracy, which, you may observe, gives zest to most of the children's games?

Little Nancy is inclined to be fretful; her nurse happens to be particularly busy this morning looking out the children's summer clothing. She is a kind-hearted woman, and fond of Nancy, but, "Why does the child whine so?" And a hasty box on the little ear emphasizes the indignant query. There is mischief already, which is the cause of the whining; and, by that concussion, Nancy is "put to death," like the people in the game; not for a year or two, though, and nobody associates nurse with the family sorrow; and she, for her part, never thinks again of that hasty blow. But, you object, nurse is ignorant, though kind; with the child's parents, it is otherwise. Yes, but not entirely otherwise. Mr. Lindsay, who is a book-lover, goes into his den to find his little boy of four, making "card-houses," with some choice volumes he has clambered after; down they go, bump, and the corners are turned, and the books unsightly objects evermore. "What are you doing here, child? Go to the nursery, and don't let me see you here again!" Ah, me! Does he know how deep it cuts? Does he know that the ten minutes' romp with "father" in his room is the supreme joy of the day for little Dick? And does he know that everything is for ever and ever to a little child, whose experience has not yet taught him the trick of hoping when things look dark? But, "It is for the child's good." Is it? Dick does not yet know what is wrong. "Never touch books which are not given you to play with," would have instructed him, and hindered similar mischief in the future.

How is it that devoted nurse and affectionate father cause injurious "concussions," moral and physical, to a child's tender nature? A good deal is to be set down to ignorance or thoughtlessness; they do not know, or they do not consider, how this and that must affect a child. But the curious thing is, that grown-up people nearly always err on the same lines.

The arbitrary exercise of authority on the part of parent, nurse, governess, whoever is set in authority over him, is the real stone of stumbling and rock of offence in the way of many a child.

Nor is there room for the tender indulgent mother to congratulate herself and say, "I always thought Mrs. Naybor was too hard on her children," for the most ruinous exercise of arbitrary authority is when the mother makes herself a law unto her child, with power to excuse him from his duties, and to grant him (more than papal) indulgences. This sort of tender parent is most tenacious of her authority, no one is permitted to interfere with her rule—for rule it is, though her children are notably unruly. She answers all advice and expostulation with one formula: "My children shall never have it to say that their mother refused them anything it was in her power to give."

"In her power." This mother errs in believing that her children are hers—in her power, body and soul. Can she not do what she likes with her own?

It is worth while to took to the springs of conduct in human nature for the source of this common cause of the mismanagement of children. There must be some unsuspected reason for the fact that persons of weak and of strong nature should err in the same direction.

In every human being there are implanted, as we know, certain so-called primary or natural desires, which are among the springs or principles out of which his action or conduct flows. These desires are neither virtuous nor vicious in themselves: they are quite involuntary: they have place equally in the savage and the savant: he who makes his appeal to any one of those primary desires is certain of a hearing. Thus, every man has an innate desire for companionship: every man wants to know, however little worthy the objects of his curiosity: we all want to stand well with our neighbours, however fatuously we lay ourselves out for esteem: we would, each of us, fain be the best at some one thing, if it be only a game of chance which excites our emulation; and we would all have rule, have authority, even if our ambition has no greater scope than the rule of a dog or a child affords. These desires being primary or natural, the absence of any one of them in a human being makes that person, so far, unnatural. The man who hates society is a misanthrope; he who has no curiosity is a clod. But, seeing that a man may make shipwreck of his character and his destiny by the excessive indulgence of any one of these desires, the regulating, balancing, and due ordering of these springs of action is an important part of that wise self-government which is the duty of every man.

It is not that the primary desires are the only springs of action; we all know that the affections, the appetites, the emotions, play their part, and that reason and conscience are the appointed regulators of machinery which may be set in motion by a hundred impulses. But the subject for our consideration is the punishments inflicted on children—and we shall not arrive at any safe conclusion unless we regard these punishments from the point of view of the punisher as well as from that of the punished.

Now every one of the primary desires, as well as of the affections and appetites, has a tendency to run riot if its object be well within its grasp. The desire for society undirected and unregulated may lead to endless gadding about and herding together. The fine principle of curiosity may issue in an inordinate love of gossip, and of poor disconnected morsels of knowledge served up in scraps, which are of the nature of gossip. Ambition, the desire of power, comes into play when we have a live thing to order; and we rule child and servant, horse and dog. And it is well that we should. The person who is (comparatively) without ambition has no capacity to rule. Have you a nurse who "manages" children well? She is an ambitious woman, and her ambition finds delightful scope in the government of the nursery. At the same time, the love of power, unless it be duly and carefully regulated and controlled, leads to arbitrary behaviour—that is, to lawless, injurious behaviour—towards those under our rule. Nay, we may be so carried away, intoxicated, by a fierce lust of power that we do some terrible, irrevocable deed of cruelty to a tender child—body or soul, and wake up to never-ending remorse. We meant no harm; we meant to teach obedience, and, good God! we have killed a child.

Within the last few years tales have been told in the newspapers of the savage abuse of power, free for the time being from external control; tales, which, be they true or not, should make us all commune with our hearts and be still. For, we may believe it, they who have done these things are no worse than we could be; they had opportunity to do ill deeds, and they did them. We have not been so far left to ourselves. But let us look ourselves in the face; let us recognise that the principle which has betrayed others into the madness of crime is inherent in us also, and that whether it shall lead us to heights of noble living or to criminal cruelty is not a matter to be left to the chapter of accidents. We have need of the divine grace to prevent and follow us, and we have need to seek consciously, and diligently use this grace to keep us who are in authority in the spirit of meekness, remembering always that the One who is entrusted with the rod of iron is meek and lowly of heart.

In proportion as we keep ourselves fully alive to our tendency in this matter of authority may we trust ourselves to administer the law to creatures so tender in body and soul as are the little children. We shall remember that a word may wound, that a look may strike as a blow. It may indeed be necessary to wound in order to heal, but we shall examine ourselves well before we use the knife. There will be no hasty dealing out of reproof and punishment, reward and praise, according to the manner of mood we are in. We shall not only be aware that our own authority is deputed, and to be used with the meekness of wisdom; but we shall be very careful indeed in our choice of the persons in whose charge we place our children. It is not enough that they be good Christian people. We all know good Christian persons of an arbitrary turn who venture to wield that rod of iron which is safe in the hands of One alone. Let them be good Christian persons of culture and self-knowledge; not the morbid self-knowledge that comes of introspection, but that wider, humbler cognisance of self that comes of a study of the guiding principles and springs of action common to us all as human beings, and which brings with it the certainty that—"I am just such an one as the rest, and might even be as the worst, were it not for the grace of God and careful walking."

It is no doubt much easier to lay down our authority and let the children follow their own lead, or be kept in order by another, than to exercise constant watchfulness in the exercise of our calling. But this is not in our option; we must rule with diligence. It is necessary for the children that we should; but we must keep ourselves continually in check, and see that our innate love of power finds lawful outlet in the building up of a child's character, and not in the rude rebuff, the jibe and sneer, the short answer and hasty slap which none of us older people could conceivably endure ourselves, and yet practise freely on the children "for their good."

"To this day," says an American author (Bits of Talk about House Matters, by Helen Hunt Jackson), "the old tingling pain burns my cheeks as I recall certain rude and contemptuous words which were said to me when I was very young, and stamped on my memory forever. I was once called 'a stupid child' in the presence of strangers. I had brought the wrong book from my father's study. Nothing could be said to me today which would give me a tenth part of the hopeless sense of degradation which came from those words. Another time, on the arrival of an unexpected guest to dinner, I was sent, in a great hurry, away from the table to make room, with the remark that 'it was not of the least consequence about the child; she could just as well have her dinner afterward.' 'The child' would have been only too happy to help in the hospitality of the sudden emergency if the thing had been differently put; but the sting of having it put that way I never forgot. Yet, in both these instances, the rudeness was so small in comparison with what we habitually see that it would be too trivial to mention, except for the bearing of the fact that the pain it gave has lasted until now."

"What, is it severity in these maudlin days to call a child 'stupid'? A pretty idiot he'll make of himself when the world comes to bandy names with him if he's to be brought up on nothing but the butter and honey of soft speeches." This is a discordant protest, not at all in harmony with the notions of perfect child-living with which we are amusing ourselves in these days; but we cannot afford to turn a deaf ear to it. "Don't make a fool of the child," was the warning young mothers used to get from their elders. But we have changed all that, and a child's paradise must be prepared for the little feet to walk in. "He's so happy at school" we are told, and we ask no more. We have reversed the old order; it used to be, "If he's good, he will be happy"; now we say, "If he's happy, he will be good." Goodness and happiness are regarded as convertible terms, only we like best to put "happy" as the cause, and "good" as the consequent. And the child brought up on these lines is both happy and good without much moral effort of self-compelling on his own part, while our care is to surround him with happy-making circumstances until he has got into the trick, as it were, of being good.

But there's something rotten in the state of Denmark. Once upon a time there was a young mother who conceived that every mother might be the means of gracing her offspring with fine teeth: "For," said she, "it stands to reason that for every year of wear and grind you save the child's teeth, the man will have a fine set a year the longer." "Nonsense, my dear madam,' said the doctor, "you are ruining the child's teeth with all this pappy food; they'll be no stronger than egg-shells. Give him plenty of hard crusts to crunch, a bone to gnaw; he must have something to harden his teeth upon." Just so, of the moral "teeth" by means of which the child must carve out a place for himself in this full world. He must endure hardness if you would make a man of him. Blame as well as praise, tears as well as smiles, are of human nature's daily food; pungent speech is a tool of the tongue not to be altogether eschewed in the building of character; let us call a spade a spade, and the child who brings the wrong book "stupid," whether before strangers or behind them. Much better, this, than a chamber-conference with "Mother" about every trifle, which latter is apt to lead to a habit of morbid introspection.

We are, in truth, between Scylla and Charybdis: on this side, the six-headed, many-toothed monster of our own unbridled love of power; on that, the whirlpool which would engulf the manly virtues of our poor little Ulysses. If we must choose, let it be Scylla rather than Charybdis; better lose something through the monster with the teeth, than lose ourselves in the whirlpool. But is there not a better way?

Weigh his estate and thine; accustomed, he,

To all sweet courtly usage that obtains
Where dwells the King. How, with thy utmost pains,
Canst thou produce what shall full worthy be?
One, 'greatest in the kingdom,' is with thee,
Whose being yet discerns the Father's face,
And, thence replenished, glows with constant grace
Take fearful heed lest he despised be!
Order thy goings softly, as before
A Prince; nor let thee out unmannerly
In thy rude moods and irritable: more,
Beware lest round him wind of words rave free.
Refrain thee; see thy speech be sweet and rare:
Thy ways, considered; and thine aspect, fair.

Chapter 6. Mrs. Sedley's Tale

It is strange how a moral weakness in her child gives a mother the same sense of yearning pity that she has for a bad bodily infirmity. I wonder if that is how God feels for us when we go on year by year doing the thing we hate? I think a mother gets to understand many things about the dealings of God that are not plain to others. For instance, how it helps me to say, "I believe in the forgiveness of sins," when I think of my poor little Fanny's ugly fault. Though there is some return of it nearly every day, what could I do but forgive?

But forgiveness that does not heal is like the wretched ointments with which poor people dress their wounds. In one thing I know I have not done well; I have hardly said a word to John about the poor little girl's failing, though it has troubled me constantly for nearly a year. But I think he suspects there is something wrong; we never talk quite freely about our shy, pretty Fanny. Perhaps that is one reason for it. She is such a nervous, timid little being, and looks so bewitching when the long lashes droop, the tender mouth quivers, and the colour comes and goes in her soft cheek, that we are shy of exposing, even to each other, the faults we see in our graceful, fragile little girl. Perhaps neither of us quite trusts the other to deal with Fanny and to use the knife sparingly.

But this state of things must not go on : it is a miserable thing to write down, but I cannot believe a word the child says! And the evil is increasing, Only now and then used Fanny to be detected in what we called a fib, but now the doubt lest that little mouth may be at any moment uttering a lie takes the delight out of life, and accounts for the pale looks which give my husband much concern.

For example, only within the last day or two I have noticed the following and other such examples:—

"Fanny, did you remember to give my message to cook?"

"Yes, mother."

"And what did she say?"

"That she wouldn't be able to make any jam to-day, because the fruit had not come."

I went into the kitchen shortly after, and found cook stirring the contents of a brass pan, and, sad to say, I asked no questions. It was one of Fanny's circumstantial statements of the kind I have had most reason to doubt. Did she lie because she was afraid to own that she had forgotten? Hardly so: knowing the child's sensitive nature, we have always been careful not to visit her small misdemeanours with any punishment whenever she "owned up." And then, cowardice would hardly cause her to invent so reasonable an answer for cook. Again—

"Did you meet Mrs. Fleming's children?"

"Oh Yes, mother! and Berty was so rude! He pushed Dotty off the curb-stone!"

Nurse, who was sitting by the fire with baby, raised her eyebrows in surprise, and I saw the whole thing was an invention. Another more extraordinary instance:—

"Mother, when we were in the park we met Miss Butler, just by the fountain, you know; and she kissed me, and asked me how my mother was";—said apropos of nothing, in the most quiet, easy way. I met Miss

Butler this morning, and thanked her for the kind inquiries she had been making through my little girl; and—"Do you think Fanny grown?"

Miss Butler looked perplexed; Fanny was a great favourite of hers, perhaps because of the loveliness of which her parents cannot pretend to be unaware.

"It is more than a month since I have seen the little maid, but I shall look in soon, and gladden her mother's heart with all the praises my sweet Fan deserves!"

Little she knew that shame, and not pride, dyed my cheek; but I could not disclose my Fanny's sad secret to even so near a friend.

But to talk it out with John is a different matter. He ought to know. There had I been thinking for months in a desultory kind of way as to the why and wherefore of this ingrained want of truthfulness in the child, and yet I was no nearer the solution, when a new departure in the way of lying made me at last break the ice with John; indeed, this was the only subject about which we had ever had reserves.

"Mother, Hugh was so naughty at lessons this morning! He went close up to Miss Clare while she was writing, nudged her elbow on purpose, and made her spill the ink all over the table-cloth."

I chanced to meet Miss Clare in the hall, and remarked that I heard she had found Hugh troublesome this morning.

"Troublesome? Not at all; he was quite industrious and obedient."

I said nothing about the ink, but went straight to the schoolroom, to find the table neat, as Miss Clare always leaves it, and no sign of even a fresh ink-spot. What possessed the child? This inveterate and inventive untruthfulness was like a form of mania. I sat in dismay for an hour or more, not thinking, but stunned by this new idea—that the child was not responsible for her words; and yet, could it be so? Not one of our children was so merry at play, so intelligent at lessons. Well, I would talk it over with her father without the loss of another day.

"John, I am miserable about Fanny. Do you know the child tells fibs constantly?"

"Call them lies; an ugly thing deserves an ugly name. What sort of lies? What tempts her to lie?"

John did not seem surprised. Perhaps he knew more of this misery than I supposed.

"That's the thing! Her fi— lies are so uncalled for, so unreasonable, that I do not know how to trust her."

"Unreasonable? You mean her tales don't hang together; that's a common case with liars. You know the saying—"Liars should have good memories'?"

"Don't call the poor child a liar, John; I believe she is more to be pitied than blamed. What I mean is, you can't find rhyme or reason for the lies she tells." And I gave my husband a few instances like those I have written above.

"Very extraordinary! There's a hint of malice in the Hugh and the ink-bottle tale, and a hint of cowardice in that about the jam; but for the rest, they are inventions pure and simple, with neither rhyme nor reason, as you say."

"I don't believe a bit in the malice. I was going to correct her for telling an unkind tale about Hugh, but you know how she hangs on her brother; and she told her tale with the most innocent face. I am convinced there was no thought of harming him."

"Are you equally sure that she never says what is false to cover a fault; in fact, out of cowardice? "

"No; I think I have found her out more than once in ingenious subterfuges; you know what a painfully nervous child she is. For instance, I found the other day a blue cup off that cabinet, with handle gone, hidden behind the woodwork. Fanny happened to come in at the moment, and I asked her if she knew who had broken it.

'No, mother, I don't know, but I think it was Mary, when she was dusting the cabinet; indeed, I'm nearly sure I heard a crash.'

"But the child could not meet my eye, and there was a sort of blanching as of fear about her."

"But, as a rule, you do not notice these symptoms? As a rule, poor Fanny's tarradiddles come out in the most quiet, easy way, with all the boldness of innocence; and even when she is found out, and the lie brought home to her, she looks bewildered rather than convicted."

"I wish you would banish the whole tribe of foolish and harmful expressions whose tendency is to make light of sin. Call a spade a spade. A 'tarradiddle' is a thing to make merry over; a fib you smile and wink at; but a lie—why, the soul is very far gone from original righteousness that can endure the name, even while guilty of the thing."

"That's just it; I cannot endure to apply so black a name to the failings of our child; for, do you know, I begin to suspect that poor little Fanny does it unawares—does not know in the least that she has departed from the fact. I have had a horrible dread upon me from time to time that her defect is a mental, and not a moral one: that she has not the clear perception of true and false with which most of us are blessed."

"Whe-ewl" from John; but his surprise was feigned. I could see now that he had known what was going on all the time, and had said nothing, because he had nothing to say; in his heart he agreed with me about our pretty child. The defect arose from a clouded intelligence, which showed itself in this way only, now; but how dare we look forward? Now I saw why poor John was so anxious to have the offence called by the blackest moral name. He wished to save us from the suspicion of an evil—worse, because less open to cure. We looked blankly at each other, he trying to carry the matter off with a light air, but his attempt failed.

I forgot to say that my sister Emma was staying with us, the 'clever woman of the family,' who was "going in" for all sorts of things, to come out, we believed, at the top of her profession as a lady doctor. She had taken no part in the talk about Fanny—which was rather tiresome of her, as I wanted to know what she thought; but now, while we were vainly trying to hide our dismay, she broke out into a long laugh, which seemed a little unfeeling

"Oh, you absurd parents! You are too good and earnest, and altogether too droll! Why in the world, instead of sitting there with blank eyes—conjuring up bogeys to frighten each other—why don't you look the thing in the face, and find out by the light of modern thought what really ails Fan? Poor pet! 'Save me from my parents!' is a rendering which might be forgiven her."

"Then you don't think there's any mental trouble?" we cried in a breath, feeling already as if a burden were lifted, and we could straighten our backs and walk abroad.

"'Mental trouble?' What nonsense! But there, I believe all you parents are alike. Each pair thinks their own experiences entirely new; their own children the first of the kind born into the world. Now, a mind that had had any scientific training would see at once that poor Fanny's lies—if I must use John's terrible bad word—inventions, I should have called them, are symptomatic, as you rightly guessed, Annie, of certain brain conditions; but of brain disease—oh, no! Why, foolish people, don't you see you are entertaining an angel unawares? This vice of 'lying' you are mourning over is the very quality that goes to the making of poets!"

"Poets and angels are well in their places," said John, rather crossly, "but my child must speak the truth. What she states for a fact, I must know to be a fact, according to the poor common-sense view of benighted parents."

"And there is your work as parents. Teach her truth, as you would teach her French or sums—a little to-day, a little more to-morrow, and every day a lesson. Only as you teach her the nature of truth will the gift she has be effectual. But I really should like to know what is your notion about truth—are we born with it, or educated up to it?"

"I am not sure that we care to be experimented upon, and held up to the world as blundering parents," said I; "perhaps we had better keep our crude notions to ourselves." I spoke rather tartly, I know, for I was more vexed for John than for myself that he should be held up to ridicule in his own house—by a sister of mine, too!

"Now I have vexed you both. How horrid I am! And all the time, as I watch you with the children, I don't feel good enough to tie your shoes. Don't I say to myself twenty times a day, 'After all, the insight and love parents get from above is worth a thousandfold more than all science has to teach'?"

"Nay, Emma, it is we who have to apologise for being jealous of science—that's the fact—and quick to take offence. Make it up, there's a good girl! and let Annie and me have the benefit of your advice about our little girl, for truly we are in a fog."

"Well, I think you were both right in considering that her failing had two sources: moral cowardice the first; she does something wrong, or wrong in her eyes, and does not tell—why?"

"Aye, there's the difficulty; why is she afraid to tell the truth? I may say that we have never punished her, or ever looked coldly on her for any fault but this of prevarication. The child is so timid that we feared severe measures might make truth-telling the more difficult."

"There I think you are right. And we have our finger on one of the weak places: Fanny tells lies out of sheer fear—moral weakness; causeless it may be, but there it is. And I'm not so sure that it is causeless; she is always in favour for good behaviour, gentleness, obedience, and that kind of thing; indeed, this want of veracity seems to me her one fault. Now, don't you think the fear of having her parents look coldly on her and think less well of her may be, to such a timid, clinging child, a great temptation to hide a fault?"

"Very likely; but one does not see how to act. Would you pass over her faults altogether without inquiry or notice?"

"I'm afraid you must use the knife there boldly, for that is the tenderest way in the end. Show little Fan your love—that there is no fault you cannot forgive in her, but that the one fault which hurts you most is, not to hear the exact truth."

"I see. Suppose she has broken a valuable vase and hides the fact, I am to unearth her secret—not, as I am very much inclined to do, let it lie buried for fear of involving her in worse falsehood, but show her the vase and tax her with hiding it."

"And her immediate impulse will be to say, 'I didn't.' No; make sure of your ground, then show her the pieces; say the vase was precious, but you do not mind about that; the thing that hurts you is that she could not trust her mother. I can imagine one of the lovely scenes you mothers have with your children, too good for outsiders to look in upon."

The tears came into my eyes, for I could imagine the scene too. I could see the way to draw my child closer and closer by always forgiving, always comprehending and loving her, and always protesting against the falsehood which would rise between us. I was lost in a happy reverie—how I might sometime come to show her that her mother's ever-ready forgiveness was but a faint picture of what someone calls the "all-forgiving gentleness of God," when I heard John break in:—

"Yes, I can see that if we both make a point of free and tender forgiveness of every fault, on condition that she owns up, we may in time cure her of lying out of sheer fear. But I don't see that she gets the principle of truth any more. The purely inventive lies go on as before, and the child is not to be trusted."

"'Purely inventive,' there you have it. Don't you see? The child is full of imagination, and figures to herself endless scenes, evolved like the German student's camel. The thousand and one things which might happen are so real to her that the child is, as you said, bewildered; hardly able to distinguish the one which has happened. Now, it's perfect nonsense to lament over this as a moral failing—it is a want of mental balance; not that any quality is deficient, but that her conceptive power runs away with her perceptive; she sees the many things that might be more readily than the thing that is. Doesn't she delight in fairy tales? "

"Well, to tell the truth, I have thought them likely to foster her failing, and have kept her a good deal on a diet of facts."

"I shouldn't wonder if you are wrong there. An imperious imagination like Fanny's demands its proper nourishment. Let her have her daily meal: 'The Babes in the Wood,' 'The Little Match-Girl,' 'The Snow-Maiden,' tales and legends half-historic; above all, the lovely stories of the Bible; whatever she can figure to herself and live over and over; but not twaddling tales of the daily doings of children like herself, whether funny or serious. The child wants an opening into the larger world where all things are possible and where beautiful things are always happening. Give her in some form this necessary food, and her mind will be so full of delightful imaginings that she will be under no temptation to invent about the commonplaces of everyday life."

My husband laughed:—"My dear Emma, you must let us do our best with the disease; the cure is too wild! 'Behold, this dreamer cometh!'—think of sending the child through life with that label."

"Your quotation is unfortunate, and you have not heard me out. I do believe that to starve her imagination would be to do real wrong to the child. But, at the same time, you must diligently cultivate the knowledge and the love of the truth. Now, the truth is no more than the fact as it is; and it is my belief that Fanny's falsehoods come entirely from want of perception of the fact through pre-occupation of mind."

"Well, what must we do?"

"Why, give her daily, or half-a-dozen times a day, lessons in truth. Send her to the window: 'Look out, Fanny, and tell me what you see.' She comes back, having seen a cow where there is a horse. She looks again and brings a true report, and you teach her that it is not true to say the thing which is not. You send a long message to the cook, requiring the latter to write it down as she receives it and send you up the slate; if it is all right, the kiss Fanny gets is for speaking the truth: gradually, she comes to revere truth, and distinguishes between the facts of life where truth is all in all, and the wide realms of make-believe, where fancy may have free play."

"I do believe you are right, Emma; most of Fanny's falsehoods seem to be told in such pure innocence, I should not wonder if they do come out of the kingdom of make-believe. At any rate, we'll try Emma's specific—shall we, John?"

"Indeed, yes; and carefully, too. It seems to me to be reasonable, the more so, as we don't find any trace of malice in Fanny's misleading statements."

"Oh, if there were, the treatment would be less simple; first, you should deal with the malice, and then teach the love of truth in daily lessons. That is the mistake so many people make. They think their children are capable of loving and understanding truth by nature, which they are not. The best parents have to be on the watch to hinder all opportunities of misstatement."

"And now, that you may see how much we owe you, let me tell you of the painful example always before our eyes, which has done more than anything to make me dread Fanny's failing. It is an open secret, I fear, but do not let it go further out of this house. You know Mrs. Casterton, our neighbour's wife? It is a miserable thing to say, but you cannot trust a word she utters. She tells you, Miss So-and-So has a bad kind of scarlet fever, and even while she is speaking you know it to be false; husband, children, servants, neighbours, none can be blind to the distressing fact, and she has acquired the sort of simpering manner a woman gets when she loses respect and self-respect. What if Fanny had grown up like her?"

"Poor woman! and this shame might have been spared her, had her parents been alive to their duty."

Chapter 7. Ability

"Be sure you call at Mrs. Milner's, Fred, for the address of her laundress."

"All right, mother!" And Fred was half-way down the path before his mother had time to add a second injunction. A second? Nay, a seventh, for this was already the sixth time of asking; and Mrs. Bruce's half-troubled expression showed she placed little faith in her son's "All right."

"I don't know what to do with Fred, doctor; I am not in the least sure he will do my message. Indeed, to speak honestly, I am sure he will not. This is a trifling matter; but when the same thing happens twenty times a day—when his rule is to forget everything he is desired to remember—it makes us anxious about the boy's future."

Dr Maclehose drummed meditatively on the table, and put his lips into form for a whistle. This remark of Mrs. Bruce's was "nuts" to him. He had assisted, professionally, at the appearance of the nine young Bruces, and the family had no more esteemed friend and general confidant. For his part, he liked the Bruces. Who could help it? The parents, intelligent and genial, the young folk well looking, well grown, and open-hearted, they were just the family to make friends. All the same, the doctor found in the Bruces occasion to mount his pet hobby:—"My Utopia is the land where the family doctor has leave to play schoolmaster to the parents. To think of a fine brood like the young Bruces running to waste in half-a-dozen different ways through the invincible ignorance of father and mother! Nice people, too!"

For seventeen years, Dr Maclehose had been deep in the family counsels, yet never till now had he seen the way to put in his oar anent any question of the bringing up of the children. Wherefore he drummed on the table, and pondered:—"Fair and softly, my good fellow; fair and softly! Make a mess of it now, and it's your last chance; hit the nail on the head, and, who knows?"

"Does the same sort of thing go on about his school work?"

"Precisely; he is always in arrears. He has forgotten to take a book, or to write an exercise, or learn a lesson; in fact, his school life is a record of forgets and penalties."

"Worse than that Dean of Canterbury, whose wife would make him keep account of his expenditure; and thus stood the entries for one week:—'Gloves, 5s.; Forgets, £4, 15s.' His writing was none too legible, so his wife, looking over his shoulder, cried, 'Faggots! Faggots! What in the world! Have you been buying wood?' 'No, my dear; those are forgets:'—his wife gave it up."

"A capital story; but what is amusing in a Dean won't help a boy to get through the world, and we are both uneasy about Fred."

"He is one of the 'School Eleven,' isn't he?"

"Oh yes, and is wild about it: and there, I grant you, he never forgets. It's, 'Mother, get cook to give us an early dinner: we must be on the field by two!' 'Don't forget to have my flannels clean for Friday, will you, mumsy?' he knows when to coax. 'Subscription is due on Thursday, mother!' and this, every day till he gets the money."

"I congratulate you, my dear friend; there's nothing seriously amiss with the boy's brain."

"Good heavens, doctor! Whoever thought there was? You take my breath away!"

"Well, well, I didn't mean to frighten you, but, don't you see, it comes to this: either it's a case of chronic disease, open only to medical treatment, if to any; or it is just a case of defective education, a piece of mischief bred of allowance which his parents cannot too soon set themselves to cure."

Mrs. Bruce was the least in the world nettled at this serious view of the case. It was one thing for her to write down hard things of her eldest boy, the pride of her heart, but a different matter for another to take her au sérieux.

"But, my dear doctor, are you not taking a common fault of youth too seriously? It's tiresome that he should forget so, but give him a year or two, and he will grow out of it, you'll see. Time will steady him. It's just the volatility of youth, and for my part I don't like to see a boy with a man's head on his shoulders." The doctor resumed his drumming on the table. He had put his foot in it already, and confounded his own foolhardiness.

"Well, I daresay you are right in allowing something on the score of youthful volatility; but we old doctors, whose business it is to study the close connection between mind and matter, see our way to only one conclusion, that any failing of mind or body, left to itself, can do no other than strengthen."

"Have another cup of tea, doctor? I am not sure I understand. I know nothing about science. You mean that Fred will become more forgetful and less dependable the older he gets?"

"I don't know that I should have ventured to put it so baldly, but that's about the fact. But, of course, circumstances may give him a bent in the other direction, and Fred may develop into such a careful old sobersides that his mother will be ashamed of him."

"Don't laugh at me, doctor; you make the whole thing too serious for a laughing matter." To which there was no answer, and there was silence in the room for the space of fully three minutes, while the two pondered.

"You say," in an imperious tone, "that 'a fault left to itself must strengthen.' What are we to do? His father and I wish, at any rate, to do our duty." Her ruffled maternal plumage notwithstanding, Mrs. Bruce was in earnest, all her wits on the alert. "Come, I've scored one!" thought the doctor; and then, with respectful gravity, which should soothe any woman's amour propre,—

"You ask a question not quite easy to answer. But allow me, first, to try and make the principle plain to you: that done, the question of what to do settles itself. Fred never forgets his cricket or other pleasure engagements? No? And why not? Because his interest is excited; therefore his whole attention is fixed on the fact to be remembered. Now, as a matter of fact, what you have regarded with full attention, it is next to impossible to forget. First, get Fred to fix his attention on the matter in hand, and you may be sure he won't forget it."

"That may be very true; but how can I make a message to Mrs. Milner as interesting to him as the affairs of his club?"

"Ah! There you have me. Had you begun with Fred at a year old the thing would have settled itself. The habit would have been formed."

To the rescue, Mrs. Bruce's woman's wit:—"I see; he must have the habit of paying attention, so that he will naturally take heed to what he is told, whether he cares about the matter or not."

"My dear madam, you've hit it; all except the word 'naturally.' At present Fred is in a delightful state of nature in this and a few other respects. But the educational use of habit is to correct nature. If parents would only see this fact, the world would become a huge reformatory, and the next generation, or, at any rate, the third, would dwell in the kingdom of heaven as a regular thing, and not by fits and starts, and here and there, which is the best that happens to us."

"I'm not sure I see what you mean; but," said this persistent woman, "to return to this habit of attention which is to reform my Fred—do try and tell me what to do. You gentlemen are so fond of going off into general principles, while we poor women can grasp no more than a practical hint or two to go on with. My boy would be cut up to know how little his fast friend, 'the doctor,' thinks of him!"

"'Poor women,' truly! and already you have thrown me with two staggering buffets. My theories have no practical outcome, and I think little of Fred, who has been my choice chum ever since he left off draperies! It remains for the vanquished to 'behave pretty.' Pray, ma'am, what would you like me to say next?"

"To 'habit,' doctor, to 'habit'; and don't talk nonsense while the precious time is going. We'll suppose that Fred is just twelve months old today. Now, if you please, tell me how I'm to make him begin to pay attention. And, by the way, why in the world didn't you talk to me about it when the child really was young?"

"I don't remember that you asked me; and who would be pert enough to think of schooling a young mother? Not I, at any rate. Don't I know that every mother of a first child is infallible, and knows more about children than all the old doctors in creation? But, supposing you had asked me, I should have said—Get him each day to occupy himself a little longer with one plaything than he did the day before. He plucks a daisy, gurgles over it with glee, and then in an instant it drops from the nerveless grasp. Then you take it up, and with the sweet coaxings you mothers know how to employ, get him to examine it, in his infant fashion, for a minute, two minutes, three whole minutes at a time."

"I see; fix his thoughts on one thing at a time, and for as long as you can, whether on what he sees or what he hears. You think if you go on with that sort of thing with a child from his infancy he gets accustomed to pay attention?"

"Not a doubt of it; and you may rely on it that what is called ability—a different thing from genius, mind you, or even talent—ability is simply the power of fixing the attention steadily on the matter in hand, and success in life turns upon this cultivated power far more than on any natural faculty. Lay a case before a successful barrister, an able man of business, notice how he absorbs all you say; tell your tale as ill as you like, he keeps the thread, straightens the tangle, and by the time you have finished, has the whole matter spread out in order under his mind's eye. Now comes in talent, or genius, or what you will, to deal with the facts he has taken in. But attention is the attribute of the trained intellect, without which genius makes shots in the dark."

"But, don't you think attention itself is a natural faculty, or talent, or whatever we should call it?"

"Not a bit of it; it is entirely the result of training. A man may be born with some faculty or talent for figures, or drawing, or music, but attention is a different matter; it is simply the power of bending such powers as one has to the work in hand; it is a key to success within the reach of every one, but the skill to turn it comes of training. Circumstances may compel a man to train himself, but he does so at the cost of great effort, and the chances are ten to one against his making the effort. For the child, on the other hand, who has been trained by his parents to fix his thoughts, all is plain sailing. He will succeed, not a doubt of it."

"But I thought school-work, Latin and mathematics, and that sort of thing, should give this kind of intellectual training? "

"They should; but it's the merest chance whether the right spring is touched, and from what you say of Fred's school-work, I should say it has not been touched in his case. It is incredible how much solid learning a boy will contrive to let slip by him instead of into him! No; I'm afraid you must tackle the difficulty yourself. It would be a thousand pities to let a fine fellow like Fred run to waste."

"What can I do?"

"Well, we must begin where we are; Fred can attend, and therefore remember: and he remembers what interests him. Now, to return to your question. How are you to make a message to Mrs. Milner as interesting to him as the affairs of his cricket club? There is no interest in the thing itself; you must put interest into it from without. There are a hundred ways of doing this: try one, and when that is used up, turn to another. Only, with a boy of Fred's age, you cannot form the habit of attention as you could with a child. You can only aid and abet; give the impulse; the training he must do for himself."

"Make it a little plainer, doctor; I have not yet reduced your remarks to the practical level of something I can do."

"No? Well, Fred must train himself, and you must feed him with motives. Run over with him what we have been saying about attention. Let him know how the land lies; that you cannot help him, but that if he wants to make a man of himself he must make himself attend and remember. Tell him it will be a stand-up fight, for this habit is contrary to nature. He will like that; it is boy nature to show fight, and the bigger and blacker you make the other side, the more will he like to pitch in. When I was a boy I had to fight this very battle for myself, and I'll tell you what I did. I stuck up a card every week, divided down the middle. One side was for 'Remembers'; the other side for 'Forgets.' I took myself to task every night—the very effort was a help—and put a stroke for every 'Remember' and 'Forget' of the day. I scored for every 'Remember,' and t'other fellow' for every 'Forget.' You don't know how exciting it got. If by Thursday I had thirty-three 'Remembers' and he thirty-six 'Forgets,' it behoved me to look alive; it was not only that 'Forget' might win the game, which was up on Saturday night, but unless 'Remember' scored ten in advance, the game was 'drawn'—hardly a remove from lost."

"That's delightful! But I wish, doctor, you would speak to Fred yourself. A word from you would go a long way."

"I'll look out for a chance, but an outsider cannot do much; everything rests with the boy himself, and his parents."

Chapter 8. Poor Mrs. Jumeau!

"Now, young people, when I go out, let there be no noise in the house; your mother is ill, so let her little folk be thoughtful for her!"

"Oh, is mother sick again?" said little Ned with falling countenance.

"Poor Neddie! he doesn't like mother to be ill. We all have to be so quiet; and, then, there's nowhere to be! It isn't like home when mother isn't about."

"Mary is right," chimed in Charlie, the eldest of the family; "if I were big enough, I should run away and go to sea, mother's so often bad! But, father, isn't it funny? Yesterday she was quite well, and doing all sorts of horrid things, helping the maids to clear out cupboards; and now, I daresay, she is too ill to move or speak, and tomorrow, perhaps, she'll be our jolly mother again, able to go shrimping with us, or anything else."

"That's because your dear mother has no self, Charlie, boy; no sooner does she feel a bit better than she does more than she can for us all, and then she is knocked up again. I wish we could teach her to be selfish, for our sakes as well as hers, for to have her with us is better than anything she can do for us; eh, Charlie?"

"Indeed, yes! We'd take lots of care of her if she'd let us. But her illness must be queer. You know when we had scarlet fever, father? Well, for weeks and weeks, after the fever was gone, I had no more strength than a tom-tit; and you know I could not go about and do things, however unselfish I was (but I'm not, though). That's what is so queer. Do you think Dr Prideau understands about mother?"

"Much better than you do, depend upon it, Charlie; but I confess your mother's illness is puzzling to all of us. There, children, off with you! I must write a letter or two before I go out."

Mr. Jumeau forgot to write his letters, and sat long, with his head between his hands, pondering the nature of his wife's ailments. What Charlie had put with a boy's rude bluntness had already occurred to him in a dim way. Mrs. Jumeau's illness certainly did not deprive her of bodily vigour; the attacks came on suddenly, left her as suddenly, and left her apparently in perfect health and gay spirits. And this was the more surprising because, while an "attack" lasted, the extreme prostration, pallid countenance and blue lips of the sufferer were painful to behold. Besides, his wife was so absolutely truthful by nature, so unselfish and devoted to her husband and family, that it was as likely she should be guilty of flagrant crime as that she should simulate illness. This sort of thing had gone on for several years. Mr. Jumeau had spent his substance on many physicians, and with little result. "No organic disease." "Overdone." "Give her rest, nourishing food, frequent change of scene and thought; no excitement; Nature will work the cure in time—in time, my good sir. We must be patient." This sort of thing he had heard again and again; doctors did not differ, if that were any consolation.

He went up to have a last look at the sufferer. There she lay, stretched out with limbs composed, and a rigidity of muscle terribly like death. A tear fell on the cold check of his wife as Mr. Jumeau kissed it, and he went out aching with a nameless dread, which, if put into words, would run—some day, and she will wake no more out of this death-like stillness.

And she? She felt the tear, heard the sigh, noted the dejected footfalls of her husband, and her weak pulse stirred with a movement of—was it joy? But the "attack" was not over; for hours she lay there rigid, speechless, with closed eyes, taking no notice of the gentle opening of the door now and then when one or another came to see how she was. Were not her family afraid to leave her alone? No; we get used to anything, and the Jumeaus, servants and children, were well used to these "attacks" in the mistress of the house. Dr Prideau came, sent by her husband, and used even violent measures to restore her, but to no effect; she was aware of these efforts, but was not aware that she resisted them effectually.

Business engagements were pressing, and it was late before Mr. Jumeau, anxious as he was, was able to return to his wife. It was one of those lovely warm evenings we sometimes get late in May, when even London windows are opened to let in the breath of the spring. Nearly at the end of the street he heard familiar strains from Parsifal, played with the vigour Wagner demands. His wife? It could be no one else. As he drew nearer, her exquisite touch was unmistakable. The attack was over, then? Strange to say, his delight was not unmixed. What were these mysterious attacks, and how were they brought on?

The evening was delightful. Mrs. Jumeau was in the gayest spirits: full of tenderness towards her husband, of motherly thought for her children, now fast asleep; ready to talk brightly on any subject except the attack of the morning; any allusion to this she would laugh off as a matter of too little consequence to be dwelt upon. The next morning she was down bright and early, having made up her mind to a giro with the children. They did not go a-shrimping, according to Charlie's forecast, but Kew was decided upon as "just the thing," and a long day in the gardens failed to tire mother or children.

"I must get to the bottom of this," thought Mr. Jumeau.

"Your question is embarrassing; if I say, Mrs. Jumeau is suffering from hysteria, you will most likely get a wrong notion and discredit my words."

Mr. Jumeau's countenance darkened. "I should still be inclined to trust the evidence of my senses, and believe that my wife is unfeignedly ill."

"Exactly as I expected: simulated ailments and hysteria are hopelessly confounded; but no wonder; hysteria is a misnomer, used in the vaguest way, not even confined to women. Why, I knew a man, a cleryman in the North, who suffered from 'clergyman's sore throat'; he was a popular evangelical preacher, and there was no end to the sympathy his case evoked; he couldn't preach, so his devoted congregation sent him, now to the South of France, now to Algiers, now to Madeira. After each delightful sojourn he returned, looking plump and well, but unable to raise his voice above a hardly audible whisper. This went on for three years or so. Then his Bishop interfered; he must provide a curate in permanent charge, with nearly the full emoluments of the living. The following Sunday he preached, nor did he again lose his voice. And this was an earnest and honest man, who would rather any day be at his work than wandering idly about the world. Plainly, too, in the etymological sense of the word, his complaint was not hysteria. But this is not an exceptional case—keep any man in his dressing-gown for a week or two—a bad cold, say—and he will lay himself out to be pitied and petted, will have half the ailments under the sun, and be at death's door with each. And this is your active man; a man of sedentary habits, notwithstanding his stronger frame, is nearly as open as a woman to the advances of this stealthy foe. Why, for what matter, I've seen it in a dog! Did you never see a dog limp pathetically on his three legs that he might be made much of for his lameness, until his master's whistle calls him off at a canter on all fours?"

"I get no nearer; what have these illustrations to do with my wife?"

"Wait a bit, and I'll try to show you. The throat would seem to be a common seat of the affection. I knew a lady—nice woman she was, too—who went about for years speaking in a painful whisper, whilst everybody said, 'Poor Mrs. Marjoribanks!' But one evening she managed to set her bed-curtains alight, and she rushed to the door, screaming, 'Ann! Ann! the house is on fire! Come at once!' The dear woman believed ever after, that 'something burst' in her throat, and described the sensation minutely; her friends believed, and her doctor did not contradict. By the way, no remedy has proved more often effectual than a house on fire, only you will see the difficulties. I knew of a case, however, where the 'house-afire' prescription was applied with great effect. It was in a London hospital for ladies; a most baffling case; patient had been for months unable to move a limb—was lifted in and out of bed like a log, fed as you would pour into a bottle. A clever young house-surgeon laid a plot with the nurses. In the middle of the night her room was filled with fumes, lurid light, etc. She tried to cry out, but the smoke was suffocating; she jumped out of bed and made for the door—more choking smoke—threw up the sash—fireman, rope-ladder—she scrambled down, and was safe. The whole was a hoax, but it cured her, and the nature of the cure was mercifully kept secret. Another example: A friend of mine determined to put a young woman under 'massage' in her own home; he got a trained operator, forbade any of her family to see her, and waited for results. The girl did not mend; 'Very odd! some reason for this,' he thought; and it came out that every night the mother had crept in to wish her child goodnight; the tender visits were put a stop to, and the girl recovered."

"Your examples are interesting enough, but I fail to see how they bear; in each case, you have a person of weak or disordered intellect simulating a disease with no rational object in view. Now the beggars who know how to manufacture sores on their persons have the advantage—they do it for gain."

"I have told my tale badly; these were not persons of weak or disordered intellect; some of them very much otherwise; neither did they consciously simulate disease; not one believed it possible to make the effort he or she was surprised into. The whole question belongs to the mysterious borderland of physical and psychological science—not pathological, observe; the subject of disease and its treatment is hardly for the lay mind."

"I am trying to understand."

"It is worth your while; if every man took the pains to understand the little that is yet to be known on this interesting subject he might secure his own household, at any rate, from much misery and waste of vital power; and not only his household, but perhaps himself—for, as I have tried to show, this that is called 'hysteria' is not necessarily an affair of sex."

"Go on; I am not yet within appreciable distance of anything bearing on my wife's case."

"Ah, the thing is a million-headed monster! hardly to be recognised by the same features in any two cases. To get at the rationale of it, we must take up human nature by the roots. We talk glibly in these days of what we get from our forefathers, what comes to us through our environment, and consider that in these two we have the sum of human nature. Not a bit of it; we have only accounted for some peculiarities in the individual; independently of these, we come equipped with stock for the business of life of which too little account is taken. The subject is wide, so I shall confine myself to an item or two.

"We all come into the world—since we are beings of imperfect nature—subject to the uneasy stirrings of some few primary desires. Thus, the gutter child and the infant prince are alike open to the workings of the desire for esteem, the desire for society, for power, etc. One child has this, and another that desire more active and uneasy. Women, through the very modesty and dependence of their nature, are greatly moved by the desire for esteem. They must be thought of, made much of, at any price. A man desires esteem, and he has meetings in the market-place, the chief-room at the feast; the pétroleuse, the city outcast, must have notoriety—the esteem of the bad—at any price, and we have a city in flames, and Whitechapel murders. Each falls back on his experience and considers what will bring him that esteem, a gnawing craving after which is one of his earliest immaterial cognitions. But the good woman has comparatively few outlets. The esteem that comes to her is all within the sphere of her affections. Esteem she must have; it is a necessity of her nature:

'Praise, blame, love, kisses, tears, and smiles,'

are truly to her, 'human nature's daily food.'

"Now, experience comes to her aid. When she is ill, she is the centre of attraction, the object of attention, to all who are dear to her; she will be ill."

"You contradict yourself, man! don't you see? You are painting, not a good woman, but one who will premeditate and act a lie!"

"Not so fast! I am painting a good woman. Here comes in a condition which hardly anyone takes into account. Mrs. Jumeau will lie with stiffened limbs and blue pale face for hours at a time. Is she simulating illness? You might as well say that a man could simulate a gunshot wound. But the thing people forget is, the intimate relation and co-operation of body and mind; that the body lends itself involuntarily to carry out the conceptions of the thinking brain. Mrs. Jumeau does not think herself into pallor, but every infinitesimal nerve fibre, which entwines each equally infinitesimal capillary which brings colour to the check, is intimately connected with the thinking brain, in obedience to whose mandates it relaxes or contracts. Its relaxation brings colour and vigour with the free flow of the blood; its contraction, pallor and stagnation; and the feeling as well as the look of being sealed in a death-like trance. The whole mystery depends on this co-operation of thought and substance of which few women are aware. The diagnosis is simply this, the sufferer has the craving for outward tokens of the esteem which is essential to her nature; she recalls how such tokens accompany her seasons of illness, the sympathetic body perceives the situation, and-she is ill; by and by, the tokens of esteem cease to come with the attacks of illness, but the habit has been set up, and she goes on having 'attacks' which bring real suffering to herself, and of the slightest agency in which she is utterly unconscious."

Conviction slowly forced itself on Mr. Jumeau; now that his wife was shown entirely blameless, he could concede the rest. More, he began to suspect something rotten in the State of Denmark, or women like his wife would never have been compelled to make so abnormal a vent for a craving proper to human nature.

"I begin to see; what must I do?"

"In Mrs. Jumeau's case, I may venture to recommend a course which would not answer with one in a thousand. Tell her all I have told you. Make her, mistress of the situation.—I need not say, save her as much as you can from the distress of self-contempt. Trust her, she will come to the rescue, and devise means to save herself; and, all the time, she will want help from you, wise as well as tender. For the rest, those who have in less measure—

"'The reason firm, the temperate will'—

'massage,' and other devices for annulling the extraordinary physical sensibility to mental conditions, and, at the same time, excluding the patient from the possibility of the affectionate notice she craves, may do a great deal. But this mischief which, in one shape or other, blights the lives of too many of our best and most highly organised women, is one more instance of how lives are ruined by an education which is not only imperfect, but proceeds on wrong lines."

"How could education help in this?"

"Why, let them know the facts, possess them of even so slight an outline as we have had before us tonight, and the best women will take measures for self-preservation. Put them on their guard, that is all. It is not enough to give them accomplishments and all sorts of higher learning; these gratify the desire of esteem only in a very temporary way. But something more than a danger-signal is wanted. The woman, as well as the man, must have her share of the world's work, whose reward is the world's esteem. She must, even the cherished wife and mother of a family, be in touch with the world's needs, and must minister of the gifts she has; and that, because it is no dream that we are all brethren, and must therefore suffer from any seclusion from the common life."

Mrs. Jumeau's life was not "spoilt." It turned out as the doctor predicted; for days after his revelations she was ashamed to look her husband in the face; but then, she called up her forces, fought her own fight and came off victorious.

Chapter 9. "A Happy Christmas To You!"

The Christmas holidays! Boys and girls at school are counting off the days till the home-coming. Young men and maidens who have put away childish things do not reckon with date-stones, but consult their Bradshaws. The little ones at home are storing up surprises. The father says genially, "We shall soon have our young folk at home again." The mother? Nobody, not the youngest of the schoolgirls, is so glad as she. She thinks of setting out for church on Christmas Day with, let us hope, the whole of her scattered flock about her. Already she pictures to herself how each has altered and grown, and yet how every one is just as of old. She knows how Lucy will return prettier and more lovable than ever; Willie, more amusing; Harry, kinder; and, "how the elders will rejoice in baby May!"

And yet, there is a shade of anxiety in the mother's face as she plans for the holidays. The brunt of domestic difficulties falls, necessarily, upon her. It is not quite easy to arrange a household for a sudden incursion of new inmates whose stay is not measured by days. Servants must be considered, and may be tiresome. Amusements, interests, must be thought of, and then—Does the mother stop short and avoid putting into shape the "and then," which belongs to the holiday weeks after Christmas Day is over?

"Let us have a happy Christmas, any way," she says, "we must leave the rest."

What is it? Pretty Lucy's face clouds into sullenness. Kind Harry is quick to take offence, and his outbursts spoil people's comfort. Willie, with all his nonsense, has fits of positive moroseness. Tom argues—is always in the right. Alice—is the child always quite straightforward? There is reason enough for the strain of anxiety that mingles with the mother's joy. It is not easy to keep eight or nine young people at their best for weeks together without their usual employments, when you consider that, wanting their elders' modicum of self-control, they may have their father's failings and their mother's failings, and ugly traits besides hardly to be accounted for. Is it a counsel of perfection that mothers should have "Quiet Days" of rest for body and mind, and for such spiritual refreshment as may be, to prepare them for the exhausting (however delightful) strain of the holidays?

Much arrears of work must fall to the heads of the house in the young folk's holidays. They will want to estimate, as they get opportunity, the new thought that is leavening their children's minds; to modify, however imperceptibly, the opinions the young people are forming. They must keep a clear line of demarcation between duties and pastimes, even in the holidays; and they must resume the work of character-training, relinquished to some extent while the children are away at school. But, after all, the holiday problem is much easier than it looks, as many a light-hearted mother knows.

There is a way of it, a certain "Open Sesame," which mothers know, or, if they do not, all the worse for the happiness of Holiday House. Occupation? Many interests? Occupation, of course; we know what befalls idle hands; but "interests" are only successful in conjunction with the password; without it, the more excitingly interesting the interests the more apt are they to disturb the domestic atmosphere and make one, sulky, and another, domineering, and a third, selfish, and each "naughty " in that particular way in which "tis his nature to."

Every mother knows the secret, but some may have forgotten the magic of it. Paradoxical as the statement may sound, there is no one thing of which it is harder to convince young people than that their parents love them. They do not talk about the matter, but supposing they did, this would be the avowal of nine children out of ten:

"Oh, of course, mother loves me in a way, but not as she loves X."

"How 'in a way'?"

"You know what I mean. She is mother, so of course she cares about things for me and all that."

"But how does she love X.?"

"Oh, I can't explain; she's fond of her, likes to look at her, and touch her, and—now don't go and think I'm saying things about mother. She's quite fair and treats us all just alike; but who could help liking X. best? I'm so horrid! Nobody cares for me."

Put most of the children (including X.) of good and loving parents into the Palace of Truth, children of all ages, from six, say, to twenty, and this is the sort of thing you would get. Boys would, as a rule, credit "mother," and girls, "father," with the more love; but that is only by comparison; the one parent is only "nicer" than the other. As for appropriating or recognising the fulness of love lavished on them, they simply do not do it.

And why? Our little friend has told us; mother and father are quite fair, there is no fault to be found in them, but "I'm so horrid, nobody cares for me." There you have the secret of "naughtiness." There is nothing more pathetic than the sort of dual life of which the young are dimly conscious. On the one hand, there are premonitions of full and perfect being, the budding of those wings of which their thoughts are full, and for which their strong sense of justice demands credit. Mother and father ought to know how great and good and beautiful they are in possibility, in prospective. They must have the comprehension, appreciation, which, if they cannot get in the drawing-room, they will seek in the kitchen or the stable-yard. Alnaschar visions? If so, it is his parents, not young Alnaschar, who kick over the basket of eggs.

If the young folk are pugnacious about their "rights," and are over-ready with their "It's not fair " "It's a shame!" it is because they reckon their claims by the great possible self, while, alas! they measure what they get by the actual self, of which they think small things. There is no word for it but "horrid"; bring them to book, and the scornful, or vain, or bumptious young persons we may know are alike in this—every one of them is "horrid" in his or her own eyes.

Now, if you know yourself to be horrid, you know that, of course, people do not love you; how can they? They are kind to you and all that, but that is because it's their business, or their nature, or their duty to be kind. It has really nothing to do with you personally. What you want is someone who will find you out, and be kind to you, and love you just for your own sake and nothing else So do we reason when we are young. It is the old story. The good that I would I do not, but the evil that I would not, that I do. Only we feel things more acutely when we are young, and take sides alternately with ourselves and against ourselves; small is the wonder that their elders find young people "difficult"; that is just what they find themselves.

"Fudge!" says the reader, who satisfies himself with the surface, and recalls the fun and frolic and gaiety of heart, the laughter and nonsense and bright looks of scores of young people he knows: of course they are gay, because they are young—but we should have many books about the sadness of youth if people in their "teens" might have the making of them. Glad and sad are not a whole octave apart.

How soon does this trouble of youth begin? That very delightful person, the Baby, is quite exempt. So, too, are the three, four, and five-year-old darlings of the nursery. They gather on your knee, and take possession of you, and make no doubt at all of your love or their deserts. But a child cannot always get out of the nursery before this doubt with two faces is upon him. I know a boy of four, a healthy intelligent child, full of glee and frolic and sense, who yet has many sad moments because one and another do not love him; and other very joyful, grateful moments because some little gift or attention assures him of love. His mother, with the delicate tact mothers have, perceives that the child needs to be continually reinstated in his own esteem. She calls him her "only boy," treats him half as her little lover, and so evens him with the two bright little sisters whom, somehow, and without any telling, poor Georgy feels to be sweeter in temper and more lovable than he. An exceedingly instructive little memorial of a child who died young came under my notice some time ago. His parents kept their children always in an atmosphere of love and gladness; and it was curious to notice that this boy, a merry, bright little fellow, was quite incapable of realising his parents' love. That they should love his sister was natural, but how could they love him?

The little ones in the nursery revel in love, but how is it with even the nursery elders? Are they not soon taught to give place to the little ones and look for small show of affection, because they are "big boys" and "big girls"? The rather sad aloofness and self-containedness of these little folk in some families is worth thinking about. Even the nursery is a microcosm, suffering from the world's ailment—love-hunger, a sickness which drives little children and grown-up people into naughty thoughts and wicked ways.

I knew a girl whose parents devoted themselves entirely to training her; they surrounded her with care and sufficient tenderness; they did not make much of her openly, because they held old-fashioned notions about not fostering a child's self-importance and vanity. They were so successful in suppressing the girl's self-esteem that it never occurred to her that all their cares meant love until she was woman-grown and could discern character, and, alas! had her parents no more to give them back love for love. The girl herself must have been unloving? In one sense, all young beings are unloving; in another, they are as vessels filled, brimming over, with love seeking an outlet. This girl would watch her mother about a room, walk behind her in the streets—adoringly. Such intense worship of their parents is more common in children than we imagine. A boy of five years was asked what he thought the most beautiful thing in the world. "Velvet," he replied, with dreamy eyes, evidently thinking of his mother in a velvet gown. His parents are the greatest and wisest, the most powerful, and the best people within the narrow range of the child's world. They are royal personages—his kings and queens. Is it any wonder he worships, even while he rebels?

But is it not more common, nowadays, for children to caress and patronise their parents, and make all too sure of their love? It may be; but only where parents have lost that indescribable attribute—dignity? authority?—which is their title to their children's love and worship; and the affection which is lavished too creaturely-wise on children fails to meet the craving of their nature. What is it they want, those young things so gaily happy with doll or bat or racquet? They want to be reinstated; they labour, some poor children almost from infancy, under a sad sense of demerit. They find themselves so little loveworthy, that no sign short of absolute telling with lip and eye and touch will convince them they are beloved.

But if one whom they trust and honour, one who knows, will, seeing how faulty they are, yet love them, regarding the hateful faults as alien things to be got rid of, and holding them, in spite of the faults, in close measureless love and confidence, why, then, the young lives expand like flowers in sunny weather; and, where parents know this secret of loving, there are no morose boys nor sullen girls.

Actions do not speak louder than words to a young heart; he must feel it in your touch, see it in your eye, hear it in your tones, or you will never convince child or boy that you love him, though you labour day and night for his good and his pleasure. Perhaps this is the special lesson of Christmas-tide for parents. The Son came—for what else we need not inquire now—to reinstate men by compelling them to believe that they—the poorest shrinking and ashamed souls of them—that they live enfolded in infinite personal love, desiring with desire the response of love for love. And who, like the parent, can help forward this "wonderful redemption"? The boy who knows that his father and his mother love him with measureless patience in his faults, and love him out of them, is not slow to perceive, receive, and understand the dealings of the higher Love.

But why should good parents, more than the rest of us, be expected to exhibit so divine a love? Perhaps because they are better than most of us; anyway, that appears to be their vocation. And that it is possible to fulfil even so high a calling we all know, because we know good mothers and good fathers.

"Parents, love your children," is, probably, an unnecessary counsel to any who read this page; at any rate, it is a presuming one. But let me say to reserved, undemonstrative parents who follow the example of righteous Abraham and rule their households,—Rule none the less, but let your children feel and see and be quite sure that you love them.

We do not suggest endearments in public, which the young folk cannot always abide. But, dear mother, take your big schoolgirl in your arms just once in the holidays, and let her have a good talk, all to your two selves; it will be to her like a meal to a hungry man. For the youths and maidens—remember, they would sell their souls for love; they do it too, and that is the reason of many of the ruined lives we sigh over. Who will break down the partition between supply and demand in many a home where there are hungry hearts on either side of the wall?

Part II Parents in Council

Chapter 1. What A Salvage!

"Now, let us address ourselves to the serious business of the evening. Here we are:

"'Six precious (pairs), and all agog,
To dash through thick and thin!'

Imprimis—our desire is for reform! Not reform by Act of Parliament, if you please; but, will the world believe?—we veritably desire to be reformed! And that, as a vicarious effort for the coming race. Why, to have conceived the notion entitles us to sit by for our term of years and see how the others do it!"

"Don't be absurd, Ned, as if it were all a joke! We're dreadfully in earnest, and can't bear to have the time wasted. A pretty President you are."

"Why, my dear, that's the joke; how can a man preside over a few friends who have done him the honour to dine at his table?"

"Mrs. Clough is quite right. It's 'Up boys, and at it!' we want to be; so, my dear fellow, don't let any graceful scruples on your part hinder work."

"Then, Henderson, as the most rabid of us all, you must begin."

"I do not know that what I have to say should come first in order; but to save time I'll begin. What I complain of, is, the crass ignorance of us—of myself, I mean. You know what a magnificent spectacle the heavens have offered these last few frosty nights. Well, one of our youngsters has, I think, some turn for astronomy. 'Look, father, what a great star! It's big enough to make the night light without the moon. It isn't always there; what's its name, and where does it go?' The boy was in the receptive 'How I wonder what you are' mood; anything and everything I could have told him would have been his—a possession for life.

"'That's not a star, it's a planet, Tom,' with a little twaddle about how planets are like our earth, more or less, was all I had for his hungry wonder. As for how one planet differs from another in glory, his sifting questions got nothing out of me; what nothing has, can nothing give. Again, he has, all of his own wit, singled out groups of stars and, like Hugh Miller, wasn't it?—pricked them into paper with a pin. 'Have they names? What is this, and this?' 'Those three stars are the belt of Orion'—the sum of my acquaintance with the constellations, if you will believe it! He bombarded me with questions all to the point. I tried bits of book knowledge which he did not want. It was a 'bowing' acquaintance, if no more, with the glorious objects before him that the child coveted, and he cornered me till his mother interfered with, 'That will do, Tom: don't tease father with your questions.' A trifling incident, perhaps, but do you know I didn't sleep a wink that night, or rather, I did sleep, and dreamt, and woke for good. I dreamt the child was crying for hunger and I had not a crust to give him. You know how vivid some dreams are. The moral flashed on me; the child had been crying to me with the hunger of the mind; he had asked for bread and got a stone. A thing like that stirs you. From that moment I had a new conception of a parent's vocation and of my unfitness for it. I determined that night to find some way to help ourselves and the thousands of parents in the same ignorant case."

"Well, but, Henderson, you don't mean to say that every parent should be an astronomer? Why, how can a man with other work tackle the study of a lifetime?"

"No, but I do think our veneration for science frightens us off open ground. Huxley somewhere draws a line between science and what he calls 'common information,' and this I take to mean an acquaintance with the facts about us, whether of Nature or of society. It's a shameful thing to be unable to answer such questions as Tom's. Every one should know something about such facts of Nature as a child is likely to come across. But how to get at this knowledge! Books? Well, I don't say but you may get to know about most things from books, but as for knowing the thing itself, let me be introduced by him that knew it before me!"

"I see what you mean; we want the help of the naturalist, an enthusiast who will not only teach but fire us with the desire to know."

"But don't you find, Morris, that even your enthusiast, if he's a man of science, is slow to recognise the neutral ground of common information?"

"That may be; but, as for getting what we want—pooh! it's a question of demand and supply. If you don't mind my talking about ourselves I should like just to tell you what we did last summer. Perhaps you may know that I dabble a little in geology—only dabble—but every tyro must have noticed how the features of a landscape depend on its geological formation, and not only the look of the landscape, but the occupations of the people. Well, it occurred to me that if, instead of the hideous 'resources'—save the word!—of a watering-place, what if we were to study the 'scape' of a single formation? The children would have that, at any rate, in visible presentation, and would hold a key to much besides.

"My wife and I love the South Downs, perhaps for auld sake's sake, so we put up at a farmhouse in one of the lovely 'Lavants' near Goodwood. Chalk and a blackboard were inseparably associated; and a hill of chalk was as surprising to the children as if all the trees were bread and cheese. Here was wonder to start with, wonder and desire to know. Truly, a man hath joy in the answer of his mouth! The delight, the deliciousness, of pouring out answers to their eager questions! and the illimitable receptivity of the children! This was the sort of thing—after scrawling on a flint with a fragment of chalk:—

"'What is that white line on the flint, Bob?'—'Chalk, father,' with surprise at my dulness; and then the unfolding of the tale of wonder—thousands of lovely, infinitely small shells in that scrawl of chalk; each had, ages and ages ago, its little inmate—and so on. Wide eyes and open mouths, until sceptical Dick—'Well, but, father, how did they get here? How could they crawl or swim to the dry land when they were dead?' More wonders, and a snub for that small boy. 'Why, this hillside we are sitting on is a bit of that old sea-bottom!' And still the marvel grew, until, trust me, there is not a feature of the chalk that is not written down in le journal intime of each child's soul. They know the soft roll of the hills, the smooth dip of the valleys, the delights of travellers' joy, queer old yews, and black-berrying in the sudden 'bottoms' of the chalk. The endless singing of the lark—nothing but larks—the trailing of cloud-shadows over the hills, the blue skies of Sussex, blue as those of Naples—these things are theirs to have and to hold, and are all associated with the chalk; they have the sense of the earth-mother, of the connection of things, which makes for poetry.

"Then their mother has rather a happy way of getting pictures printed on the 'sensitive plate' of each. She hits on a view, of narrow range generally, and makes the children look at it well and then describe it with closed eyes. One never-to-be-forgotten view was seized in this way. 'First grass, the hill-slopes below us, with sheep feeding about: and then a great field of red poppies—there's corn, but we can't see it; then fields and fields of corn, quite yellow and ripe, reaching out a long way; next, the sea, very blue, and three rather little boats with white sails; a lark a long way up in the sky singing as loud as a band of music; and such a shining sun!' No doubt our little maid will have all that to her dying day; and isn't it a picture worth having?"

"Mr. Morris's hint admits of endless expansion; why, you could cover the surface formations of England in the course of the summer holidays of a boy's school-life, and thus give him a key to the landscape, fauna, and flora of much of the earth's surface. It's admirable."

"What a salvage! The long holidays, which are apt to hang on hand, would be more fully and usefully employed than schooldays, and in ways full of out-of-door delights. I see how it would work. Think of the dales of Yorkshire, where the vivid green of the mountain limestone forms a distinct line of junction with the dim tints of the heather on the millstone grit of the moors, of the innumerable rocky nests where the ferns of the limestone—hart's-tongue, oak fern, beech fern, and the rest—grow delicately green and perfect as if conserved under glass. Think of the endless ferns and mosses and the picturesque outlines of the slate, both in the Lake Country and in Wales. What collections the children might form, always having the geological formation of the district as the leading idea."

"You are getting excited, Mrs. Tremlow. For my part, I cannot rise to the occasion. It is dull to have 'delicious' 'delightful!' 'lovely!' hailing about one's ears, and to be out of it. Pray, do not turn me out for the admission, but my own feeling is strongly against this sort of dabbling in science. In this bird's-eye view of geology, for instance, why in the world did you begin with the chalk? At least you might have started with, say, Cornwall."

"That is just one of the points where the line is to be drawn; you specialists do one thing thoroughly—begin at the beginning, if a beginning there be, and go on to the end, if life is long enough. Now, we contend that the specialist's work should be laid on a wide basis of common information, which differs from science in this amongst other things—you take it as it occurs. A fact comes under your notice; you want to know why it is, and what it is; but its relations to other facts must settle themselves as time goes on, and the other facts turn up. For instance, a child of mine should know the 'blackcap' by its rich note and black upstanding headgear, and take his chance of ever knowing even the name of the family to which his friend belongs."

"And surely, Mr. Morris, you would teach history in the same way; while you are doing a county, or a 'formation'—isn't it?—you get fine opportunities for making history a real thing. For instance, supposing you are doing the—what is it?—of Dorsetshire; you come across Corfe Castle standing in a dip of the hills, like the trough between two waves, and how real you can make the story of the bleeding prince dragged over the downs at the heels of his horse."

"Yes, and speaking of the downs, do you happen to know, Mrs. Tremlow, the glorious downs behind Lewes, and the Abbey and the Castle below, all concerned in the story of the great battle; and the ridge of Mount Harry across which De Montfort and his men marched while the royal party were holding orgies in the Abbey, and where, in the grey of the early morning, each man vowed his life to the cause of liberty, face downwards to the cool grass, and arms outstretched in the form of a cross? Once you have made a study on the spot of one of those historic sites, why, the place and the scene is a part of you. You couldn't forget it if you would."

"That is interesting, and it touches on a matter which I find very suggestive; have you noticed that in certain districts you come across, not only the spots associated with critical events, but monuments of the leading idea of centuries? Such as these are the rained abbeys which still dominate every lovely dale in Yorkshire; the twelfth-century churches, four or five of which—in certain English counties—you come across in the course of a single day's tramp, and of which there is hardly a secluded out-of-the-way nook in some counties that has not its example to show; such, again, are the endless castles on the Welsh border, the Roman camps on the downs, each bearing witness to the dominant thought, during a long period, whether of war, or, of a time when men had some leisure from fighting."

"And not only so. Think of how the better half of English literature has a local colouring; think of the thousand spots round which there lingers an aroma of poetry and of character which seems to get into your brain somehow, and leave there an image of the man, feeling of his work, which you cannot arrive at elsewhere. The Quantocks, Grasmere, Haworth Moors, the Selborne 'Hanger,' the Lincolnshire levels—it is needless to multiply examples of spots where you may see the raw material of poetry, and compare it with the finished work."

"All this is an inspiring glimpse of the possible; but surely, gentlemen, you do not suppose that a family party, the children, say, from fifteen downwards, can get in touch with such wide interests in the course of a six weeks' holiday? I doubt if, even amongst ourselves, any but you, Mr. Meredith, and Mr. Clough, have this sort of grasp of historical and personal associations."

"We must leave that an open question, Mrs. Henderson; but what I do contend for is, that children have illimitable capacity for all knowledge which reaches them in some sort through the vehicle of the senses—what they see and delight in you may pin endless facts, innumerable associations, upon, and children have capacity for them all: nor will they ever treat you to lack-lustre eye and vacant countenance. Believe me 'tis their nature to' hunger after knowledge as a labouring man hungers for his dinner; only, the thing must come in the first, the words which interpret it, in the second place."

"You mean that everything they see is to lead to a sort of object lesson?"

"Indeed I do not! Object lesson! talkee, talkee, about a miserable cut-and-dried scrap, hardly to be recognised by one who knows the thing. I should not wonder if it were better for a child to go without information than to get it in this unnatural way. No, let him see the thing big and living before him, behaving according to its wont. Specimens are of infinite use to the scientist whose business it is to generalise, but are misleading to the child who has yet to learn his individuals. I don't doubt for a minute that an intelligent family out for a holiday might well cover all the ground we have sketched out, and more; but who in the world is to teach them? A child's third question about the fowls of the air or the flowers of the field would probably floor most of us."

"That's coming to the point. I wondered if we were meant to touch our subject again to-night. To skim over all creation in an easy, airy way, is exciting, but, from an educational standpoint, it is comic to the father with a young swarm at home who care for none of these things."

"Of course they don't, Withers, if they have never been put in the way of it; but try 'em, that's all. Now, listen to my idea; I shall be too glad if any one strikes out a better, but we must come to a point, and pull up the next who wanders off on his own hobby. Each of us wishes to cover all, or more, or some of the ground suggested in our desultory talk. Difficulty, we can't teach because we don't know. We are in a corner with but one way out. We must learn what we should teach. How? Well, let us form ourselves into a college, or club, or what you like. Now, it's simply the A B C of many things we wish to learn. Once organised, we shall see our way to the next step. Even in the small party here to-night, some know something of geology, some are at home in the byways of history; what we cannot evolve from our midst we must get from outside, and either amateur recruits or professional folk must be pressed into service; recruits would be much the best, for they would learn as well as teach. Then, when we are organised, we may consider whether our desire is to exhaust a single district in the way suggested, or to follow some other plan. Only, please, if it be a district, let it be a wide one, so that our intercourse be confined to 'speaking' in passing, like ships at sea. Don't, for pity's sake, let it be a social thing, with tennis, talk, and tea!"

"Suppose we do enroll ourselves, how frequent do you think should be our meetings?"

"We'll leave that question; in the meantime, those in favour of Mr. Morris's motion that we form ourselves into a society for the consideration of matters affecting the education of children—the parents' part of the work, that is-will signify the same in the usual way."

"Carried unanimously!"

Chapter 2. Where Shall We Go This Year?

"Dost thou like fair lands?"

"Why should I not like fair lands? How? Is not that the fairest part of God's creation ?"—King Alfred (from his translation of Boetius).

Where shall we go this year? Is—the question of the day. We want to make the most of that delightful holiday month when we need do nothing but "enjoy ourselves." But, alas,

"Pleasure is spread through the earth
In stray gifts, to be claimed by whoever shall find";

and we are not always lucky. Pleasure may be spread in stray gifts, but the gifts lie in likely places, and the quest must be undertaken with circumspection. We crave "fair lands"; town dwellers, especially, sicken for "the green"; the sea, perhaps; but, any way, grass and trees. We look out for pure air and pretty country, and having secured these, we settle down and say, Let us be therewith content. For the first few days, all is delightful; we explore, we botanise, we find many interests; then, boredom sets in; and we secretly tick off the days that separate us from the labours and pleasures of our everyday lives.

Here is the whole secret of a successful holiday—the mind must be actively, unceasingly, and involuntarily engaged with fresh and ever-changing interests; and this is why, to take a holiday is by no means the easy thing it looks. The little child, indeed, is made happy day after day with spade and bucket, but that is because his unjaded imagination works without spur, and he is able to fill his sunny hours with glad interest, to make some ever new—

"Little plan or chart,
Some fragment of his dream of human life,
Shaped by himself with newly-learned art."

But the child who has outgrown spade and bucket, and who is a little fagged with school work, needs, like his elders, engrossing interests which shall compel him to think new thoughts. Fresh air for the lungs, fresh scenes for the eye, are fully healing and helpful only when the mind, too, is taken into account, and the jaded brain is spoon-fed, as it were, with new ideas. This is why foreign travel is delightful; a delight which is, alas, commonly out of the question for the parents of growing children, much more so for the children themselves; and the question is, can we stay at home, and, with the minimum of expense, and the maximum of convenience, get all the stimulus of foreign travel?

Indeed we can; disclaimers should come from those, only, who have tried the plan; I have tried it, and know it to be easy, economical, and infinitely pleasant. Treat an English county as you would a foreign country; not a district, observe, but a county: we seldom realise how individual each county is, in its landscape and history, its weather and ways;—who, for example would confound the blue skies of Sussex with the blue skies of Cambridgeshire? "There is a delicateness in the air" of each, but it is not the same delicateness. But, to be practical: we choose our county—almost any one will do, and the choice may well be influenced by the cost of taking a family far afield. We get up, roughly, in advance, its history, geology, scenery, flora; and pleasant family evenings are spent over Murray and a map: but once on our travels, nothing will satisfy us but the literature indigenous to the spot, the lives of the people who have made their dwelling-place illustrious, the books these may have written, the scenes of English history here played out. Having chosen our county, we fix upon some half-dozen centres, country towns, from which we can easily cover the interests of the whole county. Lodgings for a family can be obtained easily in towns where visitors are few and far between; we want but little luggage, for only the simplest dread-nought garments are suitable for the sort of life we have in view. It is easy to get from centre to centre; in an hour or two from leaving the last, the children are rejoicing in the investigation of new quarters. Each centre will probably afford a dozen walks and excursions of extreme interest, while the cost of the little transits is more than saved, because the rates of lodging and living in unfrequented country towns are far less than in the ordinary watering-places.

But readers are not convinced; they still think it better to settle down quietly "in a place you know," than to wander like tramps about the country, where, "What is there to see after all?" A single example is worth a peck of precepts, so let us glance at the possibilities of an English county, not a show county, either; but to know Hampshire is a liberal education in itself, and the recollection of its pleasant places and wonderfully interesting associations will stir

"Sensations sweet,
Felt in the blood, and felt along the heart,"

in many a dreary interval of life.

Are you an archaeologist? You may examine half-a-dozen churches with fragments of the original Norman structure in the course of one day's walk, and get quite new ideas of what the Norman conquerors did in scattering centres of light through the land. Are you an ornithologist? You may study the graceful ways of the swallows, and the habits of many of the "feathered nation," in Gilbert White's own "sweet Selborne." Are you a botanist? Here are rare treasures for your herbarium; in and about the Great Wood of Alton alone you may find seventeen of the thirty-eight British species of orchis. Do you care for history, for good and great men, for Miss Austen, for the Christian Year—does geology interest you? Here is a field "all dedicate" to each. Do you wish your children to enter fully upon the inheritance of culture and virtue which is theirs in right of their English birth? Bring them here, or to some other lovely and pleasant county in the three kingdoms. A month spent thus in gathering the lore of a single county is more educative than five terms of vigorous school work.

A "county" is not to be commended for the babies who must not be taught, but children of six and upwards will take in without effort many nourishing ideas in the course of such a rambling holiday as I suggest.

One thing more: it is good, doubtless, to be cosmopolitan in our tastes, liberal and unprejudiced in our judgments; but he who would love all the world must begin with the brother whom he has seen, and enlightened sympathy with other nations can coexist only with profound and instructed patriotism. In the noble character, patriotism is the warp with which every fine and delicate attribute is interwoven. The child who is not trained in patriotic feeling will not, as a man, live at the highest level possible to him; and this noblest virtue is best instilled, not by vulgar vaunting of ourselves, but by the gradual introduction of the child to the lovely lives that have been lived, the great work that has been done, in quiet places in every county of Britain through the long period of our history.

Chapter 3. The A-B-C-Darians

"We have listened to you, gentlemen, with great deference. We have profited much, and perceive a great field of work before us. I hope we may get a little outside help. I heard the other day of a young lady learned in mosses who is in the habit of taking the children she knows on 'mossing' expeditions. But what I wish to say is, education, like charity, begins at home, and you have chosen to lead us far afield at the very outset!"

"Truly, we did go off at a canter! But don't you think it is a matter for curtain discipline? If your son Tom had not 'wondered what you are' we might have begun quite at the beginning, if there be one; or, most likely, should have been till this moment wondering where to begin. We are grateful to you, Henderson, for starting us anywhere; and more so to Mrs. Henderson for her axiom, Education begins at home."

I daresay experienced people get to know all about it,' said Mrs. Clough; "but the mother of even two or three little ones has a sense of being at sea without rudder or compass. We know so little about children, or, indeed, about human beings at all!

Parents before our time had something to go upon; and the young mother could ask counsel of her elders on all matters from 'cinder tea' to the choice of a school. But now, science is abroad; many of the old wise saws turn out, not only mischievous, but ridiculous. We can't keep hold of the old, we can't get hold of the new, and there we are, like Mahomets coffin."

"You have described our quandary exactly, Mrs. Clough; and what you say accounts for many things. The older people complain that the children of these days are growing up lax, self-pleasing, disobedient, irreverent. Now, I think myself there is a great deal that's fine in our children. They are much more of persons than we were at their age; but that they do pretty much what is right in their own eyes, are neither obedient nor reverent, nor even respectful, is, I am afraid, a true bill. But don't you see how it is? We are afraid of them. We feet as a navvy might, turned in to dust the drawing-room ornaments! The mere touch of his clumsy great fingers may be the ruin of some precious thing. We parents, no doubt, get tenderness and insight from above to enable us for our delicate work; so I suppose it is our own fault that the children are beyond us."

"How do you mean, Mrs. Meredith? And if you, mothers, don't know what to do with the children, who does? The enlightened father lays himself out for a snub if he sets up for an authority at home."

"Oh yes! you men make ludicrous blunders about children. But that's no help. A young mother gets a tender human creature into her keeping, full of possibilities. Her first concern is, not only to keep it in health, but, so to speak, to fill it with reserves of health to last a lifetime. At once her perplexities begin. I shall not even ask to be excused for venturing upon details; the affairs of a young human being are important enough to engage the attention of King, Lords, and Commons, did they but know it. Well, a mother I know wished her child to be clothed delicately, as befits a first-born. She sent to Ireland for a delicious baby trousseau of lace and cambric. You, gentlemen, don't understand. Hardly had the dear little garments gone through their first wash, when somebody tells her that 'oo' a' 'oo', is the only wear for babies and grown-ups. I doubt if to this day she knows why, but there was a soupçon of science in the suggestion, so the sweet cambrics were discarded and fine woollens took their place. By-and-by, when the child came to feed like other mortals, there was a hail of pseudo-science about her ears. 'Grape-sugar,' 'farinaceous foods,' 'saliva,' and what not; but this was less simple than the wool question. She could make nothing of it, so asked her doctor how to feed the child. Further complications arose: 'the child sees everything;' 'the child knows everything'; 'what you make him now he will be through life'; 'the period of infancy is the most important in his life.' My poor friend grew bewildered, with the result that, in her ignorant anxiety to do right, she is for ever changing the child's diet, nurse, sleeping hours, airing hours, according to the last lights of the most scientific of her acquaintances; and it's my belief the little one would be a deal better off brought up like its mother before it."

"Then you would walk in the old paths?"

"Not a bit of it! Only I want to see where I'm going. I think we live in an age of great opportunities. But my contention is, that you cannot bring up children on hearsay in these days; there is some principle involved in the most everyday matter, and we must go to school to learn the common laws of healthy living and well-being."

"Mrs. Meredith is right: here is serious work sketched out for us, and of a kind as useful for ourselves as for our children. We must learn the first principles of human physiology."

"Would not it do to learn what is called Hygiene? I have a notion, that is physiology made easy; that is, you are just taught what to do, without going fully into the cause why."

"No, we must stick to physiology: I don't believe at all in learning what to do, unless founded upon a methodical, not scrappy, knowledge of why we do it. You see, all parts of the animal economy are so inter-dependent that you cannot touch this without affecting that. What we want to get at, is, the laws for the well-being of every part, for the due performance of every function."

"Why, man, you would have every one of us qualify to write M.D. to his name!"

"Not so; we shall not interfere with the doctors; we leave sickness to them; but the preservation of health, the increase in bodily vigour, must be our care. In this way; we acquaint ourselves fully with the structure of the skin, for example, with its functions, and the inter-dependence between these and the functions of certain internal organs. Now, secure vigorous action of the skin, and you gain exhilaration of spirits, absolute joy for the time, followed by a rise in the sense of general well-being, i.e., happiness. You remember how a popular American poet sat on a gate in the sun after his bath, using his flesh-brushes by the hour, until he was the colour of a boiled lobster. He might have been more seemly employed, but his joy was greater than if daily telegrams had brought him word of new editions of his poems. Well, if due action of the skin be a means to a joyous life, to health and a genial temper, what mother is there who would not secure these for her child? But the thing is not so simple as it looks. It is not merely a case of bath and flesh-brush: diet, clothes, sleep, bedroom, sunshine, happy surroundings, exercise, bright talk, a thousand things must work together to bring about this 'happy-making' condition. What is true of the skin is true all round, and we cannot go to work with a view to any single organ or function; all work together, and we must aim at a thorough grip of the subject. Is it, then, decided 'without one if or but,' that we get ourselves instructed in the science of living?"

"The 'science of living'—yes, but that covers much beyond the range of physiology. Think of the child's mind, his moral and religious potencies. It seems to me that we already make too much of the body. Our young people are encouraged to sacrifice everything to physical training; and there is a sensuousness, well hit-off in George Eliot's 'Gwendoline,' in the importance given to every detail of the bath and the toilet. One is weary of the endless magnification of the body and its belongings; and, what is more, I believe we are defeating our own ends. 'Groom' the skin, develop the muscles, by all means; but there is more to be thought of, and I doubt if to live to the flesh, even in these ways, is permissible.'

"You are right. But don't think for a moment that physiology lends itself to the cult of muscle. Here is a youth whose biceps are his better part: like most of us, he gets what he aims at—some local renown as an athlete. But what does he pay for the whistle? His violent 'sports' do not materially increase the measure of blood which sustains him: if the muscles get more than their share, their gain implies loss elsewhere, to the brain, commonly, and, indeed, to all the vital organs. By-and-by, the sports of youth over, your brawny, broad-chested young fellow collapses; is the victim of ennui, and liver, lungs, or stomach send in their requisition for arrears of nourishment fraudulently made away with."

"But, surely, Mr. Meredith, you do not think lightly of physical development? Why, I thought it one of the first duties of parents to send their offspring into the world as 'fine animals.'"

"So it is; but here, as elsewhere, there is a 'science of the proportion of things,' and the young people who go in violently and without moderation for muscular feats are a delusion and a snare: in the end, they do not prove 'fine animals'; they have little staying power."

"But a child is more than an animal; we want to know how mind and moral feelings are to be developed?"

"Even in these matters, Mrs. Tremlow, we should find much help in the study of physiology—mental physiology, if you like to call it so. I mean, the habits a child grows up with appear to leave some sort of register in his material brain, and, thus, to become part of himself in even a physical sense. Thus it rests with parents to ease the way of their child by giving him the habits of the god life in thought, feeling and action, and even in spiritual things. We cannot make a child 'good'; but, in this way, we can lay paths for the good life in the very substance of his brain. We cannot make him hear the voice of God; but, again, we can make paths where the Lord God may walk in the cool of the evening. We cannot make a child clever; but we can see that his brain is nourished with pure blood, his mind with fruitful ideas."

"I suppose all this would be encouraging if one were up to it. But I feel as if a great map of an unknown country were spread before me, where the few points one wants to make for are unmarked. How, for instance, are we to make a child obedient, kind, and true?"

"Your question, Mrs. Tremlow, suggests further ground we must cover: a few set rules will be of little service; we must know a little, at any rate, of the content of that which we call 'human nature.' We must add to our physiology, psychology, and, to psychology, moral science. Complex, yet most simple, manifold, yet one, human nature is not to be ticked off in a lecture or two as a subject we have exhausted; but there is no conceivable study which yields such splendid increase for our pains."

"And the spiritual life of the child? Does either of these 'ologies' embrace the higher life, or is it not susceptible of culture?"

"Ah, there we have new conditions—the impact of the Divine upon the human, which generates life, 'without which there is no living.' The life is there, imparted and sustained from above; but we have something to do here also. Spirit, like body, thrives upon daily bread and daily labour, and it is our part to set before the child those 'new thoughts of God, new hopes of Heaven,' which should be his spiritual diet; and to practise him in the spiritual labours of prayer, praise, and endeavour. How?—is another question for our Society to work out."

Chapter 4. "Die Neus Zeit Bedarf Der Neuen Schule" (A School-Master's Reverie)

How hard it is to turn your thoughts on! Switzerland was a mistake, so far as that goes; but to have been alive in every pore for a month is something. This night train should help, though: here goes! let us face the situation. I, Michael St. John Harrowby, aged thirty-five, have got, more by good luck than merit, the Headmastership of the Wintonley Grammar School. One's first thought is, naturally, for wife and bairns, and Fanny was sadly pinched at Appledore. Dear girl! I hope the strain is at an end for her. She will enjoy mothering the boarders along with our own five.

But here am I on the old string which we have harped upon a thousand times since I got the post—the gain to ourselves and the children. There is nothing we have not canvassed, to the Butler schoolship for baby Tim, so why go over the ground again?

Oh, shade of Jack Horner, enfant terrible, does every man-jack of us eat his plum in his corner to the tune of "What a good boy am I"? Are effort and aspiration for those others who miss the plums? Well, I have my thoughts, if I could only get at them: cakes and ale are not everything.

No cakes and ale are not the whole, and now that a fair field offers, I wonder what I shall make of the thoughts that have been working in me for these last ten years! Three months ago I could have revolutionised the whole educational system—like Moses, who was plucky enough about the exodus till his time came. Give you a chance, though, and you feel that the other men have experience on their side, and that—what is, is best. But that is laziness, cowardice. Come, Michael, man! You know in your heart that this chance has come to you just because you have thought out a few things that should be of use. That is what the world wants, for somehow, people have grown too humble and teachable to think for themselves. These are wonderful times, beautiful times! We are all so open to conviction, so agog for the right and the true; we may be gulled by false prophets, with their "Io, here!" and "Io, there!" but then, how ready we are to follow the lead of any with the least gift of insight!

In the matter of education, we are hovering round the truth: that education is not merely a preparation for life, but the work of the lifetime, is boldly announced. And, given thus much insight, is it conceivable that the education in question is no more than the cramming of a few text-books? Like religion, education is nothing or it is everything—a consuming fire in the bones. How is it that we do not see, through the hurry of eating and drinking, getting and having, that our prime business here is to raise up a generation better than ourselves?

"New schools for the new times" is the burden of an old pamphlet I picked up at Offenbach, the outcome of a congress of the "deutschen Freidenkerbundes" held a quarter of a century ago, which indicates the date when Germany first began her educational reform. It is as well to know how we stand with regard to certain burning questions, and this pamphlet rather brings us to book. "Knowledge is power" is not an alarmingly new sentiment; that the people have a right to the power which knowledge gives, that the knowledge which avails is that which qualifies a man for his life as a "social animal," we are prepared to admit. That the talent, the genius, which smoulder to-day in the heated rooms of a thousand factories, or are choked in a thousand damp cellar dwellings, must be cherished by the schools of the future to the infinite advantage of the whole commonweal—that touches a burning question. One is not sure that cellars, any more than drawing-rooms, breed geniuses by the thousand; but that is not the point; the question concerns—"the pauper population," the "criminal classes." Shame on us that such phrases are possible to our English speech; we are glad and willing to have the poor always with us to instruct us in righteousness; but what hope for us of health and beauty as a nation with this cancer at our bowels?

Apart from these, the "unspeakable" residue, how do we stand? That is, where there is work and bread, how do the people fare for education, and what are the chances for a working man's child blessed with talent or genius? Tolerably good in the large towns; in ordinary cases, the possibilities of education are limited by the length of time the parents can afford to keep their child; indeed, the law steps in to constrain the parents and to fix a minimum standard of age and attainments without which the child is not free to labour; he must read, though not fluently; write, though not easily nor correctly; must be able to add and subtract, divide and multiply with some readiness. This is not much, but it is a setting of the gates ajar for the child of genius; and, supposing that his parents are able and willing to feed and clothe him during his adolescence, his prospects are good. He wins scholarships at the primary, which carry him through the secondary school, and there he may win scholarships which will cover his University career. I know of a dozen instances of University men who have worked their way up from very low estate—the sons of journeymen labourers, of mill "hands," of petty traders—and that, with honour and consideration too, for school and college alike bid for brains, seeing that their own status depends on the men they turn out. This state of things is a mere pis aller; we are told that they manage educational matters better elsewhere: but "reform" is in the air; our whole system is being overhauled; and, meantime, it is pleasant to know that education is possible to the son of the poor man who is born a genius, and is blessed with self-denying parents, and—one more qualification—who lives in a town.

What have we here? "Nothing," says Pädagoge Diesterweg, "has more attraction for man than truth. To find it he will wander into distant lands, over desert and mountain, will search the depths of the earth, will climb into the heavens; no effort is to him too great, no obstacle too fearful, no labour too hard; his soul thirsts after truth." This is suggestive, and the conclusion that, in the schools, the children should be nourished upon truth, goes without saying. But we come back to Pilate's world-famed question.

My pedagogue means something, however, "Moses, Moses, und immer Moses," is the burden of a bitter cry. He complains that, in the Fatherland, a sixth, and sometimes more, of the time spent in school (in elementary schools) is devoted to religious instruction—Bible-lesson and psalm, catechism and hymn; and what time is left, is the cry, for literature, for metaphysics, ethics, what not, the stores of wisdom that should be laid open to poor as to rich? But this is a tale of the past, and we in England are well in advance after all. Nowhere with us are two out of twelve, much less sixteen out of twenty-four, school hours devoted to religious instruction. Psalm, hymn, and catechism have departed; the Bible lesson is pared down to a shred; and, in our zeal, we do not see that we have deprived the people of the classics, the metaphysics, the ethics—as well as the religion—peculiarly their own. Instead, we have put into their hands—"Readers"—scraps of science, of history, of geography—saw-dust, that cannot take root downwards and bear fruit upwards in human soil.

But here is matter that concerns us more closely. We learn for life, not for the schools: good and well; nothing new in that. Here we have it:—Wie?—sagt Prof. Dodel-Port in seiner neuesten Broschüre: Moses oder Darwin. Dodel-Port is plucky, or reckless, but that is the situation. What think ye of Moses? Is the crux. The worst of it is, a man may let his own thoughts simmer, but the young will have something definite, and you cannot hide anything from them. Say nothing, and they know what it means as well as if you proclaimed yourself from the housetop. Well, as a matter of fact, it is not "Moses or Darwin?" with me. I receive both, not by way of compromise, but in faith, believing that each, though in differing degree, speaks a revealed word. But, how is one to put it to the boys? They will take sides, and they doubt your sincerity if you do not.

Loyalty shall be our key-note. In a home, children are under natural conditions, and each develops on his own lines. In a school, you must have an enthusiasm, must strike a note that vibrates in every breast to secure the common feeling without which there is no life. Loyalty will do—chivalrous loyalty to each other, to the school, to their homes, to those in authority: then, the highest enthusiasm, the loyalty of Christian service; I hardly see how to work it yet, but when one is steadfastly purposed, ways arise. Supposing, then, the loyalty that does not permit itself to harbour dishonouring thoughts; suppose a passion of loyal service kindled in some breasts, and more or less affecting all—is criticism to be tabooed as disloyal? Are the boys to go into the world ignorant of the questions that are searching many hearts, to be staggered by the first shock of evidence and opinion running counter to the old thoughts? No; but how I wish I could do the boys the like inestimable service that a great teacher has done for me and many another! It is difficult to put into words, but, somehow, one is landed on the other side of the controversies of the day: they are of immense interest, but are not vital. It is just, to compare lesser things with great, as the husband of a famous woman might listen to discussions about his wife's works or published letters. Are they hers or are they not? Do they disclose facts of her life or fancies? Are the opinions put into the mouths of her best characters truly her own? It is most interesting to hear what the world says, but, for him, he knows where the world guesses; besides, these things are not vital; the vital thing is herself and their mutual relations. So, but infinitely more so, of our apprehension of the Highest, and our cognisance of the supreme relationship. Reveal to the eyes of youth the vision of the infinite Loveliness, lay bare the heart of youth to the drawings of the irresistible Tenderness, let the young know, of their own intimate knowledge, that,

"The thoughts of God are broader than the measures of man's mind,
And the heart of the Eternal is most wonderfully kind,"

and all other knowledge and relationships and facts of life will settle themselves. Thus, only, is it possible to live joyfully, purposefully, diligently. Without this—madness! or, the foolish playing of a foolish mummer's part in the presence of the "eternal verities." But, boys religiously brought up turn out indifferent or ill? Exactly so, when they have had the outward and visible signs without the inward part or thing signified; of all sawdust, this is the driest. No soul, once laid open to the touch of the divine tenderness, can go away and forget. Go away, a wilful soul may, but come back, it needs must. Well, it is something to see one's work; but, how to do it? At any rate, seeing these things, a man must go softly all his days and wait for light.

In this connection we must face the attitude of public opinion with regard to the Sacred Books. "Yea, hath God said?" is the question of the hour, and probably will be the question of the hour so long as the world endures. We who teach must hold unalterable convictions in this regard, unalterable and therefore our grounds must be deep, broad, and high, covering and underlying every point of attack. We must know with absolute certainty that here is revelation—its claim to be so resting upon internal evidence alone, the quality of that which is revealed. Let us ask what is the subject of revelation. The history of the people called Jews? The history of the beginning, and predictions of the end of all things? We are told to-day that upon the one as upon the other the light is thrown "through storied windows richly dight"; that the apple and the garden bear no more direct, material interpretation than the "tree which bears twelve manner of fruits, whose leaves are for the healing of the nations"; that, "without a parable spake he not unto them" applies more or less to what we call the history of the Bible. Perhaps the marvellous and inspired quality of the Scriptures is more brought out by attacks upon their historic truth then in any other way. Whether men choose to regard the story of the Fall as a record, a poem, a fable, a parable, a vision, its inherent teaching is the same. We have here the story of the decline and fall and hope to rise again of every soul of man.

The history of the Jews, again, what is it more, say the enlightened, than a collection of the myths of the heroic age of a nation—when the gods walked with men: myths that have their parallels, often curiously close, in the sacred legends of nations to which we do not allow divine inspiration? Here, again, the history justifies itself by its truth to human experience. The sun stands still, even now, for the finishing of our righteous acts; the Jordan parts before us in our extremities. Here we have, whether by way of historic fact or luminous fable, parables of our lives to be spiritually discerned, and, more, here we have an unfailing key to the interpretation of our times: this is by inspiration of God.

The "carnage," the "wholesale slaughterings," ascribed to Almighty God, wrought directly by His hand, or according to His will, are brought forward as irreconcilable with our conceptions of the All-good. These things happen to-day, and we have not the courage to ascribe them to God. Few amongst us are able to stand up and say, "Though He slay me and my fellows, yet will I trust in Him." We dare not say, "Here is the finger of God"; so we describe these events by a string of epithets, all of more or less pagan origin. Fortune, the stars, the fates, work us mischief. We suffer from misfortunes, mischances, casualties, catastrophes, disasters, fatalities—more reassuring, doubtless, and more scientific than the creed of the Old Testament! Is it true, then, that flood and famine, and slaughter in battle, are the will and the work of the good God? The Old Testament asserts as much, and the New has a tender word about a sparrow falling to the ground, which goes to prove that these things are, at any rate, permitted. Perhaps, life and death are less momentous than we suppose; death, conceivably, is no way final whether as regards opportunity or existence; what if it even open a chance to "try again"? We cannot know; revelation is silent; and as for science, when science has a definite utterance to make about the facts of life under her eyes, we shall be willing to hear what she says about these other mysteries. At any rate, in that Heart where every pain found its pity, there was none for the three who tasted death—only for the grief that mourned them. As for all the anguish of life, the miseries of the mind distressed, the writhings of the suffering body, who shall find his pain intolerable when he thinks upon the Cross?

We schoolmasters must face the situation; we must shirk nothing, take nothing for granted; we must fortify the boys against attack, and arm them for a chivalrous defence. As for definite tactics, suppose we concede for the moment, and for argument's sake, all that is attacked, and then see where we are. The earthworks thrown up from time to time are sadly torn up, but the fortress is intact. Panic gives way to confidence; come who may, we are ready, and not only so, we take up the offensive; our position is proof against all sallies; it is the enemy who are exposed. This seems to me important. Defensive warfare is never carried on with the enthusiasm of conviction which warms him who attacks. As a matter of fact, we are prepared to yield no iota of the Sacred Scriptures, while of the obscurities of the Old Testament, as of the Apocalypse, we say only—

"Lord, I believe what herein I do read,
But, alas, I do not understand."

But religious training, and the Bible? It is so hard to know what to teach when everything is an "open question." Courage. Nothing is lost yet, and the future is for us. We yield, not the Scriptures, but one or other of the old canons of interpretation, as Science shows it to be untenable; but we look her in the eyes and interrogate her sharply; and, above all, we are intolerant of the assumption of infallibility in a teacher who is ever (and this is her glory) smearing out with wet finger some lesson of yesterday, because it is not the truth of to-day. Are we not on the verge of a new criticism, not historical, and not natural, but personal? Is not physiology hurrying up with the announcement that to every man it is permitted to mould and modify his own brain? That, not heredity, and not environment, but education is the final and the formative power? That character is the man, and education is the maker of character, howsoever much she owe her material to the other two?

And how should this affect our study of Holy Writ? By concentrating criticism upon the personages of the Bible rather than upon the recorded events. First upon the authors—known or unknown: the instruction in righteousness is not less or more, whether Moses or another, Isaiah or another, wrote the words. Is it in human nature, is it in the nature of authors, for a man to suppress himself as do the authors here? Where do the little affectations and vanities of the man of letters crop up? Where are the turgid utterances, the egotistical, the bombastic? Even Plutarch, prince of biographers, cannot refrain himself: he gives you his opinion of his man, and illustrates it by delightful anecdotes; but, to set the man himself before you for judgment without a yea or a nay—not Plutarch or another has been able for this, least of all the biographers of to-day. Where, in the stories of Abraham, Isaac, or Jacob, of prophet, priest, or king, have we moral disquisitions? Is not rather the principle made plain all along the line that right and wrong are self-evidenced, calling for neither praise nor blame; unadorned straightforward narrative is enough when every man carries the judge in his bosom. And then the persons—how the springs of human action are laid bare in them, how they rise from out the sacred page, not a gallery of Hebrew portraits, but a procession of the living, more manifest than the people with whom you sit at table every day! Whence is this, if not by the inspiration of God? And how majestical do some of them take shape before us! How feeble are patriotism, enthusiasm, altruism, all the fine words of to-day, to express the law-giver of Israel, the prophet, the poet, the leader of men, a man of like passions with ourselves, too, but greater than we. "Moses, Moses, und immer, Moses!" Truly this one character is enough to stimulate us to the bringing up of godly and manly youth. In what two or three wonderful touches have we set before us the education that made him; and, all the time, no praises, never a story told for his exaltation, no more ever than the flow of lucid narrative showing only events in their course. Here is essential truth; here is a twofold inspiration; first, to produce the man Moses; next, to portray him. Ah, but, consider the "evolution of history"? Truly, if man is to be measured by the heaped-up praises of his biographers, every year we produce many, not only greater than Moses, but greater that Christ; for when does biography issue from the press so free of laudations as are the four evangels? Oh, "the sweet reasonableness of Christianity," the most sober sanity of that great company elected to hand on to us the counsels of God!

Do I incline with lingering fondness rather to the things of the past than to the eager stir of the present, the promise of the future? Not so; I appreciate to the full the joy of living in days characterised by childlike frankness, openness to conviction, readiness to try all things and choose that which is good. We have our faults—grave and depressing enough—but we are ready for better things, ready, indeed, for any great crusade, if some modern Luther or Savonarola should arise and tell us the thing to do. To "endeavour ourselves" to the daily effort of education, to live and act, think and speak before the children, so that they shall be hourly the better for all that we are, is harder, no doubt, than to make one enormous sacrifice. But even for this we shall be enabled in these inspiring days, when it seems to some of us that the people are being made willing in the day of His power. The outlook is very cheering: we begin to see that education is the elected handmaid of religion, and get stimulating glimpses of the stature of the perfect man, possible to redeemed humanity.

But the past offers us its accumulated treasures of wisdom and experience—

"And (we) could wish (our) days to be
Bound each to each by natural piety."

Few things could be more disastrous (as, alas, few are more imminent) than a sudden break with the traditions of the past; wherefore, let us gently knit the bonds that bind us to the generation all too rapidly dying out. Without a thought of disloyalty towards our own most earnest days, perhaps some of us feel that the cultivated men and women of the middle decades of the last century had more breadth and sweetness—any way, more delightful humour—than we perceive in our contemporaries. It is well that we gather up, with tender reverence, such fragments of their insight and experience as come in our way; for we would fain, each, be as an householder, bringing forth out of his treasures things new and old.

Chapter 5. A Hundred Years After

"It's a capital idea! the thing ought to be commemorated. At any rate, we can give a little dinner in honour of it. Whom shall we have?"

"Dr and Mrs. Oldcastle, and Harry's form-master, young Mr. Hilyard, and his wife, will represent schoolwork; we shall stand for parents in general; and, with Dr and Mrs. Brenton for our medical advisers, and the Dean and Mrs. Priestly to witness for things spiritual, we shall be quite a 'representative gathering.' Will my list do?"

"Famously! It couldn't be better. We all know the subject and each other, and I shouldn't wonder if we have some good things said."

Mr. Clough was a City merchant, as had been his fathers before him for four or five generations; he was reputed wealthy, and was a rich man, but one who held his wealth as a public trust, reserving for personal uses only what should keep his family in refined and comfortable living. Not that there was much virtue in this, for he, and others like him, held in aversion luxurious living, and whatever savoured of the "barbarous opulence" of earlier days. Dr Oldcastle was the head-master of an old-established foundation school; for the remaining guests, they have been sufficiently introduced by Mrs. Clough.

During the dinner there was the usual gay talk, and some light handling of graver subjects, until the ladies retired, with a view to the discussion of certain practical matters among themselves. Then—

"I wonder, gentlemen, has it occurred to you why my wife and I have been so pertinacious in trying to get you here to-night?"

Every one's countenance showed that he was struck by an interesting, if vague, recollection.

"A little circumstance connected with this room, and a certain date that I fear I may have mentioned more than once or twice?"

"Oh, to be sure," said the Dean; "haven't I said a dozen times to my wife, 'There's but one thing that Clough plumes himself on—that the "Fathers' and Mothers' Club" was born in his dining-room!' "

"But why to-night more than any other night?"

"Why, to-night is the hundredth anniversary of that great event!" A good-humoured smile passed round. "Yes, gentlemen, I know I'm house-proud, and give you leave to laugh. But would not you cherish an old-fashioned house in a by-street, when it's the one thing that links you to history?"

"But, my dear fellow, why in the world should this Club with the stuttering initials (how I hate initials!) be glorified? It does not get in my way, as a headmaster, it's true; but, mind you, a man can't play up to his Busby in the face of it! There was a man for his calling! How he'd walk over your 'F. M. C.'s.' Fumble! aye, that's the word. I knew 'F. M. C.' reminded me of something."

"I'm slow to see how our Club links us with history, certainly," murmured Dr Brenton reflectively.

"Why, in this way: if the Club did not initiate, it certainly marked a stage in the progress of the great educational revolution in which we have been moving for the last hundred years. Wait for two or three centuries, and you will find this revolution of ours written down as the epoch of the 'Children's Magna Charta.' "

"Sorry to disoblige you, but I'm afraid none of us sees his way to more than a century of waiting, though it be to verify the statements of his best friend. But go on, old fellow, I'm with you! Make the 'revolution' plain sailing for us."

"Thanks, Hilyard; your sanction emboldens me. But which am I to 'go on' with, the word or the thing?"

"A distinction with a difference. If I say 'the thing,' off we go to the Dark Ages themselves; and shall come out to find the ladies cloaked and hooded in the hall!"

"A thing endurable to us elder Benedicts."

"Now, Doctor! As if you weren't tied to Mrs. Oldcastle's apron-string every minute you're not in school. Fanny and I follow you for encouragement when we feel our bond growing slack."

"To order, gentlemen, to order! or we shall get neither word nor thing. We shall all want to put in a word anent 'my wife and I.' "

"Brenton's right. Seer, take up thy parable, and go ahead!"

"Who would contemn a behest of the Church?" (with a bow which threatened a candle-shade, deftly saved by Hilyard). "I go ahead; I'm not to talk about the thing, but the name. Why I call this, which has been working itself out in the last hundred years or more, an educational revolution. In the first place, what was called 'Education' a century since and what we call Education are essentially different things."

"Come, come! Isn't that rather strong? We go in for the classics and mathematics; and so did the schools of a hundred, or, for the matter of that, five hundred years ago. It is true we have to work much more with modern languages, natural science, and other subjects of which we can give but a smattering, to the confusion alike of boys and masters. Give me a classical education, or, in default, a mathematical; it's training! And, for my part, I vote for the pre-Revolutionists, if that's what you choose to call them";—said Dr Oldcastle, with a subdued snort, which epitomised much that was not civil to the reform party.

"How much clearing of the decks must take place for even a friendly discussion! Tell us, gentlemen both, what you mean by education?"

"Mean by education, Doctor? I should not have thought our united wisdoms need be called on to answer that! A boy is educated when he knows what every gentleman should know, and when he is trained to take his place in the world."

"Dr Oldcastie's definition suits me as well as another. Putting aside the polite acquirements, the question turns on the training—how much it includes, and how it is to be given."

"There you have it, Clough," put in Dr Brenton; "and my contention is, that you owe the incalulable advance in character which has taken place in the period we are considering entirely to us, doctors. Wasn't it we who found out for you that you were all blundering in the dark; that you hadn't even set your feet on the scientific basis of education; that all your doings were tentative? About a hundred years ago, men spent a third of a lifetime on mathematics. Cambridge made men Senior Wranglers in those days, and, perhaps, the distinction was worth the work. But the world said, in that weighty way in which the world likes to talk: 'Mathematics afford a mental discipline, a fortifying of character, which no other study gives.' Now I'm not denying the worth of mathematics as a factor in education; but look at your mathematician; do you find him more to the fore, more his own master, than other men? Often enough, he is irritable, obstinate, all the more wrong headed the more he's in the right. But now we (observe the we—royalty itself couldn't make more of it) find you fumbling about blindly, snatching up now this tool, now that, natural science, languages, or what not, in order to work upon material you knew nothing about, was it mind, or morals, or what? To effect issues you had not determined on—intellectual power? Force of character? In the slough we found you—parent, schoolmaster, parson—all whose business is, more or less, the bringing up of the young; and what have we done for you? Why, we've discovered to you the nature of the material you have to work upon, the laws according to which it must be wrought. We have even put it into your hands as clay in the hands of a potter, and we've shown you what is the one possible achievement before you; that is, the elevation of character. Education which fails to effect this, effects nothing. There, that's what we've done.

Every man to his trade, say I; and there's nothing like leather!"

"Well, but, but,—all this is very fine talk; but what demonstration can you give? And where in the world have I been while all this was going on? Pshaw! You delude yourselves, my dear friends. This airy talk makes flighty brains; but do you suppose I've been a schoolmaster these forty years while all this has been taking place, and yet know nothing of it?"

"That comes of fumbling over our 'F. M. C.', instead of holding us up with both hands. But, honour bright, Dr Oldcastle, do you see in these days any change in the manner of boy that comes to your hands fresh from his home?"

"Yes, yes! a thousand times, yes!"

"If Mr. Hilyard's courtesy had permitted me to answer for myself, I, also, should have said 'yes.' I see a most remarkable change, upon which society is to be congratulated. But what would you have? Civilisation and education must of necessity produce results, appreciable even within a single lifetime."

"Don't you think, Doctor, you might have made a trilogy of it, and promoted Christianity?" interposed the ever suave and gentle tones of the Dean. "I, myself, feel, with Dr Brenton, 'every man for his master,' and would fain lay every advance at the feet of mine."

"I must beg the Dean to look over a little assumed pugnacity. That we all agree with him, he may rest assured; and for this reason; every other avenue towards perfection leads you, after weeks or months or years of delightful going, to a blank wall. You see nothing beyond; all that remains is to retrace your steps, and retrogression is always bitter. You try through Christ, and find yourself in the way of endless progress cheered by perennial hope. But the talk is growing serious. We of the Club take to ourselves some of the credit of the advances Dr Oldcastle perceives, and as testimony from an alien is very valuable, perhaps he would not mind telling us in detail what differences he discerns between the young boys of to-day and their kind of forty years ago?"

"Let me consider a moment; your question is not easy to answer in a breath . . . Well, in the first place, they are more apt to learn: I conceive that there has been an extraordinary advance in intelligence during the last half-century. The work we would grind over for hours in my day, these youngsters have at their finger-ends in half an hour, and are on the alert for more. I do believe they have a real appetite for knowledge—a weakness of which not more than one or two in a hundred were guilty when I was a boy."

"Will you let me, as a parent, give you our explanation of these facts? For, with deference to Dr Brenton, who justly claims so much for his craft, I think we parents deserve a pat, too. You may bring a horse to the well, but you can't make him drink. The advance, I think, is not in intelligence, but in power of attention. This, the 'Fathers' and Mothers' Club' and its agencies recognise as the practical power of man; that which makes all the difference between the able and successful man and the poor lag-last. Attention is the power and habit of concentrating every faculty on the thing in hand. Now this habit of attention, parents, mothers especially, are taught to encourage and cultivate in their children from early infancy. What you regard with full attention, if only for a minute, you know, and remember always. Think of the few scenes and conversations we, each, have so vividly fixed that we cannot possibly forget them. Why? Because at the moment our attention was powerfully excited. You reap some benefit from this early training directly the boy goes to school. The psychologists—not your craft, this time, Doctor—tell us that enormous curiosity, a ravenous appetite for knowledge, is as natural to children as bread-and-milk hunger. Put the two together; the boy has an eager desire to know—has the power of fixing his whole mind on the new thoughts set before him, and it's as easy as A B C; of course he learns with magical quickness. The field has been ploughed by the parents, and you have only to sow your seed."

"H'm! it sounds rational; I must think it over. Anyway, the results are pleasant enough. Four hours a day instead of six or seven—and much more work done, mind you—is good for both masters and boys. Then, most of them have resources and are on nobody's hands. You'd be astonished to hear how much these fellows know, and each has his speciality. One little chap has butterflies, for instance. Ah, that reminds me! Don't tell, or I might be invited to resign; but I don't to this day know the difference between a moth and a butterfly. It's the sort of thing one ought to know, so I set up a classification of my own, no doubt correct, because it was mine! Well, this befell me. 'What have you there?' I asked a little chap, who had evidently netted a prize. 'A moth, sir, the—,' scientific name, pat. 'A moth, boy! That beautiful creature is no moth. Moths live in houses.' You should have seen the fellow suppress his grin! I couldn't ask, so don't know now, but make a point of not meeting that little chap's eye. A friend of mine, a Fellow of his College, was worse. 'I say, Oldcastle, the poets make a mighty pother about the song of the lark. Now, do tell me—do you know it when you hear it ?' But as for the boys that enter now, there's not the natural object that they don't both recognise and know all about. Their collections are of scientific worth—at least, so that fellow Hilyard thinks, so we are going in for a museum of local natural history!"

"Why, Dr Oldcastle, you're like the man in the play, who talked prose all his life, and at last found it out! You're our warmest friend, though you decline the connection. This, again, is the work of mothers working out our scheme of thought. We make a great point of giving play to the intelligent curiosity of the children about all that lives and grows within their ken. For instance, I should think most of 'our' mothers would feel disgraced if her child of six were not able to recognise any ordinary British tree from a twig with leaf-buds only. It's Nature's lore, and the children take to it like ducks to the water; the first six or seven years of their lives are spent out of doors—in possible weather—learning this sort of thing, instead of pottering over picture-books and A B C. But do fill the witness-box a minute longer. All this is delightful; an outsider who speaks with authority is worth a score of partisans."

"I bow my thanks, Clough, for the handsome things you are good enough to say. Of course my impartial witness would be quite as valuable if it told on the other side. Why, Hilyard, you're nowhere! It is I am the man of the day. But no; he's the go-ahead fellow, and I'm the drag; yet a drag has its uses."

"Granted, if you go down hill. But out of thine own mouth art thou convicted, most learned Master! What hast thou talked all this night but progress? But one thing more: tell us, do you find these Admirable Crichtons of yours the least in the world priggish? Or are they namby-pamby youths, who do as they're bid, and haven't much taste for unlawful adventure?"

"Taste for adventure! Why, little fellows of nine come, able to swim, row, ride, do everything man or boy needs do, and how are fellows of that sort to be kept out of adventures? But they do as they're bid, I grant you, and the way they do it shows fifty times the spirit of the fellows who shirked. Mind, I'm speaking of the boys who have been brought up at home, not of those who have 'growed.' But don't run away with the notion that the best of them are perfect; we must be at it all the time, or the ground gained is gone from under our feet."

"Look, look! do look at Brenton: something will happen if he doesn't get an innings."

"Gentlemen, you must, you really must, hear me on this matter! You must let me show Dr. Oldcastle the 'reason why' of what he observes."

"Hear, hear! Let's have it, Doctor. Don't spare a word."

"Well, to begin at the beginning (no! not with Adam, nor even with the Dark Ages); some five-and-twenty years or so before Clough's EVENT, men of science began to grope for a clue to the understanding of this queer riddle of human nature. That action (including speech) depends on thought, and that action—repeated action—forms character, had long ago been got at by inductive processes. Now, those meddling scientific fellows were not content with, It is, because it is! They must needs go poking round with their everlasting—'Why?' This particular 'Why' proved a most hard nut to crack; indeed, it is only within living memory that their guesses at truth have become entirely demonstrable; but, as early as I said, they had thus much ground under their feet—analogy and probability were altogether on their side, and it was impossible to prove, or even to show a fair case for, the contrary view. These scientists perceived that they were undermining the methods, the aims, the very idea of education as popularly held. They indicated new lines, suggested new principles. But their discoveries were to be like that corn of wheat—first they must fall into the ground and die. Years passed before educationalists woke up to what had been done. At last it dawned upon them that it was now possible to formulate a science of education; to propose laws which should work out definite ends with proximate, if not mathematical, certainty. The days of casual bringing-up were numbered. A basis, and that a physical basis, was found. The principle which underlies the possibility of all education was discovered to them, as it is to us to-day. They were taught that the human frame, brain as well as muscle, grows to the uses it is earliest put to. In a hundred years, we have advanced no further in principle, but we have applied the principle in many directions. It is, indeed, hardly possible to get beyond the ground covered by this so simple-sounding axiom: that is, it is hardly within our power to overstate the possibilities of education. Anything may be made of a child by those who first get him into their bands. No doubt, propagandism becomes the immediate duty of any who have perceived a saving principle for the race. And efforts were made in many directions to bring before parents of all classes the notion that the formation of habits is among the chief aims of education. Our host's *event* is one of these efforts, and the Parents' Club spread like wildfire; every one was ready for it, because people were beginning to feel the wretched uncertainty of the casual method. How is it, they asked, that, bring up two boys in the same way, and one turns out a villain, the other, a credit to his family? Now, Education as we understand it, deals entirely with individuals; not with children, but with the child; the faulty habit is supplanted, observe the word, the desirable habit produced, within a definite period, say one month or six, and then the parents' easy work is to keep the child upon the lines of habit thus produced."

"Now, stop a minute, Doctor, stop a minute! I'm afraid I'm about to lose my easily won laurels. You, who are a classical scholar, must know how familiar to the mind both of Roman and Greek was this doctrine of habit. Again, a poet of our own, an eighteenth-century man—wasn't it Dryden?—expresses capitally the time-out-of-mind English feeling on this subject—

"'Children, like tender osiers, take the bow,
And, as they first are fashion'd, always grow;
For what we learn in youth, to that alone
In age we are by second nature prone.'"

"Most happy; but don't you see, Dr Oldcastle, I began by admitting that people have always had a notion that they must bring up their children in good habits, and suppress faulty ones. But now, they have something more than a notion; they have scientific certainty. And, instead of dawdling through the whole period of childhood with spasmodic efforts to get a boy to tie his shoe-strings fast, they take it in hand once and for all, until the habit is ingrained in the stuff of the child's character. Now, don't you see that this is a very different thing from the desultory way in which a child was allowed to try off and on for a habit all his days, and never got it?"

"I admit there's a difference; it tallies, too, with what I notice in the young boys who enter with us. You mean that their mothers have definitely set themselves for one month or six, say, to form a habit—now obedience, now truthfulness, now attention, and so on—and that is why the boys come to me with character, not mere disposition?"

"Yes, that's what I mean; and it's on these lines we have been advancing for a whole century. In another direction, too, education has been going forward; but, here, we have only analogy to guide us, not yet certainty. It cannot be predicted as yet, whether we are simple or complex beings, whether in each of us is bound up one life or several. It is not impossible, for instance, that, just as our physical life is sustained because multitudinous organisms come to life, feed, grow, multiply, and die, perpetually in our substance, so, perhaps, what we may call our immaterial life is sustained by multitudinous lives such as our philosophy has never dreamed of. An idea, for instance, what is it? We don't know yet; but this we know, that every idea we get is quick within us as a living thing, that it feeds, grows, multiplies, and then, behold it is no more! There are bodies natural and there are bodies spiritual. Perhaps this sort of thing is too immature to be pressed into service; but of other parts of us to which names and ideas of something like personality are attached—conscience, will, our spiritual being—this it is quite safe to assert: they thrive upon their appropriate meat and work, they perish of inanition and idleness. This, too, we take into our scheme of education, and with great results."

The Dean took the word:—

"I, for one, must heartily thank Dr Brenton for his most suggestive lecture. No, don't look 'castigated,'

Doctor; it is a lecture for weight and worth, but of commendable brevity. Speaking for the 'cloth,' I should like to say how much we owe to this educational revolution. A century ago, our Church was supposed to show some signs of decadence; to-day she is quick to her remotest extremities. And why? simply because she has gone with the times in following up the advances of educational thought. She, with the rest of you, perceives that the world has ever one great thing to do—to bring up the young in advance of the generation before them; that the sole valuable inheritance the present has to leave behind is—exalted national character. Wherefore, she has laboured assiduously on the two lines Dr Brenton emphasises to-night—'that Habit is ten natures'; and, that the spiritual life must flourish or decay as it is duly nourished and exercised, or allowed to lie idle and unfed. Therefore is every clergyman instructed, above all, to minister to the young of his parish—of all classes. The growing soul cannot thrive upon husks—therefore must the truth be divested of the husks of the past, and clothed upon with the living thought of the present. The young soul must be taught its work, the spiritual exercises of prayer and praise, the bodily exercise of service; and as no man can teach what he does not know, the minister to the young must be qualified and ever active in these. Seeing these and kindred truths, our clergy are raising up about them a body of ardent young spirits to whom self-devotion is a law; labour in spiritual uplands a necessity. And for much of this progress, I say, we are indebted to the labours of the Educationists, whom we therefore gladly hold up with both hands."

"This is very gratifying hearing; we have all along been very sensible of the cordiality and helpfulness of the clergy, who so commonly throw in their lot with us. But that we should be doing them some service all the time—this is news indeed. May I imitate Mr. Dean, and say a word professionally? We doctors have reaped where we sowed—and abundantly. In the old days, families had each 'their doctor,' who was called in now and then to do battle with disease which had already made head way. But now, people are beginning to see that low vitality, poor physique, and even organic disease—hereditary or other—are very commonly the results of faulty education, or bringing up, if that is the better way of putting it. What is the consequence? Why, the doctor is retained, like husband or wife, for sickness and health; he is the medical adviser by the year, or usually by the lifetime. He thrives, not on sickness, but upon health. Drops in on his clients unawares, finds one girl doubled up over a book, another standing on one foot, notes the hectic flush and bright eye of this child, the tendency to drowsiness in that— the flabby arms and quick intelligence of the little town-bred family, the stolid dulness of the farmer's boy—for rich and poor come in course to him. He does not wait for disease to be set up, but averts the tendency; and though he has found no elixir of life, nor means of averting death—this, he may almost venture to promise his clients, that so long as they live, they shall live with eye not waxed dim, nor natural force abated. And—all this, because he knows that the body, too, must have its education, its careful regulation, and that bone and muscle and vital organs alike grow to the habits you set up in them."

Mr. Hilyard had been using his pencil for the last few minutes, and was evidently preparing to show on what lines the schools, too, had been advancing during this age of many revolutions, when—"It's eleven o'clock, and the ladies!" brought the discussion to an end.

Part III Concerning Youths and Maidens

Chapter 1. Concerning The Schoolboy And Schoolgirl

The Relations Between School Life and Home Life-school Discipline and Home Training

School, A New Experience

When the child goes to school a new life begins for him; not only so, but no change that may come to him afterwards will be in the same sense a new life. And for this reason: socially speaking, two lives are possible to us—private and public life; we live as members of a family, and as members of a commonwealth. Hitherto, the child has lived in the family; his duties have all been pretty plain, and his affection pretty fairly bestowed. Of course he loves and obeys his parents, more or less, and is fond of his brothers and sisters—there is no choice for him; and the law of the family and the love of the family follow him when he is allowed to mix with the outside world. "Mother says" is his law, "Father told me" his supreme authority. But when he goes to school, all that is changed: though he is still loving and dutiful towards those at home, other things have come in, and the child looks upon the world from a new standpoint. Parents may think, when they send their children to school, that the masters or mistresses and the studies are the points to be considered; that the children go to learn, i.e. to learn out of books, and that the heads of the school are, for the time being, in the place of parents to the children.

How far this may be true depends on another factor, sometimes left out of count, namely, the "All the boys" and "All the girls" of schoolboy and schoolgirl phrase. The wise parent, in selecting a school for his child, is not satisfied to examine the syllabus and to know that the masters bear a high character; he sends out feelers to test the direction of public opinion in the school: if public opinion set with a strong current towards order, effort, virtue, that is the school for him; his boy, he is assured, once entered there, will be carried along towards the right. No doubt there will be a few turbulent spirits in every considerable school, and lawlessness is contagious, but the thing to find out is, how far the lead of the scapegraces is followed by the rest.

But the direction of "public opinion" it is said, rests with the master. Not altogether: he will do his best to get it on his side; but he may be, like Arnold and Thring, years before he succeeds, and that, though he may have everything in his own character to fit him for the office of schoolmaster. We know how little to be depended upon is public opinion in the world; far more, in the little world of school, it veers with every shifting of the wind, just because boys and girls are less reasonable, more emotional, than men and women. Yet, little as it is to be depended upon, this vox populi within the school governs the school, and the masters are nowhere except as they get it on their side. Now, this fact shows the real constitution and government of the school: the family is a limited monarchy, with sovereign parents; the school is a republic, with an elected president. Of course the master may hold his post in spite of the boys, but his authority and influence, the real matters in question, he only holds so far as they go with him; that is, so far as they elect him to administer their affairs.

Now, we see why it is that the child finds himself in a new and very stimulating element when he goes to school. For the first time, he has to find his footing amongst his equals. At home, he has seldom had more than one equal, and that his friend—the brother or sister next him in age. Here, he has a whole class of his fellows, some stronger, some weaker than himself, working with him, shoulder to shoulder, running neck and neck with him in lessons and games. It is very exciting and delightful. The new boy catches the tone of the school: if the boys work, he works; if they dawdle, he dawdles,—unless he have been exceptionally well brought up. Happily, it is not too much to say that, as a rule, schoolboys and schoolgirls do work, in these days. School opinion is on the side of order and effort; and this, for several reasons. It is not that the young people are better or more diligent than young people used to be, but more powerful incentives are put before them; in fact, the motives to work are stronger than the motives to idle.

Examinations

The Universities' Local Examinations, and those of other public examining bodies, have effected a great change in the feeling of middle-class schools, both public and private, in this respect: it is possible for almost any boy or girl to get a distinction worth having, and enough care to make the effort to carry the rest along. Work is the order of the day: the desire of distinction, a strong spirit of emulation, stimulated by marks and prizes, do the work of government, and the teachers have little difficulty, except with the few rebellious spirits who decline to go the way of the others.

This looks so well on the face of it, that we ask, Is there nothing to set on the other side? But thus much, at least, must be allowed by both utilitarian and moralist—that the habit of work, the power of work, rapidity in work, the set of the will to a given task, are "the making" of man and woman; that the boy who has done the definite work necessary to pass a given examination is, other things being equal, worth twenty per cent more than he who has not been able to pull his forces together. But these "other things" must be looked into. Is the boy who prepares for a public examination—we are not speaking of prizes open only to a few, such as scholarships at the Universities, but of examinations where success is open to all who are up to a certain reasonable standard—is the boy who goes in for one of these in any respect at a disadvantage compared with him who does not?

Here comes in for consideration the question of "overpressure," a possibility—too serious to be passed over without investigation—which parents naturally dread more for their girls than their boys. In the first place, work, regular disciplinary exercise, is so entirely wholesome for the brain, that girls, even more than boys, should be the better for definite work with a given object. It cannot be too strongly put that, as a matter of health, growing girls cannot afford to be idle, mentally; it is just as pernicious that they should dawdle through their lessons as that they should lounge through the day. There is no more effectual check to the tendency to hysteria and other nervous maladies common to growing girls than the habit of steady brain-work. But then, it must be work under conditions: fit quantities at fit times, with abundant leisure for exercise and recreation.

Now, the question is, Is it possible to prepare for an examination, say, the Universities' Local Examination, Junior or Senior, under these conditions? For a girl of average intelligence, who has been fairly well taught up to her thirteenth year, it certainly is. It is not the steady work during the year that produces the symptoms of "brain-fag," but a few weeks of cram at the end, the struggle to go over the work of the year in a month or so, the excessive strain on the attention, the prolonged hours of study at the expense of play. This is, indeed, overpressure, and does harm. But it is unnecessary, because, as a matter of fact, it is useless; a name, or a date, a lucky shot or two, is all that comes of this senseless "grind." It is seldom that this kind of thing is done at the instance of teachers—the pupils invent the necessity for themselves and go to work blindly; and, therefore, parents can the more easily put it down, especially in day schools. It rests with them to say that their children shall go in for any examination, public or private, only on condition that little extra time be spent in study previous to the examination. Again, it is possible to reduce or increase the time appropriated to given subjects—language or science, say, according to the power of the pupil. And with these two precautions, there is no reason why the preparation for a public examination should do more than give the pupil a year's definite and wholesome work.

The next point to be considered is the quality of the work. There is no doubt that definite work, on a well-considered programme, with a given object in view, is a clear gain, leading to definiteness of purpose and concentration of effort and attention, the qualities that go to make a successful man. But what is to be said for the style of teaching, the method of study, encouraged by the system of school-work organised with a view to public examinations? and with what is it to be compared? And, in the first place, is it not assuming too much to suppose that these examinations do tell very greatly on the general work of middle class schools? The Times, some years ago, spoke within the mark in saying that the universities had entirely revolutionised the system of education in secondary schools by their "Local Examinations." It is not as if the regulations of the examining bodies affected only the few candidates; the whole of the first division of the school is worked upon the syllabus adopted; the second, the third, down to the lowest division, is worked towards that syllabus: that is, every pupil in the school gets the sort of teaching that is supposed to tell when his time comes to be examined; and so soon as the work of the school begins to take hold of the child, he is making efforts towards this grand result.

Nor did the Times say too much in praise of the impulse these examinations have given to secondary education, nor of the practical sterling value of the work obtained. It is a rare thing, now, to meet with a school of any standing which does not do thorough work, commonly tested by the fact that it sends in candidates for some examination. One hears of schools which obtain telling results by a system of cram, of no educative worth at all; but, as a whole, middle-class schools have reached a fair average level—few are much better or much worse than the rest. It used not to be so; a school was a place of real education or of miserable sham, according to the character of its head; but now, a scheme of work is prescribed; any man can see it carried out by assistants, if not by himself, and then his school is as good as another. In a word, the standing of a school no longer depends altogether upon force of character and organising power in its principal.

This levelling tendency of our school routine has its disadvantages; it is not easy to produce individuality in either school or pupil under the present conditions. Individuality, character, culture, public examinations—and a system of school-work based on such examinations—must necessarily strike at the head of these. For what is it possible to examine upon, when the same examination is held simultaneously all over the empire—what the pupil thinks, or what he knows, what he has seen set down in black and white? The latter, plainly, for it would be unfair to allow examiner or examinee any latitude of opinion in a matter that concerns so many. Therefore, facts, examinable matter, is the mental pabulum of the school life. If the master be given to discursive teaching, he pulls himself up, and sticks to facts; it is only upon matters of fact that it is possible to examine, and, therefore, it is upon his power of receiving, retaining, classifying, and reproducing facts that the pupil's success depends. There is no doubt that this fact-lore is an invaluable possession. But it is not culture; it does not, necessarily, produce a cultivated mind, the habits of reading and reflection:—

"A primrose by the river's brim
A yellow primrose is to him,
And it is nothing more"—

he, being the boy brought up with a view to successful examinations, and who has not found for himself a way to get out of the groove of his work.

Again, the routine of school-work becomes, at the same time, so mechanical and so incessant, there is so much hurry to get over the ground, so little leisure, so little opportunity for the master to bring himself en rapport with his pupil, to feel, as it were, the moulding of the boy's character under his fingers, that there is no space for the more delicate moral training, the refining touch, which a man of superior parts should bestow upon his pupil. The work, the routine itself, affords bracing moral training. Diligence, exactness, persistence, steady concentrated effort, are not to be despised; but something more is wanted, not easy to define, to be got only in sympathetic intercourse with our betters, morally and mentally, and this something is being pushed out in the press of work.

What is to be said then? Give up examinations, and let teachers and taught dawdle on in the old vague way? By no means: too much would be lost. Let the children go to schools as they now are, but with draw them from examination? No; for the training which schools offer now all hinges more or less upon the examinations; and if you do not get that, you get nothing in its place. But the thing is, to took the matter in the face: take the good the schools provide, and be thankful; take count of what they do not provide, and see that any culture or moral training which the schools fail to offer is to be had in the home.

The Playground

This parental duty is the more to be insisted on, because school life is so exigeant that the modern schoolboy or girl is nearly as much given up by parents as was the Spartan child of whom the State took possession. The boys and girls away at school are treated very much as visitors while at home, made much of at first, and then, before the long holidays are over, found slightly in the way; but it is not often that the parents take them under training as they do the young children who have not yet left the parent wing. The day school should offer the advantage of keeping the children constantly under home influence; but does it do so? As a matter of fact, are not the children so much occupied with school tasks, and their leisure so taken up with school companions and school interests, that the parents gradually lose hold of them? Then, the young people set up a code of their own: "Oh, nobody does so!" "Nobody thinks so!" "All the boys" or, "All the girls" say so-and-so, is supposed to settle most matters of discussion. And the worst of it is, many parents, with the diffidence of good people, are ready to believe that their children get something better at school than they have power to give; that, in fact, all proper and suitable training is given there, and they just make a merit of not interfering.

This absorption in school life is the more complete because the young people are, for the time, conscious of no want which the school does not supply. Work and play, given these in due proportion and of the fitting kind, and life is delightful: and nowhere in the world are work and play so well balanced as in the school—the boys' school, at any rate; it is less easy to make provision for the play of girls. Parents prize the discipline of the playground almost as much as that of the schoolroom; and rightly so—not only for the unequalled physical training that the games afford; but for the "pluck," the "endurance, foresight, strength, and skill," the obedience to law, the deference to authority, the readiness to give place to the best man, the self-reliance, the faithfulness to each other, even in a bad cause, cultivated by means of the school games—with their laws, their captains, their contests, their rivalries. And what finer training could the boys have for a world in which pluck and temper win the prizes?

One is half inclined to regret that the games of the girls, even when they adopt the very games of the boys, can hardly be taken in such terrible earnest, and, therefore, do not exercise the same discipline; but up to the present time, at any rate, life does not offer such rough after-usage to girls as to boys, and, therefore, the same training to hardihood is not called for. The influence which these organisations for play have on the characters of boys is not to be measured. Athletic and, at the same time, thoughtful young masters perceive that, if they are to influence boys, it must be as they are able to make a good figure in the playground, and thereby show that they are in sympathy with the prime interests of a boy's life. So of friendships, comradeships; it is in the playground the boy finds his ideal of manly excellence, the example he sets himself to follow.

School Government

The playground does invaluable work, and has much to do with the making of what is best and most characteristic in Englishmen; but, indeed, the training of the playground, as that of the schoolroom, is incomplete. The fact is, that the discipline of schoolroom and playground alike is largely carried on by stimulating and balancing, one against another, those desires which are common to us all as human beings—the desires of power, of society, of esteem, of knowledge, of mere animal activity, of excelling the rest, of work, or action, even avarice—the desire of wealth. Here is a formidable list; and it is quite possible, by playing upon and adjusting these natural desires, to govern a human being so that he may make a respectable figure in the world, while yet he has little sense of duty, feeble affections, and dispositions left to run wild, wanting the culture which should train mere disposition into character. Now, this way of governing a person through his desires is the easiest in the world. The nurse knows it very well; his desire, of praise, or play, or lollipops, leaves something always in her hands wherewith to reward the child's good behaviour. When attempts are made to stimulate people en masse, it is through their desires. They want work or play or power, money or land, and whoever plays upon any one of these desires gets the popular ear. Because this government through the desires is the easiest kind of government it is the most common, in the school as elsewhere; prizes, praise, place, success, distinction, whether in games or examinations, these are enough to keep a school going with such vigour, such éclat, that nobody is conscious of the want of other springs of action.

All these desires are right in themselves, within certain limits, and we may believe they were implanted in us as spurs to progress; the man who has no desire of wealth, no ambition, does not help himself and the world forward as does he, who has these desires. Again, in the school the desires are, on the whole, well regulated, one brought into play against another, and the result is, such sturdy qualities, sterling virtues, as "make a man" of the boy brought under school discipline. The weak place is, that boys and girls are treated too much "in the rough," without regard to the particular tendencies in each which require repression, or direction, or encouragement. The vain girl is made vainer, the diffident is snubbed: there is no time to hand a crutch to the lame, to pick up the stumbling. All must keep the pace or drop out of the race. It is astonishing how crude may be the character, how unformed the principles, how undeveloped the affections towards country, kindred, or kind, after a successful school career; the reason being, that the principle of government through the desires has left these things out of count. Nor is this the whole; the successful schoolboy too often develops into a person, devoid of intelligent curiosity, who hates reading, and shirks the labour of thought. I should like, here, to say a word about that most distressful evil which exceedingly depresses the thoughtful Heads of many of our great schools, and is, to parents, a terrorising, ambushed peril. As to what parents may do to prepare their boys for the risks to be encountered, I will say no word. Every one knows what may be done, and it is possible that too much has been said already.

We are apt to forget that every manner of offence is conceived in thought before it is produced in act; that, in fact, the offence is committed potentially once it is so conceived. Therefore, there is possible danger in all teaching which tends to occupy the mind with sexual matters: we may, in our blind zeal, befoul, for the young, the beauty of flowers, besmirch the innocence of birds. If we teach with a certain object in view, we are very likely to be the unwilling suggesters of evil, because young people are always aware of the arrière pensée. The teacher who deals with scientific facts, quâ science, and caring for nothing else, does no harm; while the virtuous man, with a moral end in view, unconsciously suggests the very evil he would fight most strenuously. The boys are aware that he is aware, and that is enough. I believe that safety lies in an unsuspected quarter. The unoccupied mind offers harbourage, as we know, to the seven devils, and intellectual emptiness, inanition, is probably the provocative cause of much that we deplore. Perhaps few schoolboys give a thought to their studies beyond the mere grind necessary to get them over; and yet boys are by nature consumed with intelligent curiosity. Give them entrancing studies which shall occupy their thoughts, and afford subjects for talk, as we all talk about the book we are reading, and there is no longer a vacuum for unclean imaginings to fill.

There are schools and schools; schools where mental discipline of the highest kind is combined with conscientious development of the character of the individual boy, and with such spiritual insight and teaching as help him into the better life; but such schools are not to be found in every street, and parents would do well not to take it for granted that it is one of these their boy attends: better, to take the school for what it is worth, thankful for the training it does afford; to look its deficiencies in the face, and take pains to supply by means of home training what the school fails to give.

Girls' Schools

Girls are, on the whole, worse off than boys as regards what they get out of school life. There is an element of generosity, of free and friendly "give and take" in boys' games, which is wanting to the girls. Beautiful and lasting girl friendships are formed in most schools, but girls do not always do each other good; perhaps because they are more delicate, nervous, and, consequently, irritable by organisation than the boys, they often enough contrive to get the worst and not the best out of each other. They have not the common bond which boys find in their games, and their alliances rest upon talk, which too often turns into gossip, possibly into sentimental and unwholesome gossip. A girl of fine, pure, noble character is like salt which seasons a whole school, and such girls are, happily, plentiful enough; but it is well parents should bear the other possibility in mind, that their daughter may be thrown amongst girls, not vicious, but with nothing in them, who will bring her down to their commonplace level.

Because girls, constitutionally sensitive, are open to the small envyings, jealousies, "cliquishness," which hinder them from getting all the good they should of each other's society, they are more dependent on the character of their head, and on their opportunities of getting in touch with her. If she be a woman of clear and vigorous mind, high principles, and elevated character, it is astonishing how all that is lovely in the feminine character is drawn towards her as by a magnet, and the girls about her mould themselves, each according to her own nature, and yet each after the type of the mistress, the "sympathy of numbers" spurring them on towards virtue, and each—

"Emulously rapid in the race."

Given, to adapt words used in describing Dr. Lant Carpenter as a schoolmaster, a woman with a power of "commanding the reverence and reconstituting the wills" of her pupils, of "great and varied intellectual power, with profound sense of right pervading the whole life and conversation, with the insight derived from a thorough and affectionate sympathy with (girl) nature," and she will "daily achieve triumphs which most teachers would believe impossible"; above all, this will be true if she succeed in putting into the hands of her pupils the key to the spiritual life. Such a woman gets all that is beautiful in girl-nature on her side—its enthusiasm, humility, deference, devotion: love works wonders, and the parents see their daughter growing under their eyes into the perfect woman they long to see their child become.

But schoolmistresses, as schoolmasters, of this type are rare; and, indeed, it is as well they are, for if the parents' highest functions are to be fulfilled by outsiders, what is left for father and mother to do? Parents will, no doubt, take care to place their daughters under generally estimable women, and having done that, they will estimate the training the school affords at its value, and endeavour to supplement it at home. How great the value of school discipline is to girls, they can appreciate who have had experience of the vagueness, inaccuracy, want of application, desultoriness, want of conscience about their work, dawdling habits of young women brought up at home under the care of governesses. Of course there are exceptions, governesses and governesses, and the girl trained under a woman who delights in knowledge for its own sake, will probably surpass the schoolgirl in range of non-personal interests, delight in life, and power of initiative. Girls often fare well when their fathers have a hand in their education. The home-taught girl may, in happy circumstances, excel in intellectual keenness and moral refinement; but for habits of work, power of work, conscientious endeavour in her work, the faithful schoolgirl is, as a rule, far before the girl who has not undergone school discipline, but has been taught by a commonplace untrained governess.

Home Training—Physical

It is not necessary to discuss here the respective merits of large and small schools, of day and boarding schools. We may assume at once that the discipline of the school is so valuable, that the boy or girl who grows up without it is at a disadvantage through life; while, at the same time, the training of the school is so far defective that, left to itself, it turns out very imperfect, inadequate human beings. The point for our consideration is, that the duty of the parents to educate their child is by no means at an end when he enters upon school life; because it rests with them to supplement what is weak or wanting in the training of the school.

Now, as hitherto, education has a fourfold bearing—on the body, the mind, the moral, and the religious nature of the pupil. As far as physical education goes, the parent who has boys at school may sit at his ease; they are as fish in the water, in the native element of that well-regulated animal activity which should train them up towards a vigorous, capable, and alert manhood.

The schoolboy is so well off in the matter of physical training, that the rest of the world may envy him. But the schoolgirl is less fortunate; her chief dependence is upon gymnastics, dancing, and calisthenics; and some of the severer kinds of gymnastics cannot be attempted without risk by girls in their "teens." Little provision is made in their case, as in that of the boys, for thorough abandonment to games as part of the business of life. If they have tennis-courts, only a few can play at a time; if they have playgrounds, the games are haphazard affairs, and the girls are not encouraged to a healthful exercise of their lungs. Day schools can seldom undertake to make full provision for the physical development of girls, and, therefore, that duty falls back upon the parents. Skipping-rope, shuttle-cock, rounders, cricket, tennis, archery, hockey, cannot be too much encouraged. Long country walks with an object, say, the getting of botanical specimens, should be promoted on at least two days a week. Every day, two or three hours in the open air should be secured, and when that is not possible, on account of the weather, the evening should end with a carpet dance, or with good romping games.

Where is the time to come from? That is a question requiring serious consideration on the part of mothers, on whose good management it must depend if their children are to grow up with that sense of leisure which should be a prerogative of youth. For it is very true that the time of the girls is too fully occupied, and it is only by careful mapping out that enough growing-time can be secured for them. Say, their waking-day is fourteen hours long, from seven in the morning till nine at night: something like five hours will be spent in the schoolroom—goings and comings count for open-air exercise, though not of the best; from an hour to an hour and a half will be required for home work, "preparation"; an hour, at least, for "practice" on the piano; two hours for meals, an hour for dressing, etc.; now, three hours and a half is all that is left upon the closest calculation; and two hours and a half of this should be given up without stint to the girls' physical culture and amusement.

The younger children, who have fewer or no home tasks, and take less time for practising, will have the more for play. But, if the schoolgirl is to get two or three hours intact, she will owe it to her mother's firmness as much as to her good management. In the first place, that the school tasks be done, and done well, in the assigned time, should be a most fixed law. The young people will maintain that it is impossible, but let the mother insist; she will thereby cultivate the habit of attention, the very key to success in every pursuit, as well as secure for her children's enjoyment the time they would dissipate if left to themselves. It seldom happens that home work is given which should occupy more than an hour to an hour and a half, and a longer time is spent in the habit of mental dawdling—a real wasting of brain substance. It is a mistake to suppose that efforts in this direction run counter to the intention of the teachers; on the contrary, the greatest impediment they meet with is that mental inertness in the children, who will rather dawdle for an hour over a task than brace the attention for five minutes' steady effort. There is promise that a certain strain will, by-and-by, be taken off home life by the removal of homework or evening 'preparation' from the school curriculum. Teachers will gradually discover that if they let their pupils work from fitting books in the three or four school hours, more ground will be covered in less time, and the occasion for home tasks (or evening work in schools) will disappear.

Firmness on the mother's part in enforcing promptness in the taking off and putting on of outdoor clothes, etc., and punctuality at meals, and in not allowing one occupation to overlap another, secures many a half-hour of pleasant leisure for the young people, and has the double advantage of also making them feel themselves under a firm home rule.

Home Training—Intellectual

The intellectual training of the young people must be left, in the main, to the school authorities. It is useless to remark further upon the subjects or the methods of study; the schoolmaster settles all that, and he, as we have seen, is greatly influenced by the lines laid down by certain examining bodies. Even where the teaching of the school is not satisfactory, there is little to be done: there is neither time nor opportunity for any other direct mental training; and to attempt it, or to criticise unfavourably the working of the school, has a bad effect on the pupil—he learns to undervalue what his school has to give him, but gets nothing else. But though parents can, and should, do nothing counter to the teachers, they may do much by playing into their hands.

It is important that parents should, so far as possible, keep up with their children, should know where they are and how they are getting on in their studies, should look into their books, give an eye to their written work, be ready with an opinion, a hint, a word of encouragement. They may feel and show hearty interest in the matter of their children's studies, and when the subject is less dry than the declension of a Latin noun may throw side-lights upon it by making it matter of table-talk. And this, for a double reason,—both as holding up the hands of the schoolmaster, and as strengthening their own. Parents do not always consider how far a word of interest from them goes to convert the dead words or a lesson into a living idea, never to be lost; and there is no excuse left for getting rusty in these days of many books. The schoolmaster reaps the benefit of such efforts—his task is lightened; he has to teach boys capable of responding; but of more consequence is it that the parents themselves keep their place as heads of the family. They keep the respect of their children; for once a boy begins to look down on the intellectual status of his parents, the entire honour and deference he owes them are at an end. Any pains taken to keep ahead should be repaid by the glow of honest pride the young people feel at every proof of intellectual power in their parents.

Home Training—Moral

(a) Honour towards Parents.—This brings us to the consideration of that education in morals which the young people must get at home, or not at all. The chief of their duties, that which should be kept always before the young, is the duty they owe to their parents: from this stem, all their other duties, to kindred, commonwealth, and neighbours, branch out; and more, they only perceive their obligations to Almighty God in proportion as they know what they owe to their human parents.

Now, parents do not always think wisely on this subject. There is a feeling abroad, that the behaviour of a child to his parent is a matter between those two alone; that if the parent choose to absolve his child from any close confidence, from obedience, respectful demeanour,—that is his business: he has as much right to do so as the slave-owner has to manumit his slaves. At the same time, two other notions prevail,—that the kindest and best thing parents can do by their children is to give them "a good time," as the Americans put it; and, that the children of these days are so much in advance of anything that went before them, that it is rather absurd to keep them in subordination to parents not half so clever as themselves. The outcome of these three popular fallacies is, that many parents give up the government of their children at a very early age—so soon, that is, as the school steps in to take possession: lax discipline, imperfect confidence, free and easy manners, the habit of doing that which is right in their own eyes, are permitted to grow up.

That school boys and girls should be thus thrown upon their own government is a blow to the interests of society, and a great loss to themselves—the loss of that careful moral training which it is the bounden duty of their parents to afford, throughout school life, at any rate, and through the two or three years that follow it. The problem is, how to maintain due parental dignity, to repress anything like a "hail, fellow, well met!" style of address, and yet to keep up the flow of affectionate intimacy, confidence, and friendly playfulness. Now, here is the secret of home government—put the child into the attitude of a receiver, the parent into that of an imparter, not merely of physical care and comfort, but of a careful and regular training for the responsibilities of life, and the rest comes easy. The difficulty is, that many parents find it hard to maintain this superiority to their children as the latter advance in age and set up other standards than those of home. They possibly feel themselves less clever, less worthy, than some others with whom their children come in contact; they are too honest to assume a dignity to which they doubt their right, so they step down from the rostrum, and stand on the same level as their children, willing to owe to affection and good-nature the consideration which is their lawful due.

Very likely such parents are not less, but more worthy than the persons they give place to; but that is not the question; they are invested with an official dignity; it is in virtue of their office, not of personal character, that they are and must remain superior to their children, until these become of an age to be parents in their turn. And parents are invested with this dignity, that they may be in a position to instruct their children in the art of living. Now, office in itself adds dignity, irrespective of personal character; so much so, that the judge, the bishop, who does not sustain his post with becoming dignity has nothing to show for himself. So of the parent; if he forego the respectful demeanour of his children, he might as well have disgraced himself before their eyes; for in the one case as in the other, he loses that power to instruct them in the art and science of living, which is his very raison d'être in the Divine economy.

If parents put it to themselves that their relation to their children is not an accident, but is a real office which they have been appointed to fill, they would find it easier to assume the dignity of persons called upon to represent a greater than themselves. The parent who feels that he has a Power behind him,—that he is, strictly, no more than the agent of Almighty God, appointed to bring the children under the Divine government, does not behave with levity and weakness; and holds his due position in the family as a trust which he has no right to give up.

And now, given the parents in their due position as heads of the family, and all the duties and affections which belong to the family flow out from that one principle as light from a sun. The parents are able to show continual tenderness and friendliness towards their children, without partiality and without weak indulgence. They expect, and therefore get, faithful and ready obedience. Their children trust them entirely, and therefore bestow confidence, and look for counsel; and, of course, treat their parents with due honour and respect. There is a spurious dignity which sometimes brings the parental character into discredit; a selfish and arbitrary parent requires much from, and gives little to, his children, treating them de haut en bas; and the children rebel, setting up their claims in opposition to those of their parents. But cases of this kind do not touch the point. Few children resist the authority of a parent who consistently and lovingly acts as the agent of a higher Authority. He is all the more a sovereign because he is recognised as a deputy sovereign.

But there are times when the "relations are strained"; and of these, the moment when the child feels himself consciously a member of the school republic is one of the most trying. Now, all the tact of the parents is called into play. Now, more than ever, is it necessary that the child should be aware of the home authority, just that he may know how he stands, and how much he is free to give to the school. "Oh, mither, mither why gar ye no' mak' me do it?" was the cry of a poor ne'er-do-weel Scotch laddie who had fallen into disgrace through neglect of his work; and that is just what every schoolboy or schoolgirl has a right to say who does not feel the pressure of a firm hand at home during the period of school life. They have a right to turn round and reproach their parents for almost any failure in probity or power in after-life. But no mere assertion of authority will do: it is the old story of the sun and the wind and the traveller's cloak. It is in the force of all-mighty gentleness that parents are supreme; not feebleness, not inertness—there is no strength in these; but purposeful, determined gentleness, which carries its point, only "for it is right." "The servant of God must not strive," was not written for bishops and pastors alone, but is the secret of strength for every "bishop," or overlooker, of a household.

(b) Gratitude towards Parents.—The parent will find that, for the sake of his child, tasks of some delicacy fall to him, which would be almost impossible as between man and man, and even in the relations of parent and child require tact and discrimination. For instance, he must foster gratitude in his child. There is nothing left to be said for the ungrateful person; even amongst the ancients, ingratitude was held heinous; and yet, what in the world is more natural than to take benefits as matters of course, our own due, and the duty of those who bestow them? We think so highly of our own deservings, are so unready to put ourselves in the place of another and see at what cost he is kind, that, certainly, gratitude is not to be held a wild fruit native to the soil of the human heart. Now, no one can ever owe so much to any living soul as to devoted parents; and if the man is to experience the holy emotion of gratitude, it is as these same parents cultivate in him the delightful sense of their love and their never-failing kindness.

It is a pity, but so it is; the children are so obtuse that they think no more of their parents' kindness as a personal matter than they do of sunshine or flowers, or any other pleasant thing in life. A mother sits up till midnight darning stockings for her boys; she says nothing about it, and the boys put their stockings on, scarcely knowing whether they are in holes or not. But "how hateful to be always reminding the children of such things, with a 'There now, see how I've had to work for you! I hope the time will come when you will do as much for me.'" Hateful, indeed, and most mischievous; that sort of thing not only irritates the hearer, but cancels the debt. But gentle rallying on "those great holes which kept mother up till midnight," with a "Never mind, my boy; you know, work for you is pleasure to your mother," sinks deep; and the boy is not worth his salt who, after that, does not mean to buy his mother silks and satins, gold and jewels, "when I'm a man!" If ever it is necessary to pinch, to do without things for the children's sake, let them know it; but do not reproach them with it; do not treat it as a hardship, but as a pleasure, for their sakes. That is, it is lawful for parents to bring their good deeds before their children as a child offers a flower to his mother, as a show of love, but not as a demand for service. For gratitude is nothing else but a movement of love, and only love kindles love.

(c) Kindness and Courtesy.—So of the other manifestations of love—kindness, courtesy, friendliness; these the parents must get from their children, not upon demand, but as love constrains them. Make occasions for services, efforts, offerings—let the children feel that their kindness is a power in the lives of their parents. I know of a girl upon whom it dawned for the first time, when she was far in her "teens," that she had any power to gratify her mother. Do not let the little common courtesies and attentions of daily life slip,—the placing of a chair, the standing aside or failing behind at proper times, the attentive eye at table, the attentive ear and ready response to question or direction. Let the young people feel that the omission of these things causes pain to loving hearts, that the doing of them is as cheering as the sunshine; and if they forget sometimes, it will only be that they forget, not that they are unwilling, or look upon the amenities of life as "all bosh."

Again, let there be a continuous flow of friendliness, graciousness, the pleasantness of eye and lip, between parent and child Let the boy perceive that a bright eye-to-eye "Good-morning, mother," is gladness to her, and that a cold greeting with averted face is like a cloud between his mother and the sun. Parents are inclined to drop these things because they are unwilling to take even their own children by the throat, with a "Pay me that thou owest"; but that is not the way to look at the matter; it is not a personal question at all. Wordsworth has a deeply suggestive little poem illustrating what I mean:—

"There is a change—and I am poor;
Your love hath been, nor long ago,
A fountain at my fond heart's door,
Whose only business was to flow;
And flow it did; not taking heed
Of its own bounty, or my need.
"What happy moments did I count I
Blest was I then, all bliss above I
Now, for this consecrated fount
Of murmuring, sparkling, living love,

What have I—shall I dare to tell?
A comfortless and hidden *well.*
"A well of love—it may be deep;
I trust it is—and never dry;
What matter? if the waters sleep
In silence and obscurity.
Such change, and at the very door
Of my fond heart, hath made me poor."
There is in the heart of every child a fountain of love,
"Whose only business is to flow";

and this it is the part of the parents to keep unsealed, unchoked, and flowing forth perennially in the appointed channels of kindness, friendliness, courtesy, gratitude, obedience, service. Keep the fountain flowing, and it will gladden not only the parents, towards whom is the first rush of the current, but all about them and beyond them—the family, the household, friends, kindred, schoolfellows, neighbours, the needy, the world, so far as it can reach. But let the spring be choked in its rise, in its natural outlet towards parents, and the chances are, it is lost, a mere buried well of love. How is the fountain to be kept aflow? Partly by this method of the poet's Complaint. Let son and daughter perceive the gladness which every outgoing of their love produces—the cloud that falls on the parent's heart when the love of the child is restrained. Natural reticence and pride incline us to take the "bounty" of the children's love for granted, and to make no sign of the pain caused by their thoughtless omissions. But these barriers of reserve should be broken down for the sake of the children, and they should be permitted to see, so far as possible, what is in the hearts of their parents towards them. And this, because no education tells so much, Godward or manward, as this education of the power of loving.

Another point to be borne in mind is, that love grows, not by what it gets, but by what it gives. Therefore, the young people must not get out of the habit of rendering services of love. There is danger of confounding mere affection, a more or less animal emotion, showing itself in coaxing and fondling, in "Mother, darling," "Father, dear," and—no more, with love, which, however affectionate it be in word and gesture, does not rest in these, but must exhibit itself in service. The little children are demonstrative, ready to give and take caresses, "loving" in their ways; but the boys and girls have, partly out of gaucherie, partly from a growing instinct of reticence, changed all that. They want at this awkward stage of life a great deal of tact and tenderness at the hands of their parents, and the channels of service, friendliness, and obedience must be kept visibly open for the love which will no longer flow in endearments.

The Awkward Age

Indeed, this, of the growing boy or girl, is not only an awkward, but a critical stage of life. For the first time, the young people are greatly occupied with the notion of their own rights: their duties are nowhere. Not what they owe, but what is due to them, it is, that oppresses their minds. "It's a shame," "It's not fair," "It's too bad," are muttered in secret, when no one ventures to murmur aloud,—and this, with aggravating unreasonableness, and a "one-sidedness" which grown-up people can hardly understand. But this tiresome behaviour does not arise from any moral twist in the young people; they really have more right than reason on their side: their claims might often be yielded, if there were none but themselves to consider. What they want, is, to have their eyes opened that they may see the rights of others as clearly as their own; and their reason cultivated, that they may have power to weigh the one against the other. This aggressiveness is not mere naughtiness. They must be met on their own ground. Care must be taken not to offend their exaggerated sense of justice as to all that affects themselves. They must get the immunities they can fairly claim; and their parents must be at the trouble to convince them, with good humour, when they are clearly in the wrong.

In the meantime, the state of feeling must be dealt with which would lead a boy to say, "I shan't," if he dared. He must be reached through his affections; the very feelings which make him offensive when centred upon himself, are beautiful and virtuous when they flow in the channels of justice and benevolence towards others. And this is a change not only possible, but easy and pleasant for parents to bring about. The feelings are there already; the strong sense of justice; and the love, which has become exaggerated self-love only because the attention has been allowed to fix upon self and its claims to the exclusion of others. It rests with the parent to turn the attention from self to other people, and the affections will flow in that direction to which the attention is turned.

For instance, let the young people feel that the happiness of home is a trust which every member of it has in charge; that the child who sits down to table with a sullen face destroys for the time the happiness of his whole family, just as a hand's-breadth held close to the eyes will shut out the whole light of the sun. What is it that makes the happiness of every day—great treats, great successes, great delights? No, but constant friendly looks and tones in those about us, their interest and help in our pursuits, their service and pity when we are in difficulty and trouble. No home can be happy if a single member of it allow himself in ugly tempers and bad behaviour. By degrees, great sensitiveness to the moral atmosphere of the home will be acquired; the happiness of a single day will come to be regarded as a costly vase which any clumsy touch may overthrow. Now, the attention is taken off self and its claims, and fixed upon brother and sister, father and mother, servants and neighbours; so slight a thing as a friendly look can add to the happiness of every one of these.

Affection flows naturally towards those to whom we can give happiness. A boy who feels himself of little account in his family will give all his heart to his dog; he is necessary to Puck's happiness, at any rate; and, as for the dog,—"I think it is wrong to let children have dogs. It spoils them for mankind," said the late Lord Lytton. Let the boy have his dog, but let him know to how many others even a pleasant word from him gives happiness for the moment. Benevolence, the delight in giving happiness, is a stream which swells as it flows. The boy who finds he really can make a difference to his home is on the look-out for chances. A hint as to what father or sister would like is not thrown away. Considerate obliging behaviour is no hardship to him when he is not "bothered" into it, but produces it of his own free will. Like begets like. The kindliness he shows is returned to him, and, by him, returned again, full measure, pressed down, and running over. He looks, not on his own things, but on the things of others.

His love of justice shows in the demand for "fair play" for others now; he will not hear others spoken ill of in their absence, will not assign unworthy motives, or accuse another easily of unworthy conduct; he is just to the conduct, the character, the reputation of others. He puts himself involuntarily in the place of the other, and judges as he would be judged.

"Teach me to feel another's woe,
To hide the faults I see;
That mercy I to others show,
That mercy show to me,"

is his unformed, unconscious prayer. His benevolence, again, his kindness, will reach, not only to the distresses of others, but will show itself in forbearance towards tiresome tempers, in magnanimity in the forgiveness of injuries. His habits of kind and friendly behaviour will, by degrees, develop into principles of action; until at last his character is established, and he comes to be known as a just and virtuous man. Towards this great result the parents can do little more than keep the channels open, and direct the streams; they draw the attention of their son to the needs and claims of others, and point out to him from time to time the ways in which he holds the happiness of others in his hands. It is needless to say how a selfish or worldly maxim thrown in—"Take care of yourself," "Look after your own interests," "Give tit for tat,'—may obstruct the channel or choke the spring. Does, then, the whole of moral training resolve itself into the culture of the affections? Even so; it is no new thing to us to learn that—

"As every rainbow hue is light,
so every grace is love,"

Home Training—Religious

With regard to the training, of the young in the religious life, I am chiefly anxious to call the reader's attention to the power and beauty of a holy youth. We are content, in this matter, with too low a standard for the children as for ourselves, looking for less than that which many a beautiful child attains in his degree—a life, "holy, harmless, undefiled, separate from sinners":—

"Who aimeth at a star,
Shoots higher, far,
Than he who means a tree."

For the few practical hints I shall venture to offer, they are in this, as in other matters of education, only what thoughtful mothers already carry out.

In the first place, "every word of God" is the food of the spiritual life; and these words come to us most freely in the moments we set apart in which to recollect ourselves, read, say our prayers. Such moments in the lives of young people are apt to be furtive and hurried; it is well to secure for them the necessary leisure—a quiet twenty minutes, say—and that, early in the evening; for the fag end of the day is not the best time for its most serious affairs. I have known happy results where it is the habit of the young people to retire for a little while, when their wits are fresh, and before the work or play of the evening has begun.

Again, the Christian life should be a progressive life. The boy should not be allowed to feel himself like a door on its hinges, always swinging over the same ground. New and definite aims, thoughts, subjects of prayer should be set before him week by week, that "something attempted, something done," may give him courage; and that, suppose he is harassed by failure, he may try in a new direction with new hope. Even those who do not belong to the Church of England would find her Sunday Collects, Epistles, and Gospels helpful, as giving the young people something definite to think about, week by week. We can hardly hope in this life to grow up to all there is in those weekly portions, but the youngest Christian finds enough to go on with, and has the reposing sense of being led, step by step, in his heavenward progress. I am not suggesting this as a substitute for wider reading of the Bible, only as a definite thought, purpose, and prayer for every week as it comes, in addition to whatever other prayers general or special needs may call for. The bringing of the thought of the collect and its accompanying scriptures home will afford occasion for a few earnest words, week by week, not to be readily forgotten. And this in itself is a gain, for we all experience some difficulty in speaking of the best things to the people we live amongst, especially to the young people.

Only one point more—a word as to the manner of keeping Sunday in the family. Do not let the young people feel themselves straitened by narrow views: give them freely the broad principle that what is right on Saturday is right on Sunday—right, but not in all things convenient; the Sunday has pursuits of its own; and we are no more willing to give up any part of it to the grind of the common business or the common pleasures of life, than the schoolboy is to give up a holiday to the grind of school-work. Even for selfish reasons of health and comfort we cannot afford to give up the repose to body, mind, and spirit which we owe to the change of thought and occupations the day brings.

Having made the principle of Sunday-keeping plain, make the practice pleasant. Let it be a joyous day—everybody in his best temper and gentlest manners. Put anxious cares aside on Sunday, for the children's sake; and if there be no "vain deluding mirth," let there be gaiety of heart and talk.

Let the day be full of its own special interests and amusements. An hour's reading aloud, from Sunday to Sunday, of a work of real power and interest, might add to the interest of Sunday afternoon; and this family reading should supply a pleasant intellectual stimulus.

A little poetry may well be got in: there is time to digest it on Sunday; not only George Herbert, Vaughan, Keble, and the like, but any poet who feeds the heart with wise thoughts, and does not too much disturb the peace of the day with the stir of life and passion. The point in the Sunday readings and occupations, is, to keep the heart at peace and the mind alive and receptive, open to any holy impression which may come from above, it may be in the fields or by the fireside. It is not that we are to be seeking, making efforts all day long, in church and out of it. We may rest altogether, in body and spirit; on condition that we do not become engrossed, that we keep ourselves open to the influences which fall in unexpected ways. This thought determines the choice of the Sunday story-book. Any pure, thoughtful study of character, earnest picture of life, will do to carry our thoughts upward, though the Divine Name be not mentioned; but tales full of affairs and society, or tales of passion, are hardly to be chosen.

It is inadvisable to put twaddling "goody-goody" story-books into the hands of the young people: a revulsion of taste will come, and then, the weakness of this sort of literature will be laid to the charge of religion. Music in the family is the greatest help towards making Sunday pleasant; but here, again, it is, perhaps, well to avoid music which carries associations of passion and unrest. There can, however, be little difficulty in making a suitable choice, when it is hardly too much to say that the greatest works of the greatest masters are consecrated to the service of religion.

"The liberal soul deviseth liberal things" is a safe rule once the principle is recognised, the purpose and meaning of the Sunday rest. I venture to enter so fully into this subject because the question of Sunday observances is one which comes up to be settled between the parents and every growing-up family.

Home Culture—Books

Although any attempt at intellectual training must be abandoned by the parents when once their children have gone to school, intellectual culture is a different matter, and this the young people must get at home, or nowhere. By this sort of culture I mean, not so much the getting of knowledge, nor even getting the power to learn, but the cultivation of the power to appreciate, to enjoy, whatever is just, true, and beautiful in thought and expression. For instance, one man reads—

"... He lay along,
Under an oak, whose antique root peeps out
Upon the brook that brawls along this wood;
To the which place a poor sequester'd stag,
That from the hunter's aim had ta'en a hurt,
Did come to languish;"—

and gets no more out of it than the four facts of the reclining man, the oak, the brook, and the wounded stag. Another reads, and gets these and something over—a delicious mental image, and a sense of exquisite pleasure in the putting of the thought, the mere ordering of the words. Now, the second has, other things being equal, a hundredfold the means of happiness which the first enjoys; he has a sixth sense, a new inlet of pleasure, which adds enjoyment to every hour of his life. If people are to live in order to get rich, rather than to enjoy satisfaction in the living, they can do very well without intellectual culture; but if we are to make the most of life as the days go on, then it is a duty to put this power of getting enjoyment into the hands of the young.

They must be educated up to it. Some children, by right of descent, take to books as ducks to the water; but delight in a fine thought, well set, does not come by nature. Moreover, it is not the sort of thing that the training of the schools commonly aims at; to turn out men and women with enough exact knowledge for the occasions of life, and with wits on the alert for chances of promotion, that is what most schools pretend to, and, indeed, do, accomplish. The contention of scholars is, that a classical education does more, turns out men with intellects cultivated and trained, who are awake to every refinement of thought, and yet ready for action. But the press and hurry of our times and the clamour for useful knowledge are driving classical culture out of the field; and parents will have to make up their minds, not only that they must supplement the moral training of the school, but must supply the intellectual culture, without which knowledge may be power, but is not pleasure, nor the means of pleasure.

The habit of casual reading, about which Sir John Lubbock says such wise and pleasant words, is a form of mild intellectual dissipation which does more harm than we realise. Many who would not read even a brilliant novel of a certain type, sit down to read twaddle without scruple. Nothing is too scrappy, nothing is too weak to "pass the time!" The "Scraps" literature of railway bookstalls is symptomatic. We do not all read scraps, under whatever piquant title, but the locust-swarm of this class of literature points to the small reading power amongst us. The mischief begins in the nursery. No sooner can a child read at all than hosts of friendly people show their interest in him by a present of a "pretty book." A "pretty book" is not necessarily a picture-book, but one in which the page is nicely broken up in talk or short paragraphs. Pretty books for the schoolroom age follow those for the nursery, and, nursery and schoolroom outgrown, we are ready for "Mudie's" lightest novels; the succession of "pretty books" never fails us; we have no time for works of any intellectual fibre, and we have no more assimilating power than has the schoolgirl who feeds upon cheese-cakes. Scott is dry as dust, even Kingsley is "stiff." We remain, though in another sense than that of the cottage dame, "poor readers" all our days. Very likely these strictures do not touch a single reader of this page, and I am like a parson of the three-decker age inveighing against the ways of the thieves and drunkards who were not in the pews. But the mischief is catching, and the children of even reading parents are not safe.

Guard the nursery; let nothing in that has not the true literary flavour; let the children grow up on a few books read over and over, and let them have none, the reading of which does not cost an appreciable mental effort. This is no hardship. Activity, effort, whether of body or mind, is joyous to a child. We older people who went out of our Robinson Crusoe into our Scott did not find the strong meat too much for us. I wonder does any little girl in these days of many books experience the keen joy of the girl of eleven I can recall, crouching by the fireside, clasping her knees, and listening, as she has never listened since, to the reading of Anne of Geierstein? Somehow, the story has never been re-read; but to this day, no sense impressions are more vivid than those of the masked faces, the sinking floor, the weird trial, the cold bright Alpine village—and no moral impression stronger than that made by the deferential behaviour of "Philip" to his father. Perhaps the impression made later by the Heir of Redelyffe ranks next in intensity. But we must adapt ourselves to new conditions; "books for the young" used to be few and dull; now, they are many and delightful.

In connection with this subject let me add a word about story-telling. Here are some of the points which make a story worth studying to tell to the nestling listeners in many a sweet "Children's Hour";—graceful and artistic details; moral impulse of a high order, conveyed with a strong and delicate touch; sweet human affection; a tender, fanciful link between the children and the Nature-world; humour, pathos, righteous satire, and last, but not least, the fact that the story does not turn on children, and does not foster that self-consciousness, the dawn of which in the child is, perhaps, the individual "Fall of Man." But children will not take in all this? No; but let it be a canon that no story, nor part of a story, is ever to be explained. You have sown the seed; leave it to germinate.

Every father and mother should have a repertoire of stories—a dozen will do, beautiful stories beautifully told; children cannot stand variations. "You left out the rustle of the lady's gown, mother!" expresses reasonable irritation; the child cannot endure a suggestion that the story he lives in is no more than the "baseless fabric of a vision." Away with books, and "reading to"—for the first five or six years of life. The endless succession of story-books, scenes, shifting like a panorama before the child's vision, is a mental and moral dissipation; he gets nothing to grow upon, or is allowed no leisure to digest what he gets. It is contrary to nature, too. "Tell us about the little boy who saved Haarlem!" How often do the children who know it ask for that most hero-making of all tales! And here is another advantage of the story told over the story read. Lightly come, lightly go, is the rule for the latter. But if you have to make a study of your story, if you mean to appropriate it as bread of life for your children, why, you select with the caution of the merchantman seeking goodly pearls. Again, in the story read, the parent is no more than the middleman; but the story told is food as directly and deliberately given as milk from the mother's breast. Wise parents, whose children sit with big eyes pondering the oft-told tale, could tell us about this. But it must be borne in mind that the story told is as milk to the child at the breast. By-and-by comes the time when children must read, must learn, and digest for themselves. By the way, before a child begins school work may be the time to give a little care to a subject of some importance.

We are in a bad way for epithets: there are hardly more than a dozen current amongst us; and of these one person has seldom more than one or two in everyday use. A cup of tea, a dress, a picture, a book, a person,—is "nice," "perfect," "delicious," "delightful," "jolly," according to the speaker; not at all according to the thing spoken of. Adverbs help a little; a thing may be "nice," "how nice!" or "too awfully nice!" but the help is rather in the way of force than of variety. J. finds all agreeable things "too awfully nice!" while B. finds the same things only "nice" As a rule, things and persons have each one distinctive quality; to see what that is in a flash, and to express it in the fittest word, is a proof of genius, or of the highest culture. "That abysmal question, the condition of East London":—if one had not known that the speaker was a man of just perceptions and wide range of thought, intimately conversant with the questions of the day, that one phrase of a short conversation would have conveyed all that and more. The fitness of this use of "abysmal" stamped the speaker. Little children often surprise and amuse their elders by the fitness and elegance of their phraseology. We have only to foster this power of theirs, to put good words in their way, to treat the perpetual use of "jolly" or "delicious" as rather idiotic, and we are not only fitting our children to shine in society, but doing something to conserve the treasures of the beautiful mother-tongue of our inheritance. It might be worthwhile to hunt up good strong Saxon epithets for everyday use from the writers of the sixteenth and seventeenth centuries. Milton alone affords a treasure-trove. In the hymn beginning,

"Let us with a gladsome mind,"

there are half-a-dozen adjectives used with original force; perhaps half-a-dozen peculiar to that hymn, in their use if not in their form. We cannot go about talking of the "golden-tressed sun"; that is too good for us;

but to get "gladsome" into our common speech is worth an effort. "Happy-making" again, in the wonderful Ode to Time,—could we have a fitter word for our best occasions?

Letter-Writing

Is it true that the charming art of letter-writing has gone out with the introduction of the halfpenny post-card? "There is a great deal to be said on both sides" would, doubtless, be Sir Roger de Coverley's decision; anyway, if we do not write letters, the useful little post-card is not to blame. But, do we not? Have we not all correspondents whose epistles are delightful in their rippling, sparkling flow of talk, with just the little touches of tenderness and confidence which make a letter a personal thing? Do we not know what it is to open an envelope with the certainty that we shall take pure delight in every line of its enclosure? Because we love the writer? Not necessarily. The morning's post may bring you an epistle from an unknown correspondent which shall captivate you, fill you with a sense of well-being for a whole day; and this, not because of the contents, but simply because the gracious courtesy of it puts you on good terms with yourself and the world. One man may refuse a favour and another grant it; and the way in which the refusal is couched may give you more pleasure than the concession.

Possibly, sincere deference is the ingredient which gives flavour to a gracious letter; and if we do not write epistles as charming as those of our grandfathers and grandmothers, is it because we do not think enough of one another to make a spontaneous outpouring worth while? The children of parents living in India usually write and receive interesting letters, and this, because children and parents are glad to make the most of the only means of knowing each other. Perhaps no opportunity of writing detailed, animated letters to children should be omitted. Let them grow up with the idea that it is worth while to write good letters. That schoolboy whose correspondence for a term was comprised in two post-cards, "All right:" "Which train?" is not a good model, except as brevity is the soul of wit!

Reading Aloud

There is little opportunity to give intellectual culture to the boy taken up with his school and its interests; the more reason, therefore, to make the most of that little; for when the boy leaves school, he is in a measure set; his thoughts will not readily run in new channels. The business of the parent is to keep open right-of-way to the pleasant places provided for the jaded brain. Few things help more in this than a family habit of reading aloud. Even a dry book is readable when everybody listens, while a work of power and interest becomes delightful when eye meets eye at the telling bits. To read The Newcomes to yourself is like sitting down to a solitary feast of strawberries and cream; every page has that in it which demands to be shared.

There are few stronger family bonds than this habit of devoting an occasional hour to reading aloud, on winter evenings, at any rate. The practice is pleasant at the time, and pleasant in the retrospect, it gives occasion for much bright talk, merry and wise, and quickens family affection by means of intellectual sympathy. Indeed, the wonder is that any family should neglect such a simple means of pure enjoyment, and of moral, as well as intellectual culture. But this, of reading aloud, is not a practice to be taken tip and laid down at pleasure. Let the habit drop, and it is difficult to take it up again, because every one has in the meantime struck a vein of intellectual entertainment for himself—trashy stuff, it may be,—which makes him an unwilling listener to the family "book." No; let an hour's reading aloud be a part of the winter evening at home—on one or two evenings a week, at any rate—and everybody will look forward to it as a hungry boy looks for his dinner.

If reading is to be pleasant to the listeners, the reading itself must be distinct, easy, and sympathetic. And here is something more which parents must do for their children themselves, for nobody else will get them into the habit of reading for the pleasure of other people from the moment when they can read fluently at all. After indistinct and careless enunciation, perhaps the two most trying faults in a reader are, the slowness which does not see what is coming next, and stumbles over the new clause, and the habit of gasping, like a fish out of water, several times in the course of a sentence.

The last fault is easy of cure: "Never breathe through the lips, but always through the nostrils, in reading," is a safe rule: if the lips be closed in the act of taking breath, enough air is inhaled to inflate the lungs, and supply "breath" to the reader: if an undue supply is taken in by mouth and nostrils both, the inconvenience is caused which relieves itself in gasps.

The stumbling reader spoils his book from sheer want of attention. He should train himself to look on, to be always a line in advance, so that he may be ready for what is coming. Faults in enunciation should be dealt with one by one. For instance, one week the reader takes pains to secure the "d" in "and"; the other letters will take care of themselves, and the less they are heard the better. Indeed, if the final consonants are secured, d, t, and ng especially, the reading will be distinct and finished.

Another advantage of the family lecture is, that it enables parents to detect and correct provincialisms; and, however anxious we may be, on historical grounds, to preserve dialect, few people desire to preserve it in the persons of their own children. For the rest, practice makes perfect. Let everybody take his night or his week for reading, with the certainty that the pleasure of the whole family depends on his reading well.

The Book for the Evening Lecture

To attempt a list of books suitable for the family lecture would be as hopeless as it is unnecessary; but it is possible to discuss the principles on which the selection should be made. In the first place, to get information is not the object of the family reading, but to make the young people acquainted with the flavour of, to give them a taste for a real "book"—that is, roughly speaking, a work of so much literary merit, that it should be read and valued for the sake of that alone, whatever its subject-matter.

This rule makes a clean sweep of the literature to be found in nine houses out of ten—twaddling story-books, funny or "good"; worthless novels; second-rate writing, whether in works of history or of general literature; compendiums, abstracts, short sketches of great lives, useful information in whatever form. None of these should be admitted to the evening lecture, and, indeed, the less they are read at all, the better. A good encyclopaedia is an invaluable storehouse of facts, and should be made use of to elucidate every difficulty that occurs in general reading; and information got in this way, at the moment it is wanted, is remembered but it is a mistake to read for information only.

Next, the book must be as interesting, amusing, or pathetic, as may be, but not too profound; the young people have been grinding all day, and now they want relaxation. One is sorry for girls and boys who do not hear the Waverley Novels read at home; nothing afterwards can make up for the delight of growing up in the company of Peveril of the Peak, Meg Merrilees, Jonathan Oldbuck, the Master of Ravenswood, Caleb Baiderstone, and the rest; and every page is a training in righteous living and gentlemanlike feeling. But novels are not the only resource; well-written books of travel are always charming; and, better than anything, good biographies of interesting people; not any of the single-volume series of "Eminent" persons, but a big two-volume book that gives you time to become at home with your man.

Important historical works had better be reserved for the holiday, but historical and literary essays by men of letters afford very delightful reading. There is no hurry. The evening reading is not task work. It is not important that many books should be read; but it is important that only good books should be read; and read with such ease and pleasant leisure, that they become to the hearers so much mental property for life.

The introduction to a great author should be made a matter of some ceremony. I do not know whether a first introduction to Ruskin, for instance, is the cause of such real emotion now as it was to intelligent young people of my generation; but the Crown of Wild Olive still, probably, marks a literary epoch for most young readers.

One other point: it is hopeless and unnecessary to attempt to keep up with current literature. Hereafter, it may be necessary to make some struggle to keep abreast of the new books as they pour from the press; but let some of the leisure of youth be spent upon "standard" authors, that have lived through, at least, twenty years of praise and blame.

Poetry as a Means of Culture

Poetry takes first rank as a means of intellectual culture. Goethe tells us that we ought to see a good picture, hear good music, and read some good poetry every day; and, certainly, a little poetry should form part of the evening lecture. "Collections" of poems are to be eschewed; but some one poet should have at least a year to himself, that he may have time to do what is in him towards cultivating the seeing eye, the hearing ear, the generous heart.

Scott, of course, here as before, opens the ball, if only for the chivalry, the youthful enthusiasm of his verse. Then, there is always a stirring story in the poem, which is a recommendation to the young reader. Cowper, who does not tell many stories, is read with pleasure by boys and girls almost as soon as they begin to care for Scott; the careful, truthful word-painting of The Task, unobscured by poetic fancies, appears to suit the matter-of-fact young mind. It is pleasant, too, to know poetry which there are frequent opportunities of verifying:—

"Now from the roost, or from the neighb'ring pale,
Come trooping, at the housewife's well-known call,
The feather'd tribes domestic:"—

who that has ever been in the country has not seen that? Goldsmith, and some others, take their places beside Cowper, to be read or not, as occasion offers. It is doubtful if Milton, sublime as he is, is so serviceable for the culture of the "unlearned and ignorant" as are some less distinguished poets; he gets out of reach, into regions of scholarship and fancy, where these fail to follow. Nevertheless, Milton must be duly read; the effort to follow his "high themes" is culture in itself. Also, "Christopher North" is right; good music and fine poetry need not be understood to be enjoyed:—

Together both, ere the high lawns appeared
Under the opening eyelids of the morn,
We drove a-field, and both together heard
What time the gray-fly winds her sultry horn,
Battening our flocks with the fresh dews of night,
Oft till the star, that rose at evening bright,
Toward heaven's descent had sloped his westering wheel:"—

the youth who carries about with him such melodious cadences will not readily be taken with tinsel. The epithets of Lycidas alone are an education of the poetic sense.

Many of us will feel that Wordsworth is the poet to read, and grow thereby. He, almost more than any other English poet of the last century, has proved himself a power, and a power for good, making for whatever is true, pure, simple, teachable; for what is supersensuous, at any rate, if not spiritual.

The adventures of Una and her tardy, finally victorious knight offer great food for the imagination, lofty teaching, and fine culture of the poetic sense. It is a misfortune to grow up without having read and dreamt over the Faerie Queene.

There is no space to glance at even the few poets each of whom should have his share in the work of cultivating the mind. After the ploughing and harrowing, the seed will be appropriated by a process of natural selection; this poet will draw disciples here, that, elsewhere; but it is the part of parents to bring the minds of their children under the influence of the highest, purest poetic thought we have. As for Coleridge, Keats, Shelley, and others of the "lords of language," it may be well to let them wait this same process of selection.

And Shakespeare? He, indeed, is not to be classed, and timed, and treated as one amongst others,—he, who might well be the daily bread of the intellectual life; Shakespeare is not to be studied in a year; he is to be read continuously throughout life, from ten years old and onwards. But a child of ten cannot understand Shakespeare. No; but can a man of fifty? Is not our great poet rather an ample feast of which every one takes according to his needs, and leaves what he has no stomach for? A little girl of nine said to me the other day that she had only read one play of Shakespeare's through, and that was A Midsummer Night's Dream. She did not understand the play, of course, but she must have found enough to amuse and interest her. How would it be to have a monthly reading of Shakespeare—a play, to be read in character, and continued for two or three evenings until it is finished? The Shakespeare evening would come to be looked on as a family festa; and the plays, read again and again, year after year, would yield more at each reading, and would leave behind in the end rich deposits of wisdom.

It is unnecessary to say a word about the great later poets, Browning, Tennyson, and whoever else stands out from the crowd; each will secure his own following of young disciples from amongst those who have had the poetic taste developed; and to develop this appreciative power, rather than to direct its use, is the business of the parents.

So much for the evening readings, which will in themselves carry on the intellectual culture we have in view: given, the right book, family sympathy in the reading of it, and easy talk about it, and the rest will take care of itself.

The evening readings should be entertaining, and not of a kind to demand severe mental effort; but the long holidays are too long for mere intellectual dawdling. Every Christmas and summer vacation should be marked by the family reading of some great work of literary renown, whether of history, or purely of belles lettres. The daily reading and discussion of one such work will give meaning and coherence to the history "grind" of the school, will keep up a state of mental activity, and will add zest to the general play and leisure of the holidays.

Yet be it confessed, that in the matter of reading, this sort of spoon-feeding is not the best thing, after all. Far better would it be that the young people should seek out their own pastures, the parents doing no more than keep a judicious eye upon their rovings. But the fact is, young people are so taken up with living, that, as a rule, they do not read nowadays; and it is possible that a course of spoon-meat may help them over an era of feeble digestive power, and put them in the way of finding their proper intellectual nourishment.

Table-Talk

The character of the family reading will affect that of the talk; but considering how little parents see of young people once entered on their school career, it is worth while to say a few words of the table-talk which affords parents their best opportunity of influencing the opinions of the young. Every one is agreed that animated table-talk is a condition of health. No one excuses the churlish temper which allows a member of a family to sit down absorbed in his own reflections, and with hardly a word for his neighbours. But conversation at table is something more than a means of amusement and refreshment. The career of many a young person has turned upon some chance remark made at the home table. Do but watch the eagerness with which the young catch up every remark made by their elders on public affairs, books, men, and you will see they are really trying to construct a chart to steer by; they want to know what to do, it is true, but they also want to know what to think about everything.

Parents sometimes forget that it is their duty to give their children grounds for sound opinions upon many questions which concern us as human beings and as citizens; and then they are scandalised when the young folk air audacious views picked up from some advanced light of their own age and standing. But they will have views; the right to have and to hold an opinion is one of those points on which the youth makes a stand.

A few parents are unjust in this matter. It is not only the right, but the duty of the growing intelligence to consider the facts that come before it, and to form conclusions; and the assumption that parents have a right to think for their children, and pass on their own views unmodified upon literature and art, manners and morals, is exceedingly trying to the young; the headstrong resent it openly, the easy-going avoid discussion, and take their own way. But, it is said, the young are in no condition to form sound opinions; they have neither the knowledge nor the experience which should guide them. That is true, and they know it, and hang on the lips of their elders for what may help them to adjust their views of life. Here is the opportunity of parents: the young people will not take ready-made opinions, therefore suppress yours; put the facts before them in the fairest, fullest light, and leave them to their own conclusions. The more you withhold your opinions, the more anxious they are to get at them. People are, for them, sharply divided into good and bad; actions are vicious or virtuous; events come as blessings or misfortunes. They have not arrived at the "years that bring the philosophic mind"; they are inclined to be severe, and have no notion of a middle view.

Now, this period in the life of a boy or girl, when he or she feels the necessity of having an opinion upon every subject under the sun, is a critical one—a turning-point, for better or worse, in the lives of many young people, and for this reason; they will find somewhere the confidant who is to mould their opinions for them. Many a mother can put her finger on the moment when her boy or girl came under the influence of So-and-so, and took to giddy or godless courses. The culture of judgment in the crude mind of the youth is one of the most delicate tasks inposed on the parent. He must not be arbitrary, as we have seen. He must not be negligent. He must not be didactic; the young cannot stand preaching. He should be liberal, gentle, just, inclined to take large kindly views, to praise rather than to blame, but uncompromising on questions of principle, quick to put his finger on the blot, ready to forgive, but not to excuse; and, at the same time, ready to allow virtues to the man who exhibits one vice.

This last is important: the young, with their sharp demarcations, when they find themselves in his company, discover that the devil is not so black as he was painted, and, forthwith, conclude that he is a very good fellow, and that the bad things said of him are mere slanders. This is the natural history of half the ruinous companionships young people form. If, on the contrary, they come forth armed with this sort of opinion,—"So-and-so is a forward girl; she is really honest and good-natured, but her lawlessness makes her an undesirable companion,"—the case is altered; the girl has had fair play; and no further drawings are felt towards her companionship.

Allowing that it rests with the parents to give their children grounds for sound opinions on men and movements, books and events, when are they to get opportunity for this sort of culture? Whenever they fall into talk with, or in the presence of, their children; but especially at table—other opportunities come by chance, but this is to be relied on. I was once spending an evening in company with a wise and learned man, and had much delightful talk until he unfortunately said, "I jotted down so-and-so as a subject of conversation"; that spoiled it. But, indeed, it is very well worth while for parents to lay themselves out for conversation with their children, and to store up from day to day a few subjects of general interest, only they must not reveal the "jotting down." If the parents come to table with preoccupied minds, the young people either remain silent, or get the talk into their own hands; in which case, it is either the "shop" of school and playground, or the

"Who danced with whom, and who is like to wed,"

of a more advanced age.

This is the opportunity to keep the young people informed upon the topics of the day,—who has made a weighty speech; who has written a book, what its merits and defects; what wars and rumours of wars are there; who has painted a good picture, and what are the characteristics of his style. The Times newspaper and a good weekly or monthly review will furnish material for talk every day in the week. The father who opens the talk need not be afraid he will have to sustain a monologue; indeed, he had better avoid prosing; and nothing is more delightful than the eager way the children toss the ball to and fro. They want to know the inns and outs of everything, recollect something which illustrates the point, and inevitably corner the thing talked about for investigation—is it "right," or "wrong," "good," or "bad"; while the parents display their tact in leading their children to form just opinions without laying down the law for them. The boys and girls are engaged with the past, both in their school-work and their home reading, and any effort to bring them abreast of the times is gratifying to them; and it has a vivifying effect on their studies.

Aesthetic Culture

In venturing to discuss the means of aesthetic culture, I feel that to formulate canons of taste is the same sort of thing as to draw up rules of conscience; that is, to attempt to do for other people what every one must do for himself. It may be vicious to have a flower pattern on our carpet, and correct to have such a pattern on our curtains; but if so, the perception of the fact must be the result of growth under culture. If it come to us as an edict of fashion that we adorn our rooms with bulrushes and peacocks' feathers; that we use geometrical forms in decorative art, rather than natural forms conventionally treated; that we affect sage-green and terra-cotta,—however good may be the effect of room or person, there is little taste displayed in either. For taste is the very flower, the most delicate expression of individuality, in a person who has grown up amidst objects lovely and befitting, and has been exercised in the habit of discrimination. Here we get a hint as to what may and what may not be done by way of cultivating the aesthetic sense in young people. So far as possible, let their surroundings be brought together on a principle of natural selection, not at haphazard, and not in obedience to fashion. Bear in mind, and let them often hear discussed and see applied, the three or four general principles which fit all occasions of building, decorating, furnishing, dressing: the thing must be fit for its purpose, must harmonise with both the persons and the things about it; and, these points considered, must be as lovely as may be in form, texture, and colour; one point more—it is better to have too little than too much. The child who is accustomed to see a vase banished, a chintz chosen, on some such principles as these, involuntarily exercises discriminating power; feels the jar of inharmonious colouring, rejects a bedroom water-jug all angles for one with flowing curves, and knows what he is about. It may not be possible to surround him with objects of art, nor is it necessary; but, certainly, he need not live amongst ugly and discordant objects; for a blank is always better than the wrong thing. "Nothing can be a work of art which is not useful, that is to say, which does not minister to the body when well under the command of the mind, or which does not amuse, soothe, or elevate the mind in a healthy state. What tons upon tons of unutterable rubbish, pretending to be works of art in some degree, would this maxim clear out of our London Houses."—William Morris

It is a pity that, in pictures and music, we are inclined to form "collections," just as in poetry. Let us eschew collections. Every painter, every composer, worth the name, has a few master ideas, which he works out, not in a single piece, but here a little and there a little, in a series of studies. If we accept the work of the artist as a mere external decoration, why, a little of one and a little of another does very well; but if we accept the man as a teacher, who is to have a refining, elevating effect upon our coarser nature, we must study his lessons in sequence, so far as we have opportunity. A house with one or two engravings from Turner in one room, from Millet in another, from Corot's pictures in a third, would be a real school of art for the child; he would have some little opportunity of studying, line by line, three masters at least, of comparing their styles, getting their characteristics by heart, perceiving what they mean to say by their pictures, and how they express their meaning. And here is a sound foundation for art-education, which should perhaps, for most of us, consist rather in drawing out the power to appreciate than the power to produce. At the same time, give the young people one or two good water-colour sketches to grow upon, to show them what to see in landscape.

It is not, however, always possible to choose pictures according to any such plan; but in default of more, it is something to get so thoroughly acquainted with even a good engraving of any one picture, that the image of it retained by the brain is almost as distinct as the picture itself. All that the parents can do is to secure that the picture be looked at; the refining influence, the art-culture, goes on independently of effort from without. The important thing is, not to vitiate the boy's taste; better to have a single work of art in the house upon which his ideas form themselves, than to have every wall covered with daubs. That the young people must commonly wait for opportunities afforded by picture-galleries to learn how the brush can catch the very spirit and meaning of nature, is not so great a loss as it would seem at first sight. The study of landscape should, perhaps, prepare them for that of pictures: no one can appreciate the moist solid freshness of the newly ploughed earth in Rosa Bonheur's pictures who has not himself been struck by the look of the clods just turned up by the plough. But, on the other hand, what is to be said to this, from Fra Lippo Lippi?—

"Don't you mark, we're made so that we love
First when we see them painted, things we have passed
Perhaps a hundred times, nor cared to see:
And so they are better painted—better to us,
Which is the same thing. Art was given for that—
God uses us to help each other so,
Lending our minds out. Have you noticed now
Your cullion's hanging face? A bit of chalk,
And, trust me, but you should though. How much more
If I drew higher things with the same truth!
That were to take the prior's pulpit-place—
Interpret God to all of you!"

Pictures or landscape, all the parents can do is to put their children in the way of seeing, and, by a suggestive word, get them to look. The eye is trained by seeing, but also by instruction; and I need hardly call attention to Mr. Ruskin's Modern Painters, as the book which makes art-education possible to outsiders.

If culture flows in through the eye, how much more through the ear, the organ of that blessed sixth sense, which appears to be distributed amongst us with partial favour. A great deal of time and a good deal of money is commonly spent to secure to the young people the power of performing indifferently upon an instrument; nor is even an indifferent performance to be despised: but it is not always borne in mind that to listen with discriminating delight is as educative and as "happy-making" as to produce; and that this power might, probably, be developed in everybody, if only as much pains were spent in the cultivation of the musical sense as upon that of musical facility. Let the young people hear good music as often as possible, and that under instruction. It is a pity we like our music, as our pictures and our poetry, mixed, so that there are few opportunities of going through, as a listener, a course of the works of a single composer. But this is to be aimed at for the young people; let them study occasionally the works of a single great master until they have received some of his teaching, and know his style.

Chapter 2. Concerning The Young Maidens At Home

Young Maidenhood—the Formation of Character and Opinions

"For life in general there is but one decree. Youth is a Blunder."—Disraell.

The idea of staying at home "for good" is delightful to the schoolgirl, and her parents look forward with equal pleasure to having their daughter about them in her bright fresh youth. If the young girl be docile and gentle, and ready to fall into the relation of pupil-friend to her parents, and if they be wise and kind enough to put themselves in the place of their daughter, and realise how much teaching and counsel she still requires of them, the relation is a very sweet one. If, on the other hand, the parents are content to let their young daughter shake down into her place with the notion that all they have to do now is to give her a fair share of whatever "home" offers, the relation is found embarrassing, both by the girl and her parents. Her maiden sweetness notwithstanding, the parents are disappointed to find their daughter so little formed. She is not an interesting companion at present, poor child! Her talk is full of "oh," "well," "you know." She has many unreasoning enthusiasms and aversions, and these are her opinions, such as they are. She has brought some little knowledge out of the schoolroom, but this appears to do little towards giving her soundness of judgment.

Her affections are as lawless as her opinions: all the emotional sentiment in her is bestowed on some outsider, girl or woman friend, most likely, while the people who have claims on her are overlooked royally. So of her moral sense: duties she acknowledges, and will move heaven and earth to fulfil them—overstrained loyalty to a friend, excessive religious observances, perhaps; while she is comically blind to duty as her elders see it; does not scruple about disobedience, evasions, even deliberate fibs. She could do great things in a great cause, so she thinks, but the trivial round, the common task, afford her occasions of stumbling. She likes to talk about herself—what she feels, thinks, purposes, and her talk is pathetic, as showing how far she is in the dark as to the nature of the self about which her thoughts are playing curiously. And this is a thoroughly nice girl, a girl who will make something of herself at last, even if left to her own devices, but whom a little friendly help may save from much blundering and sadness.

There are girls of another pattern, who have no enthusiasms—other than a new "frock" excites; who do not "gush," have no exaggerated notions of duty or affection, but look upon the world as a place wherein they are to have and to get, but not, save under compulsion, to do, to bear, and to give—these three, which make up the ideal of a noble life, have no part in their thoughts. Girls of this sort are easier to get on with than the others, because they have marked out a line for themselves, and know what they are about; but there is no principle of growth in such natures. Then, there are maidens so sweet, that, like the lilies of the field, they seem in need of no human culture. But the average nice girl, who leaves school with her education "finished," so she thinks and is yet in a crude, unformed state, what is to be done with her?

The very insufficiency of her young daughter appeals as strongly to the mother as does the helplessness of her infant. The schools have not finished, but begun the education of the girl, and now she has come home to be taught how to make the best of herself, and how she is to succeed in life,—for that is the problem before her. The girl who has been brought up at home, under her mother's eye, is, in this respect, in very much the same case as the school-girl; she, too, has yet to learn to live. Rich or poor, married or single, she may be, but it is not upon these that the success of a woman's life depends. Many a rich woman, whose children run over her, whose husband slights her, knows sorrowfully that she has made a failure of life; while many a poor woman is a queen in her own house, or is "made much of" in a house that is not hers. The woman who has herself well in hand, who thinks her own thoughts, reserves her judgments, considers her speech, controls her actions—she is the woman who succeeds in life, with a success to be measured by her powers of heart, brain, and soul.

Culture of Character

(a) By Instruction.—A woman's success in life depends on what force of character is in her; and character is to be got, like any other power, by dint of precept and practice: therefore, show the girl what she is, what she is not, how she is to become what she is not, and give her free scope to act and think for herself. What she is, is an exceedingly interesting study to the young girl, and open discussion on this subject helps her out of foolish and morbid feeling. She is full of vague self-consciousness, watching curiously the thoughts and emotions within her—an extraordinary spectacle to her inexperienced mind, leading her to the secret conviction that she is some great one, or, at any rate, is peculiar, different from the people about her. Hence arises much mauvaise honte, shyness, awkwardness; she feels herself the ugly duckling, unappreciated by the waddling ducks about her. She is clumsy enough at present, and is ready to own it; but wait a bit until the full-grown swan appear, and then they will see!

Now, this stage of self-consciousness and ignorant much-doubting self-exaltation, this "awkward age," as people call it, is common to all thoughtful girls who have the wit to perceive that there is more in them than meets the eye, but have not begun to concern themselves about what may or may not be in other people. It is a moral complaint, in which the girl requires treatment and tender nursing—only of a moral kind—as truly as she did when she had measles. If left to herself, she may become captious, morbid, hysterical; the years in which the foundations of sound character should be laid are wasted; and many a peevish, jealous, exacting woman owes the shipwreck of her life to the fact that nobody in her youth taught her to think reasonably of herself and of other people. It is only a few who founder; many girls are graciously saved: but this does not make it the less imperative on the mother to see her child safely through the troublous days of her early youth.

The best physic for the girl is a course of moral and mental science; not necessarily a profound course, but just enough to let her see where she is; that her noble dream of doing something great or good by-and-by—for which achievement she is ready to claim credit beforehand—is shared, in one form or other, by every human being; because the desire of power, the desire of goodness, are common to us all; that the generous impulse, which makes her stand up for her absent friend, and say fierce things in her behalf, is no cause for elation and a sense of superior virtue, for it is but a movement of those affections of benevolence and justice which are implanted in every human breast.

By the time the girl has discovered how much of her is common to all the world, she will be prepared to look with less admiring wonder at her secret self, and with more respect upon other people. For it is not that she has been guilty of foolish pride; she has simply been filled with honest and puzzled wonder at the fine things she has discovered in human nature as seen in herself. All her fault has been the pardonable mistake of thinking herself an exceptional person; for how is it possible that the people about her should have so much in them and so little come of it? Let her know that she is quite right about herself—that she has within her the possibilities she dreams of, and more; but that so have others, and that upon what she makes of herself, not upon what is in her, judgment will be passed.

It is true that a life of stirring action and great responsibility is the readiest means of developing character—better or worse: but not one woman in a thousand leads such a life; and then, not until she has reached maturity. Put into the hands of the girl the means of doing for herself what only exceptional circumstances will do for her; teach her, that is, the principles and methods of self-culture, seeing that you cannot undertake to provide for her the culture of circumstances. To point out these principles and methods in detail would be to go over the ground I have attempted to cover in a former volume. By the time the girl has some insight into the nature of those appetites, affections, emotions, desires, which are the springs of human action; into the extraordinary power of habit, which, though acquired by us, and not born in us, has more compelling force than any or all of the inborn principles of action; into the imperious character of the will, which rules the man, and yet is to be ruled and trained by the man; into the functions of conscience, and into the conditions of the spiritual life,—by the time she has some practical, if only fragmentary, notions on these great subjects, she may be led to consider her own nature and disposition with profit. So far from encouraging the habit of morbid introspection, such a practical dealing with herself is the very best cure for it. She no longer compares herself with herself, and judges herself by herself; but, knowing what are the endowments and what the risks proper to human nature, she is able to think soberly of, and to deal prudently with, herself, and is in a position to value the counsels of her parents.

(b) By Training, in Practical Affairs.—These counsels come to her aid in the small practical affairs of life, as telling her, not what she must do, but the principles on which she should act. Thus: she goes to the draper's; looks at this stuff, at that, at the other; now she will have this, now the other; no, neither will do; and at last she turns to her mother in despair and says, "You choose." That will not do; that is, by so much, a failure in life. Her mother takes her to task. Before she goes "shopping," she must use her reason, and that rapidly, to lay down the principles on which she is to choose her dress—it is to be pretty, becoming, suitable for the occasions on which it is to be worn, in harmony with what else is worn with it. Now, she goes to the shop; is able to describe definitely what she wants; to say "No" instantly to the wrong thing, "Yes" to the right; judgment is prompt to decide upon the grounds already laid down by reason; and what is more, the will steps in to make the decision final, not allowing so much as a twinge of after-regret for that "sweet thing" which she did not buy. For the sake of cultivating decision of character, even a leap in the dark, like that of Sydney Smith's little maid, Bunch, when she chose, quick as thought, between venison and wild duck, having never tasted either, is to be preferred to the endless dilly-dallying, deliberation, taking of advice here and there, in which the lives of some women are passed—to the trial of their friends.

Again, she is given to dawdling: a letter, some slight household task, "lasts out"; an hour is spent on what should be done in fifteen minutes. Want of attention is, probably, the failing her mother comes down upon. Many a mother of energetic character brings up for herself a dawdling daughter, for this reason—the mother is so "managing," so ready to settle the employments and amusements of everybody about her, that the girl's only chance of getting a few minutes at her own disposal is to dawdle; and this leads to small deceptions, furtive readings of story-books, any of the subterfuges of the weak in dealing with the strong.

The mother's task in dealing with her growing daughter is one of extreme delicacy. It is only as her daughter's ally and confidante she can be of use to her now. She will keep herself in the background, declining to take the task of self-direction out of her daughter's hands. She will watch for opportunities to give word or look of encouragement to every growing grace. She will deal with failings with a gentle hand, remembering that even failures in veracity or integrity, distressing as they are, arise usually from the very moral weakness which she is setting herself to strengthen.

On discovering such fault, the mother will not cover her daughter with shame; the distress she feels she will show, but so that the girl perceives her mother is sharing her sorrow, and sorrowing for her sake. What is the root of the error? No due sense of the sanctity of truth, an undue fear of consequences, chiefly of loss of esteem. The girl is betrayed into a deliberate lie; she has not, she says, written such and such a letter, said such and such words, you knowing all the time that she has done this thing. Deal gently with her: she is no longer a child to be punished or "disgraced" at her parents' pleasure; it is before her own conscience she must stand or fall now. But do not let her alone with the hopeless sense that there is no more to be done for her. Remember that conscience and intellect are still immature, that will is feeble. Give her simple sincere teaching in the nature of truth. Let her know what truth is—the simple statement of facts as they are; that all our spoken words deal with facts, and that, therefore, the obligation of truth is laid upon them all; we should never open our lips without speaking the truth. That even a jest which misleads another is a lie; that perfect truthfulness, in thought, speech and act, is an obligation laid upon us by God. That the duty is binding, not only with regard to our friends, but towards every one with whom we hold speech.

The Christian mother will add deeper teaching about the Truth from Whom all truth proceeds. She will caution her daughter as to the need of self-recollectedness in speech. She says she is "quite well, thank you" when she has a headache; that she "will be done in a minute" when the minute means half an hour; these departures from fact slip out, without thought—therefore, think first, and speak after. But such trifles surely do not matter? if so, who may cast a stone? Most of us might mend our ways in this matter; but every guard she can place upon herself is of real value to the girl with an inadequate sense of truth, as a means of training herself in the truthful habits which go to form a truthful character. Then, train her by trusting her. Believe her always; give her opportunities to condemn herself in speaking the truth, and her courage will answer the demand upon it.

A bare enumeration of the duties which truthfulness comprehends, of the vices which are different forms of lying, is helpful and instructive. The heart rises and resolves upon the mere hearing that veracity is that truthfulness in common talk which is careful to state the least important fact as it is; that simplicity tells its tale without regard to self, without any thought of showing self to advantage in the telling; that sincerity tells the whole truth purely, however much it might be to the speaker's advantage to keep any part back; that frankness is the habit of speaking of our own affairs openly and freely—a duty we owe to the people we live amongst; that fidelity, the keeping of our trusts, in great things and small, belongs to the truthful character.

Liberty and Responsibility

"Without household motions light and free,

And steps of virgin liberty,"

says Wordsworth of the girl who was to become that "perfect woman." Now, it sometimes happens that the mothers who take most pains to make their daughters deft and capable in "household motions," forget the "steps of virgin liberty." If the girl is to become a free woman with the courage of her opinions, she must grow up to the habit of liberty—not license, but liberty, for the use of which she is open to be called to account. Let her distribute her time as she likes, but count her tale of bricks; let her choose books for her own reading, but know what she chooses; let her choose her own companions, but put before her the principles on which to choose, and the home duties which should prevent their having too much of her time. Let her have the spending of money,—first, a small allowance out of which certain necessary expenses must come, as well as spendings for her pleasure, and a reserve for gifts and alms; and as soon as she can be trusted with it, an allowance large enough to dress herself out of,—that she may learn prudence by doing without necessaries when she wastes on fancies. One reason why she should have the spending of her own allowance is, that she may learn early the delight and the cost of giving, and may grow up in the habit of appropriating a fixed part of her little income to the help of the needy.

The care of her own health is another responsibility which should be made over to the young maiden. She cannot learn too soon that good health is not only a blessing, but a duty; that we may all take means to secure more or less vigorous health, and that we are criminal in so far as we fail to make use of these means. Any little book on the laws of health will put her in possession of the few simple principles of hygiene: the daily bath, attended with much friction of the skin; regular and sufficient exercise in the open air; the vigorous use of all the limbs; exercise of moderation in diet and in sleep; the free admission of fresh air to the bedroom; the due airing of the underclothing taken off at night; the necessity for active habits, for regular and hard, but not excessive brain-work; the resolute repression of ugly tempers and unbecoming thoughts—all of these are conditions of a sound mind in a sound body.

And for keeping ourselves in this delightful state of existence we are all more or less responsible. The girl who eats too much, or eats what does not suit her, and is laid up with a bilious attack; the girl who sits for hours poring over a novel, to the damage of her eyes, her brain, and her general nervous system, is guilty of a lesser fault of the nature of suicide. We are all apt, especially in youth, to overlook our accountability in the matter of health, and to think we may do what we like with our own; but, indeed, no offences are more inevitably and severely punished by the action of natural law than the neglect of the common principles of hygiene.

"Thine own friend and thy father's friend forsake not." The responsibility of keeping up courteous and kindly relations, by letter, call, or little attentions, with near and distant neighbours and friends is wholesome for the young people, and is a training in that general kindliness of spirit in which the ardour of their particular affections sometimes causes them to fail.

Conduct

The conduct of a well-brought-up girl—that is, her behaviour in various circumstances—will, on the whole, take care of itself. But in this, as in greater matters,

"More harm is wrought through want of thought,

Than e'er through want of heart";

and the mother will find opportunities to bring before her daughter the necessity for circumspection, reticence, self-control, the duty of consideration for others. Conduct at home is regulated by such plain principles of duty, that I need do no more than say a word as to the proprieties of life which should be kept up in the home circle as in any other society: behaviour which would be unbecoming in any drawing-room, is unbecoming in that of home.

In the street, the concert-room, the shop, in whatever public places she frequents, the young maiden has a distinct rôle, and must give a little study to her part. It will not do for her to go through the world with open mouth, wide-gazing eyes, head turned to this side and that, heedless tongue, like a child at a fair. But should not the girl behave naturally in public as in private? Alas! the fact is, that none of us, not even the little children, can afford to behave quite naturally, except in so far as use has become second nature to us in the acquired art of conducting ourselves becomingly. Noblesse oblige: maidenly dignity requires the modest eye, the quiet, retiring mien, subdued tones, reticence in regard to emotions of wonder, pleasure, interest, the expression of which might make the young girl a spectacle in the public streets—that is, might cause a passer-by to look at her a second time. For, excepting the children, there is nothing so interesting to be seen in public places as the young maidens approaching womanhood. They cannot fail to attract attention, but they owe it to themselves not to lay themselves open to this attention.

One claim, however, the public, in the shape of the casual passer-by, certainly has; he has a right to a gentle, not repellent, if retiring, expression of countenance, and to courtesy, even deference, of tone and manner in any chance encounter; and this, even more if he be in the garb of a working man than if in that of a gentleman. It is worth while to bear in mind the "Madam, respect the burden," with which Napoleon Bonaparte moved out of the path of a charcoal-carrier. This propriety of behaviour is mincing affectation if it be no more than a manner put on with the girl's out-of-door garments: it must be the outcome of what her mother has brought her up to think that she owes to herself and to other people; and from few but a mother can a girl acquire this mark of a gentlewoman.

How to conduct herself in society is a question of enormous interest to the maiden making her début. The subject is so large as to have called forth a literature of its own; but the principle lies in a nutshell. In society, as in the streets and public places, the girl whose mother has caused her to comprehend the respect due to herself, and the respect due to other people, will not make any grave faux pas. She goes into a room persuaded that she has claims upon the respect and consideration of the persons she may meet there; and she moves with ease, talks with quiet confidence, possesses herself in repose of manner. She is persuaded that her rights in this respect are not a matter of successful rivalry, but that each person in the room has equal claims upon her courtesy, and upon that of every other; and that her entertainers for the time being are entitled to peculiar deference. She will preserve self-possession and self-respect in intercourse with those who are socially her superiors, and will behave with deference to her inferiors. So of her intercourse with gentlemen: due self-respect and due respect for them will cause her to conduct herself with the simplicity, courtesy, and ease which she shows in her intercourse with women. In fact, these two principles will carry her with dignity and grace through all social occasions and in all social relations.

And how is the mother to enhance her daughter's self-respect? Is she to tell her, never so indirectly, that she is clever, pretty, charming, that no one can fail to admire her? If she do, her daughter may, not impossibly, become a forward young woman. No; she must put forward none but common claims. Because she is a woman, because she is a lady, because she is a guest, a fellow guest, because she is a stranger, or because she is a friend—these, and such as these, are incontestable claims upon the courteous attention of every person she meets in society. One quietly confident in such claims as these seldom experiences a rebuff. Whatever she may receive or give, over and above, on the score of personal merit, settles itself; but the thing to be established in a girl's mind is a due sense of the claims she has and of the claims she must yield.

Pleasure and Duty

We now come to consider a perplexing question which comes up for settlement upon the close of a girl's school career. Two rival claimants upon her time and interest are in the field—pleasure and duty; the question is, what is to be allowed to each, and how far may they clash. Kind-hearted parents, who find that their daughter is continually wanted for picnic or tennis, ball or concert, for morning lounge or evening party, withdraw the claims of duty, and leave the field to giddy pleasure. They say, "Poor child, she will never have a second youth." "Every dog must have its day." "We have been young ourselves; let her have a 'good time' and enjoy herself while she can.'" "If we hold her back from taking her pleasure, she will only crave for it the more; let her have a surfeit—she will settle down the more readily to a quiet life afterwards," and so on.

But before they launch their daughter—

"Youth at the prow, and Pleasure at the helm,"

it behoves parents to look into the matter. In the first place, the result, the gain of the girl's whole education hitherto is at stake. She might as well have been allowed to play ever since she was born as to play uninterruptedly now. For the gain of her education is not the amount of geography, science, and French that she knows; she will forget these soon enough unless well-trodden tracks be kept up to the brain-growth marking these acquirements. But the solid gain education has brought her lies in the powers and habits of attention, persistent effort, intellectual and moral endeavour, it has educed. Now, habits which are allowed to fall into disuse are all the same as though they had never been formed; powers not exercised grow feeble and are lost. The ground which has been gained in half-a-dozen years may be lost in a single one. And here we have the reason why many girls who have received what is called a good education read nothing weightier than a feeble or trashy novel, are not intelligent companions, and show little power of moral effort.

As for settling down by-and-by, that is not the question: if she is to recover the ground lost, she must begin all over again, and at an age when it is far more difficult to acquire habits and develop powers than in childhood. Again, the taste for parties of pleasure, for what may be called organised amusement, is an ever-growing taste, and dislodges the habit of taking pleasure in the evening reading, the fireside games with the children, the home music, the chat with friendly neighbours, the thousand delights that home should afford. For

"Pleasure is spread through the earth
In stray gifts, to be claimed by whoever shall find";

and not the least evil of incessant party-going and pleasure-seeking is, that it blinds people to the nature and conditions of pleasure; pure and true pleasure is of impromptu occurrence, a stray gift, to be found not sought; it is just a thing to happen upon by the way.

What, then, of those parents who take the opposite line,—ordain that their daughters shall stay at home and help their mothers? They did not run after pleasure, and neither shall their girls; they had home duties to attend to when they were young, and so shall their daughters, "for no good comes of gadding about"

Well, to turn the tables, it is well these should remember that you cannot put an old head on young shoulders; that young things will frolic, whether they be kittens or lambs or maidens; that what becomes deliberate pleasure-seeking in older people, comes to the girls as—

"Stray gifts to be claimed by whoever shall find";

that parties of pleasure are delightful just because they give the girls opportunities of meeting their kind, other young people, in whom they rejoice, "as 'tis their nature to." Prospero was not sufficient for Miranda. Birds of a feather flock together, and, the young to the young.

The thing then is, to draw the line wisely. Either extreme is mischievous. The girl must have definite duties on which pleasure schemes are rarely allowed to encroach—a rule, for going out once, twice, a week?—some evenings reserved for home pleasures, the mornings for regular occupations and duties, and, so far as the unfortunate habits of society allow, evening amusements avoided which spoil the following morning. But to suggest rules on this subject would be presumptuous; every mother ordains for her own daughters, remembering how—

"All work and no play makes Jack a dull boy;
All play and no work makes Jack a mere toy."

Opinions

Let us turn to a question too often overlooked in the bringing up of girls. A girl may have opinions upon questions of figure and style, fashion and furniture, but who cares what she thinks about public men and questions, books and events? All the same, what she thinks is of consequence to the world; even if she is not to be the mother of future fathers and mothers, she will make her mark somehow.

The young maiden should have a general and a special preparation towards the forming of just opinions. For the first, she should be made to use her common-sense upon the questions that occur. "What do you think of so-and-so?" says the parent, making a little wholesome fun if her thinking be foolish. But the special preparation requires more thought. What are the subjects upon which thinking persons generally must have opinions? It is upon these the girl should be qualified to judge.

In the first place, her success in life will depend greatly upon the relations with other people into which she lets herself be drawn. She must have some knowledge of character, human motives; and, therefore, as much as for the sake of her own development, every girl ought, as I have said, to go through some easy course of moral philosophy. We know how easily a girl is carried away by plausible ways of putting things, until she may find herself bound to a worthless friend or unworthy lover. And what is the poor girl to do if she have nothing to oppose to—"Oh, everybody thinks so now!" "That's a mere old-world grandmother's notion of propriety"; "A man's first duty is to look after himself, and it stands to reason that if everybody does that, nobody need trouble himself about other people"?

Again, women should know something of the principles of political economy. How many ladies are ready to decide off-hand that "it would be good for trade if an earthquake shook down all the houses in London"; that, "if all the landowners in England excused their tenants paying rent, bread would be cheaper"; or, that "the wealth of England would have been increased if the country had contained gold-mines, instead of our iron and coal"; in fact, to fall into any one of the little traps which Mrs. Fawcett sets for the unwary in her Political Economy for Beginners,—which is, by the way, as interesting as it is instructive, and the girl who studies it with thoughtful attention will be in a position to form sensible opinions on some of those questions of the day which come up to be dealt with, not as matters of opinion, but as causes, powerful to set class against class. It would be for the welfare of the country if educated women had just ideas on subjects of this nature, not only that they should share the interests of husband and brothers, but in order that they should see, and keep before the men of their families, the other side of questions which the press of affairs would incline the latter to look at from a personal standpoint.

Possibly, a mission is devolving upon educated women. A mediator is wanted between labour and capital, not only to persuade the master to endure in gentleness, but to open the eyes of the men to the difficulties and responsibilities of the masters; and this mediator, the lady, with her tact, sympathy, and quick intuitions, is fitted to become, if she will take pains to get the necessary knowledge. Not that she need step out of her proper sphere to meddle with public matters; only that she should qualify herself to speak an understanding and kindly word on these subjects to the wife, if not to the husband, in her cottage visitings. A single sentence, showing a mastery of the subject in question, spoken in one cottage may go far to turn the tide of feeling in a whole community of work-people.

Women have been clamorous for their rights, and men have, on the whole, been generous and gentle in meeting their demands. So much has been granted, that we have no right to claim immunities which belong to the seclusion of the harem. We are not free to say, "Oh, these things are beyond me; I leave such questions to the gentlemen." It is not impossible that, in the course of Providence, women have of late been brought so much to the front, that they may be in a condition to play the part of mediators in these times of dangerous alienation between class and class. That we are in the early stages of a revolution, is patent to thinking persons; and whether this revolution is to be bloodless, unmarked by the horrors which have attended others we know of, rests, more than they realise, with the women of Britain. It is time for them, at any rate, to away with the frivolous temper which "cares for none of these things."

Nor is a social revolution the only one pending: there is a horror of great darkness abroad; Christianity is on its trial; and more than that, the most elementary belief in, and worship of, Almighty God. The judgment to come, the resurrection of the body, the life everlasting,—these fundamental articles of a Christian's faith have come to be pooh-poohed; and this, not only amongst profane persons and ungodly livers, but amongst people of reputation both for goodness and wisdom.

And how are the young girls to be prepared to meet this religious crisis? In the first place, it is unwise to keep them in the dark as to the anxious questions stirring. Their zeal and love will be quickened by the knowledge that once again Christianity and infidelity are in the way to be brought into agonising conflict at our doors. But let their zeal be according to knowledge. Lay the foundations of their faith. It matters less that the lines between Church and Dissent, or between High and Low and Broad Church, be well defined, than that they should know fully in Whom they have believed, and what are the grounds of their belief. Put earnest, intellectual works into their hands. Let them feel the necessity of bracing up every power of mind they have to gain comprehension of the breadth and the depth of the truths they are called to believe. Let them not grow up with the notion that Christian literature consists of emotional appeals, but that intellect, mind, is on the other side. Supply them with books of calibre to give the intellect something to grapple with—an important consideration, for the danger is, that young people in whom the spiritual life is not yet awakened should feel themselves superior to the vaunted simplicity of Christianity.

One more point: let them not run away with the fallacy that no one is responsible for what he believes, but only for what he does. Try this principle for a moment by applying it to our social relations—say, that no man is bound to believe in the fidelity of his wife, in the dutifulness of his child, in the common integrity of the people he has dealings with—and the whole framework of society is broken up. For, indeed, our whole system, commercial and social, is nothing else than a system of credit, kept up by the unbounded faith man reposes in man. That every now and then there is hue and cry after a defaulter, is only one way of proving how true are men in general to the trusts reposed in them. Does a countryman hide away his sovereigns in an old stocking because he puts no faith in banks? He is laughed at as a miser. Will he have nothing to do with his neighbours because he is mistrustful of them? He is a misanthrope, only fit to live by himself. And if the man who does not place due and necessary faith in his fellows, however much his trust has been abused, is an outcast, what is to be said of him who lifts up his face to Almighty God, his Maker, Father, Preserver, Redeemer, sole intimate Friend, and ever-present judge, and says, "I do not believe, because I can neither see nor understand"?

I am not going out of my way to speak strongly as to the necessity of taking a firm stand here. For the sake of the children yet to be born, let the girls be brought up in abhorrence and dread of this black offence of unbelief. On points not vital, let them think gently and tolerantly, having a firm grasp of the truth as they hold it themselves, but leaving others to choose their ways of approach and service. But on questions that trench on the being, nature, and work of Almighty God, Father, Son, and Holy Ghost, and our relations of love and service towards Him, there is no room for toleration of adverse opinions: though we may have much cause to esteem the holders of such opinions. "His (creed) must be true whose life is in the right," is precisely one of those fallacies which young people should be taught to examine.

As for proofs, this is no question for proof. Every pulse that beats in the universe is, if we will have it so, a witness for God, being inexplicable without Him; but who goes about to prove that the sun is shining? At the same time, such works as Paley's Natural Theology, possibly, and Butler's Analogy most certainly, have their use, if only as showing how many plausible arguments have long ago been answered.

Pursuits and Occupations

I have left little space to glance at the pursuits and occupations proper for young women at home. It is becoming rather usual on the Continent, and, to some extent at home, for the schools to instruct young ladies in the duties of household economy—an invasion, perhaps, of the mother's province. Every woman should understand, and know how to perform, every duty of cooking or cleaning, mending or making, proper to a house; and a regular, practical course of training under her mother's eye might well occupy an hour or two of the girl's morning. May I suggest the great use and value of a household book, in which the young housekeeper notes down exactly how to do everything, from the scouring of a floor to the making of an omelet, either as she has done it herself, or has watched it being done, with the little special wrinkles that every household gathers. Such an "Enquire Within" should be invaluable hereafter, as containing personal experiences, and should enable her to speak with authority to cook or housemaid who "Never saw it done like that, ma'am." The ordering of dinners, setting of tables, entire management for a short time of the affairs of a house, will all have place in this training in domestic economy.

Where there is still a nursery, the home daughter has a great advantage, for the right regulation of the nursery in all that pertains to cleanliness, ventilation, brightness, health, happiness is a science in itself; and where there is no longer one at home, it is worth while for her to get some practical knowledge of details at the hands of a friend who has a well-regulated nursery. As for sewing, every woman should know how to cut out and make all garments for herself and her children up to a full-grown dress, and it is worth while to learn how to cut out and make even that scientifically; so here is another art in which the young lady at home must needs serve her apprenticeship. At the same time, an hour's brisk needlework at a time is as much as should commonly be expected of her; for while almost every other sort of household occupation affords, healthful muscular action, to sit long at her needle is not good for a young girl.

Besides, she has not unlimited time to sew; her education has only been begun so far, and must be kept up, and she must acquire habits of intellectual effort on her own account. She should have an hour or two in the morning for solid reading. English literature is almost an untrodden field for her; she has much history to read—ancient, mediaeval, modern,—all of which would be read the more profitably in the light of current history. She has learnt to read French and German, and now is her time to get some acquaintance with French and German literature. She will probably find it necessary to limit the reading of novels to the best, those which have become classics, except on occasion of a bad cold, or toothache, or for an idle half-hour after dinner. It is very helpful to read with a commonplace book or reading-diary, in which to put down any striking thought in your author, or your own impression of the work, or of any part of it; but not summaries of facts. Such a diary, carefully kept through life, should be exceedingly interesting as containing the intellectual history of the writer; besides, we never forget the book that we have made extracts from, and of which we have taken the trouble to write a short review.

Two or three hours of the afternoon should be given to vigorous out-of-door exercise, to a long country walk, if not to tennis, cricket, etc. The walk is interesting in proportion as it has an object, and here the student of botany has a great advantage. At almost every season there is something to be seen in some out-of-the-way spot, to make up the list of specimens illustrating an order. The girl who is neither a botanist nor an artist may find an object for her walk in the catching of some aspect of nature, some bit of landscape, to describe in writing. The little literary effort should be both profitable and pleasant, and such a record should be a dear possession in after days.

It is evident that the young lady at home has so much in hand, without taking social claims into consideration, that she can have no time for dawdling, and, indeed, will have to make a time-table for herself and map out her day carefully to get as much into it as she wishes.

The pursuits we have indicated are all, more or less, with a view to self-culture; but they will become both more profitable and more pleasant if they can be proposed to the girl as labours of love and service. Household duties and needlework will, of course, be helpful in the home; but all her occupations, and especially her music, even her walks and reading, can be laid under contribution for the family good, or for that of her neighbours, rich or poor. The girl who knows something of wild-flowers or birds, for example, is popular as a walking companion with persons of all sorts and conditions. Sunday-school teaching, cottage visiting, some sort of regular, painstaking, even laborious effort for the ignorant, the distressed, should be a part of every girl's life, a duty not to be put aside lightly for other claims. For it is only in doing, that we learn to do; through service, that we learn to serve; and it is more and more felt that a life of service is the Christian, and even the womanly, ideal life.

I shall notice, later, the importance of qualifying a girl, by means of definite training, for a particular line of service—for teaching, or nursing, or for general work in a parish, for instance; but in default of such training, as giving her an object in life apart from social success, the mother may do much to make "Ich dien" the motto of her daughter's life, marking out some special line of helpfulness into which she may throw her youthful energy.

"Abou Ben Adhem (may his tribe increase)
Awoke one night from a deep trance of peace,
And saw within the moonlight of his room,
Making it rich and like a lily in bloom,
An angel writing in a book of gold.
Exceeding peace had made Ben Adhem bold,
And to the presence in the room he said,—
'What writest thou?' The vision raised his head,
And in a voice, made all of sweet accord,
Answered, 'The names of all who love the Lord!'
'And is mine one?' Ben Adhem asked. 'Nay, not so,'
Replied the angel. Abou spoke more low, '
But cheerful still,—' I pray thee, then,
Write me as one who loves his fellow-men.'
The angel wrote and vanished. The next night
He came again, with a great wakening light,
And showed the names whom love of God had blessed,
And lo! Ben Adhem's led the rest"

"Write me as one who loves his fellow-men!" is, indeed, the cry of the earnest-minded amongst ourselves; and to qualify her for some definite line of service, in the workhouse, the infirmary, amongst the blind or the mute, to give her some object in life beyond herself, and having no bearing on her own advancement, is, perhaps, the kindest and wisest thing the mother can do for her daughter.

Objects in Life-Value of Special Training

This consideration brings me to a question sufficiently puzzling to the heads of households: What is to be done with the girls? About the boys there is less difficulty—they go to college, or they go to learn their profession; they are set to work at once, to prepare for that "opening" which, it is hoped, will introduce them to a profitable career.

Suppose a girl leave school in her eighteenth year;—her eldest sister being already at home for good, her mother's right hand, and so much identified with all the interests of the family that her career is marked out. The sense of leisure and irresponsibility is delightful at first, and every girl should have a taste of it, just as a grocer is said to give his new apprentices the run of the shop, that they may long no more for figs and raisins. She plays tennis, goes to dances, is allowed to go as much into society as her parents can conveniently arrange for. In her leisure, she paints a little, works a little, practises a little, reads a little French and a good many novels. Her mother assigns her some domestic duties, which she fulfils with more or less care; but these are seldom important enough to call forth all her energy and will. Perhaps she is to sew for the family; but then, the stress of work comes only now and then, in spurts, when everybody helps, and to be regularly and laboriously employed as a sempstress would be intolerable to a girl of spirit and education. She is not exactly idle; her occupations spread fairly well over the day, though they might all be easily crushed into the spare hour or two of a busy woman; she enjoys a good deal of leisure and pleasure, and her parents look on good-naturedly, glad that she should have her day.

For a few months, perhaps for a year or two, this is delightful; but in a year or two life becomes a burden. To dance with the same people, to play in the same set, to make or listen to the same talk month after month, becomes intolerable. But then, it is objected, she has her home-work, and additional duties can easily be made for her. Not so easily; the mother of the family clings to her own duties, having discovered that, of the two delights of life, work—the duties of our calling—is to be preferred to play. Besides, the girl wants more than work—she wants a career; she wants work that depends upon her, that cannot be done without her, and the doing of which will bring her honour, and, possibly, pay. Let her "improve her mind," you say? It is hardly the tendency of modern education to make girls in love with knowledge for its own sake, and what they do for their own sakes is too fitful and desultory to yield much profit or pleasure, unless the old spur is applied—the hope of distinction in some public examination.

Now, what is the poor girl to do under this craving for a career, which is natural to every adult human being, woman as much as man? Hard things are said of the "girl of the period"; but she deserves more consideration than she gets. People do not allow that she has erred because there has been no such outlet for her energy as her nature demands. In the 'sixties,' say, there was, practically, but one career open to the young woman of the lower and upper middle classes. She must wait until the prince comes by, and—throws the handkerchief. The girl with more energy and ambition than modesty and breeding sees her opportunity here. What if that foolish prince should throw the handkerchief to the wrong maiden, and leave her out in the cold, with nothing to do, nothing to look forward to, all the rest of her life? The thing is not to be thought of; she will make it her business to let him know where his favours should fall. And then begins a career indeed, a "hunt," people call it, exhibiting a very ugly phase of young womanhood on which there is no occasion to dwell.

The well-brought-up girl will hardly own to herself that she dreams of this best of all careers for a woman, that of wifehood and motherhood. Maidenliness will not let her put it before her as the thing of which she lives in hope. Indeed, it is not so; her fate in this respect depends so entirely on the mood of some other, that it is impossible for her to allow herself in serious anticipation, though maiden meditation may dwell innocently upon Romeo and Juliet and their kind. Except for these sweet fancies, half illicit in the eyes of many a pure-minded girl, and not too wholesome, the future is a blank; she is in real need of something beyond

"Human nature's daily food "

of common duties, pleasures, home affections. It is natural for the human brood, as for every other, to leave the parent nest; and when the due time comes, and the overgrown nestling has not taken flight, it is but a comfortless bird.

The girl wants a career, a distinct path of life for her own feet to tread, quite as much as does the boy. But the girl will be provided for, it is said, while the boy must be made able to support himself and a family by his labour of head or hands. That is not the point: people are beginning to find out that happiness depends fully as much upon work as on wages. It is work, work of her very own, that the girl wants; and to keep her at home waiting for a career which may come to her or may not, but which it is hardly becoming in her to look forward to, is, to say the least of it, not quite fair. The weak girl mopes and grows hysterical; the strong-minded girl strikes out erratic lines for herself; the good girl makes the most of such employments as are especially hers, but often with great cravings for more definite, recognised work.

The worst of it is, these home-bred daughters are not being fitted to fill a place in this workaday world at any future time. Already, amateur work is at a discount; nobody is wanted to do what she has not been specially trained for. Here seems to me to be the answer to the perplexing question, What is to be done with a family of grown-up daughters? It is not enough that they learn a little cooking, a little dressmaking a little clear-starching. Every one of them should have a thorough recognised training for some art or profession whereby she may earn her living, doing work useful to the world, and interesting and delightful to herself, as is all skilled labour of head or hands. It appears to me that parents owe this to their girls as much as to their boys. And valuable training in many branches of woman's work is to be had, at so low a charge as hardly to cost more than would keep a lady fittingly at home. Whether the girl makes use of her training, and practises the art she has acquired, depends upon circumstances, and—the handkerchief! But in no case is the training thrown away. To say nothing of the special aptitude she has acquired, she has increased in personal weight, force of character, and fitness for any work. It is not necessary to specify the lines for which women may qualify by thorough training—art, music, teaching, nursing, loftier careers for the more ambitious and better educated; but may I say a word for teaching in elementary schools—a lowly labour of quite immeasurable usefulness.

May I urge, too, the advantage of training, for work which has been too long the refuge of the destitute—I mean, the truly honourable, and often exceedingly pleasant, post of governess in a family? In proportion as parents awake to the necessity for all-round training for their children, this profession of governess will open a more and more delightful and remunerative career to the trained woman able to develop character on right lines, and to teach on rational methods. (Already this awakening has taken place so far that perhaps no woman's work is more in request or better paid than that of the specially trained governess.)

I fear the reader may think of that fox who left his tail in a trap, and advised all the foxes he met to cut off theirs—"so pleasant," says he," to be without the incumbrance of a tail!" But, indeed, I do not speak without book on this subject, having had opportunities of learning the views of many women who have placed themselves under training, partly as feeling the need of the discipline it affords, and partly out of a great craving to take some active recognised share in the work of the world. The mistress of a house and mother of a family is—unless she be a lawless, self-indulgent woman—under a discipline of circumstances which should bring out whatever is strong and lovely in the female character; but in the case of grown-up daughters at home, the difficulty parents labour under is just that of keeping up wholesome discipline. They cannot be for ever struggling against the dawdling, procrastinating, self-indulgent habits girls will fall into when not under the stimulus of pressing duties; for parents must needs admit their grown-up daughters to a friendly footing which makes an over-strict government out of the question.

The young women want scope, and they want the discipline of work, their own work, for which they alone are responsible; not of home tasks, which may be done or left undone, or which are sure to be done by somebody if the right person neglect her duty. A year or two of home life, in the interval between school and such training as I propose, is very desirable, both that parents may enjoy their daughters, and the daughters their homes, and also that parents may have an opportunity of dealing with the crude characters the girls bring home from school. But with work of their own in view, the girls will live under the stimulus of a definite future, their present work being to make the very best of themselves with a view to that future. Here is a motive for effort, and the important thing is, to keep up the habit of effort, intellectual, moral, spiritual, bodily. Nor need such regular training and regular work stand in the way of matrimony. In the first place, early marriages are far less frequent than they were, so there is time to get in some special training and some special work before the final step be taken; and, in the next place, the girl who is only occasionally at home, with fresh interests, greater force of character, is a more attractive person than her sister, who has become a little stale because she is always on hand.

Forgive me if I make use of this opportunity to press home what may seem to the reader a one-sided view of an important question. I am by no means alone in the view I advocate; seeing that many enlightened men are causing their daughters to undergo as regular a professional training as their sons, not because their means are inadequate to portion the girls, but because they feel it a duty to open a career of usefulness to these as much as to the boys of their families. Besides, I know of no other way of answering the question, What is to be done with the girls? Families of grown-up daughters at home are simply in the way. They are in an anomalous position, with no scope to produce the best that is in them; and unless they have an unusually wisely ordered home, some deterioration in character is almost a necessary consequence of the life they lead.

Part IV

"It is Written"

Some Studies in the Evolution of Character

"I too acknowledge the all-but omnipotence of early culture and nurture."—Sartor Resartus

"Of a truth, it is the duty of all men, especially philosophers, to note down with accuracy the characteristic circumstances of their education, what furthered, what hindered, what in any way modified."—Sartor Resartus.

Chapter 1. Two Peasant Boys

I

Jörn Uhl (Jörn Uhl, by Gustav Frenssen.) and Wilhelm Meister are books that parents should read. To mention a book of yesterday in the same breath as a world's classic is bold, perhaps foolhardy, but in the two we get the two sides of the shield. Wilhelm Meister becomes, passively; circumstances play upon him, and he yields himself to this formative play. Jörn Uhl also is the creature of his circumstances, but only in so far as they give impulse to his personality. Meister is, as we know, a highly emotional being in whom rank sentiment chokes out personality. The peasant boy, reared in a rougher school, becomes a person, or rather, is a person from the first. We get in these two the hint of a line of demarcation which divides the world into the people who, for one cause or another, are at the mercy of circumstances, and those others able to order their lives.

Jörn Uhl was the son of a peasant-proprietor whose farm (in Schleswig-Holstein) had been in the family some three hundred years. Klaus Uhl is a man worth considering as a father. He is notable for a hearty, jovial laugh, tells a good story, discusses politics, drinks, plays cards, is a popular person among the fast spirits of the country-side, doubly popular because he is a sort of headman among them and can always claim the flattery of a ready laugh at his jokes.

His wife, a woman of another mould, dies in giving birth to a little daughter—Elsbe, her fifth child,—chiefly because her husband would not be persuaded to send for the doctor. At last he comes to weep over her as 'Mutter, Mutter'; he has forgotten her in the relation of wife. She, a daughter of a peasant of the heath, brought the qualities of her own people into her husband's family. The three eldest sons took after their father, while the two younger children, Jörn and the little Elsbe, were Thiessens, of their mother's blood. Jörn was four years old when his mother died. The mother had the gift to attach to her, at any rate, one faithful friend, in Wieten, a serving-woman whom she charged with the care of her children.

This is how the story opens; and the scenes and circumstances of peasant life are bitten in as with an engraver's tool. Without any word to that effect, the reader feels that here is the little, bright-haired, straight-featured, handsome Jörn set down to a problem. Here are the factors of his life. What answer will come out?

This is why I venture to call this story of Jörn Uhl a companion piece to Wilhelm Meister. In both cases, we have a boy set down with the problem of life before him. Will he cry I 'check' to circumstances, or will they checkmate him? This is the anxious question that presents itself now and then to every mother when she goes up for the last good-night; to every father when the curious children gather round to see what he would show: and the children exhibit themselves in far more distinct and diverse colours than would so many neutral-tinted men and women.

The little Jörn's first essays at life afford delightful reading. Everything is so big—the house, the barn, the home-fields go on without end. Great big people come out of doors and go about their various work in a grave, puzzling way. There is no one just like Jörn but Spitz, and they two make experiments together. One day they both go into a ditch after a rat, and together are they fetched home, put into the wash-tub, whipped, and put to bed, where together they cry and comfort one another. Another day they think to make a friend of another young thing which they recognise as one of their kind—a little foal not long arrived. They know that the horse belongs to the grave, grown-up world, but the foal is another thing, and the two venture near to make acquaintance, Spitz, of course, making the opening remarks; but the mare kicks up her heels and they fly. Another day they peer down a cellar, a dark world which for them has no bottom; but beetroots and turnips come flying up at them, and, tumbling in, they find themselves on the head of a labourer. All the while the child was another Robinson Crusoe, and the world was his island. There was no one to tell him the meanings of things; Wieten was too busy, and no one else cared.

The little soul had to build its own habitation, fashion its own tools, find its own meat: 'so best,' says the author, and perhaps he is right. Little children must needs ruminate. We tease and distract them by our pestilent explanations, our continual calls upon attention already fully occupied, because we find it difficult to realise that even young children have need of a separate life. It is one thing to give a little child two or three lessons in attention in the day by inducing him to look a little longer at something he has already begun to regard with interest, but quite another to make him name a statue of Achilles or the portraits of the kings of England. Of course he can do these things; children are not stupid, but preoccupied, and the occupation they find for themselves is good for them. A clamorous forcing of his attention in many directions is apt to leave a child incapable of answering the demands which are rightly made upon him at a later date.

But little Jörn ran no risks of this sort. He and Spitz had it to themselves, running in many times a day to see that other soft young thing, the baby. And one day a strange thing happened; they found the baby standing at the door. It was very odd; but they took the little Elsbe into their company, and made their researches thenceforth in a party of three. By and by, Spitz fell to the second place, and became only a plaything where he had been companion and leader, and the children learned from each other. A little sister teaches a boy tenderness and valour, and learns from him confidence and love and that pride in him which makes a boy a hero.

Later, we get a group of three children sitting round Wieten's work-table of an evening. Fiete Krey, whose father and mother work about the place, has much to say. The Kreys, almost a clan in the village, are an ingenious folk given to petty trade and not bearing a very good name for honesty. Fiete has the family traits; he romances, tells of hidden pots of gold and of strange underground folk who guard the treasures. Wieten too tells of a rich merchant who threw all his money into a well, and of a little gray man in a three-cornered hat who sate at the bottom minding it. She tells, too, of one Theodor Storm, a student, who meant to write a book of the folk-tales.

All these things go to Jörn's education.

Here is a matter which sometimes causes uneasiness to parents: they are appalled when they think of the casual circumstances and chance people that may have a lasting effect upon their children's characters. But their part is, perhaps, to exercise ordinary prudence and not over-much direction. They have no means of knowing what will reach a child; whether the evil which blows his way may not incline him to good, or whether the too-insistent good may not predispose him to evil. Perhaps the forces of life as they come should be allowed to play upon the child, who is not, be it remembered, a product of educational care, but a person whose spiritual nurture is accomplished by that wind which bloweth whither it listeth.

Meanwhile, the father was not unaware of his fourth son, who had come to be known as a promising boy; but his concern was shown only by boastful talk in the ale-house. He should be a scholar—Klaus himself remembered tags of Latin learned at school,—should be a land-agent, should somehow bring grist to his father's pride.

One day Jörn went to school—such a pleasant schoolhouse under the lindens, where the bees came buzzing through the open windows. Lehrer Peters, the old schoolmaster, was a kindly human soul, who scanned the red heads of the Kreys and the fair heads of the Uhls with the sense that the children came to school with the makings of all they would become. The young scholars made sentences that day. "We have heard about King David," said Peters. "Who is our king?" And a small child replied: "Our king is called Klaus Uhl," for, was not Klaus the head man of the village? Then an unexpected thing happened; Jörn, the little new boy, stood up flushed and wrathful, and said: "My father is no king"; little Elsbe sobbing, "But my father is a king." When the other children had gone, the schoolmaster asked Jörn: Why did you say your father was not a king? "He often can't stand." "What? he can't stand!" "No, because he is often drunk."

This is what the child had learned for himself,—that a king must at least be able to control his own life, and that self-rule is a sort of kingship. Already had evil, passing through the alembic of a child's mind, brought forth some knowledge of good. But at what a cost! 'Experience teaches,' we say. We say too, 'Experience makes fools wise,' but that is an error. The fools are the people who get nothing from experience but the confirmed habit of things as they are. If they have done amiss and suffer for it, why, they go on doing amiss, and suffer again. If they see others do amiss, they practise the ill-doing they see, taking no heed to penalties. Fools of this sort, who do not learn from experience, were Jörn's elder brothers.

It is because the little boy was no fool that he was able to draw that tragic deduction from his experience of life—"My father is no king." Experience truly teaches the wise-hearted, whether child or man, but at so heavy a cost that the lessons are apt to leave the learner bankrupt for the remainder of his days. Reverence and the sense of filial dependence were gone out of Jörn's life; so too was the love of his mother, with all its tender teachings; and the little Crusoe was isolated from all the natural good that the filial relation includes. How soon may it dawn upon a child that his father is no king, his mother no queen! We elders are never safe. A child's eyes are ubiquitous. They see everywhere and all the time, but it is only at some small crisis in his life that the child's knowledge takes shape even in thought. Poor little Jörn! He had probably seen his father in a besotted state a thousand times without any inward comment; but this thought of a king reduced his vague ideas to clear knowledge—overwhelming, shameful knowledge.

It was the fact that they were aware of the child as a judge that caused the parents of an earlier generation to sit in state, august, unapproachable; but this was a futile endeavour to blind the child-judge who sees, however gradually, through all seeming, and arrives at the simplicity of being, worthy or unworthy. He knows what his parents are for better for worse, though it may be years before he realises that he knows.

It is instructive to compare the beginnings of Jörn Uhl with those of another peasant boy of a rather lower class. How did Diogenes Teufelsdröckh begin the world in the village of Entepfühl; or rather, to look through a transparent veil, how did Thomas Carlyle begin in the village of Ecclefechan? First, as to his father: "Andreas Futteral" was "in very deed a man of order, courage, downrightness, that understood Büsching's Geography, had been in the victory of Rossbach and left for dead in the Camisarde of Hochkirch." For Andreas had been grenadier-sergeant and even regimental schoolmaster under Frederick the Great. He was a diligent man who cultivated a little orchard and lived on its produce 'not without dignity.' On evenings, he smoked and read (had he not been a schoolmaster?), and talked to neighbours about the wars and told how Frederick had once said to him—'Peace, hound!' as a king should.

To begin with, Diogenes, or Gneschen, as they called him, had a better chance of learning reverence in the contemplation of an upright man, and obedience from an old soldier, than fell to a son of that facile good-fellow, Klaus Uhl. Then, Gneschen had a mother, a notable housewife and kind and loving mother who provided for the young child "a soft swathing of Love and infinite Hope wherein he waxes and slumbers, danced round by sweetest dreams." To such a pair, living in a roomy painted cottage surrounded by fruit-trees, with flowers looking in at the windows, came "one meek, yellow evening," a Stranger of reverend aspect. He met the pair with grave salutation and deposited before them "what seemed some basket overhung with green Persian silk, saying only, 'Good Christian people, here lies for you an invaluable Loan; take all heed thereof, in all carefulness employ it: with high recompense, or else with heavy penalty, will it one day be required back."

Here we get the true note of parenthood, the sense of a loan, a trust, containing great possibilities and involving great responsibilities. The mysterious Stranger may indicate the advent of the august Angel of Life; the roll of notes he left behind for the nurture of the child may mean such things as the love, integrity, dignity, simplicity of the pair to whom the infant arrived; for such things as these are possessions well expended on the nurture of a child. Anyhow, these were not casual parents like the one left to the little Jörn.

"Meanwhile the incipient Diogenes, like others, all ignorant of his Why, his How or whereabout, was opening his eyes to the kind light; sprawling out his ten fingers and toes; listening, tasting, feeling; in a word, by all his five senses, still more by his Sixth Sense of Hunger, and a whole infinitude of inward, spiritual, half-awakened senses, endeavouring daily to acquire for himself some knowledge of this strange universe where he had arrived, be his task therein what it might. Infinite was his progress; thus in some fifteen months he could perform the miracle of—Speech!

". . . . I have heard him noted as a still infant, that kept his mind much to himself; above all, that he seldom or never cried. He already felt that time was precious; that he had other work cut out for him than whimpering." Thus the young Gneschen grew in the paternal cottage, with a father in whom he had "as yet a prophet, priest, and king and an obedience that made him free."

As for his education, he listened to the talk of the old men under the shadow of the linden in the middle of the village. He played, and his plays were his lessons; for, says our author, "in all the sports of Children, were it only in their wanton breakages or defacements, you shall discern a creative instinct: the Mankin feels that he is born Man, that his vocation is to work. The choicest present you can make him is a Tool; be it knife or pen-gun, for construction or for destruction; either way it is for work, for change. In gregarious sports of skill or strength, the Boy trains himself to co-operation, for war or peace, as governor or governed: the little Maid again, provident of her domestic destiny, takes with preference to dolls."

Here is a thing to ponder, a word of wisdom, which should clear our nurseries of mechanical toys, and of all toys which have no use but that of being looked at. In this regard the two little boys, Jörn and Gneschen, had fairly equal opportunities. Both grew up in open places where they had the good of heaven and earth. We read how little Gneschen took out his porringer of bread and milk and ate it on the coping of the wall, from which he could see the sunset behind the western mountains. He made friends with cattle and poultry and much besides. While his sports made the boy active and sharpened his wits, "his imagination was stirred up and an historical tendency given him" by the reminiscences of his father Andreas, who had tales of battle and adventure to tell, wonderful to the child. "Eagerly I hung upon his tales, when listening neighbours enlivened the hearth; from these perils and these travels, wild and far almost as Hades itself, a dim world of adventure expanded itself within me. Incalculable also was the knowledge I acquired in standing by the old men under the linden tree: the whole of Immensity was yet new to me; and had not these reverend seniors, talkative enough, been employed in partial surveys thereof for nigh fourscore years? With amazement I began to discover that Entepfühl stood in the middle of a country, of a world; that there was such a thing as History, as Biography; to which I also, one day, by hand and tongue might contribute."

It would appear that nature opens to all children, one way or other, a perception of time past, History, and of space remote, Geography, as if these ideas were quite necessary nutriment for the mind of a child; and what is to be said for a school education that either eliminates this necessary food altogether, or serves it up in dry-as-dust morsels upon which the imagination cannot work?

These two, History and Geography, were let in upon Jörn too, though by other ways. There were the inscriptions upon the house-front telling of all the Uhls for the past three hundred years; and there was an old oak chest which gradually discovered its significance to the little boy. As for Geography, that was associated with the wide heath where his uncle Thiess Thiessen lived, an odd, solitary peasant of the heath who slept much among his piles of turf, but who had also an intellectual outlet. His cherished possession was an old atlas, and his whitewashed walls were covered with his own rough scrawls of journeys from China to Peru, from Hamburg, the outlet of Schleswig-Holstein, to all places everywhere. Here was Geography, as a child should get at it! Of all our sins of omission and commission, none perhaps are worse than the way we defraud children of those living ideas which are their right.

Here is a delightful description of how, and how slowly, a fundamental geographical idea reached the young Gneschen. (By the way, it should be enough to give chapter and verse, and not to quote at length; but Sartor Resartus is not a new book, and, do people read any but new books?) "In a like sense worked the Post-wagon, which, slow rolling under its mountains of men and luggage, wended through our Village: northwards, truly, in the dead of night; yet southwards visibly at eventide. Not till my eighth year did I reflect that this Post-wagon could be other than some terrestrial Moon, rising and setting by mere Law of Nature, like the heavenly one; that it came on made highways, from far cities towards far cities; weaving them like a monstrous shuttle into closer and closer union. It was then that . . . . I made this not quite insignificant reflection (so true also in spiritual things): Any road, this simple Entepfühl road, will lead you to the end of the World!" Even so said an Irish peasant the other day, when asked where a certain road led to.

Then, too, had he not the swallows which came year after year all the way from Africa and built in the 'cottage lobby,' and from these he learned, too, the sweet ways of the feathered nations. "Thus encircled by the mystery of existence; under the deep heavenly firmament; waited on by the four golden Seasons, with their vicissitudes of contribution,—for even grim winter brought its skating matches and shooting matches, its snow-storms and Christmas carols—did the Child sit and learn. These things were the Alphabet, whereby in after-time he was to syllable and partly read the grand volume of the World; what matters it whether such

Alphabet be in large gilt letters or in small ungilt ones, so you have an eye to read it? For Gneschen, eager to learn, the very act of looking thereon was a blessedness that gilded all: his existence was a bright, soft element of Joy; out of which, as in Prospero's Island, wonder after wonder bodied itself forth, to teach by charming."

Jörn, too, grew up in a world of wide spaces, and for him also was the ministration of the seasons. But neither of the little boys had a quite happy childhood. Indeed, childhood is quite happy only from the point of view of the elders. The pains of little children are as acute as their pleasures, and, what is more, they are eternal. Experience has not begotten hope, and every grief and disappointment is final. Besides, there probably grows about all children, as about Gneschen, "a dark ring of Care as yet no thicker than a thread and often quite over-shone," yet always reappearing and always waxing broader. "It was the Ring of Necessity whereby we are all begirt. Happy he for whom the Ring of Necessity is brightened into a Ring of Duty."

In this, Gneschen had an advantage over Jörn. Tender care and wise teaching made the needs-must of his life merge into the 'I can, I ought, I will' of duty. It was not that Jörn did not learn duty; he did, in that hard school of experience wherein he learned the meaning of kingship; but duty remained to him necessity, without the sense of joyful election on his own part.

Thus, one day Wieten sends the three children in the waggon on a picnic over the heath to the little uncle, Thiess Thiessen; and on the way back they talk. Thiess says: "The best in the world is to live on the heath and sleep and eat schwarzbrot and pig's head; and little Elsbe cries: "Love is the best in the world." "No," says Jörn, "work is the best." How had he learned it? Day by day, with solemn, childish eyes, he had watched the fruits of idleness and neglect about the homestead; neglected cattle, neglected crops, neglected out-buildings taught their lesson to the wise-hearted child, and this was the creed he got out of it—work is the best thing in the world. He never forgot it; hardly for a day did he relax the plodding, patient toil that the neglect of others had laid upon him.

Another thing he learned: "Elsbe and I will never go into an alehouse." "But when there is a ball?" said Elsbe. "I, never in my whole life," said he. The little Jörn was left to develop himself without much fostering or much hindrance, whereas Gneschen says: "I was forbid much; wishes, in any measure bold, I had to renounce. Everywhere a strait bond of Obedience inflexibly held me down.—In which habituation to Obedience, truly, it was beyond measure safer to err by excess than by defect. Obedience is our universal duty and destiny; wherein whoso will not bend must break: too early and too thoroughly we cannot be trained to know that would, in this world of ours, is as mere zero to should, and for the most part as the smallest of fractions even to shall. Hereby was laid for me the basis of worldly Discretion, nay, of Morality itself. Let me not quarrel with my upbringing!"

But the protest is well founded. Passivity is not the sole quality to be cultivated in children. It is by their self-ordered activities they develop, and they require more scope for these than an orderly house affords. An attic, a garden, a yard, a field, wherein to do as they will, is necessary to the free growth of children. If we could rid ourselves of the notion that children are somewhat imbecile, incapable of understanding principles and ordering themselves wisely, a child in a family might grow up with as little sense of collision as most of us are aware of in regard to the laws of the State to which we belong. We obey without knowing it; but when our obedience is challenged, we give it loyally.

For one other thing Diogenes blesses his parents in words so stimulating that they must be quoted:—

"My kind mother . . . did me one altogether invaluable service: she taught me, less indeed by word than by act and daily reverent look and habitude, her own simple version of the Christian Faith. Andreas too attended Church; yet more like a parade-duty, for which he in the other world expected pay with arrears,—as, I trust, he has received; but my mother, with a true woman's heart, and fine though uncultivated sense, was in the strictest acceptation Religious. How indestructibly the Good grows, and propagates itself, even among the weedy entanglements of Evil! The highest whom I knew on Earth I here saw bowed down, with awe unspeakable, before a Higher in Heaven: such things, especially in infancy, reach inwards to the very core of your being; mysteriously does a Holy of Holies build itself into visibility in the mysterious depths; and Reverence, the divinest in man, springs forth undying from its mean envelopment of Fear. Wouldst thou rather be a peasant's son that knew, were it never so rudely, there was a God in Heaven and in Man; or a duke's son that only knew there were two-and-thirty quarters on the family coach?"

This intimate sense of the presence of God was not for little Jörn.

II

"Jörn shall study," said his father; "that is understood. He shall be a land-agent. Let us drink to Jörn Uhl, the land-agent." And they drank. So the notion got about the village that Jörn was destined for high things. He went to school to Lehrer Peters to be prepared for the gymnasium. It must have been good to see him on the sofa with the old teacher, the little lad with fair hair standing on end, and deep-set, eager eyes devouring the book he held; an English book it was, for Lehrer Peters was a man of notions. He himself knew a little English, and held that English was the key to all wisdom, and indeed to the meaning of the world. A little Latin also was got in, but that was by the way.

Here follows a pretty episode. A charming child, Lisbeth Junker, the schoolmaster's niece, woos Jörn to go out fishing with her in the master's absence; and while they sit dangling their lines Jörn overhears a conversation between the schoolmaster and the magistrate, and gathers from it that his father's affairs are in a bad way. This is how another of life's lessons came to Jörn, and very admirably does the old schoolmaster bring it home to the boy, who owns frankly that he has overheard the talk. He tells him a tale of the successful career of an ancestor of Jörn's, and ends with a wise word of 'that great thinker, Goethe'—that what you inherit from your fathers you must labour in order to possess. This seed of thought sank deep. Thenceforth the little boy felt that he was responsible when there was no other to take responsibility. The child's eye kept the farm-labourers at work; and two horse-dealers, who came to traffic with his brothers, were abashed by his gaze.

But how is a person to prepare for the gymnasium with so many affairs on hand?

The time came when he must go to the neighbouring town to try his chances. Thiess Thiessen took him and his books in the waggon. The boy went in at the great gates; and Thiess, meanwhile, made acquaintance with an old shoemaker, who cheered him by saying that of five who go in, only one comes out successful. "But," says Thiess, "Jörn is clever, sits the whole day over his book and sees and hears nothing; he must succeed." But, alas! Lehrer Peter's English teaching somehow did not qualify him for a pass in Latin, and Jörn and Thiess went home crestfallen. This was the end of the boy's definite schooling.

His religious teaching fared no better; the preparation for Confirmation should have been much to him, but Jörn was told of justification by faith, that he should do no murder, and the like. The confirmation classes, though conducted by a diligent and kindly man, were a source of torment to him because he did not understand the teaching. By the way, his confirmation is a very definite era in the life of a German boy (or girl). So soon as he is fourteen he leaves school (if he be a child of the people), and, before he takes up tiny employment, is under the instruction of his pastor for six weeks, and works three hours a day in the church, besides writing and learning at home. Before his confirmation, he may not even run an errand for a neighbour for the usual penny. The practical and purposeful Jörn knew all about the concerns of the Uhl and of the whole village, but knew nothing of either the sin or the mercy about which he was taught. The list of sins began too far down, with theft, robbery, and murder, and the mercy came all too soon to satisfy his young sense of justice,—as soon as a man should throw his sins upon the Lord. God appeared to him an unpractical judge, who kept his books in fine order in his office and allowed himself to be deceived by the people without.

Meantime Jörn took his place steadily, of his own accord, as a farm labourer. He would do what he could to right matters in the neglected homestead. His step became heavy through following the plough in the heavy furrows; he had little to say, because he was more used to cattle than men; it seemed that his intellectual life had gone out, and he was in a fair way to become as one of the farm-hands. This is what the schooling of life had brought to Jörn Uhl.

Young Teufelsdröckh also goes to school and learns to handle his 'earliest tools'—his class-books. He cannot remember ever to have learned to read, which is true of many young scholars. He speaks of his education got in schools as 'insignificant.' He learned what others learned, seeing no use for it. His schoolmaster did little for him, and knew it, but thought him a genius, and said that he must be sent to the gymnasium and afterwards to a university. Meanwhile he read, eagerly as Cervantes, any scrap of page or printed paper he came across, including 'stall literature' bought out of his copper pocket-money and sewed into volumes by his own hands.

He got something out of this random reading, bits of history and bits of fable, real, both of them, out of which his mind got its necessary food. Now, here is a point worth attention. How seldom do we hear of a famous man who got that food for his mind which enabled him out of his school studies! And how often, on the other hand, do we read of those whose course of life has been determined by the random readings of boyhood! We go on blindly and stubbornly with our school curriculum, as if this were a fact of no significance, because, say we, the boy will have chances after his school-days to get such pabulum as he needs; but life is not long enough to afford the waste of some dozen years, its freshest and most intelligent period. And, what is more, the boy who has not formed the habit of getting nourishment out of his books in school-days does not, afterwards, see the good of reading. He has not acquired, in an intellectual sense, the art of reading, so he cannot be said to have lost it; and he goes through life an imperfect person, with the best and most delightful of his powers latent or maimed. Why in the world should we not give children, while they are at school, the sort of books they can live upon; books alive with thought and feeling, and delight in knowledge, instead of the miserable cram-books on which they are starved?

In spite of his school, Gneschen developed some power of thought:—"It struck me much" (he was in his twelfth year), "as I sat by the Kuhbach, one silent noontide, and watched it flowing, gurgling, to think how this same streamlet had flowed and gurgled, through all the changes of weather and of fortune, from beyond the earliest date of history"—a type of the thoughts, original so far as they are concerned, which strike all children of average intelligence.

Things went no better with Diogenes at the gymnasium; he was home-sick, the boys were rough and rude, he hated fighting and thought it disgraceful to be beaten, but also disgraceful to fight; so he wept a good deal, which did not help him with his school-fellows. Then, as for the teaching he got; Greek and Latin, he says, were mechanically taught, while, "what they called history, cosmography, philosophy and so forth, no better than not at all." Still, he learned something by watching the craftsmen who came in his way, and from some odds and ends of reading he lighted upon at his lodgings.

He complains that his teachers were hidebound pedants with no knowledge of boys' nature or of anything but their lexicons. "Innumerable dead vocables (no dead language, for they themselves knew no language) they crammed into us, and called it 'fostering the growth of mind'; " and he asks how can a mechanical gerund-grinder foster the growth of mind, which grows, not like a vegetable, by having 'etymological composts' laid upon it, but like a spirit, by contact of spirit, 'thought kindling itself at the fire of living thought.'

His years at the gymnasium brought him one idea, fertile for good and evil—"I was like no other." Here we have one of those words of profound educational insight with which Sartor Resartus abounds. There comes an epoch in every young life when the person discovers himself to be an individual. He perceives that he is like no other. It is this notion working in them which makes the captious girl and headstrong youth 'neither to have nor to hold'; and 'education' leaves young people absolutely unprepared for an era so important in their lives. The arrogant young man is apt to suppose he is individual in all that he is, and, by consequence, that in everything he is superior. No wonder he is unmanageable and infallible! But give him a ground-plan of human nature, let him know what he has in common with all men, and he is able to understand and to make use of his individual quota for the general good.

In due time Teufelsdröckh goes to the university. Being fairly perfect in 'dead vocables,' he believes he is set down "by the living Fountain there to superadd Ideas and capabilities." But, alas! it was true for him as for others that 'the pear-tree he had climbed at twelve he was still climbing at twenty.' Also, grinding poverty oppressed and distracted him, for he had lost his father.

He discovers that his university is the worst in the world for his needs. Among other defects, where all was defective, he tells us that "we boasted ourselves a Rational University; in the highest degree hostile to Mysticism; thus was the young vacant mind furnished with much talk about Progress of the Species, Dark Ages, Prejudice, and the like; so that all were quickly enough blown out into a state of windy argumentativeness; which by the better sort had soon to end in sick impotent Scepticism; the worser sort explode in finished self-conceit, and to all spiritual intents become dead."

This invective discovers a mistake in our educational methods. From the time a child is able to parse an English sentence till he can read Thucydides, his instruction is entirely critical and analytic. Does he read "The Tempest," the entrancing whole is not allowed to sink into, and become a part of him, because he is vexed about the 'vexed Bermoothes' and the like. His attention is occupied with linguistic criticism, not especially useful, and, from one point of view, harmful to him because it is distracting. It is as though one listened to "Lycidas," beautifully read, subject to the impertinence of continual interruptions in the way of question and explanation. We miss the general principle that critical studies are out of place until the mind is so 'throughly furnished' with ideas that, of its own accord, it compares and examines critically. "The hungry young," says Teufelsdröckh, "looked up to their spiritual Nurses; and, for food, were bidden to eat the east-wind"—"vain jargon of controversial Metaphysic, Etymology, and mechanical Manipulation falsely named science." Worse happened to him. Besides his wants and distresses—want of money, sympathy, hope—this manner of education resulted in 'fever paroxysms of doubt.' and he tells of cries for light in the silent watches of the night, of distresses of mind and heart, which it took long years to soothe under "the nightmare, Unbelief."

This malady of unbelief, again, is common to serious minds, educated to examine all things before they know the things they criticise by the slow, sure process of assimilating ideas. If we would but receive it, we are not capable of examining that which we do not know; and knowledge is the result of a slow, involuntary process, impossible to a mind in the critical attitude. Let us who teach spend time in the endeavour to lay proper and abundant nutriment before the young, rather than in leading them to criticise and examine every morsel of knowledge that comes their way. Who could live if every mouthful of bodily food were held up on a fork for critical examination before it be eaten?

Meantime, Teufelsdröckh got what served him, not out of the class-rooms but out of the chaos of the University library. "The foundation of a literary life was hereby laid: I learned, on my own strength, to read fluently in almost all cultivated languages, on almost all subjects and sciences; further, as man is ever the prime object to man, already it was my favourite employment to read character in speculation, and from the Writing to construe the Writer."

To Jörn, who had the makings of a man of science as had the other of a philosopher, all intellectual avenues save one were closed. In that chest, itself a page of history, he found an old book on astronomy (Littrow's). He had always liked solid knowledge, and, later in life, he explained that he had in child-hood been so overfed by Wieten and Fiete Krey upon romantic legends that he had no more appetite for poetry or fiction. Littrow was his solitary outlet; in course of time, he was able to indulge himself in the luxury of a telescope, the one luxury of his life; he contrived a revolving roof to an old arbour; made observations and recorded them on his own charts; and found in the heavens solace and relief from the manifold distresses of life. So, in spite of hindrances, we may consider that the two arrived at education. The one had reached the infinite solace and content of books; the other found for himself a single intellectual pursuit upon which the whole force of his mind could spend itself. But it is a pitiful thing when his education leaves a youth without the power or habit of reading, and also without an absorbing intellectual interest. Some men, as these two, get such gains in spite of their schooling; but how good it would be if we could devise an education which should be not only serviceable in making a living, but should enable young people to realise, use, and enjoy fulness of life! "The life is more than meat."

We read next, how Teufelsdröckh tried at various points to open that oyster of the world, and how Jörn Uhl was compelled to drive doggedly at a single point, and how each of them imagined, "it was with Work alone, and not also with Folly and Sin, in myself and others, that I had been appointed to struggle," and how folly and sin overcame them both.

Jörn Uhl forgot, just for once, his childish vow never to enter a Wirtshaus. He drank and was ashamed; and, in his shame, was thrown into a worse temptation—he learned the meaning of lust. But the woman was older than he, and had come out of the same fire herself, and taught him—Chastity. This lesson he learned so well that, later, he would not touch the hand of the woman he was about to marry until he had arranged for their nuptials.

We cannot follow Teufelsdröckh through his love-sicknesses and sorrows; but we know how it went with him, on the whole. To both young men life was a dour, hand-to-hand conflict, both set their teeth and fought it out, and both carried to the end the hardening or the softening, the sweetening or the souring of the lessons that had arrived to them during their education. For the most part, these two learned in the hard school of experience. For the one, Nature herself was a hard mistress, though passionately beloved; but each accomplished his 'pilgrim's progress' by the aid of things and of the ways of men; it is distressing to note how little help either got from direct teaching.

The problem before us all is, how far direct teaching and training may help in the evolution of character; and perhaps few things should be of more use to us than the study of such veracious records as we have in Sartor Resartus and Jörn Uhl. It were profitable to consider what might have been done here, and here, and here, for the guidance, help, and inspiration of either lonely and courageous young pilgrim. I venture to call these two veracious records, though Jörn Uhl is a novel and Sartor Resartus offers us much the same thing, that is, facts seen through a veil of romance; because we perceive that both are essentially true, and are profitable for our instruction in righteousness.

We have been told so much of the sournesses and sorenesses of Thomas Carlyle that we are in danger of forgetting how much we owe to the philosopher who, more than any other, has put hope and purpose into the adverse conditions of modem life; and, what is more to our present purpose, we overlook the lesson that the gloom and bitterness we condemn were the inevitable results of the upbringing sketched for us in the assumed experiences of Diogenes Teufelsdröckh; and that the strong virtues we admire came also out of that upbringing. So too of Jörn Uhl. Things went well with him in the end; but it took all the skill of the wise wife whom he loved to tide him over periods of dour gloom not unlike those which fell upon Carlyle.

This is (roughly) how the brave record ends:—Your life, Jörn Uhl, has not been an insignificant one. Your boyhood was tranquil, your youth, lonely; and you wrestled bravely and single-handed with the riddles of life; even if you could guess only at a few of them, your labour was not in vain. You went to the front for the land that lies about this well; you have been hardened by fire and frost and have made progress in the most important study—that of distinguishing things according to their value. You have learnt to know the passionate love of woman, and in that you gained the second great experience that life can give. You have buried Lena Tarn as well as your father and brothers, and in those hours of human grief you have peered into the eyes of knowledge and have become humble. You have fought with adverse fate and not given way; you plodded on, though it was long before help came. You worked your way into knowledge with clenched teeth and a lofty courage at an age when most men expect to repose. And, now that building and measuring and the like have been your work and joy for some years, you have not got into a groove: you take thought for all the land on each side of your measuring chain, and even consider the books which a friend of yours called Heim Heidreter writes.

"What shall a man write about, Jörn, if a life of so much meaning is not worth recording?"

Chapter 2. A Genius At "School"

"Minds like Goethe's are the common property of all nations."—Carlyle.

I

Every intimate and penetrating book has something of the nature of an autobiography. If it do not tell us what happened to the writer in the actual circumstances, it reveals what, in his idea, would have come to pass under such and such conditions. If this be true, how is it possible for one man to produce, not fifty men and women, as Browning claims to have done, but hundreds of actual persons behaving as they must because of the character that is in them? To realise this possibility is indeed as amazing and confounding as a fixed regard upon the Milky Way. Does it mean that all things are possible to all men? Anyway, Goethe confessedly images himself more or less in all his written work; and one failure especially, that of moral instability, is writ large for our instruction in "Wilhelm Meister."

It may not be unprofitable to compare this hero with another of whom we possess the journal intime, our old friend and favourite Arthur Pendennis. How far "Pendennis" is consciously an autobiography we need not inquire, for Thackeray takes no pains to tell us. Goethe, on the contrary, is at the greatest pains to trace the influences that result in himself, not only in his Dichtung und Wahrheit, an Autobiography, but in "Werther," "Wilhelm Meister," "Faust"; he is at pains to tell us, in fact, over and over again, that all he wrote was a record of himself. He tells us of the astrological influences under which he was born, and of the incidents of his birth, and he analyses his own nature with immense care, traces this to his father and the other to his mother, further traits to great-grandfather and great-grandmother. As Goethe says, he got his tall, strongly built frame and a certain earnestness in living from his father, a 'man of laws' who had also a taste for art: he married a wife not half his own age, who felt that she and her son were better mated in years and tastes than were she and her husband: "I and my Wolfgang were both young."

Catherine Goethe was a person of distinction, a correspondent of various learned ladies who, like herself, belonged to the Kultur Kampf. She appears to have been a delightful woman, full of gaiety, feeling, and imagination. "Joyousness," she writes, "is the mother of all virtues; when we are content and cheerful we wish to see all people gratified and gay, and do all we can to make them so." And again: "I have it by God's grace that no living soul ever went from me dissatisfied. I love humankind, old and young feel it." She tells us that she tried to reform no one, saw the good side of her neighbours, and left the bad to Him who made men, and "by this means I am content and happy." All this sounds well; but in practice it meant that Madame was an eclectic who chose only what she would out of her life; for example, she must not on any account be perturbed— a sentiment shared by her great son. She would say, we are told, on hiring a servant: "You shall tell me nothing terrifying, disquieting, or disagreeable, whether it happens in my own house, the neighbourhood, or the town. Once for all, I will know nothing of it. If it concerns me, I shall bear it soon enough. If it does not concern me, I have nothing to do with it. Even if a fire were to break out in the street where I am living, I will not hear of it sooner than I can help." It was not that she could not feel, but that she would not. During her son's acute illness in 1805, she would not allow herself to be told of what was going on. When it was over, she said: "I have known it all along . . . Now we may again talk about him without my feeling a stab in the heart at every mention of his name"; "stab in the heart"—in the phrase we find her excuse. She would not 'dree her weird,' would not endure the share of poignant feeling that fell to her.

To her influence and example, as well as to the nature inherited from her, we owe the limitation which must always distress the disciples of Goethe. Finding him so great, it is to them 'a stab in the heart' that he has not the added greatness of one who cared for his country and his kind. If only he had let himself care, when his country was going through one acute crisis after another! If only he had helped when men looked to him as the one wise man! But his mother saw about that. Anyway, she has left a lesson to mothers of the future. The idea of personal culture is so fascinating, and appears under so bewildering a disguise of pseudo-virtue, that high-minded women are apt to be deceived. They believe that to cultivate their minds and conserve their feelings is the best they can do not only for themselves but the world, on the principle that, if every man sweep before his own door, the street will be clean; and they bring up their children with the same desire for and effort after personal culture, and the same aloofness from the lives of other men. It is well we should clear our thoughts on this subject, and recognise, once for all, that personal culture is hardly a legitimate aim. We are allowed to seek knowledge for the sake of knowledge, culture of body and mind for the sake of serviceableness; and, recognising this, we give our lives an impersonal aspect. We look at pictures and read books for the sake of the pictures and the books, and not at all for our sakes. Our children carry forward this larger view of life. They feel, think, and labour without sparing as occasion calls upon them; they live, that is, the common life, and are not stranded in an inlet of individual culture.

We hear of the little Goethe's horror of ugliness as early as his third year,—"The dark child must be taken away. I can't endure it"; and here we get the key to much that came after. He was never taught to endure as a child, because his mother understood and shared his sensibility; and therefore endurance, the manly and cheerful acceptance of the inevitable, was never made a part of his life. Who will not endure must needs evade, and we find, let us say, Wilhelm Meister evading obligations as they occurred with a hardihood worthy of a better cause. We are shy of criticising a poet—above all, one of the world's few great poets. I once heard a distinguished man, who had had the honour of knowing Goethe, lecture upon him. His praises were fervent; and why not? But he could not bring himself to blame the poet for any failure, and said at the end to a friend, 'Have I not whitewashed him well?' Now, Goethe was too great for this process. He has offered himself as a beacon to mankind, indicating not only harbourage but rocks ahead; and we do not dishonour a great genius by considering why, in certain aspects, he was less than other men how he might have become greater all round.

His grandmother's large room upstairs was the favourite playing place for himself and his little sister Cornelia, always tenderly cherished by her brother; and one Christmas Eve this grandmother invented an amusement which gave direction to the boy's whole after-life. This was the famous puppet-show. We get full details of the incident in Wilhelm Meister. "How often," Wilhelm's mother is made to say, "have I been upbraided with that miserable puppet-show which I was unlucky enough to provide for you at Christmas, twelve years ago! It was the first thing that put these plays into your head." "Oh, do not blame the poor puppets; do not repent of your love and motherly care! It was the only happy hour I had enjoyed in the new, empty house. I never can forget that hour; I see it still before me; I recollect how surprised I was, when, after we had got our customary presents, you made us seat ourselves before the door that leads to the other room. The door opened; but not as formerly, to let us pass and repass: the entrance was occupied by an unexpected show. Within it rose a porch, concealed by a mysterious curtain. All of us were standing at a distance; our eagerness to see what glittering or jingling article lay behind the half-transparent veil was mounting higher and higher, when you bade us each sit down upon his stool and wait with patience. At length we were all seated and silent; a whistle gave the signal; the curtain rolled aloft, and showed us the interior of the Temple, painted in deep red colours. The high priest Samuel appeared with Jonathan, and their strange alternating voices seemed to me the most striking thing on earth. Shortly after entered Saul, overwhelmed with confusion at the impertinence of that heavy-limbed warrior who had defied him and all his people. But how glad was I when the little, dapper son of Jesse, with his crook and shepherd's pouch and sling, came hopping forth and said: 'Dread king and sovereign lord! let no one's heart sink down because of this; if your Majesty will grant me leave, I will go out to battle with this blustering giant'! Here ended the first act, leaving the spectators more curious than ever to see what further would happen, each praying that the music might soon be done. At last the curtain rose again. David devoted the flesh of the monster to the fowls of the air and the beasts of the field; the Philistine scorned and bullied him, stamped mightily with both his feet, and at length fell like a mass of clay, affording a splendid termination to the piece. And then the virgins sang: 'Saul hath slain his thousands, but David his ten thousands!' The giant's head was borne before his little victor, who received the king's beautiful daughter to wife." (Carlyle's Translation) Here we get the first indication of a career, the moment of vocation which came to the poet-child, as to many another, casually and without warning. Henceforth he lived in the dramatising of situations that came in his way, in the conception of situations worthy of being dramatised, and we are able to understand how, until the end of his life, the direction of the princely theatre at Weimar was his congenial and delightful occupation. We get many details in Wilhelm Meister showing how the child became possessed more and more completely by this one idea; how, prying about as children will, he found, laid by in the store-room, the puppets which had given him such joy; how he begged his mother to give them to him; how he contrived various costumes for them, and caused them to play many parts; how by and by he wrote plays for the puppets to act, speaking their several parts himself with such just expression and delicate enunciation that his sterner father, who looked askance at this new delight, felt that it was after all an instrument of education.

Many parents, who do not imagine their children to be embryo poets, are a little perplexed by the delight they take in any manner of acting, from Punch and Judy up, and they wonder how far it is well to encourage a taste which may come to interfere with serious pursuits. Children are born poets, and they dramatise all the life they see about them, after their own hearts, into an endless play. There is no reason why this natural gift should not be pressed into the service of education. Indeed, it might be safe to go further: the child who does not dramatise his lessons, who does not play at Richard and Saladin, who does not voyage with Captain Cook and excavate with Mr. Flinders Petrie, is not learning. The knowledge he gets by heart is not assimilated and does not become part of himself.

Therefore it is well that children should, at any rate, have the outlet of narration, that they should tell the things they know in full detail; and, when the humour takes them, 'play' the persons, act the scenes that interest them in their reading. On the other hand, there is the danger that their representation of facts may become more to them than the facts themselves, that the show of things may occupy their whole minds. For this reason it may be well not to indulge children with anything in the form of a stage or stage properties, not with so much as a puppet-show. They will find all they want in the chair which serves as a throne, the sofa which behaves as a ship, the ruler which plays the part of rapier, gun, or sceptre, as occasion demands. In fact, preoccupation with tawdry and trivial things will be avoided if children are let alone: imagination will furnish them with ample properties, delightful scenes, upon the merest suggestion of reality. Bottom the weaver and his crew furnish the prototype for children's plays,—

"This lantern doth the hornéd moon present,"

and there is a hint of Shakespeare's earnest in this broad jest, for do we not get the same idea amplified in the prologue to Henry V.?

II

Young Goethe's father, who delighted in teaching, instructed his children himself; and there are still exercises of the boy preserved in the Frankfort library, in German, Latin, Greek, and French, written between his seventh and ninth years. These exercises show that the manner of instruction was immediate and interesting; the father dictating what had struck himself—some news of the day or some story of 'old Fritz'; or the boy chose his own subject. He never seems to have gone to school, except on one occasion, when the family house was being rebuilt and the children were sent out of the way. Their school experience appears to have offended the two fastidious children: they were not accustomed to the turbulent life of a school, and possibly, in this first experience of a public of his own age and status, was sown the seed of that indifference to the public welfare which continued with Goethe through life. But it is easy to err in emphasising this seeming defect in the poet's character; is it not conceivable that his philosophic mind put in the balances the sorts of service it was possible for him to render, and that he recognised the impossibility of bestowing upon mankind any gifts comparable with those he has left us?

Possibly it was while he was at school that be learned to hate grammar—and, curiously enough, on the very grounds which made this subject repellent to Herbert Spencer; he could not put up with arbitrary rules. Both thinkers might have been the better for some grammatical grind; both, indeed, took their education into their own hands, as is rather the way of persons of genius.

If the analysis of language teased him, the analysis of human nature occupied young Goethe at a very early age. He tells us a curious anecdote in which he appears in the attitude proper to a child, that of curious interest and suspended judgment. He and some young friends joined in a verse competition:—"And here occurred something strange, which long troubled me. I could not help regarding my own poems, be they what they might, as the best. But I soon perceived that my competitors, who produced very poor things, were in the same case, and thought no less of themselves; nay, what struck me as still more curious, a good, though for-work-incapable, lad, who got the tutor to make his rhymes, not only held these to be the best, but was fully convinced he had himself made them, as he in perfect honesty declared to me."

Already, in his eighth or ninth year, has he observed, and that without censure or comment, one of the most baffling complexities of human nature—that the attempt to appear other than we are is rather an intellectual than a moral vice, and that the hypocrite is commonly a person who, through bad intellectual habits, is able to deceive himself. This reminiscence of Goethe's childhood reminds us that the clearsighted child, not blinded by habits of conventional usage, is with us, taking curious and amazed, if unconscious, note of all our small hypocrisies of opinion and action.

It is good to know that the sort of books all children love were dear to this poet-child. Telemachus, he tells us, had 'a sweet and beneficent influence upon him'; and that Anson's Voyage round the World combined for him 'the dignity of truth with the rich fancy of fiction,' and that he delighted in Robinson Crusoe, in folk-tales and fairy-tales.

It was a fitting thing that Goethe's home was in an ancient city, rich in traditions and associations, in all of which he took passionate delight. What was it not to him to stand in the hall in which emperors had been crowned, on the spot where once was a castle occupied by Charlemagne himself! How good, too, to think as he looked up at the vault of the Rathaus, how, for ages past, the fathers of the city had deliberated there! Then there were the picturesque houses of the Römer-Platz, and, not least significant, the stately old dwelling with projecting gables occupied by the Goethes themselves. These things he tells us of at length in his Dichtung and Walirheit, wherein he gathers up at great length the impressions of his early childhood; and, certainly, Frankfort, with its long historic perspective and stirring modern life, proved itself 'meet nurse for a poetic child.'

A child's first impressions of his native place are such a precious and rare possession that it will repay us to follow this boy in the pursuit of such ideas as his Vaterstadt had to offer him.

"It was just about this time that I first awoke to my Vaterstadt, as I wandered up and down, more and more freely and uncontrolled, now alone, now with my playfellows. In order to some extent to explain the impression which these solemn and revered surroundings made upon me, I must begin with the impression I received of my birthplace as it gradually disclosed itself to me in its many parts. Above all I liked to walk on the Mainz bridge. Its length, its strength, its handsome appearance made it a noticeable structure; it was also a very notable memorial of that foresight in years gone by which the world owes to its burghers.

"The beautiful river drew my gaze with it up and down stream, and when the golden cock on the cross on the bridge glittered in the sunshine, I had a delightful sensation. We then usually went through Sachsenhausen, and, for a kreuzer, enjoyed the ferry across. Then, again, on this side, we stole along to the wine market, gazed at the cranes at work unloading goods, but were especially entertained by the arrival of the market boats, whence we saw many strange figures descend. Then we went into the city, and, every time, paid our respects to the "Saalhof," which was, at any rate, on the very spot where the castle of Charles and his successors is said to have stood. We lost ourselves in the old trading quarter, and only too gladly found ourselves in the throng that gathered round the church of St Bartholomew on market days.

". . . I remember, too, the horror with which I fled past the closely packed, narrow, and hideous meat-stalls. The Römerberg was a quite delightful place to walk in. But what most drew the attention of the Boy were the many little towns within the town, the fortresses within the fortress; for example, the walled cloisters remaining from earlier times, and other more or less castle-like buildings transformed into dwellings and warehouses."

Frankfort had at that time no modern architecture of importance, but everywhere was evidence of 'old, unhappy, far-off times, and battles long ago.' Forts, towers, fortifications, moats, enclosed the new town, and all spoke of the necessity for providing for the common safety in troublous times. "A certain inclination towards the antique took fast hold of the boy, which was especially nourished and favoured by old chronicles and woodcuts, as, for example, those of Grave relating to the siege of Frankfort: to this another taste was added, that of observing the common circumstances of life in all their natural complexity, without any regard to interest or beauty. One of our favourite walks, which we tried to take several times in the year, was the round of the city walls. Gardens, courts, back buildings stretch to the Livinger; and we saw many thousand people in their domestic, narrow, shut-off, hidden conditions of life. From the ornamental show gardens of the rich to the orchards of the burgher who grows for his own needs, from thence to the factories, bleaching grounds, and similar workshops, to the churchyard itself (for a little world lay within the town boundary) we wandered on past a most varied, most wonderful, ever-changing spectacle, of which our childish curiosity was never weary.

"Within the Römer, . everything that concerned the election and coronation of the emperors had the greatest charm for us. We knew how to get round the keepers in order to get permission to go up the gaily painted imperial staircase, otherwise shut off by an iron gate. The Hall of Election, hung with purple, decorated with gold fringes, inspired us with awe. The door-hangings—on which little children or genii dressed in imperial colours and bearing the royal insignia play a wonderful part—we examined with great attention, and longed to see a coronation with our own eyes.

"It was only with great difficulty they got us out of the imperial hall once we had succeeded in slipping in, and we considered those our truest friends who could tell us of the deeds of the emperors whose halflength figures were painted at some height all round. Of Charlemagne we heard many a tale, but the historic interest began for us with Rudolf of Hapsburg, who by his courage put an end to so much strife. Charles the Fourth also drew our attention to himself . . . Maximilian we heard praised as the friend of man and of the burghers, and that it was prophesied that he would be the last emperor of his house; which was, alas! indeed the case, for after his death the choice lay only between the King of Spain, Charles the Fifth, and the King of France, Francis the First."

All this intimacy with his native town 'the Boy' would seem to have got before his seventh year, or possibly a little later, during the period in which the family house was being rebuilt, and the children were with friends—a time when they seem to have been left more to their own devices than was customary.

This knowledge of the Vaterstadt appears to have been picked up by the way—from children like themselves, for example, who had heard it from curators, workpeople, and the like. Where there is avidity for any sort of knowledge, it comes from chance sources. It is lamentable that this kind of lore is not much sought after by English children; and, seeing that every English county, and almost every town, is wonderfully rich in associations, historical and personal, there must be some reason why we are wanting in the local patriotism with which most Continental nations succeed in imbuing their children. I have heard a father in a valley of the Harz telling his little boy of five that here was the scene of Tilly's famous march; and, of course, the child saw the valley filled with armed men with waving plumes on pawing horses: he would never forget it. Again, a small streeturchin in Bruges will tell you where such and such a picture by Memling is to be found; or at the Hague you meet a working man taking his children round the picture-galleries, and explaining, you do not know how or what, but certainly the children are interested. Now, this sort of interest is as though it did not exist for, let us say, eighty per cent of British-born children. There appear to be two or three reasons for our defective education in this respect. In the first place, we have been brought up to believe in what is 'useful' in education: it may help us to gain a living if we can read and write and cast accounts; may help us in society if we can play and sing and chatter French; or in a career, if we can scrape up enough classical and mathematical knowledge to win a scholarship. But where's the good of knowing what happened in the past, even at the next streetcorner! What's the good of having an imagination furnished with pictures that open out in long perspective, and enrich and ennoble life?

It is the old story; utilitarian education is profoundly immoral, in that it defrauds a child of the associations which should give him intellectual atmosphere.

Another notion that stands between us and any vital appreciation of the past is, that—'we are the people!' We are cocksure that we know all that is to be known, that we do all that is worth while; and we are able to regard the traditions and mementoes of the past with a sort of superior smirk, a notion that, if the book-writers have not made it all up, this story of the past is no such great thing after all: that 'a fellow I know' could do as much any dayl There are few things more unpleasant than to see the superior air, and hear the cheap sneers, with which well-dressed people, not to say 'Arry and 'Arriet, disport themselves in the presence of any monument of antiquity they may make holiday to go and see. We have lost the habit of reverence.

A third, and perhaps more amiable trait, tells against our due delight in the past. It is strongly borne in upon us that bragging is odious. We do not choose to make much of our private possessions, and unconsciously apply the same principle to whatever might tend to magnify the past we own as a people. It is well we should know that this sort of knowledge of, and intimacy with, the associations of the past is every child's right, whatever be his class. Once we perceive the defectiveness of the education we give children in this respect, we shall no doubt find ways to remedy it.

III

Another fragment of his early education Goethe describes in words that must be quoted in order to do justice to the strength of the impression made on the little boy's mind:

"In the house, my gaze was chiefly attracted by a row of Roman views with which my father had decorated an ante-room. Here I daily saw the Piazza del Popolo, the Colosseum, the Piazza of St Peter's, St Peter's, exterior and interior, the Castle of St Angelo, and much else. These pictures made a deep impression on me, and my father, otherwise a very laconic man, was often pleased to volunteer descriptions of the subjects. His love for the Italian language, and for everything concerning that land, was very outspoken. He often showed us a little collection of marbles and natural objects which he had brought away with him, and he spent a great part of his time in writing up a diary of his travels.'

Here we get a hint as to what may be done for a child by the pictures we surround him with. This row of engravings and his father's talk about them gave Goethe practically a second fatherland. The speech of Italy, the sun of Italy, the past of Italy, became a home for his thoughts; and we know how profoundly his late long sojourn in Italy affected his style as a poet—for good or ill.

Our first idea is that all we can do for children is to give them a correct feeling for art; to surround them, for example, with the open spaces and simple, monumental figures we get in Millet's pictures: we cannot do better, but we can do more. Some, at any rate, of our pictures should be like the little windows, showing a landscape beyond, which the Umbrian Masters loved to introduce. That is just what the children want, an outlook. Every reminiscence of travel in the way of post-card or photograph will almost certainly bring about some preoccupation of a child's mind with the country his parents have seen and known; and will, as certainly, end in the child's seeking these same places when he becomes a man, not so much because his parents have been there, as because his own childish imagination has been there, and because, there, he has furnished a home for his thoughts.

IV

We find that public events, which must needs rouse reflection in all men, had their share in the education of 'the Boy': notable amongst these was the extraordinary calamity which, he tells us, deeply, for the first time, troubled his peace of mind. On 1st November 1755 occurred the earthquake of Lisbon, falling as a terrific shock upon a peaceful world. The earth shook, opened, and a large, beautiful city, with its houses, towers, walls, churches, royal palaces, and 60,000 of its people, was swallowed up by the gaping earth, while smoke and flames enveloped the ruins.

"'The Boy' who heard all this talked over was not a little troubled. God, the Creator and Upholder of heaven and earth, as the explanation of the first article of the Creed so wisely and mercifully declares, had shown Himself in no fatherly guise in rewarding the just and the unjust with destruction. In vain the young spirit sought to free itself from impressions, the more difficult to get rid of, since wise men and scholars could not agree as to the way in which such a phenomenon should be regarded."

Then he tells us that the following summer gave him another opportunity of becoming acquainted with the angry God of the Old Testament. A terrific hailstorm broke the windows of the new house, flooded the rooms, and sent the maids, shrieking, to their knees, that God would have mercy upon them. His faith was doubly shaken; he doubted both the fatherhood of God and the filial confidence of men—a seed-thought to bear fruit in the future.

Unforeseen and unpreventable natural calamities cannot occur without stirring profound reflections in the minds of thoughtful children. They think more and not less of such things than their elders, because to them they are new. A child's faith may be undermined, and no word said, by the news of some such catastrophe, and the casual way in which it is talked about; but after all, such occurrences are opportunities rather than hindrances. Every day of our lives we are face to face with the 'providential' and with the unaccountable; we cannot make the one idea fit the other; and in these contradictions consists for us much of the 'mystery of godliness.' It might be well to bring a child to face the fact of mystery when first his mind is greatly agitated by some public or private calamity. We do not know; we are not meant to know; we have our limitations. If we understood everything, there would be no room left for faith in God, because we should only believe what we could quite well see and understand. But it is just possible that the sudden loss of all these precious lives may mean that life and death are not the great and final things in the eyes of God that they are in our eyes. We are sure that people go on existing; and how they do so, we must trust to our Father, because He is our Father and theirs. Such opportunities for the exercise of a strong faith should be a means of fortifying rather than enfeebling the religious life.

Later, we get a curious account of how 'the Boy,' dissatisfied with the religious teaching he got, determined to make a religion for himself, and, like many another child, made for himself an altar (out of a lacquered music-stand of his father's), and offered natural productions thereupon over which a constant flame was to burn, signifying how man's heart rises in desire for his Maker. The flame was produced by burning pastilles, lighted at a burning-glass heated by the sun. But, at the second sacrifice, the altar caught fire, and the poetic child was diverted from the notion of inventing his own religion.

Through hard work, he tells us, he soon learned to understand what his father, and the teachers he employed, would have him learn; but he was not grounded well in anything. Grammar, as we have seen, he disliked; but he forgave the Latin grammar, because the rhymes assisted his memory. The children had a rhymed geography, too, which helped them to retain facts and names; but that following of Anson's voyages with finger on the globe, together with their father's travels, probably constituted their real knowledge.

'The Boy's' gifts of language and rhetoric were greatly cherished by his father, who made many plans for the future, turning on these gifts. He should, for example, go to two universities—Leipsic first; the other he should choose,—and then he should travel in Italy: whereupon the father would talk of Naples—talk the children delighted in more than in prospects too far in the future to attract them.

The great folio Bible, Comenius' Orbis Pictus, Gottfried's Chronicle, with cuts, taught them the principal facts of the world's history. Fables, mythology, and Ovid's Metamorphoses, the first book of which he diligently studied, all went to the nourishment of the boy.

V

His seventh year (1756) brought a new public interest to the boy, the opening of the war which, he tells us, had for the next seven years great influence on his life. Frederick the Second, king of Prussia, had with 60,000 men fallen upon Saxony; and, instead of leaving the war to account for itself, had issued a manifesto showing why he invaded Saxony. This astute move divided men into two parties, and the Goethe family was divided like the rest. The grandfather, who had assisted at the coronation of Francis I. and received a golden chain from the Empress, took, with several of the family, the side of Austria.

His father, whose sympathies had been with the unlucky Charles VII., adopted the cause of Prussia. There followed endless feuds in a hitherto united family, for all other interests gave place to the passionate partisanship stirred up by the war; and, "so was I;" he says, "also Prussian, or, to speak more exactly, Fritzisch; that was what made us Prussians: it was the personality of the great king that worked on all minds. I rejoiced with my father over our victories, wrote with delight songs of triumph, and with even more delight songs of derision upon our opponents, however feeble the rhymes.

"As the eldest grandson and godson, I had, since childhood, dined with my grandparents on Sunday; and the hours spent with them were the happiest of my week. But now the food revolted me, for I had to listen to the most horrible calumnies upon my hero. Here another wind blew, here was another manner of speech than at home. My affection, indeed even my respect, for my grandparents was lessened. I could not disclose any of this to my parents; my instinct, as well as a warning from my mother, forbade me. So I was thrown back upon myself, and as in my sixth year, after the earthquake at Lisbon, I became somewhat sceptical of the goodness of God, so now, on account of Frederick the Second, I began to doubt the justice of public opinion. I was by nature reverently inclined, and it took a great shaking to make my faith waver on any matter worthy of reverence."

How far, we are inclined to ask, should children be allowed to share in the party spirit and party strife on questions of Church and State which agitate their elders? Probably we are all agreed that young children should be kept out of this sort of turmoil. We keep the little ones in the kingdom of heaven; and, certainly, the virulence and bitterness of party do not belong to the blessed state. For another reason, too, we should do well to reserve before the children our opinions on burning questions. We naturally wish them to embrace our own views; but, if too great an emotional pressure has been put upon them as children, their tendency when they are older is to react in the opposite direction. They are apt to become indifferent or hostile where once they had been jealous and bigoted. Perhaps this is why we hear now and then of the children of Unitarians becoming Roman Catholics, of the Radical son of a Tory father, and the like. We must, for all reasons, refrain ourselves before the children; and, indeed, it is not bad for us to have their moderating influence among us. But a boy must, sooner or later, take sides, and must take the side he has a mind to, be it right or wrong; to do so is part of his initiation.

We are surprised that 'the Boy,' in the glow of his poetic sensibility, did not embrace the cause of Maria Theresa, the good and gracious empress, who certainly had a claim on chivalric devotion. But here, again, we may read between the lines. It was not only that his father's sympathies were with Frederick; it was that that astute monarch had stated his case, and a statement is, of its nature, convincing to the logical mind. This is a point we are apt to miss in dealing with questions of religion and the philosophy of life. We leave it to the dissentients to state the case, and the first statement almost inevitably carries conviction. Perhaps this is why atheistical teaching spreads so rapidly among intelligent artisans. For the first time they have received the intellectual compliment of a logical statement. As, probably, most statements can be proved to the hilt, the mind of the neophyte is stirred with sudden joy. 'I have thought,' he says to himself, for perhaps the first time; and his reason enjoys the satisfaction of logical demonstration. No wonder that it is not easy to shake what are, in such a case, primal convictions; and especially is it difficult to supplant them by means of emotional appeals. Pride of intellect is legitimate. Where we err is, in not enlisting it on the side of right thinking and right living. We seldom trouble ourselves to offer young people the intellectual grounds for any opinions we propose to them; everything is casual; and then we are discomforted when children of this world, wiser than we, make an appeal to the mind in behalf of views which are repugnant to us, and which we believe to be wrong.

Another point to be noted in this connection is the cocksureness of the young person. All young persons are cocksure, not at all because they are foolish and arrogant, but because they are unaware of the fact that equally reasonable and equally intelligent persons are capable of holding opposite views on any given question. In this, as in so many other ways, we feel the lack of what must be the rational basis of a sound education—that is, an ordered study of human nature.

Goethe's remarks on the subject are profoundly instructive:—"Thinking now carefully over the matter, I find here the germ of the indifference, indeed even contempt, of the public which influenced a period of my life, and was only late brought within bounds through greater insight and cultivation. The consciousness of party injustice was uncomfortable enough even then—was, indeed, injurious, for it accustomed the Boy to a barrier between himself and those he loved and valued.

"The battles and events quickly following each other left the parties neither rest nor peace. We took a malicious pleasure in stirring up again every imagined evil, and magnifying every trick of the opposition; and so we went on tormenting each other till a few years later, when the French took possession of Frankfort and brought real discomfort into our houses."

The elders of the house, fearing, perhaps, the mischief that a zealous young partisan might do in a divided town, kept the young people more at home, and devised schemes for their amusement and occupation. The grandmother's puppet-show was once more in use and plays on a larger scale were produced. One boy friend after another was brought in to see the show, and thus, says Goethe, he made many friends. But boys are restive, and the young actors were obliged to fall back on a younger public, with their attendants to keep them in order. We get a detailed account of this period in Wilhelm Meister—of the plays the young poet wrote, to the wonder of his companions, of how these plays never came to a point and disgusted the author, of the elaborate staging attempted, and much besides.

"I surrendered myself to my imagination; I rehearsed and prepared for ever, built a thousand castles in the air and saw not that I was at the same time undermining the foundation of these little edifices." He it was who made the necessary equipments for the boy actors, manufactured the swords, gilded and decorated the scabbards, furnished helmets with plumes of paper, made shields, even coats of mail. "We marched about the courtyards and gardens, and smote fearfully upon each other's shields and heads. Many flaws of discord rose among us, but none that lasted." The other boys were happy in this warlike display; not so 'Wilhelm.' "The aspect of so many armed figures naturally stimulated in my mind those ideas of chivalry which for some time, since I had commenced the reading of old romances, were filling my imagination." He was particularly influenced by a translation of Jerusalem Delivered which he came across, and lived long in the atmosphere of the poem. Of Clorinda he says: "The masculine womanhood, the peaceful completeness of her being had a great influence upon my mind, just beginning to unfold itself . . . A hundred and a hundred times have I repeated to myself the history of the mournful duel between Tancred and Clorinda."

"However strongly I inclined by nature to the party of the Christians, I could not help declaring for the Paynim heroine with all my heart, when she engaged to set on fire the great tower of the besiegers. And when Tancred in the darkness met the supposed knight, and the strife began between them under that veil of gloom, and the two battled fiercely, I could never pronounce the words—

'But now the sure and fated hour is nigh,
Clorinda's course is ended, she must die!'

without tears rushing into my eyes, which flowed plentifully, when the hapless lover, plunging sword into her breast, opened the departing warrior's helmet, recognised the lady of his heart, and, shuddering, brought water to baptise her. How did my heart run over, when Tancred struck with his sword that tree in the enchanted wood; when blood flowed from the gash, and a voice sounded in his ears, that now again he was wounding Clorinda; that destiny had marked him out ever unwittingly to injure what he loved beyond all else! The recital took such hold of my imagination, that the passages I had read of the poem began dimly, in my mind, to conglomerate into a whole; wherewith I was so taken that I could not but propose to have it in some way represented. I meant to have Tancred and Rinaldo acted; and for this purpose, two coats of mail, which I had before manufactured, seemed expressly suitable. The one, formed of dark-gray paper with scales, was to serve for the solemn Tancred; the other, of silver and gilt paper, for the magnificent Rinaldo. In the vivacity of my anticipations, I told the whole project to my comrades, who felt quite charmed with it, only could not well comprehend how so glorious a thing could be exhibited, and, above all, exhibited by them."

VI

Thus, for the second time, circumstances compelled the young poet on the lines of his vocation. We hear, too, of his success as a story-teller, and the youth of Frankfort wondered at his tale of The New Paris.

At this time 'the Boy' appears to have had lessons with other youths; but things did not go well with him. The teacher was harsh and cruel, and the use his best pupil made of his persecutions was to set himself definitely to bear pain without wincing. He tells us, too, how, on one occasion, three of the most ill-conditioned of his comrades fell upon him. He bore their cruel slashing of his legs with rods until the clock struck the hour which should dismiss the boys; then he turned upon the three and came off victor. In the end this attempt at companionship at lessons fell through, and he was kept more at home. He appears to have been entirely friendly with his boy comrades, but took rather an en haut de bas attitude which was no doubt exasperating to his less gifted companions. Perhaps, had he worked steadily at the gymnasium of his native town, things would have gone otherwise with him. He would have learnt something of the give and take of life, how far to bear and when not to bear, and, especially, how to bear with good-humour. He would have learned, too, that other boys have brains, would have laid a foundation of sound scholarship, and would not in the end have had to confess that he had not been grounded in anything.

All of this is true, at any rate, of an ordinarily clever boy; but we cannot predicate about a poet. It is true that we should not have had Milton had not the scholar been superadded to the poet. Byron and Shelley, on the other hand, are quoted as showing how little effect Eton and Harrow had upon poets that were to be; and perhaps it is a fact that, the more original the mind, the less it is capable of working in grooves, and the more tiresome are grammatical and even mathematical studies. But it must not be supposed that what may be all right for a genius is the best thing for persons of ordinary intellectual powers. The fact is, the genius cannot accept of the intellectual discipline of the schools, not so much out of lawlessness, as because his constructive mind is for ever busy in evolving a mental discipline of its own. It is in this sense that a genius is a law unto himself. He is not lawless, but has singular powers of self-education. The parents of the young genius will probably do him an injury if they do not give him the chance of the school-training in habits of clear thinking and right judgment, as well as in the invaluable power of sustaining relations with his fellows—a power often wanting in persons of casual education. They need not fear the undue fettering of the gifts they prize in their son. Your genius has an amazing and sufficiently irritating way of evading that which bothers him; and assuredly he will be thankful in after days for any such tincture of scholarship as his masters are able to get into him.

Goethe himself throws as much light as may be on the subject of the evolution of the man from the child. "Who is able to speak worthily of the fulness of childhood? We cannot watch the little creatures play before us without delight and admiration, for indeed the promise of childhood is usually greater than the fulfilment, as if Nature, among other of her tricks, here also specially designs to make sport of us . . .

"But growth is not merely development: the various organic systems which go to make a man, spring from each other, follow each other, change into each other, press upon each other, even swallow each other up, so that after a certain time there is scarcely a trace left of many activities, many indications of power. Even if, on the whole, the talent of a man appears to have a certain bent, it would be hard for the greatest and most experienced philosopher to trace it with any degree of certainty; and yet it is quite possible to perceive the underlying indication of a tendency."

Among the conditions which moulded 'the Boy,' was undoubtedly the restless temper of the burghers of Frankfort during the seven years of the war. Even when the town was not directly affected, every family, every citizen, as we have seen, took sides. Frankfort, divided as it was already by three religious parties, was peculiarly disturbed. At first Goethe's father, notwithstanding his (Fritzisch) sympathies, continued, with the few friends he had gathered about him, to live his life of quietness and culture. We get the names of a whole row of the beautifully-bound works of poets whose names are little known to-day, outside of Germany at any rate; these the father read constantly and knew well, and so did the boy, who could recite many passages for the pleasure of his elders.

But all of these recognised poetry as an art in which the form was of at least as much consequence as the substance; and upon this formal character of poetry the elder Goethe insisted with passionate intensity when an intimate friend, who was greatly influenced by Klopstock's Messias, endeavoured to win his sympathy. But the lover of poetry which conformed to given rules could not away with Klopstock, who not only wrote in unrhymed hexameters, but was somewhat reckless about metre. The friend retired from the controversy and read his Klopstock on Sundays; but he had gained disciples—the mother and children borrowed the volume and got it by heart during the week days. We have an amusing scene when the mystery of these secret readings transpired. The father of the family was being shaved, and the two children sat on stools somewhat out of sight and harangued each other in such strong language, Satan being one of the speakers, that the barber lost his presence of mind and upset the bowl of lather over his patron.

VII

The year 1759 was eventful for all the families in Frankfort, for then began the French occupation which lasted for a couple of years. Herr Goethe was especially afflicted. His new, or rather his restored, house was not yet completed, and, behold, billeted upon him were Count Thorane, the King's Lieutenant, with his staff. He could not reconcile himself to this invasion. The very first night, on the occasion of the distribution of the rooms, the Lieutenant made overtures of good-will. There was chance mention of the decoration of one of the reception-rooms, and Thorane, who was interested in matters of art, insisted upon seeing the pictures immediately, admired them, inquired who were the artists, and did his best to keep the careful hand of a master upon the treasures of the house. Notwithstanding this community of tastes, the elder Goethe could not accommodate himself to the new situation. He became more and more morose, and difficulties were barely smoothed over by the efforts of the house mistress, who set herself to learn French from a common friend, who represented to the Count the difficulties of the situation.

But the children had fine times. The Lieutenant had a sort of civil jurisdiction over the troops, and there was a constant coming and going of officers and men; and as the children were always peering about on the common stairway, they got to know a great deal about military matters and many military persons. The young Goethe made himself a persona grata with the Count in a remarkable way. He, at this time a child of ten, knew the haunts and homes of the artists of the city,—those artists to whose work his father had introduced the Lieutenant. Nay, more, the boy had been in the habit of attending auctions, and had always been able to describe, rightly or wrongly, the subjects of the pictures for sale. He had written an essay containing suggestions for twelve pictures illustrating the history of Joseph, and some of these had been painted. In a word, the young Goethe, child as he was, appears to have been regarded as a connoisseur; and Thorane not only took him about with him, but took his advice regarding decorative pictures for the chateau of his eldest brother, for which he was arranging.

A sort of little studio was set up in the house, where one and another artist worked for the great man, and these seemed to have liked to have the boy with them. This anecdote is interesting as offering a hint of the marvellous versatility of the poet, who would have been great as a scientist, and conceivably as an artist, had not poetry laid compelling hands upon him.

It would seem as if rather familiar intercourse with such a man as Count Thorane must in itself have been an important factor in the education of Goethe. He appears to have been the type of French officer with whom history has made us familiar, a man of dignified and reserved manners, who maintained good humoured relations with the persons under him partly by means of his shrewd and caustic wit. One circumstance appears specially to have impressed the boy. For a day, perhaps days, at a time this accessible chief was invisible. It appears he was subject to fits of hypochondriacal depression, and while they lasted he would see no one but his valet—an impressive piece of self-control.

"But now it seems necessary to set forth more circumstantially and to explain how, in the midst of such events, I got hold of French, more or less easily, though I had not learned it. My inborn gifts came to my aid, so that I easily grasped the sound and ring of a language; the movements, accent, tone, and other external peculiarities. Many words were familiar from my knowledge of Latin, Italian helped still more, and in a short time I heard so much from servants and soldiers, sentries and visitors, that though I could not start a conversation, I could at least understand questions and answers." But he tells us that all this was nothing compared with the help which the theatre brought him. His grandfather had given him a free pass, and every day found him there, against the will of his father, but with the connivance of his mother. At first his entertainment consisted only in catching the accent and watching the gestures of the players. Then he found a volume of Racine at home, and hit upon the plan of learning long speeches by heart and delivering these, so far as he could, as he had heard them, though without understanding their drift.

And now he made a friend—a nice boy connected with the theatre. The two became inseparable companions, for in the dearth of boy companionship the stranger managed to understand young Goethe's French, and by aid of familiar intercourse with him 'the Boy' made progress that surprised his friend. The two haunted the theatre, and presently found their way into what served as a greenroom, where Goethe saw (hardly comprehending much) what he described as taking place in the scratch company whose doings he chronicles in Wilhem Meister. He and his friend discussed many things, and "in four weeks (I) learned more than could have been imagined; so that no one knew how I suddenly, as if by inspiration, had acquired a foreign language."

Possibly, when the entente cordiale has become acclimatised, let us say, children belonging to the two countries may come to visit each other's families, and more French may yet be learned in a month from the companionship of a nice French boy than the best master in the world would succeed in teaching in a year. The desire to communicate with each other would doubtless bring about the power.

The French boy, whom he chooses to name Derones, introduced young Goethe to his sister, a grave maiden, who did not forget that she was much older than he; otherwise, no doubt, we should have had the first of a long series of love interludes. But he complains that young maidens treat boys younger than themselves as if they were their aunts, and his offerings of fruit and flowers made little impression.

By and by the two young friends must needs fight a duel; provocation was there none, but that did not matter. Derones called young Goethe out, and they went to a lonely place and wielded their mock swords, and the honour of the Frenchman was satisfied when he stuck his dagger into a ribbon on the enemy's equipment; and they went to a coffee-house and received each other into a closer friendship than ever.

These days of the occupation of Frankfort offered continual festival to the children and young people. Theatre and ball, parade and march drew the children hither and thither, and the life of a soldier seemed to them very delightful. The fact that the King's Lieutenant dwelt in their house made the Goethe children familiar, by sight at any rate, with all the persons of distinction in the French army.

But the war had other things in store. "A camp of the French, a flight, a defence of the town, intended only to cover a retreat in order to hold the bridge, a bombardment, plundering—all this excited the imagination and brought sorrow to both parties." Easter week of 1759 saw the event. A great stillness preceded the storm. The children were forbidden to go out of the house; and after some hours, waggon-loads of the wounded on both sides were brought into the town, proclaiming that the action was over. By and by the victorious Count Thorane returned on horseback; the children sprang towards him, kissed his hands and showed their joy, which appeared to please him, and he ordered that a collation of sweetmeats should be made for them to celebrate the event. But the father behaved quite otherwise. He met the victorious General with insult and violence: the consternation in the household was great, for it appeared certain that its head would be committed to prison; but the intervention of a friend saved the bitter and somewhat eccentric man, and things went on as before.

VIII

The children's interest in the theatre continued; many half-historical, half-mythological pieces were played then, and it came into 'the Boy's' head that he himself could write such a piece. He did so, made a clean copy, and laid it before his friend Derones, who read it with great attention, and, in answer to a modest question, conceived that it was not impossible that the piece should be played; but, first of all, he would go over it carefully with the author. "Although my friend was otherwise easy-going, the opportunity, long wished for, of playing the master seemed now to have come. He read the piece attentively, and while he sat down with me to correct a few trifles, he so altered the piece in the course of this performance that scarcely one stone was left upon another. He crossed out, added, took away a character, substituted another; in fact, he carried on the wildest career in the world, so that my hair stood on end. He even grudged to have to allow me any authorship whatever; for he had so often told me of the three unities of Aristotle, of the regularity of the French drama, of probability, of the harmony of the verse, and the rest, that I must acknowledge him as builder and founder of my play. He abused the English and despised the Germans; in fact, he brought the whole dramatic litany before me as indeed during my life I have heard it constantly repeated."

The poor boy took back his work in pieces and tried in vain to put it together again. Once more he had a fair copy made of the piece as it stood originally and showed it to his father; this time he got something in the shape of a reward; for his father no longer grumbled when he came home from the theatre.

His friend's opposition made the boy think. He determined not again to have his work shipwrecked on theories which he did not understand, so he read Corneille's work on the Unities. He read, too, in great perplexity, the criticisms and counter-criticisms on The Cid, and found that even Corneille and Racine were obliged to defend themselves from the attacks of the critics. He laboured honestly to understand what they would be at, and this famous law of the three unities became as distasteful to him as he had already found grammatical rules. Again he was a law unto himself; nor did he, for many years, reconsider his decision.

In course of time Count Thorane was transferred to another post, and the Chancellor Moritz took his place in the Goethe household. All was fish that came to the young Goethe's net. The Chancellor had a brother, the Councillor of the Legation, whose love for mathematics amounted to a hobby, and who helped the boy in this study, which he considered was of use to him in the drawing lessons which now occupied an hour daily. Of his drawing master he says, "This good man was indeed only half an artist: we had to make lines and place them together, and out of these, eyes, noses, lips and ears, and at length whole faces and heads were to grow; but there was no thought of either natural or artistic form. We were tormented for a time with this quid pro quo of the human figure, and were thought at last to have been carried so far that we received the so-called 'Passions' of Le Brun to copy; but these pictures did not appeal to us. We went on to landscapes, to all those things which are practised in the usual system of teaching without aim and without method. At last we attained to close imitation, and dropped into exactness of line without troubling ourselves about the worth or artistic value of the original."

Then, as now, art was supposed to be assisted by mechanical devices. Then, as now, children were taught to draw, not from objects, but from drawings of those objects; that is, they were and are taught to imitate lines rather than to receive and record impressions of things. The father, who held that nothing was so stimulating to young pupils as for their elders to learn with them, also laboured at this unprofitable copying; and with an English pencil on fine Dutch paper he not only copied the lines of the composition but the strokes of the engraver. "Everybody must learn to draw," the Emperor Maximilian is reported to have said; a maxim which the elder Goethe had seized upon with the avidity of one feeling in the dark for guidance in the puzzling and difficult business of education.

Charlotte Bronté tells us how Lucy Snowe exercised herself in this same laborious way, and conceived that she was learning to draw; and probably Lucy's experience is a reminiscence of "Currer Bell's" own efforts. We are not told that Charlotte Bronté ever learned to draw, but we know that all his life Goethe had a great hankering after this art; and as an old man we still find him copying a detail of some picture, line by line, shade by shade. It would appear as if we are always handicapped by the faults of our education, not merely in a general way, but subject by subject, method by method, we are only able to go on with that which has had a living beginning in our youth.

It was always the intention for the children to learn music; but not until the boy took the matter in hand himself did the right man appear to teach them. He chanced to hear a companion taught by a master who had little jokes for every finger, facetious names for every line and note, and for the moment this took with even so able a boy as the young Goethe. However, the jokes came to an end so soon as the teacher was employed; and the music lessons were deadly dry and dull, until that enterprising educationalist, the father, set up a young man who had been his secretary, and who spoke French well, and could teach it, as a schoolmaster; for the town was not satisfied with the public teaching, and there appeared to be an opening for private enterprise. This young man set to work to learn music so zealously that in a few weeks he had accomplished wonders; and not only so, he became acquainted with a maker of first-rate instruments, which he introduced to his house. This man's enthusiasm gave that impetus to the family in the direction of music for which they had been waiting.

IX

"The more I was allowed to work in this way the more I wanted to, and even my leisure hours were spent in all sorts of wonderful occupations. Already, since my earliest days, I had felt a strong impulse towards finding out about natural objects.

"I remember that as a child I often picked flowers to pieces to see how the petals were fixed in the cup, and even plucked birds to see how the feathers were fastened into the wings. Children should not be blamed for this, for even naturalists often think they will learn more from rending and parting than from connecting and uniting, from the dead than from the living.

"An armed loadstone, sewn up daintily in a piece of scarlet cloth, must needs one day experience the result of such desire for discovery. For the secret attractive power which it not only exercised on the little iron bar attached to it, but had this further quality that it increased in strength, could daily bear a heavier weight,—this secret virtue filled me with delight, so that I spent a long time in merely wondering at this power. At last I thought I should make a closer acquaintance with it if I took away the outer covering. This was done without making me any wiser, for the naked iron taught me nothing further. I took this off also and held the bare stone in my hands, with which I was never weary of experimenting with filings and needles, experiments from which my young mind drew no advantage but a manifold experience. I did not know how to put the arrangement together again, the parts got destroyed, and I lost the striking phenomena as well as the apparatus."

An electric machine, too, the property of a friend, was a source of much interest to the children, and a further means of awakening the boy's scientific imagination.

Two occupations laid upon them by their father fell as hardships upon the young people. The one was the care of silkworms, to the rearing of which a room was appropriated; but it was difficult to keep the worms in health under such artificial conditions, thousands died, and the removal of these and the efforts to keep the rest cleanly and in good condition fell to the children. The other task which they did not love was connected with the views of Rome, the source of so many early impressions. The engravings which had been so long exposed on the walls of the old house were no longer in a condition to decorate the new one, and the task which fell to the children was to keep the sheet, to which a copperplate was attached, constantly moist for a considerable time, until it could be easily removed from that which was mounted upon it. As there were a good many engravings, this was not a slight labour, and the reader hails with pleasure a mention of tiresome tasks which must be performed. That such tasks were rare is evident enough; but the meaning of must can only be learned by means of a duty which it would be agreeable to shirk.

"Lest we children should lack anything of all that life and learning have to give, it happened at that time that an English language master presented himself, who undertook to teach English to anyone not quite raw to language study in four weeks—enough, that is, to enable him to continue his study by himself. He asked a moderate fee; the number of pupils for the lesson was of no consequence.

"My father resolved on the spot to make the attempt, and took lessons with me and my sister from this expeditious master.

"The lessons were faithfully given and there was no lack of repetition, and for the four weeks some other studies were laid by. The master parted from us and we from him with satisfaction. As he stayed in the town and found plenty of employment, he came to see and help us from time to time, thankful that we were among the first who had trusted him, and proud to show us as models to the others."

It would be pleasant to know if this unnamed English teacher anticipated the conversational methods of to-day.

But new acquisitions were new responsibilities, for the father was anxious that the newly acquired English should be kept up as fully as the other languages at which the children had worked; and now we get from 'the Boy,' weary of many grammars, each with many lists of exceptions, a scheme which, though we had not the wit to originate, we might at any rate follow with advantage.

"Thereupon the thought occurred to me of settling the matter once and for all, and I invented a story about six or seven brothers and sisters who, scattered over the world at some distance from each other, mutually exchange news of their various conditions and sentiments." The eldest brother gives in good German news of all the circumstances and events of his journey. The sister, in a feminine manner, with full stops and short sentences, tells now him, now the others of the family, what she has to say as to her domestic life, as well as of her love affairs. One brother studies Latin, and writes very formal Latin, adding occasionally a postscript in Greek. Another brother, an agent in Hamburg, had to manage the English correspondence; a younger brother, in Marseilles, the French. As for Italian, one brother, a musician, was making his first essay in the world; and the youngest, cut off from the other languages, had taken refuge in Juden-Deutsch, and with his fearful lingo threw the others into despair. "The idea made my parents laugh. For this extraordinary arrangement I had to find a format, and I studied the geography of the places where my creations lived, and invented for these bare localities all sorts of human interests, in fact whatever had any relation to the character and business of my people. In this way my exercises became much more voluminous, my father was more contented, and I perceived much more quickly what was necessary in the way of revision and completion."

X

There is an unfortunate tendency at the present time to depreciate knowledge, which is indeed the chief instrument of education. Bible knowledge especially is discountenanced for several reasons. The utilitarian asks, "What is the use of teaching a child the more or less fabulous 'history' of the earlier books and the insignificant later records of one of the least among the nations?" while religious parents are inclined to pick and choose and teach only such parts of the Bible as seem to them likely to give the religious impulse. Today we are confronted with the new difficulties raised by the Higher Criticism. "How far," we ask, "is it safe to offer Bible knowledge to a child when we have by no means come to the end of the critical study of the Bible, and he may, later, hear what we have taught him controverted point by point?" If we could only know how such knowledge affects a child; could we know how the critical acumen, with which clever children are endowed, plays of itself round the sacred text; and could we know what is left of solid possession after childish scepticism has had full play!

Goethe offers us precisely such a test case in Aus

Heinem Leben. He gives us the minutest details of his own Bible studies, tells us with what temper he came to these studies, and how, by degrees, his Bible knowledge became the most precious of his intellectual possessions. This is how it came about. As a child of about ten or so he was already embarrassed by the possession of several languages which his father expected him to keep up, so he hit, as we have seen, on the plan of keeping a family diary, the brothers and sisters writing each in the language of the country where he or she lived. He had some knowledge of Juden-Deutsch, and one brother was set to correspond in that tongue.

This brilliant idea, as is the way with ideas, produced after its kind. The boy's synthetic mind found the Juden-Deutsch fragmentary and unsatisfactory. He must needs add Hebrew to his list of languages, and his father succeeded in securing lessons from Dr Albrecht, the Rector of the Gymnasium. This Rector seems to have been a man of original mind, whimsical, satirical, little understood by his fellow-townsmen. Naturally, he took to the young genius who came to him to be taught.

The Hebrew lessons went delightfully, no doubt, to both master and pupil, and the impression made upon the latter by the Hebrew Scriptures is of singular interest to us today when the question of teaching Old Testament history to children is much agitated. The boy was already able to read the Greek of the New Testament, and appears to have been in the habit of following, in the original, the Epistles and Gospels as they were read in church. Of course, a boy of his power, with both a logical and a scientific turn, ferreted out difficulties enough. "For already the contradictions between tradition and the actual and possible had struck me much, and I had put my tutors in many a corner as to the sun which stood still for Gibcon, and the moon which did likewise in the valley of Ajalon, to say nothing of other improbabilities and inconsistencies. All this was now stirred up again, for while I sought to master Hebrew, I worked entirely with the Old Testament, and this studied through, no longer in Luther's translation, but in the interlinear version of Sebastian Schmid, printed under the text, which my father had procured for me. Reading, translation, grammar, copying and repeating words seldom lasted half-an-hour; then I began immediately to attack the meaning of the passage; and although we were working at the first book of Moses, I introduced the discussion of many points which I remembered in the later books. At first the good old man tried to dissuade me from such exertions, but after a time they seemed to entertain him. He continued his tricks of coughing and laughing, and however much he coughed, as a hint to me that I might compromise him, I persisted, and was even more insistent in setting forth my doubts than in getting them answered. I became ever more lively and bolder, and he only seemed to justify me by his behaviour. I could get nothing out of him but, now and again, a laugh which shook him, and 'foolish rascal, foolish rascal.'"

All the same, his master was not blind to the boy's difficulties, and was willing to help him in the best way. He referred him to a great English 'Biblework' in his library, which attempted the interpretation of difficult passages in a thoughtful and judicious way. The German divines who translated the book had improved upon it. Various opinions and interpretations were cited, and, finally, a line was taken which preserved the dignity of the Book, made evident the grounds of religion, and gave free play to the human understanding. Now, when the boy brought out his doubts and questions towards the end of a lesson, the master pointed to the Commentary. The pupil took the volume and read while his master turned over the pages of his Lucian, and sagacious comments were answered only by the master's peculiar laugh. "In the long summer days he let me sit as long as I could read, often alone, and later he let me take one volume after another home with me."

It would be good to know all about that Commentary which satisfied so keen a young mind. Anyway, we can commend and imitate the wisdom of Dr Albrecht. Of all ways of attempting to arrive at truth, perhaps discussion is the most futile, because the disputants are bent upon fortifying their own doubts, and by no means upon solving them. The will unconsciously takes a combative attitude, adopts the doubt as a possession, a cause to be fought for; and reason is, as we know, ready with arguments in support of any position the will has taken up. But, give the young sceptic a good book bearing on the questions he has raised, let him digest it at his leisure without comment or discussion, and, according to his degree of candour and intelligence, he will lay himself open to conviction. The silence and the chuckle of this good professor are worth remembering when we are shocked by the daring announcements of the young sceptics who belong to us. So, too, is the wise passiveness which put a solution of his difficulties in the boy's way, but made no attempt to convince him.

"Man may turn where he will; he may undertake whatever he will; but he will yet return to that road which Nature has laid down for him. So it happened to me in the present case. My efforts with the language, with the contents of the Holy Scriptures, resulted in a most lively presentation to my imagination of that beautiful much-sung land, and of the countries which bordered it, as well as of the people and events which have glorified that spot of earth for thousands of years."

Those timorous but not unbelieving parents who hesitate to make their children familiar with the Old Testament Scriptures because of the difficult problems they suggest, or of the lax morality they now and then record, or because of a hundred vexed questions concerning authorship and inspiration, will find this episode in the young Goethe's education very full of interest and instruction. Here was a boy prone to doubt, quick to criticise, whose eager intellect tore the heart out of whatever subject was presented to him, and who appears, from his own confession, to have made merry over certain scientific difficulties which the Bible narrative offered; but what was the net result? This: that nowhere, so far as I know, does there exist a more valuable defence of Bible teaching than Goethe has drawn up from his boyish reminiscences.

"This little spot was to see the origin and growth of the human race; from there, the first and only news of the primeval history of the world was to reach us; a setting was presented to the imagination, simple and easy to be conceived, and adapted to manifold and wonderful wanderings and settlements. Here, between four named rivers, was chosen out of the whole habitable earth a little, wholly pleasant spot for the youth of man. Here he was to develop his activities, and here meet the fate that was allotted to his posterity—to lose his peace in striving after knowledge. Paradise was closed; men increased and grew more wicked; God, not yet accustomed to the evil deeds of this race, became impatient and annihilated it. Only a few were saved from the overwhelming flood; and hardly had those awful waters gone down, when there, before the eyes of those grateful saved souls, lay the familiar ground of their fatherland. Two rivers of the four, the Euphrates and Tigris, flowed yet in their beds. The name of the first remains, the second is indicated by its course: it could not be expected that exact traces of Paradise would remain after such a catastrophe. Now the new human race began for the second time; it found various means of getting food and work, chiefly by collecting great herds of tame beasts and travelling with them in all directions. This manner of life, as well as the increase of the families, soon made it necessary for the peoples to part. They could not resolve at once to let their relations and friends journey away not to return, so they hit upon the plan of building a high tower, which should from a distance show them the way back. But this attempt, like their first endeavour, failed. They were not to be happy and wise, numerous and united. God sent confusion amongst them; the building was stopped, the people were scattered; the world was peopled, but divided. But our gaze is fixed upon, our concern remains with, this region. At last, the founder of a race goes out again from here who is so happy as to stamp a decided character on his posterity, and by this means to unite them for all time, a great nation, inseparable through all changes.

"From the Euphrates, not without the divine guidance, Abraham wanders to the west. The desert offers no insurmountable barrier to his journey; he reaches the Jordan, crosses the river, and spreads over the beautiful southern region of Palestine. This land was already in other hands and fairly well populated. Mountains, not too high, but rocky and unfruitful, were cut through by many well-watered, pleasant valleys; towns, encampments, single settlements lay scattered over the plain on the sides of the great valley whose waters flow into Jordan. Though the land was inhabited, built upon, the world was still big enough; and men were not careful as to space, nor necessarily active enough to make themselves masters of adjacent country.

"Between their possessions lay great spaces, by which grazing herds could easily pass up and down. In such spaces Abraham and his 'brother' Lot encamped, but they could not stay long on these pastures. The very condition of a land whose population fluctuates, and whose resources are never in proportion to its needs, brings unexpected famine, and the immigrant suffers with the native, whose own supplies he has lessened by his chance presence. The two Chaldean brothers went to Egypt; and thus the stage is brought before us on which for some thousands of years the most important events of the world took place. From the Tigris to the Euphrates, from the Euphrates to the Nile, we see the earth peopled; and in this spot a man, known and loved of Heaven, and already honoured by us, goes up and down with his herds and possessions, and in a short time increases abundantly. The brothers come back, but, compelled by necessity, decide to part. Both indeed journey on to southern Canaan; but while Abraham remains at Hebron, near the plain of Mamre, Lot goes to the valley of Siddim, which—if our imagination is bold enough to give the Jordan an underground outlet, so that we should have dry ground where the Dead Sea at present lies—must appear to us a second Paradise; so much the more so because the inhabitants and surrounding nations, notorious for their effeminacy, lead us to the conclusion that life to them was comfortable and merry. Lot lived amongst them, but was not of them. But Hebron and the plain of Mamre appear before us as the important spots where the Lord spoke with Abraham and promised him all the land as far as his eyes could see in four directions.

"From these quiet dwellings, from these shepherd people who walk with angels, entertain them as guests and converse with them, we must turn our eyes again to the East and think of the settlement of the neighbouring tribes, which was probably like that of Canaan. Families held together, they united, and the manner of life of the tribe was settled by the locality which they held or had seized. On the mountains which send down their waters to the Tigris we find the warlike peoples who already very early foreshadow the brigands and war-lords of the future, and who give us in a campaign, stupendous for those times, a foretaste of wars to come . . . Now the prophecy of unending heirs was renewed, a prophecy ever enlarged in scope. From the waters of the Euphrates to the river of Egypt the whole extent of land is promised; but as Abraham has no heir, fulfilment seems doubtful. He is eighty years old and has no son. Sara, with less trust in the gods than her husband, becomes impatient; she desires, according to oriental custom, to have offspring by a maid. But scarcely is Hagar given over to her lord and there is hope of a son when division enters the house. The wife treats her own substitute ill, and Hagar flees in order to find a better position with another tribe. By divine guidance she is led back and Ishmael is born.

"Abraham is now ninety-nine years old; the promise of numerous posterity is again and again repeated, and at last both husband and wife begin to be contemptuous; and yet to Sara comes the hoped for good and she brings forth a son, who is called Isaac. The history of the human race rests on a regulated growth. The most important world-events must be traced to the domestic life of the family, and therefore the marriage of the father of the race gives us pause for reflection. It is as if the Godhead which loves to guide the fate of man wished to set forth as in a picture every aspect of marriage. Abraham having lived so long with a beautiful and much-sought-after but childless wife, finds himself in his hundredth year the husband of two wives, the father of two sons, and at this point his domestic peace goes. Two wives together, as well as two sons of two mothers in opposition, make matters impossible. The one who is less favoured by law, by descent, by disposition must yield. Abraham must sacrifice any feeling for Hagar and Ishmael; both are forsaken, and Hagar is compelled against her will to set forth again upon the road she had taken in her wilful flight, at first, as it seems, to the destruction of herself and her child; but the angel of the Lord, who had before sent her back, saves her again, this time that Ishmael may become a great people, and that the most improbable of all promises should be more than fulfilled. Two parents far on in years and a single late-born son: surely here, indeed, is cause for domestic peace and earthly happiness! But no. Heaven is preparing for the patriarch the hardest trial yet. But we cannot enter upon this without many previous considerations.

"If a natural universal religion were to rise, and a special revealed religion were to develop from it, these lands in which our imagination has lingered, the manner of life, the very people themselves, were the most entirely suited for it; any way, we do not find in the whole world anything more favourable.

"If we assume that the natural religion rose earlier, in the mind of man, we must grant the clearness of perception which belongs to it, for it rests upon the conviction of a universal providence which rules the whole world. A particular religion leads belief to a special providence which the Divine Being extends to certain favoured men, families, tribes and peoples. This could hardly be developed from the human spirit. It implies tradition, descent, custom, carried forward from the oldest times. . . . . The first men seem closely related, but their divers occupations soon part them. The hunter was the freest of all, and from him the warrior and ruler is developed. Those who wielded the plough and devoted themselves to the soil built dwellings and barns to hold their possessions, and could think well of themselves, because their circumstances promised permanence and safety. The shepherd at his post seemed to have the most limited and yet boundless possessions. The increase of flocks went on for ever, and the land on which they fed extended its boundaries on all sides. These three callings seem at first to have looked at each other with contempt and suspicion; and because the shepherd was hated by the townsfolk, he kept his distance from them. The hunter disappears from our eyes into the mountains, and only appears again as the brigand. The first fathers belong to the shepherd ranks. Their mode of life in the wide stretches of desert and pasture gave their minds breadth and freedom; the vault of heaven under which they lived, with its stars at night, gave them a sense of awe and dependence, and they were more in need than the active, resourceful hunter, or than the secure, careful, home-keeping ploughman, of the unshaken belief that a god went beside man, that he visited them, took their part, guided and saved them.

"One more consideration before we go on with the history. However human, beautiful, and cheering the religion of these first fathers appears, there are traces of savagery and cruelty out of which men rise, or into which they may again sink. That hatred should be avenged by the blood, by the death of the defeated enemy is natural; that a peace should be concluded between the rows of the dead is readily imagined; that man should think of confirming a covenant by the slaughter of animals is a natural consequence; also, there is nothing to wonder at in the fact that mankind should try to appease and win over by sacrifices the gods, who were always regarded as taking sides, as their opponents or helpers . . ."

Here follows a very interesting disquisition upon the ideas which men expressed by means of sacrifices, to introduce the story of the supreme sacrifice demanded of Abraham, the final test of his faith.

"Without a shudder Abraham blindly sets himself to carry out the command; but, to God, the will is enough. Now Abraham's trials are over, for they cannot be heightened. But Sarah dies, and this gives opportunity for Abraham, as in a figure, to take possession of the land of Canaan. He must have a grave, and this is the first time he looks round for the possession of land on this earth. A double cave towards the grove of Mamre he may have already sought for. He buys this, with the adjoining field, and the legal forms which he observes show how important this possession is for him. It was more so than perhaps even he could imagine, for he, his sons and grandsons, were to rest there, and the claim to the whole land, as well as the ever-growing inclination of his descendants to settle here, were thus founded in the most special way.

"From this time the manifold scenes of domestic life come and go. Abraham still keeps himself isolated from the inhabitants of the land; and even if Ishmael, son of an Egyptian woman, has married a daughter of the people, Isaac must marry with his own kin and one of equal birth.

"Abraham sends his servant to Mesopotamia, to his kin whom he had left behind. The wise Eleazer arrives, unrecognised; and in order to take the right bride home, he tests the serviceableness of the girl at the well. He asks for water, and, unasked, Rebecca waters also his camels. He makes her a present; he offers for her, and she is not refused to him. So he takes her to his master's house and she is betrothed to Isaac. Here also heirs were long expected.

Rebecca is only blessed after some years of trial, and the same division which resulted from the two mothers in Abraham's double marriage springs here from one. The two boys, of opposite characters, already strove beneath the mother's heart. They reach the light of day, the elder lusty and strong, the younger delicate and wise; the former his father's darling, the latter his mother's. The strife for precedence, begun already at birth, continues. Esau is calm and indifferent as to the birthright which fate granted him, but Jacob does not forget that his brother forced him back. Watchful for any opportunity of gaining this longed-for advantage, he trades with his brother for the birthright, and is beforehand in getting his father's blessing. Esau, in a rage, swears he will kill his brother. Jacob flees, in order to try his fortune in the land of his ancestors.

"Now, for the first time in so noble a family, appears a trait which hardly bears dwelling upon—that of gaining by cunning and strategy the advantages denied by nature and circumstances. It has often been remarked and discussed that the Holy Scriptures do not in any way set forth our first fathers and other men favoured by God as models of virtue. They also are men, various in character, with many deficiencies and failings, but there is one special quality in which men after God's own heart may not be wanting—it is the unshaken belief that God hears and cares for them and theirs.

"A universal, natural religion requires no special belief; for the conviction that a great governing, ordering, ruling personality hides behind nature in order to make it possible for us to comprehend Him—such a conviction forces itself upon everyone; even, indeed, if a man drop the clue which leads him through life, he will be able to pick it up again at any time. Quite otherwise is it with a particular religion which tells us that this Great Being distinctly interests Himself for one person, one family, one nation, one country. This religion is founded on faith which must be unshaken if the religion is not to be entirely destroyed. Every doubt is fatal: a man may get back to conviction, but not to faith. This is the reason of the endless trials, the tardy fulfilment of oft-repeated promises, by which the living faith of the patriarchs is brought into play.

"Jacob also had his share of this faith; and if he does not gain our respect by his strategy and deception, he wins it by his lasting, unbroken love for Rachel, whom he wins for himself as Eleazer had won Rebecca for his father. In him is the promise of a numerous posterity first fulfilled; he was to see many sons around him, but his heart suffered many pangs on their account and that of their mothers.

"Seven years he served for his loved one, without impatience or any hesitation. His stepfather, like him in cunning, like-minded in thinking the end justifies the means, deceived him, serving him just as he had served his brother. Jacob finds a wife whom he does not love in his arms. It is true that in order to pacify him Laban gives him also the one he loves, but on the condition of seven more years of service; then follows disappointment after disappointment. The unloved wife is fruitful, the loved one has no children, and she, like Sara, desires motherhood by a maid; but the first wife grudges her even this advantage, and she also gives a maid to her husband; and now the good father of the race is the most persecuted man in the world; four wives, children by three, and none by the beloved wife! But she at last is favoured and Joseph comes into the world, a lateborn child of sorrowful love . . . There is strife. Jacob flees with all his possessions and encounters the pursuing Laban, partly by luck, partly by cunning. Now Rachel presents him with another son, but she dies at his birth; the son of sorrow, Benjamin, lives; but the old father is to suffer yet greater pain at the apparent loss of his son Joseph.

"Perhaps someone may ask why I set forth here in such detail this universally known history, so oft repeated and expounded. This answer may serve: that in no other way could I show how, with the distractions of my life and my irregular education, I concentrated my mind and my emotions in quiet activity on one point; because I can in no other way account for the peace which enveloped me, however disturbed and unusual the circumstances of my life. If an ever-active imagination, of which the story of my life may bear witness, led me here and there, if the medley of fable, history, mythology, and religion threatened to drive me to distraction, I betook myself again to those morning-lands, I buried myself in the first books of Moses, and there, amongst the widespreading shepherd people, I found the greatest solitude and the greatest company."

Here we have set forth a full and sufficient reason for giving children a profound acquaintance with the Old Testament Scriptures. It will be said that in Goethe's case such an acquaintance did not result in religion. No, he was never religious in the usual sense of the word; and at the time when he recites the above confession of faith—the faith acquired in his child hood, and probably little affected by after events—he had paid that momentous visit to Italy, had returned to the classicism of his earliest years, and classic paganism had become so strong in him that he practically ceased to be a believer in God as we understand the phrase. But religion has two aspects. There is the attitude of the will towards God, which we understand by Christianity: in this sense Goethe was never religious, any more than he was moral in the accepted sense. How to set his will right towards the relations of life, whether human or divine, formed no part of his manifold culture. But religion has another aspect: that conception of God which comes from a gradual slow-growing comprehension of the divine dealings with men. This repose of the soul, this fresh background for the thoughts, Goethe tells us he got from his study of the books of Moses; tells us, too, that he could have got it in no other way (and, indeed, he tried all ways); and in all the errors of his wilful life this innermost repose appears never to have left him. "His eyes were tranquil as those of a god," says Heine; and here is revealed the secret of that large tranquillity. Here Goethe unfolds for us a principle of education which those who desire their children to possess the passive as well as the active principle of religion would do well to consider; for it is probably true that the teaching of the New Testament, not duly grounded upon that of the Old, fails to result in such thought of God—wide, all-embracing, all-permeating—as David, for example, gives constant expression to in the Psalms.

Let us have faith to give children such a full and gradual knowledge of Old Testament history that they unconsciously perceive for themselves a panoramic view of the history of mankind—typified by that of the Jewish nation—as it is unfolded in the Bible. And we need not be frightened off this field by the doubts and difficulties that clever children will raise. Let us, as did that good Dr Albrecht, not try to put down or evade their questions or pretend to offer them a final answer, but introduce them to some thoughtful commentator (what, we wonder, was that 'big English book' to which Dr Albrecht referred his pupil?) who weighs difficult questions with modesty and scrupulous care. If we do this, difficulties will assume their due measure of importance; that is to say, they will be lost sight of in the gradual unfolding of the great scheme whereby the world was educated.

XI

As my point is to indicate how the education of the boy told in the life of the man, it is not necessary to follow further these most instructive records Aus Meinem Leben. Nowhere else, so far as I know, have we a minute, almost impersonal consideration of all the influences that went to the making of a man. That this was a man of genius, a great poet, is not important to us from the educational standpoint; the noticeable fact is that no single fragment of his education, hardly a book that he read or hobby that he pursued, above all, hardly a single subject in all his numerous studies, but bore directly and obviously on the man that he became. But there is another side to the question: with all his intellect, his mighty genius, he possessed nothing as a man the seed of which had not been sown in the course of his education. The examples of both parents, the unresting efforts of his father, were all in the direction of culture; and he died with the exclamation, "More light!" The very subjects of his study as a boy, and no other subjects, fired and stimulated him to the end. His English put him in sympathy with Shakespeare, who became a passion and power in his life. His scientific interests remained with him to the end. He is allowed to have been in some respects a precursor of Darwin: he it was who discovered that all plant forms are modifications of the leaf, and arrived at the certainty that there must have been an original plant from which all plants were developed. The cathedral of Strasburg led him in his student days to the study of Gothic architecture, and in late life to the study of architecture in Italy. We hear of him saying, towards the end, that there were other contemporary poets, that there had been greater poets than he, but that no other person had promulgated his theory of colour. He spent his time in Rome in drawing, learning perspective, instructing himself in architecture, practising composition in landscape, and modelling the human form, limb by limb. His drawing never came to more than a taste for the art, but he himself perceived that the value of his study lay in teaching him to appreciate the work of others. His study of music was a parallel case of painstaking endeavour. In his eightieth year we find him taking daily music lessons from Felix Mendelssohn, and the lessons were of a kind we should do well to imitate: he would retire into a dark corner and listen for an hour to the playing of Mendelssohn. He rather shrank from Beethoven, but his master insisted on introducing him to the great composer, without any very marked result. But in his notes on these two subjects of study, as throughout the autobiography, we find repeated what we might well take as a canon of education in these subjects; that is, that a power of appreciation in both arts is of more value to many, perhaps to most of us, than the power of production, and should be as deliberately and as regularly cultivated.

The puppet-show of his childhood developed, as we know, a ruling penchant, if not passion, of his life; and the direction of the theatre at Weimar in middle life and old age was removed in degree but not in kind from the management of the puppet-plays of his early boyhood.

The enormous industry, or rather the multifarious occupations of his boyhood were continued until the closing years of his life; and even then he rejoiced that he had learned to play cards at Frankfort, because "a day is infinitely long, and you can get so much into it." Card games he regarded as a means of making himself pleasant in society; as did the late Professor Jewett, whose parting counsel to a child of his acquaintance was, "Be a good girl, my dear, read the Waverley novels and learn to play whist"; but it is a question whether the risk of developing the gambling instinct, common to us all, is not to be set against the social equipment which a knowledge of card games affords.

Again, as a child he was brought up upon the classics. The first Book of Ovid's Metamorphoses appears to have been the first book he appropriated in an intellectual sense; and though he is strongly attracted by the romanticism of the period, again and again he reverts to his old faith. We find him, while at the University of Leipsic, exchanging all his collection of modern authors with a fellow-student for a few volumes of the classics, in which for a period he lived entirely. Later, he is brought under the dominion of Shakespeare, whom he hails as his father and invokes as his inspiration; and his greatest work, no doubt, belongs to the period when he discarded the trammels of the 'Unities,' and surrendered himself to the guidance of Nature. But the old predisposition returned upon him after his two years' sojourn in Italy, and astonished Germany was required to assist at a complete overthrow of former theories.

We have just seen, too, how his Bible studies remained with him as a green background for all his thoughts. In a word, no single branch or department of his early education but bore fruit in kind all through his life and to extreme old age.

If we look, on the other hand, at the records of most English men of renown, we find their school studies have passed into oblivion, as matters that had no serious effect upon their after career. The random reading that they do for themselves becomes a power in their lives, but their set studies simply do not count. This is a point that invites reflection. Goethe's education was, as we know, casual and very faulty. We have heard him lament that he was thoroughly grounded in nothing, and yet this defective education enriched him with the seed thoughts which produced his after development in every kind. Was it that he came to each study, even on account of the very imperfection and inadequacy of the teaching equipment, as if it were a fresh field in which his own intellect had ample play? If so, it behoves us perhaps to add this freshness of outlook, this scope for the individual, to the disciplinary value of our ordered school studies.

It is perhaps a fact that each of us should, as was Goethe, be able to discern the crop yielded by every sowing, of our childhood's studies. Instead of which, we put away our school-work as if its intention had been entirely disciplinary and it would be idle to look for the maturing of any seeds of knowledge sown in the days of childhood or school-life. Surely this is a lamentable and reckless waste of intellectual gains.

Another not less vital lesson presents itself in this invaluable record. There is another side to the shield. Everything which had been initiated in Goethe's education came to conspicuous development; but, also, nothing which had been overlooked in his education arrived to him in after life. The indiscipline of his early education remained always as a defect of character, as well as lost ground which he failed to make up in his university career. Neither at Leipsic nor at Strasburg did he distinguish himself. The provincialisms, both of manner and accent, which he owed to his upbringing in a burgher family in Frankfort, were not only a constant detriment to him, but affected, so to speak, his pose of character. He always remained impressed with the fact that only persons of noble birth enjoyed the possibility of complete culture; an idea which he did not lose, notwithstanding his intimacy with the grand-ducal family at Weimar. The circumstances of his birth were no doubt fixed, but his own outlook upon these circumstances depended upon the family point of view. Had some idea of manhood other than that of culture been always present to his thought, comparisons of this sort would not have occurred to him, nor would he have been distressed or annoyed by a sense of inequality.

This consideration brings us to the grand omission in the education of this highly cultured boy. Of religious impressions, presented with enough freshness and power to reach him, he got, as we have seen, vivid ideas from the Mosaic books, and, so far as he tells us, nothing more; nothing, we should imagine, from the atmosphere of his home, his parents being occupied with the single ideal of culture. The enthusiastic reading of Klopstock's Messias appears to have left none but a literary impression. His moral education, like that of most of us, seems to have been pretty much left to chance. He appears to have received no instruction and few impressions as to his relations with, and duties towards, the persons with whom he came in contact, his country or his kind. He does not appear to be aware that he has the power of regulating his emotions, or that his moral life should be under the direction of his will. Hence, Goethe as a man is disappointing. He is like a city laid out on a grand scale, but only half built according to the plan, and the rest left waste or overrun with wretched shanties. Goethe should have been a great man as well as a great poet. He had every possibility of greatness, moral as well as intellectual; and we find him running to waste in endless puerilities of the affections, transient loves, inconstant friendships, personal aims, illiberal thoughts upon public questions other than those which affected his art. A man of mighty intellect, who should have been a great example and a great teacher of his kind, is hemmed in by narrow limitations, marred by moral defects. We are inclined to say—'But a poet is not to be judged as other men; his emotional nature runs away with him; we cannot always look for the poet and moralist in one, so let us take what we get and be thankful.' This manner of reasoning, and the careless living that proceeds from it, arises from the notion that morals and religion are independent of intellect, are, in fact, matters with which the mind is little concerned. When we perceive that the truly moral life depends upon the breadth of the intellectual outlook, upon strenuousness of intellectual effort, we shall understand that taking pains in these directions also is the concern of genius.

Probably there never was a great man who lent himself more to support the theory that genius itself is the faculty of taking pains; he had the most extraordinary patience and talent for detail; and, that he did not employ these gifts in building up a moral greatness equal to his greatness as a poet, seems to be solely the result of a defective education which did not present this manner of effort to him in his eager childhood and boyhood. What his early education did not initiate his mature life failed to accomplish.

In another point of view, too, this educational study should be profitable to us. However far back Goethe goes in recovering recollections, we never find him less than himself. He is always capable of an immense number of interests, of an immense number of studies carried on at the same time, but never interfering with one another; of aesthetic insight, of the power of generalising, of taking delight in poetic form; in fact, all that the man became the child was, not only potentially but actively. Here is where we err in our dealings with children. We regard them as persons of immature and feeble intellect, and deliberately deprive them of the scope and activities proper to an able and active mind. Every child has not in him the makings of a Goethe, but every child has the degree of power to deal with knowledge which will belong to himself as a man. His limitations are not those of incapacity, but of ignorance and of physical feebleness. Therefore our business is to feed him daily with the knowledge proper for him—in small portions, because he is a child, but of the finest intellectual quality, because he is a person—rather than to furnish him with the tools for dealing with knowledge, or even to make him an expert in the use of these tools: and of all the knowledge which a child should get, the knowledge of God is first in importance, and the knowledge of himself, next. It is not necessary to send forth any normal child as a moral or intellectual runagate.

Chapter 3. Pendennis Of Boniface

"When, like a heavenly sign
Compact of many golden stars, the princely child did shine."—
(Iliads, Book Six (Chapman's Trs.).)

I

Arthur Pendennis is as real a person as Wilhelm Meister, and, as a companion study, is not without instruction for us. What an Admirable Crichton he is, to be sure! He carried himself down Main Street with a lordly grace, for was he not the Prince of Fairoaks! The young lords themselves were content to be his followers, and of so fine a nature was he that he did not distinguish between gentle and simple. How princely his tastes were in wines, repasts, trinkets, and how many tastes he enjoyed! Horses, books, pictures, nothing came amiss to him so long as it was of the best. His copious shelves were filled with rare editions and choice bindings, his walls hung with rare prints (first proofs, of course). Nay, Alcibiades himself could not have outdone him in the elegance of his personal habits. The perfumed bath was a necessity to him as to his witty prototype, especially after any contact with the canaille, in the persons of less distinguished men. Then, too, what a name he had for intellectual prowess: "Pendennis could do anything if—momentous syllable—"if he would only work." But, really, why work? He had tried the schools—"During the first term of Mr Pen's academical life he attended classical and mathematical lectures with tolerable assiduity; but discovering before very long time that he had little taste or genius for the pursuing of the exact sciences, and being perhaps rather annoyed that one or two very vulgar young men, who did not even use straps to their trousers, so as to cover the abominably thick and coarse shoes and stockings which they wore, beat him completely in the lecture-room, he gave up his attendance at that course, and announced to his fond parent that he proposed to devote himself exclusively to the cultivation of Greek and Roman literature . . . Presently he began, too, to find that he learned little good in the classical lecture. His fellow-students there were too dull, as in mathematics they were too learned for him. Mr Buck, the tutor, was no better a scholar than many a fifth-form boy at Grey Friars—might have some stupid humdrum notions about the metre and grammatical construction of a passage of AEschylus or Aristophanes, but had no more notion of poetry than Mrs Binge, his bedmaker; and Pen grew weary of hearing the dull students and tutor blunder through a few lines of a play, which he could read in a tenth part of the time they gave to it."

We know the rest. The time came when this golden youth got somewhat haggard, absent-minded, and cynical. By the way, is debt only one cause of cynicism, or is it our chiefest and bitterest grievance against the world that it does not understand our prerogatives, does not see that we have a right to the free enjoyment of our elegant tastes, no matter at whose cost? This is a blundering world. A day of ignominy is at hand for the Prince of Fairoaks. After a brilliant and admired career, regardless of the schools, he, Pendennis of Boniface, no less, is plucked, runs out of Oxbridge like a beaten cur, with a pack of creditors at his heels.

He picks himself up, we know, at last (at the cost of those pinched and impoverished ladies, his mother and Laura), because he has some good stuff in him. He finds his feet and a friend, and earns his bread; and is, at last saved, as by fire, by the two women who loved him. But he never loses the cynicism of the whipped cur; and a certain brand of the world, which he bore when he went to college, remains with him to the last. It is well for those who have the bringing up of golden lads and girls, to bear in mind always that the leopard does not change his spots. Our facile faith in a regeneration to be brought about somehow, at school; at college, by a profession, by family ties, by public work, is really born of our laziness. That which will be done somehow for young people, we do not take the trouble to do ourselves; we shift our responsibility, and the young bear our sins and their own till the end of the chapter.

The literary parent of 'Pen' takes great pains to tell us how it all came about; and such things are, if we will receive it, written for our instruction; but it would be interesting to know how many parents and masters could stand a searching examination upon the lessons proposed to us by Thackeray alone upon the upbringing of youth.

In the first place, Arthur was the Prince of Fairoaks; and what, indeed, was Fairoaks? It was a petty estate, worth about five hundred a year; but any dunghill is high enough to crow from if we have a mind to; and the author's shrewd wit, and keen but not unkindly satire, make great play about this princely family, whose ancient glories, like their family portraits, were more or less faked up, but as firmly believed in as if Debrett were the authority.

The Pendennises are by no means solitary as the bringers-up of pseudo-princes. It begins often enough with the 'princely heart of innocence,' manifested by the little son in the way he carries his head, the fearless glance of his eye, and the frank simplicity with which he takes possession of the world which is indeed his. The parents look on and admire, and begin to suspect that this fine bearing of their child's is a family, and not a human, inheritance. A certain sense, not of greatness or scope, but of superiority, is a part of the child's nurture; and when he leaves home, either he behaves himself en prince, as did young Pendennis, at anybody's cost who will pay the piper; or he awakes to the humbug of the thing, and becomes unduly depressed and reckless; or, like the young Goethe, who never got over a certain sense of disqualification on account of his burgher birth, he attaches undue importance to class distinctions.

At the very outset of a child's career there is a role waiting for his parents. This is how a person arrives to us:—

"Those pure and virgin apprehensions I had in my infancy, and that divine light wherewith I was born, are the best unto this day wherein I can see the universe . . . Certainly Adam in Paradise had not more sweet and curious apprehensions of the world than I when I was a child.

"All appeared new and strange at first, inexpressibly rare and delightful and beautiful. I was a little stranger, which at my entrance into the world was saluted and surrounded with innumerable joys. My knowledge was divine; I knew by intuition those things which, since my apostasy, I collected again by the highest reason . . . All things were spotless and pure and glorious; yea, and infinitely mine, and joyful and precious . . . I was entertained, like an angel, with the works of God in their splendour and glory; I saw all in the peace of Eden . . .

"The corn was orient and immortal wheat, which never should be reaped nor was ever sown. I thought it had stood from everlasting to everlasting. The dust and stones of the streets were as precious as gold: the gates" (of Hereford, where he was born) "were at first the end of the world. The green trees, when I saw them first through one of the gates, transported and ravished me their sweetness and unusual beauty made my heart to leap, and almost mad with ecstasy, they were such strange and wonderful things. The Men! O what venerable and reverend creatures did the aged seem! Immortal Cherubims! And young men glittering and sparkling angels, and maids strange seraphic pieces of life and beauty! Boys and girls tumbling in the street were moving jewels: I knew not that they were born or should die. But all things abided eternally as they were in their proper places. Eternity was manifest in the Light of the Day, and something infinite behind everything appeared, which talked with my expectation and moved my desire. The City seemed to stand in Eden, or to be built in Heaven. The streets were mine, the temple was mine, the people were mine, their clothes and gold and silver were mine, as much as their sparkling eyes, fair skins, and ruddy faces. The skies were mine, and so were the sun and moon and stars, and all the world was mine; and I the only spectator and enjoyer of it." —Thomas Traherne

Or, to quote from the same writer's verse:—
How like an angel I came down!
How bright are all things here!
When first among His works I did appear
O how His glory did me crown!
The world resembled His eternity,
In which my soul did walk;
And everything that I did see
Did with me talk.
. . . . . .
The streets were paved with golden stones,
The boys and girls were mine,
O how did all their faces shine!
The sons of men were holy ones,
In joy and beauty they appeared to me,
And everything which here I found,
While like an angel I did see,
Adorned the ground."

Now, if such be the child's natural estate, what is our part? Parents are right enough in thinking that this fine sense of dignity, this luminous intelligence, grace their child, should help him through life, and are by all means to be preserved. But they make a fool of the child when the magnification of his family are the method they adopt. Whatever elements of dignity and greatness do exist in a family will have, we may be sure, enormous influence on its young scions; and the less said the better. But young Pendennis was brought up in an atmosphere of spurious dignity, none the less false because it was believed in by 'our family.' As a consequence, he was always superior to his situation, and, indeed, that is a human propensity which needs not be accentuated: at school, at college, in the world, notwithstanding a kindly and generous nature, he was never quite genial and simple, and when he had outgrown 'airs,' he took on the superiority of the cynic.

How fine a start, on the other hand, would the child have whose parents recognised his distinction as that of a human being; for this, after all, is no common state; it is distinction in each case. And what a world of persons, sweet and serviceable, we should have if each child were brought up to be all that is in him!

II

Is it ill-natured to suggest, as second amongst the causes which sent Pen astray, the influence of that consummate personage, Major Pendennis? How great he is in his own line, how absurd and how respectable; how one likes him in spite of himself, and how convincing is the neatness and finish of his unworthy code! Is the title of the novel in truth a conundrum, and which of the Pendennises is the hero? This is the reader's point of view; but what if we had been brought up to reverence this old worldling, had been placed solemnly under his guardianship? What if, on our first going forth into life, such an one accompanied us as Mentor?

"God bless you, my dear boy," Pendennis said to Arthur, as they were lighting their candles in Bury Street before going to bed . . . "I beseech you, my dear Arthur, to remember through life that with an entrée—with a good entrée, mind—it is just as easy for you to have good society as bad, and that it costs a man, when properly introduced, no more trouble or soins to keep a good footing in the best houses in London than to dine with a lawyer in Bedford Square. Mind this when you are at Oxbridge pursuing your studies, and for heaven's sake be very particular in the acquaintances which you make. The premier pas in life is the most important of all. Did you write to your mother to-day?—No?—Well, do, before you go, and call and ask Mr Foker for a frank—they like it. Good-night. God bless you."

We find the old fellow's twaddle exquisitely absurd, but all the same we lodge his maxims in our memory; they may be of use some day. As for Pen, he was with the man whom his family had delighted to honour all his life, the man who had succeeded in that emprise upon which all young people set out—the conquest of the world; especially that enchanting social world of which young persons dream.

We elders are hardly aware of the ingenuousness of the young mind, of the ignorance and simplicity of youth; and, at the same time, we fail to realise the reverence in which young people hold us just for our experience' sake. They say pert, clever, and flippant things, and we take it for granted that they are up to everything,—are, in fact, more men and women of the world than we simple elders; so we produce our little share of worldly wisdom,—they must not think us quite simpletons,—and they are far more taken in than we suppose. They seize upon every scrap of talk which shows familiarity with the ways of the world—the rather wicked world, be it said—and from these construct a whole which is, in truth, widely different from our simple experience.

Dr Portman, the excellent rector of Clavering, will not be behindhand. He, too, has seen the world. Pen must order his wine, and that of the best, from a London vintner; and he does, and improves on his instructions. The Major praises a little dinner given in his honour, supposing the occasion to be a rare one. "Poor Pen! the worthy uncle little knew how often those dinners took place, while the reckless young Amphitryon delighted to show his hospitality and skill in gourmandise. There is no art than that (so long to learn, so difficult to acquire, so impossible and beyond the means of many unhappy people!) about which boys are more anxious to have an air of knowingness. A taste in and knowledge of wines and cookery appears to them to be the sign of an accomplished roué and manly gentleman."

What is to be done? The young folk will have a knowledge of what they call 'life.' If we offer them our scraps of, perhaps, secondhand experience, they generalise and conclude that we are not really the worthy and perhaps rather saintly persons they had taken us for. We, too, have had experiences, they think, of the sort they mean to try. Here we perceive the cause of the incomprehensible attractiveness of bad companions—they know life. Here are words of wisdom worth pondering—"What young men like in their companions is what had got Pen a great part of his own repute and popularity—a real or supposed knowledge of life. A man who has seen the world, or can speak of it with a knowing air—a roué, Lovelace, who has his adventures to relate—is sure of an audience among boys. It is hard to confess, but so it is. We respect that sort of prowess. From our school-days we have been taught to admire it."

The young man who has a motive stronger than those which assail him because he is a youth among youths, if it be only that of winning academic distinction, gets through somehow. But a good many young fellows of parts, power, and generous temper, men like Pen himself, come to grief; and it is a serious question, what can be done to fortify these against the special temptations that belong to their time of life. Excellent help is to be found in novels. Here is the very knowledge of life the young person craves; the personages of the novel play their parts before him, and he is admitted to greater intimacy with them than we often arrive at with our fellows; there is no personal attack upon the reader, no preaching. If the novelist moralise a little here and there, it is but to relieve his own feelings. He is not preaching to the young reader, to whom the lessons of life come home with illustrations never to be forgotten. It is told that Mr Meredith was accused by a neighbour of caricaturing him in the character of 'Willoughby Patterne,' and that he replied—'Why, I am Willoughby Patterne, everybody is Willoughby Patterne! We are all Egoists.' In like manner, every young man who reads of Arthur Pendennis, or Edward Waverley, or Fred Vincey, or, alas, of Tito Melema, or of Darsie Latimer, George Warrington, or Martin Chuzzlewit—the list is endless, of course—finds himself in the hero. Novels are our lesson— books only so far as we give thoughtful, considerate reading to such novels as are also literature. The young person who reads three books a week from Mudie's, or elsewhere, is not likely to find in any of them 'example of life and instruction in manners.' These things arrive to us after many readings of a book that is worth while; and the absurdity of saying, 'I have read' Jane Austen or the Waverley novels should be realised. We do not say 'I have read' Shakespeare, or even Browning or Tennyson; but to 'have read' any of the great novels is also a mark of ignorance.

How many parents see to it that their sons and daughters read, mark, learn, and inwardly digest this one novel Pendennis before they go to college, or otherwise go out into life? It is stupid to disregard such a means of instruction; and yet, judicious parents either 'disapprove of novel reading for their young people' or let them read freely the insipid trash of the circulating library until they are unable to discern the flavour of a good book. 'But,' says a good mother, 'I disapprove of novels for another reason besides that they are a waste of time. I have striven to bring up my family in innocence, and wish to keep them still from that very knowledge of life which novels offer.' There is a good deal to be said for this point of view; but the decisions of life are not simple, and to taboo knowledge is not to secure innocence.

We must remember that ignorance is not innocence, and also that ignorance is the parent of insatiable curiosity. But I do not offer a plea for indiscriminate novel reading. Novels are divisible into two classes—sensational, and, to coin a word, reflectional. Narrations of hairbreadth escapes and bold adventures need not be what I should call sensational novels; but those which appeal, with whatever apparent innocence, to those physical sensations which are the begetters of lust,—the 'his lips met hers,' 'the touch of her hand thrilled him in every nerve' sort of thing which abounds in goody-goody storybooks, set apart in many families for Sunday reading, but the complete absence of which distinguishes our best English novels. To read that a girl has been betrayed by no means affects an innocent mind; but to allow oneself to thrill with the emotions which led to the betrayal is to get into the habit of emotional dram-drinking—a habit as enervating and as vitiating as that of the gin-shop. By the reflectional novel I mean, not that which makes reflections for us, after the manner of a popular lady-writer of the day. He who would save us the trouble of reflection ministers to the intellectual slothfulness which lies at the bottom of the poverty of our thoughts and the meanness of our lives. The reflectional novel is one which, like this of Pendennis, awakens reflection with every page we read; offers in every character and in every situation a criterion by which to try our random thoughts or our careless conduct. If we bear in mind that the obvious reflection proposed to us is as vicious in its way as the sensation suggested, we shall find that this test—the property of arousing reflection—eliminates all flimsy work, and confines us to the books of our great novelists.

We must record another step of this young 'rake's progress' in Thackeray's own words. To comment is, here as elsewhere, as superfluous as it is impertinent. "Mr Bloundell playfully took up a green wineglass from the supper-table, which had been destined to contain iced cup, but into which he inserted something still more pernicious—namely, a pair of dice, which the gentleman took out of his waistcoat pocket and put into the glass. Then giving the glass a graceful wave, which showed that his hand was quite experienced in the throwing of dice, he called Seven's the main, and whisking the ivory cubes gently on the table, swept them up again lightly from the cloth, and repeated this process two or three times . . . Presently, instead of going home, most of the party were seated round the table playing at dice, the green glass going round from hand to hand, until Pen finally shivered it after throwing six mains. From that night Pen plunged into the delights of hazard as eagerly as it was his custom to pursue any new pleasure."

III

Pen was, like young Goethe, a mother's boy; the son of a fonder, sweeter, less humorous mother; but he, too, was the son of parents of unequal age, and was his mother's companion. We get charming glimpses of this companionship. There was that evening when the two walked on the lawn of Fairoaks, and watched the trees in the opposite park of Clavering put on a rich golden tinge, and the little river run off brawling to the west, where was a sombre wood and the towers of the old abbey church. "Little Arthur's figure and his mother's cast long blue shadows over the grass; and he would repeat in a low voice (for a scene of great natural beauty always moved the boy, who inherited this sensibility from his mother) certain lines beginning, 'These are Thy glorious works, Parent of Good; Almighty, Thine this universal frame,' greatly to Mrs Pendennis's delight. Such walks and conversation generally ended in a profusion of filial and maternal embraces, for to love and to pray were the main occupations of this dear woman's life; and I have often heard

Pendennis say, in his wild way, that he felt that he was sure of going to heaven, for his mother could never be happy there without him."

What a pretty picture, and how every mother's heart responds! just so would she have it with her little son. He should love her, and through her should learn to love the best and the highest—Nature, and the God of Nature. And the embraces, how sweet to the mother's heart! We read later how, during his childhood and youth, Arthur thought of his mother as little less than an angel, as a supernatural being, all wisdom, love, and beauty; and indeed she was, not only a perfectly well-bred and handsome woman, but, pure and heavenly-minded in no common degree. If she had faults, they were the rather insane family pride which produced the young 'prince' and her inordinate worship of that same prince. It is a curious fact, which would seem at first sight to challenge the justice with which the world is governed, that the small failings of the good, those very failings which appear to lean to virtue's side, and are scarce discernible from virtues by the people who fall into them—these faults of the good appear to produce a more abundant crop of misfortunes than the glaring vices of the unworthy: to whom much is given, of him much will be required. The careless mother who spends her days in pleasure-seeking will sometimes have more duty-doing children than that mother whose only fault is that she loves her family, not wisely but too well. But nothing is in more urgent need of rectification than our moral code. Thackeray, tender as he is to Helen Pendennis, speaks of this same family pride and mother-rapture as "this unfortunate superstition and idol worship"; and frankly tells us that these were the causes of "a great deal of the misfortune which befell the young gentleman."

We have already considered the pride which made a prince of Arthur; and is not every mother's son a prince, and is it not the hardest thing in the world to see our son as others see him? It is less easy to understand that the maternal fondness, the unrestrained mutual embraces of mother and child, are also a danger, because they exceed that temperance, soberness, and chastity which is our duty. By and by this excess of tenderness becomes a counterfeit coin. The mother offers it to her child, and the child to his mother, in lieu of the only sterling currency amongst us—our duty. Do we not find Helen, later, hanging over her son as he lolls on the sofa reading a French novel, and handing him a cigar, which she lights, although she detests and condemns smoking? Nay, does he not tell her himself that he knows she would burn the house down to give him pleasure?

"I could not love thee, dear, so well
Loved I not honour more,"

is true of mother-love as well as of other affections. This holy passion, too, is for service, and not for gratification; and the boy who knows that his mother will do anything for him, knows also that he stands in the place of duty, is more to his mother than her duty to him and to others; he grows up without learning the meaning of two chief words in our use—must and ought are to him terms capable of being explained away.

And this pious mother did her son a greater injury yet—she taught him religion, it is true, but the religion she taught was a sentiment, and not a duty. The boy loved the sound of the church-going bells, the echo of psalm and canticle, as he loved to watch the sunset from the lawn. Sacred poems and hymns, too, he loved to learn at his mother's knee. All holy associations were with him. But what Helen failed to teach him was his duty towards God; and is not this just where many a tender mother fails? She is so anxious to present the beauty of holiness, the love of the All-Father; she herself takes such joy in the sentiment of religion, that, that 'stern Daughter of the voice of God' whose mandate is the only one that human beings obey in the face of resistance, is not allowed a hearing. Religion, service to God, is made to the child a matter of his own election and delight, and not a duty which he has no choice but to fulfil. He is taught that he may love and serve God, but not that he must do so; that this is the one duty he is in the world to fulfil. Parents have a unique opportunity to present the thought of duty to their children; and if they let this occasion pass, it is in vain to try to make up by religious feeling, sentiment, emotion. All these are passing phases, and do not belong to that tie which binds us to our God. Pen, we know failed to say his prayers on that first evening in London when he was going up to Oxbridge with his uncle; and later, Laura tells him that she dare not inquire what he has kept of his faith.

IV

Like Goethe, again, Pen was a person of casual education. It is quite open to contention that persons thus educated do a good deal of the work of the world; that, indeed, men and women of great parts and original mind are often persons who have managed to evade the regular routine of the schools. Like Pen, they have got out of working through that Greek play, line by line and word by word, on which 'the Doctor' sat such store, and have, like him, read ten times as much in the time. Allowing the genius to be a law unto himself, we must be on the watch lest the ordinarily clever boy slip the yoke; indeed, as we have seen in Goethe's case, the genius might well have been the better for the common grind. Pen, anyway, would probably not have run that disastrous course at Oxbridge had he acquired the habit of working under rule and towards an end.

It is well to consider this matter at a time when we are casting about rather wildly to find out what education is, and what it is to effect. There is certain knowledge, no doubt, which it is shameful not to possess, and, wanting which, the mind is as limp, feeble, and incapable as an ill-nourished body. There is also a time for sowing the seed of this knowledge, an intellectual as well as a natural springtime; and it would be interesting to examine the question, how far it is possible to prosecute any branch of knowledge, the sowing and germination of which has not taken place in early youth. It follows that the first three lustres belong to what we may call the synthetic stage of education, during which his reading should be wide and varied enough to allow the young scholar to get into living touch with earth-knowledge, history, literature, and much besides. These things are necessary for his intellectual life, and are especially necessary to give him material for the second stage of his education, the analytic, which, indeed, continues with us to the end. It is in this second stage that the value of the classical and mathematical grind comes in. It produces a certain sanity of judgment, and therefore a certain capacity for affairs, an ability for the examination of questions, which are rather the distinguishing marks of the public schoolman,—not merely the university man, that is another matter, but the man who has ground through that Greek play which both Pen and the young Goethe contrived to get out of. Whatever be the faults of the public school, it is not a manufactory of 'cranks'; and the danger of a transition period like the present is that it may produce a crop of these persons of unbalanced judgment and undisciplined will.

"'O friend,' said he, 'hold up your mind; strength is but strength of will;
Reverence each other's good in fight, and shame at things done ill.'"

This exordium of "Atrides" might well be the motto of our public schools; it sums up with curious exactness that which they accomplish,—the steady purpose, public spirit, and fine sense of honour which adorn our public services, recruited for the most part from our public schools.

But these fine qualities, of which we are proud, may co-exist with ignorance; and ignorance is the mother of prejudice and the obstinate foe of progress. The task before us in setting in order the house of our national education is a delicate one. We must guard those assets of character which the education of the past affords us, and recover, if we may, the passionate love of knowledge for its own sake which brought about an earlier Renaissance. To regard education as disciplinary only is as though a man sowed ploughs and harrows instead of seed-corn; but an eager, wilful, desultory pursuit of knowledge brings with it serious risks to character. There is much talk of reading in these days, of the use of public libraries to further education, and young students are taking up this cry of 'general reading.' We hear of 'three books a week' as a usual thing, and rather a matter of pride. But this, again, comes of our tendency to depreciate knowledge, and to lose sight of its alimentary character. If we perceive that knowledge, like bread, is necessary food, we see also that it must be taken in set portions, fitly combined, duly served, and at due intervals, in order to induce the digestive processes without which, knowledge, like meat, gives us labour rather than strength. In other words, desultory reading affords entertainment, and perhaps an occasional stimulus to thought. Casual reading—that is, vague reading round a subject without the effort to know—is not in much better case: if we are to read and grow thereby, we must read to know, that is, our reading must be study—orderly, definite, purposeful. In this way, what I have called the two stages of education, synthetic and analytic, coalesce; the wide reading tends to discipline, and in the disciplinary or analytic stage the mind of the student is well nourished by the continued habit of wide reading.

Arthur Pendennis made a failure of his college career, and only a qualified success of his after life, through one other cause which affects most young students. He went to college absolutely without moral instruction other than that of certain virtuous traditions and tendencies imbibed from his parents, together with tendencies quite other than virtuous. But no map of life had been presented to his view showing, the heights whose ascent should reward the wayfarer with a noble outlook, the pitfalls and morasses in which many a gallant young traveller disappears. This, too, belongs to the disrespect in which we, as a nation, hold knowledge. To know is not synonymous with to do; but we should not leave our young people to stumble on right action without any guiding philosophy of life; the risks are too great. We who bear the name of Christ do not always give ourselves the trouble to realise how His daily labour was to make the Jews know; how 'ye will not understand' was the reproach He cast upon them. Even with the example of our Master before us, we take small pains to make our young people realise the possibilities of noble action that lie in them and in everyone. We give them certain warnings, it is true, for fear of ruin and loss of reputation, but do we warn them against that deadly dull failure which is implied in a career of commonplace success? Pen was 'plucked'; but how many a man who takes his degree, let us say, does so through the continual prodding of a petty ambition, without drawing from his labour knowledge or love or strength of will towards duty! If the worlds you conquer be those of academic distinction, why, there is no spirit in you for further labours, unless as more such worlds present themselves.

In some ways the Greeks had a more adequate view of education than ourselves: they seem to have held that, along with gymnastic and music, philosophy is the chief concern of every youth. "A freeborn boy," says Plutarch, "must neglect no part of the cycle of knowledge, but he must run through one (subject) after another, so that he may get a taste of each of them—for to be perfect in all is impossible—but philosophy he must pursue in earnest. I can make this clear by a figure. it is delightful and entertaining to travel through many cities, but only profitable to linger in the best.

The philosopher Bion has well said: 'As the suitors of Penelope, when they could not obtain her, made free use of all that belonged to her, so also they who find philosophy too hard occupy themselves with other branches of knowledge, worth nothing by comparison. For this reason, philosophy must be put first in all education.

"For the nurture and development of the body men have invented two instruments, the study of medicine and gymnastic, of which one makes for the health of the body, the other for its strength. But for the sicknesses and sorrows of the soul, philosophy is the only cure.

"Through philosophy, man arrives at the knowledge of what is good and what is bad, what is just and what is unjust; most especially he learns what he should endeavour after, and what he should avoid; how he should order himself towards God, towards father and mother, towards his elders, towards the laws, towards strangers and superiors, towards his friends, towards wife and child and slave. She teaches humility towards God, reverence for parents, respect for the aged, obedience to law; to be in submission to authority, to love friends, to be chaste towards women. She teaches tenderness towards children and gentleness towards slaves; she exhibits to us the highest good, that in happiness our joy be measured, and in misfortune our grief restrained; in order that we be not as the beasts, unrestrained in desire as in rage. These are, I hold, some of the benefits we owe to the teaching of philosophy. For to be modest in good fortune, to be without envy, gentle in mind, to know how to extinguish evil desires, is wisdom; and the ruling of an angry spirit is the sign of no common understanding."

The functions which Plutarch claims for philosophy we ascribe to religion, and by so doing, we place life on a higher level. There is this fundamental difference between the two: while philosophy instructs, religion both instructs and enables. But it is a question whether that science of life or art of living which philosophy should teach had not better be made a distinct study, with its own methods, classifications, rules of progress, under the sanction of religion, and tried at every step by a religious standard.

As it is, the moral and philosophical training we give is random and scrappy to a pitiable degree. The very sincerity of our dependence upon God has resulted in a criminal ignorance about ourselves, our possibilities and our risks, and this in despite, as I have said, of the teaching of our Master. No one person should be launched upon life without an ordered knowledge of himself; he should know, for example, that he has certain appetites, servants, whose business is the upkeep of the body, and, when the time comes, the propagation of the race; that the manly part is never, in small things or great, to yield ourselves to the rule of any one of these appetites, which are so constituted that, treated as servants, they serve with diligence and obedience, but allowed to encroach, rule with relentless tyranny. To know such matters in detail may not save a youth, but should certainly give him pause—give him that moment in which to listen to the divine Counsellor who is able to save him.

Then, how many youths go into the arena of life armed with the knowledge that they are equipped with desires whose chief function seems to be to provide for the nurture of the mind and the propagation of ideas, in much the same way as the bodily appetites have their particular uses? How many know that to become the slave of a single desire, as ambition or emulation, for example, results in as truly, though not as obviously, ill-balanced and ill-governed a person as does the inordinate gratification of any one appetite? How many know that health is a duty, and not merely an advantage; that a serviceable body, strong and capable, is a debt we owe to ourselves, our kin, and our kind? A few are aware of the advantage of, at any rate, a fit body; but how many know that to possess an alert, intelligent, and reflective mind is also among our duties? How many are aware of the incalculable joys of knowledge, of imagination, of reasoned thought, and that these are a patrimony in readiness for each of us? Do young people, again, realise that they enter on life with two great affections capable of ordering all the bonds which unite them to their fellow-men in just degree—capital, as it were, for an outlay of continual serviceableness? Do they know how conscience may be played with, how reason may be suborned, how the right function of the will may give place to unreasoning wilfulness? Have they adequate thoughts of the Supreme relation? Are they aware of owing aught to man or to God? Does not our teaching of religion fall short just because we have allowed ourselves to become ignorant of ourselves? And are we not therefore in danger of losing that conception of God which should keep us in due equipoise? Are we not so much in the habit of hearing of the love and care and saving power of our God that we accept ourselves as the objects of His infinite tenderness, and gradually lose the point of view which makes men heroes and saints in the service of a Master? In a word, do we not implicitly teach our youth that meat is more than life, that getting on is the chief thing, that having is more than being or doing? No doubt there are noble youths who somehow seem to get themselves into right relations, as there are noble men and women to live with whom is continual inspiration; but, perhaps, these would be usual, and not exceptional, if we could arrive at a profounder and truer outlook upon life. Everything that need be taught to a youth is no doubt explicit or implicit in the Christian religion, but I cannot help thinking that we should make more progress in the way of that perfection which is commanded us if we set ourselves to the study of life with the method and purpose we give to other studies—pursuing this, however, with the sense, of quite peculiar divine support and direction.

Chapter 4. "Young Crossjay"

A gold thread running through a sombre stuff, a streak of sunlight in a lurid sky,—something like these is the fitful appearance of young Crossjay in that rather dreary study wherein a 'Patterne' English gentleman is exhibited, resting, fold upon fold, upon himself, every serpentine movement, stealthy, sudden, even vindictive, betraying the wiles and ways of the Egoist. But it is not as a mere foil to Sir Willoughby that Crossjay is introduced. He, with his frank outgoing boy nature, does, indeed, show up by sharp contrast the unhappy, self-involved, self-concerned, and self-adoring man. But Mr. Meredith is a profound student of that one of the 'mysteries' which we call education. He has made a study of boys and of the way to handle them; and has set forth in big letters so that they who run may read, in more than one book, how not to handle them.

But we take no heed; we discuss the plot of this novel or that, allow the author to be a master of style, quote him against persons who say we have no great novelists now, have remarks to make about the characters. What we do not perceive is, that philosophy as found written in books of philosophy to-day has become more or less academic; she no longer "cries at the gates, at the entry of the city, at the coming in at the doors, Unto you, O men, I call; and my voice is to the sons of men."

She has become an affair of the Schools. Men meet with her there, not to their souls' profit so much as for the joy of intellectual gymnastic.

But philosophy keeps to herself still two or three resorts from which we may hear her voice, 'Unto you, O men, I call.' The poets entertain her; through them she still calls to men; but her message is often implicit, and only the attentive ear may hear. Those who do hearken at the coming in of this door get oracles of price, luminous words for the interpretation of their days.

In the novel, however, she is explicit, takes up every one of the functions which we have seen Plutarch assign her; unfolds ourselves to us as poor things, most likely, and flashes a search-light upon our innocent little ways, our much-to-be-condoned moods. Also, as philosophy is for our instruction in life, and as our chief business is the bringing up of the generation to follow, the great novelists offer us a key to the vexed problem of education.

Young Crossjay is an example of this. We are told that a 'real and sunny pleasure befell Laetitia' when young Crossjay Patterne came to live with her. The phrase is delightfully just, as of course, seeing whose phrase it is. A real and sunny pleasure gleams out of every page on which Crossjay appears. The reader smiles at the mention of him as we do when a charming child crosses our path. This is how it came about. Sir Willoughby was, as we know, a mighty orb, environed by satellites, and with the gift of drawing into his sphere and causing to revolve round him whatsoever body chances to pass his way. Such a body is his cousin Lieutenant Patterne of the Marines: that he should not be of the regular Services was a mere eccentricity of English blood and ways, quite a pleasant thing to talk about, when he had distinguished the name of Patterne by an heroic action. So he is duly invited to Patterne Hall, and on a day when Sir Willoughby was spreading his glorious tail of many eyes upon the lawn before an admiring audience, and more, before the lady of his choice, he spies in the distance a rather common-looking thickset man carrying a valise, whom he discovers, by quick intuition of the folded creature, to be that cousin of his in the Marines. 'Not at home' is the answer when the footman produced the Lieutenant's card. And upon this answer turns the fiery trial between young Crossjay's lower and his higher nature, upon which much of the story hangs.

'Charming' is not at all the epithet most people would apply to Crossjay. "He was a boy of twelve, with the sprights of twelve boys in him"; and again "a rosy-cheeked, round-bodied rogue of a boy, who fell upon meats and puddings and defeated them with the captivating simplicity of his confession that he had never had enough to eat in his life." And he told of his four sisters and three brothers, 'all hungry!' How he came to live with Laetitia must be recalled to the reader. This lady was one of several persons who had been drained of their vitality by the absorbing egoist, who drew his sustenance from the vital forces of those about him. Vernon Whitford, as the reader will remember, was a cousin of Sir Willoughby's, who declined to be absorbed, and who received a small salary from him for his help in managing the estates; and it seems that this man, as outgoing a person as Crossjay himself, had heard of Captain Patterne's large family, knew, no doubt, of that 'not at home,' and felt it a shame which he must obliterate. So he went off to Devonport and brought back Crossjay, because, we are told, "Vernon was one of your men that had no occupation for their money, no bills to pay for repair of their property, and an insane desire to spend!" He had thought to have the boy at the Hall that he might prepare him for the Navy, but he counted without his host. Sir Willoughby would run no such risk. The boy's hair would be red, he said, his skin eruptive. So Vernon arranged for him to live at the Dales' cottage, and that was how this 'sunny pleasure' came to Laetitia. "The pranks of the little fellow and his revel in a country life, and muddy wildness in it, amused Laetitia from morning to night." She taught him in the morning when she could catch him, and Vernon in the afternoon if he could catch him, but there was the if. The boy was not only idle, but he hated knowledge as it was to be got out of books; and 'but I don't want to' was his answer to all persuasions. He had to be dug out of the earth, with a good deal of it upon him, when his lesson-hours arrived.

This steady hatred of books would seem rather a bad symptom in young Crossjay, only we get a key to it later on. When Clara Middleton, that 'dainty rogue in porcelain,' arrives on the scene, she and the boy become great friends, and she takes his idleness seriously to heart. Like a wise pedagogue, she set herself to find out what he did like. Having raced him and beaten him without panting, to his vast surprise, she was in a position to bring him to his bearings. He is asked to own that girls are better than boys, that they can run faster, that they learn their lessons, and so on. 'But,' says be, 'You can't make soldiers or sailors of them, though.' But she quotes Mary Ambree to him, and Mistress Hannah Snell of Pondicherry, and other little-known heroines, to say nothing of Joan of Arc and Boadicea; and it all ends up in a serious talk. "'Somebody spoils you: Miss Dale or Mr. Whitford?' 'Do they?' was the answer. 'Sir Willoughby does?' 'I don't know about spoil; I can come round him.'" Here we have the secret many a child discovers about Father or Mother, master or governess; and we ask ourselves—'How is it the young urchins can come round us?'

We pat ourselves on the back and say—'Oh, I'm a good-natured fellow, I know; I can't be hard on the young monkeys.' Now, it seems to me, Crossjay has been evoked just that we may not deceive ourselves in this matter. It is not because of some amiable trait in us that children can come round us, but because we are tarred with the same brush as that most fatiguing and intolerable person in all fiction—Sir Willoughby Patterne. It would be a wholesome and rather solemn exercise for those of us who have to deal with young folk to get by heart all the 'Willoughby and Crossjay' scenes in the novel. Who knows but the best of us might cry 'Lord, is it I?' before he is half-way through. By such light touches as this talk with Clara are the grave problems of education brought up for solution and—this is the point—offered with a key.

A few pages back we have been told that Crossjay was steadily "opposed to the acquisition of knowledge by means of books." But a few questions about Nelson, and he produces knowledge got out of books promptly, ready as the guns of a good ship. He has not been told or taught the knowledge of naval history he shows; 'he' (that is, Vernon) 'bought me the books' is all the account he gives of it. There are, then, two sorts of knowledge to be had out of books, that which he is 'opposed to' and that which he takes to; and here, in what seems no more than a pretty, gracefully told incident, we have the rock indicated upon which our good ship, National Education, comes to grief. We offer children in books the knowledge they are 'opposed to,' and not that which they take to.

'It does not do to make education too interesting,' we say; 'they must learn to grind, to work against the grain'; but we forget about that horse who won't be made to drink; and the boy never takes into him that knowledge which, according to Crossjay, 'I don't want to.' He certainly does get it into that Lethe of the mind we call the verbal memory, out of which it can shortly be reproduced on call without having under-one any 'mind-change,' untouched by ideas, unwarmed by imagination, mere dead matter, an excretion of the mind. This is what we gain for our pains in getting into a boy that knowledge which he 'does not want to' learn. No wonder he throws it all up as soon as he can, and has a sick distaste for more of the kind.

But is there any knowledge he does want to know? Plainly, Crossjay anyway found such knowledge in books, and had it pat, telling, and to the point as gunnery practice. He was being coached for the Navy entrance examination, so probably the two sorts of books dealt with the same subjects. It is not the subjects a boy hates. He wants to know about other lands and other times, about great persons, and, in fact, about everything we want to teach him. He would rather get his knowledge out of books than have it poured into him by speech; the book is more terse, graphic, satisfying to the mind than the talk of any but very rare people. The boy has really an immense appetite for knowledge, and when he does not want to learn, it is because he does not get the right books.

We give children a diet of facts, either condensed or diluted, unaware that the mind has really no use for facts uninformed by intelligence. It takes ideas to evoke ideas, intelligence to awaken intelligence, and the heavy compendiums of the schoolroom are of no use in education. An encyclopaedia is another matter, because it is when our intelligence has been awakened, our curiosity excited, that we consult it, and no school (or family) should be without a good encyclopedia, which every scholar is free to use. If we could awake to the right use of the right books in education, we should find that, as Goethe said, 'a day is infinitely long,' and we should cease to hear of an overcrowded curriculum. By the way, Nemesis is upon us: we have brought up children so long on a diet of facts that we have come to believe what we teach. We travel with Baedeker instead of the old, red, Murray's handbooks, and are becoming informed and bored rather than intelligent and alert travellers. Our notion of history is—ordered facts; though the narrations of three persons who have seen the same thing happen round the corner might show us that there is nothing so little to be depended upon as circumstantial evidence, whether historical or other. Books are a weariness to us, and no wonder, seeing the manner of books we elect.

But there's a good time coming. Crossjay would have been a good candidate as the entrance examination for the Navy is conducted to-day. He liked and knew how to get knowledge of a sort of which the world is learning the value. He knew the habits of birds, where to look for their eggs; all about fish, and how to catch them; how to manage rabbits. He had soon tramped the country about for an extraordinary number of miles. Someone had shown him a collection of stuffed birds of every English kind, and after once seeing, he could describe "goat-sucker owls, more mouth than head, with dusky dark-spotted wings like moths, all very circumstantial." We are awaking to the use of nature-knowledge, but how we spoil things by teaching them! We are not content that children should know the things of nature as we know our friends, by their looks and ways, an unconscious comprehensive knowledge which sinks in by dint of much looking, but we set them to fragmentary scraps of scientific research. They intend investigation, and lose the joy of seeing. Their attention is concentrated upon this or that, and they lose the all-round alertness which is the chief equipment of the nature-student. We shall awake some day and find that nature-study, as we have taught it, adds not at all to the joy of life. The child of the future will feel no thrill at the disclosure of the red under the tail of a little brown bird; now, every small boy likes to know such things, and it will be a weary day when we have 'nature-studied' such knowledge out of existences.

Crossjay has his loyalties, as what boy has not? He has a passion for our Naval Service, and can be even got through the lesson-grind for the sake of it. Then, 'my father's the one to lead an army'; and here comes in a problem which he pondered, boy-fashion, bringing it out again and again, to the dismay of his friends, always in the same words, always leading up to the same climax ('ten miles in the rain'), never apparently coming to a conclusion, but turning the thing over in his mind, it seems, until some day the conclusion should arrive. That, too, is the way of young people: they observe, they retain, they hold moral questions in solution, so to say, until some crisis or some slight event precipitates a conclusion, which remains from henceforth part of their moral outfit, for better, for worse. Here is Crossjay's moral problem:—"My father's the one to lead an army! . . . I say, Mr. Whitford, Sir Willoughby's kind to me, and gives me crown-pieces; why wouldn't he see my father, and my father came here ten miles in the rain to see him, and had to walk ten miles back and sleep at an inn?"

But we may postpone the consideration of Sir Willoughby; for the present, it is enough to see why he was not among Crosssjay's loyalties. Vernon Whitford, however, was, notwithstanding all his cousin's gay attempts to present him as a dour taskmaster.

Crossjay tells Clara Middleton that he would go to the bottom of the river for him. The boy is shrewd, too; all boys are; he believes that Whitford is paying for him by way of making up for that grievous sending of his father back in the rain. How that offence rankled, and how justly angry the boy was! Then, as for Clara, why, he was her knight, chivalric in his obedience (to the loss of his dinner!), giving her unbounded love, admiration, and reverence, along with a gay comradeship which she encouraged. They both loved wild-flowers, and games and open dealings, birds and all living things. Here was foundation enough for friendship!

We get, in connection with this friendship, a peep into boy nature that it behoves us to regard. Clara was reclining on the grass, with half-closed eyes, as she talked to him. We are told that had she been sitting up he would have sprung at her and kissed her.

Here we get a nice boy's unconscious reverence for the holy mystery of sex; and few things are more offensive and more likely to be disastrous than the way we set ourselves to dissipate this heaven-implanted reverence in our rash attempts to give knowledge of matters which are not for the mind. Chivalry, honour, delicacy and obedience, impassioned obedience, to the divine law, these are the chords to play upon if we are to have pure youths and maidens. But we must believe that chivalry and chastity are there, and are not foreign ideas to be introduced by our talk; and this is where many a parent fails. He is aware of evil in his child, and makes deadly allowance for it; and his suspicions create the very evils he dreads. We know how Helen Pendennis believed the worst of her son when the worst was not there, in order, one would think, that she might make occasion for self-sacrifice. It is well we should understand that suspicion also is sin, and begets mistrust and offence.

I think we should have the Utopia our hearts desire if we realised what springs of good are in our children waiting the right touch. Crossjay, who is no more than an ordinary, nice boy, has, we observe, everything he wants for noble living excepting knowledge, and certain habits of mind and body. How like a man of honour he behaves after the talk he overhears when he awakes under the sofa-rug: with a burning sense of the wrong done to his lady, he has the shrewdness and delicacy of a gentleman. He knew that this offer made to another lady was a matter not to be talked about, a matter requiring action, too, beyond his own powers. Here we get a hint as to why it is so good for boys to go to school. They get freer play for common-sense, shrewdness, discrimination, gentlemanly feeling, in the school democracy than they can find under the home autocracy, be it ever so benign.

Thus we get Crossjay presented to us with consummate art, a 'human boy,' to quote the immortal Mr. Chadband. We find the 'human boy' delightful, and perceive all that he is as a person; and we see also the safeguards he needs that he may have room for due development.

We have hardly made Crossjay's acquaintance before he comes to a parting of the ways—a moral crisis, which we watch with some anxiety. Because we are studying a lesson set by a master, the temptation is one we are not at all prepared for, and yet it is a very common one, and perhaps more 'golden lads and girls' are spoiled through this than through any other cause. Here we have it in a nutshell. Willoughby, we know, declined to receive the boy into his house, but, all the same, took upon him the airs of a patron—naturally, inevitably. It is good to see him with young Crossjay. A casual observer would think him perfect with the boy—'amused, indulgent, almost frolicsome.' He has ever a joke and a jibe for him, catches him by the elbows and gives him a leap in the air, laughs at his idleness and mischief, is altogether in fine contrast with Mr. Whitford's 'tutorly sharpness.' "He had the English father's tone of a liberal allowance for boys' tastes and pranks, and he ministered to the partiality of the genus for pocket-money." And, again, he was in contrast to Vernon Whitford: "he did not play the schoolmaster like hookworms who get poor little lads in their grasp." Willoughby poses, and his pose is admirable, one which all who have the bringing up of youth are tempted to affect; and still more those, be they fathers or schoolmasters, who wash their hands of responsibility and play to a gallery in the good-natured ways they adopt towards the young folk. It is surprising that Crossjay was not taken in; he liked it all, 'tis human nature so to do; he would run to his patron, take jumps, jokes, and tips with genuine delight,—"half-a-crown generally, but he had had a sovereign,"—and yet—was it always that question of his father being sent back to walk ten miles in the rain, or was it that he was constantly reminded of this treatment of his father by other slight circumstances which he hardly knew he observed? The latter seems to be the way in which we remember or forget the failings of those about us; faults are forgiven and forgotten until we are reminded of them by some new evidence of the same defect. But Willoughby would have been too much for the boy if his friends had not come to his aid. Crossjay wanted to be a gentleman; to shirk work, to play, ride, and generally to take life easily. He could not do these things and go into the Navy; and Willoughby, simply for the glorification of having one more hanger-on, deliberately chose that the boy should not work, but should depend upon him for all his chance preferments and pleasures. The title of the novel tells us why: was he not The Egoist, and therefore were not all his actions and intentions designed for his own magnification? Crossjay, we know, went to the crammer at last and was saved; but only at the cost of a veritable earthquake at Patterne Hall, a bouleversement of all the views of all the persons who revolved about the Patterne gentleman. But the lesson remains for us.

There are many ways of playing the egoist with the young people about us, but this of 'the English father's tone of a liberal allowance for boys' tastes and pranks' is distinctly the most fatal. For the sake of popularity we make our appeal to a boy's lower nature; and because he has that lower nature also our appeal is very seldom in vain. If we trust him as a creature who is to be won by tips and toffee, we find him as we treat him, and in the end it will be our turn as well as his to reap as we sowed. Egotism is a subtle snare, hard to be aware of; but the single eye will save us. If we regard children for themselves and as themselves, without any reflex thought as to what we do for them, what they think of us, what other people think of what we are to the children, and so on through the endless chain of self-involved motives; if we look out upon the children, and not in upon ourselves, we shall see them as they are—with the great possibilities proper to them as persons, and with the fearful hazards which it is our part to steer them through.

But we all have need of instruction in the fine art of bringing up children, and are therefore grateful to the philosopher to whom we owe 'young Crossjay.'

Chapter 5. Better-Than-My-Neighbour

Two persons meet in the porch of the King Archon; the one brings a suit, and the other appears to answer to a very serious charge. We know the impeached man and the charge brought against him. Socrates was charged by Meletus, a young man who was little known, with corrupting the youth of the city, and with inventing new gods and denying the existence of old ones. He says that Meletus shows a good deal of character in the charge he makes; and, "I fancy that he must be a wise man; and seeing that I am the reverse of a wise man, he has found me out . . . Of all our political men, he is the only one who seems to me to begin in the right way with the cultivation of virtue in youth."

But Euthyphro, the other speaker, who has come to bring a suit, declines this explanation, and thinks that Socrates is to be brought before the court as a Nealogian, such as he is himself. Socrates considers that danger lies, not in being thought wise, but in the attempt to impart wisdom to others,—"I have a benevolent habit of pouring out myself to everybody, and would even pay for a listener, and I am afraid that the Athenians may think me too talkative." Then the dialogue goes on:—

"Soc. And what is your suit, Euthyphro? are you the pursuer or the defendant?
Euth. I am the pursuer.
Soc. Of whom?
Euth. You will think me mad when I tell you.
Soc. Why, has the fugitive wings?
Euth. Nay, he is not very volatile at his time of life.
Soc. Who is he?
Euth. My father.
Soc. Your father! my good man?
Euth. Yes.
Soc. And of what is he accused?
Euth. Of murder, Socrates.
Soc. By the powers, Euthyphro! how little does the common herd know of the nature of right and truth. A man must be an extraordinary man, and have made great strides in wisdom, before he could have seen his way to bring such an action.
Euth. Indeed, Socrates, he must.
Soc. I suppose that the man whom your father murdered was one of your relatives—clearly he was; for if he had been a stranger you would never have thought of prosecuting him.
Euth. I am amused, Socrates, at your making a distinction between one who is a relation and one who is not a relation; for surely the pollution is the same in either case if you knowingly associate with the murderer, when you ought to clear yourself and him by proceeding against him.'

Then the case is stated more fully. The dead man "worked for us as a field labourer on our farm in Naxos," and in a fit of drunken passion slew a fellow-servant. "My father bound him hand and foot and threw him into a ditch" to await inquiry into the case. Meanwhile the man, being neglected, died. "And my father and family are angry with me for taking the part of the murderer and prosecuting my father. They say that he did not kill him; and that if he did, the dead man was but a murderer, and I ought not to take any notice, for that a son is impious who prosecutes his father. Which shows, Socrates, how little they know what the gods think about piety and impiety."

"Soc. And what is piety, and what is impiety? Euth. Piety is doing as I am doing; that is to say, prosecuting anyone who is guilty of murder, sacrilege, or of any similar crime—whether he be your father or mother, or whoever he may be—that makes no difference; and not to prosecute them is impiety."

Euthyphro is with us to-day, a familiar figure, mentioned in every newspaper, talked over at every table, having disciples in pretty nearly every house. We may know him as Pro-Pigtails (Punch), or Pro-pease; he may go without a hat or disport himself in sandals,—things innocent enough,—but he has this in common with his prototype: he may not indict his father, but every Euthyphrodite is ready with—'What is piety? you ask. To do as I do,' whether he malign his country or feed upon nuts. By the way, he generally does both.

We complain that the Euthyphrodite is narrow, one-sided, illiberal, unnatural, undutiful—he is unreasonable, we say, silly, a fool. But he does not regard us. Piety, he says, is doing as I am doing, and it is piety because it is pleasing to the gods. If you be another Socrates you propose yourself to him as a disciple, with wily tact, that he may give you an opportunity to confute the fallacies he unfolds. But it is of no use. 'Another time, Socrates; for I am in a hurry, and must go now.'

We call him a crank, and he gets many disciples because anybody who is cocksure brings relief to the hesitancy of the general mind. For himself, he is not to be convinced. However outrageous his conduct, whether he light the fires of persecution, make himself an exception to common law, say 'Corban' of the dues he owes to country or kin, or limit himself to such small pieties as 'I always wear' this or that; 'buy my tea' at so-and-so's, or 'spend the summer' here or there (the piety lying in the always), he has an infallible creed. We, like Socrates, if we may presume to say so, are tolerant of the 'crank': 'he is not a bad fellow,' we say, 'but he has a bee in his bonnet'; and when we do not take up his religion, he ministers to our vanity, for it is not unpleasant to feel superior to his oddities.

Where is the harm in him? we ask; if he prosecute his own father, he does it with really pious intention. Well, it is a pity that a narrow-minded, illiberal, unjust person should exist; and it is a very great pity that he should be free to propagate those pious doctrines of his,—for this reason, that every foolish little piety we accept as the whole duty of man makes us the less capable of just, liberal, and reverent thought; and we cannot be more in any situation than our own conception of what that situation requires. However likeable he may be, the crank is not a harmless person. He is bad for himself and bad for other people.

But Euthyphro is not open to conviction. The whole field of his mind is occupied by his own fallacious reasoning: there is no getting at him later, so we must catch him before he becomes a tiresome person, and, in order to do so, must find out what there is in him (and in us) that goes to the making of a crank.

An incident is told in Lavengro full of instruction on this point. We remember how Preacher Williams, who went about, with his wife Winifred, doing good, was subject to fits of spiritual despair, which came upon him especially of a Saturday because he was going to preach the next day. 'Pechod Ysprыyd Glan' (which is the Welsh for 'the sin against the Holy Ghost'), he would be heard to cry in a paroxysm of grief and terror; and 'Lavengro,' who overheard this, asked him to tell the story of his life. It appeared that when he was a child of seven he had wilfully and intentionally said certain awful words (we are not told what they were), and this was the unpardonable sin. His sweet wife was right when she told him that pride was, in truth, his sin; but 'Lavengro' made the matter plain to him. "You said that after you had committed this same sin of yours you were in the habit, at school, of looking upon your schoolfellows with a kind of gloomy superiority, considering yourself a lone, monstrous being, who had committed a sin far above the daring of any of them. Are you sure that many of your schoolfellows were not looking upon you and the others with much the same eyes with which you were looking upon them? . . . All I mean to say is, they had probably secrets of their own, and who knows that the secret sin of more than one of them was not the very sin which caused you so much misery?'

"'Dost thou imagine, then,' said Peter, 'the sin against the Holy Ghost to be so common an occurrence?'

"'As you have described it: said I, 'of very common occurrence, especially amongst children, who are indeed the only beings likely to commit it.'"

Here we have the root of the matter indicated. The desire to be exceptional is in us all, and some of us prefer a bad eminence to none. Pride takes all sorts of unexpected action; and when it leads us to rest our right to distinction on some oddity proper to us, we are on the way to mania.

The thing that strikes us about the Euthyphrodite is the strength of his convictions. He may or may not consciously seek distinction that way, the question does not occur either to us or him, but the passionate energy with which he holds and propagates what seems to us some trifling article of faith is what characterises him, and distinguishes him from the prig, a person with whom he may turn out to have some things in common. He takes his own absolute conviction to be synonymous with absolute truth. We have seen how it was with Euthyphro. There was no least chink in his mind to let in light. We do not go so far, but most of us owe our failures to the fact that we will not be convinced against our convictions; and the more ardent we are, the more we err if these should be mistaken.

For this reason it is well we should make children perceive at a very early age that a man's reason is the servant of his own will, and is not necessarily an independent authority within him in the service of truth. This is one of the by-lessons of history which quite a young child is able to understand,—how a good man can, as we say, persuade himself that wrong opinions and wrong actions are reasonable and right. Not that he does persuade himself, but that his reason appears to act in an independent way, and brings forward arguments in favour of a conclusion which he has already unconsciously accepted.

This is a piece of self-knowledge upon which every child should be brought up if we would not have him at the mercy of chance convictions. Perceiving this, he would see for himself the object of his education; and young people would be eager to acquire knowledge were they brought to perceive that wide knowledge of men and events is a necessary foundation for convictions which shall be just as well as reasonable.

This is one reason why children should have a wide and generous curriculum. We try to put them off with a parcel of ready-made opinions, principles, convictions, and are astonished that these do not stick to them; but such things each of us has to get by his own labour. It is only a person of liberal mind whose convictions are to be trusted, because they are the ripe fruit of his knowledge.

But, after all, the crank (it is possible to write with impunity of cranks and prigs, because the characters do not precisely fit anyone), is a person who errs by excess. It is not always that he does not know, but that he allows one aspect of a subject to fill his mind. Euthyphro knew as well as anyone the love and reverence due to a parent, but he allowed this single conception,—of justice, without regard to persons, as pleasing to the gods,—to occupy his mind exclusively.

And this is how we bring up cranks. We magnify a single good quality or a single conviction until there is no room for anything else. We probably fail to get in either the virtue or the conviction, but we do get in the notion that some one aspect of truth is the whole truth. This mental attitude accounts for the extraordinary fitfulness of our opinions and efforts with regard to education. Now, the country is to be brought up upon nature-lore, and now upon handicrafts; now upon science, and then upon art; we will not understand that knowledge is food; and therefore we believe that the whole of education may be accomplished by means of a single subject.

The time may come when we shall consider in the ordering of our lives the Aristotelian doctrine of the Mean, not because the Mean is safe and comfortable, but because excess is injustice, and no one may allow himself to be carried away by a single idea. Those who enlist for offensive attack upon some fortress of iniquity—intemperance, unchastity, ignorance, godlessness—are of course, occupied before all things with the duty of their calling: a fighting soldier is not required to fulfil all the claims made upon the peaceable citizen. For the rest of us, excess is weakness; the ill-balanced character is harmful to society; and I venture to think that the zealous propagation of a single virtue in our schools, that of temperance or thrift, for example, to the omission or neglect of other teaching, may well do harm to the national character. We know how the inculcation of thrift has operated in France. Let us teach these (temperance and thrift) by all means; but also, and equally, diligence, candour, kindness, all the graces that go to make up love and justice, all the habits that ensue in intelligence.

To repeat what I have already insisted upon to weariness, we must teach children a definite, ordered philosophy of life. It is all in the Bible? Yes, but our teaching of the Bible is no longer of the full, exhaustive, progressive kind that should issue in a balanced character.

The school curriculum should be an exemplification of the doctrine of the Mean as regards both studies and students, and should not be allowed to depend for its success upon the extremes of emulation or ambition. We have seen that the desire for distinction which makes the conventional person come out first in sports or examinations, converts the more erratic into what we call a crank. But, indeed, he has not had fair play—neither the one nor the other boy. Many motives must be allowed due action, and many interests must make their appeal, if we would have a sane and serviceable outgoing person. We are all creatures of infinite variety. It is a wonder to some of us how the fashionable woman sustains the London season: 'excitement,' we say, and dismiss the subject; but many a lady goes through the toils of the season with ease and pleasure who is not in the least excited by any of its events, just as many a man of affairs has a bewildering number of matters to attend to, but finds the day, as Goethe did, 'infinitely long,' and is able to get them all in.

Child or man, we spend half our time in being bored; and we are bored because our thoughts wander from the thing in hand—we are inattentive. When for a moment we do brace ourselves to an act of attention, the invigorating effect of such act is surprising. We are alive; and it is so good to be alive that we seek the fitful stimulus of excitement—to be the more listless after than before, because we have been stimulated and not invigorated. Being bored becomes a habit; we secretly look forward with longing to the end of every occupation or amusement, and are ready to take up with any 'crank' that promises distraction and fuller living, for however short a time. When we have used up that interest, another may occur.

That we cannot find life enough for our living is perhaps one of these 'shoots of everlastingnesse' (not always 'bright') which remind us that we are the 'children of an infinite hope.' But we may not check these growing pains by any means which stunt our growth; and, to begin with the children, we may do something to keep them from getting into the habit of being bored. As it is, the best children pay attention probably for about one-third of a given lesson; for the rest of the time they are at the mercy of volatile thoughts, and at the end they are fagged, not so much by the lesson as by the throng of vagrant fancies which has played upon their inattentive minds.

How, if we tried the same quantity of work in one-third of the time with the interest which induces fixed attention? This would enable us to reduce working-hours by one-third, and at the same time to get in a good many more subjects, having regard to a child's real need for knowledge of many kinds: the children would not be bored, they would discover the delightfulness of knowledge, and we should all benefit, for we might hope that, instead of shutting up our books when we leave school or college, each of us, under ninety say, would have his days varied and the springs of life renewed by periods of definite study: we should all be students, the working-man as well as the man of leisure. The writer knew a man of ninety who then began to study Spanish. We know how our late Queen began the study of Hindustani at seventy, and we all know of work of great value accomplished by aged persons.

But this highly varied intellectual work must not have the passing character of an amusement (is not this the danger of lectures?). Continuation and progression must mark every study, so that each day we go on from where we left off, and know that we are covering fresh ground. Perhaps some day we shall come to perceive that moral and spiritual progression are also for us, not by way of distinction, but for us in common with all men, and because we are human beings.

Much and varied knowledge, the habit of study (begun early and continued through life), some acquaintance with the principles of an ordered moral life, some knowledge of economic science, should help in the making of well-ordered, well-balanced persons, capable of living without weariness, and without a disordered desire for notice from other people. But if, by giving them knowledge, motive power, and work, it is possible to keep the bright impulsive children from becoming erratic persons, what about the slower and less generous natures who are apt, under culture, to develop into prigs?

This letter from a boy's master to his father indicates the sort of thing:—

"Masters sometimes growl because bad boys are sent to them: am I unreasonable in complaining that Herbert is a deal too good? I have always felt it difficult to define a prig, most people find it so, but I begin to feel that the thing is developing under my eyes. Such an early growth should be easily checked. Have you any suggestions to give me?

"Herbert does everything well; is punctual, and if late, has excellent reasons for being so; he is absolutely never in the wrong; he is industrious, does his 'preps,' takes his turn in construing, even does his French exercises (!), has an orderly desk, tidy note-books, a decent necktie—what is there he does not do? He is strong in this new nature-study, turns out a decent set of verses, makes a decent score at cricket. 'Why grumble?' you will say? 'Haven't I sent you a model, dutiful schoolboy, if he is a bit conceited?' He is not exactly conceited, and he is not dutiful. What he does is just to let all those virtues shine by comparison with the rest of the boys who lack them, many of whom are really more interesting and original than this Admirable Crichton. He just surrounds himself with an atmosphere of righteousness, in which ordinary mortals can't breathe. He is most aggravating when great people and great things are being talked about. It is proper then to be humble, and he puts on the air of an Uriah Heep. If I snub him, he is silent and stubborn. He is always too busy doing his duty to be of any use to the small boys;" etc.

This sort of virtuous child is apt to be a home-product. We are not told how long Herbert had been at school, but should judge that the school was small and for young boys. Also, we should imagine that the boy's father, and perhaps his mother were persons genuinely interested in education, who set ideals before their children. We gather, too, that the boy has little originality, although he turns out decent verses.

Here we have the young prig fully accounted for; and at a time when parents and teachers are taking education very seriously, we must remember that he is a likely outcome of this very zeal. Such another wave of educational thought reached England in the eighteenth century, and we have 'Mr. Barlow's' admirable pupils, Miss Edgeworth's Frank, and all the nicely-labelled scales of virtues and vices. The child in a family with perhaps the least in him sees that his parents commend certain things—a well-cleaned bicycle, for example—and that they reprove his brothers and sisters for being late, or untidy, or careless. He is perhaps half-conscious of inferiority to the rest in many things, so he builds up an ideal of various virtues which are easily within his reach, and presents that product which we call a 'prig.' He is a very difficult person to treat. It is not easy to say to him that his virtues are a bore; that nobody cares a pin about them; and as for snubbing him, to snub a person full of conscious virtue is to awaken a slow fire of resentment, not likely soon to go out. Perhaps education should be with us (in our family life) like religion—to be acted, but not to be talked about. The danger of offering material for a false ideal is a very real one. The child with plenty of stuff in him will slip the yoke now and then, and make jokes about the ideal which, although he does not know it, is shaping him; but the good child of slow intelligence 'acquires merit,' picks up the virtues that come in his way, and makes a caddisworm case of them, an unattached integument instead of a growth from within. It is hard to get at him, because there are no depths to be sounded; even 'the sharp ingredient of a bad success' does not affect him much—he has no measure for the badness. We must recollect that his desire for distinction is as great as that of his more original brother but, with the cuteness of a small mind, he chooses to excel in being good rather than in being odd.

But this, too, is only a phase of the uneasiness of human nature. It is encouraging to reflect that a sense of deficiency may be at the bottom of it; and for the sake of this weaker brother we must be careful not to put too big a premium of praise on the little conventional virtues, as easy as they are necessary: in our readings and talk, qualities of heart and head must be emphasised, rather than all the good little virtues contained, so to speak, in our own skin. We may even be obliging and helpful, just out of virtue: really it should be possible to make children see that self-contained virtue bores other people, that kindness and service is of value only as it comes out of love, that industry and perseverance are good only when they are the outcome of duty, that there is no worth in the diligent doing of lessons unless we love knowledge. Our danger in dealing with children of this type is that we should lose sight of our own ideal, and accept the display of virtues which are certainly convenient.

It is to be hoped that Herbert will go, by and by, to a big school. Boys do not tolerate the Better-than-my-neighbour order of virtues. Goodness, for them, must be spontaneous, and not laboured; must be unconscious too; they scent a prig from afar, and have ways of their own for taking it out of him.

The prig and the crank appear to have one thing in common—the desire to be remarkable, distinguished in one way or another; this universal desire is a natural provision for the feeding of the mind, as hunger is for that of the body; but we may not bring up boys and girls to depend upon a moral tuck-shop. There are other things to live for besides the getting of praise and the shirking of blame, and every child is open to the greater considerations.

The more sincerely we face the problems of education, the more shy we become of any cut-and-dried treatment of human nature. We have an increasing sense that a person is infinite, capable of so many joys, such aspirations, such labours, such distresses and uneasiness like that of the restless sea! How shall we get tenderness enough to deal with child or youth? is a question ever present with us. We know that his distress and his uneasiness are 'growing pains,' but we know, too, that he is not always able to bear them, and finds ways to ease his aching at the cost of his growth.

Is there no peace? Goethe, we have seen, found a curious peace which lasted him all his life in the perception that "we are His people and the sheep of His pasture," which he got out of his study of the early books of the Bible.

The writer is familiar with a German watering-place much frequented by Polish Jews of the poorer sort, sent thither probably by benevolent brethren of their race. These men are by no means phlegmatic; groups of three or four will engage in talk for hours at a spell, enviably earnest talk, impersonal, one would gather, from the faces of the speakers, and not like the chatter about baths and symptoms to be heard in passing other groups of talkers. We may take it for granted that they are not notable for the conventional virtues. But the curious thing about all these men, whether of the ruddy or dark type, is their tranquility of aspect; their faces are like those of little children, simple, interested, untroubled, and very free from lines of anxiety. Is it that, like Goethe, they are aware of themselves only as "sheep of His pasture," and for the rest, take life as it comes?

This peace comes to all simple, natural persons who have faith in God—as to the great German poet,—for faith is the only key to that science of the proportion of things which enables us to take ourselves simply as part of the general scheme, sure of being duly nourished and ordered, and under no compulsion to make life too strenuous. "My peace shall flow like a river" has been said; and this is what we forget, that the peace of God is an active principle, ever-flowing, ever-going, ever-nourishing, ever-fertilising,—and not a passive state, a quiet creek, where we may stagnate at our ease.

"My peace I leave unto you" conveys a legacy to children as well as to their elders. They appropriate this peace while they are quite young, and live in gladness and at ease; but we disturb them too soon. We throw them back upon their own endeavours; convict them of naughtiness, but do not convince them of goodness; make them uneasy and unhappy, so that they wince under our touch; and fail to open to them free paths to goodness and knowledge.

That children should have the peace of God as a necessary condition of growth is a practical question. If we believe it is their right, not to be acquired by merit nor lost by demerit, we shall take less upon ourselves, and understand that it is not we who pasture the young souls. The managing mother, who interferes with every hour and every occupation of her child's life, all because it is her duty, would tend to disappear. She would see, with some amusement, why it is that the rather lazy, self-indulgent mother is often blessed with very good children. She, too, will let her children be, not because she is lazy, but being dutiful, she sees that—give children opportunity and elbow-room, and they are likely to become natural persons, neither cranks nor prigs. And here is a hope for society; children so brought up are hardly likely to become managing persons in their turn, inclined to intrude upon the lives of others, and be rather intolerable in whatever relation.

No doubt children are deeply grateful to managing parents, and we are all lazy enough to be thankful to persons who undertake our lives for us but these well-meaning persons encroach; we are required to act for ourselves, think for ourselves, and let other persons do the same.

It is our puritan way to take too much upon us for ourselves and others: we must 'acquire merit' and they must acquire merit; and the feeding in quiet pastures, the being led beside still waters, we take to be the reward of peculiar merit, and do not see that it is a natural state and condition, proper to everyone who will claim it. If we saw this, we should be less obtrusive in our dealings with children; we should study to be quiet, only seeing to it that our inactivity is masterly.

Wordsworth sums it all up in a few lines of profound insight, and adds the noble suggestion that, given elbow-room and the freedom of opportunity, we have within us natural powers whose due activity will of itself correct our failings. We may come to see that this is some part of God's way of forgiving us our sins:

"'Tis known
That when we stand upon our native soil,
Unelbowed by such objects as oppress
Our active powers, those powers themselves become
Strong to subvert our noxious qualities.
They sweep distemper from the busy day,
And make the chalice of the big round year
Run o'er with gladness; whence the Being moves
In beauty through the world; and all who see
Bless him, rejoicing in his neighbourhood."

Chapter 6. A Modern Educator: Thomas Godolphin Rooper

I cannot better conclude this volume than by adding a grateful if unworthy appreciation of a great Educator, whose sympathy and criticism stimulated, whose life and thought inspired me during about twenty years of educational work. Even so slight a notice of one who served his country with devotion may be stimulating to the reader; but I hope we shall soon have ampler materials for judging of this unusual life.

The Parents' Union sustained an immeasurable loss in the death of Mr. Thomas Godolphin Rooper on the 20th of May 1903. From the first inception of the idea he was with us. He was a member of the first committee, which (in 1887) held many meetings in Bradford, where he was Inspector of Schools, to discuss the ways and means of launching such a Society; and he went straight to the principles of the Union, and embraced them with great warmth and insight.

His power of appreciation, in the fullest sense of the word, the outcome of a fine and highly cultivated mind, of wide reading and a wide knowledge of affairs, enabled him to weigh delicately and justly the possibilities and performances of the union. He considered, for example, "that the Parents' Union is the most important society for stimulating discussion" (on educational matters). Also, I believe he thought that in proportion as parents brought themselves to take an active part in educational thought and educational schemes would schools become altogether living and serviceable. The discriminating quality, which enabled Mr. Rooper to appreciate justly and hope steadfastly both as regards this Union and an immense number of other educational efforts and outputs, made him also a keen critic. All who worked with him had the assurance that if there were a defect he would see it, and would help to mend it.

In the matters of encouragement and of just criticism his value appears to have been profoundly felt by the Board of Education, by other members of the Inspectorate, by the teachers in his district, and by many and curiously various educational bodies and associations. But we of the Parents' Union seem to have worked a new vein in that so rich mind and generous nature. One would say that he had a singular power of self-effacement, except that there appeared to be no self to efface. "It is all in the day's work," he would say to his nurses when they sympathised with his weariness in the last sad days; and the saying was a key to his life. He appeared to find no necessity for self-expression or for self-advancement; the work, and he there to do it, appeared to limit his outlook. It is here, I think, the Society in question has reason to rejoice in having drawn from him some graceful and scholarly output of his cultivated mind. He probably would never have written for the sake of literary expression, but we have obtained from him, from time to time, lectures which make up almost the whole of two volumes of essays, full of wisdom, literary charm, and profoundly philosophic teaching. The secretary of a Branch would invite him to lecture; he always appeared to think such an invitation an honour, and the address he wrote for the occasion, while touching on some question of the hour, would rifle his treasures of wisdom, scholarship, and wide reading. The essay on "Reverence, or the Ideal in Education," will occur to some readers. This sort of phrase we find in it: "Without great thoughts there are no great deeds"; "the true spirit of patriotism is . . . such an appreciation of his country's greatness as leads a man to be humble, modest, ready to sacrifice himself as an insignificant portion for the good of the whole community." I must digress here, to notice how the sterling character of Mr. Rooper's thought proceeded from the fact that it was the outcome of his life. "I feel like a soldier who has given his life for his country," he said, smilingly, towards the end, and it is curious how the fact has been recognised. It has been well said of him that "he died a martyr to the cause of education."

Another purely delightful essay is entitled "Lyonesse: Education at Home versus Education at a Public School." 'Lyonesse' is his name for the romantic land of public-school life, buried beneath the waves of this troublesome world, but by no means forgotten. 'Lyonesse,' no doubt, also, because Harrow, his school, was founded by one Lyon. Has anything more charming been written on this subject, revealing the pieties and loyalties of the public school man, things which abide with him to the end? Indeed, one wonders if anywhere but in a great English public school and in one of our old universities could a character of such modesty, culture, and capacity be produced as we have to lament in Mr. Rooper. He was a Balliol man, a fervent disciple of Jowett, to whom his loyalty was unbounded, and to him, may be, he partly owed his insight as regards the true issues of life. From him, too, came his, shall we say, Balliol way of leaving a question open—of stating both sides and every side. I think he hated dogmatism and declamation, and his quiet, tentative way of throwing out ideas and suggestions was apt to be misleading to audiences not on the look-out for Attic salt and philosophic acumen.

Perhaps an instructed reader of his essays might readily find in them the springs of thought and purpose which moved his life. Was Lord Collingwood his special hero? The essay on his 'Theory and Practice of Education' is written with what appears to me the sympathy we feel for a life which has helped to make us what we are. Speaking of the three great admirals—Jervis, Nelson, and Collingwood—he says: "It is hardly possible even to speak of these three men without our language and thoughts rising to an elevation above the common and ordinary level of social intercourse." Surely in this sentence we have a key to the fighting ardour which brought about the untimely end we mourn. But then, Collingwood too was an educationalist: "It was his character and superior education, and study of education, and its kindred study of occupation in daily life, which made possible to Collingwood such an unparalleled achievement" (to keep eight hundred men on the high seas for twenty-two months, and to keep them in health and happiness).

Indeed, what he says of Collingwood is so word for word the testimony those who knew him would bear of Mr. Rooper that I cannot help quoting further: "For it was not merely his ceaseless military (read 'educational') occupation that wore him out. His correspondence was immense, and so highly esteemed was his judgment that he was consulted from all quarters and on all occasions, and on a great variety of questions . . . He was by nature and education a man of cultivated and refined taste, and of great simplicity of character. He united great intellectual power with great amiability, and these two gifts are rarely united in a man. His occupations at home were reading, especially works on history, from which it was his habit to compose well-written abridgments. His recreations were drawing, and cultivating his garden at Morpeth . . . 'My wits,' he writes, 'are ever at work to keep my people employed, both for health's sake and to save them from mischief. We have lately been making musical instruments, and have now a very good band. Every moonlight night the sailors dance, and there seems as much mirth and festivity as if we were in Wapping itself.'

"Lord Collingwood was a saint, but he was a human, not a Puritan. Occupation of the right kind was the keynote of his educational system, and it seems the safest and most practical for all engaged in Education."

In this essay on Lord Collingwood we get several keys to Mr. Rooper's own life: for instance, the wide reading, especially in works on history, the love of a garden, and above all the stress laid on occupation in daily life. The National Handwork Union found in him a staunch supporter, as did its publication, 'Hand and Eye.' He delighted to turn out a perfect wooden spoon on his Sloyd bench, and was most keen to learn leather-work by watching the students at the House of Education. His zealous work in connection with school gardens and his report on Continental school gardens are well known.

We get another touch of Mr. Rooper's genial wisdom and of his many-sided character in his charming essay on 'Gaiety in Education,' and still another in his essay on 'Don Quixote'; and in his praise of chivalry, even reckless chivalry, a further peep into the moving springs of a life is afforded to us.

One more essay I must mention, which he sent for publication a few weeks before the end, on 'Robinson Crusoe in Education.' No other writer that I know of has seen in this delightful tale another 'Pilgrim's Progress': "But the island hermit is not alone in the spirit. He had thoughts which led him, now undisturbed by the slow stain of the world, to a more elevated frame of mind than he could find in society.

"Knowledge and truth and virtue were his theme, and thoughts the most dear to him were lofty hopes of Divine liberty.

"Robinson Crusoe saves from the wreck a Bible, which his sad life on the island leads him to appreciate. Just as Defoe describes his hero as cut off from social and political life, so he thinks of him as free from ecclesiastical controversy. As Crusoe bit by bit fights Nature and subdues her, so his spirit wins her way to religion by aid of the Bible without human intervention . . . If you overlook this passage you cannot understand the drift of Robinson Crusoe." Here we get a glimpse into a region of thought which the writer was apt to keep jealously guarded. He abhorred cant—educational, social, religious; but those who knew him best, and were continually about him, knew that he too, like Collingwood, was "a saint."

Delightful as these lectures were to his audiences, the lecturer found perhaps an equal pleasure in giving them. On his annual visits to the College at Ambleside, Mr. Rooper had always gleeful—there is no other word—reminiscences of Parents' Union meetings which he had addressed at various places. He was incapable of pettiness or ungentle criticism; and whether his audiences were small and dull, large and intellectual, or large and fashionable, he always seemed to take the same gleeful delight that such an audience (of whichever sort) should gather for the consideration of an educational topic. Indeed, the Parents' Union was always a fresh wonder to him, an extraordinary realisation of the ideal. Perhaps the same sense of gratulation, almost self-gratulation, was shown in the news he brought of students whom he had found at work here and there. In their work, too, he seemed to find the element of surprise that comes upon us in the realisation of the ideal. "Hope," says Dante, "is the mark of all the souls whom God has made His friends"; and he projected, as it were without words, hope, confidence, aspiration and humility into the young people whose work he came to criticise.

Mr. Rooper was by no means lavish of praise, and was almost austere in criticism, but the students felt rather than heard that their spirit was congenial to him and their work satisfactory. His thoroughness was remarkable: he would begin at about 8:30 and go on till 1 o'clock without pause—hear each of the mistresses lecture, and each of the second year's students give a lesson chosen from three sets of notes. The charming thing to both mistresses and students was his keen, inquiring, and personal interest in the subject taught. He had a way of leaving the household more in love with knowledge than before—now galls, now weaving, now local geography would excite his curious interest; now a passage in a French or German author, now Italian or mathematics; but he had always the happy way of making a teacher feel, whether her class were making buns or working problems, that the subject was excessively interesting in itself and for itself. We were all struck by an instance of his thoroughness worth recording.

The notes of lessons presented for his choice by the students have always covered an unusually wide range of subjects, in languages, handicrafts, art, science, and what not, but it occurred to him that he had not heard them give piano lessons, and piano lessons were crowded into the busy day. In the afternoon he would examine the various handicrafts of the students with keen interest and knowledge; then there were drills to be seen, various books to be looked at, and in the evening the students generally entertained themselves and him with some sort of impromptu acting—now and then a charade, in which that awful personage, the Inspector, would see himself taken off with rather graceful audacity. It was good to see his gleeful amusement on these occasions.

He knew people and affairs everywhere, and so was often able to have a good deal of conversation with the students on matters they knew; and certainly he took pleasure in contact with women of some culture who were preparing for that great work of education which he had so deeply at heart; their enthusiasm and their simple manners pleased him. For their part, the students held their Inspector in great reverence as well as cordial regard: they saw that he knew and that he cared. Once or twice, in his generous zeal for education, he came to us, I believe at great inconvenience, to give lessons before the students on subjects in which he knew he could help them. On one of these occasions a student was giving a rather dull history lesson before him; he took up the subject, and such an unfolding of associations, graphic pictures, living interests, perhaps we had none of us heard before. This lesson was hardly a model for general imitation, for I think there are few persons in the country who could have opened such a storehouse.

He used to cause a good deal of entertainment at table by referring with gravity to the time "when I was a governess." He really had, after he left college, undertaken the children of his friends, Dr and Mrs. Butler, during some interregnum, an experience which he greatly enjoyed; and that and his five years' tutorship of the present Duke of Bedford gave him a special interest in the education of children brought up at home, and therefore in the work of the House of Education.

It is difficult to speak of Mr. Rooper's delightful and stimulating conversation, and of his genial interest in everything. We have lost a great man, and at a moment apparently when his achievements, his gifts and his knowledge should have been of special value to the nation he served. "To me personally the loss is irreparable," writes one of his many friends; and perhaps seldom have such sorrowful words found a wider echo. His extraordinary devotion as a brother is known to many. But to all who mourn him he has left, not only the legacy of his life amongst us, but of three sayings, spoken when he was very near the end: "hope"; then, after a long interval, "press forward"; and later, "help from Him." Whether spoken consciously, to his sisters, or unconsciously, the messages are those of his life. The blood of the martyrs is the seed of the Church. May we all "hope," "press forward," and look for "help from Him."

I cannot close this inadequate notice of a great, good man better than by quoting a few phrases from an essay on The Grammarian's Funeral—with the motto "Great Men do mean what they say," by Mr. Rooper:—

"His whole life was a long ascent, in the course of which there was no level ground."

"He lived to magnify the mind."

"Left play for work, grappled with the world, bent on escaping the common life." "He had laid out his plan for his lifetime."

"A great work will require a lifetime, and its payment will never be received this side the grave."

So let us—

"Leave him still loftier than the world suspects, Living and dying."

Appendix

A Few Books Dealing with Education

It is with diffidence that the writer ventures to reprint anything so fugitive as these short notices of books, which have appeared from time to time in the Parents' Review. On the other hand, it may be well to keep certain useful books more permanently in mind, and also, each notice gives an opportunity to bring out, often in the author's words, some instruction of value.

Pastor Agnorum: A Schoolmaster's Afterthoughts, by J. Huntley Skrine, Warden of Glenalmond (Longmans, 5s. net). We have in Pastor Agnorum another very delightful and stimulating book about education; not a number of collected papers this time, but a carefully ordered work. It is addressed to schoolmasters, Headmasters for the most part, by no means an easy class to approach from the rostrum; but Mr. Skrine writes with so scholarly an ease and grace, sprinkles his matter so cunningly with the Attic salt of his wit, that we venture to predict that even his hard sayings will be genially received by the appreciative audience he has in view. But the rest of us are not to be left out in the interest of masters. This is a book for us all—fathers, mothers, teachers—whoever is interested in the bringing up, not only of boys, but of girls also. The "shepherd's" calling, he tells us, is "to nourish, rule, and lead," and he must learn his method by the study of the Incarnation. From the life of the Pastor Pastorum he must learn to teach with authority, that is, he must know and feel what he teaches, but must seek, not to reproduce himself, but to produce the pupil's self. He must teach "not without a parable," school lessons must be a parable of the art of living well; humane letters, science lessons, mathematics can be such parables. He must be a preacher of the gospel to the poor, that is, he must teach, not some of his boys, but all, only he must also "give to him that hath." As a ruler, he must deduce the government of school from the ideas of chivalry. The secrets of chivalry are (1) Truth, which must be taught without convention or class narrowness, (2) Freedom, which needs to be interpreted, (3) Courtesy, which must be popularised, (4.) Hardihood, which should not be only of the body, (5) Chastity and Woman-worship, (6) Religion, (7) Brotherliness, without exclusiveness or partiality. The richness and unusualness of this book may be judged of from the fact that, so far, we have been quoting solely from the table of contents. Seven chapters are devoted to the consideration of the shepherd as the life of the school, inspirer, teacher. Then follows the consideration of the fold. Our Round Table sets forth how chivalry can become the bond of Head and Colleagues. This is a singularly ennobling and purifying chapter and throws much light upon what is often a difficult relation, and here, especially, we admire the wit and charm which make hard things good to be listened to. The chapter on Some Knights of the Round Table, which gives us racy pictures of several types of master, and that on The Parent as a Neglected Factor, are capital reading. The subtlety with which the author justifies that old-fashioned institution, the Family, and even ventures to hold up its casual ways for the consideration, if not the imitation, of the schoolmaster, is an example of how the salt of wit may flavour discernment. The book is a witty and even worldlywise apologia for Christianity, for the high chivalry of Christianity among masters and scholars; and we earnestly commend it to those other pastors who have but a few sheep to tend in that little fold which they call home. Reverence, insight and common-sense must needs grow from the seed-thoughts the author has dropped.

School and Home Life, by T. G. Rooper, M.A., H.M.I., Balliol College, Oxford (A. Brown & Sons, London, 6s.). "I have tried to study the education of children from the age of three onwards to their coming of age; and this, I think, few have had the chance of doing both practically and theoretically. Most teachers specialise on one period, in the nursery, the 'private' school, on the 'public' school, or the university, because they have only the experience of one such period. The relation of one stage to the next has been too much neglected, with the result that in many young persons there are two or three distinct characters." We have ventured (without permission) to quote the above from a private letter from the author of School and Home Life, because we feel that the passage throws much light on the method and scope of the work before us. The casual reader might, without such a guide, say, "Oh, but the work does not deal with education at any particular stage, or even with the education of one sex or the other," and might suppose the charming classical English in which the essays are written to be the vehicle of a literary production, and that only. But parents will find here a mine of suggestions on each of the phases of educational work with which they are concerned, including the bringing up of boys and girls from three (or one!) to one-and-twenty. Perhaps the special characteristic of the work is the author's power of initiating ideas. You read one of the essays, feel that all the thoughts are your own thoughts, and that nothing new is being said; that the "art of putting" is so happy that you are carried over the ground unawares. You digest the essay, consider it in its bearings on your own children, and, behold, you find you have imbibed a number of new ideas, practical, vital, full of interest and hope. This would be something were the ideas those of a mere theorist on education; but we have in Mr. Rooper an educational expert, at home in the literature, both English and foreign, of each subject on which he touches, an adept in practical education, and, at the same time, an original thinker who passes the materials he receives through the illuminating medium of his own mind. Probably no man in England has initiated so many and so many successful new departures in education; and not the least claim on our gratitude is that, from the very first inception of the Parents' National Educational Union, Mr. Rooper has unwaveringly and actively supported the movement. Many of the lectures have been delivered to Parents' Union audiences, and those of us who have heard some of these lectures are likely to keep the impression of them at the bottom of all our educational thought. This is absolutely a book for parents and teachers, not to be borrowed, but possessed, to be at hand ready for reference at the moment.

Thoughts on Education, by Mandel Creighton, D.D. (Longmans, 5s. net). Dr Creighton's Thoughts on Education is a possession. They do not, as Mrs. Creighton remarks in her preface, propose any system of education; indeed systems failed to interest him; he was too true an educator to care for anything but the practice and principles of education. These papers have been gathered under difficulties. Many of them exist only in newspaper reports, but, such as they are, they embody the insight of the historical mind, the enthusiasm of the educator, and the serious fervour of the Christian Bishop. They deal with such questions as The Child and the Education Question; Examinations; The Training of the Schoolboy; The Art of Teaching; The Hope of the Teacher; The Use of Books;—in fact, these thirty papers cover a wide field of thought, and touch upon questions that exercise most of us. It is not too much to say that in each paper there are sentences of epigrammatic force and terseness which present the subject in a new aspect and leave nothing more to be said. From the inspiring address to Sunday School teachers on The Hope of the Teacher we get, "That our daughters may be as corner-stones polished—there is no picture here of useless grace; quiet solidity of character receives its due adornment, and while it supports the fabric, gladdens the passer-by." And this from Apollos: A Model for Sunday School Teachers:—"You must try and make them feel that Christ is knocking at the door of each of their little hearts, and you must realise with reverent awe that it is your work to help the little trembling fingers to undo the bolt and lift the latch to admit that gracious and majestic visitant." We must add two or three sentences from The Art of Teaching (which will commend themselves especially to members of the Union):—"As regards teaching itself, however, I believe it to be an incommunicable art, a gift which may best be defined as the power of showing others some reason why they should learn. . . . That is just what the good teacher does; he brings knowledge and his pupil into a vital relationship; and the object of teaching is to establish that relationship on an intelligible basis. . . The acceptance of knowledge is an internal process which no external process can achieve. . . . A child is much more idealistic than a grown-up person, and readily responds to an ideal impulse. . . . Remember that memory is a power which does not need to be especially developed. It is the most worthless of our mental powers, and a true teacher should always try and prevent his pupils from relying on it." This volume comes to us as a welcome memorial of the late Bishop of London.

Vittorino da Feltre and other Humanist Educators, by W. H. Woodward (Cambridge University Press, 6s.). This volume is something more than an interesting study in the by-ways of history. True, it treats of the schoolmasters—especially of perhaps the most famous of them, Vittorino himself—of that most fascinating period, the early days of the Renaissance, the revival of learning. But the real value of the work to us is that it shows on what liberal lines the humanist schoolmaster dealt with the questions which are debatable ground to-day. The radical fault of our English thought and opinion on the subject of education seems to be that we have somehow lost the sense of historical perspective. At each new idea, which we believe we have ourselves conceived, we cry—"We are the people"; "Never was education like unto ours." And here, towards the end of the fourteenth and early in the fifteenth centuries, we have every one of our vexed questions answered with liberality and philosophic conviction to which we have not attained. Should girls have equal advantages with boys? Vittorino taught girls and boys together. Is early education important? He laid himself out for children of five years old. Should lessons be pleasant? La Giocosa not only named but described his school. Should there be a mixture of classes in a school? He taught children whom he educated out of his large charity with the children of princes. Do we desire a wide and liberal curriculum? This was what he accomplished—Latin and Greek, Arithmetic, Geometry, Algebra, Natural Philosophy, Euclid, Astronomy, Natural History, Music, Choral Singing, Dancing, all Games for the training and exercise of the body, and a good deal besides. Plutarch was made much use of as an educational instrument, being employed with the Bible to teach morals. Does it distress many a mother that her son should wade through the pages of classic authors too apt to be unchaste ? Such authors were not admitted into the curriculum of Vittorino. Do we pride ourselves on the higher education of women? This is an old story in Italian education, where women were advanced to professorial chairs even in universities for men. Are we beginning to expect that parents should be serious students of the philosophy of education? This was a matter of course for the fifteenth-century parent, to whom the schoolmaster looked for intelligent co-operation. We owe a great debt to Mr. Woodward for focussing our loose thoughts on the subject of the Renaissance in Italy. Persons who wish to have just and liberal views of education, not limited by the last output of the last English writer on the subject, will do well to give this volume a careful and studious perusal.

Educational Studies and Addresses, by T. G. Rooper, H.M.I. (Blackie and Son). This volume of Educational Essays by Mr. Rooper is singularly refreshing. The range of the Essays is considerable. We have the treatment of mentally deficient children in the very enlightening and encouraging article on the great French educationalist, Séguin, who studied education as it were at the fountainhead by discovering the possibilities of defective children. Séguin's great discovery was that the normal intellect depends upon the interaction and proper co-ordination of various parts of the nervous system,—"Now in a normal child the various parts of the nervous organism work so rapidly and promptly that it is almost impossible to follow the process of co-ordination. It is indeed quick as thought. In the cretinous child, owing to want of co-ordination, different movements can be studied before they are combined into a whole. The method of training such children consists in doing for them artificially what in the ordinary child is done naturally."

The lecture which follows, upon Manual Training, is an application of this principle to the normal as well as the defective child. The author deplores the fact that the home has ceased to be a miniature technical school; and certainly no English person who saw the unique exhibition at Stockholm some years ago could fail to envy a people who showed so much art feeling, industry, and capacity, such genuine love of work. Again, in natural sequence, follows the essay on Obedience; for the physical possibility of obedience also depends upon the interaction and proper coordination of various parts of the nervous system. This is the rationale of military discipline. This military discipline the author accepts as the physical basis of obedience; but, he contends, obedience must be moral and rational before it is really human. The working out of this thesis is exceedingly interesting and suggestive; all the more so because, as is his custom, the author adds modern instances to his wise saws. He begins with Agnes Grey, the unfortunate governess portrayed by Acton Bell, and concludes the essay with a reference to the great speech of the late Lord Russell of Killowen, made before the American Bar in 1896, when the vast audience—many of them lawyers—were so impressed with the beauty and dignity of law that they rose to their feet at the end of the speech and cheered vociferously for a quarter of a hour. The next essay, Lord Collingwood's Theory and Practice of Education, works out the theme in that most delightful form of a practical experiment. Few people will read this essay without added reverence for a great man, increased pride in a country that has produced a Collingwood, and clearer and more forceful notions of how to bring up one's children and how to rule in one's little domain. Personally we feel that this sort of object lesson in education is worth more than many manuals of teaching and many studies in psychology. We cannot dwell on the charming essay on Gaiety in Education, nor on that on Individualisin in Education, nor on those on the teaching of special subjects, nor on the especially charming essay on Miguel de Cervantes Saavedra. But the thoughtful reader will find in this volume much food for reflection; and, always, the pleasant sense of tempered judgment, great experience, and the recognition that education is not an air-tight compartment of life, but is a part of life itself, open to all the winds that blow and to a thousand changing lights from literature, philosophy, art,—the things and thoughts which we care about. Religious Teaching in Secondary Schools, by the Rev. Geo. Bell, M.A. (Macmillan & Co., 3s. 6d.). The former Headmaster of Marlborough has done most important service in these "Suggestions to Teachers and Parents for Lessons on the Old and New Testaments, Early Church History, Christian Evidences, etc." Only those who have to do with young people know the steadily increasing ignorance on all matters connected with our faith which they manifest, whether they have been brought up at home or at school. The cause of this lack of preparation for the religious life does not, we are convinced, lie in the carelessness whether of parents or of teachers, but is due to a sort of uneasy conscientiousness; a sense that they are not qualified to deal with Biblical criticism in its present stage; they do not know what to allow or what to refute, and the shortest way on the whole seems to be to let the subject alone. But negligence on this score is alike perilous and culpable; and a grave, moderate, practical treatment of the question by an author qualified both as a scholar and as a schoolmaster is an incalculable boon. The opening chapter on the difficulties that beset the teacher of religious knowledge is very helpful. Mr. Bell shirks no difficulty, and he writes always with fervour, reverence, and unshaken faith. We cannot better indicate the aim of this work than by quoting a passage: "The true value of religious education is to supply children with that faith in man's destination for a spiritual life, which nothing can give them except a belief that the universe is under the guidance of a Divine all-powerful Spirit. Without such belief man drops into a utilitarian secularist. We need, then, to use specially for education such parts of the Bible as display the highest qualities of human character developing under the influence of a pure faith, and thus foster the germs of spiritual heroism and earnest devotion." But in this, as in other subjects, teaching must be graduated according to capacity. In the religious teaching of young children, as in other subjects, their quickness and freshness of memory will be turned to account by making them learn facts and details suited to their intelligence; but the primary aim will be to select and use facts and details as means of quickening and cultivating the germs of religious and moral feeling towards God, love, reverence, trust towards man, such emotions as are stirred by,the biographies of the Bible. The purity and equanimity of Joseph, the piety and wisdom of Samuel, the manly faith and religious earnestness of David, the heroism of Stephen, the unselfish zeal of Paul, and, far above all, the ensample of Jesus' most holy life, attract the fresh sympathies of the young, and teaching must indeed be dull which fails to draw from such sources that which stirs emotion and lifts the heart. And in the early years this will be the main object and result of religious teaching, the reason is not much exercised, the higher ideas and truths of religion—sin, atonement, judgment, heaven, eternity—are as yet almost unintelligible, dimly foreshadowed by familiar types or analogies; the difficult problems of freewill, predestination, inspiration, have not as yet taken shape in the mind; the battle-cries of sects, transubstantiation, infallibility of Pope or Church, or Bible, are unheard of or meaningless . . . . . There is, however, very serious practical difficulty in deciding at what stage in education, and by what methods and agencies, the teacher should begin to supplement instruction in the letter of Bible history and doctrine by a gradual unfolding of the principal arguments and objections that will ultimately have to be faced. There are two questions of first importance on which such supplementary teaching seems to be necessary.—(1) the historical truth and degree of inspiration of the various parts of the Bible, especially the Old Testament; (2) the evidences of the Christian religion, ie. those facts and arguments which convince an educated Christian that his faith is intellectually and spiritually more tenable than any of the rival theories of belief or unbelief that prevail in modern society." The chapters which follow are no mere disquisitions, but contain carefully ordered practical advice as to what to teach and how to teach it; with, for example, a scheme of selections from the Old Testament, or again, topics for lessons suggested by the early chapters of Genesis. The author makes frequent reference to Mr. C. G. Montefiore's invaluable Bible for Home Reading. The chapters on the "Inspiration of the Old Testament," the "Composite Character of the Books of the Old Testament" the "Resurrection of Jesus Christ," "Miracles," and the "Difficulties of Constructive Unbelief," will be found exceedingly helpful. Indeed, we have seldom met with so much guiding and stimulating counsel in so small a volume.

Special Reports on Educational Subjects, Vol. VIII.: Education in Scandinavia, Switzerland, Holland, Hungary, etc. (3S. 2d.). Mr. Sadler in these extraordinarily instructive reports is providing the country with an educational library of unique value. The essays on education in Norway and Sweden are especially interesting, and the new law for secondary schools in Norway contains important suggestions. The article which attracts us most is that upon Children's Workshops in Sweden; the Arbetsstugor appear to us to do more than indicate the right way of teaching handwork to the children of the working-classes. They strike at the root of a fallacy which tells against educational progress; that is, that educational results are in exact proportion to the elaborateness and costliness of appliances, building, etc. In the Arbetsstugor the children work in an ordinary cottage—no more and no less comfortable than a workman's dwelling. The head of every Arbetsstuga is a lady, who, as a rule, gives her time freely to the work. Practical craftsmen are engaged when necessary to work under her direction. Boys and girls attend the Arbetsstuga separately every other day for two consecutive hours; the number of children attending one such school varies from fifty to two hundred. Ten to twelve form a class. Small rooms will do for a class, because of the excellent method of ventilation employed. The work taught is of various kinds: chip and bast plaiting and needlework for the youngest children (7-9 years); for the elder pupils (10-14) fret-sawing, brush-making, weaving, netting, carpentry, bootmending. "Thus the children have made different kinds of objects. They have plaited hats, made slippers, chairs, baskets of many kinds, tables, shelves, baking troughs, mended shoes, made waistcoats with the button-holes, pantaloons, children's dresses and aprons; they have woven mats, petticoats, aprons; they have made iron and steel instruments, hammers and other tools, rakes, spades, small iron beds, sledges, etc." The work is disposed of at an annual sale, and the sales more than cover the expenses of fresh materials. The children are rewarded by a meal, either dinner or supper, and in these meals not only health and economy, but the tastes of the children are regarded. The children get to love work, and to beg to have some to do at home. The paper on The Teaching of Arithmetic, by Mr. A. Sonnenschein, is a most helpful contribution, and not less so is that on The Teaching of Latin, by Dr E. Sonnenschein. But the whole volume is too full of wise thought and suggestive practice for us to do it justice in a short notice.

Special Reports upon Educational Subjects—Supplement to Vol. 8. Report on the School Training and Early Employment of Lancashire Children (Eyre & Spottiswoode, 3d.). To quote from the prefatory note: "The following Report, prepared by Mr. E. T. Campagnac and Mr. C. E. B. Russell deals with a question of great interest and importance at the present moment: namely, how best to fit boys who are educated in primary schools for their life's work, and how to better their present haphazard method of obtaining employment." This supplement is melancholy reading. The result of the evidence given by working-class youths, teachers, inspectors, employers, and other authorities with whom the young people of the working-classes come in contact when they go out as wage earners, amounts to a strong indictment against our system of elementary education. The boys and girls turned out of the schools, even those who have passed through all their standards with credit, are glaringly deficient in intelligence, initiative, and perception. They have no interests, they do not think, and they do not care to read. More than one employer states that he would rather pick up a street gamin for work in his office or shop than the boy who has distinguished himself in passing through the sixth or seventh standard. It is hoped by the Board of Education that the publication of this Report at this time "may be of service to local educational authorities in considering what steps can be taken for securing better and more permanent results from the large sums now spent upon our elementary schools." We profoundly hope that it may, and commend the study of the authors' judicious and stimulating remarks to all teachers. Here is a passage whose insight should commend it to intelligent persons—"It may, of course, be said that work is work, and play is play, that the habit of attention is not to be easily acquired, and that labour is necessary to enjoyment. . . . This is true, but it is not a high view either of work or of its reward; and it may well be doubted whether any work which is done in this spirit is of much value, either to the man who does it or to his fellows. But as regards intellectual work, the doctrine is false and misleading, and it is peculiarly dangerous when it is applied to the work of a school. Discipline must be kept and labour must be exacted, but there should be no radical distinction between discipline and happiness, between labour and enjoyment; and we believe it is because, somehow, this distinction has been established that an antipathy to books and to reading has grown up in the minds of so many children." We have cried aloud our panacea in the market-place, and no one heeds; but it is cheering and hopeful to come upon so authoritative a condemnation of the defects we lament.

Special Reports on Educational Subjects: Education in
Germany (Eyre and Spottiswoode, 2s. 7d.). This excessively interesting volume opens with an important essay, a considerable work in itself, on The Unrest in Secondary Education in Germany and Elsewhere, by the Editor, Mr. M. E. Sadler. This essay is encouraging reading to all who recognise "Education" as a living force rather than a more or less mechanical routine. The Board of Education commissioned Mr. Sadler to visit the Paris Exibition of 1900 in order to report upon the educational section. The first thing that struck him was that "education is not a thing by itself, but one aspect of national life." It is this recognition which marks the whole essay, and is perhaps the key to the unusual discernment and breadth of view with which the subject is treated. There has never been so deep an interest shown in education, we are told, as there is to-day, but the nations differ in their aims in this matter. Here is a passage which at the same time encourages and condemns ourselves. "Some are in the habit of identifying 'education' with what is taught in schools, and, therefore, of regarding a tidily organised school system as necessarily the most fruitful kind of national education. Others have preserved a healthier sense of the truth that education is but one aspect of life, and, therefore, as varied and as long as life itself, with the result that some of their children get a very much better education than others, and that, in the community taken as a whole, the average of intellectual attainments is low." The comparison between English and Continental secondary schools is searching and suggestive, but the gist of the whole is, that, that which we have that in which we are great, is due to the free play allowed to individuality in English education. This admits of the action of an enormous force in the making of character. "We English have always believed that some of the highest kinds of learning are not necessarily printed in books, but may be embodied in institutions; that some of the noblest combinations of intellectual and spiritual power seek to revive, inspire, or create some form of corporate life." This is cheering so far; but we cannot escape the charge, brought home to us by this prophet of our own, that we are intellectually below

other nations, our compeers, and far below what is possible to ourselves. The problem is how to level up our secondary education intellectually without loss of moral force or physical fibre. If we take the author's advice, two doors are closed to us—the perpetual examinations by which school-life is made an uneasy dream, with little or no waking profit, and for which we are held in some contempt by our Continental neighbours; and that other tempting escape, by which we run in and out to this foreign system and that, snatching at a patch here and a patch there to piece up our deficiencies. We must recognise that education is organic—the outgrowth of our nationality—and we can only take in new material of thought in proportion as we can assimilate it and it becomes part of ourselves. Among the nations, two are singled out by Mr. Sadler as having characteristics which are a possession for the world, not to be endangered by rash strictures and hasty reforms. England, on the one hand, has the spirit engendered in its public schools. France, on the other hand, has that perfect instrument of thought—its literary language—the outcome of ages of education, in its secondary schools, upon literary traditions. In considering the schools of Germany, the author's view is that German thought and English thought are at opposite ends of the pole. Germany leans to the production of high attainments, England to the all-round development of character; and each country perceives that it has much to learn from the other. The rest of the volume contains deeply interesting reports of education in various parts of Germany, Primary and Secondary girls' schools and boys' schools, Realschulen, Commercial schools, Handelsschulen and what not; an examination of the provision for training teachers; and a very interesting article upon the measurement of mental fatigue in Germany, which discloses sad facts concerning 'overpressure.' It is well that the Head of the Empire is aware that the manhood of his people is being sapped in the schools. The whole volume is most interesting reading, and we commend it to teachers. Probably no step made in England in the promotion of education is more notable than the periodic production of these perfectly adequate yellow-books.

Ideals of Culture: Two Addresses to Students. By Edward A. Sonnenschein, Oxon (Swan Sonnenschain, & Co., 2s. 6d.).—Parents who have not made up their minds on the vexed question of classical or modern culture will find Professor Sonnenschein's two lectures pleasant and helpful reading. We have only room to quote his summing up of the matter of his first lecture on Science and Culture: "Let me cast a brief glance upon the general aim and purport of what I have said. The prime essentials of culture are science and poetry; and they may be cultivated without spreading ourselves impartially over the whole field of knowledge, without ascetically denying our special bent. One branch of either of the great departments, nature and literature, may give us scope for both energies of soul; but the student of nature cannot be independent of the aid of poetry, unless, indeed, he is a poet himself. Further, in resigning claims to universal knowledge, we may remember that to command one department is to command many potentially, and even involves inquiry into and partial grasp of subjects lying outside it. Finally, life is long enough to admit of our making practical experience of our fellow-men, without which we ourselves are scarcely human."

The second essay, on Ancient Greek Games, is very interesting, and tends to show that "there are many points of kinship between Greece and England: not the least is the ideal, fostered alike by ancient philosophers and by English philosophers, and by English schools and universities, of physical and intellectual education going hand in hand." We cannot refrain from giving our readers the pleasure of reading of the games of the Greek child: "The rattle, the ball, the hoop, trundled by a crooked necked iron, the swing, occupied the same position in Greece as in our nurseries; the top is as old as Homer. Boys amused themselves with a kind of stilts and with toy carts, girls with the inevitable doll, made probably of wax or clay. It is pleasing to hear of children making their own toys. Aristophanes speaks of a precocious child that carved ships for himself, and made carts out of leather, and frogs out of pomegranate peel. Lucian says that when he got out of school he used to make oxen or horses, or even men, out of wax. Plato recommends that children should have mimic tools given them, in order to amuse themselves with carpentering. But it may be gathered that he did not approve of too many toys, which are apt to discourage originality; he rather praises the natural modes of amusement which children find out for themselves when they meet."

Ethics of Citizenship, by Professor J. Maccunn, M.A. (Maclehose, Glasgow). A singularly sane, many-sided, instructive volume, which most of us would be the better for reading in this age of many open questions. Parents, whatever be their political creed, one of whose chief duties is to bring up good citizens, would, we believe, find matter for careful consideration in Professor Maccunn's book. It is probable that the education of the future will recognise, as its guiding idea, Matthew Arnold's fine saying, that "The thing best worth living for is to be of use." Every man and woman will be a candidate for service beyond the range of his or her own family. The solidarity of the nation, anyway, if not that of the race, is being pressed home upon us, and already the more thoughtful among us suffer from uneasiness if we are not engaged in some kind of public duty. It is not a new thing, by any means, for many of us to take such public service in the cause of religion, but it is a new thing, and shows a wider, deeper conception of religion, that so many of us are now zealous to serve merely as citizens.

But the public has its choice of servants who will serve without wage. It has no call for the ignorant amateur, will none of him. If our children are to be prepared for public service, they must be indoctrinated with what Professor Maccunn calls the Ethics of Citizenship. "Oh, my Brother, my Brother, why cannot I shelter thee in my bosom and wipe away all tears from thine eyes?" says Carlyle; and here perhaps we have the note of the future for whatever party or creed. But mere blundering good-will will not serve us. We must be brought up in the principles and in the methods of wise co-operation.

A Survey of English Ethics, being the first chapter of Mr. Lecky's "History of European Morals," edited by W. A. Hirst (Longmans, 3s. 6d.). We are exceedingly indebted to Mr. Hirst for the idea of publishing in this handy form the first chapter of Mr. Lecky's History of European Morals. Mr. Hirst prefaces the volume by an introduction tracing the history of English ethics from Hobbes to John Stuart Mill. It cannot be denied that our English moralists have belonged for the most part to the utilitarian school, of which it is well said that "The history of the Utilitarian principle is the history of contribution to the stock of happiness; it is the history of what has been done from time to time to improve and perfect the operations of which enjoyment is the result." Again it is said of the Utilitarians and the philosophic radicals, "Efficiency was, in fact, their watchword. The object of efficiency, of a better system of government, morals, and legislation, was happiness." At the present moment the doctrine of the man in the street, and of the thinker who represents him, is distinctly utilitarian. In religion, morals, politics, and education, happiness is his aim; his altruistic aspirations are expressed in "the greatest happiness of the greatest number," and assuredly he labours for the aim he has in view. His benevolent and socialistic enterprises show fine results, all the more so because, as compared with the intuitive moralist, his results are readily put in evidence. In face of these obvious facts, it is startling to read Mr. Lecky's statement that "the intuitive moralist (for reasons I shall hereafter explain) believes that the Utilitarian theory is profoundly immoral." This is startling, but it is also encouraging. There are still those among us who believe in the intuitive sense of obligation which we call duty; who believe that the hope of the race lies, not in the alleviation of its discontents, but in this, which they are assured is the fact—that every man has in his nature a notion of right which carries with it a feeling of obligation; that when circumstances call upon a man to express this sense of obligation (though it be at the peril of life or limb or property), that man is for the most part ready to seize such opportunity as offering a supreme good. This is the theme which Mr. Lecky works out with singular lucidity and power, and at the same time with full and fair treatment of the Utilitarian position. We strongly advise the study of this "survey" as offering a key to many questions of the hour.

Knowledge, Duty, and Faith: a Study of Principles Ancient and Modern, by Sir Thos. Dyke Acland (Kegan, Paul & CO., 3s. 6d.). Sir Thomas Acland has done a very valuable and timely public service in the production of this volume. We say valuable, because he has reduced a subject of so much inherent difficulty as philosophy to the simplest possible forms of expression, to be "understanded" by people who know nothing of the language of the schools, but who are stirred by the natural human curiosity as to what man can know and what man should do. We say timely, because, since the mind of man began to think, it has occupied itself with the real and the ideal in, so to speak, rhythmic pulsations. For fully a generation the real has been strongly in the ascendant, and science has advanced by leaps and bounds, pari passu with materialistic thought. But, according to that law of rhythmic thinking which affects the race as truly as the individual, thought is again turning to the ideal. The limitations of the real, with its one possible outcome, that man himself is a congeries of regulated atoms—that there is nothing in the universe but atoms and regulating laws—this doctrine is oppressive to the spirit of man, and there is a strong rebound towards the Platonic conception of the Idea. Thoughtful people, who feel that they know nothing of the history of thought and nothing of the laws of thinking, will find here just the help they want—an introduction to the principles taught by typical thinkers, ancient and modern. Sir Thomas Acland's chapter on Aristotle seems to us especially useful and interesting, and still more so that upon Lotze, whom he describes as having spoken the last word on knowledge and faith and the relation between them. The author has that quality of temperance in thought and word which should distinguish the philosopher. We quote a passage illustrating this quality, and showing the practical value of the work in the conduct of life:—"If we are justified in accepting this doctrine, that the validity which belongs to ideas and to laws (of nature and mind) may be distinguished from the reality which belongs to things embodied as matters of experience, some important inferences may be drawn as to modern speculation.

"One suggestion is, that we must be very careful and self-restrained in drawing logical conclusions as to matters of fact from ideas in our minds, especially on moral and spiritual realities, the bearing or relations of which we may only imperfectly grasp by the intellect. We may feel confident that ideas or conceptions in our minds involve some preceding conditions, or some succeeding conclusions. But we cannot infer the reality of such conclusions—though they may correspond to our limited thoughts—especially when they take a negative form.

"On the other hand, while experience brings home to our minds a conviction of the reality of certain facts as known to us by their appearances or phenomena, and further teaches us that facts follow one another (as far as our experience goes) in a regular order, we shall do well to remember that no length of experience amounts to demonstration, still less to the disproof of spiritual convictions resting on grounds beyond our experience."

A chronological table of modern philosophers is a valuable appendix, and so is a list of books at low prices, meant for the help of the students in University Extension Classes, for whose use the volume is intended. We hail a book setting forth a scheme of knowledge, duty, and faith, so distinctly making for righteousness, and recognising the Divine as a fundamental necessity. To criticise the limitations of the work would be to ignore its objects and to forget the class of students for whom it was written. We repeat that the venerable author has done a lasting service for those who will come after him.

Towards A Philosophy Of Education
Table of Contents

Author's Preface

It would seem a far cry from Undine to a 'liberal education' but there is a point of contact between the two; a soul awoke within a water-sprite at the touch of love; so, I have to tell of the awakening of a 'general soul' at the touch of knowledge. Eight years ago the 'soul' of a class of children in a mining village school awoke simultaneously at this magic touch and has remained awake. We know that religion can awaken souls, that love makes a new man, that the call of a vocation may do it, and in the age of the Renaissance, men's souls, the general soul, awoke to knowledge: but this appeal rarely reaches the modern soul; and, notwithstanding the pleasantness attending lessons and marks in all our schools, I believe the ardour for knowledge in the children of this mining village is a phenomenon that indicates new possibilities. Already many thousands of the children of the Empire had experienced this intellectual conversion, but they were the children of educated persons. To find that the children of a mining population were equally responsive seemed to open a new hope for the world. It may be that the souls of all children are waiting for the call of knowledge to awaken them to delightful living.

This is how the late Mrs. Francis Steinthal, who was the happy instigator of the movement in Council Schools, wrote,—"Think of the meaning of this in the lives of the children,—disciplined lives, and no lawless strikes, justice, an end to class warfare, developed intellects, and no market for trashy and corrupt literature! We shall, or rather they will, live in a redeemed world." This was written in a moment of enthusiasm on hearing that a certain County Council had accepted a scheme of work for this pioneer school; enthusiasm sees in advance the fields white to the harvest, but indeed the event is likely to justify high expectations. Though less than nine years have passed since that pioneer school made the bold attempt, already many thousands of children working under numerous County Councils are finding that "Studies serve for delight."

No doubt children are well taught and happy in their lessons as things are, and this was specially true of the school in question; yet both teachers and children find an immeasurable difference between the casual interest roused by marks, pleasing oral lessons and other school devices, and the sort of steady avidity for knowledge that comes with the awakened soul. The children have converted the school inspectors: "And the English!" said one of these in astonishment as he listened to their long, graphic, dramatic narrations of what they had heard. During the last thirty years we (including many fellow workers) have had thousands of children, in our schoolrooms, home and other, working on the lines of Dean Colet's prayer for St Paul's School,—"Pray for the children to prosper in good life and good literature;" probably all children so taught grow up with such principles and pursuits as make for happy and useful citizenship.

I should like to add that we have no axe to grind. The public good is our aim; and the methods proposed are applicable in any school. My object in offering this volume to the public is to urge upon all who are concerned with education a few salient principles which are generally either unknown or disregarded; and a few methods which, like that bathing in Jordan, are too simple to commend themselves to the 'general.' Yet these principles and methods make education entirely effectual.

I should like to add that no statement that I have advanced in the following volume rests upon opinion only. Every point has been proved in thousands of instances, and the method may be seen at work in many schools, large and small, Elementary and Secondary.

I have to beg the patience of the reader who is asked to approach the one terminus by various avenues, and I cannot do so better than in the words of old Fuller:—"Good reader. I suspect I may have written some things twice; if not in the same words yet in sense, which I desire you to pass by favourably, forasmuch as you may well think, it was difficult and a dull thing for me in so great a number of independent sentences to find out the repetitions . . . Besides the pains, such a search would cost me more time than I can afford it; for my glass of life running now low, I must not suffer one sand to fall in waste nor suffer one minute in picking of straws . . . But to conclude this, since in matters of advice, Precept must be upon Precept, Line upon Line, I apologise in the words of St. Paul, 'To write the same things to you to me indeed is not grievous, but for you it is safe.'"

I am unwilling to close what is probably the last preface I shall be called upon to write without a very grateful recognition of the co-operation of those friends who are working with me in what seems to us a great cause. The Parents' National Educational Union has fulfilled its mission, as declared in its first prospectus, nobly and generously. "The Union exists for the benefit of parents and teachers of all classes;" and; for the last eight years it has undertaken the labour and expense of an energetic propaganda on behalf of Elementary Schools, of which about 150 are now working on the programmes of the Parents' Union School. During the last year a pleasing and hopeful development has taken place under the auspices of the Hon. Mrs. Franklin. It was suggested to the Head of a London County Council School to form an association of the parents of the children in that school, offering them certain advantages and requiring a small payment to cover expenses. At the first meeting one of the fathers present got up and said that he was greatly disappointed. He had expected to see some three hundred parents and there were only about sixty present! The promoters of the meeting were, however, well pleased to see the sixty, most of whom became members of the Parents' Association, and the work goes on with spirit.

We are deeply indebted to many fellow-workers, but not even that very courteous gentleman who once wrote a letter to the Romans could make suitable acknowledgments to all of those to whom we owe the success of a movement the rational of which I attempt to make clear in the following pages.

Charlotte M. Mason,

House of Education Ambleside. 1922

A Short Synopsis

Of the Educational Philosophy Advanced in this Volume

"No sooner doth the truth ... .come into the soul's sight, but the soul knows her to be her first and old acquaintance."

"The consequence of truth is great; therefore the judgment of it must not be negligent." (Whichcote).

1. Children are born persons.

2. They are not born either good or bad, but with possibilities for good and for evil.

3. The principles of authority on the one hand, and of obedience on the other, are natural, necessary and fundamental; but—

4. These principles are limited by the respect due to the personality of children, which must not be encroached upon whether by the direct use of fear or love, suggestion or influence, or by undue play upon any one natural desire.

5. Therefore, we are limited to three educational instruments—the atmosphere of environment, the discipline of habit, and the presentation of living ideas. The P.N.E.U. Motto is: "Education is an atmosphere, a discipline, and a life."

6. When we say that "education is an atmosphere," we do not mean that a child should be isolated in what may be called a 'child-environment' especially adapted and prepared, but that we should take into account the educational value of his natural home atmosphere, both as regards persons and things, and should let him live freely among his proper conditions. It stultifies a child to bring down his world to the child's' level.

7. By "education is a discipline," we mean the discipline of habits, formed definitely and thoughtfully, whether habits of mind or body. Physiologists tell us of the adaptation of brain structures to habitual lines of thought, i.e., to our habits.

8. In saying that "education is a life," the need of intellectual and moral as well as of physical sustenance is implied. The mind feeds on ideas, and therefore children should have a generous curriculum.

9. We hold that the child's mind is no mere sac to hold ideas; but is rather, if the figure may be allowed, a spiritual organism, with an appetite for all knowledge. This is its proper diet, with which it is prepared to deal; and which it can digest and assimilate as the body does foodstuffs.

10. Such a doctrine as e.g. the Herbartian, that the mind is a receptacle, lays the stress of education (the preparation of knowledge in enticing morsels duly ordered) upon the teacher. Children taught on this principle are in danger of receiving much teaching with little knowledge; and the teacher's axiom is,' what a child learns matters less than how he learns it."

11. But we, believing that the normal child has powers of mind which fit him to deal with all knowledge proper to him, give him a full and generous curriculum; taking care only that all knowledge offered him is vital,

that is, that facts are not presented without their informing ideas. Out of this conception comes our principle that,—

12. "Education is the Science of Relations"; that is, that a child has natural relations with a vast number of things and thoughts: so we train him upon physical exercises, nature lore, handicrafts, science and art, and upon many living books, for we know that our business is not to teach him all about anything, but to help him to make valid as many as may be of—

"Those first-born affinities

"That fit our new existence to existing things."

13. In devising a *syllabus* for a normal child, of whatever social class, three points must be considered:

(a) He requires much knowledge, for the mind needs sufficient food as much as does the body.

(b) The knowledge should be various, for sameness in mental diet does not create appetite (i.e., curiosity)

(c) Knowledge should be communicated in well-chosen language, because his attention responds naturally to what is conveyed in literary form.

14. As knowledge is not assimilated until it is reproduced, children should 'tell back' after a single reading or hearing: or should write on some part of what they have read.

15. A single reading is insisted on, because children have naturally great power of attention; but this force is dissipated by the re-reading of passages, and also, by questioning, summarising. and the like.

Acting upon these and some other points in the behaviour of mind, we find that the educability of children is enormously greater than has hitherto been supposed, and is but little dependent on such circumstances as heredity and environment.

Nor is the accuracy of this statement limited to clever children or to children of the educated classes: thousands of children in Elementary Schools respond freely to this method, which is based on the behaviour of mind.

16. There are two guides to moral and intellectual self-management to offer to children, which we may call 'the way of the will' and 'the way of the reason.'

17. The way of the will: Children should be taught, (a) to distinguish between 'I want' and 'I will.' (b) That the way to will effectively is to turn our thoughts from that which we desire but do not will. (c) That the best way to turn our thoughts is to think of or do some quite different thing, entertaining or interesting. (d) That after a little rest in this way, the will returns to its work with new vigour. (This adjunct of the will is familiar to us as diversion, whose office it is to ease us for a time from will effort, that we may 'will' again with added power. The use of suggestion as an aid to the will is to be deprecated, as tending to stultify and stereotype character, It would seem that spontaneity is a condition of development, and that human nature needs the discipline of failure as well as of success.)

18. The way of reason: We teach children, too, not to 'lean (too confidently) to their own understanding'; because the function of reason is to give logical demonstration (a) of mathematical truth, (b) of an initial idea, accepted by the will. In the former case, reason is, practically, an infallible guide, but in the latter, it is not always a safe one; for, whether that idea be right or wrong, reason will confirm it by irrefragable proofs.

19. Therefore, children should be taught, as they become mature enough to understand such teaching, that the chief responsibility which rests on them as persons is the acceptance or rejection of ideas. To help them in this choice we give them principles of conduct, and a wide range of the knowledge fitted to them. These principles should save children from some of the loose thinking and heedless action which cause most of us to live at a lower level than we need.

20. We allow no separation to grow up between the intellectual and 'spiritual' life of children, but teach them that the Divine Spirit has constant access to their spirits, and is their Continual Helper in all the interests, duties and joys of life.

Book 1
Introduction

These are anxious days for all who are engaged in education. We rejoiced in the fortitude, valour and devotion shown by our men in the War and recognize that these things are due to the Schools as well as to the fact that England still breeds "very valiant creatures." It is good to know that "the whole army was illustrious." The heroism of our officers derives an added impulse from that tincture of 'letters' that every Public schoolboy gets, and those "playing fields" where boys acquire habits of obedience and command. But what about the abysmal ignorance shown in the wrong thinking of many of the men who stayed at home? Are we to blame? I suppose most of us feel that we are: for these men are educated as we choose to understand education, that is, they can read and write, think perversely, and follow an argument, though they are unable to detect a fallacy. If we ask in perplexity, why do so many men and women seem incapable of generous impulse, of reasoned patriotism, of seeing beyond the circle of their own interests, is not the answer, that men are enabled for such things by education? These are the marks of educated persons; and when millions of men who should be the backbone of the country seem to be dead to public claims, we have to ask,—Why then are not these persons educated, and what have we given them in lieu of education?

Our errors in education, so far as we have erred, turn upon the conception we form of 'mind,' and the theory which has filtered through to most teachers implies the out-of-date notion of the development of 'faculties,' a notion which itself rests on the axiom that thought is no more than a function of the brain. Here we find the sole justification of the scanty curricula provided in most of our schools, for the tortuous processes of our teaching, for the mischievous assertion that "it does not matter what a child learns but only how he learns it." If we teach much and children learn little we comfort ourselves with the idea that we are 'developing' this or the other 'faculty.' A great future lies before the nation which shall perceive that knowledge is the sole concern of education proper, as distinguished from training, and that knowledge is the necessary daily food of the mind.

Teachers are looking out for the support of a sound theory, and such a theory must recognize with conviction the part mind plays in education and the conditions under which this prime agent acts. We want a philosophy of education which, admitting that thought alone appeals to mind, that thought begets thought, shall relegate to their proper subsidiary places all those sensory and muscular activities which are supposed to afford intellectual as well as physical training. The latter is so important in and for itself that it needs not to be bolstered up by the notion that it includes the whole, or the practically important part, of education. The same remark holds good of vocational training. Our journals ask with scorn,—"Is there no education but what is got out of books at school? Is not the lad who works in the fields getting education?" and the public lacks the courage to say definitely, "No, he is not," because there is no clear notion current as to what education means, and how it is to be distinguished from vocational training. But the people themselves begin to understand and to clamour for an education which shall qualify their children for life rather than for earning a living. As a matter of fact, it is the man who has read and thought on many subjects who is, with the necessary training, the most capable whether in handling tools, drawing plans, or keeping books. The more of a person we succeed in making a child, the better will he both fulfil his own life and serve society.

Much thoughtful care has been spent in ascertaining the causes of the German break-down in character and conduct; the war scourge was symptomatic and the symptoms have been duly traced to their cause in the thoughts the people have been taught to think during three or four generations. We have heard much about Nietzsche, Treitschke, Bernhardi and the rest; but Professor Muirhead did us good service in carrying the investigation further back. Darwin's theories of natural selection, the survival of the fittest, the struggle for existence, struck root in Germany in fitting soil; and the ideas of the superman, the super state, the right of might to repudiate treaties, to eliminate feebler powers, to recognize no law but expediency—all this appears to come as naturally out of Darwinism as a chicken comes out of an egg. No doubt the same dicta have struck us in the Commentaries of Frederick the Great; "they shall take who have the power, and they shall keep who can," is ages older than Darwin, but possibly this is what our English philosopher did for Germany:—There is a tendency in human nature to elect the obligations of natural law in preference to those of spiritual law; to take its code of ethics from science, and, following this tendency, the Germans found in their reading of Darwin sanction for manifestations of brutality.

Here are a few examples of how German philosophers amplify the Darwinian text:—"In matter dwell all natural and spiritual potencies. Matter is the foundation of all being." "What we call spirit, thought, the faculty of knowledge, consists of natural though peculiarly combined forces." Darwin himself protests against the struggle for existence being the most potent agency where the higher part of man's nature is concerned, and he no more thought of giving a materialistic tendency to modern education than Locke thought of teaching principles which should bring about the French Revolution; but men's thoughts are more potent than they know, and these two Englishmen may be credited with influencing powerfully two world-wide movements. In Germany, "prepared by a quarter of a century of materialistic thought," the teaching of Darwin was accepted as offering emancipation from various moral restraints. Ernst Haeckel, his distinguished follower, finds in the law of natural selection sanction for Germany's lawless action, and also, that pregnant doctrine of the superman. "This principle of selection is nothing less than democratic; on the contrary it is aristocratic in the strictest sense of the word." We know how Buchner, again, simplified and popularised these new theories, "All the faculties which we include under the name of Psychical activities are only functions of the brain substance. Thought stands in the same relation to the brain as the gall to the liver."

What use, or misuse, Germany has made of the teaching of Darwin would not (save for the War) be of immediate concern to us, were it not that she has given us back our own in the form of that "mythology of faculty psychology" which is all we possess in the way of educational thought. English psychology proper has advanced if not to firm ground, at any rate to the point of repudiating the 'faculty' basis. "However much assailed the concept of a 'mind' is," we are told, "to be found in all psychological writers." (quote from the article on Psychology in the Encyclopadia Britannica as being the most likely to exhibit the authoritative position.) But there are but mind and matter, and when we are told again that "psychology rests on feeling," where are we? Is there a middle region?

II

We fail to recognize that as the body requires wholesome food and cannot nourish itself upon any substance so the mind too requires meat after its kind. If the War taught nothing else it taught us that men are spirits, that the spirit, mind, of a man is more than his flesh, that his spirit is the man, that for the thoughts of his heart he gives the breath of his body. As a consequence of this recognition of our spiritual nature, the lesson for us at the moment is that the great thoughts, great events, great considerations, which form the background of our national thought, shall be the content of the education we pass on.

The educational thought we hear most about is, as I have said, based on sundry Darwinian axioms, out of which we get the notion that nothing matters but physical fitness and vocational training. However important these are, they are not the chief thing. A century ago when Prussia was shipwrecked in the Napoleonic wars it was discovered that not Napoleon but Ignorance was the formidable national enemy; a few philosophers took the matter in hand, and history, poetry, philosophy, proved the salvation of a ruined nation, because such studies make for the development of personality, public spirit, initiative, the qualities of which the State was in need, and which most advance individual happiness and success. On the other hand, the period when Germany made her school curriculum utilitarian marks the beginning of her moral downfall. History repeats itself. There are interesting rumours afloat of how the students at Bonn, for example, went in solemn procession to make a bonfire of French novels, certain prints, articles of luxury and the like; things like these had brought about the ruin of Germany and it was the part of the youth to save her now as before. Are they to have another Tugendbund?

We want an education which shall nourish the mind while not neglecting either physical or vocational training; in short, we want a working philosophy of education. I think that we of the P.N.E.U. have arrived at such a body of theory, tested and corrected by some thirty years of successful practice with thousands of children. This theory has already been set forth in volumes published at intervals during the last thirty-five years; so I shall indicate here only a few salient points which seem to me to differ from general theory and practice,—

(a) The children, not the teachers, are the responsible persons; they do the work by self-effort.

(b) The teachers give sympathy and occasionally elucidate, sum up or enlarge, but the actual work is done by the scholars.

(c) These read in a term one, or two, or three thousand pages, according to their age, school and Form, in a large number of set books. The quantity set for each lesson allows of only a single reading; but the reading is tested by narration, or by writing on a test passage. When the terminal examination is at hand so much ground has been covered that revision is out of the question; what the children have read they know, and write on any part of it with ease and fluency, in vigorous English; they usually spell well.

Much is said from time to time to show that 'mere book-learning' is rather contemptible, and that "Things are in the saddle and ride mankind." May I point out that whatever discredit is due to the use of books does not apply to this method, which so far as I can discover has not hitherto been employed. Has an attempt been made before on a wide scale to secure that scholars should know their books, many pages in many books, at a single reading, in such a way that months later they can write freely and accurately on any part of the term's reading?

(d) There is no selection of studies, or of passages or of episodes, on the ground of interest. The best available book is chosen and is read through perhaps in the course of two or three years.

(e) The children study many books on many subjects, but exhibit no confusion of thought, and 'howlers' are almost unknown.

(f) They find that, in Bacon's phrase, "Studies serve for delight"; this delight being not in the lessons or the personality of the teacher, but purely in their 'lovely books,' 'glorious books.'

(g) The books used are, whenever possible, literary in style.

(h) Marks, prizes, places, rewards, punishments, praise, blame, or other inducements are not necessary to secure attention, which is voluntary, immediate and surprisingly perfect.

(i) The success of the scholars in what may be called disciplinary subjects, such as Mathematics and Grammar, depends largely on the power of the teacher, though the pupils' habit of attention is of use in these too.

(j) No stray lessons are given on interesting subjects; the knowledge the children get is consecutive.

The unusual interest children show in their work, their power of concentration, their wide, and as far as it goes, accurate knowledge of historical, literary and some scientific subjects, has challenged attention and the general conclusion is that these are the children of educated and cultivated parents. It was vain to urge that the home schoolroom does not usually produce remarkable educational results; but the way is opening to prove that the power these children show is common to all children; at last there is hope that the offspring of working-class parents may be led into the wide pastures of a liberal education.

Are we not justified in concluding that singular effects must have commensurate causes, and that we have chanced to light on unknown tracts in the region of educational thought. At any rate that *golden rule* of which Comenius was in search has discovered itself, the *Rule, "Whereby Teachers Shall Teach less and Scholars Shall Learn More."*

Let me now outline a few of the educational principles which account for unusual results.

III

Principles Hitherto Unrecognized or Disregarded

I have enumerated some of the points in which our work is exceptional in the hope of convincing the reader that unusual work carried on successfully in hundreds of schoolrooms—home and other—is based on principles hitherto unrecognized. The recognition of these principles should put our national education on an intelligent basis and should make for general stability, joy in living, and personal initiative.

May I add one or two more arguments in support of my plea,— The appeal is not to the clever child only, but to the average and even to the 'backward' child.

This scheme is carried out in less time than ordinary school work on the same subjects.

There are no revisions, no evening lessons, no cramming or 'getting up' of subjects; therefore there is much time whether for vocational work or interests or hobbies.

All intellectual work is done in the hours of morning school, and the afternoons are given to field nature studies, drawing, handicrafts, etc.

Notwithstanding these limitations the children produce a surprising amount of good intellectual work.

No homework is required.

It is not that 'we' (of the P.N.E.U.) are persons of peculiar genius; it is that, like Paley's man who found the watch, "we have chanced on a good thing."

"No gain that I experience must remain unshared."

We feel that the country and indeed the world should have the benefit of educational discoveries which act powerfully as a moral lever, for we are experiencing anew the joy of the Renaissance, but without its pagan lawlessness.

Let me trace as far as I can recall them the steps by which I arrived at some of the conclusions upon which we are acting. While still a young woman I saw a great deal of a family of Anglo-Indian children who had come 'home' to their grandfather's house and were being brought up by an aunt who was my intimate friend. The children were astonishing to me; they were persons of generous impulses and sound judgment, of great intellectual aptitude, of imagination and moral insight. These last two points were, I recollect, illustrated one day by a little maiden of five who came home from her walk silent and sad; some letting alone, and some wise openings brought out at last between sobs,— "a poor man—no home—nothing to eat—no bed to lie upon,"—and then the child was relieved by tears. Such incidents are common enough in families, but they were new to me. I was reading a good deal of philosophy and 'Education' at the time for I thought with the enthusiasm of a young teacher that Education should regenerate the world. I had an Elementary School and a pioneer Church High School at this same time so that I was enabled to study children in large groups; but at school children are not so self-revealing as at home. I began under the guidance of these Anglo-Indian children to take the measure of a person and soon to suspect that children are more than we, their elders, except that their ignorance is illimitable.

One limitation I did discover in the minds of these little people; my friend insisted that they could not understand English Grammar; I maintained that they could and wrote a little Grammar (still waiting to be prepared for publication!) for the two of seven and eight; but she was right; I was allowed to give the lessons myself with what lucidity and freshness I could command; in vain; the Nominative 'Case' baffled them; their minds rejected the abstract conception just as children reject the notion of writing an "Essay on Happiness." But I was beginning to make discoveries; the second being, that the mind of a child takes or rejects according to its needs.

From this point it was not difficult to go on to the perception that, whether in taking or rejecting, the mind was functioning for its own nourishment; that the mind, in fact, requires sustenance—as does the body, in order that it increase and be strong; but because the mind is not to be measured or weighed but is spiritual, so its sustenance must be spiritual too, must, in fact, be ideas (in the Platonic sense of images). I soon perceived that children were well equipped to deal with ideas, and that explanations, questionings, amplifications, are unnecessary and wearisome. Children have a natural appetite for knowledge which is informed with thought. They bring imagination, judgment, and the various so-called 'faculties' to bear upon a new idea pretty much as the gastric juices act upon a food ration. This was illuminating but rather startling; the whole intellectual apparatus of the teacher, his power of vivid presentation, apt illustration, able summing up, subtle questioning, all these were hindrances and intervened between children and the right nutriment duly served; this, on the other hand, they received with the sort of avidity and simplicity with which a healthy child eats his dinner.

The Scottish school of philosophers came to my aid here with what may be called their doctrine of the desires, which, I perceived, stimulate the action of mind and so cater for spiritual (not necessarily religious) sustenance as the appetites do for that of the body and for the continuance of the race. This was helpful; I inferred that one of these, the Desire of Knowledge (Curiosity) was the chief instrument of education; that this desire might be paralysed or made powerless like an unused limb by encouraging other desires to intervene between a child and the knowledge proper for him; the desire for place,—emulation; for prizes,—avarice; for power,—ambition; for praise,—vanity, might each be a stumbling block to him. It seemed to me that we teachers had unconsciously elaborated a system which should secure the discipline of the schools and the eagerness of the scholars,—by means of marks, prizes, and the like,—and yet eliminate that knowledge-hunger, itself the quite sufficient incentive to education.

Then arose the question,—Cannot people get on with little knowledge? Is it really necessary after all? My child-friends supplied the answer: their insatiable curiosity shewed me that the wide world and its history was barely enough to satisfy a child who had not been made apathetic by spiritual malnutrition. What, then, is knowledge?—was the next question that occurred; a question which the intellectual labour of ages has not settled; but perhaps this is enough to go on with;—that only becomes knowledge to a person which he has assimilated, which his mind has acted upon.

Children's aptitude for knowledge and their eagerness for it made for the conclusion that the field of a child's knowledge may not be artificially restricted, that he has a right to and necessity for as much and as varied knowledge as he is able to receive; and that the limitations in his curriculum should depend only upon the age at which he must leave school; in a word, a common curriculum (up to the age of say, fourteen or fifteen) appears to be due to all children.

We have left behind the feudal notion that intellect is a class prerogative, that intelligence is a matter of inheritance and environment; inheritance, no doubt, means much but everyone has a very mixed inheritance; environment makes for satisfaction or uneasiness, but education is of the spirit and is not to be taken in by the eye or effected by the hand; mind appeals to mind and thought begets thought and that is how we become educated. For this reason we owe it to every child to put him in communication with great minds that he may get at great thoughts; with the minds, that is, of those who have left us great works; and the only vital method of education appears to be that children should read worthy books, many worthy books.

It will be said on the one hand that many schools have their own libraries or the scholars have the free use of a public library and that children do read; and on the other that the literary language of first-rate books offers an impassable barrier to working-men's children. In the first place we all know that desultory reading is delightful and incidentally profitable but is not education whose concern is knowledge. That is, the mind of the desultory reader only rarely makes the act of appropriation which is necessary before the matter we read becomes personal knowledge. We must read in order to know or we do not know by reading.

As for the question of literary form, many circumstances and considerations which it would take too long to describe brought me to perceive that delight in literary form is native to us all until we are 'educated' out of it.

It is difficult to explain how I came to a solution of a puzzling problem,—how to secure attention. Much observation of children, various incidents from one's general reading, the recollection of my own childhood and the consideration of my present habits of mind brought me to the recognition of certain laws of the mind, by working in accordance with which the steady attention of children of any age and any class in society is insured, week-in, week out,—attention, not affected by distracting circumstances. It is not a matter of personal magnetism, for hundreds of teachers of very varying quality, working in home schoolrooms and in Elementary and Secondary Schools on this method (in connection with the Parents' Union School) secure it without effort; neither does it rest upon the 'doctrine of interest'; no doubt the scholars are interested, sometimes delighted; but they are interested in a great variety of matters and their attention does not flag in the 'dull parts.'

It is not easy to sum up in a few short sentences those principles upon which the mind naturally acts and which I have tried to bring to bear upon a school curriculum. The fundamental idea is, that children are persons and are therefore moved by the same springs of conduct as their elders. Among these is the Desire of Knowledge, knowledge-hunger being natural to everybody. History, Geography, the thoughts of other people, roughly, the humanities, are proper for us all, and are the objects of the natural desire of knowledge. So too, are Science, for we all live in the world; and Art, for we all require beauty, and are eager to know how to discriminate; social science, Ethics, for we are aware of the need to learn about the conduct of life; and Religion, for, like those men we heard of at the Front, we all 'want God.'

In the nature of things then the unspoken demand of children is for a wide and very varied curriculum; it is necessary that they should have some knowledge of the wide range of interests proper to them as human beings, and for no reasons of convenience or time limitations may we curtail their proper curriculum.

Perceiving the range of knowledge to which children as persons are entitled the questions are, how shall they be induced to take that knowledge, and what can the children of the people learn in the short time they are at school? We have discovered a working answer to these two conundrums. I say discovered, and not invented, for there is only one way of learning, and the intelligent persons who can talk well on many subjects and the expert in one learn in the one way, that is, they read to know. What I have found out is, that this method is available for every child, whether in the dilatory and desultory home schoolroom or in the large classes of Elementary Schools.

Children no more come into the world without provision for dealing with knowledge than without provision for dealing with food. They bring with them not only that intellectual appetite, the desire of knowledge, but also an enormous, an unlimited power of attention to which the power of retention (memory) seems to be attached, as one digestive process succeeds another, until the final assimilation. "Yes," it will be said, "they are capable of much curiosity and consequent attention but they can only occasionally be beguiled into attending to their lessons." Is not that the fault of the lessons, and must not these be regulated as carefully with regard to the behaviour of mind as the children's meals are with regard to physical considerations? Let us consider this behaviour in a few aspects. The mind concerns itself only with thoughts, imaginations, reasoned arguments; it declines to assimilate the facts unless in combination with its proper pabulum; it, being active, is wearied in the passive attitude of a listener, it is as much bored in the case of a child by the discursive twaddle of the talking teacher as in that of a grown-up by conversational twaddle; it has a natural preference for literary form; given a more or less literary presentation, the curiosity of the mind is enormous and embraces a vast variety of subjects.

I predicate these things of 'the mind' because they seem true of all persons' minds. Having observed these, and some other points in the behaviour of mind, it remained to apply the conclusions to which I had come to a test curriculum for schools and families. Oral teaching was to a great extent ruled out; a large number of books on many subjects were set for reading in morning school-hours; so much work was set that there was only time for a single reading; all reading was tested by a narration of the whole or a given passage, whether orally or in writing. Children working on these lines know months after that which they have read and are remarkable for their power of concentration (attention); they have little trouble with spelling or composition and become well-informed, intelligent persons. (The small Practising School attached to the House of Education—ages of scholars from six to eighteen—affords opportunities for testing the programmes of work sent out term by term and the examinations set at the end of each term. The work in each Form is easily done in the hours of morning-school.)

But, it will be said, reading or hearing various books read, chapter by chapter, and then narrating or writing what has been read or some part of it,—all this is mere memory work. The value of this criticism may be readily tested; will the critic read before turning off his light a leading article from a newspaper, say, or a chapter from Boswell or Jane Austen, or one of Lamb's Essays; then, will he put himself to sleep by narrating silently what he has read. He will not be satisfied with the result but he will find that in the act of narrating every power of his mind comes into play, that points and bearings which he had not observed are brought out; that the whole is visualized and brought into relief in an extraordinary way; in fact, that scene or argument has become a part of his personal experience; he knows, he has assimilated what he has read. This is not memory work. In order to memorise, we repeat over and over a passage or a series of points or names with the aid of such clues as we can invent; we do memorise a string of facts or words, and the new possession serves its purpose for a time, but it is not assimilated; its purpose being served, we know it no more. This is memory work by means of which examinations are passed with credit. I will not try to explain (or understand!) this power to memorise;—it has its subsidiary use in education, no doubt, but it must not be put in the place of the prime agent which is attention.

Long ago, I was in the habit of hearing this axiom quoted by a philosophical old friend: "The mind can know nothing save what it can produce in the form of an answer to a question put to the mind by itself." I have failed to trace the saying to its source, but a conviction of its importance has been growing upon me during the last forty years. It tacitly prohibits questioning from without; (this does not, of course, affect the Socratic use of questioning for purposes of moral conviction); and it is necessary to intellectual certainty, to the act of knowing. For example, to secure a conversation or an incident, we 'go over it in our minds'; that is, the mind puts itself through the process of self-questioning which I have indicated. This is what happens in the narrating of a passage read: each new consecutive incident or statement arrives because the mind asks itself,—"What next?" For this reason it is important that only one reading should be allowed; efforts to memorise weaken the power of attention, the proper activity of the mind; if it is desirable to ask questions in order to emphasize certain points, these should be asked after and not before, or during, the act of narration.

Our more advanced psychologists come to our support here; they, too, predicate "instead of a congerie of faculties, a single subjective activity, attention;" and again, there is "one common factor in all psychics activity, that is attention." (I again quote from the article on Psychology in the Encyclopedia Britannica.) My personal addition is that attention is unfailing, prompt and steady when matter is presented suitable to a child's intellectual requirements, if the presentation be made with the conciseness, directness, and simplicity proper to literature.

Another point should be borne in mind; the intellect requires a moral impulse, and we all stir our minds into action the better if there is an implied 'must' in the background; for children in class the 'must' acts through the certainty that they will be required to narrate or write from what they have read with no opportunity of 'looking 'up,' or other devices of the idle. Children find the act of narrating so pleasurable in itself that urgency on the part of the teacher is seldom necessary.

Here is a complete chain of the educational philosophy I have endeavoured to work out, which has, at least, the merit that it is successful in practice. Some few hints I have, as I have said, adopted and applied, but I hope I have succeeded in methodising the whole and making education what it should be, a system of applied philosophy; I have, however, carefully abstained from the use of philosophical terms.

This is, briefly, how it works:—

A child is a Person with the spiritual requirements and capabilities of a person.

Knowledge 'nourishes' the mind as food nourishes the body.

A child requires knowledge as much as he requires food.

He is furnished with the desire for Knowledge, i.e., Curiosity; with the power to apprehend Knowledge, that is, attention; with powers of mind to deal with Knowledge without aid from without—such as imagination, reflection, judgment; with innate interest in all Knowledge that he needs as a human being; with power to retain and communicate such Knowledge; and to assimilate all that is necessary to him.

He requires that in most cases Knowledge be communicated to him in literary form; and reproduces such Knowledge touched by his own personality; thus his reproduction becomes original.

The natural provision for the appropriation and assimilation of Knowledge is adequate and no stimulus is required; but some moral control is necessary to secure the act of attention; a child receives this in the certainty that he will be required to recount what he has read. Children have a right to the best we possess; therefore their lesson books should be, as far as possible, our best books.

They weary of talk, and questions bore them, so that they should be allowed to use their books for themselves; they will ask for such help as they wish for.

They require a great variety of knowledge,—about religion, the humanities, science, art; therefore, they should have a wide curriculum, with a definite amount of reading set for each short period of study.

The teacher affords direction, sympathy in studies, a vivifying word here and there, help in the making of experiments, etc., as well as the usual teaching in languages, experimental science and mathematics.

Pursued under these conditions, "Studies serve for delight," and the consciousness of daily progress is exhilarating to both teacher and children.

The reader will say with truth,—"I knew all this before and have always acted more or less on these principles"; and I can only point to the unusual results we obtain through adhering not 'more or less,' but strictly to the principles and practices I have indicated. I suppose the difficulties are of the sort that Lister had to contend with; every surgeon knew that his instruments and appurtenances should be kept clean, but the saving of millions of lives has resulted from the adoption of the great surgeon's antiseptic treatment; that is from the substitution of exact principles scrupulously applied for the rather casual 'more or less' methods of earlier days.

Whether the way I have sketched out is the right and the only way remains to be tested still more widely than in the thousands of cases in which it has been successful; but assuredly education is slack and uncertain for the lack of sound principles exactly applied. The moment has come for a decision; we have placed our faith in 'civilisation,' have been proud of our progress; and of the pangs that the War has brought us, perhaps none is keener than that caused by the utter breakdown of the civilisation which we have held to be synonymous with education. We know better now, and are thrown back on our healthy human instincts and the Divine sanctions. The educable part of a person is his mind. The training of the senses and muscles is, strictly speaking, training and not education. The mind, like the body, requires quantity, variety and regularity in the sustenance offered to it. Like the body, the mind has its appetite, the desire for knowledge. Again, like the body, the mind is able to receive and assimilate by its powers of attention and reflection. Like the body, again, the mind rejects insipid, dry, and unsavoury food, that is to say, its pabulum should be presented in a literary form. The mind is restricted to pabulum of one kind: it is nourished upon ideas and absorbs facts only as these are connected with the living ideas upon which they hang. Children educated upon some such lines as these respond in a surprising way, developing capacity, character, countenance, initiative and a sense of responsibility. They are, in fact, even as children, good and thoughtful citizens.

I have in this volume attempted to show the principles and methods upon which education of this sort is being successfully carried out, and have added chapters which illustrate the history of a movement the aim of which is, in the phrase of Comenius,—"All knowledge for all men." As well as these I have been permitted to use the criticisms of various teachers and Directors of education and others upon the practical working of the scheme.

It is a matter of rejoicing that the way is open to give to all classes a basis of common thought and common knowledge, including a common store of literary and historic allusions, a possession which has a curious power of cementing bodies of men, and, in the next place, it is an enormous gain that we are within sight of giving to the working-classes, notwithstanding their limited opportunities, that stability of mind and magnanimity of character which are the proper outcome and the unfailing test of *a liberal education*.

I shall confine myself in this volume to the amplification and illustration of some of the points I have endeavoured to make in this introductory statement.

Chapter 1 Self-Education

The title of this chapter may awaken some undeserved sympathy; gratifying visions of rhythmic movements, independent action, self-expression in various interesting ways, occur to the mind—for surely these things constitute 'self-education'? Most of these modern panacea are desirable and by no means to be neglected; limbs trained to grace and agility, a hand, to dexterity and precision, an eye made to see and an ear to hear, a voice taught to interpret,—we know to-day that all these possibilities of joy in living should be open to every child, and we look forward even too hopefully to the manner of citizen who shall be the outcome of our educational zeal.

Now, although we, of the Parents' Union, have initiated some of these educational outworks and have gladly and gratefully adopted others, yet is our point of view different; we are profoundly sceptical as to the effect of all or any of these activities upon character and conduct. A person is not built up from without but within, that is, he is living, and all external educational appliances and activities which are intended to mould his character are decorative and not vital.

This sounds like a stale truism; but, let us consider a few corollaries of the notion that 'a child is a person,' and that a person is, primarily, living. Now no external application is capable of nourishing life or promoting growth; baths of wine, wrappings of velvet have no effect upon physical life except as they may hinder it; life is sustained on that which is taken in by the organism, not by that which is applied from without.

Perhaps the only allowable analogy with the human mind is the animal body, especially the human body, for it is that which we know most about; the well-worn plant and garden analogy is misleading, especially as regards that tiresome busybody, the gardener, who will direct the inclination of every twig, the position of every leaf; but, even then apart from the gardener, the child-garden is an intolerable idea as failing to recognize the essential property of a child, his personality, a property all but absent in a plant. Now, let us consider for a moment the parallel behaviour of body and mind. The body lives by air, grows on food, demands rest, flourishes on a diet wisely various. So, of the mind,—(by which I mean the entire spiritual nature, all that which is not body),—it breathes in air, calls for both activity and rest and flourishes on a wisely varied dietary.

We go round the house and round the house, but rarely go into the House of Mind; we offer mental gymnastics, but these do not take the place of food, and of that we serve the most meagre rations, no more than that bean a day! Diet for the body is abundantly considered, but no one pauses to say, "I wonder does the mind need food, too, and regular meals, and what is its proper diet?"

I have asked myself this question and have laboured for fifty years to find the answer, and am anxious to impart what I think I know, but the answer cannot be given in the form of 'Do' this and that, but rather as an invitation to 'Consider' this and that; action follows when we have thought duly.

The life of the mind is sustained upon ideas; there is no intellectual vitality in the mind to which ideas are not presented several times, say, every day. But 'surely, surely,' as 'Mrs. Proudie' would say, scientific experiments, natural beauty, nature study, rhythmic movements, sensory exercises, are all fertile in ideas? Quite commonly, they are so, as regards ideas of invention and discovery; and even in ideas of art; but for the moment it may be well to consider the ideas that influence life, that is, character and conduct; these, would seem, pass directly from mind to mind, and are neither helped nor hindered by educational outworks. Every child gets many of these ideas by word of mouth, by way of family traditions, proverbial philosophy,—in fact, by what we might call a kind of oral literature. But, when we compare the mind with the body, we perceive that three 'square' meals a day are generally necessary to health, and that a casual diet of ideas is poor and meagre. Our schools turn out a good many clever young persons, wanting in nothing but initiative, the power of reflection and the sort of moral imagination that enables you to 'put yourself in his place.' These qualities flourish upon a proper diet; and this is not afforded by the ordinary school book, or, in sufficient quantity by the ordinary lesson. I should like to emphasize quantity, which is as important for the mind as the body; both require their 'square meals.'

It is no easy matter to give its proper sustenance to the mind; hard things are said of children, that they have 'no brains,' 'a low order of intellect,' and so on; many of us are able to vouch for the fine intelligence by children who are fed with the proper mind-stuff; but teachers do not usually take the trouble to find out what this is. We come dangerously near to what Plato condemns as "that lie of the soul," that corruption of the highest truth, of which Protagoras is guilty in the saying that, "Knowledge is sensation." What else are we saying when we run after educational methods which are purely sensory? Knowledge is not sensation, nor is it to be derived through sensation; we feed upon the thoughts of other minds; and thought applied to thought generates thought and we become more thoughtful. No one need invite us to reason, compare, imagine; the mind, like the body, digests its proper food, and it must have the labour of digestion or it ceases to function.

But the children ask for bread and we give them a stone; we give information about objects and events which mind does not attempt to digest but casts out bodily (upon an examination paper?). But let information hang upon a principle, be inspired by an idea, and it is taken with avidity and used in making whatsoever in the spiritual nature stands for tissue in the physical.

"Education," said Lord Haldane, some time ago, "is a matter of the spirit,"—no wiser word has been said on the subject, and yet we persist in applying education from without as a bodily activity or emollient. We begin to see light. No one knoweth the things of a man but the spirit of a man which is in him; therefore, there is no education but self-education, and as soon as a young child begins his education he does so as a student. Our business is to give him mind-stuff, and both quality and quantity are essential. Naturally, each of us possesses this mind-stuff only in limited measure, but we know where to procure it; for the best thought the world possesses is stored in books; we must open books to children, the best books; our own concern is abundant provision and orderly serving.

I am jealous for the children; every modern educational movement tends to belittle them intellectually; and none more so than a late ingenious attempt to feed normal children with the pap-meat which may be good for the mentally sick: but, "To all wildly popular things comes suddenly and inexorably death, without hope of resurrection." If Mr. Bernard Shaw is right, I need not discuss a certain popular form of 'New Education.' It has been ably said that education should profit by the divorce which is now in progress from psychology on the one hand and sociology on the other; but what if education should use her recovered liberty make a monstrous alliance with pathology?

Various considerations urge upon me a rather distasteful task. It is time I showed my hand and gave some account of work, the principles and practices of which should, I think, be of general use. Like those lepers who feasted at the gates of a famished city, I begin to take shame to myself! I have attempted to unfold (in various volumes) a system of educational theory which seems to me able to meet any rational demand, even that severest criterion set up by Plato; it is able to "run the gauntlet of objections, and is ready to disprove them, not by appeals to opinion, but to absolute truth." Some of it is new, much of it is old. Like the quality of mercy, it is not strained; certainly it is twice blessed, it blesses him that gives and him that takes, and a sort of radiancy of look distinguishes both scholar and teacher engaged in this manner of education; but there are no startling results to challenge attention.

Professor Bompas Smith remarked in an inaugural address at the University of Manchester that,—"If we can guide our practice by the light of a comprehensive theory we shall widen our experience by attempting tasks which would not otherwise have occurred to us." It is possible to offer the light of such a comprehensive theory, and the result is precisely what the Professor indicates,—a large number of teachers attempt tasks which would not otherwise have occurred to them. One discovers a thing because it is there, and no sane person takes credit to himself for such discovery. On the contrary, he recognizes with King Arthur,—"These jewels, whereupon I chanced Divinely, are for public use." For many years we have had access to a sort of Aladdin's cave which I long to throw open 'for public use.'

Let me try to indicate some of the advantages of the theory I am urging—It fits all ages, even the seven ages of man! It satisfies brilliant children and discovers intelligence in the dull. It secures attention, interest, concentration, without effort on the part of teacher or taught.

Children, I think, all children, so taught express themselves in forcible and fluent English and use a copious vocabulary. An unusual degree of nervous stability is attained; also, intellectual occupation seems to make for chastity in thought and life. Parents become interested in the schoolroom work, and find their children 'delightful companions.' Children shew delight in books (other than story books) and manifest a genuine love of knowledge. Teachers are relieved from much of the labour of corrections. Children taught according to this method do exceptionally well at any school. It is unnecessary to stimulate these young scholars by marks, prizes, etc.

After all, it is not a quack medicine I am writing about, though the reader might think so, and there is no IS. I 1/2d. a bottle in question!

Over thirty years ago I published a volume about the home education of children and people wrote asking how those counsels of perfection could be carried out with the aid of the private governess as she then existed; it occurred to me that a series of curricula might be devised embodying sound principles and securing that children should be in a position of less dependence on their teacher than they then were; in other words, that their education should be largely self-education. A sort of correspondence school was set up, the motto of which,—"I am, I can, I ought, I will," has had much effect in throwing children upon the possibilities, capabilities, duties and determining power belonging to them as persons.

"Children are born persons," is the first article of the educational credo in question. The response made by children (ranging in age from six to eighteen) astonished me; though they only shewed the power of attention, the avidity for knowledge, the clearness of thought, the nice discrimination in books, and the ability to deal with many subjects, for which I had given them credit in advance. I need not repeat what I have urged elsewhere on the subject of 'Knowledge' and will only add that anyone may apply a test; let him read to a child of any age from six to ten an account of an incident, graphically and tersely told, and the child will relate what he has heard point by point, though not word for word, and will add delightful original touches; what is more, he will relate the passage months later because he has visualised the scene and appropriated that bit of knowledge. A rhetorical passage, written in 'journalese,' makes no impression on him; if a passage be read more than once, he may become letter-perfect, but the spirit, the individuality has gone out of the exercise. An older boy or girl will read one of Bacon's Essays, say, or a passage from De Quincey, and will write or tell it forcibly and with some style, either at the moment or months later. We know how Fox recited a whole pamphlet of Burke's at a College supper though he had probably read it no more than once. Here on the very surface is the key to that attention, interest, literary style, wide vocabulary, love of books and readiness in speaking, which we all feel should belong to an education that is only begun at school and continued throughout life; these are the things that we all desire, and how to obtain them is some part of the open secret I am labouring to disclose 'for public use.'

I am anxious to bring a quite successful educational experiment before the public at a moment when we are told on authority that "Education must be . . . an appeal to the spirit if it is to be made interesting." Here is Education which is as interesting and fascinating as a fine art to parents, children and teachers.

During the last thirty years thousands of children educated on these lines have grown up in love with Knowledge and manifesting a 'right judgment in all things' so far as a pretty wide curriculum gives them data.

I would have children taught to read before they learn the mechanical arts of reading and writing; and they learn delightfully; they give perfect attention to paragraph or page read to them and are able to relate the matter point by point, in their own words; but they demand classical English and cannot learn to read in this sense upon anything less. They begin their 'schooling' in 'letters' at six, and begin at the same time to learn mechanical reading and writing. A child does not lose by spending a couple of years in acquiring these because he is meanwhile 'reading' the Bible, history, geography, tales, with close attention and a remarkable power of reproduction, or rather, of translation into his own language; he is acquiring a copious vocabulary and the habit of consecutive speech. In a word, he is an educated child from the first, and his power of dealing with books, with several books in the course of a morning's 'school,' increases with his age.

But children are not all alike; there is as much difference between them as between men or women; two or three months ago, a small boy, not quite six, came to school (by post); and his record was that he could read anything in five languages, and was now teaching himself the Greek characters, could find his way about the Continental Bradshaw, and was a chubby, vigorous little person. All this the boy brings with him when he comes to school; he is exceptional, of course, just as a man with such accomplishments is exceptional; I believe that all children bring with them much capacity which is not recognized by their teachers, chiefly intellectual capacity, (always in advance of motor power), which we are apt to drown in deluges of explanation or dissipate in futile labours in which there is no advance.

People are naturally divided into those who read and think and those who do not read or think; and the business of schools is to see that all their scholars shall belong to the former class; it is worth while to remember that thinking is inseparable from reading which is concerned with the content of a passage and not merely with the printed matter.

The children I am speaking of are much occupied with things as well as with books, because 'Education is the Science of Relations,' is the principle which regulates their curriculum; that is, a child goes to school with many aptitudes which he should put into effect. So, he learns a good deal of science, because children have no difficulty in understanding principles, though technical details baffle them. He practises various handicrafts that he may know the feel of wood, clay, leather, and the joy of handling tools, that is, that he may establish a due relation with materials. But, always, it is the book, the knowledge, the clay, the bird or blossom, he thinks of, not his own place or his own progress.

I am afraid that some knowledge of the theory we advance is necessary to the open-minded teacher who would give our practices a trial, because every detail of schoolroom work is the outcome of certain principles. For instance, it would be quite easy, without much thought to experiment with our use of books; but in education, as in religion, it is the motive that counts, and the boy who reads his lesson for a 'good mark' becomes word-perfect, but does not know. But these principles are obvious and simple enough, and, when we consider that at present education is chaotic for want of a unifying theory, and that there happens to be no other comprehensive theory in the field which is in line with modern thought and fits every occasion, might it not be well to try one which is immediately practicable and always pleasant and has proved itself by producing many capable, serviceable, dutiful men and women of sound judgment and willing mind?

In urging a method of self-education for children in lieu of the vicarious education which prevails, I should like to dwell on the enormous relief to teachers, a self-sacrificing and greatly overburdened class; the difference is just that between driving a horse that is light and a horse that is heavy in hand; the former covers the ground of his own gay will and the driver goes merrily. The teacher who allows his scholars the freedom of the city of books is at liberty to be their guide, philosopher and friend; and is no longer the mere instrument of forcible intellectual feeding.

Chapter 2 Children are Born Persons

1. The Mind Of A Child

"No sooner doth the truth . . . . come into the soul's sight, but the soul knows her to be her first and old acquaintance."

"The consequence of truth is great, therefore the judgment of it must not be negligent."

It should not surprise the reader that a chapter, designed to set forth a startling truth, should open with the weighty words of an old Divine (Whichcote). But truths get flat and wonders stale upon us. We do not care much about the starry firmament, the budding trees, the cunning architecture of the birds; and to all except young parents and young brothers and sisters a baby is no longer a marvel. The completeness of the new baby brother is what children admire most, his toes and his fingers, his ears and all the small perfections of him. His guardians have some understanding of the baby; they know that his chief business is to grow and they feed him with food convenient for him. If they are wise they give free play to all the wrigglings and stretchings which give power to his feeble muscles. His parents know what he will come to, and feel that here is a new chance for the world. In the meantime, he needs food, sleep and shelter and a great deal of love. So much we all know. But is the baby more than a 'huge oyster'? That is the problem before us and hitherto educators have been inclined to answer it in the negative. Their notion is that by means of a pull here, a push there, a compression elsewhere a person is at last turned out according to the pattern the educator has in his mind.

The other view is that the beautiful infant frame is but the setting of a jewel of such astonishing worth that, put the whole world in one scale and this jewel in the other, and the scale which holds the world flies up outbalanced. A poet looks back on the glimmering haze of his own infancy and this is the sort of thing he sees,—

"I was entertained like an angel with the works of God in their splendour and glory . . . Is it not strange that an infant should be heir of the whole world and see those mysteries which the books of the learned never unfold? . . . The corn was orient and immortal wheat which never should be reaped nor was ever sown. I thought it had stood from everlasting to everlasting. The dust and stones of the street were as precious gold. The green trees transported and ravished me. Their sweetness and unusual beauty made my heart to leap . . . Boys and girls tumbling in the streets were moving jewels. I knew not that they were born or should die . . . The streets were mine, the people were mine, their clothes and gold and silver were mine as much as their sparkling eyes, fair skins and ruddy faces. The skies were mine and so were the sun and moon and stars, and all the world was mine and I the only spectator and enjoyer of it."

It takes a poet like Traherne to retain and produce such vivid memories, though perhaps we can all recall the sense that we were spectators at the show of life, and we can recollect a sunny time before we were able to speak or tell what we knew. Punch amused us at one time with a baby's views of his nurse and his surroundings and especially of the unwarranted pulls and pushes to which he was subject; but probably an infant is no critic. His business is to perceive and receive and these he does day in and day out.

We have an idea that poets say more than they know, express more than they see, and that their version of life must be taken cum grano, but perhaps the fact is that no labour of the mind enables them to catch and put into words the full realities of which they are cognisant, and therefore we may take Wordsworth, Coleridge, Vaughan and the rest as witnesses who only hint at the glory which might be revealed. We are not poets and are disposed to discount the sayings of the poets, but the most prosaic of us comes across evidence of mind in children, and of mind astonishingly alert. Let us consider, in the first two years of life they manage to get through more intellectual effort than any following two years can show. Supposing that much-discussed Martian were at last able to make his way to our planet, think of how much he must learn before he could accommodate himself to our conditions! Our notions of hard and soft, wet and dry, hot and cold, stable and unstable, far and near, would be as foreign to him as they are to an infant who holds out his pinafore for the moon. We do not know what the Martian means of locomotion are but we can realise that to run and jump and climb stairs, even to sit and stand at will must require fully as much reasoned endeavour as it takes in after years to accomplish skating, dancing, skiing, fencing, whatever athletic exercises people spend years in perfecting; and all these the infant accomplishes in his first two years. He learns the properties of matter, knows colours and has first notions of size, solid, liquid; has learned in his third year to articulate with surprising clearness. What is more, he has learned a language, two languages, if he has had the opportunity, and the writer has known of three languages being mastered by a child of three, and one of them was Arabic; mastered, that is, so far that a child can say all that he needs to say in any one of the three—the sort of mastery most of us wish for when we are travelling in foreign countries.

Lady Mary Wortley Montagu tells us that in her time the little children of Constantinople prattled in five tongues with a good knowledge of each. If we have not proved that a child is born a person with a mind as complete and as beautiful as his beautiful little body, we can at least show that he always has all the mind he requires for his occasions; that is, that his mind is the instrument of his education and that his education does not produce his mind.

Who shall measure the range of a child's thoughts? His continual questions about God, his speculations about 'Jesus,' are they no more than idle curiosity, or are they symptoms of a God-hunger with which we are all born, and is a child able to comprehend as much of the infinite and the unseen as are his self-complacent elders? Is he 'cabined, cribbed, confined,' in our ways and does the fairy tale afford a joyful escape to regions where all things are possible? We are told that children have no imagination, that they must needs see and touch, taste and handle, in order to know. While a child's age is still counted by months, he devotes himself to learning the properties of things by touching, pulling, tearing, throwing, tasting, but as months pass into years a coup d'oeil suffices for all but new things of complicated structure. Life is a continual progress to a child. He does not go over old things in old ways; his joy is to go on. The immensity of his powers brings its own terrors. Let me again quote Traherne,—

"Another time in a lowering and sad evening being alone in the field when all things were dead and quiet a certain wanton horror fell upon me beyond imagination. The unprofitableness and silence of the place dissatisfied me: its wildness terrified me. From the utmost ends of the earth fear surrounded me . . . I was a weak and little child and had forgotten there was a man alive on the earth. Yet also something of hope and expectation comforted me from every border."

Traherne never loses the lessons that come to him and he goes on,—

"This taught me that I was concerned in all the world . . . that the beauties of the earth were made to entertain me . . . that the presence of cities, temples and kingdoms, ought to sustain me and that to be alone in the world was to be desolate and miserable."

Reason is present in the infant as truly as imagination. As soon as he can speak he lets us know that he has pondered the 'cause why' of things and perplexes us with a thousand questions. His 'why?' is ceaseless. Nor are his reasonings always disinterested. How soon the little urchin learns to manage his nurse or mother, to calculate her moods and play upon her feelings! It is in him to be a little tyrant; "he has a will of his own," says his nurse, but she is mistaken in supposing that his stormy manifestations of greed, wilfulness, temper, are signs of will. It is when the little boy is able to stop all these and restrain himself with quivering lip that his will comes into play; for he has a conscience too. Before he begins to toddle he knows the difference between right and wrong; even a baby in arms will blush at the 'naughty baby!' of his nurse; and that strong will of his acts in proportion as he learns the difficult art of obedience; for no one can make a child obey unless he wills to do so, and we all know how small a rebel may make confusion in house or schoolroom.

2. The Mind Of A School-Child

But we must leave the quite young child, fascinating as he is, and take him up again when he is ready for lessons. I have made some attempt elsewhere to show what his parents and teachers owe to him in those years in which he is engaged in self-education, taking his lessons from everything he sees and hears, and strengthen ing his powers by everything he does. Here, in a volume which is chiefly concerned with education in the sense of schooling, I am anxious to bring before teachers the fact that a child comes into their hands with a mind of amazing potentialities: he has a brain too, no doubt, the organ and instrument of that same mind, as a piano is not music but the instrument of music. Probably we need not concern ourselves about the brain which is subject to the same conditions as the rest of the material body, is fed with the body's food, rests, as the body rests, requires fresh air and wholesome exercise to keep it in health, but depends upon the mind for its proper activities.

The world has concerned itself of late so much with psychology, whose province is what has been called 'the unconscious mind,' a region under the sway of nerves and blood (which it is best perhaps to let alone) that in our educational efforts we tend to ignore the mind and address ourselves to this region of symptoms. Now mind, being spiritual, knows no fatigue; brain, too, duly nourished with the food proper for the body, allowed due conditions of fresh air and rest, should not know fatigue; given these two conditions, we have a glorious field of educational possibilities; but it rests with us to evolve a theory and practice which afford due recognition to mind. An authoritative saying which we are apt to associate with the religious life only is equally applicable to education. That which is born of the flesh, is flesh, we are told; but we have forgotten this great principle in our efforts at schooling children. We give them a 'play way' and play is altogether necessary and desirable but is not the avenue which leads to mind. We give them a fitting environment, which is again altogether desirable and, again, is not the way to mind. We teach them beautiful motion and we do well, for the body too must have its education; but we are not safe if we take these by-paths as approaches to mind. It is still true that that which is born of the spirit, is spirit. The way to mind is a quite direct way. Mind must come into contact with mind through the medium of ideas. "What is mind?" says the old conundrum, and the answer still is "No matter." It is necessary for us who teach to realize that things material have little effect upon mind, because there are still among us schools in which the work is altogether material and technical, whether the teaching is given by means of bars of wood or more scientific apparatus. The mistress of an Elementary School writes,—"The father of one of my girls said to me yesterday, 'You have given me some work to do. E. has let me have no rest until I promised to set up my microscope and get pond water to look for monads and other wonders.'" Here we have the right order. That which was born of the spirit, the idea, came first and demanded to confirm and illustrate. "How can these things be?" we ask, and the answer is not evident.

Education, like faith, is the evidence of things not seen. We must begin with the notion that the business of the body is to grow; and it grows upon food, which food is composed of living cells, each a perfect life in itself. In like manner, though all analogies are misleading and inadequate, the only fit sustenance for the mind is ideas, and an idea too, like the single cell of cellular tissue, appears to go through the stages and functions of a life. We receive it with appetite and some stir of interest. It appears to feed in a curious way. We hear of a new patent cure for the mind or the body, of the new thought of some poet, the new notion of a school of painters; we take in, accept, the idea and for days after every book we read, every person we talk with brings food to the newly entertained notion. 'Not proven,' will be the verdict of the casual reader; but if he watch the behaviour of his own mind towards any of the ideas 'in the air,' he will find that some such process as I have described takes place; and this process must be considered carefully in the education of children. We may not take things casually as we have done. Our business is to give children the great ideas of life, of religion, history, science; but it is the ideas we must give, clothed upon with facts as they occur, and must leave the child to deal with these as he chooses.

This is how he deals with Geography, for example:—

"When I heard of any new kingdom beyond the seas the light and glory of it entered into me. It rose up within me and I was enlarged by the whole. I entered into it, I saw its commodities, springs, meadows, inhabitants and became possessor of that new room as if it had been prepared for me so much was I magnified and delighted in it. When the Bible was read my spirit was present in other ages. I saw the light and splendour of them, the land of Canaan, the Israelites entering into it, the ancient glory of the Amorites, their peace and riches, their cities, houses, vines and fig trees . . . I saw and felt all in such a lively manner as if there had been no other way to those places but in spirit only. Without changing place in myself I could behold and enjoy all those. Anything when it was proposed though it was a thousand years ago being always present before me."

I venture again to quote Traherne because I know of no writer who retains so clear a memory of his infancy; but Goethe gives as full and convincing an account of his experience of the Bible; I say 'experience' advisedly, for the word denotes the process by which children get to know. They experience all the things they hear and read of; these enter into them and are their life; and thus it is that ideas feed the mind in the most literal sense of the word 'feed.'

Do our Geography lessons take the children there? Do, they experience, live in, our story of the call of Abraham?—or of the healing of the blind man on the way to Jericho? If they do not, it is not for lack of earnestness and intention on the part of the teacher; his error is rather want of confidence in children. He has not formed a just measure of a child's mind and bores his scholars with much talk about matters which they are able to understand for themselves much better than he does. How many teachers know that children require no pictures excepting the pictures of great artists, which have quite another function than that of illustration? They see for themselves in their own minds a far more glorious, and indeed more accurate, presentation than we can afford in our miserable daubs. They read between the lines and put in all the author has left out. A child of nine, who had been reading Lang's Tales Of Troy and Greece, drew Ulysses on the Isle of Calypso cutting down trees to make a raft; a child of ten, revelling in A Midsummer Night's Dream, drew that Indian Princess bringing her lovely boy to Titania. We others are content to know that Ulysses built a raft, that the boy was the child of an Indian Princess. This is how any child's mind works, and our concern is not to starve these fertile intelligences. They must have food in great abundance and variety. They know what to do with it well enough and we need not disturb ourselves to provide for the separate exercise of each so-called 'faculty'; for the mind is one and works all together; reason, imagination, reflection, judgment, what you please, are like 'all hands' summoned by the 'heave-ho!' of the boatswain. All swarm on deck for the lading of cargo, that rich and odorous cargo of ideas which the fair vessel of a child's mind is waiting to receive. Do we wish every child in a class to say,—or, if he does not say, to feel,—"I was enlarged wonderfully" by a Geography lesson? Let him see the place with the eyes of those who have seen or conceived it; your barographs, thermographs, contour lines, relief models, sections, profiles and the like, will not do it. A map of the world must be a panorama to a child of pictures so entrancing that he would rather ponder them than go out to play; and nothing is more easy than to give him this joie de vivre. Let him see the world as we ourselves choose to see it when we travel; its cities and peoples, its mountains and rivers, and he will go away from his lesson with the piece of the world he has read about, be it county or country, sea or shore, as that of "a new room prepared for him, so much will he be magnified and delighted in it." All the world is in truth the child's possession, prepared for him, and if we keep him out of his rights by our technical, commercial, even historical, geography, any sort of geography, in fact, made to illustrate our theories, we are guilty of fraudulent practices. What he wants is the world and every bit, piece by piece, each bit a key to the rest. He reads of the Bore of the Severn and is on speaking terms with a 'Bore' wherever it occurs. He need not see a mountain to know a mountain. He sees all that is described to him with a vividness of which we know nothing just as if there had been "no other way to those places but in spirit only." Who can take the measure of a child? The Genie of the Arabian tale is nothing to him. He, too, may be let out of his bottle and fill the world. But woe to us if we keep him corked up.

Enough, that the children have minds, and every man's mind is his means of living; but it is a great deal more. Working men will have leisure in the future and how this leisure is to be employed is a question much discussed. Now, no one can employ leisure fitly whose mind is not brought into active play every day; the small affairs of a man's own life supply no intellectual food and but small and monotonous intellectual exercise. Science, history, philosophy, literature, must no longer be the luxuries of the 'educated' classes; all classes must be educated and sit down to these things of the mind as they do to their daily bread. History must afford its pageants, science its wonders, literature its intimacies, philosophy its speculations, religion its assurances to every man, and his education must have prepared him for wanderings in these realms of gold.

How do we prepare a child, again, to use the aesthetic sense with which he appears to come provided? His education should furnish him with whole galleries of mental pictures, pictures by great artists old and new;—Israels' Pancake Woman, his Children by the Sea; Millet's Feeding the Birds, First Steps, Angelus; Rembrandt's Night Watch, The Supper at Emmaus; Velasquez's Surrender of Breda,—in fact, every child should leave school with at least a couple of hundred pictures by great masters hanging permanently in the halls of his imagination, to say nothing of great buildings, sculpture, beauty of form and colour in things he see. Perhaps we might secure at least a hundred lovely landscapes too,—sunsets, cloudscapes, starlight nights. At any rate he should go forth well furnished because imagination has the property of magical expansion, the more it holds the more it will hold.

It is not only a child's intellect but his heart that comes to us thoroughly furnished. Can any of us love like a little child? Father and mother, sisters and brothers, neighbours and friends, "our" cat and "our" dog, the wretchedest old stump of a broken toy, all come in for his lavish tenderness. How generous and grateful he is, how kind and simple, how pitiful and how full of benevolence in the strict sense of goodwill, how loyal and humble, how fair and just! His conscience is on the alert. Is a tale true? Is a person good?—these are the important questions. His conscience chides him when he is naughty, and by degrees as he is trained, his will comes to his aid and he learns to order his life. He is taught to say his prayers, and we elders hardly realize how real his prayers are to a child.

3. Motives For Learning

Now place a teacher before a class of persons the beauty and immensity of each one of whom I have tried to indicate and he will say, "What have I to offer them?" His dull routine lessons crumble into the dust they are when he faces children as they are. He cannot go on offering them his stale commonplaces; he feels that he may not bore them; that he may not prick the minds he has dulled by unworthy motives of greed or emulation; he would not invite a parcel of children to a Timon feast of smoke and lukewarm water. He knows that children's minds hunger at regular intervals as do their bodies; that they hunger for knowledge, not for information, and that his own poor stock of knowledge is not enough, his own desultory talk has not substance enough; that his irrelevant remarks interrupt a child's train of thought; that, in a word, he is not sufficient for these things.

On the other hand, the children, the children of the slums especially, have no vocabulary to speak of, no background of thought derived from a cultured environment. They are like goodly pitchers, capable of holding much but with necks so narrow that only the thinnest stream can trickle in. So we have thought hitherto, and our teaching has been diluted to dishwater and the pitchers have gone empty away.

But we have changed all that. Just as in the War the magnanimous, patriotic citizen was manifested in every man so in our schools every child has been discovered to be a person of infinite possibilities. I say every child, for so-called 'backward' children are no exception. I shall venture to bring before the reader some experiences of the Parents' Union School as being ground with which I am familiar. Examination papers representing tens of thousands of children working in Elementary Schools, Secondary Schools and home schoolrooms have just passed under my eye. How the children have revelled in knowledge! and how good and interesting all their answers are! How well they spell on the whole and how well they write! We do not need the testimony of their teachers that the work of the term has been joyous; the verve with which the children tell what they know proves the fact. Every one of these children knows that there are hundreds of pleasant places for the mind to roam in. They are good and happy because some little care has been taken to know what they are and what they require; a care very amply rewarded by results which alter the whole outlook on education. In our Training College, the students are not taught how to stimulate attention, how to keep order, how to give marks, how to punish or even how to reward, how to manage a large class or a small school with children in different classes. All these things come by nature in a school where the teachers know something of the capacities and requirements of children. To hear children of the slums 'telling' King Lear or Woodstock, by the hour if you will let them, or describing with minutest details Van Eyck's Adoration of the Lamb or Botticelli's Spring, is a surprise, a revelation. We take off our shoes from off our feet; we 'did not know it was in them,' whether we be their parents, their teachers or mere lookers-on. And with some feeling of awe upon us we shall be the better prepared to consider how and upon what children should be educated. I will only add that I make no claims for them which cannot be justified by hundreds, thousands, of instances within our experience.

Chapter 3 The Good and Evil Nature of a Child

Children are not born bad but with possibilities for good and for evil.

1. Well-Being of Body

A well-known educationalist has brought heavy charges against us all on the score that we bring up children as 'children of wrath.' He probably exaggerates the effect of any such teaching, and the 'little angel' theory is fully as mischievous. The fact seems to be that children are like ourselves, not because they have become so, but because they are born so; that is, with tendencies, dispositions, towards good and towards evil, and also with a curious intuitive knowledge as to which is good and which is evil. Here we have the work of education indicated. There are good and evil tendencies in body and mind, heart and soul; and the hope set before us is that we can foster the good so as to attenuate the evil; that is, on condition that we put Education in her true place as the handmaid of Religion. The community, the nation, the race, are now taking their due place in our religious thought. We are no longer solely occupied in what an Irish woman called 'saving yer dirty sowl.' Our religion is becoming more magnanimous and more responsible and it is time that a like change should take place in our educational thought.

We find ourselves in open places breathing fresher air when we consider, not the education of an individual child or of a social class or even of a given country, but of the race, of the human nature common to every class and country, every individual child. The prospect is exhilarating and the recognition of the potentialities in any child should bring about such an educational renaissance as may send our weary old world rejoicing on its way.

Physicians and physiologists tell us that new-born children start fair. A child is not born with tuberculosis, for example, if with a tendency which it is our business to counteract. In the same way all possibilities for good are contained in his moral and intellectual outfit, hindered it may be by a corresponding tendency to evil for every such potentiality. We begin to see our way. It is our business to know of what parts and passions a child is made up, to discern the dangers that present themselves, and still more the possibilities of free-going in delightful paths. However disappointing, even forbidding, the failings of a child, we may be quite sure that in every case the opposite tendency is there and we must bring the wit to give it play.

Parents have this sort of mother-wit more commonly than we outsiders, teachers and the like. Of course, we know of the mothers and fathers who can't do anything with Tom and hope the schoolmaster will lick him into shape. But how often on the other hand are we surprised to see how much more of persons Bob and

Polly are in their own homes than at school! Perhaps this is because parents know their children better than do others and for that reason believe in them more; for our faith in the divine and the human keeps pace with our knowledge. For this reason it behoves us teachers to get a bird's eye view of the human nature which is present in every child. Everybody knows that hunger, thirst, rest, chastity are those natural endowments of the body by means of which it grows and functions; but in every child there are tendencies to greediness, restlessness, sloth, impurity, any one of which by allowance may ruin the child and the man that he will be.

Again, our old friends, the five senses, require direction and practice. Smell, especially, might be made a source of delicate pleasure by the habit of discriminating the good smells of field and garden, flower and fruit, for their own sakes, not as ministering to taste, which, unduly pampered, becomes a man's master. But there is little that is new to be learned about the body and those various body-servants with which it is equipped. Education already does her part in training the muscles, cultivating the senses, ordering the nerves, of all children, rich and poor; for in these days we perceive that the development which is due to one child is due to all. If we make a mistake in regard to physical education it is perhaps in the matter of ordering the nerves of a child. We do not consider enough that the nourishment, rest, fresh air and natural exercise, proper for the body as a whole, meet the requirements of the nervous system and that the undue nervous tension which a small child suffers in carrying a cup of tea, an older boy or girl in cramming for an examination, may be the cause later of a distressing nervous breakdown. We are becoming a nervous, overstrained nation and though golf and cricket may do something for us, a watchful education, alert to arrest every symptom of nervous over-pressure, would do much to secure for every child a fine physique and a high degree of staying power.

A snare which attends the really brilliant teacher is the exhausting effect upon children of an overpowering personality. They are such ardent and responsive little souls that the teacher who gives them nods and becks and wreathed smiles may play the Pied Piper with them. But he or she should beware. The undue play of the personality of the teacher is likely to suppress and subdue that of his scholars; and, not only so, children are so eager to live up to the demands made upon them that they may be brought to a state of continual nervous over-pressure under the influence of a 'charming personality.' This sort of subjection, the Schwarmerei of the Germans, was powerfully set forth in a recent novel in which an unprincipled and fascinating mistress 'ran' her personality with disastrous results. But the danger does not lie in extreme cases. The girl who kisses the chamber door of her class mistress will forget this lady by and by; but the parasitic habit has been formed and she must always have some person or some cause on which to hang her body and soul. I speak of 'she' and 'her' perhaps unfairly, because ever since the Greek youth hung about their masters in the walks of the Academy there have been teachers who have undermined the stability of the boys to whom they devoted themselves. Were his countrymen entirely wrong about Socrates? A tendency to this manner of betrayal is the infirmity of noble minds, of those who have the most to give; and for this reason, again, it is important that we should have before us a bird's eye view, let us call it, of human nature.

2. Well-Being of Mind

There is a common notion that it is our inalienable right not only to say what we please but to think as we please, that is, we believe that while body is subject to physical laws, while the affections, love and justice, are subject to moral laws, the mind is a chartered libertine. Probably this notion has much to do with our neglect of intellect. We do not perceive that the mind, too, has its tendencies both good and evil and that every inclination towards good is hindered and may be thwarted by a corresponding inclination towards evil; I am not speaking of moral evil but of those intellectual evils which we are slow to define and are careless in dealing with. Does the teacher of a large class always perceive that intellect is enthroned before him in every child, however dull and inattentive may be his outer show? Every child in such a class is open to the wonders that science reveals, is interested in the wheeling worlds of the winter firmament. "Child after child," said a schoolmistress, "writes to say how much they have enjoyed reading about the stars." "As we are walking sometimes and the stars are shining," says a girl of eleven in an Elementary School, "I tell mother about the stars and planets and comets. She said she should think astronomy very interesting."

But we teach astronomy, no, we teach 'light and heat' by means of dessicated text-books, diagrams and experiments, which last are no more to children than the tricks of white magic. The infinitely little is as attractive to them as the infinitely great and the behavior of an atom, an ion, is a fairy tale they delight in, that is, if no semblance to a fairy tale be suggested. The pageant of history with its interplay of characters is as delightful as any tale because every child uses his own film to show the scenes and exhibit the persons. We fuss a good deal about the dress, implements and other small details of each historic period but we forget that, give the child a few fit and exact words on the subject and he has the picture in his mind's eye, nay, a series miles long of really glorious films; for a child's amazing, vivifying imagination is part and parcel of his intellect.

The way children make their own the examples offered to them is amazing. No child would forget the characterization of Charles IX as 'feeble and violent,' nor fail to take to himself a lesson in self-control. We may not point the moral; that is the work proper for children themselves and they do it without fail. The comparative difficulty of the subject does not affect them. A teacher writes (of children of eleven),—"They cannot have enough of Publicola and there are always groans when the lesson comes to an end."

I have said much of history and science, but mathematics, a mountainous land which pays the climber, makes its appeal to mind, and good teachers know that they may not drown their teaching in verbiage. As for literature—to introduce children to literature is to install them in a very rich and glorious kingdom, to bring a continual holiday to their doors, to lay before them a feast exquisitely served. But they must learn to know literature by being familiar with it from the very first. A child's intercourse must always be with good books, the best that we can find. Of course, we have always known that this is the right thing for children in cultivated homes, but what about those in whose dwellings books are little known? One of the wise teachers in Gloucestershire notes that a recognition of two things is necessary in dealing with this problem. First, that,—

"To explain the meaning of words destroys interest in the story and annoys the child. Second, that in many instances it is unnecessary. Although a child's dictionary knowledge of words is lacking it does not follow that the meaning of a sentence or paragraph is unknown to him . . . neither is the correct employment of the words beyond him in writing or narrating. Two examples of this power to sense the meaning were observed last term. There is a particular boy in Form IIB who has not hitherto been looked upon as possessing high intelligence. Classified by age he ought to be two Forms higher. Last term in taking the story of Romulus and Remus, I found that in power of narrating and degree of understanding (that is, of 'sensing' a paragraph and either translating it into his vocabulary or in using the words read to him) he stood above the others and also above the majority in the next higher Form."

"What has surprised us most," said the Headmaster of A., "is the ready way in which boys absorb information and become interested in literature, literature which we have hitherto considered outside the scope of primary school teaching. A year ago I could not have believed that boys would have read Lytton's Harold, Kingsley's Hereward, and Scott's Talisman with real pleasure and zest or would study with understanding and delight Shakespeare's Macbeth, King John and Richard II; but experience has shown us we have underrated the abilities and tastes of the lads we should have known better."

That is the capital charge against most schools. The teachers underrate the tastes and abilities of their pupils. In things intellectual, children, even backward children, have extraordinary 'possibilities for good'—possibilities so great that if we had the wit to give them their head they would carry us along like a stream in spate.

But what about intellectual tendencies, or 'possibilities for evil'? One such tendency dominates many schools notwithstanding prodigious efforts on the part of the teachers to rouse slumbering minds. Indeed, the more the teacher works, the greater the incuria of the children, so the class is prodded with marks, the boys take places, the bogie of an oncoming examination is held before them. Some spasmodic effort is the result but no vital response and, though boys and girls love school, like their teachers and even their lessons, they care not at all for knowledge, for which the school should create enthusiasm. I can touch here on no more than two potent means of creating incuria in a class. One is the talky-talky of the teacher. We all know how we are bored by the person in private life who explains and expounds. What reason have we to suppose that children are not equally bored? They try to tell us that they are by wandering eyes, inanimate features, fidgetting hands and feet, by every means at their disposal; and the kindly souls among us think that they want to play or to be out of doors. But they have no use for play except at proper intervals. What they want is knowledge conveyed in literary form and the talk of the facile teacher leaves them cold. Another soothing potion is little suspected of producing mental lethargy. We pride ourselves upon going over and over the same ground 'until the children know it'; the monotony is deadly. A child writes, "Before we had these (books) we had to read the same old lot again and again." Is it not true? In the home schoolroom books used by the grandmother are fit for the grandchildren, books used in boys' schools may be picked up at second-hand stalls with the obliterated names of half-a-dozen successive owners. And what of the compilations, neither books nor text-books, which do duty in Elementary Schools? No wonder Mr. Fisher said, in opening a public library, that he had been "surprised and pained when visiting Elementary Schools to find that there was nothing in them which could be called a book, nothing that would charm and enlighten and expand the imagination." And yet, as he went on to say, the country is "full of artistic and literary ability and always has been so." If this ability is to be brought into play we must recognise that children are not ruminants intellectually any more than physically. They cannot go over the same ground repeatedly without deadening, even paralysing results, for progress, continual progress is the law of intellectual life.

In matters of the mind again Habit is a good servant but a bad master. Specialisation, the fetish of the end of the last century, is to be deprecated because it is at our peril that we remain too long in any one field of thought. We may not, for example, allow the affairs and interests of daily life to deprive the mind of its proper range of interests and occupations. It is even possible for a person to go into any one of the great fields of thought and to work therein with delight until he become incapable of finding his way into any other such field. We know how Darwin lost himself in science until he could not read poetry, find pleasure in pictures, think upon things divine; he was unable to turn his mind out of the course in which it had run for most of his life. In the great (and ungoverned) age of the Renaissance, the time when great things were done, great pictures painted, great buildings raised, great discoveries made, the same man was a painter, an architect, a goldsmith and a master of much knowledge besides; and all that he did he did well, all that he knew was part of his daily thought and enjoyment. Let us hear Vasari on Leonardo,—

"Possessed of a divine and marvellous intellect and being an excellent geometrician, he not only worked at sculpture . . . but also prepared many architectural plans and buildings . . . he made designs for mills and other engines to go by water; and, as painting was to be his profession . . . he studied drawing from life."

Leonardo knew nothing about Art for Art's sake, that shibboleth of yesterday, nor did our own Christopher Wren, also a great mathematician and master of much and various knowledge, to whom architecture was rather a by-the-way interest, and yet he built St. Paul's. What an irreparable loss we had when that plan of his for a beautiful and spacious London was flung aside because it would cost too much to carry it out! Just so of our parsimony do we fling aside the minds of the children of our country, also capable of being wrought into pleasaunces of delight, structures of utility and beauty, at a pitifully trifling cost. It is well we should recognise that the business of education is with us all our lives, that we must always go on increasing our knowledge.

Of the means we employ to hinder the growth of mind perhaps none is more subtle than the questionnaire. It is as though one required a child to produce for inspection at its various stages of assimilation the food he consumed for his dinner; we see at once how the digestive processes would be hindered, how, in a word, the child would cease to be fed. But the mind also requires its food and leave to carry on those quiet processes of digestion and assimilation which it must accomplish for itself. The child with capacity, which implies depth, is stupified by a long rigmarole on the lines of,—"If John's father is Tom's son, what relation is Tom to John?" The shallow child guesses the riddle and scores; and it is by the use of tests of this kind that we turn out young people sharp as needles but with no power of reflection, no intelligent interests, nothing but the aptness of the city gamin.

Imagination may become like that cave Ezekiel tells of wherein were all manner of unseemly and evil things; it may be a temple wherein self is glorified; it may be a chamber of horrors and dangers; but it may also be a House Beautiful. It is enough for us to remember that imagination is stored with those images supplied day by day whether by the cinema, the penny dreadful, by Homer or Shakespeare, by the great picture or the flaming 'shocker.' We have heard of the imaginative man who conceived a passion for the Sphinx!

In these days when Reason is deified by the unlearned and plays the part of the Lord of Misrule it is necessary that every child should be trained to recognize fallacious reasoning and above all to know that a man's reason is his servant and not his master; that there is no notion a man chooses to receive which his reason will not justify, whether it be mistrust of his neighbour, jealousy of his wife, doubts about his religion, or contempt for his country.

Realising this, we 'see reason' in the fact that thousands of men go on strike because two of their body have been denied permission to attend a certain meeting. We see reason in this but the men themselves confound reason with right and consider that such a strike is a righteous protest. The only safeguard against fallacies which undermine the strength of the nation morally and economically is a liberal education which affords a wide field for reflection and comparison and abundant data upon which to found sound judgments.

As for that aesthetic 'appetency' (to use Coleridge's word) upon which so many of the gentle pleasures of life depend, it is open to many disasters: it dies of inanition when beauty is not duly presented to it, beauty in words, in pictures and music, in tree and flower and sky. The function of the sense of beauty is to open a paradise of pleasure for us; but what if we grow up admiring the wrong things, or, what is morally worse, arrogant in the belief that it is only we and our kind who are able to appreciate and distinguish beauty? It is no small part of education to have seen much beauty, to recognize it when we see it, and to keep ourselves humble in its presence.

3. Intellectual Appetite

As the body is provided with its appetites, by undue indulgence of any one of which a man may make shipwreck, but which duly ordered should result in a robust and vigorous frame; so, too, the spiritual part of us is provided with certain caterers whose business it is to secure that kind of nourishment which promotes spiritual or intellectual growth in one or another direction. Perhaps in no part of our educational service do we make more serious blunders than in our use of those desires which act as do the appetites for the body's service. Every child wants to be approved, even baby in his new red shoes; to be first in what is going on; to get what is going; to be admired; to lead and manage the rest; to have the companionship of children and grown people; and last, but not least, every child wants to know. There they are, those desires, ready to act on occasion and our business is to make due use of this natural provision for the work of education. We do make use of the desires, not wisely, but too well. We run our schools upon emulation, the desire of every child to be first; and not the ablest, but the most pushing, comes to the front. We quicken emulation by the common desire to get and to have, that is, by the impulse of avarice. So we offer prizes, exhibitions, scholarships, every incentive that can be proposed. We cause him to work for our approbation, we play upon his vanity, and the boy does more than he can. What is the harm, we say, when all those springs of action are in the child already? The athlete is beginning to discover that he suffers elsewhere from the undue development of any set of muscles; and the boy whose ambition, or emulation, has been unduly stimulated becomes a flaccid person. But there is a worse evil. We all want knowledge just as much as we want bread. We know it is possible to cure the latter appetite by giving more stimulating food; and the worst of using other spurs to learning is that a natural love of knowledge which should carry us through eager school-days, and give a spice of adventure to the duller days of mature life, is effectually choked; and boys and girls 'Cram to pass but not to know; they do pass but they don't know.' The divine curiosity which should have been an equipment for life hardly survives early schooldays.

Now it has been demonstrated very fully indeed that the delightfulness of knowledge is sufficient to carry a pupil joyfully and eagerly through his school life and that prizes and places, praise, blame and punishment, are unnecessary insofar as they are used to secure ardent interest and eager work. The love of knowledge is sufficient. Each of those other stimuli should no doubt have its natural action, but one or two springs of action seem to be played upon excessively in our schools. Conduct gives opportunity for 'virtue emulously rapid in the race' and especially that part of conduct known as 'play' in which most of the natural desires come into action; but even in play we must beware of the excess of zeal which risks the elimination of the primary feelings of love and justice. In the schoolroom, without doubt, the titillation of knowledge itself affords sufficient stimulus to close attention and steady labour; and the desire of acquisition has due play in a boy who is constantly increasing his acquirements.

4. Misdirected Affections

We are aware of more than mind and body in our dealings with children. We appeal to their 'feelings'; whether 'mind' or 'feelings' be more than names we choose to give to manifestations of that spiritual entity which is each one of us. Probably we have not even taken the trouble to analyse and name the feelings and to discover that they all fall under the names of love and justice, that it is the glory of the human being to be endowed with such a wealth of these two as is sufficient for every occasion of life. More, the occasions come and he is ready to meet them with the ease and triumph of the solvent debtor.

But this rich endowment of the moral nature is also a matter with which the educator should concern himself. Alas, he does so. He points the moral with a thousand tedious platitudes, directs, instructs, illustrates and bores exceedingly the nimble and subtle minds of his scholars. This, of the feelings and their manifestations, is certainly the field for the spare and guarded praise and blame of parent and teacher; but this praise or blame is apt to be either scrapped by children, or, taken as the sole motive for conduct, they go forth unused to do a thing 'for it is right' but only because somebody's approbation is to be won.

This education of the feelings, moral education, is too delicate and personal a matter for a teacher to undertake trusting to his own resources. Children are not to be fed morally like young pigeons with predigested food. They must pick and eat for themselves and they do so from the conduct of others which they hear of or perceive. But they want a great quantity of the sort of food whose issue is conduct, and that is why poetry, history, romance, geography, travel, biography, science and sums must all be pressed into service. No one can tell what particular morsel a child will select for his sustenance. One small boy of eight may come down late because "I was meditating upon Plato and couldn't fasten my buttons," and another may find his meat in 'Peter Pan'! But all children must read widely, and know what they have read, for the nourishment of their complex nature.

As for moral lessons, they are worse than useless; children want a great deal of fine and various moral feeding, from which they draw the 'lessons' they require. It is a wonderful thing that every child, even the rudest, is endowed with Love and is able for all its manifestations, kindness, benevolence, generosity, gratitude, pity, sympathy, loyalty, humility, gladness; we older persons are amazed at the lavish display of any one of these to which the most ignorant child may treat us. But these aptitudes are so much coin of the realm with which a child is provided that he may be able to pay his way through life; and, alas, we are aware of certain vulgar commonplace tendencies in ourselves which make us walk delicately and trust, not to our own teaching, but to the best that we have in art and literature and above all to that storehouse of example and precept, the Bible, to enable us to touch these delicate spirits to fine issues.

St. Francis, Collingwood, Father Damien, one of the V.C.'s [war veteran awarded the Victoria Cross medal for "conspicuous bravery"] among us, will do more for children than years of talk.

Then there is that other wonderful provision for right living without which no neglected or savage man-soul exists. Everyone has Justice in his heart; a cry for 'fair play' reaches the most lawless mob, and we all know how children torment us with their 'It's not fair.' It is much to know that as regards justice as well as love there exists in everyone an adequate provision for the conduct of life: general unrest, which has its rise in wrong thinking and wrong judging far more than in faulty conditions, is the misguided outcome of that sense of justice with which, thank God, we are all endued.

Here, on the face of it, we get one office of education. This, of justice, is another spiritual provision which we fail to employ duly in our schools; and so wonderful is this principle that we cannot kill, paralyse, or even benumb it, but, choked in its natural course, it spreads havoc and devastation where it should have made the soil fertile for the fruits of good living.

Few of the offices of education are more important than that of preparing men to distinguish between their rights and their duties. We each have our rights and other persons have their duties towards us as we towards them; but it is not easy to learn that we have precisely the same rights as other people and no more; that other people owe to us just such duties as we owe to them. This fine art of self-adjustment is possible to everyone because of the ineradicable principle which abides in us. But our eyes must be taught to see, and hence the need for all the processes of education, futile in proportion as they do not serve this end. To think fairly requires, we know, knowledge as well as consideration.

Young people should leave school knowing that their thoughts are not their own; that what we think of other people is a matter of justice or injustice; that a certain manner of words is due from them to all manner of persons with whom they have to deal; and that not to speak those words is to be unjust to their neighbours. They should know that truth, that is, justice in word, is their due and that of all other persons; there are few better equipments for a citizen than a mind capable of discerning the truth, and this just mind can be preserved only by those who take heed what they think. "Yet truth," says Bacon, "which only doth judge itself, teacheth that the enquiry of truth, which is the lovemaking, or wooing of it, the knowledge of truth, which is the presence of it, and the belief of truth, which is the enjoying of it, is the sovereign good of human nature."

If justice in word is to be duly learned by all scholars still more is integrity, justice in action; integrity in work, which disallows ca'canny methods, whether those of the artisan who does as little as he can in the time, or of the schoolboy who receives payment in kind—in his support, the cost of his education and the trust imposed in him by parents and teachers. Therefore he may not scamp, dawdle over, postpone, crib, or otherwise shirk his work. He learns that "my duty towards my neighbour" is "to keep my hands from picking and stealing," and, whether a man be a workman, a servant, or a prosperous citizen, he must know that justice requires from him the integrity in material which we call honesty; not the common honesty which hates to be found out, but that refined and delicate sense of values which George Eliot exhibits for us in 'Caleb Garth.'

There is another form in which the magnanimous citizen of the future must be taught the sense of justice. Our opinions show our integrity of thought. Every person has many opinions whether his own honestly thought out, or notions picked up from his pet newspaper or his companions. The person who thinks out his opinions modestly and carefully is doing his duty as truly as if he saved a life because there is no more or less about duty.

If a schoolboy is to be guided into the justice of thought from which sound opinions emanate, how much more does he need guidance in arriving at that justice in motive which we call sound principles. For what, after all, are principles but those motives of first importance which govern us, move us in thought and action? We appear to pick up these in a casual way and are seldom able to render an account of them and yet our lives are ordered by our principles, good or bad. Here, again, we have a reason for wide and wisely ordered reading; for there are always catch-words floating in the air, as,—'What's the good?' 'It's all rot,' and the like, which the vacant mind catches up for use as the basis of thought and conduct, as, in fact, paltry principles for the guidance of a life.

Here we have one more reason why there is nothing in all those spiritual stores in the world's treasury too good for the education of all children. Every lovely tale, illuminating poem, instructive history, every unfolding of travel and revelation of science exists for children. "La terre appartient à l'enfant, toujours à l'enfant," [The ground belongs to the child, always with the child] was well said by Maxim Gorky, and we should do well to remember the fact.

The service that some of us (of the P.N.E.U.) believe we have done in the cause of education is to discover that all children, even backward children, are aware of their needs and pathetically eager for the food they require; that no preparation whatever is necessary for this sort of diet; that a limited vocabulary, sordid surroundings, the absence of a literary background to thought are not hindrances; indeed they may turn out to be incentives to learning, just as the more hungry the child, the readier he is for his dinner. This statement is no mere pious opinion; it has been amply proved in thousands of instances. Children of a poor school in the slums are eager to tell the whole story of Waverly, falling continually into the beautiful language and style of the author. They talk about the Rosetta Stone and about treasures in their local museum; they discuss Coriolanus and conclude that 'his mother must have spoiled him.' They know by heart every detail of a picture by La Hooch, Rembrandt, Botticelli, and not only is no evolution of history or drama, no subtle sweetness, no inspiration of a poet, beyond them, but they decline to know that which does not reach them in literary form.

What they receive under this condition they absorb immediately and show that they know by that test of knowledge which applies to us all, that is, they can tell it with power, clearness, vivacity and charm. These are the children to whom we have been doling out the 'three R's' for generations! Small wonder that juvenile crime increases; the intellectually starved boy must needs find food for his imagination, scope for his intellectual power; and crime, like the cinema, offers, it must be admitted, brave adventures.

5. The Well-Being of the Soul

If we leave the outer courts of mind and body, the holy places of the affections and the will (we shall consider this last later) and enter that holy of holies where man performs his priestly functions, we may well ask with diffidence and humility what may education do for the Soul of a child? "What is there that outwits the understanding of a man or that is out of the range of his thoughts, the reach of his aspirations? He is, it is true, baffled on all hands by his ignorance, the illimitable ignorance of even the wisest, but ignorance is not incapacity and the wings of a man's soul beat with impatience against the bars of his ignorance. He would out, out into the universe of infinite thought and infinite possibilities. How is the soul of a man to be satisfied?

Crowned kings have thrown up dominion because they want that which is greater than kingdoms; profound scholars fret under limitations which keep them playing upon the margin of the unsounded ocean of knowledge; no great love can satisfy itself with loving; there is no satisfaction save one for the soul of a man, because the things about him are finite, measurable, incomplete and his reach is beyond his grasp. He has an urgent, incessant, irrepressible need of the infinite." "I want, am made for, and must have a God;"—not a mere serviceable religion,—because we have in us an infinite capacity for love, loyalty and service which we cannot expend upon any other.

But what sort of approaches do we prepare for children towards the God whom they need, the Saviour in Whom is all help, the King who affords all delight, commands all adoration and loyalty? Any words or thoughts of ours are poor and insufficient, but we have a treasury of divine words which they read and know with satisfying pleasure and tell with singular beauty and fitness.

"The Bible is the most interesting book I know," said a young person of ten who had read a good many books and knew her Bible. By degrees children get that knowledge of God which is the object of the final daily prayer in our beautiful liturgy—the prayer of St Chrysostom—"Grant us in this world knowledge of Thy truth," and all other knowledge which they obtain gathers round and illuminates this.

Here is an example of how such knowledge grows. I heard a class of girls aged about thirteen read an essay on George Herbert. Three or four of his poems were included, and none of the girls had read either essay or poems before. They 'narrated' what they had read and in the course of their narration gave a full paraphrase of The Elixir, The Pulley, and one or two other poems. No point made by the poet was omitted and his exact words were used pretty freely. The teacher made comments upon one or two unusual words and that was all; to explain or enforce (otherwise than by a reverently sympathetic manner, the glance and words that showed that she too, cared), would have been impertinent. It is an interesting thing that hundreds of children of this age in Secondary and Elementary Schools and in families scattered over the world read and narrated the same essay and no doubt paraphrased the verses with equal ease. I felt humbled before the children knowing myself incapable of such immediate and rapid apprehension of several pages of new matter including poems whose intention is by no means obvious. In such ways the great thoughts of great thinkers illuminate children and they grow in knowledge, chiefly the knowledge of God.

And yet this, the chief part of education, is drowned in torrents of talk, in tedious repetition, in objurgation and recrimination, in every sort of way in which the mind may be bored and the affections deadened.

I have endeavoured to sketch some of the possibilities for good and the corresponding possibilities for evil present in all children; they are waiting for direction and control, certainly, but still more for the formative influence of knowledge. I have avoided philosophical terms, using only names in common use,—body and soul, body and mind, body, soul and spirit,—because these represent ideas that we cannot elude and that convey certain definite notions; and these ideas must needs form the basis of our educational thought.

We must know something about the material we are to work upon if the education we offer is not to be scrappy and superficial. We must have some measure of a child's requirements, not based upon his uses to society, nor upon the standard of the world he lives in, but upon his own capacity and needs. We would not willingly educate him towards what is called 'self-expression'; he has little to express except what he has received as knowledge, whether by way of record or impression; what he can do is to assimilate and give this forth in a form which is original because it is modified, re-created, by the action of his own mind; and this originality is produced by the common bread and milk which is food for everyone, acting upon the mind which is peculiar to each individual child.

Education implies a continuous going forth of the mind; but whatever induces introspection or any form of self-consciousness holds up as it were the intellectual powers and brings progress to a standstill. The reader may have noticed with some disappointment that I have not invited him to the study of psychology as it is understood to-day. No doubt there exists a certain dim region described as the unconscious mind, a sort of half-way house between mind and matter, a place where the intellect is subdued to the action of nerves and blood. Mind is of its nature infinitely and always conscious and to speak of the unconscious mind is a contradiction in terms; but what is meant is that the mind thinks in ways of which we are unconscious; and that our business is to make ourselves aware by much introspection, much self-occupation, of the nature and tendencies of this 'unconscious' region. The results of this study, so far as they have been arrived at, are not encouraging. The best that is in us would appear to find its origin in 'complexes,' sensual, erotic, greedy. Granting that such possibilities are in us safely, lies in so nourishing the mind that seed of baseness may bear fruit of beauty. Researches in this region are deeply interesting no doubt, to the psychologist, and may eventually bear fruit if only as contributing a quota to the classification of knowledge; but no authority on the subject is willing to offer at present his researches as a contribution to educational lore. It may be that the mind as well as the body has its regions where noli me tangere is a counsel of expedience; and, by the time we have dealt with those functions of the mind which we know, we may find ourselves in a position to formulate that which we certainly do not possess, a Science, should it not be a Philosophy, of Education?

Chapter 4 Authority and Docility

The principles of Authority on the one hand and Docility on the other are natural, necessary and fundamental.

The War has made surprises stale but in those remote pre-war days we were enormously startled by the discovery of wireless telegraphy. That communications should pass through almost infinite space without sign or sound or obvious channel and arrive instantly at their destination took away our breath. We had the grace to value the discovery for something more than its utility; we were awed in the presence of a law which had always been there but was only now perceived. In something the same way we have been electrified by the discovery in the fields of France of heroism in the breast of every common soldier. Now, just such discoveries wait us in the field of education and any miner in this field may strike a vein of ore which shall enrich the world. The citizens of an ancient city on the shores of Gennesaret made one of those startling discoveries and knew how to give it a name; they found out that Christ 'spake with authority' and not as their scribes.

It is not ours to speak with authority; the 'verily, verily I say unto you' is a divine word not for us. Nevertheless deputed authority is among us and in us. 'He is an authority' on such and such a subject, is a correct expression because by much study he has made it his own and has a right to speak. This deputed authority appears to be lodged in everyone, ready for occasion. Benjamin Kidd has told us how the London policeman is the very embodiment of authority, implicitly obeyed in a way surprising to strangers. Every king and commander, every mother, elder sister, school prefect, every foreman of works and captain of games, finds that within himself which secures faithful obedience, not for the sake of his merits but because authority is proper to his office. Without this principle, society would cease to cohere. Practically there is no such thing as anarchy; what is so-called is a mere transference of authority, even if in the last resort the anarchist find authority in himself alone. There is an idea abroad that authority makes for tyranny, and that obedience, voluntary or involuntary, is of the nature of slavishness; but authority is, on the contrary, the condition without which liberty does not exist and, except it be abused, is entirely congenial to those on whom it is exercised: we are so made that we like to be ordered even if the ordering be only that of circumstances. Servants take pride in the orders they receive; that our badge of honour is an 'Order' is a significant use of words. It is still true that 'Order is heaven's first law' and order is the outcome of authority.

That principle in us which brings us into subjection to authority is docility, teachableness, and that also is universal. If a man in the pride of his heart decline other authority, he will submit himself slavishly to his 'star' or his 'destiny.' It would seem that the exercise of docility is as natural and necessary as that of reason or imagination; and the two principles of authority and docility act in every life precisely as do those two elemental principles which enable the earth to maintain its orbit, the one drawing it towards the sun, the other as constantly driving it into space; between the two, the earth maintains a more or less middle course and the days go on.

The same two principles work in every child, the one producing ordered life, the other making for rebellion, and the crux in bringing up children is to find the mean which shall keep a child true to his elliptical orbit. The solution offered to-day is freedom in our schools; children may be governed but they must not be aware that they are governed, and, 'Go as you please,' must be the apparent rule of their lives, while, 'Do as you're bid,' is the moving force. The result of an ordered freedom is obtained, that ordered freedom which rules the lives of 999 in 1000 of the citizens of the world; but the drawback to an indirect method of securing this result is that when, 'Do as you please,' is substituted for, 'Do as you're bid,' there is dissimulation in the air and children fail to learn that habit of 'proud subjection and dignified obedience' which distinguishes great men and noble citizens. No doubt it is pleasing that children should behave naturally, should get up and wander about, should sit still or frolic as they have a mind to, but they too, must 'learn obedience'; and it is no small element in their happiness and ours that obedience is both delightful and reposeful.

It is the part of the teacher to secure willing obedience, not so much to himself as to the laws of the school and the claims of the matter in hand. If a boy have a passage to read, he obeys the call of that immediate duty, reads the passage with attention and is happy in doing so. We all know with what a sense of added importance we say, "I must be at Mrs. Jones's by eleven." "It is necessary that I should see Brown." The life that does not obey such conditions has got out of its orbit and is not of use to society. It is necessary that we should all follow an ordered course, and children, even infant children, must begin in the way in which they will have to go on. Happily they come to us with the two inherent forces, centripetal and centrifugal, which secure to them freedom, i.e., self-authority, on the one hand, and 'proud subjection' on the other.

But parents and those who stand in loco parentis have a delicate task. There must be subjection, but it must be proud, work as a distinction, an order of merit. Probably the way to secure this is to avoid standing between children and those laws of life and conduct by which we are all ultimately ruled. The higher the authority, the greater distinction in obedience, and children are quick to discriminate between the mere will and pleasure of the arbitrary teacher or parent and the chastened authority of him who is himself under rule. That subservience should take the place of docility is the last calamity for nation, family or school. Docility implies equality; there is no great gulf fixed between teacher and taught; both are pursuing the same ends, engaged on, the same theme, enriched by mutual interests; and probably the quite delightful pursuit of knowledge affords the only intrinsic liberty for both teacher and taught. "He is the freeman whom the truth makes free," and this freedom the steady pursuit and delightful acquirement of knowledge afford to us day by day. "The mind is its own place," we are told, "and in itself can make a heaven of hell, a hell of heaven"; and that heaven of the mind, is it not continual expansion in ordered freedom? And that restless, burning, inflammatory hell, does it not come of continual chafing against natural and righteous order?

As for the superficial freedom of sitting or standing, going or coming, that is a matter which settles itself, as do all the relations between teacher and taught, once children are allowed a due share in their own education, not a benefit for us to confer but rather a provision for them to take. Our chief concern for the mind or for the body is to supply a well-ordered table with abundant, appetising, nourishing and very varied food, which children deal with in their own way and for themselves. This food must be served au naturel, without the predigestion which deprives it of stimulating and nourishing properties and no sort of forcible feeding or spoon feeding may be practised. Hungry minds sit down to such a diet with the charming greediness of little children; they absorb it, assimilate it and grow thereby in a manner astonishing to those accustomed to the dull profitless ruminating so often practised in schools. When the teacher avoids hortatory methods, his scholars change position when they have a mind to; but their mind is commonly to sit still during a lesson time because they are so intent on their work that they have no desire for small divagations; while, on the other hand, the teacher makes it his business to see that the body gets its share, and an abundant share, of gymnastics whether by way of games or drill. But this is a subject well understood in modern schools and it is only necessary to say that though mental activity promotes bodily functions in a surprising way—has not an American physiologist discovered that people may live to 160 or 1000 years (!) if they continue to use their minds?—athleticism, on the other hand, if unduly pursued, by no means promotes mental activity.

In days when the concern of educators seems to be to provide an easy option for that mental activity, the sole condition of education, it must be urged that manual dexterity, gardening, folk-dancing, and the like, while they fulfil their proper function in training nerve and muscle to ready responsiveness, do not sustain mind. Not, again, can we educate children upon the drama, even the Shakespearean drama, nor upon poetry, even the most musical and emotional. These things children must have; but they come into the world with many relations waiting to be established; relations with places far and near, with the wide universe, with the past of history, with the the social economics of the present, with the earth they live on and all its delightful progeny of beast and bird, plant and tree; with the sweet human affinities they entered into at birth; with their own country and other countries, and, above all, with that most sublime of human relationships—their relation to God. With such a programme before his pupils only the uninstructed teacher will put undue emphasis upon and give undue time to arithmetic and handicrafts, singing, acting, or any of the hundred specifics which are passed off as education in its entirety.

The sense of must should be present with children; our mistake is to act in such a way that they, only, seem to be law-compelled while their elders do as they please. The parent or teacher who is pestered for 'leave' to do this or that, contrary to the discipline of the house or school, has only himself to thank; he has posed as a person in authority, not under authority, and therefore free to allow the breach of rules whose only raison d'être is that they minister to the well-being of the children. Two conditions are necessary to secure all proper docility and obedience and, given these two, there is seldom a conflict of wills between teacher and pupils. The conditions are,—the teacher, or other head may not be arbitrary but must act so evidently as one under authority that the children, quick to discern, see that he too must do the things he ought; and therefore that regulations are not made for his convenience. (I am assuming that everyone entrusted with the bringing up of children recognises the supreme Authority to Whom we are subject; without this recognition I do not see how it is possible to establish the nice relation which should exist between teacher and taught.) The other condition is that children should have a fine sense of the freedom which comes of knowledge which they are allowed to appropriate as they choose, freely given with little intervention from the teacher. They do choose and are happy in their work, so there is little opportunity for coercion or for deadening, hortatory talk.

But the principle of authority, as well as that of docility, is inherent in children and it is only as the tact and judgment of the teacher make opportunity for its free play that they are prepared for the duties of life as citizens and members of a family. The movement in favour of prefects, as in Public Schools, is a recognition of this fact and it is well that children should become familiar with the idea of representative authority, that is, that they are governed by chosen members of their own body, a form of self-government. To give effect to the idea, the prefect should be elected and children shew extraordinary insight in choosing the right officers. But that is not enough because only a few are set in authority; certain small offices should be held in rotation by every member of a class. The office makes the man as much as the man makes the office and it is surprising how well rather incompetent children will perform duties laid on them.

All school work should be conducted in such a manner that children are aware of the responsibility of learning; it is their business to know that which has been taught. To this end the subject matter should not be repeated. We ourselves do not attend to the matters in our daily paper which we know we shall meet with again in a weekly review, nor to that if there is a monthly review in prospect; these repeated aids result in our being persons of wandering attention and feeble memory. To allow repetition of a lesson is to shift the responsibility for it from the shoulders of the pupil to those of the teacher who says, in effect,—"I'll see that you know it," so his pupils make no effort of attention. Thus the same stale stuff is repeated again and again and the children get bored and restive, ready for pranks by way of a change.

Teachers are apt to slight their high office and hinder the processes of education because they cherish two or three fallacies. They regard children as inferior, themselves as superior, beings;—why else their office? But if they recognized that the potency of children's minds is as great or greater than that of their own, they would not conceive that spoon-feeding was their mission, or that they must masticate a morsel of knowledge to make it proper for the feeble digestion of the scholar.

We depreciate children in another way. We are convinced that they cannot understand a literary vocabulary so we explain and paraphrase to our own heart's content but not to theirs. Educated mothers know that their children can read anything and do not offer explanations unless they are asked for them; and we have taken it for granted that this quickness of apprehension comes only to the children of educated parents.

Another misapprehension which makes for disorder is our way of regarding attention. We believe that it is to be cultivated, nursed, coddled, wooed by persuasion, by dramatic presentation, by pictures and illustrative objects: in fact, the teacher, the success of whose work depends upon his 'personality,' is an actor of no mean power whose performance would adorn any stage. Attention, we know, is not a 'faculty' nor a definable power of mind but is the ability to turn on every such power, to concentrate, as we say. We throw away labour in attempting to produce or to train this necessary function. There it is in every child in full measure, a very Niagara of force, ready to be turned on in obedience to the child's own authority and capable of infinite resistance to authority imposed from without. Our part is to regard attention, too, as an appetite and to feed it with the best we have in books and in all knowledge. But children do it 'on their own'; we may not play Sir Oracle any more; our knowledge is too circumscribed, our diction too poor, vague, desultory, to cope with the ability of young creatures who thirst for knowledge. We must put into their hands the sources which we must needs use for ourselves, the best books of the best writers.

I will mention only one more disability which hinders us in our work as teachers; I mean that depreciation of knowledge which is just now characteristic of Englishmen. A well-known educationalist lately nailed up the thesis that what children want in the way of knowledge is just two things,—How to do the work by which they must earn their living and how to behave as citizens. This writer does not see that work is done and duties performed in the ratio of the person who works: the more the man is as a person, the more valuable will be his work and the more dependable his conduct: yet we omit from popular education that tincture of humane letters which makes for efficiency! One hears, for instance, of an adolescent school with some nine thousand pupils who come in batches of a few hundreds, each batch to learn one or other of a score or so of admirable crafts and accomplishments; but not one hour is spent in a three or four years' course in this people's university on any sort of humane knowledge, in any reading or thinking which should make the pupils better men and women and better citizens.

To return to our method of employing attention; it is not a casual matter, a convenient, almost miraculous way of covering the ground, of getting children to know certainly and lastingly a surprising amount; all this is to the good, but it is something more, a root principle vital to education. In this way of learning the child comes to his own; he makes use of the authority which is in him in its highest function as a self-commanding, self-compelling, power. It is delightful to use any power that is in us if only that of keeping up in cup and ball a hundred times as (to the delight of small nephews and nieces), Jane Austen did. But to make yourself attend, make yourself know, this indeed is to come into a king—all the more satisfying to children because they are so made that they revel in knowledge.

Here is some notice of a day or two spent in London by a child of eleven which reaches me as I write:

"Mother took her to Westminster Abbey one afternoon and while I was seeing her to bed she told me all the things she had noticed there which they had been hearing about in 'architecture' this term. She loves 'architecture.' She also expressed her anxiety to make acquaintance with the British Museum and see the things there that they had been 'having' in their term's work. So the next morning we went there and studied the Parthanon Room in great detail. She was a most interesting companion and taught me ever so much! We also went to St. Paul's and Madame Tussaud's where she was delighted to see many people out of 'history.' The modern people did not interest her so much except Jack Cornwell and Nurse Cavell."

It will be noticed that the child is educating herself; her friends merely take her to see the things she knows about and she tells what she has read, a quite different matter from the act of pouring information down the throats of the unhappy children who are taken to visit our national treasure houses.

A short time ago when the King and Queen paid a private visit to the British Museum, in the next hall, also, no doubt, examining the Parthenon Room, were a group of children from a London County Council School, as full of information and interest as the child above mentioned because they had been doing the same work. It is not a small thing for those children to know that their interests and delights were common to them and their Sovereigns. Of such strands are formed the cord which binds society; and one of the main purposes of a 'liberal education for all' is to form links between high and low, rich and poor, the classes and the masses, in the strong sympathy of common knowledge. The Public Schools have arrived at this through the medium of the classics; an occasional 'tag' from Horace moves and unites the House of Commons, not only through the urbane thought of the poet but because it is a key to a hundred associations. If this has been effected through the medium of a dead language, what may we not hope for in the way of common thought, universal springs of action, conveyed through our own rich and inspiring literature?

Consider what this power of perfect attention and absolute recollection should be to every employer and chief, what an asset to the nation! I heard this week of a Colonel who said that his best subaltern was an old "P.U.S." (Parents' Union School) boy; and this sort of evidence reaches us continually. There are few who do not know the mischievous and baffling effects of inattention and forgetfulness on the part of subordinates; and we visualize a world of surprising achievement when children shall have been trained to quick apprehension and retention of instructions.

We may not pose before children, nor pride ourselves on dutiful getting up of knowledge in order to deliver it as emanating from ourselves. There are those who have a right to lecture, those who have devoted a life-time to some one subject about which they have perhaps written their book. Lectures from such persons are, no doubt, as full of insight, imagination and power as are their written works; but we cannot have a score of such lecturers in every school, each to elucidate his own subject, nor, if we could, would it be good for the children. The personality of the teacher would influence them to distraction from the delight in knowledge which is itself a sufficient and compelling force to secure perfect attention, and seemly discipline.

I am not figuring an 'Erewhon,' some Utopia of our dreams; we of the P.N.E.U. seem to have let loose a force capable of sending forth young people firm with the resolve—

"I will not cease from mental strife
Nor shall my sword sleep in my hand
Till we have built Jerusalem
In England's green and pleasant land."

Practically all schools are doing wonders. The schoolmaster is abroad in the land and we are educating 'our masters' with immense zeal and self-devotion. What we have reason to deplore is that after some eight or twelve years' brilliant teaching in school, the cinema show and the football field, polo or golf, satisfy the needs of our former pupils to whatever class they belong. We are filled with compassion when we detect the lifeless hand or leg, the artificial nose or jaw, that many a man has brought home as a consequence of the War. But many of our young men and women go about more seriously maimed than these. They are devoid of intellectual interests, history and poetry are without charm for them, the scientific work of the day is only slightly interesting, their 'job' and the social amenities they can secure are all that their life has for them.

The maimed existence in which a man goes on from day to day without either nourishing or using his intellect, is causing anxiety to those interested in education, who know that after religion it is our chief concern, is, indeed, the necessary handmaid of religion.

Chapter 5 The Sacredness of Personality

These principles (ie., authority and docility) are limited by the respect due to the personality of children which may not be encroached upon whether by the direct use of fear or love, suggestion or influence, or by undue play upon any one natural desire.

People are too apt to use children as counters in a game, to be moved hither and thither according to the whim of the moment. Our crying need to-day is less for a better method of education than for an adequate conception of children,—children, merely as human beings, whether brilliant or dull, precocious or backward. Exceptional qualities take care of themselves and so does the 'wanting' intelligence, and both of these share with the rest in all that is claimed for them in the previous chapters. Our business is to find out how great a mystery a person is qua person. All action comes out of the ideas we hold and if we ponder duly upon personality we shall come to perceive that we cannot commit a greater offence than to maim or crush, or subvert any part of a person.

We have many ingenious, not to say affectionate, ways of doing this, all of them more or less based upon that egoism which persuades us that in proportion to a child's dependence is our superiority, that all we do for him is of our grace and favour, and that we have a right, whether as parents or teachers, to do what we will with our own. Have we considered that in the Divine estimate the child's estate is higher than ours; that it is ours to "become as little children," rather than theirs to become as grown men and women; that the rules we receive for the bringing up of children are for the most part negative? We may not despise them, or hinder them, ("suffer little children"), or offend them by our brutish clumsiness of action and want of serious thought; while the one positive precept afforded to us is "feed" (which should be rendered 'pasture') "my lambs," place them in the midst of abundant food. A teacher in a Yorkshire Council School renders this precept as,—"I had left them in the pasture and came back and found them feeding," that is, she had left a big class reading a given lesson and found them on her return still reading with eagerness and satisfaction. Maxima reverentia debetur pueris has a wider meaning than it generally receives. We take it as meaning that we should not do or say anything unseemly before the young, but does it not also include a profound and reverent study of the properties and possibilities present in a child?

Nor need we be alarmed at so wide a programme. The vice which hinders us in the bringing up of children is that so heavily censured in the Gospel. We are not simple; we act our parts and play in an unlawful way upon motives. Perhaps after all the least reprehensible pedagogic motive is that which is most condemned and the terrorism of 'Mr. Creakle' may produce a grey record in comparison with the blackness of more subtle methods of undermining personality. We can only touch upon a few of these, but a part may stand for the whole. For the action of fear as a governing motive we cannot do better than read again our David Copperfield (a great educational treatise) and study 'Mr. Creakle' in detail for terrorism in the schoolroom and 'Mr. Murdstone' for the same vice in the home. But,—is it through the influence of Dickens?—fear is no longer the acknowledged basis of school discipline; we have methods more subtle than the mere terrors of the law. Love is one of these. The person of winning personality attracts his pupils (or hers) who will do anything for his sake and are fond and eager in all their ways, docile to that point where personality is submerged, and they live on the smiles, perish on the averted looks, of the adored teacher. Parents look on with a smile and think that all is well; but Bob or Mary is losing that growing time which should make a self-dependent, self-ordered person, and is day by day becoming a parasite who can go only as he is carried, the easy prey of fanatic or demagogue. This sort of encroachment upon the love of children offers as a motive, 'do this for my sake'; wrong is to be avoided lest it grieve the teacher, good is to be done to pleasure him; for this end a boy learns his lessons, behaves properly, shows good will, produces a whole catalogue of schoolboy virtues and yet his character is being undermined.

'Suggestion' goes to work more subtly. The teacher has mastered the gamut of motives which play upon human nature and every suggestion is aimed at one or other of these. He may not use the nursery suggestions of lollipops or bogies but he does in reality employ these if expressed in more spiritual values, suggestions subtly applied to the idiosyncrasies of a given child. 'Suggestion' is too subtle to be illustrated with advantage: Dr. Stephen Paget holds that it should be used only as a surgeon uses an anesthetic; but it is an instrument easy to handle, and unconsidered suggestion plays on a child's mind as the winds on a weathercock. "Unstable as water, thou shalt not excel" is the unfortunate child's doom; for how is it possible for stability of mind and character to evolve under a continual play of changing suggestions? But this it will be said is true of the unconsidered suggestion. What of a carefully laid train, all leading in the same direction, to produce perseverance, frankness, courage, any other excellent virtue? The child is even worse off in such a case. That particular virtue becomes detestable; no other virtue is inviting; and he is acquiring no strength to stand alone but waits in all his doings for promptings from without. Perhaps the gravest danger attending this practice is that every suggestion received lays the person open to the next and the next. A due respect for the personality of children and a dread of making them incompetent to conduct their own lives will make us chary of employing a means so dangerous, no matter how good the immediate end.

Akin to suggestion is influence, which acts not so much by well-directed word or inciting action as by a sort of atmosphere proceeding from the teacher and enveloping the taught. Late in the last century goody-goody books were written about the beauty of influence, the duty of influence, the study of the means of influence, and children were brought up with the notion that to influence other persons consciously was a moral duty. No doubt such influence is inevitable; we must needs affect one another, not so much by what we do or say as by that which we are, and so far influence is natural and wholesome. We imbibe it from persons real and imaginary and we are kept strong and upright by currents and counter-currents of unstudied influence. Supineness before a single, steady, persistent influence is a different matter, and the schoolgirl who idolises her mistress, the boy who worships his master, is deprived of the chance of free and independent living. His personality fails to develop and he goes into the world as a parasitic plant, clinging ever to the support of some stronger character.

So far we have considered incidental ways of trespassing upon those rights of personality proper to children, but we have more pervasive, if less injurious, ways of stultifying intellectual and moral growth. Our school ethic rests upon, our school discipline is supported by, undue play upon certain natural desires. It is worth while to reflect that the mind also has its appetites, better known as desires. It is as necessary that Mind should be fed, should grow and should produce, as that these things should happen to Body, and just as Body would not take the trouble to feed itself if it never became hungry, so Mind also would not take in that which it needs if it were not that certain Desires require to be satisfied. Therefore schoolmasters do not amiss in basing their practice upon the Desires whose very function appears to be to bring nourishment to Mind.

Where we teachers err is in stimulating the wrong Desires to accomplish our end. There is the desire of approbation which even an infant shows, he is not happy unless mother or nurse approve of him. Later this same desire helps him to conquer a sum, climb a hill, bring home a good report from school, and all this is grist to the mill, knowledge to the mind; because the persons whose approbation is worth having care that he should learn and know, conquer idleness, and get habits of steady work, so that his mind may be as duly nourished every day as is his body. Alas for the vanity that attends this desire of approbation, that makes the boy more solicitous for the grin of the stable-boy than for the approval of his master! Nay, this desire for approval may get such possession of him that he thinks of nothing else; he must have approval whether from the worthless or the virtuous. It is supposed that outbreaks of violence, robbery, assassinations, occur at times for the mere sake of infamy, just as deeds of heroism are done for the sake of fame. Both infamy and fame mean being thought about and talked about by a large number of people; and we know how this natural desire is worked by the daily press; how we get, now a film actress, now a burglar, a spy, a hero, or a scientist set before us to be our admiration and our praise.

Emulation, the desire of excelling, works wonders in the hands of the schoolmaster; and, indeed, this natural desire is an amazing spur to effort, both intellectual and moral. When in pursuit of virtue two or a score are 'emulously rapid in the race,' a school acquires 'a good tone' and parents are justified in thinking it the right place for their boy. In the intellectual field, however, there is danger; and nothing worse could have happened to our schools than the system of marks, prizes, place-taking, by which many of them are practically governed. A boy is so taken up with the desire to forge ahead that there is no time to think of anything else. What he learns is not interesting to him; he works to get his remove.

But emulation does not stand alone as Viceregent in our schools; another natural desire whose unvarnished name is avarice labours for good government and so-called progress cheek by jowl with emulation. "He must get a scholarship,"—is the duty of a small boy even before he goes to school, and indeed for good and sufficient reasons. Sometimes the sons of rich parents carry off these prizes but as a rule they fall to those for whom they are intended, the sons of educated parents in rather straitened circumstances, sons of the clergy, for example. The scholarship system is no more than a means of distributing the vast wealth left by benefactors in the past for this particular purpose. Every Grammar school has its own scholarships; the Universities have open scholarships and bursaries often of considerable value; and a free, or partially free, education is open to the majority of the youth of the upper middle class on one condition, that of brains. It is small wonder that every Grammar and Public School bases its curriculum upon these conditions, knows exactly what standard of merit will secure the 'Hastings,' knows the boys who have a chance, and orders their very strenuous work towards the end in view. It is hard to say what better could be done and yet this deliberate cult of cupidity is disastrous; for there is no doubt that here and there we come upon impoverishment of personality due to enfeebled intellectual life; the boy did not learn to delight in knowledge in his schooldays and the man is shallow in mind and whimsical in judgment.

It is hopeless to make war from without on a system which affords very effectual help in the education of boys who are likely later to become of service to the country; but Britain must make the most of her sons and many of these men are capable of being more than they are. It is from within the schools that help must come and the way is fairly obvious. Most schools give from eleven in the lowest to eight hours in the highest Forms to 'English' that is, from twenty to sixteen consecutive readings a week might be afforded in a wide selection of books,—literature, history, economics, etc.,—books read with the concentrated attention which makes a single reading suffice. The act of narrating what has been read might well be useful to boys who should be prepared for public speaking. By a slight alteration of this kind, in procedure rather than in curriculum or timetable, it is probable that our schools would turn out many more well-read, well-informed men and convincing speakers than they do at present. Such a method, even if applied to 'English' only, would tend to correct any tendency in schools to become mere cramming places for examinations, would infect boys with a love of knowledge and should divert the natural desire for acquisition into a new channel, for few things are more delightful than the acquisition of knowledge.

We need not delay over that desire of power, ambition, which plays its part in every life; but the educator must see that it plays no more than its part. Power is good in proportion as it gives opportunities for serving; but it is mischievous in boy or man when the pleasure of ruling, managing, becomes a definite spring of action. Like each of the other natural desires, that for power may ruin a life that it is allowed to master; ambition is the cause of half the disasters under which mankind suffers. The ambitious boy or man would as soon lead his fellows in riot and disorder as in noble effort in a good cause; and who can say how far the labour unrest under which we suffer is inspired and inflamed by ambitious men who want to rule if only for the immediate intoxication of rousing and leading men? It is a fine thing to say of a multitude of men,—"I can wind them around my little finger"; and the much-burdened Head of a school must needs beware! If the able, ambitious fellow be allowed to manage the rest, he cheats them out of their fair share of managing their own lives; no boy should be allowed to wax feeble to make another great; the harm to the ambitious boy himself must be considered too, lest he become an ignoble, manoeuvring person. It is within a teacher's scope to offer wholesome ambitions to a boy, to make him keen to master knowledge rather than manage men; and here he has wide field without encroaching on another's preserve.

Another desire which may well be made to play into the schoolmaster's hands is that of society, a desire which has much to do with the making of the naughty boys, idle youths and silly women of our acquaintance. It is sheer delight to mix with our fellows, but much depends on whom we take for our fellows and why; and here young people may be helped by finger-posts. If they are so taught that knowledge delights them, they will choose companions who share that pleasure. In this way princes are trained; they must know something of botany to talk with botanists, of history to meet with historians; they cannot afford to be in the company of scientists, adventurers, poets, painters, philanthropists or economists, and themselves be able to do no more than 'change the weather and pass the time of day'; they must know modern languages to be at home with men of other countries, and ancient tongues to be familiar with classical allusions. Such considerations rule the education of princes, and every boy has a princely right to be brought up so that he may hold his own in good society, that is, the society of those who 'know.'

We hear complaints of the cast-iron system of British society; but how much of it is due to the ignorance which makes it only possible to men and women to talk to those of their own clique, soldiers with soldiers, schoolmasters and schoolboys with their kind? The boy who wants to be able to talk to people who 'know' has no unworthy motive for working.

We have considered the several desires whose function is to stimulate the mind and save us from that vis inertiae which is our besetting danger. Each such desire has its place but the results are disastrous if any one should dominate. It so happens that the last desire we have to consider, the desire of knowledge, is commonly deprived of its proper function in our schools by the predominance of other springs of action, especially of emulation, the desire of place, and avarice, the desire of wealth, tangible profit. This divine curiosity is recognised in ordinary life chiefly as a desire to know trivial things. What did it cost? What did she say? Who was with him? Where are they going? How many postage stamps in line would go round the world? And curiosity is satisfied by incoherent, scrappy information which serves no purpose, assuredly not the purpose of knowledge whose function is to nourish the mind as food nourishes the body. But so besotted is our educational thought that we believe children regard knowledge rather as repulsive medicine than as inviting food. Hence our dependence on marks and prizes, athletics, alluring presentation, any jam we can devise to disguise the powder. The man who wilfully goes on crutches has incompetent legs; he who chooses to go blindfold has eyes that cannot bear the sun; he who lives on pap-meat has weak digestive powers, and he whose mind is sustained by the crutches of emulation and avarice loses that one stimulating power which is sufficient for his intellectual needs. This atrophy of the desire of knowledge is the penalty our scholars pay because we have chosen to make them work for inferior ends. Our young men and maidens do not read unless with the stimulus of a forthcoming examination. They are good-natured and pleasant but have no wide range of thought, lofty purpose, little of the magnanimity which is proper for a citizen. Great thoughts and great actions are strange to them, though the possibility is still there and they may yet shew in peace such action as we have seen and wondered at during the War. But we cannot always educate by means of a great war; the penalties are too heavy for human nature to endure for long. Therefore the stimuli to greatness, magnanimity, which the war afforded we must produce in the ordinary course of education.

But knowledge is delectable. We have all the 'satiable curtiosity' of Mr. Kipling's Elephant even when we content ourselves with the broken meats flung by the daily press. Knowledge is to us as our mother's milk, we grow thereby and in the act of sucking are admirably content.

The work of education is greatly simplified when we realize that children, apparently all children, want to know all human knowledge; they have an appetite for what is put before them, and, knowing this, our teaching becomes buoyant with the courage of our convictions. We know how Richelieu shut up colleges throughout France, both Jesuit and secular, "in order to prevent the mania of the poor for educating their children which distracts them from the pursuits of trade and war." This mania exists with us, not only in the parents but in the children, the mania of hungry souls clamouring for meat, and we choke them off, not by shutting up schools and colleges, but by offering matter which no living soul can digest. The complaints made by teachers and children of the monotony of the work in our schools is full of pathos and all credit to those teachers who cheer the weary path by entertaining devices. But mind does not live and grow upon entertainment; it requires its solid meals.

The Gloucestershire teachers, under Mr. Household's direction, have entered so fully into the principles implied in the method, that I am tempted to illustrate largely from their experience. But they by no means stand alone. Hundreds of other teachers have the same experiences and describe them as opportunity offers. The finding of this power which is described as 'sensing a passage,' is as the striking of a vein of gold in that fabulously rich country, human nature. Our 'find' is that children have a natural aptitude for literary expression which they enjoy in hearing or reading and employ in telling or writing. We might have guessed this long ago. All those speeches and sayings of untamed warriors and savage potentates which the historians have preserved for us, critics have declined as showing too much cultivated rhetoric to have been possible for any but highly educated persons. But the time is coming when we shall perceive that only minds like those of children are capable of producing thoughts so fresh and so finely expressed. This natural aptitude for literature, or, shall we say, rhetoric, which overcomes the disabilities of a poor vocabulary without effort, should direct the manner of instruction we give, ruling out the talky-talky of the oral lesson and the lecture; ruling out, equally, compilations and text-books; and placing books in the hands of children and only those which are more or less literary in character that is, which have the terseness and vividness proper to literary work. The natural desire for knowledge does the rest and the children feed and grow.

It must be borne in mind that in proportion as other desires are stimulated that of knowledge is suppressed. The teacher who proposes marks and places as worthy aims will get work certainly but he will get no healthy love of knowledge for its own sake and no provision against the ennui of later days. The monotony I have spoken of attends all work prompted by the stimuli of marks and places; such work becomes mechanical, and there is hardly enough of it prepared to last through the course of a boy's school life. The master of a Preparatory School remarks,—"It must be a well-known fact (I am not speaking of the exceptional but of the average boy) that new boys are placed too low. We find it is a common experience—that if we send up a boy whether he be a good mathematician, a good classic, a good English scholar or a good linguist, a couple of years will pass by before he is doing at the Public School the work he was doing when he left us." The Public School-master makes the same sort of complaint; he says, that "At twenty the boy is climbing the same pear-tree that be climbed at twelve," that is to say, work which is done in view of examinations must be of the rather narrow mechanical kind upon which it is possible to set questions and mark answers with absolute fairness. Now, definite progress, continual advance from day to day with no treading of old ground, is a condition of education.

There is an uneasy dread in some minds lest a liberal education for all, the possibility which is now before us, should cause a social bouleversement, such an upheaval as obtained in the French Revolution. But this fear arises from an erroneous conception. The doctrine of equal opportunities for all is no doubt dangerous. It is the intellectual rendering of the 'survival of the fittest' and we have had a terrible object lesson as to how that doctrine works. The uneasy, ambitious spirit comes to the front, gets all the chances, dominates his fellows, and thinks no upheaval too great a price for the advancement of himself and his notions. Men of this type come to the top through the avenue of examinations. Ambition and possibly greed are seconded by dogged perseverance. As was said of Louis xiv, such men elevate their practice into a theory and arrogate to their habits the character of principles of government. And these pseudo-principles inflame the populace because they promise place and power to every man in the state, with no sense of the proportion he bears to the rest. Probably the 'labour unrest' of to-day is not without connexion with the habit of working in our schools for prizes and places. The boy who works to be first and to get something out of it does not always become the quiet, well-ordered citizen who helps to cement society and carries on the work of the State.

Knowledge pursued for its own sake is sedative in so far as it is satisfying; and the splendid consciousness that every boy in your Form has your own delight in knowing, your own pleasure in expressing that which he knows, shares your intimacy with this and the other sage and hero, makes for good fellowship and magnanimity and should deliver the citizen from a restless desire to come to the front. It is possible that a conscientious and intelligent teacher may be a little overwhelmed when he considers all that goes to a man, all that goes to each of the boys under his care. It is true that,

"There lives
No faculty within us which the Soul
Can spare: and humblest earthly weal demands
For dignity not placed beyond her reach
Zealous co-operation of all means
Given or required to raise us from the mire
And liberate our hearts from low pursuits
By gross utilities enslaved; we need
More of ennobling impulse from the past
If for the future aught of good must come."
[from Musings Near Aquapendente, by William Wordsworth]

Wordsworth is no doubt right. There is no faculty within the soul which can be spared in the great work of education; but then every faculty, or rather power, works to the one end if we make the pursuit of knowledge for its own sake the object of our educational efforts. We find children ready and eager for this labour and their accomplishment is surprising.

Chapter 6 Three Instruments of Education

1.—Education is an Atmosphere

Seeing that we are limited by the respect due to the personality of children we can allow ourselves but three educational instruments—the atmosphere of environment, the discipline of habit and the presentation of living ideas. Our motto is,—'Education is an atmosphere, a discipline, a life.' When we say that education is an atmosphere we do not mean that a child should be isolated in what may be called a 'child environment' specially adapted and prepared, but that we should take into account the educational value of his natural home atmosphere both as regards persons and things and should let him live freely among his proper conditions. It stultifies a child to bring down his world to the 'child's' level.

Having cut out the direct use of fear or love, suggestion or influence, undue play upon any one natural desire, emulation, for example, we are no longer free to use all means in the education of children. There are but three left for our use and to each of these we must give careful study or we shall not realise how great a scope is left to us. To consider the first of these educational instruments; for a decade or two we have pinned our faith on environment as a great part of education; as, say, nine-tenths rather than a third part of the whole. The theory has been,—put a child in the right environment and so subtle is its influence, so permanent its effects that he is to all intents and purposes educated thereby. Schools may add Latin and sums and whatever else their curriculum contains, but the actual education is, as it were, performed upon a child by means of colour schemes, harmonious sounds, beautiful forms, gracious persons. He grows up aesthetically educated into sweet reasonableness and harmony with his surroundings.

"Peter's nursery was a perfect dream in which to hatch the soul of a little boy. Its walls were done in warm, cream-coloured paint and upon them Peter's father had put the most lovely patterns of trotting and jumping horses and dancing cats and dogs and leaping lambs, a carnival of beasts . . . there was a big brass fire-guard in Peter's nursery . . . and all the tables had smoothly rounded corners against the days when Peter would run about. The floor was of cork carpet on which Peter would put his toys and there was a crimson hearthrug on which Peter was destined to crawl . . . there were scales in Peter's nursery to weigh Peter every week and tables to show how much he ought to weigh and when one should begin to feel anxious. There was nothing casual about the early years of Peter."

So, Mr. [H.G.] Wells, in that inconclusive educational treatise of his, Joan and Peter. It is an accurate picture of the preparation for 'high-souled' little persons all over the world. Parents make tremendous sacrifices to that goddess who presides over Education. We hear of a pair investing more than their capital in a statue to adorn the staircase in order that 'Tommy' should make his soul by the contemplation of beauty. This sort of thing has been going on since the 'eighties at any rate and, as usual, Germany erected a high altar for the cult which she passed on to the rest of us. Perhaps it is safe to say that the Young Intelligenzia of Europe have been reared after this manner. And is the result that Neo-Georgian youth Punch presents to us with his air of weariness, condescension and self-complacency? Let us hear Professor Sir Jagadis Chandra Bose, the Indian scientist, on one of his conclusions concerning the nervous impulse in plants,

"A plant carefully protected under glass from outside shocks looks sleek and flourishing but its higher nervous function is then found to be atrophied. But when a succession of "blows" (electric shocks) "is rained on this effete and bloated specimen, the shocks themselves create nervous channels and arouse anew the deteriorated nature. Is it not the shocks of adversity and not cotton wool protection that evolve true manhood?"

We had thought that the terrible succession of blows inflicted by the War had changed all that; but, no; the errors of education still hold sway and we still have amongst us the better-than-my-neighbour folk, whose function, let us hope, is to administer the benefits of adversity to most of us. What if parents and teachers in their zeal misread the schedule of their duties, magnified their office unduly and encroached upon the personality of children? It is not an environment that these want, a set of artificial relations carefully constructed, but an atmosphere which nobody has been at pains to constitute. It is there, about the child, his natural element, precisely as the atmosphere of the earth is about us. It is thrown off, as it were, from persons and things, stirred by events, sweetened by love, ventilated, kept in motion, by the regulated action of common sense. We all know the natural conditions under which a child should live; how he shares household ways with his mother, romps with his father, is teased by his brothers and petted by his sisters; is taught by his tumbles; learns self-denial by the baby's needs, the delightfulness of furniture by playing at battle and siege with sofa and table; learns veneration for the old by the visits of his great-grandmother; how to live with his equals by the chums he gathers round him; learns intimacy with animals from his dog and cat; delight in the fields where the buttercups grow and greater delight in the blackberry hedges. And, what tempered 'fusion of classes' is so effective as a child's intimacy with his betters, and also with cook and housemaid, blacksmith and joiner, with everybody who comes in his way? Children have a genius for this sort of general intimacy, a valuable part of their education; care and guidance are needed, of course, lest admiring friends should make fools of them, but no compounded 'environment' could make up for this fresh air, this wholesome wind blowing now from one point, now from another.

We certainly may use atmosphere as an instrument of education, but there are prohibitions, for ourselves rather than for children. Perhaps the chief of these is, that no artificial element be introduced, no sprinkling with rose-water, softening with cushions. Children must face life as it is; if their parents are anxious and perturbed children feel it in the air. "Mummie, Mummie, you aren't going to cry this time, are you?" and a child's hug tries to take away the trouble. By these things children live and we may not keep them in glass cases; if we do, they develop in succulence and softness and will not become plants of renown. But due relations must be maintained; the parents are in authority, the children in obedience; and again, the strong may not lay their burdens on the weak; nor must we expect from children that effort of decision, the most fatiguing in our lives, of which the young should generally be relieved.

School, perhaps, offers fewer opportunities for vitiating the atmosphere than does home life. But teaching may be so watered down and sweetened, teachers may be so suave and condescending, as to bring about a condition of intellectual feebleness and moral softness which it is not easy for a child to overcome. The bracing atmosphere of truth and sincerity should be perceived in every School; and here again the common pursuit of knowledge by teacher and class comes to our aid and creates a Current of fresh air perceptible even to the chance visitor, who sees the glow of intellectual life and moral health on the faces of teachers and children alike.

But a school may be working hard, not for love of knowledge, but for love of marks, our old enemy; and then young faces are not serene and joyous but eager, restless, apt to look anxious and worried. The children do not sleep well and are cross; are sullen or in tears if anything goes wrong, and are, generally, difficult to manage. When this is the case there is too much oxygen in the air; they are breathing a too stimulating atmosphere, and the nervous strain to which they are subjected must needs be followed by reaction. Then teachers think that lessons have been too hard, that children should be relieved of this and that study; the doctors probably advise that so-and-so should 'run wild' for a year. Poor little soul, at the very moment when he is most in need of knowledge for his sustenance he is left to prey upon himself! No wonder the nervous symptoms become worse, and the boy or girl suffers under the stigma of 'nervous strain.' The fault has been in the atmosphere and not in the work; the teacher, perhaps, is over anxious that her children should do well and her nervous excitation is catching. "I am afraid X cannot do his examination; he loves his work but he bursts into tears when he is asked an examination question. Perhaps it is that I have insisted too much that he must never be satisfied with anything but his best." Poor little chap (of seven) pricked into over exertion by the spur of moral stimulus! We foresee happy days for children when all teachers know that no other exciting motive whatever is necessary to produce good work in each individual of however big a class than that love of knowledge which is natural to every child. The serenity and sweetness of schools conducted on this principle is surprising to the outsider who has not reflected upon the contentment of a baby with his bottle!

There are two courses open to us in this matter. One, to create by all manner of modified conditions a hot-house atmosphere, fragrant but emasculating, in which children grow apace but are feeble and dependent; the other to leave them open to all the "airts that blow," but with care lest they be unduly battered; lest, for example, a miasma come their way in the shape of a vicious companion.

2.—Education is a Discipline

By this formula we mean the discipline of habits formed definitely and thoughtfully whether habits of mind or of body. Physiologists tell us of the adaptation of brain structure to habitual lines of thought, i.e., to our habits.

Education is not after all to either teacher or child the fine careless rapture we appear to have figured it. We who teach and they who learn are alike constrained; there is always effort to be made in certain directions; yet we face our tasks from a new point of view. We need not labour to get children to learn their lessons; that, if we would believe it, is a matter which nature takes care of. Let the lessons be of the right sort and children will learn them with delight. The call for strenuousness comes with the necessity of forming habits; but here again we are relieved. The intellectual habits of the good life form themselves in the following out of the due curriculum in the right way. As we have already urged, there is but one right way, that is, children must do the work for themselves. They must read the given pages and tell what they have read, they must perform, that is, what we may call the act of knowing. We are all aware, alas, what a monstrous quantity of printed matter has gone into the dustbin of our memories, because we have failed to perform that quite natural and spontaneous 'act of knowing,' as easy to a child as breathing and, if we would believe it, comparatively easy to ourselves. The reward is two-fold: no intellectual habit is so valuable as that of attention; it is a mere habit but it is also the hall-mark of an educated person. Use is second nature, we are told; it is not too much to say that 'habit is ten natures,' and we can all imagine how our work would be eased if our subordinates listened to instructions with the full attention which implies recollection—Attention is not the only habit that follows due self-education. The habits of fitting and ready expression, of obedience, of good-will, and of an impersonal outlook are spontaneous bye-products of education in this sort. So, too, are the habits of right thinking and right judging; while physical habits of neatness and order attend upon the self-respect which follows an education which respects the personality of children.

Physiologists tell us that thoughts which have become habitual make somehow a mark upon the brain substance, but we are bold in calling it a mark for there is no discernible effect to be quoted. Whether or no the mind be served by the brain in this matter, we are empirically certain that a chief function of education is the establishment of such ways of thinking in children as shall issue in good and useful living, clear thinking, aesthetic enjoyment, and, above all, in the religious life. How it is possible that spirit should act upon matter is a mystery to us, but that such act takes place we perceive every time we note a scowling brow, or, on the other hand,—

"A sweet attractive kind of grace,
A full assurance given by looks;
Continual comfort in a face,
The lineaments of gospel books."

We all know how the physical effort of smiling affects ourselves in our sour moods,—

"Nor soul helps flesh more now, than flesh helps soul"

Both are at our service in laying down the rails, so to speak, upon which the good life must needs run.

In the past we have, no doubt, gone through an age of infant slavery, an age of good habits enforced by vigorous penalties, conscientiously by the over scrupulous eighteenth century parent, and infamously by the school masters, the 'Creakies' and the 'Squeers' who laboured only for their own ease and profit. Now, the pendulum swings the other way. We have lost sight of the fact that habit is to life what rails are to transport cars. It follows that lines of habit must be laid down towards given ends and after careful survey, or the joltings and delays of life become insupportable. More, habit is inevitable. If we fail to ease life by laying down habits of right thinking and right acting, habits of wrong thinking and wrong acting fix themselves of their own accord. We avoid decision and indecision brings its own delays, "and days are lost lamenting o'er lost days." Almost every child is brought up by his parents in certain habits of decency and order without which he would be a social outcast. Think from another point of view how the labour of life would be increased if every act of the bath, toilet, table, every lifting of the fork and use of spoon were a matter of consideration and required an effort of decision! No; habit is like fire, a bad master but an indispensable servant; and probably one reason for the nervous scrupulosity, hesitation, indecision of our day, is that life was not duly eased for us in the first place by those whose business it was to lay down lines of habit upon which our behaviour might run easily.

It is unnecessary to enumerate those habits which we should aim at forming, for everyone knows more about these than anyone practises. We admire the easy carriage of the soldier but shrink from the discipline which is able to produce it. We admire the lady who can sit upright through a long dinner, who in her old age prefers a straight chair because she has arrived at due muscular balance and has done so by a course of discipline. There is no other way of forming any good habit, though the discipline is usually that of the internal government which the person exercises upon himself; but a certain strenuousness in the formation of good habits is necessary because every such habit is the result of conflict. The bad habit of the easy life is always pleasant and persuasive and to be resisted with pain and effort, but with hope and certainty of success, because in our very structure is the preparation for forming such habits of muscle and mind as we deliberately propose to ourselves. We entertain the idea which gives birth to the act and the act repeated again and again becomes the habit; 'Sow an act,' we are told, 'reap a habit.' 'Sow a habit, reap a character.' But we must go a step further back, we must sow the idea or notion which makes the act worth while. The lazy boy who hears of the Great Duke's narrow camp bed, preferred by him because when he wanted to turn over it was time to get up, receives the idea of prompt rising. But his nurse or his mother knows how often and how ingeniously the tale must be brought to his mind before the habit of prompt rising is formed; she knows too how the idea of self-conquest must be made at home in the boy's mind until it become a chivalric impulse which he cannot resist. It is possible to sow a great idea lightly and casually and perhaps this sort of sowing should be rare and casual because if a child detect a definite purpose in his mentor he is apt to stiffen himself against it. When parent or teacher supposes that a good habit is a matter of obedience to his authority, he relaxes a little. A boy is late who has been making evident efforts to be punctual; the teacher good-naturedly foregoes rebuke or penalty, and the boy says to himself,—"It doesn't matter," and begins to form the unpunctual habit. The mistake the teacher makes is to suppose that to be punctual is troublesome to the boy, so he will let him off; whereas the office of the habits of an ordered life is to make such life easy and spontaneous; the effort is confined to the first half dozen or score of occasions for doing the thing.

Consider how laborious life would be were its wheels not greased by habits of cleanliness, neatness, order, courtesy; had we to make the effort of decision about every detail of dressing and eating, coming and going, life would not be worth living. Every cottage mother knows that she must train her child in habits of decency, and a whole code of habits of propriety get themselves formed just because a breach in any such habit causes a shock to others which few children have courage to face. Physical fitness, morals and manners, are very largely the outcome of habit; and not only so, but the habits of the religious life also become fixed and delightful and give us due support in the effort to live a godly, righteous and sober life. We need not be deterred by the fear that religious habits in a child are mechanical, uninformed by the ideas which should give them value. Let us hear what the young De Quincey felt about going to church:—

"On Sunday mornings I went with the rest of my family to church: it was a church on the ancient model of England having aisles, galleries, organ, all things ancient and venerable, and the proportions were majestic.

Here, whilst the congregation knelt through the long litany, as often as we came to that passage so beautiful amongst many that are so where God is supplicated on behalf of 'all sick persons and young children' and 'that He would show His pity upon all prisoners and captives,' I wept in secret, and raising my streaming eyes to the upper windows saw, on days when the sun was shining, a spectacle as affecting as ever prophet can have beheld . . . there were the Apostles that had trampled upon earth and the glories upon earth, there were the martyrs who had borne witness to the truth through flames . . . and all the time I saw through the wide central field of the window where the glass was uncoloured white fleecy clouds sailing over the azure depths of the sky."

And then the little boy had visions of sick children upon whom God would have pity.—

"These visions were self-sustained, the hint from the Litany, the fragment from the clouds, those and the storied windows were sufficient. God speaks to children also in dreams and by the oracles that lurk in darkness; but in solitude, above all things when made vocal to the meditative heart by the truths and services of a national church, God holds with children 'communion undisturbed.'"

With such a testimony before us, supported by gleams of recollection on our own part, we may take courage to believe that what we rightly call Divine Service is particularly appropriate to children; and will become more so as the habit of reading beautifully written books quickens their sense of style and their unconscious appreciation of the surpassingly beautiful diction of our liturgy.

We have seen the value of habit in mind and morals, religion and physical development. It is as we have seen disastrous when child or man learns to think in a groove, and shivers like an unaccustomed bather on the steps of a new notion. This danger is perhaps averted by giving children as their daily diet the wise thoughts of great minds, and of many great minds; so that they may gradually and unconsciously get the courage of their opinions. If we fail in this duty, so soon as the young people get their 'liberty' they will run after the first fad that presents itself; try it for a while and then take up another to be discarded in its turn, and remain uncertain and ill-guided for the rest of their days.

3.—Education is a Life

We have left until the last that instrument of education implied in the phrase 'Education is a life'; 'implied' because life is no more self-existing than it is self-supporting; it requires sustenance, regular, ordered and fitting. This is fully recognised as regards bodily life and, possibly, the great discovery of the twentieth century will be that mind too requires its ordered rations and perishes when these fail. We know that food is to the body what fuel is to the steam-engine, the sole source of energy; once we realise that the mind too works only as it is fed education will appear to us in a new light. The body pines and develops humours upon tabloids and other food substitutes; and a glance at a 'gate' crowd watching a football match makes us wonder what sort of mind-food those men and boys are sustained on, whether they are not suffering from depletion, inanition, notwithstanding big and burly bodies. For the mind is capable of dealing with only one kind of food; it lives, grows and is nourished upon ideas only; mere information is to it as a meal of sawdust to the body; there are no organs for the assimilation of the one more than of the other.

What is an idea? we ask, and find ourselves plunged beyond our depth. A live thing of the mind, seems to be the conclusion of our greatest thinkers from Plato to Bacon, from Bacon to Coleridge. We all know how an idea 'strikes,' 'seizes,' 'catches hold of,' 'impresses' us and at last, if it be big enough, 'possesses' us; in a word, behaves like an entity.

If we enquire into any person's habits of life, mental preoccupation, devotion to a cause or pursuit, he will usually tell us that such and such an idea struck him. This potency of an idea is matter of common recognition. No phrase is more common and more promising than, 'I have an idea'; we rise to such an opening as trout to a well-chosen fly. There is but one sphere in which the word idea never occurs, in which the conception of an idea is curiously absent, and that sphere is education! Look at any publisher's list of school books and you shall find that the books recommended are carefully dessicated, drained of the least suspicion of an idea, reduced to the driest statements of fact. Here perhaps the Public Schools have a little pull over the rest of us--the diet they afford may be meagre, meagre almost to starvation point for the average boy, but it is not destitute of ideas; for, however sparsely, boys are nourished on the best thoughts of the best minds.

Coleridge has done more than other thinkers to bring the conception of an idea within the sphere of the scientific thought of to-day; not as that thought is expressed in psychology, a term which he himself launched upon the world with an apology for it as insolens verbum ("we beg pardon for the use of this insolens verbum but it is one of which our language stands in great need." Method, S. T. Coleridge) but as shewing the re-action of mind to an idea. This is how in his Method Coleridge illustrates the rise and progress of such an idea:—

"We can recall no incident of human history that impresses the imagination more deeply than the moment when Columbus on an unknown ocean first perceived that baffling fact, the change of the magnetic needle. How many instances occur in history when the ideas of nature (presented to chosen minds by a Higher Power than Nature herself) suddenly unfold as it were in prophetic succession systematic views destined to produce the most important revolutions in the state of man! The clear spirit of Columbus was doubtless eminently methodical. He saw distinctly that great leading idea which authorised the poor pilot to become a 'promiser of kingdoms.'"

Here we get such a genesis of an idea as fits in curiously with what we know of the history of great inventions and discoveries "presented to chosen minds by a higher Power than Nature herself." It corresponds too, not only with the ideas that rule our own lives, but with the origin of practical ideas which is unfolded to us by the prophet Isaiah:—

"Doth the ploughman plough continually to . . . open and break the clods of his ground? When he hath made plain the face thereof, doth he not cast abroad the fitches and scatter the cummin and put the wheat in rows . . . for his God doth instruct him aright and doth teach him . . . Bread corn is ground for he will not ever be threshing it . . . This also cometh from the Lord of Hosts which is wonderful in counsel and excellent in working." [Isaiah xxviii.]

Let us hear Coleridge further on the subject of those ideas which may invest us as an atmosphere rather than strike as a weapon:—

"The idea may exist in a clear and definite form as that of a circle in that of the mind of a geometrician or it may be a mere instinct, a vague appetency towards something . . . like the impulse which fills a young poet's eyes with tears."

These indefinite ideas which express themselves in an 'appetency' towards something and which should draw a child towards things honest, lovely and of good report, are not to be offered of set purpose or at set times: they are held in that thought-atmosphere which surrounds him, breathed as his breath of life.

It is distressing to think that our poor words and ways should be thus inspired by children; but to recognise the fact will make us careful not to admit sordid or unworthy thoughts and motives into our dealings with them.

Coleridge treats in more detail those definite ideas which are not inhaled as air but are conveyed as meat to the mind:—

"From the first or initiative idea, as from a seed, successive ideas germinate." "Events and images, the lively and spirit-stirring machinery of the external world, are like light and air and moisture to the seed of the mind which would else rot and perish." "The paths in which we may pursue a methodical course are manifold and at the head of each stands its peculiar and guiding idea. Those ideas are as regularly subordinate in dignity as the paths to which they point are various and eccentric in direction. The world has suffered much in modern times from a subversive and necessary natural order of science . . . from summoning reason and faith to the bar of that limited physical experience to which by the true laws of method they owe no obedience. Progress follows the path of the idea from which it sets out requiring however a constant wakefulness of mind to keep it within the due limits of its course. Hence the orbits of thought, so to speak, must differ from among themselves as the initiative ideas differ." (Method, S. T. C.).

Is it not a fact that the new light which biology is throwing upon the laws of mind is bringing us back to the Platonic doctrine that "An idea is a distinguishable power, self-affirmed and seen in unity with the Eternal Essence"?

I have ventured to repeat from an earlier volume this slight exposition of Coleridge's teaching, because his doctrine corresponds with common experience and should reverse our ordinary educational practice. The whole subject is profound, but as practical as it is profound. We must disabuse our minds of the theory that the functions of education are in the main gymnastic, a continual drawing out without a corresponding act of putting in. The modern emphasis upon 'self-expression' has given new currency to this idea; we who know how little there is in us that we have not received, that the most we can do is to give an original twist, a new application, to an idea that has been passed on to us; who recognise, humbly enough, that we are but torch-bearers, passing on our light to the next as we have received it from the last, even we invite children to 'express themselves' about a tank, a Norman castle, the Man in the Moon, not recognising that the quaint things children say on unfamiliar subjects are no more than a patchwork of notions picked up here and there. One is not sure that so-called original composition is wholesome for children, because their consciences are alert and they are quite aware of their borrowings; it may be better that they should read on a theme before they write upon it, using then as much latitude as they like.

In the early days of a child's life it makes little apparent difference whether we educate with a notion of filling a receptacle, inscribing a tablet, moulding plastic matter, or nourishing a life, but as a child grows we shall perceive that only those ideas which have fed his life, are taken into his being; all the rest is cast away or is, like sawdust in the system, an impediment and an injury.

Education is a life. That life is sustained on ideas. Ideas are of spiritual origin, and God has made us so that we get them chiefly as we convey them to one another, whether by word of mouth, written page, Scripture word, musical symphony; but we must sustain a child's inner life with ideas as we sustain his body with food. Probably he will reject nine-tenths of the ideas we offer, as he makes use of only a small proportion of his bodily food, rejecting the rest. He is an eclectic; he may choose this or that; our business is to supply him with due abundance and variety and his to take what he needs. Urgency on our part annoys him. He resists forcible feeding and loathes predigested food. What suits him best is pabulum presented in the indirect literary form which Our Lord adopts in those wonderful parables whose quality is that they cannot be forgotten though, while every detail of the story is remembered, its application may pass and leave no trace. We, too, must take this risk. We may offer children as their sustenance the Lysander of Plutarch, an object lesson, we think, shewing what a statesman or a citizen should avoid: but, who knows, the child may take to Lysander and think his 'cute' ways estimable! Again, we take the risk, as did our Lord in that puzzling parable of the Unjust Steward. One other caution; it seems to be necessary to present ideas with a great deal of padding, as they reach us in a novel or poem or history book written with literary power. A child cannot in mind or body live upon tabloids however scientifically prepared; out of a whole big book he may not get more than half a dozen of those ideas upon which his spirit thrives; and they come in unexpected places and unrecognised forms, so that no grown person is capable of making such extracts from Scott or Dickens or Milton, as will certainly give him nourishment. It is a case of,—"In the morning sow thy seed and in the evening withhold not thine hand for thou knowest not whether shall prosper, either this or that."

One of our presumptuous sins in this connection is that we venture to offer opinions to children (and to older persons) instead of ideas. We believe that an opinion expresses thought and therefore embodies an idea. Even if it did so once the very act of crystallization into opinion destroys any vitality it may have had; pace Ruskin, a crystal is not a living body and does not feed men. We think to feed children on the dogmas of a church, the theorems of Euclid, mere abstracts of history, and we wonder that their education does not seem to take hold of them. Let us hear M. Fouillée [Education From a National Standpoint.] on this subject, for to him the idea is all in all both in philosophy and education. But there is a function of education upon which M. Fouillée hardly touches, that of the formation of habits, physical, intellectual, moral.

"'Scientific truths,' said Descartes, 'are battles won.' Describe to the young the principal and most heroic of these battles; you will thus interest them in the results of science and you will develop in them a scientific spirit by means of the enthusiasm for the conquest of truth . . . How interesting Arithmetic and Geometry might be if we gave a short history of their principal theorems, if the child were meant to be present at the labours of a Pythagoras, a Plato, a Euclid, or in modern times, of a Descartes, a Pascal, or a Leibnitz. Great theories instead of being lifeless and anonymous abstractions would become living human truths each with its own history like a statue by Michael Angelo or like a painting by Raphael."

Here we have an application of Coleridge's 'captain-idea' of every train of thought; that is, not a naked generalisation, (neither children nor grown persons find aliment in these), but an idea clothed upon with fact, and story, so that the mind may perform the acts of selection and inception from a mass of illustrative details. Thus Dickens makes 'David Copperfield' tell us that,—"I was a very observant child," and that "all children are very observant," not as a dry abstraction, but as an inference from a number of charming natural incidents.

All roads lead to Rome, and all I have said is meant to enforce the fact that much and varied humane reading, as well as human thought expressed in the forms of art, is, not a luxury, a tit-bit, to be given to children now and then, but their very bread of life, which they must have in abundant portions and at regular periods. This and more is implied in the phrase, "The mind feeds on ideas and therefore children should have a generous curriculum."

Chapter 7 How We Make Use of Mind

"We hold that the child's mind is no mere sac to hold ideas but is rather, if the figure may be allowed, a 'spiritual organism' with an appetite for all knowledge. This is its proper diet with which it is prepared to deal and what it is able to digest and assimilate as the body does food-stuffs."

"Such a doctrine as the Herbartian, that the mind is a receptacle, lays the stress of education, the preparation of food in enticing morsels, duly ordered, upon the teacher. Children taught on this principle are in danger of receiving much teaching but little knowledge; the teacher's axiom being 'what a child learns matters less than how he learns it.'"

I cannot resist presenting the Herbartian Psychology in the dry light of Scottish humour. [The Herbartian Psychology applied to Education, by John Adams.]

"We have failed to explain ideas by the mind, how about explaining the mind by ideas? You are not to suppose that this is exactly how Herbart puts it, Herbart is a philosopher, a German philosopher. It is true that he starts with the mind or, as he prefers to call it, a soul: but do not fear that the sport of the hunt is to be spoiled for that . . . the 'given' soul is no more a real soul than it is a real crater of a volcano. It has absolutely no content: it is not even an idea trap. Ideas can slip in and out of it as they please, or, rather, as other ideas please but the soul has no power either to call, make, keep, or recall, an idea. The ideas arrange all these matters among themselves. The mind can make no objection."

"'The soul has no capacity nor faculty whatever either to receive or produce anything: it is therefore no tabula rasa in the sense that impressions, foreign to its nature, may be made on it. Also it is no substance in Leibnitz's sense, which includes original self-activity. It has originally neither ideas, nor feelings, nor desires. Further, within it lie no forms of intuition and thought, no laws of willing and acting, nor any sort of predisposition however remote towards these. The simple nature of the soul is totally unknown and for ever remains so. It is as little a subject for speculative as for empirical psychology.' (Lehrbuch zur Psychologie, by Herbart: Part III: pp.152, 153.) Thus, a vigorous vis inertiae is the only power of the mind. Still it is subject to the action of certain forces. Nothing but ideas (Vorstellung) can attack the soul so that the ideas really make up the mind."

We are familiar with the struggle of ideas on the threshold, with the good luck of those that get in and especially of those that get in first and mount to high places; with the behaviour of ideas, very much like that of persons who fall into groups in an anarchical state. This behaviour is described as the formation of 'apperception masses' and the mass that is sufficiently strong has it all its own way and dominates the mind. Our business is not to examine the psychology of Herbart, a very serious and suggestive contribution to our knowledge of educational principles, but rather to consider how it works out practically in education. But before we examine how Herbartian psychology bears this test of experiment, let us consider what Professor William James has to say of psychology in general.

"When we talk of psychology as a natural science," he tells us, "we must not assume that that means a sort of psychology that stands at last on solid ground. It means just the reverse. It means a psychology particularly fragile and into which the waters of metaphysical criticism leak at every joint, a psychology all of whose elementary assumptions and data must be reconsidered in wider connections and translated into other terms. It is, in short, a phrase of diffidence and not of arrogance; and it is indeed strange to hear people talk triumphantly of the 'New Psychology' and write Histories of Psychology when into the real elements and forces which the word covers not the first glimpse of clear insight exists. A string of raw facts, a little gossip and wrangle about opinions, a little classification and generalisation on the mere descriptive level . . . but not a single law . . . not a single proposition from which any consequence can casually be deduced."

But Professor James went on and wrote his extraordinarily interesting book on psychology, and we must do the same though our basis is no more than the common experience of mankind so far as one mind can express the experience common to us all.

Herbart's psychology is extraordinarily gratifying and attractive to teachers who are, like other people, eager to magnify their office; and here is a scheme which shows how every child is a new creation as he comes forth from the hands of his teacher. The teacher learns how to do it; he has but to draw together a mass of those ideas which themselves will combine in the mind into which they effect an entrance, and, behold, the thing is done: the teacher has done it; he has selected. the ideas, shewn the correlation of each with the other and the work is complete! The ideas establish themselves, the most potent rule and gather force, and if these be good, the man is made.

Here, for example, is a single week's 'Correlation of Subjects' worked out by a highly qualified teacher. "Arithmetic (Decimal Fractions), Mathematics (Simple Equations, Parallelograms), Science (Latent Heat), Housecraft (Nerves, Thought, Habits), Geography (Scotland, General Industries); or, again, for another week,—under the same headings,—Metric problems, Symbols (four rules), Triangles (sum angles), Machinery, Circulation, Sculpture of the British Isles." The ideas, no doubt, have an agility and ability which we do not possess and know how to jump at each other and form the desired 'apperception masses.'

A successful and able modern educationalist gives us a valuable introduction to Herbartian Principles, and, by way of example, "A Robinson Crusoe Concentration Scheme," a series of lessons given to children in Standard I in an Elementary School. First we have nine lessons in literature and language, the subjects being such as 'Robinson climbs a hill and finds he is on an island.' Then, ten object lessons of which the first is,—The Sea, the second, A Ship from Foreign Parts, the sixth, A Life-Boat, the seventh, Shell-Fish, the tenth, A Cave. How these 'objects' are to be produced one does not see. The third series are drawing lessons, probably as many, a boat, a ship, an oar, an anchor and so on. Then follows a series on manual training, still built upon 'Robinson'; the first, a model of the seashore; then models of Robinson's island, of Robinson's house, and Robinson's pottery. The next course consists of reading, an infinite number of lessons,—'passages from The Child's Robinson Crusoe and from a general reader on the matters discussed in object lessons.' Then follows a series of writing lessons, "simple compositions on the subject of the lessons. ... the children framed the sentences which the teacher wrote on the blackboard and the class copied afterwards." Here is one composition,—"Robinson spent his first night in a tree. In the morning he was hungry but he saw nothing round him but grass and trees without fruit. On the sea-shore he found some shell-fish which he ate." Compare this with the voluminous output of children of six or seven working on the P.U.S. scheme upon any subject that they know; with, indeed, the pages they will dictate after a single reading of a chapter of Robinson Crusoe, not a 'child's edition.'

Arithmetic follows with, no doubt, as many lessons, many mental examples and simple problems dealt with Robinson"; the eighth and last course was in singing and recitation,—'I am monarch of all I survey,' etc. "The lessons lasted about forty-five minutes each... . Under ordinary conditions the story of 'Robinson Crusoe' would be the leading feature in the work of a whole year . . . in comparing the English classes with the German classes I have seen studying 'Robinson Crusoe' I was convinced that the eagerness and interest was as keen among the children here as in the German schools . . . One easily sees what a wealth of material there is in the further development of the story." One does indeed! The whole thing must be highly amusing to the teacher, as ingenious amplifications self-produced always are: that the children too were entertained, one does not doubt. The teacher was probably at her best in getting by sheer force much out of little: she was, in fact, acting a part and the children were entertained as at a show, cinema or other; but of one thing we may be sure, an utter distaste, a loathing, on the part of the children ever after, not only for 'Robinson Crusoe' but for every one of the subjects lugged in to illustrate his adventures. We read elsewhere of an apple affording a text for a hundred lessons, including the making of a ladder, (in paper), to gather the apples; but, alas, the eating of the worn-out apple is not suggested. The author whom we quote for 'Robinson Crusoe' and whom we refrain from naming because, as a Greek Chorus might say, 'we cannot praise,' follows the 'Robinson' series with another interminable series on the Armada.

The conscientious, ingenious and laborious teachers who produce these 'concentration series' are little aware that each such lesson is an act of lese majesté. The children who are capable of and eager for a wide range of knowledge and literary expression are reduced to inanities; a lifelong ennui is set up; every approach to knowledge suggests avenues for boredom, and the children's minds sicken and perish long before their school-days come to an end. I have pursued this subject at some length because we, too, believe in ideas as the proper and only diet upon which children's minds grow. We are more in the dark about Mind than about

Mars! We can but judge by effects, and these appear to point to the conclusion that mind is a 'spiritual organism.' (I need not apologise for speaking of that which has no substance as an 'organism', no greater a contradiction in terms than Herbart's 'apperception masses.') By an analogy with Body we conclude that Mind requires regular and sufficient sustenance; and that this sustenance is afforded by ideas we may gather from the insatiable eagerness with which these are appropriated, and the evident growth and development manifested under such pabulum. That children like feeble and tedious oral lessons, feeble and tedious story books, does not at all prove that these are wholesome food; they like lollipops but cannot live upon them; yet there is a serious attempt in certain schools to supply the intellectual, moral, and religious needs of children by appropriate 'sweetmeats.'

As I have said elsewhere, the ideas required for the sustenance of children are to be found mainly in books of literary quality; given these the mind does for itself the sorting, arranging, selecting, rejecting, classifying, which Herbart leaves to the struggle of the promiscuous ideas which manage to cross the threshold. Nor is this merely a nominal distinction; Herbart was a philosopher and therefore his thought embraced the universal. Probably few schools of the day are consciously following the theories of this philosopher; but in most schools, in England and elsewhere, so far as any intelligent rationale is followed it is that of Herbart. There are many reasons for this fact. A scheme which throws the whole burden of education on the teacher, which exalts the personality of the teacher as the chief agent in education, which affords ingenious, interesting, and more or less creative work to a vast number of highly intelligent and devoted persons, whose passionate hope is to leave the world a little better than they found it by means of those children whom they have raised to a higher level, must needs make a wide and successful appeal. It appeals equally to Education Committees and school managers. Consider the saving involved in the notion that teachers are compendiums of all knowledge, that they have but, as it were, to turn on the tap and the necessary knowledge flows forth. All responsibility is shifted, and the relief is very great not only so but lessons are delightful to watch and to hear; the success of jig-saw puzzles illustrates a tendency in human nature to delight in the ingenious putting together of unlikely things, as for example, a lifebuoy and Robinson Crusoe. There is a series of small triumphs to be observed any day of the week, and these same triumphs are brought about by dramatic display, so ingenious, pleasing, fascinating, are the ways in which the teacher chooses to arrive at her point. I say 'her' point because women excel in this kind of teaching, but men do not come far short. What of the children themselves? They, too, are amused and entertained, they enjoy the puzzle-element and greatly enjoy the teacher who lays herself out to attract them. There is no flaw in the practical working of the method while it is being carried out. Later, it gives rise to dismay and anxiety among thoughtful people.

Much water has run under the bridge since several years ago Mr. Alexander Paterson startled us out of self-complacency with his Across the Bridges. We as a nation were well pleased at the time with the result of our efforts; nothing could be more intelligent, alert, brighter, than the seventh standard boy about to leave school and take up his life work. Conditions were unpropitious. We know the old story of inviting blind alleys, present success and then unemployment, with resulting depreciation in character. What is to be done? The question of after conditions is now being taken up seriously.

We have Continuation Classes which even if a boy be out of work will help him to the Chinese art of 'saving his face.' But Mr. Paterson condemns the schools for the rapidity with which their best boys run to seed. He does not quote the case of the boy who gets work, earns fair wages, conducts himself respectably, goes to a 'Polytechnic,' the sort of boy with whom Mr. Pett Ridge makes us familiar, who is so much less than he might be, so crude in his notions, so unmoral in his principles, so poor in interests, so meagre if not coarse in his choice of pleasures and after all such a good fellow at bottom. He might have been taught in school to utilise his powers, to come into the enjoyment of the fine mind that is in him; but in schools,—

"There is too much learning and too little work. The teacher ready to use the powers that his training and experience have given him works too hard while the boy's share in the struggle is too light. It is possible to make education too easy for children and to rob learning of the mental discipline which often wearies but in the end produces concentration and the capacity to work alone . . . He is rarely left to himself with the book in his hands, forced to concentrate all his mind on the dull words before him with no one at hand to explain or make the memory work easier by little tricks of repetition and association . . . The boy who reaches the seventh standard with every promise and enters the service of a railway company is first required to sit down by himself and master the symbols of the telegraphic code. This he finds extremely irksome for the only work he has ever done alone before is the learning of racy poetry which is the very mildest form of mental discipline." "'Silent reading' is occasionally allowed in odd half-hours . . . it might well be a regular subject for reading aloud is but a poor gift compared with the practice of reading in private." [Across the Bridges, by A. Paterson.]

What does his curriculum do for the boy? Let us again hear Mr. Paterson:—

"What is the educational ideal set before the average boy whose school-days are to end at fourteen? What type is it that the authorities seek to produce? A glance at the syllabus will reassure the ordinary cynic who still labours under the quaint delusion that French and Algebra and violin-playing are taught in every London Elementary School at the expense of the ratepayer. The syllabus was designed to leave a boy at fourteen with a thoroughly sound and practical knowledge of reading, writing and arithmetic and with such grounding in English, geography and history, as may enable him to read a newspaper or give a vote with some idea of what he is doing. But these are all subsidiary to teaching the three 'R's' which between them occupy more than half the twenty-four hours of teaching in the week. It is certain that the present object in view is dispiriting to master and boy alike for a knowledge of reading, writing and arithmetic is no education and no training but merely the elementary condition of further knowledge. In many schools the boy is labouring on with these mere rudiments for two or more years after all reasonable requirements have been satisfied. The intelligent visitor looking at the note-books of an average class will be amazed at the high standard of the neatness and accuracy but he will find the excellence of a very visible order. The handwriting is admirable, sixteen boys out of thirty can write compositions without a flaw in grammar or spelling. Yet it will occur to him that the powers of voluntary thought and reason, of spontaneous enquiry and imagination; have not been stirred. This very perfection of form makes him suspicious as to the fundamental principles of our State curriculum. In Public Schools boys are not trained to be lawyers, or parsons, or doctors, but to be men. If they have learned to work systematically and think independently they are then fit to be trained for such life and profession as taste or necessity may dictate. But at our Elementary Schools we seem to aim at producing a nation of clerks for it is only to a clerk that this perfection of writing and spelling is a necessary training."

The very faults of his qualities nullify the work of the teacher. His failing is that he does too much. Once more we quote our authority:

"With the average boy there is a marked waste of mental capital between the ages of ten and thirteen and the aggregate of this loss to the country is heavy indeed. Ten years at school conquer many of the drawbacks of home and discover a quick, receptive mind in the normal child. Many opportunities have been lost in these years of school but after fourteen there is a more disastrous relapse. The brain is not taxed again and shrivels into a mere centre of limited formulae acting automatically in response to appetite or sensation. The boy's general education fails utterly. Asia is but a name that it is difficult to spell though at school he spoke of its rivers and ports. It is probable that the vocabulary of a working man at forty is actually smaller than it was at fourteen so shrunk is the power of the mind to feed upon the growing experience of life. Of the majority of boys it is true to say that only half their ability is ever used in the work they find to do on leaving school, the other half curls up and sleeps for ever."

Here we have a depressing prospect of grievous waste in the future. We all applaud the Education Act of 1918, are convinced that every boy and girl wilt receive education until the end of his sixteenth, possibly eighteenth, year. A wave of generous feeling passed over the nation and employers were willing to support the law; and if the eight hours conceded be spent in making the young people more reliable, intelligent and responsible persons no doubt the employers will be rewarded for their generosity.

But there are rocks ahead. The only way to take advantage of this provision is to make this an eight hours' University course. Now as Mr. Paterson happily remarks the Universities do not undertake to prepare barristers, parsons, stockbrokers, bankers, or even soldiers and sailors, with a specialised knowledge proper for each profession. Their implicit contention is, given a well-educated man with cultivated imagination, trained judgment, wide interests, and he is prepared to master the intricacies of any profession; while he knows at the same time how to make use of himself, of the powers with which nature and education have endowed him for his own happiness; the delightful employment of his leisure; for the increased happiness of his neighbours and the well-being of the community; that is, such a man is able, not only to earn his living, but to live.

The Universities fulfil this claim; the various professions abound with men who, in newspaper phrase, are 'ornaments to their professions,' and who gave up leisure and means to serve their fellow-citizens as magistrates, churchwardens, members of committees, special constables when needed, until lately, members of Parliament, holding service as an honour, and as proud as was 'Godfrey Bertram,' that unhappy laird in Guy Mannering, to write 'J.P.' after their names. The enormous amount of voluntary service rendered in such ways throughout the Empire as well as that of insufficiently, or duly, paid service justifies the Universities in their reading of their peculiar function. But not only so, generous disinterested work can never be paid for, and our great statesmen, churchmen, soldiers and civil servants, as well as the members of County, Municipal, and Urban District Councils, have done their devoir over and above the board.

To secure this same splendidly devoted voluntary service from all classes is the task set before us as a nation, a task the more easy because we have all seen it fulfilled in the War when every man was a potential hero. Now is it not the fact that the Army proved itself an unequalled University for our men, offering them increased knowledge, broad views, lofty aims, duty and discipline, along with the finest physical culture? So much so, that instead of going on from where the War left off, we have to be on the watch against retrograde movements, physical, moral, intellectual. The downward grade is always at hand and we know how easy it is. We cannot afford another great war for the education of our people but we must in some way supply the 'University' element and Mr. Fisher's great Act points out such a way. The young people are for four years (a proper academic period) to be under influences that make for 'sweetness and light.' But we must keep to the academic ideal: all preparation for specialised industries should be taboo.

Special teaching towards engineering, cotton-spinning, and the rest, is quite unnecessary for every manufacturer knows that given a 'likely' lad he will soon be turned into a good workman in the works themselves. The splendid record of women workers in the war supports our contention. The efforts of Technical Schools and the like are not greatly prized by the heads of firms so far as the technical knowledge they afford goes. Boys from them are employed rather on the off chance that they may turn out intelligent and apt than for what they know beforehand of the business. Here is one more reason for treating the Continuation School as the People's University and absolutely eschewing all money-making arts and crafts. Denmark and Scandinavia have tried this generous policy of educating young people, not according to the requirements of their trade but according to their natural capacity to know and their natural desire for knowledge, that desire to know history, poetry, science, art, which is natural to every man; and the success of the experiment now a century old is an object lesson for the rest of the world.

Germany has pursued a different ideal. Her efforts, too, have been great, unified by the idea of utility; and, if we will only remember the lesson, the war has shown us how futile is an education which affords no moral or intellectual uplift, no motive higher than the learner's peculiar advantage and that of the State. Germany became morally bankrupt (for a season only, let us hope) not solely because of the war but as the result of an education which ignored the things of the spirit or gave these a nominal place and a poor rendering in a utilitarian syllabus. We are encouraged to face the fact boldly that it is a People's University we should aim at, a University with its thousands of Colleges up and down the land, each of them the Continuation School (the name is not inviting) for some one neighbourhood.

But, it will be argued, the subject matter of a University education is conveyed for the most part through the channel of dead languages, Latin and Greek. Our contention is that, however ennobling the literature in these tongues, we cannot honestly allow our English literature to take a second place to any other, and that therefore whatever Sophocles, Thucydides, Virgil, have it in them to do towards a higher education, may be effected more readily by Milton, Gibbon, Shakespeare, Bacon, and a multitude of great thinkers who are therefore great writers. Learning conveyed in our common speech is easier come by than that secreted in a dead language and this fact will help us to deal with the in adequacy of the period allowed. Given absolute attention, and we can do much with four hundred hours a year (1,600 hours in our four years' course) but only if we go to work with a certainty that the young students crave knowledge of what we call the 'humanities,' that they read with absolute attention and that, having read, they know. They will welcome the preparation for public speaking, an effort for which everyone must qualify in these days, which the act of narration offers.

The alternative is some such concentration scheme as that indicated in Robinson Crusoe,—a year's work on soap, its manufacture, ingredients, the Soap Trade, Soap Transport, the Uses of Soap, how to make out a Soap invoice, the Sorts of Soap, and so on ad infinitum. Each process in the iron, cotton, nail, pin, engine, button,—each process in our thousand and one manufactures will offer its own ingenious Concentration

Scheme. The advocates of utilitarian education will be delighted, the young students will be kept busy and will to some extent use their wits all the time. With what result? Some two centuries ago when a movement for adolescent education agitated Europe, devastated by the Napoleonic wars, we English took our part. The current early divided into two streams, the material and the spiritual, the useful and the educative, and England, already great in manufactures, was carried along by the first of these streams, followed by Germany, France, Switzerland; while the Scandinavian group of countries learned at the lips of that 'Father of the People's High Schools' that "spirit is might, spirit reveals itself in spirit, spirit works only in freedom." We see the apotheosis of utilitarian education in the Munich schools on the one hand and in the morale of the German army on the other. But we are slow to learn because we have set up a little tin god of efficiency in that niche within our private pantheon which should be occupied by personality. We trouble ourselves about the uses of the young person to society. As for his own use, what he should be in and for himself, why, what matter? Because, say we, if we fit him to earn his living we fit him also to be of service to the world and what better can we do for him personally? We forget that it is written, Man shall not live by bread alone, but by every word that proceedeth out of the mouth of God shall man live,—whether it be spoken in the way of some truth of religion, poem, picture, scientific discovery, or literary expression; by these things men live and in all such is the life of the spirit. The spiritual life requires the food of ideas for its daily bread. We shall find, in the words of a well-known Swedish professor, that, "just as enrichment of the soil gives the best conditions for the seed sown in it so a well-grounded humanistic training provides the surest basis for a business capacity, and not the least so in the case of the coming farmer." But we need not go so far afield, we have a prophet of our own, and I will close this part of my subject by quoting certain of Mr. Fisher's words of wisdom:—

"Now let me say something about the content of education, about the things which should be actually taught in the schools, and I am only going to talk in the very broadest possible way. In my afternoon's reading I came upon another very apposite remark in the letters of John Stuart Mill. Let me read it to you:

'What the poor, as well as the rich, require is not to be taught other people's opinions, but to be induced and enabled to think for themselves. It is not physical science that will do this, even if they could learn it much more thoroughly than they are able to do.'

"The young people of this country are not to be regenerated by economic doctrine or economic history or physical science; they can only be elevated by ideas which act upon the imagination and act upon the character and influence the soul, and it is the function of all good teachers to bring those ideas before them.

"I have sometimes heard it said that you should not teach patriotism in the school. I dissent from that doctrine. I think that patriotism should be taught in the schools. I will tell you what I mean by patriotism. By patriotism I do not mean Jingoism, but what I mean by patriotism is an intelligent appreciation of all things noble in the romances, in the literature and in the history of one's own country. Young people should be taught to admire what is great while they are at school. And remember that for the poor of this country the school is a far more important factor than it is for the rich people of this country . . .

"I say that I want patriotism in the larger sense of the term taught in the schools. Of course there is a great deal to criticise in any country, and I should be the last person to suggest that the critical faculty should not be exercised and trained at school. But before we teach children to criticise the institutions of their country, before we teach them to be critical of what is bad, let us teach them to recognize and admire what is good. After all life is very short; we all of us have only one life to live, and during that life let us get into ourselves as much love, as much admiration, as much elevating pleasure as we can, and if we view education merely as discipline in critical bitterness, then we shall lose all the sweets of life and we shall make ourselves unnecessarily miserable. There is quite enough sorrow and hardship in this world as it is without introducing it prematurely to young people."

N.B.—Probably some educational authorities may decide to give one hour or two weekly to physical training and handicrafts, in which case the time-table must allow for so much the less reading. But I should like to urge that, with the long evening leisure of which there is promise, Club life will become an important feature in every village and district. Classes will certainly be arranged for military and other drills, gymnastics, dancing, singing, swimming, carpentry, cooking, nursing, dress-making, weaving, pottery, acting,—in fact, whatever the quickened intelligence of the community demands. No compulsion would be necessary to enforce attendance at classes, for which the machinery is already in existence in most places, and which, associated with Club life, would have certain social attractions in the way of public displays, prize givings and so on. The intellectual life of the Continuation School should give zest to these evening occupations as well as to the Saturday Field Club which no neighbourhood should be without.

I have put the case for Continuation Schools as strongly as may be, but there is a more excellent way. In these days of high wages it may well happen that parents will be willing to let their children remain at school until the end of their seventeenth year, in which case they will be able to go on with the 'secondary education' which they have begun at the age of six and we shall see a new thing in the world. Every man and woman will have received a liberal education; life will no longer discount the ideas and aims of the schoolroom, and, if according to the Platonic saying, "Knowledge is virtue," knowledge informed by religion, we shall see even in our own day how righteousness exalteth a nation.

Chapter 8 I—The Way of the Will

We may offer to children two guides to moral and intellectual self-management which we may call 'the Way of the Will' and 'the Way of the Reason.'

The Way of the Will: Children should be taught (a) to distinguish between 'I want' and 'I will.' (b) That the way to will effectively is to turn our thoughts away from that which we desire but do not will. (c) That the best way to turn our thoughts is to think of, or do some quite different thing, entertaining or interesting. (d) That after a little rest in this way, the will returns to its work with new vigour. (This adjunct of the will is familiar to us as diversion, whose office it is to ease us for a time from will effort that we may 'will' again with added power. The use of suggestion as an aid to the will is to be deprecated, as lending to stultify and stereotype character. It would seem that spontaneity is a condition of development, and that human nature needs the discipline of failure as well as of success.)

The great things of life, life itself, are not easy of definition. The Will, we are told, is 'the sole practical faculty of man.' But who is to define the Will? We are told again that 'the Will is the man'; and yet most men go through life without a single definite act of willing. Habit, convention, the customs of the world have done so much for us that we get up, dress, breakfast, follow our morning's occupations, our later relaxations, without an act of choice. For this much at any rate we know about the will. Its function is to choose, to decide, and there seems to be no doubt that the greater becomes the effort of decision the weaker grows the general will. Opinions are provided for us, we take our principles at second or third hand, our habits are suitable, and convenient, and what more is necessary for a decent and orderly life? But the one achievement possible and necessary for every man is character; and character is as finely wrought metal beaten into shape and beauty by the repeated and accustomed action of will. We who teach should make it clear to ourselves that our aim in education is less conduct than character; conduct may be arrived at, as we have seen, by indirect routes, but it is of value to the world only as it has its source in character.

Every assault upon the flesh and spirit of man is an attack however insidious upon his personality, his will; but a new Armageddon is upon us in so far as that the attack is no longer indirect but is aimed consciously and directly at the will, which is the man; and we shall escape becoming a nation of imbeciles only because there will always be persons of good will amongst us who will resist the general trend. The office of parents and teachers is to turn out such persons of good will; that they should deliberately weaken the moral fibre of their children by suggestion is a very grave offence and a thoughtful examination of the subject should act as a sufficient deterrent. For, let us consider. What we do with the will we describe as voluntary. What we do without the conscious action of will is involuntary. The will has only one mode of action, its function is to 'choose,' and with every choice we make we grow in force of character.

From the cradle to the grave suggestions crowd upon us, and such suggestions become part of our education because we must choose between them. But a suggestion given by intent and supported by an outside personality has an added strength which few are able to resist, just because the choice has been made by another and not by ourselves, and our tendency is to accept this vicarious choice and follow the path of least resistance. No doubt much of this vicarious choosing is done for our good, whether for our health of body or amenableness of mind; but those who propose suggestion as a means of education do not consider that with every such attempt upon a child they weaken that which should make a man of him, his own power of choice. The parasitic creatures who live upon the habits, principles and opinions of others may easily become criminal. They only wait the occasion of some popular outburst to be carried into such a fury of crime as the Gordon Riots presented: a mad fury of which we have had terrible examples in our own day, though we have failed to ascribe them to their proper cause, the undermining of the will of the people, who have not been instructed in that ordering of the will which is their chief function as men and women. His will is the safeguard of a man against the unlawful intrusion of other persons. We are taught that there are offences against the bodies of others which may not be committed, but who teaches us that we may not intrude upon the minds and overrule the wills of others; that it is indecent to let another probe the thoughts of the 'unconscious mind' whether of child or man? Now the thought that we choose is commonly the thought that we ought to think and the part of the teacher is to afford to each child a full reservoir of the right thought of the world to draw from. For right thinking is by no means a matter of self-expression. Right thought flows upon the stimulus of an idea, and ideas are stored as we have seen in books and pictures and the lives of men and nations; these instruct the conscience and stimulate the will, and man or child 'chooses.' An accomplished statesman [Memoirs of Count Witte.] exhibited to us lately how the disintegration of a great empire was brought about by the weakness of its rulers who allowed their will-power to be tampered with, their judgment suggested, their actions directed, by those who gained access to them.

There is no occasion for panic, but it is time that we realised that to fortify the will is one of the great purposes of education, and probably some study of the map of the City of Mansoul would afford us guidance: at least a bird's eye view of the riches of the City should be spread before children. They should themselves know of the wonderful capacities to enter upon the world as a great inheritance which exist in every human being. All its beauty and all its thought are open to everyone. Everyone may take service for the world's use, everyone may climb those delectable mountains from whence he gets the vision of the City of God. He must know something of his body with its senses and its appetites: of his intellect, imagination and aesthetic sense: of his moral nature, ordered by love and justice. Realising how much is possible to Mansoul and the perils that assail it, he should know that the duty of self-direction belongs to him; and that powers for this direction are lodged in him, as are intellect and imagination, hunger and thirst. These governing powers are the conscience and the will. The whole ordering of education with its history, poetry, arithmetic, pictures, is based on the assumption that conscience is incapable of ordering life without regular and progressive instruction. We need instruction also concerning the will. Persons commonly suppose that the action of the will is automatic, but no power of Mansoul acts by itself and of itself, and some little study of the 'way of the will'—which has the ordering of every other power—may help us to understand the functions of this Premier in the kingdom of Mansoul.

Early in his teens we should at least put clearly before the child the possibility of a drifting, easy life led by appetite or desire in which will plays no part; and the other possibility of using the power and responsibility proper to him as a person and willing as he goes. He must be safeguarded from some fallacies. No doubt he has heard at home that Baby has a strong will because he cries for a knife and insists on pulling down the tablecloth. In his history lessons and his readings of tale and poem, he comes across persons each of whom carries his point by strong wilfulness. He laughs at that rash boy Phaeton, measures Esau with a considering eye, finds him more attractive than Jacob who yet wins higher approval; perceives that Esau is wilful but that Jacob has a strong will, and through this and many other examples, recognises that a strong will is not synonymous with 'being good,' nor with a determination to have your own way. He learns to distribute the characters he comes across in his reading on either side of a line, those who are wilful and those who are governed by will; and this line by no means separates between the bad and the good.

It does divide, however, between the impulsive, self-pleasing, self-seeking, and the persons who have an aim beyond and outside of themselves, even though it be an aim appalling as that of Milton's Satan. It follows for him that he must not only will, but will with a view to an object outside himself. He will learn to recognise in Louis XI a mean man and a great king, because France and not himself was the object of his crooked policy. The will, too, is of slow growth, nourished upon the ideas proposed to it, and so all things work together for good to the child who is duly educated. It is well that children should know that while the turbulent person is not ruled by will at all but by impulse, the movement of his passions or desires, yet it is possible to have a constant will with unworthy or evil ends, or, even to have a steady will towards a good end and to compass that end by unworthy means. The simple rectified will, what our Lord calls 'the single eye,' would appear to be the one thing needful for straight living and serviceableness. But always the first condition of will, good or ill, is an object outside of self. The boy or girl who sees this will understand that self-culture is not to be accepted as an ideal, will not wonder why Bushido is mighty in Japan, will enter into the problem which Browning raises in The Statue and the Bust. By degrees the scholar will perceive that just as to reign is the distinctive function of a king, so to will is the function of a man. A king is not a king unless he reigns and a man is less than a man unless he wills. Another thing to be observed is that even the constant will has its times of rise and fall, and one of the secrets of living is how to tide over the times of fall in will power.

The boy must learn too that the will is subject to solicitations all round, from the lust of the flesh and the lust of the eye and the pride of life; that will does not act alone; it takes the whole man to will and a man wills wisely, justly and strongly, in proportion as all his powers are in training and under instruction. We must understand in order to will. "How is that ye will not understand?" said our Lord to the Jews; and that is the way with most of us, we will not understand. We look out for great occasions which do not come and do not see that the sphere for the action of our wills is in ourselves. Our concern with life is to be fit, and according to our fitness come our occasions and the uses we shall be put to.

Unlike every other power in the kingdom of Mansoul, the will is able to do what it likes, is a free agent, and the one thing the will has to do is to prefer. "Choose ye this day," is the command that comes to each of us in every affair and on every day of our lives, and the business of the will is to choose. But, choice, the effort of decision, is a heavy labour, whether it be between two lovers or two gowns. So, many people minimise this labour by following the fashion in their clothes, rooms, reading, amusements, the pictures they admire and the friends they select. We are zealous in choosing for others but shirk the responsibility of decisions for ourselves.

What is to be said about obedience, to the heads of the house first, to the State, to the Church, and always to the laws of God? Obedience is the test, the sustainer of personality, but it must be the obedience of choice; because choice is laborious, little children must be trained in the obedience of habit; but every gallant boy and girl has learned to choose to obey all who are set in authority.

Such obedience is of the essence of chivalry and chivalry is that temper of mind opposed to self-seeking. The chivalrous person is a person of constant will for, as we have seen, will cannot be exercised steadily for ends of personal gain.

It is well to know what it is we choose between. Things are only signs which represent ideas and several times a day we shall find two ideas presented to our minds and must make our choice upon right and reasonable grounds. We shall thus be on our guard against the weak allowance which we cause to do duty for choice and against such dishonest fallacies as, that it is our business to get the best that is to be had at the lowest price; and it is not only in matters of dress and ornament, household use and decoration, that we run after the cheapest and newest. We chase opinions and ideas with the same restlessness and uncertainty; any fad, any notion in the newspapers, we pick up with eagerness. Once again, the will is the man. The business of the will is to choose. There are many ways to get out of the task of choosing but it is always,—"Choose you this day whom ye will serve." There are two services open to us all, the service of God, (including that of man) and the service of self. If our aim is just to get on, 'to do ourselves well,' to get all possible ease, luxury and pleasure out of our lives, we are serving self and for the service of self no act of will is required. Our appetites and desires are always at hand to spur us into the necessary exertions. But if we serve God and our neighbour, we have to be always on the watch to choose between the ideas that present themselves. What the spring is to the year, school days are to our life. You meet a man whose business in the world appears to be to eat and drink, play golf and motor; he may have another and deeper life that we know nothing about, but, so far as we can see, he has enlisted in the service of self. You meet another, a man of position, doing important work, and his ideas are those he received from the great men who taught him at school and College. The Greek Plays are his hobby. He is open to great thoughts and ready for service, because that which we get in our youth we keep through our lives.

Though the will affects all our actions and all our thoughts, its direct action is confined to a very little place, to that postern at either side of which stand conscience and reason, and at which ideas must needs present themselves. Shall we take an idea in or reject it? Conscience and reason have their say, but will is supreme and the behaviour of will is determined by all the principles we have gathered, all the opinions we have formed. We accept the notion, ponder it. At first we vaguely intend to act upon it; then we form a definite purpose, then a resolution and then comes an act or general temper of mind. We are told of Rudyard Kipling that his great ambition and desire at one time was to keep a tobacconist's shop. Why? Because in this way he could get into human touch with the men who came to buy their weekly allowance of tobacco. Happily for the world he did not become a tobacconist but the idea which moved him in the first place has acted throughout his life. Always he has men, young men, about him and who knows how many he has moved to become 'Captains Courageous' by his talk as well as by his books!

But suppose an unworthy idea present itself at the postern, supported by public opinion, by reason, for which even conscience finds pleas? The will soon wearies of opposition, and what is to be done? Fight it out? That is what the medieval Church did with those ideas which it rightly regarded as temptations; the lash, the hair shirt, the stone couch, the emaciated frame told of these not too successful Armageddons.

When the overstrained will asks for repose, it may not relax to yielding point but may and must seek recreation, diversion,—Latin thought has afforded us beautiful and appropriate names for that which we require. A change of physical or mental occupation is very good, but if no other change is convenient, let us think of something else, no matter how trifling. A new tie, or our next new hat, a story book we are reading, a friend we hope to see, anything does so long as we do not suggest to ourselves the thoughts we ought to think on the subject in question. The will does not want the support of arguments but the recreation of rest, change, diversion. In a surprisingly short time it is able to return to the charge and to choose this day the path of duty, however dull or tiresome, difficult or dangerous. This 'way of the will' is a secret of power, the secret of self-government, with which people should be furnished, not only for ease in practical right doing, or for advance in the religious life, but also for their intellectual well-being. Our claim to free will is a righteous claim; will can only be free, whether its object be right or wrong; it is a matter of choice and there is no choice but free choice. But we are apt to translate free will into free thought. We allow ourselves to sanction intellectual anarchism and forget that it rests with the will to order the thoughts of the mind fully as much as the feelings of the heart or the lusts of the flesh. Our thoughts are not our own and we are not free to think as we choose. The injunction,—"Choose ye this day," applies to the thoughts which we allow ourselves to receive. Will is the one free agent of Mansoul, will alone may accept or reject; and will is therefore responsible for every intellectual problem which has proved too much for a man's sanity or for his moral probity. We may not think what we please on shallow matters or profound. The instructed conscience and trained reason support the will in those things, little and great, by which men live.

The ordering of the will is not an affair of sudden resolve; it is the outcome of a slow and ordered education in which precept and example flow in from the lives and thoughts of other men, men of antiquity and men of the hour, as unconsciously and spontaneously as the air we breathe. But the moment of choice is immediate and the act of the will voluntary; and the object of education is to prepare us for this immediate choice and voluntary action which every day presents.

While affording some secrets of 'the way of the will' to young people, we should perhaps beware of presenting the ideas of 'self-knowledge, self-reverence, and self control.' All adequate education must be outward bound, and the mind which is concentrated upon self-emolument, even though it be the emolument of all the virtues, misses the higher and the simpler secrets of life. Duty and service are the sufficient motives for the arduous training of the will that a child goes through with little consciousness. The gradual fortifying of the will which many a schoolboy undergoes is hardly perceptible to himself however tremendous the results may be for his city or his nation. Will, free will, must have an object outside of self; and the poet has said the last word so far as we yet know,–

"Our wills are ours we know not how;
Our wills are ours to make them Thine."
[Tennyson, In Memorium]

Chapter 9 —The Way of the Reason

We should teach children, also, not to lean (too confidently) unto their own understanding because the function of reason is to give logical demonstration of (a) mathematical truth and (b) of initial ideas accepted by the will. In the former case reason is, perhaps, an infallible guide but in the latter is not always a safe one, for whether the initial idea be right or wrong reason will confirm it by irrefragible proofs.

Therefore children should be taught as they become mature enough to understand such teaching that the chief responsibility which rests upon then: as persons is the acceptance or rejection of ideas presented to them.

To help them in this choice we should afford them principles of conduct and a wide range of fitting knowledge.

Every child, every man, who comes to a sudden halt watching the action of his own reason, is another Columbus, the discoverer of a new world. Commonly we let reason do its work without attention on our part, but there come moments when we stand in startled admiration and watch the unfolding before us point by point of a score of arguments in favour of this carpet as against that, this route in preference to the other, our chosen chum as against Bob Brown; because every pro suggested by our reason is opposed to some con in the background. How else should it happen that there is no single point upon which two persons may reason,—food, dress, games, education, politics, religion,—but the two may take opposite sides, and each will bring forward infallible proofs which must convince the other were it not that he too is already convinced by stronger proofs to strengthen his own argument. Every character in history or fiction supports this thesis; and probably we cannot give a better training in right reasoning than by letting children work out the arguments in favour of this or that conclusion.

Thus, Macbeth, a great general, returns after a brilliant victory, head and heart are inflated, what can he not achieve? Could he not govern a country as well as rule an army? Reason unfolds the steps by which he might do great things; great things, ay, but are they lawful, these possible exploits? And then in the nick of time he comes across the 'weird Sisters,' as we are all apt to take refuge in fatalism when conscience no longer supports us. He shall be Thane of Cawdor, and, behold, confirmation arrives on the spot. He shall also be king. Well, if this is decreed, what can he do? He is no longer a free agent. And a score of valid arguments unfold themselves showing how Scotland, the world, his wife, himself, would be enhanced, would flourish and be blessed if he had the opportunity to do what was in him. Opportunity? The thing was decreed! It rested with him to find the means, the tools. He was not without imagination, had a poetic mind and shrank before the horrors he vaguely foresaw. But reason came to his aid and step by step the whole bloody tragedy was wrought out before his prescient mind. When we first meet with Macbeth he is rich in honours, troops of friends, the generous confidence of his king. The change is sudden and complete, and, we may believe, reason justified him at every point. But reason did not begin it. The will played upon by ambition had already admitted the notion of towering greatness or ever the 'weird Sisters' gave shape to his desire. Had it not been for this countenance afforded by the will, the forecasts of fate would have influenced his conduct no more then they did that of Banquo.

But it must not be supposed that reason is malign, the furtherer of ill counsels only. Nurse Cavell, Jack Coruwell, Lord Roberts, General Gordon, Madame Curie, leave hints enough to enable us to follow the trains of thought which issued in glorious deeds. We know how Florence Nightingale received, welcomed, reasoned out the notion of pity which obsessed her, and how through many difficulties her great project for the saving of the sick and suffering of her country's army worked itself out; how she was able to convey to those in power the same convincing arguments which moved herself. That was a happy thought of the medieval church which represented the leading idea of each of the seven Liberal Arts by a chosen exponent able to convince others by the arguments which his own reason brought forward. So Priscian taught the world Grammar; Pythagoras, Arithmetic; and the name of Euclid still stands for the science which appealed to his reason. But it is not only great intellectual advances and discoveries or world-shaping events for good or evil, that exhibit the persuasive power of reason. There is no object in use, great or small, upon which some man's reason has not worked exhaustively. A sofa, a chest of drawer, a ship, a box of toy soldiers, have all been thought out step by step, and the inventor has not only considered the pros but has so far overcome the cons that his invention is there, ready for use; and only here and there does anyone take the trouble to consider how the useful, or, perhaps, beautiful article came into existence. It is worth while to ask a child, How did you think of it? when he comes to tell you of a new game he has invented, a new country of the imagination he has named, peopled and governed. He will probably tell you what first 'put it into his head' and then how the reasons one after another came to him. After,—How did you think of it?—the next question that will occur to a child is, How did he think of it?—and he will distinguish between the first notion that has put it into his head and the reasoned steps which have gone to the completion of an object, the discovery of a planet, the making of a law. Sometimes a child should be taken into the psychology of crime, and he will see that reason brings infallible proofs of the rightness of the criminal act. From Cain to the latest great offender every criminal act has been justified by reasoned arguments which come of their own accord to the criminal. We know the arguments before which Eve fell when the Serpent played the part of the 'weird Sisters.' It is pleasant to the eye; it is good for food; it shall make you wise in the knowledge of good and evil—good and convincing arguments, specious enough to overbear the counter-pleadings of Obedience. Children should know that such things are before them also; that whenever they want to do wrong capital reasons for doing the wrong thing will occur to them. But, happily, when they want to do right no less cogent reasons for right doing will appear.

After abundant practice in reasoning and tracing out the reasons of others, whether in fact or fiction, children may readily be brought to the conclusions that reasonable and right are not synonymous terms; that reason is their servant, not their ruler,—one of those servants which help Mansoul in the governance of his kingdom. But no more than appetite, ambition, or the love of ease, is reason to be trusted with the government of a man, much less that of a state; because well-reasoned arguments are brought into play for a wrong course as for a right. He will see that reason works involuntarily; that all the beautiful steps follow one another in his mind without any activity or intention on his own part; but he need never suppose that he was hurried along into evil by thoughts which he could not help, because reason never begins it. It is only when he chooses to think about some course or plan, as Eve standing before the apples, that reason comes into play; so, if he chooses to think about a purpose that is good, many excellent reasons will hurry up to support him; but, alas, if he choose to entertain a wrong notion, he, as it were, rings the bell for reason, which enforces his wrong intention with a score of arguments proving that wrong is right.

A due recognition of the function of reason should be an enormous help to us all in days when the air is full of fallacies, and when our personal modesty, that becoming respect for other people which is proper to well-ordered natures whether young or old, makes us willing to accept conclusions duly supported by public opinion or by those whose opinions we value. Nevertheless, it is something to recognise that probably no wrong thing has ever been done or said, no crime committed, but has been justified to the perpetrator by arguments coming to him involuntarily and produced with cumulative force by his own reason. Is Shakespeare ever wrong? And, if so, may we think that a Richard III who gloats over his own villainy as villainy, who is in fact no hypocrite, in the sense of acting, to himself—is hardly true to human nature? Great is Shakespeare! So perhaps Richard was the exception to the rule which makes a man go out and hang himself when at last he sees his incomparable villainy, and does not Richard say in the end, "I myself find in myself no pity for myself"? For ourselves and our children it is enough to know that reason will put a good face on any matter we propose; and, that we can prove ourselves to be in the right is no justification for there is absolutely no theory we may receive, no action we may contemplate, which our reason will not affirm. Of course we know by many infallible proofs that Bacon wrote Shakespeare, and an ingenious person has worked out a chain of arguments proving that Dr. Johnson wrote the Bible! Why not? For a nation of logical thinkers, the French made an extraordinary faux-pas when they elected the Goddess of Reason to divine honours. But, indeed, perhaps they did it because they are a logical nation; for logic gives us the very formula of reason, and that which is logically proved is not necessarily right. We need no longer wonder that two men equally upright, equally virtuous, selected out of any company, will hold opposite views on almost any question; and each will support his views by logical argument. So we are at the mercy of the doctrinaire in religion, the demagogue in politics, and, dare we say, of the dreamer in science; and we think to save our souls by being in the front rank of opinion in one or the other. But not if we have grown up cognisant of the beauty and wonder of the act of reasoning, and also, of the limitations which attend it.

We must be able to answer the arguments in the air, not so much by counter reasons as by exposing the fallacies in such arguments and proving on our own part the opposite position. For example, "that very lovable, very exasperating but essentially real, though often wrong-headed enthusiast," Karl Marx, dominates the socialistic thought of to-day. Point by point, for good or for evil, the Marxian Manifesto of 1848 is coming into force. "For the most advanced countries," we are told, "the following measures might come into very general application."

(1) "Expropriation of landed property and application of rent to State Expenditure." We have not space to examine the Marxian proposition in detail but let us consider a single fallacy. It is assumed that the rent of landed property is for the sole use, enrichment and enjoyment of the owner. Now the schedule of the Duke of Bedford, for example, published recently, shows that the income derived from park property is inadequate to its upkeep and to the taxes imposed upon the owner.

Again, landowners are not only large employers of labour, generally under favourable conditions, but they keep up a very important benefaction; most of the extensive landowners make of their places public parks kept in beautiful order at their private expense.

(2) "Heavy progressive taxation." The fallacy lies in the fact that the proletariat in whose interest the Manifesto was issued must necessarily on account of their numbers be large taxpayers. Therefore it is upon them that heavy progressive taxation will press—as we have all seen in Russia—to the point of their extinction.

(3) "Abolition of inheritance." A measure designed to reduce all persons to the same level. As we know, the abolition of class is the main object of socialism. But the underlying fallacy is the assumption that class is stable and is not in a state of continual flux, the continual upward and downward movement as of watery particles in the Ocean. The man at the bottom to-day may be at the top to-morrow, as we see, not only in Soviet Russia, but in most civilised countries. Attempts to control this natural movement are as vain as King Canute's command to the Ocean.

(4) "Confiscation of the property of all emigrants and rebels." Assumed authority must be supported by tyranny, that worst tyranny which requires all men to think to order, as they must in a Soviet State, or be penalised to make them powerless. The fallacy lies in a misconception of human nature. There is nothing that men will not sacrifice for an idea, for such an idea as that of freedom of thought and of movement

(5), (6), (7), deal with centralisation, credit, of transport, of factories, of instruments of production in the hands of the State,—the State, that is, Everyman,—the Proletariat, in fact,—in whose hands all wealth and means of obtaining wealth shall be lodged.

Here we have a logically thought-out preparation for the government of the people, by the people, for the people; but the underlying fallacy is that it makes for revolution which effects no change but a mere change of rulers, better or worse as may be. In the Soviet Republic, according to the law of perpetual social flux, new rulers would come to the top, arbitrary and tyrannical; because not hemmed in by precedent and custom; and children will be at no loss to show how the last state of a nation so governed is worse than the first.

(8) "Compulsory obligation of labour upon all." The initial idea of a Soviet State is that it shall afford due liberty and equal conditions for all. But even in the contemplation of such a State it was necessary to postulate for everybody conscription and the discipline of an army.

(9) "Joint prosecution for Agriculture and Manufacture." The aim being the gradual removal of the distinction of town and country. Here is a point in the Manifesto which we should all like to see in practice but—is it possible?

(10) "Public and gratuitous education for all children." This happily we have seen carried out with the proviso, 'for whom it may be necessary or desirable.' The difficulty lies in the conception of education formed by a Soviet community; and the plea for free education is a specious blind, the intention being such an education as shall train the coming generation in rabid revolutionary principles.

To continue our examination of the Tenth Maxim; the next clause (b) requires "abolition of children's labour in factories in its present form." So far so good. Happily we have lived to see this abolition; there may be a sinister reading of the clause but on the surface it carries the assent of all good citizens.

(c) "Union of education with material production." Here from motives of economy we are going the way of the Communists in our Continuation Schools; but a fallacy underlies the maxim which may well frustrate our efforts towards the better education of the people. The assumption is that the boy who learns, say, certain manufacturing processes, pari passu with his intellectual education does better in the future than he who gives the full period to education. There is no consensus of the opinion of employers to prove that this is the case. On the contrary, given a likely boy, and a manufacturer will be satisfied that he will soon learn his business in the 'works.' But the function of education is not to give technical skill but to develop a person; the more of a person, the better the work of whatever kind; and as I have said before, the idea of the Continuation School is, or should be, a University course in the 'humanities'; not in what have been called the 'best humanities,' i.e., the Classics, though whether these are in any sense 'best' is a moot question, but in the singularly rich 'humanities' which the English tongue affords.

These Ten Marxian Maxims give us ample ground for discussion not for lectures or for oral lessons, but for following for a few minutes any opening suggested by 'current events,' a feature in the children's programme of work. But they must follow arguments and detect fallacies for themselves. Reason like the other powers of the mind, requires material to work upon whether embalmed in history and literature, or afloat with the news of a strike or uprising. It is madness to let children face a debatable world with only, say, a mathematical preparation. If our business were to train their power of reasoning, such a training would no doubt be of service; but the power is there already, and only wants material to work upon.

This caution must be borne in mind. Reason, like all other properties of a person, is subject to habit and works upon the material it is accustomed to handle.

Plato formed a just judgment on this matter, too, and perceived that mathematics afford no clue to the labyrinth of affairs whether public or private.

We have seen that their reading and the affairs of the day should afford scope and opportunity for the delight in ratiocination proper to children. The fallacies they themselves perpetrate when exposed make them the readier to detect fallacies elsewhere.

What are we to do? Are we to waste time in discussing with children every idle and blasphemous proposition that comes their way? Surely not. But we may help them to principles which should enable them to discern these two characters for themselves. A proposition is idle when it rests on nothing and leads to nothing. Again, blasphemy is a sin, the sin of being impudent towards Almighty God, Whom we all know, without any telling, and know Him to be fearful, wonderful, loving, just and good, as certainly as we know that the sun shines or the wind blows. Children should be brought up, too, to perceive that a miracle is not less a miracle because it occurs so constantly and regularly that we call it a law; that sap rises in a tree, that a boy is born with his uncle's eyes, that an answer that we can perceive comes to our serious prayers; these things are not the less miracles because they happen frequently or invariably, and because we have ceased to wonder about them. No doubt so did the people of Jerusalem when our Lord performed many miracles in their streets.

When children perceive that,—"My Father worketh hitherto and I work"—is the law which orders nations and individuals: that "My spirit shall not always strive with man," is an awful warning to every people and every person; that to hinder the mis-doing, encourage the well-doing of men and nations is incessant labour, the work of the Father and the Son:—to a child who perceives these things miracles will not be matters of supreme moment because all life will be for him matter for wonder and adoration.

Again, if we wish children to keep clear of all the religious clamours in the air, we must help them to understand what religion is—[What Religion Is, by Bernard Bosanquet, D.C.L.]

"Will religion guarantee me my private and personal happiness? To this on the whole I think we must answer, No; and if we approach it with a view to such happiness, then most certainly and absolutely No."

Here is a final and emphatic answer to the quasi religious offers which are being clamourously pressed upon hesitating souls. Ease of body is offered to these, relief of mind, reparation of loss, even of the final loss when those they love pass away. We may call upon mediums, converse through table-rappings, be healed by faith,—faith, that is, in the power of a Healer who manipulates us. Sin is not for us, nor sorrow for sin. We may live in continual odious self-complacency, remote from the anxious struggling souls about us, because, forsooth, there is no sin, sorrow, anxiety or pain, if we will that these things shall not be. That is to say, religion will "guarantee me my private and personal happiness," will make me immune from every distress and misery of life; and this happy immunity is all a matter within the power of my own will; the person that matters in my religion is myself only. The office of religion for me in such a case is to remove all uneasiness, bodily and spiritual, and to float me into a Nirvana of undisturbed self-complacency. But we must answer with Professor Bosanquet, "absolutely NO." True religion will not do this for me because the final form of the religion that will do these things is idolatry, self-worship, with no intention beyond self.

To go on with our quotation,—"Well, but if not that then what? We esteem the thing as good and great, but if it simply does nothing for us, how is it to be anything to us? But the answer was the answer to the question and it might be that to a question sounding but slightly different, a very different answer would be returned. We might ask, for instance, 'does it make my life more worth living?' And the answer to this might be,—'It is the only thing that makes life worth living at all.'"

In a word, "I want, am made for and must have a God."

No doubt through the sweetness of their faith and love children have immediate access to God, and what more would we have? 'Gentle Jesus' is about their path and about their bed; angels minister to them; they enjoy all the immunities of the Kingdom. But we may not forget that reason is as active in them as the affections. Towards the end of the last century people had a straight and easy way of giving a reasonable foundation to a child's belief. All the articles of the Christian Faith were supported by a sort of little catechism of 'Scripture Proofs'; and this method was not without its uses. But, to-day, we have to prove the Scriptures if we rely upon Scripture proofs and we must change our point of attack. Children must know that we cannot prove any of the great things of life, not even that we ourselves live; but we must rely upon that which we know without demonstration. We know, too, and this other certainty must be pressed home to them, that reason, so far from being infallible, is most exceedingly fallible, persuadable, open to influence on this side and that; but is all the same a faithful servant, able to prove whatsoever notion is received by the will. Once we are convinced of the fallibility of our own reason we are able to detect the fallacies in the reasoning of our opponents and are not liable to be carried away by every wind of doctrine. Every mother knows how intensely reasonable a child is and how difficult it is to answer his quite logical and foolishly wrong conclusions. So we need not be deterred from dealing with serious matters with these young neophytes, but only as the occasion occurs; we may not run the risk of boring them, with the great questions of life while it is our business to send them forth assured.

We find that, while children are tiresome in arguing about trifling things, often for the mere pleasure of employing their reasoning power, a great many of them are averse to those studies which should, we suppose, give free play to a power that is in them, even if they do not strengthen and develop this power. Yet few children take pleasure in Grammar, especially in English Grammar, which depends so little on inflexion. Arithmetic, again, Mathematics, appeal only to a small percentage of a class or school, and, for the rest, however intelligent, its problems are baffling to the end, though they may take delight in reasoning out problems of life in literature or history. Perhaps we should accept this tacit vote of the majority and cease to put undue pressure upon studies which would be invaluable did the reasoning power of a child wait upon our training, but are on a different footing when we perceive that children come endowed to the full as much with reason as with love; that our business is to provide abundant material upon which this supreme power should work; and that whatever development occurs comes with practice in congenial fields of thought. At the same time we may not let children neglect either of these delightful studies. The time will come when they will delight in words, the beauty and propriety of words; when they will see that words are consecrated as the vehicle of truth and are not to be carelessly tampered with in statement or mutilated in form; and we must prepare them for these later studies. Perhaps we should postpone parsing, for instance, until a child is accustomed to weigh sentences for their sense, should let them dally with figures of speech before we attempt minute analysis of sentences, and should reduce our grammatical nomenclature to a minimum. The fact is that children do not generalise, they gather particulars with amazing industry, but hold their impressions fluid, as it were; and we may not hurry them to formulate. If the use of words be a law unto itself, how much more so the language of figures and lines! We remember how instructive and impressive Ruskin is on the thesis that 'two and two make four' and cannot by any possibility that the universe affords be made to make five or three. From this point of view, of immutable law, children should approach Mathematics; they should see how impressive is Euclid's 'Which is absurd,' just as absurd as would be the statements of a man who said that his apples always fell upwards, and for the same reason. The behaviour of figures and lines is like the fall of an apple, fixed by immutable laws, and it is a great thing to begin to see these laws even in their lowliest application. The child whose approaches to Arithmetic are so many discoveries of the laws which regulate number will not divide fifteen pence among five people and give them each sixpence or ninepence; 'which is absurd' will convict him, and in time he will perceive that 'answers' are not purely arbitrary but are to be come at by a little boy's reason. Mathematics are delightful to the mind of man which revels in the perception of law, which may even go forth guessing at a new law until it discover that law; but not every boy can be a champion prize-fighter, nor can every boy 'stand up' to Mathematics. Therefore perhaps the business of teachers is to open as many doors as possible in the belief that Mathematics is one out of many studies which make for education, a study by no means accessible to everyone. Therefore it should not monopolise undue time, nor should persons be hindered from useful careers by the fact that they show no great proficiency in studies which are in favour with examiners, no doubt, because solutions are final, and work can be adjudged without the tiresome hesitancy and fear of being unjust which beset the examiners' path in other studies.

We would send forth children informed by "the reason firm, the temperate will, endurance, foresight, strength and skill," [Wordsworth] but we must add resolution to our good intentions and may not expect to produce a reasonable soul of fine polish from the steady friction, say, of mathematical studies only.

Chapter 10 The Curriculum

We, believing that the normal child has powers of mind which fit him to deal with all knowledge proper to him, give him a full and generous curriculum, taking care only that all knowledge offered to him is vital, that is, that facts are not presented without their informing ideas. Out of this conception comes our principle that:—

"Education is the Science of Relations'; that is, a child has natural relations with a vast number of things and thoughts: so we train him upon physical exercises, nature lore, handicrafts, science and art, and upon many living books, for we know that our business is not to teach him all about anything, but to help him to make valid as many as may be of—

"Those first-born affinities
That fit our new existence to existing things."

In devising a syllabus for a normal child, of whatever social class, three points must be considered:—

(a) He requires much knowledge, for the mind needs sufficient food as much as does the body.

(b) The knowledge should be various, for sameness in mental diet does not create appetite (i.e., curiosity).

(c) Knowledge should be communicated in well-chosen language because his attention responds naturally to what is conveyed in literary form.

As knowledge is not assimilated until it is reproduced, children should "tell back" after a single reading or hearing: or should write on some part of what they have read.

A single reading is insisted on, because children have naturally great power of attention; but this force is dissipated by the re-reading of passages, and also, by questioning, summarising, and the like.

Acting upon these and some other points in the behaviour of mind, we find that the educability of children is enormously greater than has hitherto been supposed, and is but little dependent on such circumstances as heredity and environment.

Nor is the accuracy of this statement limited to clever children or to children of the educated classes: thousands of children in elementary schools respond freely to this method, which is based on the behaviour of mind.

Few things are more remiss in our schools than the curriculum which is supposed to be entirely at the option of the Head: but is it? Most Secondary schools work towards examinations which more or less afford the privilege of entry to the Universities. The standard to be reached is set by these and the Heads of schools hold themselves powerless.

Though Elementary schools no longer work with a view to examination results yet as their best pupils try for scholarships admitting them to secondary schools, they do come indirectly under the same limitations. There is, however, much less liberty in Secondary than in Primary schools with regard to the subjects taught and the time devoted to each. The result is startling. A boy of eight in an Elementary school may shew more intelligence and wider knowledge than a boy of fourteen in a Preparatory school, that is, if he have been taught on the principles I have in view, while the other boy has been instructed with a view to a given standard of scholarship. The Preparatory school boy does, however, reach that standard in Latin, if not in Greek also, and in Mathematics.

If we succeed in establishing a similar standard which every boy and girl of a given age should reach in a liberal range of subjects, a fair chance will be afforded to the average boy and girl while brilliant or especially industrious young people will go ahead.

We labour under the mistake of supposing that there is no natural law or inherent principle according to which a child's course of studies should be regulated; so we teach him those things which, according to Locke, it is becoming for a 'gentleman' to know on the one hand, and, on the other, the arts of reading, writing and summing, that he may not grow up an illiterate citizen. In both cases the education we offer is too utilitarian, an indirect training for the professions or for a craftsman's calling with efforts in the latter case to make a boy's education bear directly on his future work.

But what if in the very nature of things we find a complete curriculum suggested? "The human race has lost its title deeds," said Voltaire, and mankind has been going about ever since seeking to recover them; education is still at sea and Voltaire's epigram holds good. We have not found our title deeds and so we yield to the children no inherent claims. Our highest aim is to educate young people for their uses to society, while every faddist is free to teach what he pleases because we have no title deeds to confront him with. Education, no doubt, falls under the economic law of supply and demand; but the demand should come from the children rather than from teachers and parents; how are their demands to become articulate? We must give consideration to this question because the answer depends on a survey of the composite whole we sum up as 'human nature,' a whole whose possibilities are infinite and various, not only in a budding genius, the child of a distinguished family, but in every child of the streets.

A small English boy of nine living in Japan, remarked, "Isn't it fun, Mother, learning all these things?

Everything seems to fit into something else." The boy had not found out the whole secret; everything fitted into something within himself.

The days have gone by when the education befitting either a gentleman or an artisan was our aim. Now we must deal with a child of man, who has a natural desire to know the history of his race and of his nation, what men thought in the past and are thinking now; the best thoughts of the best minds taking form as literature, and at its highest as poetry, or, as poetry rendered in the plastic forms of art: as a child of God, whose supreme desire and glory it is to know about and to know his almighty Father: as a person of many parts and passions who must know how to use, care for, and discipline himself, body, mind and soul: as a person of many relationships,—to family, city, church, state, neighbouring states, the world at large: as the inhabitant of a world full of beauty and interest, the features of which he must recognise and know how to name, and a world too, and a universe, whose every function of every part is ordered by laws which he must begin to know.

It is a wide programme founded on the educational rights of man; wide, but we may not say it is impossible nor may we pick and choose and educate him in this direction but not in that. We may not even make choice between science and the 'humanities.' Our part it seems to me is to give a child a vital hold upon as many as possible of those wide relationships proper to him. Shelley offers us the key to education when he speaks of "understanding that grows bright gazing on many truths."

Because the relationships a child is born to are very various, the knowledge we offer him must be various too. A lady teaching in Cape Colony writes,—"The papers incorporated in the pamphlet A Liberal Education: Practice (by A. C. Drury) testify to—to me—an almost incredible standard of proficiency. The mistakes are just the kind of mistakes that children should make and no more of them than just enough to keep them from being priggish. There are none of those howlers of fact or expression that make one view one's efforts with a feeling of utter despondency."

The knowledge of children so taught is consecutive, intelligent and complete as far as it goes, in however many directions. For it is a mistake to suppose that the greater the number of 'subjects' the greater the scholar's labour; the contrary is the case as the variety in itself affords refreshment, and the child who has written thirty or forty sheets during an examination week comes out unfagged. Not the number of subjects but the hours of work bring fatigue to the scholar; and bearing this in mind we have short hours and no evening preparation.

Section I
The Knowledge of God

Of the three sorts of knowledge proper to a child, the knowledge of God, of man, and of the universe,—the knowledge of God ranks first in importance, is indispensable, and most happy-making. Mothers are on the whole more successful in communicating this knowledge than are teachers who know the children less well and have a narrower, poorer standard of measurement for their minds. Parents do not talk down to children, but we might gather from educational publications that the art of education as regards young children is to bring conceptions down to their 'little' minds. If we give up this foolish prejudice in favour of the grown-up we shall be astonished at the range and depth of children's minds; and shall perceive that their relation to God is one of those 'first-born affinities' which it is our part to help them to make good. A mother knows how to speak of God as she would of an absent father with all the evidences of his care and love about her and his children. She knows how to make a child's heart beat high in joy and thankfulness as she thrills him with the thought, 'my Father made them all,' while his eye delights in flowery meadow, great tree, flowing river. "His are the mountains and the valleys his and the resplendent rivers, whose eyes they fill with tears of holy joy," [from The Freeman, Cowper] and this is not beyond children. We recollect how 'Arthur Pendennis' walked in the evening light with his mother and recited great passages from Milton and the eyes of the two were filled 'with tears of holy joy,' when the boy was eight. The teacher of a class has not the same tender opportunities but if he take pains to get a just measure of children's minds it is surprising how much may be done.

The supercilious point of view adopted by some teachers is the cause of the small achievements of their scholars. The 'kiddies' in a big girls' school are not expected to understand and know and they live down to the expectations formed of them. We (of the P.N.E.U.) begin the definite 'school' education of children when they are six; they are no doubt capable of beginning a year or two earlier but the fact is that nature and circumstances have provided such a wide field of education for young children that it seems better to abstain from requiring direct intellectual efforts until they have arrived at that age.

As for all the teaching in the nature of 'told to the children,' most children get their share of that whether in the infant school or at home, but this is practically outside the sphere of that part of education which demands a conscious mental effort, from the scholar, the mental effort of telling again that which has been read or heard. That is how we all learn, we tell again, to ourselves if need be, the matter we wish to retain, the sermon, the lecture, the conversation. The method is as old as the mind of man, the distressful fact is that it has been made so little use of in general education. Let us hear Dr. Johnson on the subject:—

"'Little people should be encouraged always to tell whatever they hear particularly striking to some brother, sister, or servant, immediately before the impression is erased by the intervention of newer occurrences.' He perfectly remembered the first time he heard of heaven and hell because when his mother had made out such a description of both places as she thought likely to seize the attention of her infant auditor who was then in bed with her, she got up and dressing him before the usual time, sent him directly to call the favourite workman in the house to whom she knew he would communicate the conversation while it was yet impressed upon his mind. The event was what she wished and it was to that method chiefly that he owed the uncommon felicity of remembering distant occurrences and long past conversations." (from a book about Samuel Johnson by Mrs. Hester Lynch Salusbury Thrale Piozzi).

Now our objective in this most important part of education is to give the children the knowledge of God. We need not go into the question of intuitive knowledge, but the expressed knowledge attainable by us has its source in the Bible, and perhaps we cannot do a greater indignity to children than to substitute our own or some other benevolent person's rendering for the fine English, poetic diction and lucid statement of the Bible.

Literature at its best is always direct and simple and a normal child of six listens with delight to the tales both of Old and New Testament read to him passage by passage, and by him narrated in turn, with delightful touches of native eloquence. Religion has two aspects, the attitude of the will towards God which we understand by Christianity, and that perception of God which comes from a gradual slow-growing comprehension of the divine dealings with men. In the first of these senses, Goethe was never religious, but the second forms the green reposeful background to a restless and uneasy life and it is worth while to consider how he arrived at so infinitely desirable a possession. He gives us the whole history fully in Aus Meinem Leben, a treatise on education very well worth our study. There he says,—

"Man may turn where he will, he may undertake what he will but he will yet return to that road which Dante has laid down for him. So it happened to me in the present case: my efforts with the language" (Hebrew, when he was ten) "with the contents of the Holy Scriptures, resulted in a most lively presentation to my imagination of that beautiful much-sung land and of the countries which bordered it as well as of the people and events which have glorified that spot of earth for thousands of years. Perhaps someone may ask why I set forth here in such detail this universally known history so often repeated, and expounded. This answer may serve, that in no other way could I show how with the distractions of my life and my irregular education I concentrated my mind and my emotion on one point because I can in no other way account for the peace which enveloped me however disturbed and unusual the circumstances of my life. If an ever active imagination of which the story of my life may bear witness led me here and there, if the medley of fable, history, mythology, threatened to drive me to distraction, I betook myself again to those morning lands, I buried myself in the five books of Moses and there amongst the wide-spreading shepherd people I found the greatest solitude and the greatest comfort."

It is well to know how Goethe obtained this repose of soul, this fresh background for his thoughts, and in all the errors of a wilful life this innermost repose appears never to have left him. His eyes, we are told, were tranquil as those of a god, and here is revealed the secret of that large tranquility. Here, too, Goethe unfolds for us a principle of education which those who desire their children to possess the passive as well as the active principle of religion would do well to consider; for it is probably true that the teaching of the New Testament, not duly grounded upon or accompanied by that of the Old, fails to result in such thought of God, wide, all-embracing, all-permeating, as David, for example, gives constant expression to in the Psalms. Let us have faith and courage to give children such a full and gradual picture of Old Testament history that they unconsciously perceive for themselves a panoramic view of the history of mankind typified by that of the Jewish nation as it is unfolded in the Bible. Are our children little sceptics, as was the young Goethe, who take a laughing joy in pulling their teachers with a hundred difficulties? Like that wise old Dr. Albrecht, let us be in no haste to explain. Let us not try to put down or evade their questions, or to give them final answers, but introduce them as did he to some thoughtful commentator who weighs difficult questions with modesty and scrupulous care. If we act in this way, difficulties will assume their due measure of importance, that is to say, they will be lost sight of in the gradual unfolding of the great scheme whereby the world was educated. I know of no commentator for children, say, from six to twelve, better than Canon Paterson Smyth (The Bible for the Young). He is one of the few writers able to take the measure of children's minds, to help them over real difficulties, give impulse to their thoughts and direction to their conduct.

Between the ages of six and twelve children cover the whole of the Old Testament story, the Prophets, major and minor, being introduced as they come into connection with the Kings. The teacher opens the lesson by reading the passage from The Bible for the Young, in which the subject is pictorially treated; for example,—

"It is the battle field of the valley of Elah. The camp of Israel is on one slope, the big tents of the Philistines on the other. The Israelites are rather small men, lithe and clever, the Philistines are big men, big, stupid, thick-headed giants, the same as when Samson used to fool them and laugh at them long ago. There is great excitement on both sides," etc.

There will be probably some talk and discussion after this reading. Then the teacher will read the Bible passage in question which the children will narrate, the commentary serving merely as a background for their thoughts. The narration is usually exceedingly interesting; the children do not miss a point and often add picturesque touches of their own. Before the close of the lesson, the teacher brings out such new thoughts of God or new points of behaviour as the reading has afforded, emphasing the moral or religious lesson to be learnt rather by a reverent and sympathetic manner than by any attempt at personal application.

Forms III and IV (twelve to fifteen) read for themselves the whole of the Old Testament as produced by the Rev. H. Costley-White in his Old Testament History. Wise and necessary omissions in this work make it more possible to deal with Old Testament History, in the words of the Authorised Version, than if the Bible were used as a single volume. Then, "each period is illustrated by reference to contemporary literature (e.g., Prophets and Psalms and monuments)." Again, brief historical explanations and general commentary are inserted in their proper places." For example, after Genesis iii, we read, as an introduction to the story of Cain and Abel,—

"The original object of this story was to explain the development of sin amongst mankind and the origin of homicide which in this first instance was actual murder. There are difficulties in the story which do not admit of satisfactory explanation. It may be asked,—'Why did God not accept Cain's offering?' 'How was his displeasure shewn?' 'What was the sign appointed for Cain?' 'Whom did he marry?' The best way to answer such questions is to admit that we do not know, but we may add that these early stories are only a selection which do not necessarily form a consistent and complete whole, and that in this very case there are signs that the original story has been cut down and edited.

"Among the lessons taught are the following—(1) God judges man's motives rather than his acts. The service of the heart is worth more than any ceremonial. (2) It is not the sin of murder that is condemned so much as the sin of jealousy and malice: cf. the Sermon on the Mount, Matt. xxi, 6. (3) The great doctrine of the Brotherhood of Man, that each man is his brother's keeper and has his share of responsibility for the conditions of the lives of others. (4) Sin always brings its own punishment. (5) God remonstrates with man before the climax of sin is reached."

The footnotes which form the only commentary upon the text are commendably short and to the point.

Having received a considerable knowledge of the Old Testament in detail from the words of the Bible itself and having been trained to accept difficulties freely without giving place to the notion that such difficulties invalidate the Bible as the oracle of God and our sole original source of knowledge concerning the nature of Almighty God and the manner of His government of the world, children are prepared for a further study of divinity, still following the Bible text.

When pupils are of an age to be in Forms V and VI (from 15 to 18) we find that Dummelow's One Volume Bible Commentary is of great service. It is designed to provide in convenient form,—

"A brief explanation of the meaning of the Scriptures. Introductions have been supplied to the various books and Notes which will help to explain the principal difficulties, textual, moral or doctrinal, which may arise in conjunction with them. A series of articles has also been prefixed dealing with the larger questions suggested by the Bible as a whole. It is hoped that the Commentary may lead to a perusal of many of the books of Holy Scripture which are often left unread in spite of their rare literary charm and abundant usefulness for the furtherance of the spiritual life. In recent years much light has been thrown upon questions of authorship and interpretation and the contributors to this volume have endeavoured to incorporate in it the most assured results of modern scholarship whilst avoiding opinions of an extreme or precarious kind. Sometimes these results differ from traditional views but in such cases it is not only hoped but believed that the student will find the spiritual value and authority of the Bible have been enhanced rather than diminished by the change."

The Editor has in these words set forth so justly the aims of the Commentary that I need only say we find it of very great practical value. The pupils read the general articles and the introductions to the separate Books; they read too the Prophets and the poetical books with the notes supplied. Thus they leave school with a fairly enlightened knowledge of the books of the Old Testament and of the aids modern scholarship has brought towards their interpretation; we hope also with increased reverence for and delight in the ways of God with men.

The New Testament comes under another category. The same commentaries are used and the same methods followed, that is, the reverent reading of the text, with the following narration which is often curiously word perfect after a single reading; this is the more surprising because we all know how difficult it is to repeat a passage which we have heard a thousand times; the single attentive reading does away with this difficulty and we are able to assure ourselves that children's minds are stored with perfect word pictures of every tender and beautiful scene described in the Gospels; and are able reproduce the austere if equally tender teaching which enforces the object lessons of the miracles. By degrees the Person of Our Lord as revealed in His words and His works becomes real and dear to them, not through emotional appeals but through the impression left by accurate and detailed knowledge concerning the Saviour of the World, Who went about doing good. Dogmatic teaching finds its way to them by inference through a quiet realisation of the Bible records; and loyalty to a Divine Master likely to become the guiding principle of their lives.

I should like to urge the importance of what may be called a poetic presentation of the life and teaching of Our Lord. The young reader should experience in this study a curious and delightful sense of harmonious development, the rounding out of each incident, of the progressive unfolding which characterises Our Lord's teaching; and, let me say here, the custom of narration lends itself surprisingly to this sort of poetic insight. Every related incident stands out in a sort of bas-relief; every teaching so rendered unfolds its meaning; every argument convinces; and the personages reveal themselves to us more intimately than almost any persons we know in real life. Probably very little hortatory teaching is desirable. The danger of boring young listeners by such teaching is great, and there is also the further danger of provoking counter-opinions, even counter-convictions, in the innocent-looking audience. On the whole we shall perhaps do well to allow the Scripture reading itself to point the moral.

"We are at present in a phase of religious thought, Christian and pseudo-Christian, when a synthetic study of the life and teaching of Christ may well be of use. We have analysed until the mind turns in weariness from the broken fragments; we have criticised until there remains no new standpoint for the critic; but if we could only get a whole conception of Christ's life among men and of the philosophic method of His teaching, His own words should be fulfilled and the Son of Man lifted up, would draw all men unto Himself. It seems to me that verse offers a comparatively new medium in which to present the great theme. It is more impersonal, more condensed, is capable of more reverent handling than is prose; and what Wordsworth calls the 'authentic comment' may be essayed in verse with more becoming diffidence. Again, the supreme moment of a very great number of lives, that in which a person is brought face to face with Christ, comes before us with great vividness in the Gospel narratives, and it is possible to treat what we may call dramatic situations with more force, and at the same time with more reticence, in verse than in prose.

"We have a single fragment of the great epic which the future may bring forth,—

'Those holy fields
Over whose acres walked those blessed feet
Which fourteen hundred years ago were nailed
For our advantage to the bitter cross.'
[from Shakespeare's Henry IV]

"If Shakespeare had given us the whole how rich should we be! Every line of verse dealing directly with our Lord from the standpoint of His personality is greatly treasured. We love the lines in which [Richard Chenevix?] Trench tells us,—

"Of Jesus sitting by Samarian well
Or teaching some poor fishers on the shore.'
And [John] Keble's,
'Meanwhile He paces through the adoring crowd
Calm as the march of some majestic cloud.'
[from Advent Sunday]
or his,
'In His meek power He climbs the mountain's brow.'
[from Fouth Sunday After Epiphany]

Every line of such verse is precious but the lines are few, no doubt because the subject is supremely august. Meantime we are waiting for the great epic: because the need seems to be urgent the writer [i.e., Charlotte Mason] has ventured to offer a temporary stop-gap in the six volumes ofThe Saviour of the World." (From the Preface to the first volume).

A girl of thirteen and a half (Form IV) in her Easter examination tackled the question: "The people sat in darkness" . . . "I am the Light of the World." Shew as far as you can the meaning of these statements. She was not asked to write in verse, and was she not taught by a beautiful instinct to recognise that the phrases she had to deal with were essential poetry and that she could best express herself in verse?

The people sat in darkness—all was dim,
No light had yet come unto them from Him,
No hope as yet of Heaven after life,
A peaceful haven far from war and strife.
Some warriors to Valhalla's halls might go
And fight all day, and die. At evening, lo!
They'd wake again, and drink in the great hall.
Some men would sleep for ever at their fall;
Or with their fickle Gods for ever be:
So all was dark and dim. Poor heathens, see!
The Light ahead, the clouds that roll away,
The golden, glorious, dawning of the Day;
And in the birds, the flowers, the sunshine, see
The might of Him who calls, "Come unto Me.'"

A girl of seventeen (Form V) answered the question: Write an essay or a poem on the Bread of Life, by the following lines,

"'How Came He here,' ev'n so the people cried,
Who found Him in the Temple: He had wrought
A miracle, and fed the multitude,
On five small loaves and fish: so now they'd have
Him king; should not they then have ev'ry good,
Food that they toiled not for and clothes and care,
And all the comfort that they could require?—
So thinking sought the king.

Our Saviour cried:
'Labour ye not for meat that perisheth,
But rather for the everlasting bread,
Which I will give'—Where is this bread, they cry,
They know not 'tis a heavenly bread He gives
But seek for earthly food 'I am the Bread of Life
And all who come to Me I feed with Bread.
Receive ye then the Bread. Your fathers eat
Of manna in the wilderness—and died—
But whoso eats this Bread shall have his part
In everlasting life: I am the Bread,
That cometh down from Heaven; unless ye eat
Of me ye die, but otherwise ye live.'
So Jesus taught, in Galilee, long since.
"The people murmured when they heard His Word,
How can it be? How can He be our Bread?
They hardened then their hearts against His Word,
They would not hear. and could not understand,
And so they turned back to easier ways,
And many of them walked with Him no more.
May He grant now that we may hear the Word
And harden not our hearts against the Truth
That Jesus came to teach: so that in vain
He may not cry to hearts that will not hear,
'I am the Bread of Life, for all that come,
I have this gift, an everlasting life,
And room within my Heavenly Father's House."

The higher forms in the P.U.S. read The Saviour of the World volume by volume together with the text arranged in chronological order. The lower forms read in turns each of the Synoptic Gospels; Form IV adds the Gospel of St. John and The Acts, assisted by the capital Commentaries on the several Gospels by Bishop Walsham How, published by the S.P.C.K. [Anglican Church's Society for Promoting Christian Knowledge] The study of the Epistles and the Book of Revelation is confined for the most part to Forms V and VI. The Catechism, Prayer-book, and Church History are treated with suitable text-books much in the same manner and give opportunities for such summing-up of Christian teaching as is included in the so-called dogmas of the Church. We find that Sundays together with the time given to preparation for Confirmation afford sufficient opportunities for this teaching.

Section II
The Knowledge of Man; History

I have already spoken of history as a vital part of education and have cited the counsel of Montaigne that the teacher 'shall by the help of histories inform himself of the worthiest minds that were in the best ages.' To us in particular who are living in one of the great epochs of history it is necessary to know something of what has gone before in order to think justly of what is occurring to-day. The League of Nations, for example, has reminded us not only of the Congress of Vienna but of the several Treaties of Perpetual Peace which have marked the history of Europe. It is still true that,—

"Things done without example, in their issue
Are to be feared. Have you a precedent
Of this commission?" (Henry VIII.)

We applaud the bluff King's wisdom and look uneasily for precedents for the war and the peace and the depressing anxieties that have come in their train. We are conscious of a lack of sound judgment in ourselves to decide upon the questions that have come before us and are aware that nothing would give us more confidence than a pretty wide acquaintance with history. The more educated among our 'Dominion' cousins complain that their young people have no background of history and as a consequence 'we are the people' is their master thought; they would face even the loss of Westminster Abbey without a qualm. What is it to them where great events have happened, great persons lived and moved? And, alas, this indifference to history is not confined to the Dominions; young people at home are equally indifferent, nor have their elders such stores of interest and information as should quicken children with the knowledge that always and everywhere there have been great parts to play and almost always great men to play those parts: that any day it may come to anyone to do some service of historical moment to the country. It is not too much to say that a rational well-considered patriotism depends on a pretty copious reading of history, and with this rational patriotism we desire our young people shall be informed rather than with the jingoism of the emotional patriot.

If there is but little knowledge of history amongst us, no doubt our schools are in fault. Teachers will plead that there is no time save for a sketchy knowledge of English history given in a course of lectures of which the pupils take notes and work up reports. Most of us know how unsatisfying is such a course however entertaining. Not even Thackeray could introduce the stuff of knowledge into his lectures on The Four Georges. Our knowledge of history should give us something more than impressions and opinions, but, alas, the lack of time is a real difficulty.

Now the method I am advocating has this advantage; it multiplies time. Each school period is quadrupled in time value and we find that we get through a surprising amount of history in a thorough way, in about the same time that in most schools affords no more than a skeleton of English History only. We know that young people are enormously interested in the subject and give concentrated attention if we give them the right books. We are aware that our own discursive talk is usually a waste of time and a strain on the scholars' attention, so we (of the P.N.E.U.) confine ourselves to affording two things,—knowledge, and a keen sympathy in the interest roused by that knowledge. It is our part to see that every child knows and can tell, whether by way of oral narrative or written essay. In this way an unusual amount of ground is covered with such certainty that no revision is required for the examination at the end of the term. A single reading is a condition insisted upon because a naturally desultory habit of mind leads us all to put off the effort of attention as long as a second or third chance of coping with our subject is to be hoped for. It is, however, a mistake to speak of the 'effort of attention.' Complete and entire attention is a natural function which requires no effort and causes no fatigue; the anxious labour of mind of which we are at times aware comes when attention wanders and has again to be brought to the point; but the concentration at which most teachers aim is an innate provision for education and is not the result of training or effort. Our concern is to afford matter of a sufficiently literary character, together with the certainty that no second or third opportunity for knowing a given lesson will be allowed.

The personality of the teacher is no doubt of much value but perhaps this value is intellectual rather than emotional. The perception of the teacher is keenly interested, that his mind and their minds are working in harmony is a wonderful incentive to young scholars; but the sympathetic teacher who believes that to attend is a strain, who makes allowance for the hundred wandering fancies that beset a child—whom he has at last to pull up with effort, tiring to teacher and pupil—hinders in his good-natured efforts to help.

The child of six in IB has, not stories from English History, but a definite quantity of consecutive reading, say, forty pages in a term, from a well-written, well-considered, large volume which is also well-illustrated. Children cannot of course themselves read a book which is by no means written down to the 'child's level' so the teacher reads and the children 'tell' paragraph by paragraph, passage by passage. The teacher does not talk much and is careful never to interrupt a child who is called upon to 'tell.' The first efforts may be stumbling but presently the children get into their 'stride' and 'tell' a passage at length with surprising fluency. The teacher probably allows other children to correct any faults in the telling when it is over. The teacher's own really difficult part is to keep up sympathetic interest by look and occasional word, by remarks upon a passage that has been narrated, by occasionally shewing pictures, and so on. But she will bear in mind that the child of six has begun the serious business of his education, that it does not matter much whether he understands this word or that, but that it matters a great deal that he should learn to deal directly with books. Whatever a child or grown-up person can tell, that we may be sure he knows, and what he cannot tell, he does not know. Possibly this practice of 'telling' was more used in the sixteenth and seventeenth centuries than it is now. We remember how three gentlemen meet in Henry VIII and one who has just come out of the Abbey from witnessing the coronation of Anne Boleyn is asked to tell the others about it, which he does with the vividness and accuracy we obtain from children. In this case no doubt the 'telling' was a stage device, but would it have been adopted if such narration were not commonly practised? Even in our own day a good raconteur is a welcome guest; and a generation or two ago the art was studied as a part of gentlemanly equipment. The objection occurs that such a social accomplishment is unnecessary for children and is a mere exercise of memory. Now a passage to be memorised requires much conning, much repetition, and meanwhile the learners are 'thinking' about other matters, that is, the mind is not at work in the act of memorising. To read a passage with full attention and to tell it afterwards has a curiously different effect. M. Bergson makes the happy distinction between word memory and mind memory, which, once the force of it is realised, should bring about sweeping changes in our methods of education.

Trusting to mind memory we visualise the scene, are convinced by the arguments, take pleasure in the turn the sentences and frame our own upon them; in that particular passage or chapter has been received us and become a part of us just as literally as was yesterday's dinner; nay, more so, for yesterday's dinner is of little account tomorrow; but several months, perhaps hence, we shall be able to narrate the passage we had, so to say, consumed and grown upon with all the vividness, detail and accuracy of the first telling. All powers of the mind which we call faculties have brought into play in dealing with the intellectual matter thus afforded; so we may not ask questions to help the child to reason, paint fancy pictures to help him to imagine, draw out moral lessons to quicken his conscience. These things take place as involuntarily as processes of digestion.

Children of seven are promoted to Form IA in which they remain for a couple of years. They read from the same capital book, Mrs. Marshall's Our Island Story, and about the same number of pages in a term; but while the readings in IB are confined to the first third of the book embodying the simpler and more direct histories, those in IA go on to the end of the volume and children learn at any rate to love English history. "I'd a lot sooner have history than my dinner," said a sturdy boy of seven by no means inclined to neglect his dinner.

In IA the history is amplified and illustrated by short biographies of persons connected with the period studied, Lord Clive, Nelson, etc.; and Mrs. Frewen Lord's delightful Tales from Westminster Abbey and from St. Paul's help the children immensely in individualising their heroes. It is good to hear them 'tell' of Franklin, Nelson, Howard, Shaftesbury, and their delight in visiting the monuments is very great. One would not think that Donne would greatly interest children but the excitement of a small party in noticing the marks of the Great Fire still to be seen on his monument was illuminating to lookers-on.

Possibly there is no sounder method of inculcating a sane and serviceable patriotism than this of making children familiar with the monuments of the great event if they have not the opportunity to see them. Form II (ages 9 to 12) have a more considerable historical programme which they cover with ease and enjoyment. They use a more difficult book than in IA, an interesting and well-written history of England of which they read some fifty pages or so in a term. IIA read in addition and by way of illustration the chapters dealing with the social life of the period in a volume, treating of social life in England. We introduce children as early as possible to the contemporary history of other countries as the study of English history alone is apt to lead to a certain insular and arrogant habit of mind.

Naturally we begin with French history and both divisions read from the First History of France, very well written, the chapters contemporary with the English history they are reading. The readiness with which children write or tell of Richelieu, Colbert, Bayard, justifies us in this early introduction of foreign history and the lucidity and clearness with which the story is told in the book they use results on the part of the children in such a knowledge of the history of France as throws light on that of their own country and certainly gives them the sense that history was progressing everywhere much as it was at home during the period they are reading about.

The study of ancient history which cannot be contemporaneous we approach through a chronologically-arranged book about the British Museum (written for the scholars of the P.U.S. by the late Mrs. W. Epps who had the delightful gift of realising the progress of the ages as represented in our great national storehouse). I have already instanced a child's visit to the Parthenon Room and her eager identification of what she saw with what she had read, and that will serve to indicate the sort of key to ancient history afforded by this valuable book. Miss G. M. Bernau has added to the value of these studies by producing a 'Book of Centuries' in which children draw such illustrations as they come across of objects of domestic use, of art, etc., connected with the century they are reading about. This slight study of the British Museum we find very valuable; whether the children have or have not the opportunity of visiting the Museum itself, they have the hope of doing so, and, besides, their minds are awakened to the treasures of local museums.

In Form III children continue the same history of England as in II, the same French history and the same British Museum Book, going on with their 'Book of Centuries.' To this they add about twenty to thirty pages a term from a little book on Indian History, a subject which interests them greatly.

Slight studies of the history of other parts of the British Empire are included under 'Geography.'

In Form IV the children are promoted to Gardiner's Student's History of England, clear and able, but somewhat stiffer than that they have hitherto been engaged upon, together with Mr. and Mrs. Quennell's History of Everyday Things in England (which is used in Form III also). Form IV is introduced to outlines of European history. The British Museum for Children and 'Book of Centuries' are continued.

It is as teachers know a matter of extreme difficulty to find the exactly right book for children's reading in each subject and for some years we have been regretting the fact that Lord's very delightful Modern Europe has been out of print.

The history studies of Forms V and VI (ages 15 to 18) are more advanced and more copious and depend for illustration upon readings in the literature of the period. Green's Shorter History of the English People is the textbook in English history, amplified, for example, by Macaulay's Essays on Frederick the Great and the Austrian Succession, on Pitt and Clive. For the same period we use an American history of Western Europe and a very admirable history of France, well-translated from the original of M. Duruy. Possibly Madame de Staël's L'Allemagne or some other historical work of equal calibre may occur in their reading of French. It is not possible to continue the study of Greek and Roman history in detail but an admirably written survey informed with enthusiasm is afforded by Professor de Burgh's The Legacy of the Ancient World. The pupils make history charts for every hundred years on the plan either adapted or invented by the late Miss Beale of Cheltenham, a square ruled into a hundred spaces ten in each direction with the symbol in each square showing an event which lends itself to illustration during that particular ten years. Thus crossed battle axes represent a war.

The geographical aspects of history fall under 'Geography' as a subject. This course of historical reading is valued exceedingly by young people as affording a knowledge of the past that bears upon and illuminates the present. The writer recollects meeting a brilliant group of Oxford undergraduates, keen and full of interest, but lamentably ignorant, who said, "We want to know something about history. What do you advise us to read? We know nothing." Perhaps no youth should go to College without some such rudimentary course of English, European, and, especially, French history, as is afforded by the programmes. Such a general survey should precede any special course and should be required before the more academic studies designed to prepare students for 'research work.'

It will be observed that the work throughout the Forms is always chronologically progressive. The young student rarely goes over old ground; but should it happen that the whole school has arrived at the end of 1920, say, and there is nothing for it but to begin again, the books studied throw new light and bring the young students into line with modern research.

But any sketch of the history teaching in Forms V and VI in a given period depends upon a notice of the 'literature' set; for plays, novels, essays, 'lives,' poems, are all pressed into service and where it is possible, the architecture, painting, etc., which the period produced. Thus questions such as the following on a term's work both test and record the reading of the term,—"Describe the condition of (a) the clergy, (b) the army, (c) the navy, (d) the general public in and about 1685." "Trace the rise of Prussia before Frederick the Great." "What theories of government were held by Louis XIV? Give some account of his great ministers." "Describe the rise of Russia and its condition at the opening of the eighteenth century." "Suppose Evelyn (Form VI) or Pepys (Form V) in counsel at the League of Nations, write his diary for three days." "Sketch the character and manners of Addison. How does he appear in Esmond?"

It is a great thing to possess a pageant of history in the background of one's thoughts. We may not be able to recall this or that circumstance, but, 'the imagination is warmed'; we know that there is a great deal to be said on both sides of every question and are saved from crudities in opinion and rashness in action. The present becomes enriched for us with the wealth of all that has gone before.

Perhaps the gravest defect in school curricula is that they fail to give a comprehensive, intelligent and interesting introduction to history. To leave off or even to begin with the history of our own country is fatal.

We can not live sanely unless we know that other peoples are as we are with a difference, that their history is as ours, with a difference, that they too have been represented by their poets and their artists, that they too have their literature and their national life. We have been asleep and our awaking is rather terrible. The people whom we have not taught, rise upon us in their ignorance and 'the rabble,'—

"As the world were now but to begin
Antiquity forgot, custom not known.
They cry,—'Choose we!'" (Hamlet.)

Heaven help their choice for choosing is indeed with them, and little do they know of those two ratifiers and props of every present word and action, Antiquity and Custom! It is never too late to mend but we may not delay to offer such a liberal and generous diet of History to every child in the country as shall give weight to his decisions, consideration to his actions and stability to his conduct.; that stability, the lack of which has plunged us into many a stormy sea of unrest.

It is to be noted that 'stability' is the mark of the educated classes. When we reflect upon the disturbance of the national life by labour unrest and again, upon the fact that political and social power is passing into the hands of the majority, that is of the labouring classes, we cannot but feel that there is a divine fitness, a providential adaptation in the circumstance that the infinite educability of persons of all classes should be disclosed to us as a nation at a time when an emotional and ignorant labouring class is a peculiar danger. I am not sure that the education implied in the old symbol of the ladder does make for national tranquility. It is right that equal opportunity of being first should be afforded to all but that is no new thing. Our history is punctuated by men who have risen, and the Roman Church has largely founded herself as has the Chinese Empire upon this doctrine of equal opportunity. But let us remember that the men who climb are apt to be uneasy members of society; the desire for knowledge for its own sake, on the other hand, finds satisfaction in knowledge itself.

The young men see visions; the hardships of daily life are ameliorated, and while an alert and informed mind leads to decency and propriety of living it does not lead to the restless desire to subvert society for the sake of the chances offered by a general upheaval. Wordsworth is right:—

"If rightly trained and bred Humanity is humble."

We live in times critical for everybody but eminently critical for teachers because it rests with them to decide whether personal or general good should be aimed at, whether education shall be merely a means of getting on or a means of general progress towards high thinking and plain living and therefore an instrument of the greatest national good.

The Knowledge of Man; Literature

Except in Form I the study of Literature goes pari passu with that of History. Fairy tales, (Andersen or Grimm, for example), delight Form IB, and the little people re-tell these tales copiously, vividly, and with the astonishing exactness we may expect when we remember how seriously annoyed they are with the story-teller who alters a phrase or a circumstance. Aesop's Fables, too, are used with great success, and are rendered, after being once heard, with brevity and point, and children readily appropriate the moral. Mrs. Gatty's Parables From Nature, again, serve another purpose. They feed a child's sense of wonder and are very good to tell. There is no attempt to reduce the work of this form, or any other, to a supposed 'child level.' Form IA (7 to 9) hears and tells chapter by chapter The Pilgrim's Progress and the children's narrations are delightful. No beautiful thought or bold figure escapes them. Andrew Lang's Tales of Troy and Greece, a big volume, is a piece de resistance going on from term to term.

The great tales of the heroic age find their way to children's hearts. They conceive vividly and tell eagerly, and the difficult classical names instead of being a stumbling-block are a delight, because, as a Master of a Council school says,—

"Children have an instinctive power by which they are able to sense the meaning of a whole passage and even some difficult words."

That the sonorous beauty of these classical names appeals to them is illustrated by a further quotation from the same Master,—

"A boy of about seven in my school the other day asked his mother why she had not given him one of those pretty names they heard in the stories at school. He thought Ulysses a prettier name than his own, Kenneth, and that the mother of his playmate might have called him Achilles instead of Alan."

There is profound need to cultivate delight in beautiful names in days when we are threatened with the fear that London itself should lose that rich halo of historic associations which glorifies its every street and alley, that it may be made like New York, and should name a street X500,—like a workhouse child without designation; an age when we express the glory and beauty of the next highest peak of the Himalayas by naming it D2! In such an age, this, of their inherent aptitude for beautiful names, is a lode of much promise in children's minds. The Kaffir who announced that his name was' Telephone' had an ear for sound. Kingsley's Water Babies, Alice in Wonderland, Kipling's Just So Stories, scores of exquisite classics written for children, but not written down to them, are suitable at this stage.

Form IIB has a considerable programme of reading, that is, not the mere mechanical exercise of reading but the reading of certain books. Therefore it is necessary that two years should be spent in Form IA and that in the second of these two years the children should read a good deal of the set work for themselves. In IIB they read their own geography, history, poetry, but perhaps Shakespeare's Twelfth Night, say, Scott's Rob Roy, Gulliver's Travels, should be read to them and narrated by them until they are well in their tenth year. Their power to understand, visualise, and 'tell' a play of Shakespeare from nine years old and onwards is very surprising. They put in nothing which is not there, but they miss nothing and display a passage or a scene in a sort of curious relief. One or two books of the calibre of The Heroes of Asgard are also included in the programme for the term.

The transition to Form IIA is marked by more individual reading as well as by a few additional books. The children read their 'Shakespeare play' in character. Certain Council School boys, we are told, insist on dramatising Scott as they read it. Bulfinch's Age of Fable admits them to the rich imaginings of peoples who did not yet know. Goldsmith's poems and Stevenson's Kidnapped, etc., may form part of a term's work, and in each and all children shew the same surprising power of knowing, evinced by the one sure test,—they are able to 'tell' each work they have read not only with accuracy but with spirit and originality. How is it possible, it may be asked, to show originality in 'mere narration'? Let us ask Scott, Shakespeare, Homer, who told what they knew, that is narrated, but with continual scintillations from their own genius playing upon the written word. Just so in their small degree do the children narrate; they see it all so vividly that when you read or hear their versions the theme is illuminated for you too.

Children remain in Form II until they are twelve, and here I would remark on the evenness with which the power of children in dealing with books is developed. We spread an abundant and delicate feast in the programmes and each small guest assimilates what he can. The child of genius and imagination gets greatly more than his duller comrade but all sit down to the same feast and each one gets according to his needs and powers.

The surprises afforded by the dull and even the 'backward' children are encouraging and illuminating. We think we know that man is an educable being, but when we afford to children all that they want we discover how straitened were our views, how poor and narrow the education we offered. Even in so-called deficient children we perceive,—

"What a piece of work is man . . . In apprehension, how like a god!"

In Forms III and IV we introduce a History of English Literature carefully chosen to afford sympathetic interest and delight while avoiding stereotyped opinions and stale information. The portion read each term (say fifty pages) corresponds with the period covered in history studies and the book is a great favourite with children. They have of course a great flair for Shakespeare, whether King Lear, Twelfth Night, Henry V, or some other play, and The Waverleys usually afford a contemporary tale. There has been discussion in Elementary Schools as to whether an abridged edition would not give a better chance of getting through the novel set for a term, but strong arguments were brought forward at a conference of teachers in Gloucester in favour of a complete edition. Children take pleasure in the 'dry' parts, descriptions and the like, rendering these quite beautifully in their narrations. Form IV may have quite a wide course of reading. For instance if the historical period for a term include the Commonwealth, they may read L'Allegro, and Il Penseroso, Lycidas, and contemporary poets as represented in a good anthology, or, for a later period, Pope's Rape of the Lock, or Gray's poems, while Form III read poems of Goldsmith and Burns. The object of children's literary studies is not to give them precise information as to who wrote what in the reign of whom?—but to give them a sense of the spaciousness of the days, not only of great Elizabeth, but of all those times of which poets, historians and the makers of tales, have left us living pictures. In such ways the children secure, not the sort of information which is of little cultural value, but wide spaces wherein imagination may take those holiday excursions deprived of which life is dreary; judgment, too, will turn over these folios of the mind and arrive at fairly just decisions about a given strike, the question of Poland, Indian Unrest. Every man is called upon to be a statesman seeing that every man and woman, too, has a share in the government of the country; but statesmanship requires imaginative conceptions, formed upon pretty wide reading and some familiarity with historical precedents.

The reading for Forms V and VI (ages 15 to 18) is more comprehensive and more difficult. Like that in the earlier Forms, it follows the lines of the history they are reading, touching current literature in the occasional use of modern books; but young people who have been brought up on this sort of work may, we find, be trusted to keep themselves au fait with the best that is being produced in their own days. Given the proper period, Form V would cover in a term Pope's Essay on Man, Carlyle's Essay on Burns, Frankfort Moore's Jessamy Bride, Goldsmith's Citizen of the World (edited), Thackeray's The Virginians, the contemporary poets from an anthology. Form VI would read Boswell, The Battle of the Books, Macaulay's Essays on Goldsmith, Johnson, Pitt; the contemporary poets from The Oxford Book of Verse, and both Forms read She Stoops to Conquer. This course of reading, it will be seen, is suggestive and will lead to much reading round and about it in later days. As for the amount covered in each Form, it is probably about the amount most of us cover in the period of time included in a school term, but while we grown-up persons read and forget because we do not take the pains to know as we read, these young students have the powers of perfect recollection and just application because they have read with attention and concentration and have in every case reproduced what they have read in narration, or, the gist of some portion of it, in writing.

The children's answers in their examination papers, show that literature has become a living power in the minds of these young people.

The Knowledge of Man; Morals and Economics: Citizenship

Like Literature this subject, too, is ancillary to History. In Form I, children begin to gather conclusions as to the general life of the community from tales, fables and the story of one or another great citizen. In Form II, Citizenship becomes a definite subject rather from the point of view of what may be called the inspiration of citizenship than from that of the knowledge proper to a citizen, though the latter is by no means neglected. We find Plutarch's Lives exceedingly inspiring. These are read by the teacher (with suitable omissions) and narrated with great spirit by the children. They learn to answer such questions as,—"In what ways did Pericles make Athens beautiful? How did he persuade the people to help him?" And we may hope that the idea is engendered of preserving and increasing the beauty of their own neighbourhood without the staleness which comes of much exhortation. Again, they will answer,—"How did Pericles manage the people in time of war lest they should force him to act against his own judgment?" And from such knowledge as this we may suppose that the children begin to get a sympathetic view of the problems of statesmanship. Then, to come to our own time, they are enabled to answer,—"What do you know of (a) County Councils, (b) District Councils, (c) Parish Councils?"—knowledge which should make children perceive that they too are being prepared to become worthy citizens, each with his several duties. Our old friend Mrs. Beesley's Stories from the History of Rome helps us here in Form IIB instead of Plutarch, illumined by Macaulay's Lays of Ancient Rome. In giving children the knowledge of men and affairs which we class under 'Citizenship' we have to face the problem of good and evil. Many earnest-minded teachers will sympathise with one of their number who said,—

"Why give children the tale of Circe, in which there is such an offensive display of greediness, why not bring them up exclusively on heroic tales which offer them something to live up to? Time is short. Why not use it all in giving examples of good life and instruction in good manners?"

Again,—

"Why should they read any part of Childe Harold, and so become familiar with a poet whose works do not make for edification?"

Now Plutarch is like the Bible in this, that he does not label the actions of his people as good or bad but leaves the conscience and judgment of his readers to make that classification. What to avoid and how to avoid it, is knowledge as important to the citizen whether of the City of God or of his own immediate city, as to know what is good and how to perform the same. Children recognise with incipient weariness the doctored tale as soon as it is begun to be told, but the human story with its evil and its good never flags in interest. Jacob does not pall upon us though he was the elect of God. We recognise the justice of his own verdict on himself, "few and evil have been the days of my life." We recognise the finer integrity of the foreign kings and rulers that he is brought in contact with, just as in the New Testament the Roman Centurion is in every case a finer person than the religious Jew. Perhaps we are so made that the heroic which is all heroic, the good which is all virtuous, palls upon us, whereas we preach little sermons to ourselves on the text of the failings and weaknesses of those great ones with whom we become acquainted in our reading. Children like ourselves must see life whole if they are to profit. At the same time they must be protected from grossness and rudeness by means of the literary medium through which they are taught. A daily newspaper is not on a level with Plutarch's Lives, nor with Andrew Lang's Tales of Troy and Greece, though possibly the same class of incidents may appear in both. The boy, or girl, aged from ten to twelve, who is intimate with a dozen or so of Plutarch's Lives, so intimate that they influence his thought and conduct, has learned to put his country first and to see individuals only as they serve or dis-serve the State. Thus he gets his first lesson in the science of proportion. Children familiar with the great idea of a State in the sense, not of a government but of the people, learn readily enough about the laws, customs and government of their country; learn, too, with great interest something about themselves, mind and body, heart and soul, because they feel it is well to know what they have it in them to give to their country.

We labour under a difficulty in choosing books which has exercised all great thinkers from Plato to Erasmus, from Erasmus to the anxious Heads of schools to-day, I mean the coarseness and grossness which crop up in scores of books desirable otherwise for their sound learning and judgment. Milton assures us with strong asseveration that to the pure all things are pure; but we are uneasy. When pupils in the higher forms read the Areopagitica they are safeguarded in some measure because they perceive that to see impurity is to be impure. The younger children are helped by the knowledge we offer them in Ourselves, and chastely taught children learn to watch over their thoughts 'because of the angels.' So far as we can get them we use expurgated editions; in other cases the book is read aloud by the teacher with necessary omissions. We are careful not to associate the processes of nature whether in the plant or animal world with possible thoughts of impurity in the mind of a child. One point I should like to touch upon in this connection. The excessive countenance sometimes afforded to games by the Heads of schools is not altogether for the sake of distinction in the games. "I keep under my body," says St. Paul, and games which exhaust the physical powers have as their unspoken raison d'êatre the desire to keep boys and girls decent. No doubt they do so to some extent though painful occurrences come to light in even the best schools. Now a fact not generally recognised is that offences of the kind which most distress parents and teachers are bred in the mind and in an empty mind at that. That is why parents, who endeavour to save their sons from the corruption of the Public School by having them taught at home, are apt to miss their mark. The abundant leisure afforded by home teaching offers that empty chamber swept and garnished which invites sins that can be committed in thought and in solitude. Our schools err, too, in not giving anything like enough work of the kind that from its absorbing interest compels reflection and tends to secure a mind continually and wholesomely occupied. Supply a boy with abundant mental pabulum, not in the way of desultory reading, (that is a sort of idleness which leads to mischief), but in the way of matter to be definitely known, give him much and sound food for his imagination, speculation, aspiration, and you have a wholesome-minded youth to whom work is a joy and games not a strain but a healthy relaxation and pleasure. I make no apology for what may appear like a divergence from the subject of citizenship, because all boys and girls should know that they owe a sound mind and a sound body as their personal contribution alike to their city and their State.

Ourselves, our Souls and Bodies (by the Writer, i.e., Charlotte Mason) is much used in the P.U.S., as I know of no other attempt to present such a ground plan of human nature as should enable the young student to know where he is in his efforts to 'be good' as the children say. The point of view taken in this volume is, that all beautiful and noble possibilities are present in every one; but that each person is subject to assaults and hindrances in various ways of which he should be aware in order that he may watch and pray. Hortatory teaching is apt to bore both young people and their elders; but an ordered presentation of the possibilities and powers that lie in human nature and of the risks that attend these, can hardly fail to have an enlightening and stimulating effect.

But the objects we have in view in teaching 'Everyday Morals' and 'Citizenship' cannot be better illustrated than by a few papers written by children of various ages, dealing with self management, and exemplifying the virtues that help and serve city and country. "Oh dear," said a little girl coming out of a bath, "I'm just like Julius Caesar, I don't care to do a thing at all if I'm not best at it." So, in unlikely ways and from unlikely sources, do children gather that little code of principles which shall guide their lives.

The Knowledge of Man; Composition

Composition in Form I (A and B) is almost entirely oral and is so much associated with Bible history, English history, geography, natural history, that it hardly calls for a special place on the programme, where however it does appear as 'Tales.' In few things do certain teachers labour in vain more than in the careful and methodical way in which they teach composition to young children. The drill that these undergo in forming sentences is unnecessary and stultifying, as much so perhaps as such drill would be in the acts of mastication and deglutination. Teachers err out of their exceeding goodwill and generous zeal. They feel that they cannot do too much for children and attempt to do for them those things which they are richly endowed to do for themselves. Among these is the art of composition, that art of 'telling' which culminates in a Scott or a Homer and begins with the toddling persons of two and three who talk a great deal to each other and are surely engaged in 'telling' though no grown-up, not even a mother, can understand. But children of six can tell to amazing purpose. The grown-up who writes the tale to their 'telling' will cover many pages before getting to the end of "Hans and Gretel" or "The Little Match Girl" or a Bible story. The facts are sure to be accurate and the expression surprisingly vigorous, striking and unhesitating. Probably few grown-ups could 'tell' one of Aesop's Fables with the terse directness which children reproduce. Neither are the children's narrations incoherent; they go on with their book, week by week, whatever comes at a given time,—whether it be Mrs. Gatty's Parables From Nature, Andersen or Grimm or The Pilgrim's Progress, from the point where they left off,—and there never is a time when their knowledge is scrappy. They answer such questions as'—"Tell about the meeting of Ulysses and Telemachus," or, "about Jason and Hera." "Tell how Christian and Hopeful met with Giant Despair," or, "about the Shining Ones."

Children are in Form IA from 7 to 9 and their reading is wider and their composition more copious. They will 'tell' in their examinations about the Feeding of the Four Thousand, about the Building of the Tabernacle, How Doubting Castle was demolished, about the burning of Old St. Paul's, How we know that the world is round and a great deal besides; for all their work lends itself to oral composition and the power of such composition is innate in children and is not the result of instruction. Two or three points are important. Children in IB require a quantity of matter to be read to them, graduated, not according to their powers which are always present, but they require a little time to employ their power of fixed attention and that other power which they possess of fluent narration. So probably young children should be allowed to narrate paragraph by paragraph, while children of seven or eight will 'tell' chapter by chapter. Corrections must not be made during the act of narration, nor must any interruption be allowed.

Children must not be teased or instructed about the use of stops or capital letters. These things too come by nature to the child who reads, and the teacher's instructions are apt to issue in the use of a pepper box for commas. We do not say that children should never read well-intentioned second-rate books, but certainly they should not read these in school hours by way of lessons. From their earliest days they should get the habit of reading literature which they should take hold of for themselves, much or little, in their own way. As the object of every writer is to explain himself in his own book the child and the author must be trusted together, without the intervention of the middle-man. What his author does not tell him he must go without knowing for the present. No explanation will really help him, and explanations of words and phrases spoil the text and should not be attempted unless children ask, What does so and so mean? when other children in the class will probably tell.

Form II (A and B), (ages 9 to 12). Children in this Form have a wider range of reading, a more fertile field of thought, and more delightful subjects for composition. They write their little essays themselves, and as for the accuracy of their knowledge and justice of their expression, why, 'still the wonder grows.' They will describe their favourite scene from The Tempest or Woodstock. They write or 'tell' stories from work set in Plutarch or Shakespeare or tell of the events of the day. They narrate from English, French and General History, from the Old and the New Testament, from Stories from the History of Rome, from Bulfinch's Age of Fable, from, for example, Goldsmith's or Wordsworth's poems, from The Heroes Of Asgard: in fact, Composition is not an adjunct but an integral part of their education in every subject. The exercise affords very great pleasure to children, perhaps we all like to tell what we know, and in proportion as their composition is entirely artless, it is in the same degree artistic and any child is apt to produce a style to be envied for its vigour and grace. But let me again say there must be no attempt to teach composition. Our failure as teachers is that we place too little dependence on the intellectual power of our scholars, and as they are modest little souls what the teacher kindly volunteers to do for them, they feel that they cannot do for themselves. But give them a fair field and no favour and they will describe their favourite scene from the play they have read, and much besides.

Forms III and IV. In these Forms as in I and II what called 'composition' is an inevitable consequence of a free yet exact use of books and requires no special attention until the pupil is old enough to take of his own accord a critical interest in the use of words. The measured cadences of verse are as pleasing to children as to their elders. Many children write verse as readily as prose, and the conciseness and power of bringing their subject matter to a point which this form of composition requires affords valuable mental training. One thing must be borne in mind. Exercises in scansion are as necessary in English as in Latin verse. Rhythm and accent on the other hand take care of themselves in proportion as a child is accustomed to read poetry. In III and IV as in the earlier Forms, the matter of their reading during the term, topics of the day, and the passing of the Seasons, afford innumerable subjects for short essays or short sets of verses of a more abstract nature in IV than in III: the point to be considered is that the subject be one on which, to quote again Jane Austen's expression, the imagination of the children has been 'warmed.' They should be asked to write upon subjects which have interested them keenly. Then when the terminal examination comes they will respond to such a question as,—"Write twelve lines (which must scan) on 'Sir Henry Lee,' or 'Cordelia,' or Pericles, or Livingstone," or, to take a question from the early days of the War, "Discuss Lord Derby's Scheme. How is it working?"; or, (IV) an essay on "The new army in the making, shewing what some of the difficulties have been and what has been achieved."

Forms V and VI. In these Forms some definite teaching in the art of composition is advisable, but not too much, lest the young scholars be saddled with a stilted style which may encumber them for life. Perhaps the method of a University tutor is the best that can be adopted; that is, a point or two might be taken up in a given composition and suggestions or corrections made with little talk. Having been brought up so far upon stylists the pupils are almost certain to have formed a good style; because they have been thrown into the society of many great minds, they will not make a servile copy of any one but will shape an individual style out of the wealth of material they possess; and because they have matter in abundance and of the best they will not write mere verbiage. Here is an example of a programme set for a term's work in these two Forms,—"A good précis; Letters to The Times on topics of the day; subjects taken from the term's work in history and literature; or notes on a picture study; dialogues between characters occurring in your literature and history studies; ballads on current events; (VI) essays on events and questions of the day; a patriotic play in verse or prose." Here are questions set for another term,—"Write a paean, rhymed or in blank verse, on the Prince of Wales's tour in the Dominions." "An essay, dated 1930, on the imagined work of the League of Nations." Form V, "Write a woeful ballad touching the condition of Ireland, or, a poem on the King's garden party to the V.C.'s." "An essay on the present condition of England, or, on President Wilson."

The response of the young students to such a scheme of study is very delightful. What they write has literary and sometimes poetic value, and the fact that they can write well is the least of the gains acquired. They can read, appreciating every turn of their author's thought; and they can bring cultivated minds to bear on the problems of the hour and the guiding of the State; that is to say, their education bears at every point on the issues and interests of every day life, and they shew good progress in the art of becoming the magnanimous citizens of the future. Here are a few examples of the compositions of the several Forms.

(F. B. IIA. Council School.)

ARMISTICE DAY

Soldiers dying, soldiers dead,
Bullets whizzing overhead.
Tommies standing cheerily by.
Waiting for their time to die;
Soon the lull of firing comes,
And naught is heard but the roll of drums.
And now the last shell crashes 'down,
A soldier reels in pain
Too late the glad news comes to him.
He never moves again,
He is the Unknown Warrior,
A man without a name.
Two years have passed and home he comes,
To the hearts that loved him well,
Who is the Unknown Warrior?
No lips the tale can tell,
His tomb is in the Abbey,
Where the souls of Heroes dwell.
A nations sorrow and a nations tears,
Have gone with the nameless man,
Who knows, who can tell, the Warriors name,
We think that no man can,
So let our sorrow turn to joy
On the grave of the Unknown man.

(A. B. 13 3/4. III)

Write some lines, in blank verse, that must scan on one of the following: (a), Scylla and Charybdis; (b), The White Lady of Avenel; (c), The Prince of Wales in India.

THE WHITE LADY OF AVENEL

The sun had set and night was drawing on,
The hills stood black against the twilight sky.
A faint young crescent moon shone dimly forth
Casting a pale and ghostly radiance
Upon the group of pine trees on the hill,
And silvering the rivers eddying swirl.
Now all was silent, not a sound disturbed
The summer night, and not a breath of wind
Stirred in the pines. All nature slept in peace.
But what was that, standing up in the shade?
A woman, straight, and slim, all clad in white,
Upon her long soft hair a misty crown,
And ever and anon she deeply sighed,
Leaning against the rugged mountain rock,
Like to a moon beam, or a wisp of smoke.
And on her shimmering, moonlit, robe she wore
A golden girdle, in whose links was woven
The fortunes of the house of Avenel.
A cloud past o'er the moon, and the slim ghost
Faded and disappeared into the air.

A breeze sprang up among the pine trees tail;
And then the river murmuring on its way
Whispered a sad lament unto the night.
(K.L. 131/2. III.)
Write in Ballad Metre some lines on "Armistice Day" or "Echo."
ARMISTICE DAY, OR THIS UNKNOWN WARRIOR
Within the ancient Abbey's sacred pyle,
Which proudly guards the noblest of our dead.
Where kings and statesmen lie in every aisle,
And honoured poets, soldiers, priests are laid;
Behold a stranger comes. From whence is he?
Is he of noble birth; of rank or fame?
Was he as great as any whom we see
Around, who worked to make themselves a name?
Surely he is a prince. nay, e'en a king?
For see the waiting thousands gathered here;
And hear the streets of ancient London ring
To the slow tramp of men who guard his bier!
And, surely, 'tis the King himself who comes
As chiefest mourner on this solemn day,
And these who walk behind him are his sons—
All here to mourn this man. Who is he? Say!
How long the ranks of men who follow him
To his last resting-place—the House of God.
Our bishops, soldiers, statemen all are here,
Gathered to lay him in his native sod.
You ask "Is he a prince?" I answer "No
Though none could be interred with greater state!
This man went forth to guard us from a foe,
Which threatened this our land—He did his work!
He raised the flag of Liberty on high
And challenging the powers of Wrong and Might
He gave up all he had without a sigh
And died for the good cause of God and Right.
Nor is a sense of humour wanting,—
(M.O. 13. III.)
Write in Ballad Metre some lines on "Echo."
ECHO
Jupiter once went away from his
To flirt with some nymphs in a wood
But Juno, suspecting that he was with them
Came after as fast as she could.
Now Echo, a nymph, knew that Juno was there
That the nymphs they would soon be found out,
And so she kept Juno away from the wood
For if they had gone she did doubt.
But Juno knew all; and her anger was great
And Echo this dreadful thing heard
Since you are so fond of talking, from now
You only shall have the last word!"
Now Echo went far from the dwellings of men
And spent her sad life all alone

And often she'd weep and think of the past
And over her fate make her moan.
Echo loved a Greek youth, but he could not love her.
And she watched him all day from her bower
Till she pined away, all but her voice, which lives still,
And the youth was turned into a flower.
(R. C. 15. III. Elementary, Convent School.)

Write some verses on (a) 'Dandie Dinmont,' or, (b) 'Atalanta,' or, (c) Allenby.

Atlanta was a huntress,
Who dearly loved the chase.
She out-ran the deer in fleetness,
And possessed a lovely face,
Many eager suitors sought her,
But they sought her all in vain,
For she vowed she'd never marry
And her suitors all were slain.
She had heeded well the warning,
From a witch well skilled in lore,
Who had told her if she married,
Happiness was hers no more.
Then a youth whom Venus favoured,
Came one day to run the race,
And by throwing golden apples,
He out-ran her in the chase.
In their hour of joy and triumph
Venus they forget to thank,
And the goddess sore offended,
Lowered them to the wild beast's rank.
(J. T. III.)

Phaëton was a wilful youth who always got his way.
He asked to drive his father's charge upon a certain day.
But Phoebus knowing well what danger lurketh in the sky;
Implored of him to wish again and not that task to try,
But Phaëton determined was to best this dangerous way,
And leaped into the chariot to spite his father's sway.
The horses started forward at a dashing headlong pace,
Phaëton tried to hold them back and modify the race.
With dreadful swiftness on he flew, losing his proper road,
The earth and sky began to smoke in an alarming mode.
At length when all had burst in flames, Jupiter cried aloud,
Phaëton who had lost his head was killed beneath a cloud.
(H.E.M. 15 8/12. IV.)

Write thirty lines of blank verse on (a), "A Spring Morning" (following "A Winter Morning Walk"), or, (b), Pegasus, or, (c), Allenby.

A SPRING MORNING.

'Tis Spring; and now the birds with merry song
Sing with full-throated voice to the blue sky
On which small clouds float, soft as a dove's wing.
Against the blue the pale-green leaflet gleams.
The darker green of elder, further down,
Sets off the brilliance of the hawthorn-hedge.
Close to the ground, the purple violet peeps

From out its nest of overhanging leaves.
On yonder bank the daffodils toss their heads
Under the shady lichen trees so tall.
Close by a chestnut, bursting into leaf,
Drops down it's sticky calyx on the ground;
An early bumble-bee dives headlong in
To a half-opened flower of early pear.
O'erhead, in the tail beech trees, busy rooks,
With great caw-caws and many angry squawks
Build their great clumsy nests with bits of twig
And little sticks just laid upon a bough.
And by the long, straight, path tall fir trees wave
Their graceful heads in the soft whisp'ring breeze
And pressed against one ruddy trunk, an owl
In vain tries to avoid the light of day,
But blinks his wise old eyes, and shakes himself,
And nestles close amid the sheltering leaves.
Now on the rhubarb-bed we see, glad sight,
Large red buttons, which promise fruit quite soon
And further down the lettuce shoots up pale
Next to a row of parsley, getting old.
But see the peas, their curly tendrils green
Clinging to their stout pea-sticks for support.
(B. B. 15. IV.)

A SPRING MORNING

Soft on the brown woods
A pale light gleams,
And slowly spreading seems
To change the brown wood to a land of dreams,
Where beneath the trees
The great god Pan,
Doth pipe, half goat, half man,
To satyrs dancing in the dawning wan.
And then comes Phoebus,
The visions fade
And down the dewy glade
The rabbits scuttle o'er the rings they made.
In the fields near-by
The cattle rise
And where the river lies
A white mist rises to the welcoming skies.
Where the downs arise
And blue sky crowns
Their heads, fast o'er the mounds
The mist is driv'n to where the ocean sounds.
White wings against blue sky,
Gulls from the cliffs rise,
Watching, with eyes
That see from shore to where the sky line lies,
Where blue sea fades in bluer skies
Soft, doth the tide creep
O'er the golden sands

With sea-weed strands
Which, mayhap, knew the dawn of other lands.
(L B. IV.)
Write thirty lines of blank verse on "Pegasus."
The sky was blue and flecked with tiny clouds
Like sheep they ran before the driving wind
The sun was setting like a big red rose
The clouds that flew by him like rose-buds were
And as I gaz'd I saw a little cloud
White as the flower that rises in the spring
Come nearer, nearer, nearer as I looked
And as it came it took a diff'rent shape
It seemed to turn into a fairy steed.
White as the foam that rides the roaring waves
Still it flew on until it reached the earth
And galloping full lightly came to me
And then I saw it was a wondrous thing
It leapt about the grass and gently neighed
I heard its voice sound like a crystal flute
"Oh come" he said "with me ascend the sky
Above the trees, above the hills we'll soar
Until we reach the home of all the gods
There will we stay and feast awhile with them
And dance with Juno and her maidens fair
And hear dear Orpheus and the pipes of Pan
And wander, wander, wander up above"
"Oh fairy steed, oh angel steed" I said
Horse fit for Jupiter himself to ride
What is thy name I pray thee tell me this"
Then came the magic voice of him again
"If thou wilt know my name then come with me."
Yet tell me first I hesitating said
He told me and when I had heard the name
I leapt upon his back and flew with him.
(A. B. 16. V.)
Some verses, in the metre of Pope's "Essay on Man," on the meeting of the League of Nations.
From each proud kingdom and each petty state
The statesmen meet together to debate
Upon the happy time when wars shall cease
And joy shall reign, and universal peace.
No more shall day with radiance cruelly bright
Glare down upon the carnage of the fight.
No more shall night's dark cloak be rent aside
By flashing shells and searchlight's stealthy glide
No more shall weary watchers wait at home
With straining eyes for those that cannot come
The nations shall forget their strife and greed
The strong shall help the weak in time of need
May they succeed in every peaceful plan
If war can cease as long as man is man.
(B. H. 16 11/12. V.)
Gather up in blank verse the impressions you have received from your reading of Tennyson's poems.

Take up a volume of the poet's works,
Read on, lay it aside, and take thy pen,
Endeavour in a few, poor, worthless lines
To give expression of thy sentiments. . . .
Surely this man loved all the joys of life,
Saw beauty in the smallest and the least,
Put plainer things that hitherto were dim,
And lit a candle in the darkest room.
His thoughts, now sad, now gay, may surely be
The solace sweet for many a weary hour,
His words, drunk deeply, seem to live and burn
Clear, radiant, gleaming from the printed page,
Nature to him was dear and so has made
Her wiles for other men a treasure vast.
Old Books, his master mind could comprehend
Are shown to us as pictures to a child,
Read on and when the volume's put away,
Muse on the learnings thou hast found therein;
The time thus spent thou never will repent,
For love of good things all should seek and find.

(E. P. H. 16 11/12. V.)

A LULLABY SONG

The little waves are sighing on the shore,
And the little breezes sobbing in the trees;
But the little stars are shining,
In the sky's blue velvet lining,
And Lady Sleep is tapping at the door.
The little gulls are flying home to shore,
And the little lights are flashing from the ships,
But close your eyes, my sweet,
And be ready then to greet
Dear Lady Sleep who's tapping at the door.
The wind is rising all around the shore,
And the fishing boats speed home before the gale;
But hark not to the rain
That is lashing on the pane,
For Lady Sleep has entered by the door.
The storm has sunk the ships and swept the shore,
But there's weeping in the town and on the quay,
But, sweet, you're dreaming fast
Even though the dawn be past,
And Lady Sleep has gone, and closed the door.

(M. H. 17. VI.)

Write a letter in the manner of Gray on any Modern Topic.

Mr. Gray to Mr. ____ At Torquay.

M dear—

"Savez vous que je vous hais, que je vous detestevolci des termes un peu forts," still, I think that they are justified, imagine leaving a friend for two months in this place without once taking up the pen upon his behalf. If this neglect be due only to your low spirits, I will for once pardon you but only upon condition that you should come down here to visit me and at the same time strengthen your constitution. I can promise you but little diversion, but I think that the scenery will repay the journey not to speak of myself. You will also be able to study many "venerable vegetables" which are not usually to be found in England. But, I waste your time and my paper with these "betises" and I know well upon what subject your mind is at present dwelling which of us indeed is not thinking of Ireland. I would give much to hear your views upon the subject. For my part it seems to me that there can be but one true view, and it surprises me mightily to hear so much discussion upon the subject. Are we not truly a peculiar nation who pass bills of Home Rule etc with much discussion and debate, when neither of the two parties concerned will accept the conditions that we offer them? The one considering they give too little freedom, and the other too much. Accursed be the man who invented a bill which was and will be the cause of so much trouble "in saecula saeculorum." Surely we need not have any doubt as to what line of action we should adopt, surely it has not been the habit of England to let her subjects revolt without an attempt to quell them, surely the government will not stand by and see its servants murdered, and the one loyal province oppressed. But alas many things are possible with such a government. Here it is said by people who have been driven from that country by incendiaries that the Government will let things take their course till everything is in such a condition that the Premier will rise in the house and say, "You see how things stand—it is no use trying to control Ireland, let us leave it to the Seinn Feiners, and live happily ever afterwards, free from such unprofitable cares,"

Such is the talk, but I believe it not. We have as a nation always muddled things but we have muddled through triumphant in the end. It is so obvious that our interests and those of Ireland co-incide, that even to contemplate separation is to me incredible, Thus I remain your harassed friend, etc,

(N. S. 15 10/12. VI.)

Gather up in blank verse the impressions you have received from your reading of Tennyson's poem.

ON READING TENNYSON'S POEMS.

Oh! Prophet of an era yet to come,
When men shall sing where men were wont to speak
In words which even Englishmen knew not
And when I read thy songs, at once I felt
The breath of Nature that was lurking there,
And then I knew that all thy life thou dwelt
Amid the changing scenes of Nature's play,
And knew the very language of the birds,
And drank the essence of the honeysuckle.
And when thou wast but young, I knew thy thoughts,
Thy Doubts and struggles, for thou gave them me;
And yet, had I been thee, my thoughts would still
Have rested deep within my heart; but still
T'would be relief to pour out all my woes
In the sweet flow of sympathetic verse.
Thy epithets produce a vivid scene
Of knights in armour or of maiden fair,
And yet, methinks, the fairness of her face
Doth sometimes cover many a fault below.
But to thy genius and thy work for ever
Be owed a debt of thankfulness that we
No longer tread the paths of level Pope
Or read those words that are not English-born.

(K. B. 16, V.)

THE CLOUDS

Among the spirits of the nearer air
There are three children of the sun and sea—
The Genii of the clouds; it is their care
To give the ocean's bounty to the earth:
Oft they retain it in a time of dearth,
But they give all, however much it be.
The youngest of the three is very fair;

She is a maiden beautiful and sweet,
Of ever varying mood, changeful as air.
Now, plunged in merriment, she takes delight
In all she sees, now tears obscure her sight;
A breeze-swept lake shows not a change more fleet.
The fleecy clouds of April own her sway—
They, golden, lie against the golden sun,
Or sport across the blue when she is gay;
But when, anon, her girlish passions rise,
She marshalls them across the sunny skies
To flood the earth, then stops ere half begun.
Her elder brother is of different mien.
The clouds he governs are of different mould;
When the earth pants for moisture he is seen
To spread his clouds across the filmy blue.
When his rain falls, it steady is and true;
Persistent, gentle, ceaseless, yet not cold.
From the grey bowl with which he caps the earth,
It sweetly falls with earth-renewing force.
Not April's rapid change from grief to mirth
Excites its fall, but calm, determined thought
Of middle age, of deeds from judgment wrought;
He recks not blame, but still pursues his course,
Aged, yet of awesome beauty is the third,
Of flashing eye and sullen, scornful brow—
With an imperious hand she guides her herd
Of wild, tempestuous mood; quick roused to ire
Is she, slow to forgive, of vengeance dire;
Before her awful glance the tree-tops bow.
And when enraged, she stretches forth a hand—
A long, thin hand to North, South, East and West,
And draws from thence clouds num'rous as the sand;
They crowd on the horizon, and blot out
The sun's fair light; then, like a giant's shout,
The thunder booms at her dread spear's behest.
(A.P. V.)

Sketch a scene between a "Mr. Woodhouse" of to-day and a neighbour of his.

SCENE: Mr. Woodhouse's private study.

Persons present:—Owner of study, and Miss Syms, a very modern young lady.

Mr. Woodhouse—"Oh, good afternoon Miss Syms, I am charmed to see you. Dear, dear, how dark it is. One might almost think it were evening, if the clock opposite did not directly oppose the fact."

Miss S.—"Oh, I don't know, it's not so bad out. I'm awfully sorry to blow in like this, but I came to enquire after Miss Woodhouse's cold. Is she better?

Mr. W.—"How very thoughtful of you! No, I am afraid dear Emma is very indisposed. It is so trying having an invalid in the house, it makes me quite miserable when I think of my poor daughter having to stay all alone, in bed. But really, that is almost the best place in this dreadful weather. Do you really mean to say that you have been taking a walk."

Miss S.—"Yes, why on earth shouldn't I? It's about the only way to get really warm."

Mr. W." If the liberty might be allowed me, (dryly) I should say, that it was the one way in which to get a feverish cold, besides making oneself thoroughly miserable; and the ground is so damp under foot!

Miss S.—"Oh. it hasn't been raining much lately. I only got caught in a little shower, (visible start from Mr. W.). (coyly,) Excuse me, but is that a box of cigarettes up there on the mantlepiece?"

Mr. W.—"Cigarettes? Oh, no! I couldn't think of keeping them near the house. I never smoke. It irritates my throat, which is naturally weak."

Miss S.—"But don't your visitors ever take the liberty of enjoying something of the sort? Besides, what about Miss Woodhouse?"

Mr. W.—(horrified,)"Dear Emma smoke a cigarette!! Why, I never heard of such a thing. What would she say if I told her. Dear Emma smoke, no, no, certainly not".

Miss S.—(laughing,) "Oh, I am sure I'm very sorry. I didn't mean to offend. How do you think the old Johnnies in Ireland are behaving themselves?"

Mr. W.—(coldly.) "I beg your pardon."

Miss S.—(sweetly,) "I said, how do you think matters are looking, in Ireland."

Mr. W.—"I am sorry, I think I could not have heard aright before.—Matters in Ireland, yes. oh I think the Irish rebels are positively awful. To think of breaking into houses, and turning the poor inhabitants out into the cold streets, (where they probably nearly die of cold), it is too dreadful!"

Miss S.—"Oh, I s'pose they are rather brutes sometimes. But in a way I almost sympathise with them. I wouldn't like to have to knuckle under to the English (catching sight of Mr. W.'s expression of horror and pained surprise.) I really think I'd better get a move on. Please don't look at me like that! I really don't mean half I say. Cheerio!"

Mr. W.—"Good afternoon Miss Syms, it was so kind of you to come. (aside) Oh, how unfeeling of dear Emma to have a cold, if it means visitors like this every hour. (aloud,) Good afternoon, can you find your way out. I really shall catch cold if I move out of this room

(E.G. 17. V.)

Write some lines on "Spring" in the metre of "Allegro."

SPRING

Begone I for a short space
Ye whistling winds, and fogs, and snowy clouds,
And frosts that with fair lace
Each window-pane in dainty pattern shrouds,
Offsprings of Winter, ye!
Begone! find out some icy arctic land.
Upon that cheerless strand
'Mongst piercing ice, and chilling glaciers dwell
Such regions suit ye well,
Go, cold Winter, well are we rid of thee!
Come Spring, thou fairest season come!
With the bee's enchanting hum,
And the dainty blossoms swinging
On the tree, while birds are singing.
See how they clothe the branches gray
In dress of freshest pink, all day,
Then when the dewy evening falls
They close their flowers till Morning calls.
Sweet Morn! Spring leads thee by the hand
And bids thee shine o'er all the land;
Thou send'st forth beams of purest gold,
To bid the daffodils unfold,
While Spring bends down with her fresh lips
To kiss the daisie's petal tips.
And as she walks o'er the green sward
A cheerful mavis, perfect bard
Breaks into song; his thrilling notes
Are echoed from a hundred throats
Of eager birds, who love to sing

To their sweet mistress, fairest Spring.
Then as she sits on mossy throne
A scarlet lady-bird, alone,
Bids her good welcome; and above
Is heard the cooing of the dove.
Two butterflies in russet clad
Fly round her head with flutt'rings glad;
While at her side a giddy fly
Buzzes his joy that she is nigh,
Oh! Spring my heart's desire shall be
That thou wilt ever dwell with me!

The Knowledge of Man; Languages

English is rather a logical study dealing with sentences and the positions that words occupy in them than with words and what they are in their own right. Therefore it is better that a child should begin with a sentence and not with the parts of speech, that is, he should learn a little of what is called analysis before he learns to parse. It requires some effort of abstraction for a child to perceive that when we speak, we speak about something and say something about it; and he has learned nearly all the grammar that is necessary when he knows that when we speak we use sentences and that a sentence makes sense; that we can put words together so as to make utter nonsense, as,—"Tom immediately candlestick uproarious nevertheless"—a string of words making perfect nonsense and therefore not a sentence. If we use words in such a way as to make sense we get a sentence; "John goes to school" is a sentence. Every sentence has two parts, (1), the thing we speak of, and (2), what we say about it. We speak of John, we say about him that he goes to school. At this stage the children require many exercises in finding out the first and second parts of simple sentences. When they are quite familiar with the fact that the first part of a sentence is what we speak about, they may get a name for it, subject, which will be made simpler to them if they know the word subject means that which we talk about. For instance, we may say, the subject of conversation was parsley, which is another way of saying the thing we were speaking about was parsley. To sum up such a lesson, the class should learn,—Words put together so as to make sense form a sentence. A sentence has two parts, that which we speak of and what we say about it. That which we speak of is the subject.

Children will probably be slow to receive this first lesson in abstract knowledge, and we must remember that knowledge in this sort is difficult and uncongenial. Their minds deal with the concrete and they have the singular faculty of being able to make concrete images out of the merest gossamer of a fairy tale. A seven year old child sings,—

I cannot see fairies,
I dream them.
There is no fairy that can hide from me;
I keep on dreaming till I find him.
There you are, Primrose! I see you, Blackwing!"

But a child cannot dream parts of speech, and any grown-up twaddle attempting to personify such abstractions offends a small person who with all his love of play and nonsense has a serious mind. Most children can be got to take in the notion of a sentence as, words making sense, especially if they are allowed a few excursions into non-sense, the gibberish of strings of words which do not make sense. Again, by dint of many interesting exercises in which they never lose sight of the subject, they get hold of that idea also.

One more initial idea is necessary if children are not to wander blindfold through the mazes of grammar 'as she is' not 'spoke,' but writ in books. They must be familiar with verbs and perhaps the simplest way to approach this idea is to cause them to make sentences with two words, the thing they speak of and what they say about it,—Mary sings, Auntie knits, Henry runs. In each of these examples, the child will see the thing we speak of and what we say about it.

But these are matters familiar to all teachers and we have nothing new in the teaching of grammar to suggest; but we probably gain in the fact that our scholars pay full attention to grammar, as to all other lessons. We look forward hopefully to the result of efforts so to unify grammar that it will no longer perplex the student, as English, Latin, French grammar, each with its own nomenclature.

Children in Form IIB have easy French Lessons with pictures which they describe, but in IIA while still engaged on the Primary French Course children begin to use the method which is as full of promise in the teaching of languages as in English, that is, they are expected to narrate the sentence or paragraph which has been read to them. Young children find little difficulty in using French vocables, but at this stage the teacher should with the children's help translate the little passage which is to be narrated, them re-read it in French and require the children to narrate it. This they do after a time surprisingly well, and the act of narrating gives them some command of French phrases as far as they go, much more so than if they learnt the little passage off by heart. They learn French songs in both divisions and act French Fables (by Violet Partington) in Form IIA. This method of closely attentive reading of the text followed by narration is continued in each of the Forms. Thus Form II is required to "Describe in French, picture 20." "Narrate the story Esope et le Voyageur." Part of the term's work in Form III is to "Read and narrate Nouveaux Contes Français, by Marc Ceppi." Form IV is required amongst other things to "Read and narrate Moliere's Les Femmes Savantes." Forms V and VI are required to "Write a résume' of Le Misanthrope or L'Avare," "Translate into French, Modern Verse, page 50, 'Leisure.'"

We have not space to follow in detail the work of the P.U.S. in French, which of course includes the usual attention to French Grammar but it may interest the reader to see the sort of thing that students of the House of Education are able to accomplish in the way of narration. The French mistress gives, let us suppose, a lecture in history or literature lasting, say, for half an hour. At the end the students will narrate the substance of the lecture with few omissions and few errors. Here is an example of the sort of thing Mr. Household heard, on the occasion of a short visit to the House of Education, Ambleside,—

"A French lesson was given to the second-year students by the French mistress, a native of Tournal, who came to Ambleside in 1915. She had been teaching in England for some years but had not previously come into contact with Miss Mason's methods. Those methods were exactly followed during the lesson. There was the book of recognised literary merit, the single reading, and the immediate narration—of course in French. The book was Alphonse Daudet's Lettres de Mon Moulin, and the story read was 'La Chèvre de M. Seguin.' Before the reading began, a few—a very few—words of explanation were given—of course, in French. Then nine pages of the story were read straight through by the mistress, without pause or interruption of any kind, at the same pace that one would read an English story. The students followed by ear only: they had no books. As soon as the reading ended, on the instant, without hesitation of any kind, narration began in French, different members of the class taking up the story in turn till it was finished. All were good; some astonishingly good. To all French was a tongue in which they could think and speak with considerable facility. Yet the time given to French is two hours and three quarters a week only. Such results compel attention. It may be added that last year the writer heard a history lecture on the reign of Louis XI given in French by the same mistress to the then senior students, and the content of the lecture was narrated in a similar manner, with the same astonishing success."

This hitherto unused power of concentrated attention in the study of languages whether ancient or modern appears to hold promise of making us at last a nation of linguists. We have attained very good results in Italian and German by this same method, both in the House of Education and the Practising School belonging to it, and we are in a fair way to produce noticeable results in Latin. The classical mistress writes,—

"Latin is taught at the House of Education by means of narration after each section has been thoroughly studied in grammer, syntax and style. The literature studied increases in difficulty as the pupil advances in grammar, etc. Nothing but good Latin is ever narrated, so the pupil acquires style as well as structure. The substance of the passage is usually reproduced with the phraseology and style of the original and both students and children learn what is really Latin and realise that it is a language and not a mere grammar."

Here we get Grammar, that is, construction, learned as we learn it in English, at the lips of those who, know, and the extraordinary readiness in acquiring new words shewn by the scholars promises English folk the copious vocabulary in one or another foreign language, the lack of which is a national distress.

The Knowledge of Man; Art

There are few subjects regarded with more respect and less confidence in our schools than this of 'Art.' Of course, we say, children should have their artistic powers cultivated, especially those who have such powers, but how is the question. The neat solution offered by South Kensington in the sixties,—freehand drawing, perspective, drawing from the round, has long been rejected; but nothing definite has taken its place and we still see models of cones, cubes and so on, disposed so that the eye may take them in freely and that the hand may perhaps produce what the eye has seen. But we begin now to understand that art is not to be approached by such a macadamised road. It is of the spirit, and in ways of the spirit must we make our attempt. We recognise that the power of appreciating art and of producing to some extent an interpretation of what one sees is as universal as intelligence, imagination, nay, speech, the power of producing words. But there must be knowledge and, in the first place, not the technical knowledge of how to produce, but some reverent knowledge of what has been produced; that is, children should learn pictures, line by line, group by group, by reading, not books, but pictures themselves. A friendly picture-dealer supplies us with half a dozen beautiful little reproductions of the work of some single artist, term by term. After a short story of the artist's life and a few sympathetic words about his trees or his skies, his river-paths or his figures, the little pictures are studied one at a time; that is, children learn, not merely to see a picture but to look at it, taking in every detail. Then the picture is turned over and the children tell what they have seen,—a dog driving a flock of sheep along a road but nobody with the dog. Ah, there is a boy lying down by the stream drinking. It is morning as you can see by the light so the sheep are being driven to pasture, and so on; nothing is left out, the discarded plough, the crooked birch, the clouds beautiful in form and threatening rain, there is enough for half an hour's talk and memory in this little reproduction of a great picture and the children will know it wherever they see it, whether a signed proof, a copy in oils, or the original itself in one of our galleries. We hear of a small boy with his parents in the National Gallery; the boy, who had wandered off on his own account, came running back with the news,—"Oh, Mummy, there's one of our Constables on that wall." In this way children become acquainted with a hundred, or hundreds, of great artists during their school-life and it is an intimacy which never forsakes them. A group of children are going up to London for a treat. "Where would you like to go?" "Oh, Mummy, to the National Gallery to see the Rembrandts." Young people go to tea in a room strange to them and are delighted to recognise two or three reproductions of De Hooch's pictures. In the course of school-life children get an Open Sesame to many art galleries, and to many a cultivated home; and life itself is illustrated for them at many points. For it is true as Browning told us,—

For, don't you mark, we're made so that we love
First when we see them painted, things we have passed
Perhaps a hundred times nor cared to see."

Here is an example of how beautiful and familiar things give quite new delight when they are pictured. A lady writes,

"I was invited to a small village to talk about the P.U. School. Twelve really interested women came in spite of heavy rain. I suggested introducing them to some of the friends their children had made and we had a delightful picture talk with Jean B. Corot, delightful to me because of the way one woman especially narrated. She did it as if she had been set free for the first time for months. It was the 'Evening' picture with a canal on the right and that splendid mass of quiet trees in the centre. The others gave bits of the picture but she gave the whole thing. It was a green pasture to her."

The noteworthy thing is that these women were familiar with all such details as Corot offers in their own beautiful neighbourhood, but Browning is right; we learn to see things when we see them painted.

It will be noticed that the work done on these pictures is done by the children themselves. There is no talk about schools of painting, little about style; consideration of these matters comes in later life, but the first and most important thing is to know the pictures themselves. As in a worthy book we leave the author to tell his own tale, so do we trust a picture to tell its tale through the medium the artist gave it. In the region of art as else-where we shut out the middleman.

Forms V and VI are asked to,—"Describe, with study in sepia, Corot's 'Evening.'" Beyond this of a rough study from memory of a given picture or of any section of it, these picture studies do not afford much material for actual drawing; they are never copied lest an attempt to copy should lessen a child's reverence for great work. We are shy in speaking of what we do in actual drawing since Herr Cizek came among us and shewed what great things children could do with scarcely any obvious teaching and but little suggestion. But probably such work is only to be done under the inspiration of an artist of unusual powers and I am writing for teachers who depend upon their children rather than upon themselves. They illustrate favourite scenes and passages in the books read during the term and the spirit with which the illustrations are drawn and the fitting details introduced make the teacher aware of how much more the children have seen in the passage than he has himself. Their courage in grappling with points of technique is very instructive. They tackle a crowd with wonderful ingenuity, a crowd listening to Mark Antony's oration, cheering the Prince of Wales in India, in fact wherever a crowd is wanted it is suggested pretty much as an artist would give it by a show of heads. Like those Viennese children they use all their paper, whether for a landscape or the details in a room. They give you horses leaping brooks, dogs running after cats, sheep on the road, always with a sense of motion. It is evident that children study the figures they see with due attention and will give you a gardener sharpening his scythe, their mother sewing, a man rowing, or driving, or mowing. Their chairs stand on four legs and their figures on two feet in a surprising way, and they are always on the watch to correct their errors by what they see. They have a delightful and courageous sense of colour, and any child will convince you that he has it in him to be an artist. Their field studies give them great scope. The first buttercup in a child's nature note book is shockingly crude, the sort of thing to scandalise a teacher of brush-drawing, but by and by another buttercup will appear with the delicate poise, uplift and radiance of the growing flower.

Drawing is generally so well taught now that we need do no more than emphasize one or two special points in our work, such as the definite study of pictures and the illustrations of Nature Note Books.

We do what is possible to introduce children to Architecture; and we practise clay-modelling and the various artistic handicrafts, but there is nothing unusual in our work in these directions.

With Musical Appreciation the case is different; and we cannot do better than quote from an address made by Mrs. Howard Glover at the Ambleside Conference of the Parents' Union, 1922:—

"Musical Appreciation—which is so much before the eye at the present moment—originated in the P.N.E.U. about twenty-five years ago. At that time I was playing to my little child much of the best music in which I was interested, and Miss Mason happened to hear of what I was doing. She realised that music might give great joy and interest to the life of all, and she felt that just as children in the P.U.S. were given the greatest literature and art, so they should have the greatest music as well. She asked me to write an article In the Review on the result of my observations, and to make a programme of music each term which might be played to the children. From that day to this, at the beginning of every term a programme has appeared; thus began a movement which was to spread far and wide.

"Musical Appreciation, of course, has nothing to do with playing the piano. It used to be thought that 'learning music' must mean this, and it was supposed that children who had no talent for playing were unmusical and would not like concerts. But Musical Appreciation had no more to do with playing an instrument than acting had to do with an appreciation of Shakespeare, or painting with enjoyment of pictures. I think that all children should take Musical Appreciation and not only the musical ones, for it has been proved that only three per cent of children are what is called 'tone-deaf'; and if they are taken at an early age it is astonishing how children who appear to be without ear, develop it and are able to enjoy listening to music with understanding."

Section III
The Knowledge of the Universe; Science and Geography

Huxley's axiom that science teaching in the schools should be of the nature of 'common information' is of use in defining our limitations in regard to the teaching of science. We find another limitation in the fact that children's minds are not in need of the mental gymnastics that such teaching is supposed to afford. They are entirely alert and eager to know. Books dealing with science as with history, say, should be of a literary character, and we should probably be more scientific as a people if we scrapped all the text-books which swell publishers' lists and nearly all the chalk expended so freely on our blackboards. The French mind has appreciated the fact that the approach to science as to other subjects should be more or less literary, that the principles which underlie science are at the same time so simple, so profound and so far-reaching that the due setting forth of these provokes what is almost an emotional response; these principles are therefore meet subjects for literary treatment, while the details of their application are so technical and so minute as, except by way of illustration,—to be unnecessary for school work or for general knowledge. We have not a copious scientific literature in English but we have quite enough to go on with in our schools. We find an American publication called The Sciences (whose author would seem to be an able man of literary power) of very great value in linking universal principles with common incidents of every day life in such a way that interest never palls and any child may learn on what principles an electric bell works, what sound means, how a steam engine works, and many other matters, explained here with great lucidity. Capital diagrams and descriptions make experiments easy and children arrive at their first notions of science without the verbiage that darkens counsel. Form IIA read Life and Her Children by Arabella Buckley and get a surprising knowledge of the earlier and lower forms of life. IIB take pleasure in Kingsley's Madam How and Lady Why. They are expected to do a great deal of out-of-door work in which they are assisted by The Changing Year, admirable month by month studies of what is to be seen out-of-doors. They keep records and drawings in a Nature Note Book and make special studies of their own for the particular season with drawings and notes.

The studies of Form III for one term enable children to—"Make a rough sketch of a section of ditch or hedge or sea-shore and put in the names of the plants you would expect to find." "Write notes with drawings of the special study you have made this term," "What do you understand by calyx, corolla, stamen, pistil? In what ways are flowers fertilised?" "How would you find the Pole Star? Mention six other stars and say in what constellations they occur." "How would you distinguish between Early, Decorated and Perpendicular Gothic? Give drawings." Questions like these, it will be seen, cover a good deal of field work, and the study of some half dozen carefully selected books on natural history, botany, architecture and astronomy, the principle being that children shall observe and chronicle, but shall not depend upon their own unassisted observation.

The study of natural history and botany with bird lists and plant lists continues throughout school life, while other branches of science are taken term by term.

The questions for Form IV for one term illustrate the various studies of the scholars in natural history, general science, hygiene and physiology; in fact, their studies are so various that it is difficult to give each a separate title in the programme:—

Geography.

1. Write a short sketch of Central Asia with map.
2. Compare Palestine with the Yorkshire moors. Describe the valley of the Jordan.
3. "There is but one Nelson." Illustrate by half-a-dozen instances.
4. What is said in Eothen of the Church of the Holy Sepulchre?

Natural History.

1. What do you know of (a), the manatee, (b), the whale-bone whale (sketch of skeleton), (c), porpoises and dolphins?

or, 1. Describe (a), quartz crystals, (b), felspar, (c), mica, (d), hornblende. In what rock do these occur?

2. What do you know of insectivorous plants? Name those you know.
3. What circumstances strike you in a walk in summer?

General Science

1. What do you understand by,—(a), electrical attraction, (b), repulsion, (c), conductors, (d), insulators, (e), methods of obtaining electricity?
2. Prove that "you never see matter itself," and show how sight gives us knowledge.

Physiology.

1. Describe the structure of the human ear.

Perhaps Some Wonders of Matter by Bishop Mercer is the most inspiring of the half-dozen volumes in current use in Form IV for this section of their work. The questions indicate the varied nature of the work and the answers shew that in every case the knowledge is fairly wide and thorough. All the children in the school are usually ready to answer each question on the work of the term.

Forms V and VI again cover a wide field as the following questions on a term's work sufficiently indicate,—

Geography.

VI. 1. Show how the discovery of the New World affected England in commerce and war.

2. According to what general law is life distributed on the earth?

3. Describe the Siege of Mexico by Cortes, and its surrender.

VI. & V. 4. How has the war affected (a), Luxembourg, (b), the Eastern frontier of Belgium, (c), Antwerp and the Scheldt?

V. 1. Show how the Restoration affected our American possessions.

2. Show accurately how longitude is determined.

3. Sketch the history and character of Montezuma.

Geology and Science.

VI. 1. Discuss fully (a), the cause of radioactivity, (b), gravitation.

2. What have you to say of the scenic aspects of the English Trias? Name a dozen of the fossils. Sketch half-a-dozen.

V. 1. Give as full an explanation as you can of colour.

2. Describe the composition of the igneous rocks. Where do they appear?

Biology, Botany, Etc.

VI. 1. What are the characters of the backboneless animals? Describe half-a-dozen examples.

2. Describe and account for the vegetation of (a), woodlands, (b), heath, (c), moorland, (d), meadow.

V. 1. How would you classify the industries of animals? Give examples.

2. Describe the flora of the seashore.

VI. & V. 3. Describe, with drawings, the special study you have made this term.

Astronomy.

VI. 1. What do you understand by precession? Describe the precession and mutation of the earth's axis.

V. 1. Write an essay on the planet Mercury.

If we wanted an excuse for affording children a wide syllabus introducing them at any rate to those branches of science of which every normal person should have some knowledge, we find it in the deprecatory words of Sir Richard Gregory in his Presidential Address in the Education Science Section of the British Association. He said that,

"Education might be defined as a deliberate adjustment of a growing human being to its environment, and the scope and character of the subjects of instruction should be determined by this biological principle. What was best for one race or epoch need not be best for another. The essential mission of school science was to prepare pupils for civilised citizenship by revealing to them something of the beauty and the power of the world in which they lived, as well as introducing them to the methods by which the boundaries of natural knowledge had been extended. School science, therefore, was not intended to prepare for vocations, but to equip pupils for life. It should be part of a general education, unspecialised, but in no direct connexion with possible university courses to follow. Less than three per cent of the pupils from State-aided secondary schools proceeded to universities, and yet most of the science courses in these schools were based on syllabuses of the type of university entrance examinations. The needs of the many were sacrificed to the few.

"Too much importance was attached to what could be covered by personal experiment and observation. Every science examination qualifying for the first school certificate, which now represented subjects normally studied up to about sixteen years of age, was mainly a test of practical acquaintance with facts and principles encountered in particular limited fields, but not a single one afforded recognition of a broad and ample course of instruction in science such as was a necessary complement to laboratory work.

"The numbers [of examination candidates] suggested that general scientific teaching was almost non-existent. The range of instruction in the portions of subjects taken, moreover, was almost confined to what could be taught in a laboratory. Reading or teaching for interest or to learn how physical science was daily extending the power of man received little attention because no credit for knowledge thus gained was given in examinations. There was very special need for the reminder that science was not all measurement, nor all measurement science."

It is reassuring to see methods that we have pursued for over thirty years with admirable results recommended thus authoritatively. The only sound method of teaching science is to afford a due combination of field or laboratory work, with such literary comments and amplifications as the subject affords. For example, from Ethics Of the Dust children derive a certain enthusiasm for crystals as such that their own unaided observation would be slow to afford. As a matter of fact the teaching of science in our schools has lost much of its educative value through a fatal and quite unnecessary divorce between science and the 'humanities.'

The nature note books which originated in the P.U.S. have recommended themselves pretty widely as travelling companions and life records wherein the 'finds' of every season, bird or flower, fungus or moss, is sketched, and described somewhat in the manner of Gilbert White. The nature note book is very catholic and finds room for the stars in their courses and for, say, the fossil anemone found on the beach at Whitby. Certainly these note books do a good deal to bring science within the range of common thought and experience; we are anxious not to make science a utilitarian subject.

Geography

The teaching of Geography suffers especially from the utilitarian spirit. The whole tendency of modern Geography, as taught in our schools, is to strip the unfortunate planet which has been assigned to us as our abode and environment of every trace of mystery and beauty. There is no longer anything to admire or to wonder at in this sweet world of ours. We can no longer say with Jasper Petulengro,—"Sun, moon and stars are sweet things, brother; there is likewise the wind on the heath." No, the questions which Geography has to solve henceforth are confined to how and under what conditions is the earth's surface profitable to man and desirable for his habitation. No more may children conceive themselves climbing Mont Blanc or Mount Everest, skating on the Fiords of Norway or swimming in a gondola at Venice. These are not the things that matter, but only how and where and why is money to be made under local conditions on the earth's surface. It is doubtful whether this kind of teaching is even lucrative because the mind works on great ideas, and, upon these, works to great ends. Where science does not teach a child to wonder and admire it has perhaps no educative value.

Perhaps no knowledge is more delightful than such an intimacy with the earth's surface, region by region, as should enable the map of any region to unfold a panorama of delight, disclosing not only mountains, rivers, frontiers, the great features we know as 'Geography,' but associations, occupations, some parts of the past and much of the present, of every part of this beautiful earth. Great attention is paid to map work; that is, before reading a lesson children have found the places mentioned in that lesson on a map and know where they are, relatively to other places, to given parallels, meridians. Then, bearing in mind that children do not generalise but must learn by particulars, they read and picture to themselves the Yorkshire Dales, the Sussex Downs, the mysteries of a coal-mine; they see 'pigs' of iron flowing forth from the furnace, the slow accretions which have made up the chalk, the stirring life of the great towns and the occupations of the villages. Form II (A and B) are engaged with the counties of England, county by county, for so diverse are the counties in aspect, history and occupations, that only so can children acquire such a knowledge of England as will prove a key to the geography of every part of the world, whether in the way of comparison or contrast. For instance, while I write, the children in IIA are studying the counties which contain the Thames basin and "Write verses on 'The Thames'" is part of their term's work. Our Sea Power, by H. W. Household, is of extraordinary value in linking England with the world by means of a spirited account of the glorious history of our navy, while the late Sir George Parkin, than whom there is no better qualified authority, carries children round the Empire. They are thrown on their own resources or those of their teachers for what may be called current Geography. For instance, "Learn what you can about The Political Map of Europe after the Great War. (Evans, 4d.)."

In Form III the Geography is still regional, that is, children are led to form an intimate acquaintance with the countries of Europe so that the map of any country calls up in a child's imagination a wonderful panorama of the diversities of the country, of the people, their history and occupations. It is evident that this kind of geographical image cannot be secured in any other way than by considering Europe country by country. They begin with a general survey of the seas and shores of the continent, of the countries and peoples, of the diversities of tongues and their historical origin, of the plains and mountains, of the rivers and their basins a survey after which they should be able to answer such questions as,—"Name three rivers which flow into the Baltic." "What lands form the southern and eastern shores of the Mediterranean?" "What countries are washed by the Baltic?" "Between what parallels does Europe extend? What other continents lie partly within the same parallels?" The young scholars are at home with the map of Europe before they consider the countries separately.

The picture we present of the several countries is meant to be before all things interesting and at the same time to provide an intelligent and fairly exhaustive account of the given country. Whatever further knowledge a child acquires will fit in to this original scheme. For example, "The Rhône Valley and the Border lands." [The Ambleside Geography; Book IV, by the Writer.]

"The warm and fertile Rhône valley belongs in climate to the southern region, where, although the vine is grown, large plantations of olive and mulberry occupy much of the land. We are apt to think of the South of France as the sunny south, the sweet south, 'but,' says a writer whom we have already quoted, 'it is austere, grim, sombre' . . . . but the mulberry feeds the silkworm and so furnishes material for the great manufacture of France. Lyons, the second city of France, is the seat of the silk manufacture including those of velvets and satins. It is seated upon a tongue of land at the confluence of the rapid Rhône and the sluggish Saône, and along the banks of both rivers are fine quays.

This extract indicates how geographical facts are introduced incidentally, pretty much as a traveller comes across them. The work for one term includes Belgium, Holland, Spain and Portugal, and the interests connected with each of these countries are manifold. For example,—

"On the seashore near Leyden is Katwyck where the expiring Rhine is helped to discharge itself into the sea by means of a wide artificial channel provided with no less than thirteen pairs of enormous floodgates. These are shut to keep out the sea when the tide is coming in, and open to let the streams pass out during ebb tide. Notwithstanding these great works the once glorious Rhine makes but an ignoble exit. The delta of this river may be said to include the whole breadth of Holland." [Ambleside Geography: Book IV, by the Writer.]

It will be noticed that an attempt is made to shew the romance of the natural features, the history, the industries, so that a country is no more a mere matter of names on a map, or of sections shewn by contour lines. Such generalisations are not Geography but are slow conclusions which the mind should come to of itself when it acquires intimacy with a region. Something of a literary character is preserved in the Geography lessons. The new feature in these is the study of maps which should be very thorough. For the rest the single reading and narration as described in connection with other work is sufficient in this subject also. Children cannot tell what they have not seen with the mind's eye, which we know as imagination, and they cannot see what is not told in their books with some vividness and some grasp of the subject. The thoroughness of the map study is shewn by such a question to be answered from memory as,—"What part of Belgium does the Scheldt drain? Name any of its feeders. Name ten famous places in its basin. What port stands at the head of its estuary?" We find great light thrown upon the geography of the Empire in a little book of literary quality, Fighting for Sea Power in The Days of Sail.

There are two rational ways of teaching Geography. The first is the inferential method, a good deal in vogue at the present time; by it the pupil learns certain geographical principles which he is expected to apply universally. This method seems to me defective for two reasons. It is apt to be misleading as in every particular case the general principle is open to modifications; also, local colour and personal and historical interests are wanting and the scholar does not form an intellectual and imaginative conception of the region he is learning about. The second which might be called the panoramic method unrolls the landscape of the world, region by region, before the eyes of the scholar with in every region its own conditions of climate, its productions, its people, their industries and their history. This way of teaching the most delightful of all subjects has the effect of giving to a map of a country or region the brilliancy of colour and the wealth of detail which a panorama might afford, together with a sense of proportion and a knowledge of general principles. I believe that pictures are not of very great use in this study. We all know that the pictures which abide with us are those which the imagination constructs from written descriptions.

The Geography for Form IV [The Ambleside Geography: Book V, by the Writer.] includes Asia, Africa, America and Australasia. But the same principle is followed: vivid descriptions, geographical principles, historical associations and industrial details, are afforded which should make, as we say, an impression, should secure that the region traversed becomes an imaginative possession as well as affording data for reasonable judgments. The pupil begins with a survey of Asia followed by a separate treatment of the great countries and divisions and of the great physical features. Thus of Siberia we read,—

"All travellers unite in praise of the free Siberian peasant. As soon as one crosses the Urals one is surprised by the extreme friendliness and good nature of the inhabitants as much as by the rich vegetation of the well-cultivated fields and the excellent state of the roads in the southern part of the government of Tobolsk."

or,—

"The glossy jet black soft thick fur of the sea-otter is the most valuable of all the Russian skins. Next ranks the skin of the black fox. But though a thousand of its skins are worth no more than one skin of the sea-otter, the little grey squirrel whose skins are imported by the million really plays the most important part in the Siberian fur trade."

Of Further India,—

"Pigou, the middle division, is really the vast delta of the Irrawaddy, a low-lying country which yields enormous quantities of rice while on the higher grounds which wall in the great river are the finest teak forests in the world."

Africa follows Asia with the discoveries of Livingstone, Speke, Burton, Grant, etc. We get an account of African village life and among the chapter headings are Abyssinia, Egypt, Up the Nile, The Soudan, The Sahara, The Barbary States, South Africa, Cape Colony, The Islands. America follows with an account of the progress of discovery, a geographical sketch of South America, the Andes and the Mountain States, Chili, Peru, Bolivia, etc., the Great Plains of South America, Central America, North America, Canada, a historical sketch of the United States, the Eastern States, States of the Mississippi valley, the prairies, the Western States and territories, California. In the section on the Eastern States we read,

"Stretching from this chain (the Alleghanies) is the great Appalachian coalfield which extends through Pennsylvania, Virginia and Ohio, with a length of 720 miles containing, it is said, coal enough to supply the world for four thousand years! Iron occurs with the coal in great abundance. Most of this coal is of the kind called Anthracite. It is extremely slow in burning, emits no smoke, but has a painfully drying effect upon the air of a room. Sir Charles Lyall speaking of Pottsville on this coal-field says,—'Here I was agreeably surprised to see a flourishing manufacturing town with the tall chimneys of a hundred furnaces burning night and day, yet quite free from smoke. Leaving this clear atmosphere and going down into one of the mines it was a no less pleasing novelty to find that we could handle the coal without soiling our fingers.'"

But enough has been said to indicate the sort of intimacy that scholars in Form IV get with all quarters of the world, their geography, landscape, histories and industries, together with the study of the causes which affect climate and industries. Geikie's Physical Geography affords an admirable introduction to the principles of physical geography.

Forms V and VI are expected to keep up with the newspapers and know something about places and regions coming most into note in the current term. Also, in connection with the history studied, Seeley's Expansion of England, The Peoples and Problems of India, Geikie's Elementary Lessons in Physical Geography, Mort's Practical Geography, and Kipling's Letters of Travel are included in the reading of one term. In these Forms the young students are expected to apply their knowledge to Geography, both practical and theoretical, and to make much use of a good Atlas without the map questions which have guided the map work of the lower Forms.

The Knowledge of the Universe; Mathematics

The question of Arithmetic and of Mathematics generally is one of great import to us as educators. So long as the idea of 'faculties' obtained no doubt we were right to put all possible weight on a subject so well adapted to train the reasoning powers, but now we are assured that these powers do not wait upon our training. They are there in any case; and if we keep a chief place in our curriculum for Arithmetic we must justify ourselves upon other grounds. We take strong ground when we appeal to the beauty and truth of Mathematics; that, as Ruskin points out, two and two make four and cannot conceivably make five, is an inevitable law. It is a great thing to be brought into the presence of a law, of a whole system of laws, that exist without our concurrence,—that two straight lines cannot enclose a space is a fact which we can perceive, state, and act upon but cannot in any wise alter, should give to children the sense of limitation which is wholesome for all of us, and inspire that sursum corda which we should hear in all natural law.

Again, integrity in our dealings depends largely upon 'Mr. Micawber's' golden rule, while 'Harold Skimpole's' disregard of these things is a moral offence against society. Once again, though we do not live on gymnastics, the mind like the body, is invigorated by regular spells of hard exercise.

But education should be a science of proportion, and any one subject that assumes undue importance does so at the expense of other subjects which a child's mind should deal with. Arithmetic, Mathematics, are exceedingly easy to examine upon and so long as education is regulated by examinations so long shall we have teaching, directed not to awaken a sense of awe in contemplating a self-existing science, but rather to secure exactness and ingenuity in the treatment of problems.

What is better, it will be said, than a training in exactness and ingenuity? But in saying so we assume that this exactness and ingenuity brought out in Arithmetic serve us in every department of life. Were this the case we should indeed have a royal road to learning; but it would seem that no such road is open to us. The habits and powers brought to bear upon any one educational subject are exercised upon that subject simply. The familiar story of how Sir Isaac Newton teased by his cat's cries to be let in caused a large hole in the door to be made for the cat and a small one for the kitten, illustrates not a mere amusing lapse in a great mind but the fact that work upon special lines qualifies for work upon those lines only. One hears of more or less deficient boys to whom the study of Bradshaw is a delight, of an admirable accountant who was otherwise a little 'deficient.'

The boy who gets 'full marks' in Arithmetic makes a poor show in history because the accuracy and ingenuity brought out by his sums apply to his sums only: and as for the value of Arithmetic in practical life, most of us have private reasons for agreeing with the eminent staff officer who tells us that,—

"I have never found any Mathematics except simple addition of the slightest use in a work-a-day life except in the Staff college examinations and as for mental gymnastics and accuracy of statement, I dispute the contention that Mathematics supply either any better than any other study."

We have most of us believed that a knowledge of the theory and practice of war depended a good deal upon Mathematics, so this statement by a distinguished soldier is worth considering. In a word our point is that Mathematics are to be studied for their own sake and not as they make for general intelligence and grasp of mind. But then how profoundly worthy are these subjects of study for their own sake, to say nothing of other great branches of knowledge to which they are ancillary! Lack of proportion should be our bête noire in drawing up a curriculum, remembering that the mathematician who knows little of the history of his own country or that of any other, is sparsely educated at the best.

At the same time Genius has her own rights. The born mathematician must be allowed full scope even to the omission of much else that he should know. He soon asserts himself, sees into the intricacies of a problem with half an eye, and should have scope. He would prefer not to have much teaching. But why should the tortoise keep pace with the hare and why should a boy's success in life depend upon drudgery in Mathematics? That is the tendency at the present moment to close the Universities and consequently the Professions to boys and girls who, because they have little natural aptitude for mathematics, must acquire a mechanical knowledge by such heavy all-engrossing labour as must needs shut out such knowledge of the 'humanities' say, as is implied in the phrase 'a liberal education.'

The claims of the London Matriculation examination, for example, are acknowledged by many teachers to be incompatible with the wide knowledge proper to an educated person.

Mathematics depend upon the teacher rather than upon the text-book and few subjects are worse taught; chiefly because teachers have seldom time to give the inspiring ideas, what Coleridge calls, the 'Captain' ideas, which should quicken imagination.

How living would Geometry become in the light of the discoveries of Euclid as he made them!

To sum up, Mathematics are a necessary part of every man's education; they must be taught by those who know; but they may not engross the time and attention of the scholar in such wise as to shut out any of the score of 'subjects,' a knowledge of which is his natural right.

It is unnecessary to exhibit mathematical work done in the P.U.S. as it is on the same lines and reaches the same standard as in other schools. No doubt his habit of entire attention favours the P.U.S. Scholar.

The Knowledge of the Universe; Physical Development and Handicrafts

It is unnecessary, too, to say anything about games, dancing, physical exercises, needlework and other handicrafts as the methods employed in these are not exceptional.

Book II Theory Applied

Chapter 1 A Liberal Education in Elementary Schools

I need not waste time in attempting to convince the reader of what we all know, that a liberal education is, like justice, religion, liberty, fresh air, the natural birthright of every child. Neither need we discuss the scope of such an education. We are aware that good life implies cultivated intelligence, that, according to the Platonic axiom, 'Knowledge is virtue,' even though there be many exceptions to the rule. Educated teachers are not slow to perceive the part the Humanities play in a worthy scheme of education, but they are faced by enormous difficulties which are admirably summed up in a recent work, [Citizens to Be, by Miss M. L. V. Hughes.]

"The tragedy of modem education has been the prolonged failure of Humanism to secure conditions under which its purpose might be realised for the people at large."

It is because we (of the Parents' Union School) have succeeded in offering Humanism under such conditions that we believe the great problem of education is at last solved. We are able to offer the Humanities (in the mother tongue) to large classes of children from illiterate homes in such a way that the teaching is received with delight and freely assimilated. One swallow does not make a summer, we all know, but the experience of one school shows that it is possible to carry out a pretty full literary programme joyously and without effort while including all the usual school activities. Wireless telegraphy was, so to speak, in the air before the first Marconi message was sent, but that first wireless message made it possible for any passenger on board a Channel steamer to send such a message. Just so, the experiment in the Drighlington School (Yorkshire) placed the conditions for a humanistic education at the service of any teacher. I am much impressed by the amount of work of this kind which is already being done in our schools. I heard the other day of a man whose whole life had been elevated by a single inspiring (poetic) sentence which he heard as a schoolboy; we have been told that the 'man in the street' cannot resist a row of books; we are told, too, that the War has made us a nation of readers, both at home and in the trenches, readers largely of the best books in poetry and history; is there no credit due to the schools for these things? But teachers are not satisfied; their reach is greater than their grasp and they are more aware of the sordid lives about them, of the "dull, unfeeling, barren ignorance" which prevails, than of any success they have yet attained. Therefore they fret under the time limitations which seem to make it impossible to do anything worth while in such vast subjects as History and Literature, for example.

I wonder does this uneasiness point to a fact which we are slow to realise,—that the requirements of the mind are very much like those of the body? Both require as conditions of health,—activity, variety, rest and, above all, food. There has been some tendency among us to offer gymnastics, whether intellectual or physical, by way of a square meal of knowledge, which is as if one were to invite a boy to Swedish Drill by way of his dinner; and that wretched misnomer 'education' is partly to blame.

Now, potency, not property, is the characteristic of mind. A child is able to deal with much knowledge, but he posses none worth speaking of; yet we set to work to give him that potency which he already possesses rather than the knowledge which he lacks; we train his reason, cultivate his judgment, exercise this and the other faculty, which we have no more to do with than with the digestive processes of a healthy child; we know that the more we meddle with these the worse for the child; but what if the devitalisation we notice in so many of our young people, keen about games but dead to things of the mind, is due to the processes carried on in our schools, to our plausible and pleasant ways of picturing, eliciting, demonstrating, illustrating, summarising, doing all those things for children which they are born with the potency to do for themselves? No doubt we do give intellectual food, but too little of it; let us have courage and we shall be surprised, as we are now and then, at the amount of intellectual strong meat almost any child will take at a meal and digest at his leisure.

Perhaps the first thing for us to do is to get a just perception of what I may call the relativity of knowledge and the mind. The mind receives knowledge, not in order that it may know, but in order that it may grow, in breadth and depth, in sound judgment and magnanimity; but in order to grow, it must know.

The fact is that we are handicapped, not so much by the three or four difficulties I have already indicated, as by certain errors of judgment, forms of depreciation, which none of us escape because they are universal. We as teachers depreciate ourselves and our office; we do not realise that in the nature of things the teacher has a prophetic power of appeal and inspiration, that his part is not the weariful task of spoon-feeding with pap-meat, but the delightful commerce of equal minds where his is the part of guide, philosopher and friend. The friction of wills which makes school work harassing ceases to a surprising degree when we deal with the children, mind to mind, through the medium of knowledge.

Next, we depreciate children, even though most teachers lay down their lives for their charges with amazing devotion. We have been so long taught to regard children as products of education and environment, that we fail to realise that from the first they are persons; and, as Carlyle has well said,—

"The mystery of a person, indeed, is ever divine, to him that has a sense for the godlike."

We must either reverence or despise children; and while we regard them as incomplete and undeveloped beings who will one day arrive at the completeness of man, rather than as weak and ignorant persons, whose ignorance we must inform and whose weakness we must support, but whose potentialities are as great as our own, we cannot do otherwise than despise children, however kindly and even tenderly we commit the offence.

As soon as he gets words with which to communicate with us, a child lets us know that he thinks with surprising clearness and directness, that he sees with a closeness of observation that we have long lost, that he enjoys and that he sorrows with an intensity we have ceased to experience, that he loves with an abandon and a confidence which, alas, we do not share, that he imagines with a fecundity no artist among us can approach that he acquires intellectual knowledge and mechanical skill at a rate so amazing, that, could the infant's rate of progress be kept up to manhood, he would surely appropriate the whole field of knowledge in a single lifetime! (It is worth while in this connection to re-read the early chapters of David Copperfield.)

I am considering a child as he is, and am not tracing him, either with Wordsworth, to the heights above, or, with the evolutionist, to the depths below; because a person is a mystery, that is, we cannot explain him or account for him, but must accept him as he is. This wonder of personality does not cease, does not disappear, when a child goes to school; he is still 'all there' in quite another sense from that of the vulgar catchword. But we begin to lose the way to his mind from the day that he enters the schoolroom; the reason for this is, we have embraced the belief that 'knowledge is sensation,' that a child knows what he sees and handles rather than what he conceives in his mind and figures in his thoughts. I labour this point because our faith in a child's spiritual, i.e., intellectual educability is one of our chief assets. Having brought ourselves face to face with the wonder of mind in children, we begin to see that knowledge is the aliment of the mind as food is that of the body. In the days before the War, a lifetime ago it seems, our insular contempt for knowledge was a by-word; except for a schoolmaster or other thinker here and there, nobody took knowledge seriously; we announced boldly that it did not matter what a child learned but only how he learned it. As for mere 'book-learning,' for that we had a fine contempt! But we have changed all that. We are beginning to suspect that ignorance is our national stumbling-block, a chief cause of those difficulties at home which hinder our efforts abroad. For ignorance there is only one cure, and that is, knowledge; his school is the seat of knowledge for a child, and whatever else his teachers do for him, first of all they must sustain him with knowledge, not in homeopathic doses, but in regular, generous servings. If we ask, what is knowledge?—there is no neat and ready answer at hand: Matthew Arnold, we know, classifies all knowledge under three heads,—the knowledge of God, divinity, the knowledge of man, known as the 'humanities' and the knowledge of the physical world, science, and that is enough to go on with. But I should like to question this division and to class all three parts of knowledge under the head of Humanism, which should include all knowledge that makes a direct appeal to the mind through the channel of literary form; now, the substance of Divinity is contained in one of the three great literatures of the world, and Science, in France if not usually in England, is embodied in a beautiful and poetic literature of great clarity, precision and grace. Is it not then allowable to include all knowledge of which literature is a proper medium under the head of 'Humanism'? One thing at any rate we know with certainty, that no teaching, no information becomes knowledge to any of us until the individual mind has acted upon it, translated it, transformed, absorbed it, to reappear, like our bodily food, in forms of vitality. Therefore, teaching, talk and tale, however lucid or fascinating, effect nothing until self-activity be set up; that is, self-education is the only possible education; the rest is mere veneer laid on the surface of a child's nature.

I have endeavoured to call your attention to a certain undervaluing of children and undervaluing of knowledge which seem to me to mar our twentieth century ideal of education, fine as that is. If we realise that the mind and knowledge are like two members of a ball and socket joint, two limbs of a pair of scissors, fitted to each other, necessary to each other and acting only in concert, we shall understand that our function as teachers is to supply children with the rations of knowledge which they require; and that the rest, character and conduct, efficiency and ability, and, that finest quality of the citizen, magnanimity, take care of themselves. "But how?" cries the teacher, whose life is spent in the labour of Sisyphus. I think we have chanced on a way that, at any rate, works to admiration, the principles and practice of which I am anxious to bring before you.

Let me first repeat [cf. "Introduction."] a few of the results that have been made good by thousands of children, and within the last few years by many Council Schools throughout the country:

The children, not the teachers, are the responsible persons; they do the work by self-effort.

The teachers give the uplift of their sympathy in the work and where necessary elucidate, sum up or enlarge, but the actual work is done by the scholars.

These read in a term from one thousand to between two and three thousand pages, according to age and class, in a large number of set books; the quantity set for each lesson allows of only a single reading.

The reading is tested by narration, or by writing on a test passage.

No revision is attempted when the terminal examination is at hand; because too much ground has been covered to allow of any 'looking up.'

What the children have read they know, and write on any part of it with ease and fluency, in vigorous English. They usually spell well.

During the examinations, which last a week, the children cover say from twenty to sixty sheets of Cambridge paper, according to age and class; but if ten times as many questions were set on the work studied most likely they would cover ten times as much paper.

It rarely happens that all the children in a class are not able to answer all the questions set in such subjects as history, literature, citizenship, geography, science. But here differences manifest themselves; some children do better in history, some in science, some in arithmetic, others in literature; some, again, write copious answers and a few write sparsely; but practically all know the answers to the set questions.

In the course of an examination they deal freely with a great number of substantives, including many proper names; I once had the names used by a child of ten in an examination paper counted; there were well over a hundred, of which these are the 'A's'—

Africa, Alsace-Lorraine, Abdomen, Antigonons, Antennae, Aphis, Antwerp, Alder, America, Amsterdam, Austria-Hungary, Ann Boleyn, Antarctic, Atlantic;

and these are the 'M's,'—

Megalopolis, Maximilian, Milan, Martin Luther, Mary of the Netherlands, Messina, Macedonia, Magna Charta, Magnet, Malta, Metz, Mediterranean, Mary Queen of Scots, Treaty of Madrid;

and upon all these subjects the children wrote as freely and fully as if they were writing to an absent sister about a new family of kittens!

The children write with perfect understanding as far as they go and there is rarely a 'howler' in hundreds of sets of papers. They have an enviable power of getting at the gist of a book or subject. Sometimes they are asked to write verses about a personage or an event; the result is not remarkable by way of poetry, but sums up a good deal of thoughtful reading in a delightful way; for example,—the reading of King Lear is gathered in twelve lines on 'Cordelia,'—

CORDELIA
Nobliest lady, doomed to slaughter,
An unlov'd, unpitied daughter,
Though Cordelia thou may'st be,
"Love's" the fittest name for thee;
If love doth not, maid, bestow
Scorn for scorn, and "no" for "no,"
If love loves through scorn and spite,
If love clings to truth and right,
If love's pure, maid, as thou art,
If love has a faithful heart,
Thou art then the same as love;
Come from God's own realms above!
M.K.C. l0 10/12 Form II,

A life of Livingstone (read in connection with the Geography of Africa) is thus epitomised,— Livingstone
"The whole of Africa is desert bare,
Except around the coast." So people said,
And thought of that great continent no more.
"The smoke of thousand villages I've seen!"
So cried a man. He knew no more. His words
Sank down into one heart there to remain.
The man who heard rose up and gave his all:
Into the dark unknown he went alone.
What terrors did he face? The native's hate,
The fever, tsetse-fly and loneliness.
But to the people there he brought great Light.
Who was this man, the son of some great lord?
Not so. He was a simple Scottish lad
Who learnt to follow duty's path. His name
Was Livingstone, he will not be forgot.
E. P. (15.) Form IV.

And here is a rendering of Plutarch's Life of Pericles by a girl of fourteen in Form IV,—
Oh! land, whose beauty and unrivalled fame;
Lies dead, obscure in Time's great dusty vault.
Not so in memory, for truly here,
Each and alike look up and do revere
Those heroes of the hidden past. Plato,
Who's understanding reached the wide world's end;
Aristides, that just and noble man.
And last, not least, the great wise Pericles
Who's socialistic views and clever ways
For governing the rich and poor alike
Were to be envied. In his eyes must Greece
Live for ever as the home of beauty.

So to the Gods great marble shrines he made,
Temples and theatres did he erect;
So that the beauty of his beloved Greece
Might live for ever. And now when seeing
What is left of all those wondrous sights
We think not of the works themselves
But rather of the man who had them built
J.F.

One wonders is 'socialistic' used for democratic; any way, the notion is original. There is little to be said for the technique of the verses but I think the reader will agree that each set shows thoughtful appreciation of some part of the term's reading. The verses are uncorrected.

Much use is made according to this method of the years from 6 to 8, during which children must learn to read and write; they get at the same time, however, a good deal of consecutive knowledge of history and geography, tale and fable, some of which at the end of the term they dictate in answer to questions and their answers form well-expressed little essays on the subjects they deal with.

The time appropriated in the time-table at this stage to the teaching of some half-dozen more or less literary subjects such as Scripture, and the subjects I have indicated, is largely spent by the teachers in reading, say, two or three paragraphs at a time from some one of the set books, which children, here and there in the class, narrate. The teacher reads with the intention that the children shall know, and therefore, with distinctness, force, and careful enunciation; it is a mere matter of sympathy, though of course it is the author and not himself, whom the teacher is careful to produce. This practice, of the teacher reading aloud and the class narrating, is necessarily continued through all the classes of an elementary school, because some of the books used are rather costly and only one copy is furnished. I wonder does this habit of listening with close attention to what is read aloud tend to equalise the children of the 'uneducated' with those of the educated classes? Certainly, the work of the two is surprisingly equal. By the way, there is no selection of subjects, passages or episodes on the ground of interest. The best available book is chosen and read through in the course, it may be, of two or three years.

Let me add that the appeal of these principles and this method is not to the clever child only but to the average and even to the 'backward' child; indeed we have had several marked successes with backward children. Just as we all partake of that banquet which is 'Shakespeare' according to our needs and desires, so do the children behave at the ample board set before them; there is enough to satisfy the keenest intelligence while the dullest child is sustained through his own willing effort. This scheme of fairly wide and successful intellectual work is carried out in the same or less time than is occupied in the usual efforts in the same directions; there are no revisions, no evening preparations (because far more work is done by the children in ordinary school-time than under ordinary school methods, when the child is too often a listener only): no notetaking, because none are necessary, the children having the matter in their books and knowing where to find it; and as there is no cramming or working up of subjects there is much time to spare for vocational and other work of the kind.

Such an education as I am urging should act as a social lever also; everyone is much occupied with problems concerning amelioration of life for our 'poorer classes' but do we sufficiently consider that, given a better education, the problems of decent living will for the most part be solved by the people themselves?

Like all great ventures of life this that I propose is a venture of faith, faith in the saving power of knowledge and in the assimilative power of children. Its efficacy depends upon the fact that it is in the nature of things, that is, in the nature of knowledge and in the nature of children. Bring the two together in ways that are sanctioned by the laws of mind and, to use a figure, a chemical combination takes place and a new product appears, a person of character and intelligence, an admirable citizen whose own life is too full and rich for him to be an uneasy member of society.

Education is part and parcel of religion and every enthusiastic teacher knows that he is obeying the precept, 'feed my lambs'—feed with all those things which are good and wholesome for the spirit of a man; and, before all and including all, with the knowledge of God.

I have ventured to speak of the laws of mind, or spirit, but indeed we can only make guesses here and there and follow with diffidence such light as we get from the teachings of the wise and from general experience; general experience, because peculiar experience is apt to be misleading; therefore, when I learned that long tried principles and methods were capable of application to the whole of a class of forty children in the school of a mining village, I felt assured that we were following laws whose observance results in education of a satisfying kind.

The mind requires sustenance as does the body, that it may increase and be strong; so much everybody knows. A long time ago it was perceived that the pabulum given in schools was of the wrong sort; Grammar rules, lists of names and dates and places,—the whole stock in trade of the earlier schoolmaster—was found to be matter which the minds of children reject: and, because we were wise enough to see that the mind functions for its own nourishment whether in rejecting or receiving, we changed our tactics, following, so we thought, the lead of the children. We did well, and therefore are prepared; if necessary, to do better. What, then, if our whole educational equipment, our illustrations, elucidations, questionings, our illimitable patience in getting a point into the children, were all based on the false assumption of the immature, which we take to connote the imperfect, incomplete minds of children? "I think I could understand, Mummy, if you did not explain quite so much,"—is this the inarticulate cry of the school child to-day? He really is capable of much more than he gets credit for, but we go the wrong way about getting his capable mind into action.

We err when we allow our admirable teaching to intervene between children and the knowledge their minds demand. The desire for knowledge (curiosity) is the chief agent in education: but this desire may be made powerless like an unused limb by encouraging other desires to intervene, such as the desire for place (emulation), for prizes (avarice), for power (ambition), for praise (vanity). But I am told that marks, places and prizes (except for attendance) do not figure largely in Elementary Schools, therefore the love of knowledge for its own sake is likely to have a freer course in these schools than in others.

That children are born persons,—is the first article of the educational credo which I am concerned to advance; this implies that they come to us with power of attention, avidity for knowledge, clearness of thought, nice discrimination in books even before they can read, and the power of dealing with many subjects.

Practical teachers will say, guarantee to us the attention of our scholars and we will guarantee their progress in what Colet calls 'good literature.' I have already explained how I came to a solution of this puzzling problem,—how to secure attention.

Let me add again that the principles and methods I have indicated are especially suitable for large classes; what is called the 'sympathy of numbers' stimulates the class, and the work goes with added impetus: each child is eager to take part in narration or to do written work well. By the way, only short test answers are required in writing, so that the labour of correction is minimised.

To two further points I must invite attention; the choice of books and the character of the terminal examinations. I do not know better how to describe the sort of books that children's minds will consent to deal with than by saying that they must be literary in character. A child of seven or eight will narrate a difficult passage from The Pilgrim's Progress, say, with extraordinary zest and insight; but I doubt if he or his elders would retain anything from that excellent work, Dr. Smiles's Self-Help! The completeness with which hundreds of children reject the wrong book is a curious and instructive experience, not less so than the avidity and joy with which they drain the right book to the dregs; children's requirements in the matter seem to be quantity, quality and variety: but the question of books is one of much delicacy and difficulty. After the experience of over a quarter of a century [The P.U.S. was started in 1891.] in selecting the lesson books proper to children of all ages, we still make mistakes, and the next examination paper discovers the error! Children cannot answer questions set on the wrong book; and the difficulty of selection is increased by the fact that what they like in books is no more a guide than what they like in food.

The moment has come to try the great cause of Education V. Civilisalion, with the result, let us hope, that the latter will retire to her proper sphere of service in the amelioration of life and will not intrude on the higher functions of inspiration and direction which belong to Education. Both Civilisation and Education are the handmaids of Religion, but, each in its place, and the one may not thrust herself into the office of the other. It is a gain, any way, that we are within sight of giving to all members of the working classes notwithstanding their limited opportunities that stability of mind and magnanimity of character which are the proper outcome and the unfailing test of a *Liberal Education*; also it is to the good that "the grand elementary principle of pleasure" should be discovered in unexpected places, in what is too often the drudgery of the schoolroom.

Milton's ideal of a "complete and generous education" meets our occasions;—"that which fits a man to perform justly, skilfully and magnanimously all the offices both private and public of peace and war"; and perhaps it remains for our generation to prove that this ideal is open to and necessary for persons of all sorts and conditions. It has been well said that,—

"Just as there is only one kind of truth common to us all, so there is only one education common to us all. In the case of the education of the people the only question is: How is this common education to be developed under the circumstances of simple conditions of life and large masses of people? That this should be accomplished is the decisive mark of all real education."

The writer (Eucken) offers no solution of this problem: and it remains with the reader to determine each with himself whether that solution which I here propose is or is not worth a trial.

Chapter 2 A Liberal Education in Secondary Schools

Mighty is the power of persistent advertisement. The author of The Pagan may or may not be bringing an indictment against Pelmanism, but without any doubt 'Pelmanism' is bringing an indictment against secondary education. Half a million souls, Judges and Generals, Admirals and Barristers, are protesting that they have not been educated. No doubt the spirit that informs advertisements is often a lying spirit but claims so well attested as these may have something in them, and we who are engaged in secondary education are uneasy. Again, we have the Board of Education desiring that returns should be made promptly of all schools not already in communication with the State, which, by the way, is taking paternal action in several directions to secure a liberal education for all His Majesty's lieges. "Pay the schoolmaster well and you will get education" is the panacea of the moment, and so we get in one neighbourhood a village schoolmaster with a salary of £350 and a house, and a singularly able curate, an Oxford man, with a wife and family and no house—who flourishes on £150 a year! Work, however, is more than wages, and this exclusive stress on high salaries is a tacit undervaluing of teachers. Most of us know of fine educational work being done with little inducement in the way of either pay or praise. The real drawback to a teacher's work and the stumbling-block in the way of a liberal education is the monotonous drudgery of teaching continually what no one wants to learn. Before the War, the President of the British Association complained that education was uninteresting alike to pupils, teachers and parents. That is why we are always learning and never knowing, and why teachers exert themselves to invent a 'Play Way,' why handicrafts, 'Eurhythmics' and the like are offered, not as adjuncts to, but as substitutes for, education, why our Public Schools are exhorted to change their ways and our lesser private schools are threatened with extinction.

And with all this the intelligence and devotion, the enthusiasm and self-sacrificing zeal of teachers generally is amazing. They realise that education is, not merely an interest, but a passion; and this is true not only of the heads and the staffs of great schools but of those hundreds of little private schools scattered over the country.

We have all heard of "the two Miss Prettymans, who kept a girls' school at Silverbridge. Two more benignant ladies than the Miss Prettymans never presided over such an establishment." As for Miss Annabella Prettyman, the elder, "it was considered . . . that she did all the thinking, that she knew more than any other woman in Barsetshire, and that all the Prettyman schemes for education emanated from her mind. It was said, too, by those who knew them best, that her sister's good-nature was as nothing to hers, that she was the most charitable, the most loving, the most conscientious of schoolmistresses." To be sure Miss Ann, the younger sister, knew more about Roman History and Roman Law than about current history and English Law, but what would you have?

Here was a type of school with which Trollope was familiar generations ago, and perhaps it would not be hard to find such another school in every 'Silverbridge' of to-day. To-day, however, we are uneasy, and in our unrest produce "Joan and Peter" types of education; that is, small schools indulge in freaks and great schools with much reason to believe in themselves are aware of a hitch somewhere, for they fail to turn out many boys or girls who have intellectual interests, or have that flexibility of mind which Matthew Arnold tells us their

Academy gives to our neighbours across the Channel. There is that bugbear of 'Pelmanism' urging a charge of inadequacy against our methods; there is always some new book by a man who brings railing accusations against his particular school: and here is a tempered protest from Colonel Repington which is telling:

"When I look back upon Eton schooling I regard it with mixed feelings, for I loved my five years at Eton, gloried in its beauties and traditions, and was in upper division when I left, But all the same I was conscious that Eton was not teaching me the things that I wanted to know, and was trying to teach me things that revolted me, particularly mathematics and classics. I wanted to learn history, geography, modern languages, literature, science, and political economy, and I had a very poor chance at Eton of obtaining anything but a smattering of any one of them... I do not agree that we learnt nothing or were lazy. We worked very hard, but at what, to my mind, were useless things, and, with my feet planted firmly in the ground, I resisted in a mulish way any attempts to teach me dead languages and higher mathematics, I believe that I was right. Classics have left nothing with me but some ideas that I could have learnt better from a crib."

Probably the writer is mistaken as to what he owes to Eton. Without those five years he might not have become the authority on the theory and practice of war he is admitted to be. Who knows how much 'Caesar' may have influenced him as a small boy! No doubt Public Schools have many defects but they also have the knack of turning out men who do the work of the world. We know about the 'playing fields,' but perhaps when all is said it is the tincture of the classics that every public schoolboy gets which makes him 'to differ.' Nevertheless such protests as 'Eton was not teaching me the things I wanted to know' deserve consideration.

It is easy to condemn the schools, but the fact is, a human being is born with a desire to know much about an enormous number of subjects. How is the school time table to get them all in or an adequate treatment of any one of them? Then, boys (and girls too) offer a resisting medium of extraordinary density. Every boy 'resists in a mulish way' attempts to teach him, not only dead languages and higher mathematics, but literature and science and every subject the master labours at; with the average boy a gallon of teaching produces scarce a gill of learning, and what is the master to do? It is something to know, however, that behind all this 'mulishness' there is avidity for knowledge, not so much for the right sort (every sort is the right sort), but put in the right way, and we cannot say that every way is the right way.

I put before the reader what we (of the P.N.E.U.) have done towards the solution of this educational problem with sincere diffidence, but also with courage, because I know that no persons are more open to conviction on reasonable grounds than are many distinguished Headmasters and Mistresses; may they, if convinced, have the courage of their convictions!

So little is known about the behaviour of mind that it is open to anyone to make discoveries in this terra incognita. I speak, not of psychology, of which we hear a great deal and know very little, but of mind itself, whose ways are subtle and evasive; nevertheless that education only is valid which has mind for its objective. The initial difficulty is the enormous field of knowledge to which a child ought to be introduced in right of his human nature and of those "first born affinities" which he lives to make good. First and chiefest is the knowledge of God, to be got at most directly through the Bible; then comes the knowledge of man, to be got through history, literature, art, civics, ethics, biography, the drama, and languages; and lastly, so much knowledge of the universe as shall explain to some extent the phenomena we are familiar with and give a naming acquaintance at any rate with birds and flowers, stars and stones; nor can this knowledge of the universe be carried far in any direction without the ordering of mathematics. The programme is immense and school life is limited. What we may call the 'Academic' solution of the problem is,—teach a boy to know one thing thoroughly, say, Greek or Chemistry or Mathematics, and you give him the key to all knowledge. Therefore, we are told, it is not what you know that matters, but how you learn it; and a grammar grind, a mathematics grind or a laboratory 'stunt,' with a few odd matters thrown in, is supposed to answer all the purposes of education. The plan answers fairly well with the dozen best boys or girls in any school, because these are so keen and intelligent that they forage for themselves in various directions; but it does not answer with the average pupil, and he is coming in for his share of public attention. Shortly we shall have a new rule,—every school must educate every scholar in the three sorts of knowledge proper to him as a human being. What is knowledge? some one will say, and there is no pat, neatly-framed answer to be given; only this we can assert,—Knowledge is that which we know; and the learner knows only by a definite act of knowing which he performs for himself. But appalling incuria blocks the way. Boys and girls do not want to know;

therefore they do not know; and their future intellectual requirements will be satisfied by bridge at night and golf by day.

It has come to us of the Parents' Union School to discover great avidity for knowledge in children of all ages and of every class, together with an equally remarkable power of attention, retention, and intellectual reaction upon the pabulum consumed. The power which comes into play in the first place is, of course, attention, and every child of any age, even the so-called 'backward' child seems to have unlimited power of attention which acts without mark, prize, place, praise or blame. This fact clearly recognised opens great possibilities to the teacher; though his first impulse be to deny statements which seem to him sweeping and absurd. But the education of the future will probably offer us intellectual assets in human nature as surprising as the ethical values exhibited by the War.

We have not attained but I think we are on the way to attainment. After over a quarter of a century of experiment on a wide scale and consequent research, we have discovered what children are able to know and desire to know; what their minds will act upon in the ways of judgment and imagination; what they are incapable of knowing; and under what conditions knowledge must be offered to them. We do not want a 'play-way,' nor need we substitute arts and crafts or eurhythmics or even 'rugger' and the swimming bath, as things that boys take to, whereas learning goes against the grain. Physical and mechanical training are necessary for the up-bringing of the young, but let us regard them for the moment as training rather than education,—which ought to concern itself with things of the mind. Education as we know it is admirably designed to 'develop the faculties'; but if "All that's an exploded idee," if there be no faculties to develop, but only mind,—alert, self-active, discriminating, logical, capable alike of great flights and of minute processes—we must necessarily alter our educational tactics. Mind is benefitted by occasional gymnastics just as is 'Brother Body,' but cannot subsist on these any more than 'Body' can live on Swedish drill.

As I have said, knowledge, that is, roughly, ideas clothed upon with facts, is the proper pabulum for mind. This food a child requires in large quantities and in great variety. The wide syllabus I have in view is intended in every point to meet some particular demand of the mind, and the curious thing is that in a syllabus embracing a score of subjects the young learner is quite unconfused, makes no howlers, and never mixes, say, a fact of English with a fact of French history.

Again, we have made a rather strange discovery, that the mind refuses to know anything except what reaches it in more or less literary form. It is not surprising that this should be true of children and persons accustomed to a literary atmosphere but that it should be so of ignorant children of the slums points to a curious fact in the behaviour of mind. Persons can 'get up' the driest of pulverised text-books and enough mathematics for some public examination; but these attainments do not appear to touch the region of mind. When we get a young Pascal who enters voluntarily and eagerly into the study of mathematics he finds himself in a region of high thinking and self-existent law of the very nature of poetry; minds of this calibre assert themselves; but this is a gift and does not come of plodding. For the general run of scholars probably the "Association of Head Mistresses" are right and a less exacting standard should be set for public examinations.

Of Natural Science, too, we have to learn that the way into the secrets of nature is not through the barbed wire entanglements of science as she is taught but through field work or other immediate channel, illustrated and illuminated by books of literary value.

The French Academy was founded to advance Science and Art, a fact which may account for the charming lucidity and the exquisite prose of many French books on scientific subjects. The mind is a crucible which brings enormous power to act on what is put into it but has no power to distil from sand and sawdust the pure essence of ideas. So much for the manner of food which that organism (if I may be allowed the figure) called the mind requires for its daily subsistence. How various this sustenance must be I have already indicated and we remember how urgently Dr. Arnold insisted on 'very various reading' in the three parts of knowledge, knowledge of God, of man, and of the universe.

But the mind was a deceiver ever. Every teacher knows how a class will occupy itself diligently by the hour and accomplish nothing, even though the boys think they have been reading. We all know how in we could stand an examination on the daily papers over which we pore. Details fail us, we can say,—"Did you see such and such an article?" but are not able to outline its contents. We try to remedy this vagueness in children by making them take down, and get up, notes of a given lesson: but we accomplish little. The mind appears to have an outer court into which matter can be taken and again expelled without ever having entered the inner place where personality dwells. Here we have the secret of learning by rote, a purely mechanical exercise of which no satisfactory account has been given, but which leaves the patient, or pupil, unaffected. Most teachers know the dreariness of piles of exercises into which no stray note of personality has escaped. Now there is a natural provision against this mere skimming of the ground by the educational plough. Give children the sort of knowledge that they are fitted to assimilate, served in a literary medium, and they will pay great attention. What next? A clever questionnaire? Questions, as Dr. Johnson told us, are an intrusion and a bore; but here we have a word of ancient wisdom for our guidance; "The mind can know nothing except what it can express in the form of an answer to a question put by the mind to itself." Observe, not a question put by an outsider, but, put by the mind to itself. We all know the trick of it. If we want to tell the substance of a conversation, a sermon, a lecture, we 'go over it in our minds' first and the mind puts its question to itself, the same question over and over again, no more than,—What next?—and lo, we have it, the whole thing complete! We remember how one of Burke's pamphlets, by no means light affairs, was told almost verbatim at a College supper. We admire such a feat and think it quite out of our reach but it is the sort of thing that any boy or girl of fifteen could do if allowed to read the pamphlet only once; a second reading would be fatal because no one can give full attention to that which he has heard before and expects to hear again. Attention will go halt all its days if we accustom it to the crutch. We as teachers offend deeply in this matter. We think that we shall be heard for our much speaking and we repeat and enforce, explain and illustrate, not altogether because we love the sound of our own voices, but because we depreciate knowledge, we depreciate children, and we do not understand that the mind and knowledge are as the two members of a ball and socket joint, each of them irrelevant without the other. 'Education' will have turned over a new leaf once we realise that knowledge is to the mind as food is to the body, without which the one faints and flags and eventually perishes as surely as does the other.

The way to bring this panacea into use is exceedingly simple. Let the child (up to any age while he is an infant in the eye of the law) tell what he has read in whole or in part on the instant, and again, in an examination paper months later. 'Mere verbal memory,' some reader will say, and there is no answer to be given but that which one must give to oneself. Let the objector read an essay of Lamb's, say, or of Matthew Arnold's, Lycidas or the 'raven' scene in Barnaby Rudge and then put himself to sleep or wile away an anxious or a dull hour by telling to himself what he has read. The result will be disappointing; he will have forgotten this and that turn of thought, link in the chain of argument, but he will know the whole thing in a surprising way; the incidents, the figures, the delicate play of thought in the author will be brought out in his mind like the figures in the low relief which the sculptor produces from his block. He finds he has taken in 'mind stuff' which will come into use in a thousand ways perhaps as long as he lives.

Here we get the mind forces which must act continuously in education,—attention, assimilation, narration, retention, reproduction. But what of reason, judgment, imagination, discrimination, all the corps of 'faculties' in whose behoof the teacher has hitherto laboured? These take care of themselves and play as naturally and involuntarily upon the knowledge we receive with attention and fix by narration as do the digestive organs upon duly masticated food-stuff for the body. We must feed the mind as the body fitly and freely; and the less we meddle with the digestive processes in the one as in the other the more healthy the life we shall sustain. It is an infinitely great thing, that mind of man, present in completeness and power in even the dullest of our pupils; even of him it may be said,

"Darkness may bound his Eyes, not his Imagination. In his Bed he may lie, like Pompey and his Sons, in an quarters of the Earth, may speculate the Universe, and enjoy the whole World in the Hermitage of Himself."

We are paying in our education of to-day for the wave of materialism that spread over the country a hundred years ago. People do not take the trouble to be definitely materialistic now, but our educational thought has received a trend which carries us whither we would not. Any apostle of a new method is welcome to us. We have ceased to believe in mind, and though we would not say in so many words that "the brain secretes thought as the liver secretes bile," yet the physical brain rather than the spiritual mind is our objective in education; therefore, "things are in the saddle and ride mankind," and we have come to believe that children are inaccessible to ideas or any knowledge.

The message for our age is, Believe in mind, and let education go straight as a bolt to the mind of the pupil. The use of books is a necessary corollary, because no one is arrogant enough to believe he can teach every subject in a full curriculum with the original thought and exact knowledge shown by the man who has written a book on perhaps his life-study. But the teacher is not moved by arrogance but by a desire to be serviceable. He believes that children cannot understand well-written books and that he must make of himself a bridge between the pupil and the real teacher, the man who has written the book.

Now we have proved that children, even children of the slums, are able to understand any book suitable for their age: that is, children of eight or nine will grasp a chapter in Pilgrim's Progress at a single reading; children of fourteen, one of Lamb's Essays or a chapter in Eöthen, boys and girls of seventeen will 'tell' Lycidas. Given a book of literary quality suitable to their age and children will know how to deal with it without elucidation. Of course they will not be able to answer questions because questions are an impertinence which we all resent, but they will tell you the whole thing with little touches of individual personality in the narrative. Perhaps this is the key to the enormous difficulty of humanistic teaching in English. We are no longer overpowered by the mass of the 'humanities' confronted with the slow process of getting a child to take in anything at all of the author he is reading. The slow process is an invention of our own. Let the boy read and he knows, that is, if he must tell again what he has read.

This, of telling again, sounds very simple but it is really a magical creative process by means of which the narrator sees what he has conceived, so definite and so impressive is the act of narrating that which has been read only once. I dwell on the single reading because, let me repeat, it is impossible to fix attention on that which we have heard before and know we shall hear again.

Treat children in this reasonable way, mind to mind; not so much the mind of the teacher to that of the child,—that would be to exercise undue influence but the minds of a score of thinkers who meet the children, mind to mind, in their several books, the teacher performing the graceful office of presenting the one enthusiastic mind to the other. In this way children cover an incredible amount of ground in the time at their disposal.

Perhaps there is no better way of measuring a person of liberal education than by the number of substantives he is able to use with familiarity and discrimination. We remember how Scott tried a score of openings with the man on the coach and got no further until he hit upon 'bent leather'; then the talk went merrily for the man was a saddler. We have all had such experiences and know to our shame that we ourselves have victimised interlocutors who have not been able to find our particular 'bent leather.' Now, this is a matter for teachers to consider. There are a thousand subjects on which we could have definite knowledge and be able to speak with intelligence; and, indeed, do we not set 'general knowledge' papers, with the result that boys and girls are 'out' for scrappy information and provide material for comic paragraphs? There is no remedy for this state of things but a great deal of consecutive reading from very various books, all of some literary value; and this we find can be accomplished readily in school hours because one reading is sufficient; nor should there be any revision for the distant examination. Here is an uncorrected list of 200 names, used with ease and fitness in an examination on one term's work by a child of eleven in Form II.

Abinadab, Athenian, Anne Boleyn, Act of Uniformity, Act of Supremacy, America, Austria, Alcibiades, Athens, Auckland, Australia, Alexandria, Alhambra.

Bible, Bishop of Rochester, Baron, Bean-shoots, Bluff, Bowen Falls, Bishoprics, Blind Bay, Burano.

Currants, Cupid, Catholic, Court of High Commission, Cranmer, Charles V, Colonies, Convent, Claude, Calais, Cook Strait, Canterbury Plain, Christchurch, Cathedral, Canals, Caliph of Egypt, Court of the Myrtles, Columbus, Cordova.

David, Defender of the Faith, Duke of Guise, Dunedin, Doge's Palace.

England, Emperor, Empire, Egmont (Count), English Settlement

Flour, Fruits, French, Francis I, Francis of Guise, Ferdinand, Foveau Strait, Fuchsias, Fiords, Ferns.

Greek, Germany, Gondolas, "Gates of the Damsels," Gondoliers, Granada, Gate of Justice, Gypsies.

Henry VIII, History, Hooper, Henry II, Hungary, Haeckel.

Israel, Italian (language), Italy, Infusoria.

Jesse, Jonathan, Joseph, John, Jerusalem, James, Jane Seymour.

King of Denmark, King of Scotland, Kiwi.

"Love-in-Idleness," Lord Chancellor, Lord Burleigh, Lord Robert Dudley, Lime, Lyttleton, N.Z., Lake Tango.

Mary (The Virgin), More (Sir Thomas), Music, Martyr's Memorial, Milan, Metz, Monastery, Mary, Queen of Scots, Mediterranean, Microscope, Messina, Middle Island, Mount Egmont, Mount Cook, Milford Sound, Museum, Moa, Maoris, Mussulman, Moorish King.

Naomi, Netherlands, Nice, New Zealand, North Island, Napier, Nelson.

Oberon, Oxford, Orion.

Pharisees, Plants, Parliament, Puck, Pope, Protestant, Poetry,

Philosophy, "Paix des Dames ," Philip II, Paris, Planets, "Pink Terraces," Piazetta, Philip of Burgundy.

Queen Catherine, Queen Elizabeth, Queen Mary, Queen Isabella, Queen Juana.

Ruth, Robin Goodfellow, Ridley, Reformation, Radiolaria, Rotomaliana (Lake), Rea.

Saul, Samuel, Simeon, Simon Peter, Sunshine, Sugar-cane, Spices, Sultan, Spain, St. Quentin, Socrates, Stars, Sycamore, Seed-ball, Stewart Island, Seaports, Southern Alps, Scotch Settlement, St. Mark, St. Theodore, St. Maria Formosa (Church), Sierra Navada.

Temple, Titania, Testament, Treaty, Turks, Toul, Thread Slime, Tree Ferns, Timber Trees, Trieste, Toledo.

Verdure, Venus (Planet), Volcano, Volcanic Action, Venice.

Whieat, Wiltshire, William Cecil, Walsingham, Winged Seed, Wellington, Waikato.

Zaccharias, Zebedee.

The fitness and simplicity with which these substantives are employed is evidenced in the complete sets of papers that follow.

Supposing we have succeeded in shifting a conscientious and intelligent teacher from one mental position to another, suppose that he give up the notion of developing 'faculties' because he perceives that mind is complete and sufficient and wants nothing but its proper pabulum; that, again, he yield his place as the medium of all knowledge because his boys are qualified to deal with knowledge at first hand from the right books; suppose he scrap all the text-books and compendiums he has in use, perceiving that only that curious outsider, the verbal memory, and not the mind, will consent to deal with these dry-as-dust compilations; suppose he concede that much knowledge of various sorts and therefore a wide curriculum is necessary for the production of an intelligent and magnanimous citizen; supposing he has proved that any boy can face such a curriculum because all boys have immense power of attention and are able to know their work after a single reading,—surely he has still one or two strongholds that have not been attacked! What he aims at, he will tell you, is, not to open avenues of approach to the subjects about which intelligent citizens should know something, but to give pretty thorough knowledge in two or three directions and to turn out straight Englishmen; that is, he looks upon school as a nursery for the formation of character rather than for the acquisition of knowledge. As for the one or two subjects, practically, classics and mathematics, I have nothing to say; those subjects are of real value and also under existing regulations pretty high attainments in them are necessary as a preliminary to professional advancement. It is possible that when a boy has the habit of covering the ground rapidly he may get more into the given 'period' and leave a margin for the wider range of subjects proper to a liberal education. Experiments in this direction are being tried in one of our great Grammar Schools, and how important such experiments are to us as a democracy, I need not be at pains to show. There is every promise that the 'masses' will learn to read in their schools in such wise as to produce in a terminal examination as considerable a list of names as those on the preceding page. If the masses know 'Sancho Panza,' Elsinore, 'Excalibur,' 'Rosinante,' 'Mrs. Jellaby,' redstart, 'Bevis,' bogbean, the classes must know these things too with easy intimacy. If the one class is familiar with the pictures of the Van Eycks, with 'Comus,' 'Duessa,' 'Baron of Bradwardine,' the other class must know them too, and be able to use the knowledge with such effect as does the 'Honourable Member' when he quotes a familiar tag from Horace. He touches a spring to which all hearts rise, because allusions to what we know are like the light on 'old familiar faces.' What we want is a common basis of thought, such a ground work as we get from having read the same books, grown familiar with the same pictures, the same musical compositions, the same interests; when we have such a fundamental basis, we shall be able to speak to each other whether in public speaking or common talk; we shall "all hear in our own tongue the wonderful works of God" because we have learned a common speech through those who in their books have lived to educate the race. And how persuasively shall we speak to those who know, and therefore do not present the dead front of opposition the natural resource of ignorance!

A democratic education must have new features. We must all be able to 'take the front' of men and women by speaking of that which they have known and felt and already found joy in. So shall we cease to present motives of self interest and personal advantage as incentives to public action; we shall touch springs of poetry, of heroism, to which all natures have the habit of rising; and thus shall we build "Jerusalem in England's green and pleasant land." Towards this, we must have read the same books, only in English rather than in Latin or Greek, because the people will probably never have time to attain proficiency in these; neither, as a matter of fact, has the average boy at our great schools. If we must still have an exclusive education to which only the few best in a school can attain, and it seems to me that we must, that this is in fact, the one thing we have achieved, an education that has accomplished great results in character and conduct;—but if we would keep this possession, we must at the same time broaden its base and narrow its bounds. We must give wide reading in the lower forms, reading that everybody has read, and we must so compress our classical and mathematical work in the higher Forms that much history and 'English' may be included. I speak without authority but is it not true that there is overlapping in the passage from Preparatory to Public School, from one Form to a higher, from the Sixth to the University? Probably it will be found possible to give the old training which has produced such notable results, but to make it an inclusive not an exclusive education, to take in the books which everyone should know, the pictures everyone should be familiar with, the history, the travel, in which we should all be at home, some understanding of the phenomena which come before us all. Once we give up the notion that education is a development of the 'faculties' to be accomplished by the teacher and realize that it is on the contrary an appropriation of wide knowledge which the pupil must get for himself, there is some fear that the old exclusive education must go by the board; but this would be a national calamity. We must keep that to which we have attained and add to it the wide reading of a liberal education. The careers of 'Joan' and 'Peter,' as depicted by Mr. Wells are instructive. Peter is not entered for a recognised Public School for his guardian had many things against such schools, but games are his chief concern. Later we find the two at College, and of Joan it is said, "No religion has convinced her of a purpose in her life, neither Highmorton nor Cambridge has suggested any mundane devotion to her nor pointed her ambitions to a career. The only career these feminine schools and Colleges recognised was a career of academic success and teaching." The implicit charge against the schools is that they try each in its own way to find a substitute for the saving grace of knowledge. Academic success and knowledge are not the same thing and many excellent schools fail to give their pupils delight in the latter for its own sake or to bring them in touch with the sort of knowledge that influences character and conduct. The slow, imperceptible, sinking-in of high ideals is the gain that a good school should yield its pupils.

We have, if not a higher, yet another standard which it may be interesting to consider. We offer children knowledge for its own sake and our pupils discover that 'studies serve for delight.' We do not give our best attention to brilliant children, it is not necessary; these work well on their own account and so do the average and even the dull pupils. Historical characters become real to them and a fairly wide historical field comes under their purview; they do not grow up in crass ignorance of the history of foreign countries; they understand, for example, the India of to-day the better because they have some slight intimacy with Akbar as a contemporary of Elizabeth. They take to themselves a lesson from the youthful presumption of 'Phaeton'; 'Midas' and 'Circe,' Xerxes and Pericles enrich the background of their thoughts. The several Forms get through a great deal of reading because we have discovered that a single reading suffices to secure a clear knowledge (as far as it goes) of a subject, given the right book. Therefore, many books are necessary, and each is read consecutively so that the knowledge acquired is not scrappy and insecure. I know that teachers enjoy the work set term by term fully as much as do the children and that a schoolroom life in which there is no monotony, no dulness, little or no idleness or inattention, does away with the necessity to make games the paramount interest of the school—to make them indeed a stern necessity rather than a joyous relaxation.

The introduction of the methods I advocate has a curious effect on a whole family. The old nurse and the gardener are told of the adventures of 'Waverley.' "A.B. has named a moss her father picked on the tip-top of Ben Lawers. It is very rare and only grows on Ben Lawers and one other mountain. She is so pleased," and so, no doubt, is her father! The whole household thinks of and figures to itself great things, for nothing is so catching as knowledge and that fine temper of mind that knowledge brings with it. Children so taught are delightful companions because they have large interests and worthy thoughts; they have much to talk about and such casual talk benefits society. The fine sense, like an atmosphere, of things worth knowing and worth living for, this it is which produces magnanimous citizens, and we feel that Milton was right in claiming magnanimity as the proper outcome of education.

When we compare the large number of books, of historical and literary personages, the range of natural phenomena, with which children brought up on these lines are acquainted, with the sterile syllabus, not very well mastered, which is the schoolboy's normal fare, we find matter for reflection. Yet I suppose that in few things is the general moral and intellectual progress evidenced more than in the culture common among the teachers of secondary schools. Every Head knows how to draw up the best possible syllabus and to secure good work, if upon narrow lines, but we (of the P.N.E.U.) work at an advantage when, as I have said, we recognise one or two natural laws.

I have no doubt that some of my readers are interested in the work we are doing in Elementary schools,—a work the more astonishing because children who have little vocabulary to begin with, no trace of literary background, show themselves able to hear or read a work of literary value and after a single reading to narrate pages with spirit and accuracy, not hedging at the longest names nor muddling complicated statements. This was a revelation to us, and it signifies that a literary education is open to all, not after tedious and laborious preparation, but immediately. The people wait only for the right books to be put into their hands and the right method to be employed.

Let me repeat that we live in times critical for everybody, but eminently critical for teachers, because it rests with them whether personal or general good shall be aimed at, whether education shall be merely a means of getting on, or a means of general progress towards high thinking and plain living, and therefore an instrument of the greatest national good.

Let me beg that Heads of schools, so far in sympathy with me that they perceive we are at the parting of the ways, will consider a method which brings promise of relief.

We are in a condition, for example, to answer the questions to be considered by the Departmental Committee on English:

"Can history and literature be brought into closer relations with the school curriculum than is the case at present? How much grammar is necessary? Could not oral composition and drama and debate, do something to cure our national aphasia? How can the preparatory schools improve their English teaching? How can the school essay be redeemed from barrenness? How can examinations be made a test of English without destroying the love of literature?"

These questions might have been framed with a view to bring out the attainments of the Parents' Union School. History, European as well as English, runs in harness with literature. Some Syntax is necessary and a good deal of what may be called historical Grammar, but, not in order to teach the art of correct writing and speaking; this is a native art, and the beautiful consecutive and eloquent speech of young scholars in narrating what they have read is a thing to be listened to not without envy. As to aphasia, to quote a Director of Education on this subject, "Conversational readiness becomes a characteristic. A quarter of a century of these methods with all the children of England and the strong silent Englishman should be a rare bird!" A schoolmaster remarks that his big boys are now eager to speak at some length—a thing new in his experience. Consider what an asset this should be to a country whose safety will depend more and more upon the power in the middle classes of clear and conclusive speech. Oral composition is the habit of the school from the age of six to eighteen. "Children of ten who read Shakespeare" is the heading of an article in a local newspaper which sent a reporter to investigate the P.N.E.U. method at work in a school as the result of an article in the Nineteenth Century and After written by the Headmaster. As for preparatory schools, we can do no more than offer them a method the results of which in teaching English are rather surprising. The final question as to how examinations may be made a source of intellectual profit is I think sufficiently answered in the P.U S. children's examination papers.

We do not invite Heads of schools to take up work lightly, which implies a sound knowledge of certain principles and as faithful a practice. The easy tolerance which holds smilingly that everything is as good as everything else, that one educational doctrine is as good as another, that, in fact, a mixture of all such doctrines gives pretty safe results,—this sort of complacent attitude produces lukewarm effort and disappointing progress. I feel strongly that to attempt to work this method without a firm adherence to the few principles laid down would be not only idle but disastrous. "Oh, we could do anything with books like those," said a master; he tried the books and failed conspicuously because he ignored the principles. We teachers are really modest and diffident and are not prepared to say that we are more capable of handling a subject than is a carefully chosen author who writes especially upon that subject. "Yes, but," says a young and able teacher, "we know better how to reach the minds of children than does the most eloquent author speaking through the dull pages of a book." This is a contention of which we have finally disposed. We have shown that the mass of knowledge, evoking vivid imagination and sound judgment, acquired in a term from the proper books, is many times as great, many times more thoroughly visualised by the scholars, than had they waited upon the words of the most able and effective teacher. This is why we insist upon the use of books. It is not that teachers are not eminently capable but because information does not become knowledge unless a child perform the 'act of knowing' without the intervention of another personality.

Heads of schools are a generous folk and perhaps they have some reason to think parents are niggardly, but the provision of the necessary books by the parents is a sine quâ non. It is our part to see to it that books take root in the homes of our scholars and we must make parents understand that it is impossible to give a liberal education to children who have not a due provision of very various books. Moreover, it is impossible to teach children to spell when they do not read for themselves; we hear complaints of the difficulties of spelling, of the necessity to do violence to the language which is dear to us all in order to make 'spelling made easy'; but in thousands of cases that come before us we find that children who use their books for themselves spell well because they visualise the words they read. Those who merely listen to their teacher have no guide (in English at any rate) to the spelling of the words they hear. We are, perhaps, opposed to oral lessons or lectures except by way of occasional review or introduction. For actual education children must do their own work out of their own books under the sympathetic guidance of an intelligent teacher. We find, I may add, that once parents recognise how necessary a considerable supply of books is, they make no difficulty about getting those set in our programmes. Mr. Fisher says, "there are books and text-books," and the day is at hand when we shall all see that the latter are of no educational value. We rarely use text-books in the Parents' Union School but confine ourselves as far as possible to works with the imaginative grasp, the touch of originality, which distinguish a book from a text-book. Perhaps we should apologise for ourselves as purveyors not precisely of books but of lists of books. Every headmaster or mistress is able to draw up such lists, but think of the labour of keeping some 170 books in circulation with a number of changes every term! Here is our excuse for offering our services to much-occupied teachers. There has been talk from time to time about interfering with the liberty of teachers to choose their own books, but one might as well contend for everyman's liberty to make his own boots! It is one of those questions of the division of labour which belong to our civilisation; and if the question of liberty be raised at all, why should we not go further and let the children choose their books? But we know very well that the liberty we worship is an elusive goddess and that we do not find it convenient to do all those things we are at liberty to do.

The terminal examinations are of great importance. They are not merely and chiefly tests of knowledge but records which are likely to be permanent. There are things which every child must know, every child, for the days have gone by when 'the education befitting a gentleman' was our aim.

The knowledge of God is the principal knowledge, and no teaching of the Bible which does not further that knowledge is of religious value. Therefore the children read, or if they are too young to read for themselves the teacher reads to them, a passage of varying length covering an incident or some definite teaching. If there are remarks to be made about local geography or local custom, the teacher makes them before the passage has been read, emphasizing briefly but reverently any spiritual or moral truth; the children narrate what has been read after the reading; they do this with curious accuracy and yet with some originality, conveying the spiritual teaching which the teacher has indicated. Now this is no parrot-exercise, but is the result of such an assimilation of the passage that it has become a part of the young scholar. It is only by trying the method oneself on such an incident, for example, as the visit of Nicodemus or the talk with the woman of Samaria, that we realise the wonderful clearness with which each incident is brought out, the fullness of meaning with which every phrase is invested by such personal effort. This method of teaching is especially valuable in dealing with the Gospel history, but none of us who read during the War the daily lessons appointed by the Church could fail to be struck by the fact that the law and the prophets still interpret the ways of God, and we shall not do well if we tacitly treat the Old Testament as out-of-date as a guide to life.

Next in order to religious knowledge, history is the pivot upon which our curriculum turns. History is the rich pasture of the mind—which increases upon the knowledge of men and events and, more than all, upon the sense of nationhood, the proper corrective of the intolerable individualism of modern education. Let Amyot tell us,—

"How greatly is the reading of histories to be esteemed, which is able to furnish us with more examples in one day, than the whole course of the longest life of any man is able to do. Insomuch that they which exercise themselves in reading as they ought to do, although they be but young, become such in respect of understanding of the affairs of this world, as if they were old and grayheaded and of long experience. Yea, though they never have removed out of their houses, yet are they advertised, informed and satisfied of all things in the world."

Hence, the great value of the Old Testament,—history and poetry, the law and the prophets; and perhaps no one was more sensible of this educative value of the Scriptures than Goethe, though he was little sensible of their more spiritual worth. We endeavour to bring records contemporary with the Bible before children, using the contents of certain Rooms of the British Museum as a basis. Episodes of Greek and Roman history come in, partly for their historical, partly for their distinctly ethical value. Plutarch is, of course, our great authority.

"(Plutarch) hath written the profitable story of all authors. For all other were fain to take their matter, as the fortune of the countries whereof they wrote fell out: But this man being excellent in wit, learning, and experience, hath chosen the special acts of the best persons, of the famousest nations of the world." (North).

English History is always with us, but only in the earliest years is it studied alone. It is not, as we know, possible always to get the ideal book, so we use the best we can find and supplement with historical essays of literary value. Literature is hardly a distinct subject, so closely is it associated with history, whether general or English; and whether it be contemporary or merely illustrative; and it is astonishing how much sound learning children acquire when the thought of an age is made to synchronise with its political and social developments. A point which I should like to bring before the reader is the peculiar part which poetry plays in making us aware of this thought of the ages, including our own. Every age, every epoch, has its poetic aspect, its quintessence, as it were, and happy the people who have a Shakespeare, a Dante, a Milton, a Burns, to gather up and preserve its meaning as a world possession.

Let me repeat that what is called 'composition' is an inevitable consequence of this free yet exact use of books and requires no special attention until the pupil is old enough to take naturally a critical interest in the use of words. Civics takes place as a separate subject, but it is so closely bound up with literature and history on the one hand and with ethics, or, what we call every-day morals, on the other, that the division of subjects is only nominal.

We have considered in a previous chapter what we do for children as inhabitants of a world ordered by natural law. Here we have a contention with some teachers of science who maintain that a child can only learn what he discovers for himself de novo. The theory is plausible, but the practice is disappointingly narrow and inexpansive. The teacher has got his knowledge through books; why then are they taboo for the children? Probably the reason is that text-books of science are dessicated to the last degree, so the teacher hopes to make up for their dryness by familiar talk about the Hydra, for example, as a creature capable of close friendships, about the sea-anemone as a 'Granny' of enormous longevity; that is, the interest of the subject is made to depend upon side issues. The French scientists know better; they perceive that as there is an essence of history which is poetry so there is an essence of science to be expressed in exquisite prose. We have a few books of this character in English and we use them in the P.U.S. in conjunction with field work and drawing—a great promoter of enthusiasm for nature.

I have already shown what we do, for example, in the way of affording children familiar acquaintance with great music and great pictures. An eminent art-dealer in London paid us a pretty compliment when he said,—"Lord help the children!" were our work to come to an end; and he had reason for he had just sold to P.U.S. children thousands of little exquisite reproductions of certain pictures by Velasquez which were the study of the term; no wonder that a man who loves art and believes in it should feel that something worth while was being done. In drawing, the scholars work very freely in colour from natural figures and objects and draw scenes visualised in the term's reading. We do not teach drawing as a means of self-expression; the scholars express, not themselves, but what they can see and what they conceive.

I have already gone into the teaching of languages; the habit of fixed attention and ready narration which the P.U.S. pupils acquire should be of value in this branch of work, and I believe a new era is opening for us and we English will at last become linguists. At the House of Education the students narrate in French, [See Chapter X.] more readily and copiously than they do in English,—the courses of lectures in French history and literature which form part of their work. In German and Italian they are able to read a scene in a play and 'tell' the scene in character, or a short passage from a narrative. We rather emphasise Italian, the language is so beautiful and the literature so rich, and I should like to suggest that schools should do the same. Latin and Greek we learn in the usual ways, but we apply the method of narration to the former.

I must commend any further study of the rationale of our syllabus to the reader's own kind consideration; he will perceive that we have a principle of correlation in things essential, but no fatiguing practice of it in detail. But to one more statement, a very daring one, I beg for favourable attention. The common theory and practice of education are on trial. It is idle to 'develop the faculties' if there be no faculties, but only mind, which, like Wordsworth's cloud, moves altogether when it moves at all. Therefore, those subjects whose raison d'étre is to develop this and the other faculty are practically out of court and we must seek another basis for education. Subjects of instruction which would be valuable if reason, judgment, imagination, had to be 'developed' become as meretricious, as much 'accomplishments,' as those early Victorian accomplishments over which we make merry. Education must be in touch with life. We must learn what we desire to know. Nobody talks to his friend about 'stinks,' about the niceties of Greek accents, nor, unless the two be mathematicians, about surds. But, when Jupiter is regnant, how good to tell and to learn! What a welcome companion is he who can distinguish between songs that differ in the vespers of the birds! How grateful the company of the reader of history who brings forward parallels to episodes in the great War! We are apt to work for one thing in the hope that we shall get another and a very different thing; we don't. If we work for public examinations, the questions in which must be of a narrow academic cast, we get a narrow, accurate, somewhat sterile type of mind. We reap as we have sown.

The future of England depends largely upon Secondary schools; let the Heads of these lay out a liberal field of study and astonishingly fair things will grow in that garden of mind in which we are invited to sow the seeds of all knowledge. My bold proposal is that the Heads of Secondary Schools from the least to the greatest should adopt a scheme of work following the lines I have indicated, faute de mieux, that of the Parents' Union School, and that they should do this for the nation's sake.

Mr. Masefield remarks,—

"There can be no great art without great fable. Great art can only exist where great men brood intensely on something upon which all men brood a little. Without a popular body of fable there can be no unselfish art in any country. Shakespeare's art was selfish till he turned to the great tales in the four most popular books of his time, Raphael Holinshed, Thomas North's Plutarch, Geraldi Cinthio's Hecatommithi and Francois De Belleforest's Histoires Tragiques. Since the newspaper became powerful, topic has supplanted fable and subject comes to the artist untrimmed and unlit by the vitality of many minds."

It is this vitality of many minds that we aim at securing and entreat educational workers and thinkers to join in forming a common body of thought which shall make England great in art no doubt, and also great in life.

This is the way to make great men and not by petty efforts to form character in this direction or in that. Let us take it to ourselves that great character comes out of great thoughts, and that great thought must be initiated by great thinkers; then we shall have a definite aim in education. Thinking and not doing is the source of character.

Chapter 3 The Scope of Continuation Schools

A hundred years ago, about the close of the Napoleonic wars, there was such another stirring among the dry bones as we are aware of to-day. All the world knew then, as now, that war was the outcome of the wrong thinking of ignorance, and that education was the nostrum for minds diseased.

Prussia led the way; not the children but the young people were the immediate concern of Statesmen, and, guided by the philosophy of Fichte, and organised under the statesmanship of Stein, that noble league of youth, the Tugendbund, came into being. Prussia was miserably impoverished, but her concern was not with the arts which should make her rich; her young people looked to philosophic principles for precept and to history for example, and, it was well with the land.

Not only in Prussia but throughout western Europe there was a more or less active intellectual renaissance, but, whether because the times were not ripe or the peoples were not worthy, the high ideals of the early days of the century were superseded by the utilitarian motive.

When the 'Continuation School' movement revived, envy of the commercial and manufacturing successes of England actuated the new effort; and already in 1829 a Bavarian statesman had announced that if you would have the fruit you must sow the seed, that is, manufacturing success is to be had only at the cost of technical education.

We all know the result in the great Munich schools where first-rate organisation and admirable teaching have produced an appreciable effect upon German industries. But the best German minds have long been aware that "an education which has powerful economic interests behind it is apt to become too narrowly utilitarian in motive and to lose that ideal element which gives all education its chief power over character." As Mr. Lecky has said concerning morals, "the Utilitarian theory is profoundly immoral."

The occasion brought forth the man; we know how in 1900 Dr. Kirsehensteiner chanced to see the announcement of a prize offered for an essay on the best way of training youth. He wrote the essay, was crowned by the Academy of his country, and that essay in pamphlet form has influenced opinion and directed action throughout the west: Professors Dewey and Stanley Hall in the United States, Dr. Armstrong and Sir Philip Magnus at home, are among its leading exponents.

And what was the note of this new gospel of education? Practically that same note which had proceeded from England, France, Switzerland. a century earlier: a utilitarian education should be universal and compulsory; child and adolescent should be "saturated with the spirit of service, provided with the instruments of effective self-direction." Behold, Utopia at hand! every young person fitted, body and soul, for the uses of society; as for his own uses, what he should be in and for himself—why, what matter?

It is not that the eminent educationalists I have referred to would willingly sacrifice the individual youth to society; on the contrary they would raise him, give him place and power, give him opportunity; place his feet on the rungs of that ladder we used to hear about; but we have all been misled by mistaken views as to the function of education. We have believed that knowledge may be derived from sensation, that what we have seen with our eyes and our hands have handled affords us the nutriment our souls demand. No doubt a boy uses his mind to some purpose when he makes, for example, an ingenious model; and, seeing mind at work, we run away with the notion that food and work are synonymous terms; for the body they may be so in a certain sense, for work brings pay and pay buys food, but no such indirect transaction is possible to mind; a mind perpetually at heavy work is a sort of intellectual navvy, whose food must be proportioned to his labour. Our great statesmen, Gladstone, Lord Salisbury and others, knew this, and their wide and deep reading in other matters than politics should not occasion surprise.

The War has forced new ideas upon us; we begin, for instance, to realise the avidity of the adult mind for instruction; it was startling to read of 1,500 soldier candidates for twenty vacant places in a certain class. We begin to see that mind, the mind of all sorts and conditions of men, requires its rations, wholesome and regularly served. As things are we shall have to see to it that everybody gets fed; but our hope is that henceforth we shall bring up our young people with self-sustaining minds, as well as self-sustaining bodies, by a due ordering of the process of education. We hope so to awaken and direct mind hunger that every man's mind will look after itself.

What is the proper food of mind, has already been discussed but we may assume that education should make our boys and girls rich towards God (we remember the fool of the parable who failed because he was not "rich towards God"), rich towards society and rich towards themselves. I will not press my point by urging the moral bankruptcy which has been exposed to us during recent years as co-existent with, if not caused by, utilitarian education; for the catastrophe has been accelerated by the sort of moral madness of which we too have had our seasons in the past,—witness our Barnaby Rudge and Peveril of the Peak episodes; we have indeed been carried off our feet by a fallacious notion once and again, but our national insanity has on each occasion been short-lived because our education hitherto has not taught us to believe a lie.

We are not worse than others, and if we think well of ourselves as a nation, why, national pride and personal modesty do not go ill together; in peace-time we have bitter things to say of our British working-man, but all the same he compares favourably with the somewhat sardonic Latin, the sullen Teuton, whom we all know. And the better man does the better work. We have heard much of German efficiency, and perhaps the German excels in little matters like doors that shut, blinds that draw, springs that act, things of domestic utility important in a country with a more extreme climate than ours; but these are little matters and perhaps our failing is, not to do our best except on big occasions; give us a big job or a big war and we show our mettle.

But probably in all our considerable industries we excel. German women will purr over the material of our dresses with "Ach, englisches Tuch!" Well dressed men are English tailored in English cloths. We buy, or bought, things "made in Germany" because they were cheap, but the most costly and most desired goods in German shops are advertised as "englisch."

This is a point to be borne in mind in considering the education of adolescents. We are given to depreciating ourselves and each other, but in fact we have no lee-way to make up; as both a manufacturing and commercial nation we are well in the van and are without inducement to sell the people's birthright for a mess of pottage.

Before I come to the point I desire to make, let us consider whether the problem of Continuation Schools has been attacked anywhere more successfully than in those countries of Middle Europe. Some of them, Germany especially, have done all that is to be done in response to the cry for efficiency with its resultant big returns and high wages; but from the beginning of the Continuation School movement in, say, 1806, the four north-western countries have worked towards different ends. In Denmark they have, not Continuation Schools, but People's High Schools, a pleasanter name for possibly a pleasanter thing.

Denmark, like Germany, was, as we know, devastated by the Napoleonic wars, but had been vitalised by the liberation of its serfs in 1788, and this prepared the ground for Grundtvig, that poet, historian and enthusiast, who became the "Father of the People's High Schools."

"Where there is most life, there is the victory," said he, and the immediate way to an access of life he saw in "A Danish High School accessible to young people all over the land," a school which should inspire "admiration for what is great, love for what is beautiful, faithfulness and affection, peace and unity, innocent cheerfulness, pleasure and mirth." Observe, there is no word of 'efficiency' in this poet's dream, but he did assure Charles VIII that with such a school, "a well of healing in the land," he might afford to smile at the newspapers, whether they chose to praise or blame. The King gave heed, begged for a further development of his plans than was afforded in the original pamphlet, and by 1845 the Schools he had dreamed of began to be.

We cannot follow the development of these Danish People's Schools, but in 1903-4 their pupils numbered over three thousand men and rather more women, and wise men cherished the hope that "the new Danish school for youth is to have the good fortune to blend all classes of the people into one."

All of these High Schools bear the mark of the genius of their "Father"—whose pupils have known how to sum up his teaching in three sayings,—"Spirit is might; Spirit reveals itself in spirit; Spirit works only in freedom." We are able to trace the source of these sayings, and indeed this movement seems to have been from the first profoundly Christian—Christian in no narrow sense, but sharing the wide liberality of that Allegoria filosofica della Religione Cattolica conceived by the 'Angelic Doctor' and pictured by Simone Memmi on the walls of the Spanish chapel in Santa Maria Novella (Florence): the several teachers commemorated were themselves illustrious pagans but not therefore the less under Divine teaching. Here, it seems to me, is an educational credo worth reviving in these utilitarian days, and some such creed seems to have been Grundtvig's, though probably independently conceived. His great hope is that "above all, some acquaintance with popular literature, especially with the poetry and history of one's own country, will create a brand new world of readers all over the land."

I cannot go into the question of the Agricultural Schools of which it is said that "the Danish Agricultural School is the child of the Danish Folkshöjskole, and must, like this, have Christian faith and national life for its basis." In the careless days before the War we could all testify to the excellence of Danish butter, but did we consider the "resolution and capacity" with which Danish peasants passed over from the making of poor butter in their various small holdings to the "manufacture in co-operative dairies of butter of an almost uniform fineness"? This, too, says an eminent Swedish Professor, is due to the High Schools, for, said he, "Just as the enrichment of the soil gives the best conditions for the seeds sown in it, so a well-grounded humanistic training provides the surest basis for business capacity, and not the least so in the case of the coming farmers." [cf Continuation Schools, ed. by Sir Michael Sadler, and published by the Manchester University, 1908, to which the writer is greatly indebted.] These are weighty words deserving our consideration at a moment when we, too, are on the eve of a new departure.

The three neighbouring countries watched the experiments in Denmark with keen interest, and almost simultaneously People's High Schools sprang up in all four.

These northern High Schools, necessarily winter schools, were not open at the time of my visit, but two or three things casually observed might, I think, be traced to their influence. For instance, Copenhagen itself, as compared with Munich, strikes one as a city with a soul. At the Hague, again, I saw an artisan in his working clothes shewing pictures in one of the galleries to his boy of seven who looked earnestly and listened eagerly. The young people in the great Delft porcelain works shewed traces of culture and gentleness in countenance and manner. But nothing struck me more than what I saw in the general shop of an out of the way village in Sweden; the villagers were peasants and the one shop sold cabbages and herrings, cheese and calico; but across the small-paned window was a shelf closely packed with volumes in paper covers which had not had time to get dusty; of course I could not read all the titles, but among them were translations from French, German and English. I noticed slim volumes of Scott, Dickens, Thackeray, Ruskin, Carlyle and the last thing out. One felt assured that the village was in 'kingdom come,' that of a long winter's evening, in any home, one read aloud whilst the rest worked, that there was much to talk about when friends met and lovers walked. (How sad by the way, to read that 'Tommy,' whom we all love and revere, is quick to form friendships but that these do not progress for the friends have nothing to talk about.) Think of little plays got up, of public readings given by the villagers themselves; might such things be with us, the lure of the town would cease to draw our village men and maids, for the village that can offer a happy community life, sustained by the people themselves, is able to hold its people.

Our upper and middle classes, professional and other, are singularly stable folk, and they are so, not because of their material but of their intellectual well-being; in this sense only they are most of them the 'Haves' as compared with the 'Have-nots.' The reason is not far to seek. Are there not agitators abroad whose business it is to sow seeds of discontent in the gaping minds of the multitude? The full mind passes on, but that which is empty seizes on any new notion with avidity, and is hardly to be blamed for doing so; a hungry mind takes what it can get, and the baker is apt to be lenient about prosecuting the starving man who steals a loaf. I do not hesitate to say that the constantly recurring misery of our age, 'Labour Unrest,' is to be laid at the door, not of the working man, but of the nation which has not troubled itself to consider the natural hunger of mind and the manner of meat such hunger demands.

I have tried to establish that the Kultur offered by the Munich type of Continuation School has had no good effect upon morals or manners and no conspicuously good effect upon manufactures.

That England is under no necessity to follow Germany's lead in this matter for Germany allows our superiority by paying a high price for our goods.

That Denmark and the neighbouring states, on the contrary, excel in those things in which we fall short.

That the People's High Schools of Denmark are worthier of our imitation than the Continuation Schools of Germany.

That they are so because character and conduct, intelligence and initiative, are the outcome of a humanistic education in which the knowledge of God is put first.

But we cannot take educational prescriptions designed for another patient; the Grundtvig Schools are for students ranging from eighteen to twenty-five, not for the more difficult ages from fourteen to eighteen. Again, these People's High Schools are residential. In countries so largely agricultural it is possible for a great part of the young adult population to spend the five winter months year by year at one of these People's High Schools. Their case and ours do not go on all fours. Our problem is the young adolescent in a country largely manufacturing.

Now, we have received our cloth, and not in ungenerous measure. How shall we cut our coat, that is, how shall we spend those seven or eight hours a week in which "education" is to do her part for the young citizen?

If we take the easiest way, we shall let the boy do what he is doing for the rest of the week,—work for his employer, whether directly, by way of increased output, or indirectly, by way of increased skill. This would be a betrayal. No employer wishes to take with one hand what he gives with the other; besides, what employer doubts the ability of his staff to train his young employees? Again, the technique of any employment takes but little time to understand. It is the practice that is of value, and such practice is work. Continuation Schools should not exist for technical instruction; they are established definitely for the sort of education of which such instruction forms no part; and will not the evening hours be free as they are at present for technical classes, gymnastic clubs, and various forms of recreative exercise?

This particular gift of time must be dedicated to things of the mind if we believe that mind too requires its rations and that to use the mind is by no means the same thing as to feed it.

With the best will in the world to give boys and girls something on which to chew the cud, real mind-stuff for digestion and assimilation, we find that the flood-gates are opened; an ocean of things good to know overwhelms us and we have eight hours a week! We seize on that blessed word compromise and see two possibilities: we are in a hurry to make good citizens. Now, good citizens must have sound opinions about law, duty, work, wages, what not; so we pour opinions into the young people from the lips of lecturer or teacher, his opinions, which they are intended to take as theirs. In the next place there is so much to be learned that a selection must needs be made; the teacher makes this selection and the young people are "poured into like a bucket," which, says Carlyle, "is not exhilarating to any soul." Some ground is covered; teachers and Education Authorities are satisfied; and if, when the time comes, the young people leave school discontented and uneasy, if their work bore them and their leisure bore them, if their pleasures are mean and meagre, and if they become men and women rather eager than other wise for the excitement of a strike, that is because the Continuation, as the Elementary, School will have failed to find them.

This is the real educational difficulty in schools for all classes, for pupils of all ages,—the enormous field of knowledge which it is necessary to cover in order to live with intelligence and moral insight. Know one thing well and you have the power to apprehend many things is the academic solution, which has not worked altogether badly, but it cannot be stretched to fit our present occasion, the "Enlightenment of the Masses." What we may call the 'academic' doctrine assumes that mind like body is capable of development in various directions by means of due exercise. Profounder educational thought, however, reveals mind to us as of enormous capacity, self-active, present in everyone and making but one demand—its proper pabulum. Feed mind duly and its activities take care of themselves. As the well-fed workman is fit for all his labours, so the duly nourished mind knows, thinks, feels, judges with general righteousness. The good man and magnanimous citizen is he who has been fed with food convenient for him.

Such a view of education naturally includes religion, not only "for his God doth instruct him and doth teach him," but because we may take knowledge roughly as of three sorts,—knowledge of God, to be got first-hand through the sacred writings, knowledge of man, to be arrived at through history, poetry, tale; through the customs of cities and nations, civics; through the laws of self-government, morals. One other great branch of knowledge remains. Every youth should know some thing of the flowers of the field, the birds of the air, the stars in their courses, the innumerable phenomena that come under general observation; he should have some knowledge of physics, though chemistry perhaps should be reserved for those who have a vocation that way.

Here are we on the verge of that new life for our country which we all purpose, faced with infinite possibilities on either hand,—the vast range of knowledge and the vast educability of mind. Another certainty presents itself, that we have not time for short cuts: the training of muscle and sense, however necessary, does not nourish mind; and, on the other hand, the verbiage of a lecturer is not assimilated. There is no education but self-education and only as the young student works with his own mind is anything effected.

But we are not without hope. An astounding field has been opened to us; thousands of children in Council Schools are doing incredible things with freedom and joy. They have taken in hand their own education and are greedy of knowledge for its own sake, knowledge in the three great fields that I have indicated.

The fact is that a great discovery has been vouchsafed to us, greater, I think, as concerns education, than any since the invention of the first alphabet. Let us again refer to Coleridge on the origin of great discoveries.

Coleridge gives no qualification to the minds which receive these great ideas, they are not described as great minds, but, he says, they are "previously prepared to receive them," that is, the great ideas. If the reader will forgive me for saying so I think my mind has been so prepared—by extraordinary incapacity in one direction, the direction, roughly, of academic attainments, and by some degree of capacity in other directions, and it has been gradually borne in upon me that this incapacity and this capacity are pretty general, and perhaps afford a key to the problem of education. A further preparation came to me in unusual opportunities for testing and understanding the minds of children and young people. I am anxious to bring this idea of a discovery before the reader because our methods are so simple and obvious that people are inclined to take them up at random and say that extensive reading is a "good idea which we have all tried more or less" and that free narration "is a good plan in which there is nothing new." It is true that we all read and that narration is as natural as breathing, its value depending solely upon what is narrated. What we have perhaps failed to discover hitherto is the immense hunger for knowledge (curiosity) existing in everyone and the immeasurable power of attention with which everyone is endowed; that everyone likes knowledge best in a literary form; that the knowledge should be exceedingly various concerning many things on which the mind of man reflects; but that knowledge is acquired only by what we may call "the act of knowing," which is both encouraged and tested by narration, and which further requires the later test and record afforded by examinations. This is nothing new, you will say, and possibly no natural law in action appears extraordinarily new; we take flying already as a matter of course; but though there is nothing surprising in the action of natural laws, the results are exceedingly surprising, and to that test we willingly submit these methods.

"All is not for all" was the sad conclusion of that Danish patriot and prophet. No doubt Grundtvig thought of the impassable barriers presented by a poor and mean vocabulary and a field of thought without literary background. So "all is not for all" he said, even as a prophet of our own proclaims that a worthy education is only for the élite. Books are not for the people, was Grundtvig's conclusion; wherefore those young Danes were lectured to by men of enthusiasm who had their country's literature and history at their fingers' ends and could convey the temper of their own minds. A great deal was effected, but minds nourished at the lips of a teacher have not the stability of those which seek their own meat.

But what if all were for all, if the great hope of Comenius—"All knowledge for all men"—were in process of taking shape? This is what we have established in many thousands of cases, even in those of dull and backward children, that any person can understand any book of the right calibre (a question to be determined mainly by the age of the young reader); that the book must be in literary form; that children and young persons require no elucidation of what they read; that their attention does not flag while so engaged; that they master a few pages at a single reading so thoroughly that they can 'tell it back' at the time or months later whether it be the Pilgrim's Progress or one of Bacon's Essays or Shakespeare's plays; that they throw individuality into this telling back so that no two tell quite the same tale; that they learn incidentally to write and speak with vigour and style and usually to spell well. Now this art of telling back is Education and is very enriching. We all practise it, we go over in our minds the points of a conversation, a lecture, a sermon, an article, and we are so made that only those ideas and arguments which we go over are we able to retain. Desultory reading or hearing is entertaining and refreshing, but is only educative here and there as our attention is strongly arrested. Further, we not only retain but realise, understand, what we thus go over. Each incident stands out, every phrase acquires new force, each link in the argument is riveted, in fact we have performed *the Act of Knowing*, and that which we have read, or heard, becomes a part of ourselves, it is assimilated after the due rejection of waste matter. Like those famous men of old we have found out "knowledge meet for the people" and to our surprise it is the best knowledge conveyed in the best form that they demand. Is it possible that hitherto we have all been like those other teachers of the past who were chidden because they had taken away the key of knowledge, not entering in themselves and hindering those who would enter in?

To-day we are in this position. We realise that there is an act of knowing to be performed; that no one can know without this act, that it must be self-performed, that it is as agreeable and natural to the average child or man as singing is to the song thrush, that "to know" is indeed a natural function. Yet we hear of the incuria which prevails in most schools, while there before us are the young consumed with the desire to know, can we but find out what they want to know and how they require to be taught Humanistic education, whether in English or Latin, affects conduct powerfully; knowledge of this sort is very welcome to children and young persons; a good deal of ground may be covered because a single reading of a passage suffices; this sort of humanistic work has been tried with good effect; and if our Continuation Schools are to be of value they must afford an education on some such lines.

The Parents' Union School, originally organised [1891] for the benefit of children educated at home, is worked by means of programmes followed by examination papers sent out term by term. When the same work, if not the whole of it, was taken up by Council Schools, [1913] the advantage of such an organisation was apparent, especially in that it afforded a common curriculum for children of all classes. By using this curriculum we were enabled to see that the slum child in a poor school compares quite favourably with the child of clever or opulent parents who had given heed to his education.

Now one of our national difficulties is the fact that we have no common basis of thought or ground for reflection. No doubt, by pretty copious reading, links of common interests might be established, and the schoolroom might do at least as much for the general life as does the cricket-pitch. The scheme works practically without a hitch in Council Schools; this is the sort of work that the highest class in these Schools, (in Standard VII), are doing with great success and very great delight. They read English, French and General History (three or four volumes), two or three books dealing with citizenship and morals from various points of view; Literature, contemporary with the history read (several works); natural history, physical geography and science (three or four books); Scripture (chiefly the Bible). Every term brings a new programme of work, the continuation usually of books already in reading. Children in Secondary Schools and in families remain for one year in Form IV and that work seems adapted to the status of Continuation Schools for the first year or two. After that the more advanced programme (Forms V and VI) might be used in the same way. This work would appeal to young people as being unlike the ordinary school grind, and as giving them opportunity for consecutive speaking and essay writing.

There is probably no better test of a liberal education than the number of names a person is able to use accurately and familiarly as occasion requires. We all recollect a character of Miss Austen's who had no opinion to offer as to whether the Bermudas should be described as the West Indies or not, because she had never called them anything in her life!

Now, here is an alphabetical (uncorrected) list taken from the examination papers of a girl of thirteen, containing 213 proper names, all of them used accurately, easily and with interest.

Amaziah, Ariel, Ayrshire, Arcot, America, Austrian Army, Artemidorus, Antium, Aufidius, Auditors, Apotheosis, Altai Mts., Assouan, Africa, Atbara, Annulosa, Arachnoida, Armadillo, Albumen, Abdomen, Auricles, Angle, Arc.

Burns (Robert), Bastille, Bombay, Bengal, Burke, Black Hole of Calcutta, British Museum, Benevolence, Basalt, Butterfly, Beetles, Blood-vessels, Berber, Blue Nile, Baghdad, Burne Jones.

Cowper, Calcutta, Clive, Canada, Colonel Luttrel, Cleopatra, Candace, Coriolanus, Cassowary, Cormorants, Curlews, Cranes, Calyptra, Cotton grass, Chalk, Conglomerate, Crustacea, Cheiroptera, Carnivora, Chyle, Centre of Circle, China Proper, Canton, Cairo, Cheops, Circe.

'Dick Primrose,' "Deserted Village," Dupleix, Demotic characters, Ducks, Despotic Government, Doctor Livingstone,

Deposits, Delta, diaphragm, Duodenum.

England, East India Company, Economical Reform, Europe, Emperor of Austria, Empress of Russia, Emu, Eastern Turkestan, Egypt.

France, Frederick the Great, Frederick William of Prussia, Flightless birds, First Cataract, Foraminifera.

Gadarenes, Gizeh, Great Commoner, George III, General Warrants, Governor General, Grace and Free-will, Greek language, Generosity, Gulls, Granite, Grubs, Gastric juice, Globules.

Huldah, Highlands of Scotland, Herodotus, Hieroglyphics, Herons, Hoang-ho, Hedgehog, Hydrochloric Acid, Hydrocarbons, Heart.

Isaiah, India, Influence of light.

Josiah, Judah, Jehosaphat, Jerusalem, Jonas, Jonah, Jesuits, Jansenists, Japan.

Künersdorf, Kuen Lun Mts., Kioto, Karnac, Khartum, Kolcheng, Kalabari.

Lord North, "Lords in Waiting "of Love, Land birds, Lamellae, Luxor, Lake Ngami, Loanda, Lake Nyassa.

Manasseh, Mongolia, Manchuria, Madras, Mahrattas, Member of Parliament, Middlesex, Methodists, Mississippi Company, Maria Theresa, Mummies, Microscopic Shells, Membrane.

Nagasaki, Nile, Nitrogenous food.
'Olivia Primrose,' Ostriches.
Pharisees, 'Primrose (Mrs.),' Philosophers. Plassey, Pitt, Prime Minister, Pragmatic Sanction, Prague, Peace of Hubertusburg, Pity, Puffins, Penguins, Plovers, Pelicans, Plants, Polytrichum formosum, Peristom, Porphyric, Puddingstone, Pepsin, Peptone, Pancreas, Pulmonary artery, Pamir Plateau, Prairies, Pyramid, Portuguese West Africa.
Quilemane.
Rome, Rossbach, Rosetta Stone, Rhea, Rodentia.
Sea of Galilee, 'Sophia Primrose,' Surajali Dowlali, Seven Years' War, Silesia, Saxony, Secretary, Storks, Sandpipers, Seedlings.
"The Task," Treaty of Dresden, Tullus, Trade Unions, Trustees, Treasurer, Tropical countries.
Ulysses, Ungulata.
Volcanic eruptions, Vermes, Vertebrate, Villi, Ventricles, Vernae Cavae, Vicar of Wakefield, Volscians, Vice President.
Wallace, Walpole, War of Independence, Wilkes, Whitfield, Wesley, War of the Austrian Succession, Water birds, Wady Halfa.
Yang-tse-kiang.
Zonga, Zambesi, Zorndorff.

This is 'Secondary' work, but supposing the young people of a Continuation School, who could not read all the books on the programmes, got some degree of intimacy, some association, with, say, one hundred such names in a term, we might believe that they were receiving a liberal education. This is the sort of work we hope to see done in Continuation Schools by pupils from fourteen to sixteen. The young people of the future between sixteen and eighteen should be prepared to work in Forms V and VI.

It is not the best children that answer the examination questions; the general rule is that everybody takes every question. I have touched only on the more humanistic subjects as whatever is done in Mathematics, for instance, the Head of the Continuation School will no doubt arrange; and indeed so much has been done in the Elementary School already that probably the keeping of fictitious account books would be a sufficient exercise for young people who show some mathematical talent.

No cost whatever is attached to the adoption and continued working of this method [In Elementary and Continuation Schools.] except the cost of books and of these, young wage-earners would no doubt buy their own, so that by degrees each would form his little library of books that he has read, understands and knows his way about. I should like to quote a few sentences from Professor Eucken on the education of the people:

"By education of the people it must not for a moment be supposed that we mean a special kind of education. We do not refer to a condensed preparation of our spiritual and intellectual possessions, suitable for the needs and interests of the great masses; we are not thinking of a diluted concoction of the real draught of education which we are so kind and condescending as to dispense to the majority. No! . . . . there is only one education common to us all." "We can all unite in the construction of a spiritual world over against that of petty human routine. Thus there is, in truth, a possibility of a truly human education, and therefore of a true education of the people."

The Jena Professor sees clearly enough the task before us all; but he sees, or sets forth, no possible way of accomplishing it, nor is there any other way than that which we have set forth that can afford this sort of liberal education; the electric telegraph was not discovered twice over.

After all our protests we are in our way utilitarian for no other study is so remunerative as that of the 'humanities.' Let me draw the reader's attention to one point. Instability, unrest, among our wage-earners is the serious danger threatening our social life. Now it is said that nothing can act but where it is and the class which acts steadily where it is, at some outpost of empire, on a home estate, in Parliament, where you will, is the class educated at Public Schools, that is, men brought up on the 'humanities.' Strong language will be used about the deadness and decadence of these men although they do much of our national work. Their defects are obvious and manifold, but still, as I say, the public work that is done is, for the most part, done by men whom no one could describe as progressive. Is there not some confusion of ideas about this fetish of progress? Do we not confound progress with movement, action, assuming that where these are there is necessarily advance? Whereas much of our activity is like the waves of the sea, going always and arriving never. What we desire is the still progress of growth that comes of root striking downwards and fruit urging upwards. And this progress in character and conduct is not attained through conditions of environment or influence but only through the growth of ideas, received with conscious intellectual effort.

It will be possible to have only a little of this strong meat in Continuation Schools, but a little goes a long way, how far, our Public School men illustrate; for a careful analysis will bring us to the conclusion that not Latin and Greek, Games, Athletics, or environment, but the 'humanities' in English alone will bring forth the stability and efficiency which we desire to see in all classes of society.

I have said that we have after all a generous allowance of cloth from which to cut our garment, seven or eight hours a week. In that time we may get in, page for page, book for book, as full a complement of the 'humanities,' poetry, history, essay, tragedy, comedy, philosophy, between the ages of fourteen and eighteen, as our public men have imbibed at their schools. To be sure these do it in the classic tongues while for those there is only plain English; but however duly we magnify Greek literature we cannot honestly say that that of England is second to any the world has yet seen. We can give to the people the thought of the best minds and we can secure on their part the conscious intellectual effort, the act of knowing, which bears fruit in capability, character and conduct. We cannot offer to the people the grace of scholarship in the allotted time, but no doubt earnest souls will find a way to get this surpassing excellence also; if there be profit in 'grinding at Grammar' that they must forego, too, but the inspiration and delight of entering into an intellectual world full of associations, this they should have, a well of healing and fountain of delight.

Now a common ground of thought is inestimable in what may be called its cohesive value; and what we desire to afford to the nation at large is such another background of thought, sketched in like that of the Public School man from the books men and women have read at school, books which made them intimate with Pitt and Fox, 'Dick Swiveller,' 'Mrs. Quickly,' with daffodils and clouds and nightingales as the poets have seen them, with a thousand promiscuous and seemingly purposeless scenes and sayings which somehow combine to serve the purpose of a background throwing the thoughts and incidents of to-day into clear relief. For this reason we, like the Public Schools, all read the same books, with such an intensive single reading that for the rest of the lives of these young people phrases or allusions they come across will kindle in their eyes that 'light which never was on sea or land.' We may hope that Public Schools will presently add this modicum of English to their classical studies; then the candidate for election will have something to appeal to other than the desire to better himself, which is supposed to dominate every man. By the way, is the paucity of literary or historical allusions, not in Latin, to be heard in the House due to the fact that the audience cannot be counted upon to rise to a reference not included in the well-known school books? If so, we shall change all that; once the masses read, the classes must read, too, and the Peace will be signalised by a new bond of intellectual life in common.

"There is no more dreadful sight," says Goethe, "than ignorance in action," and is not this the sight that is at the present time dismaying us all? Demos is king to-day, and who may dispute his right? But let us all give him the chance to become that philosopher/king who according to an ancient dream was to be the fit ruler, or rulers, of the people. The hopeful sign is that Demos himself perceives his lack, and clamours for the humanistic education in which he sees his salvation.

Chapter 4 The Basis of National Strength

[The Author owes to the Editor of The Times permission to reprint the chapters under this heading written in 1912; as also the happy titles of the several chapters and the general title.]

A Liberal Education from a National Standpoint: Knowledge

We have from time to time given some attention to the failure of our attempts to educate "The Average Boy," and it may be useful to look into one or two fundamental principles upon which this question and others seem to me to depend. For if our conceptions of education are heterogeneous and incoherent, naturally, we shall have a tangle of examination schemes evolved to test our ill-conceived work.

Educationally, we are in a bad way. We were told some time ago, in Across the Bridges, of the rapid deterioration of the bright intelligent responsive schoolboy who has passed through the sixth and seventh standards. Why? we ask. Industrial unrest often reveals virtue, even heroism of a sort, in the working man, but a lamentable want of knowledge—lack of education; he appears to have little insight, imagination, or power of reflection. The tendency in his class is that "dangerous tendency which we must all do our best to resist" indicated by Mr. Burns at a public meeting some few years ago; "the spirit of the horde," he said, "is being developed; and whether it is in exhibitions, sports, or legislation, the individual is becoming less and less important and the mob more and more so." And again, "the tendency of the present day in all modern movements is for great crowds to be brought together to see other people play; and that is extending not only to play, but to other fields of life." Could the industrial movement of to-day be better diagnosed? Again we ask, Why? As for those young men from Public Schools who fail in the Dominions, enough has been said about them; but those other Public School men who succeed in a measure at outposts of the Empire because of the virtue that is in them, do they not fail sometimes in an equal measure for lack of the insight, imagination, intelligence, which come of knowledge? As for the people who stay at home, "educated" men and women, I write as an old woman who remembers how in the sixties and seventies "countenance" was much talked of; "an intelligent countenance," "a fine countenance," "a noble countenance," were matters of daily comment. The word has dropped out of use; is it because the thing signified has dropped out of existence? Countenance is a manifestation of thought, feeling, intelligence; and it is none of these, but stolid indifference combined with physical well-being, that we read in many faces to-day.

If we have these grounds for discontent, education is no doubt the culprit at the bar, though there never was, I suppose, a more heroic and devoted body of teachers at work. They get for themselves the greater blessing of those who give; but the children suffer, poor little souls; "poured into like a bucket," they receive without stint, and little comes of it. There is no lack of zeal on the part of the teaching profession, but there is a tendency amongst us to depreciate knowledge and to depreciate our scholars. Now, knowledge is the material of education, as flour is the material of bread; there are substitutes for knowledge, no doubt, as there are for flour. Before the era of free meals I heard of a little girl in East London whose mother gave her a penny, to buy dinner for herself and her little sister, when the two set out for school. The child confided to her teacher that a ha'porth of aniseed drops "stays your stomach" more than a halfpenny bun. Now, our schools are worked more or less upon aniseed drops—marks, prizes, scholarships, blue ribbons, all of which "stay the stomach" of the boy who does not get the knowledge that he needs. That is the point. He needs knowledge as much as he needs bread and milk; his appetite for knowledge is as healthy as his appetite for his dinner; and an abundant regular supply at short intervals of various knowledge is a constitutional necessity for the growing youth as well as for the curious child; and yet we stay his hunger pangs upon "aniseed drops."

We do worse. We say, "What is the good of knowledge? Give a boy professional instruction, whether he is to be a barrister or a bricklayer, and strike out from his curriculum Greek or geography, or whatever is not of utilitarian value. Teach him to play the game and handle the ropes of his calling, and you have done the best for him." Now, here is a most mischievous fallacy, an assertion that a child is to be brought up for the uses of society only and not for his own uses. Here we get the answer to the repeated question that suggested itself in a survey of our educational condition. We launch children upon too arid and confined a life. Now personal delight, joy in living, is a chief object of education; Socrates conceived that knowledge is for pleasure, in the sense, not that knowledge is one source, but is the source of pleasure.

It is for their own sakes that children should get knowledge. The power to take a generous view of men and their motives, to see where the greatness of a given character lies, to have one's judgment of present events illustrated and corrected by historic and literary parallels, to have, indeed, the power of comprehensive judgment these are admirable assets within the power of every one according to the measure of his mind; and these are not the only gains which knowledge affords. The person who can live upon his own intellectual resources and never know a dull hour (though anxious and sad hours will come) is indeed enviable in these days of intellectual inanition, when we depend upon spectacular entertainments pour passer le temps.

If knowledge means so much to us, "What is knowledge?" the reader asks. We can give only a negative answer. Knowledge is not instruction, information, scholarship, a well-stored memory. It is passed, like the light of a torch, from mind to mind, and the flame can be kindled at original minds only. Thought, we know, breeds thought; it is as vital thought touches our minds that our ideas are vitalized, and out of our ideas comes our conduct of life. The case for reform hardly needs demonstration, but now we begin to see the way of reform. The direct and immediate impact of great minds upon his own mind is necessary to the education of a child. Most of us can get into touch with original minds chiefly through books; and if we want to know how far a school provides intellectual sustenance for its scholars, we may ask to see the list of books in reading during the current term. If the list be short, the scholar wilt not get enough mind-stuff; if the books are not various, his will not be an all-round development; if they are not original, but compiled at second hand, he will find no material in them for his intellectual growth. Again, if they are too easy and too direct, if they tell him straight away what he is to think, he will read, but he will not appropriate. Just as a man has to eat a good dinner in order that his physical energies may be stimulated to select and secrete that small portion which is vital to him, so must the intellectual energies be stimulated to extract what the individual needs by a generous supply, and also by a way of presentation that is not obvious. We have the highest authority for the indirect method of teaching proper to literature, and especially to poetry. The parables of Christ remain dark sayings; but what is there more precious in the world's store of knowledge?

How injurious then is our habit of depreciating children; we water their books down and drain them of literary flavour, because we wrongly suppose that children cannot understand what we understand ourselves; what is worse, we explain and we question. A few pedagogic maxims should help us, such as, "Do not explain." "Do not question," "Let one reading of a passage suffice," "Require the pupil to relate the passage he has read." The child must read to know; his teacher's business is to see that he knows. All the acts of generalization, analysis, comparison, judgment, and so on, the mind performs for itself in the act of knowing. If we doubt this, we have only to try the effect of putting ourselves to sleep by relating silently and carefully, say, a chapter of Jane Austen or a chapter of the Bible, read once before going to bed. The degree of insight, the visualization, that comes with this sort of mental exercise is surprising.

As I have said, a child in his seventh year will relate The Pilgrim's Progress, chapter by chapter, though he cannot read it, and some half-dozen other books of the best we can find for him. In his eighth or ninth year he works happily with a dozen books at a time, books of history, adventures, travels, poems. From his tenth to his twelfth year he reads considerable books of English and French history, seriously written, Shakespeare's historical plays, North's Plutarch's Lives, and a dozen other worthy books. As he goes up the school, his reading becomes wider and more difficult, but every one knows the reading proper at the ages of fifteen, seventeen, eighteen. The right books are given, but not enough of them. The reading dietary is too meagre for the making of a full man. A score of first-rate books should appear in the school curriculum term by term. The point that I insist upon, however, is that from his sixth year the child should be an "educated child" for his age, should love his lesson books, and enjoy a terminal examination on the books he has read. Children brought up largely on books compare favourably with those educated on a few books and many lectures; they have generous enthusiasms, keen sympathies, a wide outlook and sound judgment, because they are treated from the first as beings of "large discourse looking before and after." They are persons of leisure too, with time for hobbies, because their work is easily done in the hours of morning school.

It is not necessary to speak of modern languages and mathematics, field work in natural history, handiwork, etc. Schools are pretty much agreed about the treatment of these subjects. As for Latin and Greek, the teaching of these and the possibility of getting in any work beyond these is a crucial question; but I think it is open to Public Schoolmasters to discover that, given boys who have read and thought, and who have maintained the habit of almost perfect attention that a child begins with, the necessary amount of work in the Classics may be done in a much shorter time, and that the mind of the pupil is the more alert because it is engaged in handling various subjects.

Perhaps, too, some enlightened Headmaster may come to distinguish between scholarship and knowledge—a distinction which practical men, like Napoleon, for example, have known how to draw. Probably there never was a life on which the 'humanities' exercised a more powerful influence; rarely has there been such an example of the power of the informed mind to conquer the world. Napoleon is the final answer to the contention that a knowledge of books has no practical value, for there was, perhaps, no incident in his career that was not suggested, inspired, illustrated by some historical precedent, some literary apophthegm. He was, as we know, no scholar, but he read diligently, even in the midst of absorbing affairs, Homer, the Bible, the Koran, poetry, history, Plutarch.

Nations grow great upon books as truly as do individuals. We know how that heroic young Queen, Louisa of Prussia, perceived that the downfall of her country was not due to Napoleon alone, but also to national ignorance, and that if Prussia were to rise it must be through the study of history. So she set herself to work at the history of modern Europe during that sojourn at Memel, when she knew poverty as a peasant woman knows it. The disciples of Kant founded a league of virtue to arouse Prussian students to the duty of patriotism; Fichte knew how to issue a trumpet call; the nation became a nation of students, and the son of Queen Louisa established the German Empire! Alas, that an age should have come when the 'humanities' were proscribed on German soil—and humanity followed them into exile! A noble view of education was as righteousness exalting a nation; but, alas, we all know what universal havoc and disaster have proceeded from the debased and materialised theory of education promulgated at Munich.

The Danes, again, as we all know, owe their rise out of illiteracy to the Napoleonic impulse. After we had seized their battleships, by way of clipping the claws of Bonaparte, they set to work to make themselves the first farmers in Europe; this they have done in and through their schools and their continuation schools, where they get, not technical instruction, but a pretty wide course in history and literature. As for the Japanese revolution of some fifty years ago, history has little to show of a finer quality; and this, again, was the work of a literary people.

If we would not be left behind by the East and the West we must, as other nations have done, "add to our virtue, knowledge"; and we are still competent, as some of these are not, to mount from the bottom rung of the Apostolic educational ladder. It rests with us to add to our faith, virtue, and to our virtue, knowledge. It is an unheard of thing that the youth of a great nation should grow up without those ideals, slow enough in maturing, which are to be gathered for the most part from wide and wisely directed reading.

II Letters, Knowledge and Virtue

The following fragments of a valuable letter illustrate the contention of the foregoing chapter:—

"There is one thing, however, one note of regret, and that is that one paragraph, that on classical education, was not more expanded. I am satisfied that your central view covers the whole truth; and I am going to give you a small individual experience illustrating this fact—viz., that an early education in the great books of our own language, read, with enjoyment, by children and appropriately given to them from year to year, is the true groundwork of later expansion. Here is the story: My three daughters were suckled on Walter Scott and Shakespeare. Later, about the ages of from ten to twelve, off their own, they took up Plutarch's Lives, Bunyan, Defoe, and in the same period they refused to learn arithmetic and geography, the former on the ground of its monotony, and the latter, because, although they loved it, they held that the existing system of teaching geography was 'rotten,' and that geography ought to be learnt by going to the places. I knew better than to remonstrate. I meekly suggested that perhaps they would substitute something else in their curriculum, and they said at once, in an obviously prepared sentence, 'That's just it, we want to learn Latin and harmony.' Now here comes your point (in that lamentably abbreviated paragraph):

'Given boys (or girls) who have read and thought, and who have maintained the habit of almost perfect attention that a child begins with, the necessary amount of work in the classics may be done in a much shorter time, and the mind of the pupil is the more alert because it is engaged in handling various subjects.'

Six months later these girls knew more Latin than I learnt in six years under distinguished scholars with very eminent names. They could sling passages from Horace appropriately; they knew the first two Eclogues and half the Aeneid by heart; they regarded Cicero's Letters to Atticus as a 'penny post' affair, and were quite unduly familiar with the private life of Seneca. But all this did not interfere with their painting or their horsemanship, and better authorities on cricket and the Turf I don't happen to know. That is the illustrative episode. The point, in my mind, is that an early education from great books with the large ideas and the large virtues is the only true foundation of knowledge—the knowledge worth having."

This interesting letter brings us straight to a question which I thought had been pretty fully threshed out; and I tackle it with diffidence, only because an outsider may see aspects overlooked by experts. The gist of the charges brought against Public Schools is, Classics take up so much time that there is no opportunity for Litterae Humaniores in any other form. It is easy to say, Gain time by giving up Greek; but, in the first place, Public Schools, with our old Universities in sequence, are our educational achievement. Other efforts are experimental, but this one thing we know—that men are turned out from this course who are practically unmatched for quality, culture, and power; even the average B.A. shows up better than his compeers, and a degree in Arts signifies more than one in any other faculty.

We return thus to my original contention—that letters, primarily, are the content of knowledge; that if Wellington ever said how Waterloo was won, it was not on the playing-fields only, but in the class-rooms of Eton; that Caesar, Thucydides, Prometheus Bound, have won more battles than we know on fields civil and military. A little strong meat goes a long way, and even the average Public School boy turns out a capable man. But, alas, if capable, he is also ignorant; he does not know the history and literature of his own country or any other. He has not realised that knowledge is, not a store, but rather a state that a person remains within or drops out of. His degree taken, he shuts his books, reads the newspapers a little, perhaps a magazine or two, but otherwise occupies himself with the interests of sports, games, shows, or his employment. What is to be done, we wonder vaguely, to secure to this average boy some tincture of knowledge and some taste for knowledge? The expedient of dropping Greek to make room for other things recurs; but on reflection we say, "No"; for culture begins with the knowledge that everything has been known and everything has been perfectly said these two thousand years ago and more. This knowledge, slowly drummed into a youth, should keep him from swelled head, from joining in the "We are the people" cry of the blatant patriot; and there is no better way of knowing a people than to know something of their own words in their own speech.

It is well, by the way, that we should remember that we have as a nation an enormous loss to make good; time was, and not so long ago, when rich and poor were intimately familiar with one of the three great classical literatures. Men's thoughts were coloured, their speech moulded, their conduct more or less governed, by the pastoral idylls called "Genesis," the impassioned poetry of Isaiah, the divine philosophy of John, the rhetoric of Paul—all, writings, like the rest of the Bible, in what Matthew Arnold calls "the grand manner." Here is the well of English undefiled from which men have drawn the best that our literature holds, as well as their philosophy of life, their philosophy of history, and that principal knowledge we are practising to do without—the knowledge of God. And we wonder that the governing classes should forget how to rule as those who serve; and that the working man, brought up on "Readers" in lieu of a great literature, should act with the obstinate recklessness proper to ignorance.

But to return to the main issue. How shall we instruct the ignorance and yet retain the classical culture of the average Public School boy? I should like to suggest, again, with diffidence, that he, like his more brilliant compeer, is driven through a mill the outpour of which should be scholarship. Now, scholarship is an exquisite distinction which it would be ill for us as a nation to miss; but if all the men in an assemblage were decorated, who would care to wear an order? Some things are precious for their rarity, and to put a school in the running for this goal is as absurd as the ambition of the little boy who meant to be a Knight of the Garter when he grew up. The thing is not to be done; some men are born to be scholars, as the shape of their heads testifies. The rest of us take pleasure in their decoration, but are not envious, for scholarship is not the best thing, and does not necessarily imply that vital touch of mind upon mind out of which is got knowledge. As for erudition, we may leave that out of count, it is hardly even an aim at the present time. The geniuses, as one to some thousands, say, of our best, do not trouble themselves much about the regimen we offer classics or modern languages, or what not; an idle tale, a puppet show, the meanest flower that blows, is enough for them. Anyway, they take care of themselves, and we come back to the average boy.

He must learn his Greek and Latin, but there is an easier way; the girls mentioned in the letter I cite had hit upon it. That favourite girl pupil of Vittorino's who spoke and wrote Greek with "remarkable purity" at twelve, having, so to speak, done with Latin at an earlier age—she, we may be sure, had not been through the grammar school grind. Nor had any of the learned ladies of the Italian and the French Renaissance, the list of whose accomplishments leaves us breathless. While still children, we know how early they married, their knowledge of the classics was copious (and not too wholesome), they knew two or three modern languages, could treat the wounded, nurse the sick, prepare simples, govern great households, ride to chase, yes, and kill too! and do exquisite embroidery. Our own women of the Tudor times appear likewise to have been "infinitely informed" and to have carried their learning gaily; Maria Theresa, by no means a learned lady, could make speeches and converse with her Magyar nobles in Latin, and they could respond, neither knowing the native speech of the other. If these things were true of girls and women, how much more was expected of boys and men!

Are we persons of less intelligence, or how did they do it all? Every preparatory school knows how. Perhaps few boys enter Public Schools who could not pass "Responsions," that is, who are not, as far as Greek goes, ready for Oxford. I once heard a Headmaster say:—

"A boy does as much Latin now by the age of twelve as he will ever need for examination purposes, and he spends the next eight years in doing over again and again the same work. A clever boy of twelve could easily pass Responsions."

A headmaster in Newfoundland mentions in his school report for 1905 a boy who "began Greek in October and passed the Oxford Responsions in January."

There is a leakage somewhere, and there is overlapping, and both are due to the examinations upon which scholarships are awarded. Something must be done, because Public Schools, with all their splendid records, are not effective in the sense that they turn out the average boy a good all-round man. For better or for worse, who knows? the Democracy is coming in like a flood, and our old foundations will be tossed about in the welter unless we make haste to strengthen our weak places. Might not a commission—consisting of two or three headmasters, as many preparatory school masters, University "Dons," and public men (once public school boys and now the fathers of such boys) look into the question and devise examination tests which shall safeguard Letters, ancient and modern, without putting too high a premium upon scholarship?

Once the hands of schoolmasters were united, they would no doubt devise means by which our friend, the average boy, would get such a knowledge of the classics as should open life-long resources to him. Like the 'Baron of Bradwardine' he would go about with a pocket Livy (as he would say, "Titus Livius,") to be read, not laboured at a few lines at a time: The Seven against Thebes, Iphigenia in Aulis, the few tragedies left to us by the great dramatists would form part of the familiar back ground of his thoughts. He would know somewhat of the best that has been written in Greek and Latin, whether through printed translations or through the text itself rendered in the sort of running translation which some masters know how to give. Pari passu, he would do his share of gerund-grind, and construe the two or three books of his present limited acquaintance. But his limitations would be recognised, and he would not be required to turn out Greek and Latin verse.

Meantime his master wilt require him to know pretty intimately a hundred worthy books in addition to the great novels—to be read in class periods, in vacation, and in leisure time—his knowledge of each to be tested by a single bit of oral description or written work in verse or prose. "Ground he at Grammar," sums up every successful school boy's record as it did that of the dead "Grammarian"; but the ten or twelve years of school life should yield more than this.

I say nothing now about the teaching of science, for which most schools provide, except that for our generation, science seems to me to be the way of intellectual advance. All the same, the necessity incumbent upon us at the moment is to inculcate a knowledge of Letters. Men and their motives, the historical sequence of events, principles for the conduct of life, in fact, practical philosophy, is what the emergencies of the times require us to possess, and to be able to communicate. These things are not to be arrived at by any short cut of economics, eugenics, and the like, but are the gathered harvests of many seasons' sowing of poetry, literature, history. The nation is in sore need of wise men, and these must be made out of educated boys.

III Knowledge, Reason, and Rebellion

We have been very busy about education these sixty years or more diligently digging, pruning, watering; but there is something amiss with our tree of knowledge; its fruits, both good and evil, are of a mean, crabbed sort, with so little to choose between them that superior persons find it hard to determine which is which. To examine the individual apples would be a long process, but let me take one at a venture: is it not true that a conviction of irresponsibility characterises our generation?

If this be true, seeing that we all think as we have been brought up to think, our education is at fault. Faulty education is to blame if private property be recklessly injured in broad day, if working men do vital injury to their country thinking to serve their caste, if there be people who love to have it so, as long as their own interests are immune. The melancholy fact is that the people who do damage to private property, to public interests, and to that more delicate asset of a nation, public opinion, are all by way of being educated in their several degrees. All of them can write and speak clearly, think logically if not sincerely, and exhibit a certain practical ability. It is true that the War has changed much and has brought us a temporary salvation, but education must secure to us our gains or the last state of the nation may be worse than the first.

No doubt we are better and not worse than our forefathers; and, where we err, it is through ignorance. "Through ignorance ye did it," was said of the worst crime that men have done; and that appalling offence was wrought for no worse reason than because it is the habit of more or less lettered ignorance to follow specious arguments to logical conclusions. The sapient East knows all about it. Lady Lugard tells us how "the Copts have a saying that 'in the beginning when God created things He added to everything its second.' 'I go to Syria,' said Reason; 'I go with you,' said Rebellion." We need not follow the other pairs that went forth, but stern Reason is apt to be accompanied by Rebellion when it sets out in search of a logical issue.

For it is a fatal error to think that reason can take the place of knowledge, that reason is infallible, that reasonable conclusions are of necessity right conclusions. Reason is a man's servant, not his master; and behaves like a good and faithful servant—a sort of 'Caleb Balderstone,' ready to lie royally in his master's behoof—and bring logical demonstration of any premiss which the will chooses to entertain. But the will is the man, the will chooses; and the man must know, if the will is to make just and discriminating decisions. This is what Shakespeare, as great a philosopher as a poet, set himself to teach us, line upon line, precept upon precept. His 'Leontes,' 'Othello,' 'Lear,' 'Prospero,' 'Brutus,' preach on the one text—that a man's reason brings certain infallible proofs of any notions he has wilfully chosen to take up. There is no escape for us, no short cut; art is long, especially the art of living.

In the days when the working man represented only the unit of his family he picked up enough knowledge to go on with at church and chapel, by scrutinizing his neighbour's doings, in the village parliament, held at pump or "public," from the weekly news-sheet. But we have changed all that: bodies of working men have learned by means of union to act with a momentum which may be paralysing or propelling according to whether the men have or have not knowledge. Without knowledge, Reason carries a man into the wilderness and Rebellion joins company. The man is not to be blamed: it is a glorious thing to perceive your mind, your reasoning power, acting of its own accord as it were and producing argument after argument in support of any initial notion; how is a man to be persuaded, when he wakes up to this tremendous power he has of involuntary reasoning, that his conclusions are not necessarily right, but rather that he who reasons without knowledge is like a child playing with edged tools? Following his reason, he acquires this and the other sort of freedom; but is it not written:—

"Nor yet
(Grave this upon thy heart!) if spiritual things
Be lost through apathy, or scorn, or fear,
Shalt thou thy humbler franchises support,
However hardly won or justly dear."
[Wordsworth, from Obligations of Civil to Religious Liberty]

If, then, the manners and the destinies of men are shaped by knowledge, it may be well to inquire further into the nature of that evasive entity. Matthew Arnold helps us by offering a threefold classification which appeals to common sense--knowledge of God, knowledge of men, and knowledge of the natural world; or, as we should say, Divinity, the Humanities, and Science. But I think we may go further and say that Letters, if not (as I said before) the main content of knowledge, constitute anyway the container—the wrought salver, the exquisite vase, even the alabaster box to hold the ointment.

If a man cannot think without words, if he who thinks with words will certainly express his thoughts, what of the monosyllabic habit that is falling upon men of all classes? The chatter of many women and some men does not count, for thought is the last thing it is meant to express. The Greeks believed that a training in the use and power of words was the chief part of education, recognising that if the thought fathers the word, so does the word in turn father the thought. They concerned themselves with no language, ancient or modern, save their own, but of that they acquired a consummate appreciation. With the words came the great thoughts, expressed in whatever way the emergencies of the State called for—in wise laws, victorious battles, glorious temples, sculpture, drama. For great thoughts anticipate great works; and these come only to a people conversant with the great thoughts that have been written and said. In what strength did the youngest and greatest of our Premiers bring about the "revival of England"? He was fortified by illimitable reading, by a present sense of a thousand impossibilities that had been brought to pass—of a thousand things so wisely said that wise action was a necessary outcome. To say that we as a nation are suffering from our contemptuous depreciation of knowledge is to say that we scorn Letters, the proper vehicle of all knowledge.

Let us glance at the three departments of knowledge to see in regard to which of the three we are most in error. Some of us are content with such knowledge of Divinity as is to be picked up from the weekly sermon heard in church, but even with the qualification of a degree in Arts I wonder do our divines lift us as much as they might into that serener region where words fitly spoken beget thoughts of peace and holy purpose? That worship is the main end of our church services is a sublime ideal, but, "The Way, without which there is no going, the Truth, without which there is no knowing, the Life, without which there is no living," must needs be set before us in "words that burn," and we wait for preachers like those of a bygone day, "Whose pulpit thunders shook a nation's soul."

It is possible that the Church may err in keeping us underfed upon that knowledge which is life, but she does not send us away empty. We get some little share, too, of literature, poetry, history: a phrase, a line, lights up a day for us; to read of Charles Fox's having said, "Poetry's everything," of that black conqueror of the Soudan who said, "Without learning life would have neither pleasure nor savour"—these things do us good, we cannot tell why.

But there is a region of apparent sterility in our intellectual life. Science says of literature, "I'll none of it," and science is the preoccupation of our age. Whatever we study must be divested to the bone, and the principle of life goes with the flesh we strip away: history expires in the process, poetry cannot come to birth, religion faints; we sit down to the dry bones of science and say, Here is knowledge, all the knowledge there is to know. "I think that is very wonderful," a little girl wrote in an examination paper after trying to explain why a leaf is green. That little girl had found the principle—admiration, wonder—which makes science vital, and without wonder her highest value is, not spiritual, but utilitarian. A man might as well collect matchboxes, like those charming people in one of Anatole France's novels, as search for diatoma, unless the wonder of the world be ever fresh before his eyes. In the eighteenth century science was alive, quick with emotion, and therefore it found expression in literature. Still, a Lister, a Pasteur, moves us, and we feel that in one department of science, anyway, men stirred by the passion of humanity ("letters" at the fountain head?) are doing monumental work.

But for the most part science as she is taught leaves us cold; the utility of scientific discoveries does not appeal to the best that is in us, though it makes a pretty urgent and general appeal to our lower avidities. But the fault is not in science—that mode of revelation which is granted to our generation, may we reverently say?—but in our presentation of it by means of facts and figures and demonstrations that mean no more to the general audience than the point demonstrated, never showing the wonder and magnificent reach of the law unfolded. The Hebrew poet who taught us that "Breadcorn is bruised . . . because his God doth instruct him and doth teach him," glorified life. Coleridge has revealed the innermost secret, whether of science or literature: speaking on the genesis of an idea, he says, "When the idea of Nature (presented to chosen minds by a Higher Power than Nature herself)," etc. The man who would write for us about the true inwardness of wireless telegraphy, say, how truly it was a discovery, a revealing of that which was there and had been there all along, might make our hearts burn within us. No doubt there are many scientific men who are also men of letters, and some scientific books as inspiring as great poems—but science is waiting for its literature; and, though we cannot live in shameful ignorance and must get what we can out of the sources open to us, science as it is too commonly taught tends to leave us crude in thought and hard and narrow in judgment.

We are told that in times of great upheaval it profits not to cast blame on this or that section of the community; that we are all to blame even for the offences of individuals; and we partly believe it because our fathers have told us; thus did the prophets humble themselves before God, and bemoaned each his exceeding great sin in the sin of his people. We, too, are meek under chastisements, but we are vague and, to that extent, insincere.

Perhaps our duty is to give serious thought to the problems of our national life; then we may come to realise that man does not live by bread alone; we may perceive that "bread" (or cake!) is our sole and final offer to all persons of all classes; that we are losing our sense of any values excepting money values; that our young men no longer see visions, and are attracted to a career in proportion as "there's money in it." Nothing can come out of nothing, and, if we bring up the children of the nation on sordid hopes and low ambitions, need we be surprised that every man plays for his own hand?

We recognise now and then, when the shoe pinches, that the nation is in the throes of a revolution, but do we take trouble to find out the cause of "industrial unrest" and the correct attitude of the public towards that unrest? The revolution which is in progress may, it seems to me, develop on either of two lines: the men may get those "humbler franchises" they covet, but at the loss of "spiritual things"—such as the character for fair play, straight dealing, and loyalty to contract, which we like to think of as distinctively English. But what about the warning that these "humbler franchises" will be likewise lost? Trade unionism is no new thing; centuries ago and for centuries, as we know, England and Europe were under the dominion of those states within the State—the Trades Guilds. At this distance of time we can afford to admire these for the spiritual things to which they held fast; their religious organisation, the thorough training they afforded to their apprentices, and the obligation every member of a guild was under to use just weights and measures and to turn out first rate work of whatever kind. But, notwithstanding these moral safeguards, the tyranny of the guilds became insupportable, and they disappeared into the limbo of things no longer serviceable. Could any dream of Socialism, again, offer more perfect conditions than did the Russian village communes? But these too established a tyranny which was felt to be more oppressive than serfdom itself: the Mir disappeared, lost in that Gahenna which engulfed the guilds.

Wordsworth's prophetic lines should instruct us. "However hardly won or justly dear" those humbler franchises for which men are standing out in their tens of thousands with unanimity, courage, devotion to a cause justified by their *reason*, they wilt not be able to support those same franchises if spiritual things, the real things of life, be lost in gaining them. Therefore we may predict that the present movement may well issue in worse things but will not issue in the triumph of either trade unionism or syndicalism.

Here is our opportunity. We blame the workmen for their irresponsible action, for what seems to us the reckless way in which the poorest are impoverished and multitudes of workers are compelled to unwilling idleness. But those of us who are neither miners nor owners may not allow ourselves irresponsible thought or speech, and we may contribute our quota towards appeasement. It is within everybody's province to influence public opinion, if it be only the opinion of two or three; we may raise the whole question to a higher plane, the plane of those spiritual things—duty, responsibility, brotherly love (towards all men) which make the final appeal. We could not, and we need not try to, obstruct the revolution of which we are vaguely conscious, but we may help to make it a turn of the wheel which shall bring us out of the darkness of a Simplon Tunnel into the light and glory of a Lombard plain. We may, respecting the claims of working men, perceive that they demand so little, and that the things they demand are not those which matter. Even the shock of a revolution is not too high a price for an experience which should convince us that knowledge is the basis of a nation's strength.

IV New and Old Conceptions of Knowledge

I have so far advanced that "knowledge" is undefined and probably indefinable; that it is a state out of which persons may pass and into which they may return, but never a store upon which they may draw; that knowledge-hunger is as universal as bread-hunger; that our best provision for conveying knowledge is marvellously successful with the best men, but rather futile with the second best; that persons whose education has not enriched them with knowledge store up information (statistics and other facts), upon which they use their reasoning powers; that the attempt to reason without knowledge is disastrous; and that, during the present distress, England is, for various economical reasons, in a condition of intellectual inanition consequent upon a failure in her food supply, in this case the supply of food proper for the mind. I have glanced at Knowledge under the three headings suggested by one who speaks with authority, and have contended that, even if the knowledge be divisible, the vehicle by which it is carried is one and indivisible, and that it is generally impossible for the mind to receive knowledge except through the channel of letters.

But the medieval mind had, as we know, a more satisfactory conception of knowledge than we have arrived at. Knowledge is for us a thing of shreds and patches, knowledge of this and of that, with yawning gaps between.

The scholastic mediaeval mind, probably working on the scattered hints which the Scriptures offer, worked out a sublime Filosofica della Religione Cattolica, pictured, for example, in the great fresco painted by Simone Memmi and Taddeo Gaddi (which Ruskin has taught us to know), and implied in "The Adoration of the Lamb" painted by the two Van Eycks. In the first picture we get a Pentecostal Descent, first, upon the cardinal virtues and the Christian graces, then, upon prophets and apostles, and below these upon the seven Liberal Arts represented each by its captain figure, Cicero, Aristotle, Zoroaster, etc., none of them Christian, not one of them a Hebrew. Here we get the magnificent idea that all knowledge (undebased) comes from above and is conveyed to minds which are, as Coleridge says, previously prepared to receive it; and, further, that it comes to a mind so prepared, without question as to whether it be the mind of pagan or Christian; a truly liberal catholic idea, it seems to me, corresponding marvellously with the facts of life. As sublime and even more explicit is the Promethean fable which informed the Greek mind. With the sense of a sudden plunge we come down to our own random and ineffectual notions, and are tempted to cry with Wordsworth,—

"Great God! I'd rather be
A Pagan suckled in a creed outworn,"

and know that God had brought gifts of knowledge to men at awful cost, than to sit serene in the vague belief that knowledge arrives in incoherent particles, no one knows how and no one knows whence; or that it is self-generated in a man here and there who gets out of himself new insight into the motions of mind and heart, a new perception of the laws of life, the hint of a new amelioration in the condition of men.

Because the notion that we entertain of knowledge as being heterogeneous lies at the root of our heterogeneous theories of education, it may be as well to quote a passage from Ruskin's description of that picture in the chapel of the Church of Santa Maria Novella to which I have referred:—

". . . On this side and the opposite side of the Chapel are represented by Simon Memmi's hand, the teaching power of the Spirit of God and the saving power of the Christ of God in the world according to the understanding of Florence in his time.

"We will take the side of intellect first. Beneath the pouring forth of the Holy Spirit in the point of the arch beneath are the three Evangelical Virtues. Without these, says Florence, you can have no science. Without Love, Faith and Hope no intelligence. Under these are the four Cardinal Virtues— Temperance, Prudence, Justice, Fortitude. Under these are the great Prophets and Apostles . . . Under the line of Prophets, as powers summoned by their voices are the mythic figures of the seven theological or spiritual and the seven geological or natural sciences; and under the feet of each of them the figure of its Captain-teacher to the world." (Mornings in Florence.)

That is, the Florentines of the Middle Ages believed in "the teaching power of the Spirit of God," believed not only that the seven Liberal Arts were fully under the direct outpouring of the Holy Ghost, but that every fruitful idea, every original conception, be it in geometry, or grammar, or music, was directly derived from a Divine source.

Whether we receive it or not, and the Scriptures abundantly support such a theory regarding the occurrence of knowledge, we cannot fail to perceive that here we have a harmonious and ennobling scheme of education and philosophy. It is a pity that the exigencies of his immediate work prevented Ruskin from inquiring further into the origin, the final source, of knowledge, but we may continue the inquiry for ourselves. In "the teaching power of the Spirit of God" we have a pregnant and inspiring phrase. Supposing that we accept this medieval philosophy tentatively for present relief, what would be our gains?

First, the enormous relief afforded by a sense of unity of purpose, of progressive evolution, in the education of the race. It induces great ease of mind to think that knowledge is dealt out to us according to our preparedness and according to our needs; that God whispers in the ear of the man who is ready in order that he may be the vehicle to carry the new knowledge to the rest of us. "God has a few of us whom He whispers in the ear," 'Abt Vogler' is made to say; and another poet causes his Explorer to cry:—

"God chose me for His whisper, and I've found it, and it's yours!"

Next, that knowledge, in this light, is no longer sacred and secular, great and trivial, practical and theoretical. All knowledge, dealt out to us in such portions as we are ready for, is sacred; knowledge is, perhaps, a beautiful whole, a great unity, embracing God and man and the universe, but having many parts which are not comparable with one another in the sense of less or more, because all are necessary and each has its functions. Next, we perceive that knowledge and the mind of man are to each other as are air and the lungs. The mind lives by means of knowledge; stagnates, faints, perishes, deprived of this necessary atmosphere.

That, it is not for a man to choose, "I will learn this or that, the rest is not my concern"; still less is it for parent or schoolmaster to limit a child to less than he can get at of the whole field of knowledge; for, in the domain of mind at least as much as in that of morals or religion, man is under a Divine Master; he has to know as he has to eat.

That, there is not one period of life, our school days, in which we sit down to regular meals of intellectual diet, but that we must eat every day in order to live every day.

That, knowledge and what is known as "learning" are not to be confounded; learning may still be an available store when it is not knowledge; but by knowledge one grows, becomes more of a person, and that is all that there is to show for it. We sometimes wonder at the simplicity and modesty of persons whose knowledge is matter of repute; but they are not hiding their light; they are not aware of any unusual possessions; they have nothing to show but themselves, but we feel the force of their personalities. Now, forceful personalities, persons of weight and integrity, of decision and sound judgment, are what the country is most in need of; and, if we propose to bring such persons up for the public service, the gradual inception of knowledge is one condition amongst others.

There are various delightfully "new" educational systems in favour, in all of which a grain of knowledge is presented in a gallon of warm diluent. We have the theory that it does not matter what a child learns, but only how he learns it; which is as sound as, It does not matter what a child eats, but only how he eats it, therefore feed him on sawdust! Then, we have Rousseau's primitive man theory, that a child must get all his knowledge through his own senses and by his own wits, as if there were no knowledge waiting to be passed on by the small torch-bearer; and there is the theory which obtained in Catholic England, exemplified in more than one of the Waverley Novels, in the sports purveyed for her tenantry by 'Lady Margaret Bellenden,' for example. Those men and maidens had been trained as children to be "supple, active, healthy, with senses alert, ready for dance and song, with an eye and ear ready for the beautiful, intelligent, happy, capable." (I quote from a valuable letter in The Times). What with our morris-dances, pageants, living pictures, miracle plays, and so on, we are reviving the Stuart educational ideals, and no doubt we do well to aim at increasing the general joy. But our age requires more of us; in the sort of self-activity and self-expression implied in these and in half a dozen other educational theories, knowledge plays no part, and the city gamin exhibits in perfection every quality of gaiety, alert intelligence, delight in shows, which we set ourselves to cultivate.

"With all thy getting, get understanding," is the message for our needs, and understanding is, in one sense, the conscious act of the mind in apprehending knowledge, which is in fact relative, and does not exist for any person until that person's mind acts upon the intellectual matter presented to it "Why will ye not understand?" is the repeated and poignant question of the Gospels.

That is what ails us as a nation, we do not understand; not ignorant persons only, but educated men and women, employ fallacious arguments, offer prejudices for principles, and platitudes for ideas. If it be argued that these failures are due less to ignorance than to insincerity, I should reply that insincerity is an outcome of ignorance; the darkened intelligence cannot see clearly. "The day is unto them that know," but knowledge is by no means the facile acquirement of those who, according to Ruskin, "cram to pass and not to know."

I would not be understood as passing strictures upon the vast and excellent educational work nearly all teachers are doing; it is impossible to go into an Elementary School without being impressed by the competence of the teachers and the intelligence of the children, I have already paid a worthless tribute to Public Schools, and should like here to add a word of affectionate and hearty appreciation of the High School girl as I know her, thoughtful and well educated—a person quite undeserving of the slings and arrows of outrageous criticism too freely aimed at her. As for our new Universities, they remove the stigma under which many of us have suffered in presence of the numerous centres of intellectual life which add dignity and grace to continental cities. The new Universities are full of promise for the land.

We have, no doubt, arrived at a good starting place, but we may not consider that the journey is accomplished, I need not repeat the charges to which we have laid ourselves open because of our ignorance, but I shall endeavour to take a closer survey of the field of education as regarded from the standpoint of knowledge and the innate affinities existing in the mind with that knowledge which is proper for it. For the present the need is that "abstract knowledge" should present itself to practical persons as the crying demand of the nation; the "mandate," let us say, pronounced by certain general failures to understand the science of relations, and that other neglected form of knowledge, "the science of the proportion of things."

V Education and the Fullness of Life

"I must live my life!" said the notorious bandit who before the War terrorized Paris; and we have heard the sort of cant often, even before The Doll's House gave to "self-expression" the dignity of a cult; nevertheless, the brigand Bonnot has done an ill turn to society, for a misguiding theory neatly put is more dangerous than an ill-example.

We are tired of the man who claims to live his life at the general expense, of the girl who will live hers to her family's annoyance or distress; but there really is a great opportunity open to the nation which will set itself to consider what the life of a man should be and will give each individual a chance to live his life.

We are doing something; we are trying to open the book of nature to children by the proper key—knowledge, acquaintance by look and name, if not more, with bird and flower and tree; we see, too, that the magic of poetry makes knowledge vital, and children and grown-ups quote a verse which shall add blackness to the ashbud, tender wonder to that "flower in the crannied wall," a thrill to the song of the lark. As for the numerous field clubs of the northern towns, the members of which, weavers, miners, artisans, reveal themselves as accomplished botanists, birdmen, geologists, their Saturday rambles mean not only "life," but splendid joy. It is to be hoped that the opportunities afforded in the schools will prepare women to take more part in these excursions; at present the work done is too thorough for their endurance and for their slight attainments.

In another direction we are doing well; we are so made that every dynamic relation, be it leap-frog or high-flying, which we establish with Mother Earth, is a cause of joy; we begin to see this and are encouraging swimming, dancing, hockey, and so on, all instruments of present joy and permanent health. Again, we know that the human hand is a wonderful and exquisite instrument to be used in a hundred movements exacting delicacy, direction and force; every such movement is a cause of joy as it leads to the pleasure of execution and the triumph of success. We begin to understand this and make some efforts to train the young in the deft handling of tools and the practice of handicrafts. Some day, perhaps, we shall see apprenticeship to trades revived, and good and beautiful work enforced. In so far, we are laying ourselves out to secure that each shall "live his life"; and that, not at his neighbour's expense; because, so wonderful is the economy of the world that when a man really lives his life he benefits his neighbour as well as himself; we all thrive in the well-being of each. We are perceiving, too, that a human being is endowed with an ear attuned to harmony and melody, with a voice from which music may issue, hands whose delicate action may draw forth sounds in enthralling sequence. With the ancient Greeks, we begin to realise that music is a necessary part of education. So, too, of pictorial art; at last we understand that every one can draw, and that, because to draw is delightful, every one should be taught how; that every one delights in pictures, and that education is concerned to teach him what pictures to delight in.

A person may sing and dance, enjoy music and natural beauty, sketch what he sees, have satisfaction in his own good craftsmanship, labour with his hands at honest work, perceiving that work is better than wages; may live his life in various directions, the more the merrier. A certain pleasant play of the intellect attends the doing of all these things; his mind is agreeably exercised; he thinks upon what he is doing, often with excitement, sometimes with enthusiasm. He says, "I must live my life," and he lives it—in as many of these ways as are open to him; no other life is impoverished to supply his fullness, but, on the contrary, the sum of general joy in well-being is increased both through sympathy and by imitation.

This is the sort of ideal that is obtaining in our schools and in the public mind, so that the next generation bid fair to be provided with many ways of living their lives, ways which do not encroach upon the lives of others. Here is the contribution of our generation to the science of education, and it is not an unworthy one; we perceive that a person is to be brought up in the first place for his own uses, and after that for the uses of society; but, as a matter of fact, the person who "lives his life" most completely is also of most service to others because he contains within him provision for many serviceable activities which are employed in living his life; and, besides, there is a negative advantage to the community in the fact that the man is able to live on his own resources.

But a man is not made up only of eyes to see, a heart to enjoy, limbs delightful in the using, hands satisfied with perfect execution: life in all these kinds is open more or less to all but the idly depraved. But what of man's eager, hungry, restless, insatiable mind? True, we teach him the mechanical art of reading while he is at school, but we do not teach him to read; he has little power of attention, a poor vocabulary, little habit of conceiving any life but his own; to add to the gate-money at a football match is his notion of adventure and diversion.

We are, in fact, only taking count of the purlieus of that vast domain which pertains to every man in right of his human nature. We neglect mind. We need not consider brain; a duly nourished and duly exercised mind takes care of its physical organ provided that organ also receives its proper material nourishment. But our fault, our exceeding great fault, is that we keep our own minds and the minds of our children shamefully underfed. The mind is a spiritual octopus, reaching out limbs in every direction to draw in enormous rations of that which under the action of the mind itself becomes knowledge. Nothing can stale its infinite variety; the heavens and the earth, the past, the present, and future, things great and things minute, nations and men, the universe, all are within the scope of the human intelligence. But there would appear to be, as we have seen, an unsuspected unwritten law concerning the nature of the "material" which is converted into knowledge during the act of apprehension. The idea of the Logos did not come by chance to the later Greeks; "The Word" is not a meaningless title applied to the second Person of the Trinity; it is not without significance that every utterance which fell from Him is marked by exquisite literary fitness; (a child's comment on a hymn that was read to her was, "that is not poetry, Jesus would have said it much better"); in rendering an account of His august commission Christ said: "I have given unto them the words which Thou gavest me"; and one disciple voiced the rest when he said, "Thou hast the words of eternal life." The Greeks knew better than we that words are more than things, more than events; with all primitive peoples rhetoric appears to have been a power; the grand old sayings which we have scorned as inventions are coming to their own again, because, what modern is capable of such inventions? Men move the world, but the motives which move men are conveyed by words. Now, a person is limited by the number of things he is able to call by their names, qualify by appropriate epithets; this is no mere pedantic ruling, it belongs to that unfathomable mystery we call human nature; and the modern notion of education, with its shibboleth of "things not words," is intrinsically demoralizing. The human intelligence demands letters, literature, with a more than bread-hunger. It is almost within living memory how the newly emancipated American negroes fell upon books as the famished Israelites fell upon food in the deserted camp of Sennacherib.

Only as he has been and is nourished upon books is a man able to "live his life." A great deal of mechanical labour is necessarily performed in solitude; the miner, the farm-labourer, cannot think all the time of the block he is hewing, the furrow he is ploughing; how good that he should be figuring to himself the trial scene in the Heart of Midlothian, the "high-jinks" in Guy Mannering, that his imagination should be playing with 'Ann Page' or 'Mrs. Quickly,' or that his labour goes the better "because his secret soul a holy strain repeats." People, working people, do these things. Many a one can say out of a rich experience, "My mind to me a kingdom is"; many a one cries with Browning's 'Paracelsus,' "God! Thou art mind! Unto the master-mind, Mind should be precious. Spare my mind alone!" We know how "Have mynde" appears on the tiles paving the choir of St. Cross; but "mynde," like body, must have its meat.

Faith has grown feeble in these days, hope faints in our heavy ways, but charity waxes strong; we would make all men millionaires if we could, or, at any rate, take from the millionaires to give to the multitude. No doubt some beneficent and venturous Robin Hood of a minster will arise (has arisen?) to take steps in that direction; but when all has been done in the way of social amelioration we shall not have enabled men to "live their lives" unless we have given them a literary education of such sort that they choose to continue in the pleasant places of the mind. "That is all very well in theory," some one objects, "but look at the Masses, are they able to receive Letters? When they talk it is in journalese and anything in the nature of a book must be watered down and padded to suit their comprehension." But is it not true that working men talk in "journalese" because it is only the newspapers that do them the grace to meet them frankly on their own level? Neither school education nor life has put books in their way, and their adoption of the only literary speech that offers but proves a natural aptitude for Letters. One cannot always avoid appeal to the authority one know to be final, and I will not apologise for citing the fact at which no doubt we have wondered that Christ should expose the profoundest philosophy to the multitude the "Many," whom even Socrates contemns.

May I quote, with apologies to the writer, a letter signed "A Working Man," written in answer to one of mine which was honoured by being reprinted in The Times Weekly Edition? (It is good, by the way, that such a journal should be in the hands of working men). My correspondent "thanks Heaven that there are still a few persons left in this country who regard education as somewhat different from the means of keeping a shop." We may all thank Heaven that there are working men who value knowledge for its own sake and hate to have it presented to them as a means of getting on.

The fact is, Letters make a universal appeal because they respond to certain innate affinities: young Tennysons, De Quinceys, and the like, are, as we all know, inordinate readers, but these are capable of foraging on their own account; it is for the average, the dull and the backward boy I would lay urgent claim to a literary education; the minds of such as these respond to this and to no other appeal, and they turn out perfectly intelligent person, open to knowledge by many avenues. For working men whose intelligence is in excess of their education, Letters are the accessible vehicle of knowledge; having learned the elements of reading, writing, and summing, it is unnecessary to trouble them with any other "beggerly elements"; their natural intelligence and mature minds make them capable of dealing with difficulties as they occur; and for further elucidation every working men's club should have an encyclopaedia. Some men naturally take to learning, and will struggle manfully with their Latin grammar, and Cicero, their Euclid and trigonometry. Happy they! But the general conclusion remains, that for men and women of all ages, all classes, and all complexions of mind, Letters are an imperative and daily requirement to satisfy that universal mind-hunger, the neglect of which gives rise to emotional disturbances, and, as a consequence, to evils that dismay us.

VI Knowledge in Literary Form

I have so far urged that knowledge is necessary to men and that, in the initial stages, it must be conveyed through a literary medium, whether it be knowledge of physics or of Letters, because there would seem to be some inherent quality in mind which prepares it to respond to this form of appeal and no other. I say in the initial stages, because possibly, when the mind becomes conversant with knowledge of a given type, it unconsciously translates the driest formulae into living speech; perhaps it is for some such reason that mathematics seem to fall outside this rule of literary presentation; mathematics, like music, is a speech in itself, a speech irrefragibly logical, of exquisite clarity, meeting the requirements of mind.

To consider Letters as the staple of education is no new thing; nor is the suggestion new that to turn a young person into a library is to educate him. But here we are brought to a stand; the mind demands method, orderly presentation, as inevitably as it demands knowledge; and it may be that our educational misadventures are due to the fact that we have allowed ourselves to take up any haphazard ordering that is recommended with sufficient pertinacity.

But no one can live without a philosophy which points out the order, means and end of effort, intellectual or other; to fail in discovering this is to fall into melancholia, or more active madness: so we go about picking up a maxim here, a motto there, an idea elsewhere, and make a patchwork of the whole which we call our principles; beggarly fragments enough we piece together to cover our nakedness and a hundred phrases which one may hear any day betray lives founded upon an ignoble philosophy. No doubt people are better than their words, better than their own thoughts; we speak of ourselves as "finite beings," but is there any limit to the generosity and nobility of almost any person? The hastily spoken "It is the rule at sea," that distressed us a while ago, what a vista does it disclose of chivalric tenderness, entire self-sacrifice! Human nature has not failed—what has failed us is philosophy, and that applied philosophy which is called education. Philosophy, all the philosophies, old and new, land us on the horns of a dilemma; either we do well by ourselves and seek our own perfection of nature or condition, or we do well by others to our own loss or deterioration. If there is a mean, philosophy does not declare it.

There are things of which we have desperate need: we want a new scale of values: I suppose we all felt when, in those days before the War, we read how several millionaires went down in the "Titanic" disaster, not only that their millions did not matter, but that they did not matter to them; that possibly they felt themselves well quit of an incessant fatigue. We want more life: there is not life enough for our living; we have no great engrossing interests; we hasten from one engagement to another and glance furtively at the clock to see how time, life, is getting on; we triumph if a week seems to have passed quickly; who knows but that the approach of an inevitable end might find us glad to get it all over? We want hope: we busy ourselves excitedly about some object of desire, but the pleasure we get is in effort, not in attainment; and we read, before the War, of the number of suicides among Continental schoolboys, for instance, with secret understanding; what is there to live for? We want to be governed: servants like to receive their "orders"; soldiers and schoolboys enjoy discipline; there is satisfaction in stringent Court etiquette; the fact of being "under orders" adds dignity to character. When we revolt it is only that we may transfer our allegiance. We want a new start: we are sick of ourselves and of knowing in advance how we shall believe and how we shall feel on all occasions; the change we half-unconsciously desire is to other aims, other ways of looking at things. We feel that we are more than there is room for; other conditions might give us room; we don't know; any way, we are uneasy. These are two or three of the secret matters that oppress us, and we are in need of a philosophy which shall deal with such things of the spirit. We believe we should be able to rise to its demands, however exigeant, for the failure is not in us or in human nature so much as in our limited knowledge of conditions.

The cry of decadence is dispiriting, but is it well-founded? The beautiful little gowns that have come down as heirlooms would not fit the "divinely tall" daughters of many a house where they are treasured. We have become frank, truthful, kind; our conscientiousness and our charity are morbid; we cannot rest in our beds for a disproportionate anxiety for the well-being of everybody; we even exceed the generous hazard, that, peradventure for a good man one might be found to die; almost any man will risk his life for the perishing without question of good or bad; and we expect no less from firemen, doctors, life-boatmen, parsons, the general public. And what a comment on the splendid magnanimity of men does the War afford!

An annoying inquiry concerning risks at sea almost resulted in a ruling that no one should let himself be saved so long as others were in danger; it is preposterous, but is what human nature expects of itself. No, we are not decadent on the whole, and our uneasiness is perhaps caused by growing pains. We may be poor things, but we are ready to break forth into singing should the chance open to us of a full life of passionate devotion. Now, all our exigeant demands are met by words written in a Book, and by the manifestations of a Person; and we are waiting for a Christianity such as the world has not yet known. Hitherto, Christ has existed for our uses; but what if a time were coming when we, also, should taste the "orientall fragrancie" of, "My Master!" So it shall be when the shout of a King is among us, and are there not premonitions? But these things come not by prayer and fasting, by good works and self-denial, alone; there is something prior to all these upon which our Master insists with distressful urgency, "Why will ye not know? Why will ye not understand?"

My excuse for touching upon our most intimate concerns is that this matter, too, belongs to the domain of Letters; if we propose to seek knowledge we must proceed in an orderly way, recognising that the principal knowledge is of most importance; the present writer writes and the reader reads, because we are all moved by the spirit of our time; these things are our secret pre-occupation, for we have come out of a long alienation as persons "wearied with trifles," and are ready and anxious for a new age. We know the way, and we know where to find our rule of the road; but we must bring a new zeal and a new method to our studies; we may no longer dip here and there or read a perfunctory chapter with a view to find some word of counsel or comfort for our use. We are engaged in the study of, in noting the development of, that consummate philosophy which meets every occasion of our lives, all demands of the intellect, every uneasiness of the soul.

The arrogance which pronounces judgment upon the written "Word" upon so slight an acquaintance as would hardly enable us to cover a sheet or two of paper with sayings of the Master, which confines the Divine teaching to the great Sermon, of which we are able to rehearse some half-dozen sentences, is as absurd as it is blameworthy. Let us give at least as profound attention to the teaching of Christ as the disciples of Plato, say, gave to his words of wisdom. Let us observe, notebook in hand, the orderly and progressive sequence, the penetrating quality, the irresistible appeal, the unique content of the Divine teaching; (for this purpose it might be well to use some one of the approximately chronological arrangements of the Gospel History in the words of the text). Let us read, not for our profiting, though that will come, but for love of that knowledge which is better than thousands of gold and silver. By and by we perceive that this knowledge is the chief thing in life; the meaning of Christ's saying, "Behold, I make all things new," dawns upon us; we get new ideas as to the relative worth of things; new vigour, new joy, new hope are ours.

If we believe that knowledge is the principal thing, that knowledge is tri-partite, and that the fundamental knowledge is the knowledge of God, we shall bring up our children as students of Divinity and shall pursue our own life-long studies in the same school. Then we shall find that the weekly sermons for which we are prepared are as bread to the hungry; and we shall perhaps understand how enormous is the demand we make upon the clergy for living, original thought. It is only as we are initiated that science and "Nature" come to our aid in this chief pursuit; then, they "their great Original proclaim"; but while we are ignorant of the principal knowledge they remain dumb. Literature and history have always great matters to speak of or suggest, because they deal with states or phases of moral government and moral anarchy, and tacitly indicate to us the sole key to all this unintelligible world; and literature not only reveals to us the deepest things of the human spirit, but it is profitable also "for example of life and instruction in manners."

We are at the parting of the ways; our latest educational authority, one who knows and loves little children, would away with all tales and histories that appeal to the imagination; let children learn by means of things, is her mandate; and the charm and tenderness with which it is delivered may well blind us to its desolating character. We recognise Rousseau, of course, and his Emile, that self-sufficient person who should know nothing of the past, should see no visions, allow no authority. But human nature in children is stronger than the eighteenth century philosopher and the theories which he continues to inform. Whoever has told a fairy tale to a child has been made aware of that natural appetency for letters to which it is our business to minister. Are we not able to believe that words are more than meat, and, so believing, shall we not rise up and insist that children shall have a liberal diet of the spirit? Rousseau, in spite of false analogies, fallacious arguments, was able to summon fashionable mothers and men of the world throughout Europe to the great task of education, because his eloquence convinced them that this was their assigned work and a work capable of achievement; and we who perhaps see with clearer eyes should do well to cherish this legacy the conviction that the education of the succeeding generation is the chief business of every age.

Nevertheless, though we are ourselves emerging from the slough of materialism, we are willing to plunge children into its heavy ways through the agency of a "practical" and "useful" education; but children have their rights, and among these is the freedom of the city of mind. Let them use things, know things, learn through things, by all means; but the more they know Letters the better they will be able, with due instruction, to handle things. I do not hesitate to say that the whole of a child's instruction should be conveyed through the best literary medium available. His history books should be written with the lucidity, concentration, personal conviction, directness, and admirable simplicity which characterizes a work of literary calibre. So should his geography books; the so-called scientific method of teaching geography now in vogue is calculated to place a child in a somewhat priggish relation to Mother Earth; it is impossible, too, that the human intelligence should assimilate the sentences one meets with in many books for children, but the memory retains them and the child is put in the false attitude of one who offers pseudo-knowledge. Most of the geography books, for example, require to be translated into terms of literature before they can be apprehended. Great confidence is placed in diagrammatic and pictorial representation, and it is true that children enjoy diagrams and understand them as they enjoy and understand puzzles; but there is apt to be in their minds a great gulf between the diagram and the fact it illustrates. We trust much to pictures, lantern slides, cinematograph displays; but without labour there is no profit, and probably the pictures which remain with us are those which we have first conceived through the medium of words; pictures may help us to correct our notions, but the imagination does not work upon a visual presentation; we lay the phrases of a description on our palette and make our own pictures; (works of art belong to another category). We recollect how Dr. Arnold was uneasy until he got details enough to form a mental picture of a place new to him. So it is with children and all persons of original mind: a map to put the place in position, and then, all about it, is what we want.

Readings in literature, whether of prose or poetry, should generally illustrate the historical period studied; but selections should be avoided; children should read the whole book or the whole poem to which they are introduced. Here we are confronted by a serious difficulty. Plato, we know, determined that the poets in his "Republic" should be well looked after lest they should write matter to corrupt the morals of youth; aware of what happened in Europe when the flood-gates of knowledge were opened, Erasmus was anxiously solicitous on this score, and it is a little surprising to find that here, Rossetti was on the side of the angels. Will the publishers, who, since Friedrich Perthes discovered their educational mission, have done so much for the world, help us in this matter also? They must excise with a most sparing hand, always under the guidance of a jealous scholar; but what an ease of conscience it would be to teachers if they could throw open the world of books to their scholars without fear of the mental and moral smudge left by a single prurient passage! Many, too, who have taken out their freedom in the republic of letters would be well content to keep complete library editions in costly bindings in their proper place, while handy volumes in daily use might be left about without uneasiness.

The Old Testament itself after such a (very guarded) process would be more available for the reading of children; and few persons would feel that Shakespeare's plays suffered from the removal of obscenities here and there. In this regard we cherish a too superstitious piety. In another matter, let that great "remedial thinker," Dr. Arnold, advise us:—"Adjust your proposed amount of reading to your time and inclination; but whether that amount be large or small let it be varied in its kind and widely varied. If I have a confident opinion on any one point connected with the improvement of the human mind it is on this." Here we get support for a varied and liberal curriculum; and, as a matter of fact, we find that the pupil who studies a number of subjects knows them as well as he who studies a few knows those few.

Children should read books, not about books and about authors; this sort of reading may be left for the spare hours of the dilettante. Their reading should be carefully ordered, for the most part in historical sequence; they should read to know, whether it be Robinson Crusoe or Huxley's Physiography; their knowledge should be tested, not by questions, but by the oral (and occasionally the written) reproduction of a passage after one reading; all further processes that we concern ourselves about in teaching, the mind performs for itself; and, lastly, this sort of reading should be the chief business in the class room.

We are at a crucial moment in the history of English education. John Bull is ruminating. He says, "I have laboured at the higher education of women; let them back to the cooking-pot and distaff and learn the science (!) of domestic economy. I have tried for these forty years to educate the children of the people. What is the result? Strikes and swelled head! Let them have 'prentice schools and learn what will be their business in life!" John Bull is wrong. In so far as we have failed it is that we have offered the pedantry, the mere verbiage, of knowledge in lieu of knowledge itself; and it is time for all who do not hold knowledge in contempt to be up and doing; there is time yet to save England and to make of her a greater nation, more worthy of her opportunities. But the country of our love will not stand still; if we let the people sink into the mire of a material education our doom is sealed; eyes now living will see us take even a third-rate place among the nations, for it is knowledge that exalteth a nation, because out of duly-ordered knowledge proceedeth righteousness and prosperity ensueth.

"Think clear, feel deep, bear fruit well," says our once familiar mentor, Matthew Arnold, and his monition exactly meets our needs.

Supplementary; Too Wide a Mesh

"The wide world dreaming on things to come" is concentrating on a luminous figure of education which it beholds, dimly, emerging from a cloudy horizon. This gracious presence is to change the world, to give to all men wide possibilities, other thoughts, aims: but, alas, this Education which is to be open to all promises no more on a nearer view than to make Opportunity universal—that is, in spiritual things, he may take who has the power and he may keep who can.

The net is cast wide no doubt and brings in a mighty haul but the meshes are so wide that it will only retain big fishes. Now this is the history of education since the world was and is no new thing. The medeival schools of castle or abbey, the Renaissance schools, the very schools of China, have all been conducted upon this plan. Education is for him who wants it and can take it but is no universal boon like the air we breathe or the sunshine we revel in.

We are a little sorry for the effect of this limitation upon the 'working classes': only a small percentage of the children of these are 'big' enough to be retained in the examination net which, to do it justice, explores all waters. A few of the pass men may do big things and fill big posts, but for the rest, a large percentage is, in practice, illiterate except for the spelling out of a local 'rag' for football and parish news.

But is the mischief confined to what we call the 'working classes'? Is it not a fact that in most schools the full force of instruction is turned on upon a few boys who are likely to distinguish themselves? While for the rest of the school teaching is duly given no doubt but the boys find they may take it or leave it as the humour takes them.

We were all fascinated a while ago by the story of a pair of charming 'Twins'; these went through the usual preparatory school education and then passed on to a great Public School where they remained until they were nineteen; that is, they had ten or twelve good years among most excellent opportunities. As they were attractive boys we may take it that their masters were not at any rate unwilling to teach them. Their record should have been quite a good one, and, though it is the fashion to sneer a little at Public Schools, we know that these have turned out and do turn out the best and most intellectual men the country has occasion for. Therefore what happened in the case of these 'Twins' does not cast any reflection upon Public Schools but solely upon the system of the Big Mesh. Here are some of the things we read in that delightful biography:—

"While in hospital after a smash at polo R— wrote to F—: 'I enjoyed it immensely. What lucky people we are taking an interest in so many things!'"

Surely here was material for a schoolmaster to work upon! Again, we read:—

"They never ceased to wonder at the magnificence of the world and they carried a divine innocence into soldiering and travel and sport and business and, not least,—into the shadows of the Great War."

And this 'wonder' of theirs was the note that marked them at school. Again, what material for their instructors!

"But," we read, "at X— they showed little interest in books and, later, were wont to lament to each other that 'They had left school wholly uneducated.'" (The italics are ours.)

Their kindly biographer and dear friend goes on to say:—

"But they learnt other things,—the gift of leadership, for instance, and the power of getting alongside all varieties of human nature."

But was not this nature rather than nurture, school nurture at any rate, for these gifts seem to have been a family inheritance? Born in 1880, they left school in 1899, when there follows a delightful record for the one brother of successful and adventurous sport while

"R— was soon absorbed in the city . . . and beginning to lament his want of education." "F—, while in Egypt was greatly impressed by Lord Cromer and writes to R—, 'he is quite the biggest man we have! . . . to hear him talk is worth hearing.'"

The two brothers correspond constantly and R— takes the part of mentor to his brother. He advises him to learn The Times leaders by heart to improve his style,—"because they are very good English." Again,

"I will send you out next mail a very good book, Science and Education, by Professor Huxley which I have marked in several places, the sort of book you can read over again." R— "had discovered that he was very badly educated and was determined to remedy this defect:—'It don't matter . . . I do believe not having learned at X— so long as one does so now.'"

See the fine loyalty of the young man; his failures were not to be put down to his school!

If the schools take credit for any one thing it is that they show their pupils 'how to learn'; but do they? We are told that R— set to work at a queer assortment of books and writes to F—:

"Anyone can improve his memory: the best way is by learning by heart—no matter what—and then when you think you know it, say it or write it. After two or three days you are sure to forget it again and then instead of looking at the book 'strain your mind' and try to remember it. Above all things always keep your mind employed. One great man (I forget which) used to see a number on a door, say 69, and tried to remember all that had happened in the years ending in 69.

Or, see a horse and remember how many you have seen that day. Asquith always learns things by heart, he never wastes a minute; as soon as he has nothing to do he picks up some book. He reads till 1-30 every night. When driving to the Temple next morning he thinks over what he has read. Result: he has a marvellous memory and knows everything."

Think of the Herculean labours the poor fellow set for both himself and his brother! They ran an intellectual race across a ploughed field after heavy rain and the marvel is that they made way at all. Yet these two brothers had sufficient intellectual zeal to have made them great men as Ambassadors, Governors of Dominions, Statesmen, what not; whereas so far as things of the mind go, they spent their days in a hopeless struggle, alert for any indication which might help them to make up lee-way, and all because, according to their own confession, they 'had learned nothing at school.' Here are further indications of R—'s labours in the field of knowledge:

"I am reading Rosebery's Napoleon and will send it to you. What a wonder he was! Never spent a moment of his life without learning something . . . I enclose an essay from Bacon's book. Learn it by heart if you can. I have and think it a clinker. I have also finished Life of Macaulay. I have always wondered how our great politicians and literary chaps live. I also send you a Shakespeare. I learnt Antony's harangue to the Romans after Caesar's death; I am also trying to learn a little about electricity and railroad organization, so have my time filled up. Pickwick Papers I also send to you. I have always avoided this sort of books but Dickens' works are miles funnier than the rotten novels one sees . . . I have learnt one thing by my reading and my conversation with Professors,—you and I go at a subject all wrong." (Italics ours.)

These letters are pathetic documents and, that they are reassuring also, let us be thankful. They do go to prove that the desire of knowledge is inextinguishable whatever schools do or leave undone; but have these nothing to answer for when a pursuit which should yield ever recurring refreshment becomes dogged labour over heavy roads with little pleasure in progress?

Here, again, is another evidence of the limitations attending an utter absence of education. A cultivated sense of humour is a great factor in a joyous life, but these young men are without it. Perhaps the youth addicted to sports usually fails to appreciate delicate nonsense; sports are too strenuous to admit of a subtler, more airy kind of play and we read:

R— heard Mr. Balfour and Lord Reny praising Alice in Wonderland. Deeply impressed he bought the book as soon as he returned to London and read it earnestly. To his horror he saw no sense in it. Then it struck him that it might be meant as nonsense and he had another try, then he concluded that it was rather funny but he remained disappointed."

We need not follow the career of these interesting men further. Both fell early before they were forty. Their fine qualities and their personal fascination remained with them to the end, as did also, alas, their invincible ignorance. They laboured indefatigably, but, as R— remarked,—"You and I go at a subject all wrong!"

The schools must tell us why men who attained mediocre successes and the personal favour due to charming manners and sweet natures were yet somewhat depressed and disappointed on account of the ignorance which they made blind and futile efforts to correct; but they never got so far as to learn that knowledge is delightful because one likes it; and that no effort at self-education can do anything until one has found out this supreme delightfulness of knowledge.

It must be noted that this failure of a great school to fulfil its purpose occurred twenty years ago, and that no educational body has made more well-considered and enlightened advances than have the Headmasters of the great Public Schools. Probably that delightful group of Eton boys in Coningsby has always been and is to-day typical, there is a certain knightly character in the fine bearing and intelligent countenances of the Head Boys one comes across there which speaks well for their intellectual activity. The question is whether more might not be done with the average boy.

The function of the schools is no doubt to feed their scholars on knowledge until they have created in them a healthy appetite which they will go on satisfying for themselves day by day throughout life. We must give up the farce of teaching young people how to learn, which is just as felicitous a labour and just as necessary as to teach a child the motions of eating without offering him food; and studies which are pursued with a view to improve the mind must in future take a back seat.

The multitudinous things that every person wants to know must be made accessible in the schoolroom, not by diagrams, digests, and abstract principles; but boys and girls, like 'Kit's little brother,' must learn 'what oysters is' by supping on oysters. There is absolutely no avenue to knowledge but knowledge itself, and the schools must begin, not by qualifying the mind to deal with knowledge, but by affording all the best books containing all the sorts of knowledge which these 'Twins,' like everyone else, wanted to know. We have to face two difficulties. We do not believe in children as intellectual persons nor in knowledge as requisite and necessary for intellectual life. It is a pity that education is conducted in camera save for the examination lists which shew how the best pupils in a school have acquitted themselves, the half-dozen or dozen best in a big school. Finely conscientious as teachers are they can hardly fail to give undue importance to their group of candidates for examination and a school of four or five hundred stand or falls by a dozen head boys.

www.ingramcontent.com/pod-product-compliance
Lightning Source LLC
LaVergne TN
LVHW031150200826
846147LV00014B/91